NOT TO BE REMOVED
FROM THE LIBRARY

KT-551-784

WITHDRAWN FROM
THE LIBRARY
UNIVERSITY OF
WINCHESTER

KA 0141495 X

# the POEMS of JOHN KEATS

# the POEMS of JOHN KEATS

*edited by*

Jack Stillinger

HEINEMANN
LONDON

Heinemann Educational Books Ltd
LONDON EDINBURGH MELBOURNE AUCKLAND
HONG KONG SINGAPORE KUALA LUMPUR IBADAN NAIROBI
JOHANNESBURG LUSAKA NEW DELHI KINGSTON

ISBN 0 435 14850 8

Copyright © 1978 by the President and Fellows of Harvard College
All rights reserved

First published 1978

KING ALFRED'S COLLEGE
WINCHESTER
REF
821.7
KEA
73823

Published by
Heinemann Educational Books Ltd
48 Charles Street, London W1X 8AH
Printed in the United States of America
Bound in Great Britain

# Preface

THIS EDITION presents the texts of the 150 "poetical works" —148 poems of various degrees of seriousness and in various states of completion plus the collaborative play *Otho the Great* and the dramatic fragment *King Stephen*—that can reasonably be assigned to Keats at the present time, with an apparatus recording all known substantive variants that have any claim to be considered authoritative and full textual notes that give dates of composition, describe the relationships among the extant MSS and early printings, explain the choices of copy-text, and discuss matters of special interest or difficulty.

From a textual point of view, it represents the third major editing of Keats's poems in the last hundred years, the first being that in H. B. Forman's *Poetical Works and Other Writings* published in 1883 (the texts reissued, frequently with corrections and additions, in many successive editions between 1884 and 1938–39), the second being that in H. W. Garrod's Oxford English Texts *Poetical Works* published in 1939 (corrected and revised in a second edition of 1958). As a one-volume edition with apparatus at the foot of the page it will, in its formal features, most closely resemble Garrod's work among previous editions, but it differs from Garrod's in canon, in arrangement, in substantive readings in eighty-five of the 150 texts, and in several thousand particular details of information in the apparatus. All of these differences are intended to be improvements.

Some sixty MSS or parts of MSS, holograph and transcript, have come to light since Garrod did his work, as well as a number of additional first and early printings that he either overlooked or chose to ignore. These have been collated and (as appropriate) noticed in the apparatus. A fresh collation of the rest of the MSS and printed sources has made possible the correction of a great many details in both texts and annotation. But the principal novelty of the present edition is that it is the first in the history of Keats scholarship to be based on a systematic investigation of the transmission of the texts.

In *The Texts of Keats's Poems*, published by Harvard University Press in 1974, I undertook to determine the relationships among the extant MSS (who copied what from whom), the sources of the earliest published versions (how the poems first got into print), and the relative authoritativeness of the various texts that might have claims to be the standard (which versions are "the best"). The introductory section on "The Current State of Keats's Texts," while acknowledging that our modern texts of the forty-five poems in Keats's three original volumes are in reasonably sound condition, viewed the editing of the posthumously published pieces with some dismay:

> [Modern editors] take a number of their texts . . . from inferior MS or printed sources, combine states of text, and occasionally rewrite Keats's lines. . . . They often misunderstand the evidence that the various MSS provide and give a great deal of misinformation about the texts. As a result, no one working on Keats these days, unless he does the collating and works out the relationships for himself, can tell how Keats's texts were copied from one MS to another, or in which order the various texts were written, or from what sources the poems were first put into print, or which are authoritative and which are corrupt readings in any particular text. (pp. 4–5)

The rest of the book attempted to remedy this situation by listing and describing the surviving holographs, transcripts, and early printed texts (Sections II and III) and devising a "history," frequently diagramed, of the transmission of text for each of Keats's 150 pieces (Section IV). A brief final section offered suggestions for a new edition.

When I wrote the book (on sabbatical leave in 1971–72) I had no intention of editing the poems myself. My object was to point out the need for a new edition, explain in general terms how to do it, and leave the drudgery of collating, typing, checking, and proofreading to some other scholar or a committee of scholars. Then while the book was in press (in the summer of 1973) I was persuaded to change my mind and take on the job. I was thus in the rather anomalous position of having just written a book of advice addressed, in effect, to myself ("the next serious editor of Keats's poems"!). What was of much graver concern, I was also in the position of having to do the work all over again, recollating the texts from the beginning with the greater attention to accuracy and minuteness of detail that an edition requires.

The original research (as I made clear in my Preface) was done in Urbana, Illinois, on the basis of photocopies and correspondence, and it was only after the book was published that I went to the libraries in various parts of the United States and Great Britain to examine or reexamine the MSS firsthand. My travels and subsequent investigations have resulted in some losses and gains of MSS. On the debit side, Keats's drafts of *I stood tip-toe* 11–18, *Unfelt, unheard, unseen,* and *Isabella* 193–200,

216–224 are not at Harvard, the British Library, and Welbeck Abbey (as reported in *Texts*, pp. 122, 139, 183), but instead are apparently no longer extant anywhere. On the credit side, the following have surfaced or been called to my attention since publication of the book: a holograph fair copy of *To Hope* ("formerly in the possession of M. B. Forman and since disappeared" in *Texts*, p. 100, but now owned by Abel E. Berland, of Chicago), a holograph fair copy of *O Solitude* (the Lyte–Philpotts–Bromley Martin MS, also "since disappeared" in *Texts*, p. 106, but in fact all the while in the William Andrews Clark Memorial Library), the draft of *Robin Hood* (the Townshend Mayer MS, in the Isabella Stewart Gardner Museum), a facsimile of the otherwise unknown draft of *Isabella* 73–80 plus discarded lines (at Harvard), the draft of *Isabella* 481–488, 504 (in the Martin Bodmer Foundation), the draft of *Otho the Great* IV.i.74–75 (in the Philip H. and A. S. W. Rosenbach Foundation), the draft of *Lamia* I.386b–397 (also in the Rosenbach Foundation), a transcript of *Addressed to the Same* by B. R. Haydon (in a letter to Wordsworth in the Wordsworth Library, Grasmere), another transcript of *On the Sea* by Coventry Patmore (at Harvard), eight more transcripts by Richard Woodhouse (also at Harvard – these were made for Severn and are described as "since . . . lost" in *Texts*, p. 30), and Elizabeth Stott Clarke's two transcripts in Isabella Towers' copy of *1817* (at Keats House, Hampstead – last heard of in 1932 in *Texts*, p. 62). At the very last moment (middle of May 1978, after my Textual Notes and Appendix V have been set and made into pages) I learn that Woodhouse's shorthand transcript of *The Eve of St. Mark* is available for examination after all, in the Adelman Collection at Bryn Mawr. Its readings (in a photocopy very kindly supplied by Bryn Mawr's Librarian, James Tanis) bear out my speculations in *Texts*, pp. 220–222, and in the Textual Notes below.

The principles and procedures in this edition, basically a refinement and expansion of those set forth in *Texts*, are fully expounded in the Introduction. Here I would emphasize that the apparatus is intended for practical use by the general reader and beginning student of Keats as well as by the textual scholar. Essentially the reader should know the following. (1) All MSS and printed versions that are collated in the apparatus (these are routinely listed, along with the abbreviations used to designate them, in the first apparatus note to each poem) may be understood to have the same wording as the text of the present edition except where a variant is recorded. (2) Variants and other readings following the square bracket in an apparatus note are substitutable equivalents (that is, they hold the same position relative to the surrounding words) of the text represented by the word or words preceding the bracket. (3) Emendations are indicated by the presence of one or more source abbreviations or "ed" immediately after the square bracket. Thus in Book I of *Hyperion*, where the present text is based on *1820*, "6 above] *D*, *W*[2]; about *W*[1], *1820*" shows that *1820*'s "about" has been rejected in favor of the draft's and *W*[2]'s "above," and in *On Peace*, where the text is based on *W*[3], "14 horrors] *ed*; Honors *W*[3]" shows that *W*[3]'s "Honors" has been emended to "horrors." (4) A caret ∧ on either side of the square bracket calls attention to the absence of punctuation, and a wavy dash ~ on the right side of the bracket stands for the repetition of a text word on the left side that is associated with a punctuation variant. (5) Angle brackets ⟨ ⟩ enclose deleted text, and curly braces { } enclose earlier deletions made separately within a deleted passage. The rest of the procedures should be pretty much self-explanatory.

At one time I planned to include a section of Commentary giving circumstances of composition and relevant passages from the letters, identifying quotations and allusions that Keats expected the reader to recognize, and glossing hard words and expressions, but this resulted in several hundred additional pages of typescript, and there simply was no room for it. For sources and critical comment the fullest annotations are those by Ernest de Selincourt (*The Poems*, 5th ed., 1926), Douglas Bush (*Selected Poems and Letters*, Boston, 1959), Miriam Allott (*The Poems*, 1970), and John Barnard (*The Complete Poems*, Harmondsworth, 1973). I do regret being unable to reproduce some of Reginald Spofforth's *Julia to the Wood Robin, A favorite Canzonet, with an Accompaniment for the Piano Forte* (the song underlying Keats's *Stay, ruby breasted warbler, stay*), which my colleague Nicholas Temperley located for me in the Pendlebury Library of Music, Cambridge, and having to omit information sent me by R. S. Sincock, Secretary of the Teignbridge District Council, concerning the identity of certain place names in *For there's Bishop's Teign*.

For permission to examine, describe, and quote MSS and MS materials in their possession I wish to thank the Adelman Collection, Bryn Mawr College; Abel E. Berland, of Chicago; the Martin Bodmer Foundation, Cologny-Geneva; the Bristol Central Library; the University of Bristol Library; the British Library; the Buffalo and Erie County Public Library; the William Andrews Clark Memorial Library, University of California, Los Angeles; the Cornell University Libraries; the Fitzwilliam Museum, Cambridge; the Isabella Stewart Gardner Museum, Boston; the Houghton Library, the Harry Elkins Widener Memorial Collection, and the Dumbarton Oaks Research Library, Harvard University; the Henry E. Huntington Library and Art Gallery; the University of Illinois Library; Keats House, Hampstead; the Keats-Shelley Memorial House, Rome; the Pierpont Morgan Library; the Henry W. and Albert A. Berg Collection, New York Public Library, Astor, Lenox and Tilden Foundations; the Historical Society of Pennsylvania; the Carl H. Pforzheimer Library; the Free Library of Philadelphia; Dallas Pratt, of New York; the Philip H. and A. S. W. Rosenbach Foundation, Philadelphia; the National Library of Scotland; the Scottish National Portrait Gallery; the Robert H. Taylor Collection, Princeton University; the Humanities Research Center, University of Texas at Austin; the Mary Couts Burnett Library, Texas Christian University; Trinity College Library, Cambridge; Tulane University Library; the Victoria and Albert Museum; the Wisbech and Fenland Museum; Dorothy Withey, of Stratford-upon-Avon; Yale University Library; and the Wordsworth Library, Grasmere.

For various courtesies, information, and assistance I am indebted to the staffs of all the institutions just named. My greatest single obligation of this sort is to Rae Ann Nager, Curator of the Harvard Keats Collection, who good-naturedly answered hundreds of (additional) queries from me during the past four years, but I should also like to acknowledge the special help of W. H. Bond, Librarian of the Houghton Library; Hans Braun, Director of the Bodmer Foundation; William E. Conway, Librarian of the Clark Library; Clive E. Driver, Director of the Rosenbach Foundation; Christina M. Gee, Assistant Curator of Keats House, Hampstead; Stephen Gill, Honorary Librarian of the Wordsworth Library, Grasmere; Frank M. Halpern, Reference Librarian, the Free Library of Philadelphia; William H. Loos, Curator of Rare Books, Buffalo and Erie County Public Library; Ann D. McDermott, Special Collections Librarian, Texas Christian University; Paul Needham, Curator of Printed Books, the Morgan Library; Lola L. Szladits, Curator of the Berg Collection; and Daniel H. Woodward, Librarian of the Huntington Library.

I have received considerable advice and encouragement from Stuart M. Sperry, of Indiana University, Donald H. Reiman, of the Pforzheimer Library, and W. J. Bate, of Harvard, and especially helpful particular information from Walter H. Evert, of the University of Pittsburgh, Barbara Rosenbaum, compiler of the Keats section (among others) in the forthcoming second volume of *Index of English Literary Manuscripts*, Charles E. Robinson, of the University of Delaware, Wilfred S. Dowden, of Rice University, and the late J. C. Maxwell, of Oxford. G. Thomas Tanselle, of the University of Wisconsin, very graciously lent me prepublication copies of his *SB* articles referred to in the Introduction. The American Council of Learned Societies and the University of Illinois Research Board provided grants to pay for some of my travel expenses. My colleague-wife, Nina Baym, read the Introduction and put up with a lot of other trouble besides. To her especially I am very grateful.

J. S.

# Contents



## POEMS

# Abbreviations

(In references to books here and throughout this edition, the place of publication is given only when it is not London.)

| | |
|---|---|
| *1817* | John Keats, *Poems,* 1817 |
| *1818* | John Keats, *Endymion: A Poetic Romance,* 1818 |
| *1820* | John Keats, *Lamia, Isabella, The Eve of St. Agnes, and Other Poems,* 1820 |
| *1848* | *Life, Letters, and Literary Remains, of John Keats,* edited by Richard Monckton Milnes, 2 vols., 1848 |
| *1857* | R. M. Milnes, "Another Version of Keats's 'Hyperion,'" *Miscellanies of the Philobiblon Society,* 3 (1856–57) |
| *1876* | *The Poetical Works of John Keats,* edited by Lord Houghton [R. M. Milnes], 1876 |
| Allott | *The Poems of John Keats,* edited by Miriam Allott, 1970 |
| Bate | Walter Jackson Bate, *John Keats,* Cambridge, Mass., 1963 |
| Clarke | Charles Cowden Clarke, "Recollections of John Keats," in Charles and Mary Cowden Clarke, *Recollections of Writers,* 1878, pp. 120–157 |
| Colvin | Sidney Colvin, *John Keats: His Life and Poetry, His Friends, Critics, and After-Fame,* 1917 |
| Finney | Claude Lee Finney, *The Evolution of Keats's Poetry,* 2 vols., Cambridge, Mass., 1936 |
| Forman (1883) | *The Poetical Works and Other Writings of John Keats,* edited by Harry Buxton Forman, 4 vols., 1883 |
| Galignani (1829) | *The Poetical Works of Coleridge, Shelley, and Keats,* published by A. and W. Galignani, Paris, 1829 |
| Garrod | *The Poetical Works of John Keats,* edited by H. W. Garrod, 2nd ed., Oxford, 1958 |
| Gittings | Robert Gittings, *John Keats,* Boston, 1968 |
| Hampstead Keats | *The Poetical Works and Other Writings of John Keats,* edited by H. Buxton Forman, revised by Maurice Buxton Forman, 8 vols., New York, 1938–39 |

| | |
|---|---|
| *HLB* | *Harvard Library Bulletin* |
| *KC* | *The Keats Circle: Letters and Papers, 1816–1878,* edited by Hyder Edward Rollins, 2 vols., Cambridge, Mass., 1948 |
| *K-SJ* | *Keats-Shelley Journal* |
| *Letters* | *The Letters of John Keats, 1814–1821,* edited by Hyder Edward Rollins, 2 vols., Cambridge, Mass., 1958 |
| Lowell | Amy Lowell, *John Keats,* 2 vols., Boston, 1925 |
| *N&Q* | *Notes and Queries* |
| *NMM* | *The New Monthly Magazine* |
| *OED* | *The Oxford English Dictionary,* 12 vols. with supplement, 1933 |
| O.S.A. ed. | Oxford Standard Authors edition—*The Poetical Works of John Keats,* originally edited by H. B. Forman, Oxford, 1906, and many times reissued; subsequently edited by H. W. Garrod, 1956 |
| *PBSA* | *The Papers of the Bibliographical Society of America* |
| *PDWJ* | *The Plymouth and Devonport Weekly Journal* |
| Ridley | M. R. Ridley, *Keats' Craftsmanship: A Study in Poetic Development,* Oxford, 1933 |
| *SB* | *Studies in Bibliography* |
| s.d. | Stage direction |
| Sharp | William Sharp, *The Life and Letters of Joseph Severn,* 1892 |
| s.p. | Speech prefix |
| Sperry | Stuart M. Sperry, Jr., "Richard Woodhouse's Interleaved and Annotated Copy of Keats's *Poems* (1817)," *Literary Monographs,* 1 (Madison, 1967), 101–164, 308–311 |
| *Texts* | Jack Stillinger, *The Texts of Keats's Poems,* Cambridge, Mass., 1974 |
| *TLS* | *The Times Literary Supplement* |
| $W^1$ | Transcripts in the smaller of two volumes of Woodhouse copies of poems at Harvard (on this and the next two items see Appendix V) |
| $W^2$ | Transcripts in the larger of two volumes of Woodhouse copies of poems at Harvard |
| $W^3$ | Woodhouse transcripts in the Morgan Library |
| Ward | Aileen Ward, *John Keats: The Making of a Poet,* New York, 1963 |

# the POEMS of JOHN KEATS

# Introduction

JOHN KEATS, born in London on 31 October 1795, wrote his first poem at the age of eighteen, produced a score of occasional pieces during the next two years while finishing an apprenticeship to an apothecary-surgeon at Edmonton and taking a year's course in medicine at Guy's Hospital in London, but did not seriously begin his career as poet until after he passed his apothecary's examination toward the end of July 1816, three months before his twenty-first birthday. During his lifetime he published forty-five poems in three volumes—*Poems* (1817), *Endymion* (1818), and *Lamia, Isabella, The Eve of St. Agnes, and Other Poems* (1820)—plus nine more (not counting five that he had reprinted in the volumes) in periodicals and an annual, and he wrote ninety-six other pieces that were first published posthumously, between 1822 and 1939. He died at Rome, at the age of twenty-five, on 23 February 1821, but his long illness had terminated virtually all poetic activity more than a year earlier. He had the shortest writing career of any of the major poets in English, and without question the fastest development. It is a main purpose of the present edition, by means of the chronological arrangement of poems and the detailed record of variants and MS alterations, to display that development as clearly and comprehensively as possible.

The texts are edited according to the ideal of "final authorial intentions"; that is, they are supposed to represent for each poem, as exactly as can be determined, the form that Keats himself would have sanctioned and preferred over all others. But some special explanations are immediately necessary to relate "authorial intentions" to the scope and scholarly furnishings of this edition. We might in the first place think that Keats would not have allowed the printing of a sizable proportion of the poems that are given here. He did not want the unfinished *Hyperion* included in *1820*; he said of *Give me your patience, sister,* in writing it out for his brother and sister-in-law, "I would not copy it if I thought it would ever be seen by any but yourselves" (*Letters,* II, 195); he judged *This mortal body of a thousand days* so bad an effort that he would not transcribe it for J. H. Reynolds or his brother Tom (*Letters,* I, 324, 332). Many other poems obviously were written only for the private amusement of relatives and friends, and there are several fragments besides *Hyperion* that he never considered publishable. We might think that he would have objected to the present chronological arrangement, and to the giving of equal status to all the pieces, so that, for example, *Stay, ruby breasted warbler,* an inane set of lyrics that (as Richard Woodhouse noted opposite the $W^2$ transcript) he dashed off for some friends "in a few Minutes," looks as much like a seriously considered poem as *Ode to a Nightingale.* We might think that he would not have had the lines numbered by fives in the left margin (though in the original printing of *Endymion* the lines were numbered by tens in the right margin); that he would not have had textual apparatus at the foot of the page (or anywhere else, for that matter); and that he would not have had all the editorial paraphernalia of textual notes and appendixes that add considerably to the length and weight of this volume.

But Keats had high aims. On 14 October 1818, about two-thirds of the way through his brief career as a serious writer, he quietly predicted to his brother and sister-in-law, "I think I shall be among the English Poets after my death" (*Letters,* I, 394), and it is easily demonstrable that, while he occasionally wrote for money and immediate popularity (as with *Otho the Great* and *Lamia*), his larger goal from the beginning was immortal fame. It is a consequence of his success in this endeavor that his development is studied and restudied with attention to the minutest details; that his earliest and most trivial pieces, as well as the fragments, are looked at again and again for clues to help us understand the ideas and artistry of the mature poems; that his MSS with all their false starts, cancellations, and revisions (not to mention misspellings and wild punctuation) are scrutinized for indications of how he composed his poems and what he meant to achieve—by the line and by the whole—in them; and that the transcripts and early printings are combed for variants and other evidences that illuminate the process by which his poems came to be known publicly.

Keats could have foreseen the character, if not the specific methodological procedures, of the treatment given his poems here, and I do not think he would have been dismayed. In the early nineteenth century the standard scholarly edition of the chiefest of "English Poets" was *The Poetical Works of John Milton. In Six Volumes. With the Principal Notes of Various Commentators. To Which Are Added Illustrations, with Some Account of the Life of Milton. By the Rev. Henry John Todd, M.A.* (1801). Todd's first volume contains a life of Milton (160 pages), a separate discussion of his nuncupative will (29 pages), a list of editions and translations of his poems (20 pages), a list of "detached pieces of criticism" (4 pages), the texts of various commendatory verses (21 pages), Addison's critique of *Paradise Lost* (171 pages), Johnson's remarks on Milton's versification (53 pages), and finally "An Inquiry into the Origin of *Paradise Lost*" (56 pages). The poems themselves do not appear until Volume II, and there and in the succeeding volumes Todd's apparatus of textual and interpretive commentary frequently occupies more space on the page than the lines that he is annotating. In the second edition of this work (1809), expanded to seven volumes, a 400-page "Verbal Index"—in effect a concordance to the poems—is added to Volume I, and the commendatory verses, Addison, Johnson, and the "Inquiry" are moved to Volume II, where Milton's poems first begin on page 275. Todd's eight-volume edition of Spenser (1805) is on the same scale, and there were many similarly elaborate editions of other writers, especially Shakespeare. This is what it meant in Keats's time to be "among the English Poets." There was also, much more so then than now, a keen interest in nonliterary items associated with great writers of the past—witness Todd's inclusion of the twenty-nine pages on Milton's will or, closer to home, Keats's rapture in *Lines on Seeing a Lock of Milton's Hair* or his and B. R. Haydon's excitement over the discovery of a seal ring thought to have belonged to Shakespeare (*Letters,* I, 239–240, 248–249).

The editorial features of the present volume are much more to the point than a will, a lock of hair, or a seal ring, and are designed throughout for practical use in criticism and literary history. The chronological arrangement, for example, besides being a cumulative record of his productivity, shows what Keats had to choose from when he came to make up his first and third volumes. The apparatus and Textual Notes reveal a great deal about his characteristic methods of writing—for example that he rarely composed (as against copying for friends and relatives) more than two versions of a poem, and that, except in a handful of works, most notably *Otho the Great* and *Lamia,* he revised mainly to polish and clarify (improving wording, sound, meter, and the like), and not to change any large element of structure, narrative detail, characterization, or theme. In general the evidence of the MSS perfectly accords with Woodhouse's observation that Keats was "impatient of correcting" and "would rather burn the piece in question" and write a new poem instead (see *KC,* I, 128–129).

MS variants and alterations frequently illuminate Keats's meaning in a line or passage or even an entire work. "The real grass" in the draft and fair copy of *Endymion* IV.622 clinches the symbolism of the printed text's "The grass"; "Was it a vision real" in the draft of *Ode to a Nightingale* 79 helps clarify the difference between "vision" and "waking dream" in the revised text; the canceled first stanza of *Ode on Melancholy* sets a dramatic situation and a tone that may make the opening lines of the final text more intelligible (they also may complicate our interpretation, but in any case have to be taken into account); the "suppressed" revisions of *The Eve of St. Agnes* at 54/55 and 314–322 certainly clarify (as Keats meant that they should) the goings-on in that poem. The record of variants in successive versions and of MS changes by other hands than the poet's provides ample material for the study of the multiple or composite authorship of the first printed texts of some of the best known poems: the publisher John Taylor contributed to the wording of *Endymion,* and he and Woodhouse were initially responsible for some of the final readings of *Isabella, The Eve of St. Agnes, Hyperion,* and *Lamia.* We need not apologize to Keats for this late twentieth-century prying into and behind the texts. His highest "authorial intention" was to be a famous English poet, and the present edition is one more manifestation of his fulfillment of that intention.

THE PRIMARY materials on which this edition is based are (1) Keats's three original volumes, (2) the earliest printed texts of the poems published in periodicals and an annual while he was alive, (3) the earliest printed texts of the rest of the poems, all first published after his death, (4) the more than five hundred extant holograph and transcript versions underlying or otherwise associated with the printings in the first three categories, and (5) facsimiles and other records (in scholars' reports of readings) of a handful of additional MSS that were known in the later nineteenth century or more recently but have since disappeared. Secondary materials include several marked (corrected and/or annotated) copies of *1817, 1818,* and *1820,* a marked set of proof-sheets for the first poem in *1820,* Keats's and others' letters concerning corrections and alterations in various texts, and of course the significant reprintings and editings of the poems from Keats's time up to the 1970s. The primary materials are enumerated and characterized at length in Sections II and III of *The Texts of Keats's Poems* (pp. 14–83), and they and the secondary materials are listed for each poem in the individual histories in Section IV (pp. 91–271). In the present volume these materials (both primary and secondary) are again listed and described for each poem in the Textual Notes; the contents of *1817* and *1820* are listed in Appendix III; and the locations of the transcripts (along with brief identifications of the transcribers and comments on the importance of their MSS) are given in Appendix V. The main purpose of this introduction is to explain and where necessary offer some justification for the editorial procedures.

*Arrangement.* The poems are arranged in chronological order according to the known or conjectured dates of composition or (for works written over a long period) substantial completion. Many of the pieces can be dated by the exact day (or span of days) on which Keats wrote them. For a number of others, however, we know only the year, and for a very few we have no clue at all. Consequently any attempt at a chronological arrangement can at best only approximate the order in which the works were actually composed; poems that are datable only by the year and those that are not datable at all have to be intercalated among those for which we have more specific dates, and a number of the positionings here (for example, among important works, those of *Hyperion* and some of the 1819 odes) are necessarily arbitrary. I have used the internal evidences of style, subject, and allusion to season, weather, and the like only as a last resort (these are never reliable—for instance, one might suppose on internal evidence that *Lines on the Mermaid Tavern* and *Bards of passion* date from about the same time when in fact they were composed ten or eleven months apart).

There is the further problem of intermingling short poems written on a single day with long poems written over a period of weeks or even months. The position of *Endymion,* for example—determined according to "substantial completion" (as of 28 November 1817, the date at the end of the draft)—hides the facts that Keats wrote several, perhaps all, of the seven short pieces preceding it in the present arrangement after he began the long poem, and that his major effort during January–March 1818 was the revision of this same long poem and not the twenty or so short pieces of the period that are here printed after it. There are similar difficulties with other long works, especially those of the summer and autumn of 1819 (some of which themselves overlap). The precise details are given in the discussions of dating in the Textual Notes; a bare list, such as that in the Contents of this volume, will be misleading.

In *Texts,* p. 283, I remarked that "Chronological ordering sometimes brings together the memorable with the much less memorable pieces and the serious with the light-hearted, but these juxtapositions do not falsify Keats's development or his temperament." It might be noted that the alternative arrangement suggested there—printing the poems of *1817, 1818,* and *1820* in order, just as in the original volumes, and then the rest of the works chronologically (essentially a two-part division like that between Wallace Stevens' *Collected Poems* and *Opus Posthumous*)—would have much the same result. In the present arrangement, to give but a single example, *Otho the Great* is followed by *Lamia, Pensive they sit, To Autumn,* and *The Fall of Hyperion.* If *Lamia* and *To Autumn* were removed to an earlier section of *1820* poems, the "nonsense verses" *Pensive they sit* (*Letters,* II, 188) would still come between *Otho* and *The Fall.*

*Copy-texts.* The copy-text for each poem—the base-text used in the preparation of this edition—is identified in the first apparatus note

("Text from . . . ") and again, whenever there are competing sources, in the Textual Notes. For the forty-five poems included in Keats's three original volumes, the copy-texts are the printed texts of *1817, 1818,* and *1820.* For the remaining 105 pieces, the copy-texts have been chosen individually from a variety of holograph, transcript, and printed sources. The principal criterion employed throughout is authoritativeness.

The most serious problem in the selection of copy-texts has to do with eight poems of *1817, 1818,* and *1820*—*To My Brother George* (sonnet), *O Solitude, Addressed to the Same, Endymion, Lamia, Isabella, The Eve of St. Agnes,* and *Hyperion*—for which there exist competing versions in MS. (There are also significant MSS, including drafts and holograph fair copies, for most of the other poems in *1817* and *1820,* but the authority of these MSS is indisputably superseded by that of the printed texts.) For the first five items—*To My Brother George* through *Lamia*—we have Keats's fair copies from which the poems were actually set in type. In these instances the choice of copy-text lies between the printer's copy MSS and the printed texts made from them. For *Isabella* and *Hyperion* the printer's copy MSS were transcripts rather than holographs, and we have not only the transcript in each case but the holograph from which the transcript ultimately derives. Keats went over and corrected the transcript of *Isabella* before it was given to the printer, and thus both it and the holograph have claims, along with *1820,* to be the copy-text. He apparently never saw the transcript of *Hyperion,* and so in this instance the choice of copy-text lies between the holograph and *1820.* For *The Eve of St. Agnes* we lack the printer's copy MS, but George Keats's extant transcript is a highly accurate representation of the minute details—punctuation, spelling, and the like—of the lost MS from which the poem (after much editing) most probably was printed, and consequently has some claims to be considered a more authoritative text than *1820.*

One current theory of copy-text editing, if rigidly applied, would demand that MSS rather than the printed texts be used as copy-texts for most or all of these eight poems—certainly Keats's fair copies for the printer in the first five instances, probably his fair copy of *Isabella* and the extant holograph of *Hyperion,* and possibly George Keats's transcript of *The Eve of St. Agnes.* This theory, originally proposed by W. W. Greg (*SB,* 3 [1950–51], 19–36) and championed and developed by Fredson Bowers (in *Modern Philology,* 48 [1950–51], 12–20, and numerous subsequent publications), requires some explanation. In essence it is a theory concerning the best source of accidentals for a scholarly text (the routine punctuation, spelling, capitalization, word-division, and paragraphing), and has nothing to do with the substantives (the actual wording, along with punctuation of such a character that it affects essential meaning).

Greg set out to overthrow the then prevailing idea that when a literary work exists in a series of printed editions, each of which, after the first, was set from the preceding, and there is no surviving MS, the copy-text should be the latest edition published during the author's lifetime. This idea was based on the assumption that the author *might* have had a hand in the text of each successive edition; it seemed reasonable, especially in cases where later editions showed changes in wording that could be attributed to the author, to take the latest text as the most authoritative, and, because the prevailing theory made no distinction between substantives and accidentals, to take it as authoritative not only in wording but in all other respects as well. Greg countered this view by separating the components of a text into two classes, substantives (which the printer would have attempted to follow faithfully) and accidentals (which the printer would have treated more freely), and by arguing that, even if an author did revise his wording in one or more subsequent printed versions, he is not likely to have attended to the accidentals, which themselves would be subject to increasing corruption (nonauthorial alteration) each time the work was reprinted. Greg proposed instead that we use the first rather than a later edition as copy-text. This in normal circumstances will be the version that is closest to the author's lost MS, and will therefore reflect more accurately than any later text the author's own punctuation, spelling, and the like. The wording of the first edition can be emended where there is reason to think that the author himself was responsible for substantive changes in a later text, but the accidentals should remain those of the first edition.

Greg arrived at his theory in connection with the editing of sixteenth- and seventeenth-century English plays (specifically while studying the texts of Jonson's *Masque of Gipsies,* as he explains in the preface to his 1952 edition of that work), and it seems entirely sound and appropriate for the purposes that he had in mind. I do not think there is any opposition nowadays to his theory as it applies generally to the scholarly editing of Renaissance dramatic texts or any others where only a single edition was set from an author's MS and the MS itself has not survived. Beginning in the 1960s, however (with the 1962 paper published in *SB,* 17 [1964], 223–228, and the "Preface to the Text" in the first volume of the Centenary Edition of the Works of Nathaniel Hawthorne, *The Scarlet Letter,* Columbus, 1962, specifically pp. xxxiii–xxxiv), Bowers has extended Greg's theory to the editing of works of more recent periods and has argued for the use, where it is available, of the author's fair copy MS rather than a printed edition as copy-text. This development, unlike the original theory of which it is sometimes thought to be a "logical extension," has become a point of considerable controversy (see G. Thomas Tanselle, *SB*, 28 [1975], 167–229, for the most comprehensive recent survey of the debate).

It is well known from the printer's manuals of the time (especially since the facsimile reprinting of several of them in the English Bibliographical Sources series edited by D. F. Foxon, 1965–66) that in the eighteenth and nineteenth centuries it was, at least in the printer's view of the matter, the printer rather than the author who was chiefly responsible for the correctness and consistency of the accidentals of a text. According to John Smith, *The Printer's Grammar* (1755), p. 199, for example, "most Authors expect the Printer to spell, point, and digest their Copy, that it may be intelligible and significant to the Reader; which is what a Compositor and the Corrector jointly have regard to, in Works of their own language." Smith's words are repeated verbatim in Philip Luckombe's *The History and Art of Printing* (1771), p. 377, and John Johnson's *Typographia* (1824), II, 127, and there are several other statements to the same effect in these works (Smith, pp. 200, 274; Luckombe, p. 441; Johnson, II, 209, 230–231) and also in Caleb Stower's *The Printer's Grammar* (1808), pp. 80–81, 389–391, and Thomas C. Hansard's *Typographia* (1825), pp. 434–435, 742, 749–750. In this situation, when the author's fair copy MS is extant, a difficult question arises as to which version—the MS itself or the house-styled printed text set from the MS—better accords with the author's intentions in the work.

Bowers and his followers, on the one hand, feel that the author is misrepresented in a text that takes its accidentals from a printed version. "When an author's manuscript is preserved, this has paramount authority, of course. . . . if an author's habits of expression go beyond words and into the forms that these take, together with the punctuation that helps to shape the relationships of these words, then one is foolish to prefer a printing-house style to the author's style" (Bowers, *SB*, 17 [1964], 226). Opponents of the Bowers school, on the other hand, feel that the author is misrepresented in a text that takes its accidentals from a prepublication form of the work. This is a view expressed by several reviewers of the Centenary Hawthorne and other editions sponsored by the Modern Language Association Center for Editions of American Authors, and also by more general theorists such as James Thorpe and Philip Gaskell. Thorpe, after surveying the printer's manuals cited above, writes as follows:

> In many cases, probably in most cases, [the author] expected the printer to perfect his accidentals; and thus the changes introduced by the printer can be properly thought of as fulfilling the writer's intentions. To return to the accidentals of the author's manuscript would, in these cases, be a puristic recovery of a text which the author himself thought of as incomplete or unperfected: thus, following his own manuscript would result in subverting his intentions. (*Principles of Textual Criticism,* San Marino, 1972, p. 165)

Gaskell independently comes to the same conclusion:

At first glance it might seem that the manuscript will be the obvious choice for copy-text, for it is what the author actually wrote. But does it represent the text as the author wanted it to be read? As far as substantives are concerned (saving later corrections) it certainly does; but this is hardly the case with the accidentals. Most authors, in fact, expect their spelling, capitalization, and punctuation to be corrected or supplied by the printer, relying on the process to dress the text suitably for publication, implicitly endorsing it (with or without further amendment) when correcting proofs. . . . It would normally be wrong, therefore, rigidly to follow the accidentals of the manuscript, which the author would himself have been prepared—or might have preferred—to discard. (*A New Introduction to Bibliography,* New York and Oxford, 1972, p. 339)

Both sides are in agreement on the basic goal—in Thorpe's words above, "fulfilling the writer's intentions"—but are thus in direct opposition concerning how to achieve that goal. The Bowers school takes the stand that we can never really know an author's intentions, for even if he requests, endorses, or expresses gratitude for the printer's styling of his accidentals he may merely be rationalizing or acquiescing rather than expressing a genuine preference (see especially Tanselle, *SB,* 29 [1976], 167–211, on this point); the only "safe" course is to go by what the author himself actually wrote, and therefore to rely on a MS rather than a printed text. Opponents of the Bowers school think that it is unrealistic to equate the author's MS with the intended final form of the work; since house styling appears to have been the normal and expected procedure, it is safer to follow the printed text. (It might be repeated that none of this affects the substantives. The Bowers school, editing a work from MS, would emend substantively to include authorial revisions in a printed text, while the opponents, editing the same work from a printed text, would emend substantively to restore the author's MS wording where the printed text is corrupt; if there were no question about the authoritativeness of individual substantive readings, the two edited texts would be substantively identical, and the differences would lie entirely in the accidentals.)

Fortunately this ongoing debate does not have to be settled here. Both sides are attempting to arrive at a general theory to be used when there is insufficient information concerning the individual case, and neither side would (or should) insist on applying its theory to all authors at all times. Thorpe specifies "many cases, probably . . . most" in the passage cited above, Gaskell speaks of "most authors," and Bowers, reviewing Gaskell's book in *PBSA,* 67 (1973), 122, is willing to allow that "Gaskell's rejection of an author's manuscript in favor of the first edition as copy-text is perfectly sound for a handful of distinct exceptions," though he of course goes on to condemn "the mistake of formulating general principles from these exceptions instead of from normality." Obviously some authors preferred (or would have preferred) their own accidentals and, just as obviously, others preferred the printer's or someone else's styling. Where evidence indicates that a particular author did in fact have a preference, then the relative numbers of "some authors" and "others"—indeed the entire argument about what is normal and what exceptional—must be set aside, and the editor must act according to the requirements of the specific situation at hand. With Keats we do have such evidence to act on.

In general terms Keats was a writer who prepared copy for his volumes, read proofs, was free to make changes and react to the publishers' and printers' changes while the works were in press, and was grateful to the publishers for their help in making the poems presentable. As evidence of his preparation of copy we have three holograph leaves from the printer's copy MS for *1817*—the three sonnets mentioned above at the beginning of this discussion of copy-texts—foliated "53," "59," and "66" and pretty clearly parts of a MS that was entirely in the poet's hand; the holograph printer's copy MS for the whole of *Endymion*; and the holograph printer's copy MS for *Lamia* in *1820* plus the $W^1$ transcript, with Keats's corrections and revisions, that was used for *Isabella.* The printer's copy MSS for *The Eve of St. Agnes* and the shorter poems in *1820* have not survived, but they were either holographs in every case or else some combination of holographs and transcripts made with the poet's approval by Charles Brown (see *Texts,* pp. 67–68); the extant holograph fair copy of *Song of Four Fairies,* which was once a part of the MS for *1820* (Woodhouse calls it "Keats's copy for the press") and consists of four leaves foliated "8" through "11," shows that Keats wrote out at least some of the shorter poems for the printer. It is likely that *Hyperion,* the final poem in *1820,* set from a transcript that he apparently never saw, is the only poem in the three volumes for which he did not prepare, or directly supervise the preparation of, printer's copy.

As evidence for the proofreading we have C. C. Clarke's mention of Keats's receiving "the last proof-sheet [of *1817*] . . . from the printer" (Clarke, p. 137), Keats's letter to Taylor of 27 February 1818 concerning the proofs of the first book of *Endymion* (*Letters,* I, 238–239), his markings and revisions in the extant proofs of *Lamia,* and his letter to Taylor of June 1820 commenting on the proofs of *The Eve of St. Agnes* (II, 294–295). It is a reasonable supposition that he read the proofs of *1817* and *1820* (including *Hyperion*) all the way through. For *Endymion,* however, he probably read only the first two books, leaving proof correction of the remainder to Clarke and Taylor (*KC,* I, 12; *Letters,* I, 270–271).

We know almost nothing about his relationship with the publishers of

*1817,* Charles and James Ollier (Charles Ollier is mentioned several times in Keats's letters, and Clarke apparently includes him among a gathering of friends at Keats's lodgings when the last proof-sheet was sent over; the printer of the volume, Charles Richards, was the brother of a close friend of Clarke and Brown). The presence or absence of knowledge is not crucial because, on the evidence of the three extant leaves of printer's copy, the *1817* printer reproduced Keats's texts with a high degree of fidelity (almost all the changes are simply reductions of Keats's erratic capitals to lowercase), and therefore the choice of copy-text for the three *1817* poems in question is of little practical, as opposed to academic, significance. On the other hand, for *1818* and *1820,* where knowledge *is* crucial, we have a great deal of information, in letters and other documents, about his relationship with the publishers Taylor and Hessey and their legal and literary adviser Woodhouse, and it is clear that they worked closely together and that the interaction was considered beneficial by all sides. Two passages from Keats's letters to Taylor concerning *Endymion*—the first when he was reading proofs, the second after he had received an advance copy of the book—convey the spirit of the relationship: "Your alteration strikes me as being a great improvement—the page looks much better. And now I will attend to the Punctuations you speak of. . . . I am extremely indebted to you for this attention and also for your after admonitions"; "the book pleased me much. . . . I see in many places an improvement greatly to the purpose" (*Letters,* I, 238, 270–271). The independence with which he responded to Taylor's markings in the fair copy of *Endymion* and to Woodhouse's changes in the printer's copy MS of *Isabella,* the tone of his letters requesting alterations in *Endymion* and *The Eve of St. Agnes,* and especially the presence of many MS alterations of wording and accidentals suggested by Taylor and Woodhouse for *Endymion, Isabella, Hyperion,* and *Lamia* that did *not* get into the printed texts attest to the fact that (except in the special case of *The Eve of St. Agnes,* which his revisions had rendered "unfit for ladies"—*Letters,* II, 163) Keats was allowed to have his way in things that mattered to him.

This is not, however, to say that he kept a sharp eye on the minor details of his poems while they were being printed (a number of errors in the printed texts of *1817* and the early books of *Endymion* suggest that he was a careless proofreader) or, for that matter, at any other time. On the contrary, what is most pertinent to the issue at hand is the extraordinary degree to which, even in prepublication stages, he entrusted the preservation and refining of his texts to others. His apparent abandoning of the later books of *Endymion* while they were in press to the care of Clarke and Taylor is one example. But even before that, J. H. Reynolds had gone through the now lost draft of the poem to help in revision. We do not know what Reynolds contributed—"I had little to do in revising," he told Milnes much later (*KC,* II, 178)—but may infer that to some extent, however small, he altered both accidentals and substantives in the text (there would have been no reason to mention revising had he altered only accidentals), and therefore that the surviving fair copy was already a collaborative product when Taylor and the printer went to work on it.

With the later poems Keats seems regularly to have handed his MSS over to Brown and Woodhouse for transcribing, and then to have considered the transcripts, especially Brown's, the principal authorial MS versions. Brown's statement to Milnes in October 1840—"most of the originals were scrambled away to America by his brother, after I had made copies of them for the press" (*KC,* II, 37–38)—tends to support this, as does Keats's remark on 12 June 1819 to James Elmes, who wished to publish *Ode to a Nightingale* in his *Annals of the Fine Arts*: "I have but just received the Book which contains the only copy of the verses in question" (*Letters,* II, 118; the "Book" was almost certainly Brown's rather than Keats's). This situation explains how Keats could give away his fair copy of *Isabella* to his brother George in January 1820, before he had assembled his texts for *1820*—Woodhouse and probably Brown as well had transcribed it by then—and also why it is that, except for a dozen copies that Keats made for acquaintances or sent in letters and two MSS intended for the printer (*Song of Four Fairies* and *Lamia*), the extant holographs of poems written after December 1818, when he moved in with Brown at Wentworth Place, Hampstead, are all drafts rather than fair copies. The presence of his hand in Brown's transcripts of *Lines on the Mermaid Tavern, To the Nile, To Homer, Ode to Psyche, Otho the Great,* and *To Autumn* shows that the poet read over and used the transcripts for further revision; and it appears likely that at least some of the now lost MSS that he wrote out for the printer of *1820* (like the extant holograph fair copy of *Song of Four Fairies*) were copied from Brown's transcripts rather than from holographs, since the *1820* texts of the shorter poems are, where Brown's MSS survive, very close to Brown's in minor details.

This reliance on transcripts, with the transcribers' frequently extensive refinement of accidentals—much needed, it might be added, since Keats took a very casual attitude toward them himself—means that many of the poems in the printed volumes, probably most or all in *1818* and *1820* and perhaps (by extrapolation from the existing evidence) some or all in *1817* as well, became collaborative efforts not just in the printing but at a much earlier stage. (It also means that for many of the poems, including *Endymion* and possibly all the others for which we have finished fair copies in Keats's hand, it is virtually impossible to isolate every particular detail initiated by the poet himself.) Such collaboration, since it was carried on regularly and was in no sense enforced on him, has to be considered an essential element in the fulfillment of the poet's intentions, and it ought to be obvious that the publishers' and printers' additional refinements of minor details are simply a further fulfilling of those intentions. Tanselle (*SB*, 29 [1976], 186–191) poses the question of whether it is "conceivable that the author's intention may sometimes be fulfilled by other persons" and, after considering the example of Pound's alterations and deletions in the revised MS of *The Waste Land*, allows that "it is possible for someone other than the 'author' to make alterations which are identical with the intention of the 'author,' when the relationship partakes of the spirit of collaboration. . . . if an author accepts what someone else has done not in a spirit of acquiescence but of active collaboration, the result does represent his active intention." Reynolds, Clarke, Brown, Woodhouse, and Taylor were not, like Pound, literary geniuses, but they were good friends of Keats, and they all, like Keats himself, wanted to see him "among the English Poets." I think we clearly have the requisite "spirit of collaboration" here, and that it would be a violation of Keats's intentions to prefer MSS to printed versions as copy-texts for any of the poems in the three original volumes.

None of the other printed texts, except by coincidence (as when they faithfully reproduce an authoritative MS version), can be said to represent the same "spirit of collaboration." This is true even of the nine additional poems (besides those in *1817, 1818,* and *1820*) published while Keats was alive—*After dark vapours, This pleasant tale, On Seeing the Elgin Marbles, To Haydon with a Sonnet Written on Seeing the Elgin Marbles, On the Sea, Four seasons, To Ailsa Rock, As Hermes once,* and *La Belle Dame.* While it is fair to assume that Keats himself furnished copy for at least some or most of these, the periodical and annual texts differ so frequently and extensively from the other known versions that one suspects the editors of having tinkered with and even sometimes having rewritten lengthy passages of the poems that they printed (see *Texts,* pp. 72–73). Most of the nine were published by Leigh Hunt, who was, for a time at least, a close associate of the poet. But Keats's relationship with Hunt was of a different character from that with his other helpers—Hunt was the master, Keats the pupil and protégé—and in any case he did not have control over Hunt's and the other periodical texts in the same way that, in proofreading and in correspondence and consultation with his publishers, he did in his three original volumes. Consequently the periodical texts do not seem as reliably authoritative as others that are available for these poems, and I have, as for all but four of the rest of the pieces (*The Gothic looks solemn, This mortal body, What can I do to drive away,* and *The Jealousies*), preferred MS to printed versions as copy-texts.

In making my choices for these nine and the posthumously published poems I have been concerned first to discriminate between texts that have some degree of independent authority and those that derive from other texts now extant, and then, in cases where we have two or more authoritative versions, to decide which of them better or best represents Keats's considered intentions in the work (ideally, the version that he himself, if he had to select among the alternatives now available, would recommend as the basis for a standard text). This latter task is occasionally difficult, and in a few instances is impossible to carry out except by an editorial judgment that is to some extent necessarily subjective. Where two or more holographs of a poem exist, it is usually (but not always) possible to order the MSS chronologically, showing that one preceded the other. It will not do, however, simply to choose the later or latest MS as copy-text. In some of these later holographs Keats was still creating or perfecting the poem, while in others (as in letters and MSS that he sent to relatives and friends) he was mechanically copying out already finished work; the difficulty lies in distinguishing between the two situations by assessing the seriousness of the changes that he made in the later copies. We have, for example, two holograph versions of *Give me your patience, sister, There is a joy in footing slow, Not Aladdin magian,* and *The Eve of St. Mark,* and in each case the later version is a letter copy showing several substantive differences from the earlier version. I have taken Keats's changes in the later texts of *Give me your patience* and *There is a joy* to be considered revisions, and therefore have chosen the later MSS as copy-texts. The later holographs of the other two poems seem more casually written, and the substantive changes in them, including the omission of several lines from each, may be owing more to carelessness than to conscious artistry (see *Texts,* pp. 19–21); in these instances I have preferred the earlier MSS as copy-texts.

When a holograph text and a transcript or early printed text are in competition, the main question is of course the relative authority of the nonholograph version. Most of these cases are resolved by choosing the holograph as copy-text, but I have usually taken Brown's transcripts, especially those of poems written in 1819, to be authoritative, and have not hesitated to use them instead of holographs when they appear to represent the more considered version. Where it is impossible to apply general principles—as when we have differing versions whose relative degrees of authority cannot be established, or two or more equally authoritative versions but no clear indication of Keats's intentions in the texts—the choice of copy-text is necessarily my own critical preference. There does not seem to be any other way to settle the matter in these cases.

*Substantive Emendations.* A recurring fault in previous editions of Keats's poems has been the intermixing of two or more discrete states of text (for example, those of a draft and a fair copy) so as to create combinations of words that never existed in any MS or in the poet's mind. I have considered it desirable, so far as the substantives are concerned, to reproduce a single state of text for each poem—the most authoritative state available—and therefore, apart from headings (separately discussed below), have emended the copy-texts' wording only to correct certain or probable errors. All substantive emendations are recorded in the apparatus and again (along with the alterations of accidentals) in Appendix I, and the sources of the emendations and my reasons for making them are, when they are not obvious, given in the Textual Notes.

Keats's three original volumes contain a sizable number of readings that do not appear in any of the surviving MSS. Many of those in *1818* and *1820* were no doubt suggested by Taylor or Woodhouse, but in the present edition they are everywhere (except when they appear likely to be the result of a copyist's or printer's mistake) retained as authoritative. There is plentiful evidence (see the preceding section concerning the use of *1817, 1818,* and *1820* as copy-texts) that Keats had a hand in the texts of these three volumes while they were being printed and that, with the exception of certain passages in *The Eve of St. Agnes,* he was free to accept or reject his friends' changes in them. We must, therefore, operate on the assumption that these new readings—even those in *Endymion, Isabella, Hyperion,* and *Lamia* for which we know Taylor or Woodhouse to have been initially responsible—represent Keats's preferred wording. We cannot reject them all, and there is no reasonable principle on which to make choices among them.

This last statement applies also to *The Eve of St. Agnes,* the one poem among those in the three original volumes where it appears that changes were made against the poet's wishes. It is clear that the publishers insisted on the restoration of the original, more innocent version of 314–322, and highly probable that they made other alterations and omissions not in accord with Keats's considered intentions. On several occasions—in *SB,* 16 (1963), 207–212; *The Hoodwinking of Madeline* (Urbana, 1971), pp. 158–166; *Texts,* p. 219—I have argued that a standard text of the poem should incorporate the readings of Keats's now lost fair copy (via George Keats's transcript and Woodhouse's record of the fair copy variants) in 98, 143, 145–147, 314–322, as well as the added stanza following 54, and I originally constructed a text along these lines for the present edition. But, while I have not changed my mind about the faultiness of the *1820* text as a fulfillment of Keats's intentions, another conviction—that we should avoid combining readings of discrete states of text—has arisen that seriously complicates the matter. As I now see it, the second consideration outweighs the first in this case, and so the text given here is, after all, that of *1820* without substantive alteration.

The posthumously published poems are emended more frequently than those taken from the three original volumes, but only because the copy-texts have a higher frequency of apparent error. Obviously a great many of the decisions to emend or not to emend, like some of the choices of copy-text in the first place, have had to be based on the editor's personal judgment. As Thorpe reminds us (*Principles of Textual Criticism,* p. 197), "Emendation . . . is essentially guesswork of a high order, by its nature unverifiable."

*Headings.* Practical considerations—mainly the need to provide distinctive titles that can be used for scholarly and critical reference—have dictated a more liberal policy in the treatment of headings. Where the copy-text has none, a heading has been supplied in the form of the first line of the poem. First lines are also used for three poems taken from *1817* and *1820* (*Had I a man's fair form, Hadst thou liv'd in days of old,* and *Bards of passion,* titled in the copy-texts "To * * * * * *," "To * * * *," and "Ode"), for twenty-two posthumously published poems where the copy-text heading is simply "Song," "Sonnet," "To ——," "Fragment," or "Stanzas," and for five others where the copy-text heading is clearly or probably nonauthoritative. Most of these nondescriptive headings in the posthumous poems ("Song" and similar wordings) originated with the copyists and early editors, and none contributes to the understanding or aesthetic appreciation of a text. "Sonnet" has been regularly dropped (seven times) from titles like "Sonnet / To Lord Byron" and "Sonnet / Written in disgust of vulgar superstition" when the copy-text is a transcript. In the *1817* texts and surviving holographs Keats almost never used this form of heading for a sonnet, preferring instead to begin with the preposition or participle (the fair copy title "Sonnet to Sleep" is of course authoritative, and is retained in the present edition; but this MS was written in special circumstances—Keats copied a Woodhouse transcript—and is not indicative of his general practice).

While Woodhouse and most other transcribers dated the poems, when they dated them at all, at the end of the text, Brown and George Keats (the latter frequently copying the former) consistently positioned their dates after the headings—thus "Song. 1818" in their transcripts of *Hence burgundy, claret, and port.* In the texts taken from Brown and in the record of variants from Brown's and George Keats's MSS in the apparatus and Textual Notes these dates are omitted. Clearly they are not authoritative elements of the text, and in any case the inclusion of them would give the wrong impression that Brown and George Keats were the only transcribers who dated the poems that they copied.

*Treatment of Accidentals.* Obviously some degree of normalization is unavoidable in an edition that reproduces its copy-texts, printed texts and a variety of MS texts alike, in a uniform typography, and several kinds of silent change have been introduced in what might be called the presentational features of the texts—such things as the style of headings, numbering of stanzas, positioning of speech prefixes (these are detailed in a series of statements at the beginning of Appendix I). But no attempt has been made to impose a strict consistency on the accidentals of the texts themselves.

A great deal of punctuation has been added, especially in poems taken from holographs (Keats frequently omitted punctuation at the end of the line, and in some of the copy-text MSS he used almost no punctuation at all). A number of Brown's commas between clauses have been changed to heavier punctuation—semicolons, colons, or periods—and Woodhouse's and other transcribers' dashes after semicolons and periods at the end of the line have been regularly omitted (Keats rarely used this style). Otherwise copy-text punctuation has been emended only to correct or clarify syntax.

Many capitalized nouns and other words have been lowercased, again especially in poems taken from holographs (Keats capitalized ordinary nouns and even adjectives and verbs seemingly at random), and a few lowercased proper names and personifications have been capitalized. Misspellings have been corrected, and spellings that were archaic or obsolete in Keats's time have been modernized except where it appears that the old spelling was intended for special effect—humor, atmosphere, or unusual pronunciation. A few nonarchaic spellings have also been altered to avoid ambiguity—for example, "mask" has been changed to "masque," "veiled" to "vailed," "dies" to "dyes"—but generally the copy-text spelling has been retained for forms that were current at the beginning of the nineteenth century. Different forms of a word have been allowed to stand within a longer work when they are widely separated; in a shorter work, where the inconsistency might be distracting (as with the several variations of "bag-pipe" in *Of late two dainties*), a single form has been imposed on all occurrences.

Syncopated spellings as well as "-'d" verb endings have usually been reproduced just as they appear in the copy-texts. The various individual forms of compounds—for example, "out-spread" and "outspread," "sun-beams" and "sunbeams," "sun-beamy" and "moon beamy"—have also been preserved except in a few instances where the form might hinder understanding. Thus "hour glass" is retained in *Fragment of Castle-builder* 44, but the last two words in "A spacious looking glass" eight lines later are emended to "looking-glass" to make perfectly clear that Castle-builder is describing a large mirror rather than some other kind of glass that looked spacious.

All emendations of punctuation, capitalization, spelling, word-division, and paragraphing are listed in Appendix I. Those that affect the meaning of the text and therefore are substantive in character are also recorded in the apparatus.

*Apparatus.* The first apparatus note to each poem identifies the copy-text used in the present edition and specifies the other texts, if any, that are collated in the apparatus. Subsequent notes record, in a single series, all substantive emendations of the copy-text, all substantive variants in the collated texts, and (where holographs survive) the substantive alterations—cancellations, interlineations, marginal additions, and the like—that Keats made in the process of writing and perfecting a MS. (The rationale for combining variants and MS alterations in one list is that Keats sometimes revised his text within a single MS, as by deletion and interlineation, and at other times introduced changes in the process of making a copy; both types of revision ought logically to have the same status—the rejected words in each case are readings preliminary to the final text—and it would be misleading to separate them by giving the first type in a list of MS alterations and the second by means of the record of variants.) Alterations in the transcripts are also noticed in a few instances where it is possible that the initial transcript reading represents deleted wording in a now lost holograph, and nonsubstantive spelling variants are included when the spelling affects the sound or meter of a line (as with the fair copy's "speakst" for "speakest" in *Endymion* IV.127 and the many occurrences of "e'en" for "even").

In constructing the apparatus I have (just as in choosing the copy-texts) been concerned to distinguish between texts of primary authority and those that derive from other texts now extant. The derivative texts are described in the Textual Notes but (with a few special exceptions) are omitted from the apparatus. The texts of primary authority are always included in the apparatus when they contain one or more readings that differ substantively from the text of the present edition. Misspellings, slips of the pen, and compositor's errors that produce new words are ignored when the new word cannot possibly fit the context (for example, "Knight" for "night" in the draft of the sonnet *To My Brother George* 11, "Though" for "Through" in the fair copy and first printed text of *Endymion* III.811, "thrice" for "trice" in both letter texts of *Not Aladdin magian* 24); these are considered to represent accidental rather than substantive differences, because they do not produce alternative meanings. But variants in collated texts that make sense in their context are always recorded, even those that are clear errors (like Tom Keats's "incantations" in *Had I a man's fair form* 14). The object has been to make possible the reconstruction of the substantive features of every text that is included in the apparatus. All collated texts may be understood to agree substantively with the text of the present edition unless a variant is noted. (Where the substantiveness of a variant is in question, the rule has been to include it in the apparatus and then discuss it in the Textual Notes.) All readings given from a MS may be understood to be in ink and in the hand of the principal writer of the MS unless pencil or another hand is indicated.

The illustrations that follow are from Book I of *Hyperion* except where another source is specified. The copy-text for *Hyperion* is *1820,* and the apparatus records variants and MS alterations from Keats's draft (cited as *D*), Woodhouse's $W^2$ transcript, and his clerks' transcript in $W^1$. The notes describing Keats's alterations in the draft may be checked against the reproduction of the MS in de Selincourt's *Hyperion: A Facsimile* (Oxford, 1905).

Basically two types of note are employed to show variants. The first, which is used when the variant takes the form of one or more complete or partial lines that were subsequently omitted and therefore have no counterpart in the final text, consists simply of a between-lines reference ("21/22" meaning "between line 21 and line 22") followed by the additional line or lines that constitute the variant. The second, which is used when the variant does have a counterpart in the final text, consists of a line reference, a lemma (one or more words from the text, with passages of several words usually represented by the first and last words separated by three ellipsis dots), a square bracket, the variant(s), and then the siglum or sigla identifying the text(s) containing the variant(s). For example, "48 tone] tune *D*, $W^2$, $W^1$" means that *1820* (the copy-text) reads "tone" and the draft, $W^2$, and $W^1$ vary from the copy-text in reading "tune"; "81 falling] fallen *D*" means that *1820,* $W^2$, and $W^1$ have "falling" ($W^2$'s and $W^1$'s agreement with *1820* being understood by the absence of any reference to these transcripts in the note) and the draft alone has "fallen." Except where some special circumstance is described, variants and other readings following the bracket in this type of note are always substitutable equivalents (that is, they hold the same position relative to the surrounding words) of the text represented by the lemma preceding the bracket. When the same variant occurs in two or more collated texts, the accidentals of the variant are (with a few exceptions individually noted) those of the first text cited; thus the reading "Tune" in $W^2$ or $W^1$ would not be specially recorded in the first note above, and if the draft had "Tune" then the note would be "48 tone] Tune *D*, $W^2$, $W^1$" regardless of the presence or absence of a capital in $W^2$ and $W^1$. Multiple readings in a series are separated by semicolons ("16 stray'd] stay'd *D*, $W^1$; stay'd *altered to* stray'd $W^2$"). The sigla representing the collated texts are identified in the first note to each poem.

When the variant involves a significant difference in punctuation, a caret calls attention to the absence of punctuation: "209 And‸] Yes, *D*, $W^2$, $W^1$" emphasizes that *1820* has no comma (or other punctuation) after "And." If the variant is entirely a matter of punctuation, a wavy dash is used on the right side of the bracket in place of the lemma word associated with the punctuation variant; thus "267–268 wide‸ . . . streams.] ~: . . . ~. $W^2$; ~: . . . ~, $W^1$" shows that *1820* and the draft have no punctuation after "wide" while the two transcripts have a colon, and that *1820,* the draft, and $W^2$ have a period after "streams" while $W^1$ has a comma. (Three dots, when they appear in both lemma and variant, always indicate the same ellipsis on both sides of the bracket—that is, the omitted words represented by the dots are the same in both the text and the variant.) One might have given these as separate variants ("267 wide‸] ~: $W^2$, $W^1$" and "268 streams.] ~, $W^1$"), but the principal substantive matter at hand—that $W^1$ connects 268 with the following lines rather than the preceding—is better shown by combining the variants in a single note.

For practical reasons (mainly the saving of space), the elements of hyphenated compounds are treated as separate words, and the hyphens are omitted from the lemmas (they are retained in Appendixes I and II); thus "oaks, branch-charmed" in 74 is represented by the lemma "oaks . . . charmed" and the second part of "dove-wings" in 217 is represented by "wings" (the presence or absence of a hyphen in the three MSS cited in the latter instance is not considered a substantive matter, and the information is not recorded). Also for practical reasons (in this case readability), italics and small capitals in the texts—for example, in *Endymion* III.689–711, 1022–27, and the speech prefixes and stage directions of *Otho* and *King Stephen* when they are cited independently of the speeches—are changed to roman and lowercase in the lemmas, and variants and other readings are regularly given in roman; where a MS has underscoring for emphasis, the fact is specially noticed by means of prose description. Other silent changes (see the list at the beginning of Appendix I) include the standardizing of ordinary quotation marks to double quotes, the expansion of some of Woodhouse's and other transcribers' abbreviations, and the regular capitalizing of any variant to the first word of a line (this last specifically in Woodhouse's notation of draft variants to *Endymion,* which he frequently wrote with initial lowercase).

The basic emendation note consists of a line reference, a lemma (in this case the emended text), a square bracket, the source or sources of the emendation, and then, after a semicolon, the copy-text reading along with any other information that needs to be recorded. Thus "6 above] *D*, $W^2$; about $W^1$, *1820*" indicates that the draft's and $W^2$'s "above" has been substituted in the text for the copy-text's (*1820*'s) "about," which originated as a copying error in $W^1$. (Peculiarities in accidentals are ignored in such notes; if the draft or $W^2$ had "Above" the capital would not be specially recorded.) When the emended reading does not appear in any of the collated texts, "ed" is cited in the apparatus note and the source, if the emendation has been made before, is explained in the Textual Notes (for example, *On Peace* "14 horrors] *ed*; Honors $W^3$," with Textual Note crediting the emendation to H. B. Forman).

All of the above (save perhaps the ascription of other people's emendations to "ed") is pretty much standard practice in current scholarly editing. For the describing of MS alterations, however, there is at present no agreed on methodology, and each editor has to devise his or her own according to the purposes and the character of the materials at hand. The most scientific and precise systems so far developed—the prose descriptions employed by Bowers in *Whitman's Manuscripts: "Leaves of Grass" (1860), A Parallel Text* (Chicago, 1955), the elaborate series of symbols invented to construct the "genetic text" in the edition of Melville's *Billy Budd* by Harrison Hayford and Merton M. Sealts, Jr. (Chicago, 1962), and the methodology combining elements of both of these recently proposed by Bowers in *SB,* 29 (1976), 212–264—either require too much space or are too complicated for use by any but the most advanced textual specialists. Among simpler systems the practices vary idiosyncratically (angle brackets, for example, have been employed in modern editions to indicate deletions, interlineations, illegible text, damage to the MS, text omitted in ellipses, and editorial interpolations), and none of these simpler systems is adequate to describe the many complex situations presented by Keats's MSS.

The apparatus of this edition records all recoverable substantive alterations in holograph MSS except (1) deletions where the deleted text is replaced (currently, interlineally, or in the following line) by the same word or words that were deleted and (2) alterations in fair copies (such as the interlineation of an omitted word) that clearly represent the correction of copying errors rather than fresh composition. As stated above, transcript alterations are also recorded when there is a chance that the transcript reading represents the same alteration in a now lost holograph. Markings and alterations by other hands than the principal writer of a MS are divided between the apparatus and the Textual Notes: those that led to changes in a subsequent authoritative text (as with some of Taylor's markings in the fair copy of *Endymion*) are included in the apparatus; the rest are described in the Textual Notes.

Angle brackets ⟨ ⟩ enclose deleted text, and curly braces { } enclose separate deletions *within* a deleted passage. The simplest types of note using angle brackets show a deletion replaced currently—for example, "3 eve's] ⟨evening⟩ Eve's *D*," where Keats first wrote "evening," then marked through the word and continued the line with "Eve's"—and a deletion appearing between lines—for example, "12/13 ⟨Shading across it⟩ *D*," where he started the next line after 12 with "Shading across it," then marked through the words and began again on a new line. Both kinds of bracket appear in "6/7 ⟨Like Clouds {that} whose {bosoms} thundrous bosoms⟩ *D*," where "that" and the first "bosoms" were separately deleted in an incomplete line that was finally deleted altogether. These brackets and the caret and wavy dash mentioned earlier are the only special devices that are used; all other kinds of alteration are described in ordinary words ("interlined above," "written beneath," "made out of," "squeezed in," and the like). The one potential ambiguity occurs with "written over," which here must be understood to mean "written in the same space as" (for example, "21 His] *written over* ⟨The⟩," where Keats first wrote "The" and then wrote "His" on top of—in the same space as—the original word). There is no single term for this kind of superimposition that does not at the same time suggest "written above" and therefore "interlined" ("superimposed" itself, meaning both "over" and "above," is as ambiguous as any of the others). In recording this type of alteration I have regularly enclosed the original text in angle brackets, considering it to be deleted by the text that is written over it. It will be no great mistake if "written over" is confused with "interlined above"—the results of the two kinds of alteration and the relationships of the original and revised text to the surrounding words are the same in each case.

Complex alterations are sometimes described in lengthy detail, but where the progress of revision can be worked out with certainty or a high degree of probability the successive versions are usually given (in the form "—— altered to ——," "successively [a] —— [b] —— [c] ——," and the like) without specific explanation of how the revision was effected. Thus in 27—"By her in stature the tall Amazon"—Keats first wrote "Placed by her side, the tallest Amazon" and then deleted the first five words, replacing them above the line with "By her in stature the," and at the same time (as we know by analyzing the meter) deleted "est" in "tallest." Rather than describe these revisions at length, as in the preceding sentence, the note reads "27 By . . . tall] Placed by her side, the tallest *altered to* By her in stature the tall *D*." In 178—"And touch'd with shade of bronzed obelisks"—he first wrote "And," then deleted the word and continued "With chequer black of bronsed Obelisks." Subsequently he deleted "chequer," replacing it above the line with "shading" (to produce "With shading black of bronsed Obelisks"); then deleted "shading" and "black of" and interlined "Touched" at the beginning of the line and "with the shade of" above the middle of the line (to produce "Touched with the shade of bronsed Obelisks"); and finally added "and" in the margin before "Touched" and deleted "the" in the later interlineation (to produce "and Touched with shade of bronsed Obelisks"). Garrod's description (using square brackets to enclose deletions, *over* to mean *above,* and *A* as the siglum for the draft MS)—"178 and (*marg.*) Touched with [the] shade of *over* [And With chequer black of] bronsed Obelisks *A* (*above* chequer *is written* shading)"—is in this case accurate, but it does not clearly indicate the order in which the revisions were made, and therefore is less helpful than the note in the present edition: "178 And . . . of] *successively* (*a*) ⟨And⟩ With chequer black of (*b*) With shading black of (*c*) Touched with the shade of (*d*) and Touched with shade of *D.*"

Alterations not associated with one another in a line are given in separate notes. Thus Keats's substitution of "Tall" for "The" at the beginning of 74 is recorded independently of the revision of "Oaks stand charmed" first to "Oaks dream charmed" and then to "Oaks, branch-charmed" later in the same line. The change to "Tall" could have been made separately at any stage of composition or revision in the MS, and it would be a mistake (since Keats frequently revised by deletion and interlineation before continuing currently on the original line) to connect "The" with any of the versions of the rest of the line or "Tall" with any version earlier than the final text. The combining of such independent alterations with variants from several sources of text has occasionally produced as many as half a dozen separate notes to a single line (as in *Blue!—'Tis the life of heaven* 6).

IN ORDER to avoid repeating earlier editors' errors I have taken my texts as directly as was practically possible from the copy-text documents. Those from *1817, 1818,* and *1820* were typed out from three University of Illinois copies (shelfmarks x821/K22/1817, x821/K22e/1818a, and x821/K22la, respectively) and then collated against half a dozen other copies at Illinois and Harvard. (In *1818* the second line on p. 112 is numbered "140" in some copies, "1 40" in others, and in examples of each kind the dash is sometimes missing at the end of III.394; but apart from the changes in the errata leaf that distinguish the successive issues or states of *1818,* no other typographical variant has been found among copies of the three original volumes.) Those from other sources were usually typed out from photocopies and then checked against the originals. The texts and the apparatus notes have of course been rechecked many times. It would be foolish to claim that they are free from error (in particular, there is no easy way to detect errors of omission); the practical procedures are, however, designed to guarantee that whatever errors exist are my own and not someone else's.

# Poems

## *Imitation of Spenser*

* * * * * * *

Now Morning from her orient chamber came,
And her first footsteps touch'd a verdant hill;
Crowning its lawny crest with amber flame,
Silv'ring the untainted gushes of its rill;
5 Which, pure from mossy beds, did down distill,
And after parting beds of simple flowers,
By many streams a little lake did fill,
Which round its marge reflected woven bowers,
And, in its middle space, a sky that never lowers.

10 There the king-fisher saw his plumage bright
Vieing with fish of brilliant dye below;
Whose silken fins and golden scalès light
Cast upward, through the waves, a ruby glow:
There saw the swan his neck of arched snow,
15 And oar'd himself along with majesty;
Sparkled his jetty eyes; his feet did show
Beneath the waves like Afric's ebony,
And on his back a fay reclined voluptuously.

Ah! could I tell the wonders of an isle
20 That in that fairest lake had placed been,
I could e'en Dido of her grief beguile;
Or rob from aged Lear his bitter teen:
For sure so fair a place was never seen,
Of all that ever charm'd romantic eye:
25 It seem'd an emerald in the silver sheen
Of the bright waters; or as when on high,
Through clouds of fleecy white, laughs the cœrulean sky.

And all around it dipp'd luxuriously
Slopings of verdure through the glassy tide,

*Imitation of Spenser.* Text (including heading) from *1817*. Emendations and other readings from Tom Keats's transcript (*TK*). 12 scalès] *ed*; scalés *TK*; scales' *1817* 20 that (*third word*)] *made out of* the *TK* 28 dipp'd] *interlined above* ⟨mixed⟩ *TK* 29 glassy] *TK*; glossy *1817*

30 Which, as it were in gentle amity,
Rippled delighted up the flowery side;
As if to glean the ruddy tears, it tried,
Which fell profusely from the rose-tree stem!
Haply it was the workings of its pride,
35 In strife to throw upon the shore a gem
Outvieing all the buds in Flora's diadem.

* * * * * * *

## *On Peace*

Oh Peace! and dost thou with thy presence bless
The dwellings of this war-surrounded isle;
Soothing with placid brow our late distress,
Making the triple kingdom brightly smile?
5 Joyful I hail thy presence; and I hail
The sweet companions that await on thee;
Complete my joy—let not my first wish fail,
Let the sweet mountain nymph thy favorite be,
With England's happiness proclaim Europa's liberty.
10 Oh Europe, let not sceptred tyrants see
That thou must shelter in thy former state;
Keep thy chains burst, and boldly say thou art free;
Give thy kings law—leave not uncurbed the great;
So with the horrors past thou'lt win thy happier fate.

## *Lines Written on 29 May, the Anniversary of Charles's Restoration, on Hearing the Bells Ringing*

Infatuate Britons, will you still proclaim
His memory, your direst, foulest shame?
Nor patriots revere?
Ah! when I hear each traitorous lying bell,
5 'Tis gallant Sydney's, Russell's, Vane's sad knell,
That pains my wounded ear.

*On Peace.* Text (including heading) from Woodhouse's $W^3$ transcript. 13 the great] *added in pencil in* $W^3$ 14 horrors] *ed*; Honors $W^3$

*Lines Written on 29 May.* Text (including heading) from Woodhouse's transcript in $W^3$, fol. 70 ($w^3$). Heading variant from Woodhouse's transcript in $W^3$, fol. 69 ($W^3$). *Heading* Lines . . . Ringing] Written on 29 May, the anniversary of the Restoration of Charles the 2$^d$ $W^3$

## *Stay, ruby breasted warbler, stay*

TUNE—"Julia to the Wood Robin"

1

Stay, ruby breasted warbler, stay,
And let me see thy sparkling eye;
Oh brush not yet the pearl strung spray,
Nor bow thy pretty head to fly.

2

5 Stay while I tell thee, fluttering thing,
That thou of love an emblem art;
Yes! patient plume thy little wing,
Whilst I my thoughts to thee impart.

3

When summer nights the dews bestow,
10 And summer suns enrich the day,
Thy notes the blossoms charm to blow,
Each opes delighted at thy lay.

4

So when in youth the eye's dark glance
Speaks pleasure from its circle bright,
15 The tones of love our joys enhance,
And make superiour each delight.

5

And when bleak storms resistless rove,
And ev'ry rural bliss destroy,
Nought comforts then the leafless grove
20 But thy soft note—its only joy.

6

E'en so the words of love beguile,
When pleasure's tree no longer bears,
And draw a soft endearing smile,
Amid the gloom of grief and tears.

*Stay, ruby breasted warbler.* Text from Georgiana Wylie's transcript (*GAW*). Variants from the two Woodhouse transcripts in $W^3$, fols. 78, 69 ($w^3$ and $W^3$, respectively). *Heading* Stay . . . stay] *ed*; Song (*followed by* Tune . . . Robin *as in the present text*) $w^3$, $W^3$, *GAW* 8 Whilst . . . thoughts] While . . . thought $w^3$, $W^3$ 19 leafless] hapless $W^3$ 20 soft] sweet $w^3$, $W^3$ 21 E'en] Even $w^3$, $W^3$ 22 longer] flower $w^3$, $W^3$

## *Fill for me a brimming bowl*

"What wondrous beauty! From this moment I efface from my mind all women." Terence's *Eunuch.* Act 2. Sc. 4

Fill for me a brimming bowl,
And let me in it drown my soul:
But put therein some drug design'd
To banish Woman from my mind.
5 For I want not the stream inspiring,
That heats the sense with lewd desiring;
But I want as deep a draught
As e'er from Lethe's waves was quaft,
From my despairing breast to charm
10 The image of the fairest form
That e'er my rev'ling eyes beheld,
That e'er my wand'ring fancy spell'd!

'Tis vain—away I cannot chace
The melting softness of that face—
15 The beaminess of those bright eyes—
That breast, earth's only paradise!

My sight will never more be blest,
For all I see has lost its zest;
Nor with delight can I explore
20 The classic page—the muse's lore.

Had she but known how beat my heart
And with one smile reliev'd its smart,
I should have felt a sweet relief,
I should have felt "the joy of grief"!
25 Yet as a Tuscan 'mid the snow
Of Lapland thinks on sweet Arno;
So for ever shall she be
The halo of my memory.

*Fill for me a brimming bowl.* Text from the extant holograph fair copy (*FC*). Variants from the two Woodhouse transcripts in $W^3$, fols. 64, 65 ($W^3x$ and $W^3y$, respectively). *Heading* Fill . . . bowl] *ed*; *no heading in FC*, $W^3x$, $W^3y$ *Epigraph* women] ⟨other⟩ Women *FC*; *no epigraph in* $W^3x$, $W^3y$ 1 a] the $W^3x$, $W^3y$ 6 heats . . . lewd] fills the Mind with fond $W^3x$, $W^3y$ 8 waves] wave $W^3y$ 9 breast] heart $W^3y$ 13 'Tis] In $W^3x$, $W^3y$ 18 zest] *Woodhouse notes in* $W^3x$ "*originally* rest" 20 the muse's] or Muse's $W^3y$ 22 one] a $W^3x$, $W^3y$ 27 So] Even so $W^3x$, $W^3y$

## *As from the darkening gloom a silver dove*

As from the darkening gloom a silver dove
Upsoars, and darts into the eastern light,
On pinions that nought moves but pure delight;
So fled thy soul into the realms above,
5 Regions of peace and everlasting love;
Where happy spirits, crowned with circlets bright
Of starry beam, and gloriously bedight,
Taste the high joy none but the bless'd can prove.
There thou or joinest the immortal quire
10 In melodies that even heaven fair
Fill with superior bliss, or, at desire
Of the omnipotent Father, cleavest the air,
On holy message sent.—What pleasures higher?
Wherefore does any grief our joy impair?

## *To Lord Byron*

Byron, how sweetly sad thy melody,
Attuning still the soul to tenderness,
As if soft Pity with unusual stress
Had touch'd her plaintive lute; and thou, being by,
5 Hadst caught the tones, nor suffered them to die.
O'ershading sorrow doth not make thee less
Delightful: thou thy griefs dost dress
With a bright halo, shining beamily;
As when a cloud a golden moon doth veil,
10 Its sides are tinged with a resplendent glow,
Through the dark robe oft amber rays prevail,
And like fair veins in sable marble flow.
Still warble, dying swan,—still tell the tale,
The enchanting tale—the tale of pleasing woe.

*As from the darkening gloom.* Text from Woodhouse's $W^3$ transcript. Variants from Woodhouse's $W^2$. *Heading* As . . . dove] *ed*; Sonnet $W^3$, $W^2$ 13 pleasures] pleasure's $W^2$

*To Lord Byron.* Text from Woodhouse's $W^2$ transcript. *Heading* To] *ed*; Sonnet / To $W^2$

## *Oh Chatterton! how very sad thy fate*

Oh Chatterton! how very sad thy fate!
Dear child of sorrow! son of misery!
How soon the film of death obscur'd that eye,
Whence genius wildly flash'd, and high debate!
5 How soon that voice, majestic and elate,
Melted in dying murmurs! O how nigh
Was night to thy fair morning! Thou didst die
A half-blown flower, which cold blasts amate.*
But this is past. Thou art among the stars
10 Of highest heaven; to the rolling spheres
Thou sweetly singest—nought thy hymning mars
Above the ingrate world and human fears.
On earth the good man base detraction bars
From thy fair name, and waters it with tears!

* Affright—Spenser.

## *Written on the Day That Mr. Leigh Hunt Left Prison*

What though, for showing truth to flatter'd state,
Kind Hunt was shut in prison, yet has he,
In his immortal spirit, been as free
As the sky-searching lark, and as elate.
5 Minion of grandeur! think you he did wait?
Think you he nought but prison walls did see,
Till, so unwilling, thou unturn'dst the key?
Ah, no! far happier, nobler was his fate!
In Spenser's halls he strayed, and bowers fair,
10 Culling enchanted flowers; and he flew
With daring Milton through the fields of air:
To regions of his own his genius true
Took happy flights. Who shall his fame impair
When thou art dead, and all thy wretched crew?

*Oh Chatterton.* Text from the unidentified transcript in Woodhouse's *W*[3] scrapbook (*Tr*). *Heading* Oh . . . fate] *ed*; Sonnet *Tr*

*Written on the Day That Mr. Leigh Hunt Left Prison.* Text (including title but omitting sonnet number) from *1817*.

## *To Hope*

When by my solitary hearth I sit,
  And hateful thoughts enwrap my soul in gloom;
When no fair dreams before my "mind's eye" flit,
  And the bare heath of life presents no bloom;
5    Sweet Hope, ethereal balm upon me shed,
    And wave thy silver pinions o'er my head.

Whene'er I wander, at the fall of night,
  Where woven boughs shut out the moon's bright ray,
Should sad Despondency my musings fright,
10  And frown, to drive fair Cheerfulness away,
    Peep with the moon-beams through the leafy roof,
    And keep that fiend Despondence far aloof.

Should Disappointment, parent of Despair,
  Strive for her son to seize my careless heart;
15 When, like a cloud, he sits upon the air,
  Preparing on his spell-bound prey to dart:
    Chace him away, sweet Hope, with visage bright,
    And fright him as the morning frightens night!

Whene'er the fate of those I hold most dear
20  Tells to my fearful breast a tale of sorrow,
O bright-eyed Hope, my morbid fancy cheer;
  Let me awhile thy sweetest comforts borrow:
    Thy heaven-born radiance around me shed,
    And wave thy silver pinions o'er my head!

25 Should e'er unhappy love my bosom pain,
  From cruel parents, or relentless fair;
O let me think it is not quite in vain
  To sigh out sonnets to the midnight air!
    Sweet Hope, ethereal balm upon me shed,
30  And wave thy silver pinions o'er my head!

In the long vista of the years to roll,
  Let me not see our country's honour fade:

*To Hope.* Text (including heading and end-date) from *1817*. Variants and other readings from the extant holograph fair copy (*FC*). 8 shut out] exclude *FC* 10 frown,] wish‸ *FC* 14 careless] careless *altered to* reckless *FC* 28 To] I *FC*

O let me see our land retain her soul,
Her pride, her freedom; and not freedom's shade.
35 From thy bright eyes unusual brightness shed—
Beneath thy pinions canopy my head!

Let me not see the patriot's high bequest,
Great Liberty! how great in plain attire!
With the base purple of a court oppress'd,
40 Bowing her head, and ready to expire:
But let me see thee stoop from heaven on wings
That fill the skies with silver glitterings!

And as, in sparkling majesty, a star
Gilds the bright summit of some gloomy cloud;
45 Brightening the half veil'd face of heaven afar:
So, when dark thoughts my boding spirit shroud,
Sweet Hope, celestial influence round me shed,
Waving thy silver pinions o'er my head.

February, 1815

## *Ode to Apollo*

1

In thy western halls of gold
When thou sittest in thy state,
Bards, that erst sublimely told
Heroic deeds, and sung of fate,
5 With fervour seize their adamantine lyres,
Whose cords are solid rays, and twinkle radiant fires.

2

There Homer with his nervous arms
Strikes the twanging harp of war,
And even the western splendour warms
10 While the trumpets sound afar;
But, what creates the most intense surprize,
His soul looks out through renovated eyes.

33 O‸] Ah! *FC* 33 her] ⟨our⟩ her *FC* 48 silver] silver *altered to* silken *FC*
*Ode to Apollo.* Text (including heading) from Woodhouse's $W^3$ transcript.

3

Then, through thy temple wide, melodious swells
The sweet majestic tone of Maro's lyre;
15 The soul delighted on each accent dwells,—
Enraptured dwells,—not daring to respire,
The while he tells of grief, around a funeral pyre.

4

'Tis awful silence then again:
Expectant stand the spheres;
20 Breathless the laurel'd peers;
Nor move, till ends the lofty strain,
Nor move till Milton's tuneful thunders cease,
And leave once more the ravish'd heavens in peace.

5

Thou biddest Shakspeare wave his hand,
25 And quickly forward spring
The Passions—a terrific band—
And each vibrates the string
That with its tyrant temper best accords,
While from their master's lips pour forth the inspiring words.

6

30 A silver trumpet Spenser blows,
And as its martial notes to silence flee,
From a virgin chorus flows
A hymn in praise of spotless chastity.
'Tis still!—Wild warblings from the Æolian lyre
35 Enchantment softly breathe, and tremblingly expire.

7

Next, thy Tasso's ardent numbers
Float along the pleased air,
Calling youth from idle slumbers,
Rousing them from pleasure's lair:—
40 Then o'er the strings his fingers gently move,
And melt the soul to pity and to love.

8

But when *Thou* joinest with the Nine,
And all the powers of song combine,

We listen here on earth:
45 The dying tones that fill the air,
And charm the ear of evening fair,
From thee, great God of Bards, receive their heavenly birth.

## *To Some Ladies*

What though while the wonders of nature exploring,
I cannot your light, mazy footsteps attend;
Nor listen to accents that, almost adoring,
Bless Cynthia's face, the enthusiast's friend:

5 Yet over the steep, whence the mountain stream rushes,
With you, kindest friends, in idea I muse;
Mark the clear tumbling crystal, its passionate gushes,
Its spray that the wild flower kindly bedews.

Why linger you so, the wild labyrinth strolling?
10 Why breathless, unable your bliss to declare?
Ah! you list to the nightingale's tender condoling,
Responsive to sylphs, in the moon beamy air.

'Tis morn, and the flowers with dew are yet drooping,
I see you are treading the verge of the sea:
15 And now! ah, I see it—you just now are stooping
To pick up the keep-sake intended for me.

If a cherub, on pinions of silver descending,
Had brought me a gem from the fret-work of heaven;
And, smiles with his star-cheering voice sweetly blending,
20 The blessings of Tighe had melodiously given;

It had not created a warmer emotion
Than the present, fair nymphs, I was blest with from you,

*To Some Ladies.* Text (including heading) from *1817*. Variants and other readings from the extant holograph fair copy (*FC*). The apparatus also includes variants from a now lost source noted by Woodhouse in his interleaved *1817* (*RW var*). *Heading* Some Ladies] the Misses M—— (*with* at Hastings *added in another hand*) *FC*. *In his interleaved 1817 Woodhouse inserted a comma after the title and then added* who were at Hastings, in return for a present of some shells (*he identifies the ladies in shorthand as "the Misses Mathew"*) 5 rushes] gushes *FC* 6 muse] *FC* (⟨rove⟩ muse); rove *1817* 8 Its] In *FC* 9 Why . . . so] Ah! why do you start *RW var*

Than the shell, from the bright golden sands of the ocean
Which the emerald waves at your feet gladly threw.

25 For, indeed, 'tis a sweet and peculiar pleasure,
(And blissful is he who such happiness finds,)
To possess but a span of the hour of leisure,
In elegant, pure, and aerial minds.

## *On Receiving a Curious Shell, and a Copy of Verses, from the Same Ladies*

Hast thou from the caves of Golconda, a gem
Pure as the ice-drop that froze on the mountain?
Bright as the humming-bird's green diadem,
When it flutters in sun-beams that shine through a fountain?

5 Hast thou a goblet for dark sparkling wine?
That goblet right heavy, and massy, and gold?
And splendidly mark'd with the story divine
Of Armida the fair, and Rinaldo the bold?

Hast thou a steed with a mane richly flowing?
10 Hast thou a sword that thine enemy's smart is?
Hast thou a trumpet rich melodies blowing?
And wear'st thou the shield of the fam'd Britomartis?

What is it that hangs from thy shoulder, so brave,
Embroidered with many a spring peering flower?

24 Which . . . threw] Oh down by yon bank, where the waves gently flow *RW var* (*but written in different ink from the rest of the variants and possibly Woodhouse's own suggested revision*) 24 gladly] kindly *RW var* (*a separate variant from the preceding*) 25 peculiar] superior *RW var* 27 possess] have *RW var* 27 span of] span in *RW var, FC* (san *for* span in *FC*) 28 In] Of *RW var, FC*

*On Receiving a Curious Shell.* Text (including heading) from *1817*. Variants and other readings from the transcripts by George Keats (*GK*) and Georgiana Wylie (*GAW*—extant for 1–12 only), the extant holograph fair copy (*FC*), and Tom Keats's transcript (*TK*). *Heading* On . . . Ladies] Written on receiving a Copy of Tom Moore's "Golden Chain," and a most beautiful Dome shaped Shell from a Lady *GK* (*the title written at the end of the text*); Eric, / Written on his receiving a Copy of T. Moore's "Golden Chain" and a dome Shaped Shell from a Lady *GAW*; On receiving a curious Shell and a copy of verses *TK* 2 drop] drops *GAW* 4 shine] shines *TK* 5 for] of *FC* 5 wine] wines *TK* 6 right] full *GK, GAW* 7 mark'd] wrought *GK, GAW* 9 with a] with his *GK, GAW, FC* 9 richly] thickly *GK, GAW* 10 that] which *GK, GAW* 10 thine] thy *GAW* 13 thy] the *FC* 14 peering] peering *altered to* opening *FC*

15 Is it a scarf that thy fair lady gave?
And hastest thou now to that fair lady's bower?

Ah! courteous Sir Knight, with large joy thou art crown'd;
Full many the glories that brighten thy youth!
I will tell thee my blisses, which richly abound
20 In magical powers to bless, and to sooth.

On this scroll thou seest written in characters fair
A sun-beamy tale of a wreath, and a chain;
And, warrior, it nurtures the property rare
Of charming my mind from the trammels of pain.

25 This canopy mark: 'tis the work of a fay;
Beneath its rich shade did King Oberon languish,
When lovely Titania was far, far away,
And cruelly left him to sorrow, and anguish.

There, oft would he bring from his soft sighing lute
30 Wild strains to which, spell-bound, the nightingales listened;
The wondering spirits of heaven were mute,
And tears 'mong the dewdrops of morning oft glistened.

In this little dome, all those melodies strange,
Soft, plaintive, and melting, for ever will sigh;
35 Nor e'er will the notes from their tenderness change;
Nor e'er will the music of Oberon die.

So, when I am in a voluptuous vein,
I pillow my head on the sweets of the rose,
And list to the tale of the wreath, and the chain,
40 Till its echoes depart; then I sink to repose.

Adieu, valiant Eric! with joy thou art crown'd;
Full many the glories that brighten thy youth;
I too have my blisses, which richly abound
In magical powers, to bless and to sooth.

17 Knight . . . large] Eric! with *GK* 19 I . . . thee] I too, have *GK* 23 warrior . . . the] lo! it possesses this *GK* 28 cruelly] ruthlessly *FC* 29 There] Then *GK*, *FC* 29 sighing] speaking *GK* 31 wondering . . . were] Hymns of the wondering Spirits were *GK*; wandering spirits of Heaven are *TK* 37 So] And *GK*, *FC* 39 tale] song *GK* 42 Full] And *FC* 43 blisses] bliss *TK*

## *O come, dearest Emma! the rose is full blown*

1

O come, dearest Emma! the rose is full blown,
And the riches of Flora are lavishly strown;
The air is all softness, and chrystal the streams,
And the west is resplendently cloathed in beams.

2

5 We will hasten, my fair, to the opening glades,
The quaintly carv'd seats, and the freshening shades;
Where the fairies are chaunting their evening hymns,
And in the last sun-beam the sylph lightly swims.

3

And when thou art weary, I'll find thee a bed,
10 Of mosses, and flowers, to pillow thy head;
There, beauteous Emma, I'll sit at thy feet,
While my story of love I enraptur'd repeat.

4

So fondly I'll breathe, and so softly I'll sigh,
Thou wilt think that some amorous zephyr is nigh;
15 Ah! no—as I breathe it, I press thy fair knee,
And then, thou wilt know that the sigh comes from me.

5

Then why, lovely girl, should we lose all these blisses?
That mortal's a fool who such happiness misses;
So smile acquiescence, and give me thy hand,
20 With love-looking eyes, and with voice sweetly bland.

*O come, dearest Emma.* Text from the extant holograph fair copy (*FC*). Variants from the two Woodhouse transcripts in *W*³, fols. 77, 78 (*w*³ and **w**³, respectively), and the transcript by George Keats (*GK*). *Heading* O . . . blown] *ed*; To Emma **w**³; Song *FC*; *no heading in w*³, *GK* 1 dearest Emma] my dear Emma *w*³, **w**³; Georgiana *GK* 2, 4 And the] The *w*³, **w**³, *GK* 5 We . . . glades] Oh! come let us haste to the freshening shades *w*³, **w**³, *GK* 6 freshening shades] opening glades *w*³, **w**³, *GK* 11 There . . . Emma] And there Georgiana *GK* 13 fondly] softly *w*³, **w**³ 15 Ah . . . I] Yet, no! as I breathe, I will *w*³, **w**³, *GK* 17 Then . . . lovely] Ah! why, dearest *w*³, **w**³, *GK*

## *Woman! when I behold thee flippant, vain*

Woman! when I behold thee flippant, vain,
 Inconstant, childish, proud, and full of fancies;
 Without that modest softening that enhances
The downcast eye, repentant of the pain
5 That its mild light creates to heal again:
 E'en then, elate, my spirit leaps, and prances,
 E'en then my soul with exultation dances
For that to love, so long, I've dormant lain:
But when I see thee meek, and kind, and tender,
10 Heavens! how desperately do I adore
Thy winning graces;—to be thy defender
 I hotly burn—to be a Calidore—
A very Red Cross Knight—a stout Leander—
 Might I be loved by thee like these of yore.

15 Light feet, dark violet eyes, and parted hair;
 Soft dimpled hands, white neck, and creamy breast,
 Are things on which the dazzled senses rest
Till the fond, fixed eyes forget they stare.
From such fine pictures, heavens! I cannot dare
20 To turn my admiration, though unpossess'd
 They be of what is worthy,—though not drest
In lovely modesty, and virtues rare.
Yet these I leave as thoughtless as a lark;
 These lures I straight forget,—e'en ere I dine,
25 Or thrice my palate moisten: but when I mark
 Such charms with mild intelligences shine,
My ear is open like a greedy shark,
 To catch the tunings of a voice divine.

Ah! who can e'er forget so fair a being?
30 Who can forget her half retiring sweets?
 God! she is like a milk-white lamb that bleats
For man's protection. Surely the All-seeing,
Who joys to see us with his gifts agreeing,
 Will never give him pinions, who intreats
35 Such innocence to ruin,—who vilely cheats
A dove-like bosom. In truth there is no freeing
One's thoughts from such a beauty; when I hear

*Woman! when I behold thee.* Text from *1817*. Heading supplied by editor.

A lay that once I saw her hand awake,
Her form seems floating palpable, and near;
40 Had I e'er seen her from an arbour take
A dewy flower, oft would that hand appear,
And o'er my eyes the trembling moisture shake.

## *O Solitude! if I must with thee dwell*

O Solitude! if I must with thee dwell,
Let it not be among the jumbled heap
Of murky buildings; climb with me the steep,—
Nature's observatory—whence the dell,
5 Its flowery slopes, its river's crystal swell,
May seem a span; let me thy vigils keep
'Mongst boughs pavillion'd, where the deer's swift leap
Startles the wild bee from the fox-glove bell.
But though I'll gladly trace these scenes with thee,
10 Yet the sweet converse of an innocent mind,
Whose words are images of thoughts refin'd,
Is my soul's pleasure; and it sure must be
Almost the highest bliss of human-kind,
When to thy haunts two kindred spirits flee.

## *To George Felton Mathew*

Sweet are the pleasures that to verse belong,
And doubly sweet a brotherhood in song;
Nor can remembrance, Mathew! bring to view
A fate more pleasing, a delight more true
5 Than that in which the brother Poets joy'd,
Who with combined powers, their wit employ'd
To raise a trophy to the drama's muses.
The thought of this great partnership diffuses

*O Solitude.* Text from *1817*. Variants and other readings from the holograph fair copies in the Morgan and Clark libraries ($FC^1$ and $FC^2$, respectively), the *Examiner* version (*Ex*), and Tom Keats's transcript (*TK*). *Heading* O . . . dwell] *ed*; Sonnet $FC^1$; To Solitude *Ex*; Sonnet to Solitude *TK*; *no heading* (*other than sonnet number*) *in* $FC^2$, *1817* 9–10 But . . . Yet] Ah! fain would I frequent such scenes with thee; / But *Ex* 9 I'll] I'd $FC^1$, *TK*; I'd *altered to* I'll $FC^2$ 10 innocent] elegant $FC^1$ 11 are] as $FC^2$ 12 pleasure . . . sure] Pleasure. It certainly $FC^1$

*To George Felton Mathew.* Text (including heading and end-date) from *1817*.

Over the genius loving heart, a feeling
10 Of all that's high, and great, and good, and healing.

Too partial friend! fain would I follow thee
Past each horizon of fine poesy;
Fain would I echo back each pleasant note
As o'er Sicilian seas, clear anthems float
15 'Mong the light skimming gondolas far parted,
Just when the sun his farewell beam has darted:
But 'tis impossible; far different cares
Beckon me sternly from soft "Lydian airs,"
And hold my faculties so long in thrall,
20 That I am oft in doubt whether at all
I shall again see Phœbus in the morning:
Or flush'd Aurora in the roseate dawning!
Or a white Naiad in a rippling stream;
Or a rapt seraph in a moonlight beam;
25 Or again witness what with thee I've seen,
The dew by fairy feet swept from the green,
After a night of some quaint jubilee
Which every elf and fay had come to see:
When bright processions took their airy march
30 Beneath the curved moon's triumphal arch.

But might I now each passing moment give
To the coy muse, with me she would not live
In this dark city, nor would condescend
'Mid contradictions her delights to lend.
35 Should e'er the fine-eyed maid to me be kind,
Ah! surely it must be whene'er I find
Some flowery spot, sequester'd, wild, romantic,
That often must have seen a poet frantic;
Where oaks, that erst the Druid knew, are growing,
40 And flowers, the glory of one day, are blowing;
Where the dark-leav'd laburnum's drooping clusters
Reflect athwart the stream their yellow lustres,
And intertwined the cassia's arms unite,
With its own drooping buds, but very white;
45 Where on one side are covert branches hung,
'Mong which the nightingales have always sung
In leafy quiet: where to pry, aloof,
Atween the pillars of the sylvan roof,
Would be to find where violet beds were nestling,

50 And where the bee with cowslip bells was wrestling.
There must be too a ruin dark, and gloomy,
To say "joy not too much in all that's bloomy."

Yet this is vain—O Mathew, lend thy aid
To find a place where I may greet the maid—
55 Where we may soft humanity put on,
And sit, and rhyme and think on Chatterton;
And that warm-hearted Shakspeare sent to meet him
Four laurell'd spirits, heaven-ward to intreat him.
With reverence would we speak of all the sages
60 Who have left streaks of light athwart their ages:
And thou shouldst moralize on Milton's blindness,
And mourn the fearful dearth of human kindness
To those who strove with the bright golden wing
Of genius, to flap away each sting
65 Thrown by the pitiless world. We next could tell
Of those who in the cause of freedom fell;
Of our own Alfred, of Helvetian Tell;
Of him whose name to ev'ry heart's a solace,
High-minded and unbending William Wallace.
70 While to the rugged north our musing turns
We well might drop a tear for him, and Burns.

Felton! without incitements such as these,
How vain for me the niggard muse to tease:
For thee, she will thy every dwelling grace,
75 And make "a sun-shine in a shady place":
For thou wast once a flowret blooming wild,
Close to the source, bright, pure, and undefil'd,
Whence gush the streams of song: in happy hour
Came chaste Diana from her shady bower,
80 Just as the sun was from the east uprising;
And, as for him some gift she was devising,
Beheld thee, pluck'd thee, cast thee in the stream
To meet her glorious brother's greeting beam.
I marvel much that thou hast never told
85 How, from a flower, into a fish of gold
Apollo chang'd thee; how thou next didst seem
A black-eyed swan upon the widening stream;
And when thou first didst in that mirror trace
The placid features of a human face:
90 That thou hast never told thy travels strange,

And all the wonders of the mazy range
O'er pebbly crystal, and o'er golden sands;
Kissing thy daily food from Naiad's pearly hands.

November, 1815

## *Had I a man's fair form, then might my sighs*

Had I a man's fair form, then might my sighs
  Be echoed swiftly through that ivory shell
  Thine ear, and find thy gentle heart; so well
Would passion arm me for the enterprize:
5 But ah! I am no knight whose foeman dies;
  No cuirass glistens on my bosom's swell;
  I am no happy shepherd of the dell
Whose lips have trembled with a maiden's eyes.
Yet must I dote upon thee,—call thee sweet,
10 Sweeter by far than Hybla's honied roses
    When steep'd in dew rich to intoxication.
Ah! I will taste that dew, for me 'tis meet,
  And when the moon her pallid face discloses,
    I'll gather some by spells, and incantation.

## *Hadst thou liv'd in days of old*

Hadst thou liv'd in days of old,
O what wonders had been told
Of thy lively countenance,
And thy humid eyes that dance

*Had I a man's fair form.* Text from *1817*. Variants from Tom Keats's transcript (*TK*). *Heading* Had . . . sighs] *ed*; Sonnet *TK*; To * * * * * * (*preceded by sonnet number*) *1817* 14 incantation] incantations *TK*

*Hadst thou liv'd in days of old.* Text from *1817*. Variants and other readings from the two Woodhouse transcripts in *W*³, fols. 89, 85 (*w*³ and *W*³, respectively), and the extant holograph fair copy (*FC*). *Heading* Hadst . . . old] *ed*; To Miss —— *FC*; To * * * * *1817*; *no heading in w*³, *W*³ 3–36 Of . . . ten]

Of thy lively dimpled face,
Of thy footsteps full of grace;
Of thy hair's luxurious darkling,
Of thine eyes' expressive sparkling,
And thy voice's swelling rapture,
Taking hearts a ready capture.
Oh! if thou had'st breathed then,
Thou hadst made the Muses ten *w*³, *W*³

(*W*³ *has* And *for* Of *in the second of these lines*)

5 In the midst of their own brightness;
In the very fane of lightness.
Over which thine eyebrows, leaning,
Picture out each lovely meaning:
In a dainty bend they lie,
10 Like to streaks across the sky,
Or the feathers from a crow,
Fallen on a bed of snow.
Of thy dark hair that extends
Into many graceful bends:
15 As the leaves of hellebore
Turn to whence they sprung before.
And behind each ample curl
Peeps the richness of a pearl.
Downward too flows many a tress
20 With a glossy waviness;
Full, and round like globes that rise
From the censer to the skies
Through sunny air. Add too, the sweetness
Of thy honied voice; the neatness
25 Of thine ankle lightly turn'd:
With those beauties, scarce discern'd,
Kept with such sweet privacy,
That they seldom meet the eye
Of the little loves that fly
30 Round about with eager pry.
Saving when, with freshening lave,
Thou dipp'st them in the taintless wave;
Like twin water lillies, born
In the coolness of the morn.
35 O, if thou hadst breathed then,
Now the Muses had been ten.
Couldst thou wish for lineage higher
Than twin sister of Thalia?
At least for ever, evermore,
40 Will I call the Graces four.

Hadst thou liv'd when chivalry
Lifted up her lance on high,
Tell me what thou wouldst have been?
Ah! I see the silver sheen
45 Of thy broidered, floating vest

16 Turn] Turn⟨s⟩ *FC* 28 seldom] never *FC* 28 eye] Eye⟨s⟩ *FC* 38 twin] the *FC*

Cov'ring half thine ivory breast;
Which, O heavens! I should see,
But that cruel destiny
Has placed a golden cuirass there;
50 Keeping secret what is fair.
Like sunbeams in a cloudlet nested
Thy locks in knightly casque are rested:
O'er which bend four milky plumes
Like the gentle lilly's blooms
55 Springing from a costly vase.
See with what a stately pace
Comes thine alabaster steed;
Servant of heroic deed!
O'er his loins, his trappings glow
60 Like the northern lights on snow.
Mount his back! thy sword unsheath!
Sign of the enchanter's death;
Bane of every wicked spell;
Silencer of dragon's yell.
65 Alas! thou this wilt never do:
Thou art an enchantress too,
And wilt surely never spill
Blood of those whose eyes can kill.

## *I am as brisk*

I am as brisk
As a bottle of whisk-
Ey and as nimble
As a milliner's thimble.

49 Has] Hast *FC*  51 sunbeams . . . cloudlet] light in wreathed cloudlets $w^3$, $W^3$  51 nested] rested *FC*  52 locks . . . are] hair in gilden casque is $w^3$, $W^3$  52 are] *interlined above* ⟨is⟩ *FC*  53 O'er . . . bend] From the which $W^3$, *FC* (*and also as a variant in* $w^3$*—see Textual Note*)  54 gentle lilly's] fleur-de-luce's $w^3$, $W^3$, *FC*  55 a costly] an Indian $w^3$, $W^3$  57 Comes] Moves $w^3$, $W^3$ (⟨Comes⟩ Moves *in* $W^3$)  59–60 O'er . . . snow.] *written in the margin in FC with a mark for insertion after 58*  59 loins] limbs $w^3$, $W^3$  59 his trappings] the Trappings *FC*  62 enchanter's] Magician's $w^3$, $W^3$ (*interlined above* ⟨Enchanter's⟩ *in* $W^3$)  63–64 Bane . . . yell.] *written vertically in the margin in FC and followed by a line of x's and dashes (65–68 are not in FC)*  63 every wicked] the Enchanter's $w^3$, $W^3$  65 Alas] But ah $w^3$, $W^3$  67 wilt surely] thou sure wilt $w^3$, $W^3$  *After* 68

Ah me! whither shall I flee?
Thou hast metamorphosed me!
Do not let me sigh and pine,
'Prythee, be my Valentine! $w^3$, $W^3$

*I am as brisk.* Text from the extant holograph. Heading supplied by editor.

## *Give me women, wine, and snuff*

Give me women, wine, and snuff
Untill I cry out "hold, enough!"
You may do so sans objection
Till the day of resurrection;
5 For, bless my beard, they aye shall be
My beloved Trinity.

## *Specimen of an Induction to a Poem*

Lo! I must tell a tale of chivalry;
For large white plumes are dancing in mine eye.
Not like the formal crest of latter days:
But bending in a thousand graceful ways;
5 So graceful, that it seems no mortal hand,
Or e'en the touch of Archimago's wand,
Could charm them into such an attitude.
We must think rather, that in playful mood,
Some mountain breeze had turned its chief delight,
10 To show this wonder of its gentle might.
Lo! I must tell a tale of chivalry;
For while I muse, the lance points slantingly
Athwart the morning air: some lady sweet,
Who cannot feel for cold her tender feet,
15 From the worn top of some old battlement
Hails it with tears, her stout defender sent:
And from her own pure self no joy dissembling,
Wraps round her ample robe with happy trembling.
Sometimes, when the good knight his rest would take,
20 It is reflected, clearly, in a lake,
With the young ashen boughs, 'gainst which it rests,
And th' half seen mossiness of linnets' nests.
Ah! shall I ever tell its cruelty,
When the fire flashes from a warrior's eye,

*Give me women, wine, and snuff.* Text from the extant holograph (arbitrarily cited as *D*). Heading supplied by editor. 4 the] *ed*; y$^{e}$ *D*

*Specimen of an Induction.* Text (including heading) from *1817*. Variants and other readings from Tom Keats's transcript (*TK*). *Heading* Specimen . . . Poem] Induction *TK* 8 think] say *TK* 9 its] his *TK* 10 this . . . its] the . . . his *TK* 17 from . . . dissembling] now, no more her anxious grief remembring *TK*

25 And his tremendous hand is grasping it,
And his dark brow for very wrath is knit?
Or when his spirit, with more calm intent,
Leaps to the honors of a tournament,
And makes the gazers round about the ring
30 Stare at the grandeur of the ballancing?
No, no! this is far off:—then how shall I
Revive the dying tones of minstrelsy,
Which linger yet about lone gothic arches,
In dark green ivy, and among wild larches?
35 How sing the splendour of the revelries,
When butts of wine are drunk off to the lees?
And that bright lance, against the fretted wall,
Beneath the shade of stately banneral,
Is slung with shining cuirass, sword, and shield,
40 Where ye may see a spur in bloody field?
Light-footed damsels move with gentle paces
Round the wide hall, and show their happy faces;
Or stand in courtly talk by fives and sevens:
Like those fair stars that twinkle in the heavens.
45 Yet must I tell a tale of chivalry:
Or wherefore comes that steed so proudly by?
Wherefore more proudly does the gentle knight
Rein in the swelling of his ample might?

Spenser! thy brows are arched, open, kind,
50 And come like a clear sun-rise to my mind;
And always does my heart with pleasure dance,
When I think on thy noble countenance:
Where never yet was ought more earthly seen
Than the pure freshness of thy laurels green.
55 Therefore, great bard, I not so fearfully
Call on thy gentle spirit to hover nigh
My daring steps: or if thy tender care,
Thus startled unaware,
Be jealous that the foot of other wight
60 Should madly follow that bright path of light
Trac'd by thy lov'd Libertas; he will speak,

34 among] among⟨st⟩ *TK* 35 splendour] grandeur *TK* 37 that . . . lance] this . . . spear (this *made out of* the) *TK* 40 ye] you *TK* 44 that] which *TK* 46 steed] *TK*; knight *1817* 57 tender] gentle *TK* 59 other] living *TK*

And tell thee that my prayer is very meek;
That I will follow with due reverence,
And start with awe at mine own strange pretence.
65 Him thou wilt hear; so I will rest in hope
To see wide plains, fair trees and lawny slope:
The morn, the eve, the light, the shade, the flowers;
Clear streams, smooth lakes, and overlooking towers.

## *Calidore:*
## *A Fragment*

Young Calidore is paddling o'er the lake;
His healthful spirit eager and awake
To feel the beauty of a silent eve,
Which seem'd full loath this happy world to leave;
5 The light dwelt o'er the scene so lingeringly.
He bares his forehead to the cool blue sky,
And smiles at the far clearness all around,
Until his heart is well nigh over wound,
And turns for calmness to the pleasant green
10 Of easy slopes, and shadowy trees that lean
So elegantly o'er the waters' brim
And show their blossoms trim.
Scarce can his clear and nimble eye-sight follow
The freaks, and dartings of the black-wing'd swallow,
15 Delighting much, to see it half at rest,
Dip so refreshingly its wings, and breast
'Gainst the smooth surface, and to mark anon,
The widening circles into nothing gone.

And now the sharp keel of his little boat
20 Comes up with ripple, and with easy float,
And glides into a bed of water lillies:
Broad leav'd are they and their white canopies
Are upward turn'd to catch the heavens' dew.
Near to a little island's point they grew;

*Calidore.* Text (including heading) from *1817*. Variants from Tom Keats's transcript (*TK*). *Subtitle* A Fragment] *not in TK* 6 cool] clear *TK* 8 is] was *TK* 10 that] which *TK* 16 its] his *TK*

25 Whence Calidore might have the goodliest view
Of this sweet spot of earth. The bowery shore
Went off in gentle windings to the hoar
And light blue mountains: but no breathing man
With a warm heart, and eye prepared to scan
30 Nature's clear beauty, could pass lightly by
Objects that look'd out so invitingly
On either side. These, gentle Calidore
Greeted, as he had known them long before.

The sidelong view of swelling leafiness,
35 Which the glad setting sun in gold doth dress;
Whence ever and anon the jay outsprings,
And scales upon the beauty of its wings.

The lonely turret, shatter'd, and outworn,
Stands venerably proud; too proud to mourn
40 Its long lost grandeur: fir trees grow around,
Aye dropping their hard fruit upon the ground.

The little chapel with the cross above
Upholding wreaths of ivy; the white dove,
That on the window spreads its feathers light,
45 And seems from purple clouds to wing its flight.

Green tufted islands casting their soft shades
Across the lake; sequester'd leafy glades,
That through the dimness of their twilight show
Large dock leaves, spiral foxgloves, or the glow
50 Of the wild cat's eyes, or the silvery stems
Of delicate birch trees, or long grass which hems
A little brook. The youth had long been viewing
These pleasant things, and heaven was bedewing
The mountain flowers, when his glad senses caught
55 A trumpet's silver voice. Ah! it was fraught
With many joys for him: the warder's ken
Had found white coursers prancing in the glen:
Friends very dear to him he soon will see;
So pushes off his boat most eagerly,

28 mountains: but] ~. But sure *TK* 29 and] an *TK* 38 shatter'd] shuttered *TK* (*but see Textual Note*) 40 fir trees] Laburnums *TK* 41 Aye . . . upon] And bow their golden honors to *TK* 42 the cross] its cross *TK* 44 window . . . its] *TK*; windows . . . his *1817* 48 That] Which *TK* 57 found] seen *TK*

60 And soon upon the lake he skims along,
Deaf to the nightingale's first under-song;
Nor minds he the white swans that dream so sweetly:
His spirit flies before him so completely.

And now he turns a jutting point of land,
65 Whence may be seen the castle gloomy, and grand:
Nor will a bee buzz round two swelling peaches,
Before the point of his light shallop reaches
Those marble steps that through the water dip:
Now over them he goes with hasty trip,
70 And scarcely stays to ope the folding doors:
Anon he leaps along the oaken floors
Of halls and corridors.

Delicious sounds! those little bright-eyed things
That float about the air on azure wings,
75 Had been less heartfelt by him than the clang
Of clattering hoofs; into the court he sprang,
Just as two noble steeds, and palfreys twain,
Were slanting out their necks with loosened rein;
While from beneath the threat'ning portcullis
80 They brought their happy burthens. What a kiss,
What gentle squeeze he gave each lady's hand!
How tremblingly their delicate ancles spann'd!
Into how sweet a trance his soul was gone,
While whisperings of affection
85 Made him delay to let their tender feet
Come to the earth; with an incline so sweet
From their low palfreys o'er his neck they bent:
And whether there were tears of languishment,
Or that the evening dew had pearl'd their tresses,
90 He feels a moisture on his cheek, and blesses
With lips that tremble, and with glistening eye,
All the soft luxury
That nestled in his arms. A dimpled hand,
Fair as some wonder out of fairy land,
95 Hung from his shoulder like the drooping flowers
Of whitest cassia, fresh from summer showers:
And this he fondled with his happy cheek
As if for joy he would no further seek;

60 upon] across *TK* 69 goes] flies *TK* 70 stays] stops *TK* 74 about] along *TK* 78 with] from *TK* 85 tender] pretty *TK*

When the kind voice of good Sir Clerimond
100 Came to his ear, like something from beyond
His present being: so he gently drew
His warm arms, thrilling now with pulses new,
From their sweet thrall, and forward gently bending,
Thank'd heaven that his joy was never ending;
105 While 'gainst his forehead he devoutly press'd
A hand heaven made to succour the distress'd;
A hand that from the world's bleak promontory
Had lifted Calidore for deeds of glory.

Amid the pages, and the torches' glare,
110 There stood a knight, patting the flowing hair
Of his proud horse's mane: he was withal
A man of elegance, and stature tall:
So that the waving of his plumes would be
High as the berries of a wild ash tree,
115 Or as the winged cap of Mercury.
His armour was so dexterously wrought
In shape, that sure no living man had thought
It hard, and heavy steel: but that indeed
It was some glorious form, some splendid weed,
120 In which a spirit new come from the skies
Might live, and show itself to human eyes.
'Tis the far-fam'd, the brave Sir Gondibert,
Said the good man to Calidore alert;
While the young warrior with a step of grace
125 Came up,—a courtly smile upon his face,
And mailed hand held out, ready to greet
The large-eyed wonder, and ambitious heat
Of the aspiring boy; who as he led
Those smiling ladies, often turned his head
130 To admire the visor arched so gracefully
Over a knightly brow; while they went by
The lamps that from the high-roof'd hall were pendent,
And gave the steel a shining quite transcendent.

Soon in a pleasant chamber they are seated;
135 The sweet-lipp'd ladies have already greeted
All the green leaves that round the window clamber,

101 His] This *TK* 103 gently] meekly *TK* 122 'Tis . . . Gondibert] Tis brave Sir Gondibert the far fame'd *marked for alteration to* Tis the far fame'd the brave Sir Gondibert *TK*

To show their purple stars, and bells of amber.
Sir Gondibert has doff'd his shining steel,
Gladdening in the free, and airy feel
140 Of a light mantle; and while Clerimond
Is looking round about him with a fond,
And placid eye, young Calidore is burning
To hear of knightly deeds, and gallant spurning
Of all unworthiness; and how the strong of arm
145 Kept off dismay, and terror, and alarm
From lovely woman: while brimful of this,
He gave each damsel's hand so warm a kiss,
And had such manly ardour in his eye,
That each at other look'd half staringly;
150 And then their features started into smiles
Sweet as blue heavens o'er enchanted isles.

Softly the breezes from the forest came,
Softly they blew aside the taper's flame;
Clear was the song from Philomel's far bower;
155 Grateful the incense from the lime-tree flower;
Mysterious, wild, the far heard trumpet's tone;
Lovely the moon in ether, all alone:
Sweet too the converse of these happy mortals,
As that of busy spirits when the portals
160 Are closing in the west; or that soft humming
We hear around when Hesperus is coming.
Sweet be their sleep. * * * * * * * * *

## *To one who has been long in city pent*

To one who has been long in city pent,
'Tis very sweet to look into the fair
And open face of heaven,—to breathe a prayer
Full in the smile of the blue firmament.
5 Who is more happy, when, with heart's content,
Fatigued he sinks into some pleasant lair
Of wavy grass, and reads a debonair

139 airy] easy *TK* 147 warm] sweet *TK* 158 these] those *TK* 160 that] the *TK*
*To one who has been long in city pent.* Text from *1817*. Variants from the transcripts by Georgiana Wylie (*GAW*) and Tom Keats (*TK*). *Heading* To . . . pent] *ed*; Sonnet. Written in the Fields June 1816 *GAW*; Sonnet *TK*; *no heading* (*other than sonnet number*) *in 1817* 2 into] upon *GAW* 4 blue] bright *GAW, TK* 5 heart's] *TK*; hearts' *GAW*; hearts *1817* 6 into some] upon a *GAW* 7 a] some *GAW*

And gentle tale of love and languishment?
Returning home at evening, with an ear
10 Catching the notes of Philomel,—an eye
Watching the sailing cloudlet's bright career,
He mourns that day so soon has glided by:
E'en like the passage of an angel's tear
That falls through the clear ether silently.

## *Oh! how I love, on a fair summer's eve*

Oh! how I love, on a fair summer's eve,
When streams of light pour down the golden west,
And on the balmy zephyrs tranquil rest
The silver clouds, far—far away to leave
5 All meaner thoughts, and take a sweet reprieve
From little cares:—to find, with easy quest,
A fragrant wild, with Nature's beauty drest,
And there into delight my soul deceive.
There warm my breast with patriotic lore,
10 Musing on Milton's fate—on Sydney's bier—
Till their stern forms before my mind arise:
Perhaps on the wing of poesy upsoar,—
Full often dropping a delicious tear,
When some melodious sorrow spells mine eyes.

## *To a Friend Who Sent Me Some Roses*

As late I rambled in the happy fields,
What time the sky-lark shakes the tremulous dew
From his lush clover covert;—when anew
Adventurous knights take up their dinted shields:
5 I saw the sweetest flower wild nature yields,

9 home at evening] thoughtful, homeward *GAW* 11 Watching . . . bright] Following the wafted Cloudlets' light *GAW* 14 falls . . . clear] droppeth through the *GAW*

*Oh! how I love.* Text from Woodhouse's $W^2$ transcript. Variants from his $W^3$. *Heading* Oh . . . eve] *ed*; Sonnet $W^2$, $W^3$ 5 thoughts] thought⟨s⟩ $W^3$

*To a Friend.* Text (including title but omitting sonnet number) from *1817*. Variants and other readings from the extant holograph fair copy (*FC*) and Tom Keats's transcript (*TK*). *Heading* To . . . Roses] To Charles Wells on receiving a bunch of ⟨full blown⟩ roses—Sonnet *TK*; *no heading in FC* 1 rambled] wanderd *FC* 2 shakes] *made out of* shook *FC*

A fresh-blown musk-rose; 'twas the first that threw
Its sweets upon the summer: graceful it grew
As is the wand that queen Titania wields.
And, as I feasted on its fragrancy,
10 I thought the garden-rose it far excell'd:
But when, O Wells! thy roses came to me
My sense with their deliciousness was spell'd:
Soft voices had they, that with tender plea
Whisper'd of peace, and truth, and friendliness unquell'd.

## *Happy is England! I could be content*

Happy is England! I could be content
To see no other verdure than its own;
To feel no other breezes than are blown
Through its tall woods with high romances blent:
5 Yet do I sometimes feel a languishment
For skies Italian, and an inward groan
To sit upon an Alp as on a throne,
And half forget what world or worldling meant.
Happy is England, sweet her artless daughters;
10 Enough their simple loveliness for me,
Enough their whitest arms in silence clinging:
Yet do I often warmly burn to see
Beauties of deeper glance, and hear their singing,
And float with them about the summer waters.

## *To My Brother George*

Many the wonders I this day have seen:
The sun, when first he kist away the tears
That fill'd the eyes of morn;—the laurel'd peers

7 sweets] sweet *FC* 9 on] in *FC* 12 spell'd] *interlined above* ⟨quell'd⟩ *FC* 14 peace . . . truth] truth, Humanity *TK*

*Happy is England.* Text from *1817*. Heading supplied by editor.

*To My Brother George* (sonnet). Text (including title but omitting sonnet number) from *1817*. Variants and other readings from Keats's draft (*D*) and the transcripts by George Keats (*GK*) and Tom Keats (*TK*). *Heading* To . . . George] Sonnet / To my Brother George *TK*; *no heading in D, GK* 3 fill'd . . . morn] hung on Mornings Cheek *D, GK* (*written beneath* ⟨trembled in the Eye{s} of Morn⟩ *in D, with* in *interlined above an original* {on} *and* Eye{s} of Morn *above* {Mornings Eye})

Who from the feathery gold of evening lean;—
5 The ocean with its vastness, its blue green,
Its ships, its rocks, its caves, its hopes, its fears,—
Its voice mysterious, which whoso hears
Must think on what will be, and what has been.
E'en now, dear George, while this for you I write,
10 Cynthia is from her silken curtains peeping
So scantly, that it seems her bridal night,
And she her half-discover'd revels keeping.
But what, without the social thought of thee,
Would be the wonders of the sky and sea?

## *To My Brother George*

Full many a dreary hour have I past,
My brain bewilder'd, and my mind o'ercast
With heaviness; in seasons when I've thought
No spherey strains by me could e'er be caught
5 From the blue dome, though I to dimness gaze
On the far depth where sheeted lightning plays;
Or, on the wavy grass outstretch'd supinely,
Pry 'mong the stars, to strive to think divinely:
That I should never hear Apollo's song,
10 Though feathery clouds were floating all along
The purple west, and, two bright streaks between,
The golden lyre itself were dimly seen:
That the still murmur of the honey bee
Would never teach a rural song to me:
15 That the bright glance from beauty's eyelids slanting
Would never make a lay of mine enchanting,
Or warm my breast with ardour to unfold
Some tale of love and arms in time of old.

4 Who] That *D, GK* 4 from] in *D* 4 feathery] *interlined above* ⟨Paleing⟩ *D* 6 rocks] *interlined above* ⟨Dangers⟩ *D* 8 think . . . be] muse on whats to come *D, GK* 10 silken] silver *D* 10 curtains] curtain *TK* 10/11 ⟨Giving the World but snatches of delight⟩ *D* 11 that] *added above the line in D* 12/13 ⟨The Sights have warmd me but without thy love / What Joy in Earth or Sea or Heavn above?⟩ *D* 13 thought] thoughts *GK*

*To My Brother George* (epistle). Text (including heading and end-date) from *1817*. Variants from the extant holograph fair copy (*FC*). *Heading* To . . . George] *no heading in FC* 12 dimly] faintly *FC*

But there are times, when those that love the bay,
20 Fly from all sorrowing far, far away;
A sudden glow comes on them, nought they see
In water, earth, or air, but poesy.
It has been said, dear George, and true I hold it,
(For knightly Spenser to Libertas told it,)
25 That when a Poet is in such a trance,
In air he sees white coursers paw, and prance,
Bestridden of gay knights, in gay apparel,
Who at each other tilt in playful quarrel,
And what we, ignorantly, sheet-lightning call,
30 Is the swift opening of their wide portal,
When the bright warder blows his trumpet clear,
Whose tones reach nought on earth but Poet's ear.
When these enchanted portals open wide,
And through the light the horsemen swiftly glide,
35 The Poet's eye can reach those golden halls,
And view the glory of their festivals:
Their ladies fair, that in the distance seem
Fit for the silv'ring of a seraph's dream;
Their rich brimm'd goblets, that incessant run
40 Like the bright spots that move about the sun;
And, when upheld, the wine from each bright jar
Pours with the lustre of a falling star.
Yet further off, are dimly seen their bowers,
Of which no mortal eye can reach the flowers;
45 And 'tis right just, for well Apollo knows
'Twould make the Poet quarrel with the rose.
All that's reveal'd from that far seat of blisses,
Is, the clear fountains' interchanging kisses,
As gracefully descending, light and thin,
50 Like silver streaks across a dolphin's fin,
When he upswimmeth from the coral caves,
And sports with half his tail above the waves.

These wonders strange he sees, and many more,
Whose head is pregnant with poetic lore.
55 Should he upon an evening ramble fare
With forehead to the soothing breezes bare,
Would he naught see but the dark, silent blue

19 that] who *FC* 20 Fly] Glide *FC* 37 fair] bright *FC* 48 fountains'] fountains, *FC* 51 upswimmeth] upspringeth *FC*

With all its diamonds trembling through and through?
Or the coy moon, when in the waviness
60 Of whitest clouds she does her beauty dress,
And staidly paces higher up, and higher,
Like a sweet nun in holy-day attire?
Ah, yes! much more would start into his sight—
The revelries, and mysteries of night:
65 And should I ever see them, I will tell you
Such tales as needs must with amazement spell you.

These are the living pleasures of the bard:
But richer far posterity's award.
What does he murmur with his latest breath,
70 While his proud eye looks through the film of death?
"What though I leave this dull, and earthly mould,
Yet shall my spirit lofty converse hold
With after times.—The patriot shall feel
My stern alarum, and unsheath his steel;
75 Or, in the senate thunder out my numbers
To startle princes from their easy slumbers.
The sage will mingle with each moral theme
My happy thoughts sententious; he will teem
With lofty periods when my verses fire him,
80 And then I'll stoop from heaven to inspire him.
Lays have I left of such a dear delight
That maids will sing them on their bridal night.
Gay villagers, upon a morn of May,
When they have tired their gentle limbs with play,
85 And form'd a snowy circle on the grass,
And plac'd in midst of all that lovely lass
Who chosen is their queen,—with her fine head
Crowned with flowers purple, white, and red:
For there the lily, and the musk-rose, sighing,
90 Are emblems true of hapless lovers dying:
Between her breasts, that never yet felt trouble,
A bunch of violets full blown, and double,
Serenely sleep:—she from a casket takes
A little book,—and then a joy awakes
95 About each youthful heart,—with stifled cries,
And rubbing of white hands, and sparkling eyes:

60 does] doth *FC* 65 see] view *FC* 65–66 you . . . you] ye . . . ye *FC* 86 And . . . lovely] Placing in midst thereof, that happy *FC*

For she's to read a tale of hopes, and fears;
One that I foster'd in my youthful years:
The pearls, that on each glist'ning circlet sleep,
100 Gush ever and anon with silent creep,
Lured by the innocent dimples. To sweet rest
Shall the dear babe, upon its mother's breast,
Be lull'd with songs of mine. Fair world, adieu!
Thy dales, and hills, are fading from my view:
105 Swiftly I mount, upon wide spreading pinions,
Far from the narrow bounds of thy dominions.
Full joy I feel, while thus I cleave the air,
That my soft verse will charm thy daughters fair,
And warm thy sons!" Ah, my dear friend and brother,
110 Could I, at once, my mad ambition smother,
For tasting joys like these, sure I should be
Happier, and dearer to society.
At times, 'tis true, I've felt relief from pain
When some bright thought has darted through my brain:
115 Through all that day I've felt a greater pleasure
Than if I'd brought to light a hidden treasure.
As to my sonnets, though none else should heed them,
I feel delighted, still, that you should read them.
Of late, too, I have had much calm enjoyment,
120 Stretch'd on the grass at my best lov'd employment
Of scribbling lines for you. These things I thought
While, in my face, the freshest breeze I caught.
E'en now I'm pillow'd on a bed of flowers
That crowns a lofty clift, which proudly towers
125 Above the ocean-waves. The stalks, and blades,
Chequer my tablet with their quivering shades.
On one side is a field of drooping oats,
Through which the poppies show their scarlet coats;
So pert and useless, that they bring to mind
130 The scarlet coats that pester human-kind.
And on the other side, outspread, is seen
Ocean's blue mantle streak'd with purple, and green.
Now 'tis I see a canvass'd ship, and now
Mark the bright silver curling round her prow.
135 I see the lark down-dropping to his nest,
And the broad winged sea-gull never at rest;
For when no more he spreads his feathers free,

118 should] will *FC* 124 crowns . . . clift] crown . . . Cliff *FC* 135 his] her *FC*

His breast is dancing on the restless sea.
Now I direct my eyes into the west,
140 Which at this moment is in sunbeams drest:
Why westward turn? 'Twas but to say adieu!
'Twas but to kiss my hand, dear George, to you!

August, 1816

## *To Charles Cowden Clarke*

Oft have you seen a swan superbly frowning,
And with proud breast his own white shadow crowning;
He slants his neck beneath the waters bright
So silently, it seems a beam of light
5 Come from the Galaxy: anon he sports,—
With outspread wings the Naiad Zephyr courts,
Or ruffles all the surface of the lake
In striving from its crystal face to take
Some diamond water drops, and them to treasure
10 In milky nest, and sip them off at leisure.
But not a moment can he there insure them,
Nor to such downy rest can he allure them;
For down they rush as though they would be free,
And drop like hours into eternity.
15 Just like that bird am I in loss of time,
Whene'er I venture on the stream of rhyme;
With shatter'd boat, oar snapt, and canvass rent,
I slowly sail, scarce knowing my intent;
Still scooping up the water with my fingers,
20 In which a trembling diamond never lingers.

By this, friend Charles, you may full plainly see
Why I have never penn'd a line to thee:
Because my thoughts were never free, and clear,
And little fit to please a classic ear;
25 Because my wine was of too poor a savour

139 into] towards *FC*

*To Charles Cowden Clarke.* Text (including heading and end-date) from *1817*. Variants and other readings from the extant holograph fair copy (*FC*). *Heading* Charles . . . Clarke] Mr C—C—Clarke *FC* 5 Come] Shot *FC* 14 hours] time *FC*

For one whose palate gladdens in the flavour
Of sparkling Helicon:—small good it were
To take him to a desert rude, and bare,
Who had on Baiæ's shore reclin'd at ease,
30 While Tasso's page was floating in a breeze
That gave soft music from Armida's bowers,
Mingled with fragrance from her rarest flowers:
Small good to one who had by Mulla's stream
Fondled the maidens with the breasts of cream;
35 Who had beheld Belphœbe in a brook,
And lovely Una in a leafy nook,
And Archimago leaning o'er his book:
Who had of all that's sweet tasted, and seen,
From silv'ry ripple, up to beauty's queen;
40 From the sequester'd haunts of gay Titania,
To the blue dwelling of divine Urania:
One who, of late, had ta'en sweet forest walks
With him who elegantly chats, and talks—
The wrong'd Libertas,—who has told you stories
45 Of laurel chaplets, and Apollo's glories;
Of troops chivalrous prancing through a city,
And tearful ladies made for love, and pity:
With many else which I have never known.
Thus have I thought; and days on days have flown
50 Slowly, or rapidly—unwilling still
For you to try my dull, unlearned quill.
Nor should I now, but that I've known you long;
That you first taught me all the sweets of song:
The grand, the sweet, the terse, the free, the fine;
55 What swell'd with pathos, and what right divine:
Spenserian vowels that elope with ease,
And float along like birds o'er summer seas;
Miltonian storms, and more, Miltonian tenderness;
Michael in arms, and more, meek Eve's fair slenderness.
60 Who read for me the sonnet swelling loudly
Up to its climax and then dying proudly?
Who found for me the grandeur of the ode,
Growing, like Atlas, stronger from its load?
Who let me taste that more than cordial dram,
65 The sharp, the rapier-pointed epigram?
Shew'd me that epic was of all the king,

44 has] hath *FC*

Round, vast, and spanning all like Saturn's ring?
You too upheld the veil from Clio's beauty,
And pointed out the patriot's stern duty;
70 The might of Alfred, and the shaft of Tell;
The hand of Brutus, that so grandly fell
Upon a tyrant's head. Ah! had I never seen,
Or known your kindness, what might I have been?
What my enjoyments in my youthful years,
75 Bereft of all that now my life endears?
And can I e'er these benefits forget?
And can I e'er repay the friendly debt?
No, doubly no;—yet should these rhymings please,
I shall roll on the grass with two-fold ease:
80 For I have long time been my fancy feeding
With hopes that you would one day think the reading
Of my rough verses not an hour misspent;
Should it e'er be so, what a rich content!
Some weeks have pass'd since last I saw the spires
85 In lucent Thames reflected:—warm desires
To see the sun o'er peep the eastern dimness,
And morning shadows streaking into slimness
Across the lawny fields, and pebbly water;
To mark the time as they grow broad, and shorter;
90 To feel the air that plays about the hills,
And sips its freshness from the little rills;
To see high, golden corn wave in the light
When Cynthia smiles upon a summer's night,
And peers among the cloudlet's jet and white,
95 As though she were reclining in a bed
Of bean blossoms, in heaven freshly shed.
No sooner had I stepp'd into these pleasures
Than I began to think of rhymes and measures:
The air that floated by me seem'd to say
100 "Write! thou wilt never have a better day."
And so I did. When many lines I'd written,
Though with their grace I was not oversmitten,
Yet, as my hand was warm, I thought I'd better
Trust to my feelings, and write you a letter.
105 Such an attempt required an inspiration

83 it . . . so] I e'er hear it *FC* 87 streaking] stretching *FC* 88 and] or *FC* 94 peers] *interlined above* ⟨play⟩ *FC* 94 cloudlet's] Cloudlets *FC* 95 in] on *FC* 98 rhymes] Verse *FC* 103 warm] in *FC*

Of a peculiar sort,—a consummation;—
Which, had I felt, these scribblings might have been
Verses from which the soul would never wean:
But many days have past since last my heart
110 Was warm'd luxuriously by divine Mozart;
By Arne delighted, or by Handel madden'd;
Or by the song of Erin pierc'd and sadden'd:
What time you were before the music sitting,
And the rich notes to each sensation fitting;
115 Since I have walk'd with you through shady lanes
That freshly terminate in open plains,
And revel'd in a chat that ceased not
When at night-fall among your books we got:
No, nor when supper came, nor after that,—
120 Nor when reluctantly I took my hat;
No, nor till cordially you shook my hand
Mid-way between our homes:—your accents bland
Still sounded in my ears, when I no more
Could hear your footsteps touch the grav'ly floor.
125 Sometimes I lost them, and then found again;
You chang'd the footpath for the grassy plain.
In those still moments I have wish'd you joys
That well you know to honour:—"Life's very toys
With him," said I, "will take a pleasant charm;
130 It cannot be that ought will work him harm."
These thoughts now come o'er me with all their might:—
Again I shake your hand,—friend Charles, good night.

September, 1816

## *How many bards gild the lapses of time*

How many bards gild the lapses of time!
  A few of them have ever been the food
  Of my delighted fancy,—I could brood
Over their beauties, earthly, or sublime:
5 And often, when I sit me down to rhyme,
  These will in throngs before my mind intrude:
  But no confusion, no disturbance rude

112 song] Songs *FC*    127 those] these *FC*
*How many bards.* Text from *1817*. Heading supplied by editor.

Do they occasion; 'tis a pleasing chime.
So the unnumber'd sounds that evening store;
10 The songs of birds—the whisp'ring of the leaves—
The voice of waters—the great bell that heaves
With solemn sound,—and thousand others more,
That distance of recognizance bereaves,
Make pleasing music, and not wild uproar.

## *On First Looking into Chapman's Homer*

Much have I travell'd in the realms of gold,
And many goodly states and kingdoms seen;
Round many western islands have I been
Which bards in fealty to Apollo hold.
5 Oft of one wide expanse had I been told
That deep-brow'd Homer ruled as his demesne;
Yet did I never breathe its pure serene
Till I heard Chapman speak out loud and bold:
Then felt I like some watcher of the skies
10 When a new planet swims into his ken;
Or like stout Cortez when with eagle eyes
He star'd at the Pacific—and all his men
Look'd at each other with a wild surmise—
Silent, upon a peak in Darien.

## *Keen, fitful gusts are whisp'ring here and there*

Keen, fitful gusts are whisp'ring here and there
Among the bushes half leafless, and dry;
The stars look very cold about the sky,

*On First Looking into Chapman's Homer.* Text (including title but omitting sonnet number) from *1817*. Variants and other readings from the holograph draft or fair copy at Harvard (arbitrarily cited as *D*), the holograph fair copy in the Morgan Library (*FC*), Tom Keats's transcript (*TK*), and the *Examiner* version (*Ex*). *Heading* On First . . . Homer] On the first . . . Homer *D*; Sonnet On . . . Homer *TK*; *no heading in FC* 5 Oft] But *TK*, *Ex* 6 That] Which *D* 6 deep] *interlined above* ⟨low⟩ *D* 7 did . . . serene] could I never judge what Men could mean *D, FC, TK, Ex* 11 eagle] wond'ring *D* 13 Look'd] Look *FC*

*Keen, fitful gusts.* Text from *1817*. Heading supplied by editor.

And I have many miles on foot to fare.
5 Yet feel I little of the cool bleak air,
Or of the dead leaves rustling drearily,
Or of those silver lamps that burn on high,
Or of the distance from home's pleasant lair:
For I am brimfull of the friendliness
10 That in a little cottage I have found;
Of fair-hair'd Milton's eloquent distress,
And all his love for gentle Lycid drown'd;
Of lovely Laura in her light green dress,
And faithful Petrarch gloriously crown'd.

## *On Leaving Some Friends at an Early Hour*

Give me a golden pen, and let me lean
On heap'd up flowers, in regions clear, and far;
Bring me a tablet whiter than a star,
Or hand of hymning angel, when 'tis seen
5 The silver strings of heavenly harp atween:
And let there glide by many a pearly car,
Pink robes, and wavy hair, and diamond jar,
And half discovered wings, and glances keen.
The while let music wander round my ears,
10 And as it reaches each delicious ending,
Let me write down a line of glorious tone,
And full of many wonders of the spheres:
For what a height my spirit is contending!
'Tis not content so soon to be alone.

*On Leaving Some Friends.* Text (including title but omitting sonnet number) from *1817*. Variants and other readings from Keats's draft (*D*). *Heading* On . . . Hour] *no heading in D* *Before* 1

⟨Give me a golden Pen and let me lean
On heap'd up flowers in regions clear and calm
Bring me a tablet whiter than the palm
Of a young Angel what time it is seen⟩ *D*

2 clear] *interlined above* ⟨calm⟩ *D* 2 far] *interlined above* ⟨clear⟩ *D* 4 hand] palm *D* 4 hymning] *interlined above* ⟨young eyed⟩ *D* 7 Pink robes] *interlined above* ⟨Bright Looks⟩ *D* 7 wavy] *interlined above* ⟨floating⟩ *D* 7 diamond] *interlined above* ⟨sapphire⟩ *D* 8 discovered] *interlined above* ⟨seen⟩ *D* 9 round] *interlined above* ⟨here w⟩ *D* 10 ending] *interlined above* ⟨close⟩ *D* 12/13 ⟨I needs m⟩ *D*

## *To My Brothers*

Small, busy flames play through the fresh laid coals,
And their faint cracklings o'er our silence creep
Like whispers of the household gods that keep
A gentle empire o'er fraternal souls.
5 And while, for rhymes, I search around the poles,
Your eyes are fix'd, as in poetic sleep,
Upon the lore so voluble and deep,
That aye at fall of night our care condoles.
This is your birth-day, Tom, and I rejoice
10 That thus it passes smoothly, quietly.
Many such eves of gently whisp'ring noise
May we together pass, and calmly try
What are this world's true joys,—ere the great voice,
From its fair face, shall bid our spirits fly.

November 18, 1816

## *Addressed to Haydon*

Highmindedness, a jealousy for good,
A loving-kindness for the great man's fame,
Dwells here and there with people of no name,
In noisome alley, and in pathless wood:
5 And where we think the truth least understood,
Oft may be found a "singleness of aim,"
That ought to frighten into hooded shame

*To My Brothers.* Text (including title and end-date but omitting sonnet number) from *1817*. Variants and other readings from Keats's draft (*D*, extant for 1–8 only), the dated and undated holograph fair copies at Harvard ($FC^1$ and $FC^2$, respectively), and Tom Keats's transcript (*TK*). *Heading* To My Brothers] Sonnet / Written to his Brother Tom on his Birthday *TK*; *no heading in D* 1 busy . . . play] flames are peeping (*the first* p *written over* ⟨g⟩) *D* 2 And . . . creep] With a faint Crackling head distinct *altered to* And their faint Crackling o'er our Silence creeps *D* 2 faint] light $FC^2$ 2 cracklings] *interlined above* ⟨whispe⟩ $FC^2$ 3 whispers] Whisper *D*; Whisperings $FC^1$ 3 gods . . . keep] God . . . keeps *D* 4/5 ⟨And while I am searching of a Rhyme⟩ (searching *interlined above* {thinking}) *D* 5 for . . . search] I search for Rhyme $FC^2$ 7 lore so] Pages *D* 8 That] Which $FC^2$ 13 this] the $FC^1$, $FC^2$ 13 ere] ⟨till⟩ ere $FC^2$ 14 face] place *TK*

*Addressed to Haydon.* Text (including title but omitting sonnet number) from *1817*. Variants from the unidentified transcript at Harvard (*Tr*). *Heading* Addressed to Haydon] High Mindedness *Tr* 7 That] Which *Tr*

A money mong'ring, pitiable brood.
How glorious this affection for the cause
10 Of stedfast genius, toiling gallantly!
What when a stout unbending champion awes
Envy, and Malice to their native sty?
Unnumber'd souls breathe out a still applause,
Proud to behold him in his country's eye.

## *Addressed to the Same*

Great spirits now on earth are sojourning;
He of the cloud, the cataract, the lake,
Who on Helvellyn's summit, wide awake,
Catches his freshness from archangel's wing:
5 He of the rose, the violet, the spring,
The social smile, the chain for freedom's sake:
And lo!—whose stedfastness would never take
A meaner sound than Raphael's whispering.
And other spirits there are standing apart
10 Upon the forehead of the age to come;
These, these will give the world another heart,
And other pulses. Hear ye not the hum
Of mighty workings?——
Listen awhile ye nations, and be dumb.

## *To G. A. W.*

Nymph of the downward smile, and sidelong glance,
In what diviner moments of the day
Art thou most lovely? When gone far astray
Into the labyrinths of sweet utterance?

*Addressed to the Same.* Text (including title but omitting sonnet number) from *1817*. Variants from the two holograph fair copies sent to Haydon in letters of 20 and 21 November 1816 (*FC*[1] and *FC*[2], respectively), Tom Keats's transcript (*TK*), and the extant holograph used as printer's copy for *1817* (*FC*[3]). *Heading* Addressed . . . Same] Sonnet *TK*; *no heading in FC*[1], *FC*[2] 1 now] *underscored in FC*[3] 9 there are] are there *FC*[1], *FC*[2] 13 workings?——] Workings in a distant Mart? *FC*[1]

*To G. A. W.* Text (including title but omitting sonnet number) from *1817*. Variants and other readings from the extant holograph fair copy (*FC*) and the transcripts by Tom Keats (*TK*) and W. P. Woodhouse (*WPW*). *Heading* To G. A. W.] To Miss Wylie *FC*; Sonnet / To a Lady *TK*; Sonnet *WPW*

5 Or when serenely wand'ring in a trance
Of sober thought? Or when starting away,
With careless robe, to meet the morning ray,
Thou spar'st the flowers in thy mazy dance?
Haply 'tis when thy ruby lips part sweetly,
10 And so remain, because thou listenest:
But thou to please wert nurtured so completely
That I can never tell what mood is best.
I shall as soon pronounce which Grace more neatly
Trips it before Apollo than the rest.

## *To Kosciusko*

Good Kosciusko, thy great name alone
Is a full harvest whence to reap high feeling;
It comes upon us like the glorious pealing
Of the wide spheres—an everlasting tone.
5 And now it tells me, that in worlds unknown,
The names of heroes, burst from clouds concealing,
Are changed to harmonies, for ever stealing
Through cloudless blue, and round each silver throne.
It tells me too, that on a happy day,
10 When some good spirit walks upon the earth,
Thy name with Alfred's and the great of yore
Gently commingling, gives tremendous birth
To a loud hymn, that sounds far, far away
To where the great God lives for evermore.

11 wert] were *WPW* 12 what] which *WPW* 13 which] what *TK* 13 Grace] *interlined above* ⟨Nymph⟩ *FC*

*To Kosciusko.* Text (including title but omitting sonnet number) from *1817*. Emendation and a variant from the *Examiner* version (*Ex*). 7 Are] *Ex*; And *1817* 8 and round] around *Ex*

## *Sleep and Poetry*

> "As I lay in my bed slepe full unmete
> Was unto me, but why that I ne might
> Rest I ne wist, for there n'as erthly wight
> [As I suppose] had more of hertis ese
> Than I, for I n'ad sicknesse nor disese."
>
> Chaucer

What is more gentle than a wind in summer?
What is more soothing than the pretty hummer
That stays one moment in an open flower,
And buzzes cheerily from bower to bower?
5 What is more tranquil than a musk-rose blowing
In a green island, far from all men's knowing?
More healthful than the leafiness of dales?
More secret than a nest of nightingales?
More serene than Cordelia's countenance?
10 More full of visions than a high romance?
What, but thee, Sleep? Soft closer of our eyes!
Low murmurer of tender lullabies!
Light hoverer around our happy pillows!
Wreather of poppy buds, and weeping willows!
15 Silent entangler of a beauty's tresses!
Most happy listener! when the morning blesses
Thee for enlivening all the cheerful eyes
That glance so brightly at the new sun-rise.

But what is higher beyond thought than thee?
20 Fresher than berries of a mountain tree?
More strange, more beautiful, more smooth, more regal,
Than wings of swans, than doves, than dim-seen eagle?
What is it? And to what shall I compare it?
It has a glory, and nought else can share it:
25 The thought thereof is awful, sweet, and holy,
Chacing away all worldliness and folly;
Coming sometimes like fearful claps of thunder,
Or the low rumblings earth's regions under;
And sometimes like a gentle whispering
30 Of all the secrets of some wond'rous thing
That breathes about us in the vacant air;
So that we look around with prying stare,

*Sleep and Poetry.* Text (including heading and epigraph) from *1817*.

Perhaps to see shapes of light, aerial lymning,
And catch soft floatings from a faint-heard hymning;
35 To see the laurel wreath, on high suspended,
That is to crown our name when life is ended.
Sometimes it gives a glory to the voice,
And from the heart up-springs, rejoice! rejoice!
Sounds which will reach the Framer of all things,
40 And die away in ardent mutterings.

No one who once the glorious sun has seen,
And all the clouds, and felt his bosom clean
For his great Maker's presence, but must know
What 'tis I mean, and feel his being glow:
45 Therefore no insult will I give his spirit,
By telling what he sees from native merit.

O Poesy! for thee I hold my pen
That am not yet a glorious denizen
Of thy wide heaven—Should I rather kneel
50 Upon some mountain-top until I feel
A glowing splendour round about me hung,
And echo back the voice of thine own tongue?
O Poesy! for thee I grasp my pen
That am not yet a glorious denizen
55 Of thy wide heaven; yet, to my ardent prayer,
Yield from thy sanctuary some clear air,
Smoothed for intoxication by the breath
Of flowering bays, that I may die a death
Of luxury, and my young spirit follow
60 The morning sun-beams to the great Apollo
Like a fresh sacrifice; or, if I can bear
The o'erwhelming sweets, 'twill bring to me the fair
Visions of all places: a bowery nook
Will be elysium—an eternal book
65 Whence I may copy many a lovely saying
About the leaves, and flowers—about the playing
Of nymphs in woods, and fountains; and the shade
Keeping a silence round a sleeping maid;
And many a verse from so strange influence
70 That we must ever wonder how, and whence
It came. Also imaginings will hover
Round my fire-side, and haply there discover
Vistas of solemn beauty, where I'd wander

In happy silence, like the clear Meander
75 Through its lone vales; and where I found a spot
Of awfuller shade, or an enchanted grot,
Or a green hill o'erspread with chequered dress
Of flowers, and fearful from its loveliness,
Write on my tablets all that was permitted,
80 All that was for our human senses fitted.
Then the events of this wide world I'd seize
Like a strong giant, and my spirit teaze
Till at its shoulders it should proudly see
Wings to find out an immortality.

85 Stop and consider! life is but a day;
A fragile dew-drop on its perilous way
From a tree's summit; a poor Indian's sleep
While his boat hastens to the monstrous steep
Of Montmorenci. Why so sad a moan?
90 Life is the rose's hope while yet unblown;
The reading of an ever-changing tale;
The light uplifting of a maiden's veil;
A pigeon tumbling in clear summer air;
A laughing school-boy, without grief or care,
95 Riding the springy branches of an elm.

O for ten years, that I may overwhelm
Myself in poesy; so I may do the deed
That my own soul has to itself decreed.
Then will I pass the countries that I see
100 In long perspective, and continually
Taste their pure fountains. First the realm I'll pass
Of Flora, and old Pan: sleep in the grass,
Feed upon apples red, and strawberries,
And choose each pleasure that my fancy sees;
105 Catch the white-handed nymphs in shady places,
To woo sweet kisses from averted faces,—
Play with their fingers, touch their shoulders white
Into a pretty shrinking with a bite
As hard as lips can make it: till agreed,
110 A lovely tale of human life we'll read.
And one will teach a tame dove how it best
May fan the cool air gently o'er my rest;
Another, bending o'er her nimble tread,
Will set a green robe floating round her head,

115 And still will dance with ever varied ease,
Smiling upon the flowers and the trees:
Another will entice me on, and on
Through almond blossoms and rich cinnamon;
Till in the bosom of a leafy world
120 We rest in silence, like two gems upcurl'd
In the recesses of a pearly shell.

And can I ever bid these joys farewell?
Yes, I must pass them for a nobler life,
Where I may find the agonies, the strife
125 Of human hearts: for lo! I see afar,
O'er sailing the blue cragginess, a car
And steeds with streamy manes—the charioteer
Looks out upon the winds with glorious fear:
And now the numerous tramplings quiver lightly
130 Along a huge cloud's ridge; and now with sprightly
Wheel downward come they into fresher skies,
Tipt round with silver from the sun's bright eyes.
Still downward with capacious whirl they glide;
And now I see them on a green-hill's side
135 In breezy rest among the nodding stalks.
The charioteer with wond'rous gesture talks
To the trees and mountains; and there soon appear
Shapes of delight, of mystery, and fear,
Passing along before a dusky space
140 Made by some mighty oaks: as they would chase
Some ever-fleeting music on they sweep.
Lo! how they murmur, laugh, and smile, and weep:
Some with upholden hand and mouth severe;
Some with their faces muffled to the ear
145 Between their arms; some, clear in youthful bloom,
Go glad and smilingly athwart the gloom;
Some looking back, and some with upward gaze;
Yes, thousands in a thousand different ways
Flit onward—now a lovely wreath of girls
150 Dancing their sleek hair into tangled curls;
And now broad wings. Most awfully intent,
The driver of those steeds is forward bent,
And seems to listen: O that I might know
All that he writes with such a hurrying glow.

155 The visions all are fled—the car is fled
Into the light of heaven, and in their stead

A sense of real things comes doubly strong,
And, like a muddy stream, would bear along
My soul to nothingness: but I will strive
160 Against all doubtings, and will keep alive
The thought of that same chariot, and the strange
Journey it went.

Is there so small a range
In the present strength of manhood, that the high
Imagination cannot freely fly
165 As she was wont of old? prepare her steeds,
Paw up against the light, and do strange deeds
Upon the clouds? Has she not shewn us all?
From the clear space of ether, to the small
Breath of new buds unfolding? From the meaning
170 Of Jove's large eye-brow, to the tender greening
Of April meadows? Here her altar shone,
E'en in this isle; and who could paragon
The fervid choir that lifted up a noise
Of harmony, to where it aye will poise
175 Its mighty self of convoluting sound,
Huge as a planet, and like that roll round,
Eternally around a dizzy void?
Ay, in those days the Muses were nigh cloy'd
With honors; nor had any other care
180 Than to sing out and sooth their wavy hair.

Could all this be forgotten? Yes, a schism
Nurtured by foppery and barbarism,
Made great Apollo blush for this his land.
Men were thought wise who could not understand
185 His glories: with a puling infant's force
They sway'd about upon a rocking horse,
And thought it Pegasus. Ah dismal soul'd!
The winds of heaven blew, the ocean roll'd
Its gathering waves—ye felt it not. The blue
190 Bared its eternal bosom, and the dew
Of summer nights collected still to make
The morning precious: beauty was awake!
Why were ye not awake? But ye were dead
To things ye knew not of,—were closely wed
195 To musty laws lined out with wretched rule
And compass vile: so that ye taught a school
Of dolts to smooth, inlay, and clip, and fit,

Till, like the certain wands of Jacob's wit,
Their verses tallied. Easy was the task:
200 A thousand handicraftsmen wore the mask
Of Poesy. Ill-fated, impious race!
That blasphemed the bright Lyrist to his face,
And did not know it,—no, they went about,
Holding a poor, decrepid standard out
205 Mark'd with most flimsy mottos, and in large
The name of one Boileau!

O ye whose charge
It is to hover round our pleasant hills!
Whose congregated majesty so fills
My boundly reverence, that I cannot trace
210 Your hallowed names, in this unholy place,
So near those common folk; did not their shames
Affright you? Did our old lamenting Thames
Delight you? Did ye never cluster round
Delicious Avon, with a mournful sound,
215 And weep? Or did ye wholly bid adieu
To regions where no more the laurel grew?
Or did ye stay to give a welcoming
To some lone spirits who could proudly sing
Their youth away, and die? 'Twas even so:
220 But let me think away those times of woe:
Now 'tis a fairer season; ye have breathed
Rich benedictions o'er us; ye have wreathed
Fresh garlands: for sweet music has been heard
In many places;—some has been upstirr'd
225 From out its crystal dwelling in a lake,
By a swan's ebon bill; from a thick brake,
Nested and quiet in a valley mild,
Bubbles a pipe; fine sounds are floating wild
About the earth: happy are ye and glad.

230 These things are doubtless: yet in truth we've had
Strange thunders from the potency of song;
Mingled indeed with what is sweet and strong,
From majesty: but in clear truth the themes
Are ugly clubs, the poets Polyphemes
235 Disturbing the grand sea. A drainless shower
Of light is poesy; 'tis the supreme of power;
'Tis might half slumb'ring on its own right arm.
The very archings of her eye-lids charm

A thousand willing agents to obey,
240 And still she governs with the mildest sway:
But strength alone though of the Muses born
Is like a fallen angel: trees uptorn,
Darkness, and worms, and shrouds, and sepulchres
Delight it; for it feeds upon the burrs,
245 And thorns of life; forgetting the great end
Of poesy, that it should be a friend
To sooth the cares, and lift the thoughts of man.

Yet I rejoice: a myrtle fairer than
E'er grew in Paphos, from the bitter weeds
250 Lifts its sweet head into the air, and feeds
A silent space with ever sprouting green.
All tenderest birds there find a pleasant screen,
Creep through the shade with jaunty fluttering,
Nibble the little cupped flowers and sing.
255 Then let us clear away the choaking thorns
From round its gentle stem; let the young fawns,
Yeaned in after times, when we are flown,
Find a fresh sward beneath it, overgrown
With simple flowers: let there nothing be
260 More boisterous than a lover's bended knee;
Nought more ungentle than the placid look
Of one who leans upon a closed book;
Nought more untranquil than the grassy slopes
Between two hills. All hail delightful hopes!
265 As she was wont, th' imagination
Into most lovely labyrinths will be gone,
And they shall be accounted poet kings
Who simply tell the most heart-easing things.
O may these joys be ripe before I die.

270 Will not some say that I presumptuously
Have spoken? that from hastening disgrace
'Twere better far to hide my foolish face?
That whining boyhood should with reverence bow
Ere the dread thunderbolt could reach? How!
275 If I do hide myself, it sure shall be
In the very fane, the light of Poesy:
If I do fall, at least I will be laid
Beneath the silence of a poplar shade;
And over me the grass shall be smooth shaven;
280 And there shall be a kind memorial graven.
But off, Despondence! miserable bane!

They should not know thee, who, athirst to gain
A noble end, are thirsty every hour.
What though I am not wealthy in the dower
285 Of spanning wisdom; though I do not know
The shiftings of the mighty winds that blow
Hither and thither all the changing thoughts
Of man: though no great minist'ring reason sorts
Out the dark mysteries of human souls
290 To clear conceiving: yet there ever rolls
A vast idea before me, and I glean
Therefrom my liberty; thence too I've seen
The end and aim of Poesy. 'Tis clear
As any thing most true; as that the year
295 Is made of the four seasons—manifest
As a large cross, some old cathedral's crest,
Lifted to the white clouds. Therefore should I
Be but the essence of deformity,
A coward, did my very eye-lids wink
300 At speaking out what I have dared to think.
Ah! rather let me like a madman run
Over some precipice; let the hot sun
Melt my Dedalian wings, and drive me down
Convuls'd and headlong! Stay! an inward frown
305 Of conscience bids me be more calm awhile.
An ocean dim, sprinkled with many an isle,
Spreads awfully before me. How much toil!
How many days! what desperate turmoil!
Ere I can have explored its widenesses.
310 Ah, what a task! upon my bended knees,
I could unsay those—no, impossible!
Impossible!

For sweet relief I'll dwell
On humbler thoughts, and let this strange assay
Begun in gentleness die so away.
315 E'en now all tumult from my bosom fades:
I turn full hearted to the friendly aids
That smooth the path of honour; brotherhood,
And friendliness, the nurse of mutual good;
The hearty grasp that sends a pleasant sonnet
320 Into the brain ere one can think upon it;
The silence when some rhymes are coming out;
And when they're come, the very pleasant rout:

The message certain to be done to-morrow—
'Tis perhaps as well that it should be to borrow
325 Some precious book from out its snug retreat,
To cluster round it when we next shall meet.
Scarce can I scribble on; for lovely airs
Are fluttering round the room like doves in pairs;
Many delights of that glad day recalling,
330 When first my senses caught their tender falling.
And with these airs come forms of elegance
Stooping their shoulders o'er a horse's prance,
Careless, and grand—fingers soft and round
Parting luxuriant curls;—and the swift bound
335 Of Bacchus from his chariot, when his eye
Made Ariadne's cheek look blushingly.
Thus I remember all the pleasant flow
Of words at opening a portfolio.

Things such as these are ever harbingers
340 To trains of peaceful images: the stirs
Of a swan's neck unseen among the rushes:
A linnet starting all about the bushes:
A butterfly, with golden wings broad parted,
Nestling a rose, convuls'd as though it smarted
345 With over pleasure—many, many more,
Might I indulge at large in all my store
Of luxuries: yet I must not forget
Sleep, quiet with his poppy coronet:
For what there may be worthy in these rhymes
350 I partly owe to him: and thus, the chimes
Of friendly voices had just given place
To as sweet a silence, when I 'gan retrace
The pleasant day, upon a couch at ease.
It was a poet's house who keeps the keys
355 Of pleasure's temple. Round about were hung
The glorious features of the bards who sung
In other ages—cold and sacred busts
Smiled at each other. Happy he who trusts
To clear futurity his darling fame!
360 Then there were fauns and satyrs taking aim
At swelling apples with a frisky leap
And reaching fingers, 'mid a luscious heap
Of vine leaves. Then there rose to view a fane
Of liny marble, and thereto a train

365 Of nymphs approaching fairly o'er the sward:
One, loveliest, holding her white hand toward
The dazzling sun-rise: two sisters sweet
Bending their graceful figures till they meet
Over the trippings of a little child:
370 And some are hearing, eagerly, the wild
Thrilling liquidity of dewy piping.
See, in another picture, nymphs are wiping
Cherishingly Diana's timorous limbs;—
A fold of lawny mantle dabbling swims
375 At the bath's edge, and keeps a gentle motion
With the subsiding crystal: as when ocean
Heaves calmly its broad swelling smoothness o'er
Its rocky marge, and balances once more
The patient weeds, that now unshent by foam
380 Feel all about their undulating home.

Sappho's meek head was there half smiling down
At nothing; just as though the earnest frown
Of over thinking had that moment gone
From off her brow, and left her all alone.

385 Great Alfred's too, with anxious, pitying eyes,
As if he always listened to the sighs
Of the goaded world; and Kosciusko's worn
By horrid suffrance—mightily forlorn.

Petrarch, outstepping from the shady green,
390 Starts at the sight of Laura; nor can wean
His eyes from her sweet face. Most happy they!
For over them was seen a free display
Of out-spread wings, and from between them shone
The face of Poesy: from off her throne
395 She overlook'd things that I scarce could tell.
The very sense of where I was might well
Keep Sleep aloof: but more than that there came
Thought after thought to nourish up the flame
Within my breast; so that the morning light
400 Surprised me even from a sleepless night;
And up I rose refresh'd, and glad, and gay,
Resolving to begin that very day
These lines; and howsoever they be done,
I leave them as a father does his son.

# *I stood tip-toe upon a little hill*

"Places of nestling green for Poets made."
*Story of Rimini*

I stood tip-toe upon a little hill,
The air was cooling, and so very still,
That the sweet buds which with a modest pride
Pull droopingly, in slanting curve aside,
5 Their scantly leaved, and finely tapering stems,
Had not yet lost those starry diadems
Caught from the early sobbing of the morn.
The clouds were pure and white as flocks new shorn,
And fresh from the clear brook; sweetly they slept
10 On the blue fields of heaven, and then there crept
A little noiseless noise among the leaves,
Born of the very sigh that silence heaves:
For not the faintest motion could be seen
Of all the shades that slanted o'er the green.
15 There was wide wand'ring for the greediest eye,
To peer about upon variety;
Far round the horizon's crystal air to skim,
And trace the dwindled edgings of its brim;
To picture out the quaint, and curious bending

*I stood tip-toe.* Text (including epigraph) from *1817.* Variants and other readings from Keats's original draft (*D,* available from various sources—see Textual Note—for 1–27, 38–48, 53–64, 69–112, 116–173, 181–192, 215–242 only), W. H. Prideaux's transcript of missing draft text following 64 and 112 (*WHP*), Keats's revised draft of 25b–28 (*RD*), the extant holograph fair copy (*FC*), and Tom Keats's transcript (*TK*). *Heading* I . . . hill] *ed*; Endymion *TK*; *no heading in D, FC, 1817* *Epigraph* "Places . . . *Rimini*] What more felicity can fall to creature, / Than to enjoy delight with liberty— / Fate of the Butterfly *TK*; *no epigraph in D, FC* *Before* 1 ⟨He who has lingerd in a⟩ *D* 2 The] *deleted in D and nothing substituted* 2 cooling] *interlined above* ⟨silent⟩ *D* 2/3

⟨That Leaves, and buds that curve their slender stems
They had not⟩
⟨That Leaves and buds on slim⟩

(and *interlined above* {the}, that curve *above* {upon}, *and* stems *above* {stalks} *in the first line*) *D* 3 with . . . pride] *successively* (*a*) gently pu (*b*) in a modest pride (*c*) with a modest pride *D* 4 droopingly] *interlined above* ⟨their slim stems⟩ *D* 5 finely] *interlined above* ⟨gently⟩ *D* 6 those] *made out of* their *D* 9 the . . . brook] Rivers Brim *interlined above* ⟨the clear Stream⟩ *D* 13 faintest] gentlest *D* 14 all the] *interlined above* ⟨the cool⟩ (cool *apparently made out of* coll *or* cold) *D* 14 slanted o'er] slant along *altered to* slanted o'er *D* 16 upon] *interlined above* ⟨for all⟩ *D* 17 Far . . . skim] Far round the crystal horison to swim *squeezed in beneath* ⟨To leap into the crystal Horison⟩ *D* 17 horizon's . . . air] crystal Horison *FC* (*D also—see preceding note*) 18 dwindled] little *D* 18/19 ⟨Or picture out the man⟩ (man *presumably the beginning of* many) *D* 19 To] Or *D*

20 Of a fresh woodland alley, never ending;
Or by the bowery clefts, and leafy shelves,
Guess where the jaunty streams refresh themselves.
I gazed awhile, and felt as light, and free
As though the fanning wings of Mercury
25 Had played upon my heels: I was light-hearted,
And many pleasures to my vision started;
So I straightway began to pluck a posey
Of luxuries bright, milky, soft and rosy.

A bush of May flowers with the bees about them;
30 Ah, sure no tasteful nook would be without them;
And let a lush laburnum oversweep them,
And let long grass grow round the roots to keep them
Moist, cool and green; and shade the violets,
That they may bind the moss in leafy nets.

35 A filbert hedge with wild briar overtwined,
And clumps of woodbine taking the soft wind
Upon their summer thrones; there too should be
The frequent chequer of a youngling tree,
That with a score of light green brethren shoots
40 From the quaint mossiness of aged roots:
Round which is heard a spring-head of clear waters
Babbling so wildly of its lovely daughters
The spreading blue bells: it may haply mourn

20/21
⟨Or follow through the woods a li⟩
Or ⟨guess where little Streams embowered sing⟩
⟨By winding Clefts along the tops of Trees⟩
(where *interlined above* {the} {a} *in the second line, and* along *interlined above* {about} *in the third*; them, *probably the beginning of* themselves, *interlined and deleted above* sing *in the second line*) *D*  21 bowery] *interlined above* ⟨winding⟩ *D*  22 jaunty] *interlined above* ⟨nestling⟩ *D*  22 refresh] embower *D, FC, TK*  25 played upon] started to *D, FC*  25–28 I . . . rosy] *in RD this passage is preceded by two fragmentary half-lines* ⟨and thoughts delightful / Came⟩ roung about me *and is followed, after a line space, by the draft of 151–156*  25–27 I . . . began] This pleasant Earth / Is filled with ⟨In⟩ Loveliness of glorious birth / Nor were it a bad Task *D*  26 pleasures] Danties *RD*; Sweetings *FC*  27–28 So . . . rosy.] *not in TK*  28 and] or *RD, FC*  37/38 ⟨The delicate Ash⟩ (delicate *interlined above* {birch}; *the last word is also readable as* Asp, *the beginning of* Aspen) *D*  38 a] *interlined above* ⟨some⟩ *D*  38/39 ⟨Of livelier green⟩ *D*  39 with . . . shoots] *written beneath* ⟨sprouts with many of its light green peer⟩ (sprouts *interlined above* {shoots}) *D*  39 score] store *TK*  41 heard] *interlined above* ⟨found⟩ *D*  41 a] *interlined above* ⟨the⟩ *D*  41 of . . . waters] *interlined above* ⟨of a Stream⟩ *D*  42 Babbling so wildly] That Babbles sweetly *D*  42 lovely] *successively* (*a*) blue eyed (*b*) fragrant (*c*) blooming *D*  42/43 ⟨The woodland Hyacynths⟩ *D*

That such fair clusters should be rudely torn
45 From their fresh beds, and scattered thoughtlessly
By infant hands, left on the path to die.

Open afresh your round of starry folds,
Ye ardent marigolds!
Dry up the moisture from your golden lids,
50 For great Apollo bids
That in these days your praises should be sung
On many harps, which he has lately strung;
And when again your dewiness he kisses,
Tell him, I have you in my world of blisses:
55 So haply when I rove in some far vale,
His mighty voice may come upon the gale.

Here are sweet peas, on tip-toe for a flight:
With wings of gentle flush o'er delicate white,
And taper fingers catching at all things,
60 To bind them all about with tiny rings.

Linger awhile upon some bending planks
That lean against a streamlet's rushy banks,
And watch intently Nature's gentle doings:
They will be found softer than ring-dove's cooings.
65 How silent comes the water round that bend;
Not the minutest whisper does it send
To the o'erhanging sallows: blades of grass
Slowly across the chequer'd shadows pass.
Why, you might read two sonnets, ere they reach
70 To where the hurrying freshnesses aye preach
A natural sermon o'er their pebbly beds;
Where swarms of minnows show their little heads,

46 infant hands] Urchin's Hand *D* 46/47 ⟨Come ye bright Marigolds⟩ *D* 47 round] *successively (a)* congregrated *(b)* Crown *(c)* cirques *(d)* round *(both* cirques *and* round *left undeleted) D* 49 from] of *FC, TK* 52 On] By *FC* 52 which] that *FC* 55 rove] roam *D, FC* 56/57 ⟨Sweet Peas with gentle flush o'er delicate white⟩ *D* 57 Here . . . peas,] Sweet peas that seem‸ *D* 58 o'er] or *TK* 58/59 ⟨And slender hands catching⟩ (slender *interlined above* {twining}) *D* 59 catching] ⟨cl⟩ catching *FC* 60 all . . . rings] *written beneath* ⟨with neat encircleings⟩ (neat *interlined above* {small}) *D* 60 with] in *TK* 61 some] *interlined above* ⟨a⟩ *D* 62 lean] *interlined above* ⟨rest upo⟩ *D* 62 rushy] dasied *D* 63 gentle doings] *successively (a)* Happiness *(b)* goings on *(c)* gentle doings *D* 64 softer than] as soft as *D* *After* 64 *WHP* adds *(from a missing part of D)* The inward ear will ear her and be blest / And tingle with ⟨w⟩ a joy too light for rest (her *interlined above* ⟨them⟩ *in the first line*; light *underscored in the second*) 66 does] will *FC* 69 Why,] And‸ *D* 69 you] ye *D, FC* 69 might] may *D* 71 o'er] on *D* 72 minnows] Minnow *D*

Staying their wavy bodies 'gainst the streams,
To taste the luxury of sunny beams
75 Temper'd with coolness. How they ever wrestle
With their own sweet delight, and ever nestle
Their silver bellies on the pebbly sand.
If you but scantily hold out the hand,
That very instant not one will remain;
80 But turn your eye, and they are there again.
The ripples seem right glad to reach those cresses,
And cool themselves among the em'rald tresses;
The while they cool themselves, they freshness give,
And moisture, that the bowery green may live:
85 So keeping up an interchange of favours,
Like good men in the truth of their behaviours.
Sometimes goldfinches one by one will drop
From low hung branches; little space they stop;
But sip, and twitter, and their feathers sleek;
90 Then off at once, as in a wanton freak:
Or perhaps, to show their black, and golden wings,
Pausing upon their yellow flutterings.
Were I in such a place, I sure should pray
That nought less sweet might call my thoughts away,
95 Than the soft rustle of a maiden's gown
Fanning away the dandelion's down;
Than the light music of her nimble toes
Patting against the sorrel as she goes.
How she would start, and blush, thus to be caught
100 Playing in all her innocence of thought.

73 Staying] And stay *D* 73–74 streams . . . beams] Stream . . . Beam *FC*; *in D the last letters of both words are lost through damage to the MS* 74 To . . . luxury] That they may taste the warmth *D* 75 coolness . . . ever] coolness—and still they *D* 75 ever] ⟨still⟩ ever *FC* 76 own sweet] *added above the line in D* 77 on] *interlined above* ⟨'gainst⟩ *D* 77 pebbly] smooth pebbles and *D, FC* 78 If . . . out] And if ye do but ⟨g⟩ scarcely wave *D* 78 you] ye *FC* (*D also—see preceding note*) 82 the] their *D* 82 em'rald] *interlined above* ⟨amber⟩ *D* 83 The while] ⟨And⟩ as *D* 84 the] ⟨their⟩ the *D* 85 keeping] keep they *altered to* keeping *D* 88 branches] Branch *D* 88/89 ⟨They sip and⟩ *D* 90 at once] they go *D* 90/91 ⟨And as they come and go but mark their wings / So lovely for their yellow flutterings⟩ *D* 91 their . . . golden] the Beauty of their *D* 91 their] *made out of* the *FC* 93 should] would *D, TK* 95 rustle] Rustling *D, FC* 96 Fanning] Sweeping *D* 96/97 ⟨Than her light tripping on the⟩ *D* 98/99

⟨How she will start and blush that I should see⟩
⟨All⟩
⟨The wild o'er flowings⟩

(that . . . see *interlined above* {thus to be caught} *in the first line*) *D* 99 would] will *D, FC* 99/100 ⟨Gladdening in the freedom⟩ *D*

O let me lead her gently o'er the brook,
Watch her half-smiling lips, and downward look;
O let me for one moment touch her wrist;
Let me one moment to her breathing list;
105 And as she leaves me may she often turn
Her fair eyes looking through her locks aubùrne.

What next? A tuft of evening primroses,
O'er which the mind may hover till it dozes;
O'er which it well might take a pleasant sleep,
110 But that 'tis ever startled by the leap
Of buds into ripe flowers; or by the flitting
Of diverse moths, that aye their rest are quitting;
Or by the moon lifting her silver rim
Above a cloud, and with a gradual swim
115 Coming into the blue with all her light.
O Maker of sweet poets, dear delight
Of this fair world, and all its gentle livers;
Spangler of clouds, halo of crystal rivers,
Mingler with leaves, and dew and tumbling streams,
120 Closer of lovely eyes to lovely dreams,
Lover of loneliness, and wandering,
Of upcast eye, and tender pondering!
Thee must I praise above all other glories

102 Watch] With *D* 103 wrist] *interlined above* ⟨hand⟩ *D*; wrist *made out of* waist *TK* 104 breathing] breathings *FC* 105 may she] let her *D* 106 looking] peeping *D, FC* 107 What . . . A] Now for a *D* 108 mind may hover] *interlined above* ⟨though{s} may lean⟩ *D* 109 it well] the mind *TK* 109 take] taste *D* 110 ever . . . the] startled by the sudden *altered to* ever startled by the *D* 111 ripe] ⟨full⟩ ripe *D* 112/113 ⟨Or by the Moon {lifting} that Dipping her silver rim / {Above} Beneath a Cloud and with a gradual swim⟩ ({lifting} that Dipping *interlined above* {showering} [*the word is also readable as* streaming *and* shimmering *but not, as WHP's transcript has it,* shadowing] *in the first line, and* {Above} Beneath *interlined above* {Beneath} *in the second line*) *D, to which WHP adds* (*from a missing part of* D) ⟨Floating through space with ever loving eye / The {night} crowned queen of ocean and the sky⟩. *The replacement of these lines in D—i.e., the present 113–115—is still missing* 121/122 ⟨And⟩ *D* 122 upcast] *made out of* uptund *D* 122 eye] Eyes *D* 122/123

⟨Smiler on Lovers when they smile on thee⟩
⟨Thee must I place the first of all these Pleasures⟩
⟨Thee must I praise above all other things
That give our thought a pair of little wings⟩
Men's thoughts have sure been winged they have found
An inspiration in a pleasant sound
Or pleasant Sight and we have heard therefoe
Most dainty Tales from many Bards of yore

(our thought *successively* [*a*] to thoughts [*b*] each thought [*c*] our thought *in the fourth line*) *D* 123 glories] ⟨Brightness⟩ Glories *D*

That smile us on to tell delightful stories.
125 For what has made the sage or poet write
But the fair paradise of Nature's light?
In the calm grandeur of a sober line,
We see the waving of the mountain pine;
And when a tale is beautifully staid,
130 We feel the safety of a hawthorn glade:
When it is moving on luxurious wings,
The soul is lost in pleasant smotherings:
Fair dewy roses brush against our faces,
And flowering laurels spring from diamond vases;
135 O'er head we see the jasmine and sweet briar,
And bloomy grapes laughing from green attire;
While at our feet, the voice of crystal bubbles
Charms us at once away from all our troubles:
So that we feel uplifted from the world,
140 Walking upon the white clouds wreath'd and curl'd.
So felt he, who first told, how Psyche went
On the smooth wind to realms of wonderment;
What Psyche felt, and Love, when their full lips
First touch'd; what amorous, and fondling nips
145 They gave each other's cheeks; with all their sighs,
And how they kist each other's tremulous eyes:
The silver lamp,—the ravishment,—the wonder—
The darkness,—loneliness,—the fearful thunder;
Their woes gone by, and both to heaven upflown,
150 To bow for gratitude before Jove's throne.
So did he feel, who pull'd the boughs aside,
That we might look into a forest wide,
To catch a glimpse of Fauns, and Dryades
Coming with softest rustle through the trees;
155 And garlands woven of flowers wild, and sweet,

128 of the] of a *D, FC* 129 tale] *interlined above* ⟨Page⟩ *D* 130/131 ⟨And so⟩ *D* 133/134 ⟨And we can see them pl⟩ *D* 137–138 While . . . troubles:] *deleted in D and nothing substituted* 142 smooth] soft *D* 142 wind] winds *TK* 144 amorous . . . fondling] fondleing and tender *D*; fondling and amourous (*but marked for transposition*) *FC* 151 did he] do they *D*; do they *altered to* did he *FC* 151 pull'd the boughs] pull the Boughs *interlined above* ⟨pull aside the⟩ *D*; pull . . . *altered to* pull'd . . . *FC* 152 we] he *TK* 152 might] may *D*; may *altered to* might *FC* 152 look] peep *D, FC* 153 Fauns] *D*; Fawns *FC, TK, 1817* 154 softest] ⟨gen⟩ softest *D* 155 garlands woven] curious Garlands *D*; curious Garlands *altered to* Garlands woven *FC* 155 wild . . . sweet] sweet and wild (*but marked for transposition*) *D*

Upheld on ivory wrists, or sporting feet:
Telling us how fair, trembling Syrinx fled
Arcadian Pan, with such a fearful dread.
Poor nymph,—poor Pan,—how he did weep to find
160 Nought but a lovely sighing of the wind
Along the reedy stream; a half heard strain,
Full of sweet desolation—balmy pain.

What first inspired a bard of old to sing
Narcissus pining o'er the untainted spring?
165 In some delicious ramble, he had found
A little space, with boughs all woven round;
And in the midst of all, a clearer pool
Than e'er reflected in its pleasant cool
The blue sky here, and there, serenely peeping
170 Through tendril wreaths fantastically creeping.
And on the bank a lonely flower he spied,
A meek and forlorn flower, with naught of pride,
Drooping its beauty o'er the watery clearness,
To woo its own sad image into nearness:
175 Deaf to light Zephyrus it would not move;
But still would seem to droop, to pine, to love.
So while the Poet stood in this sweet spot,
Some fainter gleamings o'er his fancy shot;
Nor was it long ere he had told the tale
180 Of young Narcissus, and sad Echo's bale.

Where had he been, from whose warm head out-flew
That sweetest of all songs, that ever new,

156 or] and *D* 156 sporting] sportive *D, FC* *After* 156
One Sunbeam comes the Solitude to bless
Widening it slants athwart the Duskiness
And whert it plays upon the turfy Mould
There sleeps a Nest of Hair wavy and gold
(the *interlined above* ⟨a⟩ *in the third line, and* Mould *successively* [*a*] bed [*b*] Slope [*c*] Mould) *D* (*the present 157 then begins on a new page in D*) 157 fair] *interlined above* ⟨poor⟩ *D* 157 fled] *interlined above* ⟨feard⟩ *D* 159 he did] did he *D, FC* 160 of] *interlined above* ⟨in⟩ *D* 161 a . . . strain] *successively* (*a*) how desolate—how wild (*b*) how desolate—how lone (*c*) a half heard strain *D* 166 boughs] *interlined above* ⟨leaves⟩ *D* 166 all] ⟨o'er⟩ all *D* 169/170 ⟨With tendril⟩ *D* 170 wreaths] *added above the line in D* 171 a lonely] *interlined above* ⟨he saw⟩ *D* 171 spied] *interlined above* ⟨saw⟩ *D* 173 beauty] *interlined above* ⟨. . . tness⟩ (*the missing letters*—brigh?—*cut away*) *D* 173 the . . . clearness] *interlined above* ⟨the deepness fair⟩ *D* 174 sad] fair *FC*

That aye refreshing, pure deliciousness,
Coming ever to bless
185 The wanderer by moonlight? to him bringing
Shapes from the invisible world, unearthly singing
From out the middle air, from flowery nests,
And from the pillowy silkiness that rests
Full in the speculation of the stars.
190 Ah! surely he had burst our mortal bars;
Into some wond'rous region he had gone,
To search for thee, divine Endymion!

He was a Poet, sure a lover too,
Who stood on Latmus' top, what time there blew
195 Soft breezes from the myrtle vale below;
And brought in faintness solemn, sweet, and slow
A hymn from Dian's temple; while upswelling,
The incense went to her own starry dwelling.
But though her face was clear as infant's eyes,
200 Though she stood smiling o'er the sacrifice,
The Poet wept at her so piteous fate,
Wept that such beauty should be desolate:
So in fine wrath some golden sounds he won,
And gave meek Cynthia her Endymion.

205 Queen of the wide air; thou most lovely queen
Of all the brightness that mine eyes have seen!

183 pure] ⟨aye uplifting⟩ pure *D* 184 Coming ever] That ever comes *altered to* Coming ever *D* 185 to him bringing] *successively* (*a*) cheering him (*b*) bringing Shapes (*c*) to him bringing *D* 185/186 ⟨Of Light about him⟩ (*continuation of* [*b*] *in preceding note*) *D* 186 the] the *altered to* th' *FC* 186 unearthly singing] singing *D*; delicious singing (delicious *added above the line*) *FC* 187 out the] *not in D, FC* 189–192 Full . . . Endymion!]

Or slowly moves about the Heavens—Where
Where Had he been to catch a Thing so fair—
Into what Regions was his Spirit gone
When he first thought of thee Endymion?

(Where *added in the margin in the second line*) *D* 192 thee, divine] the divine *TK* 192/193

⟨Was he a⟩
⟨He was a Poet—sure a Lover too
Who stood on Latmus' top what time there blew
The softest breezes bearing moonl⟩

(*the rest of the last line cut away*) *D* 196 And] Which *FC* 199 infant's] Infants' *FC* 203 in . . . sounds] from Apollo's Lyere a Tone *FC* 204 meek] bright *FC* 206 eyes have] eye has *FC*

As thou exceedest all things in thy shine,
So every tale, does this sweet tale of thine.
O for three words of honey, that I might
210 Tell but one wonder of thy bridal night!

Where distant ships do seem to show their keels,
Phœbus awhile delayed his mighty wheels,
And turned to smile upon thy bashful eyes,
Ere he his unseen pomp would solemnize.
215 The evening weather was so bright, and clear,
That men of health were of unusual cheer;
Stepping like Homer at the trumpet's call,
Or young Apollo on the pedestal:
And lovely women were as fair and warm,
220 As Venus looking sideways in alarm.
The breezes were ethereal, and pure,
And crept through half closed lattices to cure
The languid sick; it cool'd their fever'd sleep,
And soothed them into slumbers full and deep.
225 Soon they awoke clear eyed: nor burnt with thirsting,
Nor with hot fingers, nor with temples bursting:
And springing up, they met the wond'ring sight
Of their dear friends, nigh foolish with delight;
Who feel their arms, and breasts, and kiss and stare,
230 And on their placid foreheads part the hair.
Young men, and maidens at each other gaz'd
With hands held back, and motionless, amaz'd
To see the brightness in each other's eyes;
And so they stood, fill'd with a sweet surprise,
235 Until their tongues were loos'd in poesy.
Therefore no lover did of anguish die:
But the soft numbers, in that moment spoken,
Made silken ties, that never may be broken.
Cynthia! I cannot tell the greater blisses,

217 like . . . call] with such an elegance withall *D, FC* 218 Or] Like *D, FC* 219 And] *successively* (*a*) And (*b*) Each (*c*) And *D* 219 were] *interlined above* ⟨was⟩ *D* 219/220 ⟨As Venus {step} bending from her Car dove drawn⟩ *D* 221 ethereal] ⟨so pure and⟩ ethereal *D* 223 it cool'd] cooling *D, FC* 223 sleep] *interlined above* ⟨dreams⟩ *D* 224 And soothed] Soothing *D, FC*; To sooth *TK* 224 them] ⟨their⟩ them *FC* 225 Soon] Whence *D*; When *FC* 225 nor] ⟨and⟩ nor *D* 226 with hot] ⟨heated Eyes, nor Lips⟩ with hot *D* 226 fingers] *interlined above* ⟨eyesight⟩ *D* 227 And . . . they] So up they sprung and *D, FC* (spang *for* sprung *in FC*) 230 foreheads] ⟨Temples p⟩ foreheads *FC* 236 Therefore] So that *D* 239 Cynthia] *interlined above* ⟨Alas⟩ *D*

240 That follow'd thine, and thy dear shepherd's kisses:
Was there a Poet born?—but now no more,
My wand'ring spirit must no further soar.—

## *Written in Disgust of Vulgar Superstition*

The church bells toll a melancholy round,
Calling the people to some other prayers,
Some other gloominess, more dreadful cares,
More heark'ning to the sermon's horrid sound.
5 Surely the mind of man is closely bound
In some black spell; seeing that each one tears
Himself from fireside joys, and Lydian airs,
And converse high of those with glory crown'd.
Still, still they toll, and I should feel a damp,
10 A chill as from a tomb, did I not know
That they are dying like an outburnt lamp;
That 'tis their sighing, wailing ere they go
Into oblivion;—that fresh flowers will grow,
And many glories of immortal stamp.

## *On the Grasshopper and Cricket*

The poetry of earth is never dead:
When all the birds are faint with the hot sun,
And hide in cooling trees, a voice will run
From hedge to hedge about the new-mown mead;
5 That is the Grasshopper's—he takes the lead
In summer luxury,—he has never done

*Written in Disgust.* Text from Tom Keats's transcript (*TK*). Variants and other readings from Keats's draft (*D*) and the unidentified transcript at Harvard (*Tr*). *Heading* Written . . . Superstition] *ed*; Sonnet / Written . . . superstition *TK*; Written on a Sunday Evening *Tr*; *no heading in D* 1 toll] ⟨give⟩ toll *D* 1 round] *interlined above* ⟨sound⟩ *D* 3 Some . . . dreadful] *interlined above* ⟨To fill their breasts with fear, and gloomy⟩ *D* 5 mind] Mind's *D* 6 seeing that] *interlined above* ⟨that now⟩ *D* 9/10 ⟨A Chill of⟩ *D* 10 tomb] *interlined above* ⟨sepulche⟩ *D* 11 dying] ⟨like⟩ ⟨but⟩ going *D* 12 'tis their] *interlined above* ⟨they are⟩ *D* 12 ere . . . go] *interlined above* ⟨in their woe⟩ *D* 12 ere] as *Tr*

*On the Grasshopper.* Text (including title and end-date but omitting sonnet number) from *1817*. Heading variant from the extant holograph fair copy (*FC*). *Heading* and] & the *FC*

With his delights; for when tired out with fun
He rests at ease beneath some pleasant weed.
The poetry of earth is ceasing never:
10 On a lone winter evening, when the frost
Has wrought a silence, from the stove there shrills
The Cricket's song, in warmth increasing ever,
And seems to one in drowsiness half lost,
The Grasshopper's among some grassy hills.

December 30, 1816

## *After dark vapours have oppressed our plains*

After dark vapours have oppressed our plains
For a long dreary season, comes a day
Born of the gentle south, and clears away
From the sick heavens all unseemly stains.
5 The anxious month, relieving from its pains,
Takes as a long lost right the feel of May,
The eyelids with the passing coolness play,
Like rose-leaves with the drip of summer rains.
And calmest thoughts come round us—as, of leaves
10 Budding—fruit ripening in stillness—autumn suns
Smiling at eve upon the quiet sheaves—
Sweet Sappho's cheek—a sleeping infant's breath—
The gradual sand that through an hour glass runs—
A woodland rivulet—a poet's death.

## *To a Young Lady Who Sent Me a Laurel Crown*

Fresh morning gusts have blown away all fear
From my glad bosom—now from gloominess
I mount for ever—not an atom less
Than the proud laurel shall content my bier.
5 No! by the eternal stars! or why sit here

*After dark vapours.* Text from Woodhouse's $W^2$ transcript. Variants from the *Examiner* version (*Ex*). *Heading* After . . . plains] *ed*; Sonnet *Ex, $W^2$* 5 from] of *Ex* 9 And] The *Ex* 12 sleeping] smiling *Ex*

*To a Young Lady.* Text from Woodhouse's $W^2$ transcript with a missing word taken over from $W^1$. *Heading* To] *ed*; Sonnet. To $W^2$

In the sun's eye, and 'gainst my temples press
Apollo's very leaves—woven to bless
By thy white fingers, and thy spirit clear.
Lo! who dares say, "Do this"?—Who dares call down
10 My will from its own purpose? who say, "Stand,"
Or "Go"? This very moment I would frown
On abject Cæsars—not the stoutest band
Of mailed heroes should tear off my crown:—
Yet would I kneel and kiss thy gentle hand!

## *On Receiving a Laurel Crown from Leigh Hunt*

Minutes are flying swiftly; and as yet
Nothing unearthly has enticed my brain
Into a delphic labyrinth. I would fain
Catch an immortal thought to pay the debt
5 I owe to the kind poet who has set
Upon my ambitious head a glorious gain—
Two bending laurel sprigs—'tis nearly pain
To be conscious of such a coronet.
Still time is fleeting, and no dream arises
10 Gorgeous as I would have it—only I see
A trampling down of what the world most prizes,
Turbans and crowns, and blank regality;
And then I run into most wild surmises
Of all the many glories that may be.

## *To the Ladies Who Saw Me Crown'd*

What is there in the universal earth
More lovely than a wreath from the bay tree?
Haply a halo round the moon—a glee
Circling from three sweet pair of lips in mirth;
5 And haply you will say the dewy birth
Of morning roses—riplings tenderly

10 own] *so* $W^1$ *and originally* $W^2$*; the latter has* high *interlined above* ⟨own⟩ *(see Textual Note)* 11 very] $W^1$ *(the word penciled in a blank space)*; *blank space in* $W^2$

*On Receiving a Laurel Crown.* Text (including heading) from the extant holograph fair copy.

*To the Ladies.* Text (including heading) from the extant holograph fair copy.

Spread by the halcyon's breast upon the sea—
But these comparisons are nothing worth.
Then is there nothing in the world so fair?
10 The silvery tears of April?—Youth of May?
Or June that breathes out life for butterflies?
No—none of these can from my favorite bear
Away the palm; yet shall it ever pay
Due reverence to your most sovereign eyes.

## *God of the golden bow*

God of the golden bow,
And of the golden lyre,
And of the golden hair,
And of the golden fire,
5 Charioteer
Round the patient year—
Where, where slept thine ire,
When like a blank ideot I put on thy wreath—
Thy laurel, thy glory,
10 The light of thy story?
Or was I a worm too low-creeping for death,
O Delphic Apollo?

The Thunderer grasp'd and grasp'd,
The Thunderer frown'd and frown'd;
15 The eagle's feathery mane
For wrath became stiffened; the sound
Of breeding thunder
Went drowsily under,
Muttering to be unbound.
20 O why didst thou pity and beg for a worm?
Why touch thy soft lute
Till the thunder was mute?
Why was I not crush'd—such a pitiful germ?
O Delphic Apollo!

*God of the golden bow.* Text from the extant holograph fair copy (*FC*). Variants and other readings from Keats's draft (*D*) and *1848*. *Heading* God . . . bow] *ed*; Hymn to Apollo *1848*; *no heading in D, FC* 6 Round] Of *D* 8 wreath] *interlined above* ⟨Laurel⟩ *D* 11 creeping] crawling *D* 15 eagle's] Eagle his *altered to* Eagle's *D* 20 beg . . . worm] for a worm *interlined above* ⟨beg of thy father⟩ (beg *deleted by mistake*) *D*

25 The Pleiades were up,
Watching the silent air;
The seeds and roots in earth
Were swelling for summer fare;
The ocean, its neighbour,
30 Was at his old labor,
When—who, who did dare
To tie for a moment thy plant round his brow,
And grin and look proudly,
And blaspheme so loudly,
35 And live for that honor to stoop to thee now,
O Delphic Apollo?

## *This pleasant tale is like a little copse*

This pleasant tale is like a little copse:
The honied lines do freshly interlace,
To keep the reader in so sweet a place,
So that he here and there full hearted stops;
5 And oftentimes he feels the dewy drops
Come cool and suddenly against his face,
And by the wandering melody may trace
Which way the tender-legged linnet hops.
Oh! what a power has white simplicity!
10 What mighty power has this gentle story!
I, that do ever feel athirst for glory,
Could at this moment be content to lie
Meekly upon the grass, as those whose sobbings
Were heard of none beside the mournful robbins.

## *To Leigh Hunt, Esq.*

Glory and loveliness have passed away;
For if we wander out in early morn,

27 earth] the Earth *D* 32 for a moment] like a Madman *D*

*This pleasant tale.* Text from Woodhouse's $W^2$ transcript. Variants from the extant holograph (arbitrarily cited as *FC*) and the *Examiner* version (*Ex*). *Heading* This . . . copse] *ed*; Written on a Blank Space at the End of Chaucer's Tale of "The Floure and the Lefe" *Ex*; Sonnet. Written on the blank space of a leaf at the end of Chaucer's tale of "The flowre and the lefe" $W^2$; *no heading in FC* 9 has] hath *FC* 11 do] for *FC* 11 athirst] a thirst *Ex*

*To Leigh Hunt, Esq.* Text from *1817*. *Heading* To] *ed*; Dedication. / To *1817*

No wreathed incense do we see upborne
Into the east, to meet the smiling day:
5 No crowd of nymphs soft voic'd and young, and gay,
In woven baskets bringing ears of corn,
Roses, and pinks, and violets, to adorn
The shrine of Flora in her early May.
But there are left delights as high as these,
10 And I shall ever bless my destiny,
That in a time, when under pleasant trees
Pan is no longer sought, I feel a free,
A leafy luxury, seeing I could please
With these poor offerings, a man like thee.

## *On Seeing the Elgin Marbles*

My spirit is too weak—mortality
Weighs heavily on me like unwilling sleep,
And each imagined pinnacle and steep
Of godlike hardship tells me I must die
5 Like a sick eagle looking at the sky.
Yet 'tis a gentle luxury to weep
That I have not the cloudy winds to keep
Fresh for the opening of the morning's eye.
Such dim-conceived glories of the brain
10 Bring round the heart an undescribable feud;
So do these wonders a most dizzy pain,
That mingles Grecian grandeur with the rude
Wasting of old time—with a billowy main—
A sun—a shadow of a magnitude.

## *To Haydon with a Sonnet Written on Seeing the Elgin Marbles*

Forgive me, Haydon, that I cannot speak
Definitively on these mighty things;

*On Seeing the Elgin Marbles.* Text (including heading) from the extant holograph fair copy (*FC*). 4 hardship] ⟨diff⟩ Hardship *FC* 9 glories] ⟨motion⟩ glories *FC*

*To Haydon with a Sonnet.* Text (including heading) from the extant holograph fair copy. Variants from the versions published in the *Examiner* (*Ex*) and *Annals of the Fine Arts*. 1 Forgive me, Haydon] Haydon! forgive me *Ex, Annals*

Forgive me that I have not eagle's wings—
That what I want I know not where to seek:
5 And think that I would not be overmeek
In rolling out upfollow'd thunderings,
Even to the steep of Heliconian springs,
Were I of ample strength for such a freak.
Think too that all those numbers should be thine;
10 Whose else? In this who touch thy vesture's hem?
For when men star'd at what was most divine
With browless idiotism—o'erweening phlegm—
Thou hadst beheld the Hesperean shine
Of their star in the east and gone to worship them.

## *On a Leander Which Miss Reynolds, My Kind Friend, Gave Me*

Come hither all sweet maidens, soberly
Down-looking—aye, and with a chastened light
Hid in the fringes of your eyelids white—
And meekly let your fair hands joined be.
5 So gentle are ye that ye could not see,
Untouch'd, a victim of your beauty bright—
Sinking away to his young spirit's night,
Sinking bewilder'd mid the dreary sea:
'Tis young Leander toiling to his death.
10 Nigh swooning, he doth purse his weary lips
For Hero's cheek and smiles against her smile.
O horrid dream—see how his body dips
Dead heavy—arms and shoulders gleam awhile:
He's gone—up bubbles all his amorous breath.

7 steep] sleep *Annals* 12 o'erweening] o'erwise *Ex, Annals*

*On a Leander.* Text (including heading) from Keats's draft (*D*). Variants from the version published in *The Gem.* *Heading* Leander . . . Me] Picture of Leander *Gem* 1 maidens, soberly$_\wedge$] *successively (a)* Maidens (*b*) Maids and soberly$_\wedge$ (*c*) Maidens soberly$_\wedge$ *D*; maidens$_\wedge$ soberly, *Gem* 2 looking—aye] ~$_\wedge$~ *Gem* 2 and . . . a] with *altered to* and with a *D* 4 be.] ~, *Gem* 5 So . . . ye (*first four words*)] *successively* (*a*) Gentle are ye nor co (*b*) are ye so gentle (*c*) so gentle are ye (*the last version from a penciled transposition possibly by Woodhouse rather than Keats—see Textual Note*) *D*; As if so gentle *Gem* 6 Untouch'd] *made out of* Untearful *D* 7 away] ⟨so young⟩ away *D* 10 Nigh swooning] *interlined above* ⟨. . . temples swoon⟩ (*six or seven illegible letters before* temples) *D*

## *On* The Story of Rimini

Who loves to peer up at the morning sun,
With half-shut eyes and comfortable cheek,
Let him with this sweet tale full often seek
For meadows where the little rivers run.
5 Who loves to linger with that brightest one
Of heaven, Hesperus—let him lowly speak
These numbers to the night and starlight meek,
Or moon, if that her hunting be begun.
He who knows these delights, and, too, is prone
10 To moralize upon a smile or tear,
Will find at once a region of his own,
A bower for his spirit, and will steer
To alleys where the fir-tree drops its cone,
Where robins hop, and fallen leaves are sere.

## *On the Sea*

It keeps eternal whisperings around
Desolate shores, and with its mighty swell
Gluts twice ten thousand caverns; till the spell
Of Hecate leaves them their old shadowy sound.
5 Often 'tis in such gentle temper found
That scarcely will the very smallest shell
Be moved for days from whence it sometime fell,
When last the winds of heaven were unbound.
O ye who have your eyeballs vext and tir'd,
10 Feast them upon the wideness of the sea;
O ye whose ears are dinned with uproar rude,
Or fed too much with cloying melody—
Sit ye near some old cavern's mouth and brood
Until ye start, as if the sea nymphs quired.

*On "The Story of Rimini."* Text (including heading) from Hunt's transcript written in a copy of Galignani (1829).

*On the Sea.* Text (including heading) from Woodhouse's clerk's letterbook transcript of Keats's now lost letter to J. H. Reynolds, 17, 18 April 1817 (*WCL*). Variants from the *Champion* version (*Ch*). *Heading* On] Sonnet. On *Ch* 1 It] *Woodhouse notes in WCL that* O Sea *was "obliterated" before this word in the holograph that the clerk copied* 7 moved . . . whence] lightly moved, from where *Ch* 9 O ye who] Ye, that *Ch* 11 O . . . dinned] Or are your hearts disturb'd *Ch* 14 if] *not in Ch*

## *Unfelt, unheard, unseen*

Unfelt, unheard, unseen,
I've left my little queen,
Her languid arms in silver slumber dying:
Ah! through their nestling touch,
5 Who, who could tell how much
There is for madness—cruel or complying?

Those faery lids how sleek,
Those lips how moist—they speak,
In ripest quiet, shadows of sweet sounds;
10 Into my fancy's ear
Melting a burden dear,
How "love doth know no fulness nor no bounds."

True tender monitors,
I bend unto your laws:
15 This sweetest day for dalliance was born;
So, without more ado,
I'll feel my heaven anew,
For all the blushing of the hasty morn.

## *Hither, hither, love*

Hither, hither, love,
'Tis a shady mead;

*Unfelt, unheard, unseen.* Text from the extant holograph fair copy (*FC*). Variants and other readings from the published facsimile of Keats's now lost draft (*D*) and the transcripts by Woodhouse ($W^3$) and C. C. Clarke (*CCC*). *Heading* Unfelt . . . unseen] *ed; no heading in D, FC,* $W^3$, *CCC* 3 dying] ⟨dying⟩ ⟨Kissing⟩ (*with nothing substituted for the second deleted word*) *D*; lying $W^3$, *CCC* 4 Ah . . . touch] *interlined above* ⟨And stifling up the Vale⟩ *D* 6/7

⟨How sleek those faery lids
How moist {that} the lip that bids
E'en in⟩ *D*

9 In . . . quiet] E'en in their quiet stillness *altered to* In ripest quiet *D* 10 Into] *successively* (*a*) Of (*b*) Into (*c*) And to (*d*) Into *D* 11 Melting‸] ~, $W^3$, *CCC* 12 How . . . bounds] *interlined (with no quotation marks) above* ⟨That every Joy and Grief and Feeling drowns⟩ *D* 12/13 ⟨So that my sight is dim⟩ *D* 13 True‸] ~!— $W^3$, *CCC* 13/14 ⟨And so no faults nor flaws⟩ *D* 15 sweetest] suniest *D*

*Hither, hither, love.* Text from the extant holograph (arbitrarily cited as *D*). Heading supplied by editor. 2 mead] Mead⟨ow⟩ *D*

Hither, hither, love,
  Let us feed and feed.

5 Hither, hither, sweet,
  'Tis a cowslip bed;
Hither, hither, sweet,
  'Tis with dew bespread.

Hither, hither, dear,
10 By the breath of life,
Hither, hither, dear,
  Be the summer's wife.

Though one moment's pleasure
  In one moment flies,
15 Though the passion's treasure
  In one moment dies;

Yet it has not pass'd—
  Think how near, how near;
And while it doth last,
20 Think how dear, how dear.

Hither, hither, hither,
  Love this boon has sent;
If I die and wither
  I shall die content.

## *You say you love; but with a voice*

You say you love; but with a voice
  Chaster than a nun's, who singeth
The soft vespers to herself
  While the chime-bell ringeth—
5     O love me truly!

You say you love; but with a smile
  Cold as sunrise in September,

14 In] *interlined above* ⟨But⟩ *D*

*You say you love.* Text from Charlotte Reynolds' transcript (*CR*). Variants from John Taylor's transcript (*JT*). *Heading* You . . . voice] *ed*; Stanzas *CR*; *no heading in JT* 3 vespers] Vesper *JT* 6 with a] then you *JT*

As you were Saint Cupid's nun,
  And kept his weeks of Ember—
10     O love me truly!

You say you love; but then your lips
  Coral tinted teach no blisses,
More than coral in the sea—
  They never pout for kisses—
15     O love me truly!

You say you love; but then your hand
  No soft squeeze for squeeze returneth;
It is like a statue's, dead,—
  While mine for passion burneth—
20     O love me truly!

O breathe a word or two of fire!
  Smile, as if those words should burn me,
Squeeze as lovers should—O kiss
  And in thy heart inurn me—
25     O love me truly!

## *Before he went to live with owls and bats*

Before he went to live with owls and bats,
  Nebuchadnezzar had an ugly dream,
  Worse than a housewife's, when she thinks her cream
Made a naumachia for mice and rats:
5 So scared, he sent for that "good king of cats,"
  Young Daniel, who did straightway pluck the beam
  From out his eye, and said—"I do not deem
Your sceptre worth a straw, your cushions old door mats."

10 O . . . truly!] *not in JT*    12 no] no⟨t⟩ *JT*    22 should] would *JT*    24 thy] *made out of* thine *CR*

*Before he went to live.* Text from Brown's transcript (*CB*). Variants and other readings from Keats's draft (*D*).    *Heading* Before . . . bats] *ed*; Sonnet *CB*; *no heading in D*    1 live] feed *D*    1 with . . . bats] *interlined above* ⟨{like Bottom} on good dry hay⟩ (dry *added above the line*) *D*    3 a housewife's] an Husif's *D*    5 scared,] *interlined above* ⟨straight⟩ *D*    6 did . . . pluck] *successively* (*a*) straight pluck'd (*b*) straightway pluck'd (*c*) soon did pluck (*with interlined* way *in* straightway *inadvertently left undeleted*) *D*    7 out] ⟨his⟩ out *D*    7 I do] he did *D*    8 Your . . . your] His . . . his *D*

A horrid nightmare, similar somewhat,
10 Of late has haunted a most valiant crew
Of loggerheads and chapmen;—we are told
That any Daniel, though he be a sot,
Can make their lying lips turn pale of hue,
By drawling out—"Ye are that head of gold!"

## *The Gothic looks solemn*

1

The Gothic looks solemn,
The plain Doric column
Supports an old bishop and crosier;
The mouldering arch,
5 Shaded o'er by a larch,
Stands next door to Wilson the Hosier.

2

Vicè—that is, by turns,—
O'er pale faces mourns
The black tassell'd trencher and common hat;
10 The chantry boy sings,
The steeple-bell rings,
And as for the Chancellor—*dominat.*

3

There are plenty of trees,
And plenty of ease,
15 And plenty of fat deer for parsons;
And when it is venison,
Short is the benison,—
Then each on a leg or thigh fastens.

9 similar somewhat] somewhat similar (*but marked for transposition*) *D* 10 valiant crew] worthy Crew *interlined above* ⟨worshipful⟩ *D* 11 Of] *written over* ⟨Most⟩ (*continuation of deleted text in 10*) *D* 14 drawling] belching *D*

*The Gothic looks solemn.* Text from Brown's now lost letter to Henry Snook, 24 March 1820, as published in Forman (1883), IV, 74 n. (*CB*). Variants from Woodhouse's $W^2$ transcript. *Heading* The . . . solemn] *ed*; Lines—Rhymed in a letter to J.H.R. from Oxford $W^2$; On Oxford *CB* 6 Stands] Lives $W^2$ 8 faces] visages $W^2$ 9 tassell'd . . . and] tassel . . . or $W^2$ 18 or] *interlined above* ⟨and⟩ $W^2$

## *O grant that like to Peter I*

O grant that like to Peter I
May like to Peter B.
And tell me lovely Jesus Y
Old Jonah went to C.

## *Think not of it, sweet one, so*

Think not of it, sweet one, so;
  Give it not a tear;
Sigh thou mayest, but bid it go
  Any, any where.

5 Do not look so sad, sweet one,
  Sad and fadingly:
Shed one drop then—It is gone—
  Oh! 'twas born to die.

Still so pale?—then, dearest, weep;
10   Weep! I'll count the tears:
And each one shall be a bliss
  For thee in after years.

Brighter has it left thine eyes
  Than a sunny hill:

*O grant that like.* Text from the extant holograph fair copy (*FC*). A variant and other readings from Keats's draft (*D*) written on the same sheet as *FC*. *Heading* O . . . I] *ed*; *no heading in D, FC* 2 B] *written over* ⟨be{e}⟩ *D* 3 Y] ⟨why⟩ Y *D* 4 Old Jonah] This Peter *D*

*Think not of it.* Text from Woodhouse's $W^3$ transcript. Variants and other readings from Keats's draft (*D*). *Heading* Think . . . so] *ed*; *no heading in D, $W^3$* *Before* 1

⟨Think not of it gentle sweet
  Is it worth a tear?
Will thine heart less warmly beat
  Thy voice less dear?⟩ *D*

3 but] and *D* 7 then . . . gone] *interlined above* ⟨an only one⟩ *D* 8 Oh . . . die] *successively (a)* Sweetly did it die (*b*) For 'twas born to die (*c*) Oh 'twas born to die *D* 8/9 ⟨Wilt thou mourn and wilt thou sob / Art indeed so sad & wan⟩ *D* 10/11 ⟨And {for} each one for thee I'll keep⟩ *D* 11 And . . . be] For each will I invent *altered to* And each one shall be *D* 14 hill] rill *D*

15 And thy whispering melodies
Are tenderer still.

Yet, as all things mourn awhile
At fleeting blisses,
Let us too!—but be our dirge
20 A dirge of kisses.

18 fleeting] *interlined above* ⟨dying⟩ *D* 19 Let] E'en let *D*

# *Endymion:*
# *A Poetic Romance*

"The stretched metre of an antique song"

INSCRIBED TO THE MEMORY OF THOMAS CHATTERTON

## Preface

Knowing within myself the manner in which this Poem has been produced, it is not without a feeling of regret that I make it public.

What manner I mean, will be quite clear to the reader, who must soon perceive great inexperience, immaturity, and every error denoting a feverish attempt, rather than a deed accomplished. The two first books, and indeed the two last, I feel sensible are not of such completion as to warrant their passing the press; nor should they if I thought a year's castigation would do them any good;—it will not: the foundations are too sandy. It is just that this youngster should die away: a sad thought for me, if I had not some hope that while it is dwindling I may be plotting, and fitting myself for verses fit to live.

This may be speaking too presumptuously, and may deserve a punishment: but no feeling man will be forward to inflict it: he will leave me alone, with the conviction that there is not a fiercer hell than the failure in a great object. This is not written with the least atom of purpose to forestall criticisms of course, but from the desire I have to conciliate men who are competent to look, and who do look with a zealous eye, to the honour of English literature.

The imagination of a boy is healthy, and the mature imagination of a man is healthy; but there is a space of life between, in which the soul is in a ferment, the character undecided, the way

*Endymion.* Text (including heading, epigraph, dedication, and preface) from *1818*. Variants and other readings from Woodhouse's record of the now lost draft text of Books II–IV in his interleaved *1818* (cited as *D*), the extracts of IV.1–29 in Keats's letter to Bailey, 28–30 October 1817 (*L*[1]), IV.146–181 in his letter to Jane Reynolds, 31 October 1817 (*L*[2]), IV.146–181 in his letter to Bailey, 3 November 1817 (*L*[3]), IV.581–590 in Woodhouse's clerk's letterbook transcript of Keats's now lost letter to J. H. Reynolds, 22 November 1817 (*L*[4]), the extant holograph fair copy (*FC*), and the errata list in Keats's letter to Taylor, 24 April 1818 (*L*[5]). For the original title page, dedication, and preface see Appendix IV. *Subtitle* A Poetic Romance] *so the 1818 title page; Keats's MS title page in FC, the printed half title before the title in 1818, and a variant title page in a copy of 1818 sold at Sotheby's on 29 March 1971 all read* A Romance

of life uncertain, the ambition thick-sighted: thence proceeds mawkishness, and all the thousand bitters which those men I speak of must necessarily taste in going over the following pages.

I hope I have not in too late a day touched the beautiful mythology of Greece, and dulled its brightness: for I wish to try once more, before I bid it farewel.

Teignmouth, April 10, 1818

## BOOK I

A thing of beauty is a joy for ever:
Its loveliness increases; it will never
Pass into nothingness; but still will keep
A bower quiet for us, and a sleep
5 Full of sweet dreams, and health, and quiet breathing.
Therefore, on every morrow, are we wreathing
A flowery band to bind us to the earth,
Spite of despondence, of the inhuman dearth
Of noble natures, of the gloomy days,
10 Of all the unhealthy and o'er-darkened ways
Made for our searching: yes, in spite of all,
Some shape of beauty moves away the pall
From our dark spirits. Such the sun, the moon,
Trees old, and young sprouting a shady boon
15 For simple sheep; and such are daffodils
With the green world they live in; and clear rills
That for themselves a cooling covert make
'Gainst the hot season; the mid forest brake,
Rich with a sprinkling of fair musk-rose blooms:
20 And such too is the grandeur of the dooms
We have imagined for the mighty dead;
All lovely tales that we have heard or read:
An endless fountain of immortal drink,
Pouring unto us from the heaven's brink.

I.9 days] *made out of* ways *FC* 13 spirits . . . moon] Spirits, and before us dances / Like glitter on the points of Arthur's Lances. / [*new* ¶] Of these bright powers are the Sun and Moon *altered to* Spirits. Such the Sun, the Moon *FC* 14 old, . . . young$_{\wedge}$] *FC*, $L^5$; $\sim_{\wedge}$ . . . $\sim$, *1818* 15 and such] *interlined above* ⟨of these⟩ *FC* 16 With] *interlined above* ⟨And⟩ *FC* 20 And such] *interlined above* ⟨Of these⟩ *FC* 20 is] *interlined above* ⟨are⟩ *FC* 24 Pouring . . . from] *written* (*with* unto *made out of* into) *on the opposite verso in FC to replace* ⟨Telling us we are on⟩ (*Keats's revised text then recopied by Taylor above the deleted words in the original line*)

25 Nor do we merely feel these essences
For one short hour; no, even as the trees
That whisper round a temple become soon
Dear as the temple's self, so does the moon,
The passion poesy, glories infinite,
30 Haunt us till they become a cheering light
Unto our souls, and bound to us so fast,
That, whether there be shine, or gloom o'ercast,
They alway must be with us, or we die.

Therefore, 'tis with full happiness that I
35 Will trace the story of Endymion.
The very music of the name has gone
Into my being, and each pleasant scene
Is growing fresh before me as the green
Of our own vallies: so I will begin
40 Now while I cannot hear the city's din;
Now while the early budders are just new,
And run in mazes of the youngest hue
About old forests; while the willow trails
Its delicate amber; and the dairy pails
45 Bring home increase of milk. And, as the year
Grows lush in juicy stalks, I'll smoothly steer
My little boat, for many quiet hours,
With streams that deepen freshly into bowers.
Many and many a verse I hope to write,
50 Before the daisies, vermeil rimm'd and white,
Hide in deep herbage; and ere yet the bees
Hum about globes of clover and sweet peas,
I must be near the middle of my story.
O may no wintry season, bare and hoary,
55 See it half finished: but let autumn bold,
With universal tinge of sober gold,
Be all about me when I make an end.
And now at once, adventuresome, I send
My herald thought into a wilderness:
60 There let its trumpet blow, and quickly dress
My uncertain path with green, that I may speed
Easily onward, thorough flowers and weed.

29 The] *successively* (*a*) The (*b*) And (*c*) The *FC* 29 passion poesy] passion poetry *altered to* passion—poesy *FC* 50 daisies] *made out of* daisy *FC*

Upon the sides of Latmos was outspread
A mighty forest; for the moist earth fed
65 So plenteously all weed-hidden roots
Into o'er-hanging boughs, and precious fruits.
And it had gloomy shades, sequestered deep,
Where no man went; and if from shepherd's keep
A lamb strayed far a-down those inmost glens,
70 Never again saw he the happy pens
Whither his brethren, bleating with content,
Over the hills at every nightfall went.
Among the shepherds, 'twas believed ever,
That not one fleecy lamb which thus did sever
75 From the white flock, but pass'd unworried
By angry wolf, or pard with prying head,
Until it came to some unfooted plains
Where fed the herds of Pan: ay great his gains
Who thus one lamb did lose. Paths there were many,
80 Winding through palmy fern, and rushes fenny,
And ivy banks; all leading pleasantly
To a wide lawn, whence one could only see
Stems thronging all around between the swell
Of turf and slanting branches: who could tell
85 The freshness of the space of heaven above,
Edg'd round with dark tree tops? through which a dove
Would often beat its wings, and often too
A little cloud would move across the blue.

Full in the middle of this pleasantness
90 There stood a marble altar, with a tress
Of flowers budded newly; and the dew
Had taken fairy phantasies to strew
Daisies upon the sacred sward last eve,
And so the dawned light in pomp receive.
95 For 'twas the morn: Apollo's upward fire
Made every eastern cloud a silvery pyre
Of brightness so unsullied, that therein
A melancholy spirit well might win
Oblivion, and melt out his essence fine

71 Whither] *interlined above* ⟨To which⟩ *FC* 74 fleecy] fleecy *altered to* fleecing (*and Keats's revision then canceled by Taylor in pencil, leaving* fleec) *FC* 79 one lamb] but one (one Lamb *penciled above the words by Taylor*) *FC* 83 all around] round *altered to* all around *FC* 94 the] ⟨the coming⟩ the *FC* 99 fine] ⟨pure⟩ fine *FC*

100 Into the winds: rain-scented eglantine
Gave temperate sweets to that well-wooing sun;
The lark was lost in him; cold springs had run
To warm their chilliest bubbles in the grass;
Man's voice was on the mountains; and the mass
105 Of nature's lives and wonders puls'd tenfold,
To feel this sun-rise and its glories old.

Now while the silent workings of the dawn
Were busiest, into that self-same lawn
All suddenly, with joyful cries, there sped
110 A troop of little children garlanded;
Who gathering round the altar, seemed to pry
Earnestly round as wishing to espy
Some folk of holiday: nor had they waited
For many moments, ere their ears were sated
115 With a faint breath of music, which ev'n then
Fill'd out its voice, and died away again.
Within a little space again it gave
Its airy swellings, with a gentle wave,
To light-hung leaves, in smoothest echoes breaking
120 Through copse-clad vallies,—ere their death, o'ertaking
The surgy murmurs of the lonely sea.

And now, as deep into the wood as we
Might mark a lynx's eye, there glimmered light
Fair faces and a rush of garments white,
125 Plainer and plainer shewing, till at last
Into the widest alley they all past,
Making directly for the woodland altar.
O kindly muse! let not my weak tongue faulter
In telling of this goodly company,
130 Of their old piety, and of their glee:
But let a portion of ethereal dew
Fall on my head, and presently unmew
My soul; that I may dare, in wayfaring,
To stammer where old Chaucer used to sing.

107 the silent] these silent (*the first word altered by Taylor in pencil to* the *and then by Keats in ink back to* these) *FC* 115 ev'n] e'en *FC* 119 in] *interlined above* ⟨and⟩ (*the change made first by Taylor in pencil and then by Keats in ink*) *FC* 127–134 Making . . . sing.] *deleted* (*but restored by Taylor with a penciled "Stet" in the margin*) *in FC*

135 Leading the way, young damsels danced along,
Bearing the burden of a shepherd song;
Each having a white wicker over brimm'd
With April's tender younglings: next, well trimm'd,
A crowd of shepherds with as sunburnt looks
140 As may be read of in Arcadian books;
Such as sat listening round Apollo's pipe,
When the great deity, for earth too ripe,
Let his divinity o'er-flowing die
In music, through the vales of Thessaly:
145 Some idly trailed their sheep-hooks on the ground,
And some kept up a shrilly mellow sound
With ebon-tipped flutes: close after these,
Now coming from beneath the forest trees,
A venerable priest full soberly,
150 Begirt with ministring looks: alway his eye
Stedfast upon the matted turf he kept,
And after him his sacred vestments swept.
From his right hand there swung a vase, milk-white,
Of mingled wine, out-sparkling generous light;
155 And in his left he held a basket full
Of all sweet herbs that searching eye could cull:
Wild thyme, and valley-lilies whiter still
Than Leda's love, and cresses from the rill.
His aged head, crowned with beechen wreath,
160 Seem'd like a poll of ivy in the teeth
Of winter hoar. Then came another crowd
Of shepherds, lifting in due time aloud
Their share of the ditty. After them appear'd,
Up-followed by a multitude that rear'd
165 Their voices to the clouds, a fair wrought car,
Easily rolling so as scarce to mar
The freedom of three steeds of dapple brown:

135 Leading . . . young] *successively* (*a*) In front, some pretty (*b*) And In the front, some (*c*) Leading the way, young (*the last version written on the opposite verso*) *FC* 136 shepherd] ⟨may da⟩ shepherd *FC* 137 Each . . . white] *successively* (*a*) And each with handy (*b*) Each with a (*c*) Each with an (*d*) Each having a white (*the last version partly based on suggestions by Taylor—see Textual Note*) *FC* 153 vase . . . white] milk white vase (*altered by Taylor first in pencil and then in ink to* vase milk white) *FC* 154 wine] wine⟨s⟩ *FC* 154 generous light] like the stars (*altered by Taylor first in pencil and then in ink to* generous light) *FC* 157–158 whiter . . . rill] white as Leda's / Bosom, and choicest strips from mountain Cedars (*altered by Taylor first in pencil and then in ink to the 1818 wording, with* blossoms *initially in place of* cresses) *FC* 163 of] o' *FC*

Who stood therein did seem of great renown
Among the throng. His youth was fully blown,
170 Shewing like Ganymede to manhood grown;
And, for those simple times, his garments were
A chieftain king's: beneath his breast, half bare,
Was hung a silver bugle, and between
His nervy knees there lay a boar-spear keen.
175 A smile was on his countenance; he seem'd,
To common lookers on, like one who dream'd
Of idleness in groves Elysian:
But there were some who feelingly could scan
A lurking trouble in his nether lip,
180 And see that oftentimes the reins would slip
Through his forgotten hands: then would they sigh,
And think of yellow leaves, of owlet's cry,
Of logs piled solemnly.—Ah, well-a-day,
Why should our young Endymion pine away!

185 Soon the assembly, in a circle rang'd,
Stood silent round the shrine: each look was chang'd
To sudden veneration: women meek
Beckon'd their sons to silence; while each cheek
Of virgin bloom paled gently for slight fear.
190 Endymion too, without a forest peer,
Stood, wan, and pale, and with an awed face,
Among his brothers of the mountain chase.
In midst of all, the venerable priest
Eyed them with joy from greatest to the least,
195 And, after lifting up his aged hands,
Thus spake he: "Men of Latmos! shepherd bands!
Whose care it is to guard a thousand flocks:
Whether descended from beneath the rocks
That overtop your mountains; whether come
200 From vallies where the pipe is never dumb;
Or from your swelling downs, where sweet air stirs
Blue hare-bells lightly, and where prickly furze
Buds lavish gold; or ye, whose precious charge
Nibble their fill at ocean's very marge,
205 Whose mellow reeds are touch'd with sounds forlorn
By the dim echoes of old Triton's horn:

168 stood] *interlined above* ⟨sat⟩ *FC* 174 there] ⟨was⟩ there *FC* 178 were] ⟨was⟩ were *FC* 182 owlet's] *ed*; owlets *FC*, *1818* 191 an awed] a bowed *altered to* an awed *FC*

Mothers and wives! who day by day prepare
The scrip, with needments, for the mountain air;
And all ye gentle girls who foster up
210 Udderless lambs, and in a little cup
Will put choice honey for a favoured youth:
Yea, every one attend! for in good truth
Our vows are wanting to our great god Pan.
Are not our lowing heifers sleeker than
215 Night-swollen mushrooms? Are not our wide plains
Speckled with countless fleeces? Have not rains
Green'd over April's lap? No howling sad
Sickens our fearful ewes; and we have had
Great bounty from Endymion our lord.
220 The earth is glad: the merry lark has pour'd
His early song against yon breezy sky,
That spreads so clear o'er our solemnity."

Thus ending, on the shrine he heap'd a spire
Of teeming sweets, enkindling sacred fire;
225 Anon he stain'd the thick and spongy sod
With wine, in honour of the shepherd-god.
Now while the earth was drinking it, and while
Bay leaves were crackling in the fragrant pile,
And gummy frankincense was sparkling bright
230 'Neath smothering parsley, and a hazy light
Spread greyly eastward, thus a chorus sang:

"O thou, whose mighty palace roof doth hang
From jagged trunks, and overshadoweth
Eternal whispers, glooms, the birth, life, death
235 Of unseen flowers in heavy peacefulness;
Who lov'st to see the hamadryads dress
Their ruffled locks where meeting hazels darken;
And through whole solemn hours dost sit, and hearken
The dreary melody of bedded reeds—
240 In desolate places, where dank moisture breeds
The pipy hemlock to strange overgrowth;
Bethinking thee, how melancholy loth
Thou wast to lose fair Syrinx—do thou now,
By thy love's milky brow!
245 By all the trembling mazes that she ran,
Hear us, great Pan!

246 Hear us] *interlined above* ⟨Listen⟩ *FC*

"O thou, for whose soul-soothing quiet, turtles
Passion their voices cooingly 'mong myrtles,
What time thou wanderest at eventide
250 Through sunny meadows, that outskirt the side
Of thine enmossed realms: O thou, to whom
Broad leaved fig trees even now foredoom
Their ripen'd fruitage; yellow girted bees
Their golden honeycombs; our village leas
255 Their fairest blossom'd beans and poppied corn;
The chuckling linnet its five young unborn,
To sing for thee; low creeping strawberries
Their summer coolness; pent up butterflies
Their freckled wings; yea, the fresh budding year
260 All its completions—be quickly near,
By every wind that nods the mountain pine,
O forester divine!

"Thou, to whom every faun and satyr flies
For willing service; whether to surprise
265 The squatted hare while in half sleeping fit;
Or upward ragged precipices flit
To save poor lambkins from the eagle's maw;
Or by mysterious enticement draw
Bewildered shepherds to their path again;
270 Or to tread breathless round the frothy main,
And gather up all fancifullest shells
For thee to tumble into Naiads' cells,
And, being hidden, laugh at their out-peeping;
Or to delight thee with fantastic leaping,
275 The while they pelt each other on the crown
With silvery oak apples, and fir cones brown—
By all the echoes that about thee ring,
Hear us, O satyr king!

"O Hearkener to the loud clapping shears,
280 While ever and anon to his shorn peers
A ram goes bleating: Winder of the horn,
When snouted wild-boars routing tender corn
Anger our huntsmen: Breather round our farms,
To keep off mildews, and all weather harms:

263 faun] *ed*; fawn *FC, 1818*  271/272 ⟨To tumble them into fair Naiads {shells} Cells⟩ *FC*  283 huntsmen] *FC*; huntsman *1818*

285 Strange ministrant of undescribed sounds,
That come a swooning over hollow grounds,
And wither drearily on barren moors:
Dread opener of the mysterious doors
Leading to universal knowledge—see,
290 Great son of Dryope,
The many that are come to pay their vows
With leaves about their brows!

"Be still the unimaginable lodge
For solitary thinkings; such as dodge
295 Conception to the very bourne of heaven,
Then leave the naked brain: be still the leaven,
That spreading in this dull and clodded earth
Gives it a touch ethereal—a new birth:
Be still a symbol of immensity;
300 A firmament reflected in a sea;
An element filling the space between;
An unknown—but no more: we humbly screen
With uplift hands our foreheads, lowly bending,
And giving out a shout most heaven rending,
305 Conjure thee to receive our humble pæan,
Upon thy Mount Lycean!"

Even while they brought the burden to a close,
A shout from the whole multitude arose,
That lingered in the air like dying rolls
310 Of abrupt thunder, when Ionian shoals
Of dolphins bob their noses through the brine.
Meantime, on shady levels, mossy fine,
Young companies nimbly began dancing
To the swift treble pipe, and humming string.
315 Aye, those fair living forms swam heavenly
To tunes forgotten—out of memory:
Fair creatures! whose young children's children bred
Thermopylæ its heroes—not yet dead,
But in old marbles ever beautiful.
320 High genitors, unconscious did they cull
Time's sweet first-fruits—they danc'd to weariness,
And then in quiet circles did they press
The hillock turf, and caught the latter end

307 Even] E'en *FC*

Of some strange history, potent to send
325 A young mind from its bodily tenement.
Or they might watch the quoit-pitchers, intent
On either side; pitying the sad death
Of Hyacinthus, when the cruel breath
Of Zephyr slew him,—Zephyr penitent,
330 Who now, ere Phœbus mounts the firmament,
Fondles the flower amid the sobbing rain.
The archers too, upon a wider plain,
Beside the feathery whizzing of the shaft,
And the dull twanging bowstring, and the raft
335 Branch down sweeping from a tall ash top,
Call'd up a thousand thoughts to envelope
Those who would watch. Perhaps, the trembling knee
And frantic gape of lonely Niobe,
Poor, lonely Niobe! when her lovely young
340 Were dead and gone, and her caressing tongue
Lay a lost thing upon her paly lip,
And very, very deadliness did nip
Her motherly cheeks. Arous'd from this sad mood
By one, who at a distance loud halloo'd,
345 Uplifting his strong bow into the air,
Many might after brighter visions stare:
After the Argonauts, in blind amaze
Tossing about on Neptune's restless ways,
Until, from the horizon's vaulted side,
350 There shot a golden splendour far and wide,
Spangling those million poutings of the brine
With quivering ore: 'twas even an awful shine
From the exaltation of Apollo's bow;
A heavenly beacon in their dreary woe.
355 Who thus were ripe for high contemplating
Might turn their steps towards the sober ring
Where sat Endymion and the aged priest
'Mong shepherds gone in eld, whose looks increas'd
The silvery setting of their mortal star.
360 There they discours'd upon the fragile bar
That keeps us from our homes ethereal;
And what our duties there: to nightly call
Vesper, the beauty-crest of summer weather;

337 watch. Perhaps] watch ⟨them⟩. Perhaps *FC* 345 Uplifting . . . air,] *written vertically in the margin in FC with a mark for insertion after 344* 352 even] e'en *FC*

To summon all the downiest clouds together
365 For the sun's purple couch; to emulate
In ministring the potent rule of fate
With speed of fire-tailed exhalations;
To tint her pallid cheek with bloom, who cons
Sweet poesy by moonlight: besides these,
370 A world of other unguess'd offices.
Anon they wander'd, by divine converse,
Into Elysium; vieing to rehearse
Each one his own anticipated bliss.
One felt heart-certain that he could not miss
375 His quick gone love, among fair blossom'd boughs,
Where every zephyr-sigh pouts, and endows
Her lips with music for the welcoming.
Another wish'd, mid that eternal spring,
To meet his rosy child, with feathery sails,
380 Sweeping, eye-earnestly, through almond vales:
Who, suddenly, should stoop through the smooth wind,
And with the balmiest leaves his temples bind;
And, ever after, through those regions be
His messenger, his little Mercury.
385 Some were athirst in soul to see again
Their fellow huntsmen o'er the wide champaign
In times long past; to sit with them, and talk
Of all the chances in their earthly walk;
Comparing, joyfully, their plenteous stores
390 Of happiness, to when upon the moors,
Benighted, close they huddled from the cold,
And shar'd their famish'd scrips. Thus all out-told
Their fond imaginations,—saving him
Whose eyelids curtain'd up their jewels dim,
395 Endymion: yet hourly had he striven
To hide the cankering venom, that had riven
His fainting recollections. Now indeed
His senses had swoon'd off: he did not heed
The sudden silence, or the whispers low,
400 Or the old eyes dissolving at his woe,
Or anxious calls, or close of trembling palms,
Or maiden's sigh, that grief itself embalms:

368 pallid] pretty (*the word underscored and* pallid *and* waning *written by Taylor both in the margin and on the opposite verso*) *FC* 386 champaign] campaign *FC* 389 plenteous] *interlined above* ⟨present⟩ *FC*

But in the self-same fixed trance he kept,
Like one who on the earth had never stept—
405 Aye, even as dead-still as a marble man,
Frozen in that old tale Arabian.

Who whispers him so pantingly and close?
Peona, his sweet sister: of all those,
His friends, the dearest. Hushing signs she made,
410 And breath'd a sister's sorrow to persuade
A yielding up, a cradling on her care.
Her eloquence did breathe away the curse:
She led him, like some midnight spirit nurse
Of happy changes in emphatic dreams,
415 Along a path between two little streams,—
Guarding his forehead, with her round elbow,
From low-grown branches, and his footsteps slow
From stumbling over stumps and hillocks small;
Until they came to where these streamlets fall,
420 With mingled bubblings and a gentle rush,
Into a river, clear, brimful, and flush
With crystal mocking of the trees and sky.
A little shallop, floating there hard by,
Pointed its beak over the fringed bank;
425 And soon it lightly dipt, and rose, and sank,
And dipt again, with the young couple's weight,—
Peona guiding, through the water straight,
Towards a bowery island opposite;
Which gaining presently, she steered light
430 Into a shady, fresh, and ripply cove,

406 Frozen] *interlined above* ⟨Sitting⟩ *FC* 407–412 Who . . . curse:] *written on the opposite verso in FC to replace:*

⟨Now happily, there sitting on the grass
Was fair Peona, a most tender Lass,
And his sweet sister; who, uprising, went
With stifled sobs, and o'er his shoulder leant.
Putting her trembling hand against his cheek
She said: "My dear Endymion, let us seek
A pleasant bower where thou may'st rest apart,
And ease in slumber thine afflicted heart:
Come my own dearest brother: these our friends
Will joy in thinking thou dost sleep where bends
Our freshening River through yon birchen grove:
Do come now!" Could he gainsay her who strove,
So soothingly, to breathe away a Curse?⟩

Where nested was an arbour, overwove
By many a summer's silent fingering;
To whose cool bosom she was used to bring
Her playmates, with their needle broidery,
435 And minstrel memories of times gone by.

So she was gently glad to see him laid
Under her favourite bower's quiet shade,
On her own couch, new made of flower leaves,
Dried carefully on the cooler side of sheaves
440 When last the sun his autumn tresses shook,
And the tann'd harvesters rich armfuls took.
Soon was he quieted to slumbrous rest:
But, ere it crept upon him, he had prest
Peona's busy hand against his lips,
445 And still, a sleeping, held her finger-tips
In tender pressure. And as a willow keeps
A patient watch over the stream that creeps
Windingly by it, so the quiet maid
Held her in peace: so that a whispering blade
450 Of grass, a wailful gnat, a bee bustling
Down in the blue-bells, or a wren light rustling
Among sere leaves and twigs, might all be heard.

O magic sleep! O comfortable bird,
That broodest o'er the troubled sea of the mind
455 Till it is hush'd and smooth! O unconfin'd

432 By] *interlined above* ⟨With⟩ *FC* 440–441 When . . . took.] *written on the opposite verso in FC to replace:*

⟨When last the Harvesters rich armfuls took.
She tied a little bucket to a Crook,
Ran some swift paces to a dark wells side,
And in a sighing time return'd, supplied
With spar cold water; in which she did squeeze
A snowy napkin, and upon her Knees
Began to cherish her poor Brother's face;
Damping refreshfully his forehead's space,
His eyes, his Lips: then in a cupped shell
She brought him ruby wine; then let him smell,
Time after time, a precious amulet,
Which seldom took she from its cabinet.⟩

(*the passage marked for deletion first by Taylor in pencil and then by Keats in ink*) 441 And] *successively* (*a*) And (*b*) While (*c*) And *FC* 442 Soon was he] *successively* (*a*) Thus was he (*b*) Soon was he (*c*) And he (*d*) Soon was he (*the last also in Taylor's hand, to clarify the final text for the printer*) *FC* 451 or] *added above the line in FC* 454 of] o' *FC*

Restraint! imprisoned liberty! great key
To golden palaces, strange minstrelsy,
Fountains grotesque, new trees, bespangled caves,
Echoing grottos, full of tumbling waves
460 And moonlight; aye, to all the mazy world
Of silvery enchantment!—who, upfurl'd
Beneath thy drowsy wing a triple hour,
But renovates and lives?—Thus, in the bower,
Endymion was calm'd to life again.
465 Opening his eyelids with a healthier brain,
He said: "I feel this thine endearing love
All through my bosom: thou art as a dove
Trembling its closed eyes and sleeked wings
About me; and the pearliest dew not brings
470 Such morning incense from the fields of May,
As do those brighter drops that twinkling stray
From those kind eyes,—the very home and haunt
Of sisterly affection. Can I want
Aught else, aught nearer heaven, than such tears?
475 Yet dry them up, in bidding hence all fears
That, any longer, I will pass my days
Alone and sad. No, I will once more raise
My voice upon the mountain-heights; once more
Make my horn parley from their foreheads hoar:
480 Again my trooping hounds their tongues shall loll
Around the breathed boar: again I'll poll
The fair-grown yew tree, for a chosen bow:
And, when the pleasant sun is getting low,
Again I'll linger in a sloping mead
485 To hear the speckled thrushes, and see feed
Our idle sheep. So be thou cheered, sweet,
And, if thy lute is here, softly intreat
My soul to keep in its resolved course."

465/466
⟨A cheerfuller resignment, and a smile
For his fair Sister, flowing like the Nile
Through all the channels of her piety,⟩ *FC*
466 I . . . this] ⟨Dear Maid, may I this moment die, / If⟩ I feel ⟨not⟩ this *FC*
470–472 Such . . . haunt] *written on the opposite verso in FC to replace:*
⟨From woodbine hedges, such a morning feel,
As do those brighter drops, that twinkling steal
Through those pressed lashes, from the blossom'd plant⟩

Hereat Peona, in their silver source,
490 Shut her pure sorrow drops with glad exclaim,
And took a lute, from which there pulsing came
A lively prelude, fashioning the way
In which her voice should wander. 'Twas a lay
More subtle cadenced, more forest wild
495 Than Dryope's lone lulling of her child;
And nothing since has floated in the air
So mournful strange. Surely some influence rare
Went, spiritual, through the damsel's hand;
For still, with Delphic emphasis, she spann'd
500 The quick invisible strings, even though she saw
Endymion's spirit melt away and thaw
Before the deep intoxication.
But soon she came, with sudden burst, upon
Her self-possession—swung the lute aside,
505 And earnestly said: "Brother, 'tis vain to hide
That thou dost know of things mysterious,
Immortal, starry; such alone could thus
Weigh down thy nature. Hast thou sinn'd in aught
Offensive to the heavenly powers? Caught
510 A Paphian dove upon a message sent?
Thy deathful bow against some deer-herd bent,
Sacred to Dian? Haply, thou hast seen
Her naked limbs among the alders green;
And that, alas! is death. No, I can trace
515 Something more high perplexing in thy face!"

Endymion look'd at her, and press'd her hand,
And said, "Art thou so pale, who wast so bland

494–495 More . . . child;] *written on the opposite verso in FC to replace:*
⟨More forest-wild, more subtle-cadenced
Than can be told by mortal: even wed
The fainting tenors of a thousand Shells,
To a million whisperings of Lilly bells;
And, mingle too, the Nightingale's complain
Caught in its hundredth echo; 'twould be vain:⟩
(*the last five lines, from* even wed, *marked by Taylor in pencil, and then all six lines deleted by Keats in ink*) 496 And] *written in the margin in FC to replace* ⟨For⟩ 513 among the alders] on flags and rushes (*altered by Taylor first in pencil and then in ink to the 1818 wording*) *FC*
516–520 Endymion . . . change] *written on the opposite verso in FC to replace:*
⟨And I do pray thee by thy utmost aim
To tell me all—No little fault or blame

And merry in our meadows? How is this?
Tell me thine ailment: tell me all amiss!—
520 Ah! thou hast been unhappy at the change
Wrought suddenly in me. What indeed more strange?
Or more complete to overwhelm surmise?
Ambition is no sluggard: 'tis no prize,
That toiling years would put within my grasp,
525 That I have sigh'd for: with so deadly gasp
No man e'er panted for a mortal love.
So all have set my heavier grief above
These things which happen. Rightly have they done:
I, who still saw the horizontal sun
530 Heave his broad shoulder o'er the edge of the world,
Out-facing Lucifer, and then had hurl'd
My spear aloft, as signal for the chace—
I, who, for very sport of heart, would race
With my own steed from Araby; pluck down
535 A vulture from his towery perching; frown
A lion into growling, loth retire—
To lose, at once, all my toil breeding fire,
And sink thus low! but I will ease my breast
Of secret grief, here in this bowery nest.

540 "This river does not see the naked sky,
Till it begins to progress silverly
Around the western border of the wood,
Whence, from a certain spot, its winding flood

---

Canst thou lay on me for a teasing Girl;
Ever as an unfathomable pearl
Has been thy secrecy to me: but now
I needs must hunger after it, and vow
To be its jealous Guardian for aye.
Uttering these words she got nigh and more nigh,
And put at last her arms about his neck:
Nor was there any tart, ungentle check,
Nor any frown, or stir dissatisfied,
But smooth compliance, and tender slide
Of arm in arm, and what is written next.
"Doubtless, Peona, thou hast been perplex'd,
And pained oft, in thinking of the change⟩
(*Taylor marked the first seven lines marginally in pencil, inserted a penciled* a *before* tender *in the twelfth line, and then, after Keats deleted and rewrote the entire passage, changed* face: *in 515 to* ~!"—) 520 hast] has *FC* 530 of] o' *FC* 536 growling] *interlined above* ⟨grumbling⟩ *FC* 538–539 And . . . nest.] *written on the opposite verso in FC to replace* ⟨And come to such a Ghost as I am now! / But listen, Sister, I will tell the how.⟩

Seems at the distance like a crescent moon:
545 And in that nook, the very pride of June,
Had I been used to pass my weary eves;
The rather for the sun unwilling leaves
So dear a picture of his sovereign power,
And I could witness his most kingly hour,
550 When he doth tighten up the golden reins,
And paces leisurely down amber plains
His snorting four. Now when his chariot last
Its beams against the zodiac-lion cast,
There blossom'd suddenly a magic bed
555 Of sacred ditamy, and poppies red:
At which I wondered greatly, knowing well
That but one night had wrought this flowery spell;
And, sitting down close by, began to muse
What it might mean. Perhaps, thought I, Morpheus,
560 In passing here, his owlet pinions shook;
Or, it may be, ere matron Night uptook
Her ebon urn, young Mercury, by stealth,
Had dipt his rod in it: such garland wealth
Came not by common growth. Thus on I thought,
565 Until my head was dizzy and distraught.
Moreover, through the dancing poppies stole
A breeze, most softly lulling to my soul;
And shaping visions all about my sight
Of colours, wings, and bursts of spangly light;
570 The which became more strange, and strange, and dim,
And then were gulph'd in a tumultuous swim:
And then I fell asleep. Ah, can I tell
The enchantment that afterwards befel?
Yet it was but a dream: yet such a dream
575 That never tongue, although it overteem

545 And . . . June,] *written on the opposite verso in FC to replace:*
⟨And in that spot the most endowing boon
Of balmy Air, sweet blooms, and coverts fresh
Has been outshed; yes, all that could enmesh
Our human senses—make us fealty sware
To gadding Flora. In this grateful lair⟩
(that *made out of* this *in the first line, and* In *successively* [*a*] In [*b*] To [*c*] In *in the last line; Taylor marked and partially revised the second through fifth lines in pencil, after which Keats deleted and rewrote the entire passage*) 546 Had] *made out of* Have *FC* 546 pass] *successively* (*a*) pass (*b*) give (*c*) pass *FC* 550 tighten] *FC* (*written with the first* t *uncrossed*); lighten *1818* 561 be . . . matron] be that, ere still *altered to* be, ere matron *FC*

With mellow utterance, like a cavern spring,
Could figure out and to conception bring
All I beheld and felt. Methought I lay
Watching the zenith, where the milky way
580 Among the stars in virgin splendour pours;
And travelling my eye, until the doors
Of heaven appear'd to open for my flight,
I became loth and fearful to alight
From such high soaring by a downward glance:
585 So kept me stedfast in that airy trance,
Spreading imaginary pinions wide.
When, presently, the stars began to glide,
And faint away, before my eager view:
At which I sigh'd that I could not pursue,
590 And dropt my vision to the horizon's verge;
And lo! from opening clouds, I saw emerge
The loveliest moon, that ever silver'd o'er
A shell for Neptune's goblet: she did soar
So passionately bright, my dazzled soul
595 Commingling with her argent spheres did roll
Through clear and cloudy, even when she went
At last into a dark and vapoury tent—
Whereat, methought, the lidless-eyed train
Of planets all were in the blue again.
600 To commune with those orbs, once more I rais'd
My sight right upward: but it was quite dazed
By a bright something, sailing down apace,
Making me quickly veil my eyes and face:
Again I look'd, and, O ye deities,
605 Who from Olympus watch our destinies!
Whence that completed form of all completeness?
Whence came that high perfection of all sweetness?
Speak, stubborn earth, and tell me where, O where
Hast thou a symbol of her golden hair?
610 Not oat-sheaves drooping in the western sun;
Not—thy soft hand, fair sister! let me shun
Such follying before thee—yet she had,
Indeed, locks bright enough to make me mad;

582 appeared] seemed (*altered by Taylor first in pencil and then in ink to* appeared) *FC* 599 all were] were all *altered to* all were *FC* 600 To . . . orbs] And to commune with them (*altered by Taylor to the 1818 wording*) *FC* 601 sight] *interlined above* ⟨eyes⟩ *FC* 601 it was] *interlined above* ⟨they were⟩ *FC*

And they were simply gordian'd up and braided,
615 Leaving, in naked comeliness, unshaded,
Her pearl round ears, white neck, and orbed brow;
The which were blended in, I know not how,
With such a paradise of lips and eyes,
Blush-tinted cheeks, half smiles, and faintest sighs,
620 That, when I think thereon, my spirit clings
And plays about its fancy, till the stings
Of human neighbourhood envenom all.
Unto what awful power shall I call?
To what high fane?—Ah! see her hovering feet,
625 More bluely vein'd, more soft, more whitely sweet
Than those of sea-born Venus, when she rose
From out her cradle shell. The wind out-blows
Her scarf into a fluttering pavilion;
'Tis blue, and over-spangled with a million
630 Of little eyes, as though thou wert to shed,
Over the darkest, lushest blue-bell bed,
Handfuls of daisies."—"Endymion, how strange!
Dream within dream!"—"She took an airy range,
And then, towards me, like a very maid,
635 Came blushing, waning, willing, and afraid,
And press'd me by the hand: Ah! 'twas too much;
Methought I fainted at the charmed touch,
Yet held my recollection, even as one
Who dives three fathoms where the waters run
640 Gurgling in beds of coral: for anon,
I felt upmounted in that region
Where falling stars dart their artillery forth,
And eagles struggle with the buffeting north
That balances the heavy meteor-stone;—
645 Felt too, I was not fearful, nor alone,
But lapp'd and lull'd along the dangerous sky.
Soon, as it seem'd, we left our journeying high,
And straightway into frightful eddies swoop'd;
Such as ay muster where grey time has scoop'd
650 Huge dens and caverns in a mountain's side:

614 they] *written over* ⟨in⟩ *FC* 621 plays] *interlined above* ⟨fawns⟩ (*the original word underscored by Taylor in pencil*) *FC* 630 wert] *made out of* wast *FC* 632 daisies] bud-stars (*altered by Taylor to* daisies) *FC* 638 even] e'en *altered to* even *FC* 646 along . . . sky] *interlined above* ⟨in safe deliriousness⟩ (*the last word also readable as* deliciousness) *FC* 646/647 ⟨Sleepy with deep foretasting, that did bless / My Soul from Madness, 'twas such certainty.⟩ *FC*

There hollow sounds arous'd me, and I sigh'd
To faint once more by looking on my bliss—
I was distracted; madly did I kiss
The wooing arms which held me, and did give
655 My eyes at once to death: but 'twas to live,
To take in draughts of life from the gold fount
Of kind and passionate looks; to count, and count
The moments, by some greedy help that seem'd
A second self, that each might be redeem'd
660 And plunder'd of its load of blessedness.
Ah, desperate mortal! I ev'n dar'd to press
Her very cheek against my crowned lip,
And, at that moment, felt my body dip
Into a warmer air: a moment more,
665 Our feet were soft in flowers. There was store
Of newest joys upon that alp. Sometimes
A scent of violets, and blossoming limes,
Loiter'd around us; then of honey cells,
Made delicate from all white-flower bells;
670 And once, above the edges of our nest,
An arch face peep'd,—an Oread as I guess'd.

"Why did I dream that sleep o'er-power'd me
In midst of all this heaven? Why not see,
Far off, the shadows of his pinions dark,
675 And stare them from me? But no, like a spark
That needs must die, although its little beam
Reflects upon a diamond, my sweet dream
Fell into nothing—into stupid sleep.
And so it was, until a gentle creep,
680 A careful moving, caught my waking ears,

651 sigh'd] died (*altered by Taylor to* sigh'd) *FC* 661 ev'n] e'en *FC* 662 cheek] cheek⟨s⟩ *FC* 665–666 There . . . alp.] *written vertically in the margin in FC to replace:*
⟨Hurry o'er
O sacrilegeous tongue the—best be dumb;
For should one little accent from thee come
On such a daring theme, all other sounds
Would sicken at it, as would beaten hounds
Scare the elysian Nightingales.⟩
(*the passage canceled and rewritten by Keats after Taylor penciled an X beside the fifth line and interlined suggested revisions in pencil, subsequently deleted, above all but the final line*) 665 was store] were stores *altered to* was store *FC*

And up I started: Ah! my sighs, my tears,
My clenched hands;—for lo! the poppies hung
Dew-dabbled on their stalks, the ouzel sung
A heavy ditty, and the sullen day
685 Had chidden herald Hesperus away,
With leaden looks: the solitary breeze
Bluster'd, and slept, and its wild self did teaze
With wayward melancholy; and I thought,
Mark me, Peona! that sometimes it brought
690 Faint fare-thee-wells, and sigh-shrilled adieus!—
Away I wander'd—all the pleasant hues
Of heaven and earth had faded: deepest shades
Were deepest dungeons; heaths and sunny glades
Were full of pestilent light; our taintless rills
695 Seem'd sooty, and o'er-spread with upturn'd gills
Of dying fish; the vermeil rose had blown
In frightful scarlet, and its thorns out-grown
Like spiked aloe. If an innocent bird
Before my heedless footsteps stirr'd, and stirr'd
700 In little journeys, I beheld in it
A disguis'd demon, missioned to knit
My soul with under darkness; to entice
My stumblings down some monstrous precipice:
Therefore I eager followed, and did curse
705 The disappointment. Time, that aged nurse,
Rock'd me to patience. Now, thank gentle heaven!
These things, with all their comfortings, are given
To my down-sunken hours, and with thee,
Sweet sister, help to stem the ebbing sea
Of weary life."

710 Thus ended he, and both
Sat silent: for the maid was very loth
To answer; feeling well that breathed words
Would all be lost, unheard, and vain as swords
Against the enchased crocodile, or leaps
715 Of grasshoppers against the sun. She weeps,
And wonders; struggles to devise some blame;
To put on such a look as would say, *Shame*
*On this poor weakness!* but, for all her strife,
She could as soon have crush'd away the life
720 From a sick dove. At length, to break the pause,
She said with trembling chance: "Is this the cause?

This all? Yet it is strange, and sad, alas!
That one who through this middle earth should pass
Most like a sojourning demi-god, and leave
725 His name upon the harp-string, should achieve
No higher bard than simple maidenhood,
Singing alone, and fearfully,—how the blood
Left his young cheek; and how he used to stray
He knew not where; and how he would say, *nay*,
730 If any said 'twas love: and yet 'twas love;
What could it be but love? How a ring-dove
Let fall a sprig of yew tree in his path;
And how he died: and then, that love doth scathe
The gentle heart, as northern blasts do roses;
735 And then the ballad of his sad life closes
With sighs, and an alas!—Endymion!
Be rather in the trumpet's mouth,—anon
Among the winds at large—that all may hearken!
Although, before the crystal heavens darken,
740 I watch and dote upon the silver lakes
Pictur'd in western cloudiness, that takes
The semblance of gold rocks and bright gold sands,
Islands, and creeks, and amber-fretted strands
With horses prancing o'er them, palaces
745 And towers of amethyst,—would I so tease
My pleasant days, because I could not mount
Into those regions? The Morphean fount
Of that fine element that visions, dreams,
And fitful whims of sleep are made of, streams
750 Into its airy channels with so subtle,
So thin a breathing, not the spider's shuttle,
Circled a million times within the space
Of a swallow's nest-door, could delay a trace,

722 This . . . alas]
This all? Yet it is ⟨wonderful—exceeding—
And yet a shallow dream, for ever breeding
Tempestuous Weather in that very Soul
That should be twice content, twice smooth, twice whole,
As is a double Peach. 'Tis⟩ sad Alas
(*the canceled text first bracketed by Taylor in pencil, then deleted by Keats in ink; 1818's* strange, and *is not in the MS*) *FC* 727 blood] ⟨young⟩ blood *FC* 738 at large] *added above the line in FC* 739 Although] What though *altered to* Although *FC* 741 Pictur'd in] Pight among *altered to* Pight amid (*the revised text then deleted and* Pictur'd in *inserted above the line by Taylor*) *FC* 747 The] *made out of* That *FC*

A tinting of its quality: how light
755 Must dreams themselves be; seeing they're more slight
Than the mere nothing that engenders them!
Then wherefore sully the entrusted gem
Of high and noble life with thoughts so sick?
Why pierce high-fronted honour to the quick
760 For nothing but a dream?" Hereat the youth
Look'd up: a conflicting of shame and ruth
Was in his plaited brow: yet, his eyelids
Widened a little, as when Zephyr bids
A little breeze to creep between the fans
765 Of careless butterflies: amid his pains
He seem'd to taste a drop of manna-dew,
Full palatable; and a colour grew
Upon his cheek, while thus he lifeful spake.

"Peona! ever have I long'd to slake
770 My thirst for the world's praises: nothing base,
No merely slumberous phantasm, could unlace
The stubborn canvas for my voyage prepar'd—
Though now 'tis tatter'd; leaving my bark bar'd
And sullenly drifting: yet my higher hope
775 Is of too wide, too rainbow-large a scope,
To fret at myriads of earthly wrecks.
Wherein lies happiness? In that which becks
Our ready minds to fellowship divine,
A fellowship with essence; till we shine,
780 Full alchemiz'd, and free of space. Behold
The clear religion of heaven! Fold

756 nothing . . . engenders] nothingness engendring *FC* 757 wherefore] *made out of* why *FC* 762 plaited] pleated *FC* 764 breeze] Puff (*altered by Taylor to* Breath) *FC* 770–771 base . . . unlace] mean . . . unseam (*altered by Taylor first in pencil and then in ink to the 1818 wording*) *FC* 776–781 To . . . Fold] *copied by Taylor on the opposite verso in FC after Keats sent him the revised text of 777–781 in a letter of 30 January 1818* (*Letters*, *I, 218*). *The original passage in FC was:*

To fret at myriads of earthly wrecks.
Wherein lies happiness? In that which becks
Our ready minds to blending pleasureable:
And that delight is the most treasureable
That makes the richest Alchymy. Behold
The clear Religion of Heaven! Fold

*Taylor marked the first four lines marginally in pencil and interlined a revision of the first line in ink to produce* To fret at ⟨Sight of⟩ this World's losses. For, behold (*intending this to connect with the final line given above*). *At some point Keats changed the last line to read* Wherin lies happiness

A rose leaf round thy finger's taperness,
And soothe thy lips: hist, when the airy stress
Of music's kiss impregnates the free winds,
785 And with a sympathetic touch unbinds
Eolian magic from their lucid wombs:
Then old songs waken from enclouded tombs;
Old ditties sigh above their father's grave;
Ghosts of melodious prophecyings rave
790 Round every spot where trod Apollo's foot;
Bronze clarions awake, and faintly bruit,
Where long ago a giant battle was;
And, from the turf, a lullaby doth pass
In every place where infant Orpheus slept.
795 Feel we these things?—that moment have we stept
Into a sort of oneness, and our state
Is like a floating spirit's. But there are
Richer entanglements, enthralments far
More self-destroying, leading, by degrees,
800 To the chief intensity: the crown of these
Is made of love and friendship, and sits high
Upon the forehead of humanity.
All its more ponderous and bulky worth
Is friendship, whence there ever issues forth
805 A steady splendour; but at the tip-top,
There hangs by unseen film, an orbed drop
Of light, and that is love: its influence,
Thrown in our eyes, genders a novel sense,
At which we start and fret; till in the end,
810 Melting into its radiance, we blend,
Mingle, and so become a part of it,—
Nor with aught else can our souls interknit
So wingedly: when we combine therewith,
Life's self is nourish'd by its proper pith,
815 And we are nurtured like a pelican brood.
Aye, so delicious is the unsating food,

---

Peona! Fold *but it is not clear whether he did this before Taylor marked the MS (in which case he would have had six lines beginning* To fret . . . *and repeating* Wherein lies happiness *in the second and sixth lines) or afterward (in which case, because of the rhymes involved, he would have reduced the text to two lines consisting of Taylor's revised first line and his own revised last line); the first quotation in his letter to Taylor fits either situation* 785 with . . . unbinds] sympathetically, unconfines *altered to* with a sympathetic touch unbinds *FC* 790 trod] *interlined above* ⟨touch'd⟩ *FC* 794 place] *interlined above* ⟨spot⟩ *FC* 795 things?—] ~‸— *FC* 813 combine] amalgamate (*altered by Taylor to* combine) *FC*

That men, who might have tower'd in the van
Of all the congregated world, to fan
And winnow from the coming step of time
820 All chaff of custom, wipe away all slime
Left by men-slugs and human serpentry,
Have been content to let occasion die,
Whilst they did sleep in love's elysium.
And, truly, I would rather be struck dumb,
825 Than speak against this ardent listlessness:
For I have ever thought that it might bless
The world with benefits unknowingly;
As does the nightingale, upperched high,
And cloister'd among cool and bunched leaves—
830 She sings but to her love, nor e'er conceives
How tiptoe Night holds back her dark-grey hood.
Just so may love, although 'tis understood
The mere commingling of passionate breath,
Produce more than our searching witnesseth:
835 What I know not: but who, of men, can tell
That flowers would bloom, or that green fruit would swell
To melting pulp, that fish would have bright mail,
The earth its dower of river, wood, and vale,
The meadows runnels, runnels pebble-stones,
840 The seed its harvest, or the lute its tones,
Tones ravishment, or ravishment its sweet,
If human souls did never kiss and greet?

"Now, if this earthly love has power to make
Men's being mortal, immortal; to shake
845 Ambition from their memories, and brim
Their measure of content; what merest whim,
Seems all this poor endeavour after fame,
To one, who keeps within his stedfast aim
A love immortal, an immortal too.
850 Look not so wilder'd; for these things are true,
And never can be born of atomies
That buzz about our slumbers, like brain-flies,
Leaving us fancy-sick. No, no, I'm sure,
My restless spirit never could endure
855 To brood so long upon one luxury,

844 Men's] Man's (*altered by Taylor in pencil to* Men's) *FC* 847 Seems] *interlined above* ⟨Shews⟩ *FC* 849 an] and *FC*

Unless it did, though fearfully, espy
A hope beyond the shadow of a dream.
My sayings will the less obscured seem,
When I have told thee how my waking sight
860 Has made me scruple whether that same night
Was pass'd in dreaming. Hearken, sweet Peona!
Beyond the matron-temple of Latona,
Which we should see but for these darkening boughs,
Lies a deep hollow, from whose ragged brows
865 Bushes and trees do lean all round athwart,
And meet so nearly, that with wings outraught,
And spreaded tail, a vulture could not glide
Past them, but he must brush on every side.
Some moulder'd steps lead into this cool cell,
870 Far as the slabbed margin of a well,
Whose patient level peeps its crystal eye
Right upward, through the bushes, to the sky.
Oft have I brought thee flowers, on their stalks set
Like vestal primroses, but dark velvet
875 Edges them round, and they have golden pits:
'Twas there I got them, from the gaps and slits
In a mossy stone, that sometimes was my seat,
When all above was faint with mid-day heat.
And there in strife no burning thoughts to heed,
880 I'd bubble up the water through a reed;
So reaching back to boy-hood: make me ships
Of moulted feathers, touchwood, alder chips,
With leaves stuck in them; and the Neptune be
Of their petty ocean. Oftener, heavily,
885 When love-lorn hours had left me less a child,
I sat contemplating the figures wild
Of o'er-head clouds melting the mirror through.
Upon a day, while thus I watch'd, by flew
A cloudy Cupid, with his bow and quiver;
890 So plainly character'd, no breeze would shiver
The happy chance: so happy, I was fain
To follow it upon the open plain,
And, therefore, was just going; when, behold!
A wonder, fair as any I have told—
895 The same bright face I tasted in my sleep,

862 Beyond] *made out of* Behind *FC* 862 matron] *interlined above* ⟨little⟩ (*the original word underscored by Taylor in pencil*) *FC*

Smiling in the clear well. My heart did leap
Through the cool depth.—It moved as if to flee—
I started up, when lo! refreshfully,
There came upon my face, in plenteous showers,
900 Dew-drops, and dewy buds, and leaves, and flowers,
Wrapping all objects from my smothered sight,
Bathing my spirit in a new delight.
Aye, such a breathless honey-feel of bliss
Alone preserved me from the drear abyss
905 Of death, for the fair form had gone again.
Pleasure is oft a visitant; but pain
Clings cruelly to us, like the gnawing sloth
On the deer's tender haunches: late, and loth,
'Tis scar'd away by slow returning pleasure.
910 How sickening, how dark the dreadful leisure
Of weary days, made deeper exquisite,
By a fore-knowledge of unslumbrous night!
Like sorrow came upon me, heavier still,
Than when I wander'd from the poppy hill:

896–897 Smiling . . . depth.—] *written on the opposite verso in FC to replace:*
⟨{Deep} in the clear water smiling. Gods that keep,
Mercifully, a little strength of heart
Unkill'd in us by raving, pang and smart;
And do preserve it, like a lilly root,
That, in another spring, it may outshoot
From its wintry prison; let this hour go
Drawling along its heavy weight of woe
And leave me living! 'Tis not more than need—
Your veriest help. Ah! how long did I feed
On that crystalline life of Portraiture!
How long I hover'd round the tender lure!
How many times dimpled the watery glass
With {Kisses} maddest Kisses; and, till they did pass
And leave the liquid smooth again, how mad!
O 'twas as if the absolute sisters bad
My Life into the compass of a Nut;
Or all my breathing minished and shut
To a scanty straw. To look above I fear'd
Lest my hot eyeballs might be burnt and sear'd
By a blank naught.⟩
({Deep} . . . smiling *interlined above* {In the green opening smiling} *in the first line, and* long . . . round *made out of* hover'd breathless at *in the eleventh line; Taylor bracketed the last thirteen lines, beginning with* 'Tis not . . . , *in pencil*). *Above the final 896–897 on the opposite verso in FC appears a preliminary attempt at revision:* ⟨Was there reflected. How my heart did leap / At⟩ (Was there *interlined above* {I saw}) 897 Through] ⟨Down⟩ Through *FC*

915 And a whole age of lingering moments crept
Sluggishly by, ere more contentment swept
Away at once the deadly yellow spleen.
Yes, thrice have I this fair enchantment seen;
Once more been tortured with renewed life.
920 When last the wintry gusts gave over strife
With the conquering sun of spring, and left the skies
Warm and serene, but yet with moistened eyes
In pity of the shatter'd infant buds,—
That time thou didst adorn, with amber studs,
925 My hunting cap, because I laugh'd and smil'd,
Chatted with thee, and many days exil'd
All torment from my breast;—'twas even then,
Straying about, yet, coop'd up in the den
Of helpless discontent,—hurling my lance
930 From place to place, and following at chance,
At last, by hap, through some young trees it struck,
And, plashing among bedded pebbles, stuck
In the middle of a brook,—whose silver ramble
Down twenty little falls, through reeds and bramble,
935 Tracing along, it brought me to a cave,
Whence it ran brightly forth, and white did lave
The nether sides of mossy stones and rock,—
'Mong which it gurgled blythe adieus, to mock
Its own sweet grief at parting. Overhead,
940 Hung a lush screen of drooping weeds, and spread
Thick, as to curtain up some wood-nymph's home.
'Ah! impious mortal, whither do I roam?'
Said I, low voic'd: 'Ah, whither! 'Tis the grot
Of Proserpine, when Hell, obscure and hot,
945 Doth her resign; and where her tender hands
She dabbles, on the cool and sluicy sands:
Or 'tis the cell of Echo, where she sits,
And babbles thorough silence, till her wits
Are gone in tender madness, and anon,
950 Faints into sleep, with many a dying tone
Of sadness. O that she would take my vows,
And breathe them sighingly among the boughs,
To sue her gentle ears for whose fair head,
Daily, I pluck sweet flowerets from their bed,

915 crept] ⟨pass'd⟩ crept *FC* 926 exil'd] ⟨beguil'd⟩ exil'd *FC* 933 In] I' *FC* 940 screen] *FC*, *L*[5], *1818 errata* (*spelled* screne *in FC*, *L*[5]); scene *1818 text*

955 And weave them dyingly—send honey-whispers
Round every leaf, that all those gentle lispers
May sigh my love unto her pitying!
O charitable Echo! hear, and sing
This ditty to her!—tell her'—so I stay'd
960 My foolish tongue, and listening, half afraid,
Stood stupefied with my own empty folly,
And blushing for the freaks of melancholy.
Salt tears were coming, when I heard my name
Most fondly lipp'd, and then these accents came:
965 'Endymion! the cave is secreter
Than the isle of Delos. Echo hence shall stir
No sighs but sigh-warm kisses, or light noise
Of thy combing hand, the while it travelling cloys
And trembles through my labyrinthine hair.'
970 At that oppress'd I hurried in.—Ah! where
Are those swift moments? Whither are they fled?
I'll smile no more, Peona; nor will wed
Sorrow the way to death; but patiently
Bear up against it: so farewel, sad sigh;
975 And come instead demurest meditation,
To occupy me wholly, and to fashion
My pilgrimage for the world's dusky brink.
No more will I count over, link by link,
My chain of grief: no longer strive to find
980 A half-forgetfulness in mountain wind
Blustering about my ears: aye, thou shalt see,
Dearest of sisters, what my life shall be;
What a calm round of hours shall make my days.

961–964 Stood . . . came:] *deleted at the bottom of a recto page in FC and then rewritten on the opposite verso. The first version is the same as the second except that the original 964 reads* Most fondly lipp'd;—I kept me still—it came (*the last two letters of* came *lost through damage to the MS*). *This line is followed* (*on the next recto page*) *by four canceled attempts at continuation:*

⟨Again in passionatest syllable{s}: saying⟩
⟨And thus again it charm⟩
⟨Again in passionatest syllables;⟩
⟨And thus again that voice's tender swells:⟩

(passionatest *made out of* passionate *in the first of these lines, and the same word successively* [*a*] passionatest [*b*] passionate [*c*] passionatest *in the third; Taylor marked the last line with a penciled X in the margin*) 969 labyrinthine] labyrinthian *FC* 970 At . . . in] *deleted in FC but restored by Keats with "stet" in the margin. Two attempted revisions appear on the opposite verso:*

⟨Since then I never⟩
⟨I never saw her Beauty more. Ah Where⟩

979 longer] ⟨more⟩ longer *FC* 981 aye,] *interlined above* ⟨no more—⟩ *FC*

There is a paly flame of hope that plays
985 Where'er I look: but yet, I'll say 'tis naught—
And here I bid it die. Have not I caught,
Already, a more healthy countenance?
By this the sun is setting; we may chance
Meet some of our near-dwellers with my car."

990 This said, he rose, faint-smiling like a star
Through autumn mists, and took Peona's hand:
They stept into the boat, and launch'd from land.

## BOOK II

O sovereign power of love! O grief! O balm!
All records, saving thine, come cool, and calm,
And shadowy, through the mist of passed years:
For others, good or bad, hatred and tears
5 Have become indolent; but touching thine,
One sigh doth echo, one poor sob doth pine,
One kiss brings honey-dew from buried days.
The woes of Troy, towers smothering o'er their blaze,
Stiff-holden shields, far-piercing spears, keen blades,
10 Struggling, and blood, and shrieks—all dimly fades
Into some backward corner of the brain;
Yet, in our very souls, we feel amain
The close of Troilus and Cressid sweet.
Hence, pageant history! hence, gilded cheat!
15 Swart planet in the universe of deeds!
Wide sea, that one continuous murmur breeds
Along the pebbled shore of memory!
Many old rotten-timber'd boats there be
Upon thy vaporous bosom, magnified
20 To goodly vessels; many a sail of pride,
And golden keel'd, is left unlaunch'd and dry.

990 This . . . he] This said *interlined above* ⟨At this, he⟩ (he *deleted by mistake*) *FC*

II.5 touching] O! for *D* 7 brings] sends *D* 8 smothering] crashing *D* 9 piercing . . . keen] reaching . . . clear *D* 13 Cressid sweet] Cressida *D* 14 Hence (*first word*)] *interlined above* ⟨Away⟩ *FC* 14 history] ⟨dead and⟩ history (*Woodhouse records* ⟨dead and⟩ *interlined before* history, *but probably the words were instead written and deleted currently in the MS*) *D* 14 hence, gilded cheat] away proud star *D*; hence gilded cheat *interlined above* ⟨away proud dull feat⟩ *FC* 19 vaporous] misty *D*

But wherefore this? What care, though owl did fly
About the great Athenian admiral's mast?
What care, though striding Alexander past
25 The Indus with his Macedonian numbers?
Though old Ulysses tortured from his slumbers
The glutted Cyclops, what care?—Juliet leaning
Amid her window-flowers,—sighing,—weaning
Tenderly her fancy from its maiden snow,
30 Doth more avail than these: the silver flow
Of Hero's tears, the swoon of Imogen,
Fair Pastorella in the bandit's den,
Are things to brood on with more ardency
Than the death-day of empires. Fearfully
35 Must such conviction come upon his head,
Who, thus far, discontent, has dared to tread,
Without one muse's smile, or kind behest,
The path of love and poesy. But rest,
In chafing restlessness, is yet more drear
40 Than to be crush'd, in striving to uprear
Love's standard on the battlements of song.
So once more days and nights aid me along,
Like legion'd soldiers.

Brain-sick shepherd prince,
What promise hast thou faithful guarded since
45 The day of sacrifice? Or, have new sorrows
Come with the constant dawn upon thy morrows?
Alas! 'tis his old grief. For many days,
Has he been wandering in uncertain ways:
Through wilderness, and woods of mossed oaks;
50 Counting his woe-worn minutes, by the strokes
Of the lone woodcutter; and listening still,

27 Juliet leaning]

⟨Juliet leans
Amid her window flowers sighs,—and, as she weans,
Her maiden thoughts from their young firstling snow,
What sorrows from the melting whiteness grow.⟩
Juliet leaning

(sighs *interlined above* {sighing} *in the second line, and the entire third line written in above* {Tenderly from their first young snow her maiden breast}) *D* 34 death . . . Fearfully] death of Empires—How fearfully *D* 36 discontent] halt and lame *D* 38 But] To *D* 39 chafing] *ed*; chaffing *FC*, *1818* 39 restlessness] discontent *D* 43 legion'd] sturdy *D* 43 Brain-sick] Fainting *D*; Brain-sick *interlined above* ⟨Fainting⟩ *FC* 49 woods of] brittle *D* 51 lone] distant *D*; lone⟨ly⟩ *FC*

Hour after hour, to each lush-leav'd rill.
Now he is sitting by a shady spring,
And elbow-deep with feverous fingering
55 Stems the upbursting cold: a wild rose tree
Pavilions him in bloom, and he doth see
A bud which snares his fancy: lo! but now
He plucks it, dips its stalk in the water: how!
It swells, it buds, it flowers beneath his sight;
60 And, in the middle, there is softly pight
A golden butterfly; upon whose wings
There must be surely character'd strange things,
For with wide eye he wonders, and smiles oft.

Lightly this little herald flew aloft,
65 Follow'd by glad Endymion's clasped hands:
Onward it flies. From languor's sullen bands
His limbs are loos'd, and eager, on he hies
Dazzled to trace it in the sunny skies.
It seem'd he flew, the way so easy was;
70 And like a new-born spirit did he pass
Through the green evening quiet in the sun,
O'er many a heath, through many a woodland dun,
Through buried paths, where sleepy twilight dreams
The summer time away. One track unseams
75 A wooded cleft, and, far away, the blue
Of ocean fades upon him; then, anew,
He sinks adown a solitary glen,
Where there was never sound of mortal men,
Saving, perhaps, some snow-light cadences
80 Melting to silence, when upon the breeze
Some holy bark let forth an anthem sweet,
To cheer itself to Delphi. Still his feet
Went swift beneath the merry-winged guide,

53 Now he is] E'en now he's *D* 56 Pavilions . . . bloom] Bends lightly over him *D* 57 snares] takes *D* 58 in] i' (*altered probably by Taylor—the hand is not certain here—to* in) *FC* 59 flowers] blooms *D*; ⟨blooms⟩ flowers *FC* 60 the] its *D* 67–68 and . . . skies]

⟨and eagerly he paces
With nimble feet beneath its airy traces⟩
and eagerly he ⟨paces⟩ traces
With nimble footsteps all its airy paces *D*

67 eager] *added above the line in FC* 69 way] path *D* 75 A wooded] Through woody *D* 80 Melting] Thawing *D* 83 swift] *made out of* sweet *FC* 83 merry-winged] ⟨flutter-loving⟩ (*deleted and nothing substituted*) *D*

Until it reached a splashing fountain's side
85 That, near a cavern's mouth, for ever pour'd
Unto the temperate air: then high it soar'd,
And, downward, suddenly began to dip,
As if, athirst with so much toil, 'twould sip
The crystal spout-head: so it did, with touch
90 Most delicate, as though afraid to smutch
Even with mealy gold the waters clear.
But, at that very touch, to disappear
So fairy-quick, was strange! Bewildered,
Endymion sought around, and shook each bed
95 Of covert flowers in vain; and then he flung
Himself along the grass. What gentle tongue,
What whisperer disturb'd his gloomy rest?
It was a nymph uprisen to the breast
In the fountain's pebbly margin, and she stood
100 'Mong lilies, like the youngest of the brood.
To him her dripping hand she softly kist,
And anxiously began to plait and twist
Her ringlets round her fingers, saying: "Youth!
Too long, alas, hast thou starv'd on the ruth,
105 The bitterness of love: too long indeed,
Seeing thou art so gentle. Could I weed
Thy soul of care, by heavens, I would offer
All the bright riches of my crystal coffer
To Amphitrite; all my clear-eyed fish,
110 Golden, or rainbow-sided, or purplish,
Vermilion-tail'd, or finn'd with silvery gauze;
Yea, or my veined pebble-floor, that draws
A virgin light to the deep; my grotto-sands
Tawny and gold, ooz'd slowly from far lands
115 By my diligent springs; my level lilies, shells,
My charming rod, my potent river spells;
Yes, every thing, even to the pearly cup
Meander gave me,—for I bubbled up
To fainting creatures in a desert wild.

84 it] *squeezed in after* ⟨he⟩ *FC* 86 then high] whereat *D* 87 And] Then *D* 93/94 ⟨Endymion {pry'd} all around the welkin sped / His {eager} anxious sight—⟩ *D* 94 sought] pry'd (*Woodhouse gives this reading separately from the preceding*) *D* 96–97 Himself . . . gloomy] His sullen limbs upon the grass—What tongue, / What airy whisperer spoilt his angry *D* 99 In] I' *altered to* In *FC* 99 margin] basin *D* 102 anxiously . . . plait] carelessly . . . twine *D* 103 round] 'bout *D* 103/104 ⟨Long hast thou tasted⟩ *D* 105 bitterness] bitter ruth *D* 116 river] water *D* 117 even] e'en *FC*

120 But woe is me, I am but as a child
To gladden thee; and all I dare to say,
Is, that I pity thee; that on this day
I've been thy guide; that thou must wander far
In other regions, past the scanty bar
125 To mortal steps, before thou canst be ta'en
From every wasting sigh, from every pain,
Into the gentle bosom of thy love.
Why it is thus, one knows in heaven above:
But, a poor Naiad, I guess not. Farewel!
130 I have a ditty for my hollow cell."

Hereat, she vanished from Endymion's gaze,
Who brooded o'er the water in amaze:
The dashing fount pour'd on, and where its pool
Lay, half asleep, in grass and rushes cool,
135 Quick waterflies and gnats were sporting still,
And fish were dimpling, as if good nor ill
Had fallen out that hour. The wanderer,
Holding his forehead, to keep off the burr
Of smothering fancies, patiently sat down;
140 And, while beneath the evening's sleepy frown
Glow-worms began to trim their starry lamps,
Thus breath'd he to himself: "Whoso encamps
To take a fancied city of delight,
O what a wretch is he! and when 'tis his,
145 After long toil and travelling, to miss
The kernel of his hopes, how more than vile:
Yet, for him there's refreshment even in toil;
Another city doth he set about,
Free from the smallest pebble-bead of doubt
150 That he will seize on trickling honey-combs:
Alas, he finds them dry; and then he foams,
And onward to another city speeds.
But this is human life: the war, the deeds,

121 I . . . to] that I may *D* 128 one knows] some know *D* 129 not. Farewel] not ⟨nor tell / Farewell I must away to my hollow cell."⟩ Farewell *D* 130 I . . . a] I've a new *D* 131 Endymion's] the listner's *D* 132 Who brooded] Whose soul kept *D* 133 fount . . . its] fall . . . the *D* 134 Lay . . . in] Crept smoothly by fresh (Crept *interlined above* ⟨Slept⟩) *D* 139 smothering] drowning *D* 140 sleepy] gentle *D*; ⟨mild⟩ sleepy *FC* 143 To . . . fancied] His soul to take a *D* 144 and . . . his] *written beneath* ⟨'tis in his sight⟩ *D* 145 toil and travelling] seige and travailing *D* 147 even] e'en *D* 149 Free from] Without *D* 149 bead] *FC*, *L*[5], *1818 errata*; head *1818 text* 150 he will] there he'll *D* 153 war] acts *D*

The disappointment, the anxiety,
155 Imagination's struggles, far and nigh,
All human; bearing in themselves this good,
That they are still the air, the subtle food,
To make us feel existence, and to shew
How quiet death is. Where soil is men grow,
160 Whether to weeds or flowers; but for me,
There is no depth to strike in: I can see
Nought earthly worth my compassing; so stand
Upon a misty, jutting head of land—
Alone? No, no; and by the Orphean lute,
165 When mad Eurydice is listening to't;
I'd rather stand upon this misty peak,
With not a thing to sigh for, or to seek,
But the soft shadow of my thrice-seen love,
Than be—I care not what. O meekest dove
170 Of heaven! O Cynthia, ten-times bright and fair!
From thy blue throne, now filling all the air,
Glance but one little beam of temper'd light
Into my bosom, that the dreadful might
And tyranny of love be somewhat scar'd!
175 Yet do not so, sweet queen; one torment spar'd
Would give a pang to jealous misery,
Worse than the torment's self: but rather tie
Large wings upon my shoulders, and point out
My love's far dwelling. Though the playful rout
180 Of Cupids shun thee, too divine art thou,
Too keen in beauty, for thy silver prow
Not to have dipp'd in love's most gentle stream.
O be propitious, nor severely deem
My madness impious; for, by all the stars
185 That tend thy bidding, I do think the bars
That kept my spirit in are burst—that I
Am sailing with thee through the dizzy sky!
How beautiful thou art! The world how deep!
How tremulous-dazzlingly the wheels sweep

155 Imagination's struggles] Imaginings and searchings *D* 159 Where . . . men] Here is soil to *D* 164 No, no;] No, heavens! *D* 166 stand] bide *D* 167 not . . . sigh] nought to long for, sigh *D* 169 care] know *D* 181 keen] sharp *D* 189 tremulous-dazzlingly] *Woodhouse records* bright *interlined and deleted above* ⟨silently and⟩ *before* tremulous *in D, and* and dazzling (*in the original line*) *altered to* —dazzlingly; *a tentative order of versions would be* (*a*) silently and tremulous (*b*) bright and tremulous (*c*) tremulous and dazzling (*d*) tremulous—dazzlingly. *Woodhouse also records Keats's mark in FC* (*which can be read as either a hyphen or a dash*) *as a dash*

190 Around their axle! Then these gleaming reins,
How lithe! When this thy chariot attains
Its airy goal, haply some bower veils
Those twilight eyes? Those eyes!—my spirit fails—
Dear goddess, help! or the wide-gaping air
195 Will gulph me—help!"—At this with madden'd stare,
And lifted hands, and trembling lips he stood;
Like old Deucalion mountain'd o'er the flood,
Or blind Orion hungry for the morn.
And, but from the deep cavern there was borne
200 A voice, he had been froze to senseless stone;
Nor sigh of his, nor plaint, nor passion'd moan
Had more been heard. Thus swell'd it forth: "Descend,
Young mountaineer! descend where alleys bend
Into the sparry hollows of the world!
205 Oft hast thou seen bolts of the thunder hurl'd
As from thy threshold; day by day hast been
A little lower than the chilly sheen
Of icy pinnacles, and dipp'dst thine arms
Into the deadening ether that still charms
210 Their marble being: now, as deep profound
As those are high, descend! He ne'er is crown'd
With immortality, who fears to follow
Where airy voices lead: so through the hollow,
The silent mysteries of earth, descend!"

215 He heard but the last words, nor could contend
One moment in reflection: for he fled
Into the fearful deep, to hide his head
From the clear moon, the trees, and coming madness.

'Twas far too strange, and wonderful for sadness;
220 Sharpening, by degrees, his appetite
To dive into the deepest. Dark, nor light,
The region; nor bright, nor sombre wholly,

191 chariot attains] silent Chariot gains *D* 192 haply] ⟨haply thou veil'st thine eyes / In some fresh bower⟩ haply *D* 193 twilight] liquid *D* 195 help] Oh *D* 197 mountain'd o'er] wondering at *D* 198 hungry . . . morn] waiting . . . dawn *D* 199 deep] hollow *D* 201 plaint . . . passion'd] wild complaint nor *D* 204 Into] Spiral into *D* 208 dipp'dst . . . arms] couldst dip thy palms *D* 210 deep] *interlined above* ⟨far⟩ *FC* 211 are . . . is] were . . . was *D* 214 silent] fearful *D* 215 He . . . words] But the last Words he heard *FC* 218 moon] night *D* 220 Sharpening] Upwinding *D*

But mingled up; a gleaming melancholy;
A dusky empire and its diadems;
225 One faint eternal eventide of gems.
Aye, millions sparkled on a vein of gold,
Along whose track the prince quick footsteps told,
With all its lines abrupt and angular:
Out-shooting sometimes, like a meteor-star,
230 Through a vast antre; then the metal woof,
Like Vulcan's rainbow, with some monstrous roof
Curves hugely: now, far in the deep abyss,
It seems an angry lightning, and doth hiss
Fancy into belief: anon it leads
235 Through winding passages, where sameness breeds
Vexing conceptions of some sudden change;
Whether to silver grots, or giant range
Of sapphire columns, or fantastic bridge
Athwart a flood of crystal. On a ridge
240 Now fareth he, that o'er the vast beneath
Towers like an ocean-cliff, and whence he seeth
A hundred waterfalls, whose voices come
But as the murmuring surge. Chilly and numb
His bosom grew, when first he, far away,
245 Descried an orbed diamond, set to fray
Old darkness from his throne: 'twas like the sun
Uprisen o'er chaos: and with such a stun
Came the amazement, that, absorb'd in it,
He saw not fiercer wonders—past the wit
250 Of any spirit to tell, but one of those
Who, when this planet's sphering time doth close,
Will be its high remembrancers: who they?
The mighty ones who have made eternal day
For Greece and England. While astonishment
255 With deep-drawn sighs was quieting, he went
Into a marble gallery, passing through

227–228 Along . . . With] Whose track the venturous Latmian follows bold / Through *D* 229 Out . . . a] And sometimes like a shooting *D* 230 Through] Past *D*; Through *interlined above* ⟨Past⟩ *FC* 230 vast] *interlined above* ⟨huge⟩ *FC* 230 antre] antre's gloom *D* 231 with] o'er *D* 232 the] a *D* 236 Vexing] Dizzy *D* 240 Now . . . he] Sometimes he fares (fares *replacing* ⟨went⟩) *D* 243 the] a *D* 248 the] this *D* 253 who . . . eternal] who've shone athwart the *D* 254 For] Of *D* 256 passing] ⟨that near the roof / Of a fair mimic Temple⟩ passing (*Woodhouse records the bracketed words as uncanceled, but syntax, rhyme, and metrical considerations suggest that they were a deleted first attempt*) *D*

A mimic temple, so complete and true
In sacred custom, that he well nigh fear'd
To search it inwards; whence far off appear'd,
260 Through a long pillar'd vista, a fair shrine,
And, just beyond, on light tiptoe divine,
A quiver'd Dian. Stepping awfully,
The youth approach'd; oft turning his veil'd eye
Down sidelong aisles, and into niches old.
265 And when, more near against the marble cold
He had touch'd his forehead, he began to thread
All courts and passages, where silence dead
Rous'd by his whispering footsteps murmured faint:
And long he travers'd to and fro, to acquaint
270 Himself with every mystery, and awe;
Till, weary, he sat down before the maw
Of a wide outlet, fathomless and dim,
To wild uncertainty and shadows grim.
There, when new wonders ceas'd to float before,
275 And thoughts of self came on, how crude and sore
The journey homeward to habitual self!
A mad-pursuing of the fog-born elf,
Whose flitting lantern, through rude nettle-briar,
Cheats us into a swamp, into a fire,
280 Into the bosom of a hated thing.

What misery most drowningly doth sing
In lone Endymion's ear, now he has raught
The goal of consciousness? Ah, 'tis the thought,
The deadly feel of solitude: for lo!

260 pillar'd vista] vist' of Colums *D* 261 on] ⟨lightly diminish'd / A Dian quiver'd tiptoe, crescented—⟩ on *D* 264 sidelong] sideway *D* 266 thread] *made out of* tread *FC* 267 All] The *D* 269 to] t' *FC* 270–272 and . . . dim] until / His weary legs he rested on the sill / Of some remotest Chamber, outlet dim (outlet dim *replacing* ⟨leading in⟩) *D* 270 and] ⟨until⟩ and *FC* 272 dim,] *FC*, $L^5$; $\sim_\wedge$ *1818* 277 A] That *D* 278 briar] beds *D*; Briar *interlined above* ⟨beds⟩ *FC* 279 swamp] bog *D* 279–280 into a fire . . . thing]

cuttings and shreds
Of old vexations plaited to a rope
Wherewith to haul us from the sight of hope
And bind us to our earthly baiting ring *D*

*The original FC text (marked with a vertical line of x's in the margin) is substantively the same as D except that it has* drag *for* haul *in the third line and* fix *for* bind *in the fourth. Keats interlined* into a fire *above* cuttings and shreds *in the first line of this FC version, and then deleted the entire passage and wrote the present text on the opposite verso* 282 raught] *FC*; caught *1818*

285 He cannot see the heavens, nor the flow
Of rivers, nor hill-flowers running wild
In pink and purple chequer, nor, up-pil'd,
The cloudy rack slow journeying in the west,
Like herded elephants; nor felt, nor prest
290 Cool grass, nor tasted the fresh slumberous air;
But far from such companionship to wear
An unknown time, surcharg'd with grief, away,
Was now his lot. And must he patient stay,
Tracing fantastic figures with his spear?
295 "No!" exclaimed he, "why should I tarry here?"
No! loudly echoed times innumerable.
At which he straightway started, and 'gan tell
His paces back into the temple's chief;
Warming and glowing strong in the belief
300 Of help from Dian: so that when again
He caught her airy form, thus did he plain,
Moving more near the while. "O Haunter chaste
Of river sides, and woods, and heathy waste,
Where with thy silver bow and arrows keen
305 Art thou now forested? O woodland Queen,
What smoothest air thy smoother forehead woos?
Where dost thou listen to the wide halloos
Of thy disparted nymphs? Through what dark tree
Glimmers thy crescent? Wheresoe'er it be,
310 'Tis in the breath of heaven: thou dost taste
Freedom as none can taste it, nor dost waste
Thy loveliness in dismal elements;
But, finding in our green earth sweet contents,
There livest blissfully. Ah, if to thee
315 It feels Elysian, how rich to me,
An exil'd mortal, sounds its pleasant name!
Within my breast there lives a choking flame—
O let me cool it the zephyr-boughs among!

290 fresh slumberous] free sleepy *D* 294 Tracing] Drawing *D*; Tracing *interlined above* ⟨Drawing⟩ *FC* 297 started . . . 'gan] roused, and gan to *D* 299 glowing] growing *D* (*FC perhaps also—see Textual Note*) 301 did] gan *D* 302 Moving] Pacing *D* 302 more near] towards *FC* 304 with thy] now with *D* 305 now forested] in covert hid *D* 308 Through . . . tree] from what deep glen *D* 311 as] ⟨of⟩ as *FC* 313 in] on *D*, *FC* 318 cool it] cool't *D*, *FC* 318 the . . . among] *ed*; among the waving boughs (*but marked for transposition to* the waving boughs among) *D*; among the zephyr-boughs *FC*, *1818*

A homeward fever parches up my tongue—
320 O let me slake it at the running springs!
Upon my ear a noisy nothing rings—
O let me once more hear the linnet's note!
Before mine eyes thick films and shadows float—
O let me 'noint them with the heaven's light!
325 Dost thou now lave thy feet and ankles white?
O think how sweet to me the freshening sluice!
Dost thou now please thy thirst with berry-juice?
O think how this dry palate would rejoice!
If in soft slumber thou dost hear my voice,
330 O think how I should love a bed of flowers!—
Young goddess! let me see my native bowers!
Deliver me from this rapacious deep!"

Thus ending loudly, as he would o'erleap
His destiny, alert he stood: but when
335 Obstinate silence came heavily again,
Feeling about for its old couch of space
And airy cradle, lowly bow'd his face
Desponding, o'er the marble floor's cold thrill.
But 'twas not long; for, sweeter than the rill
340 To its old channel, or a swollen tide
To margin sallows, were the leaves he spied,
And flowers, and wreaths, and ready myrtle crowns
Up heaping through the slab: refreshment drowns
Itself, and strives its own delights to hide—
345 Nor in one spot alone; the floral pride
In a long whispering birth enchanted grew
Before his footsteps; as when heav'd anew
Old ocean rolls a lengthened wave to the shore,

319 A . . . my] A fever parches up my suppliant *altered to* An endless fever parches up my *D* 319 A] An *FC* (*D also—see preceding note*) 325 feet] ⟨hands⟩ feet *FC* 327 berry] cherry *D* 330 should] would *D* 331 Young] Oh *D* 332 Deliver . . . rapacious] Lift me, oh lift me from this horrid *D* 335 came] ⟨cloudily⟩ came *D* 336 about for] *interlined above* ⟨its way to⟩ *D* 337 lowly bow'd] he bent down *D* 339 But . . . not] ⟨Bu⟩ 'Twas not for *D*; But ⟨not⟩ 'twas not *FC* 340 old] cool *D*; cold *FC* 340 or a swollen] the oerswollen *D* 343 Up heaping] Upswelling *D* 344 Itself . . . hide] Itself lush tumbling ⟨f⟩ ⟨on⟩ down on every side *D; in FC the 1818 text is written on the opposite verso to replace* ⟨Itself, lush-tumbling on every side⟩ *with* cool *and* fragrance *separately interlined and deleted after* tumbling (*perhaps successively* [*a*] Itself, lush-tumbling on every side [*b*] Itself, lush-tumbling cool on . . . [*c*] Itself, tumbling fragrance on . . . ) 346 enchanted] ⟨before⟩ enchanted *FC* 348 rolls] sends *D*

Down whose green back the short-liv'd foam, all hoar,
350 Bursts gradual, with a wayward indolence.

Increasing still in heart, and pleasant sense,
Upon his fairy journey on he hastes;
So anxious for the end, he scarcely wastes
One moment with his hand among the sweets:
355 Onward he goes—he stops—his bosom beats
As plainly in his ear, as the faint charm
Of which the throbs were born. This still alarm,
This sleepy music, forc'd him walk tiptoe:
For it came more softly than the east could blow
360 Arion's magic to the Atlantic isles;
Or than the west, made jealous by the smiles
Of thron'd Apollo, could breathe back the lyre
To seas Ionian and Tyrian.

O did he ever live, that lonely man,
365 Who lov'd—and music slew not? 'Tis the pest
Of love, that fairest joys give most unrest;
That things of delicate and tenderest worth
Are swallow'd all, and made a seared dearth,
By one consuming flame: it doth immerse
370 And suffocate true blessings in a curse.
Half-happy, by comparison of bliss,
Is miserable. 'Twas even so with this

349 Down] *successively* (*a*) From (*b*) Oer (*c*) Down *D* 349 back] ⟨head⟩ back *D* 349 short-liv'd] gentle *D* 350 Bursts] ⟨Runs⟩ Bursts *D* 353 he scarcely] that scarce he *D* 353 wastes] waits (*underscored by Taylor in pencil*) *FC* 357 still] warm *D*; ⟨w⟩ still *FC* 359 For it] For't *FC* 363–372 To . . . miserable]

To seas Ionian and Tyrian. Dire
Was the lovelorn despair to which it wrought
Endymion—for dire is the bare thought
⟨The flame of love⟩
That among lovers things of tenderest worth
Are swallow'd all, and made a blank—a dearth
By one devouring flame: and far far worse
Blessings to them become a heavy curse
Half happy till comparisons of bliss
To misery lead them

(is . . . thought *interlined above* ⟨to {placid} quiet bosoms is the thought⟩ *in the third line and* till . . . bliss *above* ⟨will they gaze upon the sky⟩ *in the ninth*) *D* 365 Who . . . and] Whom loving *altered to* Who lov'd and *FC* 369 it] ⟨and⟩ it *FC* 371 comparison] comparisons *FC* (*D also—see note to 363–372*) 372 'Twas even] 'T e'en *FC* 372 with] *made out of* in *FC*

Dew-dropping melody, in the Carian's ear;
First heaven, then hell, and then forgotten clear,
375 Vanish'd in elemental passion.

And down some swart abysm he had gone,
Had not a heavenly guide benignant led
To where thick myrtle branches, 'gainst his head
Brushing, awakened: then the sounds again
380 Went noiseless as a passing noontide rain
Over a bower, where little space he stood;
For, as the sunset peeps into a wood,
So saw he panting light, and towards it went
Through winding alleys; and lo, wonderment!
385 Upon soft verdure saw, one here, one there,
Cupids a slumbering on their pinions fair.

After a thousand mazes overgone,
At last, with sudden step, he came upon
A chamber, myrtle wall'd, embowered high,
390 Full of light, incense, tender minstrelsy,
And more of beautiful and strange beside:
For on a silken couch of rosy pride,
In midst of all, there lay a sleeping youth
Of fondest beauty; fonder, in fair sooth,
395 Than sighs could fathom, or contentment reach:
And coverlids gold-tinted like the peach,
Or ripe October's faded marigolds,
Fell sleek about him in a thousand folds—
Not hiding up an Apollonian curve
400 Of neck and shoulder, nor the tenting swerve
Of knee from knee, nor ankles pointing light;
But rather, giving them to the filled sight
Officiously. Sideway his face repos'd
On one white arm, and tenderly unclos'd,

377 Had not a] But that some *D* 378 thick] young *D* 379 awakened: then] awaken'd him: *D* 380 Went] Came *D*; Went *interlined above* ⟨Came⟩ *FC* 380 noiseless . . . noontide] softly as a gentle evening *D* 381–383 Over . . . went]
Around a bower, where he stay'd harkening
And through whose tufted shrubby darkening
Bright starry glimmers came, towards which he went *D*
385 verdure] turf he *D* 396 coverlids gold] draperies mellow *D* 397 ripe . . . faded] lady peas entwined with *D* 399 an] *interlined above* ⟨his⟩ *FC* 402 giving] gave *FC* 402 filled] gazer's *D* 403–404 repos'd . . . unclos'd] reclined / Upon his kissing hands and arms entwined (kissing *interlined above* ⟨joined⟩) *D*

405 By tenderest pressure, a faint damask mouth
To slumbery pout; just as the morning south
Disparts a dew-lipp'd rose. Above his head,
Four lily stalks did their white honours wed
To make a coronal; and round him grew
410 All tendrils green, of every bloom and hue,
Together intertwin'd and trammel'd fresh:
The vine of glossy sprout; the ivy mesh,
Shading its Ethiop berries; and woodbine,
Of velvet leaves and bugle-blooms divine;
415 Convolvulus in streaked vases flush;
The creeper, mellowing for an autumn blush;
And virgin's bower, trailing airily;
With others of the sisterhood. Hard by,
Stood serene Cupids watching silently.
420 One, kneeling to a lyre, touch'd the strings,
Muffling to death the pathos with his wings;
And, ever and anon, uprose to look
At the youth's slumber; while another took
A willow-bough, distilling odorous dew,
425 And shook it on his hair; another flew
In through the woven roof, and fluttering-wise
Rain'd violets upon his sleeping eyes.

At these enchantments, and yet many more,
The breathless Latmian wonder'd o'er and o'er;
430 Until, impatient in embarrassment,
He forthright pass'd, and lightly treading went
To that same feather'd lyrist, who straightway,
Smiling, thus whisper'd: "Though from upper day
Thou art a wanderer, and thy presence here
435 Might seem unholy, be of happy cheer!
For 'tis the nicest touch of human honour,
When some ethereal and high-favouring donor
Presents immortal bowers to mortal sense;

405 a] his *D* 409 coronal] coronet *D* 410 tendrils] tendril *FC* 410 every bloom] pleasant lush *D* 412 glossy] purply *D* 413 Ethiop] darkling *D* 414 Of . . . blooms] With all its honey bugle tufts *D* 415 in] *interlined above* ⟨of⟩ *FC* 416 mellowing . . . autumn] blushing deep at Autumn's *D* 419 serene . . . silently] Cupids holding o'er an upward gaze / Each a slim wand tipt with a silver blaze (Each . . . wand *replacing* ⟨Each one a silver torch⟩) *D* 424 willow] myrtle *D* 426 through the woven] from the branched *D* 429 breathless] mortal *D* 436 nicest touch] highest reach *D*

As now 'tis done to thee, Endymion. Hence
440 Was I in no wise startled. So recline
Upon these living flowers. Here is wine,
Alive with sparkles—never, I aver,
Since Ariadne was a vintager,
So cool a purple: taste these juicy pears,
445 Sent me by sad Vertumnus, when his fears
Were high about Pomona: here is cream,
Deepening to richness from a snowy gleam;
Sweeter than that nurse Amalthea skimm'd
For the boy Jupiter: and here, undimm'd
450 By any touch, a bunch of blooming plums
Ready to melt between an infant's gums:
And here is manna pick'd from Syrian trees,
In starlight, by the three Hesperides.
Feast on, and meanwhile I will let thee know
455 Of all these things around us." He did so,
Still brooding o'er the cadence of his lyre;
And thus: "I need not any hearing tire
By telling how the sea-born goddess pin'd
For a mortal youth, and how she strove to bind
460 Him all in all unto her doting self.
Who would not be so prison'd? but, fond elf,
He was content to let her amorous plea
Faint through his careless arms; content to see
An unseiz'd heaven dying at his feet;
465 Content, O fool! to make a cold retreat,
When on the pleasant grass such love, lovelorn,
Lay sorrowing; when every tear was born
Of diverse passion; when her lips and eyes
Were clos'd in sullen moisture, and quick sighs
470 Came vex'd and pettish through her nostrils small.
Hush! no exclaim—yet, justly mightst thou call
Curses upon his head.—I was half glad,
But my poor mistress went distract and mad,
When the boar tusk'd him: so away she flew

442 Alive . . . sparkles] Sparkling up diamonds *D* 448 Sweeter . . . nurse] Even sweet as that which *D* 456 Still . . . of] Keeping a ravishing cadence with *D* 457 thus . . . hearing] thus it was "I'll not thy knowing *D* 461 prison'd . . . fond] bound, but, foolish *D* 462 to] ⟨t' unclasp his⟩ to *D* 462 her . . . plea] ⟨Elysium⟩ Divinity *interlined above* ⟨a fainting heaven⟩ *D* 463 Faint . . . careless] Faint gradual from his *altered to* Slip through his careless *D* 464 dying] sighing *D* 474 tusk'd] tush'd (*but see Textual Note*) *FC*

475 To Jove's high throne, and by her plainings drew
Immortal tear-drops down the thunderer's beard;
Whereon, it was decreed he should be rear'd
Each summer time to life. Lo! this is he,
That same Adonis, safe in the privacy
480 Of this still region all his winter-sleep.
Aye, sleep; for when our love-sick queen did weep
Over his waned corse, the tremulous shower
Heal'd up the wound, and, with a balmy power,
Medicined death to a lengthened drowsiness:
485 The which she fills with visions, and doth dress
In all this quiet luxury; and hath set
Us young immortals, without any let,
To watch his slumber through. 'Tis well nigh pass'd,
Even to a moment's filling up, and fast
490 She scuds with summer breezes, to pant through
The first long kiss, warm firstling, to renew
Embower'd sports in Cytherea's isle.
Look! how those winged listeners all this while
Stand anxious: see! behold!"—This clamant word
495 Broke through the careful silence; for they heard
A rustling noise of leaves, and out there flutter'd
Pigeons and doves: Adonis something mutter'd,
The while one hand, that erst upon his thigh
Lay dormant, mov'd convuls'd and gradually
500 Up to his forehead. Then there was a hum
Of sudden voices, echoing, "Come! come!
Arise! awake! Clear summer has forth walk'd
Unto the clover-sward, and she has talk'd
Full soothingly to every nested finch:
505 Rise, Cupids! or we'll give the blue-bell pinch
To your dimpled arms. Once more sweet life begin!"
At this, from every side they hurried in,

479 in] i' (*altered by Taylor in pencil to* in) *FC* 482 waned . . . tremulous] paly . . . crystal *D* 487 Us] These *D*; ⟨Us⟩ Us (*the deleted* Us *written over* {Th}) *FC* 488 slumber] winter *D* 489 Even] E'en *FC* 489 filling up] 'complishing *D* 490 with] o'er *D*; with *interlined above* ⟨o'er⟩ *FC* 491 warm firstling] sweet prologue *D* 495 for] *interlined above* ⟨and⟩ *FC* 501 echoing] echoing out *D* 503 Unto] Onto *FC* 504 Full] Most *D* 505–506 Rise . . . your] Cupids awake! or black and blue we'll pinch / Your *D and originally FC; Keats replaced the first line with the present 505 on the opposite verso in FC and then added* To *in the margin before the first word of his original 506* 506 arms.] arms—⟨for lo! your Queen, your Queen⟩ (*presumably replaced by the present text—Woodhouse gives only the deleted words*) *D*

Rubbing their sleepy eyes with lazy wrists,
And doubling over head their little fists
510 In backward yawns. But all were soon alive:
For as delicious wine doth, sparkling, dive
In nectar'd clouds and curls through water fair,
So from the arbour roof down swell'd an air
Odorous and enlivening; making all
515 To laugh, and play, and sing, and loudly call
For their sweet queen: when lo! the wreathed green
Disparted, and far upward could be seen
Blue heaven, and a silver car, air-borne,
Whose silent wheels, fresh wet from clouds of morn,
520 Spun off a drizzling dew,—which falling chill
On soft Adonis' shoulders, made him still
Nestle and turn uneasily about.
Soon were the white doves plain, with necks stretch'd out,
And silken traces tighten'd in descent;
525 And soon, returning from love's banishment,
Queen Venus leaning downward open arm'd:
Her shadow fell upon his breast, and charm'd
A tumult to his heart, and a new life
Into his eyes. Ah, miserable strife,
530 But for her comforting! unhappy sight,
But meeting her blue orbs! Who, who can write
Of these first minutes? The unchariest muse
To embracements warm as theirs makes coy excuse.

509 over head] in the air *D* 523 Soon . . . doves] Anon the doves ⟨appear'd⟩ were *D* 524 And] Their *D* 524 tighten'd] *FC* (*written with the first* t *uncrossed*); lighten'd *1818* 525 soon] *interlined above* ⟨next⟩ *FC* 526–533 Queen . . . excuse.]
⟨Queen Venus bending downward, so o'ertaken,
So suffering sweet, so blushing mad, so shaken
That the wild warmth prob'd the young sleeper's heart
Enchantingly; and with a sudden start
His trembling arms were out in instant time
To catch his fainting love.—O foolish rhyme
What mighty power is in thee that so often
Thou strivest rugged syllables to soften
Even to the telling of a sweet like this.
Away! let them embrace alone! that kiss
Was far too rich for thee to talk upon.
Poor wretch! mind not those sobs and sighs! begone!
Speak not one atom of thy paltry stuff,
That they are met is poetry enough.⟩
(*the lines deleted and nothing substituted*) *D*

O it has ruffled every spirit there,
535 Saving Love's self, who stands superb to share
The general gladness: awfully he stands;
A sovereign quell is in his waving hands;
No sight can bear the lightning of his bow;
His quiver is mysterious, none can know
540 What themselves think of it; from forth his eyes
There darts strange light of varied hues and dyes:
A scowl is sometimes on his brow, but who
Look full upon it feel anon the blue
Of his fair eyes run liquid through their souls.
545 Endymion feels it, and no more controls
The burning prayer within him; so, bent low,
He had begun a plaining of his woe.
But Venus, bending forward, said: "My child,
Favour this gentle youth; his days are wild
550 With love—he—but alas! too well I see
Thou know'st the deepness of his misery.
Ah, smile not so, my son: I tell thee true,
That when through heavy hours I used to rue
The endless sleep of this new-born Adon',
555 This stranger ay I pitied. For upon
A dreary morning once I fled away
Into the breezy clouds, to weep and pray
For this my love: for vexing Mars had teaz'd
Me even to tears: thence, when a little eas'd,
560 Down-looking, vacant, through a hazy wood,
I saw this youth as he despairing stood:
Those same dark curls blown vagrant in the wind;
Those same full fringed lids a constant blind
Over his sullen eyes: I saw him throw
565 Himself on wither'd leaves, even as though
Death had come sudden; for no jot he mov'd,
Yet mutter'd wildly. I could hear he lov'd
Some fair immortal, and that his embrace
Had zoned her through the night. There is no trace
570 Of this in heaven: I have mark'd each cheek,
And find it is the vainest thing to seek;

534 it] this *D*   538 No . . . bow] His bow no sight can bear for lightning so *FC*   541 varied] ⟨sundry⟩ *replaced by* changeful *D*   541 dyes] dies *FC*   547 begun] began *FC*   548 bending] leaning *D*   552 my son:] sweet boy! *D*   554 new-born] mad-brain'd *D*   561 this] yon *FC*   567 wildly] madly *D*

And that of all things 'tis kept secretest.
Endymion! one day thou wilt be blest:
So still obey the guiding hand that fends
575 Thee safely through these wonders for sweet ends.
'Tis a concealment needful in extreme;
And if I guess'd not so, the sunny beam
Thou shouldst mount up to with me. Now adieu!
Here must we leave thee."—At these words up flew
580 The impatient doves, up rose the floating car,
Up went the hum celestial. High afar
The Latmian saw them minish into nought;
And, when all were clear vanish'd, still he caught
A vivid lightning from that dreadful bow.
585 When all was darkened, with Etnean throe
The earth clos'd—gave a solitary moan—
And left him once again in twilight lone.

He did not rave, he did not stare aghast,
For all those visions were o'ergone, and past,
590 And he in loneliness: he felt assur'd
Of happy times, when all he had endur'd
Would seem a feather to the mighty prize.
So, with unusual gladness, on he hies
Through caves, and palaces of mottled ore,
595 Gold dome, and crystal wall, and turquois floor,
Black polish'd porticos of awful shade,
And, at the last, a diamond balustrade,
Leading afar past wild magnificence,
Spiral through ruggedest loopholes, and thence
600 Stretching across a void, then guiding o'er
Enormous chasms, where, all foam and roar,
Streams subterranean tease their granite beds,
Then heighten'd just above the silvery heads
Of a thousand fountains, so that he could dash
605 The waters with his spear; but at the splash,

584–585 A . . . darkened,] Anon and ever gleams from that dread bow. / One lightning more—then‸ *D* 587 left] shut *D* 588 He . . . stare] Nor did he rave, nor did he stare (stare *replacing* ⟨feel⟩) *D* 590 And . . . loneliness] Leaving him solitary *D* 592 prize] *replacing* ⟨joy⟩ *D* 596 porticos] porticos too *D* 597 And . . . diamond] Then diamond steps and ruby *D* 598 afar past] to fierce and *D* 599 through] by *D* 600 guiding] leading *D* 602 tease their] ⟨rage in⟩ *replaced by* wear their *D* 604 thousand] hundred *D*

Done heedlessly, those spouting columns rose
Sudden a poplar's height, and 'gan to enclose
His diamond path with fretwork, streaming round
Alive, and dazzling cool, and with a sound,
610 Haply, like dolphin tumults, when sweet shells
Welcome the float of Thetis. Long he dwells
On this delight; for, every minute's space,
The streams with changed magic interlace:
Sometimes like delicatest lattices,
615 Cover'd with crystal vines; then weeping trees,
Moving about as in a gentle wind,
Which, in a wink, to watery gauze refin'd,
Pour'd into shapes of curtain'd canopies,
Spangled, and rich with liquid broideries
620 Of flowers, peacocks, swans, and naiads fair.
Swifter than lightning went these wonders rare;
And then the water, into stubborn streams
Collecting, mimick'd the wrought oaken beams,
Pillars, and frieze, and high fantastic roof,
625 Of those dusk places in times far aloof
Cathedrals call'd. He bade a loth farewel
To these founts Protean, passing gulph, and dell,
And torrent, and ten thousand jutting shapes,
Half seen through deepest gloom, and griesly gapes,
630 Blackening on every side, and overhead
A vaulted dome like heaven's, far bespread
With starlight gems: aye, all so huge and strange,
The solitary felt a hurried change
Working within him into something dreary,—
635 Vex'd like a morning eagle, lost, and weary,
And purblind amid foggy, midnight wolds.
But he revives at once: for who beholds
New sudden things, nor casts his mental slough?

606 Done heedlessly] He playfully made (*presumably following* splash *in 605 without the comma*) *D* 607 to] *not in FC* 608 diamond . . . streaming] mid-air . . . quivering *D* 610 sweet] loud *D* 615 Cover'd . . . trees] O'erspread . . . peas *D* 616 Moving] Waving *D* 622 water] waters *D, FC* 623 oaken] rafts and *D* 625 dusk] dim *D*; dusk *made out of* dim *FC* 628 jutting] *successively* (*a*) massy (*b*) blackening (*c*) bulging *D* 629 Half . . . gloom] Hid in the dim profound *D* 629 through] *written over* ⟨in⟩ *FC* 631 far bespread] overspread *D*; ⟨oversp⟩ far bespread *FC* 632 huge and] monstrous *D* 633 hurried] dizzy *D* 635 Vex'd] Scared *D* 636 foggy,] damp and‸ *D*; ⟨damp an⟩ foggy, *FC*

Forth from a rugged arch, in the dusk below,
640 Came mother Cybele! alone—alone—
In sombre chariot; dark foldings thrown
About her majesty, and front death-pale,
With turrets crown'd. Four maned lions hale
The sluggish wheels; solemn their toothed maws,
645 Their surly eyes brow-hidden, heavy paws
Uplifted drowsily, and nervy tails
Cowering their tawny brushes. Silent sails
This shadowy queen athwart, and faints away
In another gloomy arch.

Wherefore delay,
650 Young traveller, in such a mournful place?
Art thou wayworn, or canst not further trace
The diamond path? And does it indeed end
Abrupt in middle air? Yet earthward bend
Thy forehead, and to Jupiter cloud-borne
655 Call ardently! He was indeed wayworn;
Abrupt, in middle air, his way was lost;
To cloud-borne Jove he bowed, and there crost
Towards him a large eagle, 'twixt whose wings,
Without one impious word, himself he flings,
660 Committed to the darkness and the gloom:
Down, down, uncertain to what pleasant doom,
Swift as a fathoming plummet down he fell
Through unknown things; till exhaled asphodel,

639 Forth from] From out *D*   639 rugged] *successively* (*a*) dismal (*b*) beetling (*c*) gloomy *D*; ⟨f⟩ rugged *FC*   639 dusk] *interlined above* ⟨dark⟩ *FC*   641/642
⟨About her Majesty, and her pale brow
With turrets crown'd, which forward heavily bow
Weighing her chin to the breast. Four lions draw
The wheels in sluggish time—each toothed maw
Shut patiently—eyes hid in tawny veils—
Drooping about their paws, and nervy tails
Cowering their tufted brushes to the dust.⟩ *D*
643 maned] tawny *D*   644 toothed] ⟨patient⟩ *replaced by* closed *D*   645 brow-hidden,] halfshut, their∧ *D*   646 drowsily] lazily *D*; ⟨sleepily⟩ drowsily *FC*   647 Cowering . . . brushes] Vailing . . . tufts *D*   649 In] ⟨To⟩ In *interlined above* ⟨Into⟩ *FC*   657–660 bowed . . . gloom]
bent: and there was tost
Into his grasping hands a silken cord
At which without a single impious word
He swung upon it off into the gloom *D*
662 Swift as] Dropt like *D*

And rose, with spicy fannings interbreath'd,
665 Came swelling forth where little caves were wreath'd
So thick with leaves and mosses, that they seem'd
Large honey-combs of green, and freshly teem'd
With airs delicious. In the greenest nook
The eagle landed him, and farewel took.

670 It was a jasmine bower, all bestrown
With golden moss. His every sense had grown
Ethereal for pleasure; 'bove his head
Flew a delight half-graspable; his tread
Was Hesperean; to his capable ears
675 Silence was music from the holy spheres;
A dewy luxury was in his eyes;
The little flowers felt his pleasant sighs
And stirr'd them faintly. Verdant cave and cell
He wander'd through, oft wondering at such swell
680 Of sudden exaltation: but, "Alas!"
Said he, "will all this gush of feeling pass
Away in solitude? And must they wane,
Like melodies upon a sandy plain,
Without an echo? Then shall I be left
685 So sad, so melancholy, so bereft!
Yet still I feel immortal! O my love,
My breath of life, where art thou? High above,
Dancing before the morning gates of heaven?
Or keeping watch among those starry seven,
690 Old Atlas' children? Art a maid of the waters,
One of shell-winding Triton's bright-hair'd daughters?
Or art, impossible! a nymph of Dian's,
Weaving a coronal of tender scions
For very idleness? Where'er thou art,
695 Methinks it now is at my will to start

668–670 In . . . bestrown]

Long he hung about
Before his nice enjoyment could pick out
The resting place: but at the last he swung
Into the greenest cell of all—among
Dark leaved jasmine: star flowered and bestrown *D*

679 oft . . . such] with still encreasing *D* 681 this . . . feeling] these gushing feelings *D* 681 this] *made out of* these *FC* 684 Then . . . I] Ah I shall *D* 689 those] the *D* 690 maid] nymph *D* 690 of] o' *FC* 691 bright-hair'd] floating *D* 692 Or art . . . nymph] Art thou . . . maid *D*

Into thine arms; to scare Aurora's train,
And snatch thee from the morning; o'er the main
To scud like a wild bird, and take thee off
From thy sea-foamy cradle; or to doff
700 Thy shepherd vest, and woo thee mid fresh leaves.
No, no, too eagerly my soul deceives
Its powerless self: I know this cannot be.
O let me then by some sweet dreaming flee
To her entrancements: hither, sleep, awhile!
705 Hither, most gentle sleep! and soothing foil
For some few hours the coming solitude."

Thus spake he, and that moment felt endued
With power to dream deliciously; so wound
Through a dim passage, searching till he found
710 The smoothest mossy bed and deepest, where
He threw himself, and just into the air
Stretching his indolent arms, he took, O bliss!
A naked waist: "Fair Cupid, whence is this?"
A well-known voice sigh'd, "Sweetest, here am I!"
715 At which soft ravishment, with doating cry
They trembled to each other.—Helicon!
O fountain'd hill! Old Homer's Helicon!
That thou wouldst spout a little streamlet o'er
These sorry pages; then the verse would soar
720 And sing above this gentle pair, like lark
Over his nested young: but all is dark
Around thine aged top, and thy clear fount
Exhales in mists to heaven. Aye, the count
Of mighty Poets is made up; the scroll
725 Is folded by the Muses; the bright roll
Is in Apollo's hand: our dazed eyes
Have seen a new tinge in the western skies:
The world has done its duty. Yet, oh yet,

697 the morning] among them *D* 697 o'er] ⟨to attain / The starry heights and find thee ere a breath⟩ o'er (*Woodhouse gives the bracketed words as uncanceled*) *D* 698 scud] skim *D* 701 No, no,] But ah! *D* 702 powerless] mortal *D*; ⟨reachin⟩ powerless *FC* 702 I know] O since *D* 703 let] ⟨th⟩ let *FC* 706 For . . . hours] With thy quick Magic *D* 709 searching] feeling *D*; ⟨feeling⟩ searching *FC* 713 Fair Cupid,] Good heavens! *D* 715 soft . . . cry] each uttering forth ⟨a wailful⟩ cry (⟨an anguish⟩ *interlined above* ⟨a wailful⟩—*apparently the line was left incomplete*) *D* 719 the] this *D* 720 this] the *D* 722 top] green *D* 723 mists] mist *FC* 725 bright] great *D* 726 dazed] ⟨dazzled⟩ *replaced by* mortal *D*

Although the sun of poesy is set,
730 These lovers did embrace, and we must weep
That there is no old power left to steep
A quill immortal in their joyous tears.
Long time in silence did their anxious fears
Question that thus it was; long time they lay
735 Fondling and kissing every doubt away;
Long time ere soft caressing sobs began
To mellow into words, and then there ran
Two bubbling springs of talk from their sweet lips.
"O known Unknown! from whom my being sips
740 Such darling essence, wherefore may I not
Be ever in these arms? in this sweet spot
Pillow my chin for ever? ever press
These toying hands and kiss their smooth excess?
Why not for ever and for ever feel
745 That breath about my eyes? Ah, thou wilt steal
Away from me again, indeed, indeed—
Thou wilt be gone away, and wilt not heed
My lonely madness. Speak, delicious fair!
Is—is it to be so? No! Who will dare
750 To pluck thee from me? And, of thine own will,
Full well I feel thou wouldst not leave me. Still
Let me entwine thee surer, surer—now
How can we part? Elysium! who art thou?
Who, that thou canst not be for ever here,
755 Or lift me with thee to some starry sphere?
Enchantress! tell me by this soft embrace,
By the most soft completion of thy face,
Those lips, O slippery blisses, twinkling eyes,
And by these tenderest, milky sovereignties—
760 These tenderest, and by the nectar-wine,
The passion"——"O dov'd Ida the divine!
Endymion! dearest! Ah, unhappy me!
His soul will 'scape us—O felicity!

735 every] dreaming *D* 736 soft] few *D* 743 toying] languid *D* 747 Thou wilt . . . wilt] And there must be a time when thou'lt *D* 747 and wilt] and will (will *altered by Taylor in pencil to* wilt) *FC* 748 Speak] O *D* 748 delicious] *D*, *L*[5]; my kindest *FC*, *1818* 748 fair] *replacing* ⟨maid⟩ *D* 749 Who] What *D* 751 Full well‸] I know— *D* 756 soft] mad *D* 757 most . . . thy] moist languor of thy breathing (moist *replacing* ⟨smooth⟩) *D* 760–761 nectar . . . divine] breath—the love / The passion—nectar—Heaven!"—"Jove above *D* 761 dov'd] *FC* (*the word added above the line*); lov'd *1818*

How he does love me! His poor temples beat
765 To the very tune of love—how sweet, sweet, sweet.
Revive, dear youth, or I shall faint and die;
Revive, or these soft hours will hurry by
In tranced dulness; speak, and let that spell
Affright this lethargy! I cannot quell
770 Its heavy pressure, and will press at least
My lips to thine, that they may richly feast
Until we taste the life of love again.
What! dost thou move? dost kiss? O bliss! O pain!
I love thee, youth, more than I can conceive;
775 And so long absence from thee doth bereave
My soul of any rest: yet must I hence:
Yet, can I not to starry eminence
Uplift thee; nor for very shame can own
Myself to thee. Ah, dearest, do not groan
780 Or thou wilt force me from this secrecy,
And I must blush in heaven. O that I
Had done't already; that the dreadful smiles
At my lost brightness, my impassion'd wiles,
Had waned from Olympus' solemn height,
785 And from all serious Gods; that our delight
Was quite forgotten, save of us alone!
And wherefore so ashamed? 'Tis but to atone
For endless pleasure, by some coward blushes:
Yet must I be a coward!—Horror rushes
790 Too palpable before me—the sad look
Of Jove—Minerva's start—no bosom shook
With awe of purity—no Cupid pinion
In reverence vailed—my crystalline dominion
Half lost, and all old hymns made nullity!
795 But what is this to love? O I could fly
With thee into the ken of heavenly powers,
So thou wouldst thus, for many sequent hours,
Press me so sweetly. Now I swear at once
That I am wise, that Pallas is a dunce—

770 and] yet *D*  771 to] 'gainst *D*  773/774 ⟨Listen to me if Love will let me—⟩ *D*  782 done't] *FC*, $L^5$; done it *1818*  782 already] ⟨for⟩ already *FC*  783 lost . . . my] ⟨dear weakness and⟩ (*the words deleted and nothing substituted*) *D*  785 Gods . . . our] Powers . . . my *D*  787 And] But *D*  788 by] *written over* ⟨in⟩ *FC*  789 Horror] *FC*, $L^5$, *1818 errata* (⟨the⟩ horror *in FC*); ⟨the idea⟩ *replaced by* The thing *D*; Honour *1818 text*  793 vailed] *FC* (*made out of* veiled); veiled *1818*  796 heavenly] starry *D*  798 Press] Hug *D*  799/800 ⟨Does Pallas self not love? she must—she must!⟩ *D*

800 Perhaps her love like mine is but unknown—
O I do think that I have been alone
In chastity: yes, Pallas has been sighing,
While every eve saw me my hair uptying
With fingers cool as aspen leaves. Sweet love,
805 I was as vague as solitary dove,
Nor knew that nests were built. Now a soft kiss—
Aye, by that kiss, I vow an endless bliss,
An immortality of passion's thine:
Ere long I will exalt thee to the shine
810 Of heaven ambrosial; and we will shade
Ourselves whole summers by a river glade;
And I will tell thee stories of the sky,
And breathe thee whispers of its minstrelsy.
My happy love will overwing all bounds!
815 O let me melt into thee; let the sounds
Of our close voices marry at their birth;
Let us entwine hoveringly—O dearth
Of human words! roughness of mortal speech!
Lispings empyrean will I sometime teach
820 Thine honied tongue—lute-breathings, which I gasp
To have thee understand, now while I clasp
Thee thus, and weep for fondness—I am pain'd,
Endymion: woe! woe! is grief contain'd
In the very deeps of pleasure, my sole life?"—
825 Hereat, with many sobs, her gentle strife
Melted into a languor. He return'd
Entranced vows and tears.

Ye who have yearn'd
With too much passion, will here stay and pity,
For the mere sake of truth; as 'tis a ditty
830 Not of these days, but long ago 'twas told

807 vow] swear *D*; vow *interlined above* ⟨swear⟩ *FC* 813 whispers of its] Empyrean *D* 814 My . . . love] ⟨O my mad love⟩ *replaced by* My maddest love *D* 814 happy] ⟨Love⟩ happy *FC* 816 our close] both our *D* 817 hoveringly] inextricably *D* 818 human . . . mortal] mortal words! I'll teach thee other *D* 819 empyrean] immortal *D* 820 lute] *interlined above* ⟨Gold⟩ *FC* 822 weep for fondness] shed these drops (drops *interlined above* ⟨tears⟩) *D* 823 woe! woe! is] There is a *D* 824 deeps . . . my sole] shrine . . . O my *D* 825 many] fainting *D* 826 Melted . . . a] Died into passive *D* 827–829 Entranced . . . mere]

No answer, saving tears—Ye who have burn'd
With over passion, here exclaim and pity
Even for the *D*

By a cavern wind unto a forest old;
And then the forest told it in a dream
To a sleeping lake, whose cool and level gleam
A poet caught as he was journeying
835 To Phœbus' shrine; and in it he did fling
His weary limbs, bathing an hour's space,
And after, straight in that inspired place
He sang the story up into the air,
Giving it universal freedom. There
840 Has it been ever sounding for those ears
Whose tips are glowing hot. The legend cheers
Yon centinel stars; and he who listens to it
Must surely be self-doomed or he will rue it:
For quenchless burnings come upon the heart,
845 Made fiercer by a fear lest any part
Should be engulphed in the eddying wind.
As much as here is penn'd doth always find
A resting place, thus much comes clear and plain;
Anon the strange voice is upon the wane—
850 And 'tis but echo'd from departing sound,
That the fair visitant at last unwound
Her gentle limbs, and left the youth asleep.—
Thus the tradition of the gusty deep.

Now turn we to our former chroniclers.—
855 Endymion awoke, that grief of hers
Sweet paining on his ear: he sickly guess'd
How lone he was once more, and sadly press'd
His empty arms together, hung his head,
And most forlorn upon that widow'd bed
860 Sat silently. Love's madness he had known:
Often with more than tortured lion's groan
Moanings had burst from him; but now that rage
Had pass'd away: no longer did he wage
A rough-voic'd war against the dooming stars.
865 No, he had felt too much for such harsh jars:
The lyre of his soul Eolian tun'd

831 cavern wind] Cavern's mouth *D*; Cavern's Mouth *altered to* Cavern wind *FC* 833 sleeping] slumbering *D* 837 And$_\wedge$ after, straight$_\wedge$] ~, ~$_\wedge$ ~, *FC* 849 Anon . . . upon] But after . . . on *D* 850 echo'd from] guess'd from the *D* 852 gentle] prison'd *D* 856 on] *made out of* in *FC* 860 Sat silently] Patiently sat *D* 862 Moanings] Passion *D*; *successively* (*a*) Complaints (*b*) Plainings (*c*) Moanings *FC* 865 had . . . much] ⟨was⟩ felt too divine *D*

Forgot all violence, and but commun'd
With melancholy thought: O he had swoon'd
Drunken from pleasure's nipple; and his love
870 Henceforth was dove-like.—Loth was he to move
From the imprinted couch, and when he did,
'Twas with slow, languid paces, and face hid
In muffling hands. So temper'd, out he stray'd
Half seeing visions that might have dismay'd
875 Alecto's serpents; ravishments more keen
Than Hermes' pipe, when anxious he did lean
Over eclipsing eyes: and at the last
It was a sounding grotto, vaulted, vast,
O'er studded with a thousand, thousand pearls,
880 And crimson mouthed shells with stubborn curls,
Of every shape and size, even to the bulk
In which whales harbour close, to brood and sulk
Against an endless storm. Moreover too,
Fish-semblances, of green and azure hue,
885 Ready to snort their streams. In this cool wonder
Endymion sat down, and 'gan to ponder
On all his life: his youth, up to the day
When 'mid acclaim, and feasts, and garlands gay,
He stept upon his shepherd throne: the look
890 Of his white palace in wild forest nook,
And all the revels he had lorded there:
Each tender maiden whom he once thought fair,
With every friend and fellow-woodlander—
Pass'd like a dream before him. Then the spur
895 Of the old bards to mighty deeds: his plans
To nurse the golden age 'mong shepherd clans:
That wondrous night: the great Pan-festival:
His sister's sorrow; and his wanderings all,
Until into the earth's deep maw he rush'd:
900 Then all its buried magic, till it flush'd
High with excessive love. "And now," thought he,

868 melancholy thought] thoughts of tenderest birth *D* 870–871 Loth . . . imprinted] Scarcely could he move / His limbs from the dear *D* 873 hands] arms *D* 874 Half . . . visions] Scarce . . . wonders *D* 876 Hermes'] ⟨those of⟩ Herme's *FC* 878 It was] He found *D* 878 vaulted,] $\sim_\wedge$ *FC* 879 O'er] *interlined above* ⟨And⟩ *FC* 880 crimson . . . stubborn] shells out swelling their faint tinged *D* 881 shape] *interlined above* ⟨hue⟩ *FC* 882 harbour] *ed*; arbour *FC, 1818* 884 azure] golden *D* 895 the old bards] minstrelsy *D* 897 night . . . festival] night ⟨that wean'd him⟩: great Pan's high festival *D* 899 deep] dim *D*

"How long must I remain in jeopardy
Of blank amazements that amaze no more?
Now I have tasted her sweet soul to the core
905 All other depths are shallow: essences,
Once spiritual, are like muddy lees,
Meant but to fertilize my earthly root,
And make my branches lift a golden fruit
Into the bloom of heaven: other light,
910 Though it be quick and sharp enough to blight
The Olympian eagle's vision, is dark,
Dark as the parentage of chaos. Hark!
My silent thoughts are echoing from these shells;
Or they are but the ghosts, the dying swells
915 Of noises far away?—list!"—Hereupon
He kept an anxious ear. The humming tone
Came louder, and behold, there as he lay,
On either side outgush'd, with misty spray,
A copious spring; and both together dash'd
920 Swift, mad, fantastic round the rocks, and lash'd
Among the conchs and shells of the lofty grot,
Leaving a trickling dew. At last they shot
Down from the ceiling's height, pouring a noise
As of some breathless racers whose hopes poize
925 Upon the last few steps, and with spent force
Along the ground they took a winding course.
Endymion follow'd—for it seem'd that one
Ever pursued, the other strove to shun—
Follow'd their languid mazes, till well nigh
930 He had left thinking of the mystery,—
And was now rapt in tender hoverings
Over the vanish'd bliss. Ah! what is it sings
His dream away? What melodies are these?
They sound as through the whispering of trees,
935 Not native in such barren vaults. Give ear!

"O Arethusa, peerless nymph! why fear
Such tenderness as mine? Great Dian, why,
Why didst thou hear her prayer? O that I

907 Meant] ⟨Made⟩ *replaced by* Sent *or* Lent (*Woodhouse here uncertain about Keats's initial letter*) *D*  908 a golden] their ripen'd *D*  914 but the . . . the] subtlest and (*but see Textual Note*) *D*  915 away?—] ~‸— *FC*  917 and] ⟨still⟩ and *FC*  920 lash'd] splash'd *D*  931 now] ⟨eve⟩ now *FC*  932 Over the vanish'd] O'er past and future *D*  932 is it] is't *FC*

Were rippling round her dainty fairness now,
940 Circling about her waist, and striving how
To entice her to a dive! then stealing in
Between her luscious lips and eyelids thin.
O that her shining hair was in the sun,
And I distilling from it thence to run
945 In amorous rillets down her shrinking form!
To linger on her lily shoulders, warm
Between her kissing breasts, and every charm
Touch raptur'd!—See how painfully I flow:
Fair maid, be pitiful to my great woe.
950 Stay, stay thy weary course, and let me lead,
A happy wooer, to the flowery mead
Where all that beauty snar'd me."—"Cruel god,
Desist! or my offended mistress' nod
Will stagnate all thy fountains:—tease me not
955 With syren words—Ah, have I really got
Such power to madden thee? And is it true—
Away, away, or I shall dearly rue
My very thoughts: in mercy then away,
Kindest Alpheus, for should I obey
960 My own dear will, 'twould be a deadly bane.
O, Oread-Queen! would that thou hadst a pain
Like this of mine, then would I fearless turn
And be a criminal. Alas, I burn,
I shudder—gentle river, get thee hence.
965 Alpheus! thou enchanter! every sense
Of mine was once made perfect in these woods.
Fresh breezes, bowery lawns, and innocent floods,
Ripe fruits, and lonely couch, contentment gave;
But ever since I heedlessly did lave
970 In thy deceitful stream, a panting glow
Grew strong within me: wherefore serve me so,
And call it love? Alas, 'twas cruelty.
Not once more did I close my happy eye

945 In . . . down] Amorous and slow adown *D* 947 Between her kissing] About her ⟨pouting⟩ budding *D* 948–949 Touch . . . woe] Kiss, raptur'd—even to her milky toes. / O foolish maid be gentle to my woes *D* 952 snar'd] slew *D* 954 fountains] waters *D*; fountains *interlined above* ⟨waters⟩ *FC* 960–961 bane.$_\wedge$ / $_\wedge$O] *FC*, $L^5$; ~."— / "~ *1818* 963 criminal.$_\wedge$ $_\wedge$Alas] *FC*, $L^5$; ~."—"~ *1818* 964 gentle river] for sweet mercy *D* 966 perfect] happy *D* 967 bowery] shady *D* 968 lonely] leafy *D* 969 did] gan *D* 973 Not . . . did] No longer could *D* 973 happy] *successively* (*a*) sleepless (*b*) weary (*c*) wearied *D* 973 eye] *D*; eyes *FC*, *1818*

Amid the thrush's song. Away! Avaunt!
975 O 'twas a cruel thing."—"Now thou dost taunt
So softly, Arethusa, that I think
If thou wast playing on my shady brink,
Thou wouldst bathe once again. Innocent maid!
Stifle thine heart no more;—nor be afraid
980 Of angry powers: there are deities
Will shade us with their wings. Those fitful sighs
'Tis almost death to hear: O let me pour
A dewy balm upon them!—fear no more,
Sweet Arethusa! Dian's self must feel
985 Sometimes these very pangs. Dear maiden, steal
Blushing into my soul, and let us fly
These dreary caverns for the open sky.
I will delight thee all my winding course,
From the green sea up to my hidden source
990 About Arcadian forests; and will shew
The channels where my coolest waters flow
Through mossy rocks; where, 'mid exuberant green,
I roam in pleasant darkness, more unseen
Than Saturn in his exile; where I brim
995 Round flowery islands, and take thence a skim
Of mealy sweets, which myriads of bees
Buzz from their honied wings: and thou shouldst please
Thyself to choose the richest, where we might
Be incense-pillow'd every summer night.
1000 Doff all sad fears, thou white deliciousness,
And let us be thus comforted; unless
Thou couldst rejoice to see my hopeless stream
Hurry distracted from Sol's temperate beam,
And pour to death along some hungry sands."—
1005 "What can I do, Alpheus? Dian stands
Severe before me: persecuting fate!
Unhappy Arethusa! thou wast late
A huntress free in"—At this, sudden fell
Those two sad streams adown a fearful dell.
1010 The Latmian listen'd, but he heard no more,

974 thrush's] Thrushes *FC* 977 on] by *D* 980 powers] ⟨Deities⟩ Powers *FC* 985 Sometimes] Sometime *FC* 990 Arcadian forests] Arcadia's Plains *D* 990 will] I will *FC* 996 mealy] powdery *D* 997 Buzz] Shake *D*; Buzz *interlined above* ⟨Shake⟩ *FC* 998 richest] freshest *D* 1004 some hungry] hot Afric's *D* 1006 persecuting] cruel, cruel *D*

Save echo, faint repeating o'er and o'er
The name of Arethusa. On the verge
Of that dark gulph he wept, and said: "I urge
Thee, gentle Goddess of my pilgrimage,
1015 By our eternal hopes, to soothe, to assuage,
If thou art powerful, these lovers' pains;
And make them happy in some happy plains."

He turn'd—there was a whelming sound—he stept,
There was a cooler light; and so he kept
1020 Towards it by a sandy path, and lo!
More suddenly than doth a moment go,
The visions of the earth were gone and fled—
He saw the giant sea above his head.

## BOOK III

There are who lord it o'er their fellow-men
With most prevailing tinsel: who unpen
Their baaing vanities, to browse away
The comfortable green and juicy hay
5 From human pastures; or, O torturing fact!
Who, through an idiot blink, will see unpack'd
Fire-branded foxes to sear up and singe
Our gold and ripe-ear'd hopes. With not one tinge
Of sanctuary splendour, not a sight
10 Able to face an owl's, they still are dight
By the blear-eyed nations in empurpled vests,
And crowns, and turbans. With unladen breasts,
Save of blown self-applause, they proudly mount
To their spirit's perch, their being's high account,
15 Their tiptop nothings, their dull skies, their thrones—
Amid the fierce intoxicating tones
Of trumpets, shoutings, and belabour'd drums,
And sudden cannon. Ah! how all this hums,
In wakeful ears, like uproar past and gone—

1013 said] ⟨I⟩ said *FC* 1015–23 By . . . head.] *written in FC by J. H. Reynolds (see Textual Note)* 1016 art] are *FC* 1017 some happy] their native *D* 1020 sandy] ⟨scanty path⟩ sandy *FC* *After* 1023 End of 2^d^ Book *FC*

III.5 torturing] devilish *D* 6 through] with *D* 19 past and] almost *D*

20 Like thunder clouds that spake to Babylon,
And set those old Chaldeans to their tasks.—
Are then regalities all gilded masks?
No, there are throned seats unscalable
But by a patient wing, a constant spell,
25 Or by ethereal things that, unconfin'd,
Can make a ladder of the eternal wind,
And poise about in cloudy thunder-tents
To watch the abysm-birth of elements.
Aye, 'bove the withering of old-lipp'd Fate
30 A thousand Powers keep religious state,
In water, fiery realm, and airy bourne;
And, silent as a consecrated urn,
Hold sphery sessions for a season due.
Yet few of these far majesties, ah, few!
35 Have bared their operations to this globe—
Few, who with gorgeous pageantry enrobe
Our piece of heaven—whose benevolence
Shakes hand with our own Ceres; every sense
Filling with spiritual sweets to plenitude,
40 As bees gorge full their cells. And, by the feud
'Twixt Nothing and Creation, I here swear,
Eterne Apollo! that thy Sister fair
Is of all these the gentlier-mightiest.
When thy gold breath is misting in the west,
45 She unobserved steals unto her throne,
And there she sits most meek and most alone;
As if she had not pomp subservient;
As if thine eye, high Poet! was not bent
Towards her with the Muses in thine heart;
50 As if the ministring stars kept not apart,
Waiting for silver-footed messages.
O Moon! the oldest shades 'mong oldest trees
Feel palpitations when thou lookest in:
O Moon! old boughs lisp forth a holier din
55 The while they feel thine airy fellowship.

21–22 tasks . . . masks] work.— / Are then all regal things so gone, so murk *D* 23 throned] ⟨other Thrones to mount⟩ throned *D* 30/31 ⟨In the several vastnesses of air and fire / And silent, as a corpse upon a pyre⟩ *D* 34 Yet . . . ah] How . . . how *D* 38 Shakes . . . every] Salutes our native Ceres—and each (and each *interlined above* ⟨every⟩) *D* 39 Filling . . . sweets] With spiritual honey fills *D* 44 breath . . . in] hair falls thick about *D* 49 Towards] Upon *D* 52 shades . . . oldest] shadows ⟨of⟩ 'mong old *D*

Thou dost bless every where, with silver lip
Kissing dead things to life. The sleeping kine,
Couched in thy brightness, dream of fields divine:
Innumerable mountains rise, and rise,
60 Ambitious for the hallowing of thine eyes;
And yet thy benediction passeth not
One obscure hiding-place, one little spot
Where pleasure may be sent: the nested wren
Has thy fair face within its tranquil ken,
65 And from beneath a sheltering ivy leaf
Takes glimpses of thee; thou art a relief
To the poor patient oyster, where it sleeps
Within its pearly house.—The mighty deeps,
The monstrous sea is thine—the myriad sea!
70 O Moon! far-spooming Ocean bows to thee,
And Tellus feels his forehead's cumbrous load.

Cynthia! where art thou now? What far abode
Of green or silvery bower doth enshrine
Such utmost beauty? Alas, thou dost pine
75 For one as sorrowful: thy cheek is pale
For one whose cheek is pale: thou dost bewail
His tears, who weeps for thee. Where dost thou sigh?
Ah! surely that light peeps from Vesper's eye,
Or what a thing is love! 'Tis She, but lo!
80 How chang'd, how full of ache, how gone in woe!
She dies at the thinnest cloud; her loveliness
Is wan on Neptune's blue: yet there's a stress
Of love-spangles, just off yon cape of trees,
Dancing upon the waves, as if to please
85 The curly foam with amorous influence.
O, not so idle: for down-glancing thence

56–57 every . . . life] all things—even dead things sip / A midnight life from thee *D* 63 sent] wrought *D* 63/64 ⟨Quiet behind dark ivy leaves⟩ *D* 66 art] are *FC* 69 myriad] monstrous *D* 70 far] old *D* 71 his] *FC*, *1818 errata*; her *1818 text (the erroneous word penciled by Taylor in the margin of FC)* 74 Such] *replacing* ⟨Thine⟩ *D* 77–78 dost . . . eye] art thou Ah / Surely that light is from the Evening star *D* 85/86

⟨Yet not so idle—{but} for down glancing thence
It mingles and darts about unfathomed⟩

(Yet . . . idle *interlined above* {Nor stays it}, cradled idly *interlined and deleted above* {there sleeps the idleness}, *and* for down *interlined after* {but}, *all in the first line; Woodhouse's presentation makes for several uncertainties, but a tentative order of versions would be* [*a*] Nor stays it [*b*] Nor there sleeps the idleness—but glancing thence [*c*] Nor cradled idly—but down glanc-

She fathoms eddies, and runs wild about
O'erwhelming water-courses; scaring out
The thorny sharks from hiding-holes, and fright'ning
90 Their savage eyes with unaccustomed lightning.
Where will the splendor be content to reach?
O love! how potent hast thou been to teach
Strange journeyings! Wherever beauty dwells,
In gulf or aerie, mountains or deep dells,
95 In light, in gloom, in star or blazing sun,
Thou pointest out the way, and straight 'tis won.
Amid his toil thou gav'st Leander breath;
Thou leddest Orpheus through the gleams of death;
Thou madest Pluto bear thin element;
100 And now, O winged Chieftain! thou hast sent
A moon-beam to the deep, deep water-world,
To find Endymion.

On gold sand impearl'd
With lily shells, and pebbles milky white,
Poor Cynthia greeted him, and sooth'd her light
105 Against his pallid face: he felt the charm
To breathlessness, and suddenly a warm
Of his heart's blood: 'twas very sweet; he stay'd
His wandering steps, and half-entranced laid
His head upon a tuft of straggling weeds,
110 To taste the gentle moon, and freshening beads,
Lashed from the crystal roof by fishes' tails.
And so he kept, until the rosy veils
Mantling the east, by Aurora's peering hand
Were lifted from the water's breast, and fann'd
115 Into sweet air; and sober'd morning came
Meekly through billows:—when like taper-flame
Left sudden by a dallying breath of air,
He rose in silence, and once more 'gan fare
Along his fated way.

Far had he roam'd,
120 With nothing save the hollow vast, that foam'd

---

ing thence [*d*] Yet not so idle—for down glancing thence; *the second line could have been written after any of the last three versions was arrived at*) *D* 89 The thorny] Enormous *D* 90 Their savage] The whale's large *D* 94–95 In . . . gloom] In air, or living flame—or magic shells, / In earth, or mist *D* 94 gulf or] gulph, on *altered to* gulph or *FC*

Above, around, and at his feet; save things
More dead than Morpheus' imaginings:
Old rusted anchors, helmets, breast-plates large
Of gone sea-warriors; brazen beaks and targe;
125 Rudders that for a hundred years had lost
The sway of human hand; gold vase emboss'd
With long-forgotten story, and wherein
No reveller had ever dipp'd a chin
But those of Saturn's vintage; mouldering scrolls,
130 Writ in the tongue of heaven, by those souls
Who first were on the earth; and sculptures rude
In ponderous stone, developing the mood
Of ancient Nox;—then skeletons of man,
Of beast, behemoth, and leviathan,
135 And elephant, and eagle, and huge jaw
Of nameless monster. A cold leaden awe
These secrets struck into him; and unless
Dian had chaced away that heaviness,
He might have died: but now, with cheered feel,
140 He onward kept; wooing these thoughts to steal
About the labyrinth in his soul of love.

"What is there in thee, Moon! that thou shouldst move
My heart so potently? When yet a child
I oft have dried my tears when thou hast smil'd.
145 Thou seem'dst my sister: hand in hand we went
From eve to morn across the firmament.
No apples would I gather from the tree,
Till thou hadst cool'd their cheeks deliciously:
No tumbling water ever spake romance,
150 But when my eyes with thine thereon could dance:
No woods were green enough, no bower divine,
Until thou liftedst up thine eyelids fine:
In sowing time ne'er would I dibble take,
Or drop a seed, till thou wast wide awake;
155 And, in the summer tide of blossoming,
No one but thee hath heard me blithely sing
And mesh my dewy flowers all the night.
No melody was like a passing spright
If it went not to solemnize thy reign.

128 reveller] revellers *D* 140 kept] ⟨went⟩ kept *FC* 150 eyes] Soul *D* 159 went] ⟨flew⟩ *replaced by* sought *D*

160 Yes, in my boyhood, every joy and pain
By thee were fashion'd to the self-same end;
And as I grew in years, still didst thou blend
With all my ardours: thou wast the deep glen;
Thou wast the mountain-top—the sage's pen—
165 The poet's harp—the voice of friends—the sun;
Thou wast the river—thou wast glory won;
Thou wast my clarion's blast—thou wast my steed—
My goblet full of wine—my topmost deed:—
Thou wast the charm of women, lovely Moon!
170 O what a wild and harmonized tune
My spirit struck from all the beautiful!
On some bright essence could I lean, and lull
Myself to immortality: I prest
Nature's soft pillow in a wakeful rest.
175 But, gentle Orb! there came a nearer bliss—
My strange love came—Felicity's abyss!
She came, and thou didst fade, and fade away—
Yet not entirely; no, thy starry sway
Has been an under-passion to this hour.
180 Now I begin to feel thine orby power
Is coming fresh upon me: O be kind,
Keep back thine influence, and do not blind
My sovereign vision.—Dearest love, forgive
That I can think away from thee and live!—
185 Pardon me, airy planet, that I prize
One thought beyond thine argent luxuries!
How far beyond!" At this a surpris'd start
Frosted the springing verdure of his heart;
For as he lifted up his eyes to swear
190 How his own goddess was past all things fair,
He saw far in the concave green of the sea
An old man sitting calm and peacefully.
Upon a weeded rock this old man sat,
And his white hair was awful, and a mat
195 Of weeds were cold beneath his cold thin feet;
And, ample as the largest winding-sheet,

163, 166, 167 wast . . . wast glory . . . wast my clarion's] was . . . was glory . . . was my Clarion's (*each* was *altered by Taylor in pencil to* wast) *FC* 168 topmost] highest *D* 170 harmonized] harmonizing *D* 171 struck] ⟨sung⟩ *replaced by* made *D* 176 Felicity's] dear pleasure's own *D* 180 orby] orbed *D* 183 My . . . vision] The vision of my Love *D* 188 Frosted . . . verdure] Blighted the flowing river (Blighted the *replacing* ⟨Stemm'd quick the⟩) *D*

A cloak of blue wrapp'd up his aged bones,
O'erwrought with symbols by the deepest groans
Of ambitious magic: every ocean-form
200 Was woven in with black distinctness; storm,
And calm, and whispering, and hideous roar,
Quicksand and whirlpool, and deserted shore
Were emblem'd in the woof; with every shape
That skims, or dives, or sleeps, 'twixt cape and cape.
205 The gulphing whale was like a dot in the spell,
Yet look upon it, and 'twould size and swell
To its huge self; and the minutest fish
Would pass the very hardest gazer's wish,
And shew his little eye's anatomy.
210 Then there was pictur'd the regality
Of Neptune; and the sea nymphs round his state,
In beauteous vassalage, look up and wait.
Beside this old man lay a pearly wand,
And in his lap a book, the which he conn'd
215 So stedfastly, that the new denizen
Had time to keep him in amazed ken,
To mark these shadowings, and stand in awe.

The old man rais'd his hoary head and saw
The wilder'd stranger—seeming not to see,
220 His features were so lifeless. Suddenly
He woke as from a trance; his snow-white brows
Went arching up, and like two magic ploughs
Furrow'd deep wrinkles in his forehead large,
Which kept as fixedly as rocky marge,
225 Till round his wither'd lips had gone a smile.
Then up he rose, like one whose tedious toil
Had watch'd for years in forlorn hermitage,
Who had not from mid-life to utmost age
Eas'd in one accent his o'er-burden'd soul,
230 Even to the trees. He rose: he grasp'd his stole,
With convuls'd clenches waving it abroad,
And in a voice of solemn joy, that aw'd
Echo into oblivion, he said:—

202 Quicksand . . . shore] *D*; *not in FC, 1818* (*neither of which has any punctuation at the end of 201*) 205 whale] Whale⟨s⟩ *FC* 206 it . . . size] it long, 'twould grow *D* 226 tedious] studious *D* 230 Even] Not even (*the first word deleted by Taylor in pencil*) *FC*

"Thou art the man! Now shall I lay my head
235 In peace upon my watery pillow: now
Sleep will come smoothly to my weary brow.
O Jove! I shall be young again, be young!
O shell-borne Neptune, I am pierc'd and stung
With new-born life! What shall I do? Where go,
240 When I have cast this serpent-skin of woe?—
I'll swim to the syrens, and one moment listen
Their melodies, and see their long hair glisten;
Anon upon that giant's arm I'll be,
That writhes about the roots of Sicily:
245 To northern seas I'll in a twinkling sail,
And mount upon the snortings of a whale
To some black cloud; thence down I'll madly sweep
On forked lightning, to the deepest deep,
Where through some sucking pool I will be hurl'd
250 With rapture to the other side of the world!
O, I am full of gladness! Sisters three,
I bow full hearted to your old decree!
Yes, every god be thank'd, and power benign,
For I no more shall wither, droop, and pine.
255 Thou art the man!" Endymion started back
Dismay'd; and, like a wretch from whom the rack
Tortures hot breath, and speech of agony,
Mutter'd: "What lonely death am I to die
In this cold region? Will he let me freeze,
260 And float my brittle limbs o'er polar seas?
Or will he touch me with his searing hand,
And leave a black memorial on the sand?
Or tear me piece-meal with a bony saw,
And keep me as a chosen food to draw
265 His magian fish through hated fire and flame?
O misery of hell! resistless, tame,
Am I to be burnt up? No, I will shout,
Until the gods through heaven's blue look out!—
O Tartarus! but some few days agone
270 Her soft arms were entwining me, and on
Her voice I hung like fruit among green leaves:
Her lips were all my own, and—ah, ripe sheaves
Of happiness! ye on the stubble droop,

240 When] *interlined above* ⟨Now⟩ *FC* 266 O] ⟨Of⟩ O *FC* 266 of] Oh *D* 269 days] *interlined above* ⟨hours⟩ *FC* 271 voice] *interlined above* ⟨lips⟩ *FC*

But never may be garner'd. I must stoop
275 My head, and kiss death's foot. Love! love, farewel!
Is there no hope from thee? This horrid spell
Would melt at thy sweet breath.—By Dian's hind
Feeding from her white fingers, on the wind
I see thy streaming hair! and now, by Pan,
280 I care not for this old mysterious man!"

He spake, and walking to that aged form,
Look'd high defiance. Lo! his heart 'gan warm
With pity, for the grey-hair'd creature wept.
Had he then wrong'd a heart where sorrow kept?
285 Had he, though blindly contumelious, brought
Rheum to kind eyes, a sting to humane thought,
Convulsion to a mouth of many years?
He had in truth; and he was ripe for tears.
The penitent shower fell, as down he knelt
290 Before that care-worn sage, who trembling felt
About his large dark locks, and faultering spake:

"Arise, good youth, for sacred Phœbus' sake!
I know thine inmost bosom, and I feel
A very brother's yearning for thee steal
295 Into mine own: for why? thou openest
The prison gates that have so long opprest
My weary watching. Though thou know'st it not,
Thou art commission'd to this fated spot
For great enfranchisement. O weep no more;
300 I am a friend to love, to loves of yore:
Aye, hadst thou never lov'd an unknown power,
I had been grieving at this joyous hour.
But even now most miserable old,
I saw thee, and my blood no longer cold
305 Gave mighty pulses: in this tottering case
Grew a new heart, which at this moment plays
As dancingly as thine. Be not afraid,
For thou shalt hear this secret all display'd,
Now as we speed towards our joyous task."

286 humane] *FC*; human *1818* 291 About his] The youth's *D* 294 brother's] *interlined above* ⟨father's⟩ *FC* 298 art] are (*altered probably by Taylor—the hand is not certain—to* art) *FC* 307 dancingly] youthfully *D* 309 Now as] The while *D*

310 So saying, this young soul in age's mask
Went forward with the Carian side by side:
Resuming quickly thus; while ocean's tide
Hung swollen at their backs, and jewel'd sands
Took silently their foot-prints.

"My soul stands
315 Now past the midway from mortality,
And so I can prepare without a sigh
To tell thee briefly all my joy and pain.
I was a fisher once, upon this main,
And my boat danc'd in every creek and bay;
320 Rough billows were my home by night and day,—
The sea-gulls not more constant; for I had
No housing from the storm and tempests mad,
But hollow rocks,—and they were palaces
Of silent happiness, of slumberous ease:
325 Long years of misery have told me so.
Aye, thus it was one thousand years ago.
One thousand years!—Is it then possible
To look so plainly through them? to dispel
A thousand years with backward glance sublime?
330 To breathe away as 'twere all scummy slime
From off a crystal pool, to see its deep,
And one's own image from the bottom peep?
Yes: now I am no longer wretched thrall,
My long captivity and moanings all
335 Are but a slime, a thin pervading scum,
The which I breathe away, and thronging come
Like things of yesterday my youthful pleasures.

"I touch'd no lute, I sang not, trod no measures:
I was a lonely youth on desert shores.
340 My sports were lonely, 'mid continuous roars,
And craggy isles, and sea-mew's plaintive cry
Plaining discrepant between sea and sky.
Dolphins were still my playmates; shapes unseen
Would let me feel their scales of gold and green,
345 Nor be my desolation; and, full oft,
When a dread waterspout had rear'd aloft

329 A . . . sublime] At one glance back the mistiness of time *D* 337 youthful] first youth's *D* 342 between] 'twixt the *D*; atween *FC* 346 had] has *FC*

Its hungry hugeness, seeming ready ripe
To burst with hoarsest thunderings, and wipe
My life away like a vast sponge of fate,
350 Some friendly monster, pitying my sad state,
Has dived to its foundations, gulph'd it down,
And left me tossing safely. But the crown
Of all my life was utmost quietude:
More did I love to lie in cavern rude,
355 Keeping in wait whole days for Neptune's voice,
And if it came at last, hark, and rejoice!
There blush'd no summer eve but I would steer
My skiff along green shelving coasts, to hear
The shepherd's pipe come clear from airy steep,
360 Mingled with ceaseless bleatings of his sheep:
And never was a day of summer shine,
But I beheld its birth upon the brine:
For I would watch all night to see unfold
Heaven's gates, and Æthon snort his morning gold
365 Wide o'er the swelling streams: and constantly
At brim of day-tide, on some grassy lea,
My nets would be spread out, and I at rest.
The poor folk of the sea-country I blest
With daily boon of fish most delicate:
370 They knew not whence this bounty, and elate
Would strew sweet flowers on a sterile beach.

"Why was I not contented? Wherefore reach
At things which, but for thee, O Latmian!
Had been my dreary death? Fool! I began
375 To feel distemper'd longings: to desire
The utmost privilege that ocean's sire
Could grant in benediction: to be free
Of all his kingdom. Long in misery
I wasted, ere in one extremest fit
380 I plung'd for life or death. To interknit
One's senses with so dense a breathing stuff
Might seem a work of pain; so not enough
Can I admire how crystal-smooth it felt,
And buoyant round my limbs. At first I dwelt

353 utmost] tip-top *FC* (*also in L*[5], *but Keats changed his mind and deleted the request there*) 358 coasts] coast *FC* 359 airy] *FC*; aery *1818* 367 spread out] out spead *altered to* spead out *FC* 377 be] ⟨become⟩ be *FC*

385 Whole days and days in sheer astonishment;
Forgetful utterly of self-intent;
Moving but with the mighty ebb and flow.
Then, like a new fledg'd bird that first doth shew
His spreaded feathers to the morrow chill,
390 I tried in fear the pinions of my will.
'Twas freedom! and at once I visited
The ceaseless wonders of this ocean-bed.
No need to tell thee of them, for I see
That thou hast been a witness—it must be—
395 For these I know thou canst not feel a drouth,
By the melancholy corners of that mouth.
So I will in my story straightway pass
To more immediate matter. Woe, alas!
That love should be my bane! Ah, Scylla fair!
400 Why did poor Glaucus ever—ever dare
To sue thee to his heart? Kind stranger-youth!
I lov'd her to the very white of truth,
And she would not conceive it. Timid thing!
She fled me swift as sea-bird on the wing,
405 Round every isle, and point, and promontory,
From where large Hercules wound up his story
Far as Egyptian Nile. My passion grew
The more, the more I saw her dainty hue
Gleam delicately through the azure clear:
410 Until 'twas too fierce agony to bear;
And in that agony, across my grief
It flash'd, that Circe might find some relief—
Cruel enchantress! So above the water
I rear'd my head, and look'd for Phœbus' daughter.
415 Ææa's isle was wondering at the moon:—
It seem'd to whirl around me, and a swoon
Left me dead-drifting to that fatal power.

"When I awoke, 'twas in a twilight bower;
Just when the light of morn, with hum of bees,
420 Stole through its verdurous matting of fresh trees.
How sweet, and sweeter! for I heard a lyre,
And over it a sighing voice expire.

395 these I know] such a drink *D* 404 bird] mew *D* 412 find some] afford *D* 415 wondering] looking *D* 417 to] to⟨wards⟩ *FC* 419 Just when] What time *D* 420/421 ⟨How sweet to me! and then I heard a Lyre / With which a sighing voice⟩ *FC*

It ceased—I caught light footsteps; and anon
The fairest face that morn e'er look'd upon
425 Push'd through a screen of roses. Starry Jove!
With tears, and smiles, and honey-words she wove
A net whose thraldom was more bliss than all
The range of flower'd Elysium. Thus did fall
The dew of her rich speech: 'Ah! Art awake?
430 O let me hear thee speak, for Cupid's sake!
I am so oppress'd with joy! Why, I have shed
An urn of tears, as though thou wert cold dead;
And now I find thee living, I will pour
From these devoted eyes their silver store,
435 Until exhausted of the latest drop,
So it will pleasure thee, and force thee stop
Here, that I too may live: but if beyond
Such cool and sorrowful offerings, thou art fond
Of soothing warmth, of dalliance supreme;
440 If thou art ripe to taste a long love dream;
If smiles, if dimples, tongues for ardour mute,
Hang in thy vision like a tempting fruit,
O let me pluck it for thee.' Thus she link'd
Her charming syllables, till indistinct
445 Their music came to my o'er-sweeten'd soul;
And then she hover'd over me, and stole
So near, that if no nearer it had been
This furrow'd visage thou hadst never seen.

"Young man of Latmos! thus particular
450 Am I, that thou may'st plainly see how far
This fierce temptation went: and thou may'st not
Exclaim, How then, was Scylla quite forgot?

"Who could resist? Who in this universe?
She did so breathe ambrosia; so immerse
455 My fine existence in a golden clime.
She took me like a child of suckling time,
And cradled me in roses. Thus condemn'd,
The current of my former life was stemm'd,

425 Starry] Mighty *D* 431 I am] I'm *FC* 432 though] if *D* 436 will] would *D* 441 ardour] rapture *D* 445 soul] *interlined above* ⟨sense⟩ *D* 445/446 ⟨And then I felt a hovering influence / A breathing on my forehead⟩ *D* 451 and thou] that thou *D*; thou (& *inserted before the word in pencil, presumably by Taylor*) *FC*

And to this arbitrary queen of sense
460 I bow'd a tranced vassal: nor would thence
Have mov'd, even though Amphion's harp had woo'd
Me back to Scylla o'er the billows rude.
For as Apollo each eve doth devise
A new appareling for western skies;
465 So every eve, nay every spendthrift hour
Shed balmy consciousness within that bower.
And I was free of haunts umbrageous;
Could wander in the mazy forest-house
Of squirrels, foxes shy, and antler'd deer,
470 And birds from coverts innermost and drear
Warbling for very joy mellifluous sorrow—
To me new born delights!

"Now let me borrow,
For moments few, a temperament as stern
As Pluto's sceptre, that my words not burn
475 These uttering lips, while I in calm speech tell
How specious heaven was changed to real hell.

"One morn she left me sleeping: half awake
I sought for her smooth arms and lips, to slake
My greedy thirst with nectarous camel-draughts;
480 But she was gone. Whereat the barbed shafts
Of disappointment stuck in me so sore,
That out I ran and search'd the forest o'er.
Wandering about in pine and cedar gloom
Damp awe assail'd me; for there 'gan to boom
485 A sound of moan, an agony of sound,
Sepulchral from the distance all around.
Then came a conquering earth-thunder, and rumbled
That fierce complain to silence: while I stumbled
Down a precipitous path, as if impell'd.
490 I came to a dark valley.—Groanings swell'd
Poisonous about my ears, and louder grew,
The nearer I approach'd a flame's gaunt blue,
That glar'd before me through a thorny brake.
This fire, like the eye of gordian snake,

461 even] e'en *FC* 465 spendthrift] passing *D* 466 balmy consciousness] nectarous Influence *D* 477 morn] *interlined above* ⟨day⟩ *FC* 492/493 ⟨This fire like the eye of gordian Snake⟩ *FC*

495 Bewitch'd me towards; and I soon was near
A sight too fearful for the feel of fear:
In thicket hid I curs'd the haggard scene—
The banquet of my arms, my arbour queen,
Seated upon an uptorn forest root;
500 And all around her shapes, wizard and brute,
Laughing, and wailing, groveling, serpenting,
Shewing tooth, tusk, and venom-bag, and sting!
O such deformities! Old Charon's self,
Should he give up awhile his penny pelf,
505 And take a dream 'mong rushes Stygian,
It could not be so phantasied. Fierce, wan,
And tyrannizing was the lady's look,
As over them a gnarled staff she shook.
Oft-times upon the sudden she laugh'd out,
510 And from a basket emptied to the rout
Clusters of grapes, the which they raven'd quick
And roar'd for more; with many a hungry lick
About their shaggy jaws. Avenging, slow,
Anon she took a branch of mistletoe,
515 And emptied on't a black dull-gurgling phial:
Groan'd one and all, as if some piercing trial
Was sharpening for their pitiable bones.
She lifted up the charm: appealing groans
From their poor breasts went sueing to her ear
520 In vain; remorseless as an infant's bier
She whisk'd against their eyes the sooty oil.
Whereat was heard a noise of painful toil,
Increasing gradual to a tempest rage,
Shrieks, yells, and groans of torture-pilgrimage;
525 Until their grieved bodies 'gan to bloat
And puff from the tail's end to stifled throat:
Then was appalling silence: then a sight
More wildering than all that hoarse affright;
For the whole herd, as by a whirlwind writhen,
530 Went through the dismal air like one huge Python
Antagonizing Boreas,—and so vanish'd.
Yet there was not a breath of wind: she banish'd
These phantoms with a nod. Lo! from the dark

495 Bewitch'd me towards] Drew me towards it *D* 498 The . . . arms] My beatiful rose bud *D* 500 around] about *D* 506 phantasied] peopled *D* 511 raven'd] gobbled *D* 525 grieved] ⟨stif⟩ grieved *FC*

Came waggish fauns, and nymphs, and satyrs stark,
535 With dancing and loud revelry,—and went
Swifter than centaurs after rapine bent.—
Sighing, an elephant appear'd and bow'd
Before the fierce witch, speaking thus aloud
In human accent: 'Potent goddess! chief
540 Of pains resistless! make my being brief,
Or let me from this heavy prison fly:
Or give me to the air, or let me die!
I sue not for my happy crown again;
I sue not for my phalanx on the plain;
545 I sue not for my lone, my widow'd wife;
I sue not for my ruddy drops of life,
My children fair, my lovely girls and boys!
I will forget them; I will pass these joys;
Ask nought so heavenward, so too—too high:
550 Only I pray, as fairest boon, to die,
Or be deliver'd from this cumbrous flesh,
From this gross, detestable, filthy mesh,
And merely given to the cold bleak air.
Have mercy, Goddess! Circe, feel my prayer!'

555 "That curst magician's name fell icy numb
Upon my wild conjecturing: truth had come
Naked and sabre-like against my heart.
I saw a fury whetting a death-dart;
And my slain spirit, overwrought with fright,
560 Fainted away in that dark lair of night.
Think, my deliverer, how desolate
My waking must have been! disgust, and hate,
And terrors manifold divided me
A spoil amongst them. I prepar'd to flee
565 Into the dungeon core of that wild wood:
I fled three days—when lo! before me stood
Glaring the angry witch. O Dis, even now,
A clammy dew is beading on my brow,

537 Sighing, an] For a large *D*; Seeing an *FC* 539 In . . . Potent] With human voice O Potent (*Woodhouse does not record any punctuation*) *D* 540 pains] ⟨spells⟩ *replaced by* charms *D* 541 me] it *D* 545 lone, my widow'd] lonely, my dear *D* 546 ruddy] hearts blood *D* 547 children fair] sweetest babes *D* 548 I . . . I will] Ah, likely they are dead—I *D* 554 Circe,] feel oh$_\wedge$ *D* 554/555 (*continuing the address begun in 539*) Pity great Circe!'—Nor sight nor syllable / Saw I or heard I more of this sick spell— *D* 560 dark lair] dull realm *D* 567 even] e'en *FC*

At mere remembering her pale laugh, and curse.
570 'Ha! ha! Sir Dainty! there must be a nurse
Made of rose leaves and thistledown, express,
To cradle thee, my sweet, and lull thee: yes,
I am too flinty-hard for thy nice touch:
My tenderest squeeze is but a giant's clutch.
575 So, fairy-thing, it shall have lullabies
Unheard of yet; and it shall still its cries
Upon some breast more lily-feminine.
Oh, no—it shall not pine, and pine, and pine
More than one pretty, trifling thousand years;
580 And then 'twere pity, but fate's gentle shears
Cut short its immortality. Sea-flirt!
Young dove of the waters! truly I'll not hurt
One hair of thine: see how I weep and sigh,
That our heart-broken parting is so nigh.
585 And must we part? Ah, yes, it must be so.
Yet ere thou leavest me in utter woe,
Let me sob over thee my last adieus,
And speak a blessing: Mark me! Thou hast thews
Immortal, for thou art of heavenly race:
590 But such a love is mine, that here I chase
Eternally away from thee all bloom
Of youth, and destine thee towards a tomb.
Hence shalt thou quickly to the watery vast;
And there, ere many days be overpast,
595 Disabled age shall seize thee; and even then
Thou shalt not go the way of aged men;
But live and wither, cripple and still breathe
Ten hundred years: which gone, I then bequeath
Thy fragile bones to unknown burial.
600 Adieu, sweet love, adieu!'—As shot stars fall,
She fled ere I could groan for mercy. Stung
And poisoned was my spirit: despair sung
A war-song of defiance 'gainst all hell.
A hand was at my shoulder to compel
605 My sullen steps; another 'fore my eyes
Moved on with pointed finger. In this guise

570 Ha! ha!] ⟨O! O!⟩ *replaced by* Ha! He! *D*; Ah Ah, *FC* 575 fairy] tender *D* 577 lily] Zephyr *D* 579 trifling] little *D* 581–583 Sea . . . sigh] Great Jove / What fury of the three could harm this dove / Dear Youth! see how I weep, hear how I sigh *D* 588 hast] hadst *FC* 595 even] e'en *FC*

Enforced, at the last by ocean's foam
I found me; by my fresh, my native home.
Its tempering coolness, to my life akin,
610 Came salutary as I waded in;
And, with a blind voluptuous rage, I gave
Battle to the swollen billow-ridge, and drave
Large froth before me, while there yet remain'd
Hale strength, nor from my bones all marrow drain'd.

615 "Young lover, I must weep—such hellish spite
With dry cheek who can tell? While thus my might
Proving upon this element, dismay'd,
Upon a dead thing's face my hand I laid;
I look'd—'twas Scylla! Cursed, cursed Circe!
620 O vulture-witch, hast never heard of mercy?
Could not thy harshest vengeance be content,
But thou must nip this tender innocent
Because I lov'd her?—Cold, O cold indeed
Were her fair limbs, and like a common weed
625 The sea-swell took her hair. Dead as she was
I clung about her waist, nor ceas'd to pass
Fleet as an arrow through unfathom'd brine,
Until there shone a fabric crystalline,
Ribb'd and inlaid with coral, pebble, and pearl.
630 Headlong I darted; at one eager swirl
Gain'd its bright portal, enter'd, and behold!
'Twas vast, and desolate, and icy-cold;
And all around—But wherefore this to thee
Who in few minutes more thyself shalt see?—
635 I left poor Scylla in a niche and fled.
My fever'd parchings up, my scathing dread
Met palsy half way: soon these limbs became
Gaunt, wither'd, sapless, feeble, cramp'd, and lame.

"Now let me pass a cruel, cruel space,
640 Without one hope, without one faintest trace
Of mitigation, or redeeming bubble
Of colour'd phantasy; for I fear 'twould trouble
Thy brain to loss of reason: and next tell

621 Could . . . be] Was not thine harshest avengeance *D*, *FC* (avengeance *replacing* ⟨wrath with me⟩ *in D*) 626 waist] waist and dived *D* 629 coral,] ~‸ *FC*

How a restoring chance came down to quell
One half of the witch in me.

645 "On a day,
Sitting upon a rock above the spray,
I saw grow up from the horizon's brink
A gallant vessel: soon she seem'd to sink
Away from me again, as though her course
650 Had been resum'd in spite of hindering force—
So vanish'd: and not long, before arose
Dark clouds, and muttering of winds morose.
Old Eolus would stifle his mad spleen,
But could not: therefore all the billows green
655 Toss'd up the silver spume against the clouds.
The tempest came: I saw that vessel's shrouds
In perilous bustle; while upon the deck
Stood trembling creatures. I beheld the wreck;
The final gulphing; the poor struggling souls:
660 I heard their cries amid loud thunder-rolls.
O they had all been sav'd but crazed eld
Annull'd my vigorous cravings: and thus quell'd
And curb'd, think on't, O Latmian! did I sit
Writhing with pity, and a cursing fit
665 Against that hell-born Circe. The crew had gone,
By one and one, to pale oblivion;
And I was gazing on the surges prone,
With many a scalding tear and many a groan,
When at my feet emerg'd an old man's hand,
670 Grasping this scroll, and this same slender wand.
I knelt with pain—reached out my hand—had grasp'd
These treasures—touch'd the knuckles—they unclasp'd—
I caught a finger: but the downward weight
O'erpowered me—it sank. Then 'gan abate
675 The storm, and through chill aguish gloom outburst
The comfortable sun. I was athirst
To search the book, and in the warming air
Parted its dripping leaves with eager care.
Strange matters did it treat of, and drew on

644 restoring] ⟨small⟩ restoring *FC* 650 Had . . . hindering] She would resume in spite of adverse *D* 655 the silver] their silver *D*, *FC* 678 Parted its dripping] Unfolded its damp *D*

680 My soul page after page, till well-nigh won
Into forgetfulness; when, stupefied,
I read these words, and read again, and tried
My eyes against the heavens, and read again.
O what a load of misery and pain
685 Each Atlas-line bore off!—a shine of hope
Came gold around me, cheering me to cope
Strenuous with hellish tyranny. Attend!
For thou hast brought their promise to an end.

*"In the wide sea there lives a forlorn wretch,*
690 *Doom'd with enfeebled carcase to outstretch*
*His loath'd existence through ten centuries,*
*And then to die alone. Who can devise*
*A total opposition? No one. So*
*One million times ocean must ebb and flow,*
695 *And he oppressed. Yet he shall not die,*
*These things accomplish'd:—If he utterly*
*Scans all the depths of magic, and expounds*
*The meanings of all motions, shapes, and sounds;*
*If he explores all forms and substances*
700 *Straight homeward to their symbol-essences;*
*He shall not die. Moreover, and in chief,*
*He must pursue this task of joy and grief*
*Most piously;—all lovers tempest-tost,*
*And in the savage overwhelming lost,*
705 *He shall deposit side by side, until*
*Time's creeping shall the dreary space fulfil:*
*Which done, and all these labours ripened,*
*A youth, by heavenly power lov'd and led,*
*Shall stand before him; whom he shall direct*
710 *How to consummate all. The youth elect*
*Must do the thing, or both will be destroy'd."—*

"Then," cried the young Endymion, overjoy'd,
"We are twin brothers in this destiny!
Say, I intreat thee, what achievement high
715 Is, in this restless world, for me reserv'd.
What! if from thee my wandering feet had swerv'd,
Had we both perish'd?"—"Look!" the sage replied,

685–686 a . . . cope] sweet rays of hope / Glanc'd round me cheering me at once to ⟨hope⟩ cope *D* 686 around] round *altered to* around *FC* 689 In] Listen! In (*the first word deleted in pencil, presumably by Taylor*) *FC* 697 Scans] Sounds *D* 702 joy and] heaviest *D*

"Dost thou not mark a gleaming through the tide,
Of divers brilliances? 'tis the edifice
720 I told thee of, where lovely Scylla lies;
And where I have enshrined piously
All lovers, whom fell storms have doom'd to die
Throughout my bondage." Thus discoursing, on
They went till unobscur'd the porches shone;
725 Which hurryingly they gain'd, and enter'd straight.
Sure never since king Neptune held his state
Was seen such wonder underneath the stars.
Turn to some level plain where haughty Mars
Has legion'd all his battle; and behold
730 How every soldier, with firm foot, doth hold
His even breast: see, many steeled squares,
And rigid ranks of iron—whence who dares
One step? Imagine further, line by line,
These warrior thousands on the field supine:—
735 So in that crystal place, in silent rows,
Poor lovers lay at rest from joys and woes.—
The stranger from the mountains, breathless, trac'd
Such thousands of shut eyes in order plac'd;
Such ranges of white feet, and patient lips
740 All ruddy,—for here death no blossom nips.
He mark'd their brows and foreheads; saw their hair
Put sleekly on one side with nicest care;
And each one's gentle wrists, with reverence,
Put cross-wise to its heart.

"Let us commence,"
745 Whisper'd the guide, stuttering with joy, "even now."
He spake, and, trembling like an aspen-bough,
Began to tear his scroll in pieces small,
Uttering the while some mumblings funeral.
He tore it into pieces small as snow
750 That drifts unfeather'd when bleak northerns blow;
And having done it, took his dark blue cloak
And bound it round Endymion: then struck
His wand against the empty air times nine.—
"What more there is to do, young man, is thine:

719 divers] diverse (*the last letter deleted in pencil, presumably by Taylor*) *FC* 745 even] e'en *FC* 750 unfeather'd] all shatter'd *D* 751 done it, took] don't, he took *FC* 752 struck] stroke *FC* 753 against the empty] at something in the *D*

755 But first a little patience; first undo
This tangled thread, and wind it to a clue.
Ah, gentle! 'tis as weak as spider's skein;
And shouldst thou break it—What, is it done so clean?
A power overshadows thee! Oh, brave!
760 The spite of hell is tumbling to its grave.
Here is a shell; 'tis pearly blank to me,
Nor mark'd with any sign or charactery—
Canst thou read aught? O read for pity's sake!
Olympus! we are safe! Now, Carian, break
765 This wand against yon lyre on the pedestal."

'Twas done: and straight with sudden swell and fall
Sweet music breath'd her soul away, and sigh'd
A lullaby to silence.—"Youth! now strew
These minced leaves on me, and passing through
770 Those files of dead, scatter the same around,
And thou wilt see the issue."—'Mid the sound
Of flutes and viols, ravishing his heart,
Endymion from Glaucus stood apart,
And scatter'd in his face some fragments light.
775 How lightning-swift the change! a youthful wight
Smiling beneath a coral diadem,
Out-sparkling sudden like an upturn'd gem,
Appear'd, and, stepping to a beauteous corse,
Kneel'd down beside it, and with tenderest force
780 Press'd its cold hand, and wept,—and Scylla sigh'd!
Endymion, with quick hand, the charm applied—
The nymph arose: he left them to their joy,
And onward went upon his high employ,
Showering those powerful fragments on the dead.
785 And, as he pass'd, each lifted up its head,
As doth a flower at Apollo's touch.
Death felt it to his inwards: 'twas too much:
Death fell a weeping in his charnel-house.
The Latmian persever'd along, and thus
790 All were re-animated. There arose
A noise of harmony, pulses and throes
Of gladness in the air—while many, who
Had died in mutual arms devout and true,

758 is it] is't *FC* 768 "Youth] ⟨'Tis⟩ "Youth *FC* 780 Scylla‸ sigh'd!] ~! ~. *FC* 787 to] at *D* 791 noise of] hum, a *D*

Sprang to each other madly; and the rest
795 Felt a high certainty of being blest.
They gaz'd upon Endymion. Enchantment
Grew drunken, and would have its head and bent.
Delicious symphonies, like airy flowers,
Budded, and swell'd, and, full-blown, shed full showers
800 Of light, soft, unseen leaves of sounds divine.
The two deliverers tasted a pure wine
Of happiness, from fairy-press ooz'd out.
Speechless they eyed each other, and about
The fair assembly wander'd to and fro,
805 Distracted with the richest overflow
Of joy that ever pour'd from heaven.

——"Away!"

Shouted the new born god; "Follow, and pay
Our piety to Neptunus supreme!"—
Then Scylla, blushing sweetly from her dream,
810 They led on first, bent to her meek surprise,
Through portal columns of a giant size,
Into the vaulted, boundless emerald.
Joyous all follow'd, as the leader call'd,
Down marble steps; pouring as easily
815 As hour-glass sand,—and fast, as you might see
Swallows obeying the south summer's call,
Or swans upon a gentle waterfall.

Thus went that beautiful multitude, nor far,
Ere from among some rocks of glittering spar,
820 Just within ken, they saw descending thick
Another multitude. Whereat more quick
Moved either host. On a wide sand they met,
And of those numbers every eye was wet;
For each their old love found. A murmuring rose,
825 Like what was never heard in all the throes
Of wind and waters: 'tis past human wit
To tell; 'tis dizziness to think of it.

This mighty consummation made, the host
Mov'd on for many a league; and gain'd, and lost

795 high] sweet *D* 796 Enchantment] *interlined above* ⟨Ravishment⟩ *FC* 802 from . . . ooz'd] not from earthly grapes press'd *D*

830 Huge sea-marks; vanward swelling in array,
And from the rear diminishing away,—
Till a faint dawn surpris'd them. Glaucus cried,
"Behold! behold, the palace of his pride!
God Neptune's palaces!" With noise increas'd,
835 They shoulder'd on towards that brightening east.
At every onward step proud domes arose
In prospect,—diamond gleams, and golden glows
Of amber 'gainst their faces levelling.
Joyous, and many as the leaves in spring,
840 Still onward; still the splendour gradual swell'd.
Rich opal domes were seen, on high upheld
By jasper pillars, letting through their shafts
A blush of coral. Copious wonder-draughts
Each gazer drank; and deeper drank more near:
845 For what poor mortals fragment up, as mere
As marble was there lavish, to the vast
Of one fair palace, that far far surpass'd,
Even for common bulk, those olden three,
Memphis, and Babylon, and Nineveh.

850 As large, as bright, as colour'd as the bow
Of Iris, when unfading it doth shew
Beyond a silvery shower, was the arch
Through which this Paphian army took its march,
Into the outer courts of Neptune's state:
855 Whence could be seen, direct, a golden gate,
To which the leaders sped; but not half raught
Ere it burst open swift as fairy thought,
And made those dazzled thousands veil their eyes
Like callow eagles at the first sunrise.
860 Soon with an eagle nativeness their gaze
Ripe from hue-golden swoons took all the blaze,
And then, behold! large Neptune on his throne
Of emerald deep: yet not exalt alone;

832 dawn . . . Glaucus] dawning bloom'd—And Glaucus *D* 834 God . . . palaces] Of God Neptunus pride (pride *interlined above* ⟨palace⟩) *D* 834 noise] hum *D*; noise *interlined above* ⟨hum⟩ *FC* 835 They shoulder'd] The host moved *D* 836 At . . . step] And as it moved along *D* 838–839 'gainst . . . spring] leveling against their faces / With expectation high, and hurried paces *D* 842 letting] giving *D* 845 fragment] *interlined above* ⟨treasure⟩ *FC* 847 far far surpass'd] to nothing cast *D*; far far surpast (*the first* far *interlined above* ⟨as⟩) *FC* 860 Soon . . . nativeness] But soon like Eagles natively *D*

At his right hand stood winged Love, and on
865 His left sat smiling Beauty's paragon.

Far as the mariner on highest mast
Can see all round upon the calmed vast,
So wide was Neptune's hall: and as the blue
Doth vault the waters, so the waters drew
870 Their doming curtains, high, magnificent,
Aw'd from the throne aloof;—and when storm-rent
Disclos'd the thunder-gloomings in Jove's air;
But sooth'd as now, flash'd sudden everywhere,
Noiseless, sub-marine cloudlets, glittering
875 Death to a human eye: for there did spring
From natural west, and east, and south, and north,
A light as of four sunsets, blazing forth
A gold-green zenith 'bove the Sea-God's head.
Of lucid depth the floor, and far outspread
880 As breezeless lake, on which the slim canoe
Of feather'd Indian darts about, as through
The delicatest air: air verily,
But for the portraiture of clouds and sky:
This palace floor breath-air,—but for the amaze
885 Of deep-seen wonders motionless,—and blaze
Of the dome pomp, reflected in extremes,
Globing a golden sphere.

They stood in dreams
Till Triton blew his horn. The palace rang;
The Nereids danc'd; the Syrens faintly sang;
890 And the great Sea-King bow'd his dripping head.
Then Love took wing, and from his pinions shed
On all the multitude a nectarous dew.
The ooze-born Goddess beckoned and drew
Fair Scylla and her guides to conference;
895 And when they reach'd the throned eminence
She kist the sea-nymph's cheek,—who sat her down
A toying with the doves. Then,—"Mighty crown
And sceptre of this kingdom!" Venus said,
"Thy vows were on a time to Nais paid:

864–865 and . . . paragon] elate / And ⟨at⟩ on his left Love's fairest mother sate *D* 869 vault] *interlined above* ⟨canopy⟩ *FC* 876 and south . . . north] and north, and south *altered to* and South, and north *FC* 889 faintly] sweetly *D*

900 Behold!"—Two copious tear-drops instant fell
From the God's large eyes; he smil'd delectable,
And over Glaucus held his blessing hands.—
"Endymion! Ah! still wandering in thc bands
Of love? Now this is cruel. Since the hour
905 I met thee in earth's bosom, all my power
Have I put forth to serve thee. What, not yet
Escap'd from dull mortality's harsh net?
A little patience, youth! 'twill not be long,
Or I am skilless quite: an idle tongue,
910 A humid eye, and steps luxurious,
Where these are new and strange, are ominous.
Aye, I have seen these signs in one of heaven,
When others were all blind; and were I given
To utter secrets, haply I might say
915 Some pleasant words:—but Love will have his day.
So wait awhile expectant. Pr'ythee soon,
Even in the passing of thine honey-moon,
Visit my Cytherea: thou wilt find
Cupid well-natured, my Adonis kind;
920 And pray persuade with thee—Ah, I have done,
All blisses be upon thee, my sweet son!"—
Thus the fair goddess: while Endymion
Knelt to receive those accents halcyon.

Meantime a glorious revelry began
925 Before the Water-Monarch. Nectar ran
In courteous fountains to all cups outreach'd;
And plunder'd vines, teeming exhaustless, pleach'd
New growth about each shell and pendent lyre;
The which, in disentangling for their fire,
930 Pull'd down fresh foliage and coverture
For dainty toying. Cupid, empire-sure,
Flutter'd and laugh'd, and oft-times through the throng
Made a delighted way. Then dance, and song,
And garlanding grew wild; and pleasure reign'd.
935 In harmless tendril they each other chain'd,
And strove who should be smother'd deepest in
Fresh crush of leaves.

907 harsh] rough *D* 913 were all] sight was *D* 915 pleasant] honey *D* 917 Even] E'en *FC* 919 well-natured] a treasure *D* 922 fair] blithe *D* 930 fresh] full *D* 934–935 pleasure . . . chain'd] wildness reigns. / They bound each other up in tendril chains *D* 937 crush of] crushing *D*

O 'tis a very sin
For one so weak to venture his poor verse
In such a place as this. O do not curse,
940 High Muses! let him hurry to the ending.

All suddenly were silent. A soft blending
Of dulcet instruments came charmingly;
And then a hymn.

"King of the stormy sea!
Brother of Jove, and co-inheritor
945 Of elements! Eternally before
Thee the waves awful bow. Fast, stubborn rock,
At thy fear'd trident shrinking, doth unlock
Its deep foundations, hissing into foam.
All mountain-rivers lost in the wide home
950 Of thy capacious bosom ever flow.
Thou frownest, and old Eolus thy foe
Skulks to his cavern, 'mid the gruff complaint
Of all his rebel tempests. Dark clouds faint
When, from thy diadem, a silver gleam
955 Slants over blue dominion. Thy bright team
Gulphs in the morning light, and scuds along
To bring thee nearer to that golden song
Apollo singeth, while his chariot
Waits at the doors of heaven. Thou art not
960 For scenes like this: an empire stern hast thou;
And it hath furrow'd that large front: yet now,
As newly come of heaven, dost thou sit
To blend and interknit
Subdued majesty with this glad time.
965 O shell-borne King sublime!
We lay our hearts before thee evermore—
We sing, and we adore!

"Breathe softly, flutes;

945–946 before . . . bow] in awe / Of thee the waves bow down *D*, *FC* (*altered by Taylor in pencil to the 1818 wording in the latter MS*) 949 All mountain] A thousand *D* 949–950 rivers∧ lost∧ . . . bosom∧] $L^5$; ~, ~∧ . . . ~, *D*; ~∧ ~∧ . . . ~, *FC*; ~∧ ~, . . . ~∧ *1818* 952 complaint] complaint⟨s⟩ *FC* 954 When . . . diadem,] When thy bright diadem∧ *D* 955 Slants . . . bright] O'er blue dominion slants.—Thy finny (slants *replacing* ⟨casts⟩) *D* 956 Gulphs] Snorts *D* 960 this] *made out of* these *FC* 962 As . . . come] Like a young child *D* 968 "Breathe . . . flutes;] *indented as a half-line* (*combining with 967 to make a full pentameter*) *in FC*

Be tender of your strings, ye soothing lutes;
970 Nor be the trumpet heard! O vain, O vain;
Not flowers budding in an April rain,
Nor breath of sleeping dove, nor river's flow,—
No, nor the Eolian twang of Love's own bow,
Can mingle music fit for the soft ear
975 Of goddess Cytherea!
Yet deign, white Queen of Beauty, thy fair eyes
On our souls' sacrifice.

"Bright-winged Child!
Who has another care when thou hast smil'd?
980 Unfortunates on earth, we see at last
All death-shadows, and glooms that overcast
Our spirits, fann'd away by thy light pinions.
O sweetest essence! sweetest of all minions!
God of warm pulses, and dishevell'd hair,
985 And panting bosoms bare!
Dear unseen light in darkness! eclipser
Of light in light! delicious poisoner!
Thy venom'd goblet will we quaff until
We fill—we fill!
And by thy Mother's lips——"

990 Was heard no more
For clamour, when the golden palace door
Opened again, and from without, in shone
A new magnificence. On oozy throne
Smooth-moving came Oceanus the old,
995 To take a latest glimpse at his sheep-fold,
Before he went into his quiet cave
To muse for ever—Then a lucid wave,
Scoop'd from its trembling sisters of mid-sea,
Afloat, and pillowing up the majesty
1000 Of Doris, and the Egean seer, her spouse—
Next, on a dolphin, clad in laurel boughs,
Theban Amphion leaning on his lute:
His fingers went across it—All were mute

978 "Bright . . . Child!] *indented as a half-line in FC* 979 has . . . care] is not full of heaven *D* 983 sweetest of all] essence of all sweetest (*but see Textual Note*) *D*

To gaze on Amphitrite, queen of pearls,
And Thetis pearly too.—

1005 The palace whirls
Around giddy Endymion; seeing he
Was there far strayed from mortality.
He could not bear it—shut his eyes in vain;
Imagination gave a dizzier pain.
1010 "O I shall die! sweet Venus, be my stay!
Where is my lovely mistress? Well-away!
I die—I hear her voice—I feel my wing—"
At Neptune's feet he sank. A sudden ring
Of Nereids were about him, in kind strife
1015 To usher back his spirit into life:
But still he slept. At last they interwove
Their cradling arms, and purpos'd to convey
Towards a crystal bower far away.

Lo! while slow carried through the pitying crowd,
1020 To his inward senses these words spake aloud;
Written in star-light on the dark above:
*Dearest Endymion! my entire love!*
*How have I dwelt in fear of fate: 'tis done—*
*Immortal bliss for me too hast thou won.*
1025 *Arise then! for the hen-dove shall not hatch*
*Her ready eggs, before I'll kissing snatch*
*Thee into endless heaven. Awake! awake!*

The youth at once arose: a placid lake
Came quiet to his eyes; and forest green,
1030 Cooler than all the wonders he had seen,
Lull'd with its simple song his fluttering breast.
How happy once again in grassy nest!

1007 there far strayed] there, a stray lamb *D* 1012 I hear . . . wing—"] love calls me hence"—thus muttering *D* 1015 spirit] spirits *D* 1016 But . . . slept] They gave him nectar—shed bright drops, and strove / Long time in vain *D* 1017–18 purpos'd . . . away] carefully conveyed / His body towards a quiet bowery shade *D* 1017 purpos'd to convey] *interlined above* ⟨did his⟩ ⟨carried him str⟩ *FC* 1019 pitying] parting *D* 1019 crowd] *interlined above* ⟨throng⟩ *FC* 1022 my] my own *D* 1024 hast] has *FC* 1025 Arise] ⟨Awak⟩ Arise *FC* 1026 kissing] madly *D*

## BOOK IV

Muse of my native land! loftiest Muse!
O first-born on the mountains! by the hues
Of heaven on the spiritual air begot:
Long didst thou sit alone in northern grot,
5 While yet our England was a wolfish den;
Before our forests heard the talk of men;
Before the first of Druids was a child;—
Long didst thou sit amid our regions wild
Rapt in a deep prophetic solitude.
10 There came an eastern voice of solemn mood:—
Yet wast thou patient. Then sang forth the Nine,
Apollo's garland:—yet didst thou divine
Such home-bred glory, that they cry'd in vain,
"Come hither, Sister of the Island!" Plain
15 Spake fair Ausonia; and once more she spake
A higher summons:—still didst thou betake
Thee to thy native hopes. O thou hast won
A full accomplishment! The thing is done,
Which undone, these our latter days had risen
20 On barren souls. Great Muse, thou know'st what prison,
Of flesh and bone, curbs, and confines, and frets
Our spirit's wings: despondency besets
Our pillows; and the fresh to-morrow morn
Seems to give forth its light in very scorn
25 Of our dull, uninspired, snail-paced lives.
Long have I said, how happy he who shrives
To thee! But then I thought on poets gone,
And could not pray:—nor can I now—so on
I move to the end in lowliness of heart.——

30 "Ah, woe is me! that I should fondly part
From my dear native land! Ah, foolish maid!
Glad was the hour, when, with thee, myriads bade

IV.2 first . . . on the] *interlined above* ⟨mountain born⟩ *D* 2 on] of *L*[1] 2 by] *interlined above* ⟨while⟩ *D* 6 talk] voice *D* 7 child] *replacing* ⟨babe⟩ *D* 10 an eastern] a hebrew *D*, *L*[1]; a hebrew *altered to* an eastern *FC* 11 the] those *D* 13 they . . . vain] in vain they cry'd *FC* 14 of] from *D* 16 A higher] In self surpassing *D* 17 thy native] thyself and to thy *D*; thyself and to thy *altered to* thy darling *L*[1]; thyself and to thy *altered to* thy native *FC* 17 hast] has *L*[1] 19 undone . . . risen] wanting all these latter days had dawnd *D* 20 Great] Oh *D*, *L*[1] 29 lowliness] Humbleness *L*[1] 31 From] With *D*

Adieu to Ganges and their pleasant fields!
To one so friendless the clear freshet yields
35 A bitter coolness; the ripe grape is sour:
Yet I would have, great gods! but one short hour
Of native air—let me but die at home."

Endymion to heaven's airy dome
Was offering up a hecatomb of vows,
40 When these words reach'd him. Whereupon he bows
His head through thorny-green entanglement
Of underwood, and to the sound is bent,
Anxious as hind towards her hidden fawn.

"Is no one near to help me? No fair dawn
45 Of life from charitable voice? No sweet saying
To set my dull and sadden'd spirit playing?
No hand to toy with mine? No lips so sweet
That I may worship them? No eyelids meet
To twinkle on my bosom? No one dies
50 Before me, till from these enslaving eyes
Redemption sparkles!—I am sad and lost."

Thou, Carian lord, hadst better have been tost
Into a whirlpool. Vanish into air,
Warm mountaineer! for canst thou only bear
55 A woman's sigh alone and in distress?
See not her charms! Is Phœbe passionless?
Phœbe is fairer far—O gaze no more:—
Yet if thou wilt behold all beauty's store,
Behold her panting in the forest grass!

34 To . . . clear] Where no friends are, the very *D* 36 Yet . . . but] Then take my life, great Gods! for *D* 36 Yet] *interlined above* ⟨And⟩ *FC* 41 thorny-green] ever rough *D* 42 Of underwood] ⟨Of br⟩ In the ⟨thick⟩ briar'd wood *D* 45 life] hope *D* 49–54 No . . . mountaineer]

false! twas false
They said how beautiful I was! who calls
Me now divine? Who now knells down and dies
Before me till from these enslaving eyes
Redemption sparkles—Ah me how sad I am!
Of all the Poisons sent to make us mad
Of all Death's overwhelmings"—Stay Beware
Young Mountaineer *D*

51 I . . . lost] Sad and lost I am (*but marked for transposition*) *FC* 55 alone and in] in the luxury of *D*

60 Do not those curls of glossy jet surpass
For tenderness the arms so idly lain
Amongst them? Feelest not a kindred pain,
To see such lovely eyes in swimming search
After some warm delight, that seems to perch
65 Dovelike in the dim cell lying beyond
Their upper lids?—Hist!

"O for Hermes' wand,
To touch this flower into human shape!
That woodland Hyacinthus could escape
From his green prison, and here kneeling down
70 Call me his queen, his second life's fair crown!
Ah me, how I could love!—My soul doth melt
For the unhappy youth—Love! I have felt
So faint a kindness, such a meek surrender
To what my own full thoughts had made too tender,
75 That but for tears my life had fled away!—
Ye deaf and senseless minutes of the day,
And thou, old forest, hold ye this for true,
There is no lightning, no authentic dew
But in the eye of love: there's not a sound,
80 Melodious howsoever, can confound
The heavens and earth in one to such a death
As doth the voice of love: there's not a breath
Will mingle kindly with the meadow air,
Till it has panted round, and stolen a share
Of passion from the heart!"—

85 Upon a bough
He leant, wretched. He surely cannot now

63 swimming] fruitless *D* 70 life's fair] living's *D* 72 For . . . have] After some beauteous Youth—Who, who hath *D* 73 So . . . kindness] ⟨As I do now⟩ So warm a faintness *D* 74 full] fair *D* 76–77 Ye . . . for] Sweet shadow, be distinct awhile and stay / While I speak to thee—trust me it is *D* 79 the] a *D*; the *written over* ⟨a⟩ *FC* 79 eye of love] lover's eye *D*; ⟨Lover's e⟩ eye of Love *FC* 82 doth . . . love] will a lover's voice *D* 85–87 Of . . . love:]

Of passion from the heart—Where love is not
Only is solitude—poor Shadow! what
I say thou hearest not! away begone,
And leave me prythee with my grief alone."
The Latmian lean'd his arm upon a bough,
A wretched Mortal: what can he do now?
Must he another Love? *D*

Thirst for another love: O impious,
That he can even dream upon it thus!—
Thought he, "Why am I not as are the dead,
90 Since to a woe like this I have been led
Through the dark earth, and through the wondrous sea?
Goddess! I love thee not the less: from thee
By Juno's smile I turn not—no, no, no—
While the great waters are at ebb and flow.—
95 I have a triple soul! O fond pretence—
For both, for both my love is so immense,
I feel my heart is cut for them in twain."

And so he groan'd, as one by beauty slain.
The lady's heart beat quick, and he could see
100 Her gentle bosom heave tumultuously.
He sprang from his green covert: there she lay,
Sweet as a muskrose upon new-made hay;
With all her limbs on tremble, and her eyes
Shut softly up alive. To speak he tries.
105 "Fair damsel, pity me! forgive that I
Thus violate thy bower's sanctity!
O pardon me, for I am full of grief—
Grief born of thee, young angel! fairest thief!
Who stolen hast away the wings wherewith
110 I was to top the heavens. Dear maid, sith
Thou art my executioner, and I feel
Loving and hatred, misery and weal,
Will in a few short hours be nothing to me,
And all my story that much passion slew me;
115 Do smile upon the evening of my days:
And, for my tortur'd brain begins to craze,
Be thou my nurse; and let me understand
How dying I shall kiss that lily hand.—
Dost weep for me? Then should I be content.

92 Goddess] Mine own (Mine *made out of* My) *D* 94 While . . . flow.—]
While the fair Moon gives light, or rivers flow
My adoration of thee is yet pure
As infants prattling—How is this—why sure$_\wedge$ *D*
97 for . . . twain] *ed*; in twain for them *FC, 1818* 104–105 To . . . damsel]
Ye harmonies
Ye tranced visions—ye flights ideal
Nothing are ye to life so dainty real
O Lady *D*

120 Scowl on, ye fates! until the firmament
Outblackens Erebus, and the full-cavern'd earth
Crumbles into itself. By the cloud girth
Of Jove, those tears have given me a thirst
To meet oblivion."—As her heart would burst
125 The maiden sobb'd awhile, and then replied:
"Why must such desolation betide
As that thou speakest of? Are not these green nooks
Empty of all misfortune? Do the brooks
Utter a gorgon voice? Does yonder thrush,
130 Schooling its half-fledg'd little ones to brush
About the dewy forest, whisper tales?—
Speak not of grief, young stranger, or cold snails
Will slime the rose to night. Though if thou wilt,
Methinks 'twould be a guilt—a very guilt—
135 Not to companion thee, and sigh away
The light—the dusk—the dark—till break of day!"
"Dear lady," said Endymion, " 'tis past:
I love thee! and my days can never last.
That I may pass in patience still speak:
140 Let me have music dying, and I seek
No more delight—I bid adieu to all.
Didst thou not after other climates call,
And murmur about Indian streams?"—Then she,
Sitting beneath the midmost forest tree,
145 For pity sang this roundelay——

122 By] ⟨for⟩ By (*the deleted word originally following a colon*) *FC* 127 speakest] speakst *FC* 137–138 "Dear . . . last] (*continuing the maiden's speech begun in 126*)
Canst thou do so? Is there no balm, no cure
Could not a beckoning Hebe soon allure
Thee into Paradise? What sorrowing
So weighs thee down what utmost woe could bring
This madness—Sit thee down by me, and ease
Thine heart in whispers—haply by degrees
I may find out some soothing medicine."—
"Dear Lady, said Endymion I pine
I die—the tender accents thou has spoken,
Have finish'd all—my heart is lost and broken *D*
143 streams . . . she]
streams—now, now—
I listen—it may save me—O my vow—
Let me have music dying! The ladye *D*
145 For] With tears of *D*

"O Sorrow,
Why dost borrow
The natural hue of health, from vermeil lips?—
To give maiden blushes
150 To the white rose bushes?
Or is't thy dewy hand the daisy tips?

"O Sorrow,
Why dost borrow
The lustrous passion from a falcon-eye?—
155 To give the glow-worm light?
Or, on a moonless night,
To tinge, on syren shores, the salt sea-spry?

"O Sorrow,
Why dost borrow
160 The mellow ditties from a mourning tongue?—
To give at evening pale
Unto the nightingale,
That thou mayst listen the cold dews among?

"O Sorrow,
165 Why dost borrow
Heart's lightness from the merriment of May?—
A lover would not tread
A cowslip on the head,
Though he should dance from eve till peep of day—
170 Nor any drooping flower
Held sacred for thy bower,
Wherever he may sport himself and play.

"To Sorrow,
I bade good-morrow,
175 And thought to leave her far away behind;
But cheerly, cheerly,

145–146 roundelay . . . Sorrow] Roundelay. "O Sorrow (*originally one line—the last two words deleted by Taylor in pencil and rewritten as a separate line*) *FC* 146–290 "O . . . shade."] *the stanza spacings and most of the indentions are the result of Taylor's pencil in FC; Keats himself indicated stanza divisions (by paragraph indentions) only at 193, 209, 218, 228, 239, 251, and 257* 151 is't] *D*, $L^2$, $L^3$, *FC*, $L^5$; is it *1818* 154 a falcon-eye] a lover's eye *D*, $L^2$; an orbed eye $L^3$ 157 tinge, on] tinge ⟨the⟩ on $L^2$ 160 mellow] ⟨me⟩ tender $L^3$ 161 give] give't $L^2$ 171 for] to $L^3$ 172 Wherever] However *D*

She loves me dearly;
She is so constant to me, and so kind:
I would deceive her
180 And so leave her,
But ah! she is so constant and so kind.

"Beneath my palm trees, by the river side,
I sat a weeping: in the whole world wide
There was no one to ask me why I wept,—
185 And so I kept
Brimming the water-lily cups with tears
Cold as my fears.

"Beneath my palm trees, by the river side,
I sat a weeping: what enamour'd bride,
190 Cheated by shadowy wooer from the clouds,
But hides and shrouds
Beneath dark palm trees by a river side?

"And as I sat, over the light blue hills
There came a noise of revellers: the rills
195 Into the wide stream came of purple hue—
'Twas Bacchus and his crew!
The earnest trumpet spake, and silver thrills
From kissing cymbals made a merry din—
'Twas Bacchus and his kin!
200 Like to a moving vintage down they came,
Crown'd with green leaves, and faces all on flame;
All madly dancing through the pleasant valley,
To scare thee, Melancholy!
O then, O then, thou wast a simple name!
205 And I forgot thee, as the berried holly
By shepherds is forgotten, when, in June,
Tall chesnuts keep away the sun and moon:—
I rush'd into the folly!

"Within his car, aloft, young Bacchus stood,
210 Trifling his ivy-dart, in dancing mood,

178 so . . . me] to me so constant $L^2$, $L^3$ (so *interlined above* ⟨too⟩ *in* $L^2$) 181 so . . . so] too . . . too *D*, $L^2$, $L^3$ 187 Cold as my] Chill'd with strange *D* 190 wooer] lover *D* 202 through] down *D* 203 thee,] my$_\wedge$ *D*; thee$_\wedge$ *FC* 207 chesnuts] Beeches *D*

With sidelong laughing;
And little rills of crimson wine imbrued
His plump white arms, and shoulders, enough white
For Venus' pearly bite:
215 And near him rode Silenus on his ass,
Pelted with flowers as he on did pass
Tipsily quaffing.

"Whence came ye, merry Damsels! whence came ye!
So many, and so many, and such glee?
220 Why have ye left your bowers desolate,
Your lutes, and gentler fate?—
'We follow Bacchus! Bacchus on the wing,
A conquering!
Bacchus, young Bacchus! good or ill betide,
225 We dance before him thorough kingdoms wide:—
Come hither, lady fair, and joined be
To our wild minstrelsy!'

"Whence came ye, jolly Satyrs! whence came ye!
So many, and so many, and such glee?
230 Why have ye left your forest haunts, why left
Your nuts in oak-tree cleft?—
'For wine, for wine we left our kernel tree;
For wine we left our heath, and yellow brooms,
And cold mushrooms;
235 For wine we follow Bacchus through the earth;
Great God of breathless cups and chirping mirth!—
Come hither, lady fair, and joined be
To our mad minstrelsy!'

"Over wide streams and mountains great we went,
240 And, save when Bacchus kept his ivy tent,
Onward the tiger and the leopard pants,
With Asian elephants:
Onward these myriads—with song and dance,
With zebras striped, and sleek Arabians' prance,
245 Web-footed alligators, crocodiles,
Bearing upon their scaly backs, in files,

212 rills] Streaks *D* 213 enough] dainty *D* 214 Venus'] any *D* 221/222 We follow Bacchus from a far country *D* 225 before] beside *D* 232 kernel tree] *replacing* ⟨forest meat⟩ *D* 236 chirping] endless *D*

Plump infant laughers mimicking the coil
Of seamen, and stout galley-rowers' toil:
With toying oars and silken sails they glide,
250 Nor care for wind and tide.

"Mounted on panthers' furs and lions' manes,
From rear to van they scour about the plains;
A three days' journey in a moment done:
And always, at the rising of the sun,
255 About the wilds they hunt with spear and horn,
On spleenful unicorn.

"I saw Osirian Egypt kneel adown
Before the vine-wreath crown!
I saw parch'd Abyssinia rouse and sing
260 To the silver cymbals' ring!
I saw the whelming vintage hotly pierce
Old Tartary the fierce!
The kings of Inde their jewel-sceptres vail,
And from their treasures scatter pearled hail;
265 Great Brahma from his mystic heaven groans,
And all his priesthood moans;
Before young Bacchus' eye-wink turning pale.—
Into these regions came I following him,
Sick hearted, weary—so I took a whim
270 To stray away into these forests drear
Alone, without a peer:
And I have told thee all thou mayest hear.

"Young stranger!
I've been a ranger
275 In search of pleasure throughout every clime:
Alas, 'tis not for me!
Bewitch'd I sure must be,
To lose in grieving all my maiden prime.

"Come then, Sorrow!
280 Sweetest Sorrow!
Like an own babe I nurse thee on my breast:

247 Plump . . . mimicking] Arch infant crews in mimic of *D* 254 always] alway *D* 263 jewel] jewel'd *D* 267/268 ⟨All City gates were opened to his pomp⟩ *D* 272 thou mayest] that thou canst *D* 277 I . . . must] must I sure *D* 278 lose] loose *FC*

I thought to leave thee
And deceive thee,
But now of all the world I love thee best.

285 "There is not one,
No, no, not one
But thee to comfort a poor lonely maid;
Thou art her mother,
And her brother,
290 Her playmate, and her wooer in the shade."

O what a sigh she gave in finishing,
And look, quite dead to every worldly thing!
Endymion could not speak, but gazed on her;
And listened to the wind that now did stir
295 About the crisped oaks full drearily,
Yet with as sweet a softness as might be
Remember'd from its velvet summer song.
At last he said: "Poor lady, how thus long
Have I been able to endure that voice?
300 Fair Melody! kind Syren! I've no choice;
I must be thy sad servant evermore:
I cannot choose but kneel here and adore.
Alas, I must not think—by Phœbe, no!
Let me not think, soft Angel! shall it be so?
305 Say, beautifullest, shall I never think?
O thou could'st foster me beyond the brink
Of recollection! make my watchful care
Close up its bloodshot eyes, nor see despair!
Do gently murder half my soul, and I
310 Shall feel the other half so utterly!—
I'm giddy at that cheek so fair and smooth;
O let it blush so ever! let it soothe
My madness! let it mantle rosy-warm
With the tinge of love, panting in safe alarm.—
315 This cannot be thy hand, and yet it is;

291 sigh] sob *D* 292 look,] look'd$_\wedge$ *D* 304 shall it] shall't *FC* 307 care] care⟨s⟩ *FC* 311–314 I'm . . . alarm]
That—oh how beautiful—how giddy smooth!
Blush so for ever! let those glances soothe
My madness, for did I no mercy spy
Dear lady I should shudder and then die *D*

And this is sure thine other softling—this
Thine own fair bosom, and I am so near!
Wilt fall asleep? O let me sip that tear!
And whisper one sweet word that I may know
320 This is this world—sweet dewy blossom!"—*Woe!*
*Woe! Woe to that Endymion! Where is he?*—
Even these words went echoing dismally
Through the wide forest—a most fearful tone,
Like one repenting in his latest moan;
325 And while it died away a shade pass'd by,
As of a thunder cloud. When arrows fly
Through the thick branches, poor ring-doves sleek forth
Their timid necks and tremble; so these both
Leant to each other trembling, and sat so
330 Waiting for some destruction—when lo,
Foot-feather'd Mercury appear'd sublime
Beyond the tall tree tops; and in less time
Than shoots the slanted hail-storm, down he dropt
Towards the ground; but rested not, nor stopt
335 One moment from his home: only the sward
He with his wand light touch'd, and heavenward
Swifter than sight was gone—even before
The teeming earth a sudden witness bore
Of his swift magic. Diving swans appear
340 Above the crystal circlings white and clear;
And catch the cheated eye in wide surprise,
How they can dive in sight and unseen rise—
So from the turf outsprang two steeds jet-black,
Each with large dark blue wings upon his back.
345 The youth of Caria plac'd the lovely dame
On one, and felt himself in spleen to tame
The other's fierceness. Through the air they flew,
High as the eagles. Like two drops of dew
Exhal'd to Phœbus' lips, away they are gone,
350 Far from the earth away—unseen, alone,
Among cool clouds and winds, but that the free,
The buoyant life of song can floating be
Above their heads, and follow them untir'd.—
Muse of my native land, am I inspir'd?
355 This is the giddy air, and I must spread

316 is . . . this] thine other softling—and is this *D* 317 I . . . near!] am I so near? *D* 341 wide] *D*, *FC*; wild *1818* 343 jet] coal *D* 349 they are] they're *FC*

Wide pinions to keep here; nor do I dread
Or height, or depth, or width, or any chance
Precipitous: I have beneath my glance
Those towering horses and their mournful freight.
360 Could I thus sail, and see, and thus await
Fearless for power of thought, without thine aid?—

There is a sleepy dusk, an odorous shade
From some approaching wonder, and behold
Those winged steeds, with snorting nostrils bold
365 Snuff at its faint extreme, and seem to tire,
Dying to embers from their native fire!

There curl'd a purple mist around them; soon,
It seem'd as when around the pale new moon
Sad Zephyr droops the clouds like weeping willow:
370 'Twas Sleep slow journeying with head on pillow.
For the first time, since he came nigh dead born
From the old womb of night, his cave forlorn
Had he left more forlorn; for the first time,
He felt aloof the day and morning's prime—
375 Because into his depth Cimmerian
There came a dream, shewing how a young man,
Ere a lean bat could plump its wintery skin,
Would at high Jove's empyreal footstool win
An immortality, and how espouse
380 Jove's daughter, and be reckon'd of his house.
Now was he slumbering towards heaven's gate,
That he might at the threshold one hour wait
To hear the marriage melodies, and then
Sink downward to his dusky cave again.
385 His litter of smooth semilucent mist,
Diversely ting'd with rose and amethyst,
Puzzled those eyes that for the centre sought;
And scarcely for one moment could be caught
His sluggish form reposing motionless.
390 Those two on winged steeds, with all the stress
Of vision search'd for him, as one would look

362 ¶There . . . ] $L^5$; *new page but no ¶ indention in FC; no ¶ in 1818* 366 Dying . . . native] Seeming but embers to their former *D* 367 curl'd] comes *D* 368 new] half *D* 369 willow] willow⟨s⟩ *FC* 370 journeying] voyaging *D* 374 aloof] on high *D* 384 Sink . . . dusky] Betake him downward to his *D* 385 smooth] pale *D* 387 those] the *D* 388 for one] one short *D*

Athwart the sallows of a river nook
To catch a glance at silver throated eels,—
Or from old Skiddaw's top, when fog conceals
395 His rugged forehead in a mantle pale,
With an eye-guess towards some pleasant vale
Descry a favourite hamlet faint and far.

These raven horses, though they foster'd are
Of earth's splenetic fire, dully drop
400 Their full-veined ears, nostrils blood wide, and stop;
Upon the spiritless mist have they outspread
Their ample feathers, are in slumber dead,—
And on those pinions, level in mid air,
Endymion sleepeth and the lady fair.
405 Slowly they sail, slowly as icy isle
Upon a calm sea drifting: and meanwhile
The mournful wanderer dreams. Behold! he walks
On heaven's pavement; brotherly he talks
To divine powers: from his hand full fain
410 Juno's proud birds are pecking pearly grain:
He tries the nerve of Phœbus' golden bow,
And asketh where the golden apples grow:
Upon his arm he braces Pallas' shield,
And strives in vain to unsettle and wield
415 A Jovian thunderbolt: arch Hebe brings
A full-brimm'd goblet, dances lightly, sings
And tantalizes long; at last he drinks,
And lost in pleasure at her feet he sinks,
Touching with dazzled lips her starlight hand.
420 He blows a bugle,—an ethereal band
Are visible above: the Seasons four,—
Green-kyrtled Spring, flush Summer, golden store
In Autumn's sickle, Winter frosty hoar,
Join dance with shadowy Hours; while still the blast,
425 In swells unmitigated, still doth last
To sway their floating morris. "Whose is this?
Whose bugle?" he inquires: they smile—"O Dis!
Why is this mortal here? Dost thou not know

394 top] front *D*  401 mist] air *D*; ⟨mists⟩ mist *FC*  418 And . . . he] With pleasure at her knees he swoons and *D*  420 blows . . . ethereal] takes a bugle blows it, an aerial *D*  421 above] oerhead *D*  424 with] with the *D*  425 In] Echoed in *D*  428 this] a *D*

Its mistress' lips? Not thou?—'Tis Dian's: lo!
430 She rises crescented!" He looks, 'tis she,
His very goddess: good-bye earth, and sea,
And air, and pains, and care, and suffering;
Good-bye to all but love! Then doth he spring
Towards her, and awakes—and, strange, o'erhead,
435 Of those same fragrant exhalations bred,
Beheld awake his very dream: the gods
Stood smiling; merry Hebe laughs and nods;
And Phœbe bends towards him crescented.
O state perplexing! On the pinion bed,
440 Too well awake, he feels the panting side
Of his delicious lady. He who died
For soaring too audacious in the sun,
When that same treacherous wax began to run,
Felt not more tongue-tied than Endymion.
445 His heart leapt up as to its rightful throne,
To that fair shadow'd passion puls'd its way—
Ah, what perplexity! Ah, well a day!
So fond, so beauteous was his bed-fellow,
He could not help but kiss her: then he grew
450 Awhile forgetful of all beauty save
Young Phœbe's, golden hair'd; and so 'gan crave
Forgiveness: yet he turn'd once more to look
At the sweet sleeper,—all his soul was shook,—
She press'd his hand in slumber; so once more
455 He could not help but kiss her and adore.
At this the shadow wept, melting away.
The Latmian started up: "Bright goddess, stay!
Search my most hidden breast! By truth's own tongue,
I have no dædale heart: why is it wrung
460 To desperation? Is there nought for me,
Upon the bourne of bliss, but misery?"

These words awoke the stranger of dark tresses:

429 'Tis . . . lo] Ah Ah, Ah Ah! / Tis Dian's, here she comes, look out afar *D*, *FC* 430 looks] *made out of* look'd *FC* 432 care] cares *D* 442–444 For . . . Endymion]

Because in sunshine treacherous wax would melt,
Even at the fatal melting thereof, felt
Not more tongue-tied than did Endymion

(melt *interlined above* ⟨run⟩ *in the first line*) *D* 443 When] *FC*; Where *1818* 449 kiss . . . grew] kiss—then did he grow *D* 451 so 'gan] humbly *D* 455 kiss her] kiss, kiss *D* 458 hidden] *interlined above* ⟨inmost⟩ *FC* 462 stranger] lady *D*

Her dawning love-look rapt Endymion blesses
With 'haviour soft. Sleep yawned from underneath.
465 "Thou swan of Ganges, let us no more breathe
This murky phantasm! thou contented seem'st
Pillow'd in lovely idleness, nor dream'st
What horrors may discomfort thee and me.
Ah, shouldst thou die from my heart-treachery!—
470 Yet did she merely weep—her gentle soul
Hath no revenge in it: as it is whole
In tenderness, would I were whole in love!
Can I prize thee, fair maid, all price above,
Even when I feel as true as innocence?
475 I do, I do.—What is this soul then? Whence
Came it? It does not seem my own, and I
Have no self-passion or identity.
Some fearful end must be: where, where is it?
By Nemesis, I see my spirit flit
480 Alone about the dark—Forgive me, sweet:
Shall we away?" He rous'd the steeds: they beat
Their wings chivalrous into the clear air,
Leaving old Sleep within his vapoury lair.

The good-night blush of eve was waning slow,
485 And Vesper, risen star, began to throe
In the dusk heavens silverly, when they
Thus sprang direct towards the Galaxy.
Nor did speed hinder converse soft and strange—
Eternal oaths and vows they interchange,
490 In such wise, in such temper, so aloof
Up in the winds, beneath a starry roof,
So witless of their doom, that verily
'Tis well nigh past man's search their hearts to see;
Whether they wept, or laugh'd, or griev'd, or toy'd—
495 Most like with joy gone mad, with sorrow cloy'd.

Full facing their swift flight, from ebon streak,
The moon put forth a little diamond peak,
No bigger than an unobserved star,

463 look] glance *D* 465 swan of Ganges] wandering fair one *D* 483 within his] to sail in *D* 484 blush] hush *D* 485 Vesper . . . star] Vesper's timid pulse *D* 486 silverly] *FC*; silvery *1818* 487 towards] up to *D* 492 their doom] all things *D* 495 Most like] *successively* (*a*) Haply (*b*) Until (*c*) Most like *D* 495 joy] *replacing* ⟨woe⟩ *D*

Or tiny point of fairy scymetar;
500 Bright signal that she only stoop'd to tie
Her silver sandals, ere deliciously
She bow'd into the heavens her timid head.
Slowly she rose, as though she would have fled,
While to his lady meek the Carian turn'd,
505 To mark if her dark eyes had yet discern'd
This beauty in its birth—Despair! despair!
He saw her body fading gaunt and spare
In the cold moonshine. Straight he seiz'd her wrist;
It melted from his grasp: her hand he kiss'd,
510 And, horror! kiss'd his own—he was alone.
Her steed a little higher soar'd, and then
Dropt hawkwise to the earth.

There lies a den,
Beyond the seeming confines of the space
Made for the soul to wander in and trace
515 Its own existence, of remotest glooms.
Dark regions are around it, where the tombs
Of buried griefs the spirit sees, but scarce
One hour doth linger weeping, for the pierce
Of new-born woe it feels more inly smart:
520 And in these regions many a venom'd dart
At random flies; they are the proper home
Of every ill: the man is yet to come
Who hath not journeyed in this native hell.
But few have ever felt how calm and well
525 Sleep may be had in that deep den of all.
There anguish does not sting; nor pleasure pall:
Woe-hurricanes beat ever at the gate,
Yet all is still within and desolate.
Beset with plainful gusts, within ye hear
530 No sound so loud as when on curtain'd bier
The death-watch tick is stifled. Enter none
Who strive therefore: on the sudden it is won.

505 had yet] slept or *D* 506 This . . . birth] Such beauty being born *D* 507 fading] faded *D* 508 he . . . wrist] her wrist he seized *D* 509 her . . . kiss'd] his lips were teazed / To Madness—for his—— (*see Textual Note*) *D* 513 Beyond] ⟨Of misery⟩ Beyond (*Woodhouse records* Of misery *as uncanceled*) *D* 518 doth linger] lingers *D* 520 venom'd] random *D* 522 the man] that Soul *D* 526 does . . . pleasure] stings not —sweetness cannot *D* 527 Woe-hurricanes] Dark hurricanes of woe *D* 531 stifled] muffled *D*

Just when the sufferer begins to burn,
Then it is free to him; and from an urn,
535 Still fed by melting ice, he takes a draught—
Young Semele such richness never quaft
In her maternal longing! Happy gloom!
Dark paradise! where pale becomes the bloom
Of health by due; where silence dreariest
540 Is most articulate; where hopes infest;
Where those eyes are the brightest far that keep
Their lids shut longest in a dreamless sleep.
O happy spirit-home! O wondrous soul!
Pregnant with such a den to save the whole
545 In thine own depth. Hail, gentle Carian!
For, never since thy griefs and woes began,
Hast thou felt so content: a grievous feud
Hath led thee to this Cave of Quietude.
Aye, his lull'd soul was there, although upborne
550 With dangerous speed: and so he did not mourn
Because he knew not whither he was going.
So happy was he, not the aerial blowing
Of trumpets at clear parley from the east
Could rouse from that fine relish, that high feast.
555 They stung the feather'd horse: with fierce alarm
He flapp'd towards the sound. Alas, no charm
Could lift Endymion's head, or he had view'd
A skyey masque, a pinion'd multitude,—
And silvery was its passing: voices sweet
560 Warbling the while as if to lull and greet
The wanderer in his path. Thus warbled they,
While past the vision went in bright array.

"Who, who from Dian's feast would be away?
For all the golden bowers of the day

534 Then it] This den *D* 537 longing!] *FC*, *L*[5]; ~. *1818* 539 Of . . . due] The rightful tinge of health *D* 542 shut] close *D* 546 woes] joys *D* 548 led] *D*, *FC* (*made out of* let *in FC*); let *1818* 550 With . . . speed] On dangerous Winds *altered to* With dangerous speed *FC* 550 and . . . not] nor did he sigh and *D* 554–556 from . . . sound]

⟨him⟩ from ⟨that⟩ inward feast—and yet to hear't
'Twas like a gift of Prophecy—alert
The feather'd horse he snorted with alarm
And towards it flapp'd away *D*

554 from] ⟨him⟩ from *FC* 558 masque] *ed*; Mask *FC, 1818* 563 from . . . away] would absent be from Dian's feast *D* 564 bowers . . . day] chambers . . . East *D*

565 Are empty left? Who, who away would be
From Cynthia's wedding and festivity?
Not Hesperus: lo! upon his silver wings
He leans away for highest heaven and sings,
Snapping his lucid fingers merrily!—
570 Ah, Zephyrus! art here, and Flora too!
Ye tender bibbers of the rain and dew,
Young playmates of the rose and daffodil,
Be careful, ere ye enter in, to fill
Your baskets high
575 With fennel green, and balm, and golden pines,
Savory, latter-mint, and columbines,
Cool parsley, basil sweet, and sunny thyme;
Yea, every flower and leaf of every clime,
All gather'd in the dewy morning: hie
580 Away! fly, fly!—
Crystalline brother of the belt of heaven,
Aquarius! to whom king Jove has given
Two liquid pulse streams 'stead of feather'd wings,
Two fan-like fountains,—thine illuminings
585 For Dian play:
Dissolve the frozen purity of air;
Let thy white shoulders silvery and bare
Shew cold through watery pinions; make more bright
The Star-Queen's crescent on her marriage night:
590 Haste, haste away!—
Castor has tamed the planet Lion, see!
And of the Bear has Pollux mastery:
A third is in the race! who is the third,
Speeding away swift as the eagle bird?
595 The ramping Centaur!
The Lion's mane's on end: the Bear how fierce!
The Centaur's arrow ready seems to pierce
Some enemy: far forth his bow is bent
Into the blue of heaven. He'll be shent,
600 Pale unrelentor,
When he shall hear the wedding lutes a playing.—
Andromeda! sweet woman! why delaying

566/567 Who who would be? *D* 569/570 He stay behind—he glad of lazy plea? / Not he! not he! *D* 573 Be . . . to] Mind ere ye enter in to oppress and *D* 576 latter] early *D*; ⟨early⟩ latter *FC* 577 basil . . . and] dripping cresses, *D* 582 has] ha'th *L*[4] 583/584 ⟨Thine illuminings⟩ *FC* 589 Star] Night *D* 592 has] hath *D* 593 A third is] Ay three are *D*

So timidly among the stars: come hither!
Join this bright throng, and nimbly follow whither
605 They all are going.
Danae's Son, before Jove newly bow'd,
Has wept for thee, calling to Jove aloud.
Thee, gentle lady, did he disenthral:
Ye shall for ever live and love, for all
610 Thy tears are flowing.—
By Daphne's fright, behold Apollo!—"

More
Endymion heard not: down his steed him bore,
Prone to the green head of a misty hill.

His first touch of the earth went nigh to kill.
615 "Alas!" said he, "were I but always borne
Through dangerous winds, had but my footsteps worn
A path in hell, for ever would I bless
Horrors which nourish an uneasiness
For my own sullen conquering: to him
620 Who lives beyond earth's boundary, grief is dim,
Sorrow is but a shadow: now I see
The grass; I feel the solid ground—Ah, me!
It is thy voice—divinest! Where?—who? who
Left thee so quiet on this bed of dew?
625 Behold upon this happy earth we are;
Let us ay love each other; let us fare
On forest-fruits, and never, never go
Among the abodes of mortals here below,
Or be by phantoms duped. O destiny!
630 Into a labyrinth now my soul would fly,
But with thy beauty will I deaden it.
Where didst thou melt to? By thee will I sit
For ever: let our fate stop here—a kid
I on this spot will offer: Pan will bid
635 Us live in peace, in love and peace among
His forest wildernesses. I have clung
To nothing, lov'd a nothing, nothing seen
Or felt but a great dream! O I have been

607–608 aloud . . . lady,] aloud$_\wedge$ / For thee—thee gentle$_\wedge$ *D* 622 grass . . . the] real grass, the *D*; real Grass; I feel the *FC* 624 quiet on] safe upon *D* 629 O destiny] Alas! alas *D* 630 fly] pass *D*; ⟨pass⟩ fly *FC* 632 to] *ed*; too *FC*, *1818*

Presumptuous against love, against the sky,
640 Against all elements, against the tie
Of mortals each to each, against the blooms
Of flowers, rush of rivers, and the tombs
Of heroes gone! Against his proper glory
Has my own soul conspired: so my story
645 Will I to children utter, and repent.
There never liv'd a mortal man, who bent
His appetite beyond his natural sphere,
But starv'd and died. My sweetest Indian, here,
Here will I kneel, for thou redeemed hast
650 My life from too thin breathing: gone and past
Are cloudy phantasms. Caverns lone, farewel!
And air of visions, and the monstrous swell
Of visionary seas! No, never more
Shall airy voices cheat me to the shore
655 Of tangled wonder, breathless and aghast.
Adieu, my daintiest Dream! although so vast
My love is still for thee. The hour may come
When we shall meet in pure elysium.
On earth I may not love thee; and therefore
660 Doves will I offer up, and sweetest store
All through the teeming year: so thou wilt shine
On me, and on this damsel fair of mine,
And bless our simple lives. My Indian bliss!
My river-lily bud! one human kiss!
665 One sigh of real breath—one gentle squeeze,
Warm as a dove's nest among summer trees,
And warm with dew at ooze from living blood!
Whither didst melt? Ah, what of that!—all good
We'll talk about—no more of dreaming.—Now,
670 Where shall our dwelling be? Under the brow
Of some steep mossy hill, where ivy dun
Would hide us up, although spring leaves were none;
And where dark yew trees, as we rustle through,
Will drop their scarlet berry cups of dew?
675 O thou wouldst joy to live in such a place;
Dusk for our loves, yet light enough to grace

641 each to each] to each other *D* 642 flowers] roses *D* 643 his] its *D* 646 There] Has *D* 649 Here will] Will *FC* 650 life . . . breathing] spirit . . . a breath *D* 653 No, never] No more, no *D* 656 although so] how vast how *D* 660 up] thee *D* 661 shine] *interlined above* ⟨smile⟩ *FC* 664 human] mortal *D*

Those gentle limbs on mossy bed reclin'd:
For by one step the blue sky shouldst thou find,
And by another, in deep dell below,
680 See, through the trees, a little river go
All in its mid-day gold and glimmering.
Honey from out the gnarled hive I'll bring,
And apples, wan with sweetness, gather thee,—
Cresses that grow where no man may them see,
685 And sorrel untorn by the dew-claw'd stag:
Pipes will I fashion of the syrinx flag,
That thou mayst always know whither I roam,
When it shall please thee in our quiet home
To listen and think of love. Still let me speak;
690 Still let me dive into the joy I seek,—
For yet the past doth prison me. The rill,
Thou haply mayst delight in, will I fill
With fairy fishes from the mountain tarn,
And thou shalt feed them from the squirrel's barn.
695 Its bottom will I strew with amber shells,
And pebbles blue from deep enchanted wells.
Its sides I'll plant with dew-sweet eglantine,
And honeysuckles full of clear bee-wine.
I will entice this crystal rill to trace
700 Love's silver name upon the meadow's face.
I'll kneel to Vesta, for a flame of fire;
And to god Phœbus, for a golden lyre;
To Empress Dian, for a hunting spear;
To Vesper, for a taper silver-clear,
705 That I may see thy beauty through the night;
To Flora, and a nightingale shall light
Tame on thy finger; to the River-gods,
And they shall bring thee taper fishing-rods
Of gold, and lines of Naiads' long bright tress.
710 Heaven shield thee for thine utter loveliness!
Thy mossy footstool shall the altar be
'Fore which I'll bend, bending, dear love, to thee:
Those lips shall be my Delphos, and shall speak

680 little . . . go] river at its flow *D* 682 hive] nest *D* 687 mayst always] by ear mayst *D* 691 prison me] weigh me down *D* 693–694 tarn . . . barn] tarns . . . barns *D* 697 I'll] I *FC* 699 I . . . to] Aye, I will make this crystal rillet *D*; And I will make this crystal rillet *altered to* I will entice this crystal rill to *FC* 700/701 And by it shalt thou sit and sing, hey nonny! / While doves coo to thee for a little honey. *FC* 709 and] with *D* 709 Naiads'] Naiad's *FC*

Laws to my footsteps, colour to my cheek,
715 Trembling or stedfastness to this same voice,
And of three sweetest pleasurings the choice:
And that affectionate light, those diamond things,
Those eyes, those passions, those supreme pearl springs,
Shall be my grief, or twinkle me to pleasure.
720 Say, is not bliss within our perfect seisure?
O that I could not doubt!"

The mountaineer
Thus strove by fancies vain and crude to clear
His briar'd path to some tranquillity.
It gave bright gladness to his lady's eye,
725 And yet the tears she wept were tears of sorrow;
Answering thus, just as the golden morrow
Beam'd upward from the vallies of the east:
"O that the flutter of this heart had ceas'd,
Or the sweet name of love had pass'd away.
730 Young feather'd tyrant! by a swift decay
Wilt thou devote this body to the earth:
And I do think that at my very birth
I lisp'd thy blooming titles inwardly;
For at the first, first dawn and thought of thee,
735 With uplift hands I blest the stars of heaven.
Art thou not cruel? Ever have I striven
To think thee kind, but ah, it will not do!
When yet a child, I heard that kisses drew
Favour from thee, and so I kisses gave
740 To the void air, bidding them find out love:
But when I came to feel how far above
All fancy, pride, and fickle maidenhood,
All earthly pleasure, all imagin'd good,
Was the warm tremble of a devout kiss,—
745 Even then, that moment, at the thought of this,
Fainting I fell into a bed of flowers,

716 of . . . the] the most velvet peaches to my *D*; ⟨the most velvet⟩ of three sweetest pleasurings the *FC* 720 Say, is not] Is not, then, *D* 721 doubt!"] *FC*, $L^5$; ~ ?" *1818* 723 His] The *D* 724–725 It . . . sorrow;] *Woodhouse notes that these lines (with the variant given in the next note) were written in D at the end of Book IV and "Probably intended for this place"* 724 It . . . to] There was rejoicing in *D* 726 just as] what time *D* 728 had] has *FC* 734 dawn and thought] thought and dawn *D* 739 kisses gave] $L^5$, *1818 errata*; gave gave *FC*; gave and gave *1818 text* 744 warm . . . devout] moist music of a single *D*

And languish'd there three days. Ye milder powers,
Am I not cruelly wrong'd? Believe, believe
Me, dear Endymion, were I to weave
750 With my own fancies garlands of sweet life,
Thou shouldst be one of all. Ah, bitter strife!
I may not be thy love: I am forbidden—
Indeed I am—thwarted, affrighted, chidden,
By things I trembled at, and gorgon wrath.
755 Twice hast thou ask'd whither I went: henceforth
Ask me no more! I may not utter it,
Nor may I be thy love. We might commit
Ourselves at once to vengeance; we might die;
We might embrace and die: voluptuous thought!
760 Enlarge not to my hunger, or I'm caught
In trammels of perverse deliciousness.
No, no, that shall not be: thee will I bless,
And bid a long adieu."

The Carian
No word return'd: both lovelorn, silent, wan,
765 Into the vallies green together went.
Far wandering, they were perforce content
To sit beneath a fair lone beechen tree;
Nor at each other gaz'd, but heavily
Por'd on its hazle cirque of shedded leaves.

770 Endymion! unhappy! it nigh grieves
Me to behold thee thus in last extreme:
Ensky'd ere this, but truly that I deem
Truth the best music in a first-born song.
Thy lute-voic'd brother will I sing ere long,
775 And thou shalt aid—hast thou not aided me?
Yes, moonlight Emperor! felicity
Has been thy meed for many thousand years;
Yet often have I, on the brink of tears,
Mourn'd as if yet thou wert a forester;—
Forgetting the old tale.

780 He did not stir

748 wrong'd] ⟨serv'd⟩ wrong'd *FC* 750 With . . . of] My own imaginations to *D* 751 shouldst . . . of] would'st o'ertop them *D* 754 trembled] tremble *FC* 766 Far] Long *D* 769 cirque of shedded] carpet of shed *D* 771 extreme] extreme⟨s⟩ *FC* 772 Ensky'd . . . truly] Thou hadst been high ere this, but *D* 778 on . . . of] mid some foolish *D*

His eyes from the dead leaves, or one small pulse
Of joy he might have felt. The spirit culls
Unfaded amaranth, when wild it strays
Through the old garden-ground of boyish days.
785 A little onward ran the very stream
By which he took his first soft poppy dream;
And on the very bark 'gainst which he leant
A crescent he had carv'd, and round it spent
His skill in little stars. The teeming tree
790 Had swollen and green'd the pious charactery,
But not ta'en out. Why, there was not a slope
Up which he had not fear'd the antelope;
And not a tree, beneath whose rooty shade
He had not with his tamed leopards play'd:
795 Nor could an arrow light, or javelin,
Fly in the air where his had never been—
And yet he knew it not.

O treachery!
Why does his lady smile, pleasing her eye
With all his sorrowing? He sees her not.
800 But who so stares on him? His sister sure!
Peona of the woods!—Can she endure—
Impossible—how dearly they embrace!
His lady smiles; delight is in her face;
It is no treachery.

"Dear brother mine!
805 Endymion, weep not so! Why shouldst thou pine
When all great Latmos so exalt will be?
Thank the great gods, and look not bitterly;
And speak not one pale word, and sigh no more.
Sure I will not believe thou hast such store
810 Of grief, to last thee to my kiss again.
Thou surely canst not bear a mind in pain,

783 wild] perchance *D* 785 onward] onwards *D* 791 ta'en out] effaced *D* 792 fear'd] chaced *D* 794 tamed leopards] jessied falcon's *D* 796 the] that *D* 801 of the woods] kind and fair *D* 805 Endymion,] Dear Endy: (*see Textual Note*) *D* 808 and sigh no] nor sigh once *D* 811–813 Thou . . . pull]

Were this sweet damsel like a long neck'd crane
Or an old rocking barn owl half asleep
Some reason would there be for thee to keep
So dull-eyed—but thou knows ⟨shell⟩ she's beautiful
Yes, Yes! and thou dost love her—well I'll pull *D*

Come hand in hand with one so beautiful.
Be happy both of you! for I will pull
The flowers of autumn for your coronals.
815 Pan's holy priest for young Endymion calls;
And when he is restor'd, thou, fairest dame,
Shalt be our queen. Now, is it not a shame
To see ye thus,—not very, very sad?
Perhaps ye are too happy to be glad:
820 O feel as if it were a common day;
Free-voic'd as one who never was away.
No tongue shall ask, whence come ye? but ye shall
Be gods of your own rest imperial.
Not even I, for one whole month, will pry
825 Into the hours that have pass'd us by,
Since in my arbour I did sing to thee.
O Hermes! on this very night will be
A hymning up to Cynthia, queen of light;
For the soothsayers old saw yesternight
830 Good visions in the air,—whence will befal,
As say these sages, health perpetual
To shepherds and their flocks; and furthermore,
In Dian's face they read the gentle lore:
Therefore for her these vesper-carols are.
835 Our friends will all be there from nigh and far.
Many upon thy death have ditties made;
And many, even now, their foreheads shade
With cypress, on a day of sacrifice.
New singing for our maids shalt thou devise,
840 And pluck the sorrow from our huntsmen's brows.
Tell me, my lady-queen, how to espouse
This wayward brother to his rightful joys!
His eyes are on thee bent, as thou didst poise
His fate most goddess-like. Help me, I pray,
845 To lure—Endymion, dear brother, say
What ails thee?" He could bear no more, and so
Bent his soul fiercely like a spiritual bow,
And twang'd it inwardly, and calmly said:
"I would have thee my only friend, sweet maid!
850 My only visitor! not ignorant though,

815 Pan's holy] Great Pan's high *D* 816 And . . . is] This Shepherd Prince *D* 819 are . . . glad] feel too much joy—too overglad *D* 825 hours] long hours *D* 827 O . . . night] Why! hark ye! on this very eve *D* 840 sorrow] Cypress *D*

That those deceptions which for pleasure go
'Mong men, are pleasures real as real may be:
But there are higher ones I may not see,
If impiously an earthly realm I take.
855 Since I saw thee, I have been wide awake
Night after night, and day by day, until
Of the empyrean I have drunk my fill.
Let it content thee, sister, seeing me
More happy than betides mortality.
860 A hermit young, I'll live in mossy cave,
Where thou alone shalt come to me, and lave
Thy spirit in the wonders I shall tell.
Through me the shepherd realm shall prosper well;
For to thy tongue will I all health confide.
865 And, for my sake, let this young maid abide
With thee as a dear sister. Thou alone,
Peona, mayst return to me. I own
This may sound strangely: but when, dearest girl,
Thou seest it for my happiness, no pearl
870 Will trespass down those cheeks. Companion fair!
Wilt be content to dwell with her, to share
This sister's love with me?" Like one resign'd
And bent by circumstance, and thereby blind
In self-commitment, thus that meek unknown:
875 "Aye, but a buzzing by my ears has flown,
Of jubilee to Dian:—truth I heard?
Well then, I see there is no little bird,
Tender soever, but is Jove's own care.
Long have I sought for rest, and, unaware,
880 Behold I find it! so exalted too!
So after my own heart! I knew, I knew
There was a place untenanted in it:
In that same void white Chastity shall sit,
And monitor me nightly to lone slumber.
885 With sanest lips I vow me to the number
Of Dian's sisterhood; and, kind lady,
With thy good help, this very night shall see
My future days to her fane consecrate."

853 there are] I have *D* 862 shall] will *D* 864 all . . . confide] *successively* (*a*) all health confide (*b*) confide all health (*c*) all health confide *FC* 866 as a dear] ev'n as a *D* 874 meek] mild *D* 876 heard?] *FC*, *L*[5]; ~! *1818* 882 place] void *D* 888 to] in *D*

As feels a dreamer what doth most create
890 His own particular fright, so these three felt:
Or like one who, in after ages, knelt
To Lucifer or Baal, when he'd pine
After a little sleep: or when in mine
Far under-ground, a sleeper meets his friends
895 Who know him not. Each diligently bends
Towards common thoughts and things for very fear;
Striving their ghastly malady to cheer,
By thinking it a thing of yes and no,
That housewives talk of. But the spirit-blow
900 Was struck, and all were dreamers. At the last
Endymion said: "Are not our fates all cast?
Why stand we here? Adieu, ye tender pair!
Adieu!" Whereat those maidens, with wild stare,
Walk'd dizzily away. Pained and hot
905 His eyes went after them, until they got
Near to a cypress grove, whose deadly maw,
In one swift moment, would what then he saw
Engulph for ever. "Stay!" he cried, "ah, stay!
Turn, damsels! hist! one word I have to say.
910 Sweet Indian, I would see thee once again.
It is a thing I dote on: so I'd fain,
Peona, ye should hand in hand repair
Into those holy groves, that silent are
Behind great Dian's temple. I'll be yon,
915 At Vesper's earliest twinkle—they are gone—
But once, once, once again—" At this he press'd
His hands against his face, and then did rest
His head upon a mossy hillock green,
And so remain'd as he a corpse had been
920 All the long day; save when he scantly lifted
His eyes abroad, to see how shadows shifted
With the slow move of time,—sluggish and weary
Until the poplar tops, in journey dreary,
Had reach'd the river's brim. Then up he rose,
925 And, slowly as that very river flows,

889 doth] can *D* 891 knelt] ⟨to⟩ knelt *FC* 892 he'd pine] at strife *D* 899 housewives] Huswives *FC* 904 dizzily] patiently *D* 906 maw] *replacing* ⟨shade⟩ *D* 918–919 head . . . been] hands upon a pillow of green moss / And so remained, without impatient toss (*Woodhouse also records* hands *for* head *in a separate note, making clear that the variant word is Keats's slip rather than his own*) *D* 920 long day] day long *D* 922 With . . . weary] And note the weary time.—Ah weary, weary *D*

Walk'd towards the temple grove with this lament:
"Why such a golden eve? The breeze is sent
Careful and soft, that not a leaf may fall
Before the serene father of them all
930 Bows down his summer head below the west.
Now am I of breath, speech, and speed possest,
But at the setting I must bid adieu
To her for the last time. Night will strew
On the damp grass myriads of lingering leaves,
935 And with them shall I die; nor much it grieves
To die, when summer dies on the cold sward.
Why, I have been a butterfly, a lord
Of flowers, garlands, love-knots, silly posies,
Groves, meadows, melodies, and arbour roses;
940 My kingdom's at its death, and just it is
That I should die with it: so in all this
We miscal grief, bale, sorrow, heartbreak, woe,
What is there to plain of? By Titan's foe
I am but rightly serv'd." So saying, he
945 Tripp'd lightly on, in sort of deathful glee;
Laughing at the clear stream and setting sun,
As though they jests had been: nor had he done
His laugh at nature's holy countenance,
Until that grove appear'd, as if perchance,
950 And then his tongue with sober seemlihed
Gave utterance as he entered: "Ha! I said,
King of the butterflies; but by this gloom,
And by old Rhadamanthus' tongue of doom,
This dusk religion, pomp of solitude,
955 And the Promethean clay by thief endued,
By old Saturnus' forelock, by his head
Shook with eternal palsy, I did wed
Myself to things of light from infancy;
And thus to be cast out, thus lorn to die,
960 Is sure enough to make a mortal man
Grow impious." So he inwardly began
On things for which no wording can be found;
Deeper and deeper sinking, until drown'd
Beyond the reach of music: for the choir

926 with . . . lament:] lamenting, "O‸ *D*   927 breeze is sent] breezes blow *D*   949 that . . . appear'd] he saw that grove *D*   949/950 ⟨And then his soul was changed⟩ *D*   955 the] *written over* ⟨by⟩ *FC*   955/956 ⟨And by old Saturn's single forelock—⟩ *D*   959 thus . . . out] to be cast out thus *D*   964 reach] ⟨distant⟩ reach *D*

965 Of Cynthia he heard not, though rough briar
Nor muffling thicket interpos'd to dull
The vesper hymn, far swollen, soft and full,
Through the dark pillars of those sylvan aisles.
He saw not the two maidens, nor their smiles,
970 Wan as primroses gather'd at midnight
By chilly finger'd spring. "Unhappy wight!
Endymion!" said Peona, "we are here!
What wouldst thou ere we all are laid on bier?"
Then he embrac'd her, and his lady's hand
975 Press'd, saying: "Sister, I would have command,
If it were heaven's will, on our sad fate."
At which that dark-eyed stranger stood elate
And said, in a new voice, but sweet as love,
To Endymion's amaze: "By Cupid's dove,
980 And so thou shalt! and by the lily truth
Of my own breast thou shalt, beloved youth!"
And as she spake, into her face there came
Light, as reflected from a silver flame:
Her long black hair swell'd ampler, in display
985 Full golden; in her eyes a brighter day
Dawn'd blue and full of love. Aye, he beheld
Phœbe, his passion! joyous she upheld
Her lucid bow, continuing thus: "Drear, drear
Has our delaying been; but foolish fear
990 Withheld me first; and then decrees of fate;
And then 'twas fit that from this mortal state
Thou shouldst, my love, by some unlook'd for change
Be spiritualiz'd. Peona, we shall range
These forests, and to thee they safe shall be
995 As was thy cradle; hither shalt thou flee
To meet us many a time." Next Cynthia bright
Peona kiss'd, and bless'd with fair good night:
Her brother kiss'd her too, and knelt adown
Before his goddess, in a blissful swoon.
1000 She gave her fair hands to him, and behold,
Before three swiftest kisses he had told,
They vanish'd far away!—Peona went
Home through the gloomy wood in wonderment.

967 vesper] prelude *D* 974 Then he embrac'd] Her brother kiss'd *D*; ⟨Her⟩ Then he embrac'd *FC* 975 Press'd . . . Sister] Saying, Sweet sister *D* 977 At . . . eyed] Then that dark-tressed *D* 984–986 in . . . blue] while it turned / Golden—and her eyes of jet dawned ⟨forth a⟩ / Blue—blue *D*

## *In drear nighted December*

In drear nighted December,
  Too happy, happy tree,
Thy branches ne'er remember
  Their green felicity—
5 The north cannot undo them
With a sleety whistle through them,
Nor frozen thawings glue them
  From budding at the prime.

In drear nighted December,
10   Too happy, happy brook,
Thy bubblings ne'er remember
  Apollo's summer look;
But with a sweet forgetting
They stay their crystal fretting,
15 Never, never petting
  About the frozen time.

Ah! would 'twere so with many
  A gentle girl and boy—
But were there ever any
20   Writh'd not of passed joy?
The feel of not to feel it,
When there is none to heal it,
Nor numbed sense to steel it,
  Was never said in rhyme.

*In drear nighted December.* Text from the extant holograph fair copy (*FC*). Variants and other readings from a now lost earlier holograph as reported by H. B. Forman in Hampstead Keats, IV, 61–62 n. (*Law MS*), two Woodhouse transcripts ($W^3$, $W^2$), and the versions published in the *Literary Gazette* (*Gaz*) and *The Gem*. *Heading* In . . . December] *ed*; Song $W^3$, $W^2$; Stanzas *Gaz, Gem*; *no heading in Law MS, FC* 1, 9 In] In a *Gaz, Gem* 2 happy (*third word*)] *added above the line in Law MS* 5 The] ⟨But w⟩ The *FC* 18 gentle] *interlined above* ⟨happy⟩ *Law MS* 20 of] at *Law MS*, $W^3$, $W^2$, *Gaz, Gem* 21 The . . . to] To know the change and *Gaz, Gem* 21 not] *underscored in* $W^2$ 23 steel] $W^3$, $W^2$, *Gaz, Gem*; steal *FC* 24 said] told *Gem*

## *Apollo to the Graces*

APOLLO

Which of the fairest three
To-day will ride with me?
My steeds are all pawing on the thresholds of morn:
Which of the fairest three
5 To-day will ride with me
Across the gold autumn's whole kingdoms of corn?

THE GRACES *all answer*

I will, I—I—I—
O young Apollo, let me fly along with thee;
I will, I—I—I—
10 The many, many wonders see,
I—I—I—I—
And thy lyre shall never have a slacken'd string;
I—I—I—I—
Through the golden day will sing.

## *To Mrs. Reynolds's Cat*

Cat! who hast past thy grand climacteric,
How many mice and rats hast in thy days
Destroy'd?—how many tit bits stolen? Gaze
With those bright languid segments green and prick
5 Those velvet ears—but prythee do not stick
Thy latent talons in me—and upraise
Thy gentle mew—and tell me all thy frays
Of fish and mice and rats and tender chick.
Nay, look not down, nor lick thy dainty wrists—

*Apollo to the Graces.* Text (including heading) from the extant holograph (arbitrarily cited as *D*). Variants from Woodhouse's $W^2$ transcript. *Heading* Graces] Graces. / written to the Tune of the air "[*blank space*] in Don Giovanni $W^2$ 3 on] *written over* ⟨at⟩ *D*; at $W^2$ 7 I—I—I] I—I, ⟨I⟩ I *D* 12 And] ⟨I f⟩ And *D* 14 golden] ⟨whole⟩ golden *D*

*To Mrs. Reynolds's Cat.* Text (including heading) from the extant holograph fair copy (*FC*). Variants from Woodhouse's $W^2$ transcript and the version published in Hood's *The Comic Annual* (*Ann*). *Heading* To . . . Cat] Sonnet / On M[rs] Reynolds's Cat $W^2$; Sonnet to a Cat *Ann* 1 hast] has *Ann* 1 grand] *added above the line in FC* 9 dainty] gentle $W^2$

10 For all the wheezy asthma—and for all
Thy tail's tip is nicked off—and though the fists
Of many a maid have given thee many a maul,
Still is that fur as soft as when the lists
In youth thou enter'dst on glass bottled wall.

## *Lines on Seeing a Lock of Milton's Hair*

Chief of organic numbers!
Old scholar of the spheres!
Thy spirit never slumbers,
But rolls about our ears
5 For ever, and for ever:
O, what a mad endeavour
Worketh he,
Who, to thy sacred and ennobled hearse,
Would offer a burnt sacrifice of verse
10 And melody.

How heavenward thou soundedst,
Live temple of sweet noise;
And discord unconfoundedst,—
Giving delight new joys,
15 And pleasure nobler pinions—
O, where are thy dominions?
Lend thine ear,
To a young Delian oath—aye, by thy soul,
By all that from thy mortal lips did roll;
20 And by the kernel of thine earthly love,
Beauty, in things on earth and things above;
When every childish fashion

10 the wheezy] thou hast *altered to* the weezy *FC* 12 have] $W^2$; has *FC*, *Ann* 14 bottled] bottle $W^2$

*Lines on Seeing a Lock of Milton's Hair.* Text (including heading) from the holograph fair copy at Keats House, Hampstead (*FC*). Variants and other readings from Keats's draft (*D*), his letter to Bailey, 23 January 1818 (*L*), and Brown's transcript (*CB*). *Heading* Lines . . . Hair] *so FC* (*the first three words a later addition by Keats*); On seeing a Lock of Milton's Hair— / Ode (*the last word underscored*) *L*; *no heading in D* *Before* 1 ⟨Father of⟩ *D* 6 O] Ah *D* 7 Worketh] Macketh *D* 11 heavenward] heavenly *D* 11 soundedst] soundest *CB* 11/12 ⟨O living fane of Sounds⟩ *D* 13 unconfoundedst] unconfoundest *CB* 18 Delian] *interlined above* ⟨phœbean⟩ *D* 20 thine] thy *D*, *CB* 20 earthly] earthy *D* 21/22 I swear *added in pencil by Woodhouse in L*, *CB*, *and written over in ink by Brown in CB* (*see Textual Note*)

Has vanish'd from my rhyme,
Will I, grey-gone in passion,
25 Leave to an after time
Hymning and harmony
Of thee, and of thy works, and of thy life;
But vain is now the burning, and the strife,
Pangs are in vain—until I grow high-rife
30 With old philosophy;
And mad with glimpses at futurity!

For many years my offerings must be hush'd.
When I do speak, I'll think upon this hour,
Because I feel my forehead hot and flush'd—
35 Even at the simplest vassal of thy power;
A lock of thy bright hair—
Sudden it came,
And I was startled, when I caught thy name
Coupled so unaware;
40 Yet at the moment, temperate was my blood—
Methought I had beheld it from the Flood.

25 Leave] Give *L* 26 Hymning and] A Hymn and *D*; A Hymn, a *altered to* Hymning and *FC* 29 Pangs . . . vain] *interlined above* ⟨In vain the Pang⟩ *D* 31 And . . . futurity] *interlined above:*

⟨Till then⟩
⟨And so presumptuous tongue in rest⟩ *D*

31 at] of *CB* 32 For . . . hush'd] Then will I speak—but now my voice is hush⟨d⟩ *D* 33 When . . . I'll] Then will I speak and *D* 33/34 ⟨For at this hour am I⟩ (am I *written over* {is my}) *D* 34 flush'd] flush *D* 35 Even . . . simplest] Aye from the simplest *D*; At the most simple *altered to* Even at the simplest *FC* 36–37 A . . . came, (*two lines*)] *D, L*; *one line in FC*; *originally one line but rewritten as two lines in CB* 36 A] One *D* 38 And . . . name] Before me—and I started at thy name (*the last six words written beneath a series of deletions*—⟨and cold {death} death⟩ *on the original line, with* ⟨constant⟩ *and* ⟨hand⟩ *or* ⟨head⟩ *above the line and* ⟨touch its gold⟩ *and* ⟨kiss'd⟩ *beneath; a tentative reconstruction of the successive endings of the line before the final version would be* [*a*] and cold death [*b*] and constant death [*c*] and death hand *or* head [*d*] and cold death touch its gold [*e*] and cold death kiss'd its gold, *but the order of readings and the relationships of words in them are quite uncertain*) *D* 38 caught] heard *L* 40 moment, temperate] time unheated *D* 41 Methought] It seem'd *D*

## *On Sitting Down to Read* King Lear *Once Again*

O golden-tongued Romance, with serene lute!
Fair plumed syren, queen of far-away!
Leave melodizing on this wintry day,
Shut up thine olden pages, and be mute.
5 Adieu! for, once again, the fierce dispute
Betwixt damnation and impassion'd clay
Must I burn through; once more humbly assay
The bitter-sweet of this Shaksperean fruit.
Chief Poet! and ye clouds of Albion,
10 Begetters of our deep eternal theme!
When through the old oak forest I am gone,
Let me not wander in a barren dream:
But, when I am consumed in the fire,
Give me new phœnix wings to fly at my desire.

## *When I have fears that I may cease to be*

When I have fears that I may cease to be
Before my pen has glean'd my teeming brain,
Before high piled books, in charactry,
Hold like rich garners the full ripen'd grain;
5 When I behold, upon the night's starr'd face,
Huge cloudy symbols of a high romance,
And think that I may never live to trace
Their shadows, with the magic hand of chance;
And when I feel, fair creature of an hour,

*On Sitting Down to Read "King Lear."* Text (including heading) from the extant holograph fair copy (*FC*). Variants and other readings from Keats's draft (*D*), Woodhouse's $W^2$ transcript, and Jeffrey's transcript of Keats's now lost letter to George and Tom Keats, 23, 24 January 1818 (*JJ*). *Heading* On] Sonnet. On $W^2$ 2 queen of] Queen of *altered to* Queen! if *JJ* 4 thine] *made out of* thy *D* 4 pages] ⟨Books⟩ Pages *D*; volume *JJ* 6 damnation] Hell-torment $W^2$, *JJ* 7 humbly] *interlined above* ⟨must I⟩ *D*; *the word omitted in JJ* 8/9 ⟨Chief! what a gloom thine old oak forest hath!⟩ (thine *made out of* thy) *D* 9 Chief Poet] ⟨O⟩ Chief Poet *interlined above* ⟨Chieftain⟩ *D* 10 our] this *D*, $W^2$; our *interlined above* ⟨this⟩ *FC* 11 through . . . am] I am through the old oak forest *JJ* 13 in] with *JJ* 14 at] to *D*, $W^2$; at *written over* ⟨to⟩ *FC*

*When I have fears.* Text from Brown's transcript (*CB*). Variants from Charlotte Reynolds' transcript (*CR*) and Woodhouse's clerk's letterbook transcript (*WCL*), both made from Keats's now lost letter to J. H. Reynolds, 31 January 1818. *Heading* When . . . be] *ed*; Sonnet *CB*; *no heading in CR, WCL* 4 rich] full *WCL* 7 think] feel *CR, WCL*

10 That I shall never look upon thee more,
Never have relish in the fairy power
Of unreflecting love;—then on the shore
Of the wide world I stand alone, and think
Till love and fame to nothingness do sink.

## *O blush not so! O blush not so*

1

O blush not so! O blush not so!
Or I shall think you knowing;
And if you smile, the blushing while,
Then maidenheads are going.

2

5 There's a blush for won't, and a blush for shan't,
And a blush for having done it;
There's a blush for thought, and a blush for nought,
And a blush for just begun it.

3

O sigh not so! O sigh not so!
10 For it sounds of Eve's sweet pippin;
By those loosen'd hips, you have tasted the pips,
And fought in an amorous nipping.

4

Will you play once more, at nice cut-core,
For it only will last our youth out;
15 And we have the prime of the kissing time,
We have not one sweet tooth out.

5

There's a sigh for yes, and a sigh for no,
And a sigh for I can't bear it!
O what can be done? Shall we stay or run?
20 O cut the sweet apple and share it!

*O blush not so.* Text from Brown's transcript (*CB*). Variants from Woodhouse's $W^3$ transcript and his clerk's letterbook transcript of Keats's now lost letter to J. H. Reynolds, 31 January 1818 (*WCL*). *Heading* O . . . so] *ed*; Song $W^3$, *CB*; *no heading in WCL* 2, 3, 13 you] ye $W^3$, *WCL* 5 won't] want $W^3$; wont *altered to* want *WCL* 9 sigh . . . sigh] say . . . say $W^3$ 15 of the] of our $W^3$ 17 yes . . . no] aye . . . nay $W^3$

## *Hence burgundy, claret, and port*

Hence burgundy, claret, and port,
  Away with old hock and madeira!
Too earthly ye are for my sport;
  There's a beverage brighter and clearer!
5 Instead of a pitiful rummer,
My wine overbrims a whole summer;
    My bowl is the sky,
    And I drink at my eye,
    Till I feel in the brain
10 A Delphian pain—
Then follow, my Caius, then follow!
    On the green of the hill,
    We will drink our fill
    Of golden sunshine,
15 Till our brains intertwine
With the glory and grace of Apollo!

## *God of the meridian*

God of the meridian!
  And of the east and west!
To thee my soul is flown,
  And my body is earthward press'd:
5 It is an awful mission,
A terrible division,
And leaves a gulf austere
To be fill'd with worldly fear.
Aye, when the soul is fled
10 Too high above our head,
Affrighted do we gaze
After its airy maze—
As doth a mother wild
When her young infant child
15 Is in an eagle's claws.
And is not this the cause

*Hence burgundy.* Text from Brown's transcript (*CB*). Variants from Woodhouse's $W^2$ transcript and his clerk's letterbook transcript (*WCL*), both made from Keats's now lost letter to J. H. Reynolds, 31 January 1818. *Heading* Hence . . . port] *ed*; Song *CB*; *no heading in* $W^2$, *WCL* 3 earthly] courtly $W^2$; couthly *WCL*

*God of the meridian.* Text from Woodhouse's $W^2$ transcript. Heading supplied by editor. 10 Too] *ed*; To $W^2$

Of madness?—God of Song,
Thou bearest me along
Through sights I scarce can bear;
20 O let me, let me share
With the hot lyre and thee
The staid philosophy.
Temper my lonely hours
And let me see thy bowers
25 More unalarmed! * * *

## *Robin Hood*

### TO A FRIEND

No! those days are gone away,
And their hours are old and gray,
And their minutes buried all
Under the down-trodden pall
5 Of the leaves of many years:
Many times have winter's shears,
Frozen north, and chilling east,
Sounded tempests to the feast
Of the forest's whispering fleeces,
10 Since men knew nor rent nor leases.

No, the bugle sounds no more,
And the twanging bow no more;
Silent is the ivory shrill
Past the heath and up the hill;
15 There is no mid-forest laugh,
Where lone Echo gives the half
To some wight, amaz'd to hear
Jesting, deep in forest drear.

*Robin Hood.* Text (including heading and dedication) from *1820.* Variants and other readings from Keats's draft (*D*) and transcripts by Woodhouse (*W*²), Brown (*CB*), and George Keats (*GK*). *Heading and dedication* Robin . . . Friend] To John H. Reynolds / In answer to his Robin Hood Sonnets *W*²; To John Reynolds, in answer to his Robin Hood Sonnets *CB*; To John Reynolds in answer to his Sonnets on Robin Hood *GK*; *no heading or dedication in D* 6 have] *interlined above* ⟨old⟩ *D* 7 chilling] chilly *D* 10 knew nor . . . nor] paid no Rent and *D*, *W*² 12/13 ⟨And the whistle shrill is⟩ *D* 15/16 ⟨No old Hermit with his⟩ *D* 18 Jesting . . . in] Jests deep in a (deep in *made out of* within) *D*

On the fairest time of June
20 You may go, with sun or moon,
Or the seven stars to light you,
Or the polar ray to right you;
But you never may behold
Little John, or Robin bold;
25 Never one, of all the clan,
Thrumming on an empty can
Some old hunting ditty, while
He doth his green way beguile
To fair hostess Merriment,
30 Down beside the pasture Trent;
For he left the merry tale
Messenger for spicy ale.

Gone, the merry morris din;
Gone, the song of Gamelyn;
35 Gone, the tough-belted outlaw
Idling in the "grenè shawe";
All are gone away and past!
And if Robin should be cast
Sudden from his turfed grave,
40 And if Marian should have
Once again her forest days,
She would weep, and he would craze:
He would swear, for all his oaks,
Fall'n beneath the dockyard strokes,
45 Have rotted on the briny seas;
She would weep that her wild bees

18/19 ⟨No more barbed arrows fly / Through one's own roof to the Sky⟩ *D* 19 On] In *made out of* On *D* 19 time] *interlined above* ⟨day⟩ *D* 21 seven] ⟨Planet⟩ seven *D* 22 Or] And *D* 22 ray] ⟨beam⟩ ray *D* 25 one, of all] any of $W^2$ 25 one] ⟨meet⟩ one *D* 26 Thrumming] ⟨Rattling⟩ Thrumming *D* 27 Some] An *D* 29 hostess] *interlined above* ⟨Mistress⟩ *D*; Hostess' $W^2$ 31–32 For . . . ale] *written vertically in the margin in D* 31 For] *interlined above* ⟨When⟩ *D* 32 for] to *D*, $W^2$, *CB*, *GK* (*interlined above* ⟨for⟩ *in D*) 33–41 Gone . . . days,] *written on the reverse side of the sheet in D. The original passage in D is uncanceled:*

No, those times are flown and past.
What if Robin should be cast
Sudden From his turfed grave?
How would Marian behave
In the forest now a days?

(Sudden *added in the margin in the third line*) 37 away and] and all is *D* 38 should be] *underscored in* $W^2$, *CB* 39 turfed] tufted *D* 40 should have] *underscored in CB* (*the first word only also underscored in* $W^2$) 44 dockyard] Woodma's *D* 46 her] his *GK*

Sang not to her—strange! that honey
Can't be got without hard money!

So it is: yet let us sing,
50 Honour to the old bow-string!
Honour to the bugle-horn!
Honour to the woods unshorn!
Honour to the Lincoln green!
Honour to the archer keen!
55 Honour to tight little John,
And the horse he rode upon!
Honour to bold Robin Hood,
Sleeping in the underwood!
Honour to maid Marian,
60 And to all the Sherwood-clan!
Though their days have hurried by
Let us two a burden try.

## *Lines on the Mermaid Tavern*

Souls of poets dead and gone,
What elysium have ye known,
Happy field or mossy cavern,
Choicer than the Mermaid Tavern?
5 Have ye tippled drink more fine
Than mine host's Canary wine?
Or are fruits of Paradise
Sweeter than those dainty pies
Of venison? O generous food!
10 Drest as though bold Robin Hood
Would, with his maid Marian,
Sup and bowse from horn and can.

47–48 ‸strange . . . money!‸] "~ . . . ~." $W^2$ 49 yet] *interlined above* ⟨Then⟩ *D* 50/51 ⟨Though the Glories⟩ *D* 61 days] ⟨Pleasures⟩ days *D* 62 Let . . . burden] You and I a stave will *D*

*Lines on the Mermaid Tavern.* Text (including heading) from *1820.* Variants and other readings from the holograph fair copies at Harvard and the British Library ($FC^1$ and $FC^2$, respectively) and transcripts by Woodhouse ($W^2$) and Brown (*CB*). *Heading* Lines . . . Tavern] Lines to the Mermaid Tavern *CB*; Ode (*added in George Keats's hand*) $FC^2$; *no heading in* $FC^1$ (*but see Textual Note*) 4 Choicer] Fairer $FC^1$, $W^2$, *and originally CB*; Fairer *altered to* Choicer *by Keats in CB* 7 Or are] Are the *interlined above* Or are (*left undeleted*) $FC^1$ 8 Sweeter] Richer $FC^2$ 9 O generous] Old generous $FC^1$; delicious $FC^2$ 12 bowze] bouze $FC^1$, *CB*; booze $W^2$; bouse $FC^2$

  I have heard that on a day
Mine host's sign-board flew away,
15 Nobody knew whither, till
An astrologer's old quill
To a sheepskin gave the story,
Said he saw you in your glory,
Underneath a new old sign
20 Sipping beverage divine,
And pledging with contented smack
The Mermaid in the zodiac.

  Souls of poets dead and gone,
What elysium have ye known,
25 Happy field or mossy cavern,
Choicer than the Mermaid Tavern?

## *Welcome joy, and welcome sorrow*

"Under the flag
Of each his faction, they to battle bring
Their embryo atoms."

Milton

Welcome joy, and welcome sorrow,
  Lethe's weed, and Hermes' feather,
Come to-day, and come to-morrow,
  I do love you both together!
5 I love to mark sad faces in fair weather,
And hear a merry laugh amid the thunder;
  Fair and foul I love together;
Meadows sweet where flames burn under;
And a giggle at a wonder;
10 Visage sage at pantomime;
Funeral and steeple-chime;

18 Said] Says $FC^1$, $W^2$, *CB*, $FC^2$ 19 new$_\wedge$ old$_\wedge$ sign] $W^2$, $FC^2$; ~ -~$_\wedge$ ~ $FC^1$; ~$_\wedge$ ~ -~ *CB*, *1820* 20 Sipping] Lipping $W^2$ 24–26 What . . . Tavern]
Are the Winds a sweeter Home
Richer is uncellar'd Cavern
Than the merry Mermaid Tavern $FC^1$, $W^2$, *CB*

*Welcome joy.* Text (including epigraph) from Brown's transcript (*CB*). Variants from the fair copy in the possession of Dorothy Withey (*Withey MS*). *Heading* Welcome . . . sorrow] *ed*; Fragment *Withey MS, CB*

Infant playing with a skull;
Morning fair and storm-wreck'd hull;
Night-shade with the woodbine kissing;
15 Serpents in red roses hissing;
Cleopatra, regal drest,
With the aspics at her breast;
Dancing music, music sad,
Both together, sane and mad;
20 Muses bright and Muses pale;
Sombre Saturn, Momus hale,
Laugh and sigh, and laugh again,
Oh! the sweetness of the pain!
Muses bright and Muses pale,
25 Bare your faces of the veil,
Let me see, and let me write
Of the day, and of the night,
Both together,—let me slake
All my thirst for sweet heart-ache!
30 Let my bower be of yew,
Interwreath'd with myrtles new,
Pines, and lime-trees full in bloom,
And my couch a low grass tomb.

## *Time's sea hath been five years at its slow ebb*

Time's sea hath been five years at its slow ebb;
  Long hours have to and fro let creep the sand,
Since I was tangled in thy beauty's web,
  And snared by the ungloving of thy hand:
5 And yet I never look on midnight sky,
  But I behold thine eyes' well-memoried light;
I cannot look upon the rose's dye,
  But to thy cheek my soul doth take its flight:
I cannot look on any budding flower,
10   But my fond ear, in fancy at thy lips,
And hearkening for a love-sound, doth devour

13 storm-wreck'd] shipwreck'd *Withey MS*

*Time's sea hath been.* Text from Woodhouse's $W^2$ transcript. Variants from the version published in *Hood's Magazine.* *Heading* Time's . . . ebb] *ed*; To —— $W^2$; Sonnet *Hood's* 1 Time's . . . years] Life's . . . times *Hood's* 7 cannot look] never gaze *Hood's* 9 cannot] never *Hood's*

Its sweets in the wrong sense.—Thou dost eclipse
Every delight with sweet remembering,
And grief unto my darling joys dost bring.

## *To the Nile*

Son of the old moon-mountains African!
Chief of the pyramid and crocodile!
We call thee fruitful, and, that very while,
A desert fills our seeing's inward span;
5 Nurse of swart nations since the world began,
Art thou so fruitful? or dost thou beguile
Such men to honor thee, who, worn with toil,
Rest for a space 'twixt Cairo and Decan?
O may dark fancies err! they surely do;
10 'Tis ignorance that makes a barren waste
Of all beyond itself: thou dost bedew
Green rushes like our rivers, and dost taste
The pleasant sun-rise; green isles hast thou too,
And to the sea as happily dost haste.

## *Spenser, a jealous honorer of thine*

Spenser, a jealous honorer of thine,
A forester deep in thy midmost trees,
Did last eve ask my promise to refine
Some English that might strive thine ear to please.
5 But Elfin-Poet, 'tis impossible
For an inhabitant of wintry earth

13 Every . . . sweet] Other delights with thy *Hood's* 14 grief unto] sorrow to *Hood's*

*To the Nile.* Text from Brown's transcript with 6–8 in Keats's hand (*CB*). Variants from Woodhouse's $W^2$ transcript. The apparatus also includes the variants recorded by Brown in two notes at the end of his transcript (*CB var*). *Heading* To] *ed*; Sonnet. To $W^2$; Sonnet, / To *CB* 2 Chief] Stream $W^2$, *CB var* 6–7 fruitful . . . with] beautiful, or a wan smile, / Pleasant but to those Men who, sick with $W^2$; beautiful? or a wan smile / Pleasing but to those men, who, after *CB var* 7 Such] *interlined above* ⟨Those⟩ *CB* (*both original and revised words in Keats's hand*) 8 for] them $W^2$ 10 'Tis . . . makes] And ignorance doth make $W^2$

*Spenser, a jealous honorer.* Text from the extant holograph fair copy (*FC*). Canceled readings from Keats's draft (*D*). *Heading* Spenser . . . thine] *ed*; *no heading in D, FC* 2 forester] *interlined above* ⟨Wanderer⟩ *D* 2 deep in] *interlined above* ⟨in thy⟩ ⟨among⟩ *D* 2 trees] *interlined above* ⟨Wood{s}⟩ *D* 3 ask my] *interlined above* ⟨make⟩ *D*

To rise like Phœbus with a golden quell,
  Fire-wing'd, and make a morning in his mirth:
It is impossible to escape from toil
10  O' the sudden, and receive thy spiriting:—
The flower must drink the nature of the soil
  Before it can put forth its blossoming.
Be with me in the summer days, and I
Will for thine honor and his pleasure try.

## *Blue!—'Tis the life of heaven—the domain*

Blue!—'Tis the life of heaven—the domain
  Of Cynthia:—the wide palace of the sun;
The tent of Hesperus and all his train;
  The bosomer of clouds gold, grey, and dun.
5 Blue!—'Tis the life of waters—Ocean,
  And all its vassal streams, pools numberless,
May rage, and foam, and fret, but never can
  Subside, if not to dark blue nativeness.
Blue!—gentle cousin to the forest green,
10  Married to green in all the sweetest flowers—
Forget-me-not—the blue-bell—and, that queen
  Of secrecy, the violet:—What strange powers
Hast thou, as a mere shadow?—But how great,
When in an eye thou art, alive with fate!

8 in] ⟨f⟩ in *FC*   9 escape . . . toil] *interlined above* ⟨leave this world⟩ *D*   11 The flower] ⟨Thy⟩ The flower *D*

*Blue!—'Tis the life.* Text from Woodhouse's $W^2$ transcript. Variants and other readings from the published facsimile of Keats's now lost draft (*D*, available for 2–14 only), a lost transcript by J. H. Reynolds as given in the *Athenaeum,* 3 June 1876 (*JHR*), and Woodhouse's copy for Severn (*late W*).   *Heading* Blue . . . domain] *ed*; Answer. J. Keats $W^2$; After an argument with a friend on the Question whether black or blue eyes were preferable *late W*; *no heading in JHR*   1 life] hue *JHR, late W* (*interlined above* ⟨life⟩ *in late W*)   2 wide] bright *JHR, late W*   6 And] With *JHR, late W*   6 its] his *D, JHR, late W* (*the word added above the line in D*)   6 vassal] tributary *JHR, late W*   6 streams,] ~ : *D*   6 pools] *interlined above* ⟨Lakes,⟩ *D*   6 numberless,] *successively* (*a*) Pools and Seas$_{\wedge}$ (*b*) Waterfalls$_{\wedge}$ (*c*) numbeless$_{\wedge}$ (*the first version and perhaps also the second following* Lakes,—*see preceding note*) *D*   6/7 ⟨And Waterfalls and Fountans never ran / Or swell'd or slep't but still⟩ (swell'd *interlined above* {flow'd}) *D*   8 if not to] but to a *D*; unless to (⟨if not⟩ unless *interlined above* ⟨unless⟩) *late W*   11 Forget-me-not] *interlined above* ⟨The Violet⟩ *D*   12 secrecy] *interlined above* ⟨Hiddenness⟩ *D*   13 But how great] *interlined above* ⟨then how high⟩ *D*   14 When in an] Trembling in *altered to* When in an *D*   14 art,] ~$_{\wedge}$ *D*

## *O thou whose face hath felt the winter's wind*

O thou whose face hath felt the winter's wind,
Whose eye has seen the snow clouds hung in mist,
And the black-elm tops 'mong the freezing stars,
To thee the spring will be a harvest-time.
5 O thou whose only book has been the light
Of supreme darkness which thou feddest on
Night after night, when Phœbus was away,
To thee the spring shall be a tripple morn.
O fret not after knowledge—I have none,
10 And yet my song comes native with the warmth;
O fret not after knowledge—I have none,
And yet the evening listens. He who saddens
At thought of idleness cannot be idle,
And he's awake who thinks himself asleep.

## *Extracts from an Opera*

O were I one of the Olympian twelve,
Their godships should pass this into a law;
That when a man doth set himself in toil
After some beauty veiled far-away,
5 Each step he took should make his lady's hand
More soft, more white, and her fair cheek more fair;
And for each briar-berry he might eat,
A kiss should bud upon the tree of love,
And pulp, and ripen, richer every hour,
10 To melt away upon the traveller's lips.

* * * * * * *

DAISY'S SONG

1

The sun, with his great eye,
Sees not so much as I;
And the moon, all silver proud,
Might as well be in a cloud.

*O thou whose face.* Text from Keats's letter to J. H. Reynolds, 19 February 1818 (*L*). Heading supplied by editor. 6 supreme] *added above the line in L*

*Extracts from an Opera.* Text (including heading and the separate titles to the second, third, and fifth songs) from Brown's transcript.

2

5 And O the spring—the spring!
I lead the life of a king!
Couch'd in the teeming grass,
I spy each pretty lass.

3

I look where no one dares,
10 And I stare where no one stares,
And when the night is nigh,
Lambs bleat my lullaby.

* * * * * * *

FOLLY'S SONG

When wedding fiddles are a playing,
Huzza for folly O!
And when maidens go a maying,
Huzza etc.
5 When a milk-pail is upset,
Huzza etc.
And the clothes left in the wet,
Huzza etc.
When the barrel's set abroach,
10 Huzza etc.
When Kate Eyebrow keeps a coach,
Huzza etc.
When the pig is overroasted,
Huzza etc.
15 And the cheese is overtoasted,
Huzza etc.
When Sir Snap is with his lawyer,
Huzza etc.
And Miss Chip has kiss'd the sawyer,
20 Huzza etc.

* * * * * * *

O, I am frighten'd with most hateful thoughts!
Perhaps her voice is not a nightingale's,
Perhaps her teeth are not the fairest pearl;
Her eye-lashes may be, for ought I know,

5 Not longer than the May-fly's small fan-horns;
There may not be one dimple on her hand,
And freckles many; ah! a careless nurse,
In haste to teach the little thing to walk,
May have crumpt up a pair of Dian's legs,
10 And warpt the ivory of a Juno's neck.

* * * * * * *

SONG

1

The stranger lighted from his steed,
  And ere he spake a word,
He seiz'd my lady's lily hand,
  And kiss'd it all unheard.

2

5 The stranger walk'd into the hall,
  And ere he spake a word,
He kiss'd my lady's cherry lips,
  And kiss'd 'em all unheard.

3

The stranger walk'd into the bower,—
10   But my lady first did go,—
Aye hand in hand into the bower,
  Where my lord's roses blow.

4

My lady's maid had a silken scarf,
  And a golden ring had she,
15 And a kiss from the stranger as off he went
  Again on his fair palfrey.

* * * * * * *

Asleep! O sleep a little while, white pearl,
And let me kneel, and let me pray to thee,
And let me call heaven's blessing on thine eyes,
And let me breathe into the happy air,
5 That doth enfold and touch thee all about,
Vows of my slavery, my giving up,
My sudden adoration, my great love!

## *Four seasons fill the measure of the year*

Four seasons fill the measure of the year;
  Four seasons are there in the mind of man.
He hath his lusty spring, when fancy clear
  Takes in all beauty with an easy span:
5 He hath his summer, when luxuriously
  He chews the honied cud of fair spring thoughts,
Till, in his soul dissolv'd, they come to be
  Part of himself. He hath his autumn ports
And havens of repose, when his tired wings
10 Are folded up, and he content to look
On mists in idleness: to let fair things
  Pass by unheeded as a threshold brook.
He hath his winter too of pale misfeature,
Or else he would forget his mortal nature.

## *For there's Bishop's Teign*

1

For there's Bishop's Teign
And King's Teign
And Coomb at the clear Teign head—
Where close by the stream
5 You may have your cream
All spread upon barley bread.

2

There's Arch Brook
And there's Larch Brook,
Both turning many a mill,

*Four seasons.* Text from Keats's letter to Bailey, 13 March 1818 (*L*). Variants from the version published in Hunt's *Literary Pocket-Book* (*P-B*). *Heading* Four . . . year] *ed*; The Human Seasons *P-B*; *no heading in L* 2 Four . . . there] There are four seasons *P-B* 3, 5, 13 hath] has *P-B* 6–10 He . . . look]
  Spring's honied cud of youthful thought he loves
To ruminate, and by such dreaming nigh
  His nearest unto heaven: quiet coves
His soul has in its Autumn, when his wings
  He furleth close; contented so to look *P-B*

*For there's Bishop's Teign.* Text from Keats's letter to Haydon, 21 March 1818 (*L*). Heading supplied by editor.

10 And cooling the drouth
Of the salmon's mouth,
And fattening his silver gill.

3

There is Wild Wood,
A mild hood
15 To the sheep on the lea o' the down,
Where the golden furze
With its green thin spurs
Doth catch at the maiden's gown.

4

There is Newton Marsh
20 With its spear grass harsh—
A pleasant summer level
Where the maidens sweet
Of the Market Street
Do meet in the dusk to revel.

5

25 There's the barton rich
With dyke and ditch
And hedge for the thrush to live in,
And the hollow tree
For the buzzing bee,
30 And a bank for the wasp to hive in.

6

And O, and O
The daisies blow,
And the primroses are waken'd,
And the violet white
35 Sits in silver plight,
And the green bud's as long as the spike end.

7

Then who would go
Into dark Soho
And chatter with dack'd hair'd critics,

30 in] *interlined above* ⟨him⟩ *L*

40 When he can stay
For the new mown hay
And startle the dappled prickets?

## *Where be ye going, you Devon maid*

1

Where be ye going, you Devon maid,
 And what have ye there i' the basket?
Ye tight little fairy, just fresh from the dairy,
 Will ye give me some cream if I ask it?

2

5 I love your meads and I love your flowers,
 And I love your junkets mainly;
But 'hind the door, I love kissing more—
 O look not so disdainly!

3

I love your hills and I love your dales,
10 And I love your flocks a bleating—
But O on the hether to lie together
 With both our hearts a beating.

4

I'll put your basket all safe in a nook
 And your shawl I hang up on this willow,
15 And we will sigh in the daisy's eye
 And kiss on a grass green pillow.

## *Over the hill and over the dale*

Over the hill and over the dale,
 And over the bourn to Dawlish—
Where gingerbread wives have a scanty sale,
 And gingerbread nuts are smallish.

*Where be ye going.* Text from Keats's letter to Haydon, 21 March 1818 (*L*). Heading supplied by editor. 6 mainly] *interlined above* ⟨huge⟩ly *L*

*Over the hill.* Text from Keats's letter to Rice, 24 March 1818 (*L*). Heading supplied by editor.

5 Rantipole Betty she ran down a hill,
  And kick'd up her petticoats fairly.
Says I, I'll be Jack if you will be Gill—
  So she sat on the grass debonnairly.

Here's somebody coming, here's somebody coming!
10   Says I, 'tis the wind at a parley.
So without any fuss, any hawing and humming,
  She lay on the grass debonnairly.

Here's somebody here and here's somebody there!
  Says I, hold your tongue, you young gipsey.
15 So she held her tongue and lay plump and fair
  And dead as a venus tipsy.

O who wouldn't hie to Dawlish fair,
  O who wouldn't stop in a meadow?
O who would not rumple the daisies there,
20   And make the wild fern for a bed do?

## *Dear Reynolds, as last night I lay in bed*

Dear Reynolds, as last night I lay in bed,
There came before my eyes that wonted thread
Of shapes, and shadows, and remembrances,
That every other minute vex and please:
5 Things all disjointed come from north and south,
Two witch's eyes above a cherub's mouth,
Voltaire with casque and shield and habergeon,
And Alexander with his night-cap on—
Old Socrates a tying his cravat;
10 And Hazlitt playing with Miss Edgeworth's cat;
And Junius Brutus pretty well so so,
Making the best of 's way towards Soho.

  Few are there who escape these visitings—
P'rhaps one or two, whose lives have patient wings,
15 And through whose curtains peeps no hellish nose,

19 O who] *ed*; O *L*

*Dear Reynolds.* Text from Woodhouse's $W^2$ transcript. *Heading* Dear . . . bed] *ed*; To J. H. Reynolds Esq[r] $W^2$ 14 patient] *ed*; patent $W^2$

No wild boar tushes, and no mermaid's toes:
But flowers bursting out with lusty pride,
And young Æolian harps personified,
Some, Titian colours touch'd into real life.
20 The sacrifice goes on; the pontif knife
Gleams in the sun, the milk-white heifer lows,
The pipes go shrilly, the libation flows:
A white sail shews above the green-head cliff,
Moves round the point, and throws her anchor stiff.
25 The mariners join hymn with those on land.
You know the Enchanted Castle—it doth stand
Upon a rock on the border of a lake
Nested in trees, which all do seem to shake
From some old magic like Urganda's sword.
30 O Phœbus, that I had thy sacred word
To shew this castle in fair dreaming wise
Unto my friend, while sick and ill he lies.

You know it well enough, where it doth seem
A mossy place, a Merlin's hall, a dream.
35 You know the clear lake, and the little isles,
The mountains blue, and cold near neighbour rills—
All which elsewhere are but half animate,
Here do they look alive to love and hate,
To smiles and frowns; they seem a lifted mound
40 Above some giant, pulsing underground.

Part of the building was a chosen see
Built by a banish'd santon of Chaldee:
The other part two thousand years from him
Was built by Cuthbert de Saint Aldebrim;
45 Then there's a little wing, far from the sun,
Built by a Lapland witch turn'd maudlin nun—
And many other juts of aged stone
Founded with many a mason-devil's groan.

The doors all look as if they oped themselves,
50 The windows as if latch'd by fays and elves—
And from them comes a silver flash of light

29 Urganda's] *interlined above* ⟨the Witch's⟩ *W*[2] 42/43 ⟨Poor Man he left the Terrace Walls of Ur.⟩ *W*[2] (*Woodhouse gives this line on the opposite verso in W*[2], *marking its position in the text with a cross and noting "Here the following line is written and erased"*)

As from the westward of a summer's night;
Or like a beauteous woman's large blue eyes
Gone mad through olden songs and poesies.

55 See what is coming from the distance dim!
A golden galley all in silken trim!
Three rows of oars are lightening moment-whiles
Into the verdurous bosoms of those isles.
Towards the shade under the castle wall
60 It comes in silence—now 'tis hidden all.
The clarion sounds; and from a postern grate
An echo of sweet music doth create
A fear in the poor herdsman who doth bring
His beasts to trouble the enchanted spring:
65 He tells of the sweet music and the spot
To all his friends, and they believe him not.

O that our dreamings all of sleep or wake
Would all their colours from the sunset take:
From something of material sublime,
70 Rather than shadow our own soul's daytime
In the dark void of night. For in the world
We jostle—but my flag is not unfurl'd
On the admiral staff—and to philosophize
I dare not yet!—Oh never will the prize,
75 High reason, and the lore of good and ill,
Be my award. Things cannot to the will
Be settled, but they tease us out of thought.
Or is it that imagination brought
Beyond its proper bound, yet still confined,—
80 Lost in a sort of purgatory blind,
Cannot refer to any standard law
Of either earth or heaven?—It is a flaw
In happiness to see beyond our bourn—
It forces us in summer skies to mourn:
85 It spoils the singing of the nightingale.

Dear Reynolds, I have a mysterious tale
And cannot speak it. The first page I read
Upon a lampit rock of green sea weed
Among the breakers.—'Twas a quiet eve;
90 The rocks were silent—the wide sea did weave
An untumultuous fringe of silver foam

Along the flat brown sand. I was at home,
And should have been most happy—but I saw
Too far into the sea; where every maw
95 The greater on the less feeds evermore:—
But I saw too distinct into the core
Of an eternal fierce destruction,
And so from happiness I far was gone.
Still am I sick of it: and though to-day
100 I've gathered young spring-leaves, and flowers gay
Of periwinkle and wild strawberry,
Still do I that most fierce destruction see,
The shark at savage prey—the hawk at pounce,
The gentle robin, like a pard or ounce,
105 Ravening a worm.—Away ye horrid moods,
Moods of one's mind! You know I hate them well,
You know I'd sooner be a clapping bell
To some Kamschatkan missionary church,
Than with these horrid moods be left in lurch.
110 Do you get health—and Tom the same—I'll dance,
And from detested moods in new romance
Take refuge.—Of bad lines a centaine dose
Is sure enough—and so "here follows prose."

## *To J. R.*

O that a week could be an age, and we
Felt parting and warm meeting every week;
Then one poor year a thousand years would be,
The flush of welcome ever on the cheek.
5 So could we live long life in little space;
So time itself would be annihilate;
So a day's journey, in oblivious haze
To serve our joys, would lengthen and dilate.
O to arrive each Monday morn from Ind,
10 To land each Tuesday from the rich Levant,
In little time a host of joys to bind,
And keep our souls in one eternal pant!
This morn, my friend, and yester evening taught
Me how to harbour such a happy thought.

98 far was] was far *altered to* far was $W^2$

*To J. R.* Text (including heading) from the extant holograph (arbitrarily cited as *D*). 12 keep] *written over* ⟨wrap⟩ *D* 12/13 ⟨This morn and yester eve my friend has taught / Such Greediness of Pleasure⟩ *D*

# *Isabella;*
# *or,*
# *The Pot of Basil*

A STORY FROM BOCCACCIO

1

Fair Isabel, poor simple Isabel!
  Lorenzo, a young palmer in Love's eye!
They could not in the self-same mansion dwell
  Without some stir of heart, some malady;
5 They could not sit at meals but feel how well
  It soothed each to be the other by;
They could not, sure, beneath the same roof sleep
But to each other dream, and nightly weep.

2

With every morn their love grew tenderer,
10 With every eve deeper and tenderer still;
He might not in house, field, or garden stir,
  But her full shape would all his seeing fill;
And his continual voice was pleasanter
  To her, than noise of trees or hidden rill;
15 Her lute-string gave an echo of his name,
She spoilt her half-done broidery with the same.

3

He knew whose gentle hand was at the latch,
  Before the door had given her to his eyes;

*Isabella.* Text (including heading) from *1820.* Variants and other readings from Keats's draft (*D*, available from various sources—see Textual Note—for 1–96, 113–120, 193–200, 216–326, 337–342, 345–352, 361–366, 385–392, 411–504 only), the brief extracts included in Woodhouse's clerk's letterbook transcript of Keats's now lost letter to J. H. Reynolds, 27 April 1818 ($L^1$, cited for 233 and 237 only), the extant holograph fair copy (*FC*), three Woodhouse transcripts ($W^3$, $W^2$, $W^1$), and the brief extract included in Keats's lost letter to Fanny Brawne, February (?) 1820, as published in Forman (1883), IV, 153 ($L^2$, cited for 319). *Heading* Isabella . . . Boccaccio] *so 1820* (*the last four words appearing only on the half title preceding the first page of text*); The Pot of Basil *FC*, $W^3$ (*shorthand*), $W^2$; Isabella / or / The Pot of Basil $W^3$ (*longhand*), $W^1$ (*but the longhand title in* $W^3$ *and the first two words in* $W^1$ *are later additions to these MSS*); *no heading in D* 1 Fair Isabel] Fair Isabel⟨1a⟩ *D* 2 in] *interlined above* ⟨to⟩ *D* 2 eye] *interlined above* ⟨dream⟩ *D* 5 not] *added above the line in D* 6 the] each *D, FC*, $W^3$, $W^2$, $W^1$ 7 not, sure,] not sure *interlined above* ⟨not sleep⟩ *D* 9 every morn] *interlined above* ⟨restless nights⟩ *D* 10 eve] night *D* 11 He] *interlined above* ⟨They⟩ *D* 14 noise] *interlined above* ⟨sigh⟩ *FC* 15/16 ⟨She mar'd her half done broidery with his⟩ *D* 16 spoilt] ⟨mar'd⟩ spoit *D* 17 at] on *D*

And from her chamber-window he would catch
20 Her beauty farther than the falcon spies;
And constant as her vespers would he watch,
Because her face was turn'd to the same skies;
And with sick longing all the night outwear,
To hear her morning-step upon the stair.

4

25 A whole long month of May in this sad plight
Made their cheeks paler by the break of June:
"To-morrow will I bow to my delight,
To-morrow will I ask my lady's boon."—
"O may I never see another night,
30 Lorenzo, if thy lips breathe not love's tune."—
So spake they to their pillows; but, alas,
Honeyless days and days did he let pass;

5

Until sweet Isabella's untouch'd cheek
Fell sick within the rose's just domain,
35 Fell thin as a young mother's, who doth seek
By every lull to cool her infant's pain:
"How ill she is," said he, "I may not speak,
And yet I will, and tell my love all plain:
If looks speak love-laws, I will drink her tears,
40 And at the least 'twill startle off her cares."

6

So said he one fair morning, and all day
His heart beat awfully against his side;
And to his heart he inwardly did pray
For power to speak; but still the ruddy tide
45 Stifled his voice, and puls'd resolve away—
Fever'd his high conceit of such a bride,

19 her] his *D* 20 farther] farer *D* 23–24 outwear . . . stair] outwear⟨s⟩ . . . stair⟨s⟩ *D* 25 A . . . long] Through the whole *altered to* A whole long *D* 25 sad] *interlined above* ⟨sweet⟩ *D* 26 Made . . . cheeks] Made their lips *interlined above* ⟨Their cheeks were⟩ *D* 26 paler by] pale upon *altered to* paler by *D*; paler ⟨than⟩ by *FC* 26 break] *interlined above* ⟨first⟩ *D* 28/29 ⟨Said he⟩ *D* 30 lips] tongue *D*, *FC*, $W^3$; lips *interlined above* ⟨tongue⟩ $W^1$ 30 breathe] play *D*; speak *FC*, $W^3$, $W^2$, $W^1$; breathe *interlined by Taylor above* speak (*not deleted*) *in* $W^1$ 32 he] *interlined above* ⟨they⟩ *D* 33 sweet] *interlined above* ⟨young⟩ *D* 34 sick] *interlined above* ⟨thin⟩ *D* 34 within] *interlined above* ⟨upon⟩ *D* 40 least] worst *D*, *FC*, $W^3$ 40 startle] ⟨mak⟩ startle *D* 44 still] no *D*

Yet brought him to the meekness of a child:
Alas! when passion is both meek and wild!

7

So once more he had wak'd and anguished
50 A dreary night of love and misery,
If Isabel's quick eye had not been wed
To every symbol on his forehead high;
She saw it waxing very pale and dead,
And straight all flush'd; so, lisped tenderly,
55 "Lorenzo!"—here she ceas'd her timid quest,
But in her tone and look he read the rest.

8

"O Isabella, I can half perceive
That I may speak my grief into thine ear;
If thou didst ever any thing believe,
60 Believe how I love thee, believe how near
My soul is to its doom: I would not grieve
Thy hand by unwelcome pressing, would not fear
Thine eyes by gazing; but I cannot live
Another night, and not my passion shrive.

9

65 "Love! thou art leading me from wintry cold,
Lady! thou leadest me to summer clime,

48 Alas . . . wild] *written at the top of the opposite recto leaf to replace* ⟨How nigh is Love to death, both meek and wild⟩ *D* 49 So . . . he] Yet he once more (Yet *interlined above* ⟨And⟩) *D* 49 wak'd and anguished] anguished and wak'd (*but marked for transposition*) *D* 54 lisped] said too *D*; ⟨said⟩ lisped *FC* 55–56 "Lorenzo . . . rest.] "Lorenzo I would clip my ringlet hair / To make thee laugh again & debonnair— *D, FC,* $W^3$, $W^2$, *and originally* $W^1$; *Taylor deleted these lines in* $W^1$ *and substituted the 1820 wording (which he took from a pencil version by Woodhouse on the opposite verso) above them* 56/57

"Then should I be," said he, "full deified
And yet I would not have it clip it not—
For Lady I do love it, where 'tis tied
About the Neck I dote on—and that spot
That anxious dimple it doth take a pride
To play about—Aye Lady I have got
Its shadow in my heart and every sweet
Its Mistress owns there summed all complete—

*D, FC,* $W^3$, $W^2$, $W^1$ (anxious *interlined above* ⟨snowy⟩ *in the fifth line in D*); *the stanza is canceled with a light pencil stroke in* $W^2$ *and crossed out in both pencil and ink in* $W^1$ 61 My . . . its] This moment's to my *D* 62 Thy] Thine *D, FC,* $W^3$ (*made out of* This *in D*) 63 Thine] Those *D, FC,* $W^3$; Thine *made out of* Those $W^1$ 64 Another] ⟨Without their⟩ Another *D*

And I must taste the blossoms that unfold
  In its ripe warmth this gracious morning time."
So said, his erewhile timid lips grew bold,
70 And poesied with hers in dewy rhyme:
Great bliss was with them, and great happiness
Grew, like a lusty flower in June's caress.

10

Parting they seem'd to tread upon the air,
  Twin roses by the zephyr blown apart
75 Only to meet again more close, and share
  The inward fragrance of each other's heart.
She, to her chamber gone, a ditty fair
  Sang, of delicious love and honey'd dart;
He with light steps went up a western hill,
80 And bade the sun farewell, and joy'd his fill.

11

All close they met again, before the dusk
  Had taken from the stars its pleasant veil,
All close they met, all eves, before the dusk
  Had taken from the stars its pleasant veil,
85 Close in a bower of hyacinth and musk,
  Unknown of any, free from whispering tale.
Ah! better had it been for ever so,
Than idle ears should pleasure in their woe.

12

Were they unhappy then?—It cannot be—
90 Too many tears for lovers have been shed,
Too many sighs give we to them in fee,
  Too much of pity after they are dead,
Too many doleful stories do we see,
  Whose matter in bright gold were best be read;
95 Except in such a page where Theseus' spouse
Over the pathless waves towards him bows.

67 taste . . . unfold] feast on fruitage that unfolds *altered to* taste the blossoms that unfold *D* 67/68 ⟨Its blossoms young⟩ (*continuation of the original text of 67*) *D* 68 this] *made out of* the *D* 75 more] all *D*, *FC*, $W^3$, $W^2$, $W^1$ 77/78 ⟨Of happy Love sang in its⟩ *D* 78 Sang, of delicious] Did sing of happy *D*; Sung of delicious *FC* 79 a western] an western (western *made out of* eastern) *D* 86/87 ⟨O that unto the end it had been so⟩ *D* 87 Ah] O *D*

13

But, for the general award of love,
The little sweet doth kill much bitterness;
Though Dido silent is in under-grove,
100 And Isabella's was a great distress,
Though young Lorenzo in warm Indian clove
Was not embalm'd, this truth is not the less—
Even bees, the little almsmen of spring-bowers,
Know there is richest juice in poison-flowers.

14

105 With her two brothers this fair lady dwelt,
Enriched from ancestral merchandize,
And for them many a weary hand did swelt
In torched mines and noisy factories,
And many once proud-quiver'd loins did melt
110 In blood from stinging whip;—with hollow eyes
Many all day in dazzling river stood,
To take the rich-ored driftings of the flood.

15

For them the Ceylon diver held his breath,
And went all naked to the hungry shark;
115 For them his ears gush'd blood; for them in death
The seal on the cold ice with piteous bark
Lay full of darts; for them alone did seethe
A thousand men in troubles wide and dark:
Half-ignorant, they turn'd an easy wheel,
120 That set sharp racks at work, to pinch and peel.

16

Why were they proud? Because their marble founts
Gush'd with more pride than do a wretch's tears?—
Why were they proud? Because fair orange-mounts
Were of more soft ascent than lazar stairs?—
125 Why were they proud? Because red-lin'd accounts
Were richer than the songs of Grecian years?—
Why were they proud? again we ask aloud,
Why in the name of Glory were they proud?

102 this] the *FC*, *W*[3], *W*[2], *W*[1] (the *made out of* this *in W*[1]; the *subsequently altered in pencil to* this *in W*[2]) 117 alone] *interlined above* ⟨in woe⟩ *D* 117 seethe] seath *D*, *FC*; scath *W*[3], *W*[2]; scathe *originally W*[1] (*deleted there and replaced by* seeth *in an unidentified hand*)

17

130 Yet were these Florentines as self-retired
In hungry pride and gainful cowardice,
As two close Hebrews in that land inspired,
Paled in and vineyarded from beggar-spies;
The hawks of ship-mast forests—the untired
And pannier'd mules for ducats and old lies—
135 Quick cat's-paws on the generous stray-away,—
Great wits in Spanish, Tuscan, and Malay.

18

How was it these same ledger-men could spy
Fair Isabella in her downy nest?
How could they find out in Lorenzo's eye
140 A straying from his toil? Hot Egypt's pest
Into their vision covetous and sly!
How could these money-bags see east and west?—
Yet so they did—and every dealer fair
Must see behind, as doth the hunted hare.

19

145 O eloquent and famed Boccaccio!
Of thee we now should ask forgiving boon,
And of thy spicy myrtles as they blow,
And of thy roses amorous of the moon,
And of thy lilies, that do paler grow
150 Now they can no more hear thy ghittern's tune,
For venturing syllables that ill beseem
The quiet glooms of such a piteous theme.

136/137
⟨Two young Orlandos far away they seem'd,
But on a near inspect their vapid Miens—
Very alike,—at once themselves redeem'd
From all suspicion of Romantic spleens—
No fault of theirs, for their good Mother dream'd
In the longing time of Units in their teens
Of proudly-bas'd addition and of net—
And both their backs were mark'd with tare and tret.⟩
*FC, W*[3] (of *inserted above the line before* net *in the seventh line in FC*; proudly base *in the same line in W*[3]) 144 the] a *FC, W*[3] 145 and . . . Boccaccio] Boccace of green Arno *FC, W*[3], *W*[2], *and originally W*[1]; *Keats deleted the entire line in W*[1] *and substituted the 1820 wording on the opposite verso* 147 spicy] *added above the line in FC* 151–152 syllables . . . piteous] one word unseemly mean / In such a place on such a daring *FC, W*[3], *W*[2], *and originally W*[1]; *Keats canceled all of the original 151–152 in W*[1] *and substituted the 1820 wording on the opposite verso*

20

Grant thou a pardon here, and then the tale
  Shall move on soberly, as it is meet;
155 There is no other crime, no mad assail
  To make old prose in modern rhyme more sweet:
But it is done—succeed the verse or fail—
  To honour thee, and thy gone spirit greet;
To stead thee as a verse in English tongue,
160 An echo of thee in the north-wind sung.

21

These brethren having found by many signs
  What love Lorenzo for their sister had,
And how she lov'd him too, each unconfines
  His bitter thoughts to other, well nigh mad
165 That he, the servant of their trade designs,
  Should in their sister's love be blithe and glad,
When 'twas their plan to coax her by degrees
To some high noble and his olive-trees.

22

And many a jealous conference had they,
170   And many times they bit their lips alone,
Before they fix'd upon a surest way
  To make the youngster for his crime atone;
And at the last, these men of cruel clay
  Cut Mercy with a sharp knife to the bone;
175 For they resolved in some forest dim
To kill Lorenzo, and there bury him.

23

So on a pleasant morning, as he leant
  Into the sun-rise, o'er the balustrade
Of the garden-terrace, towards him they bent
180   Their footing through the dews; and to him said,
"You seem there in the quiet of content,
  Lorenzo, and we are most loth to invade
Calm speculation; but if you are wise,
Bestride your steed while cold is in the skies.

159 To . . . tongue] *Keats deleted this line in W*[1]*, substituting* Thy Muse's Vicar in the english tongue *on the opposite verso; then Taylor canceled Keats's revision, penciled "Stet" beside the deleted text, and (to make it clearer for the printer) rewrote the original line in ink above the deleted text* 168 olive] *interlined above* ⟨forest⟩ *FC*

24

185 "To-day we purpose, ay, this hour we mount
To spur three leagues towards the Apennine;
Come down, we pray thee, ere the hot sun count
His dewy rosary on the eglantine."
Lorenzo, courteously as he was wont,
190 Bow'd a fair greeting to these serpents' whine;
And went in haste, to get in readiness,
With belt, and spur, and bracing huntsman's dress.

25

And as he to the court-yard pass'd along,
Each third step did he pause, and listen'd oft
195 If he could hear his lady's matin-song,
Or the light whisper of her footstep soft;
And as he thus over his passion hung,
He heard a laugh full musical aloft;
When, looking up, he saw her features bright
200 Smile through an in-door lattice, all delight.

26

"Love, Isabel!" said he, "I was in pain
Lest I should miss to bid thee a good morrow:
Ah! what if I should lose thee, when so fain
I am to stifle all the heavy sorrow
205 Of a poor three hours' absence? but we'll gain
Out of the amorous dark what day doth borrow.
Good bye! I'll soon be back."—"Good bye!" said she:—
And as he went she chanted merrily.

27

So the two brothers and their murder'd man
210 Rode past fair Florence, to where Arno's stream

187 pray thee] pry'thee *FC*; prythee *altered to* praythee *W*³; pry thee *altered to* pray thee (*the first word apparently changed before the second was written*) *W*² 189 courteously] courteous *FC*, *W*³, *W*², *W*¹ 194 oft] soft *D* (*but see Textual Note*) 196 footstep] footsteps *D*, *FC*, *W*³ 197 thus . . . passion] *interlined above* ⟨stood from the gallery she⟩ *D* 199–200 When . . . delight.] And looking up he saw her smiling through / A little indoor Lattice, morning new— *D*; And looking up he saw her smiling through / A little indoor Lattice—— *FC*, *W*³ (smiling *interlined above* ⟨laughing⟩ *in FC*); *Woodhouse omitted both lines* (*leaving space for them*) *in W*² *and W*¹, *and in the latter MS Keats wrote in the 1820 wording, with* ⟨fair⟩ bright *at the end of 199 and* ⟨debonair⟩ all delight *at the end of 200* (*see Textual Note*) 207 I'll] I *FC*

Gurgles through straiten'd banks, and still doth fan
  Itself with dancing bulrush, and the bream
Keeps head against the freshets. Sick and wan
  The brothers' faces in the ford did seem,
215 Lorenzo's flush with love.—They pass'd the water
Into a forest quiet for the slaughter.

28

There was Lorenzo slain and buried in,
  There in that forest did his great love cease;
Ah! when a soul doth thus its freedom win,
220 It aches in loneliness—is ill at peace
As the break-covert blood-hounds of such sin:
  They dipp'd their swords in the water, and did tease
Their horses homeward, with convulsed spur,
Each richer by his being a murderer.

29

225 They told their sister how, with sudden speed,
  Lorenzo had ta'en ship for foreign lands,
Because of some great urgency and need
  In their affairs, requiring trusty hands.
Poor Girl! put on thy stifling widow's weed,
230 And 'scape at once from Hope's accursed bands;
To-day thou wilt not see him, nor to-morrow,
And the next day will be a day of sorrow.

30

She weeps alone for pleasures not to be;
  Sorely she wept until the night came on,
235 And then, instead of love, O misery!
  She brooded o'er the luxury alone:
His image in the dusk she seem'd to see,
  And to the silence made a gentle moan,
Spreading her perfect arms upon the air,
240 And on her couch low murmuring "Where? O where?"

213 Sick] *interlined above* ⟨Pale⟩ *FC* 220 is] *interlined above* ⟨as⟩ *D* 221 break] ⟨dull⟩ break *D* 221 such] *interlined above* ⟨the⟩ *D* 222 water] River *D*, *FC*, *W*[3] 228 requiring] ⟨and ba⟩ requiring *D* 228/229 ⟨And that he⟩ *D* 229 stifling] doleful *D* 233 weeps] wept *D*, *L*[1], *FC*, *W*[3] 237 His . . . to] What might have been too plainly did she *D*, *L*[1]

31

But Selfishness, Love's cousin, held not long
  Its fiery vigil in her single breast;
She fretted for the golden hour, and hung
  Upon the time with feverish unrest—
245 Not long—for soon into her heart a throng
  Of higher occupants, a richer zest,
Came tragic; passion not to be subdued,
And sorrow for her love in travels rude.

32

In the mid days of autumn, on their eves
250 The breath of Winter comes from far away,
And the sick west continually bereaves
  Of some gold tinge, and plays a roundelay
Of death among the bushes and the leaves,
  To make all bare before he dares to stray
255 From his north cavern. So sweet Isabel
By gradual decay from beauty fell,

33

Because Lorenzo came not. Oftentimes
  She ask'd her brothers, with an eye all pale,
Striving to be itself, what dungeon climes
260 Could keep him off so long? They spake a tale
Time after time, to quiet her. Their crimes
  Came on them, like a smoke from Hinnom's vale;
And every night in dreams they groan'd aloud,
To see their sister in her snowy shroud.

34

265 And she had died in drowsy ignorance,
  But for a thing more deadly dark than all;
It came like a fierce potion, drunk by chance,

242 single] ⟨native Mind⟩ single *D* 242/243 ⟨For Joy escap'd she moun'd⟩ *D* 247 passion] Passion⟨s⟩ *D* 248 And . . . rude] *successively* (*a*) Exalting her to patient Fortitude (*b*) A yearning for her Love (*c*) And Sorrow for her Love in travels rude *D* 251 the sick] from the *altered to* the sick *D* 252 Of . . . tinge] Some golden touching *altered to* Of Some gold tinge (Some *interlined above* ⟨Let [*or possibly* Set] af⟩) *D* 260 keep] bind *D* 261 Time . . . time] Month . . . Month *D*, *FC*, $W^3$ 262 on] ⟨heavy⟩ on *D* 263 night] *added above the line in D* 267 drunk] drank *D*, *FC*, $W^3$ (darank *in D*); drank *altered to* drunk $W^1$

Which saves a sick man from the feather'd pall
For some few gasping moments; like a lance,
270 Waking an Indian from his cloudy hall
With cruel pierce, and bringing him again
Sense of the gnawing fire at heart and brain.

35

It was a vision.—In the drowsy gloom,
The dull of midnight, at her couch's foot
275 Lorenzo stood, and wept: the forest tomb
Had marr'd his glossy hair which once could shoot
Lustre into the sun, and put cold doom
Upon his lips, and taken the soft lute
From his lorn voice, and past his loamed ears
280 Had made a miry channel for his tears.

36

Strange sound it was, when the pale shadow spake;
For there was striving, in its piteous tongue,
To speak as when on earth it was awake,
And Isabella on its music hung:
285 Languor there was in it, and tremulous shake,
As in a palsied Druid's harp unstrung;
And through it moan'd a ghostly under-song,
Like hoarse night-gusts sepulchral briars among.

37

Its eyes, though wild, were still all dewy bright
290 With love, and kept all phantom fear aloof
From the poor girl by magic of their light,
The while it did unthread the horrid woof
Of the late darken'd time,—the murderous spite
Of pride and avarice,—the dark pine roof

268 a . . . feather'd] the sick some moments from the *altered to* a sick man from the featherd *D* 273 drowsy] heavy *D* 275 wept: the] wept. His *D* (*but see Textual Note*) 276 which] that *D*, *FC*, *W*[3] 277 Lustre] Bright gold *D* 277 put cold] *interlined above* ⟨stampd his⟩ *D* 278 lips] ⟨soiled⟩ lips *D* 278 taken the soft] *interlined above* ⟨took the mellow⟩ *D* 279 lorn] deep *D* 279 past] ⟨down⟩ past *D* 281 sound it was] was the sound *altered to* sound it was *D* 281 pale] poor *D*, *FC*, *W*[3] 284 And] *successively* (*a*) And (*b*) When (*c*) And *D* 285 Languor . . . was] Passion there was *interlined above* ⟨And there was Love⟩ *D* 287 And] But *D*, *FC*; But *deleted and replaced in the margin by* And *W*[3]; And *written over* ⟨But⟩ *W*[2] 288 hoarse] *added above the line in D* 289 though wild] *added above the line in D* 290 fear] fears *D*

295 In the forest,—and the sodden turfed dell,
Where, without any word, from stabs he fell.

38

Saying moreover, "Isabel, my sweet!
  Red whortle-berries droop above my head,
And a large flint-stone weighs upon my feet;
300 Around me beeches and high chestnuts shed
Their leaves and prickly nuts; a sheep-fold bleat
  Comes from beyond the river to my bed:
Go, shed one tear upon my heather-bloom,
And it shall comfort me within the tomb.

39

305 "I am a shadow now, alas! alas!
  Upon the skirts of human-nature dwelling
Alone: I chant alone the holy mass,
  While little sounds of life are round me knelling,
And glossy bees at noon do fieldward pass,
310 And many a chapel bell the hour is telling,
Paining me through: those sounds grow strange to me,
And thou art distant in Humanity.

40

"I know what was, I feel full well what is,
  And I should rage, if spirits could go mad;
315 Though I forget the taste of earthly bliss,
  That paleness warms my grave, as though I had
A Seraph chosen from the bright abyss
  To be my spouse: thy paleness makes me glad;
Thy beauty grows upon me, and I feel
320 A greater love through all my essence steal."

302 river] Ano (*for* Arno) *D* 303 one] a *D*, *FC*, $W^3$ 304 it] I *D*, *FC*, $W^3$ (*the word underscored in* $W^3$, *with "q. it" in the margin*) 304 comfort me within] turn a diamond in *D*, *FC*, $W^3$, $W^2$, $W^1$ 304 the] my *D* 306/307 ⟨I moun alone⟩ *D* 306–307 dwelling‸ / Alone:] ~‸ / ~, *D*, $W^2$, $W^1$; ~; / ~, *FC*; ~‸ / ~. $W^3$ 309 And] While *D*, *FC*, $W^3$ 311 grow . . . me] to me grow strange (*but marked for transposition*) *D* 312 distant] ⟨far beyond them⟩ distant *D* 313 I feel] ⟨and now⟩ I feel *D* 314 rage] rave *D*; rage *interlined above* ⟨weep⟩ *FC* 314 spirits] shadows *D* 315 the . . . bliss] what Pleasure was a kiss *D*; the heaven of a Kiss *FC*, $W^3$, $W^2$, *and originally* $W^1$; *Keats deleted the last four words in* $W^1$ *and substituted the 1820 wording above them* 319 Thy] Your $L^2$ 320/321 ⟨The Spirit mourn'd Adieu and slow dissol'd / Into the darkness, staring the black voild⟩ (slow *interlined above* {quick}) *D*

41

The Spirit mourn'd "Adieu!"—dissolv'd, and left
The atom darkness in a slow turmoil;
As when of healthful midnight sleep bereft,
Thinking on rugged hours and fruitless toil,
325 We put our eyes into a pillowy cleft,
And see the spangly gloom froth up and boil:
It made sad Isabella's eyelids ache,
And in the dawn she started up awake;

42

"Ha! ha!" said she, "I knew not this hard life,
330 I thought the worst was simple misery;
I thought some Fate with pleasure or with strife
Portion'd us—happy days, or else to die;
But there is crime—a brother's bloody knife!
Sweet Spirit, thou hast school'd my infancy:
335 I'll visit thee for this, and kiss thine eyes,
And greet thee morn and even in the skies."

43

When the full morning came, she had devised
How she might secret to the forest hie;
How she might find the clay, so dearly prized,
340 And sing to it one latest lullaby;
How her short absence might be unsurmised,
While she the inmost of the dream would try.
Resolv'd, she took with her an aged nurse,
And went into that dismal forest-hearse.

44

345 See, as they creep along the river side,
How she doth whisper to that aged Dame,
And, after looking round the champaign wide,
Shows her a knife.—"What feverous hectic flame
Burns in thee, child?—What good can thee betide,
350 That thou should'st smile again?"—The evening came,

321 dissolv'd . . . left] *interlined above* ⟨and slow dissolv'd⟩ *D* 322 The . . . darkness] ⟨To gloom⟩ The Atom⟨s of⟩ Darkness *D* 334 hast] has *FC* 342 the dream] her dream *D* 347 champaign] Campaign *D*, *FC*, $W^2$, $W^1$; Champaign (*longhand, the* h *added afterward*) $W^3$ 350 should'st] dost *D*, *FC*, $W^3$; ⟨dost⟩ should'st $W^1$

And they had found Lorenzo's earthy bed;
The flint was there, the berries at his head.

45

Who hath not loiter'd in a green church-yard,
  And let his spirit, like a demon-mole,
355 Work through the clayey soil and gravel hard,
  To see scull, coffin'd bones, and funeral stole;
Pitying each form that hungry Death hath marr'd,
  And filling it once more with human soul?
Ah! this is holiday to what was felt
360 When Isabella by Lorenzo knelt.

46

She gaz'd into the fresh-thrown mould, as though
  One glance did fully all its secrets tell;
Clearly she saw, as other eyes would know
  Pale limbs at bottom of a crystal well;
365 Upon the murderous spot she seem'd to grow,
  Like to a native lily of the dell:
Then with her knife, all sudden, she began
To dig more fervently than misers can.

47

Soon she turn'd up a soiled glove, whereon
370   Her silk had play'd in purple phantasies,
She kiss'd it with a lip more chill than stone,
  And put it in her bosom, where it dries
And freezes utterly unto the bone
  Those dainties made to still an infant's cries:
375 Then 'gan she work again; nor stay'd her care,
But to throw back at times her veiling hair.

48

That old nurse stood beside her wondering,
  Until her heart felt pity to the core
At sight of such a dismal labouring,

352 at] o'er *D*  359 this] that *FC*, *W*[3]  365 murderous] fatal *D*  373–374 unto . . . cries] *Keats deleted* unto the bone *in W*[1], *substituting* Love's sighful throne *in the margin, and deleted all of 374 without rewriting the line; then Taylor canceled Keats's revision, penciled "Stet" beside the deleted W*[1] *text, and rewrote Keats's original lines in ink on the opposite verso*  376 veiling] vailing *W*[2], *W*[1]

380 And so she kneeled, with her locks all hoar,
And put her lean hands to the horrid thing:
Three hours they labour'd at this travail sore;
At last they felt the kernel of the grave,
And Isabella did not stamp and rave.

49

385 Ah! wherefore all this wormy circumstance?
Why linger at the yawning tomb so long?
O for the gentleness of old Romance,
The simple plaining of a minstrel's song!
Fair reader, at the old tale take a glance,
390 For here, in truth, it doth not well belong
To speak:—O turn thee to the very tale,
And taste the music of that vision pale.

50

With duller steel than the Perséan sword
They cut away no formless monster's head,
395 But one, whose gentleness did well accord
With death, as life. The ancient harps have said,
Love never dies, but lives, immortal Lord:
If Love impersonate was ever dead,
Pale Isabella kiss'd it, and low moan'd.
400 'Twas love; cold,—dead indeed, but not dethroned.

51

In anxious secrecy they took it home,
And then the prize was all for Isabel:
She calm'd its wild hair with a golden comb,
And all around each eye's sepulchral cell
405 Pointed each fringed lash; the smeared loam
With tears, as chilly as a dripping well,

382 they labour'd] were they *FC*, $W^3$, *and originally* $W^2$ *and* $W^1$; *Woodhouse altered the* $W^2$ *text in pencil to read* they labored *and Keats made the same change in ink in* $W^1$ (*see Textual Note*) 388 a] *interlined above* ⟨the⟩ *D* 392 that] this *D* 393 steel] sliver *FC*, $W^3$, $W^2$, *and originally* $W^1$; *Keats deleted* sliver than the *in* $W^1$ *and substituted* Steel than the *above the line* 394 formless monster's] foul Medusa's *FC*, $W^3$, $W^2$, *and originally* $W^1$; *Keats deleted the two words in* $W^1$ *and substituted* formless monster's *above the line* 395 one] one's *FC*, $W^3$, $W^2$, *and originally* $W^1$; *either Woodhouse or Taylor altered the* $W^1$ *text in pencil to read* one 398 Love . . . ever] ever any piece of Love was *FC*, $W^3$, $W^2$, *and originally* $W^1$; *Taylor canceled the entire line in* $W^1$, *writing* With fond caress as if it were not dead *above the line* (*see Textual Note*) 405 fringed] single *FC*, $W^3$

She drench'd away:—and still she comb'd, and kept
Sighing all day—and still she kiss'd, and wept.

52

Then in a silken scarf,—sweet with the dews
410 Of precious flowers pluck'd in Araby,
And divine liquids come with odorous ooze
Through the cold serpent-pipe refreshfully,—
She wrapp'd it up; and for its tomb did choose
A garden-pot, wherein she laid it by,
415 And cover'd it with mould, and o'er it set
Sweet basil, which her tears kept ever wet.

53

And she forgot the stars, the moon, and sun,
And she forgot the blue above the trees,
And she forgot the dells where waters run,
420 And she forgot the chilly autumn breeze;
She had no knowledge when the day was done,
And the new morn she saw not: but in peace
Hung over her sweet basil evermore,
And moisten'd it with tears unto the core.

54

425 And so she ever fed it with thin tears,
Whence thick, and green, and beautiful it grew,
So that it smelt more balmy than its peers
Of basil-tufts in Florence; for it drew
Nurture besides, and life, from human fears,
430 From the fast mouldering head there shut from view:
So that the jewel, safely casketed,
Came forth, and in perfumed leafits spread.

55

O Melancholy, linger here awhile!
O Music, Music, breathe despondingly!

414 wherein . . . by] *written beneath* ⟨that she might ever be⟩ *D* 414/415 ⟨{Close} To it and to herself⟩ (*continuation of deleted text in 414, with* To *made out of* to) *D* 415 o'er] over *D* 416 Sweet . . . wet.] *the single word* tombs (*see 413*) *appears in the margin of D beside this line* 417 and sun] the Sun *D, FC* 423 her] the *D* 425–432 And . . . spread.] *written after 504 on the last page of D* 425 And . . . ever] *interlined above* ⟨For many a day she⟩ (For *written over* {She}) *D* 426 thick] tall *D* 427 smelt . . . than] flourish'd sweet above *D* 428 in . . . drew] *interlined above* ⟨that florence nights bedew⟩ *D* 430 mouldering] moulding *D* 431 the jewel] her ⟨treasure⟩ jewel *D*

435 O Echo, Echo, from some sombre isle,
Unknown, Lethean, sigh to us—O sigh!
Spirits in grief, lift up your heads, and smile;
Lift up your heads, sweet Spirits, heavily,
And make a pale light in your cypress glooms,
440 Tinting with silver wan your marble tombs.

56

Moan hither, all ye syllables of woe,
From the deep throat of sad Melpomene!
Through bronzed lyre in tragic order go,
And touch the strings into a mystery;
445 Sound mournfully upon the winds and low;
For simple Isabel is soon to be
Among the dead: She withers, like a palm
Cut by an Indian for its juicy balm.

57

O leave the palm to wither by itself;
450 Let not quick Winter chill its dying hour!—
It may not be—those Baälites of pelf,
Her brethren, noted the continual shower
From her dead eyes; and many a curious elf,
Among her kindred, wonder'd that such dower
455 Of youth and beauty should be thrown aside
By one mark'd out to be a noble's bride.

58

And, furthermore, her brethren wonder'd much
Why she sat drooping by the basil green,
And why it flourish'd, as by magic touch;
460 Greatly they wonder'd what the thing might mean:
They could not surely give belief, that such
A very nothing would have power to wean

435 sombre] lonely *D* 436 Unknown, Lethean, sigh] Ionian—unknown—⟨one⟩ sigh *D* 437 in] of *D* 438 heads] eyes *D* 440 Tinting] *interlined above* ⟨Endging⟩ *D* 443 bronzed] *interlined above* ⟨the large⟩ *D* 450 quick . . . chill] Hot lightning sear *D* 452 noted] *interlined above* ⟨marking⟩ *D* 453 From] Of *D*, *FC*, $W^3$ 456 a] a⟨n⟩ *D* 457 wonder'd] marvel'd *D* 460 Greatly] ⟨Util no⟩ Greatly *D* 461 They] *interlined above* ⟨Perplex'ed⟩ *D* 461 give] *interlined above* ⟨have⟩ *D* 462 would] could *D* 462 power] *added above the line in D*

Her from her own fair youth, and pleasures gay,
And even remembrance of her love's delay.

59

465 Therefore they watch'd a time when they might sift
  This hidden whim; and long they watch'd in vain;
For seldom did she go to chapel-shrift,
  And seldom felt she any hunger-pain;
And when she left, she hurried back, as swift
470   As bird on wing to breast its eggs again;
And, patient as a hen-bird, sat her there
Beside her basil, weeping through her hair.

60

Yet they contriv'd to steal the basil-pot,
  And to examine it in secret place:
475 The thing was vile with green and livid spot,
  And yet they knew it was Lorenzo's face:
The guerdon of their murder they had got,
  And so left Florence in a moment's space,
Never to turn again.—Away they went,
480 With blood upon their heads, to banishment.

61

O Melancholy, turn thine eyes away!
  O Music, Music, breathe despondingly!
O Echo, Echo, on some other day,
  From isles Lethean, sigh to us—O sigh!
485 Spirits of grief, sing not your "Well-a-way!"
  For Isabel, sweet Isabel, will die;
Will die a death too lone and incomplete,
Now they have ta'en away her basil sweet.

463 her own] own *D*  463 gay] *interlined above a short deleted word ending in* er—*possibly* ⟨ever⟩ *D*  464 remembrance] Rembrance *interlined above* ⟨Lorenzo's⟩ *D*  464 of . . . delay] *interlined above* ⟨of Lorenzo's stay⟩ *D*  465 sift] *interlined above* ⟨seach⟩ *D*  471 sat] set $W^2$, $W^1$  471 there] *successively* (*a*) down (*b*) still (*c*) there *D*  472 her basil] the basil *D*, *FC*, $W^3$  475 thing] *interlined above* ⟨head⟩ *D*  476 And yet they] But they well *D*  478–479 space, . . . again.—Away] ~∧ . . . ~∧ away *D*; ~— . . . ~∧ away *FC*; ~∧ . . . ~. Away $W^3$  482 breathe despondingly] slumber silently *D*  484 Lethean] hesperrian *D*  485 your] you *FC*, $W^3$, $W^2$, $W^1$ (*a pencil note by Woodhouse*—"*q* your"—*appears on the opposite verso in* $W^2$)  486 sweet] ⟨bereft of⟩ sweet *D*  488 Now] For *D*  488 ta'en] stolen *D*

62

Piteous she look'd on dead and senseless things,
490 Asking for her lost basil amorously;
And with melodious chuckle in the strings
Of her lorn voice, she oftentimes would cry
After the pilgrim in his wanderings,
To ask him where her basil was; and why
495 'Twas hid from her: "For cruel 'tis," said she,
"To steal my basil-pot away from me."

63

And so she pined, and so she died forlorn,
Imploring for her basil to the last.
No heart was there in Florence but did mourn
500 In pity of her love, so overcast.
And a sad ditty of this story born
From mouth to mouth through all the country pass'd:
Still is the burthen sung—"O cruelty,
To steal my basil-pot away from me!"

489 on] at *D*, *FC*, $W^3$ 490 lost] sweet *D* 492 lorn . . . cry] *interlined above* ⟨dissolving accents would she cry⟩ *D* 494/495 ⟨They kept it from her⟩ *D* 495 her] *added above the line in D* (*and the preceding word* from *written over what appears to have been* ⟨for me⟩) 496/497 ⟨And so folorn she was and so she pind⟩ (folorn she was *made out of* she died folorn) *D* 499 No . . . Florence] *deleted in D and nothing substituted* 499 did mourn] *interlined above* ⟨well mournd⟩ *D* 500 In] for *written over* ⟨At⟩ *D*; At *FC*, $W^3$ 500 of] at *D* 501 ditty‸ . . . born‸] ~, . . . ~, *FC*, $W^2$ 502 through] *written over* ⟨o'er⟩ *D* 503 the] that *D* 503 burthen] Ditty *D*; Burden *FC*, $W^3$, $W^2$ *After* 504 end of The Pot of Basil *FC*

## *Mother of Hermes! and still youthful Maia*

Mother of Hermes! and still youthful Maia!
May I sing to thee
As thou wast hymned on the shores of Baiæ?
Or may I woo thee
5 In earlier Sicilian? or thy smiles
Seek, as they once were sought, in Grecian isles,
By bards who died content in pleasant sward,
Leaving great verse unto a little clan?
O give me their old vigour, and unheard,
10 Save of the quiet primrose, and the span
Of heaven, and few ears
Rounded by thee, my song should die away,
Content as theirs,
Rich in the simple worship of a day.

## *To Homer*

Standing aloof in giant ignorance,
Of thee I hear and of the Cyclades,
As one who sits ashore and longs perchance
To visit dolphin-coral in deep seas.
5 So wast thou blind;—but then the veil was rent,
For Jove uncurtain'd heaven to let thee live,
And Neptune made for thee a spumy tent,
And Pan made sing for thee his forest-hive;
Aye on the shores of darkness there is light,
10 And precipices show untrodden green,
There is a budding morrow in midnight,
There is a triple sight in blindness keen;
Such seeing hadst thou, as it once befel
To Dian, Queen of Earth, and Heaven, and Hell.

*Mother of Hermes.* Text from Woodhouse's clerk's letterbook transcript of Keats's now lost letter to J. H. Reynolds, 3 May 1818. Heading supplied by editor.

*To Homer.* Text from Brown's transcript (*CB*). Variants from Woodhouse's $W^2$ transcript. *Heading* To] *ed*; Sonnet, / To *CB*, $W^2$ 3 sits . . . perchance] *interlined by Keats above* ⟨strives against a level glance⟩ *CB* 6 For] And $W^2$

## *Give me your patience, sister, while I frame*

Give me your patience, sister, while I frame
Exact in capitals your golden name:
Or sue the fair Apollo and he will
Rouse from his heavy slumber and instill
5 Great love in me for thee and Poesy.
Imagine not that greatest mastery
And kingdom over all the realms of verse
Nears more to heaven in aught than when we nurse
And surety give to love and brotherhood.

10 Anthropophagi in Othello's mood,
Ulysses stormed, and his enchanted belt
Glow with the muse, but they are never felt
Unbosom'd so and so eternal made,
Such tender incense in their laurel shade,
15 To all the regent sisters of the Nine,
As this poor offering to you, sister mine.

Kind sister! aye, this third name says you are;
Enchanted has it been the Lord knows where.
And may it taste to you like good old wine,
20 Take you to real happiness and give
Sons, daughters, and a home like honied hive.

## *Sweet, sweet is the greeting of eyes*

Sweet, sweet is the greeting of eyes,
And sweet is the voice in its greeting,
When adieux have grown old and goodbyes
Fade away where old time is retreating.

*Give me your patience.* Text from Keats's letter to George and Georgiana Keats, 17–27 September 1819 ($L^2$). Variants and other readings from his letter to the same recipients, 27, 28 June 1818 ($L^1$). *Heading* Give . . . frame] *ed; no heading in* $L^1$, $L^2$ 2 Exact in capitals] Enitials vese-wise of $L^1$ 4 heavy slumber] Slumber heavy $L^1$ 9 And . . . to] *interlined above* ⟨In its vast safety⟩ $L^1$ 11/12 ⟨By the sweet Muse are never never felt⟩ $L^1$ 14 tender] selfsame $L^1$ 16 you] thee $L^1$ 18 Enchanted] Enhanced $L^1$ 19 And‸] Ah! $L^1$ 20 to] ⟨the⟩ to $L^1$

*Sweet, sweet is the greeting.* Text from Keats's letter to George and Georgiana Keats, 27, 28 June 1818 (*L*). Heading supplied by editor. There is a stanza division between 4 and 5.

5 Warm the nerve of a welcoming hand,
And earnest a kiss on the brow,
When we meet over sea and o'er land
Where furrows are new to the plough.

## *On Visiting the Tomb of Burns*

The town, the churchyard, and the setting sun,
  The clouds, the trees, the rounded hills all seem,
  Though beautiful, cold—strange—as in a dream
I dreamed long ago. Now new begun,
5 The short-lived, paly summer is but won
  From winter's ague, for one hour's gleam;
  Though saphire warm, their stars do never beam;
All is cold beauty; pain is never done
For who has mind to relish, Minos-wise,
10 The real of beauty, free from that dead hue
    Sickly imagination and sick pride
  Cast wan upon it! Burns! with honour due
    I have oft honoured thee. Great shadow, hide
Thy face—I sin against thy native skies.

## *Old Meg she was a gipsey*

Old Meg she was a gipsey,
  And liv'd upon the moors;
Her bed it was the brown heath turf,
  And her house was out of doors.

5 Her apples were swart blackberries,
  Her currants pods o' broom,

7 o'er] *added above the line in L*

*On Visiting the Tomb of Burns.* Text (including heading) from Jeffrey's transcript of Keats's now lost letter to Tom Keats, 29 June–2 July 1818 (*JJ*). 4 ago. Now new begun,] *ed*; ~, now ~ ~^ *JJ* 7 Though] *ed*; Through *JJ* 11 Sickly] *ed*; Fickly *JJ* 12 Cast] *ed*; *blank space in JJ, with the note "An illegible word occurs here"* 13 thee. Great shadow,] *originally* ~, great ~; *JJ* (*Jeffrey then changed the comma after* thee *to a full stop, but did not alter the rest of the line*)

*Old Meg.* Text from Keats's letter to Fanny Keats, 2–5 July 1818 (*L*[1]). Variants from his letter to Tom Keats, 3–9 July 1818 (*L*[2]), and the version published in *PDWJ*, 22 November 1838. *Heading* Old . . . gipsey] *ed*; Meg Merrilies. A Ballad, written for the amusement of his young sister *PDWJ*; *no heading in L*[1], *L*[2]

Her wine was dew o' the wild white rose,
  Her book a churchyard tomb.

Her brothers were the craggy hills,
10  Her sisters larchen trees—
Alone with her great family
  She liv'd as she did please.

No breakfast had she many a morn,
  No dinner many a noon,
15 And 'stead of supper she would stare
  Full hard against the moon.

But every morn of woodbine fresh
  She made her garlanding,
And every night the dark glen yew
20  She wove and she would sing.

And with her fingers old and brown
  She plaited mats o' rushes,
And gave them to the cottagers
  She met among the bushes.

25 Old Meg was brave as Margaret Queen
  And tall as Amazon:
An old red blanket cloak she wore;
  A chip hat had she on.
God rest her aged bones somewhere—
30  She died full long agone!

## *There was a naughty boy*

There was a naughty boy
  A naughty boy was he
He would not stop at home
  He could not quiet be—
5    He took

7 o'] of *PDWJ*  13 had] $L^2$, *PDWJ*; has $L^1$  13 morn] *interlined above* ⟨day⟩ $L^1$  21 with] ⟨sometimes⟩ with $L^1$  22 o'] of *PDWJ*

*There was a naughty boy.* Text from Keats's letter to Fanny Keats, 2–5 July 1818 (*L*). Heading supplied by editor.

In his knapsack
A book
Full of vowels
And a shirt
10 With some towels—
A slight cap
For night cap—
A hair brush
Comb ditto
15 New stockings
For old ones
Would split O!
This knapsack
Tight at 's back
20 He rivetted close
And follow'd his nose
To the north
To the north
And follow'd his nose
25 To the north—

There was a naughty boy
And a naughty boy was he
For nothing would he do
But scribble poetry—
30 He took
An inkstand
In his hand
And a pen
Big as ten
35 In the other
And away
In a pother
He ran
To the mountains
40 And fountains
And ghostes
And postes
And witches
And ditches
45 And wrote
In his coat
When the weather

Was cool
Fear of gout
50 And without
When the weather
Was warm—
Och the charm
When we choose
55 To follow one's nose
To the north
To the north
To follow one's nose to the north!

There was a naughty boy
60 And a naughty boy was he
He kept little fishes
In washing tubs three
In spite
Of the might
65 Of the maid
Nor afraid
Of his granny-good—
He often would
Hurly burly
70 Get up early
And go
By hook or crook
To the brook
And bring home
75 Miller's thumb
Tittlebat
Not over fat
Minnows small
As the stall
80 Of a glove
Not above
The size
Of a nice
Little baby's
85 Little finger—
O he made
'Twas his trade

48 cool] ⟨warm⟩ cool *L* 52 warm] *interlined above* ⟨cool⟩ *L*

Of fish a pretty kettle
A kettle—a kettle
90 Of fish a pretty kettle
A kettle!

There was a naughty boy
And a naughty boy was he
He ran away to Scotland
95 The people for to see—
There he found
That the ground
Was as hard
That a yard
100 Was as long,
That a song
Was as merry,
That a cherry
Was as red—
105 That lead
Was as weighty
That fourscore
Was as eighty
That a door
110 Was as wooden
As in England—
So he stood in
His shoes
And he wonder'd
115 He wonder'd
He stood in his
Shoes and he wonder'd—

## *Ah! ken ye what I met the day*

Ah! ken ye what I met the day
Out owre the mountains,
A coming down by craggis grey
An' mossie fountains?

*Ah! ken ye what.* Text from Keats's letter to Tom Keats, 10–14 July 1818 (*L*). Heading supplied by editor. 3 by] *written over* ⟨the⟩ *L*

5 Ah goud hair'd Marie, yeve I pray
Ane minute's guessing—
For that I met upon the way
Is past expressing.
As I stood where a rocky brig
10 A torrent crosses,
I spied upon a misty rig
A troup o' horses—
And as they trotted down the glen
I sped to meet them,
15 To see if I might know the men,
To stop and greet them.
First Willie on his sleek mare came
At canting gallop—
His long hair rustled like a flame
20 On board a shallop.
Then came his brother Rab and then
Young Peggy's mither,
And Peggy too—adown the glen
They went togither.
25 I saw her wrappit in her hood
Fra wind and raining—
Her cheek was flush wi' timid blood
'Twixt growth and waning.
She turn'd her dazed head full oft,
30 For thence her brithers
Came riding with her bridegroom soft
An' mony ithers.
Young Tam came up an' eyed me quick
With reddened cheek—
35 Braw Tam was daffed like a chick,
He coud na speak.
Ah Marie, they are all gane hame
Through blustring weather,
An' every heart is full on flame
40 An' light as feather.
Ah! Marie, they are all gone hame
Fra happy wedding,
Whilst I—Ah is it not a shame?
Sad tears am shedding.

26/27 ⟨There was a blush upon her⟩ *L* 33 Young] *written over* ⟨An⟩ *L* 39 full] *interlined above* ⟨light on⟩ *L*

## *To Ailsa Rock*

Hearken, thou craggy ocean pyramid,
Give answer by thy voice, the sea fowls' screams!
When were thy shoulders mantled in huge streams?
When from the sun was thy broad forehead hid?
5 How long is't since the mighty power bid
Thee heave to airy sleep from fathom dreams—
Sleep in the lap of thunder or sunbeams,
Or when grey clouds are thy cold coverlid?
Thou answer'st not, for thou art dead asleep;
10 Thy life is but two dead eternities,
The last in air, the former in the deep—
First with the whales, last with the eagle skies;
Drown'd wast thou till an earthquake made thee steep—
Another cannot wake thy giant size!

## *This mortal body of a thousand days*

This mortal body of a thousand days
Now fills, O Burns, a space in thine own room,
Where thou didst dream alone on budded bays,
Happy and thoughtless of thy day of doom!
5 My pulse is warm with thine old barley-bree,
My head is light with pledging a great soul,
My eyes are wandering, and I cannot see,
Fancy is dead and drunken at its goal;
Yet can I stamp my foot upon thy floor,
10 Yet can I ope thy window-sash to find
The meadow thou hast tramped o'er and o'er,—
Yet can I think of thee till thought is blind,—
Yet can I gulp a bumper to thy name,—
O smile among the shades, for this is fame!

*To Ailsa Rock.* Text (including heading) from Keats's letter to Tom Keats, 10–14 July 1818 (*L*). Variants from the version published in Hunt's *Literary Pocket-Book* (*P-B*). *Heading* To] Sonnet to *P-B* 2 by] from *P-B* 10 is but] *interlined above* ⟨has been⟩ ⟨will be⟩ *L*

*This mortal body.* Text from *1848*. *Heading* This . . . days] *ed*; Sonnet *1848*

## *All gentle folks who owe a grudge*

All gentle folks who owe a grudge
  To any living thing,
Open your ears and stay your trudge
  Whilst I in dudgeon sing.

5 The gadfly he hath stung me sore—
  O may he ne'er sting you!
But we have many a horrid bore
  He may sting black and blue.

Has any here an old grey mare
10   With three legs all her store?
O put it to her buttocks bare
  And straight she'll run on four.

Has any here a lawyer suit
  Of 1743?
15 Take lawyer's nose and put it to't
  And you the end will see.

Is there a man in Parliament
  Dumfounder'd in his speech?
O let his neighbour make a rent
20   And put one in his breech.

O Lowther, how much better thou
  Hadst figur'd t' other day,
When to the folks thou mad'st a bow
  And hadst no more to say,

25 If lucky gadfly had but ta'en
  His seat upon thine a—e,
And put thee to a little pain
  To save thee from a worse.

Better than Southey it had been,
30   Better than Mr. D——,

*All gentle folks.* Text from Keats's letter to Tom Keats, 17–21 July 1818 (*L*). Heading supplied by editor. 15 nose] *added above the line in L*

Better than Wordsworth too, I ween,
Better than Mr. V——.

Forgive me pray, good people all,
For deviating so;
35 In spirit sure I had a call—
And now I on will go.

Has any here a daughter fair
Too fond of reading novels,
Too apt to fall in love with care
40 And charming Mister Lovels?

O put a gadfly to that thing
She keeps so white and pert—
I mean the finger for the ring—
And it will breed a wert.

45 Has any here a pious spouse
Who seven times a day
Scolds as King David pray'd, to chouse
And have her holy way?

O let a gadfly's little sting
50 Persuade her sacred tongue
That noises are a common thing
But that her bell has rung.

And as this is the summum bo-
Num of all conquering,
55 I leave withouten wordes mo
The gadfly's little sting.

## *Of late two dainties were before me plac'd*

Of late two dainties were before me plac'd,
Sweet, holy, pure, sacred, and innocent,
From the ninth sphere to me benignly sent
That gods might know my own particular taste.

*Of late two dainties.* Text from Keats's letter to Tom Keats, 17–21 July 1818 (*L*). Heading supplied by editor.

5 First the soft bag-pipe mourn'd with zealous haste;
The Stranger next with head on bosom bent
Sigh'd; rueful again the piteous bag-pipe went;
Again the Stranger sighings fresh did waste.
O bag-pipe, thou didst steal my heart away;
10 O Stranger, thou my nerves from pipe didst charm;
O bag-pipe, thou didst reassert thy sway;
Again thou Stranger gav'st me fresh alarm—
Alas! I could not choose. Ah! my poor heart,
Mumchance art thou with both obliged to part.

## *There is a joy in footing slow across a silent plain*

There is a joy in footing slow across a silent plain,
Where patriot battle has been fought, when glory had the gain;
There is a pleasure on the heath where Druids old have been,
Where mantles grey have rustled by and swept the nettles green:
5 There is a joy in every spot made known by times of old,
New to the feet, although the tale a hundred times be told:
There is a deeper joy than all, more solemn in the heart,
More parching to the tongue than all, of more divine a smart,
When weary feet forget themselves upon a pleasant turf,
10 Upon hot sand, or flinty road, or sea shore iron scurf,
Toward the castle or the cot where long ago was born
One who was great through mortal days and died of fame unshorn.
Light hether-bells may tremble then, but they are far away;
Woodlark may sing from sandy fern,—the sun may hear his lay;
15 Runnels may kiss the grass on shelves and shallows clear,

8 sighings . . . waste] sigh'd in discontent *altered to* sighings fresh did waste *L*

*There is a joy.* Text from Keats's letter to Bailey, 18, 22 July 1818 (*L*). Variants and other readings from the earlier extant holograph (arbitrarily cited as *D*) and the *Examiner* version (*Ex*). *Heading* There . . . plain] *ed*; Lines written in the highlands after a visit to Burns's Country *D* (*the title written at the end of the text*); Lines Written in the Scotch Highlands *Ex*; *no heading in L* 1 joy] charm *D*, *Ex* 1 silent] ⟨grand camp [*the beginning of* campaign]⟩ silent *D* 2 when] where *Ex* 5 There . . . spot] In every spot there is a Joy (*but marked for transposition*) *D* 5 by times] in days *Ex* 6 the tale] each tale *D*, *Ex* 8 the] *not in D* 9 feet] steps *D*, *Ex* 9 upon] ⟨towards⟩ upon *D* 13 Light] *interlined above* ⟨Blue⟩ *D* 15 shelves and] *added above the line in D*

But their low voices are not heard, though come on travels dear;
Blood-red the sun may set behind black mountain peaks;
Blue tides may sluice and drench their time in caves and weedy creeks;
Eagles may seem to sleep wing-wide upon the air;
20 Ring doves may fly convuls'd across to some high cedar'd lair;
But the forgotten eye is still fast wedded to the ground—
As palmer's that with weariness mid-desert shrine hath found.
At such a time the soul's a child, in childhood is the brain;
Forgotten is the worldly heart—alone, it beats in vain.
25 Aye, if a madman could have leave to pass a healthful day,
To tell his forehead's swoon and faint when first began decay,
He might make tremble many a man whose spirit had gone forth
To find a bard's low cradle place about the silent north.
Scanty the hour and few the steps beyond the bourn of care,
30 Beyond the sweet and bitter world—beyond it unaware;
Scanty the hour and few the steps, because a longer stay
Would bar return and make a man forget his mortal way.
O horrible! to lose the sight of well remember'd face,
Of brother's eyes, of sister's brow, constant to every place;
35 Filling the air, as on we move, with portraiture intense,
More warm than those heroic tints that fill a painter's sense,
When shapes of old come striding by and visages of old,
Locks shining black, hair scanty grey, and passions manifold.
No, no, that horror cannot be—for at the cable's length
40 Man feels the gentle anchor pull and gladdens in its strength.
One hour, half ideot, he stands by mossy waterfall,
But in the very next he reads his soul's memorial:
He reads it on the mountain's height, where chance he may sit down
Upon rough marble diadem, that hill's eternal crown.
45 Yet be the anchor e'er so fast, room is there for a prayer
That man may never lose his mind on mountains bleak and bare;

16 on] *interlined above* ⟨from⟩ *D* 21 is] ⟨keeps⟩ is *D* 21 wedded] lidded *D, Ex* 25 if a] if the *altered to* if a *D* 26 forehead's] forehead *Ex* 27 man] one *D, Ex* (*interlined above* ⟨Man⟩ *in D*) 28 bard's] *Ex adds an asterisk and a footnote:* *Burns. 29 Scanty] *made out of* Short is (canty *interlined above* ⟨hort is⟩) *D* 36 fill] pain *D, Ex* 38 Locks] *interlined above* ⟨Hair⟩ *D* 44 rough] *interlined above* ⟨its⟩ *D* 45 the] his *D, Ex* (*interlined above* ⟨the⟩ ⟨our⟩ *in D*) 46 lose] *Ex*; loose *D, L* 46 bleak] black *D, Ex*

That he may stray league after league some great birthplace
to find,
And keep his vision clear from speck, his inward sight unblind.

## *Not Aladdin magian*

Not Aladdin magian
Ever such a work began;
Not the Wizard of the Dee
Ever such a dream could see;
5 Not St. John in Patmos' isle,
In the passion of his toil,
When he saw the churches seven,
Golden aisled, built up in heaven,
Gazed at such a rugged wonder.
10 As I stood its roofing under,
Lo! I saw one sleeping there
On the marble cold and bare,
While the surges washed his feet
And his garments white did beat
15 Drench'd about the sombre rocks;
On his neck his well-grown locks,
Lifted dry above the main,
Were upon the curl again.
"What is this and what art thou?"
20 Whisper'd I and touch'd his brow.
"What art thou and what is this?"
Whisper'd I and strove to kiss
The spirit's hand to wake his eyes.
Up he started in a trice.

47 birthplace] *D*, *Ex* (bithplace *in D*); Berthplace *L* 48 speck] *added above the line in D*

*Not Aladdin magian.* Text from Keats's letter to Tom Keats, 23, 26 July 1818 ($L^1$). Variants and other readings from Woodhouse's $W^2$ transcript, Keats's letter to George and Georgiana Keats, 17–27 September 1819 ($L^2$), Brown's transcript for Severn (*CB*), and the versions published in *PDWJ* and *1848*. *Heading* Not . . . magian] *ed*; ⟨Lycidas's⟩ Lines / On visiting "Staffa"—⟨the Giant's Causeway in Ireland⟩ (*the last five words deleted in pencil*) $W^2$; On Fingal's Cave. A Fragment *CB*; Fingal's Cave in Staffa.—A Fragment *PDWJ*; *no heading in* $L^1$, $L^2$, *1848* (*in* $L^2$ *the lines are introduced with the sentence "Incipit Poema Lyrica de Staffa tractans"*) 4 such a] $W^2$, $L^2$, *CB*, *PDWJ*, *1848*; such $L^1$ 7–8 When . . . heaven,] *not in* $L^2$ 9 at] on $L^2$, *CB* 17 dry] ⟨high⟩ dry $L^2$ 19 what art] who art $L^2$ 23 his eyes] *interlined above* ⟨him up⟩ $L^1$

25 "I am Lycidas," said he,
"Fam'd in funeral minstrelsy.
This was architected thus
By the great Oceanus;
Here his mighty waters play
30 Hollow organs all the day;
Here by turns his dolphins all,
Finny palmers great and small,
Come to pay devotion due—
Each a mouth of pearls must strew.
35 Many a mortal of these days
Dares to pass our sacred ways,
Dares to touch audaciously
This cathedral of the sea.
I have been the pontif priest
40 Where the waters never rest,
Where a fledgy sea bird choir
Soars for ever; holy fire
I have hid from mortal man;
Proteus is my sacristan.
45 But the stupid eye of mortal
Hath pass'd beyond the rocky portal;
So for ever will I leave
Such a taint, and soon unweave
All the magic of the place.
50 'Tis now free to stupid face,
To cutters and to fashion boats,
To cravats and to petticoats.
The great sea shall war it down,
For its fame shall not be blown
55 At every farthing quadrille dance."
So saying with a spirit's glance
He dived—

27 architected] architectur'd *CB, PDWJ, 1848* 29 Here] He $L^2$ 31 by . . . dolphins] his dolphins, one and *CB* 34/35 ⟨Many a Mortal comes to see / This Cathedrall of the S⟩ $L^1$ 35–37 a mortal . . . Dares . . . Dares to touch] Mortals . . . Dare . . . Dare to see $L^2$ 39–40 I . . . rest,] *not in CB* 40 the] these *PDWJ* 41 Where] Here *CB* 43 I have] Have I $L^2$ 44 Proteus] ⟨Old⟩ Proteus $L^1$ 45–57 But . . . dived—] *not in* $L^2$ 45 stupid] dulled *CB, PDWJ, 1848* 46 Hath] Has $W^2$, *CB* 46 pass'd beyond] dar'd to pass *CB* 46 beyond] *added above the line in* $L^1$ 50–55 'Tis . . . dance."] *not in CB, PDWJ, 1848 (56–57 were also originally not in CB; these have been added by another hand in pencil)*

## *Read me a lesson, Muse, and speak it loud*

Read me a lesson, Muse, and speak it loud
  Upon the top of Nevis, blind in mist!
I look into the chasms, and a shroud
  Vaprous doth hide them; just so much I wist
5 Mankind do know of hell: I look o'erhead,
  And there is sullen mist; even so much
Mankind can tell of heaven: mist is spread
  Before the earth beneath me; even such,
Even so vague is man's sight of himself.
10  Here are the craggy stones beneath my feet;
Thus much I know, that, a poor witless elf,
  I tread on them; that all my eye doth meet
Is mist and crag—not only on this height,
But in the world of thought and mental might.

## *Upon my life, Sir Nevis, I am piqu'd*

MRS. C——

Upon my life, Sir Nevis, I am piqu'd
That I have so far panted, tugg'd, and reek'd
To do an honor to your old bald pate
And now am sitting on you just to bate,
5 Without your paying me one compliment.
Alas, 'tis so with all, when our intent
Is plain, and in the eye of all mankind
We fair ones show a preference, too blind!
You gentlemen immediately turn tail—
10 O let me then my hapless fate bewail!
Ungrateful baldpate, have I not disdain'd
The pleasant valleys—have I not, mad brain'd,
Deserted all my pickles and preserves,
My china closet too—with wretched nerves

*Read me a lesson.* Text from Keats's letter to Tom Keats, 3, 6 August 1818. Heading supplied by editor.

*Upon my life.* Text from Keats's letter to Tom Keats, 3, 6 August 1818 (*L*). Heading supplied by editor. 8 a] *added above the line in L* 9 gentlemen] *ed*; Gentleman *L*

15 To boot—say, wretched ingrate, have I not
Left my soft cushion chair and caudle pot?
'Tis true I had no corns—no! thank the fates,
My shoemaker was always Mr. Bates.
And if not Mr. Bates, why I'm not old!
20 Still dumb, ungrateful Nevis—still so cold!

(Here the lady took some more whiskey and was putting even more to her lips when she dashed it to the ground, for the mountain began to grumble; which continued for a few minutes before he thus began,)

BEN NEVIS

What whining bit of tongue and mouth thus dares
Disturb my slumber of a thousand years?
Even so long my sleep has been secure,
And to be so awaked I'll not endure.
25 Oh pain—for since the eagle's earliest scream
I've had a damn'd confounded ugly dream,
A nightmare sure—What, madam, was it you?
It cannot be! My old eyes are not true!
Red-Crag,* my spectacles! Now let me see!
30 Good heavens, lady, how the gemini
Did you get here? O I shall split my sides!
I shall earthquake——

MRS. C——

Sweet Nevis, do not quake, for though I love
Your honest countenance all things above,
35 Truly I should not like to be convey'd
So far into your bosom—gentle maid
Loves not too rough a treatment, gentle sir;
Pray thee be calm and do not quake nor stir,
No, not a stone, or I shall go in fits—

* A domestic of Ben's.

15 wretched] *added above the line in L* 16 Left] *ed*; Let *L* 16 cushion] ⟨ch⟩ cushion *L* *Prose after* 20 dashed it] *ed*; dashed *L* 21 bit] *interlined above* ⟨burst⟩ *L* 27 you] *interlined above* ⟨true⟩ *L*

BEN NEVIS

40 I must—I shall—I meet not such tit bits,
I meet not such sweet creatures every day.
By my old night cap, night cap night and day,
I must have one sweet buss—I must and shall!
Red-Crag!—What, madam, can you then repent
45 Of all the toil and vigour you have spent
To see Ben Nevis and to touch his nose?
Red-Crag, I say! O I must have you close!
Red-Crag, there lies beneath my farthest toe
A vein of sulphur—go, dear Red-Crag, go—
50 And rub your flinty back against it—budge!
Dear madam, I must kiss you, faith I must!
I must embrace you with my dearest gust!
Blockhead,* d'ye hear—Blockhead, I'll make her feel.
There lies beneath my east leg's northern heel
55 A cave of young earth dragons—well, my boy,
Go thither quick and so complete my joy.
Take you a bundle of the largest pines,
And where the sun on fiercest phosphor shines
Fire them and ram them in the dragons' nest;
60 Then will the dragons fry and fizz their best,
Until ten thousand now no bigger than
Poor alligators, poor things of one span,
Will each one swell to twice ten times the size
Of northern whale; then for the tender prize—
65 The moment then—for then will Red-Crag rub
His flinty back, and I shall kiss and snub
And press my dainty morsel to my breast.
Blockhead, make haste!

O Muses, weep the rest—
The lady fainted and he thought her dead,
70 So pulled the clouds again about his head
And went to sleep again. Soon she was rous'd
By her affrighted servants. Next day, hous'd
Safe on the lowly ground, she bless'd her fate
That fainting fit was not delayed too late.

* Another domestic of Ben's.

## *On Some Skulls in Beauley Abbey, near Inverness*

"I shed no tears;
Deep thought, or awful vision, I had none;
By thousand petty fancies I was crossed."
Wordsworth

"And mock'd the dead bones that lay scatter'd by."
Shakspeare

1

In silent barren synod met
Within these roofless walls, where yet
The shafted arch and carved fret
Cling to the ruin,
5 The brethren's skulls mourn, dewy wet,
Their creed's undoing.

2

The mitred ones of Nice and Trent
Were not so tongue-tied,—no, they went
Hot to their Councils, scarce content
10 With orthodoxy;
But ye, poor tongueless things, were meant
To speak by proxy.

3

Your chronicles no more exist,
Since Knox, the revolutionist,
15 Destroy'd the work of every fist
That scrawl'd black letter;
Well! I'm a craniologist,
And may do better.

4

This skull-cap wore the cowl from sloth,
20 Or discontent, perhaps from both;
And yet one day, against his oath,
He tried escaping,

*On Some Skulls.* Text (including heading and epigraphs) from Brown's fair copy (*CB*). Variants from the version published in *NMM*. *Heading* On] Stanzas on *NMM* *Epigraphs* "I . . . Shakspeare] *not in NMM* 3 shafted] sever'd *NMM* 14 Since] For *NMM*

For men, though idle, may be loth
To live on gaping.

5

25 A toper this! he plied his glass
More strictly than he said the mass,
And lov'd to see a tempting lass
Come to confession,
Letting her absolution pass
30 O'er fresh transgression.

6

This crawl'd through life in feebleness,
Boasting he never knew excess,
Cursing those crimes he scarce could guess,
Or feel but faintly,
35 With prayers that heaven would cease to bless
Men so unsaintly.

7

Here's a true churchman! he'd affect
Much charity, and ne'er neglect
To pray for mercy on th' elect,
40 But thought no evil
In sending heathen, Turk, and sect
All to the devil!

8

Poor skull, thy fingers set ablaze,
With silver saint in golden rays,
45 The holy missal; thou didst craze
'Mid bead and spangle,
While others pass'd their idle days
In coil and wrangle.

9

Long time this sconce a helmet wore,
50 But sickness smites the conscience sore;
He broke his sword, and hither bore
His gear and plunder,

47 idle] idler *NMM*

Took to the cowl,—then rav'd and swore
At his damn'd blunder!

10

55 This lily colour'd skull, with all
The teeth complete, so white and small,
Belong'd to one whose early pall
A lover shaded;
He died ere superstition's gall
60 His heart invaded.

11

Ha! here is "undivulged crime"!
Despair forbad his soul to climb
Beyond this world, this mortal time
Of fever'd sadness,
65 Until their monkish pantomime
Dazzled his madness!

12

A younger brother this! a man
Aspiring as a Tartar khan,
But, curb'd and baffled, he began
70 The trade of frightening;
It smack'd of power!—and here he ran
To deal heaven's lightning.

13

This ideot-skull belong'd to one,
A buried miser's only son,
75 Who, penitent ere he'd begun
To taste of pleasure,
And hoping heaven's dread wrath to shun,
Gave hell his treasure.

14

Here is the forehead of an ape,
80 A robber's mark,—and near the nape
That bone, fie on't, bears just the shape
Of carnal passion;

55 colour'd] ⟨liver'd⟩ colour'd *CB*

Ah! he was one for theft and rape,
In monkish fashion!

15

85 This was the porter!—he could sing,
Or dance, or play, do any thing,
And what the friars bade him bring,
They ne'er were balk'd of;
Matters not worth remembering,
90 And seldom talk'd of.

16

Enough! why need I further pore?
This corner holds at least a score,
And yonder twice as many more
Of reverend brothers;
95 'Tis the same story o'er and o'er,—
They're like the others!

## *Nature withheld Cassandra in the skies*

Nature withheld Cassandra in the skies
For meet adornment a full thousand years;
She took their cream of beauty, fairest dyes,
And shaped and tinted her above all peers.
5 Love meanwhile held her dearly with his wings,
And underneath their shadow charm'd her eyes
To such a richness, that the cloudy kings
Of high Olympus utter'd slavish sighs.
When I beheld her on the earth descend,
10 My heart began to burn—and only pains,

91 further] farther *NMM*

*Nature withheld Cassandra.* Text from the extant holograph (arbitrarily cited as *FC*). Variants from two Woodhouse transcripts (*W*³, *W*²), the transcript by Charlotte Reynolds (*CR*), and *1848*. *Heading* Nature . . . skies] *ed*; Sonnet 2ᵈ *W*³; Sonnet translated from Ronsard *CR*; *no heading in FC, W*², *1848* 2 meet] more *W*³, *W*², *CR, 1848* 3 beauty,] Beauty's‸ *1848* 5 Love . . . held] Meanwhile Love kept *W*³, *W*², *CR, 1848* 6 charm'd] filled *W*³, *W*², *CR, 1848* 7 To] With *W*³, *W*², *CR, 1848* 7 richness] ⟨dea [*or possibly* hea]⟩ richness *FC* 9 I . . . earth] from the heavens I saw her first *W*³, *W*², *CR, 1848* 9 descend] descend⟨ed⟩ *FC* 10 began . . . only] took fire—and only burning *W*³, *W*², *CR, 1848* 10 and . . . pains] *interlined above* ⟨my head to daze⟩ *FC*

They were my pleasures, they my sad life's end;
Love pour'd her beauty into my warm veins.

## *Fragment of Castle-builder*

CASTLE-BUILDER

* * * * * * *

In short, convince you that however wise
You may have grown from convent libraries,
I have, by many yards at least, been carding
A longer skein of wit in Convent Garden.

BERNADINE

5 A very Eden that same place must be!
Pray what demesne? Whose lordship's legacy?
What, have you convents in that Gothic isle?
Pray pardon me, I cannot help but smile—

* * * * * * *

CASTLE-BUILDER

Sir, Convent Garden is a monstrous beast;
10 From morning, four o'clock, to twelve at noon,
It swallows cabbages without a spoon,
And then, from twelve till two, this Eden made is
A promenade for cooks and ancient ladies;
And then for supper, 'stead of soup and poaches,
15 It swallows chairmen, damns, and hackney coaches.
In short, sir, 'tis a very place for monks,
For it containeth twenty thousand punks,
Which any man may number for his sport,
By following fat elbows up a court.

* * * * * * *

20 In such like nonsense would I pass an hour
With random friar, or rake upon his tour,

11 sad life's] life's sad *W*[3], *W*[2], *CR, 1848* *After* 12 ⟨feelt it in my sacred⟩ *FC*

*Fragment of Castle-builder.* Text (including heading) from Woodhouse's *W*[2] transcript. Variants from *1848* (heading and 24–71 only). *Heading* of] of the *1848* 1 *s.p.* Castle-builder] *ed*; *not in W*[2]

Or one of few of that imperial host
Who came unmaimed from the Russian frost.
To-night I'll have my friar,—let me think
25 About my room,—I'll have it in the pink;
It should be rich and sombre, and the moon,
Just in its mid-life in the midst of June,
Should look through four large windows, and display
Clear, but for golden fishes in the way,
30 Their glassy diamonding on Turkish floor;
The tapers keep aside an hour and more,
To see what else the moon alone can shew;
While the night breeze doth softly let us know
My terrace is well bowered with oranges.
35 Upon the floor the dullest spirit sees
A guitar-ribband—and a lady's glove
Beside a crumple-leaved tale of love;
A tambour frame, with Venus sleeping there,
All finish'd but some ringlets of her hair;
40 A viol, bow strings torn, cross-wise upon
A glorious folio of Anacreon;
A skull upon a mat of roses lying,
Ink'd purple with a song concerning dying;
An hour glass on the turn, amid the trails
45 Of passion-flower;—just in time there sails
A cloud across the moon,—the lights bring in!
And see what more my phantasy can win.
It is a gorgeous room, but somewhat sad;
The draperies are so as though they had
50 Been made for Cleopatra's winding sheet;
And opposite the stedfast eye doth meet
A spacious looking-glass, upon whose face,
In letters raven-sombre, you may trace
Old "Mene, Mene, Tekel, Upharsin."
55 Greek busts and statuary have ever been
Held by the finest spirits fitter far
Than vase grotesque and Siamesian jar;
Therefore 'tis sure a want of Attic taste,
That I should rather love a Gothic waste
60 Of eye-sight on cinque coloured potter's clay
Than on the marble fairness of old Greece.
My table coverlets of Jason's fleece

29 golden fishes] gold-fish vases *1848* 31 and] *interlined above* ⟨or⟩ $W^2$ 44 on] ⟨up⟩on $W^2$

And black Numidian sheep wool should be wrought,
Gold, black, and heavy, from the lama brought.
65 My ebon sofa should delicious be
With down from Leda's cygnet progeny:
My pictures all Salvator's, save a few
Of Titian's portraiture, and one, though new,
Of Haydon's in its fresh magnificence.
70 My wine—O good! 'tis here at my desire,
And I must sit to supper with my friar.

* * * * * * *

## *And what is Love?—It is a doll dress'd up*

And what is Love?—It is a doll dress'd up
For idleness to cosset, nurse, and dandle;
A thing of soft misnomers, so divine
That silly youth doth think to make itself
5 Divine by loving, and so goes on
Yawning and doating a whole summer long,
Till Miss's comb is made a pearl tiara,
And common Wellingtons turn Romeo boots;
Till Cleopatra lives at Number Seven,
10 And Anthony resides in Brunswick Square.
Fools! if some passions high have warm'd the world,
If queens and soldiers have play'd high for hearts,
It is no reason why such agonies
Should be more common than the growth of weeds.
15 Fools! make me whole again that weighty pearl
The Queen of Egypt melted, and I'll say
That ye may love in spite of beaver hats.

## *'Tis the "witching time of night"*

'Tis the "witching time of night"—
Orbed is the moon and bright,

65 sofa] sofa⟨s⟩ $W^2$; sofas *1848*   69 fresh] *added above the line in* $W^2$

*And what is Love.* Text from Woodhouse's $W^2$ transcript. Variants from *1848*.   *Heading* And . . . up] *ed*; Modern Love *1848*; *no heading in* $W^2$   9 Till] Then *1848*   12 high] deep *1848*

*'Tis the "witching time."* Text from Keats's letter to George and Georgiana Keats, 14–31 October 1818 (*L*). Heading supplied by editor.

And the stars they glisten, glisten,
Seeming with bright eyes to listen.
5 For what listen they?
For a song and for a charm—
See they glisten in alarm,
And the moon is waxing warm
To hear what I shall say.
10 Moon, keep wide thy golden ears;
Hearken, stars, and hearken, spheres;
Hearken, thou eternal sky—
I sing an infant's lullaby,
A pretty lullaby!
15 Listen, listen, listen, listen,
Glisten, glisten, glisten, glisten,
And hear my lullaby!
Though the rushes that will make
Its cradle still are in the lake;
20 Though the linnen then that will be
Its swathe is on the cotton tree;
Though the woollen that will keep
It warm is on the silly sheep;
Listen, stars' light, listen, listen,
25 Glisten, glisten, glisten, glisten,
And hear my lullaby!
Child, I see thee! Child, I've found thee,
Midst of the quiet all around thee!
Child, I see thee! Child, I spy thee,
30 And thy mother sweet is nigh thee!
Child, I know thee! Child no more,
But a Poet *ever*more.
See, see the lyre, the lyre,
In a flame of fire,
35 Upon the little cradle's top
Flaring, flaring, flaring,
Past the eyesight's bearing—
Awake it from its sleep,
And see if it can keep
40 Its eyes upon the blaze.
Amaze, amaze!
It stares, it stares, it stares;
It dares what no one dares;

20 linnen] ⟨f⟩ linnen *L*   28 the . . . all] *successively* (*a*) quiet all (*b*) quiet all the (*c*) the quiet all *L*   29 see thee] see you *altered to* see thee *L*

It lifts its little hand into the flame
45 Unharm'd, and on the strings
Paddles a little tune and sings
With dumb endeavour sweetly!
Bard art thou completely!
Little child
50 O' the western wild,
Bard art thou completely!—
Sweetly, with dumb endeavour,
A Poet now or never!
Little child
55 O' the western wild,
A Poet now or never!

## *Where's the Poet? Show him! show him*

Where's the Poet? Show him! show him!
Muses nine, that I may know him!
'Tis the man who with a man
  Is an equal, be he king,
5 Or poorest of the beggar-clan,
  Or any other wondrous thing
A man may be 'twixt ape and Plato;
  'Tis the man who with a bird,
Wren or eagle, finds his way to
10   All its instincts;—he hath heard
The lion's roaring, and can tell
  What his horny throat expresseth;
And to him the tiger's yell
  Comes articulate, and presseth
15 On his ear like mother-tongue;
* * * * * * * * *

## *Fancy*

Ever let the Fancy roam,
Pleasure never is at home:

*Where's the Poet.* Text from Brown's transcript (*CB*). *Heading* Where's . . . show him] *ed*; Fragment *CB*

*Fancy.* Text (including heading) from *1820*. Variants and other readings from Keats's letter to George and Georgiana Keats, 16 December 1818–4 January 1819 (*L*), and the transcripts by Dilke (*CWD*) and Brown (*CB*). *Heading* Fancy] Ode, to Fancy *CB*; *no heading in L, CWD*

At a touch sweet Pleasure melteth,
Like to bubbles when rain pelteth;
5 Then let winged Fancy wander
Through the thought still spread beyond her:
Open wide the mind's cage-door,
She'll dart forth, and cloudward soar.
O sweet Fancy! let her loose;
10 Summer's joys are spoilt by use,
And the enjoying of the spring
Fades as does its blossoming;
Autumn's red-lipp'd fruitage too,
Blushing through the mist and dew,
15 Cloys with tasting: What do then?
Sit thee by the ingle, when
The sear faggot blazes bright,
Spirit of a winter's night;
When the soundless earth is muffled,
20 And the caked snow is shuffled
From the ploughboy's heavy shoon;
When the Night doth meet the Noon
In a dark conspiracy
To banish Even from her sky.
25 Sit thee there, and send abroad,
With a mind self-overaw'd,
Fancy, high-commission'd:—send her!
She has vassals to attend her:
She will bring, in spite of frost,
30 Beauties that the earth hath lost;
She will bring thee, all together,
All delights of summer weather;
All the buds and bells of May,
From dewy sward or thorny spray;
35 All the heaped autumn's wealth,
With a still, mysterious stealth:
She will mix these pleasures up
Like three fit wines in a cup,
And thou shalt quaff it:—thou shalt hear
40 Distant harvest-carols clear;

6 Through the thought] Towards heaven *L, CWD, CB* 12 does] doth *L, CB* 15 tasting] kissing *L, CWD, CB* 16 by the] in an *L, CWD* 18 winter's] winter *L* 20 snow] show *CB* 24 Even . . . her] vesper . . . the *L* 28 She has] She'll have *L, CWD, CB* 29 bring, in] bring thee *L, CWD* 30 hath] has *L* 33 buds and bells] faery buds *L* 34 From] On *L, CWD, CB* 34 dewy . . . thorny] sping turf or scented *L* 38 a] *interlined above* ⟨one⟩ *CB*

Rustle of the reaped corn;
Sweet birds antheming the morn:
And, in the same moment—hark!
'Tis the early April lark,
45 Or the rooks, with busy caw,
Foraging for sticks and straw.
Thou shalt, at one glance, behold
The daisy and the marigold;
White-plum'd lilies, and the first
50 Hedge-grown primrose that hath burst;
Shaded hyacinth, alway
Sapphire queen of the mid-May;
And every leaf, and every flower
Pearled with the self-same shower.
55 Thou shalt see the field-mouse peep
Meagre from its celled sleep;
And the snake all winter-thin
Cast on sunny bank its skin;
Freckled nest-eggs thou shalt see
60 Hatching in the hawthorn-tree,
When the hen-bird's wing doth rest
Quiet on her mossy nest;
Then the hurry and alarm
When the bee-hive casts its swarm;
65 Acorns ripe down-pattering,
While the autumn breezes sing.

Oh, sweet Fancy! let her loose;
Every thing is spoilt by use:
Where's the cheek that doth not fade,
70 Too much gaz'd at? Where's the maid
Whose lip mature is ever new?
Where's the eye, however blue,
Doth not weary? Where's the face
One would meet in every place?

43–44 hark! / 'Tis] $\sim_\wedge$ / To *L, CWD*; ~! / To *CB* 45 Or] And *L, CWD, CB* 50 Hedge-grown] Hedgerow *L, CWD* 54 self-same] same soft *L, CWD* 55 peep] creep *L* 57–58 thin . . . skin] shrank / Cast its skin on sunny bank *L, CWD, CB* 59 thou shalt] shalt thou *L* 62 her] its *L* 63 Then] When *CWD* 66/67 For the same sleek throated mouse / To store up in its winter house. (*following a comma or no punctuation at the end of 66*) *L, CWD, CB* 68 thing] joy *L*; sweet *CWD, CB* 68/69 Every pleasure, every joy— / Not a Mistress but doth cloy. *L, CWD, CB* 73 Doth] Does *CWD*

75 Where's the voice, however soft,
One would hear so very oft?
At a touch sweet Pleasure melteth
Like to bubbles when rain pelteth.
Let, then, winged Fancy find
80 Thee a mistress to thy mind:
Dulcet-eyed as Ceres' daughter,
Ere the God of Torment taught her
How to frown and how to chide;
With a waist and with a side
85 White as Hebe's, when her zone
Slipt its golden clasp, and down
Fell her kirtle to her feet,
While she held the goblet sweet,
And Jove grew languid.—Break the mesh
90 Of the Fancy's silken leash;
Quickly break her prison-string
And such joys as these she'll bring.—
Let the winged Fancy roam,
Pleasure never is at home.

76 so very] too oft and *L, CWD, CB* 89 And . . . mesh]
And Jove grew languid—Mistress fair,
Thou shalt have that tressed hair
Adonis tangled all for spite;
And the mouth he would not kiss,
And the treasure he would miss;
And the hand he would not press,
And the warmth he would distress,
O the Ravishment—the Bliss!
Fancy has her there she is—
Never fulsome, ever new,
There she steps! and tell me who
Has a Mistress to divine?
Be the palate ne'er so fine
She cannot sicken.
Break the Mess *L*
*CWD and CB agree substantively with L except in the third line from the end (where they have* so divine); *they present the final two half-lines as a single line, and have* mesh (*which is presumably what Keats intended in L*) *at the end* 90/91 Where she's tether'd to the heart— (*following a comma or no punctuation at the end of 90*) *L, CWD, CB* 91 Quickly] Quick *CWD*

## *Bards of passion and of mirth*

Bards of passion and of mirth,
Ye have left your souls on earth!
Have ye souls in heaven too,
Double-lived in regions new?
5 Yes, and those of heaven commune
With the spheres of sun and moon;
With the noise of fountains wond'rous,
And the parle of voices thund'rous;
With the whisper of heaven's trees
10 And one another, in soft ease
Seated on Elysian lawns
Brows'd by none but Dian's fawns;
Underneath large blue-bells tented,
Where the daisies are rose-scented,
15 And the rose herself has got
Perfume which on earth is not;
Where the nightingale doth sing
Not a senseless, tranced thing,
But divine melodious truth;
20 Philosophic numbers smooth;
Tales and golden histories
Of heaven and its mysteries.

Thus ye live on high, and then
On the earth ye live again;
25 And the souls ye left behind you
Teach us, here, the way to find you,
Where your other souls are joying,
Never slumber'd, never cloying.
Here, your earth-born souls still speak
30 To mortals, of their little week;

*Bards of passion.* Text from *1820.* Variants and other readings from the holograph at Keats House, Hampstead (arbitrarily cited as *D*), Keats's letter to George and Georgiana Keats, 16 December 1818–4 January 1819 (*L*), and transcripts by Brown (*CB*) and Woodhouse ($W^2$). *Heading* Bards . . . mirth] *ed*; Ode *CB*, $W^2$, *1820*; *no heading in D, L* 4/5 ⟨With the earth ones I am talking⟩ *D* 5–6 those . . . commune . . . sun and moon] that . . . communes . . . Suns and Moons *altered to* those . . . commune . . . Sun and Moon *D* 10 another] another's *D*, *L*, *CB*, $W^2$ 13 Underneath] ⟨Where⟩ Underneath *D* 16 which] that *L* 19–20 divine . . . smooth] melodious truth divine / Philosophic numbers fine *D*, *L*, *CB*, $W^2$ 21 Tales] *interlined above* ⟨Stories⟩ *D* 23 high] Earth *L* 29 souls] *interlined above* ⟨lives⟩ *D* 30 their] the *D*, *L*, *CB*, $W^2$

Of their sorrows and delights;
Of their passions and their spites;
Of their glory and their shame;
What doth strengthen and what maim.
35 Thus ye teach us, every day,
Wisdom, though fled far away.

Bards of passion and of mirth,
Ye have left your souls on earth!
Ye have souls in heaven too,
40 Double-lived in regions new!

## *Spirit here that reignest*

Spirit here that reignest!
Spirit here that painest!
Spirit here that burneth!
Spirit here that mourneth!
5 Spirit! I bow
My forehead low,
Enshaded with thy pinions!
Spirit! I look,
All passion struck,
10 Into thy pale dominions!

Spirit here that laughest!
Spirit here that quaffest!
Spirit here that danceth!
Noble soul that pranceth!
15 Spirit! with thee
I join in the glee,
While nudging the elbow of Momus!
Spirit! I flush
With a Bacchanal blush,
20 Just fresh from the banquet of Comus!

30/31 They must sojourn with their cares; *D*, *L*, *CB*, *W*² 39 have] ***underscored in W***²

*Spirit here that reignest.* Text from Brown's transcript (*CB*). Variants and a canceled reading from the extant holograph (arbitrarily cited as *D*). *Heading* Spirit . . . reignest] *ed*; Song *CB*; *no heading in D* 7 pinions] *interlined above* ⟨wings⟩ *D* 17 While] A *D*

## *I had a dove, and the sweet dove died*

I had a dove, and the sweet dove died,
And I have thought it died of grieving;
O what could it grieve for? Its feet were tied
With a silken thread of my own hand's weaving:
5 Sweet little red feet! why would you die?
Why would you leave me, sweet bird, why?
You liv'd alone on the forest tree,
Why, pretty thing, could you not live with me?
I kiss'd you oft, and gave you white pease;
10 Why not live sweetly as in the green trees?

## *Hush, hush, tread softly, hush, hush, my dear*

1

Hush, hush, tread softly, hush, hush, my dear,
All the house is asleep, but we know very well
That the jealous, the jealous old baldpate may hear,
Though you've padded his night-cap, O sweet Isabel.
5 Though your feet are more light than a fairy's feet,
Who dances on bubbles where brooklets meet—
Hush, hush, tread softly, hush, hush, my dear,
For less than a nothing the jealous can hear.

2

No leaf doth tremble, no ripple is there
10 On the river—all's still, and the night's sleepy eye

*I had a dove.* Text from Woodhouse's $W^2$ transcript. Variants from Keats's letter to George and Georgiana Keats, 16 December 1818–4 January 1819 (*L*). *Heading* I . . . died] *ed*; Song $W^2$; *no heading in L* 3 grieve . . . were] mourn for? it was *L* 5 would] did *L* 6 bird] dove *L* 9 gave] I gave *L*

*Hush, hush, tread softly.* Text from Fanny Brawne's transcript (*FB*). Variants and other readings from the extant holograph (arbitrarily cited as *D*), the transcripts by Brown (*CB*, with 21–24 in Milnes's hand), Dilke (*CWD*, lacking the last word of 22 and the final two lines), and Woodhouse ($W^3$, $W^2$), and the versions published in *Hood's Magazine* and *1848*. *Heading* Hush . . . dear] *ed*; Song *CB, CWD,* $W^2$, *FB, Hood's, 1848*; *no heading in D,* $W^3$ 1 softly, hush] softly! ⟨breathe lightly!⟩ hush *D* 1 hush, hush, my] tread gently, my $W^3$ 2 but we] and you $W^3$ 3 jealous old] jealous, ⟨the jealous⟩ old *D* 3 may] can *Hood's* 4 O] my $W^3$, $W^2$ 6 Who] That $W^3$, *Hood's* 7 Hush, hush (*first two words*)] Yet hush $W^3$ 7 tread softly] soft tiptoe *D, CB, CWD,* $W^3$, $W^2$, *1848* (⟨tread tiptoe!⟩ soft tiptoe *in D*) 9 No leaf] No leaf *altered to* Not a leaf $W^3$ 9 doth] ⟨in the tree⟩ doth *D* 10 On] In $W^3$ 10 still] hush'd $W^3$

Closes up, and forgets all its Lethean care,
  Charmed to death by the drone of the humming may fly.
    And the moon, whether prudish or complaisant,
    Hath fled to her bower, well knowing I want
15 No light in the darkness, no torch in the gloom,
But my Isabel's eyes and her lips pulped with bloom.

3

Lift the latch, ah gently! ah tenderly, sweet,
  We are dead if that latchet gives one little chink.
Well done—now those lips and a flowery seat:
20 The old man may sleep, and the planets may wink;
    The shut rose shall dream of our loves and awake
    Full blown, and such warmth for the morning take;
The stockdove shall hatch her soft brace and shall coo,
While I kiss to the melody, aching all through.

## *Ah! woe is me! poor Silver-wing*

Ah! woe is me! poor Silver-wing!
  That I must chaunt thy lady's dirge,
And death to this fair haunt of spring,
  Of melody, and streams of flowery verge,—
5   Poor Silver-wing! Ah! woe is me!
      That I must see
These blossoms snow upon thy lady's pall!
  Go, pretty page, and in her ear
  Whisper that the hour is near!

11 all] *not in Hood's* 11 Lethean] ⟨empire and⟩ lethean *D* 14 Hath] Has *D, CB, CWD, $W^{2}$, 1848* 14 her] the $W^{2}$ 15 light] torch $W^{3}$ 15 darkness] dusk *D, CB, CWD, $W^{3}$, $W^{2}$, 1848* (*interlined above* ⟨dark⟩ *in $W^{3}$*) 15 no torch] and no light $W^{3}$ 15 gloom] ⟨warm summer⟩ gloom (*the deletion made in pencil*) *D* 16 eyes] eye $W^{3}$, $W^{2}$ 16 lips] lip $W^{2}$ 17 ah . . . ah] oh . . . oh *Hood's* 17 gently! ah] gently! ⟨Ah softly!⟩ O *D* 18 chink] clink *D, CB, CWD, $W^{3}$, $W^{2}$, 1848* 19 lips and] lips, ⟨now those eyes⟩ and *D* 20 sleep] *D, CB, CWD, $W^{3}$, $W^{2}$, 1848* (*in $W^{3}$ all of 20 is written in pencil*); dream *FB, Hood's* 21 shall] *D, CB* (*in Milnes's hand*), *CWD, $W^{3}$, $W^{2}$, 1848*; may *FB, Hood's* 21 our] *interlined above* ⟨her⟩ *FB* 22 morning] morning's *D, CWD, $W^{3}$, $W^{2}$* (mornings *in D*) 23 hatch . . . coo] ⟨hatch her soft brace and {above our heads}⟩ coo (*the deletions made in pencil*) *D*; hatch her soft twin-eggs and coo $W^{3}$, $W^{2}$ (soft *added above the line in $W^{2}$*); hatch his soft twin-eggs and coo *CB* (*in Milnes's hand*), *1848*

*Ah! woe is me.* Text from Brown's transcript (*CB*). *Heading* Ah . . . wing] *ed*; Faery Song *CB*

10 Softly tell her not to fear
Such calm favonian burial!
Go, pretty page, and soothly tell,—
The blossoms hang by a melting spell,
And fall they must, ere a star wink thrice
15 Upon her closed eyes,
That now in vain are weeping their last tears,
At sweet life leaving, and these arbours green,—
Rich dowry from the spirit of the spheres,—
Alas! poor queen!

## *The Eve of St. Agnes*

1

St. Agnes' Eve—Ah, bitter chill it was!
The owl, for all his feathers, was a-cold;
The hare limp'd trembling through the frozen grass,
And silent was the flock in woolly fold:
5 Numb were the Beadsman's fingers, while he told
His rosary, and while his frosted breath,
Like pious incense from a censer old,
Seem'd taking flight for heaven, without a death,
Past the sweet Virgin's picture, while his prayer he saith.

2

10 His prayer he saith, this patient, holy man;
Then takes his lamp, and riseth from his knees,
And back returneth, meagre, barefoot, wan,
Along the chapel aisle by slow degrees:
The sculptur'd dead, on each side, seem to freeze,
15 Emprison'd in black, purgatorial rails:
Knights, ladies, praying in dumb orat'ries,
He passeth by; and his weak spirit fails
To think how they may ache in icy hoods and mails.

3

Northward he turneth through a little door,
20 And scarce three steps, ere Music's golden tongue
Flatter'd to tears this aged man and poor;
But no—already had his deathbell rung;
The joys of all his life were said and sung:
His was harsh penance on St. Agnes' Eve:
25 Another way he went, and soon among

*The Eve of St. Agnes.* Text (including heading) from *1820.* Variants and other readings from Keats's draft (*D*, extant for 64–378 only), two Woodhouse transcripts ($W^2$ and $W^1$, our source for the draft's missing 1–63), and George Keats's transcript (*GK*). The apparatus also includes Woodhouse's variants (cited as $W^a$) noted in $W^2$ from the lost fair copy that George Keats subsequently transcribed. *Heading* The . . . Agnes] Saint Agnes' Eve $W^2$, $W^1$, *GK* 1 chill] cold $W^2$, $W^1$ 4 was] were $W^1$ 4 woolly] sheltered $W^2$ ($W^1$ *has* woolly *penciled in a blank space in the text and* sheltered? *penciled on the opposite verso*) 7 pious] *not in GK* (*only*) 7 from] in $W^2$, $W^1$ (*GK only* = *1820*) 9 while] as $W^a$, *GK* 9, 10 prayer] prayers $W^2$, $W^1$ 14 seem] seem'd $W^1$ 25 went] turn'd $W^2$, $W^1$

Rough ashes sat he for his soul's reprieve,
And all night kept awake, for sinners' sake to grieve.

4

That ancient Beadsman heard the prelude soft;
And so it chanc'd, for many a door was wide,
30 From hurry to and fro. Soon, up aloft,
The silver, snarling trumpets 'gan to chide:
The level chambers, ready with their pride,
Were glowing to receive a thousand guests:
The carved angels, ever eager-eyed,
35 Star'd, where upon their heads the cornice rests,
With hair blown back, and wings put cross-wise on their breasts.

5

At length burst in the argent revelry,
With plume, tiara, and all rich array,
Numerous as shadows haunting fairily
40 The brain, new stuff'd, in youth, with triumphs gay
Of old romance. These let us wish away,
And turn, sole-thoughted, to one Lady there,
Whose heart had brooded, all that wintry day,
On love, and wing'd St. Agnes' saintly care,
45 As she had heard old dames full many times declare.

26 Rough] Black *W*², *W*¹ 27 sake] souls *W*², *W*¹ 27/28

But there are ears may hear sweet melodies,
And there are eyes to brighten festivals,
And there are feet for nimble minstrelsies,
And many a lip that for the red wine calls.—
Follow, then follow to the illumined halls,
Follow me youth—and leave the Eremite—
Give him a tear—then trophied banneral,
And many a brilliant tasseling of light,
Shall droop from arched ways this high Baronial night.

*W*², *W*¹; *subsequently canceled with a single vertical stroke in W*² (= *W*ᵃ *reading) and omitted in GK* 30 fro . . . up] fro:—and now *W*², *W*¹ 32 The level] The high-lamp'd *W*ᵃ; High-lamped *GK* 33 Were glowing] Seem'd anxious *W*², *W*¹ 37 burst . . . revelry] step . . . revelers *W*², *W*¹ 38 plume . . . all] tiara, and plume, and *W*ᵃ, *GK* (tiard *in GK*) 39–42 Numerous . . . there]

Ah what are they? the idle pulse scarce stirs,
The muse should never make the spirit gay,
Away, bright dulness, laughing fools, away,—
And let me tell of one sweet lady there *W*², *W*¹

45 times] time *W*ᵃ, *GK*

6

They told her how, upon St. Agnes' Eve,
Young virgins might have visions of delight,
And soft adorings from their loves receive
Upon the honey'd middle of the night,
50 If ceremonies due they did aright;
As, supperless to bed they must retire,
And couch supine their beauties, lily white;
Nor look behind, nor sideways, but require
Of heaven with upward eyes for all that they desire.

7

55 Full of this whim was thoughtful Madeline:
The music, yearning like a god in pain,
She scarcely heard: her maiden eyes divine,
Fix'd on the floor, saw many a sweeping train
Pass by—she heeded not at all: in vain
60 Came many a tiptoe, amorous cavalier,
And back retir'd, not cool'd by high disdain;
But she saw not: her heart was otherwhere:
She sigh'd for Agnes' dreams, the sweetest of the year.

8

She danc'd along with vague, regardless eyes,
65 Anxious her lips, her breathing quick and short:
The hallow'd hour was near at hand: she sighs
Amid the timbrels, and the throng'd resort
Of whisperers in anger, or in sport;

48 from] of $W^2$, $W^1$ 48 loves] Love's $W^2$; love *GK* (*there is no* $W^a$ *reading*) 52 couch] lay $W^2$, $W^1$ 53 require] enquire *GK* (*only*) 54/55
'Twas said her future lord would there appear
Offering, as sacrifice—all in the dream—
Delicious food, even to her lips brought near,
Viands, and wine, and fruit, and sugar'd cream,
To touch her palate with the fine extreme
Of relish: then soft music heard, and then
More pleasures follow'd in a dizzy stream
Palpable almost: then to wake again
Warm in the virgin morn, no weeping Magdalen. $W^a$, *GK*
57 She . . . heard] Touch'd not her heart $W^2$, $W^1$ 64 regardless] uneager *D*, $W^2$, $W^1$, *GK* 64 eyes] *interlined above* ⟨look⟩ *D* 65 Anxious . . . short] *interlined above* ⟨Her anxious {lips} mouth full pulp'd with rosy thought{s}⟩ *D* 66 hallow'd] *added above the line in D* 66 she] ⟨and⟩ she *D* 67 resort] report $W^2$, $W^1$ (*both subsequently corrected to* resort) 68 or] and $W^a$, *GK*

'Mid looks of love, defiance, hate, and scorn,
70 Hoodwink'd with faery fancy; all amort,
Save to St. Agnes and her lambs unshorn,
And all the bliss to be before to-morrow morn.

9

So, purposing each moment to retire,
She linger'd still. Meantime, across the moors,
75 Had come young Porphyro, with heart on fire
For Madeline. Beside the portal doors,
Buttress'd from moonlight, stands he, and implores
All saints to give him sight of Madeline,
But for one moment in the tedious hours,
80 That he might gaze and worship all unseen;
Perchance speak, kneel, touch, kiss—in sooth such things have
been.

10

He ventures in: let no buzz'd whisper tell:
All eyes be muffled, or a hundred swords
Will storm his heart, Love's fev'rous citadel:
85 For him, those chambers held barbarian hordes,
Hyena foemen, and hot-blooded lords,
Whose very dogs would execrations howl
Against his lineage: not one breast affords
Him any mercy, in that mansion foul,
90 Save one old beldame, weak in body and in soul.

70 Hoodwink'd . . . faery] She was hoodwink'd *altered to* hoodwink'd with faerry *D* 70 all amort] all a mort *D*; à-la-mort $W^a$; a la mort *GK* 74 still] *interlined above* ⟨fearful who might cl⟩ (*the rest of the line written beneath the deletion*) *D* 75 Porphyro] Lionel *D*, $W^2$, $W^1$ (*interlined above* ⟨Porphyro⟩ *in D*; *subsequently altered to* Porphyro *in* $W^2$) 75 on fire] afire *D*, $W^2$, $W^1$, *GK* 76 Beside . . . doors] *successively* (*a*) Most piteous he implores (*b*) Within the Portal Doors (*c*) Beside the Portal Doors *D* 76/77 ⟨All saints⟩ (*continuation of* [*a*] *in preceding note*) *D* 77 he] *added above the line in D* 80 and . . . unseen] *interlined above* ⟨or speak or knell⟩ *D* 81/82

⟨He ventures in cloak'd up in dark disguise
Let no Man see him—or a hundred Swords
Will storm his heart for all his amorous sighs⟩

(cloak'd up in *interlined above* {wrapped in a}) *D* 82 He . . . in] In ventures he (*but marked for transposition*) *D* 82 buzz'd] damn'd *D*, $W^2$, $W^1$ 83 a] an $W^2$, $W^1$ 86 hot] ⟨bloo⟩ hot *D* 87 dogs] *added above the line in D* 87 howl] ⟨bark⟩ howl *D* 87/88 ⟨'Gainst his Name and Lineage⟩ ('Gainst *made out of* Against *and the first letter of* Name *written over* {Ho}) *D* 88 one breast] a soul *D*, $W^2$, $W^1$ 89 foul] *interlined above* ⟨dark⟩ *D* 90 weak] ⟨nigh to loose the⟩ weak *D*

11

Ah, happy chance! the aged creature came,
Shuffling along with ivory-headed wand,
To where he stood, hid from the torch's flame,
Behind a broad hall-pillar, far beyond
95 The sound of merriment and chorus bland:
He startled her; but soon she knew his face,
And grasp'd his fingers in her palsied hand,
Saying, "Mercy, Porphyro! hie thee from this place;
They are all here to-night, the whole blood-thirsty race!

12

100 "Get hence! get hence! there's dwarfish Hildebrand;
He had a fever late, and in the fit
He cursed thee and thine, both house and land:
Then there's that old Lord Maurice, not a whit
More tame for his gray hairs—Alas me! flit!
105 Flit like a ghost away."—"Ah, Gossip dear,
We're safe enough; here in this arm-chair sit,
And tell me how"—"Good Saints! not here, not here;
Follow me, child, or else these stones will be thy bier."

13

He follow'd through a lowly arched way,
110 Brushing the cobwebs with his lofty plume,
And as she mutter'd "Well-a—well-a-day!"
He found him in a little moonlight room,
Pale, lattic'd, chill, and silent as a tomb.
"Now tell me where is Madeline," said he,
115 "O tell me, Angela, by the holy loom

91 the] that $W^1$ 91 creature] Beldam *D*, $W^2$, $W^1$ 92 Shuffling] *interlined above* ⟨Tottering⟩ *D* 92 wand] *interlined above* ⟨staff⟩ *D* 93 torch's] Torches *D*, $W^1$, *GK*; torches' *altered to* torch's $W^2$ (*there is no* $W^a$ *reading*) 94 broad] *interlined above* ⟨huge⟩ *D* 98 Porphyro] Jesu *D*, $W^2$, $W^1$, *GK* (Porphyro *penciled by Woodhouse on the opposite verso in* $W^1$) 100 Hildebrand] *interlined above* ⟨Ferdinand⟩ *D* 101 the] *interlined above* ⟨his⟩ *D* 103 Then] *interlined above marginally added* ⟨And⟩ *D* 103 there's that] There's *D*; there is $W^2$, $W^1$ 103 Lord Maurice] Lord Maurice ⟨Lacey⟩ *interlined above* ⟨Francisco Mendez⟩ *D* 103/104 ⟨Tamer for all his Palsy⟩ *D* 106 in] *written over* ⟨on⟩ *D* 107 Saints] *interlined above* ⟨Gods⟩ *D* 108 or] ⟨hush hush⟩ or *D* 109 through . . . way] *interlined above* ⟨her along a passage dark⟩ *D* 111 mutter'd] utter'd *GK* (*only*) 113 lattic'd, chill] latticed high *D*, $W^2$, $W^1$ (*interlined above* ⟨casemented⟩ *in D*) 113 a] the *D*, $W^2$, $W^1$ (*GK only = 1820*) 115 Angela] Goody *D*, $W^2$, $W^1$, *GK*

Which none but secret sisterhood may see,
When they St. Agnes' wool are weaving piously."

14

"St. Agnes! Ah! it is St. Agnes' Eve—
Yet men will murder upon holy days:
120 Thou must hold water in a witch's sieve,
And be liege-lord of all the Elves and Fays,
To venture so: it fills me with amaze
To see thee, Porphyro!—St. Agnes' Eve!
God's help! my lady fair the conjuror plays
125 This very night: good angels her deceive!
But let me laugh awhile, I've mickle time to grieve."

15

Feebly she laugheth in the languid moon,
While Porphyro upon her face doth look,
Like puzzled urchin on an aged crone
130 Who keepeth clos'd a wond'rous riddle-book,
As spectacled she sits in chimney nook.
But soon his eyes grew brilliant, when she told
His lady's purpose; and he scarce could brook
Tears, at the thought of those enchantments cold,
135 And Madeline asleep in lap of legends old.

116 secret] holy *D*, $W^2$, $W^1$ (*GK only = 1820*) 117 are weaving] do weave full *altered to* are weaving *D* 119 holy days] holidays *D*, $W^2$, $W^1$ (*GK only = 1820*) 122 so . . . amaze] so about these thorny ways $W^a$, *GK* 122 it . . . with] *interlined above* ⟨in truth it doth⟩ *D* 123 To . . . Porphyro] ⟨Young Signor Porphyro⟩ (*the words deleted and nothing substituted*) *D*; To see thee, Lionel $W^2$, $W^1$ (Lionel *subsequently altered to* Porphyro *in* $W^2$); A-tempting Beelzebub $W^a$; A tempting Be'lzebub *GK* 126 But] Yet $W^2$, $W^1$ 127 laugheth in the] *in D Keats first wrote* laugheth in the bright *and then made various attempts to get rid of the extra syllable: the MS shows* laugheth *altered to* laughs (s *interlined above* ⟨e⟩, *actually producing* laughsth), the *and* bright *both deleted, and* bright *restored above the line and again deleted; a tentative ordering of versions would be* (*a*) laugheth in the bright (*b*) laugheth in the (*c*) laugheth in bright (*d*) laughs in bright (*e*) laughs in (*the last two both incomplete*) $W^2$ *has* laughs in the *altered to* laugheth in the 128 Porphyro] Lionel $W^2$, $W^1$ (*subsequently altered to* Porphyro *in* $W^2$) 129 Like] As *D*, $W^2$ (*GK and* $W^1$ *= 1820*; *there is no* $W^a$ *reading*) 129 puzzled] *interlined above* ⟨doth an⟩ *D* 132 But soon] Sudden $W^a$, *GK* 133–134 and . . . Tears] *deleted in D and nothing substituted* 134 Tears] Sighs $W^a$, *GK* 135 And] Sweet *D*, $W^2$, *GK* ($W^1$ *only = 1820*) 135 in lap of] *interlined above* ⟨among those⟩ *D*

16

Sudden a thought came like a full-blown rose,
Flushing his brow, and in his pained heart
Made purple riot: then doth he propose
A stratagem, that makes the beldame start:
140 “A cruel man and impious thou art:
Sweet lady, let her pray, and sleep, and dream
Alone with her good angels, far apart
From wicked men like thee. Go, go!—I deem
Thou canst not surely be the same that thou didst seem.”

17

145 “I will not harm her, by all saints I swear,”
Quoth Porphyro: “O may I ne’er find grace
When my weak voice shall whisper its last prayer,
If one of her soft ringlets I displace,
Or look with ruffian passion in her face:
150 Good Angela, believe me by these tears;
Or I will, even in a moment’s space,
Awake, with horrid shout, my foemen’s ears,
And beard them, though they be more fang’d than wolves
and bears.”

136 thought . . . rose] rosy thought ⟨more rosy than the rose⟩ (*the undeleted* rosy *added above the line, and nothing substituted for the deleted words*) *D*; $W^2$ *and* $W^1$ *have* thought *with the rest of the line originally left blank* (*in* $W^1$ *Woodhouse penciled in* more rosy than the Rose, *and in* $W^2$ *he subsequently completed the line from the lost fair copy*) 136 like . . . blown] full blown like a $W^a$, *GK* 137 Flushing his brow] Heated his Brow *D*, $W^2$, $W^1$, *GK* (*interlined above* ⟨Flush’d his young Cheek⟩ *in D*) 137 pained] painful *D*, $W^2$, $W^1$ (painfle *in D*) 138 Made . . . riot:] *interlined above* ⟨Made riot fierce—and⟩ *D* 139 A] *written over* ⟨Her⟩ *D* 143 Go, go] O Christ *D*, $W^2$, $W^1$, *GK* (O *written over* ⟨by⟩ *in D*) 144 canst] *interlined above* ⟨art⟩ *D* 144 surely] *added above the line in D* 144 same] ⟨Youth⟩ same *D* 144 that] *interlined above* ⟨as⟩ *D* 145 by . . . swear] by the great $S^t$ Paul *D*, $W^2$, $W^1$, *GK* (By the Saints I swear *penciled by Woodhouse on the opposite verso in* $W^1$) 146 Quoth] Swear’th *D*, $W^a$ (*interlined above* ⟨Says⟩ *in D*); Swears $W^2$, $W^1$ (Quoth *penciled by Woodhouse on the opposite verso in* $W^1$); Sweareth *GK* 146 Porphyro] Lionel $W^2$, $W^1$ (*subsequently altered to* Porphyro *in* $W^2$; Porphyro *penciled by Woodhouse on the opposite verso in* $W^1$) 147 whisper . . . prayer] unto heaven call *D*, $W^2$, $W^1$, *GK* (send to Heaven its prayer *penciled by Woodhouse on the opposite verso in* $W^1$) 148 displace] misplace *D*, $W^2$, $W^1$ 150 believe . . . tears] *written beneath* ⟨thou hearest how I swear⟩ *D* 152 foemen’s] foeman’s *GK* (*only*)

18

"Ah! why wilt thou affright a feeble soul?
155 A poor, weak, palsy-stricken, churchyard thing,
Whose passing-bell may ere the midnight toll;
Whose prayers for thee, each morn and evening,
Were never miss'd."—Thus plaining, doth she bring
A gentler speech from burning Porphyro;
160 So woful, and of such deep sorrowing,
That Angela gives promise she will do
Whatever he shall wish, betide her weal or woe.

19

Which was, to lead him, in close secrecy,
Even to Madeline's chamber, and there hide
165 Him in a closet, of such privacy
That he might see her beauty unespied,
And win perhaps that night a peerless bride,
While legion'd fairies pac'd the coverlet,
And pale enchantment held her sleepy-eyed.
170 Never on such a night have lovers met,
Since Merlin paid his Demon all the monstrous debt.

20

"It shall be as thou wishest," said the Dame:
"All cates and dainties shall be stored there
Quickly on this feast-night: by the tambour frame
175 Her own lute thou wilt see: no time to spare,
For I am slow and feeble, and scarce dare

154 Ah . . . affright] How canst thou terrify $W^a$, *GK* 154 wilt thou] *made out of* will you *D* 156 midnight] *interlined above* ⟨morning⟩ *D* 158 never] neer *D* 158 doth she] she did $W^2$, $W^1$ 159–162 from . . . woe.] *Woodhouse originally omitted this passage in* $W^1$, *filling in the blank space with a pencil version based on D (see the notes to 160, 161, 162); apparently he did the same in* $W^2$, *for the text there, substantively agreeing with GK and 1820, is written in lighter ink over erased pencilings* 159 Porphyro] Lionel *interlined above* Porphyro (*undeleted*) *D* 160 woful] gentle *D*, $W^1$ (*the latter in pencil*) 161 Angela . . . do] the old Dame ⟨promises to do⟩ (Dame *interlined above* ⟨Beldam⟩ *and nothing substituted for the rest of the deleted text*) *D*; the old beldame promises to do $W^1$ (*in pencil*) 162 wish] say *D*, $W^1$ (*the latter in pencil*) 162/163 ⟨Which was, as all who ever lov'd will guess⟩ *D* 163 lead] *interlined above* ⟨guide⟩ *D* 164 Even . . . chamber] To Madeline's Bedchamber *altered to* Even To Madeline's chamber *D* 165 of . . . privacy‸] if such one there be—*D*, $W^2$, $W^1$, *GK* ($W^a$ *only* = *1820*) 167 And] Or *D*, $W^2$, $W^1$, *GK* 167 perhaps . . . night] that night perhaps $W^1$ 168 pac'd the coverlet] *written beneath* ⟨cl⟩ ⟨round her pillow flew⟩ *D* 170 Never] *interlined above* ⟨O when⟩ *D* 171 his Demon] *interlined above* ⟨the demons⟩ *D* 176 For] *interlined above* ⟨And⟩ *D*

On such a catering trust my dizzy head.
Wait here, my child, with patience; kneel in prayer
The while: Ah! thou must needs the lady wed,
180 Or may I never leave my grave among the dead."

21

So saying, she hobbled off with busy fear.
The lover's endless minutes slowly pass'd;
The dame return'd, and whisper'd in his ear
To follow her; with aged eyes aghast
185 From fright of dim espial. Safe at last,
Through many a dusky gallery, they gain
The maiden's chamber, silken, hush'd, and chaste;
Where Porphyro took covert, pleas'd amain.
His poor guide hurried back with agues in her brain.

178 Wait . . . patience] But wait an hour's passing *D*, *W*², *W*¹ (passing *interlined above* ⟨time—{as the} and⟩ *in D*) 179 Ah] Sooth *W*ᵃ, *GK* 181 off . . . fear] out busily *altered to* off with busy fear *D* 182 The . . . pass'd] *interlined (with the variant given in the next note) above* ⟨And we will pass the Lover's endless hour⟩ *D* 182 slowly] quickly *D*, *W*², *W*¹, *GK* (slowly *penciled by Woodhouse in the margin of W*¹) 185 dim espial] *interlined above* ⟨any noise⟩ *D* 186 many . . . gallery] *in D Keats first wrote* loneliest passages and *and then changed* loneliest *to* lonely, *deleted* passages and, *interlining and deleting* arras *above the words, and further added* oaken *and* Galleries *above the line; a tentative ordering of versions would be* (*a*) loneliest passages and (*b*) lonely arras (*c*) lonely Galleries (*d*) lonely oaken Galleries. *W*² *and W*¹ *have* lonely oaken galleries 186–189 gain . . . brain.] *as with 159–162, the W*¹ *text, a composite version of readings in D (see the notes to 186, 188, 189), is in pencil; the W*² *text, which beginning in 187 substantively agrees with GK and 1820, is written in lighter ink over erased pencilings* 186 gain] *successively* (*a*) gaind (*b*) came (*c*) reach *D*; reach *W*² (*W*¹ [*in pencil*], *W*ᵃ, *GK* = *1820*) 186/187 ⟨To⟩ ⟨The Maiden Chamber⟩ (The *made out of* the—*the original text following* [*b*] *in the preceding note and the revised version following* [*c*]) *D* 188 Where . . . amain.]

⟨Whre closeted he⟩
⟨There in a panting covert to remain,⟩
Where he in panting covert will remain,

(he *made out of* his *in the last line, and* will *interlined above* ⟨must⟩) *D*; There he in panting covert will remain *W*¹ (*in pencil*) 189 His . . . brain] ⟨I purgatory sweet or what may he attain⟩ (I [*for* In] *interlined above* {From} *and* or . . . attain *above* {to view love's own domain}; *this text, which Keats left canceled, appears at the top of a new page in the MS, and follows several fragmentary attempts, all deleted, at the bottom of the preceding page—successively* [*a*] Love [*b*] In purgatory sweet [*c*] A purgatory sweet [*d*] Upon the frontier [*e*] In purgatory sweet [*f*] From purgatory sweet) *D*; From Purgatory sweet to view what he may attain *W*¹ (*in pencil*) 189/190

⟨There secreted⟩
⟨Scace had old Angela the Stair case found
Ere Madeline, like an affrighted Swan

22

190 Her falt'ring hand upon the balustrade,
Old Angela was feeling for the stair,
When Madeline, St. Agnes' charmed maid,
Rose, like a mission'd spirit, unaware:
With silver taper's light, and pious care,
195 She turn'd, and down the aged gossip led
To a safe level matting. Now prepare,
Young Porphyro, for gazing on that bed;
She comes, she comes again, like ring-dove fray'd and fled.

23

Out went the taper as she hurried in;
200 Its little smoke, in pallid moonshine, died:
She clos'd the door, she panted, all akin
To spirits of the air, and visions wide:
No uttered syllable, or, woe betide!
But to her heart, her heart was voluble,
205 Paining with eloquence her balmy side;
As though a tongueless nightingale should swell
Her throat in vain, and die, heart-stifled, in her dell.

---

Flew past her⟩
⟨Scarce had⟩
(Swan *interlined above* {Bird} *in the third line, and* Scarce *written over* {Old An} *in the last line*) *D* 190 Her] *interlined above* ⟨With⟩ *D* 193 mission'd spirit] spirit to her *altered to* mission'd spirit *D*; spirit to her $W^a$, *GK* 194 With silver] And with her *altered to* With silver *D* 194 taper's] taper $W^a$, *GK* 194 pious] gentle *D*, $W^2$, $W^1$ 194/195 ⟨Guided her⟩ *D* 195 down . . . led] *interlined above* ⟨led the aged gossip down⟩ *D* 196 a] *interlined above* ⟨the⟩ *D* 197 Porphyro] Lionel *D*, $W^2$, $W^1$ (*interlined above* ⟨Porphyro⟩ *in D; subsequently altered to* Porphyro *in* $W^2$) 197 for] a *D*, $W^2$, $W^1$, *GK* 198 again] *added above the line in D* 199 hurried] floated $W^a$, *GK* 205 Paining] *written over* ⟨And⟩ *D* 207 throat] ⟨barren⟩ throat *D* 207/208
⟨A Casement {ach'd} tripple arch'd and diamonded
With many coloured glass fronted the Moon
In midst wereof a shilded scutcheon shed
High blushing gules; {upon} {she kneeled saintly down}
And inly prayed for grace and heavenly boon;
The blood red gules fell on her silver cross
And {her} whitest hands devout⟩

⟨There was A Casement tipple archd and high
All garlanded with carven imageries
Of fruits & {trailing} flowers and sunny corn ears parchd⟩
(wereof *interlined above* {of which} *in the third line of the first passage,* kneeled *made out of* kneeld *in the fourth line,* whitest *made out of* white *in the seventh line*; There was *added above in the first line of the second passage*) *D*

24

A casement high and triple-arch'd there was,
All garlanded with carven imag'ries
210 Of fruits, and flowers, and bunches of knot-grass,
And diamonded with panes of quaint device,
Innumerable of stains and splendid dyes,
As are the tiger-moth's deep-damask'd wings;
And in the midst, 'mong thousand heraldries,
215 And twilight saints, and dim emblazonings,
A shielded scutcheon blush'd with blood of queens and kings.

25

Full on this casement shone the wintry moon,
And threw warm gules on Madeline's fair breast,
As down she knelt for heaven's grace and boon;
220 Rose-bloom fell on her hands, together prest,
And on her silver cross soft amethyst,
And on her hair a glory, like a saint:
She seem'd a splendid angel, newly drest,
Save wings, for heaven:—Porphyro grew faint:
225 She knelt, so pure a thing, so free from mortal taint.

209 garlanded] gardended (*or* gardneded) *D* 213 As . . . wings] *interlined* (*with the readings given in the next three notes*) *above* ⟨As is the wing of evening tiger-moths⟩ *D* 213 are] is *D*, $W^2$, $W^1$ 213 deep] ⟨rich⟩ deep *D* 213 damask'd] sunset *D*, $W^2$, $W^1$ (*interlined above* ⟨damasked⟩ *in D*; *GK has* damask'd *but there is no* $W^a$ *reading*) 214 And . . . midst] And in the midst *altered to* in midst whereft *D*; In midst whereof $W^2$, $W^1$ 214 thousand] *interlined above* ⟨man⟩ (*the beginning of* many) *D* 215 twilight] ⟨dim⟩ ⟨twilight⟩ twilight *D* 218 warm] rich *D*, $W^2$, $W^1$ (⟨wam⟩ rich *interlined above* ⟨red⟩ *in D*) 218 breast] *interlined above* ⟨face⟩ *D* 219 knelt] kneel'd *D*, $W^2$, $W^1$ (*GK only = 1820*) 220 Rose . . . together] ⟨And⟩ rose ⟨with red⟩ bloom fell on her hands togeth (fell *added above*) *interlined above* ⟨Tinging her pious⟩ hands ⟨together⟩ (*the apparent order of versions is* [*a*] Tinging her pious hands together [*b*] Tinging with red her hands together [*c*] And rose bloom on her hands togeth[er] [*d*] rose bloom fell on her hands togeth[er]) *D* 221 on her] *added above the line in D* 222 saint] Saint⟨'s⟩ *D* 223 a . . . drest] silvery angel newly drest *written beneath* ⟨like an immortal agel drest⟩ *D*; like silver Angel newly dress'd $W^2$, $W^1$ 224 Save] *written over* ⟨In⟩ *D* 224 Porphyro] Lionel *D*, $W^2$, $W^1$ (*interlined above* ⟨Porphyro⟩ *in D*; *subsequently altered to* Porphyro *in* $W^2$) 225 knelt] pray'd *GK* (*only*) 225 so . . . so] too . . . too *D*, $W^2$, $W^1$, *GK* 225/226

⟨But soon his heart revives—her prayers said
  She {lays aside her necl} strips her hair of all its pearled wreathes
{Unclasps her bosom jewels}
And twist it in one knot upon her head⟩

⟨But soon his heart revives—her praying done
  Of all its wreathed pearl she strips her hair

26

Anon his heart revives: her vespers done,
Of all its wreathed pearls her hair she frees;
Unclasps her warmed jewels one by one;
Loosens her fragrant boddice; by degrees
230 Her rich attire creeps rustling to her knees:
Half-hidden, like a mermaid in sea-weed,
Pensive awhile she dreams awake, and sees,
In fancy, fair St. Agnes in her bed,
But dares not look behind, or all the charm is fled.

27

235 Soon, trembling in her soft and chilly nest,
In sort of wakeful swoon, perplex'd she lay,
Until the poppied warmth of sleep oppress'd
Her soothed limbs, and soul fatigued away;
Flown, like a thought, until the morrow-day;
240 Blissfully haven'd both from joy and pain;
Clasp'd like a missal where swart Paynims pray;

---

Unclasps her warmed jewels one by one
Loosens her fragrant boddice and doth bare⟩
(necl *in the second line of the first passage also readable as both* perl *and* veil, *and* pearled wreathes *in the same line made out of* wreathed pearl; praying *in the first line of the second passage made out of* prayers, *a second* soon *interlined and deleted before* done *in the same line, and* its *written over* {her} *in the next line; the last line, which appears at the top of a new page in the MS, follows several attempts, all deleted, at the bottom of the preceding page—successively* [*a*] Loosens the boddice from her [*b*] Loosens her bursting [*c*] Loosens her Boddice lace string [*d*] Loosens her Boddice; and her bosom bar [*e*] Loosens her) *D* 226 Anon] *interlined above* ⟨But soon⟩ *D* 226 vespers] praying *D*, $W^2$, $W^1$ (*GK only = 1820*) 227 pearls] pearl *D*, $W^1$; pearl *altered to* pearls $W^2$ 227 frees] *interlined above* ⟨strips⟩ *D* 229 by degrees] *successively* (*a*) and down slips (*b*) to her knees (*c*) by degrees *D* 230 rich] sweet *D*, $W^2$, $W^1$ 230 creeps] ⟨falls light⟩ ⟨creeps down by⟩ creeps *D* 231 mermaid] *interlined above* ⟨Syren⟩ *D* 231 in sea-weed] *interlined above* ⟨of the Sea⟩ *D* 231/232 ⟨And more melodious⟩ *D* 232 Pensive . . . awake] She stands awhile in dreaming thought *D*, $W^2$, $W^1$ (dreaming *added above the line in D*) 233 in her] on her *D*, $W^2$, $W^1$ (on *interlined above* ⟨in⟩ *in D*) 234 fled] ⟨fl⟩ dead *D* 234/235
⟨Then stepping forth she slips⟩
⟨The charm fled not—she did not look behind;⟩ *D*
235 Soon] *written over* ⟨But⟩ *D* 235/236
⟨She lay and had not seen her⟩
⟨She lay; {and as} and till the poppied wamth of sleep⟩ *D*
236 In . . . lay] She lay, in sort of wakeful swoon perplext (*but marked for transposition*) *D* 239 morrow] morrow's *altered to* morrow $W^2$; morrow's $W^1$ 241 Clasp'd . . . a] *successively* (*a*) Shut like a (*b*) like a shut (*c*) like a clasp'd (*d*) clasp'd like a *D*

Blinded alike from sunshine and from rain,
As though a rose should shut, and be a bud again.

28

Stol'n to this paradise, and so entranced,
245 Porphyro gazed upon her empty dress,
And listen'd to her breathing, if it chanced
To wake into a slumberous tenderness;
Which when he heard, that minute did he bless,
And breath'd himself: then from the closet crept,
250 Noiseless as fear in a wide wilderness,
And over the hush'd carpet, silent, stept,
And 'tween the curtains peep'd, where, lo!—how fast she slept.

29

Then by the bed-side, where the faded moon
Made a dim, silver twilight, soft he set
255 A table, and, half anguish'd, threw thereon
A cloth of woven crimson, gold, and jet:—
O for some drowsy Morphean amulet!
The boisterous, midnight, festive clarion,
The kettle-drum, and far-heard clarionet,

242 Blinded] ⟨Dead to⟩ Blinded *D* 243 shut] *successively* (*a*) shut (*b*) close (*c*) shut *D* 243/244
⟨Her slumbrous breathing⟩
⟨The listning Porphyro her breathing heard
And when⟩
⟨The entranced Porphyro stol'n to Paradise⟩ *D*
245 Porphyro] Lionel *W*², *W*¹ (*subsequently altered to* Porphyro *in W*²) 248 that] ⟨he breath'd himself⟩ that *D* 250 Noiseless] *successively* (*a*) Silent (*b*) Noiseless (*c*) Silent (*but* Noiseless *left undeleted*) *D* 250 in . . . wilderness] ⟨amid⟩ in a wide (wide *made out of* wild) *interlined above* ⟨and frozen [?] not with⟩ a wildeness (*a tentative reconstruction of successive versions would be* [*a*] and frozen [?] not with [*b*] amid a wildeness [*c*] in a wild wildeness [*d*] in a wide wildeness) *D* 251 over the hush'd] oer the silent *altered to* over the hush'd *D* 251 silent] ⟨hushing⟩ silent *D* 252 where] and *D*, *W*², *W*¹ 253 by] ⟨on⟩ by *D* 253 faded] fading *D*, *W*², *W*¹ 254 a . . . silver] an illumed *D*, *W*²; an illumin'd *W*¹ 255 and . . . threw] and with anguish spread *interlined above* ⟨light, and stilly threw⟩ (*both original and revised text following* Table *without a comma*) *D*; and with care quick spread *W*², *W*¹ (*GK only = 1820*) 258 midnight] braying *GK* (*only*) 258 festive clarion] Clarions of the Ball (Ball *interlined above* ⟨feast⟩) *altered to* festive Clarion⟨s⟩ (*with* of the *left undeleted*) *D* 258/259
⟨Sounded though faint and far away⟩
⟨Came⟩ ⟨Sound in his ears⟩ *D*
259 The] And *D*, *W*², *W*¹ (*GK only = 1820*) 259 drum] drum⟨s⟩ *D* 259 clarionet] clarinet *D*, *W*², *W*¹, *GK*

260 Affray his ears, though but in dying tone:—
The hall door shuts again, and all the noise is gone.

30

And still she slept an azure-lidded sleep,
In blanched linen, smooth, and lavender'd,
While he from forth the closet brought a heap
265 Of candied apple, quince, and plum, and gourd;
With jellies soother than the creamy curd,
And lucent syrops, tinct with cinnamon;
Manna and dates, in argosy transferr'd
From Fez; and spiced dainties, every one,
270 From silken Samarcand to cedar'd Lebanon.

31

These delicates he heap'd with glowing hand
On golden dishes and in baskets bright
Of wreathed silver: sumptuous they stand
In the retired quiet of the night,
275 Filling the chilly room with perfume light.—
"And now, my love, my seraph fair, awake!
Thou art my heaven, and I thine eremite:

259/260 ⟨Reach'd his scar'd ears⟩ *D* 260 Affray] Affray⟨'d⟩ *D* 260 in] *interlined above* ⟨with⟩ *D* 260 dying] faintest *D*, $W^2$, $W^1$ (*GK only = 1820*) 260 tone] tone⟨s⟩ *D* 261 shuts] shut⟨s⟩ *D* 261 is] *successively* (*a*) is (*b*) was (*c*) is *D* 261/262 ⟨But still she slept⟩ (But *interlined above* {And}) *D* 264 from . . . brought] brought from the cabinet $W^a$, *GK* 265 apple, quince] *successively* (*a*) sweets (*b*) fruits (*c*) sweets with (*d*) apple Quince *D* 266 creamy] creamed *D*, $W^2$, $W^1$ (*interlined above* ⟨dairy⟩ *in D*) 267 syrops] syrup *GK* (*only*) 267 tinct] *interlined above* ⟨smooth⟩ *D* 267/268 ⟨And sugar'd dates from that oer Euphrates fard⟩ *D* 268 Manna . . . transferr'd] *the D text represents the most worked over line in all of Keats's MSS* (*there are five levels of writing plus the word* argosy *written vertically in the margin and the deleted text given in the preceding and following notes*); *a tentative reconstruction of successive versions would include:* (*a*) And Manna wild (*b*) and manna wild transferrd (*c*) And Manna wild and sugar'd dates transferred (*d*) Manna and daites in Brigantine transferrd (*e*) Manna and daites in argosy transferred ([*a*] *is a fragmentary beginning of the line, and* [*b*] *a fragmentary ending*) 268/269 ⟨In Brigantine from Fez⟩ (*continuation of* [*c*] *in preceding note*) *D* 270 silken] *successively* (*a*) wealthy (*b*) glutted (*c*) silken *D* 271 he heap'd] *added above the line* (*and wrongly marked for insertion after* with) *in D* 272 dishes] salvers *D*, $W^2$, $W^1$ (*GK only = 1820*) 273 wreathed] ⟨twisted⟩ wreathed *D* 274 In . . . of the] Amid the quiet of S$^t$ Agenes' *D*, $W^2$, $W^1$ (*GK only = 1820, but* In the retired quiet of the *is penciled by Woodhouse on the opposite verso in* $W^2$) 275 Filling . . . room] *successively* (*a*) And now, saith he, my Seraph (*b*) Teeming (*c*) Filling the chilly room *D* 276 my love] *interlined above* ⟨saith he⟩ *D* 276 fair] *interlined above* ⟨may [*or* pray] awake⟩ (awake *mistakenly left deleted*) *D* 277 Thou] *written over* ⟨My⟩ *D* 277 thine] thy $W^2$, $W^1$

Open thine eyes, for meek St. Agnes' sake,
Or I shall drowse beside thee, so my soul doth ache."

32

280 Thus whispering, his warm, unnerved arm
Sank in her pillow. Shaded was her dream
By the dusk curtains:—'twas a midnight charm
Impossible to melt as iced stream:
The lustrous salvers in the moonlight gleam;
285 Broad golden fringe upon the carpet lies:
It seem'd he never, never could redeem
From such a stedfast spell his lady's eyes;
So mus'd awhile, entoil'd in woofed phantasies.

33

Awakening up, he took her hollow lute,—
290 Tumultuous,—and, in chords that tenderest be,
He play'd an ancient ditty, long since mute,
In Provence call'd, "La belle dame sans mercy":
Close to her ear touching the melody;—
Wherewith disturb'd, she utter'd a soft moan:
295 He ceased—she panted quick—and suddenly
Her blue affrayed eyes wide open shone:
Upon his knees he sank, pale as smooth-sculptured stone.

34

Her eyes were open, but she still beheld,
Now wide awake, the vision of her sleep:

279/280
⟨So whispring, his warm unnerved arm
Sunk in her pillow. Shaded was her sleep
By the dusk curtains; {f} dreamless of alarm
And vis⟩
(So *written over* {Thus} *in the first line*) *D* 280 Thus] *written over* ⟨So⟩ *D* 281 Sank] Sunk *D*, $W^1$, *GK*; Sunk *altered to* Sank $W^2$ 281 was her dream] were her dreams *altered to* was her dream *D* 284 in] *written over* ⟨on⟩ *D* 285 Broad . . . lies] *interlined above* ⟨Broad golden fringe lies wealthy on the f⟩ *D* 286 seem'd] *made out of* seems *D*; seems $W^2$, $W^1$ (*GK = 1820*) 286 could] *made out of* can *D* 288 So] And *D*, $W^2$, $W^1$ 288 mus'd] ⟨stood⟩ mus'd *D* 289 Awakening] Awaking $W^2$, $W^1$ 292 mercy] mercie $W^2$; merci *GK* 293 touching] *successively* (*a*) he held (*b*) he touch'd (*c*) touching *D* 295 she . . . quick] *interlined above* ⟨her breathing ceasd⟩ *D* 296 affrayed] half-frayed *D*, $W^2$, $W^1$ 297 sank] sunk *D*, $W^2$, $W^1$, *GK* 297 smooth] fair $W^a$, *GK* 299 Now . . . sleep] The vision of her sleep, now wide awake (*but marked for transposition*) *D* 299 vision] vision⟨s⟩ $W^2$; visions $W^1$

300 There was a painful change, that nigh expell'd
The blisses of her dream so pure and deep:
At which fair Madeline began to weep,
And moan forth witless words with many a sigh;
While still her gaze on Porphyro would keep;
305 Who knelt, with joined hands and piteous eye,
Fearing to move or speak, she look'd so dreamingly.

35

"Ah, Porphyro!" said she, "but even now
Thy voice was at sweet tremble in mine ear,
Made tuneable with every sweetest vow;
310 And those sad eyes were spiritual and clear:
How chang'd thou art! how pallid, chill, and drear!
Give me that voice again, my Porphyro,
Those looks immortal, those complainings dear!
Oh leave me not in this eternal woe,
315 For if thou diest, my love, I know not where to go."

300 a] *interlined above* ⟨some⟩ *D* 301 deep:] *D*, *GK*; ~ ; $W^2$; ~ , $W^1$; ~‸ *1820* 302 fair] ⟨she shighd⟩ fair *D* 303 moan] mourn *GK* (*only*) 303 witless] *written in the margin to replace* little (*left undeleted*) *D*; little $W^2$, $W^1$ 304 Porphyro] Lionel $W^2$, $W^1$ (*subsequently altered to* Porphyro *in* $W^2$) 305 knelt . . . hands] with an aching brow *D*, $W^2$, $W^1$ 305 eye] eyes *GK* (*only*) 306 Fearing to move] Feared to move *D*; Fear'd to remove $W^2$, $W^1$ 307 "Ah . . . but] ⟨At length⟩ she speaks, "Ah Porpyro but *interlined above* ⟨"Ah Porphyro, saith she but⟩ *D*; She speaks—"Ah Lionel; but $W^2$, $W^1$ (Lionel *subsequently altered to* Porphyro *in* $W^2$) 308 was] *added above the line in D* 308 in] ⟨by⟩ in *D* 309 Made tuneable] And tun'd devout $W^a$; And tim'd, devout, *GK* 309 with] by *D*, $W^2$, $W^1$ 309 sweetest] softest $W^a$, *GK* 310 those sad] thy kind *D*, $W^2$, $W^1$ 311 thou art] art thou *D*, $W^2$, $W^1$ (at *for* art *in D*; *GK only = 1820*) 311 how (*fifth word*)] *added above the line in D* 311 chill] cold $W^a$, *GK* 312 that] the $W^1$ 312 my Porphyro] *Woodhouse originally omitted these words in* $W^2$ *and* $W^1$; *he penciled* sweet Prospero *in the blank space in* $W^1$, *and subsequently entered* my Porphyro *from the lost fair copy in* $W^2$ 313 those (*fourth word*)] ⟨and that⟩ those *D* 314–322 Oh . . . blows‸]

See, while she speaks his arms encroaching slow,
Have zoned her, heart to heart,—loud, loud the dark winds blow!

For on the midnight came a tempest fell;
More sooth, for that his quick rejoinder flows
Into her burning ear: and still the spell
Unbroken guards her in serene repose.
With her wild dream he mingled, as a rose
Marrieth its odour to a violet.
Still, still she dreams, louder the frost wind blows,

$W^a$, *GK* (*the latter with* close *for* quick *in the second line of the new stanza*) 315 For‸] Ah! *D*, $W^2$, $W^1$ (*no punctuation in* $W^2$, *and* For *penciled above the word and then erased in the same MS*)

36

Beyond a mortal man impassion'd far
At these voluptuous accents, he arose,
Ethereal, flush'd, and like a throbbing star
Seen mid the sapphire heaven's deep repose;
320 Into her dream he melted, as the rose
Blendeth its odour with the violet,—
Solution sweet: meantime the frost-wind blows
Like Love's alarum pattering the sharp sleet
Against the window-panes; St. Agnes' moon hath set.

37

325 'Tis dark: quick pattereth the flaw-blown sleet:
"This is no dream, my bride, my Madeline!"
'Tis dark: the iced gusts still rave and beat:
"No dream, alas! alas! and woe is mine!
Porphyro will leave me here to fade and pine.—
330 Cruel! what traitor could thee hither bring?
I curse not, for my heart is lost in thine,
Though thou forsakest a deceived thing;—
A dove forlorn and lost with sick unpruned wing."

38

"My Madeline! sweet dreamer! lovely bride!
335 Say, may I be for aye thy vassal blest?
Thy beauty's shield, heart-shap'd and vermeil dyed?
Ah, silver shrine, here will I take my rest

316 Beyond . . . far] Impassion'd far beyond a mortal man (*but marked for transposition*) *D* 316 impassion'd far] in passioned fear $W^2$, $W^1$ (*subsequently corrected to* impassioned far *in* $W^2$) 317 accents] ⟨words⟩ accents *D* 318/319 ⟨Was either⟩ *D* 320 Into her] *successively* (*a*) With her bright (*b*) In her bright (*c*) Into her *D* 321 its] her its (*both words undeleted*) *D* 321 odour] *interlined above* ⟨perfume⟩ *D* 321/322 ⟨An as one⟩ *D* (*also in the same MS,* tenderness *appears vertically in the margin with a mark for insertion after 321—perhaps as a preliminary attempt at, or trial replacement of, the first word of 322—but both the word and the mark are deleted*) 322 Solution sweet] *deleted in D and nothing substituted* (*but see preceding note*) 322/323 ⟨Darkness⟩ *D* 324 Against . . . panes;] *successively* (*a*) Against the Casement gloom— (*b*) Against the Window's gloom— (*c*) Against the casement dark. (*d*) Against the windows dark. *D*; Against the windows—dark$_\wedge$ $W^2$, $W^1$ (*GK only = 1820*) 324 hath] had *D*, $W^2$, $W^1$ (*GK only = 1820*) 325 quick] still *D*, $W^2$, $W^1$, *GK* 329 Porphyro] Lionel $W^2$, $W^1$ (*subsequently altered to* Porphyro *in* $W^2$) 330 Cruel] ⟨Ah⟩ cruel *D* 332 forsakest] *successively* (*a*) forsakest (*b*) shoudst leave (*c*) forsakest *D* 333 A] ⟨To⟩ A *D* 333 dove . . . lost] *interlined above* ⟨silent mateless dove⟩ *D* 334 sweet . . . bride] *written beneath* ⟨Dark is this wintry night⟩ *D* 336 beauty's] beauty $W^2$, $W^1$ 337 here . . . my] by thee will I take *altered to* here will ⟨I⟩ take my (I *mistakenly deleted in the revision*) *D*

After so many hours of toil and quest,
A famish'd pilgrim,—saved by miracle.
340 Though I have found, I will not rob thy nest
Saving of thy sweet self; if thou think'st well
To trust, fair Madeline, to no rude infidel.

39

"Hark! 'tis an elfin-storm from faery land,
Of haggard seeming, but a boon indeed:
345 Arise—arise! the morning is at hand;—
The bloated wassaillers will never heed:—
Let us away, my love, with happy speed;
There are no ears to hear, or eyes to see,—
Drown'd all in Rhenish and the sleepy mead:
350 Awake! arise! my love, and fearless be,
For o'er the southern moors I have a home for thee."

40

She hurried at his words, beset with fears,
For there were sleeping dragons all around,
At glaring watch, perhaps, with ready spears—
355 Down the wide stairs a darkling way they found.—
In all the house was heard no human sound.

339 A . . . miracle] *successively (a)* With tearful features (*b*) With features pale and mounful Pilgrim's weeds (*c*) Pale feautred and in weeds of Pilgrimage (*actually written* ⟨Pilgrim's⟩age) *D*; Pale featured, and in weeds of pilgrimage *W*², *W*¹ 340 Though . . . thy] *successively* (*a*) I have found, but will not rob thy downy (*b*) Though I have found, I can not rob thy (*c*) Though I have found, but can not rob thy *D*; I have found but cannot rob thy downy *W*², *W*¹ 341–342 Saving . . . infidel.] Soft Nightingale, I'll keep thee in a cage / To sing to me—but hark! the blended tempests' rage! *D*, *W*², *W*¹ (I'll *written over* ⟨but⟩ *in D*; *W*² *has* tempests *and W*¹ tempest's) 343 'tis] ⟨the⟩ 'tis *D* 344 but . . . indeed] *written beneath* ⟨but, my love, to us⟩ (indeed *in the revised text made out of* in truth) *D* 345 arise (*second word*)] *interlined above* ⟨my Love⟩ *D* 347/348 ⟨Over the moors⟩ *D* 349 and] or *W*¹ 349 the . . . mead] *interlined above* ⟨the drenching mead⟩ (drenching *made out of* drench of) *D* 350 Awake . . . love] Put on warm cloathing, sweet *D*, *W*², *W*¹ 351 For . . . moors] Over the dartmoor blak *D*, *W*², *W*¹ (black *in W*², *W*¹; the . . . blak *interlined above* ⟨the bleak Dartmoor⟩ *in D*) 353 around] *interlined above* ⟨about⟩ *D* 354 At . . . perhaps] ⟨Or⟩ perhaps at glaring watch (*but marked for transposition*) *D* 355 Down] ⟨Well⟩ Down *D* 356 heard no] *interlined above* ⟨not a⟩ *D* 356 heard] found *GK* (*only*) 356/357
⟨But⟩
⟨Though every⟩
⟨But noise of winds besieging the high doors⟩
⟨But the b⟩
⟨But the besieging Storm⟩

A chain-droop'd lamp was flickering by each door;
The arras, rich with horseman, hawk, and hound,
Flutter'd in the besieging wind's uproar;
360 And the long carpets rose along the gusty floor.

41

They glide, like phantoms, into the wide hall;
Like phantoms, to the iron porch, they glide;
Where lay the Porter, in uneasy sprawl,
With a huge empty flaggon by his side:
365 The wakeful bloodhound rose, and shook his hide,
But his sagacious eye an inmate owns:
By one, and one, the bolts full easy slide:—
The chains lie silent on the footworn stones;—
The key turns, and the door upon its hinges groans.

42

370 And they are gone: ay, ages long ago
These lovers fled away into the storm.
That night the Baron dreamt of many a woe,

---

⟨The Lamps were flickeing death shads on the wall⟩
⟨Without, the Tempest kept a hollow roar⟩
⟨The Lamps were flickeing⟩
⟨The Lamps were dying in⟩
⟨But here and there a Lamp was flickeing out⟩ *D*
357 chain-droop'd] *interlined above* ⟨drooping⟩ *D* 357 by . . . door] *interlined above* ⟨here and there⟩ *D* 358 arras, rich] Arras ⟨flutterd⟩ rich *D* 359 in] ⟨with cold⟩ in *D* 361 They . . . hall] *interlined above* ⟨Like Spirits, into the wide-paven hall⟩ *D* 362 Like . . . glide] They glide,—and to the iron porch in haste (*continuation of deleted text in 361*) *altered to* Like Phantoms to the iron porch they glide *D* 363 lay] *successively* (*a*) lay (*b*) slept (*c*) lay *D* 364 huge] large *D*, *W*², *W*¹ 364 flaggon] beaker *D*, *W*², *W*¹, *GK* 365 wakeful] *added above the line in D* 366 But . . . owns] *successively* (*a*) And paced round Madeline all angerless (*b*) But with a calmed eye his Mistress owns (*c*) But his unangerd eye an inmate owns *D*; But quick his calmed eye its mistress owns *W*², *W*¹ (quick his calmed *squeezed in over some erased words in W*² *and into a blank space in W*¹) 366/367
⟨The Chains are loos'd—the⟩
⟨The Chains are⟩ *D*
367 bolts . . . easy] *successively* (*a*) easy bolts back (*b*) bolts full eas (*c*) easy bolts (*d*) ⟨bolts⟩ full easy (bolts *mistakenly deleted in the final version*) *D* 367/368
⟨Silent⟩
⟨Unon the pavement lie the heavvy chains⟩ *D*
368 chains] chain *W*¹ 368 lie] lay *D*, *W*², *W*¹, *GK* 368 footworn] footway *W*², *W*¹ 371 away . . . storm] into a night of Storms *altered to* into the Storm (away *is not in the MS*) *D*; into the night of storm *W*², *W*¹ 372 night] Morn *D*, *W*², *W*¹ (*interlined above* ⟨night⟩ *in D*; *GK = 1820*) 372 dreamt] dream'd *W*², *W*¹

And all his warrior-guests, with shade and form
Of witch, and demon, and large coffin-worm,
375 Were long be-nightmar'd. Angela the old
Died palsy-twitch'd, with meagre face deform;
The Beadsman, after thousand aves told,
For aye unsought for slept among his ashes cold.

373 guests] *interlined above* ⟨sav [?]⟩ *D* 373 shade and form] Shade⟨s⟩ and form⟨s⟩ *D* 374 witch . . . demon] Witches Deamons *altered to* Witche and Deamon *D* 374 coffin] ⟨chanal⟩ coffin *D*; coffin'd *W*[1] 374 worm] worm⟨s⟩ *D* 375 long] all *D*, *W*[2], *W*[1], *GK* (*interlined above* ⟨long⟩ *in D*; *W*[a] = *1820*) 375–378 Angela . . . cold]

Angela went off
Twitch'd by the palsy:—and with face deform
The Beadsman stiffen'd—'twixt a sigh and laugh,
Ta'en sudden from his beads by one weak little cough

*W*[a], *GK* (*the latter having* with *for* by *in the second line*) 375 the] ⟨ne'er told⟩ the *D* *After* 378 End of S[t] Agnes' Eve. *GK*

## *The Eve of St. Mark*

Upon a Sabbath day it fell;
Twice holy was the Sabbath bell,
That call'd the folk to evening prayer.
The city streets were clean and fair
5 From wholesome drench of April rains,
And on the western window panes
The chilly sunset faintly told
Of unmatur'd green vallies cold,
Of the green thorny bloomless hedge,
10 Of rivers new with springtide sedge,
Of primroses by shelter'd rills,
And daisies on the aguish hills.
Twice holy was the Sabbath bell:
The silent streets were crowded well
15 With staid and pious companies,
Warm from their fireside orat'ries,
And moving with demurest air
To even song and vesper prayer.
Each arched porch and entry low
20 Was fill'd with patient folk and slow,
With whispers hush and shuffling feet,
While play'd the organs loud and sweet.

The bells had ceas'd, the prayers begun,
And Bertha had not yet half done
25 A curious volume, patch'd and torn,
That all day long, from earliest morn,
Had taken captive her two eyes
Among its golden broideries;
Perplex'd her with a thousand things—
30 The stars of heaven, and angels' wings,

*The Eve of St. Mark.* Text (including heading) from Keats's draft in the British Library (*D*). Variants and other readings from the preliminary draft fragment of 99–114 in the Morgan Library (*DF*), Brown's transcript (*CB*), and Keats's letter to George and Georgiana Keats, 17–27 September 1819 (*L*). *Before* 1
⟨It was on a twice holiday⟩
⟨Twice holy was the sabbath-day bell⟩ *D*
2, 13 Twice] Thrice *L* 7 faintly] ⟨blaz'd⟩ faintly *D* 8 unmatur'd] immaturd *L* 17 moving] ⟨pacing⟩ moving *D* 20 patient] *added above the line in D* 20 folk] crowd *L* 22 organs] organ *CB* 25 A] *interlined above* ⟨The⟩ *D* 26 all] *interlined above* ⟨from the⟩ *D* 27 two] fair *written over* ⟨two⟩ *L*

Martyrs in a fiery blaze,
Azure saints mid silver rays,
Aaron's breastplate, and the seven
Candlesticks John saw in heaven,
35 The winged Lion of St. Mark,
And the Covenantal Ark,
With its many mysteries,
Cherubim and golden mice.

Bertha was a maiden fair
40 Dwelling in the old Minster Square;
From her fireside she could see
Sidelong its rich antiquity,
Far as the bishop's garden wall,
Where sycamores and elm trees tall,
45 Full leav'd, the forest had outstript,
By no sharp north wind ever nipt,
So shelter'd by the mighty pile.
Bertha arose and read awhile,
With forehead 'gainst the window pane;
50 Again she tried, and then again,
Until the dusk eve left her dark
Upon the legend of St. Mark.
From pleated lawn-frill fine and thin
She lifted up her soft warm chin,
55 With aching neck and swimming eyes,
And dazed with saintly imageries.

All was gloom, and silent all,
Save now and then the still footfall
Of one returning townwards late,
60 Past the echoing minster gate.
The clamorous daws, that all the day

33 Aaron's] Moses' *CB* 41 From] ⟨And⟩ From (And *added in the margin and then deleted*) *D* 45 Full . . . outstript,] ⟨Green⟩ ⟨Full leave'd the forest had outsript—⟩ (*the line deleted and nothing substituted*) *D* 50 Again . . . again,] *inserted afterward between 49 and 51 in D* 52 Upon] *interlined above* ⟨Amid⟩ *D* 52/53

⟨She {look abrod} rais'd her head and all was gloom⟩
⟨Se rai'd her swimming eyes and all
Was hidden in a cloudy pall—⟩ *D*

53 pleated] *interlined above* ⟨wide⟩ *D*; plaited *CB* 55 With] *interlined above* ⟨And swim⟩ *D* 56 And] *added in the margin in D*; All *L* 59 townwards] homewards *CB*, *L* 59/60 ⟨By the echoing Minster gate⟩ (By *interlined above* {Through}) *D*

Above tree tops and towers play,
Pair by pair had gone to rest,
Each in its ancient belfry nest,
65 Where asleep they fall betimes
To music of the drowsy chimes.

All was silent, all was gloom,
Abroad and in the homely room;
Down she sat, poor cheated soul,
70 And struck a lamp from the dismal coal,
Leaned forward, with bright drooping hair,
And slant book full against the glare.
Her shadow in uneasy guise
Hover'd about, a giant size,
75 On ceiling beam and old oak chair,
The parrot's cage and pannel square,
And the warm angled winter screen,
On which were many monsters seen,
Call'd doves of Siam, Lima mice,
80 And legless birds of paradise,
Macaw, and tender av'davat,
And silken furr'd Angora cat.
Untired she read; her shadow still
Glower'd about as it would fill
85 The room with wildest forms and shades,
As though some ghostly queens of spades
Had come to mock behind her back,

63 Pair (*first word*)] *successively* (*a*) Were gone long ago (*b*) Had gone long ago (*c*) Pair *D* 64 its] their *L* 66 of] and *CB* 68 Abroad . . . homely] Both abroad and in the *altered to* abroad and in the homely *D* 69–70 Down . . . coal,] *written vertically in the margin in D to replace:*

⟨The Maiden lost in dizzy maze
Tun'd to the fire and made a blaze;⟩

*Three intermediate attempts at the revised 69 also appear in the margin:*

⟨She broke the coal crust⟩
⟨She broke the crusted coal⟩
⟨Down she sat with⟩

70 lamp . . . dismal] swart Lamp from the *L* 71 Leaned] ⟨B⟩ Leaned *D* 71/72 ⟨Against the⟩ *D* 75 ceiling$_\wedge$ beam$_\wedge$] ~-~, *CB*; ~, ~, *L* 76 The parrot's] *interlined above* ⟨And homey [?]⟩ *D* 76/77 ⟨And angled screene⟩ *D* 79 doves . . . mice] *written beneath* ⟨Java Pheasants, Doves of Siam⟩ *D* 83 Untired she read] *interlined above* ⟨She read untir'd⟩ *D* 83 her . . . still] *successively* (*a*) and still her shadow (*b*) her image still (*c*) her shadow still *D* 85 wildest] gastly *L* 86 some] *interlined above* ⟨three⟩ *D* 86 queens] Queen *CB*, *L*

And dance, and ruffle their garments black.<br>
Untir'd she read the legend page<br>
90 Of holy Mark from youth to age;<br>
On land, on seas, in pagan-chains,<br>
Rejoicing for his many pains.<br>
Sometimes the learned eremite,<br>
With golden star, or dagger bright,<br>
95 Referr'd to pious poesies<br>
Written in smallest crow-quill size<br>
Beneath the text; and thus the rhyme<br>
Was parcel'd out from time to time:<br>
——"Als writith he of swevenis<br>
100 Men han beforne they wake in bliss,<br>
Whanne thate hir friendes thinke hem bound<br>
In crimpid shroude farre under grounde;<br>
And how a litling child mote be<br>
A saint er its nativitie,<br>
105 Gif thate the modre (God her blesse)<br>
Kepen in solitarinesse,<br>
And kissen devoute the holy croce.<br>
Of Goddis love and Sathan's force<br>
He writith; and thinges many mo:<br>
110 Of swiche thinges I may not shew;<br>
Bot I must tellen verilie<br>
Somdel of Saintè Cicilie;<br>
And chieflie whate he auctorethe<br>
Of Saintè Markis life and dethe."

115 At length her constant eyelids come<br>
Upon the fervent martyrdom;<br>
Then lastly to his holy shrine,<br>
Exalt amid the tapers' shine<br>
At Venice

88 their] *successively* (*a*) their (*b*) her (*c*) their *D*; her *CB*, *L* 89 page] ⟨tale⟩ page *D* 91 seas] sea *CB*, *L* 93 eremite] *interlined above* ⟨Monk referr'd⟩ *D* 95 poesies] *successively* (*a*) Poesies (*b*) Poesy (*c*) Madrigal (*d*) poesies *D* 95/96

⟨Small characterd⟩<br>
⟨Below the text⟩

(Below *made out of* Ben, *the beginning of* Beneath) *D* 99/100 ⟨That han the devels⟩ *DF* 100 beforne . . . bliss] *written beneath* ⟨who sleep to waken in Bliss⟩ *DF* 100 wake] waken *DF*, *L* 103 how a] ⟨of⟩ how a⟨n⟩ a *DF* 105 Gif] *made out of* If *DF*, *D* 110 Of] *interlined above* ⟨Bot⟩ *DF* 115–119 At . . . Venice] *not in L* 117/118 ⟨In Venice⟩ *D* 118 tapers'] taper's *altered to* tapers' *D*

## *Why did I laugh tonight? No voice will tell*

Why did I laugh tonight? No voice will tell:
  No god, no demon of severe response,
Deigns to reply from heaven or from hell.
  Then to my human heart I turn at once—
5 Heart! thou and I are here sad and alone;
  Say, wherefore did I laugh? O mortal pain!
O darkness! darkness! ever must I moan,
  To question heaven and hell and heart in vain!
Why did I laugh? I know this being's lease—
10 My fancy to its utmost blisses spreads:
Yet could I on this very midnight cease,
  And the world's gaudy ensigns see in shreds.
Verse, fame, and beauty are intense indeed,
But death intenser—death is life's high meed.

## *When they were come unto the Faery's court*

When they were come unto the Faery's court
They rang—no one at home—all gone to sport
And dance and kiss and love as faeries do,
For faeries be as humans, lovers true.
5 Amid the woods they were, so lone and wild,
Where even the robin feels himself exil'd,
And where the very brooks as if afraid
Hurry along to some less magic shade.
"No one at home!" the fretful Princess cry'd,
10 "And all for nothing such a dreary ride,
And all for nothing my new diamond cross,
No one to see my Persian feathers toss,
No one to see my Ape, my Dwarf, my Fool,
Or how I pace my Otaheitan mule.
15 Ape, Dwarf, and Fool, why stand you gaping there?
Burst the door open, quick—or I declare
I'll switch you soundly and in pieces tear."

*Why did I laugh.* Text from Keats's letter to George and Georgiana Keats, 14 February–3 May 1819 (*L*). Heading supplied by editor. 9 lease—] *ed*; ~$_\wedge$ *L* 14 death is] *ed*; Deaths is *L*

*When they were come.* Text from Keats's letter to George and Georgiana Keats, 14 February–3 May 1819 (*L*). Heading supplied by editor.

The Dwarf began to tremble and the Ape
Star'd at the Fool, the Fool was all agape;
20 The Princess grasp'd her switch, but just in time
The Dwarf with piteous face began to rhyme.
"O mighty Princess, did you ne'er hear tell
What your poor servants know but too, too well?
Know you the three 'great crimes' in faery land?
25 The first, alas! poor Dwarf, I understand—
I made a whipstock of a faery's wand;
The next is snoring in their company;
The next, the last, the direst of the three,
Is making free when they are not at home.
30 I was a prince—a baby prince—my doom
You see: I made a whipstock of a wand;
My top has henceforth slept in faery land.
He was a prince, the Fool, a grown up prince,
But he has never been a king's son since
35 He fell a snoring at a faery ball.
Your poor Ape was a prince, and he, poor thing,
Picklock'd a faery's boudoir—now no king,
But ape. So pray your highness stay awhile;
'Tis sooth indeed, we know it to our sorrow—
40 Persist and *you* may be an ape tomorrow."
While the Dwarf spake the Princess all for spite
Peel'd the brown hazel twig to lilly white,
Clench'd her small teeth, and held her lips apart,
Try'd to look unconcern'd with beating heart.
45 They saw her highness had made up her mind,
A quavering like three reeds before the wind—
And they had had it, but, O happy chance,
The Ape for very fear began to dance,
And grinn'd as all his ugliness did ache.
50 She staid her vixen fingers for his sake,
He was so very ugly: then she took
Her pocket mirror and began to look
First at herself and at him and then
She smil'd at her own beauteous face again.
55 Yet for all this—for all her pretty face—
She took it in her head to see the place.

22 ne'er] never *altered to* ne'er *L* 28 the (*third word*)] *written over* ⟨at⟩ *L* 33 He] *made out of* The *L* 46 A] *successively* (*a*) They (*b*) And (*c*) A *L* 46 quavering] *made out of* quaver'd *L* 46 three] *ed*; thee *L* 52 mirror] ⟨glass⟩ mirror *L*

Women gain little from experience
Either in lovers, husbands, or expence.
The more the beauty, the more fortune too:
60 Beauty before the wide world never knew—
So each Fair reasons—though it oft miscarries.
She thought *her* pretty face would please the faeries.
"My darling Ape, I won't whip you to-day—
Give me the picklock, sirrah, and go play."
65 They all three wept—but counsel was as vain
As crying cup biddy to drops of rain.
Yet lingeringly did the sad Ape forth draw
The picklock from the pocket in his jaw.
The Princess took it and, dismounting straight,
70 Tripp'd in blue silver'd slippers to the gate
And touch'd the wards; the door full courteously
Opened—she enter'd with her servants three.
Again it clos'd and there was nothing seen
But the Mule grasing on the herbage green.

End of Canto xii

Canto the xiii

75 The Mule no sooner saw himself alone
Than he prick'd up his ears and said, "Well done;
At least, unhappy Prince, I may be free—
No more a princess shall side saddle me.
O king of Otaheitè—though a mule,
80 'Aye every inch a king'—though 'Fortune's fool,'
Well done—for by what Mr. Dwarfy said,
I would not give a sixpence for her head."
Even as he spake he trotted in high glee
To the knotty side of an old pollard tree
85 And rubb'd his sides against the mossed bark
Till his girths burst and left him naked stark
Except his bridle—how get rid of that,
Buckled and tied with many a twist and plait?
At last it struck him to pretend to sleep,
90 And then the thievish monkies down would creep
And filch the unpleasant trammels quite away.

59 the beauty] the⟨ir⟩ beauty *L* 65 as] *written over* ⟨in⟩ *L* 71 full] *interlined above* ⟨opes⟩ *L* 90 then] *added above the line in L*

No sooner thought of than adown he lay,
Shamm'd a good snore—the monkey-men descended,
And whom they thought to injure they befriended.
95 They hung his bridle on a topmost bough,
And off he went, run, trot, or any how.

## *As Hermes once took to his feathers light*

As Hermes once took to his feathers light,
When lulled Argus, baffled, swoon'd and slept,
So on a Delphic reed, my idle spright
So play'd, so charm'd, so conquer'd, so bereft
5 The dragon-world of all its hundred eyes;
And, seeing it asleep, so fled away—
Not to pure Ida with its snow-cold skies,
Nor unto Tempe, where Jove griev'd a day,
But to that second circle of sad hell,
10 Where in the gust, the whirlwind, and the flaw
Of rain and hail-stones, lovers need not tell
Their sorrows. Pale were the sweet lips I saw,
Pale were the lips I kiss'd, and fair the form
I floated with, about that melancholy storm.

## *Character of C. B.*

He was to weet a melancholy carle,
Thin in the waist, with bushy head of hair,
As hath the seeded thistle, when in parle
It holds the zephyr, ere it sendeth fair

*As Hermes once.* Text from Brown's transcript (*CB*). Variants and other readings from Keats's draft (*D*), his letter to George and Georgiana Keats, 14 February–3 May 1819 (*L*), Woodhouse's $W^2$ transcript, and the *Indicator* version (*Ind*). *Heading* As . . . light] *ed*; Sonnet, / On a Dream *CB*; A Dream, after Reading Dante's Episode of Paulo and Francesca *Ind*; *no heading in D, L,* $W^2$ 6/7 ⟨Not⟩ ⟨But not olympus-ward to serene skies⟩ *D* 7 to pure] unto *Ind* 8 a] *interlined above* ⟨that⟩ *CB*; that *D, L,* $W^2$ 9 to] ⟨in⟩to *D* 10 in] *interlined above* ⟨on⟩ *D*; 'mid *Ind* 10 whirlwind] world-wind *Ind* 10–11 the flaw / Of] *divided* the / Flaw of *in D* 11 rain and] rain (*added above the line*; and *does not appear to be in the MS*) *D*

*Character of C. B.* Text (including heading) from Brown's transcript (*CB*). Variants and other readings from Keats's letter to George and Georgiana Keats, 14 February–3 May 1819 (*L*). *Heading* Character of C. B.] *no heading in L* 1 was] is *L*

5 Its light balloons into the summer air;
Thereto his beard had not begun to bloom,
No brush had touch'd his chin or razor sheer;
No care had touch'd his cheek with mortal doom,
But new he was and bright as scarf from Persian loom.

10 Ne cared he for wine, or half and half,
Ne cared he for fish, or flesh, or fowl,
And sauces held he worthless as the chaff;
He 'sdeign'd the swine-herd at the wassel bowl,
Ne with lewd ribbalds sat he cheek by jowl,
15 Ne with sly lemans in the scorner's chair;
But after water-brooks this pilgrim's soul
Panted, and all his food was woodland air,
Though he would ofttimes feed on gillyflowers rare.

The slang of cities in no wise he knew,
20 Tipping the wink to him was heathen Greek;
He sipp'd no olden Tom, or ruin blue,
Or nantz, or cherry brandy, drank full meek
By many a damsel hoarse and rouge of cheek;
Nor did he know each aged watchman's beat,
25 Nor in obscured purlieus would he seek
For curled Jewesses with ancles neat,
Who as they walk abroad make tinkling with their feet.

## *Bright star, would I were stedfast as thou art*

Bright star, would I were stedfast as thou art—
Not in lone splendor hung aloft the night,
And watching, with eternal lids apart,
Like nature's patient, sleepless eremite,
5 The moving waters at their priestlike task
Of pure ablution round earth's human shores,
Or gazing on the new soft-fallen mask

6 begun] began *L* 8 doom] *made out of* gloom *CB* 13 'sdeign'd] *interlined above* ⟨scorn'd⟩ *L* 18 feed] feast *L* 20 Tipping the wink] *underscored in L* 22 cherry] cheery *L*

*Bright star.* Text from the extant holograph fair copy (*FC*). Variants from Brown's transcript (*CB*). *Heading* Bright . . . art] *ed*; Sonnet *CB*; *no heading in FC* 2 aloft] amid *CB* 3 And] Not *CB* 4 patient] devout *CB* 5 moving] morning *CB* 7 mask] *CB*; masque *FC*

Of snow upon the mountains and the moors;
No—yet still stedfast, still unchangeable,
10 Pillow'd upon my fair love's ripening breast,
To feel for ever its soft swell and fall,
Awake for ever in a sweet unrest,
Still, still to hear her tender-taken breath,
And so live ever—or else swoon to death.

10 Pillow'd . . . love's] Cheek-pillow'd on my Love's white *CB* 11 feel . . . fall] touch, for ever, its warm sink and swell *CB* 13 Still, still to hear] To hear, to feel *CB* 14 And . . . swoon] Half passionless, and so swoon on *CB*

# *Hyperion:*
# *A Fragment*

## BOOK I

Deep in the shady sadness of a vale
Far sunken from the healthy breath of morn,
Far from the fiery noon, and eve's one star,
Sat gray-hair'd Saturn, quiet as a stone,
5 Still as the silence round about his lair;
Forest on forest hung above his head
Like cloud on cloud. No stir of air was there,
Not so much life as on a summer's day
Robs not one light seed from the feather'd grass,
10 But where the dead leaf fell, there did it rest.
A stream went voiceless by, still deadened more
By reason of his fallen divinity
Spreading a shade: the Naiad 'mid her reeds
Press'd her cold finger closer to her lips.

15 Along the margin-sand large foot-marks went,
No further than to where his feet had stray'd,
And slept there since. Upon the sodden ground
His old right hand lay nerveless, listless, dead,
Unsceptred; and his realmless eyes were closed;
20 While his bow'd head seem'd list'ning to the Earth,
His ancient mother, for some comfort yet.

*Hyperion.* Text (including heading) from *1820.* Variants and other readings from Keats's draft (*D*), Woodhouse's $W^2$ transcript, and Woodhouse's clerks' transcript in $W^1$. *Subtitle* A Fragment] *so 1820* (*in the Contents and on the half title preceding the first page of text*); *no subtitle in D,* $W^2$, $W^1$

I.3 eve's] ⟨evening⟩ Eve's *D* 6 above] *D*, $W^2$; about $W^1$, *1820* 6/7 ⟨Like Clouds {that} whose {bosoms} thundrous bosoms⟩ *D* 8–9 Not . . . grass] *written* (*with the variant given in the next note*) *vertically in the margin in D to replace* ⟨Not so much Life as a young vultur's wing / Would spread upon a field of green ear'd corn⟩ (a young vultur's *interlined above* {what an eagle's}) 9 one . . . grass] at all the dandelion's fleece *D*, $W^2$, $W^1$ (*the 1820 wording penciled above the line by Woodhouse in* $W^2$) 12/13 ⟨Shading across it⟩ *D* 16 stray'd] stay'd *D*, $W^1$; stay'd *altered to* stray'd $W^2$ 17 there . . . ground$_\wedge$] *successively* (*a*) without a motion since that time. (*b*) without a motion: on the ground$_\wedge$ (*c*) there since: upon the sodden ground$_\wedge$ *D* 18 listless, dead] *successively* (*a*) on the ground (*b*) dead, supine (*c*) listless, dead *D* 19 realmless] ⟨ancient⟩ realmless *interlined above* ⟨white brow'd⟩ *D* 21 His] *written over* ⟨The⟩ (*and another* The *added and deleted in the margin*) *D*

It seem'd no force could wake him from his place;
But there came one, who with a kindred hand
Touch'd his wide shoulders, after bending low
25 With reverence, though to one who knew it not.
She was a Goddess of the infant world;
By her in stature the tall Amazon
Had stood a pigmy's height: she would have ta'en
Achilles by the hair and bent his neck;
30 Or with a finger stay'd Ixion's wheel.
Her face was large as that of Memphian sphinx,
Pedestal'd haply in a palace court,
When sages look'd to Egypt for their lore.
But oh! how unlike marble was that face:
35 How beautiful, if sorrow had not made
Sorrow more beautiful than Beauty's self.
There was a listening fear in her regard,
As if calamity had but begun;
As if the vanward clouds of evil days
40 Had spent their malice, and the sullen rear
Was with its stored thunder labouring up.
One hand she press'd upon that aching spot
Where beats the human heart, as if just there,
Though an immortal, she felt cruel pain:
45 The other upon Saturn's bended neck
She laid, and to the level of his ear
Leaning with parted lips, some words she spake
In solemn tenour and deep organ tone:
Some mourning words, which in our feeble tongue
50 Would come in these like accents; O how frail
To that large utterance of the early Gods!
"Saturn, look up!—though wherefore, poor old King?
I have no comfort for thee, no not one:
I cannot say, 'O wherefore sleepest thou?'

21/22

Thus the old Eagle drowsy with great grief
Sat moulting his weak Plumage never more
To be restored or soar against the Sun,
While his three Sons upon Olympus stood—

*D*, *W*[2], *W*[1] (*the lines bracketed in pencil in W*[2] *and deleted in both pencil and ink in W*[1]; *D has* with ⟨his grief⟩ great ⟨woes⟩ grief *in the first line*) 27 By . . . tall] Placed by her side, the tallest *altered to* By her in stature the tall *D* 28 pigmy's height] *interlined above* ⟨little child⟩ *D* 30 stay'd . . . wheel] eased . . . toil *D*, *W*[2], *W*[1] 33 sages] ⟨Egyp⟩ Sages *D* 46 ear] hollow ear *D*, *W*[2] (*also "The Fall of Hyperion" I.348*); ⟨hollow⟩ ear *W*[1] 48 tone] tune *D*, *W*[2], *W*[1] (*also "The Fall" I.350*)

55 For heaven is parted from thee, and the earth
Knows thee not, thus afflicted, for a God;
And ocean too, with all its solemn noise,
Has from thy sceptre pass'd; and all the air
Is emptied of thine hoary majesty.
60 Thy thunder, conscious of the new command,
Rumbles reluctant o'er our fallen house;
And thy sharp lightning in unpractised hands
Scorches and burns our once serene domain.
O aching time! O moments big as years!
65 All as ye pass swell out the monstrous truth,
And press it so upon our weary griefs
That unbelief has not a space to breathe.
Saturn, sleep on:—O thoughtless, why did I
Thus violate thy slumbrous solitude?
70 Why should I ope thy melancholy eyes?
Saturn, sleep on! while at thy feet I weep."

As when, upon a tranced summer-night,
Those green-rob'd senators of mighty woods,
Tall oaks, branch-charmed by the earnest stars,
75 Dream, and so dream all night without a stir,
Save from one gradual solitary gust
Which comes upon the silence, and dies off,
As if the ebbing air had but one wave;
So came these words and went; the while in tears
8 She touch'd her fair large forehead to the ground,
Just where her falling hair might be outspread,
A soft and silken mat for Saturn's feet.
One moon, with alteration slow, had shed
Her silver seasons four upon the night,
85 And still these two were postured motionless,
Like natural sculpture in cathedral cavern;

62 unpractised] *interlined above* ⟨a⟩ ⟨impetuous⟩ *D* 65 All] Each *D*, $W^2$, $W^1$ 65 swell] ⟨the⟩ swell *D* 65 monstrous] *interlined above* ⟨rebel⟩ *D* 67/68 ⟨Or a brief dream to find its way to heaven.⟩ (*originally following* breathe *without punctuation at the end of 67*) *D* 73 Those] *made out of* The *D* 74 Tall] *interlined above* ⟨The⟩ *D* 74 oaks . . . charmed] *successively* (*a*) Oaks stand charmed (*b*) Oaks dream charmed (*c*) Oaks, branch-charmed *D* 75 Dream . . . stir] And thus all night without a stir ⟨they rest⟩ remain *altered to* Dream And so dream all night without a stir *D* 76 gradual] sudden *D*, $W^2$, $W^1$ (gradual *penciled above the line in* $W^1$) 76 solitary] *interlined above* ⟨momentary⟩ *D* 78 ebbing] *interlined above* ⟨Sea of⟩ *D* 81 falling] fallen *D* (*also "The Fall" I.380*) 81 be outspread] make spread *altered to* be outspread *D*

The frozen God still couchant on the earth,
And the sad Goddess weeping at his feet:
Until at length old Saturn lifted up
90 His faded eyes, and saw his kingdom gone,
And all the gloom and sorrow of the place,
And that fair kneeling Goddess; and then spake,
As with a palsied tongue, and while his beard
Shook horrid with such aspen-malady:
95 "O tender spouse of gold Hyperion,
Thea, I feel thee ere I see thy face;
Look up, and let me see our doom in it;
Look up, and tell me if this feeble shape
Is Saturn's; tell me, if thou hear'st the voice
100 Of Saturn; tell me, if this wrinkling brow,
Naked and bare of its great diadem,
Peers like the front of Saturn. Who had power
To make me desolate? whence came the strength?
How was it nurtur'd to such bursting forth,
105 While Fate seem'd strangled in my nervous grasp?
But it is so; and I am smother'd up,
And buried from all godlike exercise
Of influence benign on planets pale,
Of admonitions to the winds and seas,
110 Of peaceful sway above man's harvesting,
And all those acts which Deity supreme
Doth ease its heart of love in.—I am gone
Away from my own bosom: I have left
My strong identity, my real self,
115 Somewhere between the throne, and where I sit
Here on this spot of earth. Search, Thea, search!
Open thine eyes eterne, and sphere them round

87 earth] *interlined above* ⟨sand⟩ *D*   90 faded . . . his] *successively* (*a*) Eyes and saw his royal (*b*) faint blue Eyes and saw his (*c*) faded Eyes and saw his *D*   91 gloom and] gloom ⟨of⟩ and *D*   92 then] ⟨he said⟩ then *D*   98 tell] ⟨see if thou⟩ tell *D*   100 wrinkling] ⟨f⟩ wrinkling *D*   102 Who] What dost think? / Am I that same—O Chaos who *D*, $W^2$, $W^1$ (What . . . Chaos *subsequently deleted in both pencil and ink in* $W^1$)   106 But] ⟨And yet⟩ But *D*   106 it is so] *interlined above* ⟨so it is⟩ *D*   108 on] ⟨on Sun⟩ on *D*   111/112 ⟨Must do to ease itself, lest two hot grown⟩ *D*   112 Doth . . . gone]

Doth ease its heart of Love in ⟨just as tears
Leave a calm pleasure in the human breast.—
O Thea I must burn—my Spirit gasps⟩
I am gone *D*

115 the] *interlined above* ⟨my⟩ *D*   116 spot] bit *D*, $W^2$, $W^1$

Upon all space: space starr'd, and lorn of light;
Space region'd with life-air; and barren void;
120 Spaces of fire, and all the yawn of hell.—
Search, Thea, search! and tell me, if thou seest
A certain shape or shadow, making way
With wings or chariot fierce to repossess
A heaven he lost erewhile: it must—it must
125 Be of ripe progress—Saturn must be King.
Yes, there must be a golden victory;
There must be Gods thrown down, and trumpets blown
Of triumph calm, and hymns of festival
Upon the gold clouds metropolitan,
130 Voices of soft proclaim, and silver stir
Of strings in hollow shells; and there shall be
Beautiful things made new, for the surprise
Of the sky-children; I will give command:
Thea! Thea! Thea! where is Saturn?"

135 This passion lifted him upon his feet,
And made his hands to struggle in the air,
His Druid locks to shake and ooze with sweat,
His eyes to fever out, his voice to cease.
He stood, and heard not Thea's sobbing deep;
140 A little time, and then again he snatch'd
Utterance thus.—"But cannot I create?
Cannot I form? Cannot I fashion forth
Another world, another universe,
To overbear and crumble this to nought?
145 Where is another Chaos? Where?"—That word
Found way unto Olympus, and made quake
The rebel three.—Thea was startled up,
And in her bearing was a sort of hope,
As thus she quick-voic'd spake, yet full of awe.

150 "This cheers our fallen house: come to our friends,
O Saturn! come away, and give them heart;
I know the covert, for thence came I hither."

118 lorn] *made out of* lone *D* 119 life-air] life Air (Air *added above the line*) *D* 125 of . . . must] going on—Saturn must ⟨Vic⟩ still *altered to* of ripe progress—Saturn must *D* 126 Yes] *written over* ⟨Aye⟩ (*but see Textual Note*) *D*; Aye *interlined above* ⟨Yes⟩ $W^2$ 134 where is] *interlined above* ⟨Am I⟩ *D* 139 and . . . not] *interlined above* ⟨not hearing⟩ *D* 145 word] word—⟨that Sound⟩ *D* 147 startled] started *D*

Thus brief; then with beseeching eyes she went
With backward footing through the shade a space:
155 He follow'd, and she turn'd to lead the way
Through aged boughs, that yielded like the mist
Which eagles cleave upmounting from their nest.

Meanwhile in other realms big tears were shed,
More sorrow like to this, and such like woe,
160 Too huge for mortal tongue or pen of scribe:
The Titans fierce, self-hid, or prison-bound,
Groan'd for the old allegiance once more,
And listen'd in sharp pain for Saturn's voice.
But one of the whole mammoth-brood still kept
165 His sov'reignty, and rule, and majesty;—
Blazing Hyperion on his orbed fire
Still sat, still snuff'd the incense, teeming up
From man to the sun's God; yet unsecure:
For as among us mortals omens drear
170 Fright and perplex, so also shuddered he—
Not at dog's howl, or gloom-bird's hated screech,
Or the familiar visiting of one
Upon the first toll of his passing-bell,
Or prophesyings of the midnight lamp;
175 But horrors, portion'd to a giant nerve,
Oft made Hyperion ache. His palace bright,
Bastion'd with pyramids of glowing gold,
And touch'd with shade of bronzed obelisks,
Glar'd a blood-red through all its thousand courts,
180 Arches, and domes, and fiery galleries;
And all its curtains of Aurorian clouds
Flush'd angerly: while sometimes eagle's wings,
Unseen before by Gods or wondering men,
Darken'd the place; and neighing steeds were heard,

154 shade] *interlined above* ⟨gloom⟩ *D* 156 that . . . the] that gave to them like *D*, *W*², *W*¹ (that . . . them *interlined above* ⟨which to them gave⟩ *in D*) 156 mist] ⟨Air⟩ Mist *D* 157 upmounting] ⟨to⟩ upmounting *D* 158 in] ⟨were⟩ in *D* 159 such like] suchlike *D* 173 Upon . . . bell] *interlined above* ⟨Just at the tolling of his passing bell⟩ *D* 175 horrors] *interlined above* ⟨warnings⟩ *D* 175 a] *interlined above* ⟨his⟩ *D* 175 nerve] *interlined above* ⟨sense⟩ *D* 176 made] ⟨made his Chin⟩ ⟨pressed his curly chin upon his Breast⟩ made *D* 178 And . . . of] *successively* (*a*) ⟨And⟩ With chequer black of (*b*) With shading black of (*c*) Touched with the shade of (*d*) and Touched with shade of *D* 181 all its] *interlined above* ⟨through⟩ *D* 182 eagle's] Eagles' *W*² 183 Unseen before] *interlined above* ⟨Darkened the place⟩ *D*

185 Not heard before by Gods or wondering men.
Also, when he would taste the spicy wreaths
Of incense, breath'd aloft from sacred hills,
Instead of sweets, his ample palate took
Savour of poisonous brass and metal sick:
190 And so, when harbour'd in the sleepy west,
After the full completion of fair day,—
For rest divine upon exalted couch
And slumber in the arms of melody,
He pac'd away the pleasant hours of ease
195 With stride colossal, on from hall to hall;
While far within each aisle and deep recess,
His winged minions in close clusters stood,
Amaz'd and full of fear; like anxious men
Who on wide plains gather in panting troops,
200 When earthquakes jar their battlements and towers.
Even now, while Saturn, rous'd from icy trance,
Went step for step with Thea through the woods,
Hyperion, leaving twilight in the rear,
Came slope upon the threshold of the west;
205 Then, as was wont, his palace-door flew ope
In smoothest silence, save what solemn tubes,
Blown by the serious Zephyrs, gave of sweet
And wandering sounds, slow-breathed melodies;
And like a rose in vermeil tint and shape,
210 In fragrance soft, and coolness to the eye,

185 Gods or wondering] either Gods or *altered to* Gods or wondring *D* 186 Also] *interlined above* ⟨Sometimes⟩ *D* 186 taste] *successively* (*a*) taste (*b*) take (*c*) taste *D* 189 Savour of poisonous] A poison feel of *D*, $W^2$, $W^1$ (*altered by Woodhouse to the 1820 wording in* $W^1$; poison *interlined above* ⟨nausea⟩ ⟨nauseous feel⟩ *in D*) 190 And so] *interlined above* ⟨So that⟩ *D* 190 harbour'd . . . sleepy] he had harbour'd in the *altered to* harbour'd in the sleepy *D* 191 full] ⟨gradual⟩ full *D* 192 For . . . divine] Instead of rest *altered to* For rest divine *D* 193 slumber in] slumber⟨ing to b⟩ in (*with* bla *or* ble *interlined and deleted above* ing) *D* 196 each] *interlined above* ⟨deep⟩ *D* 196 deep] *interlined above* ⟨wide⟩ *D* 198 Amaz'd . . . fear] *successively* (*a*) In fear and sad amaze (*b*) In fear and sad surprise (*c*) Amazed and full of fear *D* 198 anxious men] *successively* (*a*) men at gaze (*b*) trooped men (*c*) anxious men *D* 199 wide . . . panting] *successively* (*a*) a wide plain gather in sad (*b*) wide plain gather in sad eyed (*c*) wide plain gather in panting *D* 199 plains] plain $W^2$, $W^1$ (*D also—see preceding note—and "The Fall" II.43*) 200 earthquakes . . . and] an Earthquake hath shook their city *D*, $W^2$, $W^1$ (*altered by Woodhouse to the 1820 wording in* $W^1$) 202/203 ⟨He of the Sun just lighted from the Air⟩ *D* 205 Then, as] *interlined above* ⟨As it⟩ *D*; There, as $W^2$ 205 door] door⟨s⟩ *D*, $W^2$, $W^1$ (s *deleted in all three MSS*) 205/206 Most like a Rose bud to a faery's Lute *D*, $W^2$, $W^1$ (farae's *in D*; *earlier versions of the first five words in D were, successively,* [*a*] As opes a Rose bud [*b*] As open Rose buds [*c*] As doth a Rose bud) 209 And‸] Yes, *D*, $W^2$, $W^1$ 209 in] ⟨in tint and⟩ ⟨in vermeil⟩ in *D*

That inlet to severe magnificence
Stood full blown, for the God to enter in.

He enter'd, but he enter'd full of wrath;
His flaming robes stream'd out beyond his heels,
215 And gave a roar, as if of earthly fire,
That scar'd away the meek ethereal Hours
And made their dove-wings tremble. On he flared,
From stately nave to nave, from vault to vault,
Through bowers of fragrant and enwreathed light,
220 And diamond-paved lustrous long arcades,
Until he reach'd the great main cupola;
There standing fierce beneath, he stampt his foot,
And from the basements deep to the high towers
Jarr'd his own golden region; and before
225 The quavering thunder thereupon had ceas'd,
His voice leapt out, despite of godlike curb,
To this result: "O dreams of day and night!
O monstrous forms! O effigies of pain!
O spectres busy in a cold, cold gloom!
230 O lank-eared Phantoms of black-weeded pools!
Why do I know ye? why have I seen ye? why
Is my eternal essence thus distraught
To see and to behold these horrors new?
Saturn is fallen, am I too to fall?
235 Am I to leave this haven of my rest,
This cradle of my glory, this soft clime,
This calm luxuriance of blissful light,
These crystalline pavilions, and pure fanes,
Of all my lucent empire? It is left
240 Deserted, void, nor any haunt of mine.
The blaze, the splendor, and the symmetry,

211 That] The Sun's *altered to* That *D* 214 flaming] *interlined above* ⟨fiery⟩ *D* 217 their] *made out of* the *D* 217 wings] wing *D*, $W^2$, $W^1$ (s *added marginally in pencil in* $W^1$) 217 flared] ⟨went⟩ flar'd *D* 217/218

⟨From georgeous vault to vault, from space to space
Untill he reached the great main Copula:
{And} there standing fierce beneath, he stampt his foot⟩

(standing fierce *interlined above* {he stood} *in the last line*) *D* 219 fragrant] ⟨wreathed fragrant light u⟩ fragrant *D* 223 And] ⟨The⟩ And *D* 223 basements deep] deep foundations *altered to* basements deep *D* 233 see] *interlined above* ⟨mark⟩ *D* 236–239 this soft . . . empire?] *added (with the readings given in the next three notes) on the opposite verso in D with a mark for insertion after* glory *in 236* 236 this soft] This soft *altered to* The soft *D* 236/237 ⟨Unknow elsewhere but⟩ *D* 238 These] *made out of* This *D*

I cannot see—but darkness, death and darkness.
Even here, into my centre of repose,
The shady visions come to domineer,
245 Insult, and blind, and stifle up my pomp.—
Fall!—No, by Tellus and her briny robes!
Over the fiery frontier of my realms
I will advance a terrible right arm
Shall scare that infant thunderer, rebel Jove,
250 And bid old Saturn take his throne again."—
He spake, and ceas'd, the while a heavier threat
Held struggle with his throat but came not forth;
For as in theatres of crowded men
Hubbub increases more they call out "Hush!"
255 So at Hyperion's words the Phantoms pale
Bestirr'd themselves, thrice horrible and cold;
And from the mirror'd level where he stood
A mist arose, as from a scummy marsh.
At this, through all his bulk an agony
260 Crept gradual, from the feet unto the crown,
Like a lithe serpent vast and muscular
Making slow way, with head and neck convuls'd
From over-strained might. Releas'd, he fled
To the eastern gates, and full six dewy hours
265 Before the dawn in season due should blush,
He breath'd fierce breath against the sleepy portals,
Clear'd them of heavy vapours, burst them wide
Suddenly on the ocean's chilly streams.
The planet orb of fire, whereon he rode
270 Each day from east to west the heavens through,
Spun round in sable curtaining of clouds;

243 into my] *successively* (*a*) into my (*b*) in my old (*c*) into my *D* 243 centre] *interlined above* ⟨sanctuary⟩ *D* 247 Over] *interlined above* ⟨Upon⟩ *D* 248 I will] I⟨'ll⟩ will *D* 248 a] ⟨and⟩ ⟨my ar⟩ a *D* 250 take] *interlined above* ⟨seize⟩ *D* 255 So] *interlined above* ⟨So as wind⟩ (*the deleted* So *written over* {Or}) *D* 256 horrible] *made out of* horibly *D* 257 mirror'd] *interlined above* ⟨glossy⟩ *D* 257 where] ⟨of⟩ where *D* 258 scummy] *interlined above* ⟨stagnant⟩ *D* 259 through all] *added above the line in D* 260 Crept gradual] *successively* (*a*) From the (*b*) Crept slowly (*c*) Crept gradual *D* 261 lithe] *interlined above* ⟨vast⟩ *D* 263 From] ⟨With spite⟩ From *D* 263 might] ⟨gripe⟩ might *D* 264 six] *interlined above* ⟨three⟩ *D* 267 vapours,] *interlined above* ⟨clouds, and⟩ *D* 267–268 wide$_\wedge$ . . . streams.] ~: . . . ~. $W^2$; ~: . . . ~, $W^1$ 268 Suddenly] And sudden *D*, $W^2$, $W^1$ 271–283 Spun . . . fled.—] *written on the opposite verso in D to replace:*

⟨Spun {at his} round in darkest curtaining of clouds
Not therefore hidden up and muffled quite

Not therefore veiled quite, blindfold, and hid,
But ever and anon the glancing spheres,
Circles, and arcs, and broad-belting colure,
275 Glow'd through, and wrought upon the muffling dark
Sweet-shaped lightnings from the nadir deep
Up to the zenith,—hieroglyphics old,
Which sages and keen-eyed astrologers
Then living on the earth, with labouring thought
280 Won from the gaze of many centuries:
Now lost, save what we find on remnants huge
Of stone, or marble swart; their import gone,
Their wisdom long since fled.—Two wings this orb
Possess'd for glory, two fair argent wings,
285 Ever exalted at the God's approach:
And now, from forth the gloom their plumes immense
Rose, one by one, till all outspreaded were;
While still the dazzling globe maintain'd eclipse,
Awaiting for Hyperion's command.
290 Fain would he have commanded, fain took throne
And bid the day begin, if but for change.
He might not:—No, though a primeval God:
The sacred seasons might not be disturb'd.
Therefore the operations of the dawn
295 Stay'd in their birth, even as here 'tis told.
Those silver wings expanded sisterly,
Eager to sail their orb; the porches wide
Open'd upon the dusk demesnes of night;

---

But ever and anon the glancing spheres
{Shot through} Glow'd through and still about the sable shroud
Made sweet-shap'd light{ning:}⟩

(darkest *interlined above* {blackest} *in the first line,* But *interlined above* {For} *in the third, and* about *successively* [*a*] upon [*b*] within [*c*] about *in the fourth; see Textual Note to I.283*) 272 hid] *successively* (*a*) dusk (*b*) dim (*c*) veil'd (*d*) hid *D* 274 broad] ⟨zones⟩ broad *D* 275 wrought] *interlined above* ⟨shot⟩ ⟨struck⟩ *D* 275 upon] *interlined above* ⟨throughout⟩ *D* 275 muffling] muffling *altered to* muffle *D* 275 dark] *successively* (*a*) blast (*b*) grim (*c*) dark *D* 281 save] ⟨with all their Wisdom and import⟩ save *D* 283 Their] *interlined above* ⟨And all ther⟩ *D* 283 Two . . . this] Wings this ⟨splendent⟩ (*see Textual Note*) *D* 285 Ever] *interlined above* ⟨Always⟩ *D* 285 approach] came near *interlined above* approach (*undeleted*) *D* 287 Rose] *interlined above* ⟨Came⟩ *D* 288 maintain'd] ⟨kept⟩ maintain'd *D* 292 though] ⟨not even⟩ though *D* 293 The] *successively* (*a*) Break through the (*b*) Disturb the (*c*) The (*all three versions following* God *without punctuation at the end of 292*) *D* 293 might] *interlined above* ⟨could⟩ *D* 295 here] ⟨it is writ⟩ here *D* 296 wings . . . sisterly] *interlined above* ⟨wings of the Sun were full outspead⟩ *D* 297 Eager] *interlined above* ⟨Ready⟩ *D* 298 Open'd upon] Were opened on *altered to* opened upon *D* 298 demesnes] *made out of* domain *D*

And the bright Titan, phrenzied with new woes,
300 Unus'd to bend, by hard compulsion bent
His spirit to the sorrow of the time;
And all along a dismal rack of clouds,
Upon the boundaries of day and night,
He stretch'd himself in grief and radiance faint.
305 There as he lay, the heaven with its stars
Look'd down on him with pity, and the voice
Of Cœlus, from the universal space,
Thus whisper'd low and solemn in his ear.
"O brightest of my children dear, earth-born
310 And sky-engendered, Son of Mysteries
All unrevealed even to the powers
Which met at thy creating; at whose joys
And palpitations sweet, and pleasures soft,
I, Cœlus, wonder, how they came and whence;
315 And at the fruits thereof what shapes they be,
Distinct, and visible; symbols divine,
Manifestations of that beauteous life
Diffus'd unseen throughout eternal space:
Of these new-form'd art thou, oh brightest child!
320 Of these, thy brethren and the Goddesses!
There is sad feud among ye, and rebellion
Of son against his sire. I saw him fall,
I saw my first-born tumbled from his throne!
To me his arms were spread, to me his voice
325 Found way from forth the thunders round his head!
Pale wox I, and in vapours hid my face.
Art thou, too, near such doom? vague fear there is:
For I have seen my sons most unlike Gods.
Divine ye were created, and divine
330 In sad demeanour, solemn, undisturb'd,
Unruffled, like high Gods, ye liv'd and ruled:
Now I behold in you fear, hope, and wrath;
Actions of rage and passion; even as
I see them, on the mortal world beneath,

299 bright] *interlined above* ⟨enraged⟩ *D* 300 hard] *interlined above* ⟨stern⟩ *D* 304 stretch'd] *interlined above* ⟨laid⟩ *D* 304 in . . . and] *interlined above* ⟨supine, {and} in⟩ *D* 306 Look'd] Look *D* 307 from] ⟨born of⟩ from *D* 314 came] could come *altered to* came *D* 316 Distinct, and] Distinct ⟨in form;⟩ and *D* 317 beauteous] ⟨Life and Beauty⟩ beauteous *D* 331 Unruffled] ⟨Passionless⟩ Unruffled *D* 332 Now] ⟨An aw⟩ Now *D* 332 you] *made out of* ye *D*; ye $W^2$, $W^1$ 333/334 ⟨In widest speculation I do see⟩ *D* 334 them] ⟨upon⟩ them *D*

335 In men who die.—This is the grief, O Son!
Sad sign of ruin, sudden dismay, and fall!
Yet do thou strive; as thou art capable,
As thou canst move about, an evident God;
And canst oppose to each malignant hour
340 Ethereal presence:—I am but a voice;
My life is but the life of winds and tides,
No more than winds and tides can I avail:—
But thou canst.—Be thou therefore in the van
Of circumstance; yea, seize the arrow's barb
345 Before the tense string murmur.—To the earth!
For there thou wilt find Saturn, and his woes.
Meantime I will keep watch on thy bright sun,
And of thy seasons be a careful nurse."—
Ere half this region-whisper had come down,
350 Hyperion arose, and on the stars
Lifted his curved lids, and kept them wide
Until it ceas'd; and still he kept them wide:
And still they were the same bright, patient stars.
Then with a slow incline of his broad breast,
355 Like to a diver in the pearly seas,
Forward he stoop'd over the airy shore,
And plung'd all noiseless into the deep night.

## BOOK II

Just at the self-same beat of Time's wide wings
Hyperion slid into the rustled air,
And Saturn gain'd with Thea that sad place
Where Cybele and the bruised Titans mourn'd.

343 But] ⟨Yet⟩ But *D* 345 murmur] murmurs *D*; murmur⟨s⟩ $W^2$ ($W^1$ *has* murmur *altered by Woodhouse to* murmurs) 347–348 Meantime . . . nurse."—] *written on the opposite verso in D with a mark for insertion after 346* 349 come down] *written above and beside* ⟨gone by⟩ *D* 351 Lifted] *interlined above* ⟨Opened⟩ *D* 353 they . . . bright] *successively* (*a*) they all were the same (*b*) he saw the same bright (*c*) they were the same bright *D* 356 over] ⟨into⟩ over *D*

II *heading* Book] Canto *D* *Before* 1
⟨Upon the very point of winged time
That saw Hyperion⟩
⟨Hyperion slid⟩
(the *made out of* that *in the first line*) *D* 1 beat] move *interlined above* ⟨beat⟩ *D*; beat *interlined above* move (*undeleted*) $W^2$ 4 the] *written over* ⟨her⟩ *D* 4 Titans] *interlined above* ⟨Children⟩ *D*

5 It was a den where no insulting light
Could glimmer on their tears; where their own groans
They felt, but heard not, for the solid roar
Of thunderous waterfalls and torrents hoarse,
Pouring a constant bulk, uncertain where.
10 Crag jutting forth to crag, and rocks that seem'd
Ever as if just rising from a sleep,
Forehead to forehead held their monstrous horns;
And thus in thousand hugest phantasies
Made a fit roofing to this nest of woe.
15 Instead of thrones, hard flint they sat upon,
Couches of rugged stone, and slaty ridge
Stubborn'd with iron. All were not assembled:
Some chain'd in torture, and some wandering.
Cœus, and Gyges, and Briareüs,
20 Typhon, and Dolor, and Porphyrion,
With many more, the brawniest in assault,
Were pent in regions of laborious breath;
Dungeon'd in opaque element, to keep
Their clenched teeth still clench'd, and all their limbs
25 Lock'd up like veins of metal, crampt and screw'd;
Without a motion, save of their big hearts
Heaving in pain, and horribly convuls'd
With sanguine feverous boiling gurge of pulse.
Mnemosyne was straying in the world;
30 Far from her moon had Phœbe wandered;
And many else were free to roam abroad,
But for the main, here found they covert drear.
Scarce images of life, one here, one there,
Lay vast and edgeways; like a dismal cirque

5 den] *interlined above* place (*undeleted*) *D*, $W^2$ 8 and] ⟨pouring⟩ and *D* 16 Couches] ⟨Rough stones⟩ Couches *D* 16 slaty ridge] *successively* (*a*) edge of Slate (*b*) sharpedgd Slate (*c*) sharpedgd ridge (*d*) Slaty ridge *D* 17 All . . . assembled] *written on the opposite verso in D to replace* ⟨All were not here hidden⟩ (*the last two words successively* [*a*] here hidden [*b*] hidden here [*c*] here hidden) 20–21 Typhon . . . assault,] *added on the opposite verso in D* 21 brawniest] *interlined above* ⟨hugest⟩ *D* 21 in] of *D*, $W^2$ (*written over* ⟨in⟩ *in* $W^2$) 23–28 Dungeon'd . . . pulse.] *added on the opposite verso in D* 23 to] ⟨that kept⟩ to *D* 24 and] *written over* ⟨all⟩ *D* 25 veins of metal] *successively* (*a*) veins of Metal (*b*) Metal veins, with (*c*) veins of Metal *D* 27 Heaving] *interlined above* ⟨Labouring⟩ *D* 28 boiling . . . of] *marked for transposition to* gurge of boiling $W^2$ 28 boiling] ⟨whelming⟩ boiling *added above the line in D* 30 Far] *interlined above* ⟨And⟩ *D* 31 And . . . abroad,] *added on the opposite verso in D with a mark for insertion after 30* 31/32 ⟨But for the rest⟩ *D* 32 But for] *added in the margin in D* 32 main] *successively* (*a*) others (*b*) rest (*c*) main *D* 32 they . . . drear] *interlined above* ⟨grief and respite sad⟩ *D*

35 Of Druid stones, upon a forlorn moor,
When the chill rain begins at shut of eve,
In dull November, and their chancel vault,
The heaven itself, is blinded throughout night.
Each one kept shroud, nor to his neighbour gave
40 Or word, or look, or action of despair.
Creüs was one; his ponderous iron mace
Lay by him, and a shatter'd rib of rock
Told of his rage, ere he thus sank and pined.
Iäpetus another; in his grasp,
45 A serpent's plashy neck; its barbed tongue
Squeez'd from the gorge, and all its uncurl'd length
Dead; and because the creature could not spit
Its poison in the eyes of conquering Jove.
Next Cottus: prone he lay, chin uppermost,
50 As though in pain; for still upon the flint
He ground severe his skull, with open mouth
And eyes at horrid working. Nearest him
Asia, born of most enormous Caf,
Who cost her mother Tellus keener pangs,
55 Though feminine, than any of her sons:
More thought than woe was in her dusky face,
For she was prophesying of her glory;
And in her wide imagination stood
Palm-shaded temples, and high rival fanes,
60 By Oxus or in Ganges' sacred isles.
Even as Hope upon her anchor leans,
So leant she, not so fair, upon a tusk
Shed from the broadest of her elephants.
Above her, on a crag's uneasy shelve,
65 Upon his elbow rais'd, all prostrate else,
Shadow'd Enceladus; once tame and mild
As grazing ox unworried in the meads;
Now tiger-passion'd, lion-thoughted, wroth,
He meditated, plotted, and even now
70 Was hurling mountains in that second war,

35 stones] ⟨stones⟩ ⟨temple⟩ stones *D* 38 throughout] *successively* (*a*) through long (*b*) the long (*c*) throughout *D* 43 sank] sunk *D*, $W^2$, $W^1$ 46 the] *written over* ⟨its⟩ *D*, $W^2$, $W^1$ (*the same alteration in all three MSS*) 50 As . . . pain] *interlined above* ⟨Pained he seemd⟩ *D* 51 severe] *added above the line in D* 59/60 ⟨From Tigris unto Ganges, and far north⟩ *D* 60 Oxus] *interlined above* ⟨Tigris⟩ *D* 60 sacred] shaded *D*, $W^2$, $W^1$ 62 a] *interlined above* ⟨the⟩ *D*, $W^2$; *written over* ⟨the⟩ $W^1$ 63 Shed] Sled $W^2$, $W^1$ (*made out of* Shed *by Woodhouse in both MSS*) 68 wroth] ⟨scar'd⟩ wrath *D*; wroth *made out of* wrath $W^2$

Not long delay'd, that scar'd the younger Gods
To hide themselves in forms of beast and bird.
Not far hence Atlas; and beside him prone
Phorcus, the sire of Gorgons. Neighbour'd close
75 Oceanus, and Tethys, in whose lap
Sobb'd Clymene among her tangled hair.
In midst of all lay Themis, at the feet
Of Ops the queen all clouded round from sight;
No shape distinguishable, more than when
80 Thick night confounds the pine-tops with the clouds:
And many else whose names may not be told.
For when the Muse's wings are air-ward spread,
Who shall delay her flight? And she must chaunt
Of Saturn, and his guide, who now had climb'd
85 With damp and slippery footing from a depth
More horrid still. Above a sombre cliff
Their heads appear'd, and up their stature grew
Till on the level height their steps found ease:
Then Thea spread abroad her trembling arms
90 Upon the precincts of this nest of pain,
And sidelong fix'd her eye on Saturn's face:
There saw she direst strife; the supreme God
At war with all the frailty of grief,
Of rage, of fear, anxiety, revenge,
95 Remorse, spleen, hope, but most of all despair.
Against these plagues he strove in vain; for Fate
Had pour'd a mortal oil upon his head,
A disanointing poison: so that Thea,
Affrighted, kept her still, and let him pass
100 First onwards in, among the fallen tribe.

As with us mortal men, the laden heart
Is persecuted more, and fever'd more,
When it is nighing to the mournful house
Where other hearts are sick of the same bruise;

72 themselves] *made out of* themself *D* 74 Neighbour'd close] Next neighbour'd *altered to* Neighbour'd close *D* 81 else] *interlined above* ⟨more⟩ *D* 83 chaunt] ⟨trill⟩ chaunt *D* 85 With] *written over* ⟨Up⟩ *D* 86 Above] ⟨and now was slowly come⟩ Above (*the deleted text originally following* still *without punctuation*) *D* 86 sombre] *interlined above* ⟨clifted⟩ ⟨gnarled⟩ *D* 88 Till] ⟨Till their feet⟩ Till *D* 90 Upon . . . pain,] *written on the opposite verso in D with a mark for insertion after 89* 91 eye] eyes *D* 95 of all] *added above the line in D* 101 with us] *interlined above* ⟨among⟩ *D* 103 house] ⟨spot⟩ House *D*

105 So Saturn, as he walk'd into the midst,
Felt faint, and would have sunk among the rest,
But that he met Enceladus's eye,
Whose mightiness, and awe of him, at once
Came like an inspiration; and he shouted,
110 "Titans, behold your God!" at which some groan'd;
Some started on their feet; some also shouted;
Some wept, some wail'd, all bow'd with reverence;
And Ops, uplifting her black folded veil,
Show'd her pale cheeks, and all her forehead wan,
115 Her eye-brows thin and jet, and hollow eyes.
There is a roaring in the bleak-grown pines
When Winter lifts his voice; there is a noise
Among immortals when a God gives sign,
With hushing finger, how he means to load
120 His tongue with the full weight of utterless thought,
With thunder, and with music, and with pomp:
Such noise is like the roar of bleak-grown pines;
Which, when it ceases in this mountain'd world,
No other sound succeeds; but ceasing here,
125 Among these fallen, Saturn's voice therefrom
Grew up like organ, that begins anew
Its strain, when other harmonies, stopt short,
Leave the dinn'd air vibrating silverly.
Thus grew it up—"Not in my own sad breast,
130 Which is its own great judge and searcher out,
Can I find reason why ye should be thus:
Not in the legends of the first of days,
Studied from that old spirit-leaved book
Which starry Uranus with finger bright
135 Sav'd from the shores of darkness, when the waves
Low-ebb'd still hid it up in shallow gloom;—

108 mightiness] mightliness *D*, $W^2$, $W^1$ (*but see Textual Note*) 112 some wail'd] ⟨some sat up,⟩ some wail'd *D* 115 eye . . . eyes] hollow eyes and eyebrows thin and jet (*but marked for transposition*) *D* 121 and (*third word*)] *successively* (*a*) and (*b*) or (*c*) and *D* 123 when] *written over* ⟨in⟩ *D* 123 ceases] ceacest *D*; ceaseth $W^2$; ceases *made out of* ceaseth $W^1$ 124 succeeds] is heard *D*, $W^2$, $W^1$ (⟨there⟩ is heard *in D*) 127 stopt short] *interlined above* ⟨stop short⟩ *D* 127/128 ⟨And thus it grew:⟩ *D* 128 Leave . . . silverly] *written on the opposite verso in D to replace* ⟨Leaving⟩ ⟨And leave {the Air} vibrations silver in the roof⟩ *D* 128 Leave the dinn'd] And leave the *altered to* leave the din'd *D* 128 vibrating] vibrated *D* (*see Textual Note*) 129 Not] ⟨Not in my own⟩ Not (*the undeleted* Not *made out of* Nor) *D* 132 Not] *made out of* Nor *D* 134 starry . . . with] starr'd Uranus with his *D*, $W^2$, $W^1$ (*altered by Woodhouse in pencil to the 1820 wording in* $W^1$) 136 hid . . . gloom] *successively* (*a*) scantly touch'd it (*b*) hid it in shallow gloom (*c*) hid it up in shallow gloom *D*

And the which book ye know I ever kept
For my firm-based footstool:—Ah, infirm!
Not there, nor in sign, symbol, or portent
140 Of element, earth, water, air, and fire,—
At war, at peace, or inter-quarreling
One against one, or two, or three, or all
Each several one against the other three,
As fire with air loud warring when rain-floods
145 Drown both, and press them both against earth's face,
Where, finding sulphur, a quadruple wrath
Unhinges the poor world;—not in that strife,
Wherefrom I take strange lore, and read it deep,
Can I find reason why ye should be thus:
150 No, no-where can unriddle, though I search,
And pore on Nature's universal scroll
Even to swooning, why ye, Divinities,
The first-born of all shap'd and palpable Gods,
Should cower beneath what, in comparison,
155 Is untremendous might. Yet ye are here,
O'erwhelm'd, and spurn'd, and batter'd, ye are here!
O Titans, shall I say 'Arise!'—Ye groan:
Shall I say 'Crouch!'—Ye groan. What can I then?
O Heaven wide! O unseen parent dear!
160 What can I? Tell me, all ye brethren Gods,
How we can war, how engine our great wrath!
O speak your counsel now, for Saturn's ear
Is all a-hunger'd. Thou, Oceanus,
Ponderest high and deep; and in thy face
165 I see, astonied, that severe content
Which comes of thought and musing: give us help!"

So ended Saturn; and the God of the Sea,
Sophist and sage, from no Athenian grove,
But cogitation in his watery shades,
170 Arose, with locks not oozy, and began,

136/137 ⟨Nor in that Book, nor in the⟩ (that *made out of* the) *D* 139 sign,] ⟨the⟩ sign‸ *D*; sign‸ *interlined above and after* ⟨the⟩ $W^2$; the sign‸ $W^1$ 141 At (*first word*)] *written over* ⟨In⟩ *D* 141 or] *written over* ⟨at⟩ *D*; *interlined above* ⟨at⟩ $W^2$ 144 loud warring] *interlined above* ⟨engaging⟩ *D* 146 finding] ⟨these then⟩ finding (*the second deleted word also readable as* these *and* there) *D* 150 unriddle] ⟨discover⟩ unriddle *interlined above* ⟨I find it⟩ *D* 151 universal] ⟨wide⟩ universal *D* 153 of] ⟨and⟩ of *D* 156 spurn'd] spur'd *D*; spur'd *altered to* spurn'd $W^2$ 157 groan:] groan—⟨Alas!⟩ *D* 161 we can] can we *altered to* we can *D* 165 astonied] *made out of* astonish'd *D* 167 of] o' *D*, $W^2$, $W^1$ 169 in his] *interlined above* ⟨beneath⟩ *D* 169 shades] *interlined above* ⟨glooms⟩ *D*

In murmurs, which his first-endeavouring tongue
Caught infant-like from the far-foamed sands.
"O ye, whom wrath consumes! who, passion-stung,
Writhe at defeat, and nurse your agonies!
175 Shut up your senses, stifle up your ears,
My voice is not a bellows unto ire.
Yet listen, ye who will, whilst I bring proof
How ye, perforce, must be content to stoop:
And in the proof much comfort will I give,
180 If ye will take that comfort in its truth.
We fall by course of Nature's law, not force
Of thunder, or of Jove. Great Saturn, thou
Hast sifted well the atom-universe;
But for this reason, that thou art the King,
185 And only blind from sheer supremacy,
One avenue was shaded from thine eyes,
Through which I wandered to eternal truth.
And first, as thou wast not the first of powers,
So art thou not the last; it cannot be:
190 Thou art not the beginning nor the end.
From Chaos and parental Darkness came
Light, the first fruits of that intestine broil,
That sullen ferment, which for wondrous ends
Was ripening in itself. The ripe hour came,
195 And with it Light, and Light, engendering
Upon its own producer, forthwith touch'd
The whole enormous matter into life.
Upon that very hour, our parentage,
The Heavens and the Earth, were manifest:
200 Then thou first-born, and we the giant-race,
Found ourselves ruling new and beauteous realms.
Now comes the pain of truth, to whom 'tis pain;
O folly! for to bear all naked truths,
And to envisage circumstance, all calm,

173 who . . . stung] who⟨m⟩ passion ⟨stings⟩ stung *D* 173/174 ⟨Shut up your senses⟩ *D* 177 whilst] while *W*², *W*¹ (*altered by Woodhouse to* whilst *in W*¹) 178/179 ⟨Healthy content⟩ *D* 179 will I give] *interlined above* ⟨may be felt⟩ *D* 185 And . . . supremacy,] *inserted afterward in D between 184 and 186* 185 only] *interlined above* ⟨being⟩ *D* 188 wast] was *D* 190/191

⟨Darkness was first and then a light there was;
From Chaos came the Heavens and the Earth
The first grand Parent⟩ *D*

192 the] ⟨'twas the first of all⟩ ⟨at⟩ the *D* 193 which . . . ends] *interlined above* ⟨grown unto its height⟩ *D* 194 ripening] ⟨at strange boil⟩ ripening *D*

205 That is the top of sovereignty. Mark well!
As Heaven and Earth are fairer, fairer far
Than Chaos and blank Darkness, though once chiefs;
And as we show beyond that Heaven and Earth
In form and shape compact and beautiful,
210 In will, in action free, companionship,
And thousand other signs of purer life;
So on our heels a fresh perfection treads,
A power more strong in beauty, born of us
And fated to excel us, as we pass
215 In glory that old Darkness: nor are we
Thereby more conquer'd, than by us the rule
Of shapeless Chaos. Say, doth the dull soil
Quarrel with the proud forests it hath fed,
And feedeth still, more comely than itself?
220 Can it deny the chiefdom of green groves?
Or shall the tree be envious of the dove
Because it cooeth, and hath snowy wings
To wander wherewithal and find its joys?
We are such forest-trees, and our fair boughs
225 Have bred forth, not pale solitary doves,
But eagles golden-feather'd, who do tower
Above us in their beauty, and must reign
In right thereof; for 'tis the eternal law
That first in beauty should be first in might:
230 Yea, by that law, another race may drive
Our conquerors to mourn as we do now.
Have ye beheld the young God of the Seas,
My dispossessor? Have ye seen his face?
Have ye beheld his chariot, foam'd along
235 By noble winged creatures he hath made?
I saw him on the calmed waters scud,
With such a glow of beauty in his eyes,
That it enforc'd me to bid sad farewell
To all my empire: farewell sad I took,
240 And hither came, to see how dolorous fate
Had wrought upon ye; and how I might best

207 chiefs] ⟨Kings⟩ Chiefs *D* 209 beautiful,] ~‸ $W^2$ 210 action‸ free,] action, voice, *altered to* action‸ free, *D*; action, free‸ $W^2$, $W^1$ 214 pass] ⟨di⟩ pass *D* 216 than] *made out of* that *D* 217 Say] ⟨Strife indeed there was⟩ Say *D* 217 doth] *interlined above* ⟨shall⟩ *D* 217 dull soil] *written beneath* ⟨lifel⟩ ⟨senseless soil⟩ *D* 219 feedeth‸ still,] ~, ~‸ $W^2$ 231 we] ye *D* 232 of] o' *D* 237 of] *not in D* 239 took] *interlined above* ⟨gave⟩ *D*

Give consolation in this woe extreme.
Receive the truth, and let it be your balm."

Whether through poz'd conviction, or disdain,
245 They guarded silence, when Oceanus
Left murmuring, what deepest thought can tell?
But so it was, none answer'd for a space,
Save one whom none regarded, Clymene;
And yet she answer'd not, only complain'd,
250 With hectic lips, and eyes up-looking mild,
Thus wording timidly among the fierce:
"O Father, I am here the simplest voice,
And all my knowledge is that joy is gone,
And this thing woe crept in among our hearts,
255 There to remain for ever, as I fear:
I would not bode of evil, if I thought
So weak a creature could turn off the help
Which by just right should come of mighty Gods;
Yet let me tell my sorrow, let me tell
260 Of what I heard, and how it made we weep,
And know that we had parted from all hope.
I stood upon a shore, a pleasant shore,
Where a sweet clime was breathed from a land
Of fragrance, quietness, and trees, and flowers.
265 Full of calm joy it was, as I of grief;
Too full of joy and soft delicious warmth;
So that I felt a movement in my heart
To chide, and to reproach that solitude
With songs of misery, music of our woes;
270 And sat me down, and took a mouthed shell
And murmur'd into it, and made melody—
O melody no more! for while I sang,
And with poor skill let pass into the breeze
The dull shell's echo, from a bowery strand
275 Just opposite, an island of the sea,
There came enchantment with the shifting wind,
That did both drown and keep alive my ears.
I threw my shell away upon the sand,
And a wave fill'd it, as my sense was fill'd

246 deepest] deep *altered to* deepest *D* 260 Of] O *D* 263 was] ⟨came breathing from inland⟩ was *D* 265 Full . . . joy] *deleted in D and nothing substituted* 266 delicious] deligh⟨t⟩ cious *D* 271 and made] ⟨and⟩ ⟨made what till then⟩ and made *D* 273 into] *interlined above* ⟨unto⟩ *D*

280 With that new blissful golden melody.
A living death was in each gush of sounds,
Each family of rapturous hurried notes,
That fell, one after one, yet all at once,
Like pearl beads dropping sudden from their string:
285 And then another, then another strain,
Each like a dove leaving its olive perch,
With music wing'd instead of silent plumes,
To hover round my head, and make me sick
Of joy and grief at once. Grief overcame,
290 And I was stopping up my frantic ears,
When, past all hindrance of my trembling hands,
A voice came sweeter, sweeter than all tune,
And still it cried, 'Apollo! young Apollo!
The morning-bright Apollo! young Apollo!'
295 I fled, it follow'd me, and cried 'Apollo!'
O Father, and O Brethren, had ye felt
Those pains of mine; O Saturn, hadst thou felt,
Ye would not call this too indulged tongue
Presumptuous, in thus venturing to be heard."

300 So far her voice flow'd on, like timorous brook
That, lingering along a pebbled coast,
Doth fear to meet the sea: but sea it met,
And shudder'd; for the overwhelming voice
Of huge Enceladus swallow'd it in wrath:
305 The ponderous syllables, like sullen waves
In the half-glutted hollows of reef-rocks,
Came booming thus, while still upon his arm
He lean'd; not rising, from supreme contempt.
"Or shall we listen to the over-wise,
310 Or to the over-foolish, Giant-Gods?
Not thunderbolt on thunderbolt, till all
That rebel Jove's whole armoury were spent,
Not world on world upon these shoulders piled,
Could agonize me more than baby-words

281 gush] ⟨pour⟩ gush *D* 292–293 A . . . Apollo!] *missing from D* (*cut away at the bottom of the page*) 294 morning] ⟨bright Apollo⟩ morning *D* 300 like] ⟨like⟩ ⟨in⟩ like *D* 306 of] ⟨of a⟩ of *D* 308 supreme contempt] contempt of that mild speech *altered to* supreme contempt (*and* Of that mild speech *then written again and deleted as the next line, 308/309*) *D* 310 foolish, Giant-Gods] *ed*; ∼‸ ∼-∼ *D*, $W^2$; ∼‸ ∼,—∼ $W^1$; ∼‸ ∼, ∼ *1820* 312 were] was *D*, $W^2$, $W^1$ 313 piled] pour'd *D*, $W^2$, $W^1$ (⟨lain⟩ poure'd *in D*)

315 In midst of this dethronement horrible.
Speak! roar! shout! yell! ye sleepy Titans all.
Do ye forget the blows, the buffets vile?
Are ye not smitten by a youngling arm?
Dost thou forget, sham Monarch of the Waves,
320 Thy scalding in the seas? What, have I rous'd
Your spleens with so few simple words as these?
O joy! for now I see ye are not lost:
O joy! for now I see a thousand eyes
Wide glaring for revenge!"—As this he said,
325 He lifted up his stature vast, and stood,
Still without intermission speaking thus:
"Now ye are flames, I'll tell you how to burn,
And purge the ether of our enemies;
How to feed fierce the crooked stings of fire,
330 And singe away the swollen clouds of Jove,
Stifling that puny essence in its tent.
O let him feel the evil he hath done;
For though I scorn Oceanus's lore,
Much pain have I for more than loss of realms:
335 The days of peace and slumberous calm are fled;
Those days, all innocent of scathing war,
When all the fair Existences of heaven
Came open-eyed to guess what we would speak:—
That was before our brows were taught to frown,
340 Before our lips knew else but solemn sounds;
That was before we knew the winged thing,
Victory, might be lost, or might be won.
And be ye mindful that Hyperion,
Our brightest brother, still is undisgraced—
345 Hyperion, lo! his radiance is here!"

All eyes were on Enceladus's face,
And they beheld, while still Hyperion's name
Flew from his lips up to the vaulted rocks,
A pallid gleam across his features stern:
350 Not savage, for he saw full many a God

316 yell] *added above the line in D* 316 sleepy] *added above the line in D* 320 the] *added above the line in D* 323 thousand] *interlined above* ⟨hundred⟩ *D* 325 lifted] ⟨arose⟩ lifted *D* 325/326 ⟨And {standing} stood, continuing thus:⟩ *D* 327 you] ye $W^2$, $W^1$ 330 singe] ⟨lick⟩ singe *D* 330 swollen clouds] cloudy tent *altered to* swollen clouds *D* 335 The] *written over* ⟨O⟩ *D* 340 lips] *added above the line in D* 347/348 ⟨Flew through⟩ *D*

Wroth as himself. He look'd upon them all,
And in each face he saw a gleam of light,
But splendider in Saturn's, whose hoar locks
Shone like the bubbling foam about a keel
355 When the prow sweeps into a midnight cove.
In pale and silver silence they remain'd,
Till suddenly a splendour, like the morn,
Pervaded all the beetling gloomy steeps,
All the sad spaces of oblivion,
360 And every gulf, and every chasm old,
And every height, and every sullen depth,
Voiceless, or hoarse with loud tormented streams:
And all the everlasting cataracts,
And all the headlong torrents far and near,
365 Mantled before in darkness and huge shade,
Now saw the light and made it terrible.
It was Hyperion:—a granite peak
His bright feet touch'd, and there he stay'd to view
The misery his brilliance had betray'd
370 To the most hateful seeing of itself.
Golden his hair of short Numidian curl,
Regal his shape majestic, a vast shade
In midst of his own brightness, like the bulk
Of Memnon's image at the set of sun
375 To one who travels from the dusking east:

351 Wroth] Wrath *D*; Wroth *made out of* Wrath $W^2$ 355 sweeps] *interlined above* ⟨turns⟩ *D* 356 In] ⟨Then⟩ In *D* 356/357
⟨Till suddenly a full-blown Splendour fill'd
Those native spaces of oblivion
And every glulph was seen and {every} chasm old
And every height and every sullen depth
Voiceless or filled with hoarse tormented Streams;
And all the everlasting Cataracts
And all the headlong Torrents far and near,
And all the Caverns soft with moss and weed
Or blazon'd with clear spar and barren gems;
And all the {giant-}Gods. It was Hyperion:
He stood upon a granite peak aloof
With golden hair of short numidian curl,
Rich as the colchian fleece,⟩
(was seen *in the third line, the second* every *in the fourth line, and* headlong *in the seventh all added above the line*; blazon'd *interlined above* {dazzling} *and* clear spar *above* {bright} *in the ninth line*) *D* 365 Mantled] ⟨Hid⟩ Mantled *D* 366 saw] ⟨showed⟩ saw *D* 368 view] *written over* ⟨see⟩ *D* 373 bulk] *interlined above* ⟨shade⟩ *D*

Sighs, too, as mournful as that Memnon's harp
He utter'd, while his hands contemplative
He press'd together, and in silence stood.
Despondence seiz'd again the fallen Gods
380 At sight of the dejected King of Day,
And many hid their faces from the light:
But fierce Enceladus sent forth his eyes
Among the brotherhood; and, at their glare,
Uprose Iäpetus, and Creüs too,
385 And Phorcus, sea-born, and together strode
To where he towered on his eminence.
There those four shouted forth old Saturn's name;
Hyperion from the peak loud answered, "Saturn!"
Saturn sat near the Mother of the Gods,
390 In whose face was no joy, though all the Gods
Gave from their hollow throats the name of "Saturn!"

## BOOK III

Thus in alternate uproar and sad peace,
Amazed were those Titans utterly.
O leave them, Muse! O leave them to their woes;
For thou art weak to sing such tumults dire:
5 A solitary sorrow best befits
Thy lips, and antheming a lonely grief.
Leave them, O Muse! for thou anon wilt find
Many a fallen old Divinity
Wandering in vain about bewildered shores.
10 Meantime touch piously the Delphic harp,
And not a wind of heaven but will breathe
In aid soft warble from the Dorian flute;
For lo! 'tis for the Father of all verse.
Flush every thing that hath a vermeil hue,

376 as . . . as that] *interlined above* ⟨melodious as⟩ *D* 386/387 ⟨Their whispered they bewildered, while despise [*or possibly* despire]⟩ *D* 389 sat] *interlined above* ⟨put for⟩ ⟨stood⟩ *D*

III *heading* Book] Canto *D* 2 Amazed] *interlined above* ⟨Perplexed⟩ *D* 3 O leave them to . . . woes] *written beneath* ⟨for they have succour none⟩ *D* 4 art] ⟨canst⟩ art *D* 5/6 ⟨Thy⟩ ⟨Thine anthem'd lips⟩ *D* 7 O Muse] O ⟨for many⟩ Muse (O *squeezed in before* ⟨for many⟩) *D* 8 fallen] ⟨mateless⟩ fallen *interlined above* ⟨lonely⟩ *D* 10 piously] ⟨deftly⟩ piously *D* 13 'tis] ⟨thou sing'st th⟩ 'tis *D* 13/14 ⟨Let a wam rosy hue distain⟩ *D* 14 vermeil] *interlined above* ⟨rosy⟩ *D*

15 Let the rose glow intense and warm the air,
And let the clouds of even and of morn
Float in voluptuous fleeces o'er the hills;
Let the red wine within the goblet boil,
Cold as a bubbling well; let faint-lipp'd shells,
20 On sands, or in great deeps, vermilion turn
Through all their labyrinths; and let the maid
Blush keenly, as with some warm kiss surpris'd.
Chief isle of the embowered Cyclades,
Rejoice, O Delos, with thine olives green,
25 And poplars, and lawn-shading palms, and beech,
In which the Zephyr breathes the loudest song,
And hazels thick, dark-stemm'd beneath the shade:
Apollo is once more the golden theme!
Where was he, when the Giant of the Sun
30 Stood bright, amid the sorrow of his peers?
Together had he left his mother fair
And his twin-sister sleeping in their bower,
And in the morning twilight wandered forth
Beside the osiers of a rivulet,
35 Full ankle-deep in lilies of the vale.
The nightingale had ceas'd, and a few stars
Were lingering in the heavens, while the thrush
Began calm-throated. Throughout all the isle
There was no covert, no retired cave
40 Unhaunted by the murmurous noise of waves,
Though scarcely heard in many a green recess.
He listen'd, and he wept, and his bright tears
Went trickling down the golden bow he held.
Thus with half-shut suffused eyes he stood,
45 While from beneath some cumbrous boughs hard by
With solemn step an awful Goddess came,
And there was purport in her looks for him,
Which he with eager guess began to read
Perplex'd, the while melodiously he said:

15/16 ⟨And the corn-haunting poppy⟩ *D* 19 faint] *interlined above* ⟨red⟩ *D* 22 keenly, as] as she did *altered to* keenly as *D* 27 hazels] Hyle's *W*[2], *W*[1] 28 once] ⟨the⟩ once *D* 33 wandered] ⟨roamed⟩ wanderd (*with* was *interlined and deleted above* ⟨roamed⟩) *D* 38 all the] *deleted in D and nothing substituted* 39 covert, no] covert, ⟨which⟩ no *D* 40 Unhaunted] *written over* ⟨Whi⟩ *D* 40 murmurous] ⟨Sea's⟩ murmurous *D* 43/44 ⟨So kept his with his eyes suffus'd halfshut⟩ (suffus'd *added above the line*) *D* 44 Thus] ⟨While from⟩ Thus (*the deleted words a continuation of 43/44*) *D* 45 boughs] ⟨oaks⟩ boughs *interlined above* ⟨shade⟩ *D* 47 And] *deleted in D and nothing substituted* 49 the] and *D*, *W*[2], *W*[1]

50 "How cam'st thou over the unfooted sea?
Or hath that antique mien and robed form
Mov'd in these vales invisible till now?
Sure I have heard those vestments sweeping o'er
The fallen leaves, when I have sat alone
55 In cool mid-forest. Surely I have traced
The rustle of those ample skirts about
These grassy solitudes, and seen the flowers
Lift up their heads, as still the whisper pass'd.
Goddess! I have beheld those eyes before,
60 And their eternal calm, and all that face,
Or I have dream'd."—"Yes," said the supreme shape,
"Thou hast dream'd of me; and awaking up
Didst find a lyre all golden by thy side,
Whose strings touch'd by thy fingers, all the vast
65 Unwearied ear of the whole universe
Listen'd in pain and pleasure at the birth
Of such new tuneful wonder. Is't not strange
That thou shouldst weep, so gifted? Tell me, youth,
What sorrow thou canst feel; for I am sad
70 When thou dost shed a tear: explain thy griefs
To one who in this lonely isle hath been
The watcher of thy sleep and hours of life,
From the young day when first thy infant hand
Pluck'd witless the weak flowers, till thine arm
75 Could bend that bow heroic to all times.
Show thy heart's secret to an ancient Power
Who hath forsaken old and sacred thrones
For prophecies of thee, and for the sake
Of loveliness new born."—Apollo then,
80 With sudden scrutiny and gloomless eyes,
Thus answer'd, while his white melodious throat
Throbb'd with the syllables.—"Mnemosyne!

50 unfooted] *interlined above* ⟨pathless⟩ *D* 51 and] ⟨and those⟩ and *D* 52 Mov'd] *interlined above* ⟨Walked⟩ *D* 53 o'er] ⟨by⟩ o'er *D* 55 cool] ⟨the m⟩ cool *D* 56 ample . . . about] ⟨skirts⟩ ample skirts ⟨along⟩ About *D* 57 grassy . . . flowers] Solitudes, and seen the grass and flowers (seen *made out of* seeing) *altered to* grassy Solitudes, and seen the flowers *D* 58 their] the *D* 58 pass'd] ⟨went⟩ pass'd *D* 61 dream'd] dreamm'd *altered to* dreampt *D* 62 hast dream'd] *interlined above* ⟨dreamedst⟩ *D* 63 lyre] ⟨golden⟩ Lyre *D* 64 Whose] ⟨The whi⟩ Whose *D* 64 touch'd] *interlined above* ⟨swept⟩ *D* 69 thou canst] canst thou (*but marked for transposition*) *D* 74 weak] *interlined above* ⟨mead⟩ *D* 75/76 ⟨Devellop⟩ *D* 79 Apollo then] *interlined above* ⟨To whom the God⟩ *D* 81 Thus] This *D*, *W*², *W*¹ (*added in the margin in D*) 82/83 ⟨That sound⟩ *D*

Thy name is on my tongue, I know not how;
Why should I tell thee what thou so well seest?
85 Why should I strive to show what from thy lips
Would come no mystery? For me, dark, dark,
And painful vile oblivion seals my eyes:
I strive to search wherefore I am so sad,
Until a melancholy numbs my limbs;
90 And then upon the grass I sit, and moan,
Like one who once had wings.—O why should I
Feel curs'd and thwarted, when the liegeless air
Yields to my step aspirant? why should I
Spurn the green turf as hateful to my feet?
95 Goddess benign, point forth some unknown thing:
Are there not other regions than this isle?
What are the stars? There is the sun, the sun!
And the most patient brilliance of the moon!
And stars by thousands! Point me out the way
100 To any one particular beauteous star,
And I will flit into it with my lyre,
And make its silvery splendour pant with bliss.
I have heard the cloudy thunder: Where is power?
Whose hand, whose essence, what divinity
105 Makes this alarum in the elements,
While I here idle listen on the shores
In fearless yet in aching ignorance?
O tell me, lonely Goddess, by thy harp,
That waileth every morn and eventide,
110 Tell me why thus I rave, about these groves!
Mute thou remainest—mute! yet I can read
A wondrous lesson in thy silent face:
Knowledge enormous makes a God of me.
Names, deeds, gray legends, dire events, rebellions,
115 Majesties, sovran voices, agonies,
Creations and destroyings, all at once
Pour into the wide hollows of my brain,

83/84 ⟨Thou {knowst} knowest better⟩ *D* 84 thee] *added above the line in D* 84 seest] *interlined above* ⟨knowest⟩ *D* 87 And] ⟨Are⟩ And *D* 90 the grass] *added above the line in D* 94 hateful] ⟨pa⟩ hateful *D* 100 any] any any *D* 102 its silvery] its silverly *D*, *W*[1] (it's silverrly *made out of* it pant *in D*); its silverly *altered to* its silvery *W*[2] 106 here] *interlined above* ⟨am⟩ *D* 107 yet] *interlined above* ⟨but⟩ *D* 112 A] ⟨Matte⟩ A *D* 113 Knowledge] *written over* ⟨M⟩ (*the beginning of* Matter) *D* 114 dire] ⟨fier⟩ dire *D* 114 rebellions] *interlined above* ⟨loud voices⟩ *D* 116 and] ⟨visages of⟩ and *D* 116 all at once] *interlined above* ⟨and calm peace⟩ *D* 117 hollows] ⟨hide⟩ hollows *D*

And deify me, as if some blithe wine
Or bright elixir peerless I had drunk,
120 And so become immortal."—Thus the God,
While his enkindled eyes, with level glance
Beneath his white soft temples, stedfast kept
Trembling with light upon Mnemosyne.
Soon wild commotions shook him, and made flush
125 All the immortal fairness of his limbs;
Most like the struggle at the gate of death;
Or liker still to one who should take leave
Of pale immortal death, and with a pang
As hot as death's is chill, with fierce convulse
130 Die into life: so young Apollo anguish'd:
His very hair, his golden tresses famed,
Kept undulation round his eager neck.
During the pain Mnemosyne upheld
Her arms as one who prophesied.—At length
135 Apollo shriek'd;—and lo! from all his limbs
Celestial * * * * * * * * * *
* * * * * * * * * * * * *

118 deify] ⟨like some⟩ deify (deify *made out of* deifies) *D* 119 drunk] drank *D* 120/121 ⟨While {his} level glanced beneath his temples soft / His eyes were stedfast on Mnemosyne;⟩ *D* 123 Trembling . . . light] *added in the margin in D* 123 Mnemosyne.] Mnemosyne: ⟨and⟩ *D* 123/124

⟨And while {a s} through all his frame⟩
⟨and wild commotion throughout⟩

(frame *interlined above* {limbs} *in the first line*) *D* 124 Soon wild] *interlined above* ⟨And his⟩ ⟨while⟩ *D* 125 the] ⟨his white⟩ the *D* 125/126

⟨Roseate and pained as a ravish'd nymph—⟩
Into a hue more roseate than sweet-pain
Gives to a ravish'd Nymph ⟨new-r⟩ when her warm tears
Gush luscious with no sob. ⟨Or 'twas⟩ Or more severe;—

(a *interlined above* {any} *in the first line, and* ravish'd *and* warm *added above the line in the third*) *D. Both $W^2$ and $W^1$ have the uncanceled text of D* (Into . . . severe;—); *in $W^1$ the three lines are deleted in pencil* 126 Most] More *D*, $W^2$, $W^1$ (*altered by Woodhouse in pencil to* And *in* $W^1$) 131 His very] Even his *altered to* his very *D* 132 Kept] Keep $W^2$, $W^1$ 132 undulation] *Keats interlined and deleted* graceful *before this word in D* 134 prophesied] prohesies *altered to* prohesie'd *D* 134/135 ⟨Phœbus⟩ *D* 135 from . . . limbs] *written beneath* ⟨he was the God!⟩ *D* 135/136 ⟨And godlike⟩ (*continuation of deleted text in 135*) *D*

## *La Belle Dame sans Merci: A Ballad*

1

O what can ail thee, knight at arms,
  Alone and palely loitering?
The sedge has wither'd from the lake,
    And no birds sing.

2

5 O what can ail thee, knight at arms,
  So haggard and so woe-begone?
The squirrel's granary is full,
    And the harvest's done.

3

I see a lily on thy brow
10 With anguish moist and fever dew,
And on thy cheeks a fading rose
    Fast withereth too.

4

I met a lady in the meads,
  Full beautiful, a fairy's child;
15 Her hair was long, her foot was light,
    And her eyes were wild.

5

I made a garland for her head,
  And bracelets too, and fragrant zone;
She look'd at me as she did love,
20 And made sweet moan.

*La Belle Dame.* Text (including heading) from Brown's transcript (*CB*). Variants and other readings from Keats's letter to George and Georgiana Keats, 14 February–3 May 1819 (*L*), Woodhouse's $W^2$ transcript, and the *Indicator* version (*Ind*). *Heading* Merci] Mercy $W^2$, *Ind* *Subtitle* A Ballad] *not in L, Ind* 1, 5 O . . . knight at arms] Ah . . . wretched wight *Ind* 3 has] is *Ind* 9, 11 a] *interlined above* ⟨death's⟩ (*the same alteration in both lines*) *L* 11 cheeks] cheek *Ind* 12 Fast] *added in the margin in L* 13 meads] ⟨Wilds⟩ Meads *L* 17–20 I . . . moan.] *transposed to follow 21–24 in Ind* 18 zone] Zone⟨s⟩ *L*

6

I set her on my pacing steed,
  And nothing else saw all day long,
For sidelong would she bend, and sing
    A fairy's song.

7

25 She found me roots of relish sweet,
  And honey wild, and manna dew,
And sure in language strange she said—
    I love thee true.

8

She took me to her elfin grot,
30 And there she wept, and sigh'd full sore,
And there I shut her wild wild eyes
    With kisses four.

9

And there she lulled me asleep,
  And there I dream'd—Ah! woe betide!
35 The latest dream I ever dream'd
    On the cold hill's side.

10

I saw pale kings, and princes too,
  Pale warriors, death pale were they all;
They cried—"La belle dame sans merci
40     Hath thee in thrall!"

11

I saw their starv'd lips in the gloam
  With horrid warning gaped wide,

23 sidelong . . . bend] sideways . . . lean *Ind*  26 manna] *interlined above* ⟨honey⟩ *L*  30 wept . . . sore] gaz'd and sighed deep *Ind*  30 sigh'd . . . sore] *successively* (*a*) there she sighed (*b*) sighed sore (*c*) sigh'd full sore *L*  31 wild wild] wild sad *Ind*  32 With . . . four] So kiss'd to sleep *Ind*  33 she . . . asleep] we slumber'd on the moss *Ind*  35 dream'd] dreamt *L*  36 hill's] hill *L*, *Ind*; hill *altered to* hill's *CB*  39 They] Who *Ind*  39 merci] merci *altered to* mercy *W*[2]; mercy *Ind*  40 Hath thee] Thee hath *L*  41 gloam] gloom *Ind*  41/42 ⟨All tremble⟩ *L*  42 gaped wide] wide agape *altered to* gaped wide *L*

And I awoke and found me here
On the cold hill's side.

12

45 And this is why I sojourn here,
Alone and palely loitering,
Though the sedge is wither'd from the lake,
And no birds sing.

## *Song of Four Fairies: Fire, Air, Earth, and Water*

SALAMANDER, ZEPHYR, DUSKETHA, AND BREAMA

SALAMANDER

Happy, happy glowing fire!

ZEPHYR

Fragrant air! Delicious light!

DUSKETHA

Let me to my glooms retire!

BREAMA

I to green-weed rivers bright!

SALAMANDER

5 Happy, happy glowing fire,
Dazzling bowers of soft retire,
Ever let my nourish'd wing,

44 hill's] hill *Ind* 45 sojourn] ⟨wither⟩ sojourn *L*

*Song of Four Fairies.* Text (including heading) from the extant holograph fair copy (*FC*). Variants and other readings from Keats's letter to George and Georgiana Keats, 14 February–3 May 1819 (*L*), and transcripts by Brown (*CB*) and Woodhouse ($W^2$). *Heading* Song of Four Fairies . . . Dusketha, and Breama] Chorus of Faries ⟨three⟩ 4 . . . Dusketha Breama *L* 4 *s.p.* Breama] *interlined above* ⟨Salam.⟩ *FC* 4 green] ⟨my⟩ green *L*

Like a bat's, still wandering,
Nimbly fan your fiery spaces,
10 Spirit sole in deadly places;
In unhaunted roar and blaze,
Open eyes that never daze:
Let me see the myriad shapes
Of men, and beasts, and fish, and apes,
15 Portray'd in many a fiery den
And wrought by spumy bitumen
On the deep intenser roof,
Arched every way aloof;
Let me breathe upon their skies,
20 And anger their live tapestries;
Free from cold and every care
Of chilly rain, and shivering air.

ZEPHYR

Spirit of Fire—away, away!
Or your very roundelay
25 Will sear my plumage newly budded
From its quilled sheath, and studded
With the self-same dews that fell
On the May-grown asphodel.
Spirit of Fire—away, away!

BREAMA

30 Spirit of Fire—away, away!
Zephyr, blue-eyed fairy, turn
And see my cool sedge-buried urn,
Where it rests its mossy brim
'Mid water mint and cresses dim;
35 And the flowers in sweet troubles
Lift their eyes above the bubbles,
Like our Queen when she would please
To sleep and Oberon will tease.

9 Nimbly fan] Faintly fan *L, CB, W*[2] (*interlined above* ⟨Ever beat⟩ *in L*); Faintly fan *altered to* Nimbly fan *FC*   16 bitumen‸] ~. *CB, W*[2] (*see Textual Note to 16–18*)   19 their] my *L*   23, 29, 30 Spirit] Spright *L*   25 newly] *interlined above* ⟨all⟩ *L*   26 and] all *L, CB, W*[2] (*interlined above* ⟨and⟩ *in L*)   32 buried] shaded *L*   35 And] *interlined above* ⟨Where⟩ *L*   35 in] *interlined above* ⟨amid⟩ *L*

Love me, blue-eyed fairy true,
40 Soothly I am sick for you.

ZEPHYR

Gentle Breama! by the first
Violet young nature nurst,
I will bathe myself with thee,
So you sometime follow me
45 To my home, far, far in west,
Beyond the nimble-wheeled quest
Of the golden-presenc'd sun.
Come with me, o'er tops of trees,
To my fragrant pallaces,
50 Where they ever floating are
Beneath the cherish of a star
Call'd Vesper, who with silver veil
Ever hides his brilliance pale,
Ever gently drows'd doth keep
55 Twilight for the fays to sleep.
Fear not that your watry hair
Will thirst in drouthy ringlets there;
Clouds of stored summer rains
Thou shalt taste, before the stains
60 From the mountain soil they take,
And too unlucent for thee make.
I love thee, chrystal fairy true;
Sooth I am as sick for you!

SALAMANDER

Out, ye aguish fairies, out!
65 Chilly lovers, what a rout
Keep ye with your frozen breath,
Colder than the mortal death.
Adder-eyed Dusketha, speak,
Shall we leave these and go seek

39 fairy$_\wedge$] ~, *CB* 40 Soothly I am] For in sooth I'm *altered to* soothly I am *L* 44 sometime] sometimes *CB*, *W*[2] 46 Beyond . . . wheeled] Far beyond the search and *L* 46 Beyond] Far beyond *altered to* Beyond *CB* 47 presenc'd] browed *L*, *CB*, *W*[2] 52 Call'd] *interlined above* ⟨Who with⟩ *L* 53 Ever] *added in the margin in L* 53 his] ⟨his brightness⟩ his *L* 55 for] of *L* 60 From] Of *L*, *CB*, *W*[2] 62 fairy$_\wedge$] ~, *CB*, *W*[2] 64/65 ⟨Chillier than the water⟩ *L* 69 and] ⟨spr⟩ and *L*

70 In the earth's wide entrails old
Couches warm as theirs is cold?
O for a fiery-gloom and thee,
Dusketha, so enchantingly
Freckle-wing'd and lizard-sided!

DUSKETHA

75 By thee, sprite, will I be guided!
I care not for cold or heat;
Frost or flame, or sparks, or sleet
To my essence are the same;
But I honor more the flame.
80 Sprite of Fire! I follow thee
Wheresoever it may be;
To the torrid spouts and fountains
Underneath earth-quaked mountains;
Or, at thy supreme desire,
85 Touch the very pulse of fire
With my bare unlidded eyes.

SALAMANDER

Sweet Dusketha! Paradise!
Off, ye icy spirits, fly,
Frosty creatures of the sky!

DUSKETHA

90 Breathe upon them, fiery sprite!

ZEPHYR *and* BREAMA

Away, away to our delight!

71 is] are *CB*, *W*[2] 76 care] ⟨lo⟩ care *L* 77 Frost or] Frost and *L*, *CB*, *W*[2] 82 torrid] ⟨very foun⟩ torrid *L* 82 spouts and fountains] spouts *interlined above* fountains (*undeleted*; and *is not in the MS*) *L* 89 the] *not in L* 91 *s.p.* Zephyr and Breama] *ed*; Zephyr Brema to each other *L*; *CB*, *W*[2], *FC have* Zeph. *above* Brea. (*without* and) *bracketed in the margin. Between 90 and 91, but following the s.p., L has* ⟨let us try, my love, my life⟩ (let us try *interlined above* {Ah})

SALAMANDER

Go feed on icicles, while we
Bedded in tongued flames will be.

DUSKETHA

Lead me to those fevrous glooms,
Sprite of Fire!

BREAMA

95 Me to the blooms,
Blue-eyed Zephyr, of those flowers
Far in the west where the May-cloud lowers,
And the beams of still Vesper, when winds are all whist,
Are shed through the rain and the milder mist,
100 And twilight your floating bowers.

## *Sonnet to Sleep*

O soft embalmer of the still midnight,
Shutting with careful fingers and benign
Our gloom-pleas'd eyes, embower'd from the light,
Enshaded in forgetfulness divine:
5 O soothest Sleep! if so it please thee, close,
In midst of this thine hymn, my willing eyes,
Or wait the Amen ere thy poppy throws
Around my bed its lulling charities.

92 Go‸] ~, *CB*; ~! $W^2$ 93 tongued] tongue *CB*, $W^2$ 96 Blue] *written over* ⟨Soft⟩ *L* 96 flowers] *successively* (*a*) flowers (*b*) Bowers (*c*) Flowers *FC* 97 where the] where $W^2$ 98 when] where *L*, $W^2$

*Sonnet to Sleep.* Text (including heading) from Keats's album copy in the Berg Collection (*FC*). Variants and other readings from his draft (*D*), his letter to George and Georgiana Keats, 14 February–3 May 1819 (*L*), and transcripts by Brown (*CB*) and Woodhouse ($W^2$). *Heading* Sonnet to] To *D*, *L* 3/4 ⟨Of Sun or teasing candles⟩ (*following* light *without punctuation in 3*) *D* 4 Enshaded in forgetfulness] As wearisome as darkness is *D* 6 In . . . eyes] My willing eyes in midst of this thine hymn (My *made out of* Mine) *D* 8–14 Around . . . soul]

Its sweet-death dews o'er every pulse and limb—
Then shut the hushed Casket of my soul

Then save me or the passed day will shine
10 Upon my pillow, breeding many woes:
Save me from curious conscience, that still hoards
Its strength for darkness, burrowing like the mole;
Turn the key deftly in the oiled wards,
And seal the hushed casket of my soul.

## *Ode to Psyche*

O Goddess! hear these tuneless numbers, wrung
By sweet enforcement and remembrance dear,
And pardon that thy secrets should be sung
Even into thine own soft-conched ear:
5 Surely I dreamt to-day, or did I see
The winged Psyche with awaken'd eyes?
I wander'd in a forest thoughtlessly,
And, on the sudden, fainting with surprise,
Saw two fair creatures, couched side by side
10 In deepest grass, beneath the whisp'ring roof
Of leaves and trembled blossoms, where there ran
A brooklet, scarce espied:
'Mid hush'd, cool-rooted flowers, fragrant-eyed,
Blue, silver-white, and budded Tyrian,
15 They lay calm-breathing on the bedded grass;
Their arms embraced, and their pinions too;

---

And turn the Key round in the oiled wards
And let it rest until the morn ⟨has stole⟩
Bright tressed From the grey east's shuddering bourn

(death *also readable as* dark *in the first line*; Bright tressed *added in the margin and* grey east's *interlined above* ⟨west's⟩ *in the last line*) *D* 8 lulling] dewy *L*, *CB*, *and originally* $W^2$; dewy *altered by Keats to* lulling *in the margin of* $W^2$; lulling *penciled by Woodhouse above* dewy (*left undeleted*) *in CB* 11 hoards] lords *L*, *CB*, *and originally* $W^2$; lords *altered by Woodhouse in pencil to* hoards *in* $W^2$ 12 burrowing] borrowing *L* 12 the] a *L*, *CB*, $W^2$ (*interlined above* ⟨the⟩ *in L*)

*Ode to Psyche.* Text (including heading) from *1820*. Variants and other readings from Keats's draft (*D*), his letter to George and Georgiana Keats, 14 February–3 May 1819 (*L*), and transcripts by Brown (*CB*) and Woodhouse ($W^2$). *Heading* Ode to] Ode To (Ode *added afterward*) *D* 4 into] ⟨to⟩ into *L* 5 dreamt] dreamt *altered to* dream'd $W^2$ 6 awaken'd] awaked *L* 9 couched] ⟨cl⟩ couched *L* 10 roof] fan *D*, *L*, $W^2$, *and originally CB*; fan *altered to* roof *by Keats in CB* 13 'Mid] *interlined above* ⟨In⟩ *D*; Near $W^2$ 14 silver-white] freckle pink *in the margin* (*but* silver-white *undeleted in the text*) *in D*; freckle-pink *L*; freckled, pink $W^2$ 14 Tyrian] syrian *D*, *L*, *CB*, $W^2$ 15 calm] soft *CB*

Their lips touch'd not, but had not bade adieu,
As if disjoined by soft-handed slumber,
And ready still past kisses to outnumber
20 At tender eye-dawn of aurorean love:
The winged boy I knew;
But who wast thou, O happy, happy dove?
His Psyche true!

O latest born and loveliest vision far
25 Of all Olympus' faded hierarchy!
Fairer than Phœbe's sapphire-region'd star,
Or Vesper, amorous glow-worm of the sky;
Fairer than these, though temple thou hast none,
Nor altar heap'd with flowers;
30 Nor virgin-choir to make delicious moan
Upon the midnight hours;
No voice, no lute, no pipe, no incense sweet
From chain-swung censer teeming;
No shrine, no grove, no oracle, no heat
35 Of pale-mouth'd prophet dreaming.

O brightest! though too late for antique vows,
Too, too late for the fond believing lyre,
When holy were the haunted forest boughs,
Holy the air, the water, and the fire;
40 Yet even in these days so far retir'd
From happy pieties, thy lucent fans,
Fluttering among the faint Olympians,
I see, and sing, by my own eyes inspired.
So let me be thy choir, and make a moan
45 Upon the midnight hours;
Thy voice, thy lute, thy pipe, thy incense sweet
From swinged censer teeming;

17 bade] bid *D*, *L*, *W*[2] 20 eye] ⟨dawning⟩ eye *D* 22 O happy] O ⟨p⟩ happy *L* 23 true!] ~? *L* 24 latest] lastest *L* 26 Phœbe's] *successively* (*a*) Night's ⟨wide⟩ full, (*b*) Night's orb'd (*c*) Phœbe's *D* 28 hast] hadst *L* 30 delicious] melodious *D*, *CB*, *W*[2] 32–34 No *and* no] No⟨r⟩ *and* no⟨r⟩ *in all eight places in D* 36 brightest] Bloomiest *D*, *L*, *CB*, *W*[2] 42 among] *interlined above* ⟨above⟩ *D* 43 by my] by (*corrected by Keats to* by my) *CB* 43 own] *interlined above* ⟨clear⟩ *D* 44 So] O *D*, *L*, *CB*, *W*[2] 45/46 ⟨Thy Altar heap'd with flowers,⟩ (*written vertically in the margin with a mark for insertion after 45, the line and the mark then deleted*) *D* 47 From] *interlined above* ⟨Thy⟩ *D*

Thy shrine, thy grove, thy oracle, thy heat
  Of pale-mouth'd prophet dreaming.

50 Yes, I will be thy priest, and build a fane
  In some untrodden region of my mind,
Where branched thoughts, new grown with pleasant pain,
  Instead of pines shall murmur in the wind:
Far, far around shall those dark-cluster'd trees
55 Fledge the wild-ridged mountains steep by steep;
And there by zephyrs, streams, and birds, and bees,
  The moss-lain Dryads shall be lull'd to sleep;
And in the midst of this wide quietness
A rosy sanctuary will I dress
60 With the wreath'd trellis of a working brain,
  With buds, and bells, and stars without a name,
With all the gardener Fancy e'er could feign,
  Who breeding flowers, will never breed the same:
And there shall be for thee all soft delight
65 That shadowy thought can win,
A bright torch, and a casement ope at night,
  To let the warm Love in!

## *On Fame*

Fame, like a wayward girl, will still be coy
  To those who woo her with too slavish knees,
But makes surrender to some thoughtless boy,
  And dotes the more upon a heart at ease;
5 She is a gipsey, will not speak to those
  Who have not learnt to be content without her;
A jilt, whose ear was never whisper'd close,
  Who thinks they scandal her who talk about her;

57 lull'd] *interlined above* ⟨charmd⟩ *L* 57 to sleep] asleep *altered to* to sleep *CB* 62 feign] *interlined above* ⟨frame⟩ *L* 63 breeding . . . breed] *successively* (*a*) plucks a thousand flower and never plucks (*b*) plucking flowers will never pluck (*c*) breeding flowers will ⟨never⟩ breed pluck (never *deleted by mistake instead of* pluck *in the third version*) *D* 63/64 ⟨So bower'd Goddess will I worship thee⟩ *D* 67 the . . . Love] warm Love glide *altered to* the warm Love *D*; Love $W^2$

*On Fame* ("Fame, like a waywàrd girl"). Text from Brown's transcript (*CB*). Variants from Keats's letter to George and Georgiana Keats, 14 February–3 May 1819 (*L*), and Woodhouse's $W^2$ transcript. *Heading* On] *ed*; Sonnet on *CB*, $W^2$; Another on *L* 6 learnt] learnt *altered to* learn'd $W^2$ 8 thinks] think *L*

A very gipsey is she, Nilus born,
10 Sister-in-law to jealous Potiphar;
Ye love-sick bards, repay her scorn for scorn;
Ye artists lovelorn, madmen that ye are!
Make your best bow to her and bid adieu;
Then, if she likes it, she will follow you.

## *On Fame*

"You cannot eat your cake and have it too."
Proverb

How fever'd is the man who cannot look
Upon his mortal days with temperate blood,
Who vexes all the leaves of his life's book,
And robs his fair name of its maidenhood;
5 It is as if the rose should pluck herself,
Or the ripe plum finger its misty bloom,
As if a Naiad, like a meddling elf,
Should darken her pure grot with muddy gloom;
But the rose leaves herself upon the briar,
10 For winds to kiss and grateful bees to feed,
And the ripe plum still wears its dim attire,
The undisturbed lake has crystal space;
Why then should man, teasing the world for grace,
Spoil his salvation for a fierce miscreed?

12 artists lovelorn] lovelorn Artists *L*

*On Fame* ("How fever'd is the man"). Text (including epigraph) from Brown's transcript (*CB*). Variants and other readings from Keats's letter to George and Georgiana Keats, 14 February–3 May 1819 (*L*), and Woodhouse's $W^2$ transcript. *Heading* On] *L*; Sonnet. / on *CB*; Sonnet. To $W^2$ 1 fever'd . . . man] is that Man misled *altered to* fever'd is the Man *L* (*see Textual Note*) 5 herself] *made out of* itself *CB*, $W^2$ 6 misty] *added above the line in L* 7–8 Naiad . . . with] clear Lake meddling with itself / Should Cloud its pureness with a *L and originally CB* (Cloud *interlined above* ⟨fill⟩ *in L*); *the present text then substituted by Brown above the lines in CB* 10 feed] ⟨taste⟩ feed *L* 11 still] ⟨will⟩ still *interlined above* ⟨still⟩ *L* 13 teasing . . . grace] *interlined above* ⟨his own bright name deface⟩ *L* 13/14 ⟨And {spoil} burn our pleasures in his selfish fire—⟩ *L* 14 for] by *L*

## *If by dull rhymes our English must be chain'd*

If by dull rhymes our English must be chain'd,
  And, like Andromeda, the sonnet sweet
    Fetter'd, in spite of pained loveliness;
Let us find out, if we must be constrain'd,
5  Sandals more interwoven and complete
To fit the naked foot of Poesy;
    Let us inspect the lyre, and weigh the stress
Of every chord, and see what may be gain'd
  By ear industrious, and attention meet;
10    Misers of sound and syllable, no less
Than Midas of his coinage, let us be
  Jealous of dead leaves in the bay wreath crown;
So, if we may not let the muse be free,
  She will be bound with garlands of her own.

## *Two or three posies*

Two or three posies
With two or three simples
Two or three noses
With two or three pimples—
5 Two or three wise men
And two or three ninnies
Two or three purses
And two or three guineas
Two or three raps
10 At two or three doors
Two or three naps
Of two or three hours—
Two or three cats
And two or three mice
15 Two or three sprats
At a very great price—

*If by dull rhymes.* Text from Brown's transcript (*CB*). Heading variants from Keats's letter to George and Georgiana Keats, 14 February–3 May 1819 (*L*), and Woodhouse's $W^2$ transcript. *Heading* If . . . chain'd] *ed*; Sonnet *CB*, $W^2$; *no heading in L* 4 must] *interlined above* ⟨may⟩ *CB*

*Two or three posies.* Text from Keats's letter to Fanny Keats, 1 May (?) 1819. Heading supplied by editor.

Two or three sandies
And two or three tabbies
Two or three dandies—
20 And two Mrs. ——
Two or three smiles
And two or three frowns
Two or three miles
To two or three towns
25 Two or three pegs
For two or three bonnets
Two or three dove's eggs
To hatch into sonnets—

## *Ode to a Nightingale*

1

My heart aches, and a drowsy numbness pains
  My sense, as though of hemlock I had drunk,
Or emptied some dull opiate to the drains
  One minute past, and Lethe-wards had sunk:
5 'Tis not through envy of thy happy lot,
  But being tòo happy in thine happiness,—
    That thou, light-wingèd Dryad of the trees,
      In some melodious plot
  Of beechen green, and shadows numberless,
10 Singest of summer in full-throated ease.

2

O, for a draught of vintage! that hath been
  Cool'd a long age in the deep-delved earth,
Tasting of Flora and the country green,
  Dance, and Provençal song, and sunburnt mirth!

*Ode to a Nightingale.* Text (including heading) from *1820.* Variants and other readings from Keats's draft (*D*), transcripts by Woodhouse (*W*²), Dilke (*CWD*), and George Keats (*GK*), and the version published in *Annals of the Fine Arts.* *Heading* a] the *D*, *W*², *CWD*, *GK*, *Annals* *Before* 1 Small, winged Dryad *D* (*see Textual Note*) 1 My] *deleted in D and nothing substituted* 1 drowsy] *interlined above* ⟨painful⟩ *D* 1 pains] *written beneath* ⟨falls⟩ *D* 4 past] *interlined above* ⟨hence⟩ *D* 11 hath] has *D*, *W*², *CWD*, *GK*, *Annals* 12 Cool'd a long] Cooling an *altered to* Cool'd a long *D* 14 Dance] ⟨And⟩ Dance *D*

15 O for a beaker full of the warm South,
Full of the true, the blushful Hippocrene,
With beaded bubbles winking at the brim,
And purple-stained mouth;
That I might drink, and leave the world unseen,
20 And with thee fade away into the forest dim:

3

Fade far away, dissolve, and quite forget
What thou among the leaves hast never known,
The weariness, the fever, and the fret
Here, where men sit and hear each other groan;
25 Where palsy shakes a few, sad, last gray hairs,
Where youth grows pale, and spectre-thin, and dies;
Where but to think is to be full of sorrow
And leaden-eyed despairs,
Where Beauty cannot keep her lustrous eyes,
30 Or new Love pine at them beyond to-morrow.

4

Away! away! for I will fly to thee,
Not charioted by Bacchus and his pards,
But on the viewless wings of Poesy,
Though the dull brain perplexes and retards:
35 Already with thee! tender is the night,
And haply the Queen-Moon is on her throne,
Cluster'd around by all her starry Fays;
But here there is no light,
Save what from heaven is with the breezes blown
40 Through verdurous glooms and winding mossy ways.

5

I cannot see what flowers are at my feet,
Nor what soft incense hangs upon the boughs,
But, in embalmed darkness, guess each sweet

16 true, the] true and *D*, $W^2$, *CWD*, *GK*, *Annals* 16 blushful] blissful *GK* 17 beaded] cluster'd *D* 20 away] *not in* $W^2$, *CWD, GK, Annals* 22 hast] have *CWD* 24 other] other's *CWD*, *GK*; other's *altered to* other $W^2$ 26 spectre] *added above the line (and a hyphen inserted before* thin) *in D* 26 and dies] *written beneath* ⟨and old⟩ (*another* old *is interlined and deleted before* pale *in the same line*) *D* 27 sorrow] *interlined above* ⟨grief⟩ *D* 30 new] *added above the line in D* 31 to] *interlined above* ⟨with⟩ *D* 37 Cluster'd] *deleted in D and nothing substituted* 39 heaven] *added above the line in D* 40 Through] ⟨Sidelong⟩ Through *D* 42 soft] ⟨blooms⟩ soft *D* 43/44 ⟨With with⟩ *D*

Wherewith the seasonable month endows
45 The grass, the thicket, and the fruit-tree wild;
White hawthorn, and the pastoral eglantine;
Fast fading violets cover'd up in leaves;
And mid-May's eldest child,
The coming musk-rose, full of dewy wine,
50 The murmurous haunt of flies on summer eves.

6

Darkling I listen; and, for many a time
I have been half in love with easeful Death,
Call'd him soft names in many a mused rhyme,
To take into the air my quiet breath;
55 Now more than ever seems it rich to die,
To cease upon the midnight with no pain,
While thou art pouring forth thy soul abroad
In such an ecstasy!
Still wouldst thou sing, and I have ears in vain—
60 To thy high requiem become a sod.

7

Thou wast not born for death, immortal Bird!
No hungry generations tread thee down;
The voice I hear this passing night was heard
In ancient days by emperor and clown:
65 Perhaps the self-same song that found a path
Through the sad heart of Ruth, when, sick for home,
She stood in tears amid the alien corn;
The same that oft-times hath
Charm'd magic casements, opening on the foam
70 Of perilous seas, in faery lands forlorn.

8

Forlorn! the very word is like a bell
To toll me back from thee to my sole self!

44 month] mouth *Annals* 49 dewy] sweetest *D*, *W*², *CWD*, *GK*, *Annals* 50 The] *written over* ⟨Her⟩ *D* (*but see Textual Note*) 52 been] *added above the line in D* 54 quiet] painless *D* 57 forth] thus *D*, *W*², *CWD*, *GK*, *Annals* 59 wouldst] would *D* 59/60 ⟨But requiem'd⟩ *D* 60 To] For *altered to* To (*actually producing* Fo) *D*; For *W*², *CWD*, *GK*, *Annals* 65 song] *interlined above* ⟨voice⟩ *D* 66 for] from *CWD* 69 magic] *interlined above* ⟨the wide⟩ *D* 70 perilous] ⟨Ruthless⟩ perilous *D* (*but see Textual Note*) 72 me back] *interlined above* ⟨me⟩ ⟨me⟩ (*the first deleted* me *written over* {ba}) *D* 72 to my . . . self] unto myself *D*, *W*²

Adieu! the fancy cannot cheat so well
  As she is fam'd to do, deceiving elf.
75 Adieu! adieu! thy plaintive anthem fades
  Past the near meadows, over the still stream,
    Up the hill-side; and now 'tis buried deep
      In the next valley-glades:
  Was it a vision, or a waking dream?
80   Fled is that music:—Do I wake or sleep?

## *Ode on a Grecian Urn*

1

Thou still unravish'd bride of quietness,
  Thou foster-child of silence and slow time,
Sylvan historian, who canst thus express
  A flowery tale more sweetly than our rhyme:
5 What leaf-fring'd legend haunts about thy shape
  Of deities or mortals, or of both,
    In Tempe or the dales of Arcady?
  What men or gods are these? What maidens loth?
What mad pursuit? What struggle to escape?
10   What pipes and timbrels? What wild ecstasy?

2

Heard melodies are sweet, but those unheard
  Are sweeter; therefore, ye soft pipes, play on;
Not to the sensual ear, but, more endear'd,
  Pipe to the spirit ditties of no tone:
15 Fair youth, beneath the trees, thou canst not leave
  Thy song, nor ever can those trees be bare;
    Bold lover, never, never canst thou kiss,
Though winning near the goal—yet, do not grieve;
    She cannot fade, though thou hast not thy bliss,
20   For ever wilt thou love, and she be fair!

74 deceiving] *made out of* deceitful *D* 78 valley] vally⟨'s⟩ *D* 79 vision, or a] vision real or *D* 80 music:—] ~— *D*; ~? *W*², *CWD, GK, Annals*

*Ode on a Grecian Urn.* Text (including heading) from *1820.* Variants from Brown's transcript (*CB*) and the version published in *Annals of the Fine Arts.* *Heading* Ode on] On *Annals* 1 still‸] ~, *Annals* 8 men or gods] Gods or Men *Annals* 9 mad pursuit] love? what dance *CB*, *Annals* 16 can . . . bare] bid the spring adieu *Annals* 18 yet] O *CB*, *Annals*

3

Ah, happy, happy boughs! that cannot shed
  Your leaves, nor ever bid the spring adieu;
And, happy melodist, unwearied,
  For ever piping songs for ever new;
25 More happy love! more happy, happy love!
  For ever warm and still to be enjoy'd,
    For ever panting, and for ever young;
All breathing human passion far above,
  That leaves a heart high-sorrowful and cloy'd,
30 A burning forehead, and a parching tongue.

4

Who are these coming to the sacrifice?
  To what green altar, O mysterious priest,
Lead'st thou that heifer lowing at the skies,
  And all her silken flanks with garlands drest?
35 What little town by river or sea shore,
  Or mountain-built with peaceful citadel,
    Is emptied of this folk, this pious morn?
And, little town, thy streets for evermore
  Will silent be; and not a soul to tell
40 Why thou art desolate, can e'er return.

5

O Attic shape! Fair attitude! with brede
  Of marble men and maidens overwrought,
With forest branches and the trodden weed;
  Thou, silent form, dost tease us out of thought
45 As doth eternity: Cold Pastoral!
  When old age shall this generation waste,
    Thou shalt remain, in midst of other woe
  Than ours, a friend to man, to whom thou say'st,
"Beauty is truth, truth beauty,"—that is all
50 Ye know on earth, and all ye need to know.

22 ever] never *Annals* 34 flanks] sides *CB* 40 e'er] ne'er *altered to* e'er *CB* 42 maidens‸ overwrought,] ~, ~‸ *CB* 47 shalt] wilt *CB*, *Annals* 48 a] as *CB* 49 "Beauty . . . that] ‸Beauty is Truth,—Truth Beauty,—that *CB*; ‸Beauty is Truth, Truth Beauty.—That *Annals*

## *Ode on Melancholy*

1

No, no, go not to Lethe, neither twist
Wolf's-bane, tight-rooted, for its poisonous wine;
Nor suffer thy pale forehead to be kiss'd
By nightshade, ruby grape of Proserpine;
5 Make not your rosary of yew-berries,
Nor let the beetle, nor the death-moth be
Your mournful Psyche, nor the downy owl
A partner in your sorrow's mysteries;
For shade to shade will come too drowsily,
10 And drown the wakeful anguish of the soul.

2

But when the melancholy fit shall fall
Sudden from heaven like a weeping cloud,
That fosters the droop-headed flowers all,
And hides the green hill in an April shroud;
15 Then glut thy sorrow on a morning rose,
Or on the rainbow of the salt sand-wave,
Or on the wealth of globed peonies;
Or if thy mistress some rich anger shows,
Emprison her soft hand, and let her rave,
20 And feed deep, deep upon her peerless eyes.

*Ode on Melancholy.* Text (including heading) from *1820*. Variants and other readings from the extant holograph (arbitrarily cited as *D*) and Brown's transcript (*CB*). *Heading* Ode on] On *D*; Ode, to *altered to* Ode, on *CB* *Before* 1

1

Though you should build a bark of dead men's bones,
And rear a phantom gibbet for a mast,
Stitch creeds together for a sail, with groans
To fill it out, bloodstained and aghast;
Although your rudder be a Dragon's tail,
Long sever'd, yet still hard with agony,
Your cordage large uprootings from the skull
Of bald Medusa; certes you would fail
To find the Melancholy, whether she
Dreameth in any isle of Lethe dull.

(*the stanza crossed out in pencil*) *CB*. *The remaining three stanzas in CB are numbered 2–4* 2 Wolf's] ⟨Henb⟩ Wolfs *D* 6 nor the] or the *D* 9 drowsily] *successively* (*a*) heavily (*b*) sleepily (*c*) drowsily *D* 11 fall] *interlined above* ⟨come⟩ *D* 12 a] *added above the line in D* 14 hill] hills *D*, *CB* 15 glut] *interlined above* ⟨feed⟩ *D* 16 salt] ⟨dashing⟩ salt *D*

3

She dwells with Beauty—Beauty that must die;<br>
  And Joy, whose hand is ever at his lips<br>
Bidding adieu; and aching Pleasure nigh,<br>
  Turning to poison while the bee-mouth sips:<br>
25 Ay, in the very temple of Delight<br>
  Veil'd Melancholy has her sovran shrine,<br>
    Though seen of none save him whose strenuous tongue<br>
  Can burst Joy's grape against his palate fine;<br>
His soul shall taste the sadness of her might,<br>
30     And be among her cloudy trophies hung.

## *Ode on Indolence*

"They toil not, neither do they spin."

1

One morn before me were three figures seen,<br>
  With bowed necks, and joined hands, side-faced;<br>
And one behind the other stepp'd serene,<br>
  In placid sandals, and in white robes graced:<br>
5 They pass'd, like figures on a marble urn,<br>
  When shifted round to see the other side;<br>
    They came again; as when the urn once more<br>
Is shifted round, the first seen shades return;<br>
  And they were strange to me, as may betide<br>
10     With vases, to one deep in Phidian lore.

2

How is it, shadows, that I knew ye not?<br>
  How came ye muffled in so hush a masque?<br>
Was it a silent deep-disguised plot<br>
  To steal away, and leave without a task<br>
15 My idle days? Ripe was the drowsy hour;<br>
  The blissful cloud of summer-indolence<br>
    Benumb'd my eyes; my pulse grew less and less;<br>
Pain had no sting, and pleasure's wreath no flower.

21 dwells with] lives in *D*, *CB*  27 save] but *D*  27 him] *interlined above* ⟨those⟩ *D*  29 taste] *added above the line in D*  29 sadness] anguish *D*

*Ode on Indolence.* Text (including heading and epigraph) from Brown's transcript (*CB*)  11 ye] *made out of* you *CB*

O, why did ye not melt, and leave my sense
20 Unhaunted quite of all but—nothingness?

3

A third time pass'd they by, and, passing, turn'd
Each one the face a moment whiles to me;
Then faded, and to follow them I burn'd
And ached for wings, because I knew the three:
25 The first was a fair maid, and Love her name;
The second was Ambition, pale of cheek,
And ever watchful with fatigued eye;
The last, whom I love more, the more of blame
Is heap'd upon her, maiden most unmeek,—
30 I knew to be my demon Poesy.

4

They faded, and, forsooth! I wanted wings:
O folly! What is Love? and where is it?
And for that poor Ambition—it springs
From a man's little heart's short fever-fit;
35 For Poesy!—no,—she has not a joy,—
At least for me,—so sweet as drowsy noons,
And evenings steep'd in honied indolence;
O, for an age so shelter'd from annoy,
That I may never know how change the moons,
40 Or hear the voice of busy common-sense!

5

A third time came they by;—alas! wherefore?
My sleep had been embroider'd with dim dreams;
My soul had been a lawn besprinkled o'er
With flowers, and stirring shades, and baffled beams:
45 The morn was clouded, but no shower fell,
Though in her lids hung the sweet tears of May;
The open casement press'd a new-leaved vine,
Let in the budding warmth and throstle's lay;
O shadows! 'twas a time to bid farewell!
50 Upon your skirts had fallen no tears of mine.

6

So, ye three ghosts, adieu! Ye cannot raise
My head cool-bedded in the flowery grass;

For I would not be dieted with praise,
  A pet-lamb in a sentimental farce!
55 Fade softly from my eyes, and be once more
  In masque-like figures on the dreamy urn;
    Farewell! I yet have visions for the night,
And for the day faint visions there is store;
    Vanish, ye phantoms, from my idle spright,
60 Into the clouds, and never more return!

## *Shed no tear—O shed no tear*

Shed no tear—O shed no tear!
The flower will bloom another year.
Weep no more—O weep no more!
Young buds sleep in the root's white core.
5 Dry your eyes—O dry your eyes!
For I was taught in Paradise
To ease my breast of melodies—
                Shed no tear!

Over head—look over head,
10 'Mong the blossoms white and red.
Look up, look up—I flutter now
On this flush pomgranate bough.
See me—'tis this silvery bill
Ever cures the good man's ill.
15 Shed no tear—O shed no tear!
The flower will bloom another year.
Adieu—adieu—I fly, adieu!
I vanish in the heaven's blue—
                Adieu, adieu!

*Shed no tear.* Text from the extant holograph (arbitrarily cited as *FC*). Variants from the versions in Brown's MS "The Fairies' Triumph" (*CB*) and *PDWJ*. *Heading* Shed . . . tear] *ed*; The Faery Bird's Song *PDWJ*; *no heading in FC, CB*  4 buds] birds *PDWJ*  7 my . . . of] the heart in *CB*  18 heaven's] heavens *CB*, *PDWJ*  19 Adieu, adieu] ⟨Shed⟩ Adieu Adieu *FC*

# *Otho the Great: A Tragedy in Five Acts*

## Dramatis Personæ

OTHO THE GREAT, *Emperor of Germany*
LUDOLPH, *his Son*
CONRAD, *Duke of Franconia*
ALBERT, *a Knight, favoured by Otho*
SIGIFRED, *an Officer, friend of Ludolph*
THEODORE, } *Officers*
GONFRID, }
ETHELBERT, *an Abbot*
GERSA, *Prince of Hungary*
*An Hungarian Captain*
*Physician*
*Page*
*Nobles, Knights, Attendants, and Soldiers*

ERMINIA, *Niece of Otho*
AURANTHE, *Conrad's Sister*
*Ladies and Attendants*

SCENE. *The Castle of Friedburg, its vicinity, and the Hungarian Camp*

TIME. *One Day*

## ACT I

### SCENE I. *An Apartment in the Castle.*

*Enter* CONRAD.

*Conrad.* So, I am safe emerged from these broils!
Amid the wreck of thousands I am whole;

*Otho the Great.* Text from Brown's fair copy (*CB*) except for heading, the last four items of the Dramatis Personae (plus "Scene" and "Time" details following the Dramatis Personae), and I.i.1–20, IV.ii.2–44a, V.i.30b–ii.27 (all missing from *CB*), which are taken from *1848*. Variants and other readings from Keats's first complete draft (*D*, extant for all but IV.i.71–73, 86–90, IV.ii.117–121a, V.v.11–58), Keats's revised draft of I.i.17–24, 31–44a, 55–60a, 66–68, 145–152 (*KRD*), Brown's revised draft or copy of I.i.141–144 (*BRD*), and the extract of I.iii.24–29 in Keats's letter to George and Georgiana Keats, 17–27 Sep-

For every crime I have a laurel-wreath,
For every lie a lordship. Nor yet has
5 My ship of fortune furl'd her silken sails,—
Let her glide on! This danger'd neck is saved,
By dexterous policy, from the rebel's axe;
And of my ducal palace not one stone
Is bruised by the Hungarian petards.
10 Toil hard, ye slaves, and from the miser-earth
Bring forth once more my bullion, treasured deep,
With all my jewell'd salvers, silver and gold,
And precious goblets that make rich the wine.
But why do I stand babbling to myself?
15 Where is Auranthe? I have news for her
Shall—

*Enter* AURANTHE.

*Auranthe.* Conrad! what tidings? Good, if I may guess
From your alert eyes and high-lifted brows.

---

tember 1819 (*L*). The apparatus also includes readings of *1848* where text based on it is emended from another source. *Heading* Otho . . . Acts] *so 1848* (*the subtitle appearing on the half title preceding the first page of text*); *D has* Otho *centered on an otherwise blank first page*

I.i *location and opening s.d.* An . . . Conrad]
An Apartment in the Castle of Friedborg
⟨Conrad and Auranthe meeting—⟩
Enter Conrad bristling
(*the last word also readable as* bustling *with a dotted "u"*) *D* 1 emerged] ⟨from⟩ emerged *D* 4 yet] ⟨has yet⟩ yet *D* 5 furl'd] struck *D* 6 glide . . . saved] sail . . . safe *D* 7 By . . . axe;] *not in D, but the line* (*with the last two words of 6*) *appears in a canceled passage written by Keats on the verso of the Dramatis Personae leaf in CB*:

⟨is sav'd
By dexte'rous policy from the rebel's axe
*Conrad.* Am I so welcome Sister? Your voice is tam'd
To an unusual tone of friendliness—
Say; you admire my far fore thoughted wits
My argus wacthfulness, my protean cunning
To change myself from a rank Mutineer
Into a favourite.
*Auranthe.* I must confess—
*Conrad.* Or have you {any} (seeing I have Otho's ear)
Any suit to me—Speak, for I will grant it
As you will, my liege Lady, favour me—⟩

(my *made out of* me *in the fifth line and* my protean . . . favourite *beginning in the sixth line added afterward*) 8 of] *interlined above* ⟨all⟩ *D* 10 Toil] *written over* ⟨Wor⟩ *D* 12 With] *written over* ⟨My⟩ *D* 13 rich] sweet *D* 14 But . . . myself?] *interlined above* ⟨But where's Auranthe—⟩ *D* 15 Where is] ⟨But⟩ where⟨'s⟩ (*Keats neglected to insert* is) *D* 17 what] ⟨what news?⟩ what *KRD* 18 your] *interlined above* ⟨the⟩ *KRD*

What tidings of the battle? Albert? Ludolph?
20 Otho?
*Conrad.* You guess aright. And, sister, slurring o'er
Our by-gone quarrels, I confess my heart
Is beating with a child's anxiety,
To make our golden fortune known to you.
*Auranthe.* So serious?

17–123 *Auranthe.* Conrad . . . mariners.]
*Auranthe.* Ha! Brother Conrad, ⟨s⟩ welcome from the War!
I thought I heard your Trumpet at the Gates
*Conrad.* Am I so welcome Sister—sister no more
But my liege Lady—
*Auranthe.* Liege Lady are you mad?
[5] *Conrad.* My sovran Lady what would you give now
If I would clear the puzzle from your brows?
*Auranthe.* Good Brother speak—
*Conrad.* Good Brother—will I now
Speak out since a fair Sister and an almost Queen
Commands. The Emperor—
*Auranthe.* What! Pray speak
[10] *Conrad.* Hath given consent that you should marry Ludolph
*Auranthe.* What sudden change is here—how was it Conrad?
*Conrad.* Never mind how—but let your royal blood
⟨Grown⟩ Mount in your ceeks—
*Auranthe.* I feel it mounting wam—
But it is so—Kind Brother tell me how?
[15] *Conrad.* Thank me for this;—in yesterday's hard fight
I did the Emperor service, and so help'd'
His bloostain'd Ensign to the victory
That it hath turd the edge of his sharp wrath
To overflowing kindness—now he's mine
[20] And we must take him sister in the mood
*Auranthe.* Aye this sounds well and reasonable too
*Conrad.* He will be heare this moring.
*Auranthe.* That I heard
Among the midnight tidings from the Camp—
*Conrad (going).* That is all well—Good bye my gracious Queen—
Within an hour—
[25] *Auranthe.* Conrad one word more
*Conrad.* Speak Empress!
*Auranthe.* That Letter!
*Conrad.* What Letter?
*Auranthe.* Do give it me that I may mince it up
⟨For I w⟩ Then there will be no shadow of a chance
Against my coming greatness—
*Conrad.* What dost mean—
[30] *Auranthe.* You sure received that Letter touching Albert?
*Conrad.* No—yes—
*Auranthe.* Give it me,

25 *Conrad.* Yes, so serious, that before
I utter even the shadow of a hint
Concerning what will make that sin-worn cheek
Blush joyous blood through every lineament,
You must make here a solemn vow to me.

---

*Conrad.* I have it not
*Auranthe.* Alas!
*Conrad.* At one pernicious charge of the Enemy
I for a moment whiles was Prisoner ta'en
And rifled—stuff! the horses hoof has minc'd it
*Auranthe.* Still I have half a fear:
[35] *Conrad.* Perhaps For Albert
*Auranthe.* Surely you spar'd him at my earnest prayer
*Conrad.* Spar'd him! O would to Heaven I had not—
*Auranthe.* If you do ever touch a hair of his head
I swear in your despite I will refuse
[40] Even his Highness Ludolph's sceptry hand
*Conrad.* Impossible! refuse a Prince—a Prince!
No woman, no—you dare not for yourself
You could not though it were to save your teeth
Complete for kissing, your eyes and your cheeks colour
[45] Be but a Queen and at at word you make
Pearl mouths fade out of fashion—ha ha ha,
Refuse the Prince! forgive me, I must laugh
*Auranthe.* Sir, you may laugh—but by my Life I swear—
*Conrad.* Yes, Yes I know you'll swear—do any thing
[50] To gain so poor a point as Albert's life.
Why I have known a Lady do as much
And more, fall spawling hectic on the floor
To frighten her poor lord to unstring his purse
For a new silver service—
*Auranthe.* You may find
[55] Yourself not quite so learned cunning Sir!
*Conrad.* Would you be then unqueen'd for such a dog
*Auranthe.* Aye for that word I could to torture you
*Conrad.* And this is then the fruit of all my pains
And all my risques, and all my weary plots
[60] To make thee mighty. Plot who will again
For others benefit, I'll no more of it—
The very sister of our ducal house
Will weigh a Brother and a royal Crown
Against a—
*Auranthe.* Keep the word within your lips
[65] And let it choak you! But I will be calm
To our better understanding one another—
You know some secret coverts of my heart
⟨But perh⟩
I know perhaps yours better than you mine.
Why so pathetic ⟨Brother⟩ my kind Benefactor

30 *Auranthe.* I pr'ythee, Conrad, do not overact
The hypocrite. What vow would you impose?
*Conrad.* Trust me for once. That you may be assured
'Tis not confiding in a broken reed,
A poor court-bankrupt, outwitted and lost,
35 Revolve these facts in your acutest mood,
In such a mood as now you listen to me:
A few days since, I was an open rebel,—
Against the Emperor had suborn'd his son,—
Drawn off his nobles to revolt,—and shown
40 Contented fools causes for discontent,
Fresh hatch'd in my ambition's eagle-nest;
So thrived I as a rebel,—and, behold!
Now I am Otho's favorite, his dear friend,
His right hand, his brave Conrad!

---

[70] On all the many bounties of your hand—
Sure, you forgot ⟨not self⟩ Duke Conrad all this while?
*Conrad.* By heavens, I could almost spop this match—
*Auranthe.* No, Brother, no you dare not for yourself—
Ha! ha! forgive me for I too must laugh
[75] Do you not count, when I am queen, to take
Advantage of your mean discoveries
Of my poor secrets, and so hold a rod
Over my life for your sly purposes?
*Conrad.* Now could I hear that villain—see he comes
[80] Look, woman Look your Albert is quite safe—
In haste it seems—Now shall I be in the way
And wish'd with silent curses in my grave
Or side by side with whelmed Mariners [*Enter* ALBERT.
Whisper a ⟨little⟩ Curse Auranthe in my ear
[85] 'Twill be sweet musick—Curse me far away!
For there can be no "gentle Alberts" now
No "sweet Auranthes"
*Auranthe.* Peace thou devil Peace.

(1 Brother *added above the line* 2 I . . . heard *interlined above* ⟨Am I so welcome⟩ 10 Ludolph *interlined above* ⟨Conrad⟩ 11 here *added above the line* 14 Brother *added above the line* 16 the Emperor *interlined above* ⟨him such good⟩ 22 heare *added above the line* 23 midnight *added above the line* 26 Speak *interlined above* ⟨What⟩ 28 Then *interlined above* ⟨That⟩ 28 will *interlined above* ⟨may⟩ 34 hoof has *made out of* hoofs have 35 Perhaps *added afterward* 51 Lady *interlined above* ⟨woman⟩ 52 *the fourth and fifth words written* hectic spawling *but marked for transposition* 60 mighty *interlined above* ⟨great⟩ 63 Brother . . . Crown *made out of* Brother's friendship and a Crown 75–78 Do . . . purposes? *added on the opposite verso* 79 see *interlined above* ⟨ha⟩ 80 Look . . . safe— *added on the opposite verso* 83 *s.d.* Enter Albert *inserted between the lines* 86 *the last three words actually written* 'gentle 'Alberts'! now'' 87 thou *added above the line*) *D. The draft text then continues with the variant s.d. given below at 123* 34/35 ⟨Let me impess this⟩ *KRD* 43 Now] How *KRD*

*Auranthe.* I confess
45 You have intrigued with these unsteady times
To admiration. But to be a favorite—
*Conrad.* I saw my moment. The Hungarians,
Collected silently in holes and corners,
Appear'd, a sudden host, in the open day.
50 I should have perish'd in our empire's wreck;
But, calling interest loyalty, swore faith
To most believing Otho; and so help'd
His blood-stain'd ensigns to the victory
In yesterday's hard fight, that it has turn'd
55 The edge of his sharp wrath to eager kindness.
*Auranthe.* So far yourself. But what is this to me
More than that I am glad? I gratulate you.
*Conrad.* Yes, sister, but it does regard you greatly,
Nearly, momentously,—aye, painfully!
Make me this vow—
60 *Auranthe.* Concerning whom or what?
*Conrad.* Albert!
*Auranthe.* I would enquire somewhat of him:
You had a letter from me touching him?
No treason 'gainst his head in deed or word!
Surely you spared him at my earnest prayer?
65 Give me the letter—it should not exist!
*Conrad.* At one pernicious charge of the enemy,
I, for a moment-whiles, was prisoner ta'en
And rifled,—stuff! the horses' hoofs have minced it!
*Auranthe.* He is alive?
*Conrad.* He is! but here make oath
70 To alienate him from your scheming brain,
Divorce him from your solitary thoughts,
And cloud him in such utter banishment,
That when his person meets again your eye,
Your vision shall quite lose its memory,
75 And wander past him as through vacancy.
*Auranthe.* I'll not be perjured.
*Conrad.* No, nor great, nor mighty;

51 swore faith] *interlined above* ⟨turn'd back⟩ *CB* 56 But . . . me] *interlined above* ⟨yet this not touches me⟩ *KRD* 58 it . . . greatly] *interlined above* ⟨it does, it touches you⟩ *KRD* 59 Nearly] ⟨Painfully⟩ nearly *KRD* 60 vow—] vow and you shall hear how mouch / It is a matter of Life and death with you *KRD* (*the text between these lines and 66 in KRD is missing*) 66 At] In *KRD*

You would not wear a crown, or rule a kingdom,
To you it is indifferent.
*Auranthe.* What means this?
*Conrad.* You'll not be perjured! Go to Albert then,
80 That camp-mushroom, dishonour of our house;
Go, page his dusty heels upon a march,
Furbish his jingling baldric while he sleeps,
And share his mouldy ratio in a siege.
Yet stay,—perhaps a charm may call you back,
85 And make the widening circlets of your eyes
Sparkle with healthy fevers,—the Emperor
Hath given consent that you should marry Ludolph!
*Auranthe.* Can it be, brother? For a golden crown
With a queen's awful lips I doubly thank you!
90 This is to wake in Paradise! farewell,
Thou clod of yesterday—'twas not myself!
Not till this moment did I ever feel
My spirit's faculties! I'll flatter you
For this, and be you ever proud of it;
95 Thou, Jove-like, struck'dst thy forehead,
And from the teeming marrow of thy brain
I spring complete Minerva! But the Prince—
His Highness Ludolph—where is he?
*Conrad.* I know not:
When, lackeying my counsel at a beck,
100 The rebel-lords, on bended knees, received
The Emperor's pardon, Ludolph kept aloof,
Sole,—in a stiff, fool-hardy, sulky pride;
Yet, for all this, I never saw a father
In such a sickly longing for his son.
105 We shall soon see him,—for the Emperor,
He will be here this morning.
*Auranthe.* That I heard
Among the midnight rumours from the camp.
*Conrad.* You give up Albert to me?
*Auranthe.* Harm him not!
E'en for his Highness Ludolph's sceptry hand,
110 I would not Albert suffer any wrong.
*Conrad.* Have I not labour'd, plotted—?
*Auranthe.* See you spare him;

95 struck'dst] *ed*; struck'd (st *added in pencil but probably not by Brown or Keats*) *CB* 107 rumours] *interlined above* ⟨tidings⟩ *CB* 111 See . . . him] *interlined above* ⟨Touch him not⟩ *CB*

Nor be pathetic, my kind benefactor,
On all the many bounties of your hand,—
'Twas for yourself you labour'd—not for me!
115 Do you not count, when I am queen, to take
Advantage of your chance discoveries
Of my poor secrets, and so hold a rod
Over my life?
*Conrad.* Let not this slave—this villain—
Be cause of feud between us. See! he comes!
120 Look, woman, look, your Albert is quite safe!
In haste it seems. Now shall I be in the way,
And wish'd with silent curses in my grave,
Or side by side with whelmed mariners.

*Enter* ALBERT.

*Albert.* Fair on your Graces fall this early morrow!
125 So it is like to do, without my prayers,
For your right noble names, like favorite tunes,
Have fallen full frequent from our Emperor's lips,
High commented with smiles.
*Auranthe.* Noble Albert!
*Conrad (aside).* Noble!
130 *Auranthe.* Such salutation argues a glad heart
In our prosperity. We thank you, sir.
*Albert.* Lady! O would to heaven your poor servant
Could do you better service than mere words!
But I have other greeting than mine own
135 From no less man than Otho, who has sent
This ring as pledge of dearest amity;
'Tis chosen I hear from Hymen's jewelry,
And you will prize it, lady, I doubt not,
Beyond all pleasures past, and all to come:
To you, great Duke—

112 my kind] *written over erased* ⟨Conrad⟩ *CB* 123 *s.d.* Enter Albert] Albert approaching *D* 126 like . . . tunes] *written beneath* ⟨high commented⟩ *D* 126/127 ⟨Have leap'd⟩ *D* 127 fallen . . . from] dwelt . . . on *altered to* fall'n . . . from *D* 131 sir] *not in D* 132 Lady!] *written at the right on a separate line by itself in both D (where it constitutes the last two syllables of 131—see preceding note) and CB, leaving* O . . . servant *as a tetrameter line* 134 But] Yet D 134 mine] *made out of* my *D* 137–139 'Tis . . . come:] *written on the opposite verso in D to replace* ⟨With every gratulation that can pass / From friend to friend upon a happy day—⟩ *(in the process of revising Keats also deleted and did not replace the last five words of 136)* 139 Beyond] Before *D*

140 *Conrad.* To me! What of me, ha?
*Albert.* What pleas'd your Grace to say?
*Conrad.* Your message, sir!
*Albert.* You mean not this to me?
*Conrad.* Sister, this way;
For there shall be no "gentle Alberts" now, [*Aside.*
No "sweet Auranthes"! [*Exeunt* CONRAD *and* AURANTHE.
145 *Albert* (*solus*). The Duke is out of temper; if he knows
More than a brother of a sister ought,
I should not quarrel with his peevishness.
Auranthe—heaven preserve her always fair!—
Is in the heady, proud, ambitious vein;

140–158 To you . . . *Exit.*]
The Emperor is no further from you
He is no further distant from your gates
Than what my Charger in three minutes clear'd
⟨Out⟩ galloping ⟨his slow pomp⟩ his Pomp—To you great Duke
He
*Conrad.* What of me ha?
[5] *Albert.* What pleas'd your grace to say?
*Conrad.* What matters that?
*Albert.* You mean not this to me?
*Auranthe.* My noble Brother you have grieved enough:
(*To Albert*) Lord Albert now you must not heed his words
The Duke has ever since the battle sorrow'd
[10] For one of his brave Captains slain—his friend
He was—and a most valliant—⟨Heart thou!⟩
⟨*Albert.* The Emperor's flourish!⟩
*Conrad.* Sister! would you you thrust me on—
*Auranthe.* Harst thou!
*Albert.* The Emperor's Flourish! Germany is here!
I'm sorry for his grace—
(1 The . . . you *written on the opposite verso, following the revised 137–139, and possibly intended as a replacement of the second line given here* 3 minutes clear'd *made out of* minute whiles 4 galloping *made out of* gallop'd 4 slow *interlined above* {full} 6 this *made out of* that 13 Germany *successively* [*a*] Lady he [*b*] Cæsar himself [*c*] Germany) *D* 141 message] *successively* (*a*) message (*b*) errand (*c*) message *BRD* 142 *Albert.* You . . . way]
⟨*Albert.* {The} {I understand you not, but this my errand,—}
The Emperor's prosperous wishes—nothing more.
*Conrad.* Tis well.
*Auranthe.* Dear brother let us cease—Farewell,
Most courteous Albert,—⟩
*Conrad.* Sister, this way
(Dear . . . cease *successively* [*a*] Hence! brother [*b*] Dear brother hence [*c*] Dear brother let us cease *in the second part of the third line and* this way *interlined above* ⟨come with me⟩ *in the last line; Albert's speech in the present 142*—You . . . me?—*is not in the fragment*) *BRD* 143 shall] must *BRD* 148 her] *made out of* the *KRD* 149 heady . . . vein] *written beneath* ⟨proud vein;—{he's} that man is a fool⟩ *KRD*

150 I bicker not with her,—bid her farewell!
She has taken flight from me, then let her soar,—
He is a fool who stands at pining gaze!
But for poor Ludolph, he is food for sorrow;
No leveling bluster of my licensed thoughts,
155 No military swagger of my mind,
Can smother from myself the wrong I've done him,—
Without design indeed,—yet it is so,—
And opiate for the conscience have I none! [*Exit.*

SCENE II. *The Court-yard of the Castle.*

*Martial music. Enter, from the outer gate,* OTHO, *Nobles, Knights, and Attendants. The Soldiers halt at the gate, with banners in sight.*

*Otho.* Where is my noble herald?
[*Enter* CONRAD, *from the Castle, attended by two Knights and Servants.* ALBERT *following.*
Well! hast told
Auranthe our intent imperial?
Lest our rent banners, too o' the sudden shown,
Should fright her silken casements, and dismay
5 Her household to our lack of entertainment.
A victory!
*Conrad.* God save illustrious Otho!
*Otho.* Aye, Conrad, it will pluck out all grey hairs;
It is the best physician for the spleen;
The courtliest inviter to a feast;
10 The subtelest excuser of small faults;
And a nice judge in the age and smack of wine.
[*Enter, from the Castle,* AURANTHE, *followed by Pages holding up her robes, and a train of Women. She kneels.*
Hail, my sweet hostess! I do thank the stars,
Or my good soldiers, or their ladies' eyes,
That, after such a merry battle fought,
15 I can, all safe in body and in soul,

151 She] *written over* ⟨He⟩ *KRD* 151 taken] taen *KRD* 151 then] *made out of* there *KRD* 152 who] *interlined above* ⟨that⟩ *CB* 154 leveling] *made out of* leavening *CB* 158 have] ⟨I⟩ have *CB*

I.ii *location* Castle] Castle of Friborg *D* *Opening s.d.* Otho . . . Attendants] Otho & several officers *D* Nobles, Knights] *interlined above* ⟨with Officers⟩ *CB* 1 *s.d.* Servants . . . following] servants—Albert *D* 6 illustrious] imperial *D*; illustrious *interlined above* ⟨the power of⟩ *CB* 15 and in] in and *D*

Kiss your fair hand and lady fortune's too.
My ring! now, on my life, it doth rejoice
These lips to feel't on this soft ivory!
Keep it, my brightest daughter; it may prove
20 The little prologue to a line of kings.
I strove against thee and my hot-blood son,
Dull blockhead that I was to be so blind,
But now my sight is clear; forgive me, lady.
*Auranthe.* My lord, I was a vassal to your frown,
25 And now your favour makes me but more humble;
In wintry winds the simple snow is safe,
But fadeth at the greeting of the sun:
Unto thine anger I might well have spoken,
Taking on me a woman's privilege,
30 But this so sudden kindness makes me dumb.
*Otho.* What need of this? Enough, if you will be
A potent tutoress to my wayward boy,
And teach him, what it seems his nurse could not,
To say for once I thank you. Sigifred!
35 *Albert.* He has not yet return'd, my gracious liege.
*Otho.* What then! No tidings of my friendly Arab?
*Conrad.* None, mighty Otho.
[*To one of his Knights, who goes out.*
Send forth instantly
An hundred horsemen from my honoured gates,
To scour the plains and search the cottages.
40 Cry a reward, to him who shall first bring
News of that vanished Arabian,
A full-heaped helmet of the purest gold.
*Otho.* More thanks, good Conrad; for, except my son's,
There is no face I rather would behold
45 Than that same quick-eyed pagan's. By the saints,
This coming night of banquets must not light

19 Keep] ⟨O ma⟩ Keep *D* 19 may] *interlined above* ⟨will⟩ *D* 21 thee] *added above the line in D* 31 be] *interlined above* ⟨teach⟩ *D* 33 him] *added above the line in D* 33 it] *made out of* is *D* 33 nurse] *added above the line in D* 38 An] A *D* 40 shall . . . bring] first brings news *altered to* shall first bring *D* 40/41 ⟨Of that Arabian⟩ *D* 42 A . . . purest] *successively* (*a*) Of a full heaped Helmet of bright (*b*) a full heaped Helmet of the brightest (*c*) a full heaped Helmet of the purest *D* 45 quick] *interlined above* ⟨swift⟩ *D* 45 pagan's . . . saints] *in D Keats initially ended Otho's speech with* pagan's *and wrote the s.p.* Albert *for the next line, but then canceled the s.p. and continued Otho's speech, successively* (*a*) By my Crown (*b*) By all the Saints this (*c*) By the Saints 46 coming] ⟨day of Banquets⟩ coming *D*

Her dazzling torches; nor the music breathe
Smooth, without clashing cymbal, tones of peace
And in-door melodies; nor the ruddy wine
50 Ebb spouting to the lees;—if I pledge not,
In my first cup, that Arab!
*Albert.* Mighty monarch,
I wonder not this stranger's victor-deeds
So hang upon your spirit. Twice in the fight
It was my chance to meet his olive brow,
55 Triumphant in the enemy's shatter'd rhomb;
And, to say truth, in any Christian arm
I never saw such prowess.
*Otho.* Did you ever?
O, 'tis a noble boy!—tut!—what do I say?
I mean a tripple-Saladin, whose eyes,
60 When in the glorious scuffle they met mine,
Seem'd to say—"Sleep, old man, in safety sleep;
I am the victory!"
*Conrad.* Pity he's not here.
*Otho.* And my son too, pity he is not here.
Lady Auranthe, I would not make you blush,
65 But can you give a guess where Ludolph is?
Know you not of him?
*Auranthe.* Indeed, my liege, no secret—
*Otho.* Nay, nay, without more words, dost know of him?
*Auranthe.* I would I were so over-fortunate,
Both for his sake and mine, and to make glad
70 A father's ears with tidings of his son.
*Otho.* I see 'tis like to be a tedious day.
Were Theodore and Gonfrid and the rest
Sent forth with my commands?
*Albert.* Aye, my lord.
*Otho.* And no news! No news! 'Faith! 'tis very strange
75 He thus avoids us. Lady, is't not strange?
Will he be truant to you too? It is a shame.

47 nor] ⟨nor the music sound / Softer than clashing⟩ nor *D* 47 breathe] *successively (a)* breath *(b)* smooth *(c)* breathe *D* 47/48 ⟨The indoor⟩ *D* 48 clashing] the clashing (the *added above the line*) *D* 50 pledge not] cannot pledge *altered to* pledge not *D* 51 monarch] Cæsar *D* 52 this] *interlined above* ⟨these⟩ *D* 56 And] ⟨His hair⟩ And *D* 60 glorious] *added above the line in D* 61 safety sleep] *interlined above* ⟨surety⟩ *D* 62 I] ⟨This⟩ I *D* 73 commands?] commands—⟨No news! No news⟩ *D* 73 Aye] *written over* ⟨Yes⟩ *D* 76 It . . . shame] 'Tis a shame *written beneath* ⟨What's that shout⟩ *D*

*Conrad.* Will't please your Highness enter, and accept
The unworthy welcome of your servant's house?
Leaving your cares to one whose diligence
80 May in few hours make pleasures of them all.
*Otho.* Not so tedious, Conrad. No, no, no, no,—
I must see Ludolph or the—What's that shout?
*Voices without.* Huzza! Huzza! Long live the Emperor!
*Other voices.* Fall back! Away there!
*Otho.* Say, what noise is that?
*Albert* (*advancing from the back of the stage, whither he had hastened on hearing the cheers of the soldiery*). It is young Gersa, the
85 Hungarian prince,
Pick'd like a red stag from the fallow herd
Of prisoners. Poor prince, forlorn he steps,
Slow, and demure, and proud in his despair.
If I may judge by his so tragic bearing,
90 His eye not downcast, and his folded arm,
He doth this moment wish himself asleep
Among his fallen captains on yon plains.

*Enter* GERSA, *in chains, and guarded.*

*Otho.* Well said, Sir Albert.
*Gersa.* Not a word of greeting,
No welcome to a princely visitor,
95 Most mighty Otho? Will not my great host
Vouchsafe a syllable, before he bids
His gentlemen conduct me with all care
To some securest lodging—cold perhaps!
*Otho.* What mood is this? Hath fortune touch'd thy brain?
100 *Gersa.* O kings and princes of this fevrous world,
What abject things, what mockeries must ye be,
What nerveless minions of safe palaces!
When here, a monarch, whose proud foot is used
To fallen princes' necks, as to his stirrup,

83 *s.p.* Voices without] *inserted before* ⟨Albert⟩ *D* 87 steps] ⟨walk⟩ steps *D* 88 Slow . . . his] Slow, in the demure proudness of (Slow, in *interlined above* ⟨With all⟩) *D* 93 Sir Albert] *successively* (*a*) Lord Albert (*b*) Albert (*c*) Sir Albert *D*; my Albert *altered by Keats to* Sir Albert *CB* 93 Not . . . greeting,] *successively* (*a*) Wilt not greet me—Otho? (*b*) Wilt thou not greet me—Otho? (*c*) ⟨No⟩ Not a word of greeting— (*each version connecting metrically with its counterpart in preceding note*) *D* 95 great] *interlined above* ⟨illustrious⟩ *D* 98 securest] *interlined above* ⟨convenient⟩ *D* 101 be] ⟨are⟩ *interlined above* ⟨be⟩ (*both words left deleted*) *D*

105 Must needs exclaim that I am mad forsooth,
Because I cannot flatter with bent knees
My conqueror!
*Otho.* Gersa, I think you wrong me:
I think I have a better fame abroad.
*Gersa.* I pr'ythee mock me not with gentle speech,
110 But, as a favour, bid me from thy presence;
Let me no longer be the wondering food
Of all these eyes; pr'ythee command me hence!
*Otho.* Do not mistake me, Gersa. That you may not,
Come, fair Auranthe, try if your soft hands
115 Can manage those hard rivets to set free
So brave a prince and soldier.
*Auranthe (sets him free).* Welcome task!
*Gersa.* I am wound up in deep astonishment!
Thank you, fair lady—Otho!—Emperor!
You rob me of myself; my dignity
120 Is now your infant;—I am a weak child.
*Otho.* Give me your hand, and let this kindly grasp
Live in our memories.
*Gersa.* In mine it will.
I blush to think of my unchasten'd tongue;
But I was haunted by the monstrous ghost
125 Of all our slain battalions. Sire, reflect,
And pardon you will grant, that, at this hour,
The bruised remnants of our stricken camp
Are huddling undistinguish'd, my dear friends
With common thousands, into shallow graves.
130 *Otho.* Enough, most noble Gersa. You are free
To cheer the brave remainder of your host
By your own healing presence, and that too,
Not as their leader merely, but their king;
For, as I hear, the wily enemy,

114 Come . . . hands] *accompanied by the s.d.* To Auranthe *in D* 114 try] *interlined above* ⟨thy⟩ *D* 119 of] *not in D* 125 our . . . battalions] *successively (a)* my splendent Army *(b)* the hungarian *(c)* my slain Batallions *(d)* our slain Batallions *D* 127 The . . . stricken] That the poor brused remnants of my *altered to* The brused remnants of our stricken *D* 128 huddling . . . dear] huddling unknow my dearest *D*; *successively (a)* huddling unknown, my dearest *(b)* now huddling unknown, my dearest *(c)* huddling undistinguish'd, my dear *(the alterations all by Keats) CB* 132 your] ⟨their⟩ your *D* 132 healing] *added above the line in D* 132 and] ⟨nor merely as their⟩ and *D* 133 their *(third word)*] *interlined above* ⟨a⟩ *D* 133 leader] ⟨General⟩ Leader *D* 134 the] your *D*

135 Who eas'd the crownet from your infant brows,
Bloody Taraxa, is among the dead.
*Gersa.* Then I retire, so generous Otho please,
Bearing with me a weight of benefits
Too heavy to be borne.
*Otho.* It is not so;
140 Still understand me, King of Hungary,
Nor judge my open purposes awry.
Though I did hold you high in my esteem
For your self's sake, I do not personate
The stage-play emperor to entrap applause,
145 To set the silly sort o' the world agape,
And make the politic smile; no, I have heard
How in the Council you condemn'd this war,
Urging the perfidy of broken faith,—
For that I am your friend.
*Gersa.* If ever, sire,
150 You are my enemy, I dare here swear
'Twill not be Gersa's fault. Otho, farewell!
*Otho.* Will you return, Prince, to our banquetting?
*Gersa.* As to my father's board I will return.
*Otho.* Conrad, with all due ceremony, give
155 The Prince a regal escort to his camp;
Albert, go thou and bear him company.
Gersa, farewell!
*Gersa.* All happiness attend you!
*Otho.* Return with what good speed you may; for soon
We must consult upon our terms of peace.
[*Exeunt* GERSA *and* ALBERT, *with others.*
160 And thus a marble column do I build
To prop my empire's dome. Conrad, in thee
I have another steadfast one, to uphold
The portals of my state; and, for my own
Preeminence and safety, I will strive

135 eas'd] *interlined above* ⟨took⟩ *D* 137 generous] ⟨m⟩ generous *D* 137 Otho] Cæsar *D* 139 It] ⟨Still understand / My⟩ It *D* 142 did] *interlined above* ⟨must⟩ *D* 145 set] ⟨see f⟩ set *D* 145 sort] *interlined above* ⟨store⟩ *D* 145 o'] of *D* 150 my] mine *D* 152 our] *interlined above* ⟨my⟩ *CB* 154 Conrad . . . give] Farewell! Conrad, with all due ceremony *altered to* Conrad, with all due ceremony give *D* 157/158 (*continuing Gersa's speech*) ⟨Soon my I see you⟩ *D* 158–159 *Otho.* Return . . . peace.] *added afterward at the bottom of the page in D* 159 terms] term *D* 160 marble] *interlined above* ⟨golden⟩ *D* 161 in thee] *interlined above* ⟨thou⟩ *D* 162 steadfast] *interlined above* ⟨noble⟩ *D* 164 and . . . strive] ⟨I will use a⟩ and safety I will strive *interlined above* ⟨and safety it shall be my care⟩ *D*

165 To keep thy strength upon its pedestal.
For, without thee, this day I might have been
A show-monster about the streets of Prague,
In chains, as just now stood that noble prince:
And then to me no mercy had been shown,
170 For when the conquer'd lion is once dungeoned,
Who lets him forth again? or dares to give
An old lion sugar-cates of mild reprieve?
Not to thine ear alone I make confession,
But to all here, as, by experience,
175 I know how the great basement of all power
Is frankness, and a true tongue to the world;
And how intriguing secresy is proof
Of fear and weakness, and a hollow state.
Conrad, I owe thee much.
*Conrad.* To kiss that hand,
180 My Emperor, is ample recompense
For a mere act of duty.
*Otho.* Thou art wrong;
For what can any man on earth do more?
We will make trial of your house's welcome,
My bright Auranthe!
*Conrad.* How is Friedburg honoured!

*Enter* ETHELBERT *and six Monks.*

185 *Ethelbert.* The benison of heaven on your head,
Imperial Otho!
*Otho.* Who stays me? Speak! Quick!
*Ethelbert.* Pause but one moment, mighty conqueror,
Upon the threshold of this house of joy—
*Otho.* Pray do not prose, good Ethelbert, but speak
190 What is your purpose.
*Ethelbert.* The restoration of some captive maids,
Devoted to heaven's pious ministries,
Who, driven forth from their religious cells,

168 as] ⟨and now⟩ as *D* 169 And] *interlined above* ⟨But⟩ *D* 170 For] ⟨A⟩ For *D* 170 when] *added above the line in D* 170 dungeoned] *interlined above* ⟨cag'd⟩ *D* 171 or] *written over* ⟨an⟩ *D* 171 dares] ⟨th⟩ dares *D* 172 cates] *interlined above* ⟨plums⟩ *D* 172 reprieve] *interlined above* ⟨forgiveness⟩ *D* 179 kiss] kneel and kiss *D* 180/181 ⟨For my mere duty done⟩ (my *made out of* me *and* duty *made out of* duties) *D* 186/187 (*continuing Otho's speech*) ⟨O Ethelbert⟩ *D* 189 good] old *D* 193 driven] being driven *D* 193 from] *added above the line in D*

And kept in thraldom by our enemy,
195 When late this province was a lawless spoil,
Still weep amid the wild Hungarian camp,
Though hemm'd around by thy victorious arms.
*Otho.* Demand the holy sisterhood in our name
From Gersa's tents. Farewell, old Ethelbert.
200 *Ethelbert.* The saints will bless you for this pious care.
*Otho.* Daughter, your hand; Ludolph's would fit it best.
*Conrad.* Ho! let the music sound!
[*Music.* ETHELBERT *raises his hands, as in benediction of* OTHO.
*Exeunt severally. The scene closes on them.*

SCENE III. *The Country, with the Castle in the distance.*

*Enter* LUDOLPH *and* SIGIFRED.

*Ludolph.* You have my secret, let it not be breath'd.
*Sigifred.* Still give me leave to wonder that the Prince
Ludolph and the swift Arab are the same;
Still to rejoice that 'twas a German arm
5 Death doing in a turban'd masquerade.
*Ludolph.* The Emperor must not know it, Sigifred.
*Sigifred.* I pr'ythee why? What happier hour of time
Could thy pleas'd star point down upon from heaven
With silver index, bidding thee make peace?
10 *Ludolph.* Still it must not be known, good Sigifred;
The star may point oblique.
*Sigifred.* If Otho knew
His son to be that unknown Mussleman
After whose spurring heels he sent me forth,
With one of his well-pleas'd Olympian oaths,
15 The charters of man's greatness, at this hour
He would be watching round the castle-walls,
And, like an anxious warder, strain his sight

I.iii *scene number* III] 2nd *altered to* 3nd *D. Location and opening s.d. are not in D, and 1–63 follow 64–123* (*see Textual Note to 1–63*) 1 You . . . breath'd.] *written on the opposite verso in D to replace* ⟨My {lord} friend you have the⟩ (*the original line incomplete*) 2 the] my *D*; my *altered to* the *CB* 3/4
⟨And that a cristian am⟩
⟨And still let me rejoice⟩ *D*
5 doing] ⟨giving⟩ doing *D* 7 hour] *interlined above* ⟨point⟩ *D* 8 down] ⟨out⟩ down *D* 11 star] ⟨planet⟩ Star *D* 11 If Otho] O if he *altered to* If Otho *D* 16 He] ⟨He'd act the⟩ He *D* 16 round] *interlined above* ⟨on⟩ *D*

For the first glimpse of such a son return'd;
Ludolph, that blast of the Hungarians,
20 That Saracenic meteor of the fight,
That silent fury, whose fell scymitar
Kept danger all aloof from Otho's head,
And left him space for wonder.
*Ludolph.* Say no more.
Not as a swordsman would I pardon claim,
25 But as a son. The bronz'd centurion,
Long toil'd in foreign wars, and whose high deeds
Are shaded in a forest of tall spears,
Known only to his troop, hath greater plea
Of favour with my sire than I can have.
30 *Sigifred.* My lord, forgive me that I cannot see
How this proud temper with clear reason squares.
What made you then, with such an anxious love,
Hover around that life, whose bitter days
You vext with bad revolt? Was't opium,
35 Or the mad-fumed wine—? Nay, do not frown,
I rather would grieve with you than upbraid.
*Ludolph.* I do believe you. No, 'twas not to make
A father his son's debtor, or to heal
His deep heart-sickness for a rebel child.
40 'Twas done in memory of my boyish days,
Poor cancel for his kindness to my youth,
For all his calming of my childish griefs,
And all his smiles upon my merriment.
No, not a thousand foughten fields could sponge
45 Those days paternal from my memory,
Though now upon my head he heaps disgrace.
*Sigifred.* My Prince, you think too harshly—
*Ludolph.* Can I so?

18 such] ⟨thee⟩ Such *D* 22/23 ⟨Like his good Angel⟩ *D* 23/24 ⟨I would not buy my Pardon⟩ *D* 24 claim] *interlined above* ⟨crave⟩ *D*; crave *L* 31/32
⟨What then could⟩
⟨Why {then} did you then so hover⟩ *D*
32 such] *added above the line in D* 33 bitter] *interlined above* ⟨painful⟩ *D* 35 mad-fumed] mad ⟨wine⟩-fumed *D* 37 you] *written over* ⟨thee⟩ *D* 39 His] *interlined above* ⟨The⟩ *D* 39 deep] ⟨recent wounds⟩ deep (*with* bleeding *interlined and deleted above* recent) *D* 39 for] at *written over* ⟨for⟩ *D* 40 'Twas] ⟨No⟩ 'Twas *D* 42 calming] ⟨sorrow⟩ calming *D* 43 my] *interlined above* ⟨young⟩ *D* 43/44 ⟨Ever will those bright days live in my heart / Though he still⟩ (*Keats also wrote and deleted the s.p.* Sigifre *at this point on the opposite verso, but the canceled text is a continuation of Ludolph's speech*) *D* 47 think too harshly] ⟨judge⟩ think too ⟨sadly⟩ harshly *D*

Hath he not gall'd my spirit to the quick?
And with a sullen rigour obstinate
50 Pour'd out a phial of wrath upon my faults?
Hunted me as a Tartar does the boar,
Driven me to the very edge o' the world,
And almost put a price upon my head?
*Sigifred.* Remember how he spared the rebel-lords.
55 *Ludolph.* Yes, yes, I know he hath a noble nature
That cannot trample on the fallen. But his
Is not the only proud heart in his realm.
He hath wrong'd me, and I have done him wrong;
He hath lov'd me, and I have shown him kindness;
We should be almost equal.
60 *Sigifred.* Yet, for all this,
I would you had appear'd among those lords,
And ta'en his favour.
*Ludolph.* Ha! till now I thought
My friend had held poor Ludolph's honour dear.
What! would you have me sue before his throne,
65 And kiss the courtier's missal, its silk steps?
Or hug the golden housings of his steed,
Amid a camp, whose steeled swarms I dar'd
But yesterday? And, at the trumpet sound,
Bow like some unknown mercenary's flag
70 And lick the soiled grass? No, no, my friend,
I would not, I, be pardon'd in the heap,
And bless indemnity with all that scum,—
Those men I mean, who on my shoulders propp'd
Their weak rebellion, winning me with lies,
75 And pitying forsooth my many wrongs;
Poor self-deceived wretches, who must think
Each one himself a king in embryo,
Because some dozen vassals cry'd—my lord!
Cowards, who never knew their little hearts,

49/50 ⟨Hunted me as the Tartar⟩ *D* 50 faults] ⟨head⟩ faults *D* 52 o'] of *D* 55 Yes . . . nature] *successively (a)* I know he hath a noble nature (*b*) He hath a noble nature well I know (*c*) Yes Yes I know he hath a noble nature *D* 56 That] ⟨And⟩ That *D* 56 his] *interlined above* ⟨why⟩ *D* 65 missal] *interlined above* ⟨bible⟩ *D* 66 golden] ⟨steeled⟩ golden (*both words added above the line*) *D* 66 steed] ⟨Horse⟩ Steed *D* 66/67 ⟨When through the camp he passes⟩ *D* 67 a] *interlined above* ⟨the⟩ *D* 68 sound] sound⟨'s⟩ *D* 72 bless indemnity] be indemnified *altered to* bless indemnity *D* 75 forsooth] ⟨my⟩ forsooth *D* 76 wretches, who] wretches ⟨would⟩ who *D* 76 must] *interlined above* ⟨would⟩ *D*

80 Till flurried danger held the mirror up,
And then they own'd themselves without a blush,
Curling, like spaniels, round my father's feet.
Such things deserted me and are forgiven,
While I, least guilty, am an outcast still,
85 And will be, for I love such fair disgrace.
*Sigifred.* I know the clear truth; so would Otho see,
For he is just and noble. Fain would I
Be pleader for you—
*Ludolph.* He'll hear none of it;
You know his temper, hot, proud, obstinate;
90 Endanger not yourself so uselessly.
I will encounter his thwart spleen myself,
To-day, at the Duke Conrad's, where he keeps
His crowded state after the victory.
There will I be, a most unwelcome guest,
95 And parley with him, as a son should do,
Who doubly loathes a father's tyranny;
Tell him how feeble is that tyranny,
How the relationship of father and son
Is no more valid than a silken leash
100 Where lions tug adverse, if love grow not
From interchanged love through many years.
Aye, and those turreted Franconian walls,
Like to a jealous casket, hold my pearl—
My fair Auranthe! Yes, I will be there.
105 *Sigifred.* Be not so rash; wait till his wrath shall pass,
Until his royal spirit softly ebbs
Self-influenced; then, in his morning dreams
He will forgive thee, and awake in grief
To have not thy good morrow.
*Ludolph.* Yes, to-day
110 I must be there, while her young pulses beat

80 flurried] *added above the line in D* 82 Curling] And curld *altered to* curling *D* 86 know] *interlined above* ⟨see⟩ *D* 86 so] ⟨and⟩ so (and *squeezed in afterward, then deleted*) *D* 87/88 even though the sacred ⟨na⟩ nam (*inserted in very small writing beneath the last three words of 87; the deleted and undeleted letters following* sacred *are very uncertain*) *D* 90 so] ⟨and nothin⟩ so *D* 90/91 ⟨I will break the matter to him myself⟩ *D* (*this line comes at the bottom of a page in D*; *a strip containing perhaps two more deleted lines and, on the verso, the s.p.'s and s.d. for 117–118 has been cut away from the top of the next leaf*) 93 crowded] ⟨State⟩ crowded *D* 100 grow not] grown *altered to* grown not *D* 100/101 ⟨Not from mutual benefits—⟩ *D* 101 interchanged] ⟨mutual benefits⟩ interchanged *D* 102 walls] *successively (a)* Walls *(b)* Gates *(c)* Walls *D* 107 then, in] then ⟨he⟩ in *D* 109 Yes, to-day‸] ⟨Sigifred! / Have you seen her of late—⟩ Yes to day! *D*

Among the new-plum'd minions of the war.
Have you seen her of late? No? Auranthe,
Franconia's fair sister, 'tis I mean.
She should be paler for my troublous days—
115 And there it is my father's iron lips
Have sworn divorcement 'twixt me and my right.
*Sigifred* (*aside*). Auranthe! I had hoped this whim had pass'd.
*Ludolph.* And, Sigifred, with all his love of justice,
When will he take that grandchild in his arms,
120 That, by my love I swear, shall soon be his?
This reconcilement is impossible,
For see—But who are these?
*Sigifred.* They are messengers
From our great Emperor; to you, I doubt not,
For couriers are abroad to seek you out.

*Enter* THEODORE *and* GONFRID.

125 *Theodore.* Seeing so many vigilant eyes explore

112/113 ⟨'Tis I mean, the Duke's fair sister⟩ *D* 114 She] ⟨Ha?⟩ She *D* 115 there it is] there's oppression again *altered to* there's it is *D* 115 lips] *interlined above* ⟨arm⟩ *D* 116 Have] ⟨Weighs⟩ Have *D* 117–118 *s.p.'s* Sigifred (aside) *and* Ludolph] *both s.p.'s* (*and the s.d.*) *are missing from D* (*see 90/91, above*) 118 his] *added above the line in D* 120 shall] *not in D* 120/121 ⟨Auranthe! these hash times⟩ *D* 123 to . . . not] I doubt not to you (*see Textual Note*) *D* 124 are . . . out] *written beneath* ⟨to that purpose are abroad⟩ *D* 124 seek] *successively* (*a*) seeke (*b*) search (*c*) seek *D* 125–132 *Theodore.* Seeing . . . castle.] *written by Keats on the opposite verso in CB to replace:*

⟨*Sigifred.* Pray what would you with us?
*Theodore* (*to Ludolph*). My Lord, I come
To bring you to the Presence all in haste;
No doubt you will obey the Emperor's summons.
*Ludolph.* D'ye hear this fellow how he braves his Prince!
[5] I've a shrewd guess that the Court atmosphere
Is too fine for my breathing, Sigifred,
When such an ugly vermin dares so much.
*Theodore.* Yield up your sword, my Lord, and come away.
*Ludolph.* Give him some answer, Sigifred,—or blows.
{*Sigifred*} *Theodore.* The Emperor's commands!
[10] *Sigifred.* Insolent slave!
*Gonfrid.* Nay, my good Prince, we are not warranted
Beyond a civil message, to request
Your Highness would obey great Otho's call.
*Ludolph.* This is another tune. [*To* THEODORE.
Fellow, avaunt!
[15] *Theodore.* I trust your Highness' anger will not fall
On one whose fault, if such it was, arose

The province to invite your Highness back
To your high dignities, we are too happy.
*Gonfrid.* We have no eloquence to colour justly
The Emperor's anxious wishes—
*Ludolph.* Go—I follow you.
[*Exeunt* THEODORE *and* GONFRID.

130 I play the prude: it is but venturing—
Why should he be so earnest? Come, my friend,
Let us to Friedburg castle.

## ACT II

### SCENE I. *An Antichamber in the Castle.*

*Enter* LUDOLPH *and* SIGIFRED.

*Ludolph.* No more advices, no more cautioning;
I leave it all to fate—to any thing!
I cannot square my conduct to time, place,
Or circumstance; to me 'tis all a mist!
*Sigifred.* I say no more.
5 *Ludolph.* It seems I am to wait
Here in the antiroom;—that may be a trifle.
You see now how I dance attendance here,

---

From ignorance.
*Ludolph.* Thou art right; thy plea is good;
Thou hast forgot the nature of an insult
By constant sufferance for thine own preferment.
[20] Let me not see thee more. Come, Sigifred,
I will to Friedburg Castle on the spur,
And feel the Dragon's paws. [*Exeunt.*⟩

(19 thine own *altered in pencil, possibly by Keats, to* some small). *D has the same text with the following variants and alterations*: 1 Pray] *added in the margin* 2 all in haste] *interlined above* ⟨at the Castle⟩ 4 *s.p.* Ludolph] *accompanied by s.d.* (To Sigifred) 5 that] *deleted and nothing substituted* 6 fine] *interlined above* ⟨thick⟩ 7 When] *made out of* While [?] 10 *s.p.* Theodore] *successively* (*a*) Theodore (*b*) Sigifr (*c*) Theodore 13 obey] *interlined above* ⟨but meet⟩ 17 plea] plea⟨s⟩ 19 thine own] a small 20/21 ⟨I will examine all the Dragon's paws⟩ 21 I] *successively* (*a*) I (*b*) We (*c*) I 21 to] now *interlined and deleted above this word* 21 Friedburg Castle] *interlined above* ⟨Conrad's Castle⟩ 132 Let us] *interlined above* ⟨I will⟩ *CB* (*Keats's hand*) *After* 132 End of the first Act. *CB*

II.i] *no act or scene heading in D* (*the text begins with the location*) 1 cautioning] cautions Sigifred *D*; cautions, Sigifred *altered by Keats to* cautioning *CB* 4 all] now *D* 4/5 (*continuing Ludolph's speech*) ⟨The happy⟩ *D* 5 say no more] have done Sir *D*; say no more *interlined by Keats above* ⟨have done, Sir⟩ *CB* 6 that] ⟨But⟩ That *D*

Without that tyrant temper, you so blame,
Snapping the rein. You have medicin'd me
10 With good advices; and I here remain,
In this most honourable antiroom,
Your patient scholar.
*Sigifred.* Do not wrong me, Prince.
By heavens, I'd rather kiss Duke Conrad's slipper,
When in the morning he doth yawn with pride,
15 Than see you humbled but a half degree!
Truth is, the Emperor would fain dismiss
The nobles ere he sees you.

*Enter* GONFRID, *from the Council-room.*

*Ludolph.* Well, sir! What!
*Gonfrid.* Great honour to the Prince! The Emperor,
Hearing that his brave son had reappeared,
20 Instant dismiss'd the Council from his sight,
As Jove fans off the clouds. Even now they pass. [*Exit.*

*Enter the Nobles from the Council-room. They cross the stage, bowing with respect to* LUDOLPH, *he frowning on them.* CONRAD *follows. Exeunt Nobles.*

*Ludolph.* Not the discoloured poisons of a fen,
Which he who breathes feels warning of his death,
Could taste so nauseous to the bodily sense,
25 As these prodigious sycophants disgust
The soul's fine palate.
*Conrad.* Princely Ludolph, hail!
Welcome, thou younger scepter to the realm!
Strength to thy virgin crownet's golden buds,
That they, against the winter of thy sire,
30 May burst, and swell, and flourish round thy brows,
Maturing to a weighty diadem!
Yet be that hour far off; and may he live,

9 You] ⟨Certes⟩ You *D* 15 humbled] ⟨so degraged⟩ humbled *D* 21 *s.d.* Nobles from . . . Nobles] Nobles who cross &c *D* 23/24 ⟨Not the death watch tickling a Beldam's ear⟩ *D* 24 taste so nauseous] *interlined above* ⟨nauseate me⟩ *D* 24 to] in *D*; to *written over* ⟨in⟩ *CB* 24 the] *successively (a)* the *(b)* my *(c)* the *D* 25/26 ⟨The relish of my souls invisible tongue⟩ *D* 26 The] *successively (a)* My *(b)* That *(c)* The *D* 28 virgin] *interlined above* ⟨rounded⟩ *D* 29 against the] in the last *altered to* against the *D* 31 Maturing] ⟨And⟩ Maturing *D*

Who waits for thee, as the chapp'd earth for rain.
Set my life's star! I have liv'd long enough,
35 Since under my glad roof, propitiously,
Father and son each other repossess.
*Ludolph.* Fine wording, Duke! but words could never yet
Forestall the fates; have you not learnt that yet?
Let me look well: your features are the same,
40 Your gait the same, your hair of the same shade,
As one I knew some passed weeks ago,
Who sung far different notes into mine ears.
I have mine own particular comments on't;
You have your own perhaps.
*Conrad.* My gracious Prince,
45 All men may err. In truth I was deceived
In your great father's nature, as you were.
Had I known that of him I have since known,
And what you soon will learn, I would have turn'd
My sword to my own throat, rather than held
50 Its threatening edge against a good king's quiet;
Or with one word fever'd you, gentle Prince,
Who seem'd to me, as rugged times then went,
Indeed too much oppress'd. May I be bold
To tell the Emperor you will haste to him?
55 *Ludolph.* Your dukedom's privilege will grant so much.
[*Exit* CONRAD.
He's very close to Otho, a tight leach!
Your hand—I go! Ha! here the thunder comes
Sullen against the wind! If in two angry brows
My safety lies, then, Sigifred, I'm safe.

*Enter* OTHO *and* CONRAD.

60 *Otho.* Will you make Titan play the lackey-page
To chattering pigmies? I would have you know

36 Father] ⟨Meet⟩ Father *D* 37 wording] *made out of* words *D* 37 words] *added above the line in D* 47 have] ⟨since⟩ have *CB* 51 fever'd . . . Prince] *written beneath* ⟨f⟩ ⟨put fever in your heart⟩ *D* 53 be bold] *written beneath* ⟨express⟩ *D* 55 *and s.d.* Your . . . Conrad.] *squeezed in afterward in D between 54 and 56 (D's s.d. at 59 has Conrad still on stage)* 55 dukedom's . . . grant] Dukedom privileges you to *altered to* Dukedom's privilege with [*for* will] grant *D* 56 He's] ⟨Aside⟩ He's (*the deleted s.d. added in the margin*) *D* 56 a . . . leach] Sigifred *D*; ⟨Sigifred⟩ a tight leach *CB* 58 in] *interlined above* ⟨by⟩ *D* 58 brows] *interlined above* ⟨eyes⟩ *D* 59 *s.d.* and Conrad] *not in D* 60 lackey-page] *written beneath* ⟨lackey boy⟩ *D*

That such neglect of our high Majesty
Annuls all feel of kindred. What is son,—
Or friend,—or brother,—or all ties of blood,—
65 When the whole kingdom, centred in ourself,
Is rudely slighted? Who am I to wait?
By Peter's chair! I have upon my tongue
A word to fright the proudest spirit here!—
Death!—and slow tortures to the hardy fool
70 Who dares take such large charter from our smiles!
Conrad, we would be private! Sigifred!
Off! And none pass this way on pain of death!
[*Exeunt* CONRAD *and* SIGIFRED.
*Ludolph.* This was but half expected, my good sire,
Yet I am griev'd at it, to the full height,
75 As though my hopes of favour had been whole.
*Otho.* How you indulge yourself: what can you hope for?
*Ludolph.* Nothing, my liege; I have to hope for nothing.
I come to greet you as a loving son,
And then depart, if I may be so free,
80 Seeing that blood of yours in my warm veins
Has not yet mitigated into milk.
*Otho.* What would you, sir?
*Ludolph.* A lenient banishment;
So please you let me unmolested pass
This Conrad's gates, to the wide air again.
85 I want no more. A rebel wants no more.
*Otho.* And shall I let a rebel loose again
To muster kites and eagles 'gainst my head?
No, obstinate boy, you shall be kept cag'd up,
Serv'd with harsh food, with scum for Sunday-drink.
*Ludolph.* Indeed!
90 *Otho.* And chains too heavy for your life;
I'll choose a jailor, whose swart monstrous face
Shall be a hell to look upon, and she—

63 all] of *D* 68 A] I *D* 68 proudest . . . here] Devil—Banishment *D*; proudest spirit here *interlined by Keats above* ⟨Devil—Banishment⟩ *CB* 69 and slow] slowest *altered to* and slow *D* 69 hardy] *added above the line in D* 70 our] *interlined above* ⟨my⟩ *D* 72 none] ⟨let⟩ none *D* 76 How . . . for?] *written by Keats in a blank space left by Brown in CB*; Hopes! what in your conscience can you hope for (can *added above the line, and* all *interlined and deleted before* your) *D* 77 liege] *written over* ⟨Lord⟩ *D* 89 scum . . . drink] puddle for your drink *altered to* scum for sunday drink *D* 90 And] ⟨You shall⟩ And *D* 91 whose] who *D* 92 upon . . . she] on—She (on *squeezed in afterward*) *D*

*Ludolph.* Ha!
*Otho.* Shall be your fair Auranthe.
*Ludolph.* Amaze! Amaze!
*Otho.* To-day you marry her.
95 *Ludolph.* This is a sharp jest!
*Otho.* No. None at all. When have I said a lie?
*Ludolph.* If I sleep not, I am a waking wretch.
*Otho.* Not a word more. Let me embrace my child.
*Ludolph.* I dare not. 'Twould pollute so good a father!
100 O heavy crime! that your son's blinded eyes
Could not see all his parent's love aright,
As now I see it. Be not kind to me—
Punish me not with favour.
*Otho.* Are you sure,
Ludolph, you have no saving plea in store?
*Ludolph.* My father, none!
105 *Otho.* Then you astonish me.
*Ludolph.* No, I have no plea. Disobedience,
Rebellion, obstinacy, blasphemy,—
Are all my counsellors. If they can make
My crooked deeds show good and plausible,
110 Then grant me loving pardon,—but not else,—
Good gods! not else, in any way, my liege!
*Otho.* You are a most perplexing noble boy.
*Ludolph.* You not less a perplexing noble father.
*Otho.* Well! you shall have free passport through the gates.
Farewell!
115 *Ludolph.* Farewell! and by these tears believe,
And still remember, I repent in pain
All my misdeeds!
*Otho.* Ludolph, I will! I will!
But, Ludolph, ere you go, I would enquire
If you, in all your wandering, ever met

93 *Ludolph.* Ha!] *inserted afterward in D* 94 Shall . . . Auranthe.] Shall be Your fair Auranthe—Oh! my Boy / What will you say to that? *D and originally CB*; Oh . . . that? *then deleted by Keats or Brown in CB* 95 To-day you] *interlined above* ⟨You shall⟩ *D* 96 have I said] *successively* (*a*) did I tell (*b*) did I say (*c*) have I said *D* 98 Not . . . more] No more words *altered to* No on word more *D* 100 your] *written over* ⟨a⟩ *D* 101 his . . . aright] *written beneath* ⟨the love⟩ ⟨your open nature clear⟩ *D* 105 My] *added in the margin in D* 107 blasphemy] *written beneath* ⟨Insult, Pride⟩ *D* 108 all] ⟨my⟩ all *D* 109 deeds] deed *D* 110 loving] *added above the line in D* 110 but] *added above the line in D* 111 in any way] *added above the line in D* 114 free] free⟨est⟩ *D* 119 met] meet *D*

120 A certain Arab haunting in these parts.
*Ludolph.* No, my good lord, I cannot say I did.
*Otho.* Make not your father blind before his time;
Nor let these arms paternal hunger more
For an embrace, to dull the appetite
125 Of my great love for thee, my supreme child!
Come close, and let me breathe into thine ear
I knew you through disguise. You are the Arab!
You can't deny it. [*Embracing him.*
*Ludolph.* Happiest of days!
*Otho.* We'll make it so.
*Ludolph.* 'Stead of one fatted calf,
130 Ten hecatombs shall bellow out their last,
Smote 'twixt the horns by the death-stunning mace
Of Mars, and all the soldiery shall feast
Nobly as Nimrod's masons, when the towers
Of Nineveh new kiss'd the parted clouds!
135 *Otho.* Large as a god speak out, where all is thine.
*Ludolph.* Aye, father;—but the fire in my sad breast
Is quench'd with inward tears! I must rejoice
For you, whose wings so shadow over me
In tender victory,—but for myself
140 I still must mourn. The fair Auranthe mine!
Too great a boon! I pr'ythee, let me ask
What more than I know of could so have chang'd
Your purpose touching her.
*Otho.* At a word, this:
In no deed did you give me more offence
145 Than your rejection of Erminia.
To my appalling, I saw too good proof
Of your keen-eyed suspicion,—she is naught!
*Ludolph.* You are convinc'd?
*Otho.* Aye, spite of her sweet looks.
O, that my brother's daughter should so fall!
150 Her fame has pass'd into the grosser lips
Of soldiers in their cups.
*Ludolph.* 'Tis very sad.

123 arms] ⟨hun⟩ ams *D* 126 close] near *D*; close *interlined above* ⟨near⟩ *CB* 128 *s.d.* Embracing him.] *not in D* 129 so.] so—⟨Ten Hecatombs shall fall⟩ (*the deleted words then replaced by Ludolph's speech in 129, which Keats inserted between the lines*) *D* 133 Nobly] ⟨More⟩ nobly *D* 136 sad] *added above the line in D* 143/144 ⟨First I must⟩ *D* 147 Of] O *D* 151 their] the *D*

*Otho.* No more of her. Auranthe—Ludolph, come!
This marriage be the bond of endless peace! [*Exeunt.*

SCENE II. *The entrance of* GERSA'S *Tent in the Hungarian Camp.*

*Enter* ERMINIA.

*Erminia.* Where! Where! Where shall I find a messenger?
A trusty soul? A good man in the camp?
Shall I go myself? Monstrous wickedness!
O cursed Conrad! devilish Auranthe!
5 Here is proof palpable as the bright sun!
O for a voice to reach the Emperor's ears!
[*Shouts in the Camp.*

*Enter an Hungarian Captain.*

*Captain.* Fair prisoner, you hear these joyous shouts?
The King—aye, now our King,—but still your slave,
Young Gersa, from a short captivity
10 Has just return'd. He bids me say, bright dame,
That even the homage of his ranged chiefs
Cures not his keen impatience to behold
Such beauty once again.—What ails you, lady?
*Erminia.* Say, is not that a German yonder? There!
15 *Captain.* Methinks by his stout bearing he should be—
Yes—it is Albert; a brave German knight,
And much in the Emperor's favor.
*Erminia.* I would fain
Enquire of friends and kinsfolk; how they fared
In these rough times. Brave soldier, as you pass
20 To royal Gersa with my humble thanks,
Will you send yonder knight to me?
*Captain.* I will. [*Exit.*

II.ii *location and opening s.d.* The . . . Erminia] The Hungarian Camp—the entrance of Gerza's Tent—Erminia comes out with a Letter in her hand (the entrance of *added above the line*) *D* 4/5 ⟨An Emperor is no God⟩ *D* 5 sun] *interlined above* ⟨Stars⟩ *D* 5/6 ⟨Married to day! Oh—O—O—⟩ *D* 7 you hear] you hear *altered to* hear you *D* 7 these] those *D* 10 dame] *interlined above* ⟨Lady⟩ *D* 12 keen] hot *D*; keen *interlined above* ⟨hot⟩ *CB* 16 it is] 'tis one *D* 18 friends and] *interlined above* ⟨my⟩ *D* 21 knight] *added above the line in D* 21 *s.d.* Exit] *made out of* exeunt *D*

*Erminia.* Yes, he was ever known to be a man
Frank, open, generous; Albert I may trust.
O proof! proof! proof! Albert's an honest man;
25 Not Ethelbert the monk, if he were here,
Would I hold more trustworthy. Now!

*Enter* ALBERT.

*Albert.* Good gods!
Lady Erminia! are you prisoner
In this beleaguer'd camp? Or are you here
Of your own will? You pleas'd to send for me.
30 By Venus, 'tis a pity I knew not
Your plight before, and, by her son, I swear
To do you every service you can ask.
What would the fairest—?
*Erminia.* Albert, will you swear?
*Albert.* I have. Well?
*Erminia.* Albert, you have fame to lose.
35 If men, in court and camp, lie not outright,
You should be, from a thousand, chosen forth
To do an honest deed. Shall I confide—?
*Albert.* Aye, any thing to me, fair creature. Do,
Dictate my task. Sweet woman,—
*Erminia.* Truce with that.
40 You understand me not; and, in your speech,
I see how far the slander is abroad.
Without proof could you think me innocent?
*Albert.* Lady, I should rejoice to know you so.
*Erminia.* If you have any pity for a maid,
45 Suffering a daily death from evil tongues;
Any compassion for that Emperor's niece,
Who, for your bright sword and clear honesty,
Lifted you from the crowd of common men

21/22 (*the beginning of Erminia's speech*) ⟨Albert! he was ever known a Man⟩ *D* 23 open] *successively* (*a*) open (*b*) honest (*c*) open *D* 27–28 are . . . camp] *written by Keats on the opposite verso in CB to replace* ⟨Is your Nunnery / Emptied into this Camp⟩; *D has successively* (*a*) wast your Nunnery / The old Monk win'd about (*b*) has your Nunnery / Been emptied into this unuly (*incomplete*) (*c*) is your Nunnery / ⟨To the⟩ emptied into this camp 34 Well?] *ed*; ~! *D, CB* (Well! ⟨Well!⟩ *in D*) 34 have fame to lose] *interlined above* ⟨have a good⟩ *D* 36 forth] *interlined above* ⟨out⟩ *D* 38 Aye] *added in the margin in D* 47 your] ⟨brave conduct⟩ your *D*

Into the lap of honour;—save me, knight!
50 *Albert.* How? Make it clear; if it be possible,
I by the banner of Saint Maurice swear
To right you.
*Erminia.* Possible!—Easy! O my heart!
This letter's not so soil'd but you may read it;—
Possible! There—that letter! Read—read it!
[*Gives him a letter.*
55 *Albert* (*reads it*). "To the Duke Conrad. Forget the threat you made at parting, and I will forget to send the Emperor letters and papers of yours I have become possessed of. His life is no trifle to me; his death you shall find none to yourself." (*Aside.*) 'Tis me—my life that's pleaded for! (*Reads.*) "He, for his own
60 sake, will be dumb as the grave. Erminia has my shame fix'd upon her, sure as a wen. We are safe.
"Auranthe."
A she devil! A dragon! I her imp!
Fire of hell! Auranthe—lewd demon!
65 Where got you this? Where? When?
*Erminia.* I found it in the tent, among some spoils
Which, being noble, fell to Gersa's lot.
Come in, and see. [*They go in and return.*
*Albert.* Villainy! Villainy!
Conrad's sword, his corslet, and his helm,
70 And his letter. Caitiff, he shall feel—
*Erminia.* I see you are thunderstruck. Haste, haste away!
*Albert.* O I am tortur'd by this villainy.
*Erminia.* You needs must be. Carry it swift to Otho;
Tell him, moreover, I am prisoner
75 Here in this camp, where all the sisterhood,
Forc'd from their quiet cells, are parcell'd out

54 *s.d.* Gives . . . letter.] *not in D* 55 *s.d.* reads it] coming a little forward reads the Letter *D* 55–62 Forget . . . Auranthe."] *a preliminary draft of this passage appears in D on the verso of the leaf containing II.i.97–113; apparatus readings from this earlier version are designated d* 55 Forget] ⟨Remember Conrad⟩ Forget (*the deleted words on a separate line*) *d* 56 made] *interlined above* ⟨gave⟩ *d* 56 to . . . letters] ⟨Letters and papers⟩ to send to the Emperor ⟨the⟩ Letters (to the Emperor *added above the line*) *d* 58–59 (*Aside.*) . . . for!] *not in d, D; added above the line in CB* 59 *s.d.* (Reads.)] *ed; not in d, D, CB* 60 my shame] *interlined above* ⟨the Burden of my disgrace⟩ *d* 63 she] *added above the line in D* 63 I] and I *D* 65–70 Where . . . feel—] *added on the opposite verso in D with a mark for insertion after 64* 66 it] here *D* 68 Come] *interlined above* ⟨Go⟩ *D* 68 see.] see—⟨there⟩ *D* 68 *s.d.* They] ⟨Albert—goes in and⟩ They *D* 68 Villainy! Villainy] ⟨Conrad's⟩ Villany! Villany *D* 71 I] ⟨What⟩ I *D* 71 you are] you *D and originally CB*; are *added above the line by Keats in CB* 75 the] our *D*

For slaves among these Huns. Away! Away!
*Albert.* I am gone.
*Erminia.* Swift be your steed! Within this hour
The Emperor will see it.
*Albert.* Ere I sleep:
That I can swear. [*Hurries out.*
80 *Gersa* (*without*). Brave captains, thanks! Enough
Of loyal homage now!

*Enter* GERSA.

*Erminia.* Hail, royal Hun!
*Gersa.* What means this, fair one? Why in such alarm?
Who was it hurried by me so distract?
It seem'd you were in deep discourse together;
85 Your doctrine has not been so harsh to him
As to my poor deserts. Come, come, be plain.
I am no jealous fool to kill you both,
Or, for such trifles, rob th' adorned world
Of such a beauteous vestal.
*Erminia.* I grieve, my lord,
90 To hear you condescend to ribbald-phrase.
*Gersa.* This is too much! Hearken, my lady pure,—
*Erminia.* Silence! and hear the magic of a name—
Erminia! I am she,—the Emperor's niece!
Prais'd be the heavens, I now dare own myself!
95 *Gersa.* Erminia! Indeed! I've heard of her—
Prythee, fair lady, what chance brought you here?
*Erminia.* Ask your own soldiers.
*Gersa.* And you dare own your name.
For loveliness you may—and for the rest

78 your] *added above the line in D* 78 this hour] two hours *altered to* this hour *D* 80 *s.p.* Gersa (without)] Gerza's voice without *D* 80–81 Brave . . . now] I would be private in my tent a while / Let me not be disturb'd *D and originally CB*; *Keats canceled the passage in CB, substituting* Brave Captains, thanks! now I would rest awhile *on the opposite verso, which Brown then revised to the present text* 81 *s.d.* Enter Gersa] *D*; enters *CB* 81 *s.p.* Erminia] *written beneath the canceled s.p.* ⟨Gersa⟩ *D* 82 means this] ails you *D*; means this *interlined above* ⟨ails you⟩ *CB* 83 so] ⟨in such⟩ so *D* 86 to . . . deserts] *interlined above* ⟨it has been to me⟩ *D* 88 th'] the *D* 90 hear] ⟨see⟩ hear *D* 92 the] to *D* 95–99 Erminia . . . me!] *written by Keats on the opposite verso in CB to replace:*

⟨Then you dare do no more than Women dare
Who dare the Devil on his 'vantage ground.
Yet if some strange report I heard hold good,
You are in truth no coward.⟩

*D has this same text uncanceled, with* ⟨Ha! Erminia!⟩ *after the last word and Erminia's speech then*

My vein is not censorious—
*Erminia.* Alas, poor me!
'Tis false indeed.
100 *Gersa.* Indeed you are too fair:
The swan, soft leaning on her fledgy breast,
When to the stream she launches, looks not back
With such a tender grace; nor are her wings
So white as your soul is, if that but be
105 Twin picture to your face. Erminia!
To-day, for the first day, I am a king,
Yet would I give my unworn crown away
To know you spotless.
*Erminia.* Trust me one day more,
Generously, without more certain guarantee,
110 Than this poor face you deign to praise so much;
After that, say and do whate'er you please.
If I have any knowledge of you, sir,
I think, nay I am sure, you will grieve much
To hear my story. O be gentle to me,
115 For I am sick and faint with many wrongs,
Tired out, and weary-worn with contumelies.
*Gersa.* Poor lady!

*Enter* ETHELBERT.

*Erminia.* Gentle Prince, 'tis false indeed.
Good morrow, holy father! I have had
Your prayers, though I look'd for you in vain.
120 *Ethelbert.* Blessings upon you, daughter! Sure you look
Too cheerful for these foul pernicious days.
Young man, you heard this virgin say 'twas false,—
'Tis false, I say. What! can you not employ
Your temper elsewhere, 'mong these burly tents,

---

*beginning with the present 100a* ('Tis . . . indeed) 99 vein] ⟨creed is eas⟩ vein *CB* (*Keats's hand*) 99 *s.p.* Erminia] *the canceled s.d.* ⟨enter Ethelbert⟩ *appears to the left of this s.p. in D* 100 false] ⟨all⟩ fasle *D* 100 *s.p.* Gersa] *written beneath the canceled s.p.* ⟨Ethelbert⟩ *D* 100/101 ⟨The swan leaning⟩ *D* 101 leaning] ⟨oar⟩ ⟨walking⟩ leaning *D* 102 to the stream] *successively (a)* from the bank (*b*) on the stream (*c*) to the stream *D* 107 I] ⟨I be a subject⟩ I *D* 108 know] *interlined above* ⟨see⟩ *D* 109 certain] ⟨proof⟩ certain *D* 110 deign] *interlined above* ⟨please⟩ *D* 111 After . . . whate'er] And after . . . what *altered to* after . . . whateer *D* 111 do] *interlined above* ⟨think⟩ *D* 112 sir] *interlined above* ⟨Prince⟩ *D* 117 *s.d.* Enter Ethelbert] *before adding this s.d. in D Keats wrote and deleted* Enter Ethelbert *opposite 118 and* Enter *opposite 120* (*see also the notes to 99 s.p. and 100 s.p.*) 121 for] ⟨of the time—⟩for *D* 121 these . . . days] this . . . day *altered to* these . . . days *CB* 124 'mong] *interlined above* ⟨in this⟩ *D*

125 But you must taunt this dove, for she hath lost
The eagle Otho to beat off assault.
Fie! Fie! But I will be her guard myself;
In the Emperor's name, I here demand of you
Herself, and all her sisterhood. She false!

130 *Gersa.* Peace! peace, old man! I cannot think she is.

*Ethelbert.* Whom I have known from her first infancy,
Baptis'd her in the bosom of the church,
Watch'd her, as anxious husbandmen the grain,
From the first shoot till the unripe mid-May,
135 Then to the tender ear of her June days,
Which, lifting sweet abroad its timid green,
Is blighted by the touch of calumny;
You cannot credit such a monstrous tale.

*Gersa.* I cannot. Take her. Fair Erminia,
140 I follow you to Friedburg,—is't not so?

*Erminia.* Aye, so we purpose.

*Ethelbert.* Daughter, do you so?
How's this? I marvel! Yet you look not mad.

*Erminia.* I have good news to tell you, Ethelbert.

*Gersa.* Ho! Ho, there! Guards!
145 Your blessing, father! Sweet Erminia,
Believe me, I am well nigh sure—

*Erminia.* Farewell!
Short time will show. [*Enter Chiefs.*
Yes, Father Ethelbert,
I have news precious as we pass along.

*Ethelbert.* Dear daughter, you shall guide me.

*Erminia.* To no ill.

150 *Gersa.* Command an escort to the Friedburg lines.
[*Exeunt Chiefs.*
Pray let me lead. Fair lady, forget not

125 hath] hast *D* 127 her] *written over* ⟨a⟩ *D* 129 her] *successively (a)* her *(b)* the *(c)* her *(the last perhaps in Keats's hand) CB* 130 cannot] ⟨do not⟩ cannot *D* 131 from] for *D* 134 till the unripe] untill the green *altered to* till the unripe *D* 136 sweet] ⟨light⟩ sweet *D* 137 Is] *interlined above* ⟨Was⟩ *D* 137 blighted] *interlined above* ⟨blasted⟩ *D* 137 calumny] *interlined above* ⟨infamy⟩ *D* 138 You] *preceded by* ⟨Take her⟩, *which is accompanied by the canceled s.p.* ⟨Gerza⟩ *D* 141–143 *Erminia.* Aye . . . Ethelbert.] *written on the opposite verso in D to replace* ⟨*Ethelbert.* Aye thither do we tend—⟩ *(the pentameter originally completed by the first line of Gersa's speech in 144–146)* 147 *s.d.* Chiefs] ⟨Guards⟩ Chiefs *CB* 148 news . . . along] *successively (a)* good news to make our pa *(b)* good news to tell you as we pass *(c)* news precious as we pass along *D* 149 *Ethelbert.* Dear . . . ill.] *added on the opposite verso in D*

Gersa, how he believ'd you innocent.
I follow you to Friedburg with all speed. [*Exeunt.*

## ACT III

### Scene I. *The Country.*

*Enter* Albert.

*Albert.* O that the earth were empty, as when Cain
Had no perplexity to hide his head!
Or that the sword of some brave enemy
Had put a sudden stop to my hot breath,
5 And hurl'd me down the illimitable gulph
Of times past, unremember'd! Better so
Than thus fast limed in a cursed snare,
The limbo of a wanton. This the end
Of an aspiring life! My boyhood past
10 In feud with wolves and bears, when no eye saw
The solitary warfare, fought for love
Of honour 'mid the growling wilderness.
My sturdier youth, maturing to the sword,
Won by the syren-trumpets, and the ring
15 Of shields upon the pavement, when bright mail'd
Henry the Fowler pass'd the streets of Prague.
Was't to this end I louted and became
The menial of Mars, and held a spear
Sway'd by command, as corn is by the wind?
20 Is it for this, I now am lifted up
By Europe's throned Emperor, to see
My honour be my executioner,—
My love of fame, my prided honesty
Put to the torture for confessional?
25 Then the damn'd crime of blurting to the world
A woman's secret!—though a fiend she be,
Too tender of my ignominious life;

153 to] ⟨with all the speed a Man⟩ to *D* *After* 153 End of the Second Act. *CB*

III.i.1 empty] *interlined above* ⟨desert⟩ *D* 5 hurl'd] *interlined above* ⟨left me⟩ ⟨thrown⟩ *D* 9 boyhood] *made out of* Childhood *D* 10/11 ⟨My restless warfare⟩ *D* 20 Is . . . this] *successively* (*a*) Is it for this (*b*) Ist to this end (*c*) Is it for this *D* 21 Europe's throned] a well-judging *D*; Europe's throned *interlined above* ⟨a well judging⟩ *CB*

But then to wrong the generous Emperor
In such a searching point, were to give up
30 My soul for foot-ball at hell's holiday!
I must confess,—and cut my throat,—to-day?
To-morrow? Ho! some wine!

*Enter* SIGIFRED.

*Sigifred.* A fine humour—
*Albert.* Who goes there? Count Sigifred? Ha! ha!
*Sigifred.* What, man, do you mistake the hollow sky
35 For a throng'd tavern,—and these stubbed trees
For old serge hangings,—me, your humble friend,
For a poor waiter? Why, man, how you stare!
What gipsies have you been carousing with?
No, no more wine; methinks you've had enough.
40 *Albert.* You well may laugh and banter. What a fool
An injury may make of a staid man!
You shall know all anon.
*Sigifred.* Some tavern-brawl?
*Albert.* 'Twas with some people out of common reach;
Revenge is difficult.
*Sigifred.* I am your friend;
45 We meet again to-day, and can confer
Upon it. For the present I'm in haste.
*Albert.* Whither?
*Sigifred.* To fetch King Gersa to the feast.
The Emperor on this marriage is so hot,
Pray heaven it end not in apoplexy!
50 The very porters, as I pass'd the doors,
Heard his loud laugh, and answer'd in full choir.
I marvel, Albert, you delay so long
From these bright revelries; go, show yourself,
You may be made a duke.
*Albert.* Aye, very like.

30 at] ⟨to⟩ at *D* 32 *s.d. and s.p.* Sigifred] Sigibert (*but the s.p. then corrected to* Sigifred) *D* 32 A . . . humour] Sir! Coming Sir (*the first* Sir *interlined above* ⟨Here⟩) *D*; A fine humour *written by Keats in a blank space left by Brown in CB* 33 Ha! ha!] ha ha ha *D*; Ha! ha! ⟨ha!⟩ *CB* 36 me] I *D*; me *interlined above* ⟨I⟩ *CB* 40 What] O what *altered to* What *D* 42 Some] Albert! a *D*; Some *interlined above* ⟨Albert! a⟩ *CB* 43 out . . . reach] of high consequence *D*; out of common reach *interlined above* ⟨of high consequence⟩ *CB* 43/44 ⟨With whom revenge is difficult—⟩ *D* 50 porters] *interlined above* ⟨Warders⟩ (*the* W *written over* {P}) *D* 50 doors] *interlined above* ⟨Gates⟩ *D* 53 these] those *D*; those *altered to* these *CB* 53 bright] *interlined above* ⟨ripe⟩ *D* 54 be] ⟨be outstrip⟩ be *D*

55 Pray what day has his Highness fix'd upon?
*Sigifred.* For what?
*Albert.* The marriage;—what else can I mean?
*Sigifred.* To-day! O I forgot you could not know;
The news is scarce a minute old with me.
*Albert.* Married to-day!—to-day! You did not say so?
60 *Sigifred.* Now, while I speak to you, their comely heads
Are bow'd before the mitre.
*Albert.* Oh! monstrous!
*Sigifred.* What is this?
*Albert.* Nothing, Sigifred. Farewell!
We'll meet upon our subject. Farewell, Count! [*Exit.*
*Sigifred.* Is this clear-headed Albert? He brain-turn'd!
65 'Tis as portentous as a meteor. [*Exit.*

SCENE II. *An Apartment in the Castle.*

*Enter, as from the Marriage,* OTHO, LUDOLPH, AURANTHE, CONRAD, *Nobles, Knights, Ladies, etc., etc., etc. Music.*

*Otho.* Now, Ludolph! Now, Auranthe, daughter fair!
What can I find to grace your nuptial day
More than my love, and these wide realms in fee?
*Ludolph.* I have too much.
*Auranthe.* And I, my liege, by far.
5 *Ludolph.* Auranthe! I have! O, my bride,—my love,—
Not all the gaze upon us can restrain
My eyes, too long poor exiles from thy face,
From adoration, and my foolish tongue
From uttering soft responses to the love

58 The . . . me] I heard it but an hour ago myself *D*; The news is scarce a minute old with me *interlined above* ⟨I heard it but an hour ago myself⟩ *CB* 62/63 ⟨I long to greet the happy happy pair⟩ *D* 63 *s.d.* Exit] exit Albert *D* 64–65 Is . . . meteor.] *written by Keats on the opposite verso in CB to replace* ⟨Farewell! And nothing! but this nothing is / Something, I'll take my oath on. He is mad!⟩; *D has this same text uncanceled, with* I'll *made out of* I 65 *s.d.* Exit] exit Sigifred *D*

III.ii *location* An . . . Castle.] *not in D* *Opening s.d.* the . . . Music] a marriage ceremony—Otho, Ludolph—Conrad, Auranthe and her train, Nobles, Knights Ladies & & &.—Music playing—and cease *D* 1 Auranthe] *interlined above* ⟨sweet⟩ *D* 1 fair] *written over* ⟨Now⟩ *D* 3 wide] *added above the line in D* 4 *s.p.* Ludolph] Ludolph ⟨& Auranthe together⟩ *D* 4 I have] We have *altered to* I have (*Auranthe's speech in the second half of 4 added in conjunction with this and the preceding alteration*) *D* 7 too] ⟨from adoration⟩ too *D* 7 poor exiles] *interlined above* ⟨far dongeond⟩ *D* 9 the love] *written beneath* ⟨thy mute⟩ *D*

10 I see in thy mute beauty beaming forth!
Fair creature, bless me with a single word!
All mine!
*Auranthe.* Spare, spare me, my lord; I swoon else.
*Ludolph.* Soft beauty! by to-morrow I should die,
Wert thou not mine. [*They talk apart.*
*First Lady.* How deep she has bewitch'd him!
15 *First Knight.* Ask you for her receipt for love philtres.
*Second Lady.* They hold the Emperor in admiration.
*Otho.* If ever king was happy, that am I!
What are the cities 'yond the Alps to me,
The provinces about the Danube's mouth,
20 The promise of fair sail beyond the Rhone,
Or routing out of Hyperborean hordes,
To these fair children, stars of a new age?
Unless perchance I might rejoice to win
This little ball of earth, and chuck it them
To play with!
25 *Auranthe.* Nay, my lord, I do not know.
*Ludolph.* Let me not famish.
*Otho* (*to Conrad*). Good Franconia,
You heard what oath I sware, as the sun rose,
That, unless heaven would send me back my son,
My Arab, no soft music should enrich
30 The cool wine, kiss'd off with a soldier's smack:
Now all my empire, barter'd for one feast,
Seems poverty.
*Conrad.* Upon the neighbour-plain
The heralds have prepared a royal lists;
Your knights, found war-proof in the bloody field,
Speed to the game.
35 *Otho.* Well, Ludolph, what say you?
*Ludolph.* My lord!

9/10 ⟨But eloquent Beauty⟩ (*continuation of deleted text in 9*) *D* 14 *s.d.* They . . . apart] talk aside (*written beside the s.p.'s for 12 and 13, which are bracketed*) *D* 14 *s.p.* First Lady] A Lady *written beneath the canceled s.p.* ⟨A Knight⟩ *D* 15 *s.p.* First] A *D* 15 love] her *written over* ⟨Love⟩ (*see Textual Note*) *D* 17/18 ⟨Devoted, made a slave to this day's joy!⟩ *CB*; *D has the same line uncanceled, with* ⟨to gr⟩ *before* made 19 The] What the *altered to* The *D* 20 Rhone] *made out of* rhine *D* 20/21 ⟨Or mome [?]⟩ *D* 22 stars] ⟨Unless pechance⟩ Stars *D* 24 little] *added above the line in D* 25 I . . . know] *interlined above* ⟨at your good will⟩ *D* 26 *s.d.* (to Conrad)] *not in D, which, however, has the s.d.* talk aside *after Ludolph's speech in the preceding half-line* 26 Good] ⟨Conrad⟩ Good *D* 29 enrich] *written beneath* ⟨be heard⟩ *D* 35 the game] *interlined above* ⟨this lighter game⟩ ⟨the Trumpets⟩ *D* 35 Well] ⟨It is m⟩ Well *D*

*Otho.* A tourney?
*Conrad.* Or, if't please you best—
*Ludolph.* I want no more!
*First Lady.* He soars!
*Second Lady.* Past all reason.
*Ludolph.* Though heaven's choir
Should in a vast circumference descend,
40 And sing for my delight, I'd stop my ears!
Though bright Apollo's car stood burning here,
And he put out an arm to bid me mount,
His touch an immortality, not I!—
This earth,—this palace,—this room,—Auranthe!
45 *Otho.* This is a little painful; just too much.
Conrad, if he flames longer in this wise,
I shall believe in wizard-woven loves
And old romances; but I'll break the spell.
Ludolph!
*Conrad.* He will be calm anon.
*Ludolph.* You call'd!
50 Yes, yes, yes, I offend. You must forgive me;
Not being quite recover'd from the stun
Of your large bounties. A tourney, is it not?
[*A sennet heard faintly.*
*Conrad.* The trumpets reach us.
*Ethelbert* (*without*). On your peril, sirs,
Detain us!
*First Voice* (*without*). Let not the abbot pass.
*Second Voice* (*without*). No,
On your lives!
55 *First Voice* (*without*). Holy father, you must not.
*Ethelbert* (*without*). Otho!
*Otho.* Who calls on Otho?

37 I . . . more!] *written as a separate line in D* (*the next line then consisting of the First and Second Ladies' remarks plus Ludolph's* Though heaven's choir) 37 *s.p.* First] 2nd (*added above the line*) *D* 37 *s.p.* Second] another *D* 38 Though] *written over* ⟨If⟩ *D* 42 bid me mount] *interlined by Brown above* help me in (*left undeleted*) *D* 44 Auranthe!] *written on a separate line in D and preceded by the s.d.* goes to Auranthe 48 And] *successively* (*a*) And (*b*) In (*c*) And *D* 49 He will] *D*; He ⟨wi⟩'ll *CB* 49/50 *Otho.* Come, come, a little sober reason ⟨Son⟩ Ludolph— *D* 50 You . . . me] *written beneath* ⟨I delay—people⟩ *D* 50/51 ⟨Cause an unseemly delay⟩ (*continuation of deleted text in 50?*) *D* 52 *s.d.* A . . . faintly] faint senet *D* 53 *s.p.* Ethelbert (without)] Ethelbert's voice without *D* 54 us] us ⟨not⟩ *D* 54 *s.p.* First . . . (without)] voices *altered to* 1st voice without *D* 54 *s.p.* Second . . . (without)] Other voices *D* 55 *s.p.* First . . . (without)] Other voices *D* 56 *s.p.* Ethelbert (without)] Ethelberts voice *D* (*this is the first s.p. in 56; the second s.p. for Ethelbert in the line is not in the MS*)

*Ethelbert* (*without*). Ethelbert!
*Otho.* Let him come in.
[*Enter* ETHELBERT, *leading in* ERMINIA.
Thou cursed abbot, why
Hast brought pollution to our holy rites?
Hast thou no fear of hangmen, or the faggot?
60 *Ludolph.* What portent—what strange prodigy is this?
*Conrad.* Away!
*Ethelbert.* You, Duke?
*Erminia.* Albert has surely fail'd me!
Look at the Emperor's brow upon me bent!
*Ethelbert.* A sad delay.
*Conrad.* Away, thou guilty thing!
*Ethelbert.* You again, Duke? Justice, most noble Otho!
65 You—go to your sister there and plot again,
A quick plot, swift as thought to save your heads;
For lo! the toils are spread around your den,
The world is all agape to see dragg'd forth
Two ugly monsters.
*Ludolph.* What means he, my lord?
*Conrad.* I cannot guess.
70 *Ethelbert.* Best ask your lady sister,
Whether the riddle puzzles her beyond
The power of utterance.
*Conrad.* Foul barbarian, cease;
The Princess faints!
*Ludolph.* Stab him! O sweetest wife!
[*Attendants bear off* AURANTHE.
*Erminia.* Alas!
*Ethelbert.* Your wife!
*Ludolph.* Aye, Satan, does that yerk ye?
*Ethelbert.* Wife! so soon!
75 *Ludolph.* Aye, wife! Oh, impudence!
Thou bitter mischief! Venemous bad priest!
How dar'st thou lift those beetle brows at me?

57 *s.d.* leading] forcing *D* 59 no] no⟨t⟩ *D* 59/60 (*continuing Otho's speech*) Mad Churchman wouldst thou be impal'd alive? *D* 61 Albert has surely] Sure Albert has *altered to* Albert has surely *D, CB* (*the alteration by Brown in both MSS*) 62/63 ⟨Conrad⟩ (*deleted s.p.*) *D* 63 sad] *interlined above* ⟨slight⟩ *D* 63 delay.] delay—⟨no ham—⟩ *D* 64 noble] mighty *D* 68 see . . . forth] *written beneath* ⟨see you drag'd⟩ *D* 69 ugly] *added above the line in D* 69–72 *Ludolph.* What . . . utterance.] *added on the opposite verso in D with a mark for insertion after 69a* 73 *s.d.* Attendants . . . Auranthe.] *not in D* 75 Oh] ⟨aye⟩ Oh *D* 76 bad] mad *D* 77 dar'st] dust *D*

Me—the Prince Ludolph, in this presence here,
Upon my marriage-day, and scandalise
80 My joys with such opprobrious surprise?
Wife! Why dost linger on that syllable,
As if it were some demon's name pronounc'd
To summon harmful lightning, and make yawn
The sleepy thunder? Hast no sense of fear?
85 No ounce of man in thy mortality?
Tremble! for, at my nod, the sharpen'd axe
Will make thy bold tongue quiver to the roots,
Those grey lids wink, and thou not know it, monk!
*Ethelbert.* O, poor deceived Prince, I pity thee!
Great Otho, I claim justice—
90 *Ludolph.* Thou shalt have't!
Thine arms from forth a pulpit of hot fire
Shall sprawl distracted! O that that dull cowl
Were some most sensitive portion of thy life,
That I might give it to my hounds to tear!
95 Thy girdle some fine zealous-pained nerve
To girth my saddle! And those devil's beads
Each one a life, that I might, every day,
Crush one with Vulcan's hammer!
*Otho.* Peace, my son;
You far outstrip my spleen in this affair.
100 Let us be calm, and hear the abbot's plea
For this intrusion.
*Ludolph.* I am silent, sire.
*Otho.* Conrad, see all depart not wanted here.
[*Exeunt Knights, Ladies, etc.*
Ludolph, be calm. Ethelbert, peace awhile.
This mystery demands an audience
105 Of a just judge, and that will Otho be.
*Ludolph.* Why has he time to breathe another word?
*Otho.* Ludolph, old Ethelbert, be sure, comes not
To beard us for no cause; he's not the man
To cry himself up an ambassador

82/83
⟨To rouse the sleepy Thunder⟩
⟨Which Thunder⟩ *D*
83 summon] ⟨rouse the⟩ summon *D* 83 yawn] roar *D* 86 for] *squeezed in afterward in D* 87 to] *interlined above* ⟨at⟩ *D* 96 girth] ⟨lease⟩ girth *D* 97 that] *interlined above* ⟨and⟩ *D* 97 might, every] might ⟨crush⟩ every *D* 98 one] *interlined above* ⟨one in v⟩ *D* 102 *s.d.* Exeunt . . . etc.] *not in D* 102 *s.d.* Knights] ⟨Nobles,⟩ Knights *CB*

Without credentials.
110 *Ludolph.* I'll chain up myself.
*Otho.* Old abbot, stand here forth. Lady Erminia,
Sit. And now, abbot, what have you to say?
Our ear is open. First we here denounce
Hard penalties against thee, if't be found
115 The cause for which you have disturb'd us here,
Making our bright hours muddy, be a thing
Of little moment.
*Ethelbert.* See this innocent!
Otho! thou father of the people call'd,
Is her life nothing? Her fair honour nothing?
120 Her tears from matins until even song
Nothing? Her burst heart nothing? Emperor!
Is this, your gentle niece—the simplest flower
Of the world's herbal, this fair lily blanch'd
Still with the dews of piety, this meek lady
125 Here sitting like an angel newly-shent,
Who vails its snowy wings and grows all pale—
Is she nothing?
*Otho.* What more to the purpose, abbot?
*Ludolph.* Whither, whither is he winding?
*Conrad.* No clue yet!
*Ethelbert.* You have heard, my liege, and so, no doubt, all here,
130 Foul, poisonous, malignant whisperings;
Nay open speech, rude mockery grown common,
Against the spotless nature and clear fame
Of the Princess Erminia, your niece.
I have intruded here thus suddenly,
135 Because I hold those base weeds with tight hand

110 I'll] I ⟨wi⟩'ll *D* 110 chain up myself] *interlined above* ⟨for Patience strive⟩ *D* 111 Old . . . here] Now Ethelbert stand *altered to* Old ⟨Abbot⟩ stand here (Abbot *deleted by mistake*) *D* 113 we here] *written over* ⟨I do [*or possibly* I de]⟩ *D* 118 the] *interlined above* ⟨his⟩ *D* 119 life] *interlined above* ⟨peace⟩ *D* 120 from . . . until] at matins and at *altered to* from matins until *D* 122 Is . . . niece] *successively* (*a*) She, your sweet Nie (*b*) This, your most innocent Niece (*c*) This, your most guiltless Niece (*d*) Is this your gentle Niece *D* 122 this, . . . niece—] *ed*; ~∧ . . . ~, *D*; ~∧ . . . ~? *CB* 123 herbal, this] *D*; ~? This *CB* 124/125 ⟨Who{se} {sits} now sits here folorn and⟩ *D* 126 vails] *ed*; veils *D, CB* 126 pale—] *D*; ~, *CB* (*see above for 122, 123*) 128 Whither . . . yet!] is folly's *appears in the middle of the page opposite this line in D, but Keats did not use the words anywhere in his text* 131 grown] grows *D* 132 spotless] ⟨na⟩ spotless *D* 134 I] ⟨But⟩ I *D*

Which now disfigure her fair growing stem,
Waiting but for your sign to pull them up
By the dark roots, and leave her palpable,
To all men's sight, a lady innocent.
140 The ignominy of that whisper'd tale
About a midnight-gallant, seen to climb
A window to her chamber neighbour'd near,
I will from her turn off, and put the load
On the right shoulders; on that wretch's head
145 Who, by close stratagems, did save herself,
Chiefly by shifting to this lady's room
A rope-ladder for false witness.
*Ludolph.* Most atrocious!
*Otho.* Ethelbert, proceed.
*Ethelbert.* With sad lips I shall;
For, in the healing of one wound, I fear
150 To make a greater. His young Highness here
To-day was married.
*Ludolph.* Good.
*Ethelbert.* Would it were good!
Yet why do I delay to spread abroad
The names of those two vipers, from whose jaws
A deadly breath went forth to taint and blast
This guileless lady?
155 *Otho.* Abbot, speak their names.
*Ethelbert.* A minute first. It cannot be—but may

136 fair] *interlined above* ⟨clear⟩ *D* 136 growing] growen *D* 137 Waiting] *successively* (*a*) And wait (*b*) I wait (*c*) waiting *D* 139 a . . . innocent] *written beneath* ⟨an innocent Lady⟩ *D* 140–147 The . . . atrocious!] *written on the opposite verso in D to replace:*
⟨*Otho.*⟩
⟨*Ludolph.* {I have wrong'd this man muc}
Have I not wrong'd this man?
*Conrad.* Curs'd Priest!
*Ludolph.* How!⟩
141 midnight] *added above the line in D* 141 seen to climb] *written beneath* ⟨climbing up⟩ *D* 141/142 ⟨Her chamber window⟩ *D* 145 Who . . . herself]
Who by close stratagems; ⟨especially
By shifting a Rope ladder from her room
To this much injured Lady's; has escap'd⟩
did save herself
(by *interlined above* ⟨with⟩ *in the first line*) *D* 146 to] ⟨from her⟩ to *D* 148 *s.p.* Ethelbert] *not in D* 149 in] ⟨I s⟩ ⟨though I heal one wound⟩ in *D* 150 young] *interlined above* ⟨great⟩ *D* 154 deadly] ⟨po⟩ deadly *D* 154 taint] ⟨blast and t⟩ taint *D*

I ask, great judge, if you to-day have put
A letter by unread?
*Otho.* Does't end in this?
*Conrad.* Out with their names!
*Ethelbert.* Bold sinner, say you so?
*Ludolph.* Out, tedious monk!
160 *Otho.* Confess, or by the wheel—
*Ethelbert.* My evidence cannot be far away;
And, though it never come, be on my head
The crime of passing an attaint upon
The slanderers of this virgin.
*Ludolph.* Speak aloud!
*Ethelbert.* Auranthe! and her brother there—
165 *Conrad.* Amaze!
*Ludolph.* Throw them from the windows!
*Otho.* Do what you will.
*Ludolph.* What shall I do with them?
Something of quick dispatch, for should she hear,
My soft Auranthe, her sweet mercy would
170 Prevail against my fury. Damned priest!
What swift death wilt thou die? As to the lady
I touch her not.
*Ethelbert.* Illustrious Otho, stay!
An ample store of misery thou hast,
Choak not the granary of thy noble mind
175 With more bad bitter grain, too difficult
A cud for the repentance of a man
Grey-growing. To thee only I appeal,
Not to thy noble son, whose yeasting youth
Will clear itself, and crystal turn again.
180 A young man's heart, by heaven's blessing, is
A wide world, where a thousand new-born hopes
Empurple fresh the melancholy blood:
But an old man's is narrow, tenantless

158/159 ⟨Away! or out with the names⟩ (*probably a canceled attempt at Conrad's speech in 159 rather than a continuation of Otho's in 158*) *D* 159 their] the *D* 159 sinner] *interlined above* ⟨Serpent⟩ *D* 160 Out,] *added in the margin in D* 161 My] *written over* ⟨The⟩ *D* 164 slanderers] Slanderer *D* 165 and . . . there—] *not in D; added by Keats in CB* (*the original line in both MSS consisting of Ethelbert's* Auranthe! *plus the two following speeches*) 165 *s.p.* Conrad] *written beneath the canceled s.p.* ⟨Otho⟩ *D* 171 swift] ⟨qui⟩ swift (*both added above the line*) *D* 173 An . . . store] A store *altered to* An ample store *D* 174 Choak] ⟨Suff⟩ Choak *D* 178 thy noble] thine hapless *altered to* thy noble *D* 178 son] *added above the line in D* 178 yeasting] ⟨very⟩ yeasting *D* 183 tenantless] *written beneath* ⟨stagnated⟩ *D*

Of hopes, and stuff'd with many memories,
185 Which, being pleasant, ease the heavy pulse,
Painful, clogg'd up and stagnate. Weigh this matter
Even as a miser balances his coin;
And, in the name of mercy, give command
That your knight Albert be brought here before you.
190 He will expound this riddle; he will show
A noon-day proof of bad Auranthe's guilt.
*Otho.* Let Albert straight be summon'd.
[*Exit one of the Nobles.*
*Ludolph.* Impossible!
I cannot doubt—I will not—no—to doubt
Is to be ashes!—wither'd up to death!
195 *Otho.* My gentle Ludolph, harbour not a fear;
You do yourself much wrong.
*Ludolph.* O, wretched dolt!
Now, when my foot is almost on thy neck,
Wilt thou infuriate me? Proof! Thou fool!
Why wilt thou tease impossibility
200 With such a thick skull'd persevering suit?
Fanatic obstinacy! Prodigy!
Monster of folly! Ghost of a turn'd brain!
You puzzle me,—you haunt me,—when I dream
Of you my brain will split! Bald sorcerer!
205 Juggler! May I come near you! On my soul
I know not whether to pity, curse, or laugh.
[*Enter* ALBERT, *and the Nobleman.*
Here, Albert, this old phantom wants a proof!
Give him his proof! A camel's load of proofs!
*Otho.* Albert, I speak to you as to a man
210 Whose words once utter'd pass like current gold;
And therefore fit to calmly put a close
To this brief tempest. Do you stand possess'd

186 clogg'd] *ed*; clog *D, CB* 186 Weigh] Weight *D* 189 your] *interlined above* ⟨the⟩ *D* 190 He . . . riddle;] *written on the opposite verso in D to replace* ⟨If he be not a Caitiff⟩ *D* 191 bad] *made out of* sad *D* 192 *s.d.* Exit . . . Nobles.] *not in D* 192–196 *Ludolph.* Impossible . . . O] *added on the opposite verso in D* (*the original line consisting of Otho's* Let . . . summon'd *plus Ludolph's* wretched dolt *in 196*) 194 ashes . . . death] *successively (a)* wither'd up to death (*b*) wither'd up to ashy death (*c*) ashes—wither'd up to death *D* 205 near] near⟨er⟩ *D* 206 not] *added above the line in D* 206 *s.d.* and the Nobleman] *not in D* 210 words . . . gold] word is ⟨to be taken⟩ ever counted trustworthy *D*; word is ever counted trustworthy *altered by Keats to* words once utter'd pass like current gold *CB* 211 calmly] ⟨put a⟩ calmly *D* 212 brief] day's *D*; brief *interlined by Keats above* ⟨day's⟩ *CB* 212 tempest] ⟨Storm⟩ Tempest *D*

Of any proof against the honourableness
Of Lady Auranthe, our new-spoused daughter?
215 *Albert.* You chill me with astonishment! How's this?
My liege, what proof should I have 'gainst a fame
Impossible of slur? [OTHO *rises.*
*Erminia.* O wickedness!
*Ethelbert.* Deluded monarch, 'tis a cruel lie.
*Otho.* Peace, rebel-priest!
*Conrad.* Insult beyond credence!
*Erminia.* Almost a dream!
220 *Ludolph.* We have awaken'd from!
A foolish dream that from my brow hath wrung
A wrathful dew. O folly! why did I
So act the lion with this silly gnat?
Let them depart. Lady Erminia,
225 I ever griev'd for you, as who did not?
But now you have, with such a brazen front,
So most maliciously, so madly striven
To dazzle the soft moon, when tenderest clouds
Should be unloop'd around to curtain her;
230 I leave you to the desert of the world
Almost with pleasure. Let them be set free
For me! I take no personal revenge
More than against a night-mare, which a man
Forgets in the new dawn. [*Exit* LUDOLPH.
235 *Otho.* Still in extremes! No, they must not be loose.
*Ethelbert.* Albert, I must suspect thee of a crime
So fiendish—
*Otho.* Fear'st thou not my fury, monk?
Conrad, be they in your safe custody,
Till we determine some fit punishment.
240 It is so mad a deed, I must reflect

215 chill] chill⟨d⟩ *D* 216 'gainst a fame] *interlined above* ⟨of a thing⟩ *D* 217 *s.d.* Otho rises.] *not in D* 218–220 *Ethelbert.* Deluded . . . dream!] *added on the opposite verso in D* 219 credence] *interlined above* ⟨measure⟩ *CB* 220 We . . . from] *successively (a)* Then we are quite awaken'd from this dream *(b)* That we have waken'd from *(c)* We have awaken'd from *(the first version originally following Erminia's* O wickedness! *in 217, and the line then shortened to accommodate the addition of 218–220a) D* 220 awaken'd] *D*; awak'd *CB* 221 A] *interlined above* ⟨This⟩ *D* 221 hath] has *D* 222 A] ⟨Moist⟩ a *D* 224 Lady Erminia] *written beneath* ⟨Poor lost Erminia⟩ *D* 226–227 you have, with . . . So] that you with . . . Have *altered to* you have with . . . So *D* 226 brazen] *interlined above* ⟨shameless⟩ *D* 227 so madly] most madly *D* 232 take] ⟨feel⟩ take *interlined above* ⟨have⟩ *D* 234/235 ⟨Conrad we leave them⟩ *(canceled beginning of Otho's speech) D* 236–237 *Ethelbert.* Albert . . . monk?] *added on the opposite verso in D* 238 safe] sure *D*

And question them in private; for perhaps,
By patient scrutiny, we may discover
Whether they merit death, or should be plac'd
In care of the physicians.
[*Exeunt* OTHO *and Nobles*; ALBERT *following.*
*Conrad.* My guards, ho!
245 *Erminia.* Albert, wilt thou follow there?
Wilt thou creep dastardly behind his back,
And shrink away from a weak woman's eye?
Turn, thou court-Janus, thou forget'st thyself;
Here is the Duke, waiting with open arms [*Enter Guards.*
250 To thank thee; here congratulate each other;
Wring hands; embrace; and swear how lucky 'twas
That I, by happy chance, hit the right man
Of all the world to trust in.
*Albert.* Trust! to me!
*Conrad* (*aside*). He is the sole one in this mystery.
255 *Erminia.* Well, I give up, and save my prayers for heaven!
You, who could do this deed, would ne'er relent,
Though, at my words, the hollow prison-vaults
Would groan for pity.
*Conrad.* Manacle them both!
*Ethelbert.* I know it—it must be—I see it all!
Albert, thou art the minion!
260 *Erminia.* Ah! too plain—
*Conrad.* Silence! Gag up their mouths! I cannot bear
More of this brawling. That the Emperor
Had plac'd you in some other custody!
Bring them away. [*Exeunt all but* ALBERT.
265 *Albert.* Though my name perish from the book of honour,
Almost before the recent ink is dry,

243 plac'd] *written over* ⟨put⟩ *D* 244 *s.d.* Exeunt] *made out of* exit *CB* 244 *s.d.* Nobles] Train *D* 245 *s.p.* Conrad] *written beneath the canceled s.p.* ⟨Erminia⟩ *D* 245 wilt thou] will you *D*; will you *altered to* wilt thou *CB* 246 Wilt thou] Will you *D*; Will you *altered to* Wilt thou *CB* 247 shrink] slink *D* 251 and] ⟨the gale is over blown / And you are safe: swear⟩ and *D* 252 I, by happy] ⟨I confided⟩ I by ⟨c⟩happy *D* 253 in] *written over* ⟨to⟩ *D* 253 Trust! to me!] ~‸ ~~? *D* 254 *Conrad* (*aside*). He . . . mystery.] *added on the opposite verso in D* 258 pity.] *followed by the canceled s.d.* ⟨enter Guards⟩ *D* 259 I know] ⟨Daughter!⟩ I know (know *interlined above* ⟨see⟩) *D* 259 I see it all] *interlined above* ⟨yes—'tis all out⟩ *D* 260 minion!] Minion, ⟨come⟩ *D* 260 too plain] *interlined above* ⟨I see⟩ *D* 261 up] ⟨them⟩ up *D* 264/265

⟨Albert⟩
Act 3. Scene 3rd
Manet Albert—

(*this also serves as s.p. for 265*) *D* 266 is] *interlined above* ⟨be⟩ *D*

And be no more remember'd after death,
Than any drummer's in the muster-roll;
Yet shall I season high my sudden fall
270 With triumph o'er that evil-witted Duke!
He shall feel what it is to have the hand
Of a man drowning on his hateful throat.

*Enter* GERSA *and* SIGIFRED.

*Gersa.* What discord is at ferment in this house?
*Sigifred.* We are without conjecture; not a soul
275 We met could answer any certainty.
*Gersa.* Young Ludolph, like a fiery arrow, shot
By us.
*Sigifred.* The Emperor, with cross'd arms, in thought.
*Gersa.* In one room music, in another sadness,
Perplexity every where!
*Albert.* A trifle mere!
280 Follow;—your presences will much avail
To tune our jarred spirits. I'll explain. [*Exeunt.*

## ACT IV

### SCENE I. AURANTHE'S *Apartment.*

AURANTHE *and* CONRAD *discovered.*

*Conrad.* Well, well, I know what ugly jeopardy
We are cag'd in; you need not pester that
Into my ears. Pr'ythee, let me be spared
A foolish tongue, that I may bethink me
5 Of remedies with some deliberation.
You cannot doubt but 'tis in Albert's power
To crush or save us?
*Auranthe.* No, I cannot doubt.
He has, assure yourself, by some strange means,

269 season] *interlined by Brown above* sweeten (*left undeleted*) *D* 269 sudden fall] *written beneath* ⟨evil hour⟩ *D* 270 o'er] *interlined above* ⟨over⟩ *D* 270 evil-witted] *underscored in D* 272/273 (*continuing Albert's speech*) Erminia! ⟨yet⟩ dream to night of better days / Tomorrow makes them real—once more good morrow— *D* 273, 276, 278 *s.p.* Gersa] Sigifred *D* 273 discord] ⟨ferment has⟩ discord *D* 274, 277 *s.p.* Sigifred] Gersa *D* *After* 281 End of the Third Act. *CB*

My secret; which I ever hid from him,
Knowing his mawkish honesty.
10 *Conrad.* Curs'd slave!
*Auranthe.* Aye, I could almost curse him now myself.
Wretched impediment! evil genius!
A glue upon my wings, that cannot spread,
When they should span the provinces! A snake,
15 A scorpion, sprawling on the first gold step,
Conducting to the throne high canopied.
*Conrad.* You would not hear my counsel, when his life
Might have been trodden out, all sure and hush'd;
Now the dull animal forsooth must be
20 Intreated, managed! When can you contrive
The interview he demands?
*Auranthe.* As speedily
It must be done as my bribed woman can
Unseen conduct him to me: but I fear
'Twill be impossible, while the broad day
25 Comes through the panes with persecuting glare.
Methinks, if't now were night, I could intrigue
With darkness, bring the stars to second me,
And settle all this trouble.
*Conrad.* Nonsense! Child!
See him immediately; why not now?
30 *Auranthe.* Do you forget that even the senseless door-posts
Are on the watch and gape through all the house;
How many whisperers there are about,
Hungry for evidence to ruin me;
Men I have spurn'd, and women I have taunted?
35 Besides, the foolish Prince sends, minute whiles,
His pages,—so they tell me,—to enquire
After my health, intreating, if I please,
To see me.
*Conrad.* Well, suppose this Albert here;
What is your power with him?

IV.i.11/12
⟨O wretched woman!⟩
⟨My evil genius⟩ *D*

15 sprawling] *interlined above* ⟨threatning⟩ *D* 18 sure and] *added above the line in D* 18 hush'd] hush⟨'d⟩ *D* 20 When] ⟨in⟩ when *D* 22 woman] ⟨minion⟩ woman *D* 23 conduct] ⟨him⟩ conduct *CB* 24 day] day ⟨light⟩ *D* 36 so] *squeezed in afterward in D* 37 After] *written over* ⟨Of⟩ *D* 38 this . . . here] this ⟨mongrell⟩ Albert here (this *made out of* the *and* here *apparently added afterward*) *D*

*Auranthe.* He should be<br>
40 My echo, my taught parrot! but I fear<br>
He will be cur enough to bark at me;<br>
Have his own say; read me some silly creed<br>
'Bout shame and pity.<br>
*Conrad.* What will you do then?<br>
*Auranthe.* What I shall do, I know not; what I would<br>
45 Cannot be done; for see, this chamber-floor<br>
Will not yield to the pickaxe and the spade,—<br>
Here is no quiet depth of hollow ground.<br>
*Conrad.* Sister, you have grown sensible and wise,<br>
Seconding, ere I speak it, what is now,<br>
I hope, resolv'd between us.<br>
50 *Auranthe.* Say, what is't?<br>
*Conrad.* You need not be his sexton too: a man<br>
May carry that with him shall make him die<br>
Elsewhere,—give that to him; pretend the while<br>
You will to-morrow succumb to his wishes,<br>
55 Be what they may, and send him from the castle<br>
On some fool's errand: let his latest groan<br>
Frighten the wolves!<br>
*Auranthe.* Alas! he must not die!<br>
*Conrad.* Would you were both hears'd up in stifling lead!<br>
Detested—<br>
*Auranthe.* Conrad, hold! I would not bear<br>
60 The little thunder of your fretful tongue,<br>
Though I alone were taken in these toils,<br>
And you could free me; but remember, sir,<br>
You live alone in my security:<br>
So keep your wits at work, for your own sake,<br>
Not mine, and be more mannerly.<br>
65 *Conrad.* Thou wasp!<br>
If my domains were emptied of these folk,

40 taught] *added above the line in D* 42 say] ⟨th⟩ say *D* 43 What . . . then] *written beneath* ⟨You are a Cypher then⟩ *D* 45 for] ⟨here⟩ for *D* 48 Sister] *added in the margin in D* 48 sensible and wise] *written beneath* ⟨wise and sensible⟩ *D* 49 Seconding] You second *altered to* seconding *D* 52–53 him die / Elsewhere] *divided* him / Die, elsewhere *D* 59 Detested] Detested ⟨clogs⟩ *D* 59 Conrad . . . bear] *interlined above* ⟨Hold, hold Conrad I'll not bear⟩ *D* 60 The] ⟨Your⟩ The *D* 61 taken] ⟨trammel⟩ taken *D* 63 live] ⟨fall with me⟩ live *D* 65/66<br>
⟨Who knocks!<br>
*Auranthe.* It may be Albert—hide yourself<br>
You⟩ *D*

And I had thee to starve—
*Auranthe.* O, marvellous!
But, Conrad, now be gone; the host is look'd for;
Cringe to the Emperor, entertain the lords,
70 And, do ye mind, above all things, proclaim
My sickness, with a brother's sadden'd eye,
Condoling with Prince Ludolph. In fit time
Return to me.
*Conrad.* I leave you to your thoughts. [*Exit.*
*Auranthe* (*sola*). Down, down, proud temper! down, Auranthe's pride!
75 Why do I anger him when I should kneel?
Conrad! Albert! help! help! What can I do?
O wretched woman! lost, wreck'd, swallow'd up,
Accursed, blasted! O, thou golden crown,
Orbing along the serene firmament
80 Of a wide empire, like a glowing moon;
And thou, bright sceptre, lustrous in my eyes,—
There!—as the fabled fair Hesperian tree,
Bearing a fruit more precious! graceful thing,
Delicate, godlike, magic! must I leave
85 Thee to melt in the visionary air,
Ere, by one grasp, this common hand is made
Imperial? I do not know the time
When I have wept for sorrow; but methinks
I could now sit upon the ground, and shed
90 Tears, tears of misery. O, the heavy day!
How shall I bear my life till Albert comes?
Ludolph! Erminia! Proofs! O heavy day!
Bring me some mourning weeds, that I may 'tire
Myself, as fits one wailing her own death,—
95 Cut off these curls, and brand this lily hand,
And throw these jewels from my loathing sight,—
Fetch me a missal, and a string of beads,—
A cup of bitter'd water, and a crust,—

69 lords] nobles *D* 70 proclaim] *written beneath* ⟨observe⟩ *D* 73 I . . . thoughts.] *written by Keats* (*with* you *added above the line*) *on the opposite verso in CB to replace* ⟨A sudden death light on you!⟩ 73/74 ⟨Why s⟩ 'Twere well perhaps—⟨Let me make fast the door—⟩ *D*; ⟨'Twere well perhaps!⟩ *CB* (*canceled beginning of Auranthe's speech in CB*; *the D text is missing between 70 and this line*) 75/76 ⟨To supplicate—when I should bend the knee⟩ *D* 76 help (*fourth word*)] *added above the line in D* 84 magic! must] magic—⟨handled⟩ must *D* 85 melt] ⟨the⟩ melt *D* 94 her own death] for herself *altered to* her own death *D* 98 bitter'd] *added above the line in D*

I will confess, O holy abbot!—How!
100 What is this? Auranthe, thou fool, dolt,
Whimpering ideot! up! up! and quell!
I am safe! Coward! why am I in fear?
Albert! he cannot stickle, chew the cud
In such a fine extreme,—impossible!
105 Who knocks?

[*Goes to the door, listens, and opens it. Enter* ALBERT.

Albert, I have been waiting for you here
With such an aching heart, such swooning throbs
On my poor brain, such cruel—cruel sorrow,
That I should claim your pity! Art not well?

*Albert.* Yes, lady, well.

110 *Auranthe.* You look not so, alas!
But pale, as if you brought some heavy news.

*Albert.* You know full well what makes me look so pale.

*Auranthe.* No! Do I? Surely I am still to learn
Some horror; all I know, this present, is
115 I am near hustled to a dangerous gulph,
Which you can save me from,—and therefore safe,
So trusting in thy love; that should not make
Thee pale, my Albert.

*Albert.* It doth make me freeze.

*Auranthe.* Why should it, love?

*Albert.* You should not ask me that,
120 But make your own heart monitor, and save
Me the great pain of telling. You must know.

*Auranthe.* Something has vext you, Albert. There are times
When simplest things put on a sombre cast;
A melancholy mood will haunt a man,
125 Until most easy matters take the shape
Of unachievable tasks; small rivulets
Then seem impassable.

*Albert.* Do not cheat yourself

99 abbot] father *D*; Abbot *interlined above* ⟨Father⟩ *CB* 101 and] act and *D* 102 I am] Im *interlined above* ⟨Thou art⟩ *D* 103 chew] ⟨hem and⟩ chew *D* 104 In] *written over* ⟨On⟩ *D* 104 a] ⟨extremes⟩ a *D* 105 *s.d.* Goes . . . Albert] she goes to the door, listens and lets in Albert *D* 106 been] ⟨expected you⟩ been *D* 107 swooning throbs] *interlined by Brown above* ⟨throbbing pains⟩ *D* 108 On] In *made out of* On *D* 108 cruel—cruel] ⟨a deep⟩ cruel cruel *interlined above* ⟨an expe⟩ *D* 114 this] *written over* ⟨at⟩ *D* 115 I am near] ⟨That⟩ I am ⟨in the midst⟩ near *D* 118 doth] does *D*; does *altered to* doth *CB* 120 make your] *interlined above* ⟨look'd into your⟩ *D* 125 Until] ⟨And⟩ Untill *D* 125 most easy] the easiest *altered to* most easy *D*

With hope that gloss of words, or suppliant action,
Or tears, or ravings, or self-threatened death,
Can alter my resolve.
130 *Auranthe.* You make me tremble;
Not so much at your threats, as at your voice,
Untun'd, and harsh, and barren of all love.
*Albert.* You suffocate me! Stop this devil's parley,
And listen to me; know me once for all.
135 *Auranthe.* I thought I did. Alas! I am deceiv'd.
*Albert.* No, you are not deceiv'd. You took me for
A man detesting all inhuman crime;
And therefore kept from me your demon's plot
Against Erminia. Silent? Be so still;
140 For ever! Speak no more; but hear my words,
Thy fate. Your safety I have bought to-day
By blazoning a lie, which in the dawn
I'll expiate with truth.
*Auranthe.* O cruel traitor!
*Albert.* For I would not set eyes upon thy shame;
145 I would not see thee dragg'd to death by the hair,
Penanc'd, and taunted on a scaffolding!
To-night, upon the skirts of the blind wood
That blackens northward of these horrid towers,
I wait for you with horses. Choose your fate.
Farewell!
150 *Auranthe.* Albert, you jest; I'm sure you must.
You, an ambitious soldier! I, a queen,
One who could say,—here, rule these provinces!
Take tribute from those cities for thyself!
Empty these armouries, these treasuries,
155 Muster thy warlike thousands at a nod!

131 your voice] ⟨the tone⟩ your voice *D* 132 all] *added above the line in D* 132/133 ⟨Can Ludolph's wife hold such a devil's parley! / Auranthe, listen! Know me once for all;⟩ *(beginning of Albert's speech) D* 134/135 *(continuing Albert's speech)* ⟨Sooner would I have⟩ *D* 136 No] ⟨You⟩ No *D* 141–143 Your . . . truth] To morrow to the public ear / I blazon out the Truth *D and originally CB* (To morrow *interlined above* ⟨I⟩ ⟨Tommo⟩ *and* to the . . . ear *written beneath* ⟨I discover⟩ *in D*); *Keats substituted the following on the opposite verso in CB—*

To day you are safe—
I have told a lie for you which in the Dawn
I'll expiate with truth

*—and then Brown canceled these lines and wrote the present text beneath them* 142 a lie] *interlined above* ⟨the truth⟩ *CB (final version)* 144 For] Yet *D*; For *interlined above* ⟨Yet⟩ *CB* 153/154 ⟨We want no⟩ *D*

Go! conquer Italy!

*Albert.* Auranthe, you have made

The whole world chaff to me. Your doom is fixed.

*Auranthe.* Out, villain! dastard!

*Albert.* Look there to the door!

Who is it?

*Auranthe.* Conrad,—traitor!

*Albert.* Let him in. [*Enter* CONRAD.

160 Do not affect amazement, hypocrite,

At seeing me in this chamber.

*Conrad.* Auranthe?

*Albert.* Talk not with eyes, but speak your curses out

Against me, who would sooner crush and grind

A brace of toads, than league with them t' oppress

165 An innocent lady, gull an emperor,

More generous to me than autumn-sun

To ripening harvests.

*Auranthe.* No more insult, sir.

*Albert.* Aye, clutch your scabbard; but, for prudence' sake,

Draw not the sword; 'twould make an uproar, Duke,

170 You would not hear the end of. At nightfall

Your lady sister, if I guess aright,

Will leave this busy castle. You had best

Take farewell too of worldly vanities.

*Conrad.* Vassal!

*Albert.* To-morrow, when the Emperor sends

175 For loving Conrad, see you fawn on him.

Good even!

*Auranthe.* You'll be seen!

*Albert.* See the coast clear then.

*Auranthe* (*as he goes*). Remorseless Albert! Cruel, cruel wretch!

[*She lets him out.*

*Conrad.* So, we must lick the dust?

159 *s.d.* Enter Conrad.] *not in D* 161 chamber.] Chamber;—⟨hang thyself⟩ *D* 163 Against . . . grind] *successively* (*a*) 'Gainst me who rather would grind down and crush ('Gainst *made out of* Against) (*b*) 'Gainst me who rather would crush and grind down (*c*) Against me who would sooner crush and grind *D* 164 league . . . them] *interlined above* ⟨wrong⟩ ⟨join them⟩ *D* 164 t'] to *D* 166 autumn] autum⟨s⟩ *D* 167 *s.p.* Auranthe] *written beneath the canceled s.p.* ⟨Conrad⟩ *D* 170 nightfall] ⟨the shut⟩ nightfall *D* 171 Your] ⟨Of eve⟩ your *D* 173 too of] of all *altered to* too of *D* 175 loving] ⟨loving⟩ ⟨fa⟩ loving *D* 177 *s.p. and s.d.* Auranthe (as he goes) *and* She lets him out] *D combines these in a single s.p.* Auranthe (lets him out); *in CB Brown first wrote* she lets him out *after 176, then canceled the s.d. there and added* (as he goes) *and* She . . . out *in 177*

*Auranthe.* I follow him.
*Conrad.* How? Where? The plan of your escape?
*Auranthe.* He waits
180 For me, with horses by the forest-side
Northward.
*Conrad.* Good, good; he dies. You go, say you?
*Auranthe.* Perforce.
*Conrad.* Be speedy, darkness! Till that comes,
Fiends keep you company! [*Exit.*
*Auranthe.* And you! And you!
And all men! Vanish—Oh! Oh! Oh!
[*Retires to an inner apartment.*

SCENE II. *An Apartment in the Castle.*

*Enter* LUDOLPH *and Page.*

*Page.* Still very sick, my lord; but now I went,
And there her women, in a mournful throng,
Stood in the passage whispering; if any
Moved, 'twas with careful steps, and hush'd as death:
They bade me stop.
5 *Ludolph.* Good fellow, once again
Make soft inquiry; pr'ythee, be not stay'd
By any hindrance, but with gentlest force
Break through her weeping servants, till thou com'st
E'en to her chamber-door, and there, fair boy,—
10 If with thy mother's milk thou hast suck'd in
Any diviner eloquence,—woo her ears
With plaints for me, more tender than the voice

179 Where] *interlined above* ⟨When⟩ *D* 181 Good . . . dies] *interlined above* ⟨You go?⟩ *and the rest of the line added afterward* (*Keats originally began 181 with*
Northward.
*Conrad.* You go?
*Auranthe.* Perforce—
*but then revised and expanded Conrad's speech to fill out the line and rewrote Auranthe's* Perforce *at the beginning of 182*) *D* 184 *s.d.* apartment.] *followed on a separate line by* scene draws *D*

IV.ii *opening s.d.* Page] ⟨his⟩ Page *D* 1/2 ⟨Knowing my duty to so good a Prince,⟩ *CB*; *D has the same line uncanceled* 4 careful] *interlined above* ⟨hush'd⟩ *D* 5 bade] bid *D* 6 inquiry; pr'ythee] enquiry for me *altered to* enquiry; prythee *D* 8 thou com'st] you come *altered to* thou comest *D* 9 E'en] Even *D* 11 diviner] *D*; divine *1848* (*CB missing*) 12 tender] *added above the line in D*

Of dying Echo, echoed.
*Page.* Kindest master!
To know thee sad thus, will unloose my tongue
15 In mournful syllables. Let but my words reach
Her ears, and she shall take them coupled with
Moans from my heart, and sighs not counterfeit.
May I speed better! [*Exit Page.*
*Ludolph* (*solus*). Auranthe! My life!
Long have I loved thee, yet till now not loved:
20 Remembering, as I do, hard-hearted times
When I had heard e'en of thy death perhaps,
And, thoughtless! suffer'd thee to pass alone
Into Elysium!—now I follow thee,
A substance or a shadow, wheresoe'er
25 Thou leadest me,—whether thy white feet press,
With pleasant weight, the amorous-aching earth,
Or through the air thou pioneerest me,
A shade! Yet sadly I predestinate!
O, unbenignest Love, why wilt thou let
30 Darkness steal out upon the sleepy world
So wearily, as if night's chariot-wheels
Were clogg'd in some thick cloud? O, changeful Love,
Let not her steeds with drowsy-footed pace
Pass the high stars, before sweet embassage
35 Comes from the pillow'd beauty of that fair
Completion of all delicate nature's wit!
Pout her faint lips anew with rubious health;
And, with thine infant fingers, lift the fringe
Of her sick eye-lids; that those eyes may glow
40 With wooing light upon me, ere the morn
Peers with disrelish, grey, barren, and cold!
[*Enter* GERSA *and Courtiers.*

13 echoed] echoe'd ⟨at her death⟩ *D* 14 know] *interlined above* ⟨see⟩ *D* 14 thus] ⟨touches⟩ thus *D* 15 In] *written over* ⟨To⟩ *D* 18 *s.d.* (solus)] *not in D* 19, 22 thee] *successively* (*a*) thee (*b*) her (*c*) thee *D* 21 e'en] ⟨perhaps⟩ even *D* 21 thy] *successively* (*a*) thy (*b*) her (*c*) thy *D* 23–28 now . . . predestinate!] *written on a separate leaf in D* (*a later insertion*) *to replace* ⟨Now I go with {thee} her / When heaven pleases: should it be to night.⟩ 26 pleasant] ⟨aching⟩ pleasant *D* 29 unbenignest] *interlined above* ⟨unpropitious⟩ *D* 31 wearily] *interlined above* ⟨heavily⟩ *D* 33–34 Let . . . high] *interlined above* ⟨Let her not take her drowsy-eyed watch / Among the⟩ *D* 36 delicate . . . wit] *interlined above* ⟨fairness and all form⟩ *D* 38 lift] *squeezed in afterward in D* 39 those] ⟨her⟩ those *D* 39/40 ⟨Like arking planets through⟩ (*the last three words successively* [*a*] lively barren planens [*b*] ardent barren planens [*c*] ardent planets through [*d*] arking planets through) *D* 41 Peers] ⟨Comes⟩ Peers *D*

Otho calls me his lion,—should I blush
To be so tamed? so—
*Gersa.* Do me the courtesy,
Gentlemen, to pass on.
*First Knight.* We are your servants.
[*Exeunt Courtiers.*
45 *Ludolph.* It seems then, sir, you have found out the man
You would confer with;—me?
*Gersa.* If I break not
Too much upon your thoughtful mood, I will
Claim a brief while your patience.
*Ludolph.* For what cause
Soe'er, I shall be honour'd.
*Gersa.* I not less.
50 *Ludolph.* What may it be? No trifle can take place
Of such deliberate prologue, serious 'haviour.
But, be it what it may, I cannot fail
To listen with no common interest;
For though so new your presence is to me,
55 I have a soldier's friendship for your fame.
Please you explain.
*Gersa.* As thus:—for, pardon me,
I cannot, in plain terms, grossly assault
A noble nature; and would faintly sketch
What your quick apprehension will fill up;
So finely I esteem you.
60 *Ludolph.* I attend.
*Gersa.* Your generous father, most illustrious Otho,
Sits in the banquet-room among his chiefs;
His wine is bitter, for you are not there;
His eyes are fix'd still on the open doors,
65 And ev'ry passer in he frowns upon,
Seeing no Ludolph comes.
*Ludolph.* I do neglect.
*Gersa.* And for your absence may I guess the cause?
*Ludolph.* Stay there! No—guess? More princely you must be
Than to make guesses at me. 'Tis enough.
I'm sorry I can hear no more.
70 *Gersa.* And I

44 *s.p.* First Knight] Courtier *D* 46 If] ⟨I sought you not / But as I chance to meet you here alone⟩ If *D* 46 I] *written over* ⟨it⟩ *D* 49 be] feel *D* 56 Please] ⟨I wait⟩ Please *D* 63 His] *interlined above* ⟨The⟩ *D* 68 More] ⟨this is⟩ more *D*

As griev'd to force it on you so abrupt;
Yet, one day, you must know a grief, whose sting
Will sharpen more the longer 'tis conceal'd.
*Ludolph.* Say it at once, sir! dead—dead—is she dead?
75 *Gersa.* Mine is a cruel task: she is not dead,
And would, for your sake, she were innocent.
*Ludolph.* Hungarian! Thou amazest me beyond
All scope of thought, convulsest my heart's blood
To deadly churning! Gersa, you are young,
80 As I am; let me observe you, face to face:
Not grey-brow'd like the poisonous Ethelbert,
No rheumed eyes, no furrowing of age,
No wrinkles, where all vices nestle in
Like crannied vermin,—no! but fresh, and young,
85 And hopeful featur'd. Ha! by heaven you weep!
Tears, human tears! Do you repent you then
Of a curs'd torturer's office? Why shouldst join,—
Tell me,—the league of devils? Confess—confess—
The lie!
*Gersa.* Lie!—but begone all ceremonious points
90 Of honour battailous! I could not turn
My wrath against thee for the orbed world.
*Ludolph.* Your wrath, weak boy? Tremble at mine, unless
Retraction follow close upon the heels
Of that late stounding insult! Why has my sword
95 Not done already a sheer judgment on thee?
Despair, or eat thy words! Why, thou wast nigh
Whimpering away my reason! Hark 'e, sir,—
It is no secret, that Erminia,
Erminia, sir, was hidden in your tent,—
100 O bless'd asylum! Comfortable home!
Begone! I pity thee; thou art a gull,
Erminia's fresh puppet!
*Gersa.* Furious fire!
Thou mak'st me boil as hot as thou canst flame!

72 sting] *interlined above* ⟨bulk⟩ *D* 76 your] *interlined above* ⟨thy⟩ *D* 77 Hungarian] Thou liest *D*; Hungarian *interlined by Keats above* ⟨Thou liest⟩ *CB* 77 Thou] ⟨and such a lie⟩ thou *D* 78 All . . . blood] *the canceled s.p.* ⟨Gerza⟩ *appears beside this line in D; apparently Keats intended to follow* Thou liest! *in 77 with a reply by Gersa but then deleted this s.p. and continued Ludolph's speech* 80 As] *written over* ⟨So⟩ *CB* 83 No] *added in the margin in D* 85 Ha] ⟨Ah⟩ Ha *D* 92 weak] *added above the line in D* 94 that] *interlined above* ⟨your⟩ *D* 95 already a sheer] *successively* (*a*) its (*b*) a (*c*) already a sheer *D* 97 'e] ye *D* 98 It is] Is *D*; It is *interlined by Keats above* ⟨To⟩ (To *being Brown's misreading of D*) *CB* 103 Thou] *written over* ⟨You⟩ *D*

And in thy teeth I give thee back the lie!
105 Thou liest! Thou, Auranthe's fool! A wittol!
*Ludolph.* Look! look at this bright sword;
There is no part of it, to the very hilt,
But shall indulge itself about thine heart!
Draw! but remember thou must cower thy plumes,
110 As yesterday the Arab made thee stoop.
*Gersa.* Patience! Not here; I would not spill thy blood
Here, underneath this roof where Otho breathes,—
Thy father,—almost mine.
*Ludolph.* O faltering coward! [*Enter Page.*
Stay, stay; here is one I have half a word with.
Well? What ails thee, child?
*Page.* My lord!
115 *Ludolph.* What wouldst say?
*Page.* They are fled!
*Ludolph.* They! Who?
*Page.* When anxiously
I hasten'd back, your grieving messenger,
I found the stairs all dark, the lamps extinct,
And not a foot or whisper to be heard.
120 I thought her dead, and on the lowest step
Sat listening; when presently came by
Two muffled up,—one sighing heavily,
The other cursing low, whose voice I knew
For the Duke Conrad's. Close I follow'd them
125 Through the dark ways they chose to the open air;
And, as I follow'd, heard my lady speak.
*Ludolph.* Thy life answer the truth!
*Page.* The chamber's empty!
*Ludolph.* As I will be of mercy! So, at last,
This nail is in my temples!
*Gersa.* Be calm in this.
*Ludolph.* I am.
130 *Gersa.* And Albert too has disappear'd;
Ere I met you, I sought him every where;
You would not hearken.
*Ludolph.* Which way went they, boy?

109 thy] *made out of* these *D* 113 *s.d.* Enter] reenter *D* 115 What wouldst say?] Good fellow *D*; What wouldst say? *written by Keats beneath* ⟨My good fellow!⟩ *CB* 124 Close] ⟨Curious to⟩ Close *D* 126/127 ⟨*Ludolph.* Alas!⟩ *D* 128 mercy!] mercy—⟨must I have⟩ (*the next sentence*—So . . . temples!—*added afterward*) *D* 129 temples] temple *altered to* temples *CB*

*Gersa.* I'll hunt with you.
*Ludolph.* No, no, no. My senses are
Still whole. I have surviv'd. My arm is strong,—
135 My appetite sharp—for revenge! I'll no sharer
In my feast; my injury is all my own,
And so is my revenge, my lawful chattels!
Terrier, ferret them out! Burn—burn the witch!
Trace me their footsteps! Away! [*Exeunt.*

## ACT V

### SCENE I. *A part of the Forest.*

*Enter* CONRAD *and* AURANTHE.

*Auranthe.* Go no further; not a step more. Thou art
A master-plague in the midst of miseries.
Go,—I fear thee! I tremble every limb,
Who never shook before. There's moody death
5 In thy resolved looks! Yes, I could kneel
To pray thee far away! Conrad, go! go!—
There! yonder underneath the boughs I see
Our horses!
*Conrad.* Aye, and the man.
*Auranthe.* Yes, he is there!
Go, go,—no blood! no blood!—go, gentle Conrad!
*Conrad.* Farewell!
10 *Auranthe.* Farewell! For this heaven pardon you!
[*Exit* AURANTHE.
*Conrad.* If he survive one hour, then may I die
In unimagined tortures, or breathe through
A long life in the foulest sink o' the world!

136 my injury . . . own] *successively* (*following a dash*) (*a*) Jackall lead on (*b*) My revenge is my own ⟨goods⟩ right (*c*) My injury is all my own *D* 137/138 ⟨Jackall, lead on; the Lion preys to-night!⟩ *CB*; *D has the same line uncanceled* 139 Trace] *written over* ⟨Lead⟩ *D* *After* 139 End of the Fourth Act. *CB*

V.i.1 Thou art] *interlined above* ⟨you are⟩ *D* 2 master-plague] plague-spot *altered to* master-plague *D* 3 thee] *interlined above* ⟨you⟩ *D* 6 far] *added above the line in D* 8 the] a *D* 10 (*Conrad's speech*) Farewell] Farewell ⟨then⟩ *D* 10 *s.d.* Exit Auranthe] exit *D* 11–12 survive . . . In] escape me, may I die a death / Of *altered to* survive one hour, then may I die / In *CB*; *D has the same text as the original CB, with* a *interlined above* ⟨the⟩ 13 o'] of *D*

He dies! 'Tis well she do not advertise
15 The caitiff of the cold steel at his back. [*Exit* CONRAD.

*Enter* LUDOLPH *and Page.*

*Ludolph.* Miss'd the way, boy? Say not that on your peril!
*Page.* Indeed, indeed I cannot trace them further.
*Ludolph.* Must I stop here? Here solitary die?
Stifled beneath the thick oppressive shade
20 Of these dull boughs,—this oven of dark thickets,—
Silent,—without revenge,—pshaw!—bitter end,—
A bitter death,—a suffocating death,—
A gnawing—silent—deadly, quiet death!
Escap'd?—fled?—vanish'd? melted into air?
25 She's gone! I cannot clutch her! no revenge!
A muffled death, ensnared in horrid silence!
Suck'd to my grave amid a dreary calm!

15 *s.d.* Exit Conrad] exit *D* 18–32 *Ludolph.* Must . . . *Exeunt.*] *written on the opposite verso in D to replace:*

⟨*Ludolph.* What here! here {alone} solitary must I die
Without revenge? here stifled in the shade
Of these dull Boughs? Pshaw bitter bitter end—
A bitter death! a suffocating death!
[5] A gnawing, silent deadly quiet death!
Must she escape me? Can I not clutch her fast?
She's gone—away, away, away—and now
Each moment brings its poison—I must die
As near a{s} Hermit's death as patience—Oh!
[10] War! War! War! where is that illustrious noise
{To gasp away my Life}
To smother up this sound of labouring breath
This death song of the trees—{Blow Trumpeters!
O curs'd Auranthe!} [*Enter* ALBERT *wounded.*
Albert, here is hope!
Of Glorious {illuminate} clamour yet; Thrice villainous
Tell me where that detested woman is
Or this is through thee—
[15] *Albert.* My good Prince with me
The Sword as done its worst— [*Sinks.*⟩
[AURANTHE *shrieks.*
*Page.* My Lord. A noise
This way—Hark!
*Ludolph.* Yes, a glorious clamour yet— [*Exeunt.*

(4 bitter *interlined above* {suffocating} 5 quiet *interlined above* {Silent} 13 Of *added in the margin* 15 thee *written over* {you} 17 clamour *interlined above* {skuff} *The canceled s.d.'s* ⟨sinks⟩ *and* ⟨sinking⟩ *appear beside the first half of 12,* ⟨sinks⟩ *also beside the separate cancellation in the middle of 12, and* ⟨starts up⟩ *beside the last half of 12; the last line and a half are left undeleted*) 18 Must] ⟨Am⟩ Must *D* 24 Escap'd . . . air?] *D omits the question marks and has a colon at the end of the line* 25 clutch] catch *D*; clutch *interlined above* ⟨catch⟩ *CB*

O, where is that illustrious noise of war,
To smother up this sound of labouring breath,
This rustle of the trees! [AURANTHE *shrieks at a distance.*
30 *Page.* My lord, a noise!
This way—hark!
*Ludolph.* Yes, yes! A hope! A music!
A glorious clamour! Now I live again! [*Exeunt.*

SCENE II. *Another part of the Forest.*

*Enter* ALBERT (*wounded*).

*Albert.* Oh! for enough life to support me on
To Otho's feet!

*Enter* LUDOLPH.

*Ludolph.* Thrice villanous, stay there!
Tell me where that detested woman is,
Or this is through thee!
*Albert.* My good Prince, with me
5 The sword has done its worst; not without worst
Done to another,—Conrad has it home!
I see you know it all!
*Ludolph.* Where is his sister?

*Enter* AURANTHE.

*Auranthe.* Albert!
*Ludolph.* Ha! There! there!—He is the paramour!—

28 where is] *interlined above* ⟨for⟩ *D* 30 *s.d.* at a distance] *not in D* 32 Now] *D*; How *1848* (*CB missing*)

V.ii] *continuation of scene i in D, which has here, in place of heading, location, and opening s.d.,* Scene changes to another part of the wood / enter Albert wounded and ⟨Conr⟩ Ludolph (*D then omits the s.d. in 2 and numbers the next two scenes* 2nd *and* 3rd*—see below*) 4 thee] you *D* 6 Done . . . home!] *accompanied by the s.d.* sinks *in D* 7–8 I . . . Albert!] *in D Keats originally wrote Ludolph's half-line and Auranthe's* Albert! *as the beginning of 7, but then inserted the last half-line of Albert's speech* (I . . . all) *and recopied Ludolph's and Auranthe's speeches to follow it* 7 *s.d.* Enter Auranthe] Auranthe rushes in *interlined above* ⟨enter Auranthe⟩ *D* 8 Ha! There! there] *interlined above* ⟨There he {h} is⟩ *D* 8–9 He . . . innocence]

O thou Innocence!
I see it all he is the Paramour—
There, hug him—dying—O Barbarian
(*the second line inserted afterward*) *D*

There—hug him—dying! O, thou innocence,
10 Shrive him and comfort him at his last gasp,
Kiss down his eyelids! Was he not thy love?
Wilt thou forsake him at his latest hour?
Keep fearful and aloof from his last gaze,
His most uneasy moments, when cold death
15 Stands with the door ajar to let him in?
*Albert.* O that that door with hollow slam would close
Upon me sudden! for I cannot meet,
In all the unknown chambers of the dead,
Such horrors!
*Ludolph.* Auranthe! what can he mean?
20 What horrors? Is it not a joyous time?
Am I not married to a paragon
"Of personal beauty and untainted soul"?
A blushing fair-eyed purity? A sylph,
Whose snowy timid hand has never sinn'd
25 Beyond a flower pluck'd, white as itself?
Albert, you do insult my bride—your mistress—
To talk of horrors on our wedding-night!
*Albert.* Alas! poor Prince, I would you knew my heart!
'Tis not so guilty—
*Ludolph.* Hear, he pleads not guilty!
30 You are not? or, if so, what matters it?
You have escap'd me, free as the dusk air,
Hid in the forest, safe from my revenge,
I cannot catch you! You should laugh at me,
Poor cheated Ludolph! Make the forest hiss
35 With jeers at me! You tremble—faint at once,
You will come to again. O cockatrice,
I have you! Whither wander those fair eyes
To entice the devil to your help, that he
May change you to a spider, so to crawl
40 Into some cranny to escape my wrath?
*Albert.* Sometimes the counsel of a dying man
Doth operate quietly when his breath is gone:

10 Shrive] *D*; Shrine *1848* (*CB missing*) 11 Kiss] *written over* ⟨G⟩ *D* 11 love] friend *D* 12 latest] lastest *D* 13 Keep] *interlined above* ⟨Stand⟩ *D* 16–27 *Albert.* O . . . night!] *added on the opposite verso in D with a mark for insertion after 15; above the first line of this addition appears* ⟨*Albert.* O that {that noisels} the door⟩ 17 sudden] *interlined above* ⟨I shall⟩ (*the deleted words originally following a dash*) *D* 17 meet] ⟨find⟩ meet *D* 24 sinn'd] ⟨grasp'd⟩ sin'd *D* 25 pluck'd, white] pluck'd mild *interlined above* ⟨dainty⟩ *D* 29 Hear] Hear you *D* 41–47 *Albert.* Sometimes . . . hitch'd.] *added on the opposite verso in D with a mark for insertion after 40*

Disjoin those hands—part—part—do not destroy
Each other—forget her!—Our miseries
Are equal shared, and mercy is—
45 *Ludolph.* A boon
When one can compass it. Auranthe, try
Your oratory; your breath is not so hitch'd.
Aye, stare for help! [ALBERT *dies.*
There goes a spotted soul
Howling in vain along the hollow night!
50 Hear him! He calls you—sweet Auranthe, come!
*Auranthe.* Kill me!
*Ludolph.* No! What? Upon our marriage-night?
The earth would shudder at so foul a deed!
A fair bride! A sweet bride! An innocent bride!
No! we must revel it, as 'tis in use
55 In times of delicate brilliant ceremony:
Come, let me lead you to our halls again!
Nay, linger not; make no resistance, sweet;—
Will you? Ah, wretch, thou canst not, for I have
The strength of twenty lions 'gainst a lamb!
60 Now—one adieu for Albert!—Come away! [*Exeunt.*

SCENE III. *An inner Court of the Castle.*

*Enter* SIGIFRED, GONFRID, *and* THEODORE, *meeting.*

*Theodore.* Was ever such a night?
*Sigifred.* What horrors more?
Things unbeliev'd one hour, so strange they are,
The next hour stamps with credit.
*Theodore.* Your last news?
*Gonfrid.* After the page's story of the death

43 Disjoin] ⟨If⟩ Disjoin *D* 44 equal] almost equal *D* 47 hitch'd] *interlined above* ⟨short⟩ *D* 48 *s.d.* dies] groans and dies *D* 49 along] ⟨about⟩ along *D* 55 In] ⟨On day⟩ In (On *written over* {Of}) *D*

V.iii] *headed* Scene 2nd *in D* *Location* An . . . Castle] A court yard before one of the castle doors *D* An . . . Court] The Court-yard *altered to* An inner Court *CB* *Opening s.d.* Sigifred . . . Theodore] three Gentlemen *D*; Sigifred, Gonfrid, and Theodore (Gonfrid *written over* ⟨Th⟩ *and* Theodore *interlined above* ⟨1st Knight⟩) *CB* 1, 3, 9, 13, 14 *s.p.* Theodore] *ed*; 1st Gent *D*; 1st Knight *CB* 1, 5, 13, 16 *s.p.* Sigifred] 2nd Gent *D* 2 one . . . are] *interlined above* ⟨for strangeness, {the nex} in one hour⟩ (in *added above the line*) *D* 4, 6, 10, 13, 15, 17 *s.p.* Gonfrid] 3rd Gent *D*

Of Albert and Duke Conrad?
5 *Sigifred.* And the return
Of Ludolph with the Princess.
*Gonfrid.* No more, save
Prince Gersa's freeing Abbot Ethelbert,
And the sweet lady, fair Erminia,
From prison.
*Theodore.* Where are they now? Hast yet heard?
10 *Gonfrid.* With the sad Emperor they are closeted;
I saw the three pass slowly up the stairs,
The lady weeping, the old abbot cowl'd.
*Sigifred.* What next?
*Theodore.* I ache to think on't.
*Gonfrid.* 'Tis with fate.
*Theodore.* One while these proud towers are hush'd as death.
15 *Gonfrid.* The next our poor Prince fills the arched rooms
With ghastly ravings.
*Sigifred.* I do fear his brain.
*Gonfrid.* I will see more. Bear you so stout a heart?
[*Exeunt into the Castle.*

SCENE IV. *A Cabinet, opening towards a Terrace.*

OTHO, ERMINIA, ETHELBERT, *and a Physician, discovered.*

*Otho.* O, my poor boy! My son! My son! My Ludolph!
Have ye no comfort for me, ye physicians
Of the weak body and soul?
*Ethelbert.* 'Tis not in medicine,
Either of heaven or earth, can cure, unless
5 Fit time be chosen to administer.
*Otho.* A kind forbearance, holy abbot. Come,
Erminia; here sit by me, gentle girl;
Give me thy hand; hast thou forgiven me?
*Erminia.* Would I were with the saints to pray for you!
10 *Otho.* Why will ye keep me from my darling child?

9 Where] ⟨Ah!⟩ Where *D* 11 slowly] *added above the line in D* 14 while . . . proud] minute all these *altered to* while all these poud *D* 15 fills] *added above the line in D* 17 *s.d.* Exeunt . . . Castle] they go in *D*

V.iv] *headed* Scene 3rd *in D* *Location* opening . . . Terrace] *not in D* 3 weak] *interlined above* ⟨poor⟩ *D* 3 in] the *D*

*Physician.* Forgive me, but he must not see thy face.
*Otho.* Is then a father's countenance a Gorgon?
Hath it not comfort in it? Would it not
Console my poor boy, cheer him, heal his spirits?
15 Let me embrace him; let me speak to him;
I will! Who hinders me? Who's Emperor?
*Physician.* You may not, sire; 'twould overwhelm him quite,
He is so full of grief and passionate wrath;
Too heavy a sigh would kill him, or do worse.
20 He must be sav'd by fine contrivances;
And, most especially, we must keep clear
Out of his sight a father whom he loves;
His heart is full, it can contain no more,
And do its ruddy office.
*Ethelbert.* Sage advice;
25 We must endeavour how to ease and slacken
The tight-wound energies of his despair,
Not make them tenser.
*Otho.* Enough! I hear, I hear.
Yet you were about to advise more,—I listen.
*Ethelbert.* This learned doctor will agree with me,
30 That not in the smallest point should he be thwarted,
Or gainsaid by one word; his very motions,
Nods, becks, and hints, should be obey'd with care,
Even on the moment; so his troubled mind
May cure itself.
*Physician.* There are no other means.
35 *Otho.* Open the door; let's hear if all is quiet.
*Physician.* Beseech you, sire, forbear.
*Erminia.* Do, do.
*Otho.* I command!
Open it straight;—hush!—quiet!—my lost boy!
My miserable child!
*Ludolph* (*indistinctly without*). Fill, fill my goblet,—here's a health!
40 *Erminia.* O, close the door!
*Otho.* Let, let me hear his voice; this cannot last;

22 father] *written over* ⟨B⟩ *D* 26 despair] *interlined above* ⟨hot Soul⟩ *D* 34 are] is *D* 37 it straight] *interlined above* ⟨the Door⟩ *D* 37 hush] Sh *D* 39 *Ludolph . . .* health!] *added on the opposite verso in D* (*the present 38 and 40 originally constituting a single pentameter line*) 39 *s.d.* indistinctly without] distant raving *D* 39 here's] here *D*

And fain would I catch up his dying words,
Though my own knell they be! This cannot last!
O let me catch his voice—for lo! I hear
45 A whisper in this silence that he's dead!
It is so!—Gersa?

*Enter* GERSA.

*Physician.* Say, how fares the Prince?
*Gersa.* More calm; his features are less wild and flush'd;
Once he complain'd of weariness.
*Physician.* Indeed!
'Tis good,—'tis good; let him but fall asleep,
That saves him.
50 *Otho.* Gersa, watch him like a child;
Ward him from harm,—and bring me better news!
*Physician.* Humour him to the height. I fear to go;
For should he catch a glimpse of my dull garb,
It might affright him, fill him with suspicion
55 That we believe him sick, which must not be.
*Gersa.* I will invent what soothing means I can.

[*Exit* GERSA.

*Physician.* This should cheer up your Highness; the weariness
Is a good symptom, and most favourable;
It gives me pleasant hopes. Please you, walk forth
60 Upon the terrace; the refreshing air
Will blow one half of your sad doubts away. [*Exeunt.*

44 catch] *interlined above* ⟨hear⟩ *D* 45 A . . . dead] This silence whisper me that he is dead *interlined above* ⟨A whisper in this silence that he's dead⟩ *D* 52–61 I . . . *Exeunt.*] *written on the opposite verso in D to replace:*

⟨*Gerza.* It shall be done—
But for myself I keep me from his sight. [*Exit—scene draws.*⟩

(*Keats first wrote 52b–56 as a replacement for this text and then further added 57–61 in the space above the revised lines, indicating their position with "close of this scene"*) 53 he] *squeezed in afterward in D* 56 invent . . . can] *interlined above* ⟨not be remiss—⟩ ⟨obey your wishes⟩ *D* 56 *s.d.* Exit Gersa] exit ⟨scene draws⟩ (*see note to 52–61*) *D* 57 the] *made out of* this *D* 58 good . . . favourable] most gentle symptom, of the best *altered to* good symptom, and most favourable *D* 60 Upon] Onto *D*

SCENE V. *A Banquetting Hall, brilliantly illuminated, and set forth with all costly magnificence, with supper-tables, laden with services of gold and silver. A door in the back scene, guarded by two Soldiers. Lords, Ladies, Knights, Gentlemen, etc., whispering sadly, and ranging themselves; part entering and part discovered.*

*First Knight.* Grievously are we tantalised, one and all;
Sway'd here and there, commanded to and fro,
As though we were the shadows of a sleep,
And link'd to a dreaming fancy. What do we here?
5 *Gonfrid.* I am no seer; you know we must obey
The Prince from A to Z, though it should be
To set the place in flames. I pray, hast heard
Where the most wicked Princess is?
*First Knight.* There, sir,
In the next room; have you remark'd those two
Stout soldiers posted at the door?
10 *Gonfrid.* For what? [*They whisper.*
*First Lady.* How ghast a train!
*Second Lady.* Sure this should be some splendid burial.
*First Lady.* What fearful whispering!—See, see,—Gersa there!

*Enter* GERSA.

*Gersa.* Put on your brightest looks; smile if you can;
15 Behave as all were happy; keep your eyes
From the least watch upon him; if he speaks
To any one, answer, collectedly,
Without surprise, his questions, howe'er strange.
Do this to the utmost,—though, alas! with me
20 The remedy grows hopeless! Here he comes,—
Observe what I have said,—show no surprise.

*Enter* LUDOLPH, *followed by* SIGIFRED *and Page.*

*Ludolph.* A splendid company! rare beauties here!
I should have Orphean lips, and Plato's fancy,

V.v] *two leaves containing the heading, location, and original text of 1–58 are missing from D*; *a revised 1–10 (source of the D citations below) survives on the verso of the leaf preceding the opening of the scene* *Location* A door . . . Soldiers.] *added on the opposite verso in CB* Lords] ⟨Music at intervals.⟩ Lords *CB* 1, 8 *s.p.* Knight] Lord *D* 1 Grievously] *interlined above* ⟨How⟩ *D* 1 tantalised, one] tantalized ⟨here⟩, one *D* 3 sleep] dream *D* 4 dreaming] sleeping *D* 5, 10 *s.p.* Gonfrid] 2nd Lord *D* 10 posted] ⟨pacing someti⟩ ⟨standing⟩ posted *D* 16 upon] *interlined above* ⟨of⟩ *CB*

Amphion's utterance, toned with his lyre,
25 Or the deep key of Jove's sonorous mouth,
To give fit salutation. Methought I heard,
As I came in, some whispers,—what of that?
'Tis natural men should whisper; at the kiss
Of Psyche given by Love, there was a buzz
30 Among the gods!—and silence is as natural.
These draperies are fine, and, being a mortal,
I should desire no better; yet, in truth,
There must be some superior costliness,
Some wider-domed high magnificence!
35 I would have, as a mortal I may not,
Hangings of heaven's clouds, purple and gold,
Slung from the spheres; gauzes of silver mist,
Loop'd up with cords of twisted wreathed light,
And tassell'd round with weeping meteors!
40 These pendent lamps and chandeliers are bright
As earthly fires from dull dross can be cleans'd;
Yet could my eyes drink up intenser beams
Undazzled,—this is darkness,—when I close
These lids, I see far fiercer brilliances,—
45 Skies full of splendid moons, and shooting stars,
And spouting exhalations, diamond fires,
And panting fountains quivering with deep glows!
Yes—this is dark—is it not dark?
*Sigifred.* My lord,
'Tis late; the lights of festival are ever
Quench'd in the morn.
50 *Ludolph.* 'Tis not to-morrow then?
*Sigifred.* 'Tis early dawn.
*Gersa.* Indeed full time we slept;
Say you so, Prince?
*Ludolph.* I say I quarrell'd with you;
We did not tilt each other,—that's a blessing,—
Good gods! no innocent blood upon my head!
*Sigifred.* Retire, Gersa!
55 *Ludolph.* There should be three more here:
For two of them, they stay away perhaps,
Being gloomy-minded, haters of fair revels,—
They know their own thoughts best. As for the third,

58 best . . . third]
best; ⟨tis true indeed
They fail in their allegiance to their Prince,

We'll have her presently; aye, you shall see her,
60 And wonder at her, friends, she is so fair;
Deep blue eyes, semi-shaded in white lids,
Finish'd with lashes fine for more soft shade,
Completed by her twin-arch'd ebon-brows;
White temples, of exactest elegance,
65 Of even mould, felicitous and smooth;
Cheeks fashion'd tenderly on either side,
So perfect, so divine, that our poor eyes
Are dazzled with the sweet proportioning,
And wonder that 'tis so,—the magic chance!
70 Her nostrils, small, fragrant, fairy-delicate;
Her lips—I swear no human bones e'er wore
So taking a disguise;—you shall behold her!
She is the world's chief jewel, and, by heaven,
She's mine by right of marriage!—she is mine!
75 Patience, good people, in fit time I send
A summoner,—she will obey my call,
Being a wife most mild and dutiful.
First I would hear what music is prepared
To herald and receive her; let me hear!
80 *Sigifred.* Bid the musicians soothe him tenderly.
[*A soft strain of music.*
*Ludolph.* Ye have none better? No, I am content;
'Tis a rich sobbing melody, with reliefs
Full and majestic; it is well enough,
And will be sweeter, when ye see her pace
85 Sweeping into this presence, glisten'd o'er
With emptied caskets, and her train upheld
By ladies, habited in robes of lawn
Sprinkled with golden crescents, others bright
In silks with spangles shower'd, and bow'd to
90 By duchesses and pearled margravines!

---

But if they have more urgent business,
I shall forgive them heartily⟩. As for the third
(As for *made out of* For *in the last line*) *CB* 61–72 Deep . . . her!] *written on a separate sheet in CB and marked for insertion after 60* 61 in] *interlined above* ⟨with⟩ *D* 64 of] ⟨moulded in even⟩ of (*the last two deleted words run together—in effect,* neven *with a dotted "n"*) *D* 69–70 And . . . delicate;] *marked for transposition to follow 60 in D* 80 *Sigifred.* Bid . . . tenderly.] *inserted afterward in D* 80 tenderly] ⟨with⟩ tenderly *D* 80 *s.d.* A . . . music.] *not in D* 82 with] *made out of* which *D* 85 glisten'd o'er] glistening *altered to* glisten'd o'er *D* 87–90 By . . . margravines!] *the first two words of 87 and 88 and the first three words of 89 and 90 have been torn away in D* 88 golden] *interlined above* ⟨little⟩ *D*

Sad, that the fairest creature of the earth—
I pray you mind me not—'tis sad, I say,
That the extremest beauty of the world
Should so entrench herself away from me,
95 Behind a barrier of engender'd guilt!
*Second Lady.* Ah! what a moan!
*First Knight.* Most piteous indeed!
*Ludolph.* She shall be brought before this company,
And then—then—
*First Lady.* He muses.
*Gersa.* O, Fortune, where will this end!
100 *Sigifred.* I guess his purpose! Indeed he must not have
That pestilence brought in,—that cannot be,
There we must stop him.
*Gersa.* I am lost! Hush, hush!
He is about to rave again.
*Ludolph.* A barrier of guilt! I was the fool,
105 She was the cheater! Who's the cheater now,
And who the fool? The entrapp'd, the caged fool,
The bird-lim'd raven? She shall croak to death!
Secure! Methinks I have her in my fist,
To crush her with my heel! Wait; wait! I marvel
110 My father keeps away. Good friend—ah! Sigifred?—
Do bring him to me,—and Erminia
I fain would see before I sleep,—and Ethelbert,
That he may bless me, as I know he will,
Though I have curs'd him.
*Sigifred.* Rather suffer me
To lead you to them.
115 *Ludolph.* No, excuse me,—no!
The day is not quite done. Go, bring them hither.
[*Exit* SIGIFRED.
Certes, a father's smile should, like sunlight,
Slant on my sheeved harvest of ripe bliss.
Besides, I thirst to pledge my lovely bride
120 In a deep goblet: let me see—what wine?
The strong Iberian juice? or mellow Greek?

*After* 90 e you, he bursts in tears! *interlined above* ⟨you, {he} doth he not weep?⟩ (*s.p. and the opening three or four words of both the deleted and the revised lines torn away*) *D*; *91–109 through* wait! *are not in D* (*see Textual Note to 91–109*) 112 Ethelbert] holy Ethelbert *D* 118 sheeved] sheefed *interlined above* ⟨gathed⟩ *D* 121–126 The . . . veins!] *first drafted on a separate leaf in D* (*the other side containing the added IV.ii.23b–28*), *as follows:*

Or pale Calabrian? or the Tuscan grape?
Or of old Ætna's pulpy wine-presses,
Black stain'd with the fat vintage, as it were
125 The purple slaughter-house, where Bacchus' self
Prick'd his own swollen veins! Where is my page?
*Page.* Here—here!
*Ludolph.* Be ready to obey me; anon thou shalt
Bear a soft message for me; for the hour
130 Draws near when I must make a winding up
Of bridal-mysteries—a fine-spun vengeance!
Carve it on my tomb, that, when I rest beneath,
Men shall confess,—this prince was gull'd and cheated,
But from the ashes of disgrace he rose
135 More than a fiery dragon, and did burn
His ignominy up in purging fires!
Did I not send, sir, but a moment past,
For my father?
*Gersa.* You did.
*Ludolph.* Perhaps 'twould be
Much better he came not.
*Gersa.* He enters now!

*Enter* OTHO, ERMINIA, ETHELBERT, SIGIFRED, *and Physician.*

140 *Ludolph.* Oh! thou good man, against whose sacred head
I was a mad conspirator, chiefly too
For the sake of my fair newly wedded wife,

---

Mellow greek⟨s⟩ Sir,
⟨Purple Sicilian;⟩
Or pale calabrian, or the tuscan grape
⟨Or of old Œtna's purple stained press{es}?⟩
Or of old Œtna's pulpy Winepresses
⟨Black⟩
Black stained, ⟨with⟩ ⟨and⟩ with the fat vintage as 'tis were
The purple slaughter house where Bacchus self
Prickd his own swollen veins—

(Or *made out of* Of *in the fifth of these lines, and* purple slaughter house *made out of* slaughter house of Bacchus *in the next-to-last line*) 121 Iberian] Hyberian *D*; Hyberian *altered to* Iberian *CB* 130 winding] ⟨f⟩⟨righteous⟩ winding *D* 132 it] it *altered to* 'it (*for* 't) *D* 135 dragon] Phœnix *D*; Dragon *interlined by Keats above* ⟨Phœnix⟩ *CB* 137 send,] send for my *altered to* send, *D* 138 *s.p.* Gersa] 1st Lord *D* 139 Much] *added in the margin in D* 139 *s.p.* Gersa] Lord *D* 139 *s.d.* Sigifred, and Physician] and Sigifred *altered to* Sigifred & Physician *CB* (*all of the s.d. after* Enter Otho *has been torn away in D*) 140–143 against . . . sad!] *written by Keats on the opposite verso in CB to replace* ⟨nay, do not look

Now to be punish'd,—do not look so sad!
Those charitable eyes will thaw my heart,
145 Those tears will wash away a just resolve,
A verdict ten-times sworn! Awake—awake—
Put on a judge's brow, and use a tongue
Made iron-stern by habit! Thou shalt see
A deed to be applauded, 'scribed in gold!
150 Join a loud voice to mine, and so denounce
What I alone will execute!
*Otho.* Dear son,
What is it? By your father's love, I sue
That it be nothing merciless!
*Ludolph.* To that demon?
Not so! No! She is in temple-stall
155 Being garnish'd for the sacrifice, and I,
The priest of justice, will immolate her
Upon the altar of wrath! She stings me through!—
Even as the worm doth feed upon the nut,
So she, a scorpion, preys upon my brain!
160 I feel her gnawing here!—Let her but vanish,
Then, father, I will lead your legions forth,
Compact in steeled squares, and speared files,
And bid our trumpets speak a fell rebuke
To nations drows'd in peace!
*Otho.* To-morrow, son,
Be your word law; forget to-day—
165 *Ludolph.* I will
When I have finish'd it! Now,—now, I'm pight,
Tight-footed for the deed!
*Erminia.* Alas! Alas!
*Ludolph.* What angel's voice is that? Erminia!
Ah! gentlest creature, whose sweet innocence
170 Was almost murder'd; I am penitent,
Wilt thou forgive me? And thou, holy man,
Good Ethelbert, shall I die in peace with you?
*Erminia.* Die, my lord!

so sad!⟩; *for all of 140–143 D has (as CB originally had)* O thou good Man,—nay do not look so sad! *but the revised lines also appear copied fair in Keats's hand on a separate slip that, pasted on a larger sheet, now constitutes leaf 77 of the draft MS as reconstructed in the main Textual Note* 154 Not so] *interlined above* ⟨Impossible⟩ *D* 156 The] ⟨And the⟩ The *D* 158 feed upon] feast within *D* 159 brain] Brains *D*; brain⟨s⟩ *CB* 161 lead] *interlined above* ⟨have⟩ *D* 163 trumpets] *added above the line in D*

*Ludolph.* I feel it possible.
*Otho.* Physician?
*Physician.* I fear me he is past my skill.
*Otho.* Not so!
175 *Ludolph.* I see it—I see it—I have been wandering!
Half mad—not right here—I forget my purpose.
Bestir—bestir—Auranthe! Ha! ha! ha!
Youngster! Page! go bid them drag her to me!
Obey! This shall finish it! [*Draws a dagger.*
*Otho.* Oh, my son! my son!
*Sigifred.* This must not be—stop there!
180 *Ludolph.* Am I obey'd?
A little talk with her—no harm—haste! haste! [*Exit Page.*
Set her before me—never fear I can strike.
*Several Voices.* My lord! My lord!
*Gersa.* Good Prince!
*Ludolph.* Why do ye trouble me? out—out—away!
185 There she is! take that! and that! no, no,
That's not well done.—Where is she?
[*The doors open. Enter Page. Several women are seen grouped about* AURANTHE *in the inner-room.*
*Page.* Alas! My lord, my lord! they cannot move her!
Her arms are stiff,—her fingers clench'd and cold!
*Ludolph.* She's dead! [*Staggers and falls into their arms.*
*Ethelbert.* Take away the dagger.
*Gersa.* Softly! so!
*Otho.* Thank God for that!
190 *Sigifred.* It could not harm him now.

173–174 *Otho.* Physician? . . . so!] *added (with the variant given in the next note) on the opposite verso in D* 174 Not so!] Eh! no? *D*; Not so! *interlined by Keats above* ⟨Eh? no?⟩ *CB* 178 go] *squeezed in afterward in D* 178 bid them] *interlined above* ⟨fetch her,⟩ *D* 179 *s.d.* a] his *D* 180–182 *Sigifred.* This . . . strike.] *added on the opposite verso in D with a mark for insertion after 179* 180 Am] ⟨Slaves⟩ Am *D* 181 *s.d.* Exit Page.] *not in D (but see the next note); inserted afterward in CB* 182/183 ethelbert leads off Erminia / others follow (*s.d.*) *D* 183 *s.p.'s* Several Voices *and* Gersa] *D has the single s.p.* Voices (*apparently to serve for the entire line*) *interlined between* ⟨Erminia Ethelbert⟩ *and* ⟨and the rest⟩ 184 out—out] out—out—out *D* 186 *s.d.* The . . . room] Page return with one of Auranthe's women (*this also serves as s.p. for 187*) *D* 187 Alas] *added in the margin in D* 187 they] *interlined above* ⟨we⟩ *D* 189 dead!] dead—⟨I am content—Nobles good night— / I will to bed—tomorrow—⟩ *D* 189 *s.d.* Staggers . . . arms] ⟨ falls and dies⟩ (*deleted with the text given in preceding note and nothing substituted*) *D* 190 that!] that! / ⟨*Ethelbert.* I fear the dagger⟩ *D* 190 It . . . now] I fear it could not ham him *D*; I fear it could not harm him *altered to* It could not harm him now *CB*

*Gersa.* No!—brief be his anguish!
*Ludolph.* She's gone! I am content—nobles, good night!
Where is your hand, father?—what sultry air!
We are all weary—faint—set ope the doors—
195 I will to bed!—To-morrow— [*Dies.*

THE CURTAIN FALLS.

191 No . . . anguish!] *added (without s.p.) at the bottom of the final page in D and preceded by an earlier fragmentary attempt,* He ⟨goes⟩ 193 Where . . . air!] *not in D; added by Keats on the opposite verso in CB (with* Where is *interlined above* ⟨Give me⟩ *and* what sultry air *made out of* how sultry 'tis). *Above the added line appears, in Keats's hand,* ⟨Father retire⟩ 194 set] ⟨open the⟩ set *D* *Final s.d.* The] *not in D*

# *Lamia*

## PART I

Upon a time, before the faery broods
Drove Nymph and Satyr from the prosperous woods,
Before King Oberon's bright diadem,
Sceptre, and mantle, clasp'd with dewy gem,
5 Frighted away the Dryads and the Fauns
From rushes green, and brakes, and cowslip'd lawns,
The ever-smitten Hermes empty left
His golden throne, bent warm on amorous theft:
From high Olympus had he stolen light,
10 On this side of Jove's clouds, to escape the sight
Of his great summoner, and made retreat
Into a forest on the shores of Crete.
For somewhere in that sacred island dwelt
A nymph, to whom all hoofed Satyrs knelt;
15 At whose white feet the languid Tritons poured
Pearls, while on land they wither'd and adored.
Fast by the springs where she to bathe was wont,
And in those meads where sometime she might haunt,
Were strewn rich gifts, unknown to any Muse,
20 Though Fancy's casket were unlock'd to choose.
Ah, what a world of love was at her feet!
So Hermes thought, and a celestial heat
Burnt from his winged heels to either ear,
That from a whiteness, as the lily clear,
25 Blush'd into roses 'mid his golden hair,
Fallen in jealous curls about his shoulders bare.

*Lamia.* Text (including heading and endnote) from *1820.* Variants and other readings from Keats's draft (*D*, extant for I.185–190, 324–329, 386b–397, II.26–74, 85–92, 122–147, 191–198 only), the extract of II.122–162 plus eighteen additional lines in his letter to Taylor, 5 September 1819 (*L*), and the extant fair copy (*FC*). The apparatus also includes readings of the extant proof-sheets in three places where the *1820* text apparently originated with the printer (I.132, 155, 270—further proof variants from *FC* are listed at the end of the main Textual Note), as well as all of Keats's and a selection of Woodhouse's substantive alterations *on* the proofs (those by Woodhouse that did not affect *1820* are given in separate Textual Notes). For Keats's note to the title in *FC* see below for II.311. The first division heading ("Part 1st") is a later addition in *FC*.

I.4 mantle] *interlined above* ⟨sandalls⟩ *FC*   15 At . . . white] And at whose *altered to* at whose white *FC*

From vale to vale, from wood to wood, he flew,
Breathing upon the flowers his passion new,
And wound with many a river to its head,
30 To find where this sweet nymph prepar'd her secret bed:
In vain; the sweet nymph might nowhere be found,
And so he rested, on the lonely ground,
Pensive, and full of painful jealousies
Of the Wood-Gods, and even the very trees.
35 There as he stood, he heard a mournful voice,
Such as once heard, in gentle heart, destroys
All pain but pity: thus the lone voice spake:
"When from this wreathed tomb shall I awake!
When move in a sweet body fit for life,
40 And love, and pleasure, and the ruddy strife
Of hearts and lips! Ah, miserable me!"
The God, dove-footed, glided silently
Round bush and tree, soft-brushing, in his speed,
The taller grasses and full-flowering weed,
45 Until he found a palpitating snake,
Bright, and cirque-couchant in a dusky brake.

She was a gordian shape of dazzling hue,
Vermilion-spotted, golden, green, and blue;
Striped like a zebra, freckled like a pard,
50 Eyed like a peacock, and all crimson barr'd;
And full of silver moons, that, as she breathed,
Dissolv'd, or brighter shone, or interwreathed
Their lustres with the gloomier tapestries—
So rainbow-sided, touch'd with miseries,
55 She seem'd, at once, some penanced lady elf,
Some demon's mistress, or the demon's self.
Upon her crest she wore a wannish fire
Sprinkled with stars, like Ariadne's tiar:
Her head was serpent, but ah, bitter-sweet!
60 She had a woman's mouth with all its pearls complete:
And for her eyes: what could such eyes do there
But weep, and weep, that they were born so fair?
As Proserpine still weeps for her Sicilian air.
Her throat was serpent, but the words she spake
65 Came, as through bubbling honey, for Love's sake,

27 ¶From . . . ] *FC*; *new page but no ¶ indention in 1820* 48 Vermilion] *interlined above* ⟨Cerulean⟩ *FC*

And thus; while Hermes on his pinions lay,
Like a stoop'd falcon ere he takes his prey.

"Fair Hermes, crown'd with feathers, fluttering light,
I had a splendid dream of thee last night:
70 I saw thee sitting, on a throne of gold,
Among the Gods, upon Olympus old,
The only sad one; for thou didst not hear
The soft, lute-finger'd Muses chaunting clear,
Nor even Apollo when he sang alone,
75 Deaf to his throbbing throat's long, long melodious moan.
I dreamt I saw thee, robed in purple flakes,
Break amorous through the clouds, as morning breaks,
And, swiftly as a bright Phœbean dart,
Strike for the Cretan isle; and here thou art!
80 Too gentle Hermes, hast thou found the maid?"
Whereat the star of Lethe not delay'd
His rosy eloquence, and thus inquired:
"Thou smooth-lipp'd serpent, surely high inspired!
Thou beauteous wreath, with melancholy eyes,
85 Possess whatever bliss thou canst devise,
Telling me only where my nymph is fled,—
Where she doth breathe!" "Bright planet, thou hast said,"
Return'd the snake, "but seal with oaths, fair God!"
"I swear," said Hermes, "by my serpent rod,
90 And by thine eyes, and by thy starry crown!"
Light flew his earnest words, among the blossoms blown.
Then thus again the brilliance feminine:
"Too frail of heart! for this lost nymph of thine,
Free as the air, invisibly, she strays
95 About these thornless wilds; her pleasant days
She tastes unseen; unseen her nimble feet
Leave traces in the grass and flowers sweet;
From weary tendrils, and bow'd branches green,
She plucks the fruit unseen, she bathes unseen:
100 And by my power is her beauty veil'd
To keep it unaffronted, unassail'd
By the love-glances of unlovely eyes,
Of Satyrs, Fauns, and blear'd Silenus' sighs.

69 splendid] silver *FC* 78 as a bright] as a mission'd *FC* (*altered on the proofs by Keats first to* straight as a *and then to* as a bright—*see Textual Note*) 93 Too frail] *interlined above* ⟨Superb⟩ *FC*

Pale grew her immortality, for woe
105 Of all these lovers, and she grieved so
I took compassion on her, bade her steep
Her hair in weïrd syrops, that would keep
Her loveliness invisible, yet free
To wander as she loves, in liberty.
110 Thou shalt behold her, Hermes, thou alone,
If thou wilt, as thou swearest, grant my boon!"
Then, once again, the charmed God began
An oath, and through the serpent's ears it ran
Warm, tremulous, devout, psalterian.
115 Ravish'd, she lifted her Circean head,
Blush'd a live damask, and swift-lisping said,
"I was a woman, let me have once more
A woman's shape, and charming as before.
I love a youth of Corinth—O the bliss!
120 Give me my woman's form, and place me where he is.
Stoop, Hermes, let me breathe upon thy brow,
And thou shalt see thy sweet nymph even now."
The God on half-shut feathers sank serene,
She breath'd upon his eyes, and swift was seen
125 Of both the guarded nymph near-smiling on the green.
It was no dream; or say a dream it was,
Real are the dreams of Gods, and smoothly pass
Their pleasures in a long immortal dream.
One warm, flush'd moment, hovering, it might seem
130 Dash'd by the wood-nymph's beauty, so he burn'd;
Then, lighting on the printless verdure, turn'd
To the swoon'd serpent, and with languid arm,
Delicate, put to proof the lythe Caducean charm.
So done, upon the nymph his eyes he bent
135 Full of adoring tears and blandishment,
And towards her stept: she, like a moon in wane,
Faded before him, cower'd, nor could restrain
Her fearful sobs, self-folding like a flower
That faints into itself at evening hour:

104 grew] wox *FC* (*altered on the proofs by Keats to* grew) 114 psalterian] bright-ton'd, psalterian *FC* (bright-ton'd *deleted on the proofs by Woodhouse*) · 115 lifted] lifted up *FC* (up *deleted on the proofs by Keats*) 116 a live] to live *FC* (*altered on the proofs by Keats to* living) 123 sank] sunk *FC* (*altered on the proofs by Woodhouse to* sank) 132 languid] langrous *FC* (languid *in the proofs*) 133 lythe] *deleted on the proofs by Keats and then restored there by Woodhouse*

140 But the God fostering her chilled hand,
She felt the warmth, her eyelids open'd bland,
And, like new flowers at morning song of bees,
Bloom'd, and gave up her honey to the lees.
Into the green-recessed woods they flew;
145 Nor grew they pale, as mortal lovers do.

Left to herself, the serpent now began
To change; her elfin blood in madness ran,
Her mouth foam'd, and the grass, therewith besprent,
Wither'd at dew so sweet and virulent;
150 Her eyes in torture fix'd, and anguish drear,
Hot, glaz'd, and wide, with lid-lashes all sear,
Flash'd phosphor and sharp sparks, without one cooling tear.
The colours all inflam'd throughout her train,
She writh'd about, convuls'd with scarlet pain:
155 A deep volcanian yellow took the place
Of all her milder-mooned body's grace;
And, as the lava ravishes the mead,
Spoilt all her silver mail, and golden brede;
Made gloom of all her frecklings, streaks and bars,
160 Eclips'd her crescents, and lick'd up her stars:
So that, in moments few, she was undrest
Of all her sapphires, greens, and amethyst,
And rubious-argent: of all these bereft,
Nothing but pain and ugliness were left.
165 Still shone her crown; that vanish'd, also she
Melted and disappear'd as suddenly;
And in the air, her new voice luting soft,
Cried, "Lycius! gentle Lycius!"—Borne aloft
With the bright mists about the mountains hoar
170 These words dissolv'd: Crete's forests heard no more.

Whither fled Lamia, now a lady bright,
A full-born beauty new and exquisite?
She fled into that valley they pass o'er
Who go to Corinth from Cenchreas' shore;

142 And . . . new] And she, like *altered to* And like new *FC* 155 volcanian] vulcanian *FC* (volcanian *in the proofs*) 167–168 in . . . aloft] her new voice, soft luting in the air / Cried "Lycius! gentle Lycius, where, ah where!" *FC* 173–174 pass . . . shore] must pass / Who go from Corinth out to Cencreas *FC* (*altered on the proofs by Keats to* must skirt / Who go from Corinth to Cenchrea's port, *after which Woodhouse made further changes on the proofs to produce the 1820 wording*)

175 And rested at the foot of those wild hills,
The rugged founts of the Peræan rills,
And of that other ridge whose barren back
Stretches, with all its mist and cloudy rack,
South-westward to Cleone. There she stood
180 About a young bird's flutter from a wood,
Fair, on a sloping green of mossy tread,
By a clear pool, wherein she passioned
To see herself escap'd from so sore ills,
While her robes flaunted with the daffodils.

185 Ah, happy Lycius!—for she was a maid
More beautiful than ever twisted braid,
Or sigh'd, or blush'd, or on spring-flowered lea
Spread a green kirtle to the minstrelsy:
A virgin purest lipp'd, yet in the lore
190 Of love deep learned to the red heart's core:
Not one hour old, yet of sciential brain
To unperplex bliss from its neighbour pain;
Define their pettish limits, and estrange
Their points of contact, and swift counterchange;
195 Intrigue with the specious chaos, and dispart
Its most ambiguous atoms with sure art;
As though in Cupid's college she had spent
Sweet days a lovely graduate, still unshent,
And kept his rosy terms in idle languishment.

200 Why this fair creature chose so fairily
By the wayside to linger, we shall see;
But first 'tis fit to tell how she could muse
And dream, when in the serpent prison-house,
Of all she list, strange or magnificent:
205 How, ever, where she will'd, her spirit went;
Whether to faint Elysium, or where
Down through tress-lifting waves the Nereids fair
Wind into Thetis' bower by many a pearly stair;

176 founts . . . Peræan] paps of little Perea's *FC* (paps *altered on the proofs by Woodhouse to* founts *and* little Perea's *altered by Keats to* the Peræan) 185 Ah . . . maid]

Ah! never heard of, delight never known,
Save of one happy mortal! only one;
Lycius the happy: for she was a Maid *D*, *FC*

192 its] her *FC* (*altered on the proofs by Woodhouse to* its) 196 Its] Their *FC* (*altered on the proofs by Woodhouse to* Its)

Or where God Bacchus drains his cups divine,
210 Stretch'd out, at ease, beneath a glutinous pine;
Or where in Pluto's gardens palatine
Mulciber's columns gleam in far piazzian line.
And sometimes into cities she would send
Her dream, with feast and rioting to blend;
215 And once, while among mortals dreaming thus,
She saw the young Corinthian Lycius
Charioting foremost in the envious race,
Like a young Jove with calm uneager face,
And fell into a swooning love of him.
220 Now on the moth-time of that evening dim
He would return that way, as well she knew,
To Corinth from the shore; for freshly blew
The eastern soft wind, and his galley now
Grated the quaystones with her brazen prow
225 In port Cenchreas, from Egina isle
Fresh anchor'd; whither he had been awhile
To sacrifice to Jove, whose temple there
Waits with high marble doors for blood and incense rare.
Jove heard his vows, and better'd his desire;
230 For by some freakful chance he made retire
From his companions, and set forth to walk,
Perhaps grown wearied of their Corinth talk:
Over the solitary hills he fared,
Thoughtless at first, but ere eve's star appeared
235 His phantasy was lost, where reason fades,
In the calm'd twilight of Platonic shades.
Lamia beheld him coming, near, more near—
Close to her passing, in indifference drear,
His silent sandals swept the mossy green;
240 So neighbour'd to him, and yet so unseen
She stood: he pass'd, shut up in mysteries,
His mind wrapp'd like his mantle, while her eyes
Follow'd his steps, and her neck regal white
Turn'd—syllabling thus, "Ah, Lycius bright,
245 And will you leave me on the hills alone?
Lycius, look back! and be some pity shown."

212 far] long *interlined above* ⟨far⟩ *FC* (far *then restored on the proofs by Woodhouse*) 225 In . . . Cenchreas] In harbour Cencreas *FC* (*altered on the proofs by Keats to* Close to Cenchrea) 225 Egina] *altered on the proofs by Keats to* Egina's 236 Platonic] platonian *FC* (*altered on the proofs by Woodhouse to* Platonic)

He did; not with cold wonder fearingly,
But Orpheus-like at an Eurydice;
For so delicious were the words she sung,
250 It seem'd he had lov'd them a whole summer long:
And soon his eyes had drunk her beauty up,
Leaving no drop in the bewildering cup,
And still the cup was full,—while he, afraid
Lest she should vanish ere his lip had paid
255 Due adoration, thus began to adore;
Her soft look growing coy, she saw his chain so sure:
"Leave thee alone! Look back! Ah, Goddess, see
Whether my eyes can ever turn from thee!
For pity do not this sad heart belie—
260 Even as thou vanishest so I shall die.
Stay! though a Naiad of the rivers, stay!
To thy far wishes will thy streams obey:
Stay! though the greenest woods be thy domain,
Alone they can drink up the morning rain:
265 Though a descended Pleiad, will not one
Of thine harmonious sisters keep in tune
Thy spheres, and as thy silver proxy shine?
So sweetly to these ravish'd ears of mine
Came thy sweet greeting, that if thou shouldst fade
270 Thy memory will waste me to a shade:—
For pity do not melt!"—"If I should stay,"
Said Lamia, "here, upon this floor of clay,
And pain my steps upon these flowers too rough,
What canst thou say or do of charm enough
275 To dull the nice remembrance of my home?
Thou canst not ask me with thee here to roam
Over these hills and vales, where no joy is,—
Empty of immortality and bliss!
Thou art a scholar, Lycius, and must know
280 That finer spirits cannot breathe below
In human climes, and live: Alas! poor youth,
What taste of purer air hast thou to soothe
My essence? What serener palaces,
Where I may all my many senses please,

260/261 Thou to Elysium gone, her for the vultures I. (her *corrected by Taylor in pencil to* here *and the line originally following a colon at the end of 260*) *FC* 270 Thy memory] My Memery *altered to* Their Memeries *FC* (Thy memory *in the proofs*) 272 here, upon] upon *FC* (here *added on the proofs by Woodhouse*)

285 And by mysterious sleights a hundred thirsts appease?
It cannot be—Adieu!" So said, she rose
Tiptoe with white arms spread. He, sick to lose
The amorous promise of her lone complain,
Swoon'd, murmuring of love, and pale with pain.
290 The cruel lady, without any show
Of sorrow for her tender favourite's woe,
But rather, if her eyes could brighter be,
With brighter eyes and slow amenity,
Put her new lips to his, and gave afresh
295 The life she had so tangled in her mesh:
And as he from one trance was wakening
Into another, she began to sing,
Happy in beauty, life, and love, and every thing,
A song of love, too sweet for earthly lyres,
300 While, like held breath, the stars drew in their panting fires.
And then she whisper'd in such trembling tone,
As those who, safe together met alone
For the first time through many anguish'd days,
Use other speech than looks; bidding him raise
305 His drooping head, and clear his soul of doubt,
For that she was a woman, and without
Any more subtle fluid in her veins
Than throbbing blood, and that the self-same pains
Inhabited her frail-strung heart as his.
310 And next she wonder'd how his eyes could miss
Her face so long in Corinth, where, she said,
She dwelt but half retir'd, and there had led
Days happy as the gold coin could invent
Without the aid of love; yet in content
315 Till she saw him, as once she pass'd him by,
Where 'gainst a column he leant thoughtfully
At Venus' temple porch, 'mid baskets heap'd
Of amorous herbs and flowers, newly reap'd
Late on that eve, as 'twas the night before
320 The Adonian feast; whereof she saw no more,
But wept alone those days, for why should she adore?
Lycius from death awoke into amaze,

287 arms spread] arms (*altered by Taylor to* arms spread—*see Textual Note*) *FC* 292 brighter] *added above the line in FC* 296 wakening] wakeing (*altered by Taylor in pencil to* wakening) *FC* 308 throbbing blood] throbbed in his *altered to* throbbing blood *FC* 320 whereof] of which *FC* (*altered on the proofs by Woodhouse first to* of that *and then to* whereof) 322 awoke into] woke into an *FC* (*altered on the proofs by Woodhouse to* awoke into)

To see her still, and singing so sweet lays;
Then from amaze into delight he fell
325 To hear her whisper woman's lore so well;
And every word she spake entic'd him on
To unperplex'd delight and pleasure known.
Let the mad poets say whate'er they please
Of the sweets of Fairies, Peris, Goddesses,
330 There is not such a treat among them all,
Haunters of cavern, lake, and waterfall,
As a real woman, lineal indeed
From Pyrrha's pebbles or old Adam's seed.
Thus gentle Lamia judg'd, and judg'd aright,
335 That Lycius could not love in half a fright,
So threw the goddess off, and won his heart
More pleasantly by playing woman's part,
With no more awe than what her beauty gave,
That, while it smote, still guaranteed to save.
340 Lycius to all made eloquent reply,
Marrying to every word a twinborn sigh;
And last, pointing to Corinth, ask'd her sweet,
If 'twas too far that night for her soft feet.
The way was short, for Lamia's eagerness
345 Made, by a spell, the triple league decrease
To a few paces; not at all surmised
By blinded Lycius, so in her comprized.
They pass'd the city gates, he knew not how,
So noiseless, and he never thought to know.

350 As men talk in a dream, so Corinth all,
Throughout her palaces imperial,
And all her populous streets and temples lewd,
Mutter'd, like tempest in the distance brew'd,
To the wide-spreaded night above her towers.
355 Men, women, rich and poor, in the cool hours,
Shuffled their sandals o'er the pavement white,
Companion'd or alone; while many a light
Flared, here and there, from wealthy festivals,
And threw their moving shadows on the walls,

325 whisper woman's] woman's whispers *altered to* whisper woman's *D* 326 entic'd him on] *interlined above* ⟨he nearer dr⟩ *D* 327 unperplex'd . . . known] unperplexed Bliss, and pleasure really ⟨touch'd⟩ known (really *added above the line*) *D* 328 Let the] And let *D* 329 the sweets] the ⟨loves⟩ sweets *interlined above* ⟨faery love and⟩ *D* 333 Pyrrha's] *added above the line in FC* 349 thought] *interlined above* ⟨cared⟩ *FC*

360 Or found them cluster'd in the corniced shade
Of some arch'd temple door, or dusky colonnade.

Muffling his face, of greeting friends in fear,
Her fingers he press'd hard, as one came near
With curl'd gray beard, sharp eyes, and smooth bald crown,
365 Slow-stepp'd, and robed in philosophic gown:
Lycius shrank closer, as they met and past,
Into his mantle, adding wings to haste,
While hurried Lamia trembled: "Ah," said he,
"Why do you shudder, love, so ruefully?
370 Why does your tender palm dissolve in dew?"—
"I'm wearied," said fair Lamia: "tell me who
Is that old man? I cannot bring to mind
His features:—Lycius! wherefore did you blind
Yourself from his quick eyes?" Lycius replied,
375 "'Tis Apollonius sage, my trusty guide
And good instructor; but to-night he seems
The ghost of folly haunting my sweet dreams."

While yet he spake they had arrived before
A pillar'd porch, with lofty portal door,
380 Where hung a silver lamp, whose phosphor glow
Reflected in the slabbed steps below,
Mild as a star in water; for so new,
And so unsullied was the marble hue,
So through the crystal polish, liquid fine,
385 Ran the dark veins, that none but feet divine
Could e'er have touch'd there. Sounds Æolian
Breath'd from the hinges, as the ample span
Of the wide doors disclos'd a place unknown
Some time to any, but those two alone,
390 And a few Persian mutes, who that same year
Were seen about the markets: none knew where

363 Her . . . as] And pressing hard her fingers, *FC* (*the change to the 1820 wording made partly on the proofs by Woodhouse—see Textual Note to 362–363*) 371 tell me] pray *FC* 373 features . . . you] feature: Lycius! why did you so *FC* 379 pillar'd . . . with] royal-squared, *FC* (*altered on the proofs by Woodhouse to* pillar'd porch, with) 383 was . . . hue] was the marble's hue *altered to* did the marble shew *FC* (*the original FC text, but with* marble *for* marble's, *then restored on the proofs by Woodhouse*) 386 Sounds Æolian] *written as a separate half-line in D* 389 Some time] Ever *D*; Somtime *FC* (Sometime *in the proofs altered by Woodhouse to* Some time) 390 a] some *D* 390 same] *added above the line in D*

They could inhabit; the most curious
Were foil'd, who watch'd to trace them to their house:
And but the flitter-winged verse must tell,
395 For truth's sake, what woe afterwards befel,
'Twould humour many a heart to leave them thus,
Shut from the busy world of more incredulous.

## PART II

Love in a hut, with water and a crust,
Is—Love, forgive us!—cinders, ashes, dust;
Love in a palace is perhaps at last
More grievous torment than a hermit's fast:—
5 That is a doubtful tale from faery land,
Hard for the non-elect to understand.
Had Lycius liv'd to hand his story down,
He might have given the moral a fresh frown,
Or clench'd it quite: but too short was their bliss

392/393
⟨Who strove to maze them homeward to their house
Were foild they knew not how—but what can foil
The winged verse? What Poesy not win
The humblest Muse unweried of her toil?
[5] and what can win
The scret
Were foil'd they knew not how, they could not tell—
And puzzled
Were foild, and how it was they knew not well—
[10] Perpaps this
This flitter-winged verse perhaps might tell
If it durt speak, what it should dare to speak—
But now is Poesy's long ember week
And against fashion, folly 'tis to sin,
[15] Tho over Lamia's head the faery Muse flew in.
Were foil'd. And, but this⟩

(1 maze *interlined above* {trace} 9 and *interlined above* {but} 13 now *interlined above* {this} 16 And, but *interlined above* {they knew not how.} *There are several levels of cancellation in these lines that cannot be represented by the two-bracket system used elsewhere in this apparatus. The successive versions appear to be* [*a*] *lines 1, 2, 3* [*b*] *1, 2, 4* [*c*] *1, 2a, 5, 6* [*d*] *1, 7, 8* [*e*] *1, 9, 10* [*f*] *1, 9, 11–15* [*g*] *1, 16. Keats then began again with the present 393*) *D* 393 Were foil'd] *added in the margin in FC* 393 watch'd] strove *D* 393 trace] maze *D, FC* (*altered on the proofs by Woodhouse to* trace) 393 to their] ⟨home⟩ to their *FC* 394/395 ⟨What woe⟩ *D* 396–397 leave . . . incredulous] close the door / Upon their happy days, incredulous of more *D* 396 leave . . . thus] *interlined above* ⟨close⟩ *FC*

10 To breed distrust and hate, that make the soft voice hiss.
Besides, there, nightly, with terrific glare,
Love, jealous grown of so complete a pair,
Hover'd and buzz'd his wings, with fearful roar,
Above the lintel of their chamber door,
15 And down the passage cast a glow upon the floor.

For all this came a ruin: side by side
They were enthroned, in the even tide,
Upon a couch, near to a curtaining
Whose airy texture, from a golden string,
20 Floated into the room, and let appear
Unveil'd the summer heaven, blue and clear,
Betwixt two marble shafts:—there they reposed,
Where use had made it sweet, with eyelids closed,
Saving a tythe which love still open kept,
25 That they might see each other while they almost slept;
When from the slope side of a suburb hill,
Deafening the swallow's twitter, came a thrill
Of trumpets—Lycius started—the sounds fled,
But left a thought, a buzzing in his head.
30 For the first time, since first he harbour'd in
That purple-lined palace of sweet sin,
His spirit pass'd beyond its golden bourn
Into the noisy world almost forsworn.
The lady, ever watchful, penetrant,
35 Saw this with pain, so arguing a want
Of something more, more than her empery
Of joys; and she began to moan and sigh
Because he mused beyond her, knowing well
That but a moment's thought is passion's passing bell.
40 "Why do you sigh, fair creature?" whisper'd he:
"Why do you think?" return'd she tenderly:

II.10 make] makes *FC* (*altered on the proofs by Woodhouse to* make) 29 thought . . . his] thought at work in Lycius' *altered to* thought a buzzing in his *D* 29/30
⟨For the first time since that had been his⟩
⟨For the first time since he had harbour'd in
That {happy Palace} purple-lined Palace⟩ *D*
30 first he harbour'd] he soft-harbour'd *D* 31/32 ⟨Not⟩ *D* 33 the . . . world] *successively* (*a*) the world (*b*) a world (*c*) a busy world (*d*) the busy world *D* 34 The] *interlined above* ⟨Lamia⟩ *D* 37 joys; and] Joys ⟨devote to him; and she b⟩; and *D* 38 knowing] *added above the line in D* 39 moment's] minute's *D* 40 creature?" whisper'd] Lamia? said *D*

"You have deserted me;—where am I now?
Not in your heart while care weighs on your brow:
No, no, you have dismiss'd me; and I go
45 From your breast houseless: ay, it must be so."
He answer'd, bending to her open eyes,
Where he was mirror'd small in paradise,
"My silver planet, both of eve and morn!
Why will you plead yourself so sad forlorn,
50 While I am striving how to fill my heart
With deeper crimson, and a double smart?
How to entangle, trammel up and snare
Your soul in mine, and labyrinth you there
Like the hid scent in an unbudded rose?
55 Ay, a sweet kiss—you see your mighty woes.
My thoughts! shall I unveil them? Listen then!
What mortal hath a prize, that other men
May be confounded and abash'd withal,
But lets it sometimes pace abroad majestical,
60 And triumph, as in thee I should rejoice
Amid the hoarse alarm of Corinth's voice.
Let my foes choke, and my friends shout afar,
While through the thronged streets your bridal car
Wheels round its dazzling spokes."—The lady's cheek
65 Trembled; she nothing said, but, pale and meek,
Arose and knelt before him, wept a rain
Of sorrows at his words; at last with pain

42 where . . . now] *successively* (*a*) I am a (*b*) You would (*c*) where am I now *D* 45/46 (*continuing the speech begun in 42*) Too fond was I believing; fancy fed, / In high Deliriums, and blossoms never shed"— *D, FC* (fancy⟨ing⟩ *in the first line in D, and* In high Deliriums *made out of* Deliriums eternal) 47 Where . . . small] Wherein he saw himself *D* 49 sad] ⟨for⟩ sad *FC* 50 fill] *interlined above* ⟨touch⟩ *D* 52 entangle, trammel] entangle, ⟨thee⟩ ⟨snare⟩ trammel (*the comma added afterward*) *D* 53 Your . . . you] Thy . . . thee *D, FC* 55 a . . . kiss] that was sweet *D* 58/59

⟨But shows it round⟩
⟨But triumphs {with it} it the more, the more majestical⟩

(shows *interlined above* {triumphs with it} *in the first line*) *D* 59 lets] let *D* 61 hoarse alarm] *successively* (*a*) buzzs of the Citiy's (*b*) great buzz (*c*) buzzd alam *D* 61/62

⟨Life to my friends, and to my foes a curse
O let our Marriage {march} spead brilliant as it⟩
⟨Let my friends shout and let my enemies choak⟩

(and . . . curse *interlined above* {a poison to my foes} *in the first line and* shout *added above the line in the third*) *D* 64 cheek] cheek⟨s⟩ *D* 66 a rain] a ⟨shower⟩ rain *interlined above* ⟨and look'd⟩ *D* 67 Of] *successively* (*a*) To (*b*) In (*c*) Of (*the first two versions following deleted* look'd *in 66*) *D* 67 words] ⟨purpose⟩ words *D, FC* (*the same deletion in both MSS*)

Beseeching him, the while his hand she wrung,
To change his purpose. He thereat was stung,
70 Perverse, with stronger fancy to reclaim
Her wild and timid nature to his aim:
Besides, for all his love, in self despite,
Against his better self, he took delight
Luxurious in her sorrows, soft and new.
75 His passion, cruel grown, took on a hue
Fierce and sanguineous as 'twas possible
In one whose brow had no dark veins to swell.
Fine was the mitigated fury, like
Apollo's presence when in act to strike
80 The serpent—Ha, the serpent! certes, she
Was none. She burnt, she lov'd the tyranny,
And, all subdued, consented to the hour

71 wild and] *added above the line in D* 72 in . . . despite] *interlined above* ⟨and stern against⟩ *D* 72/73 ⟨His better self⟩ (*continuation of deleted text in 72*) *D* 82–105 And . . . betray'd.] *written on an added leaf in FC* (*the present fol. 18 of the MS*) *to replace:*

⟨Became herself a flame—'twas worth an age
Of minor joys to revel in such rage.
She was persuaded, and he fixt the hour
When he should make a Bride of his fair Paramour.
[5] After the hotest day{s} comes languidest
The colour'd Eve, half-lidded in the west;
So they both look'd, so spake, if breathed sound,
That almost silence is, hath ever found
Compare with nature's quiet. Which lov'd most,
[10] Which had the weakest, strongest, heart so lost,
So ruin'd, wreck'd, destroy'd: {for certes they
Scarcely could tell} they could not guess
Whether 'twas misery or happiness.
Spells are but made to break. Whisper'd the Youth
[15] "Sure some sweet name thou hast; though by my truth
"I had not ask'd it, ever thinking thee
"Not mortal but of heavenly progeny,
"As still I do. Hast any mortal name?
"Fif silver-appellation for this dazzling frame?
[20] "Or friends, or Kinsfolks on the citied Earth,
"To share our marriage feast and nuptial mirth?"
"I have no friends," said Lamia "{as you list
"Intreat your many guests." Then all was wist
She fell asleep, and Lycius to the Shade
[25] Of deep sleep in a moment was betray'd.}
no not one;
My presence in wide Corinth is unknown;
My parent's bones are in their dusty urns
Sepulcre'd where no Kindled insence burns,

When to the bridal he should lead his paramour.
Whispering in midnight silence, said the youth,
85 "Sure some sweet name thou hast, though, by my truth,
I have not ask'd it, ever thinking thee
Not mortal, but of heavenly progeny,
As still I do. Hast any mortal name,
Fit appellation for this dazzling frame?
90 Or friends or kinsfolk on the citied earth,
To share our marriage feast and nuptial mirth?"
"I have no friends," said Lamia, "no, not one;
My presence in wide Corinth hardly known:

---

[30] Seeing all their luckless race are dead save me
And I neglect the holy rite for thee.
E'ven as you{r} list invite your many guests;
But if, as now it seems, your vision rests
With any pleasure on me, summon not
[35] Old Apollonius. Lycius ignorant what
Strange thoughts had led her to an end so blank
Made close enquiry; from whose touch she shrank
Feigning a sleep, and he to the dull shade
Of deep sleep in a moment was betray'd.⟩
(30 race *interlined above* {Kin} *15–22a, 26–39 correspond to 85–105 of the present text). Lines 5–39 of this passage, written on the versos of fols. 17 and 19, are in turn an expansion of the original passage in FC, which consisted of 1–4 of the above (at the bottom of fol. 17r) and was immediately followed by 106 ff. of the present text (beginning on fol. 19r). The earliest version of 5–25 (though it is of course later than the original passage in FC) appears on the verso of the draft of II.26–49, with variants to the above and alterations as follows*: 9 nature's] nature 11–13 destroy'd . . . happiness] destroy'd—for certes they / Scarecely could tell if this was misery 14 Whisper'd the Youth] *interlined above* ⟨said then the youth⟩ 18 still] *interlined above* ⟨now⟩ 19 Fif . . . frame] Of fit Sound for this soft ethereal frame (*the line added vertically in the margin, and* silver *interlined and deleted before* Sound) 20 friends, or] *added above the line* 22–25 I . . . betray'd.}]
"I have no fiends" said Lamia "as you list,
⟨Seeing it must be⟩
Intreat your many guests." Then all was wist—
She fell asleep, and Lycius to the Shade
⟨Of Sleep sunk with her, when his fancy stray'd
Into a Dream⟩
⟨Of Sleep went⟩
Of deep sleep in a moment was betray'd—
(Intreat *interlined above* ⟨Do with⟩ *and* many guests *interlined above* ⟨own⟩ *in the third line*; when *interlined above* {dreaming} *in the fifth line*) *The word* for *is written by itself at the top of this draft page, and upside down at the bottom appears* ⟨Mild as the⟩ (*cf. I.382*) 82 And . . . subdued] *the verso of fol. 18 in FC shows the rejected beginning* Was all subdued 83 to . . . should] he should to the bridal *altered to* to the bridal he should *FC* (*this and the next four notes cite Keats's revised text on fol. 18r of FC*) 86 have] *made out of* had *FC* 89 appellation] silver appellation (silver *deleted in pencil by Taylor*) *FC* 90 kinsfolk] Kinsfolks *FC* (*altered on the proofs by Woodhouse to* kinsfolk)

My parents' bones are in their dusty urns
95 Sepulchred, where no kindled incense burns,
Seeing all their luckless race are dead, save me,
And I neglect the holy rite for thee.
Even as you list invite your many guests;
But if, as now it seems, your vision rests
100 With any pleasure on me, do not bid
Old Apollonius—from him keep me hid."
Lycius, perplex'd at words so blind and blank,
Made close inquiry; from whose touch she shrank,
Feigning a sleep; and he to the dull shade
105 Of deep sleep in a moment was betray'd.

It was the custom then to bring away
The bride from home at blushing shut of day,
Veil'd, in a chariot, heralded along
By strewn flowers, torches, and a marriage song,
110 With other pageants: but this fair unknown
Had not a friend. So being left alone,
(Lycius was gone to summon all his kin)
And knowing surely she could never win
His foolish heart from its mad pompousness,
115 She set herself, high-thoughted, how to dress
The misery in fit magnificence.
She did so, but 'tis doubtful how and whence
Came, and who were her subtle servitors.
About the halls, and to and from the doors,
120 There was a noise of wings, till in short space
The glowing banquet-room shone with wide-arched grace.
A haunting music, sole perhaps and lone
Supportress of the faery-roof, made moan
Throughout, as fearful the whole charm might fade.
125 Fresh carved cedar, mimicking a glade
Of palm and plantain, met from either side,
High in the midst, in honour of the bride:
Two palms and then two plantains, and so on,

101 him] *interlined above* ⟨his eyes⟩ *FC* 112 was] being (*altered by Taylor first in pencil and then in ink to* was) *FC* 121 glowing] *interlined above* ⟨high-lamp'd⟩ *FC* 122 sole] *interlined above* ⟨pe⟩ ⟨lone⟩ *D* 122 and lone] *interlined above* ⟨and sole⟩ *D* 123 roof] roof-⟨ing⟩ *D* 124/125 ⟨Sweet cedar carvd there⟩ (Sweet *interlined above* {The carved}; *the successive versions appear to be* [*a*] The carved cedar [*b*] Sweet carved cedar [*c*] Sweet cedar carvd there) *D* 125 cedar, mimicking] Cedar ⟨spead a⟩ mimicking *D* 127 High in the] In the high *D*

From either side their stems branch'd one to one
130 All down the aisled place; and beneath all
There ran a stream of lamps straight on from wall to wall.
So canopied, lay an untasted feast
Teeming with odours. Lamia, regal drest,
Silently paced about, and as she went,
135 In pale contented sort of discontent,
Mission'd her viewless servants to enrich
The fretted splendour of each nook and niche.
Between the tree-stems, marbled plain at first,
Came jasper pannels; then, anon, there burst
140 Forth creeping imagery of slighter trees,
And with the larger wove in small intricacies.
Approving all, she faded at self-will,
And shut the chamber up, close, hush'd and still,
Complete and ready for the revels rude,
145 When dreadful guests would come to spoil her solitude.

The day appear'd, and all the gossip rout.
O senseless Lycius! Madman! wherefore flout
The silent-blessing fate, warm cloister'd hours,
And show to common eyes these secret bowers?
150 The herd approach'd; each guest, with busy brain,

129 From] *interlined above* ⟨On⟩ *D* 129 their . . . branch'd] ⟨a forest⟩ ⟨they⟩ their stems ⟨join⟩ branch'd *D* 130 All (*first word*)] *written over* ⟨T⟩ *D* 130 and . . . all] ⟨each⟩ and beneath all *written beneath* ⟨far as the eye could view⟩ *D* 133 with odours] a perfume *D, L*; *successively* (*a*) a perfume (*b*) wing'd odours (*c*) with odours *FC* 134 Silently] Silverly *D, L, FC* 134 as] *added above the line in D* 135 In . . . discontent,] *not in D* 137 fretted . . . each] splendid finish of each *D*; splendid cornicing of *L* 138 marbled plain] wainscoated *D, L*; marble'd plain *interlined above* ⟨wainscoated⟩ *FC* 139 Came] ⟨There⟩ Came *D* 139 jasper] *made out of* caster *or* easter *D* 140 creeping] ⟨tenderer⟩ creeping *D* 140 slighter] *interlined above* ⟨smaller⟩ *D* 141 in] *interlined above* ⟨smallest⟩ ⟨their⟩ *D* 141/142

And so till she was sated—then came down
Soft lighing on her head a brilliant crown,
Wreath'd turban-wise of tender wannish fire
And sprinkled oer with stars like Ariadnes tiar.

(on *successively* [*a*] on [*b*] oer [*c*] on *and* her *written over* ⟨the⟩ *and* head *above* ⟨Brows⟩ *in the second line,* wise *interlined above* ⟨like⟩ *in the third line, and all four lines marked with a bracket in the margin*) *D* 144 revels rude] *successively* (*a*) woeful time (*b*) woeful day (*c*) times (*d*) day of woe (*e*) revels rude *D* 146 appear'd] came soon *D, L*; appear'd *interlined above* ⟨came soon⟩ *FC* 147–148 O . . . hours] O senseless Lycius! Dolt! Fool! Madman! Lout! / Why would you murder happiness like yours *L*; *the recto of the ninth extant fragment of D ends with the first of these lines as in L* 150 approach'd;] came; and *L*; came, and *altered to* arriv'd, *FC* 150 busy] buzzy *L*

Arriving at the portal, gaz'd amain,
And enter'd marveling: for they knew the street,
Remember'd it from childhood all complete
Without a gap, yet ne'er before had seen
155 That royal porch, that high-built fair demesne;
So in they hurried all, maz'd, curious and keen:
Save one, who look'd thereon with eye severe,
And with calm-planted steps walk'd in austere;
'Twas Apollonius: something too he laugh'd,
160 As though some knotty problem, that had daft
His patient thought, had now begun to thaw,
And solve and melt:—'twas just as he foresaw.

He met within the murmurous vestibule
His young disciple. "'Tis no common rule,
165 Lycius," said he, "for uninvited guest
To force himself upon you, and infest
With an unbidden presence the bright throng
Of younger friends; yet must I do this wrong,
And you forgive me." Lycius blush'd, and led
170 The old man through the inner doors broad-spread;
With reconciling words and courteous mien
Turning into sweet milk the sophist's spleen.

152 marveling] won'dring *L*; marveling *interlined above* ⟨wondring⟩ *FC* 154 yet] but *L* 156 they hurried] went one and *L* *After* 162
Soft went the music, and the tables all
Sparkled beneath the viewless banneral
Of Magic; and dispos'd in double row
Seem'd edged Parterres of white bedded snow,
Adorne'd along the sides with living flowers
Conversing, laughing after sunny showers:
And, as the pleasant appetite entic'd,
Gush came the wine, and sheer the meats were slic'd.
Soft went the Music; the flat salver sang
Kiss'd by the emptied goblet,—and again it rang:
Swift bustled by the servants:—here's a health
Cries one—another—then, as if by stealth,
A Glutton drains a cup of Helicon,
Too fast down, down his throat the brief delight is gone.
"Where is that Music?" cries a Lady fair.
"Aye, where is it my dear? Up in the air"?
Another whispers "Poo!" saith Glutton "Mum!"
Then makes his shiny mouth a napkin for his thumb.
(shiny *in the last line also readable as* slimy) *L* 163–172 He . . . spleen.] *an added passage first written on the verso of fol. 19 in FC and then recopied* (*without substantive change*) *along with 173 and a revision of 174 on an inserted leaf* (*the present fol. 21*)

Of wealthy lustre was the banquet-room,
Fill'd with pervading brilliance and perfume:
175 Before each lucid pannel fuming stood
A censer fed with myrrh and spiced wood,
Each by a sacred tripod held aloft,
Whose slender feet wide-swerv'd upon the soft
Wool-woofed carpets: fifty wreaths of smoke
180 From fifty censers their light voyage took
To the high roof, still mimick'd as they rose
Along the mirror'd walls by twin-clouds odorous.
Twelve sphered tables, by silk seats insphered,
High as the level of a man's breast rear'd
185 On libbard's paws, upheld the heavy gold
Of cups and goblets, and the store thrice told
Of Ceres' horn, and, in huge vessels, wine
Come from the gloomy tun with merry shine.
Thus loaded with a feast the tables stood,
190 Each shrining in the midst the image of a God.

When in an antichamber every guest
Had felt the cold full sponge to pleasure press'd,
By minist'ring slaves, upon his hands and feet,
And fragrant oils with ceremony meet
195 Pour'd on his hair, they all mov'd to the feast
In white robes, and themselves in order placed
Around the silken couches, wondering
Whence all this mighty cost and blaze of wealth could spring.

Soft went the music the soft air along,
200 While fluent Greek a vowel'd undersong

173–174 Of . . . perfume:] *these lines are canceled at the bottom of fol. 20r in FC and rewritten on the inserted fol. 21 after 163–172. The first version of 174 read* Fill'd with light, music, jewels, gold, perfume; *Keats copied the first four words of this version on fol. 21r before revising the line to its present wording* 177–178 sacred . . . slender] slender . . . tripple *FC* 191–198 When . . . spring.] *an added passage in D, written on the verso of the draft of II.122–147 and probably replacing some or all of the missing draft text represented by the letter extract given above after II.162. The lines in D are preceded by two canceled fragmentary attempts:*

⟨When, in an antichamber, every guest
With fragrant oils his⟩
⟨When, in an antichamber, every guest
Tended by ministring slaves, his⟩

192 felt] *interlined above* ⟨had⟩ *D* 195 they] ⟨they all to banquet came / In white robes hymeneal,⟩ they (hymeneal *followed by several more deleted letters, possibly* her a *or* herd) *D* 195 mov'd] *interlined above* to ⟨banqu⟩ (to *left undeleted by mistake*) *D*

Kept up among the guests, discoursing low
At first, for scarcely was the wine at flow;
But when the happy vintage touch'd their brains,
Louder they talk, and louder come the strains
205 Of powerful instruments:—the gorgeous dyes,
The space, the splendour of the draperies,
The roof of awful richness, nectarous cheer,
Beautiful slaves, and Lamia's self, appear,
Now, when the wine has done its rosy deed,
210 And every soul from human trammels freed,
No more so strange; for merry wine, sweet wine,
Will make Elysian shades not too fair, too divine.

Soon was God Bacchus at meridian height;
Flush'd were their cheeks, and bright eyes double bright:
215 Garlands of every green, and every scent
From vales deflower'd, or forest-trees branch-rent,
In baskets of bright osier'd gold were brought
High as the handles heap'd, to suit the thought
Of every guest; that each, as he did please,
220 Might fancy-fit his brows, silk-pillow'd at his ease.

What wreath for Lamia? What for Lycius?
What for the sage, old Apollonius?
Upon her aching forehead be there hung
The leaves of willow and of adder's tongue;
225 And for the youth, quick, let us strip for him
The thyrsus, that his watching eyes may swim
Into forgetfulness; and, for the sage,
Let spear-grass and the spiteful thistle wage
War on his temples. Do not all charms fly
230 At the mere touch of cold philosophy?
There was an awful rainbow once in heaven:
We know her woof, her texture; she is given
In the dull catalogue of common things.
Philosophy will clip an Angel's wings,
235 Conquer all mysteries by rule and line,
Empty the haunted air, and gnomed mine—

203 the happy] *interlined above* ⟨Sicilian⟩ *FC* 213 ¶Soon . . . ] *FC*; *new page but no* ¶ *indention in 1820* 218 219 to . . . guest] of every sort / Of fragrant wreath (fragrant *added above the line*) *FC*

Unweave a rainbow, as it erewhile made
The tender-person'd Lamia melt into a shade.

By her glad Lycius sitting, in chief place,
240 Scarce saw in all the room another face,
Till, checking his love trance, a cup he took
Full brimm'd, and opposite sent forth a look
'Cross the broad table, to beseech a glance
From his old teacher's wrinkled countenance,
245 And pledge him. The bald-head philosopher
Had fix'd his eye, without a twinkle or stir
Full on the alarmed beauty of the bride,
Brow-beating her fair form, and troubling her sweet pride.
Lycius then press'd her hand, with devout touch,
250 As pale it lay upon the rosy couch:
'Twas icy, and the cold ran through his veins;
Then sudden it grew hot, and all the pains
Of an unnatural heat shot to his heart.
"Lamia, what means this? Wherefore dost thou start?
255 Know'st thou that man?" Poor Lamia answer'd not.
He gaz'd into her eyes, and not a jot
Own'd they the lovelorn piteous appeal:
More, more he gaz'd: his human senses reel:
Some hungry spell that loveliness absorbs;
260 There was no recognition in those orbs.
"Lamia!" he cried—and no soft-toned reply.
The many heard, and the loud revelry
Grew hush; the stately music no more breathes;
The myrtle sicken'd in a thousand wreaths.
265 By faint degrees, voice, lute, and pleasure ceased;
A deadly silence step by step increased,
Until it seem'd a horrid presence there,
And not a man but felt the terror in his hair.
"Lamia!" he shriek'd; and nothing but the shriek
270 With its sad echo did the silence break.
"Begone, foul dream!" he cried, gazing again
In the bride's face, where now no azure vein
Wander'd on fair-spaced temples; no soft bloom

237 Unweave] *interlined above* ⟨Destroy⟩ *FC* 237 erewhile] ⟨once w⟩ erewhile *FC* 238 melt] *written over* ⟨tu⟩ *FC* 239 her] whom *FC* 243 beseech] ⟨ensure⟩ besmeech *FC* 246–247 fix'd . . . Full] got . . . Fix'd *FC* 247 the bride] his Bride *FC* 254 thou] so *FC* 255 Know'st thou] Dost know *FC*

Misted the cheek; no passion to illume
275 The deep-recessed vision:—all was blight;
Lamia, no longer fair, there sat a deadly white.
"Shut, shut those juggling eyes, thou ruthless man!
Turn them aside, wretch! or the righteous ban
Of all the Gods, whose dreadful images
280 Here represent their shadowy presences,
May pierce them on the sudden with the thorn
Of painful blindness; leaving thee forlorn,
In trembling dotage to the feeblest fright
Of conscience, for their long offended might,
285 For all thine impious proud-heart sophistries,
Unlawful magic, and enticing lies.
Corinthians! look upon that gray-beard wretch!
Mark how, possess'd, his lashless eyelids stretch
Around his demon eyes! Corinthians, see!
290 My sweet bride withers at their potency."
"Fool!" said the sophist, in an under-tone
Gruff with contempt; which a death-nighing moan
From Lycius answer'd, as heart-struck and lost,
He sank supine beside the aching ghost.
295 "Fool! Fool!" repeated he, while his eyes still
Relented not, nor mov'd; "from every ill
Of life have I preserv'd thee to this day,
And shall I see thee made a serpent's prey?"
Then Lamia breath'd death breath; the sophist's eye,
300 Like a sharp spear, went through her utterly,
Keen, cruel, perceant, stinging: she, as well
As her weak hand could any meaning tell,
Motion'd him to be silent; vainly so,
He look'd and look'd again a level—No!
305 "A Serpent!" echoed he; no sooner said,
Than with a frightful scream she vanished:
And Lycius' arms were empty of delight,

281 thorn] ⟨ban⟩ thorn *FC*   293–294 heart . . . ghost] *a last-minute revision written by Keats (with* lay *for* sank *in 294) in Taylor's office on the back of a letter from John Clare to Taylor, 5 June 1820 (see Garrod, pp. xxxv, 213 n.); FC has* he sunk supine / Upon the Couch where Lamia's beauties pine   297–298 Of . . . prey?]

That youth might suffer have I shielded thee
Up to this very hour, and shall I see
Thee married to a Serpent? Pray you Mark,
Corinthians! A Serpent, plain and stark! *FC*

302 meaning] *made out of* motion *FC*

As were his limbs of life, from that same night.
On the high couch he lay!—his friends came round—
310 Supported him—no pulse, or breath they found,
And, in its marriage robe, the heavy body wound.*

* "Philostratus, in his fourth book *de Vita Apollonii,* hath a memorable instance in this kind, which I may not omit, of one Menippus Lycius, a young man twenty-five years of age, that going betwixt Cenchreas and Corinth, met such a phantasm in the habit of a fair gentlewoman, which taking him by the hand, carried him home to her house, in the suburbs of Corinth, and told him she was a Phœnician by birth, and if he would tarry with her, he should hear her sing and play, and drink such wine as never any drank, and no man should molest him; but she, being fair and lovely, would live and die with him, that was fair and lovely to behold. The young man, a philosopher, otherwise staid and discreet, able to moderate his passions, though not this of love, tarried with her a while to his great content, and at last married her, to whose wedding, amongst other guests, came Apollonius; who, by some probable conjectures, found her out to be a serpent, a lamia; and that all her furniture was, like Tantalus' gold, described by Homer, no substance but mere illusions. When she saw herself descried, she wept, and desired Apollonius to be silent, but he would not be moved, and thereupon she, plate, house, and all that was in it, vanished in an instant: many thousands took notice of this fact, for it was done in the midst of Greece."

Burton's "Anatomy of Melancholy." Part 3. Sect. 2. Memb. 1. Subs. 1.

## *Pensive they sit, and roll their languid eyes*

Pensive they sit, and roll their languid eyes,
Nibble their toasts, and cool their tea with sighs,
Or else forget the purpose of the night,
Forget their tea—forget their appetite.
5 See, with cross'd arms they sit—ah hapless crew,
The fire is going out, and no one rings
For coals, and therefore no coals Betty brings.

311 *note* "Philostratus . . . Subs. 1] *in place of this note at the end of the poem, FC has, at the bottom of fol. 1r, the following connected to the title with an asterisk*: The ground work of this story will be found in Burton's "Anatomy of Melancholy" Part 3. Sect 3. Memb. 1st Subs. 1st. *The printer initially set this brief note on the recto of the half-title leaf preceding the first page of text, and Woodhouse on the proofs wrote, "put this on the other side of the page.* ⟨*or else print an extract from Burton there.*⟩*" The present note was substituted at a later stage*

*Pensive they sit.* Text from Keats's letter to George and Georgiana Keats, 17–27 September 1819. Heading supplied by editor.

A fly is in the milk pot—must he die
Circled by a humane society?
10 No, no, there Mr. Werter takes his spoon,
Inverts it—dips the handle, and lo, soon
The little struggler, sav'd from perils dark,
Across the teaboard draws a long wet mark.
Romeo! Arise! take snuffers by the handle;
15 There's a large cauliflower in each candle,
A winding-sheet—Ah me! I must away
To No. 7, just beyond the Circus gay.
"Alas, my friend! your coat sits very well:
Where may your taylor live?" "I may not tell—
20 O pardon me—I'm absent now and then.
Where *might* my taylor live?—I say again
I cannot tell. Let me no more be teas'd—
He lives in Wapping, *might* live where he pleas'd."

## *To Autumn*

1

Season of mists and mellow fruitfulness,
  Close bosom-friend of the maturing sun;
Conspiring with him how to load and bless
  With fruit the vines that round the thatch-eves run;
5 To bend with apples the moss'd cottage-trees,
  And fill all fruit with ripeness to the core;
    To swell the gourd, and plump the hazel shells
  With a sweet kernel; to set budding more,
And still more, later flowers for the bees,
10 Until they think warm days will never cease,
    For summer has o'er-brimm'd their clammy cells.

*To Autumn.* Text (including heading) from *1820.* Variants and other readings from Keats's draft (*D*), his letter to Woodhouse, 21, 22 September 1819 (*L*), and transcripts by Brown (*CB*) and Woodhouse ($W^2$). *Heading* To Autumn] *no heading in D, L* 4 With . . . vines] The Vines with fruit *D, L, CB,* $W^2$ 6 fruit] fruits *D, CB* (furuits *in D*) 6 ripeness] sweetness *D, CB* (sweeness *in D*) 8 sweet] white *D, L,* $W^2$ 9 still] yet $W^2$

2

Who hath not seen thee oft amid thy store?
  Sometimes whoever seeks abroad may find
Thee sitting careless on a granary floor,
15   Thy hair soft-lifted by the winnowing wind;
Or on a half-reap'd furrow sound asleep,
  Drows'd with the fume of poppies, while thy hook
    Spares the next swath and all its twined flowers:
And sometimes like a gleaner thou dost keep
20   Steady thy laden head across a brook;
  Or by a cyder-press, with patient look,
    Thou watchest the last oozings hours by hours.

3

Where are the songs of spring? Ay, where are they?
  Think not of them, thou hast thy music too,—
25 While barred clouds bloom the soft-dying day,
  And touch the stubble-plains with rosy hue;
Then in a wailful choir the small gnats mourn
  Among the river sallows, borne aloft
    Or sinking as the light wind lives or dies;
30 And full-grown lambs loud bleat from hilly bourn;
  Hedge-crickets sing; and now with treble soft
  The red-breast whistles from a garden-croft;
    And gathering swallows twitter in the skies.

12 thee . . . store?] thee? for thy haunts are many *altered to* thee oft amid thy store⟨s⟩? *D*  12 store] stores *L*, $W^2$; store⟨s⟩ *CB* (*D also—see preceding note*)  13 abroad] *interlined above* ⟨for thee⟩ *D*  15/16

⟨While bright the Sun slants through the husky barn;—
orr on a half reap'd furrow sound asleep
Dos'd with red poppies; while thy reeping hook
Spares form Some {slumbrous} minutes while wam slumpers creep⟩

(husky *added above in the first line; the second line interlined above* {Or sound asleep in a half reaped field}) *D*  17 Drows'd] Dos'd *D*, *CB* (Dosed *in CB*); Dased *L*; Dazed $W^2$  18 Spares . . . flowers] *interlined above* ⟨Spares for some slumbrous minutes the next swath⟩ *D*  18 swath] sheath (*corrected by Keats to* swath) *CB*  18 twined] honied (*corrected by Keats to* twined) *CB*  20 laden] l⟨e⟩aden (*the correction made first by Woodhouse in pencil and then by Brown in ink*) *CB*  20 a] the *D*, *CB*  21 patient] patent *D*  22 oozings] oozing *D*, *CB*  25 While] When $W^2$  25 barred . . . bloom] a gold cloud gilds *altered to* barred clouds bloom *D*  26 And touch] ⟨And⟩ Touching *altered to* And Touch *D*  26 with] *added above the line in D*  28 borne] ⟨on the⟩ borne *D*  29 or dies] and dies *D*, *L*, $W^2$  30, 33 And] *written over* ⟨The⟩ (*the same alteration in both lines*) *D*  31 with treble] again full *D*, *CB*  32/33 ⟨And new flock still⟩ *D*  33 gathering] gather'd *D*, *L*, $W^2$ (Gather'd *made out of* Gathering *in D*)

# *The Fall of Hyperion: A Dream*

## CANTO I

Fanatics have their dreams, wherewith they weave
A paradise for a sect; the savage too
From forth the loftiest fashion of his sleep
Guesses at heaven: pity these have not
5 Trac'd upon vellum or wild Indian leaf
The shadows of melodious utterance.
But bare of laurel they live, dream, and die;
For Poesy alone can tell her dreams,
With the fine spell of words alone can save
10 Imagination from the sable charm
And dumb enchantment. Who alive can say
"Thou art no poet; may'st not tell thy dreams"?
Since every man whose soul is not a clod
Hath visions, and would speak, if he had lov'd
15 And been well nurtured in his mother tongue.
Whether the dream now purposed to rehearse
Be poet's or fanatic's will be known
When this warm scribe my hand is in the grave.

Methought I stood where trees of every clime,
20 Palm, myrtle, oak, and sycamore, and beech,
With plantane, and spice blossoms, made a screen;
In neighbourhood of fountains, by the noise
Soft showering in mine ears, and, by the touch
Of scent, not far from roses. Turning round,
25 I saw an arbour with a drooping roof
Of trellis vines, and bells, and larger blooms,
Like floral-censers swinging light in air;
Before its wreathed doorway, on a mound
Of moss, was spread a feast of summer fruits,
30 Which, nearer seen, seem'd refuse of a meal

*The Fall of Hyperion.* Text (including heading) from Woodhouse's $W^2$ transcript. Variants from the extracts of I.1–11a, 61–86 in Keats's letter to Woodhouse, 21, 22 September 1819 (*L*—the same letter also contains II.1–4 and 6 written continuously, but the text there agrees substantively with $W^2$ in these lines).

I.4 these] ⟨that⟩ these $W^2$ 10 charm] *L*; cham (*with the penciled note "probably* charm" *by Woodhouse on the opposite verso*) $W^2$ 14 lov'd] ⟨not⟩ lov'd $W^2$

By angel tasted, or our mother Eve;
For empty shells were scattered on the grass,
And grape stalks but half bare, and remnants more,
Sweet smelling, whose pure kinds I could not know.
35 Still was more plenty than the fabled horn
Thrice emptied could pour forth, at banqueting
For Proserpine return'd to her own fields,
Where the white heifers low. And appetite
More yearning than on earth I ever felt
40 Growing within, I ate deliciously;
And, after not long, thirsted, for thereby
Stood a cool vessel of transparent juice,
Sipp'd by the wander'd bee, the which I took,
And, pledging all the mortals of the world,
45 And all the dead whose names are in our lips,
Drank. That full draught is parent of my theme.
No Asian poppy, nor elixir fine
Of the soon fading jealous caliphat;
No poison gender'd in close monkish cell
50 To thin the scarlet conclave of old men,
Could so have rapt unwilling life away.
Among the fragrant husks and berries crush'd,
Upon the grass I struggled hard against
The domineering potion; but in vain:
55 The cloudy swoon came on, and down I sunk
Like a Silenus on an antique vase.
How long I slumber'd 'tis a chance to guess.
When sense of life return'd, I started up
As if with wings; but the fair trees were gone,
60 The mossy mound and arbour were no more;
I look'd around upon the carved sides
Of an old sanctuary with roof august,
Builded so high, it seem'd that filmed clouds
Might spread beneath, as o'er the stars of heaven;
65 So old the place was, I remembered none
The like upon the earth; what I had seen
Of grey cathedrals, buttress'd walls, rent towers,
The superannuations of sunk realms,
Or nature's rocks toil'd hard in waves and winds,

48 soon fading] "*originally* death doing" (*Woodhouse's note in* $W^2$) 64 spread] sail *L*
65 remembered] remember *L* 69 toil'd . . . winds] hard toil'd in winds and waves *L*, $W^2$ (*but marked for transposition to the present order in* $W^2$)

70 Seem'd but the faulture of decrepit things
To that eternal domed monument.
Upon the marble at my feet there lay
Store of strange vessels, and large draperies,
Which needs had been of dyed asbestus wove,
75 Or in that place the moth could not corrupt,
So white the linen; so, in some, distinct
Ran imageries from a sombre loom.
All in a mingled heap confus'd there lay
Robes, golden tongs, censer, and chafing dish,
80 Girdles, and chains, and holy jewelries.

Turning from these with awe, once more I rais'd
My eyes to fathom the space every way;
The embossed roof, the silent massy range
Of columns north and south, ending in mist
85 Of nothing, then to eastward, where black gates
Were shut against the sunrise evermore.
Then to the west I look'd, and saw far off
An image, huge of feature as a cloud,
At level of whose feet an altar slept,
90 To be approach'd on either side by steps,
And marble balustrade, and patient travail
To count with toil the innumerable degrees.
Towards the altar sober-pac'd I went,
Repressing haste, as too unholy there;
95 And, coming nearer, saw beside the shrine
One minist'ring; and there arose a flame.
When in mid-May the sickening east wind
Shifts sudden to the south, the small warm rain
Melts out the frozen incense from all flowers,
100 And fills the air with so much pleasant health
That even the dying man forgets his shroud;
Even so that lofty sacrificial fire,
Sending forth Maian incense, spread around
Forgetfulness of every thing but bliss,
105 And clouded all the altar with soft smoke,
From whose white fragrant curtains thus I heard
Language pronounc'd. "If thou canst not ascend
These steps, die on that marble where thou art.

70 faulture] failing *L*   81 these$_\wedge$ . . . awe,] ~, . . . ~$_\wedge$ *L*   83 massy] massive *L*
85 to] to the *L*   97 May] *ed*; way *W*[2]

Thy flesh, near cousin to the common dust,
110 Will parch for lack of nutriment—thy bones
Will wither in few years, and vanish so
That not the quickest eye could find a grain
Of what thou now art on that pavement cold.
The sands of thy short life are spent this hour,
115 And no hand in the universe can turn
Thy hour glass, if these gummed leaves be burnt
Ere thou canst mount up these immortal steps."
I heard, I look'd: two senses both at once
So fine, so subtle, felt the tyranny
120 Of that fierce threat, and the hard task proposed.
Prodigious seem'd the toil; the leaves were yet
Burning,—when suddenly a palsied chill
Struck from the paved level up my limbs,
And was ascending quick to put cold grasp
125 Upon those streams that pulse beside the throat:
I shriek'd; and the sharp anguish of my shriek
Stung my own ears—I strove hard to escape
The numbness; strove to gain the lowest step.
Slow, heavy, deadly was my pace: the cold
130 Grew stifling, suffocating, at the heart;
And when I clasp'd my hands I felt them not.
One minute before death, my iced foot touch'd
The lowest stair; and as it touch'd, life seem'd
To pour in at the toes: I mounted up,
135 As once fair angels on a ladder flew
From the green turf to heaven.—"Holy Power,"
Cried I, approaching near the horned shrine,
"What am I that should so be sav'd from death?
What am I that another death come not
140 To choak my utterance sacrilegious here?"
Then said the veiled shadow—"Thou hast felt
What 'tis to die and live again before
Thy fated hour. That thou hadst power to do so
Is thy own safety; thou hast dated on
145 Thy doom."—"High Prophetess," said I, "purge off
Benign, if so it please thee, my mind's film."
"None can usurp this height," return'd that shade,
"But those to whom the miseries of the world
Are misery, and will not let them rest.

115 turn] ⟨save⟩ turn *W*[2]  138 should] ⟨I⟩ should *W*[2]

150 All else who find a haven in the world,
Where they may thoughtless sleep away their days,
If by a chance into this fane they come,
Rot on the pavement where thou rotted'st half."—
"Are there not thousands in the world," said I,
155 Encourag'd by the sooth voice of the shade,
"Who love their fellows even to the death;
Who feel the giant agony of the world;
And more, like slaves to poor humanity,
Labour for mortal good? I sure should see
160 Other men here: but I am here alone."
"They whom thou spak'st of are no vision'ries,"
Rejoin'd that voice—"They are no dreamers weak,
They seek no wonder but the human face;
No music but a happy-noted voice—
165 They come not here, they have no thought to come—
And thou art here, for thou art less than they.
What benefit canst thou do, or all thy tribe,
To the great world? Thou art a dreaming thing;
A fever of thyself—think of the earth;
170 What bliss even in hope is there for thee?
What haven? Every creature hath its home;
Every sole man hath days of joy and pain,
Whether his labours be sublime or low—
The pain alone; the joy alone; distinct:
175 Only the dreamer venoms all his days,
Bearing more woe than all his sins deserve.
Therefore, that happiness be somewhat shar'd,
Such things as thou art are admitted oft
Into like gardens thou didst pass erewhile,
180 And suffer'd in these temples; for that cause
Thou standest safe beneath this statue's knees."
"That I am favored for unworthiness,
By such propitious parley medicin'd
In sickness not ignoble, I rejoice,
185 Aye, and could weep for love of such award."
So answer'd I, continuing, "If it please,
Majestic shadow, tell me: sure not all

164 a] *interlined above* ⟨the⟩ $W^2$ 166/167 ⟨Mankind thou lovest; many of thine hours / Have been distemper'd by their miseries;⟩ (by *interlined above* {with} *in the second line*) $W^2$ 168 To] *made out of* Do (*see Textual Note to 167–168*) $W^2$ 187–210 Majestic . . . graves.] *see Textual Note*

Those melodies sung into the world's ear
Are useless: sure a poet is a sage;
190 A humanist, physician to all men.
That I am none I feel, as vultures feel
They are no birds when eagles are abroad.
What am I then? Thou spakest of my tribe:
What tribe?"—The tall shade veil'd in drooping white
195 Then spake, so much more earnest, that the breath
Mov'd the thin linen folds that drooping hung
About a golden censer from the hand
Pendent.—"Art thou not of the dreamer tribe?
The poet and the dreamer are distinct,
200 Diverse, sheer opposite, antipodes.
The one pours out a balm upon the world,
The other vexes it." Then shouted I
Spite of myself, and with a Pythia's spleen,
"Apollo! faded, far flown Apollo!
205 Where is thy misty pestilence to creep
Into the dwellings, through the door crannies,
Of all mock lyrists, large self worshipers,
And careless hectorers in proud bad verse.
Though I breathe death with them it will be life
210 To see them sprawl before me into graves.
Majestic shadow, tell me where I am:
Whose altar this; for whom this incense curls:
What image this, whose face I cannot see,
For the broad marble knees; and who thou art,
215 Of accent feminine, so courteous."
Then the tall shade in drooping linens veil'd
Spake out, so much more earnest, that her breath
Stirr'd the thin folds of gauze that drooping hung
About a golden censer from her hand
220 Pendent; and by her voice I knew she shed
Long treasured tears. "This temple sad and lone
Is all spar'd from the thunder of a war
Foughten long since by giant hierarchy
Against rebellion: this old image here,
225 Whose carved features wrinkled as he fell,

202–204 The . . . flown Apollo!] *originally in* $W^2$ *202 read* The other vexes it." Apollo mine! *and was immediately followed by 205. Subsequently Woodhouse canceled the last two words of 202* (Apollo mine!) *and added the present 202b–204* (Then shouted I . . . flown Apollo!) *on the opposite verso. See Textual Note* 217 her] *made out of* the $W^2$

Is Saturn's; I, Moneta, left supreme
Sole priestess of his desolation."—
I had no words to answer; for my tongue,
Useless, could find about its roofed home
230 No syllable of a fit majesty
To make rejoinder to Moneta's mourn.
There was a silence while the altar's blaze
Was fainting for sweet food: I look'd thereon
And on the paved floor, where nigh were pil'd
235 Faggots of cinnamon, and many heaps
Of other crisped spice-wood—then again
I look'd upon the altar and its horns
Whiten'd with ashes, and its lang'rous flame,
And then upon the offerings again;
240 And so by turns—till sad Moneta cried,
"The sacrifice is done, but not the less
Will I be kind to thee for thy good will.
My power, which to me is still a curse,
Shall be to thee a wonder; for the scenes
245 Still swooning vivid through my globed brain
With an electral changing misery
Thou shalt with those dull mortal eyes behold,
Free from all pain, if wonder pain thee not."
As near as an immortal's sphered words
250 Could to a mother's soften, were these last:
But yet I had a terror of her robes,
And chiefly of the veils, that from her brow
Hung pale, and curtain'd her in mysteries
That made my heart too small to hold its blood.
255 This saw that Goddess, and with sacred hand
Parted the veils. Then saw I a wan face,
Not pin'd by human sorrows, but bright blanch'd
By an immortal sickness which kills not;
It works a constant change, which happy death
260 Can put no end to; deathwards progressing
To no death was that visage; it had pass'd
The lily and the snow; and beyond these
I must not think now, though I saw that face—
But for her eyes I should have fled away.
265 They held me back, with a benignant light,

236 other] *added above the line in* $W^2$  238 lang'rous] *written* (*in a blank space left for the word*) *first in pencil and then in ink in* $W^2$

Soft mitigated by divinest lids
Half closed, and visionless entire they seem'd
Of all external things—they saw me not,
But in blank splendor beam'd like the mild moon,
270 Who comforts those she sees not, who knows not
What eyes are upward cast. As I had found
A grain of gold upon a mountain's side,
And twing'd with avarice strain'd out my eyes
To search its sullen entrails rich with ore,
275 So at the view of sad Moneta's brow,
I ached to see what things the hollow brain
Behind enwombed: what high tragedy
In the dark secret chambers of her skull
Was acting, that could give so dread a stress
280 To her cold lips, and fill with such a light
Her planetary eyes; and touch her voice
With such a sorrow. "Shade of Memory!"
Cried I, with act adorant at her feet,
"By all the gloom hung round thy fallen house,
285 By this last temple, by the golden age,
By great Apollo, thy dear foster child,
And by thy self, forlorn divinity,
The pale Omega of a wither'd race,
Let me behold, according as thou said'st,
290 What in thy brain so ferments to and fro."—
No sooner had this conjuration pass'd
My devout lips, than side by side we stood,
(Like a stunt bramble by a solemn pine)
Deep in the shady sadness of a vale,
295 Far sunken from the healthy breath of morn,
Far from the fiery noon, and eve's one star.
Onward I look'd beneath the gloomy boughs,
And saw, what first I thought an image huge,
Like to the image pedestal'd so high
300 In Saturn's temple. Then Moneta's voice
Came brief upon mine ear,—"So Saturn sat
When he had lost his realms."—Whereon there grew
A power within me of enormous ken,
To see as a God sees, and take the depth
305 Of things as nimbly as the outward eye
Can size and shape pervade. The lofty theme

298 what] *ed*; was (*with the penciled query* "what?" *in the margin*) $W^2$

At those few words hung vast before my mind,
With half unravel'd web. I set myself
Upon an eagle's watch, that I might see,
310 And seeing ne'er forget. No stir of life
Was in this shrouded vale, not so much air
As in the zoning of a summer's day
Robs not one light seed from the feather'd grass,
But where the dead leaf fell there did it rest:
315 A stream went voiceless by, still deaden'd more
By reason of the fallen divinity
Spreading more shade: the Naiad mid her reeds
Press'd her cold finger closer to her lips.
Along the margin sand large footmarks went
320 No farther than to where old Saturn's feet
Had rested, and there slept, how long a sleep!
Degraded, cold, upon the sodden ground
His old right hand lay nerveless, listless, dead,
Unsceptred; and his realmless eyes were clos'd,
325 While his bow'd head seem'd listening to the Earth,
His antient mother, for some comfort yet.

It seem'd no force could wake him from his place;
But there came one who with a kindred hand
Touch'd his wide shoulders, after bending low
330 With reverence, though to one who knew it not.
Then came the griev'd voice of Mnemosyne,
And griev'd I hearken'd. "That divinity
Whom thou saw'st step from yon forlornest wood,
And with slow pace approach our fallen King,
335 Is Thea, softest-natur'd of our brood."
I mark'd the goddess in fair statuary
Surpassing wan Moneta by the head,
And in her sorrow nearer woman's tears.
There was a listening fear in her regard,
340 As if calamity had but begun;
As if the vanward clouds of evil days
Had spent their malice, and the sullen rear
Was with its stored thunder labouring up.
One hand she press'd upon that aching spot
345 Where beats the human heart; as if just there,
Though an immortal, she felt cruel pain;
The other upon Saturn's bended neck

317 more] *interlined above* ⟨a⟩ $W^2$

She laid, and to the level of his hollow ear
Leaning, with parted lips, some words she spake
350 In solemn tenor and deep organ tune;
Some mourning words, which in our feeble tongue
Would come in this-like accenting; how frail
To that large utterance of the early Gods!—
"Saturn! look up—and for what, poor lost King?
355 I have no comfort for thee, no—not one:
I cannot cry, *Wherefore thus sleepest thou?*
For heaven is parted from thee, and the earth
Knows thee not, so afflicted, for a God;
And ocean too, with all its solemn noise,
360 Has from thy sceptre pass'd, and all the air
Is emptied of thine hoary majesty.
Thy thunder, captious at the new command,
Rumbles reluctant o'er our fallen house;
And thy sharp lightning in unpracticed hands
365 Scorches and burns our once serene domain.
With such remorseless speed still come new woes
That unbelief has not a space to breathe.
Saturn, sleep on:—Me thoughtless, why should I
Thus violate thy slumbrous solitude?
370 Why should I ope thy melancholy eyes?
Saturn, sleep on, while at thy feet I weep."

As when, upon a tranced summer night,
Forests, branch-charmed by the earnest stars,
Dream, and so dream all night, without a noise,
375 Save from one gradual solitary gust,
Swelling upon the silence; dying off;
As if the ebbing air had but one wave;
So came these words, and went; the while in tears
She press'd her fair large forehead to the earth,
380 Just where her fallen hair might spread in curls,
A soft and silken mat for Saturn's feet.
Long, long, those two were postured motionless,
Like sculpture builded up upon the grave
Of their own power. A long awful time
385 I look'd upon them; still they were the same;
The frozen God still bending to the earth,
And the sad Goddess weeping at his feet;
Moneta silent. Without stay or prop

356 cry] ⟨say⟩ cry $W^2$ 382 those] *made out of* these $W^2$

But my own weak mortality, I bore
390 The load of this eternal quietude,
The unchanging gloom, and the three fixed shapes
Ponderous upon my senses a whole moon.
For by my burning brain I measured sure
Her silver seasons shedded on the night,
395 And every day by day methought I grew
More gaunt and ghostly. Oftentimes I pray'd
Intense, that death would take me from the vale
And all its burthens. Gasping with despair
Of change, hour after hour I curs'd myself:
400 Until old Saturn rais'd his faded eyes,
And look'd around, and saw his kingdom gone,
And all the gloom and sorrow of the place,
And that fair kneeling Goddess at his feet.
As the moist scent of flowers, and grass, and leaves
405 Fills forest dells with a pervading air
Known to the woodland nostril, so the words
Of Saturn fill'd the mossy glooms around,
Even to the hollows of time-eaten oaks,
And to the windings in the foxes' hole,
410 With sad low tones, while thus he spake, and sent
Strange musings to the solitary Pan.

"Moan, brethren, moan; for we are swallow'd up
And buried from all godlike exercise
Of influence benign on planets pale,
415 And peaceful sway above man's harvesting,
And all those acts which deity supreme
Doth ease its heart of love in. Moan and wail.
Moan, brethren, moan; for lo! the rebel spheres
Spin round, the stars their antient courses keep,
420 Clouds still with shadowy moisture haunt the earth,
Still suck their fill of light from sun and moon,
Still buds the tree, and still the sea-shores murmur.
There is no death in all the universe,
No smell of death—there shall be death—Moan, moan,
425 Moan, Cybele, moan, for thy pernicious babes
Have chang'd a God into a shaking palsy.
Moan, brethren, moan; for I have no strength left,

412 ¶"Moan . . . ] $W^2$ *has the quotation mark at the margin but the first word indented*
427 brethren, moan] moan, brethren (*but marked for transposition*) $W^2$

Weak as the reed—weak—feeble as my voice—
O, O, the pain, the pain of feebleness.
430 Moan, moan; for still I thaw—or give me help:
Throw down those imps and give me victory.
Let me hear other groans, and trumpets blown
Of triumph calm, and hymns of festival
From the gold peaks of heaven's high piled clouds;
435 Voices of soft proclaim, and silver stir
Of strings in hollow shells; and let there be
Beautiful things made new for the surprize
Of the sky children."—So he feebly ceas'd,
With such a poor and sickly sounding pause,
440 Methought I heard some old man of the earth
Bewailing earthly loss; nor could my eyes
And ears act with that pleasant unison of sense
Which marries sweet sound with the grace of form,
And dolorous accent from a tragic harp
445 With large limb'd visions. More I scrutinized:
Still fix'd he sat beneath the sable trees,
Whose arms spread straggling in wild serpent forms,
With leaves all hush'd: his awful presence there
(Now all was silent) gave a deadly lie
450 To what I erewhile heard: only his lips
Trembled amid the white curls of his beard.
They told the truth, though, round, the snowy locks
Hung nobly, as upon the face of heaven
A midday fleece of clouds. Thea arose
455 And stretch'd her white arm through the hollow dark,
Pointing some whither: whereat he too rose
Like a vast giant seen by men at sea
To grow pale from the waves at dull midnight.
They melted from my sight into the woods:
460 Ere I could turn, Moneta cried—"These twain
Are speeding to the families of grief,
Where roof'd in by black rocks they waste in pain
And darkness for no hope."—And she spake on,
As ye may read who can unwearied pass
465 Onward from the antichamber of this dream,
Where even at the open doors awhile
I must delay, and glean my memory
Of her high phrase: perhaps no further dare.

*After* 468 End of Canto 1.— $W^2$

## CANTO II

"Mortal, that thou may'st understand aright,
I humanize my sayings to thine ear,
Making comparisons of earthly things;
Or thou might'st better listen to the wind,
5 Whose language is to thee a barren noise,
Though it blows legend-laden through the trees.
In melancholy realms big tears are shed,
More sorrow like to this, and such-like woe,
Too huge for mortal tongue, or pen of scribe.
10 The Titans fierce, self-hid, or prison-bound,
Groan for the old allegiance once more,
Listening in their doom for Saturn's voice.
But one of our whole eagle-brood still keeps
His sov'reignty, and rule, and majesty;
15 Blazing Hyperion on his orbed fire
Still sits, still snuffs the incense teeming up
From man to the Sun's God: yet unsecure;
For as upon the earth dire prodigies
Fright and perplex, so also shudders he:
20 Nor at dog's howl, or gloom-bird's even screech,
Or the familiar visitings of one
Upon the first toll of his passing bell:
But horrors portion'd to a giant nerve
Make great Hyperion ache. His palace bright,
25 Bastion'd with pyramids of glowing gold,
And touch'd with shade of bronzed obelisks,
Glares a blood red through all the thousand courts,
Arches, and domes, and fiery galeries:
And all its curtains of Aurorian clouds
30 Flush angerly: when he would taste the wreaths
Of incense breath'd aloft from sacred hills,
Instead of sweets, his ample palate takes
Savour of poisonous brass and metals sick.
Wherefore when harbour'd in the sleepy west,
35 After the full completion of fair day,
For rest divine upon exalted couch
And slumber in the arms of melody,
He paces through the pleasant hours of ease,
With strides colossal, on from hall to hall;
40 While, far within each aisle and deep recess,

II.38 ease] *made out of* each $W^2$

His winged minions in close clusters stand
Amaz'd, and full of fear; like anxious men
Who on a wide plain gather in sad troops,
When earthquakes jar their battlements and towers.
45 Even now, while Saturn, rous'd from icy trance,
Goes, step for step, with Thea from yon woods,
Hyperion, leaving twilight in the rear,
Is sloping to the threshold of the west.
Thither we tend."—Now in clear light I stood,
50 Reliev'd from the dusk vale. Mnemosyne
Was sitting on a square edg'd polish'd stone,
That in its lucid depth reflected pure
Her priestess-garments. My quick eyes ran on
From stately nave to nave, from vault to vault,
55 Through bowers of fragrant and enwreathed light,
And diamond paved lustrous long arcades.
Anon rush'd by the bright Hyperion;
His flaming robes stream'd out beyond his heels,
And gave a roar, as if of earthly fire,
60 That scar'd away the meek ethereal hours
And made their dove-wings tremble: on he flared

* * * * * * * * * * * * *

## *The day is gone, and all its sweets are gone*

The day is gone, and all its sweets are gone!
  Sweet voice, sweet lips, soft hand, and softer breast,
Warm breath, light whisper, tender semi-tone,
  Bright eyes, accomplish'd shape, and lang'rous waist!
5 Faded the flower and all its budded charms,
  Faded the sight of beauty from my eyes,
Faded the shape of beauty from my arms,

47 leaving] *added above the line in W*[2]

*The day is gone.* Text from Brown's transcript (*CB*). Variants and other readings from Keats's draft (*D*). *Heading* The . . . are gone] *ed*; Sonnet *CB*; *no heading in D* 3 light] tranc'd *D* 5–8 Faded . . . paradise,] *these lines follow 9–12 in D* 5 and all . . . charms] *interlined above* ⟨of beuty from my {eyes} gaze⟩ (all *further added above the line in the revised wording*) *D* 6 sight . . . eyes] *successively* (*a*) voice of Love from my sad ears (*b*) sight of Love from my sad eyes (*c*) sight of Beauty from my eyes *D*

Faded the voice, warmth, whiteness, paradise,
Vanish'd unseasonably at shut of eve,
10 When the dusk holiday—or holinight—
Of fragrant curtain'd Love begins to weave
The woof of darkness, thick, for hid delight;
But, as I've read Love's missal through to-day,
He'll let me sleep, seeing I fast and pray.

## *I cry your mercy—pity—love!—aye, love*

I cry your mercy—pity—love!—aye, love,
Merciful love that tantalises not,
One-thoughted, never wand'ring, guileless love,
Unmask'd, and being seen—without a blot!
5 O, let me have thee whole,—all,—all—be mine!
That shape, that fairness, that sweet minor zest
Of love, your kiss, those hands, those eyes divine,
That warm, white, lucent, million-pleasured breast,—
Yourself—your soul—in pity give me all,
10 Withhold no atom's atom or I die,
Or living on perhaps, your wretched thrall,
Forget, in the mist of idle misery,
Life's purposes,—the palate of my mind
Losing its gust, and my ambition blind.

## *What can I do to drive away*

What can I do to drive away
Remembrance from my eyes? for they have seen,
Aye, an hour ago, my brilliant queen!
Touch has a memory. O say, Love, say,
5 What can I do to kill it and be free
In my old liberty?
When every fair one that I saw was fair,
Enough to catch me in but half a snare,
Not keep me there:
10 When, howe'er poor or particolour'd things,

8 warmth . . . paradise] ⟨the Whiteness⟩ warmth, whiteness, ⟨brilliance⟩ paradise *D* 12 woof] ⟨texture thick of darkness⟩ woof *D* 13 I've] I have *D*

*I cry your mercy.* Text from Brown's transcript (*CB*). *Heading* I . . . aye, love] *ed*; Sonnet *CB*

*What can I do.* Text from *1848*. *Heading* What . . . away] *ed*; To —— *1848*

My muse had wings,
And ever ready was to take her course
Whither I bent her force,
Unintellectual, yet divine to me;—
15 Divine, I say!—What sea-bird o'er the sea
Is a philosopher the while he goes
Winging along where the great water throes?

How shall I do
To get anew
20 Those moulted feathers, and so mount once more
Above, above
The reach of fluttering Love,
And make him cower lowly while I soar?
Shall I gulp wine? No, that is vulgarism,
25 A heresy and schism,
Foisted into the canon law of love;—
No,—wine is only sweet to happy men;
More dismal cares
Seize on me unawares,—
30 Where shall I learn to get my peace again?
To banish thoughts of that most hateful land,
Dungeoner of my friends, that wicked strand
Where they were wreck'd and live a wretched life;
That monstrous region, whose dull rivers pour
35 Ever from their sordid urns unto the shore,
Unown'd of any weedy-haired gods;
Whose winds, all zephyrless, hold scourging rods,
Iced in the great lakes, to afflict mankind;
Whose rank-grown forests, frosted, black, and blind,
40 Would fright a Dryad; whose harsh herbaged meads
Make lean and lank the starv'd ox while he feeds;
There flowers have no scent, birds no sweet song,
And great unerring Nature once seems wrong.

O, for some sunny spell
45 To dissipate the shadows of this hell!
Say they are gone,—with the new dawning light
Steps forth my lady bright!
O, let me once more rest
My soul upon that dazzling breast!
50 Let once again these aching arms be placed,

33 wretched] *ed*; wrecked *1848* 42 flowers] *ed*; bad flowers *1848*

The tender gaolers of thy waist!
And let me feel that warm breath here and there
To spread a rapture in my very hair,—
O, the sweetness of the pain!
55 Give me those lips again!
Enough! Enough! it is enough for me
To dream of thee!

## *To Fanny*

Physician Nature! let my spirit blood!
O ease my heart of verse and let me rest;
Throw me upon thy tripod, till the flood
Of stifling numbers ebbs from my full breast.
5 A theme! a theme! Great Nature! give a theme;
Let me begin my dream.
I come—I see thee, as thou standest there,
Beckon me out into the wintry air.

Ah! dearest love, sweet home of all my fears
10 And hopes and joys and panting miseries,—
To-night, if I may guess, thy beauty wears
A smile of such delight,
As brilliant and as bright,
As when with ravished, aching, vassal eyes,
15 Lost in a soft amaze,
I gaze, I gaze!

Who now, with greedy looks, eats up my feast?
What stare outfaces now my silver moon!
Ah! keep that hand unravished at the least;
20 Let, let the amorous burn—
But, prithee, do not turn
The current of your heart from me so soon:
O save, in charity,
The quickest pulse for me.

25 Save it for me, sweet love! though music breathe
Voluptuous visions into the warm air,

*To Fanny.* Text (including heading) from Milnes's transcript (*RMM*). Variants and other readings from Keats's draft (*D*, extant for 9–24, 33–56 only). 12 smile of such] smile of such *altered to* smiling *D* 14 when] *written over* ⟨e'en⟩ *D* 16/17 ⟨My temples with hot jealous pulses beat⟩ *D* 17 looks] look⟨s⟩ *D* 22 heart] *interlined above* ⟨thoughts⟩ *D* 23 O] *written over* ⟨S⟩ *D*

Though swimming through the dance's dangerous wreath,
Be like an April day,
Smiling and cold and gay,
30 A temperate lily, temperate as fair;
Then, heaven! there will be
A warmer June for me.

Why this, you'll say—my Fanny!—is not true;
Put your soft hand upon your snowy side,
35 Where the heart beats: confess—'tis nothing new—
Must not a woman be
A feather on the sea,
Swayed to and fro by every wind and tide?
Of as uncertain speed
40 As blow-ball from the mead?

I know it—and to know it is despair
To one who loves you as I love, sweet Fanny,
Whose heart goes fluttering for you every where,
Nor when away you roam,
45 Dare keep its wretched home:
Love, love alone, has pains severe and many;
Then, loveliest! keep me free
From torturing jealousy.

Ah! if you prize my subdued soul above
50 The poor, the fading, brief pride of an hour:
Let none profane my Holy See of Love,
Or with a rude hand break
The sacramental cake:
Let none else touch the just new-budded flower;
55 If not—may my eyes close,
Love, on their last repose!

33 my Fanny!] *interlined above* ⟨ah! Fanny⟩ *RMM* 34 snowy] *added above the line in D*
40/41

⟨I know it. Yet sweet Fanny I would feign
Knell for a mercy on my lonely hours⟩
⟨I know it: yet sweet fanny I would feign
Cry your soft mercy for a⟩ *D*

42 Fanny] *interlined above* ⟨Girl⟩ *D* 45 Dare] Can *D* 47 Then] *written over* ⟨Ah⟩ *D* 48/49

⟨And if you pize my subdued heart above
The poor, the fading brief pride⟩

(prized *interlined and deleted after* my—*the position is Keats's mistake—and then* pize *interlined before* my) *D* 49 Ah] *interlined above* ⟨And⟩ *D* 49 soul] heart *D* 53/54 ⟨O keep⟩ *D* 56 Love,] Now$_\wedge$ *D*

# *King Stephen:*
# *A Fragment of a Tragedy*

Dramatis Personæ

King Stephen
Earl of Glocester
Earl of Chester
Earl Baldwin de Redvers
De Kaims

The Empress Maud, *or* Matilda

## ACT I

### Scene I. *Field of Battle.*

*Alarum. Enter* King Stephen, *Knights, and Soldiers.*

*Stephen.* If shame can on a soldier's vein-swoll'n front
Spread deeper crimson than the battle's toil,
Blush in your casing helmets!—for see, see!
Yonder my chivalry, my pride of war,
5 Wrench'd with an iron hand from firm array,
Are routed loose about the plashy meads,
Of honour forfeit. O, that my known voice
Could reach your dastard ears and fright you more!
Fly, cowards, fly! Glocester is at your backs!
10 Throw your slack bridles o'er the flurried manes,
Ply well the rowel with faint trembling heels,
Scampering to death at last!
*First Knight.* The enemy
Bears his flaunt standard close upon their rear.
*Second Knight.* Sure of a bloody prey, seeing the fens
Will swamp them girth deep.
15 *Stephen.* Over head and ears,

*King Stephen.* Text of heading, Dramatis Personae, and I.i.1–ii.19a from Brown's transcript (*CB*) and of I.ii.19b–iv.58 from Keats's draft (*D*). *Dramatis Personae* Earl of Glocester] *ed*; Duke of Glocester *CB* Earl Baldwin de Redvers] *ed*; Earl Baldwin *CB* De Kaims] *ed*; *not in CB*

No matter! 'Tis a gallant enemy;
How like a comet he goes streaming on.
But we must plague him in the flank,—hey, friends?
We are well breathed,—follow!

[*Enter* EARL BALDWIN, *and Soldiers, as defeated.*

De Redvers!

20 What is the monstrous bugbear that can fright
Baldwin?

*Baldwin.* No scarecrow, but the fortunate star
Of boisterous Chester, whose fell truncheon now
Points level to the goal of victory.
This way he comes, and if you would maintain
25 Your person unaffronted by vile odds,
Take horse, my lord.

*Stephen.* And which way spur for life?
Now I thank heaven I am in the toils,
That soldiers may bear witness how my arm
Can burst the meshes. Not the eagle more
30 Loves to beat up against a tyrannous blast,
Than I to meet the torrent of my foes.
This is a brag,—be't so,—but if I fall,
Carve it upon my 'scutcheon'd sepulchre.
On, fellow soldiers! Earl of Redvers, back!
35 Not twenty Earls of Chester shall brow-beat
The diadem! [*Exeunt. Alarums.*

SCENE II. *Another part of the Field.*

*Trumpets sounding a victory. Enter* GLOCESTER,
*Knights, and forces.*

*Glocester.* Now may we lift our bruised visors up,
And take the flattering freshness of the air,
While the wide din of battle dies away
Into times past, yet to be echoed sure
5 In the silent pages of our chroniclers.

*First Knight.* Will Stephen's death be mark'd there, my good lord,
Or that we gave him lodging in yon towers?

*Glocester.* Fain would I know the great usurper's fate.

I.i.19 breathed] *ed*; breath'd *CB* 35 Earls of Chester] *ed*; Earl of Chesters *CB*

*Enter two Captains, severally.*

*First Captain.* My lord!
*Second Captain.* Most noble Earl!
*First Captain.* The King—
*Second Captain.* The Empress greets—
*Glocester.* What of the King?
10 *First Captain.* He sole and lone maintains
A hopeless bustle 'mid our swarming arms;
And with a nimble savageness attacks,
Escapes, makes fiercer onset, then anew
Eludes death, giving death to most that dare
15 Trespass within the circuit of his sword:—
He must by this have fallen. Baldwin is taken;
And for the Duke of Bretagne, like a stag
He flies, for the Welch beagles to hunt down.
God save the Empress.
*Glocester.* Now our dreaded Queen—
What message from her Highness?
20 *Second Captain.* Royal Maud
From the throng'd towers of Lincoln hath look'd down,
Like Pallas from the walls of Ilion,
And seen her enemies havock'd at her feet.
She greets most noble Glocester from her heart,
25 Intreating him, his captains, and brave knights
To grace a banquet. The high city gates
Are envious which shall see your triumph pass.
The streets are full of music—

*Enter Second Knight.*

*Glocester.* Whence come you?
*Second Knight.* From Stephen, my good Prince—Stephen—
Stephen—

I.ii.17 Bretagne] Britain *altered to* Bretagne *CB* 19 *Glocester.* Now . . . Queen] *the first surviving page of D begins:*

⟨enter another Captain⟩

⟨*Glocester.*⟩ ⟨What new⟩
⟨What ist you would say?⟩
*Glocester.* Now our dreaded Queen

(say *interlined above* {speak} *in the third line*) 20 Royal] ⟨This to thee / Most noble Gloster.⟩ Royal *D* 25 his] ⟨and⟩ his *D* 28 *s.d.* Enter . . . Knight] *ed*; a Knight *interlined above* ⟨enter another Captain⟩ *D* 28 Whence] *ed*; When *D* 28/29 ⟨3 Captain⟩ (*can-*

30 *Glocester.* Why do you make such echoing of his name?
*Second Knight.* Because I think, my lord, he is no man,
But a fierce demon 'nointed safe from wounds
And misbaptised with a Christian name.
*Glocester.* A mighty soldier. Does he still hold out?
35 *Second Knight.* He shames our victory. His valour still
Keeps elbow room amid our eager swords,
And holds our bladed falchions all aloof.
His gleaming battle axe being slaughter sick,
Smote on the morion of a Flemish knight,
40 Broke short in his hand; upon the which he flung
The heft away with such a vengeful force
It paunch'd the Earl of Chester's horse, who then
Spleen-hearted came in full career at him.
*Glocester.* Did no one take him at a vantage then?
45 *Second Knight.* Three then with tiger leap upon him flew,
Whom, with his sword swift-drawn and nimbly held,
He stung away again, and stood to breathe,
Smiling. Anon upon him rush'd once more
A throng of foes; and in this renew'd strife
50 My sword met his and snapp'd off at the hilts.
*Glocester.* Come, lead me to this Mars—and let us move
In silence, not insulting his sad doom
With clamourous trumpets. To the Empress bear
My salutation as befits the time.
[*Exeunt* GLOCESTER *and forces.*

SCENE III. *The field of Battle.*

*Enter* STEPHEN *unarm'd.*

*Stephen.* Another sword! and what if I could seize
One from Bellona's gleaming armoury,

---

*celed s.p., the* 3 *added in the margin) D* 29, 31, 35, 45 *s.p.* Second Knight] *ed*; Knight *D* 29 my good] *added above the line in D* 36 Keeps] ⟨Matains⟩ Keeps *D* 51 *s.p.* Glocester] *successively* (*a*) Glocester (*b*) 1 Knight (*c*) Glocester *D* 51 Come,] *added in the margin in D*

I.iii *before* 1
⟨*Stephen.* Another Sword! for one short minute longer
That I may pepper that De Kaimes and then
Yield to {this army} some twenty squadrons—Stephen say,
Wouldst thou exchange this helmeted renown

Or choose the fairest of her sheaved spears!
Where are my enemies? Here, close at hand,
5 Here comes the testy brood. O for a sword!
I'm faint—a biting sword! A noble sword!
A hedge-stake—or a ponderous stone to hurl
With brawny vengeance, like the labourer Cain.
Come on! Farewell my kingdom, and all hail
10 Thou superb, plum'd, and helmeted renown,
All hail—I would not truck this brilliant day
To rule in Pylos with a Nestor's beard.
Come on!

*Enter* De Kaims *and Knights, etc.*

*De Kaims.* Is't madness or a hunger after death
15 That makes thee thus unarm'd throw taunts at us?
Yield, Stephen, or my sword's point dip in
The gloomy current of a traitor's heart.
*Stephen.* Do it, De Kaims, I will not budge an inch.
*De Kaims.* Yes, of thy madness thou shalt take the meed—
*Stephen.* Darest thou?
20 *De Kaims.* How dare, against a man disarm'd?
*Stephen.* What weapon has the lion but himself?
Come not near me, De Kaims, for by the price
Of all the glory I have won this day,
Being a king, I will not yield alive
25 To any but the second man of the realm,
Robert of Glocester.
*De Kaims.* Thou shalt vail to me.
*Stephen.* Shall I, when I have sworn against it, sir?
Thou think'st it brave to take a breathing king,
That, on a court day bow'd to haughty Maud,
30 The awed presence chamber may be bold

---

To rule in quet Pylos Nestor-like?
No!—

*Enter De Kaims Knights and Soldiers dropping in.*

*De Kaims*⟩

(valliant *interlined and deleted above* army *and* Stephen say *plus comma interlined above* {This is glory!} *in the third line, and* Wouldst *made out of* Would *in the fourth; Keats then began again with I.iii.1 ff. on a new page*) *D* 1 could seize] *interlined above* ⟨took one⟩ *D* 2 One from] From forth *altered to* One From *D* 4 are my enemies] is my Enemy *altered to* are ⟨my⟩ Enemies (my *deleted by mistake*) *D* 4 Here] *interlined above* ⟨Aye⟩ *D* 16 dip] ⟨explore⟩ dip *D* 28 breathing king] King alive *altered to* breathing King *D*

To whisper, there's the man who took alive
Stephen—me—prisoner. Certes, De Kaims,
The ambition is a noble one.
*De Kaims.* 'Tis true,
And, Stephen, I must compass it—
*Stephen.* No, no—
35 Do not tempt me to throttle you on the gorge,
Or with my gauntlet crush your hollow breast,
Just when your knighthood is grown ripe and full
For lordship.
*A Soldier.* Is an honest yeoman's spear
Of no use at a need? Take that—
*Stephen.* Ah dastard!
40 *De Kaims.* What, you are vulnerable! my prisoner!
*Stephen.* No, not yet—I disclaim it, and demand
Death as a sovereign right unto a king
Who 'sdains to yield to any but his peer,
If not in title yet in noble deeds,
45 The Earl of Glocester. Stab to the hilts, De Kaims,
For I will never by mean hands be led
From this so famous field—D'ye hear! be quick!
[*Trumpets. Enter the* EARL OF CHESTER *and Knights.*

SCENE IV. *A Presence Chamber.*

QUEEN MAUD *in a chair of state. The* EARLS OF GLOCESTER *and* CHESTER, *Lords, Attendants.*

*Maud.* Glocester, no more: I will behold that Boulogne:
Set him before me. Not for the poor sake
Of regal pomp and a vainglorious hour,
As thou with wary speech, yet near enough,
Hast hinted.
5 *Glocester.* Faithful counsel have I given,
If wary, for your Highness' benefit—
*Maud.* The heavens forbid that I should not think so.
For by thy valour have I won this realm,

31 there's the man] there is he *altered to* there's the man *D* 31 who] *added above the line in D* 31/32 ⟨King⟩ ⟨The stubborn Reb⟩ *D* 47 D'ye] Do ye *altered to* D'ye *D*

I.iv *heading* Scene IV] *ed*; Scene (*without number*) *D* 2 the] *added above the line in D*

Which by thy wisdom will I ever keep.
10 To sage advisers let me ever bend
A meek attentive ear, so that they treat
Of the wide kingdom's rule and government,
Not trenching on our actions personal.
Advised, not school'd, I would be, and henceforth
15 Spoken to in clear, plain, and open terms,
Not sideways sermon'd at.
*Glocester.* Then in plain terms,
Once more for the fall'n King—
*Maud.* Your pardon, brother,
I would no more of that; for, as I said,
'Tis not for worldly pomp I wish to see
20 The rebel, but as a dooming judge to give
A sentence something worthy of his guilt.
*Glocester.* If't must be so I'll bring him to your presence.
[*Exit* GLOCESTER.
*Maud.* A meaner summoner might do as well—
My Lord of Chester, is't true what I hear
25 Of Stephen of Boulogne, our prisoner,
That he, as a fit penance for his crimes,
Eats wholesome, sweet, and palatable food
Off Glocester's golden dishes—drinks pure wine,
Lodges soft?
*Chester.* More than that, most gracious Queen,
30 Has anger'd me. The noble Earl, methinks,
Full soldier as he is, and without peer
In Council, dreams too much among his books.
It may read well, but sure 'tis out of date
To play the Alexander with Darius.
35 *Maud.* Truth! I think so—by heavens, it shall not last.
*Chester.* It would amaze your Highness now to mark
How Glocester overstrains his courtesy
To that crime-loving rebel; that Boulogne—
*Maud.* That ingrate!
*Chester.* For whose vast ingratitude

10 let me ever] ever will I *altered to* let me ever *D* 13 Not trenching] And not trench *altered to* not trenching *D* 13 actions] *added above the line in D* 15 Spoken . . . clear] *successively* (*a*) I would (*b*) Be spoken ⟨with⟩ to in (*c*) spoken to in clear *D* 29 most] *made out of* my *D* 32 too] ⟨sometimes⟩ too *D* 33 out of date] *interlined above* ⟨weak enough⟩ *D* 37/38 ⟨And finds for every one of all his⟩ *D*

40 To our late sovereign lord, your noble sire,
The generous Earl condoles in his mishaps,
And with a sort of lackeying friendliness
Talks off the mighty frowning from his brow,
Woos him to hold a duet in a smile,
45 Or if it please him play an hour at chess—
*Maud.* A perjur'd slave!
*Chester.* And for his perjury
Glocester has fit rewards—nay, I believe
He sets his bustling household's wits at work
For flatteries to ease this Stephen's hours,
50 And make a heaven of his purgatory,
Adorning bondage with the pleasant gloss
Of feasts and music, and all idle shows
Of indoor pageantry; while syren whispers,
Predestin'd for his ear, scape as half check'd
55 From lips the courtliest and the rubiest
Of all the realm, admiring of his deeds.
*Maud.* A frost upon his summer!
*Chester.* A queen's nod
Can make his June December—here he comes.

## *This living hand, now warm and capable*

This living hand, now warm and capable
Of earnest grasping, would, if it were cold
And in the icy silence of the tomb,
So haunt thy days and chill thy dreaming nights
5 That thou would wish thine own heart dry of blood,
So in my veins red life might stream again,
And thou be conscience-calm'd. See, here it is—
I hold it towards you.

43 mighty] *added above the line in D* 48 his] *squeezed in afterward in D* 58 his] ⟨cold christmas⟩ his *D*

*This living hand.* Text from the extant holograph (arbitrarily cited as *D*). Heading supplied by editor. 5 heart] *added above the line (and wrongly marked for insertion before* own*) in D*

# *The Jealousies: A Faery Tale, by Lucy Vaughan Lloyd of China Walk, Lambeth*

1

In midmost Ind, beside Hydaspes cool,
There stood, or hover'd, tremulous in the air,
A faery city, 'neath the potent rule
Of Emperor Elfinan; famed ev'rywhere
5 For love of mortal women, maidens fair,
Whose lips were solid, whose soft hands were made
Of a fit mould and beauty, ripe and rare,
To pamper his slight wooing, warm yet staid:
He lov'd girls smooth as shades, but hated a mere shade.

2

10 This was a crime forbidden by the law;
And all the priesthood of his city wept,
For ruin and dismay they well foresaw,
If impious prince no bound or limit kept,
And faery Zendervester overstept;
15 They wept, he sinn'd, and still he would sin on,
They dreamt of sin, and he sinn'd while they slept;
In vain the pulpit thunder'd at the throne,
Caricature was vain, and vain the tart lampoon.

3

Which seeing, his high court of parliament
20 Laid a remonstrance at his Highness' feet,
Praying his royal senses to content
Themselves with what in faery land was sweet,

*The Jealousies.* Text from *1848.* Variants and other readings from Keats's draft (*D*, extant for 1–729 only), Woodhouse's $W^2$ transcript, and the extract of 217–256 published in the *Indicator* (*Ind*). *Heading* The . . . Lambeth] $W^2$; The Cap and Bells; / Or, the Jealousies. / A Faëry Tale. Unfinished *1848*; *no heading in D* 9 smooth] *interlined above* ⟨soft⟩ *D* 13 If . . . kept] Where Prince religious limits overstept *altered to* If impious Prince no bound or limit kept *D* 16/17

⟨Until the faery City no more shone
{As it was wont, heaven's vengenc rubbd its bloom}
As it was wont⟩
⟨Untill the faery City no more shone
As it was wont⟩ *D*

18 tart] *interlined above* ⟨bold⟩ *D* 20 Laid] *written over* ⟨Br⟩ *or* ⟨By⟩ *D*

Befitting best that shade with shade should meet:
Whereat, to calm their fears, he promised soon
25 From mortal tempters all to make retreat,—
Aye, even on the first of the new moon,
An immaterial wife to espouse as heaven's boon.

4

Meantime he sent a fluttering embassy
To Pigmio, of Imaus sovereign,
30 To half beg, and half demand, respectfully,
The hand of his fair daughter Bellanaine;
An audience had, and speeching done, they gain
Their point, and bring the weeping bride away;
Whom, with but one attendant, safely lain
35 Upon their wings, they bore in bright array,
While little harps were touch'd by many a lyric fay.

5

As in old pictures tender cherubim
A child's soul through the sapphired canvas bear,
So, through a real heaven, on they swim
40 With the sweet Princess on her plumaged lair,
Speed giving to the winds her lustrous hair;
And so she journey'd, sleeping or awake,
Save when, for healthful exercise and air,
She chose to "promener à l'aile," or take
45 A pigeon's somerset, for sport or change's sake.

6

"Dear Princess, do not whisper me so loud,"
Quoth Corallina, nurse and confidant,
"Do not you see there, lurking in a cloud,
Close at your back, that sly old Crafticant?
50 He hears a whisper plainer than a rant:
Dry up your tears, and do not look so blue;
He's Elfinan's great state-spy militant,

23 Befitting] Befeeling *D* 29 sovereign] ⟨Emperor⟩ Sovereign *D* 32 An] *written over* ⟨The⟩ *D*; And, *W*² 33/34 ⟨Borne upon⟩ *D* 34 Whom] Who *D* 37/38 ⟨As in old Picturrese Cherubs bear aloft / The Souls of Children⟩ *D* 40 on] in *W*² 47/48 ⟨Do not you see there coming through⟩ *D* 48 a] *interlined above* ⟨that⟩ *D* 49 Crafticant] *interlined above* ⟨Crafty Cant⟩ *D* 50/51 ⟨He's Elfinan's state train and tale-bearer / His running and his flying footman⟩ *D* 52 He's] He *D*

His running, lying, flying foot-man too,—
Dear mistress, let him have no handle against you!

7

55 "Show him a mouse's tail, and he will guess,
With metaphysic swiftness, at the mouse;
Show him a garden, and with speed no less,
He'll surmise sagely of a dwelling-house,
And plot, in the same minute, how to chouse
60 The owner out of it; show him a—" "Peace!
Peace! nor contrive thy mistress' ire to rouse,"
Return'd the Princess, "my tongue shall not cease
Till from this hated match I get a free release.

8

"Ah, beauteous mortal!" "Hush!" quoth Coralline,
65 "Really you must not talk of him, indeed."
"You hush!" replied the mistress, with a shine
Of anger in her eyes, enough to breed
In stouter hearts than nurse's fear and dread:
'Twas not the glance itself made nursey flinch,
70 But of its threat she took the utmost heed;
Not liking in her heart an hour-long pinch,
Or a sharp needle run into her back an inch.

9

So she was silenced, and fair Bellanaine,
Writhing her little body with ennui,
75 Continued to lament and to complain,
That Fate, cross-purposing, should let her be
Ravish'd away far from her dear countree;
That all her feelings should be set at nought,
In trumping up this match so hastily,
80 With lowland blood; and lowland blood she thought
Poison, as every staunch true-born Imaian ought.

53 running, lying] ⟨flyin⟩ running ⟨and his⟩ lying *D* 61 thy] your $W^2$ 66 You] *underscored in* $W^2$ 66 the] *interlined above* ⟨her⟩ *D* 68/69

⟨Not for the glance itse⟩
⟨Not for the fiery glance itself perhaps⟩
⟨Nor at the glance itsef⟩

(the glance itse *interlined above* {themselves perhaps} *in the first line and* fiery *added above in the second*) *D* 69 made nursey] *interlined above* ⟨that made nurse⟩ *D* 70 its] *interlined above* ⟨the⟩ *D* 77/78 ⟨That she a highland Princess⟩ (That *successively* [*a*] That [*b*] And [*c*] That) *D*

10

Sorely she grieved, and wetted three or four
White Provence rose-leaves with her faery tears,
But not for this cause;—alas! she had more
85 Bad reasons for her sorrow, as appears
In the famed memoirs of a thousand years,
Written by Crafticant, and published
By Parpaglion and Co., (those sly compeers
Who raked up ev'ry fact against the dead,)
90 In Scarab Street, Panthea, at the Jubal's Head.

11

Where, after a long hypercritic howl
Against the vicious manners of the age,
He goes on to expose, with heart and soul,
What vice in this or that year was the rage,
95 Backbiting all the world in ev'ry page;
With special strictures on the horrid crime,
(Section'd and subsection'd with learning sage,)
Of faeries stooping on their wings sublime
To kiss a mortal's lips, when such were in their prime.

12

100 Turn to the copious index, you will find
Somewhere in the column headed letter B
The name of Bellanaine, if you're not blind;
Then pray refer to the text, and you will see
An article made up of calumny
105 Against this highland princess, rating her
For giving way, so over fashionably,
To this new-fangled vice, which seems a burr
Stuck in his moral throat, no coughing e'er could stir.

13

There he says plainly that she loved a man!
110 That she around him flutter'd, flirted, toy'd,
Before her marriage with great Elfinan;

85 reasons] *interlined above* ⟨cause of sorrow⟩ *D* 87/88 ⟨In Scarab Street Penthea⟩ *D*
91 hypercritic] hypocritic $W^2$ 107 seems] seem *D*; seem'd $W^2$ 109/110
⟨And before⟩
⟨Before her marriage used with him to flirt⟩ *D*
110 around . . . toy'd] *successively* (*a*) with him would flutter flirt and Toy (*b*) with him did flutter flirt and Toy (*c*) around him flutterd flirted toy'd *D*

That after marriage too, she never joy'd
In husband's company, but still employ'd
Her wits to 'scape away to Angle-land;
115 Where liv'd the youth, who worried and annoy'd
Her tender heart, and its warm ardours fann'd
To such a dreadful blaze, her side would scorch her hand.

14

But let us leave this idle tittle tattle
To waiting-maids, and bed-room coteries,
120 Nor till fit time against her fame wage battle.
Poor Elfinan is very ill at ease—
Let us resume his subject if you please:
For it may comfort and console him much,
To rhyme and syllable his miseries;
125 Poor Elfinan! whose cruel fate was such,
He sat and cursed a bride he knew he could not touch.

15

Soon as (according to his promises)
The bridal embassy had taken wing,
And vanish'd, bird-like, o'er the suburb trees,
130 The Emperor, empierced with the sharp sting
Of love, retired, vex'd and murmuring
Like any drone shut from the fair bee-queen,
Into his cabinet, and there did fling
His limbs upon a sofa, full of spleen,
135 And damn'd his House of Commons, in complete chagrin.

16

"I'll trounce some of the members," cried the Prince,
"I'll put a mark against some rebel names,
I'll make the opposition-benches wince,
I'll show them very soon, to all their shames,
140 What 'tis to smother up a prince's flames;
That ministers should join in it, I own,
Surprises me!—they too at these high games!
Am I an Emperor? Do I wear a crown?
Imperial Elfinan, go hang thyself or drown!

112 marriage] *added above the line in D* 115 worried and] *interlined above* ⟨ever more⟩ *D* 116 ardours] *interlined above* ⟨fires⟩ *D* 120 her] his $W^2$ 125 cruel] *added above the line in D* 127 (according] ⟨the⟩ (according *D* 130 empierced] *interlined above* ⟨tansfix'd⟩ *D* 135 damn'd] cus'd *D*

17

145 "I'll trounce 'em!—there's the square-cut chancellor,
His son shall never touch that bishopric;
And for the nephew of old Palfior,
I'll show him that his speeches made me sick,
And give the colonelcy to Phalaric;
150 The tiptoe marquis, moral and gallant,
Shall lodge in shabby taverns upon tick;
And for the Speaker's second cousin's aunt,
She sha'n't be maid of honour,—by heaven that she sha'n't!

18

"I'll shirk the Duke of A.; I'll cut his brother;
155 I'll give no garter to his eldest son;
I won't speak to his sister or his mother!
The Viscount B. shall live at cut-and-run;
But how in the world can I contrive to stun
That fellow's voice, which plagues me worse than any,
160 That stubborn fool, that impudent state-dun,
Who sets down ev'ry sovereign as a zany,—
That vulgar commoner, Esquire Biancopany?

19

"Monstrous affair! Pshaw! pah! what ugly minx
Will they fetch from Imaus for my bride?
165 Alas! my wearied heart within me sinks,
To think that I must be so near allied
To a cold dullard fay,—ah, woe betide!
Ah, fairest of all human loveliness!
Sweet Bertha! what crime can it be to glide
170 About the fragrant plaitings of thy dress,
Or kiss thine eyes, or count thy locks, tress after tress?"

145–153 "I'll . . . sha'n't!] *a preliminary draft of this stanza appears on a separate half-sheet in D; apparatus readings from this earlier version are designated d* *Before* 145 ⟨"Monstrous affair! Pshaw! Pshaw! what ugly Minx⟩ *d* 146/147 ⟨And for that tip-toe Marquis Belfior / By heavens his Nephew⟩ *d* 147 Palfior] *made out of* Palcolor *d* 148 him] *added above the line in d* 148 speeches] speech has *d*, *D* 149/150 ⟨The tiptoe Marquis moral too—by Dis / He still shall li⟩ *d* 150 moral and gallant] *successively* (*a*) moral too—good—good (*b*) moral too—God grant (*c*) moral! good—he still (*d*) moral and gallant (*e*) moral yet gallant *d* 151 lodge] live *d*; lodge *made out of* live *D* 152 second] Brother's *d*; second *interlined above* ⟨Brother's⟩ *D* 153 by heaven] *added above the line in d* 157 Viscount] *interlined above* ⟨Baron⟩ *D* 159 which] who *interlined above* ⟨that⟩ *D* 161 sets . . . as] set down every Sovereign for *interlined above* ⟨always thinks a soveeign⟩ *D* 170 plaitings] pleatings *D*

20

So said, one minute's while his eyes remain'd
Half lidded, piteous, languid, innocent;
But, in a wink, their splendour they regain'd,
175 Sparkling revenge with amorous fury blent.
Love thwarted in bad temper oft has vent:
He rose, he stampt his foot, he rang the bell,
And order'd some death-warrants to be sent
For signature:—somewhere the tempest fell,
180 As many a poor felon does not live to tell.

21

"At the same time, Eban,"—(this was his page,
A fay of colour, slave from top to toe,
Sent as a present, while yet under age,
From the Viceroy of Zanguebar,—wise, slow
185 His speech, his only words were "yes" and "no,"
But swift of look, and foot, and wing was he,)—
"At the same time, Eban, this instant go
To Hum the soothsayer, whose name I see
Among the fresh arrivals in our empery.

22

190 "Bring Hum to me! But stay—here take my ring,
The pledge of favour, that he not suspect
Any foul play, or awkward murdering,

172 said . . . remain'd] *successively* (*a*) saying (*b*) sayd his eyes one minute's while were soft (*c*) sayd one minute's while he (*d*) sayd one minute's while his eyes remaind *D* 177 rose] arose *D* 178 And . . . some] Order'd a few *altered to* And Order'd some *D* 180 felon] *D*, *W*[2]; fellow *1848* 180/181

19

⟨"{And} At the same time Amorio" said he
(This was his favourite Page a negro Fay⟩
⟨At the same time, Amorico" said he⟩
⟨At the same time Eban" (this was his Page,
A Fay of Colour, sent from Zanquebar
A Present from the Viceroy)⟩

(At *made out of* at *and* Amorio *interlined above* {Luccianal} *in the first line*) *D*. *The present stanzas 19–28 are numbered 17–26 in D* (*see Textual Note to 145–162*) 182 slave . . . toe] *interlined above* ⟨trusty secret sure⟩ (sure *successively* [*a*] close [*b*] sly [*c*] sure) *D* 184 wise] *Keats interlined and deleted* di (*the beginning of* discreet?) *above this word in D* 184 slow$_{\wedge}$] *D*; ~, *W*[2], *1848* 185 only] *added above the line in D* 187/188 ⟨To that old Fortuntellers whom I see⟩ (that *made out of* the) *D* 189 in] *interlined above* ⟨to⟩ *D* 192 murdering] handling *D*

Though I have bowstrung many of his sect;
Throw in a hint, that if he should neglect
195 One hour, the next shall see him in my grasp,
And the next after that shall see him neck'd,
Or swallow'd by my hunger-starved asp,—
And mention ('tis as well) the torture of the wasp."

23

These orders given, the Prince, in half a pet,
200 Let o'er the silk his propping elbow slide,
Caught up his little legs, and, in a fret,
Fell on the sofa on his royal side.
The slave retreated backwards, humble-eyed,
And with a slave-like silence closed the door,
205 And to old Hum through street and alley hied;
He "knew the city," as we say, of yore,
For shortest cuts and turns, was nobody knew more.

24

It was the time when wholesale houses close
Their shutters with a moody sense of wealth,
210 But retail dealers, diligent, let loose
The gas (objected to on score of health),
Convey'd in little solder'd pipes by stealth,
And make it flare in many a brilliant form,
That all the power of darkness it repell'th,
215 Which to the oil-trade doth great scaith and harm,
And supersedeth quite the use of the glow-worm.

25

Eban, untempted by the pastry-cooks,
(Of pastry he got store within the palace,)

193/194 ⟨At the same⟩ *D*  195/196 ⟨The next shall see⟩ *D*  196 that] *added above the line in D*  198 And . . . well) the] *written beneath* ⟨Or at the least put to the⟩ *D*  202 Fell] *interlined above* ⟨Lay⟩ *D*  207 For shortest] *D* (*made out of* And for short); And, for short $W^2$, *1848*  207/208

⟨His arms and wings wrapt in a crimson cloak
In cognito he makes important way
Though the Courtyard {and golden gates} whose golden Portals look
Full on a pearl-built Minster⟩

(crimson *interlined above* {purple} *in the first line; see Textual Note*) *D*  208 houses] *D*; dealers $W^2$, *1848*  211 on] on the *D*  212 pipes] tubes $W^2$  213 make] ⟨set it flaing⟩ make *D*  214 power] *D*, $W^2$; powers *1848*  214 repell'th] quite quell'th *D*  215 doth] did *D*  216 supersedeth] superseded *D*

With hasty steps, wrapp'd cloak, and solemn looks,
220 Incognito upon his errand sallies,
His smelling-bottle ready for the allies;
He pass'd the hurdy-gurdies with disdain,
Vowing he'd have them sent on board the gallies;
Just as he made his vow, it 'gan to rain,
225 Therefore he call'd a coach, and bade it drive amain.

26

"I'll pull the string," said he, and further said,
"Polluted jarvey! Ah, thou filthy hack!
Whose springs of life are all dried up and dead,
Whose linsey-wolsey lining hangs all slack,
230 Whose rug is straw, whose wholeness is a crack;
And evermore thy steps go clatter-clitter;
Whose glass once up can never be got back,
Who prov'st, with jolting arguments and bitter,
That 'tis of modern use to travel in a litter.

27

235 "Thou inconvenience! thou hungry crop
For all corn! thou snail-creeper to and fro,
Who while thou goest ever seem'st to stop,
And fiddle-faddle standest while you go;
I' the morning, freighted with a weight of woe,
240 Unto some lazar-house thou journeyest,
And in the evening tak'st a double row

219 hasty] *interlined above* ⟨measured⟩ *D* 223 on board] abord *D* 225 Therefore . . . bade] And so . . . bid *D* 227 "Polluted . . . hack] *successively* (*a*) Ah filthy Hack! Polluted Vehicle (*b*) Polluted Vehicle! Ah filthy Hack (*this is simply* [*a*] *marked for transposition*) (*c*) Polluted Jarvey! Ah thou filthy hack (*d*) In his heart Vile Javey! Ah thou filthy hack *D* 229 linsey] ⟨lining⟩ linsey *D* 231 steps] *interlined above* ⟨teeth⟩ *D* 231–234 go . . . litter] *this ending of 231* (*with* clatter clitter *written beneath* ⟨clitter clatter⟩) *and the present 233–234* (*with the variant given in the next note*) *appear in D upside down on the page containing 388–398; the original text in D is uncanceled:*

are clattering
Whose glass once up can never be got back,
Whose number stuck above my head a thing
(The number of the beast) gives trembling to my wing

(*the first six words of the last line interlined above* ⟨Gives coldness to my heart and⟩) 233 arguments] argument *D* (*revised version*) 234 modern use] vile no-use *Ind* 236 snail] *added above the line in D* 237 thou] *made out of* thy *D* 241–242 evening . . . for] Even takest in a glow / Of Beauties from *D*

Of dowdies, for some dance or party drest,
Besides the goods meanwhile thou movest east and west.

28

"By thy ungallant bearing and sad mien,
245 An inch appears the utmost thou couldst budge;
Yet at the slightest nod, or hint, or sign,
Round to the curb-stone patient dost thou trudge,
School'd in a beckon, learned in a nudge,
A dull-eyed Argus watching for a fare;
250 Quiet and plodding, thou dost bear no grudge
To whisking tilburies, or phaetons rare,
Curricles, or mail-coaches, swift beyond compare."

29

Philosophising thus, he pull'd the check,
And bade the coachman wheel to such a street,
255 Who, turning much his body, more his neck,
Louted full low, and hoarsely did him greet:
"Certes, monsieur were best take to his feet,
Seeing his servant can no further drive
For press of coaches, that to-night here meet,
260 Many as bees about a straw-capp'd hive,
When first for April honey into faint flowers they dive."

246 Yet . . . slightest] And at the least *D* 247 Round] *interlined above* ⟨Up⟩ *D* 247/248 ⟨As courteous to a Cobler as a Judge—⟩ *D* 248 School'd in] *successively* (*a*) Ever on (*b*) Up to (*c*) School'd in *D* 252/253

29

⟨Philosophising thus he check'd the d⟩
⟨Philosophising thus he pull'd the Check
{The Coachman}
And pointed⟩
Philosophisig thus he puld the Check
The Coachman turn'd and lowting down full low

(*stanza number* 29 *made out of* 27 *and* check'd the d *written beneath* {pull'd the String} *in the first line; Keats then began again with stanza 29 on a new page*) *D* 254 wheel] *interlined above* ⟨turn⟩ *D* 259/260

⟨I doubt the u⟩
⟨Thick⟩ *D*

261 faint] *added above the line in D* 261/262

30

⟨"Ho! Ho thought Eban so this Signor Hum
A Converzazione holds tonight

30

Eban then paid his fare, and tiptoe went
To Hum's hotel; and, as he on did pass
With head inclined, each dusky lineament
265 Show'd in the pearl-paved street, as in a glass;
His purple vest, that ever peeping was
Rich from the fluttering crimson of his cloak,
His silvery trowsers, and his silken sash
Tied in a burnish'd knot, their semblance took
270 Upon the mirror'd walls, wherever he might look.

31

He smiled at self, and, smiling, show'd his teeth,
And seeing his white teeth, he smiled the more;
Lifted his eye-brows, spurn'd the path beneath,
Show'd teeth again, and smiled as heretofore,

---

Whene'er he beats his literary drum
The learned muster round all light and tight
Drest in best black to talk by candle light."
{I'm at your Elbow Signor like a rocket}
E'en while he thought, for eighteen penny fare
He paid a half penny by cuning sleight
Made argent; then with self-contented Air
Broke though the Crowd to Hums, and all the world was there⟩

30

⟨So Eban paid his fare and up the Street⟩

(*the first stanza number* 30 *written over* ⟨28⟩; thought *successively* [*a*] says [*b*] said [*c*] thought *in the first line and* E'en *written over* {He} *in the seventh*) *D* 262 Eban then] So Eban *altered to* Eban then *D* 262/263 ⟨Towards Hum's⟩ *D* 263 To] To⟨wards⟩ *D* 265 in the] in *D* 270/271 (*after stanza number*)

⟨Past either Ear, half shown, his plenteous hair
{Went in a jetty wreath, and on his back
Met in curl clusters, ever shining there}
Went jetty, and in large curl clusters met
Between his shoulders, ever shining there⟩

31

⟨Past either ear, half shown, his plenteous hair
Went jetty, and in large curl-clusters fell
Between his shoulders⟩

31

⟨He smil'd thereat and⟩ *D*

272 teeth] *added above the line in D*

275 Until he knock'd at the magician's door;
Where, till the porter answer'd, might be seen,
In the clear panel, more he could adore,—
His turban wreath'd of gold, and white, and green,
Mustachios, ear-ring, nose-ring, and his sabre keen.

32

280 "Does not your master give a rout to-night?"
Quoth the dark page; "Oh, no!" return'd the Swiss,
"Next door but one to us, upon the right,
The *Magazin des Modes* now open is
Against the Emperor's wedding;—and, sir, this
285 My master finds a monstrous horrid bore;
As he retired, an hour ago I wis,
With his best beard and brimstone, to explore
And cast a quiet figure in his second floor.

33

"Gad! he's obliged to stick to business!
290 For chalk, I hear, stands at a pretty price;
And as for aqua vitæ—there's a mess!
The *dentes sapientiae* of mice
Our barber tells me too are on the rise,—
Tinder's a lighter article,—nitre pure
295 Goes off like lightning,—grains of paradise
At an enormous figure!—stars not sure!—
Zodiac will not move without a sly douceur!

275 knock'd at] *interlined above* ⟨came to⟩ *D* 275 magician's] *interlined above* ⟨Soothsay⟩ *D* 276 might be seen] he might see *altered to* might be seen *D* 277 could] *interlined above* ⟨might⟩ *D* 278/279 ⟨His ear ring, nose ring, sabre in⟩ *D* 279/280 (*after stanza number*)

⟨Does not your Master give a rout to night
Quoth Eban "every Coach in all the Town
{Is here, to} Methinks is here—⟩ *D*

283/284 ⟨And who of all the gay world now would miss / To suit each shape,⟩ *D* 286 ago] or more $W^2$ 293 me] us $W^2$ 297 sly] *D*, $W^2$; slight *1848* 297/298

34

Venus wont stir an inch without a fee—
And entre nous my master is to fond
Of—Hush, hush said Eban—sure this is he
⟨Coming down stairs, and by the Holyland,

34

"Venus won't stir a peg without a fee,
And master is too partial, *entre nous,*
300 To—" "Hush—hush!" cried Eban, "sure that is he
Coming down stairs,—by St. Bartholomew!
As backwards as he can,—is't something new?
Or is't his custom, in the name of fun?"
"He always comes down backward, with one shoe"—
305 Return'd the porter—"off, and one shoe on,
Like, saving shoe for sock or stocking, my man John!"

35

It was indeed the great magician,
Feeling, with careful toe, for every stair,
And retrograding careful as he can,
310 Backwards and downwards from his own two pair:
"Salpietro!" exclaim'd Hum, "is the dog there?
He's always in my way upon the mat!"
"He's in the kitchen, or the Lord knows where,"—
Replied the Swiss,—"the nasty, whelping brat!"
315 "Don't beat him!" return'd Hum, and on the floor came pat.

36

Then facing right about, he saw the page,
And said: "Don't tell me what you want, Eban;
The Emperor is now in a huge rage,—
'Tis nine to one he'll give you the rattan!
320 Let us away!" Away together ran
The plain-dress'd sage and spangled blackamoor,
Nor rested till they stood to cool, and fan,

---

Backwards⟩
Coming down stairs
(stir *interlined above* ⟨move⟩ *in the first line,* And entre nous *interlined above* ⟨'Tween you and me⟩ *in the second, and* said *made out of* cried *and* is *written over* ⟨was⟩ *in the third; Keats then began again with stanza 34 on a new page*) *D* 300 cried] *made out of* said *D* 300 that] *made out of* this *D* 303 fun] *interlined above* ⟨wonder⟩ *D* 304 He . . . backward] *successively* (*a*) He always comes down (*b*) The stairs he my descendeth (*c*) Hes always come down backward (*the third and fourth words and the ending of the fifth in* [*b*] *are questionable*) *D* 305 porter] *interlined above* ⟨Swiss⟩ *D* 306 Like . . . or] Like only, saving shoe for *altered to* Like, saving shoe for sock or *D* 307 It] He $W^2$ 307 magician] ⟨astrologer⟩ Magician *D* 309 careful . . . can] *written beneath* ⟨like a careful Man⟩ *D* 309/310 ⟨From the last landing of his own two Pair / And travelling backwards⟩ *D* 315 and . . . pat] *written beneath* ⟨or I will kill your Cat⟩ *D* 317 what . . . Eban] *written beneath* ⟨Eban what you want⟩ *D*

And breathe themselves at th' Emperor's chamber door,
When Eban thought he heard a soft imperial snore.

37

325 "I thought you guess'd, foretold, or prophesied,
That 's Majesty was in a raving fit."
"He dreams," said Hum, "or I have ever lied,
That he is tearing you, sir, bit by bit."
"He's not asleep, and you have little wit,"
330 Replied the page; "that little buzzing noise,
Whate'er your palmistry may make of it,
Comes from a play-thing of the Emperor's choice,
From a Man-Tiger-Organ, prettiest of his toys."

38

Eban then usher'd in the learned seer:
335 Elfinan's back was turn'd, but, ne'ertheless,
Both, prostrate on the carpet, ear by ear,
Crept silently, and waited in distress,
Knowing the Emperor's moody bitterness;
Eban especially, who on the floor 'gan
340 Tremble and quake to death,—he feared less
A dose of senna-tea, or nightmare Gorgon,
Than the Emperor when he play'd on his Man-Tiger-Organ.

39

They kiss'd nine times the carpet's velvet face
Of glossy silk, soft, smooth, and meadow-green,
345 Where the close eye in deep rich fur might trace
A silver tissue, scantly to be seen,
As daisies lurk'd in June-grass, buds in treen;
Sudden the music ceased, sudden the hand
Of majesty, by dint of passion keen,
350 Doubled into a common fist, went grand,
And knock'd down three cut glasses, and his best ink-stand.

323 th'] the *D* 325 guess'd] *interlined above* ⟨said⟩ *D* 330 little . . . noise] *successively* (*a*) noise you hear (*b*) buzzing noise you hear (*c*) little buzzing noise *D* 332 play-thing] ⟨little⟩ plaything *D* 333 prettiest . . . toys] *written beneath* ⟨King of royal toys⟩ *D* 335 ne'ertheless] *interlined above* ⟨for all that⟩ *D* 336 on] *written over* ⟨to⟩ *D* 341 senna] ⟨Phisic⟩ senna *D* 343 face] *interlined above* ⟨furr⟩ *D* 343/344 ⟨Of {green silk} {meadow} soft silk, meadow green⟩ *D* 347 treen] *D*, $W^2$; green *1848* 348/349 ⟨Of Majesty struck on the {sofa} Table⟩ *D* 349/350 ⟨Made to a⟩ *D* 351 and . . . stand] *interlined above* ⟨from his⟩ (*a third deleted word of eight or nine letters following* his *is illegible*) *D*

40

Then turning round, he saw those trembling two:
"Eban," said he, "as slaves should taste the fruits
Of diligence, I shall remember you
355 To-morrow, or the next day, as time suits,
In a finger conversation with my mutes,—
Begone!—for you, Chaldean! here remain;
Fear not, quake not, and as good wine recruits
A conjurer's spirits, what cup will you drain?
360 Sherry in silver, hock in gold, or glass'd champagne?"

41

"Commander of the faithful!" answer'd Hum,
"In preference to these, I'll merely taste
A thimble-full of old Jamaica rum."
"A simple boon!" said Elfinan, "thou may'st
365 Have nantz, with which my morning-coffee's laced."*
"I'll have a glass of nantz, then,"—said the seer,—
"Made racy—(sure my boldness is misplaced!)—
With the third part—(yet that is drinking dear!)—
Of the least drop of *crème de citron* crystal clear."

42

370 "I pledge you, Hum! and pledge my dearest love,
My Bertha!" "Bertha! Bertha!" cried the sage,
"I know a many Berthas!" "Mine's above
All Berthas!" sighed the Emperor. "I engage,"
Said Hum, "in duty, and in vassalage,
375 To mention all the Berthas in the earth;—
There's Bertha Watson,—and Miss Bertha Page,—
This famed for languid eyes, and that for mirth,—
There's Bertha Blount of York,—and Bertha Knox of Perth."

43

"You seem to know"—"I do know," answer'd Hum,
380 "Your Majesty's in love with some fine girl

* "Mr. Nisby is of opinion that laced coffee is bad for the head." *Spectator.*

353 as . . . should] *interlined above* ⟨that you may⟩ *D* 355 the next] *D*, *W*²; next *1848* 363 thimble-full] thimble full *D*; thimbleful *W*² 365 nantz . . . laced] Nantes as clear as water and as chaste *D* 365 *note* "Mr. . . . *Spectator.*] *not in D*; *W*² *omits the first* is 366 seer] *interlined above* ⟨sage⟩ *D* 369 crystal] *written beneath* ⟨bright and⟩ *D* 371 cried] said *W*² 375 mention] ⟨de⟩ mention *D*

Named Bertha; but her surname will not come,
Without a little conjuring." "'Tis Pearl,
'Tis Bertha Pearl! What makes my brains so whirl?
And she is softer, fairer than her name!"
385 "Where does she live?" ask'd Hum. "Her fair locks curl
So brightly, they put all our fays to shame!—
Live!—O! at Canterbury, with her old grand-dame."

44

"Good! good!" cried Hum, "I've known her from a child!
She is a changeling of my management;
390 She was born at midnight in an Indian wild;
Her mother's screams with the striped tiger's blent,
While the torch-bearing slaves a halloo sent
Into the jungles; and her palanquin,
Rested amid the desert's dreariment,
395 Shook with her agony, till fair were seen
The little Bertha's eyes ope on the stars serene."

45

"I can't say," said the monarch, "that may be
Just as it happen'd, true or else a bam!
Drink up your brandy, and sit down by me,
400 Feel, feel my pulse, how much in love I am;
And if your science is not all a sham,
Tell me some means to get the lady here."
"Upon my honour!" said the son of Cham,*

* Cham is said to have been the inventor of magic. Lucy learnt this from Bayle's Dictionary, and had copied a long Latin note from that work.

383 Pearl! What . . . whirl?] $\sim_{\wedge}$ what . . . ~— (what *made out of* that) *D* 383 brains] brain $W^2$ 386 they] *made out of* that *D* 386/387 ⟨She lives at Canterbury⟩ *D* 387 at] she lives at *D* 391 tiger's] tigers *D*; tigers' $W^2$ 392 halloo] *interlined above* ⟨sceaming⟩ *D* 393 jungles] Dingles *D* 393/394

⟨Rested amid the deserts dreariment
Shook with her Agony, {till fair was seen}
{The little Bertha's face} {till fair was seen}
{The little Bertha's face} till from the Screen
Of Silken⟩

(*the last two deletions on the right are successive versions of the end of the second line given here; the last three deletions on the left are attempts at the beginning of the final line of the stanza*) *D* 396 ope] ope⟨n⟩ *D* 397–398 "I . . . bam!] *written twice in D, first at the bottom of a page and then again at the top of a new page* 400 Feel, feel] *successively* (*a*) And feel (*b*) Here feel (*c*) feel, feel *D* 403 *note* Cham . . . work.] *not in D*

"She is my dainty changeling, near and dear,
405 Although her story sounds at first a little queer."

46

"Convey her to me, Hum, or by my crown,
My sceptre, and my cross-surmounted globe,
I'll knock you—" "Does your Majesty mean—*down*?
No, no, you never could my feelings probe
410 To such a depth!" The Emperor took his robe,
And wept upon its purple palatine,
While Hum continued, shamming half a sob,—
"In Canterbury doth your lady shine?
But let me cool your brandy with a little wine."

47

415 Whereat a narrow Flemish glass he took,
That since belong'd to Admiral De Witt,
Admired it with a connoisseuring look,
And with the ripest claret crowned it,
And, ere one lively bead could burst and flit,
420 He turned it quickly, nimbly upside down,
His mouth being held conveniently fit
To catch the treasure: "Best in all the town!"
He said, smack'd his moist lips, and gave a pleasant frown.

48

"Ah! good my Prince, weep not!" And then again
425 He fill'd a bumper. "Great sire, do not weep!
Your pulse is shocking, but I'll ease your pain."
"Fetch me that ottoman, and prithee keep
Your voice low," said the Emperor, "and steep
Some lady's fingers nice in Candy wine;
430 And prithee, Hum, behind the screen do peep

405 her] this $W^2$ 407 and my] and *D* 408 I'll] I *D* 409 you . . . my] I . . . your *D* 412 half a] a half *altered to* a half a (*the first* a *left undeleted by mistake*) *D* 413 doth] ⟨you to day sh⟩ doth *D* 414 cool] ⟨Tic [?]⟩ cool *D* 414/415

⟨Whereat he took a narrow flanders glass
{That once belongd to the Pensioner De Wit}
That once belong'd to Admiral de Wit⟩ *D*

415 a] *written over* ⟨he⟩ *D* 415 Flemish] flanders *D* 416 since] once *D* 419 one] *D* (*interlined above* ⟨the⟩); the $W^2$, *1848* 422 catch the treasure] save the creature *D*, $W^2$ ("the creature" *in* $W^2$) 423 smack'd his moist] and smack'd his *altered to* smack'd his most *D*

For the rose-water vase, magician mine!
And sponge my forehead,—so my love doth make me pine."

49

"Ah, cursed Bellanaine!" "Don't think of her,"
Rejoin'd the mago, "but on Bertha muse;
435 For, by my choicest best barometer,
You shall not throttled be in marriage noose;
I've said it, sire; you only have to choose
Bertha or Bellanaine." So saying, he drew
From the left pocket of his threadbare hose,
440 A sampler hoarded slyly, good as new,
Holding it by his thumb and finger full in view.

50

"Sire, this is Bertha Pearl's neat handy-work,
Her *name,* see here, *Midsummer, ninety-one.*"
Elfinan snatch'd it with a sudden jerk,
445 And wept as if he never would have done,
Honouring with royal tears the poor homespun;
Whereon were broider'd tigers with black eyes,
And long-tail'd pheasants, and a rising sun,
Plenty of posies, great stags, butterflies
450 Bigger than stags,—a moon,—with other mysteries.

51

The monarch handled o'er and o'er again
These day-school hieroglyphics with a sigh;
Somewhat in sadness, but pleas'd in the main,
Till this oracular couplet met his eye
455 Astounded,—*Cupid, I / do thee defy!*
It was too much. He shrunk back in his chair,
Grew pale as death, and fainted—very nigh!
"Pho! nonsense!" exclaim'd Hum, "now don't despair:
She does not mean it really. Cheer up, hearty—there!

436 throttled be] be confin'd *altered to* throttled be *D* 437 sire] Sir $W^2$ 440 slyly] *interlined above* ⟨clean, and⟩ *D* 441 Holding it] *successively* (*a*) And held it (*b*) And cried (*c*) And held (*d*) Holding it *D* 442 is] *not in D* 443 Midsummer . . . one] May, 1392 *altered to* Midsummer ninety one *D* 449 great] ⟨a great Stag,⟩ great *D* 452/453 ⟨With tender s⟩ (With *written over* {S}) *D* 455 Cupid, I /] *ed*; $\sim_\wedge \sim$, *D*; ~, ~— $W^2$; $\sim, \sim_\wedge$ *1848* 456 He . . . chair] *interlined above* ⟨he fell back on the couch⟩ *D* 458 Hum] *added above the line in D* 459 hearty] *added above the line in D*

52

460 "And listen to my words. You say you won't,
On any terms, marry Miss Bellanaine;
It goes against your conscience—good! Well, don't.
You say you love a mortal. I would fain
Persuade your honour's Highness to refrain
465 From peccadilloes. But, sire, as I say,
What good would that do? And, to be more plain,
You would do me a mischief some odd day,
Cut off my ears and hands, or head too, by my fay!

53

"Besides, manners forbid that I should pass any
470 Vile strictures on the conduct of a prince
Who should indulge his genius, if he has any,
Not, like a subject, foolish matters mince.
Now I think on't, perhaps I could convince
Your Majesty there is no crime at all
475 In loving pretty little Bertha, since
She's very delicate,—not over tall,—
A fairy's hand, and in the waist, why—very small."

54

"Ring the repeater, gentle Hum!" "'Tis five,"
Said gentle Hum; "the nights draw in apace;
480 The little birds I hear are all alive;
I see the dawning touch'd upon your face;
Shall I put out the candles, please your Grace?"
"Do put them out, and, without more ado,
Tell me how I may that sweet girl embrace,—
485 How you can bring her to me." "That's for you,
Great Emperor! to adventure, like a lover true."

55

"I fetch her!"—"Yes, an't like your Majesty;
And as she would be frighten'd wide awake
To travel such a distance through the sky,

461 On . . . Bellanaine] Marry Miss Bellanaine on any terms (*but marked for transposition*) *D* 466 would] will $W^2$ 468 and] *written over* ⟨or⟩ *D* 468 or] and $W^2$ 472 subject, foolish‸] ~, ~‸ *altered to* ~‸ ~, $W^2$ 477 fairy's] faëry $W^2$ 478 Ring] *interlined above* ⟨Touch⟩ *D* 479 gentle] *added above the line in D* 480 hear] heard *D* 485 you can] can you $W^2$ 486 adventure] *interlined above* ⟨fineagle⟩ *D*

490 Use of some soft manœuvre you must make,
For your convenience, and her dear nerves' sake;
Nice way would be to bring her in a swoon;
Anon, I'll tell what course were best to take;
You must away this morning." "Hum! so soon?"
495 "Sire, you must be in Kent by twelve o'clock at noon."

56

At this great Cæsar started on his feet,
Lifted his wings, and stood attentive-wise.
"Those wings to Canterbury you must beat,
If you hold Bertha as a worthy prize.
500 Look in the Almanack—*Moore* never lies—
April the twenty-fourth,—this coming day,
Now breathing its new bloom upon the skies,
Will end in St. Mark's eve;—you must away,
For on that eve alone can you the maid convey."

57

505 Then the magician solemnly 'gan frown,
So that his frost-white eyebrows, beetling low,
Shaded his deep green eyes, and wrinkles brown
Plaited upon his furnace-scorched brow:
Forth from his hood that hung his neck below,
510 He lifted a bright casket of pure gold,
Touch'd a spring-lock, and there in wool, or snow
Charm'd into ever freezing, lay an old
And legend-leaved book, mysterious to behold.

58

"Take this same book,—it will not bite you, sire;
515 There, put it underneath your royal arm;

491 your] your own *D* 491/492 ⟨This very morning Sire⟩ *D* 492 Nice] *interlined above* ⟨Best⟩ *D* 492 would] 'twould $W^2$ 492 bring] ⟨cast her⟩ bring *D* 493 I'll] I *altered to* I'll ('ll *squeezed in*) *D* 493 what] *written over* ⟨the⟩ *D* 496 great] ⟨Augus⟩ great *D* 498 Those] *made out of* Take *D* 500/501 ⟨April the twenty fifth this very morn / Is sacred to St Mark⟩ *D* 501/502 ⟨Ends quiet in St Agnes E⟩ *D* 502 breathing] *interlined above* ⟨spreading⟩ *D* 502 new] *interlined above* ⟨yong⟩ *D* 503 Will end] *interlined above* ⟨Ends⟩ *D* 504 that] *made out of* this *D* 505 'gan] *D*, $W^2$; 'gan to *1848* 506 frost] *interlined above* ⟨snow⟩ *D* 508 Plaited] Pleated *D* 508 furnace-scorched] *interlined above* ⟨weather beaten⟩ *D* 509 his hood] the Hood *D* 509/510 ⟨His lifted a bright book⟩ *D*

Though it's a pretty weight, it will not tire,
But rather on your journey keep you warm:
This is the magic, this the potent charm,
That shall drive Bertha to a fainting fit!
520 When the time comes, don't feel the least alarm;
Uplift her from the ground, and swiftly flit
Back to your palace, where I wait for guerdon fit."

59

"What shall I do with this same book?" "Why merely
Lay it on Bertha's table, close beside
525 Her work-box, and 'twill help your purpose dearly;
I say no more." "Or good or ill betide,
Through the wide air to Kent this morn I glide!"
Exclaim'd the Emperor; "When I return,
Ask what you will,—I'll give you my new bride!
530 And take some more wine, Hum;—O, heavens! I burn
To be upon the wing! Now, now, that minx I spurn!"

60

"Leave her to me," rejoin'd the magian:
"But how shall I account, illustrious fay!
For thine imperial absence? Pho! I can
535 Say you are very sick, and bar the way
To your so loving courtiers for one day;
If either of their two Archbishops' graces
Should talk of extreme unction, I shall say
You do not like cold pig with Latin phrases,
540 Which never should be used but in alarming cases."

61

"Open the window, Hum; I'm ready now!"
"Zooks!" exclaim'd Hum, as up the sash he drew,
"Behold, your Majesty, upon the brow

516 Though . . . it] It is a pretty ⟨helft⟩ weight but *altered to* Though Its a pretty weight it *D* 516/517 ⟨A Lover⟩ (*following* tire *without punctuation at the end of 516*) *D* 518/519 ⟨That shall make swoon at once⟩ *D* 519/520 ⟨Do not⟩ *D* 521 Uplift] *made out of* But lift *D*; But lift *W*², *1848* 522 where . . . fit."] *D*; *not in W*², *1848* (*W*² *leaves blank; 1848 fills out the line with asterisks*) 523 this] *D* (*made out of* that); that *W*², *1848* 526 I say] Ask me *D* 527 I] I'll *W*² 529 I'll] I *altered to* I'll ('ll *squeezed in*) *D* 531 Now, now] How, now *W*² 531 that minx] my Bride *D* 535 very] *added above the line in D* 537 Archbishops'] Archbishop's *D, W*² 540 alarming] extremest *D*

Of yonder hill, what crowds of people!" "Whew!
545 The monster's always after something new,"
Return'd his Highness; "they are piping hot
To see my pigsney Bellanaine. Hum! do
Tighten my belt a little,—so, so,—not
Too tight,—the book!—my wand!—so, nothing is forgot."

62

550 "Wounds! how they shout!" said Hum, "and there,—see, see,
Th' Ambassador's return'd from Pigmio!
The morning's very fine,—uncommonly!
See, past the skirts of yon white cloud they go,
Tinging it with soft crimsons! Now below
555 The sable-pointed heads of firs and pines
They dip, move on, and with them moves a glow
Along the forest side! Now amber lines
Reach the hill top, and now throughout the valley shines."

63

"Why, Hum, you're getting quite poetical!
560 Those *nows* you managed in a special style."
"If ever you have leisure, sire, you shall
See scraps of mine will make it worth your while,
Tit-bits for Phœbus!—yes, you well may smile.
Hark! hark! the bells!" "A little further get,
565 Good Hum, and let me view this mighty coil."
Then the great Emperor full graceful set
His elbow for a prop, and snuff'd his mignionette.

544 Whew!] *D*, $W^2$; Where? *1848* 549 so] no *D* 550 said] *interlined above* ⟨and⟩ *D*; *written over erased* ⟨says⟩ $W^2$ 551 Th' Ambassador's] The Ambassadors *interlined above* ⟨Your Embassay⟩ *D* 553 yon] *interlined above* ⟨that⟩ *D* 554 crimsons . . . below] *written beneath* ⟨purples⟩ ⟨crimsons and a glow⟩ *D* 555 sable . . . of] sable heads of pointed *altered to* sable pointed heads ⟨of⟩ (of *deleted by mistake*) *D* 555/556 ⟨They dip and fill the forest with a glow⟩ *D* 556 them] *added above the line (and the following* moves *deleted by mistake) in D* 560 you . . . in] are brough in with *altered to* you managed in *D* 562 will] shall *D* 564 get] *D*, $W^2$; yet *1848* 564/565 ⟨Good Hum I wish⟩ *D* 565 view] see $W^2$ 567/568

64

⟨And sneering look'd upon the busy scene—⟩
⟨The People⟩
⟨The merry bells with rival⟩

64

The morn was full of holiday; loud bells
With rival clamours rang from every spire;
570 Cunningly-station'd music dies and swells
In echoing places; when the winds respire,
Light flags stream out like gauzy tongues of fire;
A metropolitan murmur, lifeful, warm,
Came from the northern suburbs; rich attire
575 Freckled with red and gold the moving swarm;
While here and there clear trumpets blew a keen alarm.

65

And now the fairy escort was seen clear,
Like the old pageant of Aurora's train,
Above a pearl-built minster, hovering near;
580 First wily Crafticant, the chamberlain,
Balanced upon his grey-grown pinions twain,
His slender wand officially reveal'd;
Then black gnomes scattering sixpences like rain;
Then pages three and three; and next, slave-held,
585 The Imaian 'scutcheon bright,—one mouse in argent field.

---

⟨The merry Bells with rival clamours rang
The flags talk with their⟩

(sneering *interlined above* {smiling} *in the first line*) *D* 568 was] *D*, *W*[2]; is *1848* 569 rang] *D*, *W*[2]; ring *1848* 572 Light . . . out] *interlined above* ⟨Stream go the flags⟩ *D* 574 Came] *D*, *W*[2]; Comes *1848* 574/575

⟨Freckled the moving populace—an alarm
Of Trumpets here and there⟩
⟨Of gold and purple⟩

(an alarm *made out of* a cham *in the first line and* Of *added in the margin in the second*) *D* 575 Freckled] *D*, *W*[2]; Freckles *1848* 576 blew] *D*, *W*[2] (belw *in D*); blow *1848* 576 keen] *written beneath* ⟨lou⟩ *D* 577 was . . . clear] *successively* (*a*) in splendid (*b*) coming (*c*) floating near (*d*) floated near (*e*) was seen clear *D* 578 old] *interlined above* ⟨full⟩ *D* 579 a] *interlined above* ⟨the⟩ *D* 580 First wily] *interlined above* ⟨Sagacious⟩ *D* 581/582

⟨His slender wand{s} official slan'd wise held;
{Then Pages fluttering two and two}
Then black-gnomes slacctering six pences like rain
Upon the Populace; and next slave held
{By} The Imaian 'scutchon Bright—Six mice in silver feld.⟩

(slan'd . . . held *interlined above* {held aslant} *in the first line and* slave held *made out of* upheld *in the fourth*) *D* 582 officially] officiously *W*[2] 584 Then] *interlined above* ⟨Next⟩ *D* 584 three and three] two and too *altered to* three and three *D* 585 argent] *successively* (*a*) golden (*b*) silver (*c*) argent *D*

66

Gentlemen pensioners next; and after them,
A troop of winged janizaries flew;
Then slaves, as presents bearing many a gem;
Then twelve physicians fluttering two and two;
590 And next a chaplain in a cassock new;
Then lords in waiting; then (what head not reels
For pleasure?)—the fair Princess in full view,
Borne upon wings,—and very pleased she feels
To have such splendour dance attendance at her heels.

67

595 For there was more magnificence behind:
She waved her handkerchief. "Ah, very grand!"
Cried Elfinan, and closed the window-blind;
"And, Hum, we must not shilly-shally stand,—
Adieu! adieu! I'm off for Angle-land!
600 I say, old hocus, have you such a thing
About you,—feel your pockets, I command,—
I want, this instant, an invisible ring,—
Thank you, old mummy!—now securely I take wing."

68

Then Elfinan swift vaulted from the floor,
605 And lighted graceful on the window-sill;

587 troop] swarm [?] *interlined and deleted above* troop (*left undeleted*) *D* 587 winged] *interlined above* ⟨flying⟩ *D* 588 slaves] *Keats interlined and deleted* poor *before this word in D* 588 as] ⟨shoulder-worn⟩ as *D* 597 closed] shut *D* 598/599 ⟨Good bye⟩ *D* 600/601
⟨About you⟩
⟨In you old jewish pocket⟩ *D*
603/604

68

Then Elfinan swift vauted from the floor
⟨So saying he vaulted to the window cill
And standing like a little Mercury⟩
⟨So saying he vauted nimbly⟩ from the floor
[5] And lighted graceful on the window cill.
Under one arm the magic book he bore.
⟨The other⟩
⟨"Hum you must laugh with me, I know you will—
"More wine, old Boy! well mind it dos'ent spill⟩
(*the first line is a later insertion, and* nimbly *is interlined above* {lightly} *in the fourth; the successive versions are* [*a*] *lines 2, 3* [*b*] *4, 5* [*c*] *1, 5, 6, 7* [*d*] *1, 5, 6, 8, 9—after which Keats began again with stanza 68 on a new page*) *D*

Under one arm the magic book he bore,
The other he could wave about at will;
Pale was his face, he still look'd very ill:
He bow'd at Bellanaine, and said—"Poor Bell!
610 Farewell! farewell! and if for ever! still
For ever fare thee well!"—and then he fell
A laughing!—snapp'd his fingers!—shame it is to tell!

69

"By'r Lady! he is gone!" cries Hum, "and I,—
(I own it,)—have made too free with his wine;
615 Old Crafticant will smoke me, by-the-bye!
This room is full of jewels as a mine,—
Dear valuable creatures, how ye shine!
Sometime to-day I must contrive a minute,
If Mercury propitiously incline,
620 To examine his scrutoire, and see what's in it,
For of superfluous diamonds I as well may thin it.

70

"The Emperor's horrid bad; yes, that's my cue!"
Some histories say that this was Hum's last speech;
That, being fuddled, he went reeling through
625 The corridor, and scarce upright could reach
The stair-head; that being glutted as a leach,
And used, as we ourselves have just now said,
To manage stairs reversely, like a peach

609 at] *interlined above* ⟨to⟩ *D* 613 By'r Lady] By la⟨i⟩'kin *D* 616 This] *made out of* His *W*[2] 618 a minute] an hour *altered to* a minute *D* 621/622

70

⟨"The Emperor's horrrid bad—yes, that's my cue"
Some Histories say that this was Hum's last speech,
That being fuddled he went reeling through
The Corridor, and scace up right could reach
The Star head; that being juice ripe as a peach
He gain'd the Landing, and (as we have said,
Being usd to decend Backwards)⟩

(that *added above the line and* this . . . speech *made out of* these were Hum's last words *in the second line*; He gain'd *successively* [*a*] Gaining [*b*] Reac [*c*] He gain'd *and* Landing *interlined above* {Stair head} *in the sixth*) *D* 626 as] *interlined above* ⟨like⟩ *D* 628 manage] *interlined above* ⟨descend⟩ *D*

Too ripe, he fell, being puzzled in his head
630 With liquor and the staircase: verdict—*found stone dead.*

71

This as a falsehood Crafticanto treats;
And as his style is of strange elegance,
Gentle and tender, full of soft conceits,
(Much like our Boswell's), we will take a glance
635 At his sweet prose, and, if we can, make dance
His woven periods into careless rhyme;
O, little faery Pegasus! rear—prance—
Trot round the quarto—ordinary time!
March, little Pegasus, with pawing hoof sublime!

72

640 Well, let us see,—*tenth book and chapter nine,*—
Thus Crafticant pursues his diary:—
"'Twas twelve o'clock at night, the weather fine,
Latitude thirty-six; our scouts descry
A flight of starlings making rapidly
645 Tow'rds Thibet. Mem.:—birds fly in the night;
From twelve to half-past—wings not fit to fly
For a thick fog—the Princess sulky quite—
Call'd for an extra shawl, and gave her nurse a bite.

73

"Five minutes before one—brought down a moth
650 With my new double-barrel—stew'd the thighs,
And made a very tolerable broth—
Princess turn'd dainty, to our great surprise,

630 staircase . . . *dead*] *successively* (*a*) Stairs, and reach the bottom dead (*b*) Stairs—found at the bottom dead (*c*) Staircase—verdict—found stone dead *D* 630/631 (*after stanza number*)

⟨But Crafticant {entirely denies} denies this out and out—
And as he has an elegaince of style,
Gentle, imaginative⟩ *D*

631 This . . . treats] *successively* (*a*) This Crafticanto out and out denies (*b*) This Crafticanto out and out refutes (*c*) This Crafticanto as a blunder treats (*d*) This as a falsehood crafticanto treats *D* 632 of . . . elegance] *interlined above* ⟨pure and elegant⟩ *D* 633 and] ⟨imaginative,⟩ and *D* 634 Boswell's] Cowley's *D* 637 rear] *interlined above* ⟨pran⟩ *D* 641 diary] History *D* 650 thighs] *successively* (*a*) legs (*b*) loin (*c*) ribs (*d*) thighs *D*

Alter'd her mind, and thought it very nice:
Seeing her pleasant, tried her with a pun—
655 She frown'd; a monstrous owl across us flies
About this time,—a sad old figure of fun;
Bad omen—this new match can't be a happy one.

74

"From two to half-past, dusky way we made,
Above the plains of Gobi,—desert, bleak;
660 Beheld afar off, in the hooded shade
Of darkness, a great mountain (strange to speak),
Spitting, from forth its sulphur-baken peak,
A fan-shaped burst of blood-red, arrowy fire,
Turban'd with smoke, which still away did reek,
665 Solid and black from that eternal pyre,
Upon the laden winds that scantly could respire.

75

"Just upon three o'clock, a falling star
Created an alarm among our troop,
Kill'd a man-cook, a page, and broke a jar,

655 a . . . flies] *written beneath* ⟨and tred to beat my face and eyes⟩ *D* 657/658

74

⟨At two o'Clock we pass⟩
From two till half past, darkling way we made
Above the plains of Gobi desolate—
Beheld aftar off in the hooded Shade
Of Darkness a ⟨peak'd mountain⟩ Volcano, vast and great
⟨Sending⟩
Spitting from forth its nitrous peak elate
A fan-shap'd burst of bloodred arrowy fire
Turban'd with monstrous clouds

(darkling . . . made *is interlined above* ⟨made our darkling way⟩ *in the second line, and* Desert of Gobi, *related to the third line, appears by itself at the top of the opposite verso; Keats then began again with stanza 74 on a new page) D* 658 to] till *D* 658 dusky] *interlined above* ⟨darkling⟩ *D* 661 great . . . speak)] *successively* (*a*) Volcano smoke and reek (*b*) Volcano's fiery reek (*c*) great Mountain, strange to speak *D* 663 A . . . fire] *three preliminary attempts at this line appear in D beneath the passage given in the apparatus at 297/298:*

⟨A ruddy fan—⟩
⟨A bloodred fan of fire⟩
A fan shap'd burst of ⟨fire⟩ bloodred fire

663 fire] *interlined above* ⟨flames⟩ *D* 664 smoke . . . away] swarthy smoke, which still *altered to* smoke, which still away *D* 664/665 ⟨Upon the {laden} heavy-laden wind⟩ *D* 666 winds] wind *D* 669/670 ⟨Three Pl⟩ *D*

670 A tureen, and three dishes, at one swoop,
Then passing by the Princess, singed her hoop:
Could not conceive what Coralline was at—
She clapp'd her hands three times, and cried out 'Whoop!'—
Some strange Imaian custom. A large bat
675 Came sudden 'fore my face, and brush'd against my hat.

76

"Five minutes thirteen seconds after three,
Far in the west a mighty fire broke out—
Conjectured, on the instant, it might be
The city of Balk—'twas Balk beyond all doubt:
680 A griffin, wheeling here and there about,
Kept reconnoitring us—doubled our guard—
Lighted our torches, and kept up a shout,
Till he sheer'd off—the Princess very scared—
And many on their marrow-bones for death prepared.

77

685 "At half-past three arose the cheerful moon—
Bivouac'd for four minutes on a cloud—
Where from the earth we heard a lively tune
Of tambourines and pipes, serene and loud,
While on a flowery lawn a brilliant crowd
690 Cinque-parted danced, some half asleep reposed
Beneath the green-fan'd cedars, some did shroud
In silken tents, and 'mid light fragrance dozed,
Or on the open turf their soothed eyelids closed.

78

"Dropp'd my gold watch, and kill'd a kettle-drum—
695 It went for apoplexy—foolish folks!—
Left it to pay the piper—a good sum—
(I've got a conscience, maugre people's jokes:)
To scrape a little favour, 'gan to coax

673 hands] hand *D* 674 A . . . bat] *written beneath* ⟨Saw a Bat,—⟩ *D* 674/675 ⟨He shee'd off to the right—⟩ *D* 675 'fore] *interlined above* ⟨on⟩ *D* 678 on the] *interlined above* ⟨at the time⟩ *D* 679 beyond] *interlined above* ⟨without⟩ *D* 680 griffin] ⟨Drag⟩ Griffin *D* 687 we . . . lively] *interlined above* ⟨a most melodious⟩ *D* 692 dozed] *ed*; dos'd *D*; dosed $W^2$, *1848* 693 turf] *interlined above* ⟨green⟩ *D* 697–698 jokes:) . . . favour,] $W^2$; ~,—. . . ~$_\wedge$ *D*; ~,) . . . ~; *1848*

Her Highness' pug-dog—got a sharp rebuff—
700 She wish'd a game at whist—made three revokes—
Turn'd from myself, her partner, in a huff;
His Majesty will know her temper time enough.

79

"She cried for chess—I play'd a game with her—
Castled her king with such a vixen look,
705 It bodes ill to his Majesty—(refer
To the second chapter of my fortieth book,
And see what hoity-toity airs she took:)
At half-past four the morn essay'd to beam—
Saluted, as we pass'd, an early rook—
710 The Princess fell asleep, and, in her dream,
Talk'd of one Master Hubert, deep in her esteem.

80

"About this time,—making delightful way,—
Shed a quill-feather from my larboard wing—
Wish'd, trusted, hoped 'twas no sign of decay—
715 Thank heaven, I'm hearty yet!—'twas no such thing:—
At five the golden light began to spring,
With fiery shudder through the bloomed east;
At six we heard Panthea's churches ring—
The city all her unhived swarms had cast,
720 To watch our grand approach, and hail us as we pass'd.

81

"As flowers turn their faces to the sun,
So on our flight with hungry eyes they gaze,
And, as we shaped our course, this, that way run,
With mad-cap pleasure, or hand-clasp'd amaze:
725 Sweet in the air a mild-toned music plays,
And progresses through its own labyrinth;

700/701 ⟨When at poor Corraline she 'gan to huff⟩ *D* 707 hoity . . . airs] whim, and vagaries *D* 708 essay'd] began *D* 708 beam] *interlined above* ⟨break⟩ *D* 711 deep . . . esteem] *interlined above* ⟨mm—what can this mean⟩ *D* 713 Shed . . . feather] I shed a feather *altered to* shed a quill feather *D* 716/717 ⟨Into the⟩ *D* 717 fiery] *successively* (*a*) gleaming (*b*) tremulous (*c*) fiery *D* 717 through . . . east] *interlined above* ⟨upward throug the dark⟩ *D* 719 her] *D*, $W^2$; his *1848* 724 clasp'd] *interlined above* ⟨join'd⟩ *D* 725 in] *interlined above* ⟨through⟩ *D* 725 a] *added above the line in D*

Buds gather'd from the green spring's middle-days,
They scatter'd,—daisy, primrose, hyacinth,—
Or round white columns wreath'd from capital to plinth.

82

730 "Onward we floated o'er the panting streets,
That seem'd throughout with upheld faces paved;
Look where we will, our bird's-eye vision meets
Legions of holiday; bright standards waved,
And fluttering ensigns emulously craved
735 Our minute's glance; a busy thunderous roar,
From square to square, among the buildings raved,
As when the sea, at flow, gluts up once more
The craggy hollowness of a wild-reefed shore.

83

"And 'Bellanaine for ever!' shouted they,
740 While that fair Princess, from her winged chair,
Bow'd low with high demeanour, and, to pay
Their new-blown loyalty with guerdon fair,
Still emptied, at meet distance, here and there,
A plenty horn of jewels. And here I
745 (Who wish to give the devil her due) declare
Against that ugly piece of calumny,
Which calls them Highland pebble-stones not worth a fly.

84

"Still 'Bellanaine!' they shouted, while we glide
'Slant to a light Ionic portico,
750 The city's delicacy, and the pride
Of our Imperial Basilic; a row
Of lords and ladies, on each hand, make show
Submissive of knee-bent obeisance,
All down the steps; and, as we enter'd, lo!
755 The strangest sight—the most unlook'd-for chance—
All things turn'd topsy-turvy in a devil's dance.

85

"'Stead of his anxious Majesty and court
At the open doors, with wide saluting eyes,

729 capital] pedestal $W^2$ 730 o'er] through $W^2$

*Congées* and scrape-graces of every sort,
760 And all the smooth routine of gallantries,
Was seen, to our immoderate surprise,
A motley crowd thick gather'd in the hall,
Lords, scullions, deputy-scullions, with wild cries
Stunning the vestibule from wall to wall,
765 Where the Chief Justice on his knees and hands doth crawl.

86

"Counts of the palace, and the state purveyor
Of moth's down, to make soft the royal beds,
The Common Council and my fool Lord Mayor
Marching a-row, each other slipshod treads;
770 Powder'd bag-wigs and ruffy-tuffy heads
Of cinder wenches meet and soil each other;
Toe crush'd with heel ill-natured fighting breeds,
Frill-rumpling elbows brew up many a bother,
And fists in the short ribs keep up the yell and pother.

87

775 "A poet, mounted on the court-clown's back,
Rode to the Princess swift with spurring heels,
And close into her face, with rhyming clack,
Began a prothalamion;—she reels,
She falls, she faints! while laughter peals
780 Over her woman's weakness. 'Where,' cried I,
'Where is his Majesty?' No person feels
Inclined to answer; wherefore instantly
I plunged into the crowd to find him or to die.

88

"Jostling my way I gain'd the stairs, and ran
785 To the first landing, where, incredible!
I met, far gone in liquor, that old man,
That vile impostor Hum,——"
So far so well,—
For we have proved the mago never fell
Down stairs on Crafticanto's evidence;
790 And therefore duly shall proceed to tell,
Plain in our own original mood and tense,
The sequel of this day, though labour 'tis immense!

89

Now Hum, new fledg'd with high authority,
Came forth to quell the hubbub in the hall.

* * * * * * * * * * *

## *In after time a sage of mickle lore*

In after time a sage of mickle lore,
Yclep'd Typographus, the giant took
And did refit his limbs as heretofore,
And made him read in many a learned book,
5 And into many a lively legend look;
Thereby in goodly themes so training him,
That all his brutishness he quite forsook,
When, meeting Artegall and Talus grim,
The one he struck stone blind, the other's eyes wox dim.

793–794 Now . . . hall.] *W*[2]; *not in 1848* (*see Textual Note*)
*In after time a sage.* Text from Brown's transcript (*CB*). Heading supplied by editor. 8 grim] *interlined above* slim (*left undeleted*) *CB*

TEXTUAL NOTES

APPENDIXES

INDEX OF TITLES AND FIRST LINES

# Textual Notes

The Textual Notes give the date or dates of composition for each poem and the details of first publication, list the extant holographs and transcripts, discuss (where there is sufficient evidence) the transmission of text prior to first publication, and explain the choice of copy-text. With the exception of derivative MSS that had no influence on any subsequent text—for example, Mary Mathew's and J. C. Stephens' copies from *1817*—the notes describe the substantive peculiarities of every MS and first or early printing that is referred to; but variants recorded in the apparatus or Appendix II (a list of early emendations and errors that recur in modern editions) are here usually cited only by line number. Thus all of Tom Taylor's corruptions in 1, 2, 5, 7, 8, and 14 of the first printed text of *Where be ye going, you Devon maid* are mentioned in the Textual Note, but only those in 5, 7, and 8 are actually quoted, the rest being included in Appendix II. Locations of the transcripts are given in Appendix V.

*Imitation of Spenser*

Written probably in 1814 (Brown in *KC*, II, 55–56, calls the poem Keats's "earliest attempt" and places it after the completion of "his eighteenth year"—i.e., after October 1813). First published in *1817*, pp. 44–46. The two extant MSS are transcripts by Tom Keats and J. C. Stephens. The former, presumably from a holograph source predating *1817,* varies substantively from *1817* in 12 and 29. The latter was copied from *1817* and has no textual significance. The present text, based on *1817,* departs substantively from the copy-text (as Garrod does) in 12 and 29, and the apparatus includes Tom Keats's alterations in 20 and 28 as possible representations of earlier wording in the now lost MS that he was copying. *1817*'s asterisks at the beginning and end of the poem may be typographical ornaments, but more likely were intended as indications of fragmentariness; such asterisks appear elsewhere in *1817* only in the last line of *Calidore.*

12 scalès] The emendation (to the reading of Tom Keats's MS, but with a grave rather than an acute accent) is based on the meter of Keats's line, which calls for a two-syllable word, and the likelihood that *1817*'s "scales'" resulted from a compositor's misreading of an accent mark in the lost printer's copy. There is still some question whether the last two words of the line are to be read as plural possessive plus noun (as in *1817*) or noun plus adjective (as apparently in Tom Keats's MS), and Tom's lack of an apostrophe in the first word is no help in the matter since, like Keats, he frequently omitted apostrophes in possessives.

The emended text (with "light" as an adjective) parallels the wording and syntax of Chaucer's *The Parliament of Fowls* 187–189: "colde welle-stremes . . . That swymmen ful of smale fishes lighte, / With fynnes rede and skales sylver bryghte."

29 glassy] Though the difference is very slight, Tom Keats's "glassy" is preferred over *1817*'s "glossy" (possibly a printing error) as better according with Keats's reflection images in 8–11, 14, 28–31.

### *On Peace*

Written perhaps in April 1814 (Napoleon surrendered on 11 April and departed for Elba shortly afterward), or possibly somewhat later. First published by Ernest de Selincourt in *N&Q*, 4 February 1905, p. 82. The three extant MSS are two transcripts by Woodhouse (*W*³, *W*²) and a late copy by one of his clerks (Garrod's *T*). There are no significant differences among the transcripts (*W*² and the clerk's MS have "chains'" and "chain's," respectively, for *W*³'s "chains" in 12, but *W*²'s apostrophe is a slip of the pen and the clerk miscopied the word from *W*²). *W*³, made from a now lost transcript by Kirkman in Woodhouse's cousin Mary Frogley's album (see *Texts*, pp. 39–41, 92–93), is the earliest of the three MSS, *W*² is a copy of *W*³, and the clerk's MS derives from *W*². De Selincourt first printed the poem from the clerk's MS. The present text, based on *W*³, departs substantively from the copy-text in 14.

13 the great] In all three MSS, 13 was initially left unfinished—*W*³ ending the line with "uncurbed" and *W*² and the clerk's MS with "th" and "the"—and in all three the line and the rhyme have been completed in pencil, with "the great" in *W*³ (probably by Woodhouse) and "-e great?" and "great?" in the others (possibly by different hands). It is not clear whether this incompleteness reflects a lacuna or damage in whatever lost holograph was the original source of text or in some intermediate source before *W*³. The penciled conclusion of the line is probably a good guess rather than an authoritative reading.

14 horrors] The emendation (following H. B. Forman, O.S.A. ed.) is based on the sense of the rest of the line plus the likelihood that Kirkman or an earlier transcriber misread the word in the holograph original. Keats's "horror" and "horrors" in surviving holographs of other poems are virtually indistinguishable from "honor" and "honors"; in *Endymion* II.789 the *1818* compositor set "Honour" from the holograph fair copy's "horror," and the error was not caught until after the book was printed.

### *Lines Written on 29 May, the Anniversary of Charles's Restoration, on Hearing the Bells Ringing*

Written probably in 1814 or 1815. First published in Lowell, I, 66. The two extant MSS are transcripts by Woodhouse in *W*³, fols. 70 and 69—here and in the apparatus designated *w*³ and *W*³, respectively—which differ substantively only in heading. Woodhouse's source was a now lost transcript by Kirkman in Mary Frogley's album. It is not clear whether *w*³ or *W*³ is the earlier MS, though one of them was almost certainly copied from the other. Lowell first printed the poem (with substantive errors in 1 and 4) from *w*³. The present text is arbitrarily based on *w*³.

5 Vane's sad] In *w*³ Woodhouse put pencil marks under both the "Va" in "Vane's" and the "a" in "sad," and noted "originally and" in the margin. One supposes that his source or some other now lost version that he saw had a deleted "and" either before or after "Vane's," but Keats's initial intention (if the note reflects a reading in a lost holograph) is unrecoverable.

*Stay, ruby breasted warbler, stay*

Written probably in 1814 ("1814" in Georgiana Wylie's MS; "Ab^t 1815/6" in a note by Woodhouse originally connected with one of his earliest transcripts). First published in *1876,* p. 6. The seven extant MSS are all transcripts—three by Woodhouse (a *W*² copy plus two in *W*³, fols. 78 and 69, that here and in the apparatus are designated *w*³ and *W*³, respectively) and one each by one of his clerks (the earlier of Garrod's *T* transcripts), Patmore, Georgiana Wylie, and George Keats. These contain two principal states of text, one of them best represented by Woodhouse's *w*³ and *W*³ (from the former of which *W*², the clerk's and Patmore's MSS, and the *1876* text all derive in sequence without substantive variation) and the other by Georgiana Wylie's MS (which was probably the source of George Keats's copy). Woodhouse's initial source was a now lost Kirkman transcript in Mary Frogley's album; Georgiana Wylie's is assumed to have been a lost holograph. (Though the poem has sometimes been assigned to George Keats on the basis of a "G.K." added at the end of Georgiana Wylie's MS by an unknown hand, it seems best to accept Woodhouse's specific statement that this is one of ten poems "copied for my cousin . . . by M^r Kirkman, and said to be by Keats.") The two principal states differ substantively in 8, 20, 21, and 22, and one of the early Woodhouse transcripts (*W*³) has a further variant in 19 (see below); only Georgiana Wylie's copy has stanza numbers. It is not clear which of the two states is the earlier. The present text is arbitrarily based on Georgiana Wylie's MS.

19 leafless] Since one of the two earliest Woodhouse transcripts was almost certainly made from the other, and since Georgiana Wylie's MS confirms "leafless" as authorial, probably *W*³ (with a unique "hapless") was miscopied from *w*³ (with "leafless") rather than vice versa. But the overall evidence concerning the relationships among Woodhouse's duplicate *W*³ transcripts is ambiguous; see *Texts,* pp. 39–41.

*Fill for me a brimming bowl*

Written in August 1814 (so dated in the extant holograph and three of the transcripts, all but *W*³*x*). First published by Ernest de Selincourt in *N&Q,* 4 February 1905, p. 81. The five extant MSS are a holograph fair copy among Woodhouse's papers in the Morgan Library, three transcripts by Woodhouse (a *W*² copy plus two in *W*³, fols. 64 and 65, that here and in the apparatus are designated $W^3x$ and $W^3y$, respectively), and a late copy by one of his clerks (Garrod's *T*).

$W^3x$ and $W^3y$ lack the Morgan fair copy's epigraph and paragraph divisions and have different wording from the fair copy in 1, 6, 13, 22, and 27; $W^3y$ further varies in 8, 9, and 20. Though the evidence is ambiguous, it is probably best to take $W^3x$ as the earlier of the $W^3$ transcripts, and $W^3y$'s 8, 9, and 20 as independent errors or changes made by Woodhouse in a subsequent copying. Woodhouse's initial source was a transcript by Kirkman in Mary Frogley's album. At some later date he saw a now lost holograph MS very similar to the Morgan fair copy and entered variants from it in longhand and shorthand above the lines and marginally in both of the $W^3$ transcripts—the Morgan readings of 1, 6 (in part), and 27 (as well as a canceled reading *not* in the Morgan MS in 18) in $W^3x$, and the Morgan readings of 1, 6 (in full), and 22 (plus indications of paragraph divisions after 12, 16, and 20) in $W^3y$. (He did not record a variant in either transcript for 13, and did not comment anywhere on the transcripts' differences in 8, 9, and 20.) He transcribed $W^2$ from $W^3y$, incorporating the variants "a" and "one" in 1 and 22 and making paragraph divisions after 12 and 20 (but not after 16). His clerk copied the poem (with a substantive error in 4) from $W^2$, and de Selincourt first printed it (with a mistaken "happiness" for "beaminess" in 15) from the clerk's MS.

Apparently there are three authoritative states of text for this poem—that of the Morgan fair copy, that (very close to the fair copy) represented by the variants that Woodhouse noted in the two $W^3$'s, and that of $W^3x$ without the variants. But the order of these states is uncertain, and the fact that Woodhouse did not record a full set of variants in either of the $W^3$'s makes it difficult to reconstruct with complete accuracy the lost holograph that the variants are supposed to represent. The present text is arbitrarily based on the Morgan fair copy.

### *As from the darkening gloom a silver dove*

Written in December 1814 (the poem is dated 1816 in all MSS, but according to a shorthand note originally opposite the $W^2$ text Keats told Woodhouse in February 1819 that "he had written it on the death of his grandmother, about five days afterward"; the grandmother was buried on 19 December 1814). First published in *1876,* p. 58. The five extant MSS are transcripts—three by Woodhouse ($W^3$, $W^2$, $W^1$), a late copy by one of his clerks (the earlier of Garrod's *T* transcripts), and a copy by Patmore. Woodhouse's initial source was a now lost transcript by Kirkman in Mary Frogley's album. $W^3$ and $W^2$ are the earliest surviving MSS, but it is not clear which of the two—they vary perhaps substantively only in 13 (see below)—was made first. The clerk's and Patmore's MSS and *1876* (the last with some semisubstantive editorial tinkering in 12 to improve the meter) all derive in sequence from $W^2$; $W^1$ (with a nonauthoritative "which" for "that" in 10) probably also derives from $W^2$, even though it agrees with $W^3$ rather than with $W^2$ in 13. The present text is arbitrarily based on $W^3$.

13 pleasures] $W^2$'s "pleasure's" may simply represent an archaic form of the plural (Woodhouse occasionally elsewhere makes plurals with "'s"—e.g., "fal-

con's" in his record of the draft variant to *Endymion* IV.794 and "Titan's" in the $W^2$ text of *Hyperion* II.4) rather than a contracted form of "pleasure is" and hence may be a spelling rather than a substantive variant.

*To Lord Byron*

Written in December 1814 (so dated in both MSS). First published in *1848,* I, 13. The two extant MSS are transcripts by Woodhouse ($W^2$) and one of his clerks (Garrod's *T*). Woodhouse's source is unknown. The clerk transcribed $W^2$, and Milnes printed the poem (with a substantive error or emendation in 9) probably from an amanuensis' copy of the clerk's MS, the only source known to have been available to him. The present text is based on $W^2$. Both H. B. Forman and Garrod have suggested emendations to fill out the meter in 7—"dost ever dress" (Forman, Hampstead Keats, IV, 14 n.) and "thy thorny griefs" (Garrod, p. 477 n.).

*Oh Chatterton! how very sad thy fate*

Written in 1815 (so dated in all MSS). First published in *1848,* I, 12–13. The three extant MSS are transcripts by an unidentified copyist (Garrod's $W^3$, among Woodhouse's papers in the Morgan Library), Woodhouse ($W^2$), and one of his clerks (Garrod's *T*). The first of these is in a formal hand very much like that of George Keats in the Keats-Wylie Scrapbook and may in fact have been made by him. The only substantive differences among the MSS occur in heading ($W^2$ and the clerk's copy have "Sonnet. To Chatterton") and in the note to 8 ("amate—to affright—Spenser" in $W^2$, "'amate'. Chaucer—Affright—J.K." in Woodhouse's hand in the clerk's MS). The Morgan transcript is the likeliest source for Woodhouse's text in $W^2$, the clerk copied $W^2$, and the *1848* text (with substantive errors in 4, 6, and 8) almost certainly derives from the clerk's MS. The present text is based on the Morgan transcript, which uses—unexplainably—a superscript "4" to connect text with note in 8.

*Written on the Day That Mr. Leigh Hunt Left Prison*

Written on 2 February 1815 (the day on which Hunt was released from Horsemonger Lane Prison after serving a two-year sentence for libel against the Prince Regent). First published (as Sonnet III) in *1817,* p. 81. No MS has survived (apart from a transcript by J. C. Stephens made from *1817*), and *1817* is our sole authoritative source.

*To Hope*

Written in February 1815 (so dated in the extant holograph and *1817*). First published in *1817,* pp. 40–43. The two extant MSS are a holograph fair copy formerly owned by M. B. Forman and now in the possession of Abel E. Berland, of Chicago, and a transcript by J. C. Stephens. The former varies substantively from *1817* in six lines, and contains, written vertically by Keats on the verso, the fragment that Garrod includes on p. 554: "They weren fully glad of their gude hap / And tasten all the Pleasausnces of joy." Stephens' MS was made from *1817*. The present text is based on *1817*.

### *Ode to Apollo*

Written in February 1815 (so dated in all MSS). First published in *1848,* II, 252–254. The three extant MSS are two transcripts by Woodhouse (*W*³, *W*², to which may be added the quotation of 18–23 in a note to the sonnet *To My Brother George* 3 in his interleaved *1817*—see Sperry, p. 148) and a late copy by one of his clerks (Garrod's *T*). Woodhouse made *W*³ from a now lost transcript by Kirkman in Mary Frogley's album. *W*² (with "sang" in 4 and the more modern spelling "chords" in 6), the clerk's MS, and *1848* (with a substantive error in 7) all derive in sequence from *W*³. The present text is based on *W*³.

### *To Some Ladies*

Written in the summer of 1815 ("1815" in the extant holograph and Woodhouse's interleaved *1817*; the fair copy heading, Woodhouse's addition to the title in his *1817,* and a note by Woodhouse in *W*³ fol. 52 identify the addressees as the Mathew sisters, Caroline and Ann, who were on holiday by the sea with their cousin G. F. Mathew). First published in *1817,* pp. 29–31. The two extant MSS are a holograph fair copy in the Texas Christian University Library and a transcript by J. C. Stephens. The former varies substantively from *1817* in 5 (a copying error), 6, 8, 27, and 28. An earlier state than either of these is a version that Woodhouse saw perhaps in the possession of Mary Frogley, which can be at least partially reconstructed from variants that he recorded above and opposite the lines in his interleaved copy of *1817* (see Sperry, pp. 113, 143). Woodhouse's variants to 9, 24 (the single word "kindly"), 25, 27, and 28 are written in red ink; his addition to the title and the fuller version of 24 (as well as the date noted at the end) are all in black ink, were therefore written on a different occasion from the preceding, and may represent Woodhouse's own commentary and a suggested revision rather than readings from an authoritative source. Stephens' MS was made from *1817*. The present text, based on *1817,* incorporates a substantive correction in 6.

### *On Receiving a Curious Shell, and a Copy of Verses, from the Same Ladies*

Written in the summer of 1815 ("1815" in the extant holograph—and see note on the preceding poem). First published in *1817,* pp. 32–35. The five extant MSS are a holograph fair copy at Harvard, complete transcripts by George Keats, Tom Keats, and J. C. Stephens, and a partial copy (1–12) by Georgiana Wylie. George Keats's and Georgiana Wylie's MSS—probably made independently from a now lost holograph (see *Texts,* p. 103) and representing the earliest recoverable state of text—together vary from *1817* in title and the wording of eleven lines (Georgiana's further variants in 2 and 10 are presumably copying errors). The extant holograph is a revised version that varies from *1817* in eight lines.

Tom Keats's MS, with a shortened version of the *1817* title, is closer still to the printed text, differing significantly only in 31 ("are"); his other variants—in 4, 5, 31 ("wandering"), and 43—would appear to be simple copying errors. Stephens' MS was made from *1817*. Only Georgiana Wylie's partial copy has stanza numbers. The present text is based on *1817*.

*O come, dearest Emma! the rose is full blown*

Written probably in 1815 (though the only external evidence, not very helpful, is the presence of the sonnet *O Solitude* on the reverse side of the extant holograph). First published in Forman (1883), II, 211–212. The six extant MSS are a holograph fair copy among Woodhouse's papers in the Morgan Library, three transcripts by Woodhouse ($W^2$ plus two $W^3$ copies, fols. 77 and 78, that here and in the apparatus are designated $w^3$ and $\mathbf{w}^3$, respectively), a late copy by one of his clerks (Garrod's *T*), and a transcript by George Keats.

There are at least three, and probably are four, states of text for this poem. One of them is represented by the $W^3$ transcripts, which derive from a now lost copy by Kirkman in Mary Frogley's album and differ substantively from one another only in heading ($w^3$ has none); one of these was almost surely copied from the other, but the order is uncertain. Another state is that of George Keats's untitled copy, which is addressed not to Emma but to Georgiana Wylie. His text, which was Forman's source for the poem in 1883, differs from the $W^3$ transcripts in 1, 11, and 13. A third state is that of the Morgan fair copy, which is headed "Song" and differs from the $W^3$ transcripts in eight lines. Only the Morgan holograph has stanza numbers.

Still another state may be represented by variants to 1, 2, 4, 5 ("opening glades"), 6, 13, and 17 ("lovely") that Woodhouse entered above the lines in $\mathbf{w}^3$. These all agree with readings of the Morgan fair copy (and therefore with the present text), but since Woodhouse did not note the further variants in the Morgan MS in heading, the first five words of 5, the first, sixth, and seventh words of 15, and the first word of 17, it seems likely that, just as with *Fill for me a brimming bowl,* he took the variants from a now lost holograph rather than from the Morgan fair copy, even though at some time or other he gained possession of the Morgan MS and inserted a variant to 15 in it from his transcripts (see below). He copied $W^2$ from $\mathbf{w}^3$, incorporating the variants for 4 ("And the") and 13 ("fondly") that he had noted there and parenthetically adding "Mathews" (not "Mathew") in shorthand beside the title. The clerk made his transcript from $W^2$.

Unfortunately we have no evidence for ordering the three or four states described above. The present text is arbitrarily based on the Morgan fair copy.

2 strown] All but the first and last letters of this word (as well as some letters and the punctuation at the end of 1) are lost through damage in the Morgan fair copy. Woodhouse spells the word "strewn" and George Keats "strown."

15 it, I] The Morgan fair copy shows "I will" interlined above "it, I" (not deleted), but the inserted words are in lighter ink and are in Woodhouse's hand rather than Keats's. This is the first (in terms of the chronological order of the poems) of several instances in which Woodhouse marked and altered MSS that he was copying or collating.

*Woman! when I behold thee flippant, vain*

Written in 1815 or 1816 (there is no external evidence for dating beyond the fact that the lines were finished in time to be included in *1817*; Bate, p. 40 n., and Ward, p. 418, n. 14, assign them to 1815 on the basis of G. F. Mathew's high opinion of them in his *European Magazine* review of *1817*). First published in *1817,* pp. 47–49. No MS has survived (apart from a transcript by J. C. Stephens made from *1817*), and *1817* is our sole authoritative source. Twentieth-century editors have tended to treat the sonnet-stanzas as separate pieces, but in the format of *1817* they are clearly presented as three stanzas of a single poem.

*O Solitude! if I must with thee dwell*

Written in 1815 or 1816 (almost all scholars choose October or November 1815, a time shortly after Keats entered medical school; but the basis for this dating is rather shaky—mainly J. M. Murry's idea, in *Studies in Keats,* 1930, pp. 1–6, that G. F. Mathew's undated *To a Poetical Friend,* which seems to echo 7–8 of this poem, was written *before* Keats's November 1815 epistle *To George Felton Mathew*). First published in the *Examiner,* 5 May 1816, p. 282, and then (as Sonnet VII) in *1817,* p. 85. The four extant MSS are an early holograph fair copy among Woodhouse's papers in the Morgan Library (with *O come, dearest Emma* on the reverse side), a later holograph fair copy in the William Andrews Clark Memorial Library, U.C.L.A. (the Lyte–Philpotts–Bromley Martin MS), and transcripts by Tom Keats and J. C. Stephens.

The Morgan fair copy, apparently the earliest recoverable state of text, varies substantively from *1817* in heading (*1817* has none), 9, 10, and 12. The *Examiner* text ("To Solitude"), which comes next, has unique readings in 9 and the first word of 10 and *1817* readings later in 10 ("innocent") and 12; some or all of these revisions may represent editorial tinkering by Leigh Hunt. Tom Keats's MS ("Sonnet to Solitude"), made around the end of 1816 and containing a still later version than either of the preceding, has the Morgan MS's 9 and *1817*'s 10 and 12. The Clark Library holograph, with a last-minute revision in 9, was printer's copy for *1817* (it is headed "7"—the poem was the seventh sonnet in *1817*—and is foliated "59," the fifty-ninth leaf of Keats's complete MS for the volume); the *1817* text has lowercase for Keats's capitals in fifteen words but otherwise follows this MS fairly accurately, varying only in the insertion of a hyphen in 13 and the correction of the MS's "as" (a slip of the pen) to "are" in 11. Stephens' MS was made from *1817*.

The present text is based on *1817*.

5 river's] The Morgan fair copy, the *Examiner* text, and Tom Keats's MS all have "Rivers" or "rivers" (without the apostrophe), but this—because there is only one "dell"—has to be a spelling rather than a substantive variant.

9 But . . . thee] Woodhouse's note in his interleaved *1817,* that the line "was at first written 'Ah fain would I frequent such scenes with thee'" (Sperry, p. 149), is most probably a mistaken assumption based on the *Examiner* text.

*To George Felton Mathew*

Written in November 1815 (so dated in *1817*). First published in *1817,* pp. 53–58. Edmund Blunden, *English,* 1 (1936), 50 n., reports having seen a transcript by Mathew with a variant to 68—"name's . . . heart" for "name . . . heart's" (probably, like the variants in his quotations from the poem in *KC*, II, 186–187, 204, 215, Mathew's copying errors)—but the transcript cannot now be located, and no other MS has survived (apart from a transcript by J. C. Stephens made from *1817*). *1817* is thus our sole authoritative source. The epigraph preceding the three Epistles in *1817* (of which this is the first) is given in Appendix III.

*Had I a man's fair form, then might my sighs*

Written in 1815 or 1816 (Finney, I, 97–98, Bate, p. 54 n., Gittings, p. 58 n., and Allott, p. 32, taking a hint from two Woodhouse notes connected with *Hadst thou liv'd in days of old,* all suggest that the sonnet was written as a valentine, perhaps to Mary Frogley, in February 1816). First published (as Sonnet II, "To * * * * *") in *1817,* p. 80. The two extant MSS are transcripts by Tom Keats and J. C. Stephens. The former varies substantively from *1817* only in heading and 14 (the reading there is obviously a copying error). Stephens' MS was made from *1817.* The present text (with an emended heading for convenience of reference) is based on *1817*.

*Hadst thou liv'd in days of old*

Written on or shortly before 14 February 1816 (Woodhouse notes that the poem was composed for George Keats to send as a valentine to Mary Frogley, and that he saw a copy, apparently in George's handwriting, that was postmarked 14 February 1816—see below). First published (under the heading "To * * * *") in *1817,* pp. 36–39. The six extant MSS are a holograph fair copy in the Wisbech and Fenland Museum, four transcripts by Woodhouse ($W^2$, $W^1$, and two copies in $W^3$, fols. 89 and 85, that here and in the apparatus are designated $w^3$ and $W^3$, respectively), and a transcript by J. C. Stephens.

The earliest recoverable state of text is that represented by the $W^3$ transcripts, which differ substantively from one another only in 4 (the second line of the variant passage given in the apparatus for 3–36) and 53. One of these was almost surely copied from the other, but the order is uncertain. The $w^3$ copy contains the fullest of Woodhouse's various headnotes explaining his source: "In page 36 of Keats's poems published in 1817.—are lines, addressed 'to + + + +' (Mary).—The published lines were much altered from those originally sent, which were written at the request of Geo: Keats & sent as a Valentine to the Lady in question—The following is a Copy of the original Valentine which is now in the lady's custody—The post-brand bears date the 14 February 1816.—This was one of 3 poetical Valentines written by him at the same time." (Each of the other Woodhouse transcripts has a similar note; see Finney, I, 92–93, who gives the four notes in the order $W^3$, $w^3$, $W^1$, $W^2$.) The two $W^3$ texts vary from *1817* in heading (they are untitled) and 3–36, 51, 52, 53 ($W^3$ only—see the separate note below),

54, 55, 57, 59, 62, 63, 65, and 67, and have four additional lines after 68. $W^2$ (headed "To + + + +" and with a nonauthoritative "Hath" for "Has" in 49) was copied from $w^3$, and $W^1$ (with "From which bend" in 53, "Comes" in 57, and "Magician's" and "Enchanter's" interchanged in 62–63) derives from $W^3$.

The second state is that of the Wisbech holograph, which varies substantively from *1817* in heading, 28, 38, 49, 51 (a copying error based on the last word of 52), 53, 54, and 59, and breaks off after 64. The final state is that of *1817*. Stephens' MS was made from *1817*.

The present text (with an emended heading for convenience of reference) is based on *1817*.

53 O'er . . . bend] In $w^3$, which agrees with *1817* here, Woodhouse notes on the opposite verso, "This line I have corrected from the printed poem.—In the original it is written 'From the which four Milky plumes' &c without any verb.—The mistake was probably made by G.K. in copying it out." (Since the Wisbech holograph also has "From the which," Woodhouse is surely wrong in attributing the "mistake" to George Keats.) A marginal "from which bend &c" in $W^3$, which has "From the which" in its text, is presumably a nonauthoritative correction that Woodhouse devised on his own. $W^1$'s "From which bend" comes from this marginal correction.

### *I am as brisk*

Written probably in 1816 (on the second page of the extant holograph of *Hadst thou liv'd in days of old*). First published by Garrod in his 1939 edition, p. 567. The untitled holograph version in the Wisbech and Fenland Museum is our sole source of text.

### *Give me women, wine, and snuff*

Written toward the end of 1815 or during the first half of 1816 (while Keats was a medical student—see below). First published in H. B. Forman's one-volume *Poetical Works of John Keats* (1884), p. 558. The only authoritative source for these lines is the holograph at Trinity College, Cambridge—an untitled pencil version written on the cover of a lecture notebook that belonged to Henry Stephens, a fellow student with Keats at Guy's Hospital. The imperfect text of 1–4 quoted in an unidentified transcript of an 1847 letter from Stephens to G. F. Mathew now at Harvard (see *KC*, II, 210) represents a copy of a copy of this MS.

5 bless . . . they] The words "bless" and "they" are nearly illegible in the holograph. The present text accepts Forman's original deciphering of the line.

### *Specimen of an Induction to a Poem*

Written in 1816, probably in the spring sometime after the publication (in February) of Hunt's *The Story of Rimini,* which obviously influenced Keats's lines. First published in *1817,* pp. 15–18. The two extant MSS are transcripts by Tom Keats and J. C. Stephens. The former is written without paragraph divisions, varies from *1817* in heading and the wording of eleven lines, and shows marginal and other markings by Hunt—presumably indicating his approval or special liking—of 1–4, 14, 17 (five check marks at the right), 18 (a double dagger and a bracket in the margin as well as a line under "trembling"), 22–28, 44, 52, and 63–68. (On the relationship of this poem to *Calidore* in Tom Keats's copybook see the main note to the next poem.) Stephens' MS was made from *1817.* The present text, based on *1817,* includes a substantive emendation in 46 taken from Tom Keats's MS and confirmed by MS corrections in two presentation copies of *1817* (to George Keats and Charles Wells) at Harvard.

*Calidore*

Written in 1816, probably in the spring just after the preceding poem. First published in *1817,* pp. 19–28. The two extant MSS are transcripts by Tom Keats and J. C. Stephens. In Tom Keats's copybook *Specimen of an Induction* and *Calidore* are presented as two parts of a single fragmentary work. (All items in the copybook have the author's name at the end except for *Specimen*; all items begin on a new page except for *Calidore*; and Tom's note at the end of *Calidore,* "marked by Leigh Hunt—1816," clearly applies, since Hunt marked both texts, to the whole of *Specimen* and *Calidore.*) Tom's MS, with the title or section heading "Calidore," is written without paragraph divisions, varies substantively from *1817* in twenty-five lines, and shows marginal and other markings by Hunt of 2–3, 6–11, 24, 28, 31–32, 34, 40, 42–43, 53–55, 62–63, 65, 68, 77 ("twain" is circled), 79 ("Portcullis" is underscored), 80 ("a Kiss" is underscored), 82–83, 85–86, 88–94, 100–102, 120–123, 138–140, 144–145, and 150–151. Stephens' MS was made from *1817.* The present text, based on *1817,* contains two substantive emendations from Tom Keats's MS in 44.

38 shatter'd] The reading given for Tom Keats's MS ("shuttered") is questionable; Tom fails to close his "a" in a number of other words in the copybook transcripts.

84 affection] Woodhouse's insertion of "soft" before this word in his interleaved *1817* (Sperry, p. 143) is presumably his own suggestion to fill out the meter rather than an authoritative correction.

103 gently] Possibly a copying or printing error (from "gently" in 101); Forman (O.S.A. ed.) emends to Tom Keats's "meekly." But "gently" and "gentle" were two of Keats's favorite words, and "gentle" occurs in consecutive lines (again, however, possibly in error) in Tom Keats's transcript of *Specimen* 56–57.

*To one who has been long in city pent*

Written in June 1816 (so dated in the transcripts by Georgiana Wylie and George Keats). First published (as Sonnet X) in *1817,* p. 88. The four extant MSS are transcripts by Georgiana Wylie, George Keats, Tom Keats, and J. C. Stephens. The earliest recoverable text is that of Georgiana Wylie's MS, which varies from *1817* in heading and the wording of seven lines (two further variants—

"City's" in 1 and the omission of "of" in 3, later added in pencil—are clearly slips of the pen and are omitted from the apparatus). George Keats's copy (with "Sonnet" at the beginning of the text and the rest of Georgiana's title after the last line) has the same principal variants and probably was made from Georgiana's MS rather than the now lost holograph from which she took her text. Tom Keats copied a revised version varying significantly from *1817* only in 4. Stephens' MS was made from *1817.* The present text is based on *1817.*

5 heart's] So spelled in the MSS by George and Tom Keats; in the present context Georgiana Wylie's "hearts'" and *1817*'s "hearts" have to be considered spelling rather than substantive variants. Woodhouse corrected "hearts" to "heart's" in his interleaved *1817* (Sperry, p. 163).

11 Watching . . . bright] George Keats's MS (otherwise agreeing with Georgiana Wylie's text of this line) has the singular "Cloudlet's" as in *1817*; Tom Keats's MS (otherwise agreeing with *1817* here) has the ambiguous spelling "Cloudlets."

### *Oh! how I love, on a fair summer's eve*

Written in 1816 (so dated in all MSS), perhaps in the summer. First published in *1848,* II, 287. The six extant MSS are all transcripts—four by Woodhouse ($W^3$, $W^2$, $W^1$, and a copy in his interleaved *1817*), a late copy by one of his clerks (Garrod's *T*), and a copy by Patmore. Woodhouse's initial source was a now lost transcript by Kirkman in Mary Frogley's album. $W^3$ and $W^2$ are the earliest of the extant MSS; one of them was almost certainly copied from the other, but it is not clear which was made first. They differ substantively only in 5, where $W^3$'s original "thoughts" has been altered by erasure to "thought." ($W^3$ also contains three attempted revisions by Woodhouse, all interlined in pencil—"fire" above "warm" in 9, "Perhaps on wings of poesy upsoar" above 12, and "Or feel warm gushing a delicious tear" above 13.) The rest of the MSS apparently derive from $W^2$ (the clerk's and Patmore's in sequence), and vary substantively only in Patmore's omission of "the" (to regularize the meter) in 12. Patmore's MS was printer's copy for *1848.*

The array of MSS and their relationships are very similar to those for *As from the darkening gloom.* For the poem at hand, however, since the authoritativeness of $W^3$'s altered 5 is uncertain, the present text is based on $W^2$.

### *To a Friend Who Sent Me Some Roses*

Written on 29 June 1816 (so dated in Tom Keats's transcript). First published (as Sonnet V) in *1817,* p. 83. The three extant MSS are a holograph fair copy in the Morgan Library and transcripts by Tom Keats and J. C. Stephens. The holograph varies substantively from *1817* in heading (it has none), 1, 7, and 9. (Woodhouse saw either this MS or another early version, recording the holograph's variant to 1 in shorthand in his interleaved *1817*—see Sperry, p. 148.) Tom Keats's MS, presumably later than the preceding, varies from *1817* in heading and 14. Stephens' MS was made from *1817.* The present text is based on *1817.*

*Happy is England! I could be content*

Written perhaps in 1816 (but there is no external evidence apart from the inclusion of the poem in *1817*). First published (as Sonnet XVII) in *1817,* p. 95. The two extant MSS are an untitled holograph fair copy at Harvard and a transcript by J. C. Stephens. The holograph agrees substantively with *1817* throughout (and therefore does not appear in the apparatus). The transcript was made from *1817*. The present text is based on *1817*.

*To My Brother George* (*sonnet*)

Written at Margate in August 1816 (so placed and dated in George Keats's transcript). First published (as Sonnet I) in *1817,* p. 79. The five extant MSS are a holograph pencil draft in the so-called Severn pocketbook at Harvard, a holograph fair copy also at Harvard, and transcripts by George Keats, Tom Keats, and J. C. Stephens.

In its finished state, the much worked over first draft varies substantively from *1817* in heading (it has none), 3, 4, 8, and 10. George Keats's untitled MS, which has draft readings in 3, 4 ("That"), and 8, and revised readings in 4 ("from") and 10 (George's "thoughts" in 13 is probably a copying error), is an intermediate version between the draft and the final text, and most likely was made from a lost fair copy that Keats wrote and sent him soon after completing the draft. The later extant holograph was printer's copy for *1817* (there is a "1" between the title and the first line—the poem was the first sonnet in *1817*—and it is foliated "53," the fifty-third leaf of Keats's complete MS for the volume). Its text agrees substantively with *1817* throughout (and therefore does not appear in the apparatus), and is quite close to *1817* in all minor details except capitalization (the printer lowercased fourteen words that Keats had capitalized, added a hyphen in 12, and omitted a comma after "sky" in 14). Tom Keats's MS, varying significantly from *1817* only in 10 (probably a copying error), has the same punctuation as the holograph fair copy in twenty-one out of twenty-four places—the three differences are Tom's omissions—and may have been taken from it. Stephens' MS was made from *1817*.

The present text is based on *1817*.

*To My Brother George* (*epistle*)

Written at Margate in August 1816 (so dated in the extant holograph, George Keats's transcript, and *1817*—the first two with "Margate" before the date). First published in *1817,* pp. 59–67. The four extant MSS are a holograph "fair Coppy" at Harvard (see *Letters,* I, 105–109), complete transcripts by George Keats and J. C. Stephens, and a partial copy (through "warder" in 31) by Georgiana Wylie. A "second transcript made by George" that H. B. Forman cites for 45 and 77 (Hampstead Keats, I, 58 n., 60 n.) and Garrod (as "$a^2$") cites for 77 and 86 cannot now be located or identified, and may never have existed; its one reported reading that differs from *1817* ("just right" in 45—George's extant MS also has "just right" but the words are marked for transposition) is not noticed in the apparatus in this edition.

The holograph fair copy, with paragraph divisions just as in the printed text, varies from *1817* in heading (it has none) and the wording of fourteen lines. George's extant transcript and (as far as it goes) Georgiana's partial copy agree with the holograph text in all of these; their few variants from the holograph—George's "strokes" (11), "hear" for "ear" (32), "the" for "each" (77), and "Ocean's Waves" (125), Georgiana's "lightnings" (6), "try" for "strive" (8), and "strokes" (11)—are not significant, and it seems safe to assume, in spite of their agreement in 11, that both transcripts derive independently from the holograph, which Keats sent to George just after he wrote the poem. Stephens' MS was made from *1817*.

The present text is based on *1817*.

118 should] Possibly a compositorial error in *1817* (from "should" in 117), but it is at least equally likely that Keats altered his text (from the fair copy's "will") to avoid the repetition of sound in "still . . . will."

124 clift] Again possibly a compositorial error (the fair copy has "Cliff"), though "clift" was still current as a by-form of "cliff" in Keats's time.

### *To Charles Cowden Clarke*

Written at Margate in September 1816 (so dated in the extant holograph and *1817*—the holograph with "Margate" before the date). First published in *1817*, pp. 68–75. The three extant MSS are a holograph fair copy in the Huntington Library, a transcript of 1–20 by Thomasine Leigh, and a complete transcript by J. C. Stephens. The extant holograph, which apparently was sent in a letter to Clarke (it shows signs of having been folded several times to make an enclosure approximately 3″ × 5″), has paragraph indentions in 15, 21, 49, and 84, and varies from *1817* in heading and the wording of a dozen lines. Both transcripts are derivative texts—Thomasine Leigh's 1–20 from an extract quoted in J. H. Reynolds' review of *1817* in the *Champion*, 9 March 1817, p. 78, and Stephens' MS from *1817*. The present text is based on *1817*. For Woodhouse's suggested improvements in wording (in 94, 97, 110) and punctuation (13, 60, 61, 81, 96) marked in his interleaved *1817* see Sperry, pp. 147, 162.

84 Some . . . ] The *1817* text of 84 ff. begins at the top of a page, and since the printer did not indent new paragraphs it is possible that a paragraph division (as in the holograph) was intended. But the preceding page in *1817*, rather than shorter, is a line longer than the surrounding pages.

94 cloudlet's] It is not clear (since Keats frequently omitted apostrophes in possessives) whether the holograph's "Cloudlets" is a substantive or merely a spelling variant; Forman (1883 ed.) emends to "cloudlets."

114 fitting;] *1817*'s full stop (also in the holograph) is here emended to a semicolon to clarify the connection between "many days have past since . . . " in 109 and "Since . . . " in 115.

*How many bards gild the lapses of time*

Written probably in 1816 (but there is no external evidence apart from the inclusion of the poem in *1817*; Woodhouse's supposed date of March 1816, reported by Ernest de Selincourt in *The Poems of John Keats,* 5th ed., 1926, p. 397, does not appear in the implied source, Woodhouse's interleaved *1817*—see Sperry, pp. 110–111—and it seems unlikely that de Selincourt had access to some other Woodhouse material now lost). First published (as Sonnet IV) in *1817,* p. 82. No MS has survived (apart from a transcript by J. C. Stephens made from *1817*), and *1817* is our sole authoritative source.

*On First Looking into Chapman's Homer*

Written in October 1816 (so dated in the *Examiner*). First published in the *Examiner,* 1 December 1816, pp. 761–762, and then (as Sonnet XI) in *1817,* p. 89. The five extant MSS are a holograph draft or early fair copy at Harvard, a holograph fair copy in the Morgan Library, and transcripts by Tom Keats, Mary Strange Mathew, and J. C. Stephens.

The earliest recoverable text is that of the Harvard holograph, which may well be (as most recent scholars have agreed) Keats's first draft, even though it is fairly cleanly written and shows but a single compositional revision (in 6); it varies substantively from *1817* in heading, 6, 7, and 11. The rest of the authoritative texts are not directly relatable, and except for the last, *1817,* cannot be chronologically ordered. The Morgan holograph, which bears the inscription "To Mariane Reynolds" in an unidentified hand, varies from *1817* in heading (it has none), 7, and 13 (this last probably just a slip of the pen); Tom Keats's MS varies in heading, 5, and 7; and the *Examiner* version, with the same title as *1817,* varies also in 5 and 7 (agreeing with Tom's MS in both lines). The MSS by Mary Mathew and Stephens were both made from *1817*.

The present text is based on *1817*.

4 to] Woodhouse's marginal "of" for this word in his interleaved *1817* (Sperry, p. 150) is either an explanation or a suggested change but in any case is not an authoritative reading.

7 Yet . . . serene] Clarke, p. 130, says that "The original which [Keats] sent me had the phrase—'Yet could I never tell what men could mean'"; but since this varies in only one word ("tell" for "judge") from the reading of the holographs, Tom Keats's MS, and the *Examiner,* it may be supposed that Clarke was simply misquoting the line rather than accurately reporting from another (otherwise unknown) MS version. The Harvard holograph shows signs of having been folded for enclosure in a letter, and was almost surely the MS that Keats sent through the mail to Clarke.

*Keen, fitful gusts are whisp'ring here and there*

Written in October or November 1816 ("Very shortly after [Keats's] installation at . . . [Leigh Hunt's] cottage," says Clarke, p. 134; Keats first met Hunt in

October). First published (as Sonnet IX) in *1817,* p. 87. No MS has survived (apart from a transcript by J. C. Stephens made from *1817*), and *1817* is our sole authoritative source.

### *On Leaving Some Friends at an Early Hour*

Written in October or November 1816 ("shortly after" the preceding poem—Clarke, p. 135). First published (as Sonnet XII) in *1817,* p. 90. The two extant MSS are Keats's draft, in the Morgan Library (with early versions of *I stood tip-toe* 25b–28 and 151–156 on the reverse side), and a transcript by J. C. Stephens. The draft shows much cancellation and revision, but in its finished state varies substantively from *1817* only in heading (it has none) and 4. Stephens' MS was made from *1817.* The present text is based on *1817.*

### *To My Brothers*

Written on Tom Keats's seventeenth birthday, 18 November 1816 (so dated in one of the holograph fair copies, Tom Keats's transcript, and *1817*). First published (as Sonnet VIII) in *1817,* p. 86. The five extant MSS are a holograph pencil draft of 1–8 in the so-called Severn pocketbook at Harvard (a second leaf containing 9–14 has not survived), two holograph fair copies also at Harvard, and transcripts by Tom Keats and J. C. Stephens.

The earliest version is obviously that of the pencil draft, which in the lines that exist varies substantively from *1817* in heading (it has none), 1, 2, 3, and 7. The order of the two holograph fair copies, both of which have *1817*'s title, cannot be determined. One of them, dated "Nov$^r$ 18—" ($FC^1$ here and in the apparatus), contains a unique substantive variant in 3 and another variant from *1817* in 13; the other ($FC^2$), which is undated and has what is apparently the original draft of *I stood tip-toe* 231–235 on the reverse side, shows unique variants in 2, 5, and 8, and the same variant from *1817* that $FC^1$ has in 13. (Charles Ollier, one of the publishers of *1817,* wrote at the top of $FC^2$, "1817 This was copy for the press," but he was surely mistaken; one supposes that he came upon the MS, glanced at the title and first line, and wrongly assumed that it had been printer's copy.) $FC^1$ is closer than $FC^2$ to *1817,* but since their principal variants are unique in each case it is theoretically possible for either to have been made before the other. Tom Keats's transcript appears to be the latest of the authoritative MS texts, varying from *1817* only in heading and 14 (perhaps a copying error). Stephens' MS was made from *1817.*

The present text is based on *1817.*

### *Addressed to Haydon*

Written in 1816 (there is no evidence for a more precise dating, and scholars vary widely in their guesses). First published (as Sonnet XIII) in *1817,* p. 91. The two extant MSS are transcripts by J. C. Stephens and an unidentified copyist (the latter, at Harvard, with the sonnet *Written in Disgust of Vulgar Superstition* in the same hand on the reverse side). Stephens' MS was copied from *1817.* The unidentified transcript varies substantively (but probably not authoritatively) from *1817* in heading and 7. The source of this MS is not known, but it appears to have been made quite late, probably by a professional copyist from some now lost MS in Milnes's possession. It was the basis of a text published in *Hood's Magazine,* 3 (April 1845), 352, under the heading "Sonnet. By the Late John Keats. (Communicated by R. Monckton Milnes, Esq., M.P.)." None of the substantive variants in *Hood's* ("Adoring kindness" in 2, "Dwell" in 3, "when" in 5, "Which" in 7, "So when" in 11, and "sky" in 12) has independent authority, and they are ignored in the apparatus. The present text is based on *1817.*

*Addressed to the Same*

Written on 20 November 1816 (Keats's date at the end of the text in the earliest extant holograph—see *Letters,* I, 117). First published (as Sonnet XIV) in *1817,* p. 92. The six extant MSS are three holograph fair copies (all at Harvard) and transcripts by Haydon, Tom Keats, and J. C. Stephens.

Keats's first fair copy, in a letter to Haydon of 20 November 1816, varies substantively from *1817* in heading (it has none), 9, and 13. His second copy, sent to Haydon on the following day (*Letters,* I, 118–119), is also untitled and has the same variant as the first copy in 9 but the *1817* ellipsis (suggested by Haydon) in 13. Haydon's MS, which the painter forwarded to Wordsworth on the last day of the year, was made from this second holograph copy. Tom Keats's MS is, except in heading, substantively identical with *1817.* The final holograph was printer's copy for *1817* (it is headed "14" and "Addressed to the Same," is foliated "66"—the sixty-sixth leaf of Keats's complete MS for the volume—and is dated "Christ Day," apparently the day, 25 December 1816, on which he made the copy); the *1817* text has lowercase for Keats's capitals in twelve words but otherwise varies only in printing "*now*" (which Keats had underscored in the first line) as "now." Stephens' MS was made from *1817.*

The present text is based on *1817.*

*To G. A. W.*

Written in December 1816 (so dated in Tom Keats's transcript). First published (as Sonnet VI) in *1817,* p. 84. The four extant MSS are a holograph fair copy in the Keats-Wylie Scrapbook at Harvard and transcripts by Tom Keats, Woodhouse's brother W. P. Woodhouse, and J. C. Stephens. The holograph varies substantively from *1817* only in heading. Tom Keats's MS varies in heading and 13 (probably a copying error based on 12). W. P. Woodhouse's MS has substantive differences in heading, 11, and 12; these are very likely corruptions but nevertheless are included in the apparatus because Woodhouse's source is unknown. Stephens' MS was made from *1817.* The present text is based on *1817.*

*To Kosciusko*

Written in December 1816 (so dated in the *Examiner*). First published in the *Examiner,* 16 February 1817, p. 107, and then (as Sonnet XVI) in *1817,* p. 94. No

MS has survived (apart from a transcript by J. C. Stephens made from *1817*). The two early printed texts differ in 7 (where *1817* is clearly in error in either the first or the second word of the line) and 8. The present text, based on *1817*, incorporates the *Examiner*'s "Are" in 7.

6–7 burst . . . changed] In his interleaved *1817* Woodhouse designated "burst" as a verb and altered "changed" to "change" (which he also designated as a verb), producing "The names . . . burst . . . And change to harmonies" (Sperry, p. 152). But Woodhouse's markings in his *1817* usually represent his own interpretations or suggested revisions rather than authoritative corrections, and the *Examiner* reading has been given preference in this instance.

### *Sleep and Poetry*

Written sometime during October–December 1816 (after Keats met Hunt and before the MS for *1817* was put together). First published in *1817*, pp. 97–121. No MS has survived (apart from a transcript by J. C. Stephens made from *1817*), and *1817* is our sole authoritative source. Woodhouse added half a line to the poem's epigraph and queried "cubs" for "clubs" (234) in his interleaved *1817* (Sperry, pp. 117–118, 152, 155), but there is no reason to think that the *1817* text is faulty in either place.

### *I stood tip-toe upon a little hill*

Completed in December 1816 (the date at the end of Keats's draft, his fair copy, and Tom Keats's transcript—and see *Letters*, I, 121); possibly begun several months earlier, though the elaborate datings in Ward, pp. 420–421, n. 32, and Gittings, pp. 70, 77, 92, 93, 106, 109, are too speculative, and Leigh Hunt's statement in *Lord Byron and Some of His Contemporaries*, 2nd ed. (1828), I, 413, that the poem "was suggested to [Keats] by a delightful summer-day, as he stood beside the gate that leads from the Battery on Hampstead Heath into a field by Caen Wood" cannot be based on his own observation, since it refers to a time before he knew Keats personally (Keats could have later given him some of these details, but if Hunt's "delightful summer-day" was inferred from the poem itself then it is of course no help in dating). First published in *1817*, pp. 1–14. The five known MSS are Keats's original draft (of which about four-fifths is either extant or recoverable through facsimiles and earlier scholars' reports), a holograph fair copy at Harvard, transcripts by Tom Keats and J. C. Stephens, and a copy of the draft's 111–112 and 61–64 by W. H. Prideaux (see *KC*, II, 219–220).

The following list (updating Garrod, pp. lxxxiv–lxxxviii, and correcting some details in *Texts*, pp. 122–123) includes everything that has survived of Keats's draft (which once belonged to C. C. Clarke and was dispersed by him in fragments of a few lines each), gives the sources of apparatus readings for fragments that were once known but have since disappeared, and arranges the items according to the contents of each leaf of the MS in its finished state. (There are no folio or page numbers in the MS.)

| | *Recto* | *Verso* | *Location/source* |
|---|---|---|---|
| Leaf 1 | 1–10 | 19–27 | Extant at Harvard (in two fragments, 1–6 and 19–23 on the first, 7–10 and 24–27 on the second) |
| | 11–18 | 28–34 | Missing, but the text of the recto side is available in facsimile in Sotheby sale catalogue of 27 March 1929 |
| Leaf 2 | 35–37 | 49–52 | Missing; text unrecorded |
| | 38–48 | 53–60, 107–110 | Extant at Harvard (the lines on the verso written continuously, 107 following 60 without a break) |
| Leaf 3 | 111–112 plus a canceled version of 113–114 | 61–64 | Extant at Harvard |
| | Replacement of canceled 113 ff. plus 115 | At least two lines following 64 plus 65–68 | Missing, but W. H. Prideaux's transcript of the draft's 111–112 and 61–64 adds two more canceled lines following the draft's canceled 114 and two uncanceled lines following 64 |
| | 116–122 plus the four canceled lines given in the apparatus at 122/123 | 69–80 | Extant in the Berg Collection, New York Public Library |
| | Four uncanceled lines following the preceding | 81–86 | Extant in the Scottish National Portrait Gallery |
| Leaf 4 | 87–106 | 123–150 | Missing, but variants and other readings are given by M. B. Forman |

(*continued*)

| | *Recto* | *Verso* | *Location/source* |
|---|---|---|---|
| | | | in *TLS*, 27 August 1938, pp. 555–556 |
| Leaf 5 | 25b–28, 151–156 plus four additional lines | Draft of *On Leaving Some Friends at an Early Hour* | Extant in the Morgan Library (the first passage on the recto is a revision of lines already drafted on the verso of leaf 1; the second passage, beneath it, is apparently the original draft of lines following from the verso of leaf 4) |
| Leaf 6 | 157–173 | 181–192 plus a canceled version of 193–195 | Extant in the possession of Dallas Pratt, of New York |
| | 174–180 | Replacement of canceled 193 ff. plus 196–c. 200 | Missing; text unrecorded |
| Leaf 7 | c. 201–214 | (Presumably blank) | Missing; text unrecorded |
| Leaf 8 | 215–230 | Blank | Extant in the Free Library of Philadelphia |
| Leaf 9 | 231–235 | Fair copy of *To My Brothers* | Extant at Harvard (the passage on the recto is apparently the original draft of lines that Keats then recopied at the beginning of the next leaf) |
| Leaf 10 | 231–242 | Blank | Missing, but the text is available in facsimile in the *Sunday Times*, 12 November 1933, p. ii of "Book Exhibition Number" |

Leaves 1 and 2 were once conjugate; it is not known if any of the others were originally thus joined. The arrangement of lines in these leaves is virtually certain, except that the division of text between the verso of leaf 6 and the recto of leaf 7 is unknown (the verso of Dr. Pratt's fragment ends with lines 193–194 and part of a variant 195 all canceled; presumably Keats rewrote these lines on the missing bottom of the page before going on to 196 and the following lines). From various line numbers in Keats's hand on the rectos and versos of leaves 2, 3, and 4 it seems probable that he wrote the lines in the order in which the leaves, recto and verso, are reconstructed above—i.e., 1–60, 107–122 (plus four lines), 61–106, and 123–242—though it is of course possible that some of the fragments contain revised text that replaced earlier draft text now lost; the main question arising from the MS evidence at hand concerns the point at which Keats wrote the revised 25b–28 in the Morgan fragment (fairly obviously before he drafted 151–156).

Since the draft, the fair copy, and Tom Keats's MS are all dated December 1816, and we know that Keats was preparing copy for the printer during this month, the four texts that we have (including *1817*) belong to a very short period. The draft is untitled, has no epigraph, and except for the indention of 231 at the beginning of leaf 10 is written without paragraph divisions. In the recoverable portions its text varies substantively from *1817* in some sixty lines. The revised draft of 25b–28 on leaf 5 (cited in the apparatus as *RD*) varies in 26 and 28; the texts of 231–235 on leaves 9 and 10 do not vary substantively from *1817*.

The fair copy, which is also without title and epigraph, has slight paragraph indentions in 61, 93, 163, 181, and 211. It agrees with distinctive wording of the recoverable portions of draft text against *1817* in twenty-one lines and further varies from *1817* in fifteen others. Tom Keats's transcript, the latest of the authoritative MS texts, is headed "Endymion" (the same title that Keats refers to in *Letters,* I, 121) and contains after the title the lines from *Muiopotmos* that were used on the title page of *1817* (see Appendix III); it omits 27–28, has paragraphing more or less as in *1817* (lacking only the division between 204 and 205), and varies from the printed text in eleven lines (the omission of 27–28 and the variants in 39, 58, 109, and 152 are pretty obviously copying errors, and those in 142 and 192 may also be errors). Stephens' MS was made from *1817*.

The present text is based on *1817*.

90/91 (*apparatus*) ⟨And . . . flutterings⟩] M. B. Forman (*TLS,* 27 August 1938, p. 555) transcribes the first of these lines from the missing leaf 4 of the draft as "And as they come and go but neath their wings." The present apparatus reading incorporates Garrod's correction of the eighth word (presumably from the same photostats that Forman used) to "mark."

107 ¶What . . . ] In *1817* (in which new paragraphs are set off by line spaces but are not indented) the text of 107 ff. begins at the top of a page, but the preceding page is full (not short), and so there is some question whether a new paragraph was intended here. The present text relies on the paragraph division in Tom Keats's MS to resolve the ambiguity.

153 Fauns] "Fawns" (in the fair copy, Tom Keats's MS, and *1817*) is an archaic spelling of "fauns," and the emendation here is not substantive.

### *Written in Disgust of Vulgar Superstition*

Written on 22 December 1816 (dated "Sunday Evening Dec$^{r}$ 24 1816" in Tom Keats's transcript; the Sunday closest to this date in 1816 was 22 December). First published in *1876,* pp. 58–59. The four extant MSS are Keats's original draft, at Harvard, and transcripts by Tom Keats, J. C. Stephens, and an unidentified copyist (the last MS, also at Harvard, with the sonnet *Addressed to Haydon* in the same hand on the reverse side). The draft, written on the back of an August 1816 letter from George to John and Tom Keats, is untitled and has "they are going" in 11. Tom Keats's MS has both a title and a different reading in 11. Because C. C. Clarke told Milnes in 1846 that Keats wrote the poem "one Sunday morning as I stood by his side" (*KC*, II, 154), possibly Tom's date ("Sunday *Evening*") indicates that Keats revised 11 and Tom copied the poem later on the same day on which it was originally composed—though Clarke's statement comes long after the event, and it seems more likely that he simply misremembered the time of day. In any case, Tom added "J Keats / Written in 15 Minutes" below the last line in Keats's draft. Stephens' MS was copied from the draft.

The unidentified transcript agrees with Tom's MS rather than the draft in 11 and varies from both of these in heading and 12. The source of this MS is not known, but it appears to have been made quite late, probably by a professional copyist from some now lost MS in Milnes's possession. It was the basis of the text published in *1876,* which introduced further variants—clearly corruptions—in heading ("Written on a Summer Evening"),1 ("toll'd"), 6 ("To some blind"), and 8 ("Fond converse").

The present text is based on Tom Keats's MS.

### *On the Grasshopper and Cricket*

Written on 30 December 1816 (so dated in the extant holograph and *1817*). First published (as Sonnet XV) in *1817,* p. 93. The two extant MSS are a holograph fair copy in the Forster Collection of the Victoria and Albert Museum and a transcript by J. C. Stephens. The former varies substantively from *1817* only in title. The latter was made from *1817.* The present text is based on *1817.*

### *After dark vapours have oppressed our plains*

Written on 31 January 1817 (so dated in five of the six MSS, all but Woodhouse's last copy). First published in the *Examiner,* 23 February 1817, p. 124, and then in *1848,* II, 289. The six extant MSS are all transcripts—four by Woodhouse ($W^2$, $W^1$, a copy in his interleaved *1817,* and a late copy made for Severn) and one each by one of his clerks (Garrod's *T*) and Patmore. There are no significant variants among the MSS (in Woodhouse's copy for Severn, "relieving" in 5 is made out of an original "relieved" and a unique "rite" in 6 is preceded by "right" twice canceled, but both the original 5 and the final 6 are Woodhouse's own inventions). $W^2$, "from J.H.R."—i.e., from a now lost holograph that J. H. Reynolds had or, much more probably, from a Reynolds copy of a holograph—is almost surely the earliest of the extant MSS, and the others may be assumed to proceed from it (the clerk's and Patmore's MSS and *1848* derive from $W^2$ in sequence, *1848* with a nonauthoritative variant in 5).

Presumably Keats himself furnished a MS for the *Examiner,* but it is not clear whether this was the same MS that Reynolds had (or copied) or a different one. The *Examiner* text varies substantively from the MSS in 5, 9, and 12. Since we are in the dark concerning Woodhouse's immediate source for $W^2$, and there is always the possibility that some or all of the *Examiner* variants were the result of Hunt's editing ("smiling" in 12 very likely represents a copyist's or compositor's mistaken repetition of the same word at the beginning of 11), the authoritativeness of each distinctive reading in both of the principal versions is an open question. The present text is arbitrarily based on $W^2$.

*To a Young Lady Who Sent Me a Laurel Crown*

Written perhaps in 1816 or 1817 (but there is no external evidence for dating). First published in *1848,* II, 288. The four extant MSS are all transcripts—two by Woodhouse ($W^2$, $W^1$) and one each by one of his clerks (Garrod's *T*) and Patmore. $W^2$, "from J.K's M.S." (possibly in the possession of a Reynolds sister, if one of them was the "Young Lady" of the title), is the earliest of these, and the rest of the texts all derive from it (the clerk's and Patmore's MSS and *1848* in sequence). There is one substantive difference among the MSS—$W^2$ has "own" altered in lighter ink to "high" in 10 (the clerk and Patmore reproduce "high"), while $W^1$ reads "own"—and one other peculiarity in that all four MSS have a blank space between "This" and "moment" in 11 into which, in $W^1$ only, someone has penciled "very." The present text, based on $W^2$, follows the original rather than the altered reading of 10 and incorporates the penciled word from $W^1$ in 11.

10 own] We do not know Woodhouse's authority for the alteration of "own" to "high" in $W^2$. Since the change was made in different ink, and after he copied $W^1$ from $W^2$, most likely it is his own improvement of the text rather than an authorial revision.

11 very] The handwriting of the penciled word in $W^1$ (probably Woodhouse's) cannot be certainly identified. Since Keats did not leave blank spaces of this sort in holographs that survive, the lacuna most likely represents a word in his source that Woodhouse could not decipher and the penciled "very" a good guess rather than an authoritative reading. *1848*'s "mighty" (Milnes's addition in proofs) is clearly not authoritative.

*On Receiving a Laurel Crown from Leigh Hunt*

Written at the end of 1816 or early in 1817 (Hunt's sonnet to Keats ending "I see, ev'n now, / Young Keats, a flowering laurel on your brow" is dated 1 December 1816 in both a holograph MS and a transcript, and his two sonnets on receiving a crown of ivy from Keats are dated 1 March 1817; possibly none of these refers to the incident of the present poem, but they give an idea of when this sort of activity took place—see *The Poetical Works of Leigh Hunt,* ed. H. S. Milford, 1923, p. 720; Garrod, pp. lxxxi, 2; and Bate, pp. 138–139 n.). First published in

*The Times,* 18 May 1914, pp. 9–10. The single extant MS, a holograph fair copy written (with the next poem) on the blank page opposite Sonnet I in the copy of *1817* that Keats presented to J. H. Reynolds (at Harvard), is our sole source of text.

4 immortal] Because Keats did not dot his "i," the word in the holograph can also be read as "unmortal," and H. B. Forman (O.S.A. ed.) and Garrod both print "unmortal." But critical considerations, plus the fact that Keats used "immortal" in twenty-five or more lines elsewhere but never "unmortal," decidedly favor "immortal."

### *To the Ladies Who Saw Me Crown'd*

Written at the end of 1816 or early in 1817 (dating the same as for the preceding poem). First published in *The Times,* 18 May 1914, pp. 9–10. As for the preceding, the single extant MS, a holograph fair copy written in the copy of *1817* that Keats presented to J. H. Reynolds (at Harvard), is our sole source of text.

### *God of the golden bow*

Written at the end of 1816 or early in 1817 (Woodhouse in $W^2$ says "shortly after" the incident of the two preceding poems). First published in the *Western Messenger,* 1 (June 1836), 763, then in the *Harbinger,* 2 (21 March 1846), 234, and *1848,* II, 255–256. The seven extant MSS are Keats's original draft, at Harvard, a revised holograph fair copy in the Morgan Library (with *Unfelt, unheard, unseen* written on the first page of the same sheet), four transcripts by Woodhouse ($W^3$, $W^2$, $W^1$, and a late copy for Severn), and a transcript by Charlotte Reynolds.

The two authoritative states of text for this poem are, quite simply, those of the two extant holographs. George Keats gave the draft, which he had taken to America, to James Freeman Clarke, and Clarke printed the poem in both the *Western Messenger* and the *Harbinger* from this MS (in both periodicals omitting "beg," inadvertently deleted in the MS, in 20, and in the *Western Messenger* but not in the *Harbinger* changing the MS's "his" to "its" in 30; the two texts are titled "Ode to Apollo" and "To Apollo"). The later holograph differs substantively from the draft in 6, 11, 27, and 32; neither holograph has stanza numbers.

Woodhouse's initial source—"a M.S. in Keats's writing," as he indicates in $W^2$—was almost surely the Morgan holograph. $W^3$ was the first copy made, and the rest of the transcripts, including Charlotte Reynolds', derive from $W^3$ (see *Texts,* pp. 129–130). None of the transcripts' variants from the Morgan MS (the added title, "Ode to Apollo," in all five transcripts, the added stanza numbers in all but $W^1$, $W^2$'s "its" for "his" in 30, repeated from $W^2$ in $W^1$ and Charlotte Reynolds' MS, and two unique readings in Woodhouse's copy for Severn, "And the" in 15 and "one" for "a" in 32) is authoritative. Milnes's source for *1848* is, on the other hand, unknown (J. F. Clarke had sent him a now lost transcript of Keats's draft in 1845—see *KC,* II, 139–140—but the *1848* text agrees with the Morgan MS rather than the draft in 6, 11, 27, and 32), and consequently the *1848* title, even though probably not authoritative, is included in the apparatus.

The present text is based on the Morgan holograph.

12, 24, 36 Apollo? . . . Apollo! . . . Apollo?] The copy-text's inconsistent punctuation is retained here. Keats's draft, $W^2$ and the transcripts deriving from it, and *1848* have exclamations in all three lines, while $W^3$ has question marks in all three.

36 O . . . Apollo?] Followed by either one or two lines of crosses or x's (indicating fragmentariness) in $W^3$, $W^2$, $W^1$, and Charlotte Reynolds' MS, but there is nothing of this sort in either of the extant holographs. Woodhouse added the descriptive words "fragment of an" to a note on the poem in $W^3$ and changed the $W^1$ title to "Fragment of an Ode to Apollo" after he saw, in November 1818, a now lost Reynolds copy in which the poem was designated "a fragment" (*KC*, I, 63).

*This pleasant tale is like a little copse*

Written in February 1817 (so dated in all MSS). First published in the *Examiner,* 16 March 1817, p. 173, and then in the *Morning Chronicle,* 17 March 1817, p. 3, C. C. Clarke's *The Riches of Chaucer* (1835), I, 53, Robert Fletcher Housman's *A Collection of English Sonnets* (1835), p. 190, and *1848,* II, 290. The six extant MSS are a holograph draft or fair copy written on pp. 104–105 of Volume XII (after the end of *The Floure and the Leafe*) in Clarke's set of Chaucer's *Poetical Works* (14 vols., Edinburgh, 1782), now in the British Library, and transcripts by Woodhouse (two copies, $W^2$ and $W^1$), Isabella Towers, one of Woodhouse's clerks (Garrod's *T*), and Patmore.

Of the two principal states of text, the earlier is that of the extant holograph and the later is that represented by the *Examiner* and $W^2$. Clarke in several places describes the untitled holograph as Keats's original draft (see Clarke's *The Riches of Chaucer,* I, 52–53, "Recollections of John Keats," p. 139, and *KC*, II, 150, 170), but the MS is written out precisely and evenly, without deletion or other sign of initial composition, in Keats's smallest handwriting (1–12, on the first of the two facing pages, occupy a space $1\frac{7}{16}$ inches high by $2\frac{5}{16}$ inches wide), and it is almost surely an early fair copy in spite of Clarke's reiterated account. Clarke's sister Isabella Towers transcribed this holograph (adding a nonauthoritative title and changing "has" to "hath" in 10), and Clarke himself also took his text from this same MS when he published the poem in *The Riches of Chaucer* (adding another nonauthoritative title and changing "do" to "so" in 2, "power" to "charm" in 9, and "has" to "hath" in 10). R. F. Housman's text later in the same year is a reprint from *The Riches of Chaucer.*

Presumably Keats himself provided copy—a slightly revised now lost MS—for the *Examiner* version, which has a title and differs substantively from the extant holograph in 9 and 11. The text in the *Morning Chronicle* is a reprint from the *Examiner.* Woodhouse, who took $W^2$ from "J.K's M.S." (probably a MS in the possession of J. H. Reynolds and very likely the source from which the *Examiner*'s text derives), has a slightly different title from that in the *Examiner* but otherwise varies from this first printed text only in 11 ("athirst" where the *Examiner* reads, uniquely, "a thirst"). $W^1$ and the clerk's and Patmore's copies all derive from $W^2$ (the clerk's and Patmore's in sequence, Patmore's with a change of wording in 2), and Patmore's MS was printer's copy for *1848*.

The present text, preferring the MSS's "athirst" in 11 and disregarding the various headings in the transcripts and the *Examiner,* is based on $W^2$.

10 power] In both $W^2$ and his clerk's MS Woodhouse penciled "? magic" in the margin, suggesting a revision to avoid the repetition of "power" in 9 and 10. Clarke changed 9 in *The Riches of Chaucer* (see above) for the same reason.

### *To Leigh Hunt, Esq.*

Written in February 1817 (apparently extempore, when the final proof-sheets of *1817* were brought from the printer—see *KC,* II, 150, and Clarke, pp. 137–138). First published (as the Dedication) in *1817,* on the recto side of the leaf preceding p. 1. No MS has survived (apart from a transcript by J. C. Stephens made from *1817*), and *1817* is our sole authoritative source.

### *On Seeing the Elgin Marbles*

Written on 1 or 2 March 1817 (*Letters,* I, 122; in the three earliest printings and the extant holograph—but not in Woodhouse's transcripts or *1848*—this sonnet follows rather than precedes the next poem, but Keats's apology at the beginning of the next suggests that this was the earlier of the two to be composed). First published in the *Champion,* 9 March 1817, p. 78, and the *Examiner,* also 9 March 1817, p. 155, and then in *Annals of the Fine Arts,* 3 (April 1818), 172, and *1848,* I, 27. The seven extant MSS are a holograph fair copy written (with the next poem) on a blank page at the end of the copy of *1817* that Keats presented to J. H. Reynolds (at Harvard), four transcripts by Woodhouse ($W^3$, $W^2$, a copy in his interleaved *1817,* and a late copy for Severn), and a transcript each by Thomasine Leigh and Haydon.

There are no authoritative substantive differences among the MSS and early printed texts. The extant holograph, a now lost MS given to Hunt for the *Examiner* (see *KC,* II, 142), and a lost MS sent to Haydon (*Letters,* I, 122)—all three presumably from the same source and written about the same time—were the bases of the early printings in the *Champion,* the *Examiner,* and *Annals,* respectively. The rest of the texts apparently derive from one or another of these early printings. Thomasine Leigh copied the poem from the *Champion*; Woodhouse took his first transcript, probably $W^3$, from the *Examiner* (and the others then from $W^3$); and Haydon made his copy, which he sent to Edward Moxon, Milnes's publisher, in 1845, from the *Annals (KC,* II, 141–142). The text in *1848* most likely derives from Haydon's MS. The few substantive variants among the texts—Woodhouse's "pleasing" for "gentle" (6) in his interleaved *1817,* his "o'er" for "round" (10) in the copy for Severn, and *1848*'s "indescribable" (10)—are all assumed to be corruptions.

The present text is based on the extant holograph.

### *To Haydon with a Sonnet Written on Seeing the Elgin Marbles*

Written on 1 or 2 March 1817 (dating the same as for the preceding poem). First published in the *Champion,* 9 March 1817, p. 78, and the *Examiner,* also 9 March 1817, p. 155, and then in *Annals of the Fine Arts,* 3 (April 1818), 171–172, and *1848,* I, 27–28. As for the preceding, the seven extant MSS are a holograph fair copy written in the copy of *1817* that Keats presented to J. H. Reynolds (at Harvard), four transcripts by Woodhouse ($W^3$, $W^2$, a copy in his interleaved *1817,* and a late copy for Severn), and a transcript each by Thomasine Leigh and Haydon.

Keats made three fair copies early in March—the extant holograph in the presentation copy to Reynolds, which was the basis of the *Champion* printing; a now lost MS for Hunt, which was the source of the *Examiner* text; and a lost copy for Haydon, which the painter sent on to James Elmes for the *Annals* (*KC*, II, 141–142). The two authoritative states of text—that of the extant holograph and the *Champion,* on the one hand, and that of the *Examiner* and *Annals,* on the other—differ substantively in 1 and 12; further variants in the early printings—"sleep" for "steep" (7) in both the *Champion* and *Annals* and "where" for "when" (11) in the *Champion*—are obviously misreadings of Keats's handwriting (in the first instance, a misreading of an uncrossed "t" such as appears in the extant holograph). The rest of the texts again appear to derive from the early printings—Thomasine Leigh's MS from the *Champion,* Woodhouse's copies (beginning probably with $W^3$) from the *Examiner,* Haydon's MS from the *Annals,* and the *1848* text from Haydon. The rather considerable number of further variants in these derivative texts—differences in heading (in part referring to the spatial relationship of this poem to the preceding, e.g., "with the foregoing Sonnet" in $W^2$, "with the above" in Woodhouse's copy for Severn and *1848*), "of" for "on" (2) in Haydon's MS and *1848* (Woodhouse first wrote "of" in $W^3$ before changing it to "on," and also queried "of?" in the margin of his copy for Severn), "might" for "strength" (8) in $W^3$, Woodhouse's interleaved *1817,* and his copy for Severn, "these" for "those" (9) in *1848,* "while" for "when" (11) in Woodhouse's copy for Severn, and "brainless idiotism and o'erwise" (12) and "the full Hesperian" (13) in *1848*—are all assumed to be corruptions.

Unfortunately we do not know which of the two authoritative states, that of the extant holograph and *Champion* or that of the *Examiner* and *Annals,* is the later (slightly revised) version. The present text is arbitrarily based on the extant holograph.

### *On a Leander Which Miss Reynolds, My Kind Friend, Gave Me*

Written probably in March 1817 (the extant holograph has "March" at the end followed by a year that is best interpreted as "1817," though the last digit is difficult to make out; Woodhouse read the date as March 1816, but Keats did not meet the Reynoldses until later that year). First published in *The Gem* (1829), p. 108, and then in Galignani (1829), p. 71 of the Keats section. The four extant MSS are Keats's original draft, at Harvard (with Wordsworth's *Lines Written while Sailing in a Boat at Evening* copied in an unidentified hand on the verso), two transcripts by Woodhouse (*W*[2] and another Harvard copy—Garrod's *T*—that he made for Brown), and a transcript by J. C. Stephens. The draft and the version in *The Gem* represent the two principal states of text, differing substantively in the wording of the heading and 5 and in the punctuation of 1, 2, and 4. The rest of the texts derive from these—Woodhouse's *W*[2] (with "sight" in 2, corrected marginally in pencil to "light") from the draft, his later copy from *W*[2], and Stephens' MS (with "you could" for "ye could" in 5) and the Galignani printing from *The Gem.*

The main textual problem, apart from the reading of Keats's draft in 5 (see below), has to do with the authoritativeness of *The Gem*'s variants. It is probable that *The Gem*'s text derives from the draft—since the editor of the volume was Thomas Hood, who had married one of the Misses Reynolds, Jane, in 1825—and that the variants there are corruptions; but Hood's source is not definitely known, and the readings are accordingly included in the apparatus. The present text is based on Keats's draft.

5 So . . . ye] In the draft Keats first wrote "Gentle are ye nor co," then deleted "Gentle" and "nor co" and interlined "so gentle" above the second deletion. Someone, presumably Keats or Woodhouse (when he was copying the draft and, as *W*[2] shows, having difficulty in making out Keats's intention at this point—see *Texts,* p. 135), then marked "so gentle" in pencil for transposition to the beginning of the line. Since we cannot determine who was responsible for the penciling, and since there is an outside chance that the draft's "are ye so gentle" (the second version given in the apparatus) was all along intended to be read as "So gentle are ye" (as Woodhouse finally decided in *W*[2]), the present text follows the penciled transposition. Allott prints "Are ye so gentle" and punctuates 5–8 as a question.

### *On* The Story of Rimini

Written in March 1817 (before the 25th, when Keats mentions the poem, recently composed, in a letter to C. C. Clarke—*Letters,* I, 127). First published in *1848,* II, 292. The three extant MSS are a transcript by Brown and two transcripts by Hunt, the earlier written on a blank leaf at the end of a copy of Galignani (1829) and the later on a separate sheet, presumably the copy that Hunt sent Milnes in the 1840s (see *KC*, II, 156). There are no substantive differences among the MSS. Hunt's source, as he notes at the end of his earlier transcript, was a now lost holograph version "Written by Keats in a blank page of the 'presentation-copy' of his first volume of poems." Brown's MS, which was printer's copy for *1848* (Milnes inserting "Leigh Hunt's Poem" in the title on the MS), could have come from another lost holograph, but more likely—since Brown was a close friend of Hunt in both England and Italy—derives directly or indirectly from the holograph that Hunt possessed. The present text is based on the earlier of Hunt's extant transcripts.

### *On the Sea*

Written at Carisbrooke, Isle of Wight, probably on 17 April 1817 (the date on which Keats included the poem in a letter to J. H. Reynolds—*Letters,* I, 132; since the original MS of the letter is lost, there is no sure basis for determining whether the version there was a draft or a fair copy). First published in the *Champion,* 17 August 1817, p. 261, and then in *1848,* II, 291. The eleven extant MSS are all transcripts—five by Woodhouse (*W*³, *W*², *W*¹, a copy in his interleaved *1817,* and a late copy for Severn), two by Woodhouse's clerks (one of them in a letterbook transcript of the lost letter to J. H. Reynolds, the other—Garrod's *T*—a late copy made for Brown), two by Patmore, and one each by Charlotte Reynolds and Elizabeth Stott Clarke.

The two principal states of text, differing substantively in 7, 9, 11, and 14, are those of the clerk's letterbook transcript (the earlier) and the *Champion* (the later). The rest of the texts are derivative—Woodhouse's (apparently in this instance beginning with the MS in his interleaved *1817*) initially from the *Champion,* Charlotte Reynolds' and the later Woodhouse clerk's MSS from *W*², Patmore's first transcript (with a mistaken "who" for "whose" in 11) from the clerk's letterbook copy, Patmore's second transcript from the later clerk's copy, *1848* from Patmore's second MS (which was printer's copy), and Elizabeth Clarke's MS from *1848.* Woodhouse's transcripts show a gradual progress of change—from readings of the *Champion* to those of the letter text (which he later saw both in a now lost transcript by J. H. Reynolds—*KC*, I, 63—and in the letter itself)—that is too complicated to explain here (see *Texts,* pp. 138–139). His readings that differ from both the *Champion* and the letter text—"clamour" for "uproar" (11) in *W*³ and the copy for Severn, and "with too much" (12) in his interleaved *1817, W*³, and the copy for Severn (subsequently corrected in pencil in the first two and in ink in the third; *W*² has "⟨with⟩ too much with" written currently)—are assumed to be corruptions. The important fact is that by *W*² (if we ignore the copy for Severn) Woodhouse had arrived at a text that differs in only one word ("where" for "whence" in 7) from Keats's letter, and this is the text that, via the later clerk's MS and Patmore's second copy, was printed in *1848.*

The main unsettled textual question has to do with the source—and therefore the authoritativeness—of the *Champion*'s variant wording. Keats may have supplied a revised MS for the periodical, but it is also possible that the *Champion*'s readings in 7, 9 ("that"), and 11 are the result of Reynolds' revisions or editorial tinkering with the text that Keats had sent him in the letter (the *Champion*'s further variants, omissions in 9 and 14, are pretty obviously copying or printing errors). Because of the uncertainty concerning the *Champion*'s source, the present text is based on Woodhouse's clerk's letterbook transcript.

*Unfelt, unheard, unseen*

Written in 1817 (before 17 August, when J. H. Reynolds quoted the last four words of 9 in the *Champion*; the transcripts are dated 1817). First published in *1848,* II, 258. The three extant MSS are a holograph fair copy in the Morgan Library (on the first page of a sheet that also contains a fair copy of *God of the golden bow*) and transcripts by Woodhouse (*W*³) and C. C. Clarke. Keats's original draft survived at least into the 1880s, when it was in the possession of John Gilmer Speed, but has since disappeared (*Texts,* p. 139, is in error concerning its existence); its readings are available in the facsimile published in Speed's edition, *The Letters and Poems of John Keats* (New York, 1883), facing II, xxx.

The two authoritative states of text are those of the draft and the holograph fair copy, differing substantively in 3 (where the draft has no replacement for the second deleted word at the end of the line) and 15. Woodhouse almost surely made his transcript from the extant fair copy, adding stanza numbers, misreading or changing Keats's final word in 3, and inserting substantive punctuation in 11 and 13. Clarke's text apparently also derives from the extant fair copy, most likely by way of some now lost transcript made for him by Woodhouse; his MS agrees with $W^3$ in 3, 11, and 13 and, for $W^3$'s "Keats. 1817" written at the left margin beneath the last line of the poem, has "1817" at the left and "J Keats" at the right (it also agrees with the draft and the holograph fair copy against $W^3$ in the absence of stanza numbers, but the fact is not very significant, since Woodhouse in other poems sometimes added or omitted stanza numbers while making transcripts from his own or other people's MSS, and could have omitted them here in making a copy for Clarke). Because their sources are not known for sure, both Woodhouse's and Clarke's variants are in this instance included in the apparatus, but they are pretty clearly not authoritative (see the separate notes below). Clarke's MS was printer's copy for *1848* (Milnes wrote the heading "Lines" at the top of the transcript, and "nor" in 12 was changed to "and" in the course of printing).

The present text is based on the Morgan fair copy.

3 dying] The initial letter of this word in the Morgan fair copy is the same as that in "dear" in 11 and "day" and "dalliance" in 15, but it also somewhat resembles one of Keats's characteristic capital "L's," and Woodhouse's and Clarke's "lying," which makes better sense in the context, could easily have come directly or indirectly from this MS. The canceled "dying" in the draft is less ambiguously written.

13 True$_{\wedge}$] Woodhouse and Clarke punctuate as a separate element, an exclamation. The absence of punctuation in both the draft and the Morgan fair copy (making "True" an adjective modifying "monitors") is not decisive in the question, because Keats used very little punctuation in either holograph.

### *Hither, hither, love*

Written perhaps in 1817 or 1818 (there is no external evidence for dating). First published in the *Ladies' Companion,* 7 (August 1837), 187, and then in the *Ladies' Pocket Magazine,* Part I (1838), pp. 229–230. The single extant MS is a generally unpunctuated holograph at Yale. In giving the poem in the *Ladies' Companion,* John Howard Payne described his source as "one of these unpremeditated effusions, in the handwriting of John Keats, just scribbled as if playing with his pen, in lines sometimes crooked, sometimes straight, and sometimes with a row of words blurred out with his finger, before the ink was dry. . . . His brother gave [the MS] to me as unpublished." Though the lines in the Yale MS are "sometimes crooked, sometimes straight," there are no such blurrings as Payne commented on, and this fact led H. B. Forman (Hampstead Keats, IV, 37–38 n.) to the conclusion that Payne's MS was a now lost first draft and the Yale MS a fair copy. Possibly Payne was exaggerating. In any event, his text and that of the extant MS are substantively identical throughout. The *Ladies' Pocket Magazine* reprinted the poem (along with Payne's article) from the *Ladies' Companion.* The present text is based on the Yale MS.

### *You say you love; but with a voice*

Written perhaps in 1817 or 1818 (there is no external evidence for dating). First published by Colvin in *TLS,* 16 April 1914, p. 181. The three extant MSS are transcripts by Charlotte Reynolds, Woodhouse ($W^2$), and John Taylor (this last—Garrod's $W^3$—among Woodhouse's papers in the Morgan Library). Charlotte Reynolds' source is unknown, but presumably was either a now lost holograph given to her or someone else in the Reynolds family or a copy of one. Woodhouse's transcript, which has two shorthand notations at the end, "from Miss Reynolds" in ink followed by "and Mrs. Jones" in pencil, is substantively identical with Charlotte Reynolds' MS, and it is a fair assumption that he took his text from her album. Colvin first printed the poem from $W^2$, changing a word in 19.

John Taylor's MS differs substantively from the other two in heading (it has none), 3, 6, 10, and 22. Woodhouse subsequently saw this transcript, penciled its variants in 3, 6, and 22 into $W^2$, and at the same time entered the $W^2$ readings for these lines in pencil on Taylor's MS. His shorthand addition "and Mrs. Jones" obviously refers to Taylor's transcript, and may be taken to indicate that Taylor's text came from a MS in the possession of Isabella Jones, a friend of Taylor and other members of the Keats circle whom Joanna Richardson, *Fanny Brawne: A Biography* (1952), pp. 20, 172, and later scholars have identified as the Hastings "Lady" mentioned by Keats in *Letters,* I, 402–403, II, 65.

We do not know which of the two principal texts, Charlotte Reynolds' or Taylor's, is the later version. Charlotte's, however, may represent the more accurate copying, whether by her or in her source (Taylor's omission of 10 is evidence of carelessness somewhere along the line), and the present text is based on her MS.

### *Before he went to live with owls and bats*

Written perhaps in 1817 ("circa 1817" after the heading in Brown's transcript). First published in *Literary Anecdotes of the Nineteenth Century,* ed. W. Robertson Nicoll and Thomas J. Wise, II (1896), 277–278. The three extant MSS are Keats's original draft, in the Huntington Library, and transcripts by Brown and J. C. Stephens. (Garrod's references to a $W^3$ transcript, from which he purports to give several readings but none differing from those that he records for Stephens' MS, appear to be a mistake.)

Brown's date (see above) suggests that this may be one of the poems that he "rummaged up" in April 1819 (see *Letters,* II, 104). His transcript, presumably from some now lost revised MS, varies substantively from Keats's untitled draft in seven lines. Possibly Keats made these extensive revisions at the time Brown transcribed the poem. Stephens copied the extant draft (then in the possession of C. C. Clarke—see *KC,* II, 154); his substantive differences ("pluck away" for "pluck" in 6 and "Most" for "Of" in 11) are easily seen as misreadings of Keats's revisions in the Huntington holograph. Nicoll and Wise published the poem (with further substantive corruptions in 8, 10, and 13) from Stephens' MS, which at the time belonged to H. B. Forman.

The present text is based on Brown's MS.

*The Gothic looks solemn*

Written probably in September 1817 (either drafted or copied in a now lost letter to J. H. Reynolds from Oxford, where Keats visited Bailey from about 3 September to 5 October—*Letters,* I, 152). First published in Forman (1883), IV, 74 n. The two extant MSS, both transcripts by Woodhouse ($W^2$ and $W^1$), differ substantively from one another only in heading, where $W^1$ has "received (by J.H.R.)" for $W^2$'s "to J.H.R.," and each quotes a couple of introductory sentences from the original source of text, the lost letter to Reynolds. Woodhouse may have taken $W^2$ directly from Keats's letter (and $W^1$ from $W^2$), but, since he did not include the letter itself among his letterbook transcripts, there is a good chance that he never actually saw it, and that he transcribed the poem and the introductory sentences instead from some intermediate source, perhaps a lost copy made by Reynolds.

The other recoverable text is that of a letter from Brown to Henry Snook, 24 March 1820, which was extant when Forman published it in 1883 but has since disappeared. Brown's text, presumably a later or more accurate version transcribed from some holograph that he discovered while nursing Keats in his final illness, varies from Woodhouse's MSS in heading, 6, 8, and 9. The present text is based on Forman's 1883 printing of Brown's letter, but sets aside Brown's heading as probably nonauthoritative.

*O grant that like to Peter I*

There is no evidence for dating. First published in *The Poems & Verses of John Keats,* ed. J. M. Murry (1930), II, 592. The holograph at Harvard, our only source of text, consists of two quatrains, the second differing substantively from the first in 4. Pretty clearly the first quatrain is a preliminary version of the second, and the two are referred to in the apparatus as *D* and *FC,* respectively.

*Think not of it, sweet one, so*

Written about 11 November 1817 ("ab[t] 11 Nov[r] 1817" in $W^3$, $W^2$, and $W^1$; "Nov 11—1817" in Charlotte Reynolds' transcript). First published in *1848,* II, 257. The seven extant MSS are Keats's original draft, in the Morgan Library, four transcripts by Woodhouse ($W^3$, $W^2$, $W^1$, and a copy in his interleaved *1818*), and a transcript each by Charlotte Reynolds and C. C. Clarke.

The earlier of the two recoverable states of text is that of the extant draft, which Keats wrote on the last leaf of the original MS of *Endymion* (it was still with the *Endymion* MS when J. H. Reynolds lent it to Milnes in 1847—see *KC*, II, 228). Woodhouse's transcript in his *1818,* made at the same time that he noted variants there from the *Endymion* MS, is a painstaking copy of the draft, including most of the canceled words and interlineations. The later state is that of a now lost holograph fair copy which, as Woodhouse informed Clarke (see *Texts,* p. 145), Keats wrote out "for a Lady." This revised state, represented by the rest of the Woodhouse transcripts ($W^3$, $W^2$, $W^1$) and Charlotte Reynolds' MS, varies substantively from the draft's text in 3, 14, and 19. $W^3$ is probably the earliest surviving MS in this state and the only transcript made directly from the lost fair copy; the other three, all of which have the added heading "To ——," are assumed to derive from $W^3$ ($W^2$ directly from $W^3$, and $W^1$ and Charlotte's MS by way of $W^2$).

The subsequent history of the text is rather complicated (see *Texts,* pp. 1–2, 145–146). On the basis of his interleaved *1818* and probably also $W^2$ (in which he had recorded first in pencil and then in ink some of the cancellations and variants from Keats's draft), Woodhouse sent Clarke a now lost copy incorporating draft readings in 3 and 14 and the revised text's reading in 19, and including, in a different color of ink (and probably above the lines), readings that Keats had canceled in the draft in 7, 8, 11, and 18. Clarke's extant transcript, made for Milnes in the 1840s, reproduces Woodhouse's mixture of draft and revised readings as just described and gives the draft's canceled readings for 7, 8, 11, and 18 in parentheses in the margin. (Clarke's MS also has a variant heading, which is either Clarke's or Woodhouse's invention, and the date "Ap$^{l}$ 1817," which is an error by one or the other copyist perhaps deriving from the first word of Woodhouse's dating as it appears with an initial capital in $W^2$, "Ab$^{t}$ . . . .") Milnes used Clarke's MS as printer's copy for *1848,* marking out the main text's readings in 7 and 11 (leaving the canceled draft readings in the margin to be printed instead) and altering "tenderer" in 16 to "more tender." Thus the *1848* text has canceled draft readings in 7 and 11, distinctive uncanceled draft readings in 3 and 14, a distinctive reading of the lost revised MS in 19, and a word of Milnes's own devising in 16.

The present text is based on $W^3$.

### *Endymion*

Begun toward the end of April 1817 and first completed in draft form on 28 November 1817. Keats pretty well kept to the timetable that he announces at the outset of the poem (I.39–57). He started writing at Carisbrooke sometime after 18 April (*Letters,* I, 134, 139) and continued with Book I at Margate, Canterbury, Hastings, and Hampstead. Book II was written at Hampstead during the summer months (I, 149), Book III at Oxford in September (I, 155, 166, 168), and Book IV at Hampstead and Burford Bridge, Surrey, in October and November (I, 172, 175, 187); the date of completion is that at the end of the now lost original MS as recorded by Woodhouse in his interleaved *1818,* "Burford Bridge Nov$^{r}$ 28. 1817." Keats recopied the poem, revising as he wrote it out, in January–March 1818 (I, 196, 201–202, 206–207, 212, 213, 226, 239, 246, 253); the proofs of Book I began arriving in the middle of February, while he was still working on the later books (I, 228, 238–239). First published (toward the end of April) in *1818*.

Keats's original draft, of which Books II–IV were still extant in 1847, when J. H. Reynolds lent the MS to Milnes (*KC,* II, 227–228), has not survived, but we have Woodhouse's elaborate notation of variants and cancellations in the draft of II–IV (along with variants recorded from Keats's revised fair copy of the complete poem) in his interleaved copy of *1818* now in the Berg Collection, New York Public Library. (The first draft of Book I apparently was disposed of earlier, separately from the rest, and there is no record of it.) Keats's revised fair copy of the poem and a holograph title page, dedication, and draft of the preface (given below in Appendix IV) are all extant in the Morgan Library.

In addition to these basic materials, we have four letters of late 1817 in which Keats copied passages from Book IV (from the draft MS, but with a few otherwise unknown substantive variants)—to Bailey, 28–30 October, quoting 1–29 (MS at Harvard, cited as $L^1$ in the apparatus), to Jane Reynolds, 31 October, quoting 146–181 (Yale, $L^2$), to Bailey, 3 November, again quoting 146–181 (Harvard, $L^3$), and to J. H. Reynolds, 22 November, quoting 581–590 (surviving in a letterbook transcript by one of Woodhouse's clerks, $L^4$)—and three important letters of 1818 to Taylor giving the revised text of I.777–781 (30 January), discussing the proofs of Book I (27 February), and commenting on an advance copy of the printed poem and including a list of errata (24 April, cited as $L^5$—the MSS of all three letters to Taylor are in the Morgan Library, and Woodhouse made transcripts of the three in his letterbook).

Some derivative and nonauthoritative materials may be listed (for the record) in a long separate paragraph. Woodhouse, before he saw the draft MS in the possession of Reynolds, made several pages of notes at the end of $W^2$ recording canceled and variant readings from the extant holograph fair copy and then, after these notes, transcribed Keats's MS title page, dedication, and original preface. There is a copy of *1818* in the Tulane University Library containing corrections in Taylor's hand made from the errata list that Keats sent him on 24 April 1818 (see Robert H. Swennes, *K-SJ*, 20 [1971], 14–17). Another copy, at Keats House, Hampstead, with the signatures of two of Leigh Hunt's sons, Shelley Leigh Hunt and Henry Sylvan Leigh Hunt, on a flyleaf and the title page, has corrections and variants in one or more unidentified hands (both pencil and ink) to the wording and punctuation of some 190 lines. These notations, combining draft and fair copy readings, were clearly taken from Woodhouse's notes in his interleaved *1818,* and it is highly probable that at least some of them (especially those in pencil) are in Woodhouse's own hand. Dilke's copy of *1818,* also at Keats House, contains in Dilke's hand the five corrections specified by the errata list included in the second issue (or state) of the book, but no others. Keats's presentation copy to Leigh Hunt, in the Berg Collection, has only the correction of a misprint in I.790 ("where" for *1818*'s "were") and a presumably nonauthoritative improvement of meter in I.833 (the penciled substitution of "impassion'd" for "passionate"), both in unidentified hands. Charles Wells's copy, at Harvard, has alterations in still another unknown hand to I.348 ("waves" for *1818*'s "ways") and II.386 ("Crouch'd Cupids slumb'ring" for "Cupids a slumbering") as well as three corrections made from the published errata. A copy sold at Sotheby's on 29 March 1971 and now in private ownership and unavailable for examination is said (in the sale catalogue) to have in Keats's hand the same corrections to I.14, II.748, and IV.151 and 739 that he requested of Taylor in his letter of 24 April 1818. None of the above is noticed in the apparatus of the present edition (the readings in Woodhouse's $W^2$

notes are better taken from the extant fair copy itself, Taylor's corrections in the *1818* at Tulane are better taken from Keats's letter, and so on), but the Sotheby copy just mentioned is also reported to have an otherwise unknown state of the title page, and the variant (from Sotheby's description) is included in the apparatus note to the subtitle.

Woodhouse's notes in his interleaved *1818,* valuable as they are, present some serious problems in interpretation. He acquired the interleaved copy on 24 November 1818 (his date on a flyleaf—see also *KC*, I, 65–66), and probably shortly thereafter began collating the extant fair copy, recording variant readings and cancellations in both pencil and ink—frequently first in pencil, usually going over the note afterwards in ink, and also sometimes initially in shorthand, later rewriting the note in longhand. (He made these notes independently of those from the fair copy that he recorded at the end of $W^2$; there are fair copy readings in his *1818* that are not in $W^2$, and also readings in $W^2$ that are not in the *1818*.) At some later time he then collated the now lost draft of Books II–IV, adding further variants and cancellations to those already entered there from the fair copy and again making at least some of the notes initially in pencil. In general he used the abbreviations "o$^{l}$" and "or$^{l}$" (= "in the original") for readings taken from the fair copy and "o$^{y}$" and "or$^{y}$" (= "originally") for readings from the draft, but there are clear exceptions to this practice (e.g., the variants to II.409, 412, 567, 604, 610, 868, 996, 998, III.69, 70, 170, 180, 307, 570, IV.693–694, none of which appears in the fair copy, are accompanied by the abbreviation "o$^{l}$"), and there are also a great many readings for which there is no source designation at all—the alternative words are simply written above the line, in the margin, or on a facing page without comment, and some of them may be Woodhouse's own explanations, corrections, and suggested revisions rather than authoritative readings (these are listed below in the separate note to II.353). He sometimes indicated cancellations by marking through words in the variant reading or by using such explanations as "o$^{y}$ sundry—then changeful" (for II.541), but he also, as we can see by comparing his "o$^{l}$" and "or$^{l}$" notes with the extant fair copy (and again by comparing his duplicate notes from the draft at II.192 and 897), sometimes presented deleted text in his source as undeleted.

As a consequence, there is considerable uncertainty about (1) the cancellation status of his "o$^{y}$" and "or$^{y}$" readings taken from the draft (i.e., whether the variant words were canceled or uncanceled in the MS), (2) the authoritativeness of readings and annotations for which no source is designated, and (3) the reading of the draft text—agreement with the fair copy vs. agreement with *1818*—in places where Woodhouse gives only a variant from the fair copy (this last for the simple reason that, because he collated the fair copy first, he may well not have bothered to record, in the second collating, draft readings that were the same as variants he had already written down from the fair copy). The apparatus includes (with the siglum *D*) all of Woodhouse's readings that, on the basis of all the evidence considered at once, seem most likely to derive from the draft rather than from either the fair copy or Woodhouse's own inventiveness. Some of the more ambiguous situations are specially commented on in the apparatus entries and in separate notes below (see in particular the notes to II.5, 93/94, 240, 339, 541, 592), but in general the *D* readings in the apparatus and the absence of "*D*" where a variant is given from the fair copy alone should be viewed with some caution.

Keats's revision in January–March 1818 produced the fair copy from which the poem was set in type. Although we have no information concerning the draft text of Book I, Woodhouse's notes for the rest of the poem in his *1818* suggest that Keats changed the wording of some 660 lines in Books II–IV (between one-fifth and one-fourth of the total in these books) as he wrote out and then further revised the fair copy. J. H. Reynolds seems to have had a hand in marking and making suggestions in the original MS—"You shall see the [draft] M.S of Endymion," he told Milnes at the end of 1846, "I had little to do in revising" (*KC*, II, 178)—but Woodhouse's record of variants in this MS does not mention Reynolds or throw any light on his statement. In the fair copy, however, which Keats delivered to the publishers a book at a time, we can see Taylor at work as editor—correcting Keats's slips of the pen, underscoring and marking passages for revision or deletion, occasionally querying words and suggesting alternate words and phrases.

In Book I Taylor apparently first went over the fair copy in pencil, and then showed (or perhaps returned) the roughly edited MS to Keats, who sometimes accepted Taylor's suggestions by writing over the pencilings in ink, sometimes made further revisions and deletions in passages thus marked, and sometimes ignored the suggestions entirely. (Keats says nothing in his letters about these further revisions in reaction to Taylor's pencilings, but it seems clear that they were made before the MS was given over to the printer. Garrod, p. xxxii, on the basis of discrepancies between the printer's marking of signature C, p. 17, in the MS at I.269 and signature D, p. 33, at I.590 and the position of these lines in the printed text, fifteen lines before the beginning of p. 17 in the first instance and thirty-eight lines before the beginning of p. 33 in the second, believes that Keats made large-scale revisions after Book I was set in type. But there are no alterations before 269 extensive enough to account for the fifteen-line discrepancy in the first instance—indeed, had the printer originally omitted 127–134, which Keats marked for deletion, the first line on p. 17 would have been 292 rather than, as it now stands in the printed text, 284—and consequently these signature markings must, at least for the time being, be set aside as unexplainable.) In Books II–IV Taylor continued to mark the fair copy in pencil (and occasionally also in ink), but with many fewer alterations and corrections. There is no evidence that Keats saw the edited MS of these later books.

All of Taylor's markings that are substantive in character are either recorded in the apparatus or (where they did not influence the final text) described in separate notes below. If we include punctuation, spelling, and some corrections of grammar, the markings affect some 130 or 140 lines in the fair copy, but Taylor did not make—as opposed to suggest—significant alterations in more than about two dozen lines (see the apparatus for I.74, 79, 153, 154, 157–158, 513, 582, 600, 632, 651, 741, 770–771, 813, 844, II.58, 479, III.71, 230, 451, 689, 719, 945–946), and in at least some of these, as when he subsequently rewrote his own penciled suggestions in ink (I.153, 513, 582, 770–771), he may have been acting at Keats's request rather than on his own initiative. A typical example of his influence would be the change at I.368, where the fair copy reads "pretty" and

Taylor underscored the word and wrote "pallid" and "waning" in the margin and on the opposite verso. *1818* reads "pallid," but since Taylor did not *substitute* one of his words in the MS we are probably safe in concluding that Keats accepted the suggestion and made the change himself in proofs. In a similar instance, opposite "bob" in the MS at I.311 Taylor wrote "push" and "raise"; but *1818* has "bob," and Woodhouse noted in $W^2$, "the words raise, push, were suggested to the Author: but he insisted on retaining *bob*." The overall spirit of the relationship between author and publisher is conveyed in the opening of Keats's letter to Taylor of 27 February 1818, concerning the proofs of Book I: "Your alteration strikes me as being a great improvement—the page looks much better. And now I will attend to the Punctuations you speak of. . . . I am extremely indebted to you for this attention and also for your after admonitions" (*Letters,* I, 238). Very likely the same relationship and tone were maintained through the publication of *1820,* where both Woodhouse and Taylor queried words and lines and suggested revisions but did not, so far as we know (except in *The Eve of St. Agnes*), actually enforce any changes against Keats's objections.

As first issued, *1818* contained a single erratum (to III.71); in a second issue (or state) a five-item errata slip correcting I.940, II.149, 789, III.71, and IV.739 was tipped in to cover the single erratum, and still later a cancel leaf containing the same five errata was substituted for the original erratum leaf. If we set aside the alterations marked in Taylor's hand in the MS, *1818*'s corrections of Keats's slips of the pen, and the five errata corrections, there remain substantive differences between the fair copy and *1818* in some ninety lines. Twenty-eight of these differences have to do with the expansion of Keats's contracted forms (the MS's "e'en" becomes "even" or "ev'n" a dozen times, "o'" becomes "of" four times, "'t" becomes "it" seven times, and the other five differences are of a similar character —see the note below to II.782). Another five are *1818*'s corrections of verb forms (usually the change of a third-person form to make it agree with a second-person subject). Another eleven are fairly clearly *1818*'s errors, either in printing or in reading Keats's hand (these are specified in the emendations list in the next paragraph). The remaining forty-six may be seen in the apparatus notes to I.107, 368, 386, 722, 756, 762, 764, 849, 969, II.215, 302, 313, 319, 340, 353, 371, 402, 410, 474, 503, 538, 561, 607, 622, 723, 985, 990, III.342, 346, 353, 358, 537, 570, 588, 621, 655, 751, IV.13, 429, 622, 649, 697, 700/701, 709, 739, 754. Some of the items in this list probably or certainly were corrections of mistakes in the MS (e.g., those at I.849, II.353, 985, III.537, IV.649, 697, 739), and some of course may be further printer's errors (e.g., those at II.340, 474, 622, 723—"glowing" at II.299, where the fair copy reading is uncertain, is also possibly an error). In general, however, the responsibility for these changes cannot be ascertained. We know that Keats read the proofs of Book I, but also that he was a careless proofreader. Probably he read those of Book II as well, but early in March 1818, upon leaving London for Teignmouth, he asked the publishers to send the proofs of Book III to C. C. Clarke (*KC,* I, 12). This last fact raises the possibility that he never saw proofs of Books III and IV, and the possibility is strengthened by the opening sentence of his letter to Taylor written from Teignmouth on 24 April: "I think I Did very wrong to leave you to all the trouble of Endymion" (*Letters,* I, 270).

The present text, based on *1818,* incorporates substantive emendations in

I.182, 283, 550, II.282, 318, 524, 748, 761, 782, 973, III.202, 286, 359, IV.97, 151, 341, 443, 486, 548. Those at I.283, 550, II.282, 524, 761, III.286, 359, IV.341, 443, 486, 548 are corrections of printer's errors. Those at II.748, 782, IV.151 are based on Keats's errata list in the 24 April letter to Taylor. Those at II.973 and III.202 (where both *1818* and the fair copy are clearly in error) are taken from Woodhouse's record of draft readings. The rest (along with some nonsubstantive spelling changes) are commented on in separate notes below.

I.1 A . . . ever] According to Henry Stephens, a fellow medical student who shared lodgings with Keats in 1815–16, the original version of this line was "A thing of beauty is a constant joy." Keats recited it in this form to Stephens and then, after hearing the latter's opinion that "It has the true ring, but is wanting in some way," revised it to its present wording (see Benjamin Ward Richardson, *Asclepiad,* 1 [1884], 149). If this really happened, we must suppose (in spite of Gittings' explanation, p. 121) that an interval of perhaps a year or more passed before Keats went on with the rest of the poem.

I.29 glories] On the opposite verso in the fair copy Taylor suggested "and glories" and then "its glories"—probably an attempt to straighten out the meter —but Keats ignored the suggestion.

I.78 ay] *1818* consistently uses "ay" for the adverb ("ever") and "aye" for the interjection ("yes," "ah"). *1817* and *1820* also regularly distinguish between the two but reverse the spellings. Keats in his MSS wrote "aye" for all meanings.

I.127–134 Making . . . sing.] Keats deleted these lines in the fair copy probably in response to a penciled bracket by Taylor in the margin beside 132–134. In canceling the passage Keats also changed the punctuation after "past" (126) to a full stop.

I.135 Leading . . . young] It is not perfectly clear at what stage of revision Keats changed "some" to "young" in the fair copy (because the latter word is both interlined above the deleted "some" in the original text and also written in the final version on the opposite verso). It may be that the intermediate version given in the apparatus should read "And In the front, young."

I.137 Each . . . white] As a replacement for the original wording in the fair copy Taylor suggested on the opposite verso "Each brought a little" and "Each bringing a white." He deleted both of these after Keats revised the text (with a participle and Taylor's "white") to the *1818* reading.

I.182 owlet's] The ambiguous "owlets" in the fair copy and *1818* clearly requires emendation. The usual reading "owlets'" (e.g., in H. B. Forman's editions and Allott) goes back to Galignani (1829). The present text follows Garrod in correcting to the singular "owlet's."

I.232–306 "O . . . Lycean!"] Woodhouse dated this "Hymn to Pan" (above the beginning of it) 26 April 1817 in a copy of Galignani (1829)—now at Harvard —that Severn gave him in 1832, but his authority for this is unknown; he did not date the passage in his interleaved *1818*.

I.263 faun] See Textual Note to *I stood tip-toe* 153.

I.311 bob] On the opposite verso in the fair copy Taylor suggested "push" and "raise," but, as Woodhouse recorded in his $W^2$ notes on the poem, Keats "insisted on retaining *bob.*"

I.315 swam] On the opposite verso in the fair copy Taylor suggested "mov'd."

I.405 a] Above this word in the fair copy Taylor interlined and then deleted "the" in pencil.

I.472 those] In Keats's revised text in the fair copy, Taylor altered "those" to "thy" in pencil, but *1818* has "those."

I.509 powers] Taylor underscored this word in pencil in the fair copy.

I.511 herd] So *1818*. In the fair copy Keats seems to have written "r" over "a" in this word or "a" over "r"; it is also possible that he wrote "r" over a mistaken "rr." Garrod and Allott emend to "head," but neither Keats in his letters nor Woodhouse in his interleaved copy commented on the *1818* reading, and it is therefore retained here.

I.541 progress silverly] Keats enclosed these words in quotation marks in the fair copy (they echo Shakespeare's *King John* V.ii.46).

I.550 tighten] Keats's uncrossed "t's," fairly common in his MSS, sometimes produce ambiguous readings, but here there is none, since one does tighten rather than loosen ("lighten") the reins in the process of slowing down (see 551). The same situation occurs in II.524.

I.552 His . . . four] Taylor bracketed these words in pencil in the fair copy.

I.595 spheres] Taylor altered this word to "sphere" in pencil in the fair copy, but *1818* has "spheres."

I.698 aloe] Taylor underscored this word and marginally marked it with an X in pencil in the fair copy.

I.726 No . . . maidenhood,] Taylor penciled an X in the margin beside this line in the fair copy, probably suggesting that Keats's meaning could be clarified or better expressed.

I.813 combine] Taylor also attempted other revisions in this line in the fair copy to reduce it from six to five feet, interlining and deleting "wheneer" in pencil above "when we" and writing some now illegible word or words above "amalgamate" that he then replaced with the final choice, "combine," in ink.

I.833 passionate] Taylor inserted a penciled "the" before this word in the fair copy (ostensibly to improve the meter), but *1818* has Keats's original text.

I.849 an] The fair copy's "and" is presumably a slip of the pen. Taylor, trying to make sense of the line, revised it in pencil to read "A Love both mortal, and immortal too."

I.943–959 'Ah . . . her'] In his letter to Taylor of 24 April 1818 Keats listed this passage with two others, III.429–443 and 570–600, as "Parts that should have inverted commas [i.e., opening quotation marks] to every line" (*Letters,* I, 272), but he did not specify the same for two other passages of internal quotation, I.965–969 and III.539–554. The present text follows *1818* in all five passages.

I.972 smile] Taylor underscored this word in pencil in the fair copy.

I.977 the] Taylor underscored this word in pencil in the fair copy and wrote "this" in the margin, but *1818* has "the."

Book II] On a half-title leaf preceding the first leaf of text in the fair copy of Book II Taylor instructed the printer, "Attend to the punctuation in general as marked, and to the Elisions in the last Syllables of the participles as they are written." If more than one compositor worked on the poem, presumably only the one setting the opening pages of Book II saw this note.

II.5 touching] Woodhouse's most frequent forms for noting draft readings in his *1818*—here "or$^y$ written 'but O! for thine'" and in II.7 "o$^y$ sends"—do not reliably indicate whether the variant words that he records were deleted or undeleted in the draft. While he sometimes marked through words to show cancellation, or explained that a word or phrase was "erased," it is clear that he was not consistent in his practice. In the present apparatus his undeleted readings are regularly given as undeleted unless there is some special evidence to the contrary (see the notes below to II.93/94, 240, 592).

II.39 chafing] The fair copy–*1818* "chaffing" represents a spelling current in Keats's time, and the emendation here (for clarity) is not substantive. Woodhouse altered the word to "chafing" in his *1818*.

II.93/94 (*apparatus*) ⟨Endymion . . . sight—⟩] Woodhouse records this text, uncanceled except for the two words in curly braces, as the "original" draft text for 93, but it seems more probable that it was an incomplete attempt deleted before the present 94, and so it is given in the apparatus as a between-lines cancellation. Other uncanceled readings of this sort are interpreted in the same way in the apparatus notes for II.103/104, 799/800, IV.949/950, 955/956.

II.145 travelling] The draft's "travailing" may be merely a spelling variant, but the intention in both the draft and the later texts is still in question because "travail" was an acceptable form of modern "travel" in Keats's time (just as "travel," in the fair copy of *Isabella* 382, was a form of modern "travail"). With the later texts' "toil" in the same line, "travailing" is redundant; with the draft's "seige" (so spelled in Woodhouse's note) it seems less so. Allott emends to "travailing."

II.146 The . . . vile:] A check mark is penciled beside this line in the fair copy —possibly questioning Keats's use of "kernel."

II.165 When . . . to't;] A check mark is penciled beside this line in the fair copy—possibly questioning Keats's rhyme of "lute" and "to't."

II.192 haply] Woodhouse has two separate notes on this line in his *1818,* in one giving "haply . . . bower" as canceled and in the other giving the same words as uncanceled.

II.240 Now . . . he] In recording the draft variant Woodhouse gives both "fares" and "went" as uncanceled, simply writing "fares" above "went." In this situation (occurring again at II.419, 644, 789, III.188) the apparatus uses the phrase "replacing" or "replaced by," interprets the word written above as the later, and presents the earlier word as deleted.

II.299 glowing] The word in the fair copy is either "glowing" written with a shorter "l" than usual or "growing" (as Woodhouse recorded in the draft) with a taller "r" than usual; if the latter, then *1818*'s "glowing" may be a compositorial error.

II.318 O . . . among] Woodhouse noted on the opposite verso in the fair copy, when he was collating its text with *1818* (and before he saw Keats's draft), "Perhaps thus originally O let me cool't the Zephyr boughs among." The editorial correction here (justified by the transposition marked in the draft and also of course by the requirement of rhyme) was first made in print in Milnes's edition of 1854 (though Milnes omitted "the" in transposing the words).

II.334 alert he stood] Woodhouse marked these words for transposition to "he stood alert" in his *1818*—presumably a suggested revision rather than an authoritative reading.

II.339 But . . . not] It is possible that "⟨Bu⟩" in the draft variant represents Woodhouse's own error rather than a cancellation in the MS he was collating. The same applies to the deleted text given in the draft readings for III.52, 685–686, 864–865, IV.42 and also the alterations recorded for II.973 ("weary" to "wearied") and IV.92 ("My" to "Mine").

II.340 old] The fair copy's "cold" is clearly written; *1818*'s "old" is either a printer's error or else an intentional change (to avoid repetition of the same word already used in 338 and also perhaps to improve the sense) made by Keats or someone else while the poem was in press. Garrod emends to "cold."

II.353 he scarcely] Here and in some eighty other places in his *1818* Woodhouse does not specify "$o^l$" or "$o^y$" but simply writes the alternative wording above, beside, or opposite the text without comment. In most instances it may be supposed that these are draft readings and that he omitted the source designation either through oversight or because he had already recorded an earlier variant on the page with "$o^y$" and intended the same designation to be understood to apply to the later; but in a few it is possible that the alternative wording is Woodhouse's own explanation or suggested improvement of the text. The following (for the record) is a complete list of *D* readings included in the apparatus for which Woodhouse does not specify source: II.353, 357, 378, 596, 597, 598, 645, 647, 668–670, 692 ("maid"), 747, 748 (all three readings), 798 (the word is simply written in the margin in shorthand), 824 ("O my"), 878, III.63/64, 74, 465, 498, 500, 506, 511, 541, 650, 842, 962, 979, 983, IV.2 (both of the draft readings), 74, 76–77, 92, 236, 374, 451, 546, 592, 593, 624, 630, 643, 650, 653, 656, 660, 664, 699 (the first four words of the variant, which Woodhouse records separately from the final word "rillet"), 716, 785, 794, 796, 801, 805, 808, 811–813, 815, 816, 827 ("Why! hark ye"), 862, 866, 874, 882, 926, 927. Some other markings that seem more likely to be Woodhouse's own explanations or changes are excluded from the apparatus and commented on in separate notes above and below to II.334, 377, 852, 961, III.323, 871, 918, IV.319, 507, 566/567, 819 (another reading besides that given in the apparatus), 923.

II.376 And . . . gone,] A check mark is penciled beside this line in the fair copy—perhaps questioning the "had gone, / Had not" repetition in 376–377.

II.377 benignant] Woodhouse altered this word to "benignantly" in his *1818*—presumably his own interpretation of the syntax rather than an authoritative correction.

II.474 tusk'd] It is not clear whether Keats actually intended "tush'd" in the fair copy or simply wrote "tusk'd" with an unclosed "k." "Tushes" as a noun (the main use recognized by the *OED*) occurs in *Dear Reynolds, as last night I lay in bed* 16.

II.501 echoing] In recording the draft reading Woodhouse enclosed "out" in parentheses, possibly indicating that the word was canceled in the draft. The same occurs in his note to III.626. Other parenthetical notations at III.871, IV.319, 566/567 (see the notes below) are taken to be his own explanations or additions to the text.

II.524 tighten'd] See Textual Note to I.550.

II.541 varied] Woodhouse records "$o^y$ sundry—then changeful." In this situation (occurring again at II.602, 726, 814, 907, III.159, 171, 540, 570) the apparatus uses the phrase "replaced by" and takes the second variant to be the final (uncanceled) reading in the draft. The same type of phrasing ("replacing") is also used in apparatus notes to II.588, 748, 757, III.621, 955, IV.495, where Woodhouse gives the earlier draft reading as a cancellation but does not indicate whether the revised text was interlined above or written currently after the deleted word in the MS.

II.541 dyes] The fair copy's "dies" was a variant form of "dyes" in Keats's time. H. B. Forman (1883 ed.) took the MS word to be a verb and emended his text accordingly.

II.592 prize] Woodhouse records "o$^{y}$ joy" (uncanceled) but gives no variant for the rhyme word in 593. In this situation (occurring again at IV.7, 232, 906) the apparatus presents the variant as canceled. Probably some of the draft text at II.308 and IV.19 should also (because of the rhymes involved) have been represented as canceled.

II.641/642 (*apparatus*) ⟨About . . . dust.⟩] Woodhouse's note on the deleted lines in the draft—that they were "afterwards crossed out & the printed lines substituted"—does not make clear whether Keats rewrote the passage immediately below the last deleted line (i.e., currently) or subsequently on the opposite verso or an added leaf.

II.681 this . . . feeling] In addition to recording the variant draft reading, Woodhouse altered the printed text to "feelings" in his interleaved copy and also penciled "q feeling*s*" opposite the line in the fair copy.

II.749 Is . . . Who] Taylor altered the text in pencil in the fair copy to read "Is it to be so? No! For Who," but *1818* has Keats's original wording.

II.764–765 How . . . sweet, sweet, sweet.] Taylor bracketed these lines in pencil in the fair copy, suggesting deletion or revision of them.

II.782 done't] In requesting this correction and that at IV.151 Keats told Taylor, "Those abbreviations of *is 't* [for] *is it* and *done 't* for *done it* are of great consequence" (*Letters,* I, 273). It seems odd that he singled out just these two, while making no mention of the many other contracted forms that were expanded in the printed text—e.g., "cool't" (II.318), "For't" (II.359), "is't" (II.932 and III.758), "I'm" (III.431), "speakst" (IV.127), "shall't" (IV.304), "they're" (IV.349), and a number of instances of "e'en" for "even," "i'" for "in," "o'" for "of," and "t'" for "to" (passim). See also the apparatus for III.751.

II.793 vailed] *1818*'s "veiled" was an acceptable spelling of "vailed" in Keats's time, and the emendation here (for clarity) is not substantive.

II.852 limbs] Woodhouse penciled "arms" above this word in his *1818*—presumably a suggested revision.

II.868 O . . . swoon'd] In his *1818* Woodhouse wrote "or$^{y}$ O he had fainted the" but then deleted the note.

II.882 harbour] There is no definition in the *OED* that covers Keats's "arbour" (in the fair copy and *1818*) as a verb. The emendation here (following a correction of the text by Woodhouse in his *1818*) is based on the likelihood that Keats simply dropped an "h" by mistake (as he sometimes did elsewhere in his extant MSS). Though the same emendation was made independently of Woodhouse in Moxon's editions beginning in 1846 (and retained in *1876* and H. B. Forman's 1883 ed.), Garrod and other twentieth-century editors have reverted to "arbour."

II.889 stept] Woodhouse read and in his *1818* recorded the fair copy's word as "slept" (which is to some degree plausible in the context), but also penciled "q stept" on the opposite verso in the fair copy. The MS word is almost surely "stept" written with the first "t" uncrossed (see Textual Note to I.550).

II.897 night . . . festival] In one note in his *1818* Woodhouse gives "that wean'd him" as an undeleted draft reading, but a second note recording the full variant for the rest of the line implies that the three earlier words were canceled.

II.914 but the . . . the] There is some problem here in ascertaining just how Woodhouse's draft variant relates to the *1818* text. He underscored all four words in *1818*'s "but the ghosts, the," but "subtlest" has to be pronounced as three syllables to fit this equivalence ("Or they are subtlest and dying swells"). It seems likelier that the draft words stood in place of three words—either "the ghosts, the" or (more probably) "but the ghosts."

II.961 Oread-Queen] Woodhouse notes "Diana" in the margin of his *1818*—possibly a draft variant, but more probably his own explanatory comment.

II.974 thrush's] So *1818*. On the basis of the fair copy's ambiguous "Thrushes" Woodhouse changed the text in his *1818* to "thrushes'" (an emendation followed by H. B. Forman beginning in 1883 and more recent editors). But Woodhouse's alteration is an interpretation of Keats's MS, not an authoritative correction, and Keats could as easily have intended "Thrushes" to represent the possessive singular "thrush's."

II.1015–23 By . . . head.] These lines, written in J. H. Reynolds' hand in the fair copy, are, as Garrod observes (p. xxxi), "on a separate leaf, the only unnumbered leaf in the MS. In this connexion it is worth noticing that, writing to Reynolds on 3 February 1818, Keats says he hopes to call on him on 4 February bringing with him (the fair copy of) Book II [*Letters,* I, 225]. Did Reynolds spill the ink over, or otherwise damage, the last leaf of the MS., and atone by copying it fair in his own hand?" It is highly probable that the deleted words in the fair copy at II.1020 represent Reynolds' own error, subsequently corrected, rather than a cancellation in the MS leaf that he was copying.

III.41 'Twixt . . . swear,] Woodhouse notes in his *1818,* "At the End of this line [in the draft] is written 'Oxford Sept$^{r}$ 5.'"

III.99 thin] Garrod (p. 131 n.) queries "?thine," but presumably Keats was referring to the difference between the sulphurous fumes of Pluto's abode in Hades and the "thinner" atmosphere above. Cf. "too thin breathing" at IV.650.

III.195 were] Taylor interlined and deleted "was" above this word in pencil in the fair copy.

III.247–249 thence . . . Where] Woodhouse appears to have written "w" for the first letter of "thence" in the margin of his *1818* and "T" for the first letter of "Where," but both markings are blurred and probably should be considered canceled.

III.323 and] Woodhouse inserted "yet" above this word in his *1818*—presumably a suggested revision.

III.359 airy] Keats's word in the fair copy looks like "aery" with a dotted "e," but he uses the form "airy" everywhere else in his MSS, and *1818*'s Miltonic "aery" (which could be read or misread as a noun in a noun-adjective inversion at the end of the line) is almost surely a compositor's mistake. Woodhouse read and in his *1818* recorded the fair copy word as "airy."

III.417 to] After Keats changed "towards" to "to" in the fair copy, Taylor restored "towards" in pencil above the original word but then deleted it.

III.429–443 'Ah . . . thee.'] See Textual Note to I.943–959.

III.570–600 'Ha . . . adieu!'] See Textual Note to I.943–959.

III.620 hast] Taylor interlined "hadst" in pencil above this word in the fair copy, but *1818* has Keats's "hast."

III.626 waist] In recording the draft reading Woodhouse enclosed "and dived" in parentheses. See Textual Note to II.501.

III.665 The crew] Taylor interlined "All" in pencil above these words in the fair copy (to improve the meter), but *1818* has Keats's original text.

III.704 savage] Woodhouse queried "surges?" opposite this word in his *1818*.

III.752 struck] The fair copy's "stroke" is an archaic spelling of the past tense of "strike," not a substantive variant.

III.871 Aw'd] Woodhouse inserted a caret after this word in his *1818* and wrote "(away)" in the margin—presumably a clarification of Keats's meaning rather than a draft variant.

III.918 Visit my Cytherea] Woodhouse altered the text in his *1818* to read "Visit thou my Cythēra." This is almost certainly his own correction—a change of name plus adjustment for meter—rather than a draft reading, and the fair copy–*1818* error has been allowed to stand ("Cytherea," used correctly in II.492, III.975, is a name for Venus; "Cythera" is the island sacred to her).

III.983 sweetest of all] Woodhouse underscored only these three words in recording the variant "essence of all sweetest" in his *1818*; probably he should have also marked the preceding word, giving as the draft reading "O sweetest essence of all sweetest minions."

*After* III.1032] Woodhouse notes in his *1818,* "In the orig[l] Copy [Keats's draft], here is inserted Oxf: Sept[r] 26."

IV.9 Rapt] The extract in Keats's letter to Bailey of 28–30 October 1817 ($L^1$) has "Wrapt," and the fair copy shows "⟨W⟩rapt," but Keats frequently miswrote "rapt" in this way and the letter variant is not substantive.

IV.51 I . . . lost] After Keats marked the fair copy to read "I am Sad and lost" Taylor queried the new word order in pencil and changed the transposition marks to produce "Sad I am and lost," but *1818* follows Keats's transposition rather than Taylor's.

IV.97 for . . . twain] The fair copy is marked in faint pencil to read "for them in twain." Probably it was Woodhouse who did this, when he was collating the fair copy against the printed text. In his *1818* itself he seems to have first changed the text to read "for them in twain" and then further transposed "is cut" so as to produce "I feel my heart for them is cut in twain." Apparently neither the simpler nor the more elaborate transposition has any authority beyond the obvious requirement of rhyme. The present text follows H. B. Forman (1883 ed.) in preferring the simpler transposition.

IV.203 thee, Melancholy] Since Keats sometimes doubled the "e" in writing "the," it is possible that the fair copy's "thee melancholy" (without punctuation or capital) is a miswriting of "the melancholy." Cf. "find the Melancholy" in the ninth line of the canceled opening stanza of *Ode on Melancholy*.

IV.319 whisper] Woodhouse inserted a parenthetical "(thou)" after this word in his *1818*—pretty obviously his own clarification of Keats's ambiguous syntax.

IV.354 Muse . . . ] This line is slightly indented in the fair copy, and Woodhouse marked his *1818* (first in pencil and then in ink) for paragraph spacing and indentions both here and at 362. He also, on his own initiative (no doubt in connection with his alteration at 362), marked his *1818* to remove the indention and close up the lines at 367.

IV.507 gaunt] Woodhouse underscored this word in his *1818* and wrote "thin, meagre" in the margin—probably an explanatory gloss in this instance rather than a record of draft readings.

IV.509 her . . . kiss'd] Woodhouse does not make clear how the second line that he records from the draft connects with the *1818* text. Probably it represents either a preliminary attempt (afterwards canceled) at the present 510 or else the beginning of a full line (perhaps ending in "own" to rhyme with the now rhymeless "alone" in 510) so worked over in the MS that Woodhouse could not decipher it.

IV.550 With . . . speed] Here Woodhouse notes the draft's agreement with *1818* rather than with the original wording in the fair copy.

IV.558 masque] The fair copy–*1818* "Mask" was an acceptable form of modern "masque" in Keats's time (just as "masque" in the fair copy of *Bright star* 7 was a form of modern "mask"), and the emendation here (for clarity) is not substantive. Woodhouse altered the word to "masque" in his *1818*.

IV.566/567 (*apparatus*) Who . . . be?] Woodhouse gives the draft reading as "Who who (away?) would be?"—the parenthetical "away?" probably his own addition rather than an illegible word in the MS.

IV.632 to] The fair copy's "too" (also in *1818*) is a slip of the pen in the MS, and the emendation here is not substantive. Woodhouse corrected the word to "to" in his *1818*.

IV.739 kisses gave] The fair copy's "gave gave" is marginally corrected in pencil to "kisses gave." In this instance the hand is probably Woodhouse's, and the correction made at the time he collated the fair copy against the printed text.

IV.805 Endymion,] It is possible that "Endy:" in the draft variant is Woodhouse's abbreviation for the full name. The line would scan properly if "Dear Endymion" were elided into three syllables.

IV.819 are . . . glad] In addition to recording the draft variant given in the apparatus, Woodhouse also wrote "glad, too overglad" in the margin of his *1818* as a replacement for the last four words of the line in the printed text. This may be a separate (earlier or later) variant in the draft, but is more likely to be Woodhouse's own suggested improvement of the text.

IV.923 the . . . tops] Woodhouse penciled "shades of" beneath these words (in the last line of a page) in his *1818*—pretty clearly an explanatory gloss rather than a draft variant.

### *In drear nighted December*

Written in December 1817 (so dated in $W^2$; the extant holograph has "Dec$^{r}$" at the end). First published in the *Literary Gazette,* 19 September 1829, p. 618, and then, in order, in *The Gem* (dated 1830 but issued in October 1829), p. 80, *NMM,* 26 (November 1829), 485, and Galignani (1829), p. 75 of the Keats section. The seven extant MSS are a holograph fair copy in the University of Bristol Library, three transcripts by Woodhouse ($W^3$, $W^2$, $W^1$), a transcript by Woodhouse's brother W. P. Woodhouse, an unidentified transcript (perhaps made by someone in Leigh Hunt's family) that once belonged to Severn and is now at Keats House, Hampstead, and a transcript by Isabella Towers. Another holograph, possibly Keats's original draft, was extant as late as 13 June 1876, when it was sold at Sotheby's to Charles Law, but has since disappeared; Law lent it just after he acquired it to H. B. Forman, who reported its readings in various editions beginning in 1883 (those in the present apparatus are taken from Hampstead Keats, IV, 61–62 n.; the alterations in 2 and 18 are assumed to have been made above the line).

Essentially there are three versions of the poem—one represented by the now lost Law MS, $W^3$, $W^2$, and $W^1$; another represented by the Bristol holograph; and a third represented by the early printed texts, the unidentified transcript at Keats House, and Mrs. Towers' MS. Apart from heading, the first two versions differ significantly from the third in 1, 9, and 21; the second version (that of the Bristol MS, whose alteration in 5, where Keats began to write the fifth line of the second stanza, suggests that it is a copy rather than a draft) has, in addition, a unique "of" for the other texts' "at" in 20. (A fourth version, incorporating Woodhouse's proposed revision of the entire final stanza—see *KC,* I, 64–65—and represented by W. P. Woodhouse's MS, which, under the title "Pain of Memory," has the text of this rewritten final stanza but with "darkly" for Woodhouse's "sadly" in the third line, is clearly not authoritative. This version is ignored in the following discussion and omitted from the apparatus.)

Woodhouse's notations at the end of the $W^2$ text, "from J: H: Reynolds" and "Dec[r] 1817" followed (in shorthand) by "the date from Miss Reynolds' album," plus the variant that he entered opposite 20, "*of* in Miss R's Copy in Keats's hand writing," tell us that he got his text from Reynolds (almost certainly a now lost Reynolds copy in November 1818—see *KC*, I, 63–64), and that he subsequently saw the Bristol holograph ("Miss R's Copy in Keats's hand writing") and possibly also an otherwise unknown dated MS in "Miss Reynolds' album" (since the Bristol holograph is incompletely dated, lacking the year). $W^3$ and $W^2$ are the earliest of the transcripts, but there does not seem to be any basis for determining whether they are independent copies from Reynolds' lost MS or one was made from the other. They differ slightly in that $W^2$ has stanza numbers (the rest of the MS and printed texts do not) and reads "*not*" (underscored) for $W^3$'s "not" in 21. $W^1$ (with an erroneous "not" for "none" in 22) was made from $W^2$, and the other transcripts are also clearly derivative—the unidentified transcript at Keats House (with a miscopied "great" for "green" in 4) from the version in the *Literary Gazette* and Isabella Towers' copy from Galignani's text.

The significant early printings are those in the *Literary Gazette* and *The Gem.* Though the *Literary Gazette,* in reviewing *The Gem* on 24 October 1829 (p. 697), commented on the poem's reappearance in that annual and explained that "the proprietors [of the *Literary Gazette*] had previously printed their version from another copy," it seems fairly obvious that both texts ultimately derive from a single source. One may guess that Thomas Hood, who was editor of the preceding year's *Gem* but had quarreled with the publisher and withdrawn from the work (see Alvin Whitley, *HLB,* 5 [1951], 119), had prepared a copy for the next year's volume and then, after resigning, had offered the same poem (in "another copy") to the *Literary Gazette.* Both Hood and Reynolds had published work of their own in the *Literary Gazette* in 1828 (Peter F. Morgan, *K-SJ,* 11 [1962], 88). The two printed texts (which differ substantively from one another only in 24, where *The Gem* is presumably in error) could have been based on any of the MSS—the lost Reynolds copy, the Bristol holograph, and the lost MS in "Miss Reynolds' album" (if this in fact was a different MS from the Bristol holograph)—that Woodhouse saw, all of which belonged to members of the Reynolds family, with which Hood was connected by his marriage to Jane Reynolds in 1825. Galignani reprinted the poem from the *Literary Gazette,* and *NMM* from *The Gem.*

The authoritativeness of the printed texts' readings in 1, 9, and 21 is somewhat in question. Both the Bristol holograph and $W^3$ have part or all of the printed texts' 21—"To know the change and feel it"—written above or beside the original line, and probably not by Woodhouse in either MS, even though he objected to the third stanza and, as has been mentioned parenthetically above, attempted elsewhere to rewrite it. It is not clear whether this reading was entered in the MSS before or after the printed texts appeared; it may have been (in the Bristol MS) the source of the line in the printed texts, but more probably was added to the MSS from one of the printed texts. In any event, it seems extremely unlikely that Keats was responsible for the printed texts' 21—Woodhouse penciled "not as Keats wrote it" beside the third stanza in his copy of Galignani now at Harvard —and their reading in 1 and 9 may also be a corruption (introduced by an intervening copyist or editor) rather than an authoritative variant.

After the authoritativeness of the printed texts' variants, the remaining textual question is the order of readings in the MSS in 20. Since Forman is silent on the matter, we may assume that the Law MS, apparently earlier than the Bristol holograph, agreed with the preponderance of texts in reading "at"; the Bristol MS's "of" is therefore best taken to be a change that Keats made in the process of writing out a fair copy. The present text is based on the Bristol MS.

23 steel] The Bristol MS's "steal" (repeated independently in Galignani's text and thence in Isabella Towers' MS) is a spelling error, and the emendation here is not substantive.

### *Apollo to the Graces*

Written perhaps early in 1818 (Allott, p. 290, identifies "Don Giovanni" in Woodhouse's heading as a pantomime produced at Drury Lane in December 1817 and reviewed by Keats in the *Champion* on 4 January 1818). First published by Colvin in *TLS,* 16 April 1914, p. 181. The two extant MSS are a holograph at Harvard, possibly Keats's original draft, and a transcript by Woodhouse ($W^2$). The transcript, which according to Woodhouse's note was made "From the orig[l] in Miss Reynolds's Possession," differs from the Harvard holograph in heading and 3. Since the heading variant (the addition of "written . . . Giovanni") is simply an extension of the holograph's title—and therefore possibly Woodhouse's own explanation—and since the variant in 3 agrees with a canceled reading in the holograph, it is not clear whether Woodhouse copied the Harvard MS or another holograph not now known. Colvin first printed the poem (with substantive errors or changes in 3 and 6) from $W^2$. The present text is based on the extant holograph.

3 My . . . morn] In the holograph Keats added short horizontal lines—presumably accent marks—above "steeds" and the first syllables of "pawing" and "thresholds."

14 Through] The holograph's reading has always been reported as "Though" (Rollins, *HLB,* 6 [1952], 174; Garrod, p. 545 n.; *Texts,* p. 155). Actually Keats's word cannot be represented in conventional typography; it most nearly resembles "Ttroigh," which is as close to "Through" (the $W^2$ reading) as it is to "Though."

### *To Mrs. Reynolds's Cat*

Written on 16 January 1818 (so dated in all MSS). First published in Hood's *The Comic Annual* (1830), p. 14. The three extant MSS are a holograph fair copy in the Buffalo and Erie County Public Library and two transcripts by Woodhouse ($W^2$, $W^1$). The transcripts differ substantively from the holograph in heading, 9, 12, and 14. Woodhouse presumably took his $W^2$ text from some now lost holograph or copy in the Reynolds family, and $W^1$ (with "tender wrists" in 9, a copying error based on 8) from $W^2$. The *Comic Annual* version, also probably deriving from a MS in the Reynolds family, varies substantively from all three extant MSS in heading and 1 (very likely neither variant is authoritative), and agrees with the holograph against the transcripts in 9, 12, and 14.

There is no way of knowing whether the $W^2$ readings are earlier or later than those in the extant holograph. The present text, arbitrarily based on the holograph, incorporates Woodhouse's variant or correction (to make the verb agree with its subject) in 12.

### *Lines on Seeing a Lock of Milton's Hair*

Written on 21 January 1818 (so dated in seven of the eight MSS, all but the original draft). First published in *PDWJ,* 15 November 1838, and then in *1848,* I, 78–79. The eight extant MSS are Keats's original draft, at Harvard, a holograph fair copy written on the last page of his facsimile reprint of Shakespeare's First Folio at Keats House, Hampstead, a fair copy included in his letter to Bailey of 23 January 1818 (holograph at Harvard), and transcripts by Brown, Dilke, Woodhouse (two copies, $W^2$ and $W^1$), and Charlotte Reynolds.

Keats drafted the poem at Hunt's, the first seventeen lines in a notebook belonging to Hunt and the rest on a separate sheet. The two holograph copies (in the Hampstead Shakespeare and the letter to Bailey) show revisions from the draft in heading (the draft has none) and the wording of thirteen lines. In addition the letter text differs from the Hampstead MS in heading, 25, and 38 and in the arrangement of 36–37 (two lines in the letter, as in the draft, and one line in the Hampstead MS). Because the Hampstead MS contains internal revisions from the draft text to that of the letter in 26 and 35, it seems clear that the letter version is the later of the two fair copies. Gittings, p. 185, is probably right in thinking that Keats wrote the Hampstead MS on 22 January, one day after the draft, when he got out the Shakespeare volume to read *King Lear* (see the next poem); the letter version then followed a day later, on the 23rd.

Brown probably transcribed the Hampstead holograph, changing verb endings from past to present tense in 11 and 13 and altering the wording of 20 and 31. He miscopied Keats's "fashion" as "passion" in 22, subsequently correcting the error after someone—most likely Woodhouse—queried the word in the margin of the MS. Still later he copied over in ink a penciled "I swear" apparently added by Woodhouse after 21 (see below), and changed 36–37 from a single line (as he had originally written it) to two lines, again going over a penciled alteration in ink. Dilke copied Brown's MS in its earlier state, before "passion" was corrected to "fashion" and before "I swear" was written in and 36–37 were made into two lines; he otherwise differs substantively from Brown only in "offering" for "offerings" (32).

Though we cannot be certain about Woodhouse's source for $W^2$, his note to 36–37 gives us a clue: "In the copy from which I took this, these 2 lines were written in one: I have separated them on account of the rhyme to 'unaware.'" Among extant MSS, the only ones having 36–37 as a single line are the Hampstead holograph, Brown's transcript (before the lines were divided there), and Dilke's copy. Woodhouse took at least his date from Brown ("21 Jan$^y$ 1818. C.B."), and most probably his text as well, for in its first completed state $W^2$ had the same heading and the same substantive text as Brown's MS except for Brown's erroneous "passion" in 22. In place of this word Woodhouse wrote "fashion," noting in the margin in pencil, again obviously from Brown's MS, "originally passion"; it is not difficult to suppose that he independently guessed the correct word when he made his copy. $W^1$ has the same text as $W^2$ in the state just described (except for "thine" in 20, no doubt from the same impulse that made Woodhouse first write "thine" in $W^2$, before correcting it currently to "thy"), and was almost surely copied from $W^2$.

Upon seeing Keats's letter to Bailey, sometime in 1821, Woodhouse made a number of changes in $W^2$. He deleted "Lines" from the title and inserted "Ode" beneath it, erased and changed the verb endings to "-edst" in 11 and 13, deleted "of" and wrote in "at" in 31 (noting "BB." as his source), and recorded the letter's unique variant in 25 and the fact that 36–37 "are written separate in B.B's copy" (by which he meant the holograph letter, not a transcript by Bailey). Charlotte Reynolds' MS is substantively identical with $W^2$ in this altered state (except that she has "-est" in 11 and 13), and probably was copied from it.

The most curious feature of several of the MSS has to do with a penciled "I swear" appearing after 21 in $W^2$, $W^1$, Brown's MS (where the penciled words were subsequently inked over by Brown), and the letter to Bailey. When he first copied the poem Woodhouse noted in $W^2$, opposite 21, which comes at the bottom of a page, "Should there not be a short line to rhyme with 'ear' at the end of this page, such as—'I swear'?" It seems that Woodhouse later followed his own suggestion, inserting "I swear" not only in $W^2$ but in the other three MSS as well, for all four pencilings are in the same hand, and the hand is almost certainly Woodhouse's.

Woodhouse's "I swear" appears in both of the earliest printings of the poem. The *PDWJ* version derives from Brown's MS (with which it agrees substantively except for the omission of the sixth line, a mistake rectified in an erratum published two weeks later, on 29 November 1838). Milnes printed the poem as part of the letter to Bailey, which he took from a letterbook transcript by one of Woodhouse's clerks. His text of the poem itself, for which the clerk includes only a title and the first line in his transcript of the letter, almost surely came from Brown's MS, the only source known to have been available to him. The *1848* text is headed "On Seeing . . . Hair" (the clerk's title), but otherwise differs from Brown's MS only in 31 ("wed" for "mad," a copying or printing error) and 41 ("I thought" for "Methought," presumably a change by Milnes). Since Brown's MS shows no signs of having been handled by a printer, probably *1848* was set from a now lost copy of it.

Each of three MSS—the Hampstead holograph, the letter to Bailey (copied from the preceding but with changes of wording in heading, 25, and 38), and Brown's transcript (probably also copied from the Hampstead MS but with significant changes in 11, 13, 20, and 31)—has a claim to be the basis for a standard text. Though Woodhouse could have inserted "I swear" after 21 (and also marked 22 and 36–37) in Brown's MS while Keats was alive, Brown did not get his transcripts back from the publishers and Woodhouse until some months after Keats's death, and consequently (contrary to the suggestion offered in *Texts,* p. 159) there may not have been any occasion on which Keats could have approved or even seen Woodhouse's pencilings or Brown's response to them in ink in the transcript. While it is still possible that Brown's earlier changes were made at Keats's request, their authoritativeness has to remain in question. The present text is arbitrarily based on the Hampstead holograph, but follows Keats's draft and the letter text in presenting 36–37 as two lines.

### *On Sitting Down to Read* King Lear *Once Again*

Written on 22 January 1818 (*Letters,* I, 212, 214—also the date in the Hampstead holograph and all the transcripts except $W^1$ and Jeffrey's). First published in *PDWJ,* 8 November 1838, and then in *1848,* I, 96–97. The eight extant MSS are Keats's original draft, in the National Library of Scotland, a holograph fair copy written opposite the first page of *King Lear* in his facsimile reprint of Shakespeare's First Folio at Keats House, Hampstead, and transcripts by Brown, Dilke, Woodhouse (two copies, $W^2$ and $W^1$), Charlotte Reynolds, and Jeffrey (this last in a copy of Keats's now lost letter to George and Tom Keats of 23, 24 January 1818).

The earliest of the four recoverable states of text is obviously that of Keats's draft, but the chronological order of the three later states cannot be settled conclusively. One of them is that of the holograph fair copy, which initially had the same substantive text as the draft but shows alterations to new readings in 10 and 14. Brown transcribed this MS (with the heading "Sonnet, / On Sitting . . . "), and both Dilke's copy and the *PDWJ* text (which has "essay" in 7) derive from Brown. Another state is best represented by Woodhouse's $W^2$ transcript, which is substantively identical with the draft except in 6. Woodhouse's notations at the end of $W^2$—"J.H.R." followed by "22 Jan$^y$ 1818. C.B."—indicate that he got his text from J. H. Reynolds (most probably a lost Reynolds copy from some unknown source, ultimately of course the draft, which at one time or another came into the possession of Reynolds' sister Jane—see *The Letters of Thomas Hood,* ed. Peter F. Morgan, Toronto, 1973, p. 653) and the date from Brown (from whose MS Woodhouse also recorded variants to 6, 10, and 14 in $W^2$ and the variant to 14 in $W^1$). Both $W^1$ and Charlotte Reynolds' MS apparently derive from $W^2$. Still another state is that of the letter to George and Tom, in which Keats copied the sonnet on the day after he drafted it. The letter text, surviving only in Jeffrey's transcript, agrees with $W^2$ in 6 and with the Hampstead holograph in 10 and 14, and has unique substantive variants in 2, 4, 7, 11, and 13 (those in 2 and 7 are clearly errors, probably by Jeffrey rather than by Keats, and some of the others—perhaps all but that in 4—are of questionable authoritativeness, since Jeffrey is known to have been generally unreliable as a copyist). Milnes printed the poem in *1848* as part of the letter from an amanuensis' copy of Jeffrey's transcript.

Probably the Hampstead holograph was written earlier than the letter text—the holograph's alterations in 10 and 14 could (though they need not) have been made in the process of copying, and it is possible that Keats wrote out this MS on the same day on which he drafted the poem, and then incorporated the revised 10 and 14 when he copied it in the letter a day later—and probably the $W^2$ text also represents a version earlier than that of the letter, since it has the draft's readings in 10 and 14 rather than the revisions of the Hampstead MS and the letter. But these orderings are rather too speculative, and in any case the chronological relationship of the Hampstead MS and the $W^2$ version is not at all clear: on the evidence of 6 the Hampstead MS (agreeing with the draft against $W^2$) is earlier than $W^2$, while on the evidence of 10 and 14 $W^2$ (agreeing with the draft against the Hampstead MS) would appear to be the earlier. And one is reluctant to take the letter text, even if it is the latest of the four versions, as representing Keats's final intentions, since it is so obviously corrupt in Jeffrey's transcript. The present text is arbitrarily based on the Hampstead holograph.

### *When I have fears that I may cease to be*

Written toward the end of January 1818 (Keats calls it "my last Sonnet" in copying it out for J. H. Reynolds on 31 January; what is apparently his next-to-last, *On Sitting Down to Read "King Lear" Once Again,* was composed nine days earlier, on the 22nd—*Letters,* I, 222, 212, 214). First published in *1848,* II, 293. The seven extant MSS are all transcripts—three by Woodhouse ($W^2$, $W^1$, and a late copy for Severn) and one each by Charlotte Reynolds, one of Woodhouse's clerks (in a letterbook copy of Keats's now lost letter to J. H. Reynolds of 31 January 1818), Brown, and Dilke.

The two principal texts, one best represented by Charlotte Reynolds' MS and the other by Brown's, differ significantly only in 7. Charlotte Reynolds probably made her transcript, as she says in a note at the end of it, "From J. Keats' letter to

J H R 31 Jan 1818." Woodhouse's clerk's MS, also from the lost letter, agrees with Charlotte Reynolds' MS in 7 but has "full garners" in 4 (presumably an error based on "full" later in the same line). Woodhouse copied $W^2$, repeating "full garners," from the clerk's MS, and later noted "rich C.B." on the opposite verso; $W^1$ incorporates the correct "rich garners" from $W^2$ via this note. Brown's transcript, with a different word in 7, was the source of Dilke's MS and was printer's copy for *1848*. The most curious of the MSS is Woodhouse's late copy for Severn, which agrees with Brown rather than with Charlotte Reynolds, the clerk, and his own earlier transcripts in 7 and has unique variants in 2 ("hath"), 3 ("tomes" for "books"), 5 ("And when I see"), 9 ("think" for "feel"), 10 ("may" for "shall"), 11 ("pleasure" for "relish"), 13 ("sit" for "stand"), and 14 ("shrink"). One has to suppose that in this instance Woodhouse had no source at all, but was either writing from memory or else freely composing a sonnet of his own on the basis of Keats's text; clearly none of his unique variants in this MS is authoritative.

It is not known whether Brown's source was the same now lost MS from which Keats made the letter copy for J. H. Reynolds (in which case Keats would have altered "think" to "feel" in 7 in the process of copying the poem in the letter) or a slightly revised MS (in which case Brown's "think" would represent the later version). The present text is arbitrarily based on Brown's MS.

### *O blush not so! O blush not so*

Written probably on 31 January 1818 (it is not absolutely certain that Keats's letter version of that date represents the original draft, and the holograph of the letter has been lost—*Letters,* I, 219–220). First published in Forman (1883), II, 279–280. Each of the three extant MSS—transcripts by Woodhouse ($W^3$), Brown, and one of Woodhouse's clerks (in a letterbook copy of Keats's now lost letter to J. H. Reynolds of 31 January 1818)—gives a different version from the other two. $W^3$ (from an unknown source, possibly a copy by Reynolds) and Woodhouse's clerk's MS (from Keats's letter) agree in 2, 3, 5, and 13, but differ in heading (the clerk's MS has none), in the presence or absence of stanza numbers ($W^3$ has none), and in 9, 15, and 17. At some later time Woodhouse penciled the clerk's readings in 9 above his own in $W^3$, and interlined suggested revisions partly in shorthand above the text in 3 ("and blush the while" above "the blushing while"), 11 ("lips" above "hips"), and 15 (the penciling here is illegible). Brown's MS agrees with $W^3$ in heading, agrees with the clerk's MS in the presence of stanza numbers and in 9, 15, and 17, and varies from both in 2, 3, 5, and 13. One supposes that Brown made his transcript from a holograph; possibly this is one of the poems that he later described to Milnes as being "of an exceptionable kind . . . written and copied for the purpose of preventing the young bluestocking ladies from asking for the loan of [Keats's] MS Poems" (*KC*, II, 103). If the letter version that the clerk copied was Keats's original draft and Brown's variants are authoritative, then Brown's MS represents a slightly revised text of the poem. The authoritativeness of Woodhouse's unique variants in $W^3$ is somewhat more questionable.

Forman printed the poem from some now lost MS deriving either from Brown or from the MS that Brown copied (Forman in a note mentions the poem's having "been handed about in manuscript and more than once copied," and Brown's transcripts were not available to him at the time). His differences from Brown's text in heading (a characteristic Forman invention) and 11 (a typical misreading and a bowdlerization made independently of Woodhouse's penciling in $W^3$) are assumed to be corruptions.

The present text is arbitrarily based on Brown's MS.

### *Hence burgundy, claret, and port*

Written on 31 January 1818 (in the same letter to J. H. Reynolds in which Keats copied *When I have fears* and drafted or copied *O blush not so*—*Letters,* I, 219–222; Charlotte Reynolds' transcript assigns this and the next poem to the following Saturday, "Feb 7 1818," but her date is probably a mistake—see *Texts,* p. 164). First published in *1848,* I, 81–82. On the relationship of this to *God of the meridian* see Textual Note to the next poem.

The five extant MSS—transcripts by Woodhouse ($W^2$), one of his clerks (in a letterbook copy of the lost letter to J. H. Reynolds), Charlotte Reynolds, Brown, and George Keats—differ significantly among themselves only in 3. (Brown and George Keats add the heading "Song," and Charlotte Reynolds has a unique "the" for "my" in 8, presumably a copying error.) The authoritative texts are those of Woodhouse and his clerk—both apparently made independently from the lost letter (see discussion of the next poem)—and that of Brown, which derives from another now lost holograph. Charlotte Reynolds most probably copied $W^2$, and George Keats certainly copied Brown's MS. Milnes printed the poem in *1848* as part of the letter from an amanuensis' copy of Woodhouse's clerk's transcript, emending the clerk's 3 to the reading of Brown's MS, which he also had in his possession.

The present text is based on Brown's MS.

3 earthly] In spite of the clerk's "couthly" (which Woodhouse verified with a marginal "*so*" in the letterbook), there is a good chance that Keats all along intended "earthly" and simply wrote the word in such a way—with an unclosed "e" and a spaced out "ar"—that it looked most like "couthly." $W^2$'s "courtly" is best explained as an emendation to make sense of the lost letter's apparent "couthly."

### *God of the meridian*

Written on 31 January 1818 (dating the same as for the preceding poem). First published in *1848,* I, 82–83. This poem has frequently been printed as the final twenty-five lines of *Hence burgundy, claret, and port,* but the textual evidence (a significant amount of space between these lines and *Hence burgundy* in the transcripts deriving from Keats's lost letter to Reynolds, and the absence of these lines in Brown's transcript of *Hence burgundy*) as well as differences in tone and meter (*Hence burgundy* is in anapests, while the more serious *God of the meridian* is in iambs) decidedly favor treating them as separate pieces.

The four extant MSS—two transcripts by Woodhouse ($W^2$ and $W^1$, the latter containing 13–25 only, with the preceding leaf missing), a transcript by one of his clerks (in a letterbook copy of Keats's letter to J. H. Reynolds of 31 January 1818), and a transcript by Charlotte Reynolds—do not differ substantively among themselves. Apparently Woodhouse and his clerk took their texts independently from Keats's lost letter (Woodhouse's note in $W^2$ opposite the beginning of *Hence burgundy*—"The lines . . . are extracted from a letter to J.H.R."—applies to both that poem and *God of the meridian,* and his independence of the clerk's transcript is evidenced by the fact that he has a long dash and some crosses after "unalarmed" in the final line, indications of fragmentariness that may have been in the original MS but do not appear in the clerk's transcript). Presumably Woodhouse made $W^1$ from $W^2$, and Charlotte Reynolds probably also copied $W^2$. Milnes printed the poem in *1848* as part of the letter from an amanuensis' copy of the clerk's MS.

Both $W^2$ and the clerk's MS have claims to be the basis for a standard text. The present text, with a substantive emendation in 10, is arbitrarily based on $W^2$.

1 God . . . meridian] Garrod, p. 482 n., points out that the line would rhyme with 3 if Keats had written "meridian zone."

10 Too] $W^2$'s (and the other MSS') "To" is probably an accurate representation of what Keats wrote, but his spelling here is not necessarily to be depended on ("to" for "too" occurs at least eleven times in surviving holographs of other poems, and "too" for "to" another six times). It is also possible, but less likely in the context, that Keats intended "So," inscribing the word with a capital "S" that looked like "T" (see Textual Notes to *On Visiting the Tomb of Burns* 11 and *Fancy* 89). Charlotte Reynolds, attempting to make sense of the line in her source, wrote "So" and then changed it to "To."

### *Robin Hood*

Written at the beginning of February 1818 (copied out in a letter to J. H. Reynolds on the 3rd—*Letters,* I, 225). First published in *1820,* pp. 133–136. The six extant MSS are Keats's original draft, in the Isabella Stewart Gardner Museum, Boston (the S. R. Townshend Mayer MS), and transcripts by Woodhouse (two copies, $W^2$ and $W^1$), Brown, Dilke, and George Keats. The holograph of Keats's letter to Reynolds in which he copied the poem has disappeared, and Woodhouse's letterbook transcript of the letter includes only a heading—"To J. H. R. In answer to his Robin Hood Sonnets"—and the first line of the poem, referring to $W^2$ for the rest.

The principal recoverable states of text before *1820* are that of the draft, that represented by $W^2$, and that represented by the consensus of Brown's and George Keats's MSS. The draft varies substantively from *1820* in heading (it has none), 7, 10, 18, 19, 22, 27, 32, 37, 39, 44, and 62. $W^2$, which was taken either from the lost letter to Reynolds or, more probably, from a copy of the letter text made by Reynolds, has the draft readings in 10 and 32 but none of the others just cited; it varies substantively from *1820* in heading, 25, and 29 (this last probably a corruption). Subsequently in $W^2$ Woodhouse recorded variants from Brown's transcript in 10 and 25 (as well as Brown's omission of quotation marks in 47–48); $W^1$ differs from $W^2$ in heading ("To J. H. R. / In . . . "), 10 (see the note below), 29 ("Hostess"), 43 ("sweep" for "swear"), and 62 ("burthen"), but nevertheless was almost surely taken from $W^2$, and before Woodhouse entered the variants just described from Brown's MS. Brown and George Keats seem to have made independent copies of a now lost holograph varying from *1820* only in heading and 32 (in the latter instance agreeing with the draft and $W^2$); apart from an insignificant difference in the wording of the heading and a copying error by George Keats in 46, their transcripts are substantively the same throughout. Dilke made his copy from Brown's MS.

The present text is based on *1820*.

10 (*apparatus*) paid no Rent and] Before he saw Brown's MS Woodhouse queried "on?" for "and" in pencil beside this line in $W^2$ (suggesting "paid no Rent on leases"). In $W^1$ he left a blank space for the word, later penciling in "on" and noting "originally *and*" in the margin.

### *Lines on the Mermaid Tavern*

Written at the beginning of February 1818 (dating the same as for the preceding poem). First published in *1820,* pp. 131–132. The seven extant MSS are an early holograph fair copy at Harvard, a later holograph fair copy written in George Keats's notebook now in the British Library, a transcript by Dilke, three transcripts by Woodhouse ($W^2$ and two $W^1$ copies), and a transcript by Brown. The original of Keats's letter to J. H. Reynolds of 3 February 1818, in which he copied the poem, has disappeared, and Woodhouse's letterbook transcript of the letter includes only the first line of the poem, referring to $W^2$ for the rest.

Strictly speaking, there are four recoverable states of text before that of *1820,* represented by the Harvard holograph, Woodhouse's and Brown's MSS, Brown's MS again after Keats changed a word in it, and the British Library holograph. The Harvard holograph varies substantively from *1820* in 4, 9, 18, and 24–26. A 1-inch by 3½-inch rectangle has been cut away at the top of this MS, just above the first line, and it is not possible to determine whether it ever had a heading. Dilke took his text from this MS, presumably before the poem was published, and his transcript has no heading, but the situation is puzzling: it is unlikely that Keats himself cut away the missing part (since he did not elsewhere alter his MSS in this way); it seems equally unlikely that someone else (wanting a piece of Keats's MS to preserve as a relic) would have cut away a title at so early a date, and it is also difficult to imagine anyone's cutting up the MS if there was no writing on the missing part.

$W^2$ and Brown's MS as originally written differ significantly from the Harvard holograph only in the addition of a heading (Brown has "to" for $W^2$'s "on") and in 9 ("O" for the holograph's "Old"). Woodhouse took the $W^2$ text, just as he did that of *Robin Hood,* either from the lost letter to Reynolds or from a copy made by Reynolds (and then, if he followed what seems to have been his usual practice elsewhere, made his $W^1$ copies from $W^2$; all three Woodhouse MSS have an extra paragraph division after 4). His further variant in 20, representing a common misreading (by him or in his source) of Keats's capital "S" as "L," is not authoritative. Brown could have copied the Harvard MS, adding a title and changing 9 perhaps on Keats's authority, but it is safer to hypothesize a now lost holograph, which could have been the original draft or another fair copy, as the basis of his transcript. Since Keats's text in the lost letter was a copy rather than the original draft, and since we do not know Brown's source, it is not clear whether the state represented by $W^2$ and Brown's MS is earlier or later than the text of the Harvard holograph.

At some later time, possibly when he made the fair copy now in the British Library, Keats read over Brown's MS and changed Brown's "Fairer" to "Choicer" in 4. (Subsequently Woodhouse saw Brown's MS and noted this revised reading from it in $W^2$ as well as "Sipping" in 20 and the spelling variant in 12.) The British Library MS also has "Choicer" in 4, unique readings in 8 and 9, and the *1820* text of 24–26. Keats made this copy in or before January 1820, when George Keats wrote his transcripts in the same notebook to take back to America, and there is a good chance that he worked from Brown's transcript rather than from a MS of his own, revising 4, 8, 9, and 24–26 in the process of copying. The *1820* text combines the British Library holograph's 4 and 24–26 with the earlier MSS' 8 and $W^2$'s and Brown's 9, and has a new reading (a change of verb tense) in 18.

The present text is based on *1820*.

### *Welcome joy, and welcome sorrow*

Written in 1818 (so dated in all MSS). First published in *1848*, I, 285–286. The seven extant MSS are an unidentified fair copy, possibly a holograph, in the possession of Dorothy Withey, of Stratford-upon-Avon, and transcripts by Brown, Woodhouse (two copies, $W^2$ and $W^1$), George Keats, J. C. Stephens, and C. C. Clarke. These all have the same heading and epigraph (Woodhouse penciled "n?" after "embryo" in the margin of $W^2$ and corrected "embryo" to "embryon" in $W^1$; Clarke's MS has "embryon" altered to "embryo") and differ significantly only in 13, where Miss Withey's MS, Stephens, and Clarke agree against Brown, Woodhouse, and George Keats. The rest of the variants would appear to be corruptions: Stephens wrote "fine" instead of "fair" in 5; Clarke wrote "are" for "burn" in 8; both Stephens and Clarke have "Aspic" in 17; and George Keats transposed 14 and 15.

Miss Withey's MS (in a hand that one might identify as Woodhouse's, were it not that $W^2$ and $W^1$ have a different reading in 13 and obviously came from a different source) is pretty clearly the MS that Clarke transcribed, or else a copy of it; in both Miss Withey's MS and Clarke's transcript, 9 is first written and then canceled after 7, and Clarke notes "struck out here" beside the deleted line in his transcript. Stephens' copy almost surely derives from the same source as Clarke's (and earlier, since Clarke's MS was made for Milnes); Clarke's and Stephens' variants in 5, 8, and 17 may be taken to be independent copying errors. Clarke's MS was printer's copy for *1848*.

Brown probably copied a now lost holograph, and George Keats certainly made his transcript from Brown's (see *Texts*, p. 170). Woodhouse copied either Brown (from whom he took his date in $W^2$) or, what is perhaps more likely, the same lost MS that Brown worked from; presumably $W^2$ is the earlier of Woodhouse's transcripts, and $W^1$ a copy from $W^2$. It is not perfectly clear whether Miss

Withey's MS or the consensus of Brown's transcript and $W^2$ represents the later of the two states of text. Since MSS once in Clarke's possession tend to be early versions, probably the Brown-$W^2$ text should be considered the later. The present text is arbitrarily based on Brown's MS, with which $W^2$ agrees substantively throughout.

*Time's sea hath been five years at its slow ebb*

Written on 4 February 1818 (so dated in $W^2$, $W^1$, and Charlotte Reynolds' transcript). First published in *Hood's Magazine,* 2 (September 1844), 240, and then in *1848,* II, 297. The six extant MSS are all transcripts—three by Woodhouse ($W^2$, $W^1$, and a late copy for Severn) and one each by Charlotte Reynolds, one of Woodhouse's clerks (Garrod's *T*), and Patmore.

Woodhouse's source for $W^2$ is not known (it was probably, from the position of the poem in the $W^2$ book of transcripts, either a now lost holograph MS or a copy by J. H. Reynolds). The rest of the MSS derive from $W^2$—the $W^1$ transcript, Charlotte Reynolds' copy, and the clerk's copy all directly, Woodhouse's copy for Severn probably also directly (if Woodhouse did not write it from memory), and Patmore's from the clerk's MS. The few substantive variants among the MSS—the absence of heading in $W^1$ and Woodhouse's copy for Severn, "has" for "hath" (1) in $W^1$, "thine" for "thy" (4) in Woodhouse's copy for Severn and Patmore's MS (each independently of the other), and "eye's" for "eyes'" (6) in Woodhouse's copy for Severn—are all certainly corruptions. Patmore included a version of the note—"the Lady whom he saw for some few moments at Vauxhall"—that Woodhouse added with an asterisk above the heading in the clerk's MS, and *1848,* set from Patmore's MS, reproduces both Patmore's note and his altered wording in 4.

The *Hood's* text is a much different version, with substantive variants from $W^2$ and the other MSS in heading and 1, 7, 9, 13, and 14. Although Hood explained to W. F. Watson, in a letter of 8 October 1844, that the sonnet "was sent me, *copied,* from [Keats's] M.S." (*The Letters of Thomas Hood,* ed. Peter F. Morgan, Toronto, 1973, p. 652), nothing further is known of his source. Unfortunately the relative authoritativeness of the $W^2$ and *Hood's* texts is quite uncertain. Each of the distinctive readings in both versions may represent intervening revision by J. H. Reynolds or some other copyist, and those in the first printed text may also reflect editorial tinkering by Hood. The present text is arbitrarily based on $W^2$.

*To the Nile*

Written on 4 February 1818 (*Letters,* I, 227–228). First published in *PDWJ,* 19 July 1838, and then in *1848,* I, 99–100. The six extant MSS are all transcripts—three by Woodhouse ($W^2$, $W^1$, and a copy in his interleaved *1817*) and one each by Charlotte Reynolds, Brown, and Dilke.

The two principal states of text—the earlier best represented by $W^2$ and the later by Brown's MS with three lines in Keats's hand—differ substantively in 2, 6–7, 8, and 10. $W^2$ ("from J.K.'s M.S."), the two other Woodhouse transcripts, and Charlotte Reynolds' copy are all dated 6 February, and pretty clearly derive from a now lost holograph that had that date on it (perhaps a MS in the possession of J. H. Reynolds, since Reynolds apparently included the sonnet in his "volume of Poetry" that Woodhouse saw in November 1818—*KC*, I, 63 and n.). Most likely Woodhouse took $W^2$ from this lost holograph, and copied both $W^1$ and the version in his interleaved *1817* from $W^2$. He later in $W^2$ entered in shorthand the variant readings to 2, 6–7, 8, and 10 from Brown's MS. Charlotte Reynolds, though she has unique variants in 11 ("bestow" for "bedew"), 12 ("doth" for "dost"), and 14 ("doth" again), probably also copied $W^2$; her unique variants are assumed to be corruptions.

Brown's transcript is the real oddity among the MSS. He omitted 6–8 as he copied, and Keats wrote the revised lines in the space that Brown left for them. In the scholarly manner of Woodhouse (and *not* in the unscholarly manner of Brown, who does not elsewhere cite variants in his transcripts), Brown records in two notes the earlier readings of 2 and 6–7 (varying slightly from $W^2$ in the second line of the latter note; Brown's variants in this line may represent still another state, intermediate between $W^2$ and Brown's text in its final form, but the rest of this intermediate state cannot be recovered with certainty). And there is a penciled "them" written above "for" (8) in a hand that appears to be neither Keats's nor Brown's. The best explanation for the first of these peculiarities, Brown's leaving space for Keats's 6–8, is that Brown made his copy while Keats was attempting to reconstruct or revise his original text. The penciled word above 8 was probably written in by Woodhouse at the time that he took the variant readings from Brown's MS. Dilke made his transcript from Brown's MS. Both early printings also derive from Brown; *PDWJ* has the revised text except for "Stream" in 2 and "them" in 8, while *1848* printed both of these variants and "Those" (a canceled word in Keats's hand in the transcript) for "Such" in 7.

The present text is based on Brown's MS.

### *Spenser, a jealous honorer of thine*

Written on 5 February 1818 (so dated in all MSS). First published in *1848,* I, 11. The five extant MSS are Keats's original draft, in Harvard's Dumbarton Oaks Research Library, Washington, D.C., a holograph fair copy in the Morgan Library, and transcripts by Woodhouse ($W^2$), one of his clerks (Garrod's *T*), and W. A. Longmore.

There are no significant differences among the MSS. The Morgan fair copy has the final text of Keats's draft; $W^2$ ("f$^m$ JK's M.S.") is a copy of the Morgan MS; and Woodhouse's clerk transcribed the poem from $W^2$. Milnes printed it in *1848* (with substantive changes in 7 and 9) probably from an amanuensis' copy of the clerk's MS, the only source known to have been available to him. At the end of 1870 W. A. Longmore, son of J. H. Reynolds' sister Eliza, sent Milnes a fairly accurate copy of Keats's draft (with *1848*'s "quill," however, for the draft's "quell" in 7), and in 1875 lent him the MS itself (*KC*, II, 331–332, 334, 340); Milnes included in a note to the poem in *1876* a text representing most of the punctuation and spelling peculiarities of Longmore's transcript.

The present text is based on the Morgan holograph.

*Blue!—'Tis the life of heaven—the domain*

Written on 8 February 1818 (so dated in five MSS, all but Woodhouse's copy for Severn and Elizabeth Clarke's copy). First published in *1848,* II, 295. The seven extant MSS are all transcripts—three by Woodhouse ($W^2$, $W^1$, and a late copy for Severn) and one each by Charlotte Reynolds, one of Woodhouse's clerks (Garrod's *T*), Patmore, and Elizabeth Stott Clarke. Keats's original draft, formerly in the possession of one of George Keats's daughters in Louisville, who gave it to Oscar Wilde, has since disappeared, but its readings in 2–14 (the first line and possibly a heading having been cut away earlier) are available in the facsimile published in *Century Guild Hobby Horse,* 1 (1886), 81. A version written by J. H. Reynolds in a copy of his *The Garden of Florence* (1821), now also missing, is reported and transcribed by A. J. Horwood, *Athenaeum,* 3 June 1876, p. 764.

The two principal states of text, differing in wording in 6 and 8 (and possibly also substantively in the punctuation of 6 and 14), are those of the draft (in facsimile) and a later version best represented by $W^2$. Two other texts, in the lost transcript by J. H. Reynolds (in the *Athenaeum*) and Woodhouse's copy for Severn, are of more questionable authority. Woodhouse took $W^2$ "from K's M.S.," a now lost holograph copy written, as Woodhouse further explains in another note in $W^2$, "in a M.S. collection of the Poetry of [Reynolds,] Keats & others" compiled by Reynolds. Keats's poem is a response to the concluding lines of Reynolds' *Sweet poets of the gentle antique line,* and both Woodhouse in $W^2$ and Charlotte Reynolds copied first Reynolds' sonnet and then Keats's, heading the latter "Answer. J. Keats." Woodhouse presumably made $W^1$ (with a longer heading, "Lines / Written upon reading a Sonnet by J. H. Reynolds, which will be found p: 17," referring to a $W^1$ copy of Reynolds' poem) from $W^2$. Charlotte Reynolds' MS probably also came from $W^2$, as did the clerk's late copy ("Answer—by J Keats," to which Woodhouse added "to a Sonnet ending thus" and a quotation of the last line and a half of Reynolds' sonnet—"Dark eyes are dearer far / Than orbs that mock the hyacinthine bell"—followed by the author's initials). Patmore copied the clerk's MS, omitting "by J Keats" in the clerk-Woodhouse heading and substituting "those" for "orbs" in the quotation from Reynolds' sonnet (Woodhouse had written "those" before correcting it currently to "orbs") and "of" for "to" in 9. The *1848* text, set from Patmore's MS, reproduces Patmore's changes and adds another, misreading Patmore's "mock" in the quotation from Reynolds as "made" (an error corrected, however, in the *1848* errata). Elizabeth Clarke's MS, with "made" in the quotation from Reynolds, obviously derives from *1848.*

J. H. Reynolds' transcript written in *The Garden of Florence,* varying substantively from all the preceding texts in 1, 2, and 6, and Woodhouse's copy for Severn, with the same readings in 1, 2, and 6 and a more detailed heading and a further variant in 8, are quite puzzling. If either set of variants existed uniquely one would take them to be corruptions—nonauthoritative revisions, careless errors, or the results of copying from memory—but the fact that Reynolds and Woodhouse's late MS agree in 1, 2, and 6 demands some more elaborate explanation. The variant in 1 and part of the variant in 6 are characteristic of the literal-mindedness that we see in well-intentioned "improvements" of Keats's phrasing in some other poems ("hue" in 1 being a more accurate word for color, "tributary" in 6 a better description of the relationship between streams and the ocean), and Woodhouse's distinctive wording in 8 may well be, like his heading, his own invention (he first wrote "unless," then "if not," and finally "unless" in his text, and part of this sequence, "if not" above a deleted "unless," also appears in the margin). It may be that the variants in 1, 2, and 6 were initiated by Reynolds, and that Woodhouse subsequently saw a Reynolds text with these readings in it and then incorporated them, working from memory (as he seems to have done in some of the other copies for Severn), when he wrote out his latest transcript. But nothing of the sort can be demonstrated on the evidence that we have, and the readings are included in the apparatus as possibly authoritative, even though probably corrupt.

The present text is based on $W^2$.

### *O thou whose face hath felt the winter's wind*

Written on 19 February 1818 (drafted or else immediately copied, it is not clear which, in a letter to J. H. Reynolds of that date—*Letters,* I, 233). First published in *1848,* I, 90. The two extant MSS are the holograph version in Keats's letter to Reynolds (MS in the Robert H. Taylor Collection, Princeton University Library) and a copy of the letter by Woodhouse in his letterbook. Woodhouse wrote "hath" for Keats's "has" in 2 and 5. Milnes printed the poem as part of the letter from an amanuensis' copy of Woodhouse's transcript, incorporating Woodhouse's alterations in 2 and 5 and further changing "'mong" to "among" in 3 and "shall" to "will" in 8. The present text is based on the letter holograph.

### *Extracts from an Opera*

Written in 1818 (so dated in all MSS; several scholars place the lyrics among the "many songs & Sonnets" that Keats mentions in February 1818—*Letters,* I, 228—but this more specific dating is highly conjectural). First published in *1848,* II, 264–267. The extant MSS are transcripts of all six known songs by Brown and Woodhouse in $W^2$, and partial transcripts by Woodhouse in $W^3$ (the second and fifth songs only) and Charlotte Reynolds (the first, fifth, and sixth songs). There are no significant differences among the MSS (Charlotte Reynolds mistakenly omits "up" in the sixth line of the final lyric). We may suppose that Brown copied a lost holograph (or holographs). Woodhouse's source is unknown; he took at least his $W^2$ date from Brown, and could have taken his texts as well, since they are very close to Brown's in minor details. Charlotte Reynolds probably copied $W^2$. There seems to be no ready explanation for her selection of lyrics from the group, or for Woodhouse's in the $W^3$ scrapbook. Brown's MS was printer's copy for *1848.*

Both $W^2$ and Brown's MS have claims to be the basis for a standard text. The present text is arbitrarily based on Brown's MS.

### *Four seasons fill the measure of the year*

Written in the second week of March 1818 (after Keats's arrival at Teignmouth on the 6th or 7th and before he copied the poem in a letter to Bailey on the 13th

—*Letters,* I, 243). First published in Leigh Hunt's *Literary Pocket-Book* for 1819 (1818), p. 225, and then in Galignani (1829), p. 71 of the Keats section. The six extant MSS are the holograph fair copy in Keats's letter to Bailey (MS at Harvard), two transcripts by Woodhouse ($W^2$ and that in a letterbook copy of the letter to Bailey), and a transcript each by J. C. Stephens, one of Woodhouse's clerks (the earlier of Garrod's *T* transcripts), and Patmore.

Of the two recoverable states of text, the earlier is represented by Keats's version in the letter, which Woodhouse twice copied from the letter MS, his clerk (with "came" for "come" in 7) copied from $W^2$, and Patmore (restoring "come") copied from the clerk's MS. The other state is that of Hunt's *Pocket-Book,* which differs substantively from the first state in heading (the letter text has none), 2, 3, 5, 6–10, and 13, and leaves off the final letter in "forget" (14). Both Stephens and Galignani took their texts from the *Pocket-Book*—Stephens with independent errors in 4 ("at" for "with") and 9 ("its" for "his"), and Galignani emending a word in 8 (see below). For the *Pocket-Book*'s misprinted "forge" in 14 (corrected to "forget" in an unidentified hand in the copy at Keats House, Hampstead), Stephens wrote "forget" and Galignani wrongly guessed "forego."

The considerable problem presented by the texts of this poem is the extent to which Keats was responsible for the changes between the earlier version (the letter copy) and that of the *Pocket-Book.* If he did in fact provide the *Pocket-Book* version as we have it, then probably it should be the basis for a standard text. But the frequency with which unique readings appear elsewhere in Keats's texts published by Hunt and other periodical editors raises the possibility that some or all of the *Pocket-Book*'s distinctive readings originated with Hunt. Because of this possibility, the present text is based on the letter holograph.

6–10 He . . . look] If Keats was responsible for the *Pocket-Book* text, then its "nigh / His" in 7–8 may well be a combination of errors by Keats, Hunt, and/or the printer for "high / Is." Galignani emended the *Pocket-Book* reading to "nigh / Is," and Milnes in *1876* chose "high / Is."

*For there's Bishop's Teign*

Written at Teignmouth on 21 March 1818 (in a letter to Haydon of that date—*Letters,* I, 249–250). First published in Tom Taylor's *Life of Benjamin Robert Haydon, Historical Painter, from His Autobiography and Journals* (1853), I, 362–363. The holograph draft in Keats's letter to Haydon (MS at Harvard) is our sole authoritative source. Taylor's text (as part of the letter) includes some of Keats's introductory prose as an added opening line ("Here all the summer could I stay") and has further substantive errors in 3, 13, 19, 24, 25, 34, 35, 36, 39, and 42 (all but one of which—the omission of "the" in 25—have been repeated in one or more modern editions).

39 dack'd] So the letter holograph, but Keats frequently writes "a" for "o" in his MSS and may have intended "dock'd."

*Where be ye going, you Devon maid*

Written at Teignmouth on 21 March 1818 (in a letter to Haydon of that date—*Letters,* I, 251). First published in Tom Taylor's *Life of Benjamin Robert Haydon*

(1853), I, 363–364. As for the preceding poem, the holograph draft in Keats's letter to Haydon (MS at Harvard) is our sole authoritative source. Taylor's text (as part of the letter) has substantive errors in 1, 2, 5 ("dales" for "flowers"), 7 ("behind" for "'hind"), 8 ("divinely" for "disdainly"), and 14. In the letter holograph, both "nook" in 13 and "on this willow" in 14 are (for lack of space) written on separate lines and underscored. In other holographs Keats occasionally underscores run-over words thus separated but more often does not; in this instance he may have underscored the words to emphasize sexual punning, but his intention is not at all clear.

### *Over the hill and over the dale*

Written at Teignmouth on 23 or 24 March 1818 (Dawlish Fair was held on the 23rd; Keats either drafted or copied the poem in a letter on the 24th to James Rice—*Letters,* I, 256–257). Lines 1–4 first published in *1848,* I, 119, and the complete poem first in Lowell, I, 610–611. The three extant MSS are the holograph version in Keats's letter to Rice (MS at Harvard), a transcript of the poem by Woodhouse ($W^3$), and a copy of 1–4, with an incomplete reference to $W^3$ for the rest, in Woodhouse's letterbook transcript of the extant letter. $W^3$ ("From a letter sent by Keats to Rice") unaccountably—but certainly unauthoritatively—varies from the holograph text in 2 ("water" for "bourn") and 11 ("or" for "and"), and has "O (who) would not" for the letter's "O would not" in 19. Milnes included 1–4 as part of the letter from an amanuensis' copy of Woodhouse's transcript in the letterbook. Lowell printed the poem from the letter (but with substantive errors in 8, 11, and 19, and a bracketed "who" in 19). The present text, with a substantive emendation in 19, is based on the letter holograph.

13 there] Underscored in the letter holograph. The word is run-over (written on a separate line), and, as with 13 and 14 in the preceding poem, Keats may have intended the underscoring for emphasis.
19 O . . . not] The letter's "O would not" is clearly a mistake. The emendation here is based on Woodhouse's and Lowell's bracketed insertion of "who," but it is also possible that Keats meant to write "Or would not."

### *Dear Reynolds, as last night I lay in bed*

Written at Teignmouth on 25 March 1818 (Woodhouse's date in $W^2$ and his letterbook). First published in *1848,* I, 113–116. The single extant MS is Woodhouse's $W^2$ transcript made from a now lost holograph letter. The prose that followed these lines in the letter is also extant in a letterbook transcript by one of Woodhouse's clerks, but the clerk includes only the first line and a half of the poetry, and Woodhouse has added a note referring to $W^2$ for the rest. Though in *1848* Milnes printed the prose from the letterbook, his source for the lines themselves is unknown, since the $W^2$ book of transcripts was not available to him. The *1848* text differs substantively from $W^2$ in heading (*1848* has none) and the wording of 38, 61, 73, 75, 90 ("wave" for "weave"), 94 ("man" for "maw"), and 109, and it lacks the final four lines; it also differs substantively in the punctuation of 19 and 29, and has a new paragraph at 26. These *1848* variants are all almost certainly corruptions (Milnes himself corrected 73, 90, 94, and 109 in his one-volume *Life* of 1867). The present text, based on $W^2$ but disregarding the $W^2$ heading, which is surely Woodhouse's own addition, contains a substantive emendation in 14 suggested by S. R. Swaminathan, *N&Q,* August 1967, pp. 306–307 ("patient wing" occurs in *Endymion* III.24, and Keats wrote "patent" for "patient" in the draft of *To Autumn* 21).

21 Gleams] Woodhouse first wrote "Gloams," adding "So" in the margin, and then later, in different ink, changed the word to "Gleams." But Keats cannot have intended "Gloams" ("darkens") in this context, and Woodhouse was just recording a slip of the pen in the MS he was copying.

*To J. R.*

Written perhaps in April 1818 (Lowell, I, 615–618, and others, on the basis of the inscription in a copy of *Guzman d'Alfarache* now at Harvard, have conjectured that "J. R."—James Rice—visited Keats at Teignmouth on 18–20 April; but the poem could refer to some other occasion that we know nothing about). First published in *1848,* II, 296. The four extant MSS—a holograph at Harvard and transcripts by Woodhouse ($W^2$), one of his clerks (Garrod's *T*), and Patmore—have the same substantive text throughout. The extant holograph may be Keats's original draft, though there are signs of composition (as opposed to copying) only in 12 and the canceled line and a half before 13. Woodhouse transcribed the poem from this MS, the clerk followed $W^2$, Patmore took his text from the clerk's copy, and Patmore's MS was printer's copy for *1848.* Milnes mistakenly altered the title to "To J. H. Reynolds" (the *1848* heading) on Patmore's MS. The present text is based on the extant holograph.

*Isabella*

Written in February–April 1818 ("the first few stanzas" before Keats departed for Teignmouth on 4 March, and the rest probably late in March, after he finished revising *Endymion,* and in April; completed by 27 April—*Letters,* I, 274). First published in *1820,* pp. 47–80. The five known MSS are Keats's original draft (of which about two-thirds is either extant or recoverable through facsimiles and earlier scholars' reports), a holograph fair copy written in the notebook that George Keats later filled with transcripts to take back to America (now in the British Library), and three transcripts by Woodhouse ($W^3$, $W^2$, $W^1$—the first in shorthand). Keats's letter to J. H. Reynolds of 27 April 1818 contained the draft text of 89–104 and 233–240, but the holograph of the letter has been lost; a letterbook transcript is extant, by one of Woodhouse's clerks, but it includes only the opening lines of the three stanzas with a note by Woodhouse giving the lost letter's text of 237. A later letter to Fanny Brawne, now known only through H. B. Forman's text of it in his 1883 edition, quotes 319–320 with a unique variant in 319 (*Letters,* II, 256—the text there reprinted from Forman's edition).

Keats's draft, at least all of it after the first six stanzas, was once in the possession of Severn and was given away by him in fragments of a stanza or two apiece, as we know from the various inscriptions signed by him on one or more of the surviving fragments cut from leaves 3, 4, 6, 7, 9, 10, and 12. (The double-sheet containing the first six stanzas—leaves 1 and 2—is inscribed as having been received from Brown; it is not clear whether this was still another gift by Severn or whether Brown had it all along after he or Keats, or both, recopied its text in a fair copy.) The following list (updating Garrod's headnote, p. 215, and *Texts,* pp. 182–183) includes everything that has survived of the draft, gives the sources of apparatus readings for fragments that were once known but have since disappeared, and arranges the items according to the contents of each leaf of the MS. (There are no folio or page numbers in the MS.)

| | *Recto* | *Verso* | *Location/source* |
|---|---|---|---|
| Leaf 1 | 1–24 | 25–47 plus a canceled 48 | Extant at Texas Christian University ("the first few stanzas" referred to in *Letters,* I, 274) |
| Leaf 2 | Replacement of canceled 48 | Blank | Same as preceding (conjugate with leaf 1) |
| Leaf 3 | 49–56 plus the first line of the following stanza | 65–72 | Extant at Harvard |
| | Last seven lines of a stanza (ultimately omitted from the poem) between 56 and 57 | 73–80 | Missing, but the text of both sides is available in an unidentified facsimile among Louis A. Holman's papers at Harvard |
| | 57–64 | 81–88 | Extant in the Historical Society of Pennsylvania |
| Leaf 4 | 89–96 | 113–120 | Extant at Harvard |
| | 97–112 | 121–136 | Missing; text unrecorded |
| Leaf 5 | 137–160 | 161–184 | Missing; text unrecorded |
| Leaf 6 | 185–192 | 209–215 | Missing; text unrecorded |

| | *Recto* | *Verso* | *Location/source* |
|---|---|---|---|
| | 193–200 | 216–224 | Missing, but variants and canceled readings are given by H. B. Forman in the *Athenaeum,* 6 April 1912, pp. 389–390 (in the apparatus of the present edition, three alterations reported in 197, 220, and 221 are assumed to have been made above the line) |
| | 201–208 | Contents unknown (probably a canceled first attempt at 225–232) | Missing; text unrecorded |
| Leaf 7 | 225–232 | 249–256 | Extant at Cornell |
| | 233–248 | 257–272 | Extant at Harvard |
| Leaf 8 | 273–296 | 297–320 | Extant at Harvard |
| Leaf 9 | 321–326 | 345–352 | Extant at Harvard |
| | 327–336 | 353–360 | Missing; text unrecorded |
| | 337–339 | 361–364 | Extant at the University of Texas |
| | 340–342 | 365–366 | Extant in the Carl H. Pforzheimer Library |
| | 343–344 | 367–368 | Missing; text unrecorded |
| Leaf 10 | 369–384 | 393–410 | Missing; text unrecorded |
| | 385–392 | 411–416 | Extant in the National Library of Scotland |
| Leaf 11 | 417–424, 433–448 | 449–472 | Extant at Harvard |

(*continued*)

| | *Recto* | *Verso* | *Location/source* |
|---|---|---|---|
| Leaf 12 | 473–480 | 497–503 | Missing, but the text of both sides is available in facsimile in *The Library of Jerome Kern,* Anderson Galleries sale catalogue (New York, 1929), p. 253 |
| | 481–488 | 504 | Extant in the Martin Bodmer Foundation, Cologny-Geneva |
| | 489–496 | 425–432 | Extant at the University of Texas |

It seems safe to assume that the draft and the fair copy are the only complete versions that ever existed in the poet's own hand (Keats's promises on 27 April and 3 May 1818 to "copy the whole out" for Reynolds, *Letters,* I, 274, 283, refer to the writing of the extant fair copy, which he made apparently toward the end of August and then lent rather than gave to Reynolds in October—see *Letters,* I, 371, 366 and n., 376–377). In passages for which the draft text is available, the fair copy shows revisions from the draft in heading (the draft has none) and the wording of some fifty lines. Keats numbered only the first three stanzas in the draft; there are no stanza numbers in the fair copy (the transcripts have stanza numbers all the way through).

Woodhouse's shorthand transcript ($W^3$, "from [Keats's] own manuscript") was clearly taken from the holograph fair copy. The evidence for determining the immediate source(s) of $W^2$ and $W^1$ is less conclusive (see *Texts,* p. 184), and the situation is complicated by the fact that Woodhouse made four transcripts (*KC*, I, 79), one more than the number we now have—the lost transcript may have had an intervening role in the transmission of text from $W^3$ to the later extant transcripts—and also by the fact that $W^2$ and $W^1$ are in many places altered by erasure (rather than by deletion and interlineation) in such a way that the original readings cannot be recovered. The probability is either that both $W^2$ and $W^1$ derive independently from the shorthand transcript, or that $W^2$ derives from the shorthand and $W^1$ from $W^2$ (in any case, because the poem occurs fairly near the beginning of the $W^2$ book but is the last poem in $W^1$, $W^2$ is likely to be the earlier of the two MSS; this would certainly be true if the fourth transcript mentioned in *KC*, I, 79, written in a "Book" at the publishers', is $W^1$), but neither case can be proved. Subsequently Keats read over $W^1$ and made changes and corrections, sometimes in response to queries, suggestions, and other markings in the MS by Taylor and Woodhouse, and the transcript was then used as printer's copy for *1820.*

Keats had considerable help (amounting to coauthorship) from others in arriving at the final text of this poem. Reynolds suggested the alteration of a word—

we do not know which one—when he first read the fair copy in October 1818 (*Letters,* I, 377), Woodhouse offered a number of suggestions and introduced several changes in the course of writing his transcripts, and Taylor apparently also was responsible for a handful of readings in the printed text. In particular (to speak of substantive matters only), when he was making $W^3$ from the fair copy Woodhouse marked the holograph with pencil lines beside the stanza following 56 (also underscoring the last three words of the sixth line of this stanza) and beside 74–76, indicated the omission of a word in 346, and (again in pencil) suggested revisions on the opposite versos for 55–56 and the whole of the following stanza (56/57), 62–63, 382, 384, 430, and 460 (all of these proposed revisions by Woodhouse are given in Hampstead Keats, III, 62, 82, 85, 86 nn., and most of them—all but the stanza opposite 56/57 and the revision in 460—are reprinted in Garrod's notes; Woodhouse's stanza opposite 56/57 has also been rediscovered and taken to be Keats's by Clayton E. Hudnall in *English Language Notes,* 7 [1969], 111–114, and by Allott, pp. 330–331 n.).

In $W^3$ itself Woodhouse changed Keats's text substantively only in 207 (correcting an error by Keats), 306–307 (punctuation), 334 (correcting the grammar), 347, 417, 478–479 (punctuation), and probably also in 117 (though the $W^3$ reading is uncertain here). But in $W^2$ and $W^1$ he introduced several more changes—most of which, like those in $W^3$, were incorporated into the *1820* text—in the heading (the $W^1$ "Isabella or" is a later addition) and 30, 40, 56/57 (deleting the stanza), 62, 63, 78, 144, 187 (also altering $W^3$ when he made the $W^2$ copy), 196, 222, 233, 261, 267, 276, 281, 287 (again altering $W^3$ when he made $W^2$), 303, 304 (the change based on a marginal query in $W^3$), 309, 350, 359, 405, 453, 471, 472, 489, and 500—and he may have been responsible for further changes in 102 (where the original "the" is altered in pencil in $W^2$ to read "this"), 376 (perhaps just a spelling variant, however), 382 (where *1820*'s "they labour'd" appears as a pencil alteration in $W^2$ as well as in Keats's hand in $W^1$), 395 (where *1820*'s "one" appears as a pencil alteration—by Woodhouse or Taylor—in $W^1$), and 485 (where *1820*'s "your" appears as a pencil query in $W^2$). He also penciled suggested revisions above, beneath, and opposite the text of $W^2$ for 36, 39–40, 55–56 (five different versions plus one at the end of the $W^2$ book), 57, 63–64, 117, 131, 199–200, 237, 366, and 460, and penciled x's and queries beside or opposite 46, 151–152, 197, 241, 315, and 374; in $W^1$ he did the same for 55–56 (three more versions, the last of which is the same as the *1820* wording), 57, 70, 89–96, 97–98, 100, 199–200, 287, and 398–399, and he penciled "Stop this as you please" opposite 46 and "Please point this as you like" opposite 246–247. (Half or more of these pencil markings and revisions in $W^2$ and $W^1$ are given in Garrod's apparatus, but Garrod is usually wrong or noncommittal concerning the identity of the hand responsible for them.)

Keats himself made changes in $W^1$ in 145, 151–152, 159, 199–200 (filling in the blank there), 287 (correcting a slip in response to Woodhouse's query), 315, 373–374, 382 (again in response to Woodhouse's marking of the text), 393, and 394. And Taylor's hand is also evident in $W^1$. He interlined a new word in 30, interlined the final text of 55–56 (copying the last of Woodhouse's attempted revisions), canceled Keats's revision of 159 (restoring the original wording above the line), canceled Keats's incomplete revision of 373–374 (again restoring the original lines, this time opposite the text), perhaps made the pencil change in 395 already commented on in the preceding paragraph, and interlined a new version of 398 (again copying one of Woodhouse's suggested revisions of the line). (The hand that corrected "scathe" to "seeth" in 117 remains unidentified.) In addition to all the above, *1820* has new readings in 6, 75, 189, 304, and 398. The final responsibility for some of these changes—especially those in Taylor's hand (including his canceling of Keats's revisions) and the new readings in *1820*—cannot be definitely assigned. Even so, it appears that Woodhouse and Taylor were at least the initiators of substantive changes from the fair copy text in some forty or more lines.

The present text is based on *1820*. Woodhouse's three transcripts, even though deriving from the extant fair copy, are included in the apparatus in order to show where the changes subsequent to the fair copy in each case occurred. Some ambiguous situations are specially commented on in the notes below.

36 cool] Woodhouse suggested "calm" and "soothe" in pencil beneath this word in $W^2$.

39–40 If . . . cares."] Woodhouse marked these lines with three vertical strokes in the margin of $W^2$ and penciled "'twill scare away her tears" (apparently an incomplete attempt at revision, but possibly the last word was meant to be "fears") on the opposite verso.

46 Fever'd . . . bride,] So punctuated in Keats's fair copy and *1820* (the draft and $W^3$ have no punctuation in the line). The $W^2$ punctuation is "Fever'd, . . . bride$_\wedge$"; in $W^1$ Woodhouse originally wrote the line without punctuation, adding "Stop this as you please" in pencil on the opposite verso, and he (at the time) or someone else (later) inserted a comma in pencil at the end of the line.

55–56 "Lorenzo . . . rest.] Woodhouse made no fewer than ten attempts (one in the fair copy, six in $W^2$, and three in $W^1$) to revise the fair copy text of these lines. The *1820* wording, written into $W^1$ by Taylor, represents a copying of the last of Woodhouse's attempts. Since Keats refers to his original text here (specifically the word "debonair") in his $W^1$ note concerning 199–200 (see below), the change in 55–56 must have been made after Keats's revision of the later lines.

57 "O . . . perceive] As a suggested revision, Woodhouse altered the text in pencil in $W^2$ to produce "O Isabel, said he, I half perceive"; he apparently began the same alteration in $W^1$, marking the last two letters of "Isabella" for omission but then deleting his mark.

62–64 Thy . . . shrive] On the opposite verso in the fair copy, as a suggested revision of 62 and the first half of 63, Woodhouse penciled "Thine Eyes by gazing, nor should thy hand fear / Unwelcome pressing"; in $W^2$, for the rhyme words in 63 and 64, he suggested "dwell" and "tell."

70 rhyme] Woodhouse penciled "q *ch*ime" opposite this line in $W^1$.

78 Sang] The $W^3$ reading is ambiguous in Woodhouse's shorthand (= "sng"); $W^2$ and $W^1$ have "Sang."

89–96 Were . . . bows.] Woodhouse marked this stanza for omission in pencil in $W^1$ but then deleted his mark.

97–98 But, for . . . The] On the opposite verso in $W^1$ Woodhouse in pencil suggested revision to "Yet, 'tis . . . Whose."

100 And] Woodhouse suggested "Yet" in pencil above this word in $W^1$ but then deleted the suggestion.

102 this] Woodhouse's pencil alteration of "the" to "this" in $W^2$ may have been made from *1820,* but it is more likely that he himself initiated the change and therefore was responsible for the *1820* reading. The reverse alteration in $W^1$(in ink)—"this" to "the"—is difficult to explain.

117 seethe] The $W^3$ word, "scath" (in longhand), is also readable as "seath"; $W^2$'s "scath" and $W^1$'s "scathe" are less questionable. Apparently preferring "scath" as a noun, Woodhouse suggested "bore" in pencil above the preceding word ("did") in $W^2$, adding "q" on the opposite verso.

131 that] Woodhouse penciled "their" above this word in $W^2$.

136/137 (*apparatus*)⟨Two . . . tret.⟩] The draft is missing here; but since Keats was regularly writing three stanzas per page in the draft (see the above reconstruction of the MS), this stanza was probably not in the MS as originally written. It could of course have been added on a separate sheet inserted between leaves 4 and 5.

187 pray thee] Since both $W^3$ and $W^2$ show the fair copy's reading "pry'thee" altered in effect to *1820*'s "pray thee," it may be assumed that the $W^3$ alteration dates from the time that Woodhouse made the $W^2$ transcript rather than from his initial copying of the poem in $W^3$.

194 oft] The lost draft reading of "soft" is somewhat in question. In the *Athenaeum,* 6 April 1912, H. B. Forman records "soft," explaining that Keats first changed the word to "oft" in the fair copy; in Hampstead Keats, III, 70 n., he says that Keats made the alteration in the draft itself. His earlier report is the more circumstantial, and is probably the more accurate.

199–200 When . . . delight.] Woodhouse invented couplets to complete this stanza in both $W^2$ and $W^1$, penciling "When lo an indoor lattice met his view, / And her fair features smiling playful through" opposite the blank space in $W^1$. When Keats filled in the blank in $W^1$ he initially ended the lines with "fair" and "debonair," and added a note concerning the latter word at the bottom of the page: "as I have used this word before in the poem [in the original text of 56] you may use your judgement between your lines [i.e., Woodhouse's] and mine." He then changed the final words to "bright" and "all delight" and continued his note, "I think my last alteration will do."

237 His . . . see] Woodhouse penciled "What might have been full clearly doth she see" on the opposite verso in $W^2$, interlined "plainly" above "clearly," and then wrote "she clearly seem'd to see" beneath the last five words. The middle version (with "plainly") is the one closest to the text that Woodhouse saw in Keats's letter to Reynolds.

246–247 Of . . . subdued] Opposite these lines in $W^1$ Woodhouse penciled "Please point this as you like." Probably he was concerned with the punctuation after "tragic" in 247, though his note may also (or instead) refer to the marks before and after "a richer zest" in 246. The MSS' differences in punctuation in these lines are not significant.

275 the] The draft reading, either "His" written over "⟨The⟩" or "The" written

over "⟨His⟩," cannot be determined with certainty. Garrod, p. 226 n., thinks "His" is the later word.

287 And] Since both $W^3$ and $W^2$ show the fair copy's "But" changed to *1820*'s "And," it may be assumed that the $W^3$ alteration dates from the time that Woodhouse made the $W^2$ transcript (same situation as that in 187).

287 through] The fair copy has "though" (a characteristic slip of the pen), which Woodhouse copied in all three transcripts, underscoring the word in $W^3$ and querying it in $W^1$ ("q Is this word used in Chaucer's sense of *then*"). Keats responded to Woodhouse's query by canceling "though" and interlining "through" in $W^1$, and Woodhouse then corrected the word to "through" in $W^2$.

306–307 dwelling$_\wedge$ / Alone:] The draft's punctuation makes "Alone" a part of the clause of 305–306 (as in *1820*), while that in the fair copy connects the word instead with the clause of 307. Woodhouse's punctuation independently accords with that of the draft.

346 whisper] This word, which Keats later inserted above the line in the fair copy, was not in the fair copy when Woodhouse made his first transcript. Woodhouse indicated the omission in the fair copy by penciling a caret in the text and "(—)" on the opposite verso, and he wrote "(whisper)" in longhand in $W^3$. But "whisper" was already in the draft, and therefore the word did not originate (even if it was an independent guess in $W^3$) with Woodhouse.

366 the] Woodhouse penciled "that?" on the opposite verso in $W^2$.

376 veiling] $W^2$'s and $W^1$'s "vailing" is perhaps a spelling variant rather than a substantive change (according to the *OED,* "vail" was a spelling of the verb "veil" in the sixteenth, seventeenth, and eighteenth centuries).

382 they labour'd] Woodhouse's pencil alteration in $W^2$ may have been made from *1820*, but it is more likely that he himself initiated the change. On the opposite verso in the fair copy, in pencil, he suggested revision of the original wording to "beheld them," and in $W^1$ he called attention to the faulty meter of the line by marking "hours" as a two-syllable word ("hoürs"); Keats's revision in $W^1$ was surely a response to this marking, whether or not he got the revised wording from Woodhouse.

382 travail] The fair copy has "travel," which, however, is simply a spelling variant ($W^3$ has "trvl," $W^2$ "travail," and $W^1$ "travel" altered to "travail"). The reverse situation in *Endymion* II.145 is more ambiguous.

384 stamp and] On the opposite verso in the fair copy, in pencil, Woodhouse suggested revision to "weep or."

398–399 If . . . moan'd] On the opposite verso in $W^1$ Woodhouse penciled "With fond caress, as if it were not dead" as a suggested revision of 398, and then "The ghostly [*or* ghastly] Features of her Lover dead / Pale Isabella kissed and lowly moand" for 398–399. Taylor's interlineation above 398 in $W^1$ is simply a recopying of Woodhouse's first suggestion; it is not known who was responsible for the entirely new *1820* reading in this line.

430 From . . . mouldering] On the opposite verso in the fair copy, in pencil, Woodhouse suggested revision to "And from the mouldering."

460 the thing] On the opposite verso in the fair copy, in pencil, Woodhouse suggested revision to "it all"; in $W^2$ he suggested "such grief."

471 sat] The $W^3$ reading is ambiguous in Woodhouse's shorthand (= "st").

478–479 space . . . Away] The $W^3$ punctuation given in the apparatus is based on Woodhouse's customary use (in his shorthand) of a virgule for a full stop. The initial capital in the apparatus reading "Away" (since Woodhouse's shorthand makes no distinction between capitals and lowercase letters) is taken over from $W^2$ and $W^1$.

485 your] The fair copy's "you" for "your" represents one of the commonest slips of the pen in Keats's MSS; Garrod nevertheless emends the *1820* text to "you."

### *Mother of Hermes! and still youthful Maia*

Written at Teignmouth on 1 May 1818 (the date that Keats gives, along with a copy of the lines, in a letter to J. H. Reynolds of 3 May—*Letters,* I, 278). First published in *1848,* I, 135. The three extant MSS—a letterbook transcript by one of Woodhouse's clerks (copying the letter to Reynolds), a transcript by Woodhouse ($W^2$), and a late copy by another of Woodhouse's clerks (Garrod's $T$)—do not differ substantively except in heading (the letterbook transcript has none). The first clerk, working from the now lost holograph of the letter, wrote 11 ff. as three lines:

> Of Heaven, and few ears rounded by thee
> My song should die away content as theirs
> Rich in the simple worship of a day.—

In going over his clerk's transcript Woodhouse inserted double virgules in red ink after "span" in 10, "ears" in 11, "away" and "theirs" in the next line, and "day" at the end, and noted beside the text, "Perhaps the lines sho$^{d}$ be divided as shewn in red Ink." In $W^2$, where he added the title "Ode to May—Fragment" (based on Keats's introductory prose in the letter), he divided the last lines according to his own markings in the letterbook. Because he wrote "Perhaps . . . " in his note in the letterbook, and did not comment on the line-division in $W^2$, it seems likely that Woodhouse made $W^2$ from the first clerk's MS rather than from Keats's letter. The later clerk transcribed the lines from $W^2$, and Milnes printed them as part of the letter from an amanuensis' copy of the first clerk's MS, dividing 11 ff. according to Woodhouse's markings there. *1848* introduced a substantive corruption in 7.

The present text, based on the first clerk's MS, follows Woodhouse's suggested rearrangement of the final lines (the resulting rhymes are a reasonable indication of Keats's intentions, and if he did actually write 11 ff. as three lines he may have done so simply for lack of space on the page).

11–12 ears$_{\wedge}$ . . . thee,] The letterbook transcript has no punctuation in this part of the text, and the participle "Rounded," meaning both "whispered" and "whispered to," may be read as modifying either "song" (12) or "ears" (11). In $W^2$ Woodhouse chose the former alternative, adding a comma after "ears" (*1848's* punctuation, with commas after both "ears" and "thee," is as ambiguous as the clerk's); the present text prefers the latter alternative.

### *To Homer*

Written in 1818 (so dated in all MSS). First published in *1848,* II, 294. The four extant MSS are transcripts—one each by Brown and Dilke and two by

Woodhouse ($W^2$, $W^1$). Brown copied some now lost holograph, Keats revised 3 on Brown's MS, and Dilke transcribed Brown's MS in this revised state (long afterward changing 5 and 7 to agree with *1848*'s wording in these lines). We do not know Woodhouse's source for $W^2$, which has the revised text of 3 (with the original reading in the margin in shorthand, no doubt from Brown's MS, from which he also took the date) but a different reading in 6. Possibly Woodhouse got his text from Brown, altering 6 in the process of copying. $W^1$ was probably made from $W^2$, and *1848* almost surely derives (by way of an amanuensis' copy) from Brown's MS. The *1848* text has substantive corruptions in 5 and 7. The present text is based on Brown's MS.

### *Give me your patience, sister, while I frame*

Written at Wythburn, Cumberland, on 27 June 1818 (in a letter to George and Georgiana Keats under that date—*Letters,* I, 303–304). First published in the New York *World,* 25 June 1877, p. 2. The two extant MSS are both holographs—Keats's original draft in his letter to George and Georgiana, 27, 28 June 1818 (MS at Harvard), and a revised fair copy, made after the first letter was returned to him, in the 18 September section of his letter to George and Georgiana of 17–27 September 1819 (MS in the Morgan Library). The later letter, which was the source of the first publication of the poem in 1877, shows substantive changes by Keats in six lines. Because these all seem considered revisions, the present text is based on the later letter holograph.

### *Sweet, sweet is the greeting of eyes*

Written at Keswick on 28 June 1818 (in a letter to George and Georgiana Keats under that date—*Letters,* I, 304). First published by Lowell, II, 28. The holograph draft in Keats's letter (MS at Harvard) is our sole authoritative source.

### *On Visiting the Tomb of Burns*

Written on 1 July 1818 (the day on which Keats visited Burns's tomb at Dumfries and afterward either drafted or copied the sonnet in a now lost letter to Tom Keats—*Letters,* I, 308–309). First published in *1848,* I, 156–157. The single extant MS, a transcript by Jeffrey (in a copy of Keats's lost letter to Tom of 29 June–2 July 1818), is our sole source. Milnes printed the poem in *1848* as part of the letter from an amanuensis' copy of Jeffrey's MS, changing "Through" to "Though" in 7, "Fickly" to "Sickly" in 11, and "have oft" to "oft have" in 13, supplying a missing verb (where Jeffrey had left a blank space) in 12, and changing or adding substantive punctuation in 4 and 8. Because of Jeffrey's general unreliability as a copyist, several of his readings are in question, and modern texts differ considerably from one another according to the kind and degree of emendation that the editors allow themselves. The present text, based on Jeffrey's MS, follows Milnes's emendations in 7 and 11 and incorporates his choice of verb in 12.

4 ago . . . begun,] Because Keats and Jeffrey were very casual in their punctuation and copying, respectively, it is not clear from the transcript whether "now new begun" is supposed to modify "dream" (3) or "summer" (5). *1848*'s full stop after "begun" is certainly not authoritative.

7 Though] Jeffrey's "Through" probably represents a characteristic slip of the pen by Keats, but some scholars (e.g., J. C. Maxwell, *K-SJ,* 4 [1955], 77–80, and Allott) have printed and defended "Through."

8 done$_\wedge$] Although Jeffrey has no punctuation here, editors beginning with Milnes in *1848* have frequently supplied either a colon or a full stop. The absence of punctuation at the end of a line is not necessarily to be depended on, and "For . . . it" (9–12) can be read both as a separate statement (beginning with a conjunction) and as a prepositional phrase following "pain . . . done."

11 Sickly] The word in Jeffrey's MS—"Fickly"—occurs earlier as an adjective only in the First Folio text of *King Lear* II.iv.186, where it apparently is a misprint of the quarto reading "fickle." The First Folio text (in a facsimile reprint) is of course the one that Keats read and marked, but it seems more likely, in spite of the "Sickly . . . sick" repetition, that Jeffrey mistook Keats's "S" for an "F" (Keats's "S" has sometimes been misread as "T" and therefore might also be misread as "F"; the reverse situation occurs in the holograph fair copy of *Endymion* at II.639, where "Forth" appears to have been written "Sorth"). It is also, of course, possible that Keats wrote or meant to write "Fickle."

### *Old Meg she was a gipsey*

Written at Auchencairn, Kirkcudbrightshire, on 3 July 1818 (drafted in the morning in a letter to Fanny Keats, and copied almost immediately by both Brown in his journal and Keats in a letter to Tom Keats—see *Letters,* I, 311, 317, 437–438, and *KC,* II, 61–62; Rollins' note on the date in *Letters,* I, 312, is misleading, since the change from 2 to 3 July occurs on the preceding page a few lines before the text of the poem). First published in *PDWJ,* 22 November 1838, and then again in *PDWJ,* 22 October 1840, *Hood's Magazine,* 1 (June 1844), 562, and *1848,* I, 160–161. The two extant MSS, both holographs—Keats's draft in his letter to Fanny of 2–5 July 1818 (MS in the Morgan Library) and a fair copy that he made just afterward in his letter to Tom of 3–9 July (MS at Harvard)—do not differ significantly in wording; the earlier letter has the poem in quatrains, except for a final six-line stanza, while the second has no stanza divisions.

Though there are no extant transcripts, a now lost copy that Brown took from the draft is of considerable importance as the basis of all four of the early printings. Brown's transcript, which we can reconstruct from these early printings, corrected a slip of the pen in Keats's draft version in 13, changed "o'" to "of" in 7 and 22, and arranged the first twenty-four lines into three eight-line stanzas (this is the form that the poem has in both of the *PDWJ* printings; in *Hood's,* where it was printed probably from a copy sent in by Milnes, who was a frequent contributor to the magazine; and in *1848,* where "chip hat" in 28 was altered by mistaken emendation to "ship-hat"). Probably Brown changed 7, 22, and the stanza-arrangement on his own initiative, but the readings of the earlier *PDWJ* version (as representative of all the early printings) are included in the apparatus as possibly authoritative. None of the titles in the early printings is authoritative.

Milnes printed the letter to Tom in *1848* from an amanuensis' copy of a Jeffrey transcript, but for the poem itself, which Jeffrey omitted, he used Brown's now lost transcript as printer's copy. (This is the first of six poems from the Scottish tour that Brown at one time intended to quote in his "Life" of Keats. The other five—see *KC*, II, 62–64—are *To Ailsa Rock, This mortal body, There is a joy in footing slow, Not Aladdin magian,* and *Read me a lesson.* Milnes incorporated all six poems, clearly from Brown's texts, into letters or his narrative in Volume I of *1848,* and the disappearance of Brown's transcripts of these six along with the bulk of Milnes's MS for Volume I may be taken as evidence that the transcripts served as printer's copy.)

The present text is based on the earlier letter holograph.

*There was a naughty boy*

Written at Kirkcudbright on 3 July 1818 (in a letter to Fanny Keats on that day—*Letters,* I, 312–315). First published in Forman (1883), II, 290–294. The holograph draft in Keats's letter to Fanny of 2–5 July 1818 (MS in the Morgan Library) is our sole authoritative source. In first printing the lines Forman added a title (from Keats's introductory prose in the letter), inserted section numbers (1 through 4), misread Keats's hand in 85 and 96, and made several changes in line-division.

*Ah! ken ye what I met the day*

Written at Ballantrae, Ayrshire, on 9 or 10 July 1818 (Keats got the subject on the 9th, and either drafted or copied the poem in a letter to Tom Keats on the 10th—*Letters,* I, 327–328). First published in Forman (1883), III, 180–181. The holograph version in Keats's letter to Tom of 10–14 July 1818 (MS in the British Library) is our sole authoritative source. Forman printed the poem as part of the letter, changing "craggis" to "craggi[e]s" in 3 and "An" to "And" in 32, and preferring "there" to the present text's "thence" in 30.

30 thence] The word in the holograph is readable as both "thence" and "therere" (which could be a characteristic miswriting of "there"); the context makes it more likely that Keats intended "thence."

*To Ailsa Rock*

Written at Girvan, Ayrshire, on 10 July 1818 (*KC*, II, 62; *Letters,* I, 329). First published in Hunt's *Literary Pocket-Book* for 1819 (1818), p. 225, and then in Alaric A. Watts's *Poetical Album* (1828), p. 167, Galignani (1829), pp. 71–72 of the Keats section, *PDWJ,* 13 September 1838, and *1848,* I, 167. The three extant MSS are a holograph fair copy in Keats's letter to Tom Keats of 10–14 July 1818 (MS in the British Library) and transcripts by C. C. Clarke (Garrod's $W^3$) and J. C. Stephens.

The two principal texts of this sonnet—the first best represented by the letter copy and the second by the *Literary Pocket-Book*—differ significantly only in 2. Brown copied the poem, probably in his journal at the time Keats wrote it, and intended to include it in his "Life" of Keats (*KC*, II, 62). His now lost transcript (with the same reading as the holograph in 2) served as the basis of the *PDWJ* printing (where the poem is headed "Ailsa Rock: in height 940 feet from the sea, near the Ayrshire Coast," and "steep" in 13 is misprinted "sleep") and was printer's copy for *1848* (see Textual Note to *Old Meg*; the *1848* heading is "Sonnet on Ailsa Rock," the same that Brown uses in his "Life" of Keats). Presumably the version in the *Literary Pocket-Book* came from a MS supplied by Keats. All the remaining texts—Clarke's (copied for Woodhouse), Watts's, Stephens', and Galignani's—derive from this earliest printing, and the substantive variants in them (in 2, 7, and 13 in Stephens' MS, and in 3, 7, 10, and 14 in Watts's version—see *Texts,* p. 193) are all corruptions.

It is not known whether the *Pocket-Book*'s 2 is authoritative or the result of Hunt's editing. The present text is based on the letter holograph.

### *This mortal body of a thousand days*

Written in the cottage in which Burns was born, at Ayr, on 11 July 1818 (*Letters,* I, 322–325, 331–332). First published in *1848,* I, 159. No MS has survived, and *1848*—printed from a now lost transcript by Brown, who quoted 3–4 in an article in the *Liberal,* 1 (1822), 328, and at one time intended to include the poem in his "Life" of Keats (*KC*, II, 63)—is our sole source. In his one-volume *Life* of 1867 Milnes or the printer changed "old" (5) to "own," but this reading is almost certainly a corruption.

### *All gentle folks who owe a grudge*

Written at Cairndow, Argyllshire, on 17 July 1818 (the letter text of that date is probably the original draft, even though there are no deletions or other signs of fresh composition—*Letters,* I, 334–336). First published in Forman (1883), II, 303–306. The two extant MSS are the holograph version in Keats's letter to Tom Keats of 17–21 July 1818 (MS at Keats House, Hampstead) and an unidentified transcript of this letter at Harvard (a copy made for Milnes—see *Letters,* I, 333 n.). In first printing the poem Forman added a title, numbered the stanzas, and made substantive changes in 26 and 44. The present text is based on the letter holograph.

### *Of late two dainties were before me plac'd*

Written on 17 or 18 July 1818 (Keats saw Kotzebue's *The Stranger* at Inveraray, Argyllshire, on the evening of the 17th and wrote this sonnet about the performance either that night or the next day; probably the letter text of the 18th is the original draft—*Letters,* I, 336–337). First published in the *Athenaeum,* 7 June 1873, p. 725. As for the preceding poem, the two extant MSS are the holograph version in Keats's letter to Tom Keats of 17–21 July 1818 (MS at Keats House,

Hampstead) and an unidentified transcript of the letter at Harvard. The present text is based on the letter holograph.

### *There is a joy in footing slow across a silent plain*

Written in July 1818 (copying these lines in a letter to Bailey on the 22nd, Keats describes them as "cousin-german to the Circumstance" that produced *This mortal body* on the 11th, and says that he composed them "a few days afterwards"—*Letters,* I, 344, 343). Lines 1–6, 25–26, and 41–48 first published in *NMM,* 4 (March 1822), 252, and a complete text first in the *Examiner,* 14 July 1822, p. 445, and then in *1848,* I, 180–181. The six extant MSS are an early holograph version that may be the original draft, a revised holograph version in Keats's letter to Bailey of 18, 22 July 1818 (both holographs are at Harvard), a transcript by Dilke, two transcripts by Woodhouse ($W^3$, $W^2$), and an unidentified copy inserted in George Keats's notebook in the British Library (Garrod's *E*). The earlier holograph has a title after the last line of text. The untitled letter copy shows substantive revisions from the earlier version in 1, 6, 8 (correcting the omission of a word), 9, 21, 27, 36, 45, and 46. All subsequent texts derive from one or the other of these holographs.

Brown took a copy of the earlier holograph, probably in his journal at the time Keats wrote the lines, and intended to include a text in his "Life" of Keats (*KC*, II, 64). His now lost transcript was the source of the partial text printed at the end of his article on "Mountain Scenery" in *NMM* (where the seven-foot lines are divided into alternating tetrameters and trimeters) and was again the source of the *Examiner* text (where a headnote complains of the "mutilated" version in *NMM*). Milnes printed the letter to Bailey in *1848* from an amanuensis' copy of Woodhouse's letterbook transcript, but for the lines themselves, which Woodhouse omitted, he used Brown's MS as printer's copy (see Textual Note to *Old Meg*). The *NMM, Examiner,* and *1848* texts have in common substantive variants from the earlier holograph in 2 and 5 (*NMM* and the *Examiner* read "in days"; *1848* has "in times," a combination that Milnes may have invented after consulting the holograph, which Dilke had sent him around 1845 or 1846—see *KC*, II, 161), and they change Keats's "loose" to "lose" in 46; the *Examiner* and *1848* texts have the corrected reading of 8 (a line not included in *NMM*'s partial text) and paragraph spacings after 12, 22, 28, and 38. In addition, the *Examiner* text contains a heading (one that is different from the title at the end of the earlier holograph) and a footnote to 28, and misprints a word in 26; and *1848* has unique variants—all of which are corruptions attributable to Milnes or his printer—in 2 ("had been" for "has been"), 4, 10, and 46.

Dilke's MS is also a copy of the earlier holograph, with substantive differences in 8 ("the tongue") and 23 ("world's" for the holograph's "Soul's," a copying error based on "worldly" just beneath in 24). Woodhouse's $W^3$ and $W^2$ are independent copies taken from the letter to Bailey. The unidentified transcript in George Keats's notebook was made from the *Examiner*; like *NMM,* this transcript divides the lines into alternating tetrameters and trimeters, but it has the *Examiner*'s distinctive title and accidentals, and also the *Examiner*'s footnote to 28.

Both the earlier and the revised holograph versions could serve as the basis for a standard text, and Brown's lost transcript (reported in the apparatus from the *Examiner* printing) also has a claim, though we do not know whether his variants in heading, 2, and 5 and his division of the lines into five paragraphs are corruptions or changes that he made on Keats's authority. The choice between the two holographs depends on how seriously we think Keats was working when he altered 1, 6, 9, 21, 27, 36, 45, and 46 in the letter copy. In some other letter texts (e.g., the later holograph of *Not Aladdin magian*) Keats's substantive changes appear to be the results of careless transcribing, but here the later readings generally have the character of considered revisions, and therefore the present text is based on the letter holograph.

46 lose] Although the reading of both holographs—"loose"—makes sense in context, it is almost certainly a spelling error (or variant), and the emendation here (following Brown's text in the *Examiner*) ought not to be considered substantive. The same applies to the emendation of the letter's "Berthplace" in 47.

46 on] This word is now missing from the letter holograph owing to damage to the MS, but it was there when Woodhouse made his copies from the letter.

*Not Aladdin magian*

Written between 24 and 26 July 1818 (Keats visited Fingal's Cave on the island of Staffa on the 24th, and either drafted or, more probably, copied the poem in a letter to Tom Keats on the 26th—*Letters,* I, 349–351). First published in the *Western Messenger,* 1 (July 1836), 822–823, and then in *PDWJ,* 20 September 1838, and *1848,* I, 186–187. The six extant MSS are an earlier holograph version in Keats's letter to Tom of 23, 26 July 1818 (MS at Harvard), a later holograph version in the 18 September section of his letter to George and Georgiana Keats of 17–27 September 1819 (MS in the Morgan Library), two transcripts by Woodhouse ($W^2$, $W^1$), a transcript by Charlotte Reynolds, and a transcript by Brown. The extant Brown transcript is the one that Severn mentions having in 1845 (*KC,* II, 131), and is not the same as another transcript, now lost, from which Brown would have given the poem in his "Life" of Keats (*KC,* II, 63). This latter version can be reconstructed from the *PDWJ* and *1848* texts.

The details for this poem are almost as complicated and puzzling as those for *Hush, hush, tread softly.* There are unique substantive variants, some of them involving entire lines, in Keats's first letter (4), his second letter (19, 35–37, 43, plus a substantive-looking slip of the pen in 29), $W^1$ ("each" for "every" in 55), Brown's transcript for Severn (31, 41, 46), and *PDWJ* (40). Keats's first letter, $W^2$, $W^1$, and Charlotte Reynolds' MS have all fifty-seven lines of the present text (though in $W^1$ Woodhouse wrote the final eight lines in pencil); Keats's second letter omits 7–8 and breaks off after 44; Brown's transcript for Severn omits 39–40 and ends with 49 (another hand has added 56–57 in pencil); *PDWJ* and *1848* omit 50–55. If we set aside the unique readings (and also the various titles added by the transcribers), the principal substantive differences among the texts appear in 9, 27, 45, 46, and the presence or absence of 50–55.

Two early versions are represented by Keats's first letter and Woodhouse's and Charlotte Reynolds' MSS, which differ among themselves only in 4 (where the letter omits a word) and 46 (where the letter reads "Hath" for Woodhouse's and Charlotte Reynolds' "Has"). Woodhouse's source is unknown, but in $W^2$ the lines appear among poems taken from one or another Reynolds source, and we may guess that his text derives (probably by way of a lost copy) from some unknown letter to J. H. Reynolds or one of his sisters written about the same time as the extant letter to Tom Keats. Very likely both $W^1$ and Charlotte Reynolds' MS were made from $W^2$ (they have as heading the same four words that were left in $W^2$ after Woodhouse marked through the last five words in pencil there). George Keats lent J. F. Clarke the holograph of the letter to Tom, and Clarke published the poem in the *Western Messenger* from this MS (*KC*, II, 140); the *Western Messenger* text corrects the letter's omission in 4 but has substantive corruptions in 13 ("ocean" for "surges"), 17 ("upon" for "above"), 29 ("the" for "his"), 34 ("Each a month of mass must rue"), and 53 ("wear" for "war").

A later version is represented by the September 1819 letter to George and Georgiana, in which Keats recopied the poem from the letter to Tom, omitting several lines, making substantive changes in a number of others, and introducing paragraph divisions after 9 and 18. Since there are signs that Keats was working casually in making this copy, its variants and omissions probably should not be taken too seriously.

The main difficulties arise when we consider Brown's copies of the poem. *PDWJ* and *1848,* representing Brown's lost transcript and differing significantly from one another only in 40, agree with Keats's first letter in 9 and the form of verb in 46, but omit 50–55 and have different readings from the letter in 27 and 45. Brown's extant transcript, on paper watermarked 1822, also omits 50–55 (and 39–40, 56–57 as well), has the same readings as *PDWJ* and *1848* in 27 and 45, but agrees with Keats's later letter in 9 and with Woodhouse's and Charlotte Reynolds' form of verb in 46, and differs from all the other texts in 31, 41, and the rest of 46. These details do not fit any pattern. It may be surmised that, as with some other poems from the Scottish tour, Brown's lost transcript came from an early holograph version, possibly one earlier than those of the letter to Tom and Woodhouse's and Charlotte Reynolds' MSS, but we are in complete ignorance on the point, and the variants in the extant copy made for Severn are simply unexplainable (oddly enough, Woodhouse's most erratic MSS are also ones that he made for Severn). Milnes printed the letter to Tom from an amanuensis' copy of a Jeffrey transcript, but for the poem itself, which Jeffrey omitted, he used Brown's lost transcript as printer's copy (see Textual Note to *Old Meg*). *PDWJ*'s 40 probably represents a copying or printing error rather than an authoritative variant.

At least four texts have claims to be our basis for the standard—those of the two extant letters, Brown's lost transcript (via *PDWJ* and *1848*), and $W^2$. Because Brown's and Woodhouse's sources are not known for sure, and Keats's later letter varies so peculiarly from the others, the present text is based on the earlier letter holograph.

57 dived—] Brown calls the poem "a fragment . . . which I never could induce him to finish" (*KC*, II, 63), and Woodhouse in $W^2$ either copied or added three crosses after the final dash, indicating that it was not complete.

*Read me a lesson, Muse, and speak it loud*

Written on the top of Ben Nevis on 2 August 1818 (*Letters,* I, 352, 357; *KC*, II, 63). First published in *PDWJ,* 6 September 1838, and then in *1848,* I, 189. The single extant MS—a holograph fair copy in Keats's letter to Tom Keats of 3, 6 August 1818 (MS at Harvard)—does not differ significantly from the two earliest printed versions. Brown copied the poem, probably in his journal at the time Keats wrote it, and intended to include it in his "Life" of Keats (see *KC*, II, 63—Brown's "read" for "speak" in the first line there, which is all that he gives, is obviously a copying error). His now lost transcript was the source of the *PDWJ* version (with the nonauthoritative title "Sonnet, Written on the Summit of Ben Nivis") and was printer's copy for *1848* (see Textual Note to *Old Meg*). The present text is based on the letter holograph.

*Upon my life, Sir Nevis, I am piqu'd*

Written at Letterfinlay, Inverness-shire, on 3 August 1818 (in a letter to Tom Keats under that date—*Letters,* I, 354–357). First published in Forman (1883), III, 207–209. The holograph draft in Keats's letter to Tom of 3, 6 August 1818 (MS at Harvard) is our sole authoritative source. Forman's text (as part of the letter) emends Keats's slips of the pen in 9, 16, and the prose following 20, and has substantive misreadings in 47, 58, and 59. The present text incorporates Forman's corrections in 16 and the prose following 20 but chooses a different emendation in 9.

1 Upon . . . ] Keats introduces the dialogue by explaining that "there was one M[rs] Cameron of 50 years of age and the fattest woman in all inverness shire who got up this Mountain some few years ago. . . . 'T is said a little conversation took place between the mountain and the Lady—After taking a glass of Wiskey as she was tolerably seated at ease she thus begun" (*Letters,* I, 354).

9 gentlemen] The letter holograph clearly reads "Gentleman" (without punctuation). In context, Allott's emendation to "gentlemen" seems much preferable to Forman's "Gentle man."

56 so . . . joy.] In the letter holograph, which has no punctuation in this line, "so complete my joy" can be read as part of the imperative clause ("Go . . . and . . . complete") or as an exclamation. (It is also possible that Keats intended "*to* complete my joy," and mistakenly wrote "so" for "to.") Garrod takes the four words to be an exclamation, enclosing them in parentheses.

*On Some Skulls in Beauley Abbey, near Inverness*

Written by Keats and Brown early in August 1818 (they arrived at Inverness on the 6th, and Keats sailed for London on the 8th), or possibly some weeks or even months later. First published in *NMM,* 4 (January 1822), 47–48 (with the signature "S. Y."). The single extant MS is a fair copy by Brown among Woodhouse's papers in the Morgan Library (Garrod's $W^3$). The *NMM* text, which was supplied by Brown, has neither the epigraphs nor the stanza numbers of the extant fair copy, and differs substantively from the fair copy in heading, 3, 14, 47, and 91. A third version, that of a now lost Woodhouse transcript printed by Colvin, pp. 553–556, agrees with Brown's MS against *NMM* in the five places just cited but varies from both texts in 19, 35, 41 ("Scot" for "sect"), 64, 65, 71, and 80. Each of the Woodhouse-Colvin variants almost certainly represents either Woodhouse's misreading of Brown's hand or Colvin's miscopying of Woodhouse, since some Brown version, most likely the extant MS, must have been Woodhouse's source. Colvin's text is of some value, however, as our only source for Woodhouse's record of the lines contributed by Keats (1, the first four words of 2, and all of 7–12, 43–48, and 55–60).

Since Brown was coauthor of the poem, both the extant fair copy and the *NMM* version are authoritative, but we know nothing of the chronological relationship of the two texts or of *NMM*'s editorial handling of the poem. Because of the possibility that some of the *NMM*'s distinctive readings are corruptions (those in 47 and 91 are probably best attributed to the printer), the present text is based on the extant fair copy.

*Nature withheld Cassandra in the skies*

Translated from Ronsard's *Nature ornant Cassandre qui devoit* (in the text of 1587) on or shortly before 21 September 1818 (*Letters,* I, 369, 371). First published in *1848,* I, 241. The four extant MSS are a holograph version (written in pencil and gone over in ink by Woodhouse) on a blank page of the 1806 *Poetical Works of William Shakespeare* at Keats House, Hampstead, two transcripts by Woodhouse ($W^3$, $W^2$), and a transcript by Charlotte Reynolds.

Keats copied the lines into a letter to J. H. Reynolds of c. 22 September 1818, but the holograph of the letter has not survived, and Woodhouse in transcribing it in his letterbook includes only the first line of poetry, referring to $W^2$ for the rest. Probably both of Woodhouse's transcripts derive from this letter text ($W^3$ perhaps by way of a now lost copy made from the letter by J. H. Reynolds, and $W^2$ perhaps by way of $W^3$). Charlotte Reynolds' MS, while it is quite close to $W^2$ in accidentals, perhaps in this instance was made from the same source that Woodhouse copied rather than from $W^2$; she adds a heading not in $W^2$ (though this could have come from the beginning of a brief extract from the letter quoted by Woodhouse opposite the text, "Here is a free translation of a Sonnet of Ronsard . . ."), and gives only "1818" where Woodhouse dates the lines alternatively September and December 1818. In any case, the three transcripts do not differ substantively among themselves except in heading. Milnes printed the lines in *1848* as part of the letter to Reynolds, introducing into a copy of the letterbook transcript a text taken from some unknown source (since, so far as we can determine, none of the extant transcripts was available to him, and he clearly did not use the extant holograph). The untitled *1848* text is the same as that of the transcripts except for a unique reading in 3 (possibly an attempted improvement by Milnes, who completed the translation by adding two more lines of his own in square brackets).

The chief problem here concerns the status of the extant holograph, which has no title and differs substantively from the transcripts in seven lines. Because it was written in pencil, shows signs of composition as opposed to copying in 7, 9, and 10, and contains an attempt at an additional line following 12, one might take it to be the original draft, but the Shakespeare volume containing it bears the inscription, in Keats's hand, "John Hamilton Reynolds to John Keats 1819." While it is possible that Keats drafted the lines in the volume earlier, in September 1818, when it belonged to Reynolds (and before Reynolds formally presented it to him), it is perhaps more likely that the holograph is a later version, penciled in the volume some months or more after Keats wrote the text represented by the transcripts.

The present text is arbitrarily based on the extant holograph. Because of our uncertainty concerning their sources, all three of the transcripts and *1848* are included in the apparatus.

### *Fragment of Castle-builder*

Written in 1818 (so dated in $W^2$). Lines 24–71 first published in *1848,* I, 283–285, and 1–23 first by Colvin in *TLS,* 16 April 1914, p. 181. The single extant MS is a transcript by Woodhouse ($W^2$). Woodhouse's form of date there ("CB. 1818") indicates the existence of a now lost transcript by Brown, and it is possible that both $W^2$ and *1848* derive from this lost transcript, though we have no way of knowing for sure. The partial text in *1848* differs substantively from $W^2$ in heading, 29, and 65. Colvin printed 1–23 from $W^2$. Because there is a fair chance that *1848*'s distinctive readings are corruptions (emendations or errors by Milnes and/or his printer), the present text is based on $W^2$.

8 Pray . . . smile—] The asterisks (actually a line of small crosses) following this line are a later insertion by Woodhouse, squeezed in after he wrote the speech prefix for 9, which lacks a rhyming line.

17 For it containeth] On the opposite verso in $W^2$ Woodhouse penciled "And" and "s full," presumably suggesting a revision (to "And it contains full") rather than recording an authoritative variant.

22 of few] So $W^2$, but possibly an error by Woodhouse or in his source for "or few."

40 viol, bow strings] So punctuated in $W^2$ and *1848* (with "bow-strings" in *1848*). H. B. Forman (O.S.A. ed.) emends to "viol-bow, strings."

60 Of . . . clay] Woodhouse left a half-line of blank space after this line to indicate the absence of a rhyming line. He did the same after 69.

### *And what is Love?—It is a doll dress'd up*

Written in 1818 (so dated in $W^2$). First published in *1848,* I, 283. The single extant MS is a transcript by Woodhouse ($W^2$). As with the preceding poem, Woodhouse's form of date in $W^2$ ("C.B. 1818") indicates the existence of a now lost Brown transcript, and it is possible that both $W^2$ and *1848* derive from this lost transcript. *1848* differs substantively from $W^2$ in heading ($W^2$ has none), 9, and 12. The present text is based on $W^2$.

5 loving] In the margin of $W^2$ Woodhouse suggested the insertion of "too" ("loving too") to fill out the meter.

*'Tis the "witching time of night"*

Written on 14 October 1818 (in a letter to George and Georgiana Keats on that day—*Letters,* I, 398–399). First published in the *Ladies' Companion,* 7 (August 1837), 187, and then in the *Ladies' Pocket Magazine,* Part I (1838), pp. 231–232, and *1848,* I, 233–234. The two extant MSS are the holograph draft in Keats's journal letter of 14–31 October 1818 (MS at Harvard) and a transcript by John Howard Payne. All subsequent texts derive from the letter holograph. Payne's transcript, which he sent Milnes in 1847, was made from a now lost copy of the lines that George Keats had written out for him from the original letter (*KC,* II, 224–225). This same lost copy by George was also Payne's source for the text included in his article in the *Ladies' Companion,* and the *Ladies' Pocket Magazine* reprinted the poem (with Payne's article) from the *Ladies' Companion.* Milnes printed Keats's letter in *1848* from an amanuensis' copy of a Jeffrey transcript, but for the poem itself, which Jeffrey omitted, he apparently inserted a copy taken from Payne's transcript, the only source known to have been available to him. The *1848* text has substantive corruptions in 1 and 20. The present text is based on the letter holograph.

24 stars' light] The letter holograph reads "Stars light," which requires emendation of some sort. The present text follows Allott's correction rather than the substantive alteration in Payne's MS and the early printings ("starlight"). It is, of course, possible that Keats first wrote "Stars" by itself and then, deciding on "Starlight," wrote "Stars light" by mistake.

*Where's the Poet? Show him! show him*

Written in 1818 (so dated in all MSS). First published in *1848,* I, 282–283. The three extant MSS—transcripts by Brown, George Keats, and Woodhouse ($W^2$)—do not differ substantively except that Woodhouse has "mine" (a slip of the pen) for "nine" in 2. George Keats's and Woodhouse's transcripts were made directly from Brown's MS, and the *1848* text (agreeing substantively with Brown throughout) almost surely derives from the same source. The present text is based on Brown's MS.

*Fancy*

Written toward the end of 1818 (it is probably one of the poems that Keats promised his brother and sister-in-law on 18 December; he copied it out for them on the following 2 January—*Letters,* II, 12, 21–24). First published in *1820,* pp. 122–127. The four extant MSS are a holograph fair copy in Keats's journal letter of 16 December 1818–4 January 1819 (MS at Harvard) and transcripts by Dilke, Brown, and Woodhouse ($W^2$). Woodhouse's MS, copied "from C.B.," can be set aside as having no independent authority. The rest of the texts—the holograph letter, Dilke's and Brown's MSS, and *1820*—represent the four recoverable states for this poem, though except for *1820,* which is clearly the final state, their chronological order is uncertain.

The untitled letter text, while it contains the same number of lines as the transcripts, has unique substantive readings in 18, 24, 30, 33, 34, 55, 59, 62, and 68, and possibly also in 25 and one of the lines following 89 (see the notes below). These may derive from a lost original or early draft, or may be the result of the same kind of casual tinkering-while-copying that we see in some of Keats's other letter copies (e.g., the later holograph of *Not Aladdin magian*).

Dilke's MS, which in this instance does not derive from Brown (Dilke's source for a number of his other transcripts), was almost certainly made from a now lost holograph, though whether before or after the date of Keats's letter copy (2 January 1819) is not known. Brown's MS was also taken from a lost holograph. If we consider Dilke's distinctive readings in 63 and 91 and Brown's in 20 as simple copying errors, then Dilke's MS differs substantively from Brown's in heading (Dilke's MS has none), 12, 16, 29, 50, 54, and 73—Dilke agreeing with the letter text in the absence of heading and in 16, 29, 50, and 54, and Brown with the letter text in 12 and 73. Both may have copied the same lost holograph, but if so one has to suppose that Keats made slight revisions in the MS between the two copyings, whichever was the earlier.

*1820* omits a total of eighteen lines at 66/67, 68/69, 89, and 90/91, and further varies substantively from all earlier texts in 6, 15, 28, 34, 44, 45, 57–58, 68, and 76. Though the publishers may have been responsible for the exclusion of the couplet following 68 and some of the lines following 89, the alterations in general are so extensive that they must be attributed to the poet. The present text is based on *1820*.

25 there] The word in the letter holograph is equally readable as "there" and "then." Garrod (p. 265 n.) and Rollins (*Letters*, II, 22) both take it to be "then."

66/67 (*apparatus*) For . . . house.] These lines were at one time lightly marked out in pencil in Brown's MS (the penciling has since been erased). Woodhouse, unsure whether or not to include them, wrote them in pencil in $W^2$.

89 And . . . mesh] In the variant passage given in the apparatus it is not clear whether Keats's "to divine" (third line from the end) was intended to be "so divine," as in Dilke's and Brown's MSS, or a unique "too divine." See Textual Note to *God of the meridian* 10.

*Bards of passion and of mirth*

Written toward the end of 1818 (dating the same as for the preceding poem). First published (under the heading "Ode") in *1820*, pp. 128–130. The five extant MSS are a holograph version written opposite the first page of *The Fair Maid of the Inn* in Volume IV of the 1811 *Dramatic Works of Ben Jonson, and Beaumont and Fletcher* at Keats House, Hampstead, a holograph fair copy in the 2 January section of Keats's journal letter of 16 December 1818–4 January 1819 (MS at Harvard), a transcript by Brown, and two transcripts by Woodhouse ($W^2$, $W^1$).

Keats's untitled MS at Hampstead has deletions and revisions after 4 and in 5–6, 13, 21, and 29, but otherwise is straightforwardly written out, and without paragraph divisions. It is probably a relatively clean original draft, but could also be a revised version made from an earlier MS not now known. Keats copied this text in his journal letter, introducing paragraph divisions after 22 and 36 (as in *1820*), making a slight substantive change in 16, and miscopying a word in 23.

Brown's transcript has the same lack of paragraph divisions as the Hampstead holograph and the holograph's distinctive readings in 10, 19–20, 30, and 30/31 (and also "dasies" in 14 where Keats had written "daises"), but shows a heading not in the holograph. If the heading was added in the copying (with or without Keats's authority), then Brown probably made his transcript from the holograph. $W^2$ has the same text as the Hampstead holograph but with paragraph divisions after 4 and 36 (there is none after 22) and the heading that appears in Brown's MS. Woodhouse's note at the end of $W^2$, "from J.H.R. 26 Mar 1819," is best interpreted as referring to a now lost Reynolds copy and probably the date that Reynolds put on his MS when he copied the poem (rather than the date on which Woodhouse made the $W^2$ transcript). Because $W^2$ shows a deleted word—perhaps the Hampstead holograph's "daises" or another misspelling—before "daisies" in 14, and "sprights" with the "r" deleted in 32 (the Hampstead holograph has "spights"), it seems likely that Woodhouse's source, the lost Reynolds copy, came from the Hampstead holograph. The untitled $W^1$ (with a nonauthoritative "In Philosophic" in 20) pretty clearly derives from $W^2$. The absence of title in $W^1$ suggests the possibility that the heading in $W^2$ is a later addition (perhaps from Brown's MS).

The *1820* text has new readings in 10, 19–20 (but see the note below), and 30, and omits the earlier texts' unrhymed line after 30. The present text (with an emended heading for convenience of reference) is based on *1820*. Brown's MS and $W^2$ are included in the apparatus in order to have a record of their agreement in heading with *1820*.

19–20 But . . . smooth] In $W^2$ ("But melodious truth divine, / Philosophic numbers fine") Woodhouse marked the text in pencil in such a way as to produce "But divine melodious truth, / sophic numbers fine & sooth." Since his revision is similar to but not the same as *1820*, it may be supposed that this penciling was done before the *1820* text was arrived at and that he therefore may have had some influence on the final text.

30/31 (*apparatus*) They . . . cares;] In $W^2$ Woodhouse left a line space after this line and noted on the opposite verso, "a line is omitted here in the Copy from which I took this." In $W^1$ he wrote the unrhymed line in pencil.

### *Spirit here that reignest*

Written perhaps in 1818 (the only clue to dating is the fact that Keats drafted or copied the poem in the same volume in which he wrote the preceding poem toward the end of 1818). First published in *1848*, II, 262. The two extant MSS are a holograph draft or fair copy written on a blank page between *Cupid's Revenge* and *The Two Noble Kinsmen* in Volume IV of the 1811 *Dramatic Works of Ben Jonson, and Beaumont and Fletcher* at Keats House, Hampstead, and a transcript by Brown. The transcript differs substantively from the holograph in heading (the holograph has none) and 17. Brown either copied the extant holograph, perhaps changing 17 at Keats's request, or followed another, now lost holograph. Brown's MS was printer's copy for *1848,* which emended the verb-endings in 3, 4, 13, and 14 to "-est" but otherwise reproduced his words accurately. The present text is arbitrarily based on Brown's MS.

### *I had a dove, and the sweet dove died*

Written at the end of December 1818 or the beginning of January 1819 (Woodhouse dates the poem 1818 on the basis of a now lost Brown transcript; Keats copied it in a journal letter to George and Georgiana Keats on 2 January 1819, introducing it with the remark, "In my journal I intend to copy the poems I write the days they are written"—*Letters,* II, 26–27). First published in *1848,* II, 260. The three extant MSS are the holograph fair copy in Keats's journal letter of 16 December 1818–4 January 1819 (MS at Harvard) and transcripts by Woodhouse ($W^2$) and Milnes.

Keats's letter copy and $W^2$—the latter taken "from CB.," a lost Brown transcript deriving from some otherwise unknown holograph version—are the two authoritative states, differing substantively in heading (the letter text has none), 3, 5, 6, and 9. Milnes's transcript, which was printer's copy for *1848,* almost surely derives from the same lost Brown transcript that Woodhouse copied (Milnes's heading and date are in Brown's characteristic form, "Song. 1818"), and its substantive differences from $W^2$ in 5, 7, 8, and 10 ("lie" for "live," a slip of the pen corrected in the *1848* text) are all assumed to be corruptions.

It is not known whether $W^2$ or the letter copy represents the later (or more considered) version. The present text is arbitrarily based on $W^2$.

### *Hush, hush, tread softly, hush, hush, my dear*

Written in 1818 (so dated in Brown's transcript; a more precise dating is not possible regardless of whether Keats was providing words for Charlotte Reynolds' piano music, was dramatizing an event concerning Isabella Jones, or was doing both of these at once or something else—see Forman, 1883, I, xxix–xxx, and Bate, p. 382 n.). First published in *Hood's Magazine,* 3 (April 1845), 339, and then in *1848,* II, 259–260. The six extant MSS are a holograph version at Harvard, a partial transcript by Brown (lacking the last four lines, which are supplied in Milnes's hand on the verso), a partial transcript by Dilke (breaking off after "morning's" in 22), two transcripts by Woodhouse ($W^3$, $W^2$), and a transcript by Fanny Brawne.

Textually this is the strangest poem in the Keats canon. In addition to the peculiarities of Brown's and Dilke's MSS (see just above), the extant holograph has a line left unfinished (23); Woodhouse's $W^3$ transcript is a slapdash affair, with a number of variant readings and/or alterations and an entire line (20) written in pencil and unique readings in 1, 2, 7, 9, 10, and 15; Woodhouse's $W^2$, "from C.B.," has (uncharacteristically) four substantive variants from the stated source, two of which (in 14 and 16) are unique; and *Hood's* has unique readings in 3, 11, and 17. Except for the agreement of *1848* with Brown's MS, no two versions are substantively identical throughout.

If we set aside Woodhouse's pencilings in his transcripts (see the fourth paragraph below), the distinctive agreements among the texts may be summarized as follows. The extant holograph, Brown's MS (with Milnes's 21–24), Dilke's MS, $W^3$, $W^2$, and *1848* agree against Fanny Brawne's MS and *Hood's* in the third and fourth words of 7, the fifth word of 15, 18, 20, and 21; and all of these texts except $W^3$ agree against Fanny Brawne's MS and *Hood's* in the first word of 14. The extant holograph, Dilke's MS, $W^3$, and $W^2$ agree against Fanny Brawne's MS, *Hood's,* Milnes's completion of Brown's MS, and *1848* in 22. $W^3$ and $W^2$ agree against all other texts in 4 and the fourth word of 16. $W^3$ and *Hood's* agree in 6. $W^3$, $W^2$, Milnes's completion of Brown's MS, and *1848* agree in the last five words of 23 (the latter two texts agreeing against all other versions in the fifth word of the same line). The extant holograph and $W^3$ agree in the absence of title (the rest of the texts are headed "Song"). $W^3$ and *Hood's* agree against the rest in lacking stanza numbers (Dilke's MS omits the number for the first stanza only).

In very general terms there are two basic texts for this poem, the earlier best represented by the extant holograph and the later by Fanny Brawne's MS and the *Hood's* version. The holograph, because it has deletions in 1, 3, 7, 9, 11, 15, 17, 19, and 23, would appear at first glance to be a draft. Actually, however, the MS was initially written straight through, without any sign of original composition, and Keats made all the deletions afterward (those in 15 and 23 in pencil) when he decided to change his metrical form by dropping three syllables from the first, third, and seventh lines of each stanza. (In the holograph's 23—"The Stock dove shall hatch her soft brace and above our heads coo"—there was no handy three-syllable unit to omit; Keats separately deleted "above our heads" and then most of the rest of the line without writing in anything to replace the canceled text.) While it is still possible that the holograph is the original draft rather than a fair copy (it is arbitrarily cited as *D* in the apparatus), the question cannot be decided on the appearance of the MS.

Brown's transcript (as far as it goes) seems to be a copy of the extant holograph, and Dilke's transcript (as far as it goes) is certainly a copy made from Brown's. Perhaps the incompleteness of these MSS has to do with the state of the holograph in 23; Keats did not settle on a final version of the line, Brown may have left both 23 and 24 incomplete, and Dilke may have copied as far as Brown's MS went at the time. Milnes's source for the four lines that he added to Brown's MS is unknown; his "his" for "her" in 23 could be a misreading of Brown's hand (Brown's "s" and "r" in other MSS have been misread and interchanged by copyists and printers), but it is also possible that he took the lines partly or entirely from some other source. There is the additional complication that Woodhouse's transcripts (the $W^2$ text "from C.B.") differ in 23 from the holograph, proposed just above as Brown's source. Possibly Brown's MS did have the text of 23 that Milnes and Woodhouse agree in (apart from Milnes's "his"), perhaps even in Keats's hand as he attempted on the missing part of Brown's transcript to revise the line that he left unfinished in the extant holograph—but any answer to the puzzle of these final lines has to be very speculative. Brown's MS as completed by Milnes was printer's copy for *1848*.

Fanny Brawne's and the *Hood's* texts, agreeing against all other versions in 7, 15, 18, 20, 21, and 23 (and against all but $W^3$ in 14 and all but Milnes's completion of Brown's MS and *1848* in 22), derive from some now lost revised holograph, or possibly from two copies representing more or less the same revised state of text. Their differences from the rest of the texts in 20 and 21 look like copying errors (their distinctive readings in 18 and 22 may also be errors, but "chink" is a perfectly good word in its context and "morning" has the independent support of Milnes's completion of Brown's transcript), and it is probable that at some point along the line they had a source in common. The unique variants in *Hood's* very likely represent alterations in an intervening copy (perhaps by someone in the Reynolds family), editorial changes, printer's errors, or some combination of these.

Woodhouse's transcripts raise some further problems. He probably did take $W^2$, as he says, "from C.B.," but there seems to be no explanation for his substantive differences from Brown in 4, 14, and 16, or for his text of 23 (see above). $W^3$, with its many unique variants and also readings in common with both the earlier text of the extant holograph and the revised text represented by Fanny Brawne and *Hood's,* bears no understandable relation to $W^2$ or to any other known text. One may guess, on the basis of its appearance, that $W^3$ was written from dictation, from shorthand taken from dictation, or from memory. Subsequently in $W^2$, in pencil, Woodhouse marked "All" (2) and "That" (3) for deletion—presumably suggestions for revision rather than authoritative readings—and noted the variant "O" for his text's "my" (4). In $W^3$ he entered several more variants and/or alterations also in pencil above, below, and beside the text—"hush hush" for his "tread gently" in 1, "O" for "my" in 4, "Who" for "That" in 6, "still" for "hush'd" in 10, "Has" for "Hath" in 14, "light . . . dark, no torch" for "torch . . . dusk, and no light" in 15, "eyes" for "eye" and "lip" for "lips" in 16, the whole of 20 (penciled into a blank space that Woodhouse left for the line), and "brace and shall coo" for "twin-eggs and coo" in 23. It is not in every instance clear whether these pencilings are variant readings or alterations of the text. In general they agree with the holograph wording, and could have been taken from Brown's transcript, but the second pencil marking in 15 contains a unique reading ("dark," a word that also, however, appears deleted in the original line in $W^3$), the second marking in 16 agrees with $W^2$ only, and the marking in 23 agrees with the Fanny Brawne–*Hood's* text.

The present text is based on Fanny Brawne's MS, but incorporates readings from the earlier version in 20 and 21. Because of the complicatedness of the textual relationships, all the known versions—even those that seem clearly derivative (Brown's 1–20, Dilke's MS, and *1848*)—are included in the apparatus.

### *Ah! woe is me! poor Silver-wing*

Written in 1818 or 1819. First published in *PDWJ,* 25 October 1838, and then in *1848,* II, 263. The single extant MS, a transcript by Brown, was the basis of the *PDWJ* text (which is headed "Faery Dirge") and was printer's copy for *1848*. The present text is based on Brown's MS.

### *The Eve of St. Agnes*

Drafted mainly or entirely at Chichester and Bedhampton during the last two weeks of January and perhaps also the first few days of February 1819 (*Letters,* II,

58–59, in which it is not clear whether "the blank part of the rest" at the top of p. 59 refers to the unfinished state of the draft, to the letter that Keats has just begun, or to the notebook later given to George Keats in which the poet had already copied *Isabella* and was about to draft *The Eve of St. Mark*; for the date of Keats's return from Bedhampton to Hampstead see Rollins, *HLB,* 8 [1954], 244–245); revised at Winchester in September 1819 (*Letters,* II, 157, 162–163). First published in *1820,* pp. 81–104.

The four extant MSS are Keats's original draft, at Harvard (complete except for the missing first sheet containing 1–63), two transcripts by Woodhouse ($W^2$, $W^1$), and a transcript by George Keats. A letter from Keats to Taylor of June 1820 requests two alterations in the proofs (*Letters,* II, 294–295).

In broad outline the history of the text is simple. Keats drafted the poem early in 1819; Woodhouse transcribed the draft in April 1819; Keats revised the poem in a now lost fair copy in September; Woodhouse read the fair copy sometime between September and the following January and recorded variants from it between the lines and opposite his original text in $W^2$; George Keats transcribed the fair copy in January 1820; and this same fair copy, after further revision by Keats and editing by his publishers, was probably printer's copy for *1820.* There is, however, a degree of fluidity among the texts that we do not encounter in Keats's other poems. It is clear, for example, that Keats further worked on his original draft after Woodhouse transcribed it, and also further revised the fair copy after first Woodhouse and then George Keats saw and used it; it is also clear that Woodhouse filled in blank spaces and changed the texts of both $W^2$ and $W^1$ at various times after he took his initial transcript. We lack the all-important fair copy containing Keats's revised text, but there are plenty of complications among the MSS that we have.

Keats's draft is one of his roughest and most heavily worked over MSS, and it is a minor miracle that Woodhouse in copying it got so many of the words right. The $W^2$ transcript has a note opposite the beginning of the poem—"This Copy was taken from K's original M.S. He afterwards altered it for publication, & added some stanzas & omitted others.—His alterations are noticed here. The Published Copy differs from both in a few particulars. K. left it to his Publishers to adopt which they pleased, & to revise the Whole"—and another note at the end, "Copied from J.K's rough M.S. 20 Ap[l] 1819." But these notes do not necessarily mean that $W^2$ was taken directly from the draft. Woodhouse also copied *Hyperion* on the same 20 April, and there is abundant evidence that the $W^2$ transcript of that poem *was* made directly from a holograph MS; it seems unlikely that Woodhouse would have written out both poems in longhand on the same day, especially since he had been up playing cards "till very daylight" the night before (*Letters,* II, 93). Blank spaces in $W^2$, later filled in by Woodhouse, where Keats's draft is perfectly clear and readable (e.g., in 159–162), and a number of initial misreadings by Woodhouse—"Awaking" for Keats's "Awakening" (289), "in passioned fear" for "Impassion'd far" (316), "windows—dark S[t] Agnes' moon" for "windows dark. S[t] Agnes moon" (324), "tempests" for "tempests'" (342), "footway" for "footworn" (368), all of which could have come from the ambiguities of shorthand notation suggest that Woodhouse copied $W^2$ "from J.K's rough M.S." via an intervening shorthand transcript, in the same way that he did *Isabella* and *The Eve of St. Mark.*

$W^2$ readings like "report" (67, later corrected to "resort") where Keats had written "ressort" with a long first "s" (so that the word looks like "report") and "care quick" (255) where Keats had written "anguish" in such a way (with a space between the second and third letters) that it can be read as "cre quick" or "are quick," as well as several blank spaces (later filled in) where the draft text is almost unreadable, are unmistakable signs that Woodhouse took his first transcript from the extant draft. On the other hand, there are a few readings in $W^2$ (especially that in 123), and $W^2$'s initial substitution of "Lionel" throughout for the draft's "Porphyro," that could not have come directly from the draft; and we have to assume that Keats provided some instructions (concerning the name of the hero) before Woodhouse made his first copy, and perhaps also some help as he copied.

There are enough peculiar likenesses in wording and accidentals to suggest that one of the extant Woodhouse transcripts had to have come from the other (rather than independently from either the draft or the hypothesized shorthand transcript), and there are signs of the priority of $W^2$ (e.g., in 358–359, where Woodhouse deleted and rewrote some words and squeezed in his punctuation in $W^2$ but copied the lines more straightforwardly in $W^1$). Substantive differences between $W^2$ and $W^1$ (not counting those where Woodhouse later altered $W^2$ according to the revised text but did not change $W^1$) occur in 4, 14, 91, 129, 135, 167, 254, 312, 342, 349, 368, and 374. If we set aside 342 in this list (where both $W^2$ and $W^1$ vary from the draft), the $W^2$ text agrees with the draft against $W^1$ in every instance for which the draft MS survives, and it is probable therefore that in all these places (including 4 and 14, for which the draft is missing) the $W^1$ variant reading represents an alteration or error introduced by Woodhouse in the process of recopying the poem from $W^2$. Thus the available evidence points to Woodhouse's having first made a shorthand copy, then written out $W^2$ from the shorthand, and later copied $W^1$ from $W^2$.

Both Woodhouse's variant readings in $W^2$—the "alterations" mentioned in the $W^2$ note quoted above—and George Keats's transcript derive from the now lost fair copy that Keats made in September 1819. (Woodhouse first entered these variants in pencil in $W^2$ and then rewrote them—all but that in 45—in a lighter ink than he had used in the initial copying. These variants are designated $W^a$ in the apparatus. There are also a number of corrections and changes in $W^2$ written in the darker ink of the original copying—most notably in 93, 127, 227, 239, 281, and 299—and these are treated in the apparatus as independent changes rather than as $W^a$ variants.) From the agreement of the $W^a$ variants and George's MS we know that Keats consistently named his hero "Porphyro" in the fair copy (the name had sometimes been "Lionel" in the draft), omitted a stanza after 27, added a stanza after 54, and changed his wording from the draft text (in a few places completing text that had been left unfinished in the draft) in more than ninety lines.

There are, however, substantive differences between the $W^2$ text with its $W^a$ "alterations" and George Keats's MS (not counting George's omission of a word in 7, his further copying errors in 53, 152, 267, 305, 309, and 356, and his differences in a few places where Woodhouse changed the text on his own initiative, as in 83, 93, 158, 281, and 289) in 7, 32, 48, 111, 113, 116, 119, 129, 165, 213, 219, 225, 226, 255, 258, 259, 260, 272, 274, 286, 303, 311, 317 (see apparatus for 314–322), 324, 372, 375, and 376 (see apparatus for 375–378). These differences make it impossible to recover the lost fair copy wording completely. The agreement of *1820* with George's MS in seventeen of them (those in 7, 113, 116, 119, 129, 213, 219, 226, 255, 259, 260, 272, 274, 286, 311, 324, 372) makes it fairly certain that the George Keats–*1820* readings in these lines were in the fair copy when George transcribed it. Woodhouse could have missed some of them when he noted the $W^a$ variants in $W^2$, but it seems unlikely that he would have missed as many as seventeen, and therefore we must suppose that Keats revised some or all of these seventeen lines after Woodhouse saw the fair copy (it is on this supposition that the $W^a$ "alterations" are considered to have been entered in $W^2$ before George Keats copied the poem in January 1820). For the rest of the differences between the altered $W^2$ and George's MS listed above (those in 32, 48, 111, 165, 225, 258, 303, 317, 375, 376) the possibility exists in each case that George's text represents (1) a fair copy revision that Woodhouse overlooked when he noted the variants in $W^2$, (2) a further revision that Keats made after Woodhouse saw the fair copy (including, in 165 and 375, revision to restore the draft text), or (3) a copying error by George. George's readings in 48, 111, and 303 probably belong in this last category, but there is no way of knowing for sure, and the authority of the rest and the point at which, if authoritative, they entered the text are quite uncertain.

The lost fair copy was probably printer's copy for *1820,* but the MS was edited by Taylor and surely also by Woodhouse before it was set in type. As Woodhouse says in his $W^2$ note already quoted, "K. left it to his Publishers to adopt which [readings] they pleased, & to revise the Whole." *1820* differs from the fair copy text as represented by George Keats's MS and Woodhouse's $W^a$ readings—and from George's MS alone (again not counting the obvious errors in it listed at the beginning of the preceding paragraph) where it varies from the altered $W^2$ text —in heading, in the omission of a stanza that Keats added in revision after 54, and in the wording of fifty-seven lines. The sources of these differences may be categorized as follows. In heading, 64, 75 ("on fire"), 115, 136 ("like a full-blown"), 137 ("Flushing"), 143, 145, 147, 167, 197 ("for"), 225 ("so . . . so"), 259 ("clarionet"), 297 ("sank"), 315, 325, 364 ("flaggon"), and 368 ("lie") the *1820* text has readings not occurring earlier in any MS; in 123 and 281 *1820* has readings that first appear in $W^2$; in 165 and 375 ("long") *1820* has readings that appear earlier as $W^a$ variants but are not in George Keats's MS (the 375 reading also appears earlier as a deleted word in the draft); in 135 *1820* agrees with a change made by Woodhouse in copying $W^1$; in 98, 146, 182, and partially in 145 and 147, *1820* incorporates revisions penciled by Woodhouse in the margin and opposite the text in $W^1$ (his other proposed revisions there—for 143, 189, 312, and 378—were ignored); in the rest of these differences—in 9 ("while"), 32, 38, 45, 48, 54/55, 68, 70, 111, 122, 132, 134, 154, 179, 193, 194 ("taper's"), 199, 225 ("knelt"), 258, 264, 297 ("smooth"), 303 ("moan"), 309 ("Made tuneable" and "sweetest"), 311 ("chill"), 314–322 (except for the first word of 315), and 375–378 ("Angela . . . cold")—the *1820* text represents a return to readings of Keats's draft, which the publishers had in one of Woodhouse's transcripts (most probably $W^1$).

The extent of Keats's hand and/or approval in this final text is quite uncertain. From the exchange of letters concerning the poem between Woodhouse and

Taylor in September 1819 (see *Letters,* II, 162–163, 182–183) it is clear that the publishers forced the restoration of the original 314–322—Taylor says flatly that Keats must return to the earlier text or find another publisher—and it is almost as certain that they insisted on the omission of the added stanza following 54 and also on the rewriting, partly by Woodhouse, of 98, 143, and 145–147 (passages of the same objectionable tendency, from the point of view of the letters referred to). But we are in the dark concerning the responsibility for the many other changes from the fair copy text that appear in *1820.* Both Woodhouse's note in $W^2$ and Keats's letter to Taylor of June 1820 (*Letters,* II, 294–295) suggest that Keats did not see the poem between the time that he handed over his fair copy and the time that he read the proofs. But there is nevertheless the possibility that he interacted with the publishers and Woodhouse in the lost fair copy just as he did in the extant transcript from which *Isabella* was printed, and there is the further possibility that he made other proof corrections (in Taylor's office and/or in one or more letters now lost) than those in the surviving letter to Taylor. The present editor has long advocated the reincorporation of Keats's fair copy text of 98, 143, 145–147, 314–322, and the added stanza following 54, but this position must now be abandoned, with the admission (on the advice particularly of Stuart M. Sperry, reviewing *Texts* in *Journal of English and Germanic Philology,* 74 [1975], 452–457) that emending these passages only, and not all the others where *1820* departs from the fair copy text, would result in the same kind of subjective eclecticism that is a principal fault in the previous editing of so many other Keats poems. The present text is that of *1820* without substantive emendation.

Because Woodhouse's $W^a$ "alterations" are not a complete text of the poem but are simply a record of variant readings in the lost fair copy at the time that he saw it, special notes (usually in the form "*GK only* = *1820*") have been added in the apparatus to point out substantive differences between George Keats's readings and those of the altered $W^2$ (including differences where George Keats's MS has a new reading but there is no corresponding $W^a$ variant in $W^2$). Wherever George Keats is not cited for a variant from *1820* (as in the apparatus note to 1), and there is no explanation to the contrary, it may be assumed that both his MS *and the altered* $W^2$ agree with *1820.* $W^2$ and $W^1$, representing the missing draft text of 1–63, are included in the apparatus all the way to the end in order to show the sources of the handful of *1820* readings that came from them in the later lines of the poem.

*Heading* The . . . Agnes] Keats and Brown consistently use the form "S[t] Agnes' Eve" in their letters (*Letters,* II, 58, 62, 139, 157, 174, 234, 276, 294), while Woodhouse and Taylor usually prefer the title that the poem was given in *1820* (five times in *Letters,* II, 162–163, 182).

1 chill] The *1820* printer set "cold" (the reading of the missing draft text recoverable via $W^2$ and $W^1$). Keats requested the restoration of his revised "chill" when he read the proofs in June 1820 (*Letters,* II, 295).

4 woolly] The lost fair copy had "woolly" (the reading of the $W^a$ variant and George Keats's MS), but the missing draft reading is in question. If, as seems most likely, the draft had "sheltered" (the original $W^2$ reading), then the pencilings in $W^1$ probably should be taken to mean that Woodhouse was dissatisfied

with the draft text and so left a blank space, penciling "sheltered?" opposite as a record of the draft reading (from $W^2$) and later writing in "woolly" after he saw the fair copy.

27/28 (*apparatus*) But . . . night.] In the surviving portion of the draft Keats numbered only three of the stanzas. Since the first of these (226–234) shows the number "27" altered to "26" and the second and third (289–297, 352–360) are headed "33" and "40" without alteration, Keats probably decided to cancel this early stanza following line 27 sometime between the writing of the present stanzas 26 and 33 (cf. Ridley, p. 155 n., who does not mention the alteration in numbering of stanza 26). Woodhouse initially copied this early stanza as uncanceled in $W^2$ and $W^1$, but in other poems he occasionally transcribed canceled text as uncanceled. (For the record, $W^2$ and $W^1$ have stanza numbers throughout—1 through 43, since this early stanza is included in the numbering—while George Keats's MS has no stanza numbers.)

32 The level] Since both the $W^a$ variant ("The high-lamp'd") and George Keats's reading ("High-lamped") fit the meter, George's text probably represents a further change that Keats made after Woodhouse saw the fair copy.

45 times] The $W^a$ "alteration" ("times" to "time") is in pencil only; presumably Woodhouse simply neglected to go over it in the lighter ink that he used for rewriting the other $W^a$ variants.

48 loves] The $W^2$ "Love's" is either a slip of the pen by Woodhouse or a peculiar form of the plural noun (such as we occasionally see elsewhere in his MSS), but in any case is not a substantive variant from *1820*. Woodhouse correctly wrote "loves" in $W^1$.

57–58 divine, / Fix'd . . . saw] The *1820* printer set "incline$_\wedge$ / Still . . . while"—an alteration (presumably by Taylor) resulting from the misunderstanding of Keats's use of "train" in 58. Keats requested the restoration of his original text when he read the proofs, explaining to Taylor that "I do not use *train* for *concourse of passers by* but for *Skirts* sweeping along the floor" (*Letters,* II, 294–295).

75 Porphyro] Keats consistently first wrote "Porphyro" in the twelve places where the hero's name occurs in the draft, but here and in 159, 197, and 224 he interlined "Lionel" above the original name (in 159 without canceling the original). Woodhouse consistently wrote "Lionel" throughout (except in 159 and 312, where he initially left blank spaces in his transcripts), and then in $W^2$ changed the name in each instance to "Porphyro." Woodhouse's changes of the name could have been given in the apparatus as $W^a$ variants—they were usually made first in pencil and then in the lighter ink of the $W^a$ readings elsewhere, and obviously at the same time—but are instead considered corrections to $W^2$ because of the conflict of readings in 123 ("Lionel" corrected to "Porphyro" in $W^2$ but then an entirely different $W^a$ reading also noted) and also because Woodhouse in every case canceled his original reading in $W^2$ (rather than just noting the revised reading as a variant) when he changed the name.

93 torch's] The draft's, $W^1$'s, and George Keats's "Torches" (lowercase in the latter two MSS) is ambiguous (like "owlets" and "Thrushes" in Keats's fair copy of *Endymion* I.182 and II.974), but probably is not a substantive variant from *1820*'s "torch's." $W^2$'s "torches'" altered to "torch's" represents Woodhouse's interpretation of the draft's ambiguous spelling.

98 Porphyro] Woodhouse's penciling in $W^1$ could have been taken from *1820,* but more probably was the source of *1820*'s new reading in this line. The same applies to his pencilings in $W^1$ opposite or beside 146 ("Quoth") and 182, and in 145 and 147 his pencilings apparently provided part of the *1820* wording.

123 To . . . Porphyro] The $W^2$-$W^1$ reading, which was (with the appropriate change of name) chosen for *1820* over Keats's revised text in the fair copy, is not in the draft, and has to be taken as Woodhouse's invention, unless Keats supplied it to him orally.

129 Like] $W^1$'s "Like" is an independent change by Woodhouse; the fact that "Like" appears in George Keats's MS but is not noted as a $W^a$ variant in $W^2$ suggests that Keats altered his fair copy text after Woodhouse saw it.

135 And] The *1820* reading is apparently based on the change that Woodhouse introduced in copying $W^1$.

143 Go, go] Woodhouse penciled "Away" on the opposite verso in $W^1$, indicating his own dissatisfaction with the MSS' "O Christ"; presumably the *1820* reading originated with him or Taylor.

165 of . . . privacy] Since the *1820* reading occurs in the MSS only as a $W^a$ variant taken from the lost fair copy (George Keats's MS agreeing with the draft text), Keats must have restored his draft wording in the fair copy after Woodhouse saw it.

189 His . . . brain] Woodhouse underscored "what" in the $W^1$ version of this line (see apparatus) and penciled "q. all that?" on the opposite verso.

223 a] This word is not separately written in the draft. The last letter of the preceding word ("seem'd") is spaced apart from the rest and has a very short ascender, and Keats apparently took it to represent "a" when he revised the line in the MS.

238 fatigued‸ away;] In $W^2$ and $W^1$ Woodhouse originally punctuated this "fatigued, away‸" but he subsequently altered $W^2$ to "fatigued‸ away:" (George Keats's MS also has "fatigued‸ away:" and the draft agrees with *1820*).

254 twilight, soft‸] Punctuated "twilight‸ soft," in $W^2$ and $W^1$ (the draft has no punctuation; George Keats's MS agrees with *1820*).

312 Give . . . Porphyro] Opposite this line in $W^1$ Woodhouse penciled (as a suggested improvement), "Give me again that voice's warbling flow."

375 long] Same situation as in 165 (see the note above), except that the $W^a$ reading in this instance occurs earlier as a deleted word in the draft.

375–378 Angela . . . cold] Woodhouse reported to Taylor on 19 September 1819 that Keats had "altered the last 3 lines to leave on the reader a sense of pettish disgust, by bringing Old Angela in (only) dead stiff & ugly" (*Letters,* II, 162–163), but in all extant texts both Angela and the Beadsman are "brought in" at the end. One supposes that Woodhouse simply misunderstood the revised version here (he had heard Keats recite it when he wrote to Taylor, but had not yet actually read it). His later note in $W^2$ beneath the $W^a$ text of 375–378, "Altered 1820. / before March" (the last two words in shorthand), is best interpreted as indicating that Keats restored the original version of these lines before he handed his MS over to the publishers.

378 For aye] Woodhouse underscored these words in $W^1$ and penciled "Long Time" on the opposite verso, presumably a suggested improvement to avoid the repetition in "For . . . for."

*The Eve of St. Mark*

Written between 13 and 17 February 1819 (so dated—"13/17 Feb^y^ 1819"—in *W*²). First published in *1848,* II, 279–283. The six extant MSS are a holograph leaf containing a preliminary draft of 99–114 (Morgan Library, with an additional sixteen-line fragment on the reverse side, the text of which is given below in the note to 99–114), a holograph draft of all 119 lines in the notebook in which George Keats later made copies of Keats's poems to take back to America (British Library), a holograph fair copy of 1–114 in the 20 September section of the 17–27 September 1819 journal letter to George and Georgiana Keats (MS in the Morgan Library), a transcript by Brown, and two transcripts by Woodhouse (the earlier, in shorthand, is in private hands and unavailable for examination, but a facsimile of the first page, containing 1–50, is given in A. Edward Newton's *A Magnificent Farce and Other Diversions of a Book-Collector,* Boston, 1921, p. 121; the later, in longhand, is in the *W*² book of transcripts).

The British Library holograph is the earliest full version that we have, and, except for the preliminary draft of 99–114 in the Morgan leaf, is almost certainly Keats's original draft. Brown transcribed this MS, as his text evidences in 12 (where he first copied Keats's "dasies" and then inserted an "i"), 33 (where he wrote "Moses'"—Keats's "Aron's" is inscribed in such a way that both "Moses'" and Woodhouse's "Aaron's" could come from it), 45 (where Keats deleted but did not replace his text, and Brown originally omitted the line, later inserting it between 44 and 46), and 101 (where Keats's "hir" looks like "his" and Brown originally wrote "his" before correcting it to "hir"). Brown's transcript differs substantively from the draft in 22, 33, 53, 59, 66, 86, 88, and 91. The transcript was printer's copy for *1848,* which incorporated Brown's eight variants into its text, misread "mid" as "and" in 32 and "hem" as "him" in 101, and emended "the" to "th'" in 40 (*1848*'s "unfinished" in parentheses beneath the title was added on the MS by Milnes).

*W*², "Copied from J.K's M.S.," also came from the British Library draft, but not directly. As originally written, *W*² differs substantively from the draft in 12 ("Of" for Keats's "And"), 30 ("even" for "heaven"), 40 (the omission of "old"), 49 ("to" for "'gainst"), 60 ("Passed"), 62 ("About"), 65 ("fell"), 68 ("lonely"), 74 ("giant's"), 82 ("Angola"), 91 ("sea"), 92 ("in" for "for"), and 115 ("eye had" for "eyelids"). The transcript shows 45–46 and some words in 81 and 84 first written in pencil and later in ink, and has, uncanceled, the two lines after 68 that Keats deleted in his draft when he replaced them with the present 69–70. The blank spaces and misreadings in *W*² are best explained as deriving from Woodhouse's intervening shorthand transcript, whose known text for 1–50 agrees with the British Library draft against *W*² in 12 but omits "old" in 40 and all of 45 (with a sign marking the omission of the line), and in 49 has neither "to" nor "'gainst" but apparently "by." *W*²'s "even" in 30 clearly came from the shorthand transcript (Woodhouse's system regularly uses the same symbol for both "even" and "heaven"), and several of the other misreadings—those in 62, 65, and 115 in particular—can probably also be attributed to the ambiguities of shorthand notation.

Subsequently Woodhouse saw Brown's MS, altered his *W*² text in 22 (changing "organs" to "organ"), 30 ("even" to "heaven"), 49 ("to" to "'gainst"), and 86 ("queens" to "queen"), and recorded Brown's readings above and beside the text in 33 ("Moses"), 40 ("old"), 53 ("plaited"), 88 ("her"), 92 ("for"), and 115 ("eyelids"), and it was probably on this occasion that he filled in 45–46 and the blanks in 81 and 84. Subsequently also, when he saw the Morgan leaf containing the preliminary draft of 99–114, Woodhouse altered *W*²'s "wake" to "waken" in 100, and then at the end of his transcript, after half a page of blank space, copied the sixteen-line extra fragment ("Gif ye wol standen . . . ") from the verso of this leaf.

Keats's September 1819 letter version omits 115–119, has additional paragraph divisions after 47, 52, 82, and 88 (as well as an interruption for prose commentary between 98 and 99), and differs in wording from the British Library draft in 2, 8, 13, 20, 27, 56, 59, 64, 70, 85, 86, 88, 91, and 100, and in substantive punctuation in 75. From the agreement of the letter with Brown's MS in 59, 86, 88, and 91 (the rest of the variants except that in 100 are unique) it might be thought that Keats took his text from the transcript. But since his letter copy has the draft's readings rather than those of Brown's MS in 22, 33, 53, and 66, and since he did not anywhere correct Brown's text, as he might have done (especially in 33) had he been working from it, we must suppose instead that he copied his own draft version.

Though both the British Library draft and the letter copy have claims to be the basis for a standard text, the earlier is probably the more considered version (the letter copy appears to have been written out in the same casual manner in which Keats copied *Not Aladdin magian,* also omitting several lines, in the same letter two days earlier). For this reason the present text (which includes the canceled 45 as uncanceled) is based on the draft. Brown's MS, though a derivative text, is included in the apparatus on the chance that one or more of its variants have some degree of authority.

39 ¶Bertha . . . ] Here and at 57 and 115 the text in the draft begins on a new page without indention. The paragraphing in the present text is based primarily on these page divisions, but also has the support of Brown's MS and (in the first two instances) Keats's letter copy.

99–114 ——"Als . . . dethe."] On the reverse side of the Morgan leaf containing 99–114 Keats wrote the following passage describing a popular superstition connected with the Eve of St. Mark:

Gif ye wol stonden hardie wight—
Amiddes of the blacke night—
Righte in the churche porch, pardie
Ye wol behold a companie
5 Appouchen thee Full dolourouse
For sooth to sain from everich house
Be it in City or village
Wol come the Phantom and image
Of ilka gent and ilka carle
10 Whom coldè Deathè hath in parle
And wol some day that very year
Touchen with foulè venìme spear
And sadly do them all to die—

Hem all shalt thou see verilie—
15 And everichon shall by thee pass
All who must die that year Alas

3 Righte] *interlined above* ⟨Full⟩ 5 Appouchen thee] *added above the line* 8 Wol] ⟨From⟩ Wol (Wol *made out of* Will) 8 Phantom] *interlined above* ⟨feature⟩ 12 foulè] ⟨his⟩ foulè 14/15 ⟨And they shall passen the beside / The in the darke⟩ 15 pass] *interlined above* ⟨go⟩ 15/16 ⟨Truly mine Auctour sayset so⟩ 16 must] *the first three letters have now been lost through damage to the MS, but the entire word is visible in the facsimiles published by H. B. Forman in the "Bookman," 31 (1906), 16, and in his 1906 "Poetical Works of John Keats," after p. 342*

Though Forman (Hampstead Keats) and several more recent editors have incorporated these lines into the poem after 98, Keats himself never made use of them, and they must (even though they are physically associated with the poem and in content are related at least to the poem's title) be considered a separate fragment of his writing.

### *Why did I laugh tonight? No voice will tell*

Written in March 1819 (before the 19th, when Keats copied the poem in a letter to his brother and sister-in-law—*Letters,* II, 81). First published in *1848,* II, 301. The three extant MSS are the holograph fair copy in Keats's journal letter of 14 February–3 May 1819 (MS at Harvard) and transcripts by Jeffrey (in his copy of the letter) and Milnes. Jeffrey's text varies substantively from the letter holograph in 6 ("I say wherefore"); Milnes made his copy from Jeffrey's MS, the only source available to him, again changing 6 (to repair Jeffrey's corruption of the meter); and the *1848* printer set the poem from Milnes's MS, misreading a word in 11. The present text is based on the letter holograph.

9 lease—] The letter holograph's lack of punctuation here should not be considered a substantive matter. While it is possible to construe 9–10 without punctuation ("I know that my fancy spreads this being's lease to its [fancy's] utmost blisses"), Keats rarely wrote such convoluted sentences, and it is much more likely that he was simply using the line ending itself as punctuation.

14 death is] The present editor takes the letter reading to be a slip of the pen (the final "s" in "Deaths" anticipating the sound of the next word, "is"), but Walter H. Evert, *Aesthetic and Myth in the Poetry of Keats* (Princeton, 1965), pp. 291–292 n., interprets the first word as an intended possessive, "Death's" (with the inverted sense "life's high meed is death's," i.e., is ultimately claimed by death).

### *When they were come unto the Faery's court*

Written on 15 April 1819 ("a little extempore" in a letter to George and Georgiana Keats under that date—*Letters,* II, 85). Lines 1–17 first published by Colvin in *Macmillan's Magazine,* 58 (1888), 317–318, and a complete text first in H. B. Forman's *Poetry and Prose by John Keats: A Book of Fresh Verses and New Readings*

(1890), pp. 31–34. The holograph draft in Keats's journal letter of 14 February–3 May 1819 (MS at Harvard) is our sole source. In printing 1–17 ("by way of specimen"), Colvin misread 1 ("had come into"), 4 ("human lovers"), and 17 ("or" for Keats's "and"). Forman took over part of the corruption in 1 ("into") and made further substantive changes in 46 and 53. The present text incorporates an emendation by Allott in 46.

46 A . . . three] Forman's reading—"And quaver'd like the"—represents a misunderstanding of Keats's revisions in the first two words but also a possibly valid interpretation of the fourth word (where the letter holograph has "thee"). Since Keats so often omitted "r" from words in his MSS elsewhere ("thee" for "three" occurs four times in the holograph of *Two or three posies,* for example), Allott's choice of "three" seems much to be preferred.

53 and at] Forman's bracketed insertion of "then" ("and [then] at") is an arbitrary emendation to fill out the meter.

66 cup biddy] Garrod emends to "C'up, biddy" and quotes (p. 565 n.) an explanation sent to him by C. T. Onions, "the rustic call probably to hens and chickens."

### *As Hermes once took to his feathers light*

Written in April 1819 (on or before the 16th, when Keats copied the poem in a letter to his brother and sister-in-law—*Letters,* II, 91). First published in the *Indicator,* 28 June 1820, p. 304 (with the signature "Caviare"), and then in the *London Magazine,* 4 (November 1821), 526, the *Ladies' Companion,* 7 (August 1837), 186, the *Ladies' Pocket Magazine,* Part I (1838), pp. 228–229, and *1848,* II, 302. The nine extant MSS are a holograph draft written on a blank leaf at the end of Volume I of H. F. Cary's 1814 translation *The Vision; or, Hell, Purgatory, and Paradise, of Dante Alighieri* now at Yale, the holograph fair copy in Keats's journal letter of 14 February–3 May 1819 (MS at Harvard), and transcripts by Brown, Dilke, Woodhouse (two copies, $W^2$ and $W^1$), Hessey (Garrod's $W^3$), Payne, and Jeffrey (in his copy of the letter).

Several of the texts are untitled; Brown and Dilke head the poem "Sonnet, / On a Dream," while Hessey has "Sonnet after reading Dante," the *Indicator* "A Dream, after Reading Dante's Episode of Paulo and Francesca," and the *London Magazine* "Sonnet,—A Dream." The draft appears to lack a word (by oversight) in 11, there is a slip of the pen ("look," later corrected marginally in pencil) in the first line of $W^1$, and Jeffrey omitted the entire first line and wrote "pine" for "pure" in 7, but otherwise the MSS do not differ substantively among themselves as originally written. Brown's transcript shows "that" altered to "a" in 8 ($W^1$ has the same alteration in pencil, probably from Brown or the *Indicator*), and this is the only significant variant among the texts. The *Indicator* version also has "a" in 8, and unique variants that almost surely ought to be disregarded in 7 and 10.

The holograph in the Dante volume is pretty clearly Keats's original draft (even though it shows deletions and interlineations only in 6/7, 9, 10, and 11), and there are two fragments in Keats's hand elsewhere in the same volume that are best interpreted as rejected beginnings prior to the writing of the complete draft: "Amid a thousand" (inside the back cover, where Fanny Brawne later copied the *Bright star* sonnet) and "Full in the midst of bloomless hours, my ⟨spright⟩ soul / Seeing one night the dragon world asleep / Arose like Hermes" (inside the front cover, the last two words in pencil). We may assume that the letter copy was made soon after the draft, though whether from the draft itself or a now lost holograph copy in Keats's "book" (see *Letters,* II, 104) is not known.

Brown probably transcribed a lost holograph rather than the draft or the letter copy (this simply on the basis of what seems to have been his practice with other short poems of the spring of 1819). Dilke copied Brown's text exactly, and before Brown changed "that" to "a" in 8. Woodhouse's source in $W^2$ was probably the same lost MS posited above as Brown's source (see Textual Note to *Character of C. B.*). $W^2$ has parentheses around "baffled" (2) and a note on the opposite verso recording Brown's title and citing some illustrative passages from Cary's Dante; at some later time Woodhouse tried his hand (in pencil) at revising 12, producing "Pale was the sweet cheek I saw" (to avoid the repetition of "lips" in the next line). We may suppose that he took $W^1$ from $W^2$. Hessey's MS, certainly deriving from Woodhouse but not necessarily directly from $W^2$ or $W^1$, apparently was printer's copy for his *London Magazine* version (capital letters are underscored thrice in his MS, and there is a penciled direction at the bottom, "to follow the 'Lawyer,'" referring to a poem that appeared in the *London* in August 1821); in a footnote to 9 the *London* prints some of the Dante lines that Woodhouse had quoted in his note in $W^2$.

Presumably Keats himself supplied a text for the *Indicator* version—he was living at Hunt's at the time the poem was published—and possibly by dictation, since the erroneous "world-wind" in 10 has nearly the same sound as the correct "whirlwind." The *Indicator*'s "Not unto Ida" in 7 looks like a copyist's or printer's mistake based on the similar wording in the next line, and "'mid" in 10 perhaps represents an editorial change by Hunt. Payne's MS, which he sent Milnes in 1847, derives from a now lost copy of the poem that George Keats had written out for him from the journal letter (see *KC*, II, 224). This same George Keats copy was the basis of the version included in Payne's article in the *Ladies' Companion* (which printed "it" for "so" in 6, an independent error); the *Ladies' Pocket Magazine* reprinted the poem (with Payne's article) from the *Ladies' Companion.* Jeffrey's text of course also derives from the letter. Brown's MS was printer's copy for *1848,* and Milnes struck out "Sonnet" in the title and added the reference to his Volume I, page 270, on the MS.

Keats's letter copy, Brown's MS, $W^2$, and the *Indicator* version (if we set aside its unique readings in 7 and 10) all appear to have claims to be the basis for a standard text. The present text, disregarding the various headings in the transcripts and the *Indicator,* is arbitrarily based on Brown's MS.

### *Character of C. B.*

Written on 16 April 1819 (drafted or copied in a letter to George and Georgiana Keats on that day—*Letters,* II, 89–90). First published in *1848,* I, 269–270. The four extant MSS are the holograph draft or fair copy in Keats's journal letter of 14 February–3 May 1819 (MS at Harvard) and transcripts by Brown, Woodhouse ($W^2$), and Jeffrey (in his copy of the letter).

The two principal texts—one represented by the letter holograph and the other by Brown's and Woodhouse's MSS—differ substantively in heading (the letter text has none), 1, 18, and 22. In transcribing the letter Jeffrey changed "cheery" to "cherry" in 22 and "hoarse" to "brave" in 23. Milnes printed the stanzas as part of the letter from a now lost amanuensis' copy of Jeffrey's MS. The *1848* text has Jeffrey's readings in 22 and 23 and further substantive corruptions (an emendation and a misreading) in 3–4 and 13.

Unfortunately both the status of the letter holograph (draft vs. fair copy) and the source(s) of Brown's and Woodhouse's MSS are uncertain. The wording of Keats's introductory remark in the letter ("I shall amuse myself . . . a little," *Letters,* II, 89) suggests that his text there is the original draft, but except in 13 the lines are cleanly written out and look much more like fair copy than draft text (especially when we consider that Keats was working in the demanding form of the Spenserian stanza). Brown almost certainly made his transcript from a now lost holograph rather than from the letter text (we have no Brown transcripts of *Why did I laugh tonight* and *When they were come unto the Faery's court,* which are also in the same letter), but whether he copied a version earlier or later than that of the letter is not known. If the letter text is the original draft, then Brown's version (if his variants are authoritative) represents a lost revised MS. But if the letter text is a fair copy, then it is possible that both the letter and Brown's MS derive from a single lost source (in which case either Keats or Brown or both would have made changes in the process of copying), and also possible that the letter and Brown's MS derive from different sources (the letter from a lost draft and the transcript from a lost revised MS, or vice versa).

Woodhouse took his date from Brown ("1819 C.B."), and could have taken his text as well, which does not differ substantively from Brown's, but also could have copied the same lost holograph from which Brown worked. The situation here concerning Woodhouse's source is the same as that for seven other poems of the spring of 1819—*As Hermes once, La Belle Dame, Song of Four Fairies, Sonnet to Sleep,* the two sonnets *On Fame,* and *If by dull rhymes.* In each of the eight cases, regardless of what other authoritative sources are extant, we have a Brown transcript certainly or very probably deriving from a lost holograph and a $W^2$ transcript that (apart from headings, the few alterations made subsequently in one or the other transcript, and errors by Woodhouse in *Song of Four Fairies* 97, 98) is substantively the same as Brown's. The question of Woodhouse's sources is important because, if Woodhouse did copy the same lost holographs that Brown transcribed, then his texts confirm Brown's distinctive readings as authoritative (where otherwise we might take them to be Brown's errors or independent alterations). The question cannot be answered definitively, but Woodhouse's penciling above a word in Brown's MS of *Sonnet to Sleep* and certain peculiarities in the $W^2$ texts of *Song of Four Fairies* 16 and 98 and the second sonnet *On Fame* 5 and 12 (see Textual Notes to the three poems) suggest that Woodhouse took his copies of these from lost holographs; extrapolating from the three examples, the present editor has supposed that the $W^2$ texts of all eight poems derive from holographs rather than from Brown's MSS.

The above is regrettably inconclusive, and still does not solve the problem of which of the two principal texts of the poem at hand is the later or more considered. The present text is arbitrarily based on Brown's MS.

*Bright star, would I were stedfast as thou art*

Written in 1819 (so dated in Brown's transcript; a more precise dating is not possible, though scholars have vigorously debated in favor of various specific months and even specific days between October 1818 and the end of 1819). First published in *PDWJ,* 27 September 1838, and then in the *Union Magazine,* 1 (February 1846), 156, and *1848,* II, 306. The three extant MSS are a holograph fair copy written opposite the beginning of *A Lover's Complaint* in the 1806 *Poetical Works of William Shakespeare* at Keats House, Hampstead, and transcripts by Brown and Fanny Brawne.

The two principal versions of this poem—the earlier represented by Brown's MS (from a now lost holograph, possibly the original draft) and the later by Keats's copy in the Shakespeare volume and Fanny Brawne's MS—differ significantly in 2, 3, 4, 5 (probably a copying error in Brown's MS), 10, 11, 13, and 14. Keats made the extant holograph copy aboard ship on his way to Italy (if we can believe Severn's well-known account), at the end of September or the beginning of October 1820. Fanny Brawne, whose text agrees throughout with the fair copy, most likely made her transcript from this MS after Keats's death, though it is also possible that she copied another holograph now unknown (Sharp, p. 55, seems to say that Severn got another copy from Keats besides the one in the Shakespeare volume). The *PDWJ* version derives from Brown's MS, and the *Union Magazine* printed a facsimile of the extant holograph, sent in by Severn. The *1848* text (headed "Keats's Last Sonnet") is also based on the extant holograph, but whether from a copy by Severn, the *Union Magazine*'s facsimile, or examination of the MS itself is not certain. Milnes introduced a substantive change (presumably to improve the rhyme) in 11, and in a footnote printed the final line of Brown's text as "Another reading."

The present text is based on the extant holograph.

7 mask] See Textual Note to *Endymion* IV.558.

*Hyperion*

Begun in the closing months of 1818 (perhaps by 27 October and certainly by 18 December—*Letters,* I, 387, II, 12) and abandoned in or before April 1819 (Woodhouse copied the poem as we now have it on 20 April, and about the same time noted in his interleaved *1818,* opposite *Endymion* IV.774, "*April 1819.* K. lent me the Fragment here alluded to for perusal—It contains 2 books & ½. . . . He said he was dissatisfied with what he had done of it; and should not complete it"; though we do not usually think of *Hyperion* as a work of the spring of 1819, Keats's references in the letters from 22 December 1818 to the following 8 March are mainly comments on *not* writing it—see *Letters,* II, 14–15, 18, 21, 42, 62—and it is therefore possible that he composed some sizable portion of it between the middle of March and the middle of April). First published in *1820,* pp. 143–199.

The three principal MSS are a holograph draft (complete in the British Library except for the lower third of fol. 14, containing II.116–127, which is in the Morgan Library, and a small strip cut away from the bottom of fol. 19, containing II.292–293, which is now lost), a transcript by Woodhouse ($W^2$), and a transcript by two of his clerks ($W^1$, the first clerk copying the bulk of the poem, the second writing III.51–76—the lower five-sixths of $W^1$ p. 93—perhaps while the first clerk took a short break, and Woodhouse going over and correcting the whole). In addition to these, we have Woodhouse's extracts, probably taken from $W^2$, of II.1–18, 32–35, 39–55, 64–72 at the end of his interleaved *1818* (three unique readings there—"venom" for "poison" in 48, "floor" for "flint" in 50, "form" for "forms" in 72—are Woodhouse's own changes or errors and have no textual significance). The "copy of Hyperion" that E. L. Lushington wrote to Milnes about in 1856 (*KC,* II, 316–317) has not been identified; it seems unlikely that it was any of the extant MSS of either *Hyperion* or *The Fall of Hyperion.*

Though various writers have taken the extant holograph to be a fair copy or "second draft" (e.g., de Selincourt, *Hyperion: A Facsimile,* Oxford, 1905, p. 5; Ridley, p. 67; Ward, p. 430, n. 8), Woodhouse described it as "the original & only copy . . . composed & written down at once as it now stands" (see the next paragraph). He could have been mistaken, of course, but his description sounds like information received from the poet himself, and in general the MS is no more cleanly written than the earliest draft pages of *Otho the Great,* another long work that is also in blank verse. It seems best to accept Woodhouse's statement that the MS we have is the only holograph of the poem that ever existed, and therefore is the original draft.

Woodhouse copied the draft in $W^2$, adding after the last line "Thus the M.S. copy Ends," and below this "Copied 20 Ap[l] 1819 from J.K's Manuscript written in 1818/9" and "The Copy from which I took the above was the original & only copy—The alterations are noted in the margin—With the exception of these, it was composed & written down at once as it now stands." $W^2$ is a very painstaking copy, with many notes in the margins and on the opposite versos recording canceled readings in the draft. Woodhouse's clerks made the $W^1$ transcript from $W^2$. There is evidence (see the note to II.63, below) that Woodhouse went through the draft again on a later occasion, correcting copying errors in both $W^2$ and $W^1$ in the process. The corrected $W^1$ was printer's copy for *1820.*

If we set aside Keats's probable or certain slips of the pen in the draft (those in I.16, 147, 306, II.108, 156, 237, 260, III.100 are included in the apparatus), two grammatical errors (II.123, 188), and three places where he deleted words without replacing them (II.265, III.38, 47), *1820* differs substantively from the draft text in forty-three lines and omits nine other lines altogether. In I.9, 46, 81, 236, 275, 283, 345, II.1, 21, 68, 91, 128, 231, 232, 351, III.58, 102, 119 *1820* has readings (in most instances via $W^1$, in some others perhaps via proofreading against $W^2$) that seem to originate with Woodhouse's text and pencilings in $W^2$. In I.6, 76, 189, 200, 217, II.123, 134, 310 *1820* has readings that first appear in the clerks' text and Woodhouse's alterations and pencilings in $W^1$ (the wording in I.6 and substantive punctuation in II.310 are copying errors by the first clerk). In I.30, 48, 65, 116, 156, 199, 209, 268, II.43, 60, 124, 167, 312, 313, III.49, 81, 126 *1820* has readings that do not appear earlier in any MS. Four lines of draft text following I.21, two half-lines at I.102, and three lines following III.125 were all first deleted in $W^1$, and possibly by Taylor rather than Woodhouse (though the lines following I.21 are also bracketed in pencil in $W^2$); the MSS' line following I.205 was first omitted in the printed text. *1820*'s paragraph divisions after I.71, 134, 149, II.166, 243, 299 first appear in $W^2$; that after II.100 is new in *1820.*

As with the other long poems in *1820,* the extent of Keats's hand and/or approval in the printed text of *Hyperion* cannot be determined. As the *1820* Advertisement makes clear (see Appendix III), Keats did not want the fragment included in the volume: "it was printed at [the publishers'] particular request, and contrary to the wish of the author." Woodhouse's draft of the Advertisement (*KC,* I, 115–116) adds that "the Author's health is not at pres[t] such as to enable him to make any corrections" (i.e., revisions), but neither his statement nor the printed Advertisement can be taken to mean that Keats did not read proofs and alter the poem while it was being printed. There is no evidence that he saw either of the transcripts, but *1820* restores the text of the draft, where it had been changed in $W^2$ or $W^1$, in I.332, II.63, 139, 210 (substantive punctuation), 327, III.27, 132. If, as seems likely, Keats was responsible for these corrections, he could also have authored some or all of the new readings in *1820* and could have approved the various other changes as well. Because of our uncertainty in the matter, the present text, based on *1820,* contains substantive emendations only in I.6 and II.310. $W^2$ and $W^1$, though derivative texts, are included in the apparatus in order to show where the changes subsequent to the draft in each case occurred. A list of corresponding passages in *The Fall of Hyperion* is given in the Textual Note to I.294 of the later fragment.

I.6 above] The clerk's "about" in $W^1$ is a copying error based on the preceding line.

I.9 one . . . grass] So also *The Fall of Hyperion* I.313. Woodhouse's pencil interlineation in $W^2$ could have been made from *1820* but more likely was entered (from his transcript of *The Fall*) before *1820* was set in type. Other *1820* readings apparently based on *The Fall* occur in I.76, 189, 200, 217.

I.16 stray'd] The draft's "stay'd" is probably a slip of the pen rather than a substantive variant. *The Fall* I.321, however, has "rested" (which is closer in meaning to "stay'd"), and for this reason Ridley, p. 275, suggests that "stay'd" is what Keats meant. It may be that Keats intended "stray'd" when he wrote *Hyperion* but then, in revising the line in *The Fall,* changed his meaning (and chose "rested") on the basis of his own miswritten "stay'd." We do not know Woodhouse's source or authority for the alteration in $W^2$ (which was made after the clerk copied the line in $W^1$).

I.46 She . . . ear] Woodhouse penciled an x beside this line in Keats's draft and marked the draft text to read "and to the level of his hollow ear" (suggesting the omission of "She laid"), but also copied the full hexameter line in $W^2$. He later underscored "hollow" in pencil in $W^2$ and probably was responsible for the deletion of the word in $W^1$.

I.48 tone] In the margin of his transcript of *The Fall* (beside I.350) Woodhouse penciled "q tone," and his quotation of the line in a letter to Taylor of 31 August 1819 has "tone" rather than "tune" (*Letters,* II, 150); it seems probable that he was responsible for the *1820* reading.

I.67 has] Woodhouse underscored this word in pencil in Keats's draft and queried "have?" in the margin.

I.76 gradual] So also *The Fall* I.375 (see the note to I.9, above). The rough penciling in $W^1$ is probably Woodhouse's but cannot be certainly identified.

I.81 falling] It is not clear why Woodhouse wrote "falling" in $W^2$. Garrod emends to restore the draft's "fallen."

I.126 Yes] The draft reading is not perfectly certain (it may be "Aye" written over "⟨Yes⟩"). In any case, since $W^1$ has "Yes," Woodhouse must have altered $W^2$ after the clerk copied the line.

I.156 that . . . the] In recording the draft's canceled text on the opposite verso in $W^2$ ("form[y]—which *to them gave* like mist") Woodhouse added the explanation "i.e. yielded." We may suppose that the *1820* wording owes something to this gloss.

I.189 Savour of poisonous] So also *The Fall* II.33 (see the note to I.9, above).

I.190 And so] Woodhouse underscored these words in pencil in $W^1$ and suggested "Wherefore" on the opposite verso.

I.200 earthquakes . . . and] So also *The Fall* II.44 (see the note to I.9, above).

I.205 Then] Woodhouse wrote "There" in $W^2$ but, uncertain about Keats's word in the draft, added "or q. *then*" in the margin; the clerk apparently copied "There" in $W^1$, but then he or Woodhouse changed the word by erasure to "Then."

I.205/206 (*apparatus*) Most . . . Lute] There are penciled x's beside both this line and 209 in $W^1$ calling attention to the repetition of the rose simile. Presumably *1820*'s substitution of "And" for "Yes" in 209 was made in conjunction with the omission of this line following 205.

I.217 wings] So also *The Fall* II.61. The penciled addition in $W^1$ was made by the same hand that marked I.76 (see above).

I.268 Suddenly . . . streams.] There is a penciled x beside this line in $W^1$, questioning either the wording or the punctuation (perhaps both, since both were changed).

I.277–280 Up . . . centuries:] Woodhouse marked these lines with a pencil stroke in the margin of $W^1$ and wrote "qy" beside them.

I.283 Two] The original 283 in the draft was a full pentameter: "Made sweet-shap'd lightning: Wings this splendent orb" (see apparatus for 271–283 and 283). Though "Two" does not appear here in Keats's hand, the word was probably in his mind when he revised the line, for both the first altered version of the original ("Made sweet-shap'd light: Wings this splendent orb") and the final revised version partly written opposite ("Their wisdom long since fled.—Wings this orb") are a syllable short. Woodhouse inserted "2" in pencil before "Wings" in the revised line in the draft, and also added "Two" above the line in $W^2$; the clerk similarly wrote the word above the line in $W^1$.

I.285 at . . . approach] The interlined "came near" above "approach" in the draft apparently represents the beginning of a revision to read "as the God came near," but Keats did not change "at" or "God's" (which he wrote "Gods") and did not cancel "approach." Woodhouse recorded this intention in $W^2$, interlining "⟨as⟩" above "at" and "⟨came near⟩" above "approach" and underscoring the "'s" in "God's."

I.319–320 Of . . . Goddesses] Woodhouse had trouble with the syntax of these lines. He penciled parentheses around "new-form'd" in $W^2$, and underscored the second, third, and fourth words of both 319 and 320 in pencil in $W^1$, adding "q[y]" beside 320 and suggesting a partial revision on the opposite verso:

"q^y Of these new formd thou art one / Of these also are thy brethren & the Goddesses."

I.323 tumbled] The draft has "tumbled" interlined above a deleted word that can be read as both "tumled" and "hurrled." Woodhouse, recording the original word beside the line in $W^2$, chose "hurled."

I.345 murmur] There is a penciled x beside this line in $W^1$, but it is not clear whether it questions "murmur" before Woodhouse added the "s" there or the altered "murmurs" afterward.

II.1 beat] On the opposite verso in $W^2$ Woodhouse noted his opinion that "beat" was "a better word" than Keats's revised "move" in the draft, and the clerk copied "beat" in $W^1$ (perhaps initially leaving a blank space for the word, as he clearly did for "den" in 5, entering the word later, probably after Woodhouse told him which to choose).

II.21 in] Presumably Woodhouse restored Keats's "of" in $W^2$ after the clerk copied "in" in $W^1$.

II.28 boiling . . . of] Woodhouse's transposition in $W^2$ (which is based on a misreading of Keats's revision in the draft) must have been marked after the clerk copied the line in $W^1$. See the note to II.63, below.

II.36 When] Both $W^2$ and $W^1$ have "When" made out of "Where." Woodhouse noted in pencil on the opposite verso in $W^1$, "I think it sh^d be Where."

II.60 sacred] There is a penciled "sacred" beside this line in $W^1$, but this is in a later hand and was entered from some printed source.

II.63 Shed] The "h" is badly formed in Keats's draft, and the word could be taken to be "Sled." Both Woodhouse and the clerk first wrote "Shed," and then Woodhouse altered the word to "Sled" in the two transcripts. This is one of a dozen or more instances (most of them omitted from the apparatus) in which Woodhouse seems to have corrected—here, miscorrected—both $W^2$ and $W^1$ on the basis of a fresh collation of the draft. Some or all of his changes in $W^2$ in I.126, II.21, 28, and 139 (see the notes above and below) may also have been made on this later occasion.

II.108 mightiness] The draft reading (which Woodhouse and the clerk represent as "mightliness") could as easily be "mighttiness," and in any case "mightliness" is not recognized by the *OED*. This and the preceding and following lines (107–109) are marked in pencil in the margin of $W^2$.

II.128 vibrating] Woodhouse wrote "vibrating" in $W^2$ (recording the draft's "vibrated" on the opposite verso), and the clerk copied "vibrating" in $W^1$. Woodhouse then altered the $W^1$ reading to "vibrated" but also penciled a question mark in the margin and wrote "ing" above the corrected "ed." It is not known who (possibly the printer) made the final choice of "vibrating."

II.133–134 Studied . . . bright] The single word "footstool" (used in 138) appears in the margin of Keats's draft beside these lines.

II.139 sign] Presumably Woodhouse deleted "the" in $W^2$ after the clerk copied "the sign" in $W^1$.

II.156 spurn'd] As Woodhouse noted of the draft reading in $W^2$, "originally spur'd (by mistake)."

II.292 all] $W^2$ has "all" interlined above "⟨the⟩," possibly representing an alteration in the missing draft text.

II.310 foolish, Giant-Gods] The emendation of punctuation here (following H. B. Forman, O.S.A. ed.) is justified by the sense, in which "over-wise" (309) refers to Oceanus' speech (173–243) and "over-foolish" (310) to Clymene's (252–299). Keats's mark between "Giant" and "Gods" in the draft can be interpreted as either a hyphen or a dash, but is the same as that (in the same phrase) in the tenth line of the canceled passage following II.356.

II.366 saw] Woodhouse underscored this word in pencil in Keats's draft and queried "q caught" in the margin.

III.27 hazels] Keats's word in the draft is apparently "Hzle's" but can also be read as "Hyle's." Woodhouse wrote "Hyle's" in $W^2$, taking it to be a place-name and tentatively explaining on the opposite verso, "q. And Hyle's (olive trees, & poplars, & Palms & beech Trees) thick & dark stemm'd &c." He later added the better explanation: "N.B. K, it seems, meant to write *hazles.*"

III.77–79 Who . . . then,] The three lines are marked in pencil in the margin of $W^2$.

III.102 silvery] Presumably Woodhouse altered "silverly" to "silvery" in $W^2$ after the clerk copied "silverly" in $W^1$.

III.125/126 (*apparatus*) ⟨Roseate . . . severe;—] As a suggested revision for the first two and a half uncanceled lines ("Into . . . sob"), Woodhouse penciled in the blank space after the last line of the poem in Keats's draft, "Into a hue more roseate ⟨as⟩ than a Nymph's / By a warm kiss surprized" (cf. III.22).

III.126 Most like the] Woodhouse underscored "More like the" in $W^2$ and noted in the margin, ostensibly from Keats's draft, "originally like a dread," but there is no sign of this reading in the holograph MS. The change to "Most" in *1820* (perhaps influenced by Woodhouse's penciled "And" in $W^1$) was made in conjunction with the omission of the three lines following 125.

III.132 Kept] Woodhouse's "Keep" is a misreading of the draft's "Keept," in which, however, the "t" is written over rather than after the "p."

III.135–136 from . . . Celestial] In $W^1$ Woodhouse added "⟨he was a god!⟩" (based on the deleted wording in the draft, which he had miscopied in $W^2$) in pencil beneath "from all his limbs," and Taylor attempted, also in pencil, to complete the sentence after "Celestial": "Glory ⟨broke.⟩ dawn'd." Apparently the last two lines in Taylor's version were to read "Apollo shriek'd—And lo from all his limbs / Celestial glory dawn'd. He was a god!" but then the original "from all his limbs / Celestial" was separately marked off in pencil, and this is what the printer set in type. There are no asterisks following the last word in any of the MSS.

### *La Belle Dame sans Merci*

Written on 21 or 28 April 1819 (Keats drafted the poem in his spring 1819 journal letter to George and Georgiana on a "Wednesday Evening"—*Letters,* II, 95; the two preceding pages in Rollins' edition were written on 21 April, but the next firm date in the letter, coming ten pages later on II, 104, is "Friday—April 30," and consequently this "Wednesday Evening," since there is no earlier "Wednesday Morning" for it to relate to, could equally well be 21 or 28 April; Rollins assigns the entire span to 21 April, with a hint of uncertainty in the queried "April 20?" for "Yesterday" on II, 104, but it seems likely that there were several breaks in the writing and, whatever the date of the present poem, that *Song of Four Fairies* and the discussion of "The vale of Soul-making" in the same letter were written on two separate later occasions). First published in the *Indicator,* 10 May 1820, p. 248 (with the signature "Caviare"), and then in *Arcturus,* 3 (January 1842), 158–159, and *1848,* II, 268–270.

The four extant MSS are the holograph draft in Keats's journal letter of 14 February–3 May 1819 (MS at Harvard), a transcript by Brown, and two transcripts by Woodhouse ($W^2$, $W^1$). Brown's MS and $W^2$, which are substantively identical throughout, add a subtitle and stanza numbers not in the letter draft and differ slightly from the draft's wording in 36 and 40. We have no certain information about Brown's or Woodhouse's source, but may suppose that Brown copied a now lost holograph fair copy and that Woodhouse took his $W^2$ text independently from the same lost MS (see Textual Note to *Character of C. B.*) and then made $W^1$ (with a slip of the pen, "a" for "her" in 17) from $W^2$. Brown's MS was printer's copy for *1848.*

The *Indicator* version, for which copy was presumably supplied by Keats himself, agrees with the letter draft against the transcripts in the absence of subtitle and stanza numbers and in the wording of 36; agrees with the transcripts against the draft in 40; and varies substantively from the extant MSS in 1, 3, 5, 11, 23, 30, 31, 32, 33, 39, 41, 44, and in the transposition of the fifth and sixth stanzas. Such extensive changes are difficult to explain, and some scholars have been tempted to attribute some or all of them to Hunt's influence or even to his actual editing of the poem. In 1845 Jeffrey had in his possession a holograph beginning "Ah what can ail thee, wretched wight" (*KC,* II, 120); this agreement with the *Indicator*'s first line does not mean that Jeffrey's holograph had the *Indicator* readings throughout, or that Hunt had no influence in the alterations, but it does seem to suggest (unless Jeffrey simply quoted the first line of the printed text for convenience) that Keats had a hand in some version differing from those represented by the extant MSS. *Arcturus,* a magazine published in New York, reprinted the poem from the *Indicator.*

The present text is based on Brown's MS. The frequency with which unique readings appear elsewhere in Keats's texts published by Hunt and other periodical editors suggests that the *Indicator* version may be less reliably authoritative than any of the extant MSS. If Brown and Woodhouse did copy the same lost holograph independently (as has been supposed above), then their texts probably should be taken to represent a more considered version than the draft. The choice of Brown's MS over $W^2$ is purely arbitrary.

### *Song of Four Fairies*

Written toward the end of April 1819 (drafted in the spring 1819 journal letter to George and Georgiana Keats after the composition of *La Belle Dame* and before 30 April—*Letters,* II, 97–100, and see Textual Note to the preceding poem). First published in *1848,* II, 271–275. The four extant MSS are the holograph draft in Keats's journal letter of 14 February–3 May 1819 (MS at Harvard), a holograph fair copy (also at Harvard), and transcripts by Brown and Woodhouse ($W^2$).

The three states of text for this poem are that of the letter draft, that of

Brown's and Woodhouse's MSS, and that of the extant holograph fair copy. Brown's MS differs substantively from the letter draft in heading, 19, 23, 29, 30, 32, 44, 46, 55, 71, 82, 89, 91 s.p., and 93 (the letter's variants in 82 and 89 are inadvertent omissions by Keats). The $W^2$ text as originally written agreed with Brown in all these places and further varied in 97 and 98. Brown took his text from some now lost revised holograph, and Woodhouse apparently also copied the same lost MS (see the notes to 16 and 98, below). Brown's MS was printer's copy for *1848*.

The extant holograph fair copy, which Keats wrote out either from the lost MS that Brown and Woodhouse copied or, more probably, from Brown's transcript, shows further revisions in 9, 26, 47, 60, and 77, and a return to draft readings in 44, 71, and 93. Woodhouse subsequently made various changes in $W^2$ from this MS (altering 9, 26, 44, 47, 77, 93, 97, 98—but not 60—to the readings of the fair copy and interlining the fair copy's "is" above "are," which he did not delete, in 71), and added an important note at the end of his transcript: "Corrected, by Keats's copy for the press." His note tells us that the poem was once intended for inclusion in *1820,* and thus we have evidence that at least some of the printer's copy for the shorter pieces in the volume was in Keats's hand. Keats's foliation of the four leaves, "8" through "11," suggests that the poem would have had an early position among those shorter pieces.

The present text is based on the holograph fair copy. Keats's abbreviated speech prefixes, written in the left margin (as they are also in Brown's and Woodhouse's MSS and in 1–4 only of the letter draft), have been expanded and centered above the lines, and a small substantive change has been introduced in the speech prefix for 91. The $W^2$ readings in the apparatus represent Woodhouse's original text; his corrections from the fair copy have been ignored there.

16 wrought] Both Brown and Woodhouse first wrote "wrangle," which is what the word—actually "wraugh" or "wrough"—looks like in the letter draft, and then corrected it to "wrought" (Brown probably immediately, at the time he was making his transcript, and Woodhouse perhaps later, when he entered corrections from the holograph fair copy). The deleted reading in $W^2$ has some bearing on the question of whether Woodhouse made his transcript from Brown's MS or from the same MS that Brown copied (see Textual Note to *Character of C. B.*). Woodhouse could not have taken $W^2$ from the letter, and it is highly unlikely that he would have reproduced Brown's error and correction. The assumption therefore is that Keats also wrote "wraugh" or "wrough" looking like "wrangle" in his lost MS made after the draft, and that both Brown and Woodhouse misread the word independently from this source.

16–18 bitumen$_\wedge$ . . . roof, . . . aloof;] So punctuated in the holograph fair copy. Brown's MS and $W^2$ have a full stop at the end of 16 and a comma at the end of 17 but differ in their marks at the end of 18 (a comma in Brown, which makes sense with his punctuation of 16 and 17, and a full stop in $W^2$, which leaves 17–18 as a sentence fragment). The letter draft has no punctuation in 16–18.

47 Of . . . sun.] In $W^2$ Woodhouse left a space after this line in which he later penciled a rhyming line of his own devising, "When his arched course is run," with an alternative "done" added above the last word.

98 when] So the holograph fair copy and Brown's MS. Since Keats's "when" and "where" are frequently undistinguishable from one another, Woodhouse's "where" (later corrected to "when") is some further slight evidence of his working independently from a lost holograph rather than copying Brown's MS.

*Sonnet to Sleep*

Written probably toward the end of April 1819 (the chronological relationships of this and the next four poems, all of which Keats included in his spring 1819 journal letter to George and Georgiana on or after 30 April, are somewhat in question; presumably the present poem is one of the sonnets then "lately written," but, if so, Keats never did copy any of the "old sins" that he refers to at the beginning of the 30 April section—*Letters,* II, 104–105). First published in *PDWJ,* 11 October 1838, and then in *1848,* II, 298. The seven extant MSS are the holograph draft written on a flyleaf of Volume II of the 1807 *Paradise Lost* that Keats gave to Mrs. Dilke (Keats House, Hampstead), a holograph fair copy in his journal letter of 14 February–3 May 1819 (MS at Harvard), a holograph fair copy signed and dated June 1820 that was once in a lady's album subsequently owned by Sir John Bowring (Berg Collection, New York Public Library), and transcripts by Brown, Dilke, and Woodhouse (two copies, $W^2$ and $W^1$).

The original draft is a twelve-line version that Keats abandoned without finishing (he originally rhymed the eleventh line with the ninth, then deleted the last two words of the eleventh to make it rhyme with the twelfth, but did not replace the two missing syllables in the thus shortened eleventh line and left the tenth line unrhymed). The two authoritative states following the draft are that represented by Keats's letter copy, Brown's MS, and Woodhouse's initial text in $W^2$ (which agree in showing substantive alterations from the draft in 4 and 6 and the expansion of the draft's last five lines into a revised 8–14) and that of Keats's album copy in the Berg Collection (which shows further changes in 8, 11, and 12).

A single now lost holograph (in Keats's "book"—*Letters,* II, 104) was pretty clearly the source of Keats's letter copy and both Brown's MS and $W^2$ as well (see Textual Note to *Character of C. B.* for discussion of Woodhouse's sources). The rest of the texts derive from one or the other of these two transcripts. Brown's MS was the source of Dilke's transcript (an exact copy in every detail), was the basis of the *PDWJ* version (which has two nonauthoritative variants, "head" for "bed" in 8 and "rise"—possibly to rhyme with "eyes" and "charities"—in 9), and was printer's copy for *1848.* Woodhouse transcribed $W^1$ from $W^2$, and Keats when he made his album copy in June 1820 also wrote out the poem from $W^2$. The evidence for this last fact and the rather complicated details of two significant changes in the course of transmission are given in the notes to 8 and 11 below.

Each of four MSS—Keats's letter copy, Brown's MS, $W^2$ as originally written, and Keats's album copy in the Berg Collection—has a claim to be the basis for a standard text. Because album-copying constitutes publication of a sort, the present text is based on the Berg MS.

4 Enshaded] Woodhouse queried "q enshr*ou*ded" in pencil on the opposite verso in $W^2$.

8 lulling] Keats in his letter, Brown, and Woodhouse in $W^2$ all copied "dewy" from the lost holograph source. The change to "lulling," which Keats substituted in the margin of $W^2$ and at the same time incorporated into his album copy, is explained by Woodhouse in a note opposite the line in $W^2$: "This word '*lulling*' is in K's handwriting. The correction was made when he borrowed this book to select a small poem to write in an Album, intended to consist of original Poetry, for a lady." (Clearly the Berg MS is the album copy in question. Puttick and Simpson's sale catalogue for 9 May 1929 describes both this MS and the album from which it has been removed.) At some later time, when he was going through Brown's MSS, Woodhouse penciled "lulling" above "dewy" in Brown's transcript, and both the *PDWJ* and *1848* texts have "lulling" from this interlineation. Woodhouse's penciling in Brown's MS, since it shows that he already possessed a text of the poem before he saw Brown's MS, is one more piece of evidence that he made his texts of this and several other spring 1819 poems independently of Brown's transcripts.

11 hoards] Keats in his letter, Brown, and Woodhouse in $W^2$ all copied "lords." The new word "hoards" first appears as a pencil alteration by Woodhouse in $W^2$. Because $W^1$, made from $W^2$, has "hoards" here but also "dewy" in 8 (with no sign of the change to "lulling"), it is clear that Woodhouse substituted "hoards" in $W^2$ and then copied it into $W^1$ before Keats saw $W^2$ and revised "dewy" to "lulling." This change to "hoards," therefore, which Keats accepted when he wrote out the album copy, originated with Woodhouse.

12 burrowing] Critics sometimes defend the letter copy's "borrowing" on the basis of its metaphorical connection with "hoards" in the preceding line. But "hoards" is a later change (see just above), and the letter's "borrowing" is almost certainly just a slip of the pen.

### *Ode to Psyche*

Written probably toward the end of April 1819 ("the last I have written," Keats says on or shortly after 30 April—*Letters,* II, 105; if he copied the poem in his journal letter on 30 April then his remark overlooks the sonnets *On Fame* composed on that day, but if the line drawn across the page on II, 105, marks the beginning of a new section on a later date then possibly the ode belongs after the next two poems). First published in *1820,* pp. 117–121. The four extant MSS are a holograph draft in the Morgan Library, a holograph fair copy in Keats's journal letter of 14 February–3 May 1819 (MS at Harvard), and transcripts by Brown and Woodhouse ($W^2$).

According to a note in $W^2$ (see below), Keats gave a MS of the poem to J. H. Reynolds on 4 May 1819. This has to be the Morgan draft, which remained with Reynolds and his relatives and their descendants until 1901, when it was sold at Sotheby's; Reynolds lent it to Milnes in 1847 as "the *original*" MS (*KC,* II, 227). There ought to be no question about its chronological priority over the letter copy, which is straightforwardly written out and incorporates into its text among other things two words in 14 that Keats had added tentatively in the margin of the Morgan MS. The letter copy also shows changes in 28 and 30 and omits the paragraph or stanza division between 49 and 50; its distinctive readings in 6 and

24 appear to be copying errors, and the alterations in 57 and 62 may be taken as instances in which Keats tried out revisions and then returned to his original wording.

Brown probably copied the Morgan draft, from which his transcript varies significantly only in 15. Keats later read over this transcript, making a substantive change in 10 and correcting Brown's omission of a word in 43. Woodhouse's source is less easily determined. His note at the end of the text, "Given by J.K. to J.H.R. 4 May 1819," might suggest that he copied the Morgan draft, but the substantive variants in his transcript rule out this possibility. $W^2$ differs from the draft in 13, 14, and 67, and Woodhouse did not record, as he almost surely would have, had he seen the draft, the various cancellations and revisions in the draft, including eight changes of "nor" to "no" in 32 and 34; the one hint of the draft—a notation in the margin of $W^2$ that corresponds to an alternative reading for 14 in the draft—must have come via an intervening source: the draft reads "silver-white," with "freckle pink" in the margin, while $W^2$ has "freckled, pink" in its text and the note "originally freckle" in the margin. The most likely explanation is that Woodhouse transcribed not a holograph but a copy of the Morgan draft made (and slightly revised in the process) by Reynolds.

Subsequently, above the lines and in the margins of $W^2$, Woodhouse penciled *1820* readings for 14 ("silver white"), 17, 30, 44, and 67; those in 14, 17, and 67 could have been taken from Brown's MS, which Woodhouse undoubtedly saw (he noted Brown's lowercase "s" in "syrian" in 14 and Brown's initial error in 57 as variants in the same pencil), but that in 30 occurs earlier only in the letter copy (which Woodhouse did not see) and that in 44 is an otherwise new reading in *1820*. Possibly Woodhouse entered these variants after *1820* was published, but he did not notice other readings in 14 ("Tyrian") and 36 that also first appeared in *1820*, and so the question of his source for the variants (and his possible responsibility for *1820*'s 44) has to be left unsettled. The *1820* text has Brown's 17, the letter copy's 30, and new readings not in any MS (apart from Woodhouse's pencilings just mentioned) in 14, 36, and 44.

The present text is based on *1820*. Brown's and Woodhouse's transcripts (but not Woodhouse's pencilings) are included in the apparatus on the chance that one or more of their variant readings may be authoritative.

13 'Mid . . . ] *1820* begins a new page with this line, but H. B. Forman's introduction of a paragraph or stanza division between 12 and 13 (1883 ed., repeated in many later texts taken from Forman) is not justified by any of the MSS.

17 bade] The *OED* does not recognize "bade" (in Brown's MS and *1820*) as a past participle form, and Garrod emends to the reading of the two extant holographs ("bid"). In $W^2$ Woodhouse recorded the variant "bade" above his original "bid" and added a punning "malè" in pencil in the margin.

### *On Fame ("Fame, like a wayward girl")*

Written on 30 April 1819 ("just written" before Keats copied the poem under that date in his spring 1819 journal letter to George and Georgiana—*Letters,* II, 104). First published in the *Ladies' Companion,* 7 (August 1837), 186, and then in the *Ladies' Pocket Magazine,* Part I (1838), p. 228, the *Odd Fellow,* 8 January 1842, and *1848,* II, 299. The six extant MSS are the holograph fair copy in Keats's journal letter of 14 February–3 May 1819 (MS at Harvard) and transcripts by Brown, Dilke, Woodhouse (two copies, $W^2$ and $W^1$), and Payne. There are no significant differences among the MSS except for the transposition of the second and third words of 12 in the letter copy and Payne's MS.

Brown transcribed the poem (just after Keats wrote it) from the same source that Keats copied in his letter, a now lost holograph in Keats's "book" (*Letters,* II, 104), and Dilke took his text from Brown's MS. Woodhouse probably copied the same lost holograph that Brown worked from (see Textual Note to *Character of C. B.*) and presumably made $W^1$ from $W^2$. Payne's MS, which he sent Milnes in 1847, derives from a now lost copy that George Keats had written out for him from the letter (*KC,* II, 224). This same George Keats copy was the basis of the text included in Payne's article in the *Ladies' Companion*; the *Ladies' Pocket Magazine* reprinted the poem (with Payne's article) from the *Ladies' Companion,* and the *Odd Fellow* reprinted it (with an erroneous "love-sick" for "lovelorn" in 12) from one or the other of these magazines. Brown's MS was printer's copy for *1848.*

The letter holograph, Brown's MS, and $W^2$ all have claims to be the basis for a standard text. The present text is arbitrarily based on Brown's MS.

### *On Fame ("How fever'd is the man")*

Written on 30 April 1819 (drafted under that date in the spring 1819 journal letter to George and Georgiana Keats—*Letters,* II, 104). First published in *1848,* II, 300. The four extant MSS are Keats's original draft in his journal letter of 14 February–3 May 1819 (MS at Harvard) and transcripts by Brown, Dilke, and Woodhouse ($W^2$).

Brown's MS as originally written had the same substantive text as the letter draft except in 5 ("itself" for the draft's "herself") and 14 ("for" for "by"). Subsequently Brown altered "itself" to "herself" in 5 and interlineally substituted two new lines for the original 7–8. Dilke copied Brown's MS after these changes were made, and Woodhouse's MS also has (except for a slight difference in heading) the same text as Brown's altered MS. Like Brown's MS, $W^2$ shows "itself" in 5 changed to "herself," and in 12, where Brown had written "chrystal" and later crossed out the "h," Woodhouse began "chr" and then deleted the letters and wrote "crystal"; on the opposite verso of $W^2$ Woodhouse recorded the original text of 7–8 with the comment: "The objection to these lines was, probably, that *itself* was thus made to rhyme to itself—But the author in altering them forgot that he left an allusion in the 12th line to those thus erased."

Taking a hint from Woodhouse's note we can reconstruct the progress of composition and transmission as follows. After drafting the poem in the letter Keats wrote out a now lost fair copy (in his "book"—*Letters,* II, 104) with "itself" in 5 and "for" in 14. Brown then made his transcript from this lost holograph. At some later time (perhaps immediately afterward) Keats changed 5 in his fair copy —to avoid the rhyme "itself"/"itself" in 5 and 7—and then (since "herself"/"itself" was not much of an improvement) rewrote 7–8, again in the fair copy, and

Brown altered his transcript in 5 and 7–8 accordingly. Woodhouse then probably copied this lost holograph fair copy, recording Keats's revision in 5 in his text and the earlier wording of 7–8 on the opposite verso. (Woodhouse could have got the same text with a record of the alterations by copying Brown's MS, but his "⟨chr⟩ crystal" in 12, where the lost holograph fair copy certainly had "chrystal," is some slight evidence that he worked from the lost holograph rather than from Brown's MS; see the discussion of Woodhouse's sources in Textual Note to *Character of C. B.*) Brown's MS was printer's copy for *1848*.

Both Brown's MS and $W^2$ could serve as the basis for a standard text. The present text is arbitrarily based on Brown's MS.

1 the] Rollins prints "that" in his text of the letter draft and says in a note that the word was changed to "the" and then back to "that" (*Letters,* II, 104). But the last two letters of "that" are marked out in the MS and the interlined "e" is probably blurred rather than canceled, and so the simpler sequence of "that" altered to "the" seems the more likely reading. The word may have been changed independently of the other revisions in this line (i.e., Keats may have had an intermediate "How is the Man misled" or "How fever'd is that Man" before reaching the final "How fever'd is the Man").

13 teasing] Rollins' "leasing" is simply "teasing" written with an uncrossed "t."

### *If by dull rhymes our English must be chain'd*

Written toward the end of April or at the beginning of May 1819 (copied out in the spring 1819 journal letter to George and Georgiana Keats on or before 3 May; it is not clear, especially since the end of the letter is known only through Jeffrey's transcript, where the 3 May section actually begins—*Letters,* II, 108–109). First published in the *Plymouth, Devonport, and Stonehouse News,* 15 October 1836, and then in *1848,* II, 303. The six extant MSS are a holograph copy of 1–4 in Keats's journal letter of 14 February–3 May 1819 (MS at Harvard; the holograph of the last sheet of the letter, containing 5–14, is extant but in private ownership and unavailable for examination) and transcripts by Brown, Dilke, Woodhouse (two copies, $W^2$ and $W^1$), and Jeffrey (in his copy of the letter).

There are no substantive differences among the MSS except in heading. We may suppose that—just as with *Sonnet to Sleep* and the first sonnet *On Fame*—Keats's letter copy, Brown's transcript, and $W^2$ all derive from a single now lost holograph (see Textual Note to *Character of C. B.*), and that $W^1$ (headed "On the Sonnet") was made from $W^2$. Dilke copied Brown's MS, and Jeffrey copied the letter holograph. Brown's MS was the basis of the version in the *Plymouth News* (which has an erroneous "will" for "may" in 13), and was printer's copy for *1848*.

Brown's MS and $W^2$ are the most authoritative versions that we have. The present text is arbitrarily based on Brown's MS.

*Heading* If . . . chain'd] Woodhouse added "Irregular" in parentheses beside the heading in both $W^2$ and $W^1$; presumably this is his own comment rather than a part of the title (the same appears beside the $W^1$ heading of *Sonnet to Sleep*).

*Two or three posies*

Written probably on 1 May 1819 (Rollins' conjectural date for the letter to Fanny Keats in which the lines were drafted—see *Letters,* II, 55 n.). First published in Forman (1883), III, 298–299. Keats's draft in his letter to Fanny (MS at Harvard) is our sole authoritative source. Forman, printing the lines as part of the letter, reads "dove" in 27, but the MS clearly has "dove's" (the description in *Texts,* p. 243, based on an imperfect photocopy, is in error).

20 And two Mrs. ——] Beside this line in his letter (referring to the wife of Richard Abbey, the Keats children's guardian) Keats added a cautionary "mum!"

*Ode to a Nightingale*

Written in May 1819 (the date in Brown's now lost transcript, recorded in Dilke's and both of Woodhouse's copies). First published in *Annals of the Fine Arts,* 4 (July 1819), 354–356, and then in *1820,* pp. 107–112. The five extant MSS are the holograph draft in the Fitzwilliam Museum, Cambridge, and transcripts by Woodhouse (two copies, $W^2$ and $W^1$), Dilke, and George Keats. Brown's transcript, from which Woodhouse noted the date and a variant in $W^2$, has disappeared.

There has been considerable debate over whether the Cambridge holograph is Keats's original draft (see, e.g., Robert N. Roth, *PBSA,* 48 [1954], 91–95, also the references there, and Gittings, p. 311 n.). In his "Life" of Keats, Brown's account of how he "rescued" the ode by copying "some scraps of paper . . . four or five in number" (*KC,* II, 65) does not square with the fact that the Cambridge MS consists of two half-sheets, and neither of them "scraps." But the Cambridge MS shows an uncanceled rejected beginning (see the first separate note below) and the first thirty lines written continuously without stanza divisions (after which there are spaces between the stanzas but no stanza numbers), and in general has the appearance of other original drafts by Keats. Gittings' suggestion that Brown was remembering not *Nightingale* but the draft of *Ode on Indolence,* which probably *was* on several scraps of paper, is a good one. (In any event, Brown's lost transcript, which we can reconstruct from Dilke's and George Keats's copies and a note in $W^2$, was not taken from the extant holograph.) Keats gave the Cambridge MS to J. H. Reynolds probably not long after he wrote the poem, and it remained with Reynolds and his relatives and their descendants through the rest of the century; Reynolds lent it to Milnes in 1847, calling it "the *original*" MS (*KC,* II, 227).

The next state of text following the draft is, in general terms, that of the transcripts and *Annals,* though there are substantive differences among these in 24 and 72. Aside from copying errors, Dilke's and George Keats's MSS are substantively the same, and they agree against the Cambridge draft (not counting places —in 1 and 37—where Keats deleted words in the draft without replacing them) in 17, 20, 24, 54, 59, 60, 72, 79 (and possibly also in 50, where the draft reading is uncertain). Dilke took his text from Brown's lost transcript (he has the "CB" flourish at the end), and George Keats almost certainly also copied Brown (as he did for his texts of *Grecian Urn, Melancholy,* and *Autumn*), making his transcript specifically on 15 January 1820 (*Letters,* II, 243). We may suppose that Brown transcribed some revised holograph that Keats subsequently destroyed or gave away (possibly again to Reynolds—see the second paragraph below). Keats, writing out the poem for James Elmes, the editor of *Annals of the Fine Arts,* probably copied either this same lost holograph or else Brown's transcript; in a note to Elmes of 12 June 1819 he mentions having "just received the Book which contains the only copy of the verses in question" (*Letters,* II, 118–120), and since Brown at this time seems regularly to have made his transcripts of poems fairly soon after Keats composed them, one may guess that Keats was referring to Brown's copy rather than to any MS of his own. The *Annals* text varies significantly from the Dilke–George Keats agreement only in 24 (presumably an authoritative return to the draft reading).

$W^2$ is a sort of variorum text of the poem. In its initial state it differed substantively from Brown's text (the Dilke–George Keats agreement) only in 72, where it reads "unto myself," as in the draft, rather than "to my sole self," as in Dilke's and George Keats's MSS. Subsequently Woodhouse noted variants to 74 and 80 from "JHR" (see the notes below), added the date and the variant to 72 from "C.B.," and in a series of red-ink notations, all but one in shorthand, entered variants (in 17, 20, 54, 79) and deleted readings (in 1, 4, 12, 26, 31, 40, 42, 65, 69, 70, 74) from the Cambridge draft. He also, in black ink, changed his original "other's" in 24 to "other" (as in the draft, *Annals,* and *1820*) and on a later occasion, probably after *1820* was published, wrote the *1820* readings above his own text in title, 16, and 49 (in the last instance deleting the original word).

Woodhouse's initial source for $W^2$ is unknown. One possibility is that he originally took the poem from a lost copy made by Reynolds from the same holograph that Brown transcribed. Woodhouse's notes from "JHR" to 74 and 80 are clear evidence that he at least saw a Reynolds copy, and that this copy was virtually identical with the Dilke–George Keats agreement (were it not, Woodhouse would of course have noted other variants). The better likelihood, however, is that he transcribed the same lost holograph that Brown worked from, and that Keats revised 72 (to the reading of Dilke's and George Keats's MSS, *Annals,* and *1820*) on Brown's transcript. $W^1$ (with an independent error, "tell" for "see," in 41) was fairly certainly made from $W^2$, and after Woodhouse altered "other's" in 24 to "other."

*1820* returns to the wording of the Cambridge draft in 20 and 60, has the draft's and *Annals'* (and Woodhouse's corrected) wording in 24, incorporates Keats's revisions (in the lost holograph and Brown's lost transcript) in 17, 54, 59, 72, and 79, and has new readings not in any MS (except for Woodhouse's notations in $W^2$) in heading, 11, 16, 49, and 57.

The present text is based on *1820.* The apparatus readings for 22 and 66 in Dilke's MS and 16 in George Keats's MS are copying errors, and that for 44 in *Annals* is a misreading or printer's error. $W^2$ is cited in its original state, and Woodhouse's changes and variants are (except for 24, which is a special case) ignored in the apparatus.

*Before* 1 (*apparatus*) Small . . . Dryad] This rejected beginning appears upside down at the bottom of what is now the second page of the draft. It was of course originally written right side up at the top, but then Keats turned the sheet around when he began again on a new page.

24 other] Woodhouse's alteration of "other's" (in the lost holograph that Brown copied) to "other" was perhaps made when the *Annals* text appeared; he wrote "other" in $W^1$, but none of the other variants or corrections that he (therefore probably later) entered in $W^2$.

50 The] Actually the draft reading looks more like "The" altered to "Her" than vice versa, but "Her murmurous haunt . . . " seems an unlikely phrasing.

70 perilous] The deleted draft word (frequently reported as "keelless") is difficult to make out. The last seven letters—"uthless"—are fairly certain, and the initial letter seems to be either an imperfect "R" or an imperfect "K." Woodhouse recorded the word in shorthand in $W^2$ as "ruthless." David V. Erdman, in a letter to the present editor, has suggested "pathless" (Keats originally wrote "pathless Sea" in *Hyperion* III.50, and "pathless waves" occurs in *Isabella* 96).

74 fam'd] Woodhouse recorded "(feigned) JHR" above this word in $W^2$, and we may suppose that a Reynolds copy that Woodhouse saw had "feigned" either in the text itself or else above or beside the text as a suggested revision or query. John Jones, *John Keats's Dream of Truth* (1969), p. 167, thinks that the word in the extant draft may be "fain'd" rather than "fam'd"; while this seems doubtful, it shows how Reynolds might have interpreted the word in the draft or another holograph MS as "feigned."

80 music:—] Woodhouse noted on the opposite verso of $W^2$, referring to the punctuation in his MS ("music?"), "JHR's copy has this Note of Interrog$^{n}$—It is left out of the Printed Copy [*1820*]—(Why?)."

### *Ode on a Grecian Urn*

Written in 1819 (the date in Brown's transcript, repeated in Dilke's, George Keats's, and Woodhouse's copies; the dating is difficult to consider objectively, because virtually all scholars in the twentieth century have assigned the poem specifically to May, usually without question or qualification, and this tradition has been given the status of fact by Garrod's mistaken report of a "May 1819" date in Dilke's MS). First published in *Annals of the Fine Arts,* 4 (January 1820), 638–639, and then in *1820,* pp. 113–116. The four extant MSS are transcripts by Brown, Dilke, George Keats, and Woodhouse ($W^2$).

Brown's is the one transcript made directly from a holograph. Dilke's MS, the next written, lowercases twenty-one words that are capitalized in Brown's copy, but otherwise follows Brown almost exactly (there is but a single difference in punctuation) and has the "CB" flourish at the end. Dilke copied the poem before Brown's "ne'er" in 40 was altered by erasure to "e'er." George Keats's MS, made in January 1820, varies from Brown's text in twelve details of capitalization, three of punctuation, and one of hyphenation, but nevertheless also clearly derives from Brown; following his source mechanically, George left some extra space before "e'er" in 40 where Brown's MS, after the erasure of the initial letter in "ne'er," also has extra space. Woodhouse likewise took his copy "from C.B."; $W^2$ has "will" for "can" in 40 (a copying error) and also "e'er" in the same line.

The *Annals* text, which most likely was printed from a Keats copy transmitted by Haydon (see W. Roberts, *TLS,* 20 August 1938, p. 544), has a variant heading, new readings in 34 and 48, and unique variants that represent copying and/or printing errors in 8, 16, and 22. There is a good chance that Keats made his copy for the *Annals* from Brown's transcript rather than from a MS of his own (see Textual Note to the preceding poem).

*1820* has the *Annals* text of 34 and 48 and substantive readings that do not appear in any earlier version in 9, 18, and 47 (as well as the controversial quotation marks in 49). The present text is based on *1820*.

### *Ode on Melancholy*

Written in 1819 (the date in Brown's transcript, repeated in George Keats's and Woodhouse's copies; a more precise dating is not possible, though most scholars routinely assign the poem to May). First published in *1820,* pp. 140–142 (and the canceled opening stanza first in *1848,* I, 287). The four extant MSS are a holograph, probably Keats's original draft (the first sheet, containing stanzas 1 and 2, in the Robert H. Taylor Collection, Princeton University Library, and the second sheet, containing stanza 3, in the Berg Collection, New York Public Library), and transcripts by Brown, George Keats, and Woodhouse ($W^2$).

Brown's transcript differs from the Taylor-Berg MS in heading, in the addition of stanza numbers and a new stanza (deleted in pencil in the transcript) before the present 1, and in the wording of the present 6, 27, and 29. Brown may have copied the Taylor-Berg MS, taking the additional opening stanza from a separate now lost sheet provided by Keats as an afterthought and making changes in 6, 27, and 29 perhaps according to Keats's instructions as he copied, or he may have transcribed a later, revised MS containing the additional stanza. Clearly he did not get his text from an *earlier* version than the extant holograph, for his transcript has several readings that Keats arrived at by revisions in the Taylor-Berg MS, and Brown could not have copied these final-text readings had he been working from an earlier version.

George Keats's MS derives from Brown's. It is not known who deleted the opening stanza in Brown's MS, but George's text has only the three stanzas that were published in *1820,* and therefore the decision to omit this stanza must have been reached in or before January 1820, when George made his copy. Woodhouse also took his text "from C.B.," following Brown's minor details with an unusual fidelity and including the canceled opening stanza without any comment on its status. (In spite of the presence of this stanza, Woodhouse's transcript is almost surely later than George's. Occasionally elsewhere—e.g., in *The Eve of St. Mark* following 68—Woodhouse copied deleted text without indicating that it was deleted.)

*1820* has Brown's wording in heading, 6, 27, and 29 and new readings that do not appear in any MS in 14 and 21. The present text is based on *1820*.

*Before* 1 (*apparatus*) Though . . . dull.] Both Brown's and Woodhouse's MSS show "shrouds" penciled above or opposite "creeds" in the third line of this stanza. The penciling is almost certainly Woodhouse's in both transcripts, and is best interpreted as Woodhouse's own suggestion for revision. The *1848* text of the stanza, deriving from Brown's MS, incorporates the penciled "shrouds." Garrod, p. 504 n., suggests that "Melancholy, whether" in the ninth line is a mistake (by Keats or Brown) for "melancholy weather" (see also the elaborate explanation in Garrod's O.S.A. ed., pp. 469–470).

*Ode on Indolence*

Written in the spring of 1819 (probably after Keats described to his brother and sister-in-law on 19 March a mood of indolence in which "Poetry . . . Ambition . . . Love . . . pass by me . . . like three figures on a greek vase," and certainly before he mentioned the poem in a letter of 9 June—*Letters,* II, 78–79, 116). First published in *1848,* II, 276–278. The two extant MSS are transcripts by Brown and Woodhouse ($W^2$). Brown copied a lost holograph that apparently consisted of several separate sheets, for he initially got the stanzas in the wrong order (Gittings, p. 311 n., suggests that Brown was thinking of the MS of *Indolence* when he recalled in his "Life" of Keats how he rescued the text of *Nightingale* from "some scraps of paper . . . four or five in number"—*KC,* II, 65). His transcript presents the stanzas as follows:

| | |
|---|---|
| Stanza "1" | 1–10 |
| Stanza "2" | 11–20 |
| Stanza "3" (corrected to "4") | 31–40 |
| Stanza "4" (corrected to "6") | 51–60 |
| Stanza "5" (corrected to "3") | 21–30 |
| Stanza "5" | 41–50 |

The uncorrected "5" at the head of this final stanza shows that Brown discovered his mistake and, possibly in consultation with Keats, corrected the numbering of the preceding three stanzas before he wrote out the last stanza (Brown says that he arranged the stanzas of *Nightingale* "With [Keats's] assistance"—*KC,* II, 65). His corrected order is that of the present text. Woodhouse transcribed the stanzas in this corrected order "from C.B." (there are no substantive differences between the two texts), and Milnes used Brown's MS as printer's copy for *1848,* rewriting three words at the beginning of 41 in proofs.

The present text is based on Brown's MS.

*Shed no tear—O shed no tear*

Written probably in 1819 (but the dating is highly conjectural, since we cannot date Brown's fairy tale for which the poem was composed—see below). First published in *PDWJ,* 18 October 1838, and then in *1848,* II, 261 (with a facsimile of the extant holograph facing the title page of Volume II). The four extant MSS are a holograph version at Harvard and transcripts by Brown (included in his unfinished MS "The Faeries' Triumph," at Keats House, Hampstead), Milnes, and Frederick Locker-Lampson.

The extant holograph—very cleanly written and perhaps a fair copy rather than a draft—was made for Brown, who inscribed on the verso, "A faery Song written for a particular purpose at the request of CB." Brown's version in his fairy tale differs substantively from the holograph in 7 and 18, and may have come from another source. The *PDWJ* text, deriving from some lost copy by Brown, adds a heading, agrees with the holograph in 7 and with Brown's fairy-tale MS in 18, and has a copying or printing error (most likely a misreading of Brown's hand) in 4. Milnes's MS (headed "Fairy's Song") varies from the holograph, which was almost surely his source, only in "the" for "this" in 13; *1848* ("Faery Song"), printed from Milnes's MS, restores "this" in 13. Presumably Milnes's and *1848*'s headings derive from Brown's endorsement on the holograph. Locker-Lampson's MS was made from the text (rather than the facsimile) in *1848*.

The present text is based on the extant holograph.

### *Otho the Great*

Written by Keats and Brown at Shanklin, Isle of Wight, and Winchester in July–August 1819 (Act I completed perhaps in the first week of July; Act II begun by 11 July, after the drafting of *Lamia* Part I; Acts III and IV completed by 14 August; the whole "just finish'd" by 23 August—*Letters,* II, 128, 139, 143), with further revisions in December 1819 and January 1820 (II, 237, 241). First published in *1848,* II, 111–203, though a dozen short passages (I.i.136–137, I.ii.6–11, 40–41, 86–87a, I.iii.5, 20, 98–101, III.ii.76, 122–126, IV.ii.128b–129a, V.i.14–15, 22 and 26–27) had appeared earlier as chapter epigraphs in E. J. Trelawny's *Adventures of a Younger Son* (1831), I, 21, 262, 271, II, 67, 74, 88, 236, 243, 251, III, 124, 283.

In very general terms, we have two nearly complete MSS of the play, a draft and a fair copy, and five fragments of revised or intermediate draft for parts of the first scene of Act I. Keats quotes I.iii.24–29 at the end of his 17–27 September 1819 journal letter to George and Georgiana (MS in the Morgan Library), and Brown's copy of the extracts printed in Trelawny's *Adventures* is extant at the end of his transcript of that work (printer's copy for the first edition) now at Harvard.

The draft MS, in Keats's hand throughout except for a few interlined revisions by Brown, is mainly divided between the University of Texas (Acts I–III and the first scene of IV minus the leaf containing IV.i.71–90) and the Huntington Library (the remainder minus the leaves and parts of leaves containing, in the revised line numbering of the present edition, IV.ii.117–139, V.i.18–32, V.ii.8b–15, and V.v.11–58, 140a, 143b–164a, 173c–174, 180–182). The Texas portion of this MS consists of sixty-one leaves (the first of which served as a title page with the single word "Otho" on it), and the Huntington portion consists of fourteen leaves and parts of leaves (including a small slip containing only V.v.140–143). If we add to these the missing leaves necessary to make up a complete version of the play, this unfoliated MS once consisted of seventy-nine leaves, of which leaves 1–56 and 58–62 are at Texas and leaves 63–65, 67, 68, 70–72, 75–77, 79, and parts of 69 and 78 are at the Huntington. Leaves 73 and 74, containing a canceled first version of V.v.1–10 (rewritten on the verso of leaf 72) and the original draft of V.v.11–58, are entirely missing, and the details of their text unrecorded, but parts of leaves 57, 66, 69, and 78 are extant elsewhere and can be related to one another and to fragmentary leaves at the Huntington as follows:

| | *Recto* | *Verso* | *Location* |
|---|---|---|---|
| Leaf 57 | IV.i.71–73 | (Presumably blank) | Missing; text unrecorded |
| | 74–75 | Blank | Rosenbach Foundation |
| | 76–85 | Blank | Harvard |
| | 86–90 | (Presumably blank) | Missing; text unrecorded |
| Leaf 66 | IV.ii.117–121a | (Presumably blank) | Missing; text unrecorded |
| | 121b–126 | Blank | Harvard |
| | 127–139 | V.i.18–32 (revision of lines canceled on leaves 67r and 68r) | Harvard |
| Leaf 69 | V.ii.8b–15 | Blank | Harvard |
| | 28–40, 48–56 | Blank | Huntington Library |
| | (16–27 and 41–47 were added on the verso of leaf 68 with marks for insertion after 15 and 40 on leaf 69r.) | | |
| Leaf 78 | V.v.140a, 143b–151a (written continuously) | V.v.180–182 | Berg Collection, New York Public Library |
| | 151b–164a | 173c–174 | Harvard |
| | 164b–172 | Blank | Huntington Library |
| | (The lines on the verso are added passages written for insertion after 179 and 173b on leaf 79r.) | | |

What is missing, then, from this reconstructed draft version amounts to no more than sixty and a half lines—the text of IV.i.71–73 and 86–90 (at the top and bottom of leaf 57r), IV.ii.117–121a (at the top of leaf 66r), and V.v.11–58 (leaves 73 and 74). The first sixty-two leaves were taken to America by George Keats in January 1820 (see *KC,* II, 15–16, 23, 117, 120); leaves 63–79 were in the possession of Severn, who inscribed the various fragments that he cut off and gave away.

Not all of these leaves represent original draft, however. Keats employed four different methods of indicating speech prefixes, writing them (a) on the opposite verso (leaves 2–21, 30–52, 72, the text of I.i.1–iii.132, II.ii.1–III.ii.281, V.iv.28–52a), (b) in the center of the page above the beginning of each speech (leaves 22–29, 53–59, the text of II.i.1–153, IV.i.1–127a), (c) in the left margin with the speakers' names generally abbreviated (leaves 60–62, the text of IV.i.127b–184), and (d) in the left margin with the speakers' names generally spelled out in full (leaves 64–71, 75, 76, 78, 79, the text of IV.ii.1–V.iv.27, V.v.59–195). (Leaves 63 and 77, lacking speech prefixes altogether, are omitted from this account; and Keats used still another method in the extant fragments of revised or intermediate draft of I.i described in the second paragraph below, writing the prefixes in the left margin but on a separate line above each speech.) The leaves in category (a) are pretty clearly original draft; those in categories (b) and (c) appear to be revised or recopied leaves that replaced original text now lost, and at least some of those in category (d) also have the look of revised leaves (see the separate notes below to II.i, IV.i, IV.ii). Nevertheless all seventy-nine leaves of this reconstructed draft were Brown's initial source for the fair copy of the play. Though George Keats says that, when he brought the draft MS back with him to America, "John took some pa[ins] to get the sheets together, copied what was deficient and m[ade] the whole, as he said perfect" (*KC,* II, 15), there is no evidence that any of the extant leaves was specially made for George at that time, and plenty of evidence that they were all made earlier. It is possible that George inferred this recopying, just as in the discussion above, from the appearance of the MS itself.

The fair copy of the play, written out by Brown and showing revisions by both authors, is at Harvard except for part of a leaf containing the Dramatis Personae, which is in the Robert H. Taylor Collection at Princeton, and the title leaf, the rest of the Dramatis Personae leaf, and five leaves containing I.i.1–20, IV.ii.2–44a, and V.i.30b–ii.27, all of which are lost. In its initial state, this MS represents a further stage of composition, as Brown copied out Keats's draft text, correcting, revising, and generally tidying up as he went along. Like the draft MS, however, the fair copy also is a compound of original and revised or recopied leaves. As Brown's running total of line numbers for Act I makes clear ("155" at the end of scene i on fol. 9, "161" opposite the bottom of fol. 11, thirty-two lines into scene ii), fols. 2–9 are revised leaves in the MS. Originally the fair copy consisted of a title page, a sheet containing the Dramatis Personae (the partial leaf in the Taylor Collection, which appears to bear the canceled folio number "1"), and eight leaves (foliated 2–9) containing the text of I.i more or less as it stands in Keats's draft, which would have amounted, in Brown's numbering, to 129 lines (the "161" for fol. 11 minus the thirty-two lines of scene ii at that point). After Keats rewrote 17 ff. of the scene (see just below), Brown recopied the scene, gaining an extra page by canceling the folio number "1" on the Dramatis Personae leaf and beginning with a new "1" on the now lost leaf containing I.i.1–20.

The source of Brown's recopied text in I.i may be seen in five extant fragments of revised draft, all but the last in Keats's hand and, like the draft of IV.ii ff., once in the possession of Severn. From Keats's numbering ("1," "2," "3") in the upper lefthand corner of the first three of these fragments we can reconstruct some leaves of his revision of I.i.17 ff. (*KRD* in the apparatus) as follows:

| | *Recto* | *Verso* | *Location* |
|---|---|---|---|
| Revised leaf 1 | I.i.17–24 | Blank | Harvard |
| | 25–33 | (Presumably blank) | Missing; text unrecorded |
| Revised leaf 2 | I.i.34–44a | Blank | Harvard |
| | 44b–54 | (Presumably blank) | Missing; text unrecorded |
| Revised leaf 3 | I.i.55–60a plus additional text (see apparatus for 60) | I.i.145–152 | University of Texas |
| | 61–65 (?) | 153–158 | Missing; text unrecorded |
| | 66–68 | Blank | University of Texas |

The remainder of revised leaf 3 (probably another dozen lines) and the rest of the leaves in this series (three or four if Keats continued his revision straight through to the end of the scene, and one fewer if he rewrote only 17–123 and 140–158) are missing.

The final piece of text in this category—a fragment containing I.i.141–144 in Brown's hand (in the British Library, inserted in a copy of *The Poems of Frederick Locker,* 1883, cited as *BRD* in the apparatus)—is no doubt related to these other revised fragments, but the connection is not clear. Garrod knew of, but was not allowed to examine, a fragment in W. T. Spencer's possession containing, in Keats's hand, I.i.141 "followed by 3 lines not identified" (Garrod, pp. xliii, 311, 318 n.). Probably this now lost fragment formed some part of the revised leaves described in the preceding paragraph, and Brown's I.i.141–144 is a revision or copy of its text.

The progress of composition is thus the following: Keats drafted the play all the way through, revising some pages here and there in the process, producing the 79-leaf draft MS reconstructed above; Brown wrote out a fair copy from Keats's draft, making further revisions as he copied; then Keats rewrote I.i.17 ff. (either 17–158 or 17–123, 140–158), and Brown recopied the scene, substituting Keats's revised text for the original pages in the fair copy. It is probable that Keats rewrote I.i.17 ff. late in December 1819, when he says in a letter to Fanny Keats that he has been "hightening the interest of our Tragedy" (*Letters,* II, 237), and similarly probable that his remark to Georgiana on 13 January 1820, "Brown has just done patching up the Copy, as it is altered" (II, 241), refers to Brown's rewriting of I.i in the fair copy. At least some of the pencil markings in Brown's

MS were made in late 1819 (see the notes below to I.i.95 and I.ii.6), and one may guess that Keats's and Brown's response to them and Keats's other revisions in the fair copy were also part of the "hightening" mentioned in December 1819.

The fair copy in its final form was the source of the twelve extracts that Brown gave Trelawny for inclusion in *Adventures of a Younger Son,* and was printer's copy for *1848,* which introduced substantive corruptions in some twenty-five lines (see Appendix II). According to both Dilke (in his notes at the end of his copy of *1818* at Keats House, Hampstead) and Severn (Sharp, p. 166), Woodhouse had a copy made of this MS, but the transcript has not survived.

The present text is based on Brown's MS supplemented by *1848* for the parts of the MS that are missing (heading, the last four items of the Dramatis Personae, I.i.1–20, IV.ii.2–44a, V.i.30b–ii.27). It contains substantive emendations in I.i.95, II.ii.34 (punctuation), 59 s.d., 81 s.d., III.ii.49, 186, 220, IV.ii.11, V.i.32, V.ii.10, and V.iii.1 ff. s.p., most of which are discussed in the separate notes below.

I.i.1 ff. *Conrad.* So . . . ] The speech prefixes for the first page of text in the draft (leaf 2r, containing I.i.1–16 plus the first ten lines of the variant passage at I.i.17–123) appear at the right margin on the verso of the present leaf 21 (containing on the recto side the last fourteen lines of the variant passage at I.iii.125–132). From this peculiarity (along with those at I.iii.64–90 and II.ii.1–21—see also the apparatus for II.ii.55–62 and V.v.121–126) we may infer that Brown copied the play scene by scene as Keats drafted it, rather than all at once after the draft was complete. Keats simply made further use, for composition (and in one instance for his title page), of the blank sides of leaves that Brown had already copied.

I.i.7 (*apparatus*) ⟨is . . . me—⟩] These lines in Keats's hand on the verso of Brown's leaf containing the Dramatis Personae (the partial leaf in the Taylor Collection at Princeton) were written to replace text then existing on the facing first page of scene i in Brown's fair copy, and therefore represent intermediate text between that of the original draft (as initially transcribed by Brown in the fair copy) and the final text that Brown substituted when he recopied the scene. In this intermediate version Auranthe is apparently on stage from the beginning.

I.i.95 struck'dst] The responsibility for the various pencilings in the fair copy, probably by more than one hand, cannot be determined with certainty. Those at IV.i.63, 144, and IV.ii.102 look very much like the work of Woodhouse. For the rest, the most likely possibilities, apart from Brown, Keats, and Woodhouse, are the readers of the MS at Drury Lane (R. W. Elliston and perhaps Edmund Kean), Taylor (who surely would have read the play out of interest in Keats's work), and Milnes (when he was preparing the MS for publication in *1848*). At least some of the pencilings were entered while Keats was alive, because both he and Brown changed their text in several places in response to these markings (see the next note). The penciling here (I.i.95) is incorporated into the present text for the sake of grammar; the others are omitted from the apparatus but described in the notes below.

I.ii.6 God . . . illustrious] In the original fair copy text both "God" and "power" are underscored in pencil. Presumably Brown's "illustrious" was prompted by these markings. For other pencilings that seem to have influenced revisions in the fair copy see the notes to II.i.1, 94, II.ii.27–28, III.ii.209–210, IV.i.73, IV.ii.77, V.v.190.

I.ii.101 be] The interlined "are" in the draft apparently represents the beginning of a revision to "what mockeries ye are"; Keats changed his mind before deleting "must," but neglected to restore "be."

I.iii.1–63 *Ludolph.* You . . . dear.] Keats began scene iii in the draft with 64–123, then drew a line across the page and wrote 1–63, drew another line across the page, rewrote the last half of 123 (as a cue) and continued with 124 and the variant passage at 125–132. The first line of the scene is marked "Line 1$^{st}$," and 64 is marked "Line 64$^{th}$."

I.iii.64–90 What . . . uselessly.] These lines are on leaf 16r in the draft. The speech prefixes for 86 and 88 appear at the right margin on the verso of leaf 1 (the title leaf). See the note to I.i.1 ff.

I.iii.115 is$_{\wedge}$] So the draft and Brown's fair copy. *1848* adds a dash after this word, but the intended meaning of 115–116 is probably something like "And there is the matter concerning which my father's iron lips have sworn . . . ."

I.iii.123 to . . . not] The draft has "I doubt not to you" both in the original line and in the cue text following 63 (see the note to I.iii.1–63, above). In the original line the words are marked in pencil for transposition to the present text.

II.i] Leaves 22–29 of the draft, containing all of II.i, are separately foliated "1" through "8," and speech prefixes are centered above the lines rather than (as before and for much of the rest of the MS) written on the opposite versos. The fact that the next scene in the draft is headed "Act 2$^{nd}$—Scene 2$^{nd}$" without any alteration of the scene number suggests that these eight leaves of II.i represent revised or recopied text replacing earlier draft text now lost (rather than the later addition of the entire scene).

II.i.1 cautioning] The canceled "Sigifred" is underscored in pencil in the fair copy, presumably to point out that the original line was a hexameter.

II.i.94 Shall . . . Auranthe.] The canceled "Oh . . . that?" is underscored in pencil in the fair copy.

II.i.128 Happiest of days] Underscored in pencil in the fair copy.

II.ii.1–21 *Erminia.* Where . . . will.] These lines are on leaf 30r in the draft. The speech prefixes for them appear at the right margin on the verso of leaf 15 (containing on the recto side I.ii.183–202). See the note to I.i.1 ff.

II.ii.21 Will you send] Underscored in pencil in the fair copy.

II.ii.27–28 are . . . camp] In the original fair copy text "Nunnery" (a slang term for brothel) is underscored in pencil.

II.ii.54 it] Underscored (and an illegible word written in the margin) in pencil in the fair copy.

II.ii.59 *s.d.* (Reads.)] The additional stage direction (made necessary by Brown's interlined aside in the fair copy) is here taken over from *1848*.

II.ii.61 wen] Underscored in pencil in the fair copy.

II.ii.68 Villainy! Villainy!] There is a large X penciled beside these words and the preceding stage direction in the fair copy.

II.ii.81 *s.d.* Enter Gersa] The emendation here (for clarity) was first made independently of the draft in *1848*.

II.ii.128 of you] In the fair copy these words are lightly deleted in ink (ostensibly to improve the meter), but probably not by Brown or Keats. They were omitted in *1848*.

III.i.20 Is . . . this] Keats's final text in the draft is canceled and rewritten (for clarity) in lighter ink by another hand in the margin. The same hand also recopied Keats's alteration in 40, and made similar clarifications in a few other places in the MS. Probably all these rewritings are by Brown, whose interlineations in the draft at III.ii.42, 61, 269 and IV.i.107 are more certainly identifiable.

III.ii.15 love] Garrod reads "Love" made out of "her" in the draft, but "her" appears to be the later word. It is possible that Keats intended to add (rather than substitute) "her," so as to produce "her love philtres."

III.ii.20 sail] The word appears to be "sail" in both the draft and the fair copy. H. B. Forman's emendation to "soil" (O.S.A. ed.) has been followed by all modern editors, but "fair sail beyond the Rhone" (i.e., into the Mediterranean) makes perfectly good sense. "About the Danube's mouth" in the preceding line may be a clue to Keats's thinking here.

III.ii.49 He will] Brown's alteration to "He'll" in the fair copy is a mistake, since the meter calls for two syllables.

III.ii.49/50 (*apparatus*) *Otho.* Come . . . Ludolph—] Here and at III.ii.59/60 and 272/273 the fair copy omits lines that are uncanceled in the draft (see also the apparatus for V.ii.8–9, where the fair copy is missing). We must suppose that Brown left these out on purpose (just as, at V.iv.45, he preferred Keats's original rather than the revised line in the draft), though some or all of the omissions may in fact be simple copying errors.

III.ii.83 yawn] H. B. Forman (O.S.A. ed.) emends to the draft's nearly illegible "roar" on the grounds that the fair copy's "yawn" "is not good sense" (Hampstead Keats, V, 83 n.), and modern editors usually print "roar." But the *OED* cites many examples of "yawn" as a threatening action (including one in which a wounded lion "yawns a dreadful roar"!).

III.ii.122–126 flower / Of . . . its] In copying 122–126 for the chapter epigraph in Trelawny's *Adventures* Brown wrote "flower / In . . . his," and the printer of the work misread the first word as "flowers."

III.ii.126 vails] The emendation (for clarity) is not substantive. See Textual Note to *Endymion* II.793.

III.ii.128 Whither, whither] The second word is crossed out in pencil in the fair copy and omitted in *1848*, but the marking is clearly not by Brown or Keats and probably was made by Milnes.

III.ii.186 clogg'd] Keats frequently omitted "'d" and "ed" in past tenses and participles, and his and Brown's "clog" has to be a mistake, since memories cannot both "ease" and "clog up" a heavy pulse (184–186). The emendation here makes "Painful," "clogg'd up," and "stagnate" a series of adjectives modifying "pulse" (cf. "stagnated" modifying heart in the apparatus for 183).

III.ii.209–210 Albert . . . gold] There is a large X penciled beside these lines in the fair copy.

III.ii.220 awaken'd] Brown's two-syllable "awak'd" in the fair copy is probably a mistake, though whether for "awaked" (Milnes's emendation in *1848*) or the draft's "awaken'd" is not certain.

IV.i] In leaves 53–59 of the draft (containing IV.i.1–127a) the speech prefixes are centered above the lines, and the text shows relatively few alterations. Pretty clearly these leaves represent revised or recopied text replacing earlier text now lost (see the note to II.i, above). The next three leaves (60–62, containing 127b–184), in which the prefixes are written neither above nor opposite the lines but beside them, abbreviated, in the margin, also represent revised text. Because leaf 59 is separately foliated "3" and leaves 60–62 have folio numbers "2" through "4" altered to "3" through "6," it would appear that the revision of 127b–184 preceded that of 1–127a.

IV.i.63 You . . . security] The text has been marked and altered in pencil in the fair copy—probably by Woodhouse in this instance—to read "only in my security You live."

IV.i.73 I . . . thoughts.] The original wording in the fair copy ("A . . . you!") is underscored in pencil and marked with a large X in the margin.

IV.i.135 I am deceiv'd.] The text has been altered in pencil in the fair copy to read "am I deceiv'd?"

IV.i.144 For . . . eyes] The text has been altered in pencil in the fair copy—probably by Woodhouse—to read "For that I would not look."

IV.i.152 say . . . these] The text has been altered in pencil in the fair copy to read "say,—rule these fair."

IV.i.166 autumn] The deleted "s" in the draft's "autum⟨s⟩" probably represents a slip of the pen (anticipating "sun") rather than a singular or plural possessive.

IV.ii] Beginning with IV.ii.1 (and coincidentally with the Huntington portion of the MS), the draft has speech prefixes spelled out in full in the left margin (not abbreviated, as in IV.i.127b–184). This continues to the end of the MS, except that on leaf 72r (containing V.iv.28–52a) Keats reverted to his earlier method of writing the prefixes on the opposite verso. Much of the text in these leaves is cleanly written, and some of it may represent revision of earlier text now lost.

IV.ii.11 diviner] The fair copy is missing for 2–44a of this scene. The emendation here is based on the likelihood that it was Milnes rather than Brown who changed Keats's "diviner" to "divine." Keats probably intended "eloquence" to be pronounced as two syllables.

IV.ii.77 Hungarian . . . amazest] In the original fair copy text both "Thou liest" and "amazest" are underscored in pencil.

IV.ii.102 fresh] This word has been canceled and replaced by "last new" in pencil in the fair copy, probably Woodhouse's attempt to improve the meter. *1848* printed "last new."

IV.ii.129 temples] In copying 128b–129a for Trelawny's *Adventures* Brown wrote "temples," but the printed chapter epigraph has "temple."

V.i.32 Now] The fair copy is missing for V.i.30b–ii.27, and choices have to be made between the draft's and *1848*'s readings in V.i.32, V.ii.4, 7 s.d., 8–9, 10, 11, and 25. Most of these differences may be supposed to represent Brown's or Keats's changes in the fair copy, but *1848*'s V.i.32 and V.ii.10 seem more likely to be corruptions, and accordingly are emended to the draft readings.

V.ii.10 Shrive] See the preceding note.

V.ii.22 "Of . . . soul"] The quotation marks do not appear in the draft. Presumably they were added in the fair copy rather than in *1848*. Allott, p. 602 n., suggests that "Ludolph is referring ironically to the general estimate of Auranthe's character." The fair copy also has quotes at the beginning and end of V.ii.32, but these are deleted.

V.iii.1 ff. *s.p.* Theodore] The fair copy has "1st Knight" altered to "Theodore" in the opening stage direction but "1st Knight" unchanged in the speech prefixes that follow. The emendation here (first made by H. B. Forman, 1883 ed., before he saw the fair copy) is based on the assumption that Brown intended his first alteration to apply throughout the scene.

V.iv.24 ruddy] Underscored in pencil in the fair copy.

V.iv.39 Fill, fill] The second word in the draft, usually read as "full," is probably "fill" with an extra minim rather than "full" with a dotted "u."

V.v.91–109 Sad . . . Wait; wait!] It is not clear at what point in the composition this text was added to the play. The present leaf 75 of the draft (containing on the verso stage directions for the recto of leaf 76, which therefore immediately followed 75 from the beginning) ends with the fragmentary line given in the apparatus after 90, and leaf 76 begins with the end of 109 ("I marvel"); it appears consequently that the draft had only a single line between 90 and 110, perhaps a short speech by Sigifred—something like "Gersa, see you, he bursts in tears!"—plus Ludolph's "I marvel." Presumably Brown transcribed 91–109 from a separate sheet now lost, for the lines are cleanly written in the fair copy and without any sign that they were added afterward.

V.v.124–126 Black . . . page?] Keats enclosed these three lines in large parentheses in the draft.

V.v.167 Tight-footed] Underscored in pencil in the fair copy.

V.v.190 now] The final word in the fair copy alteration was first written in pencil (possibly by another hand than Brown's or Keats's) and then rewritten in ink by Brown.

V.v.192 nobles] Underscored in pencil in the fair copy.

### *Lamia*

Written mainly in July and August 1819 (after arriving at Shanklin on 28 June Keats drafted Act I of *Otho* and then took up *Lamia,* finishing Part I by 11 July; he resumed work on the poem at Winchester in the last week of August, and completed it sometime before 5 September—*Letters,* II, 128, 139, 157), with further revisions in March 1820 (II, 276). First published in *1820,* pp. 1–46.

The two principal MSS are Keats's original draft (of which about one-sixth is extant) and a holograph fair copy (at Harvard). Keats quotes the draft text of II.122–162 plus eighteen lines subsequently discarded in a letter to Taylor of 5 September 1819 (MS at Harvard), and we have a complete set of proof-sheets for the poem (also at Harvard).

The following list (updating Garrod's headnote, p. 191, and *Texts,* p. 255) gives the contents of the nine surviving fragments of Keats's draft, which was once in the possession of Severn, or perhaps shared by Severn and Brown (seven of the pieces are inscribed by or otherwise associated with Severn, but the third in the list was given to Mrs. Leigh Hunt by Brown and the last, which was in Milnes's possession, may be the unidentified fragment that Brown enclosed in a letter to Milnes in 1840—*KC,* II, 37).

| *Recto* | *Verso* | *Location* |
|---|---|---|
| I.185a (two and a half lines with the same wording as the fair copy text through "Lycius the happy") | Blank | University of Texas |
| I.185b–190 | Blank | Keats-Shelley Memorial House, Rome |
| I.324–329 | Blank | Berg Collection, New York Public Library |
| I.386b–397 | Blank | Rosenbach Foundation |
| II.26–49 | II.85–92, preceded and followed by eleven lines subsequently discarded and a twelfth that became II.105 | Harvard |
| II.50–61 | Blank | Robert H. Taylor Collection, Princeton |
| II.62–67a | Blank | Robert H. Taylor Collection |
| II.67b–74 | Blank | Keats-Shelley Memorial House, Rome |
| II.122–147 | II.191–198 | Harvard |

We do not have enough fragments to reconstruct the draft MS for Part I; the first and second items above are two connected pieces cut away from one leaf, while the third item appears to be the bottom one-fifth of another leaf and the fourth item most of still another leaf. For the draft of Part II, however, where Keats separately foliated at least the first five of his leaves, a partial reconstruction can be made. The fifth item above is leaf 2 of Part II, the sixth, seventh, and eighth items fit together to make leaf 3, and the ninth item is leaf 5. The missing leaf 1r contained II.1–25, and the missing leaf 4r contained II.75–81, the first four lines ("Became . . . Paramour") given in the apparatus at II.82–105, and then II.106–121. The passages on the versos of leaves 2 and 5 (the fifth and ninth items above) are both later additions, the first drafted after Keats had already incorporated the contents of leaf 4r in the fair copy and the second written probably as a replacement of some or all of the draft text recoverable via Keats's letter after II.162.

The fair copy, obviously made from the draft and at least half done by 19 September 1819 (the rest may have been copied as late as March 1820—see *Letters,* II, 164, 276), is an especially neat and well punctuated MS. Keats wrote the twenty-six numbered leaves of this copy in order except that fols. 18 and 21 (containing II.82–105 and 163–174) are inserted leaves added in each case just after the next-following leaf was written (the present fol. 19 was originally "18" and the present fol. 22 was originally "21," but fols. 20 and 23–26 had their present numbers from the beginning). The MS was printer's copy for *1820,* and apart from capitals and "-ed" vs. "-'d" verb endings the printer followed its accidental details quite closely.

*1820* is seven lines shorter than Keats's final text in the fair copy (omitting three lines at I.260/261, II.45/46, and reducing three to one at I.185 and four to two at II.297–298), differs substantively from the fair copy in close to fifty other lines, and has a much longer note explaining the poem's source in Burton. The extant proof-sheets, a set read and marked by both Keats and Woodhouse and preserved by Woodhouse in lieu of a transcript of the poem (he recorded variants from the draft passage in Keats's letter to Taylor in them, and a few also from the fair copy), show that almost all of the substantive changes between the fair copy and *1820* were introduced after the poem was first set in type. Three of them—in I.287, II.89, 112 (plus the nonsubstantive correction of "wakeing" to "wakening" in I.296)—were made by Taylor in the fair copy before it was given to the printer. Two others—in I.132, 270 (plus the respelling of "vulcanian" in I.155)—were made by the printer in the initial setting of the poem. A number of others resulted from alterations marked on the proofs by Keats (in I.78, 104, 115), by Woodhouse (I.114, 123, 192, 196, 212, 236, 272, 320, 322, 379, 383, 389, 393, II.10), and by Keats and Woodhouse collaboratively (I.173–174, 176). The omission and reduction of lines at I.185, 260/261, II.45/46, 297–298, the changes in wording in I.69, 116, 167–168, 185, 225, 363, 371, 373, II.53, 134, 150, 177–178, 218–219, 239, 246–247, 254, 255, 293–294, and the expansion and repositioning of the endnote were all done further along the line by some combination of Keats (who we know rewrote II.293–294 in Taylor's office), Woodhouse (who had made suggestions for I.69, 167–168, 363, and other lines on the proofs and elsewhere), and Taylor (who worried over the text at II.297–298)—probably in many cases by all three working together.

The present text is based on *1820.* The apparatus includes the printed text of the proof-sheets only at I.132, 155, 270, 389 (this last simply in order to record Woodhouse's proof correction); the printed proofs also vary substantively from Keats's fair copy text in seven places where the printer followed Taylor's alterations in the MS (I.287, II.89, 112, plus the four mentioned in the notes below to II.88, 90, 96–97, 200) and in five others where the printer misinterpreted Keats's handwriting (setting "lonely" for "lovely" in I.198, "hue" for "live" in I.281, "caught" for "laught" in II.159, "shining" for "shrining" in II.190, and "tree's" for "trees" in II.216, all of which Woodhouse corrected on the proofs).

I.27 ¶From . . . ] Initially the *1820* printer did not indent paragraphs, simply using a line space to mark each division. But I.27 and II.213 came at the top of new pages, and consequently all record of the divisions here (the spacings being between pages) was lost. When paragraph indentions were subsequently introduced into the text (most of those in Part I were marked on the proofs by Woodhouse), these two were overlooked. (For the record, the extant draft fragment of II.122–147 has no paragraph indention at 146; the letter extract of II.122–162 has indentions at both 146 and 150.)

I.57–58 fire . . . tiar] Woodhouse on the proofs suggested the transposition of "fire" and "tiar," but then he or Keats marked out the suggestion.

I.69 splendid] As a replacement for the original "silver" Woodhouse on the proofs suggested "shadowy."

I.78 as a bright] The fair copy wording of the line—"And, swiftly as a mission'd Phœbean dart"—requires "Phœbean" to be mispronounced as two syllables. Both Keats and Woodhouse worked over the line on the proofs, Keats first deleting "mission'd" and inserting "straight" to come after "swiftly," and then deleting "straight" and interlining "bright" above "⟨mission'd⟩." Above Keats's "straight," Woodhouse suggested "sped," "shot," and "launch'd," each apparently to come after "swiftly" ("And, swiftly sped as a Phœbean dart"), but it is not clear whether he wrote these words before or after Keats arrived at the final text. Keats's jottings on the half title of the proofs (see William Allan Coles, *HLB,* 8 [1954], 115 n.) show him questioning the accenting of "Phœbean" and also "Circean," "Caducean," "Cenchrea," and "Peræa," and the text was altered where each of these occurs (see the apparatus for I.115, 133, 173–174, 176, 225). Similar changes to reduce "Lamia" from three to two syllables were made in I.272, 371.

I.104 grew] After Keats changed "wox" to "grew" on the proofs, Woodhouse wrote "stet *wox*" in the margin, but the final printed text has Keats's revision.

I.133 lythe] Both Keats's deletion and Woodhouse's restoration of this word on the proofs relate to the accenting of the next word, "Caducean," which appears with "pen. incert." (penultimate uncertain) in Keats's list of Greek names on the half title of the proofs (see note to I.78).

I.155 volcanian] The fair copy's "vulcanian" has the same meaning ("volcanic").

I.167–168 And . . . aloft] The last three words of the original 168 are lightly marked out in pencil in the fair copy (probably by Taylor) and deleted in ink on the proofs (probably by Woodhouse, who also marked 167–168 with an X and the comment "Rhymes," perhaps objecting to the juxtaposition of "air"/"where" and "hoar"/"more" in successive couplets). In a note to Taylor of June (?) 1820 Woodhouse suggested substituting "And a soft voice was heard upon the air / Muttering, 'Where art thou, Lycius! Ah Where?'" ("was heard" interlined above "swell'd out," which is marked for deletion—*KC,* I, 112).

I.185 Ah . . . maid] Woodhouse on the proofs marked the first line of the original passage to read "Ah! rapture, rarely heard of, never known." The passage was reduced to a single line at a later stage.

I.203 when in the] Woodhouse on the proofs changed these words to "while in her," but then he or Keats canceled the alteration.

I.206 faint] Woodhouse on the proofs queried this word in the margin.

I.224 her] Woodhouse on the proofs suggested "its?"

I.230 For . . . retire] Woodhouse on the proofs altered the line to read "And by some freakful chance made him retire."

I.244 Turn'd . . . thus] Woodhouse on the proofs revised the words to read "She turn'd—thus syllabling."

I.255–256 Due . . . sure] There is a large X opposite these lines on the proofs, perhaps questioning Keats's wordplay in 255 or the rhyme of "sure" with "adore."

I.287 Tiptoe . . . spread] In the fair copy Taylor first changed Keats's text in pencil to read "On Tiptoe with white arms," then canceled "On" and inserted "spread" both before and after "arms," and finally rewrote the second interlined "spread" in ink.

I.335 a fright] Woodhouse on the proofs changed the two words to "affright."

I.362–363 Muffling . . . as] Keats's wording in the fair copy (see apparatus for 363) has two participles and a prepositional phrase all modifying "one" (Apollonius) rather than Lycius. The *1820* text is partly the work of Woodhouse, who revised the lines on the proofs to read "He hid his face . . . And pressed her fingers hard, as."

II.29 thought, a buzzing] The *1820* comma was added by the printer. Garrod and Allott emend to "thought a-buzzing."

II.88 Hast] Taylor changed this word in pencil in the fair copy to "Is," which the printer set in the proofs. Here and in 90, 96–97, Woodhouse noted the MS's "original" readings on the proofs, and his markings may have influenced the final printed text, which restores Keats's words in all three places.

II.90 Or . . . earth] Taylor revised this line in pencil in the fair copy to read "Or hast thou friends, or Kinsfolks on the earth," which the printer set (omitting the comma and lowercasing "Kinsfolks"). See the preceding note.

II.96–97 me . . . neglect] Taylor revised the text in pencil in the fair copy to read "she, / Who now neglects," which the printer set. See the note to II.88.

II.106 ¶It . . . ] The fair copy text begins on a new page but without indention. The paragraph division in *1820* (made after the poem was in proofs) may have been introduced by the printer in order to realign his pages (which would have been running short after the omission of two lines at II.45/46).

II.190 shrining] Taylor penciled "shriving" beneath this word in the fair copy. The printer set "shining," which Woodhouse then corrected on the proofs to "shrining."

II.200 a] Taylor changed this word in pencil in the fair copy to "its," which the printer set. Woodhouse restored "a" on the proofs.

II.213 ¶Soon . . . ] See the note to I.27.

II.297–298 Of . . . prey?"] At the end of the extant proof-sheets Taylor made two attempts to revise Keats's original lines, writing "Thee married to a Serpent? Mark the Cheat, / Corinthians! a Serpent, I repeat" and then "That youth might suffer have I shielded thee / And married to a Serpent shalt thou be! / Then Lamia &c." Apparently his main concern was to get rid of Keats's "stark" (in the fourth line of the original passage). Opposite Taylor's lines Woodhouse copied two passages using "stark" from Shelley's *The Revolt of Islam,* 2792–93 and 1218, and in the note to Taylor of June (?) 1820 he cites a line from *The Faerie Queene* I.i.44 for the same word (*KC,* I, 113).

*Pensive they sit, and roll their languid eyes*

Written at Winchester on 17 September 1819 (in the opening section of Keats's 17–27 September journal letter to George and Georgiana—*Letters,* II, 188). First published in the New York *World,* 25 June 1877, p. 2. The holograph draft in Keats's letter (MS in the Morgan Library) is our sole authoritative source. The *World*'s text (as part of the letter) omitted "Circled" in 9 and "Romeo" in 14 and misread other words substantively in 2, 5, 11, and 12.

*To Autumn*

Written at Winchester on 19 September 1819 (*Letters,* II, 167). First published in *1820,* pp. 137–139. The five extant MSS are Keats's original draft (at Harvard), a holograph fair copy in his letter to Woodhouse of 21, 22 September 1819 (MS also at Harvard), and transcripts by Brown, George Keats, and Woodhouse ($W^2$).

Brown's MS, though as originally written it differed from the draft text in the addition of a heading and stanza numbers and in the wording of 8, 18, 20, 29, and 33, was nevertheless almost certainly made from the draft. The transcript's two variants in 18 are easily seen as misreadings of Keats's handwriting in the draft, that in 20 is a slip of the pen, and that in 33 represents the original reading of the draft (which Keats may have altered after Brown took his copy). Those in 8 and 29 are more difficult to account for; possibly they are changes requested by Keats at the time Brown made his transcript. George Keats copied Brown's MS in this initial state in January 1820, incorporating Brown's distinctive errors in 18 and 20 (and also writing a unique "a" for "the" in 17). Sometime afterward, probably when he was preparing copy for *1820,* Keats read over Brown's MS and corrected the two miscopied words in 18 (but allowed 8, 20, 29, and 33 to stand), and on still another occasion Woodhouse, collating his $W^2$ text with Brown's, made pencil changes in Brown's MS in 17 (altering Brown's "Dosed" to "Dased") and 20 (correcting "leaden" to "laden" and changing "the" to "a") and Brown himself rewrote the first pencil change in 20 ("leaden" to "laden") in ink.

Keats's untitled letter copy for Woodhouse, made two days after the initial composition of the poem, differs substantively from the draft in 6, 12, 17, 20, 22, and 31. Woodhouse transcribed this letter text in $W^2$, adding a heading and stanza numbers and miscopying two words in 9 and 25. He later, in red ink, entered variants from Brown's MS to 6 ("sweetness"—he did not notice Brown's "fruits" in the same line), 8, 9 (Woodhouse here in effect correcting his own copying error), 17, 20, 29, 31, and 33, and either then or on one or more other occasions, in black ink, changed "stores" to "store" in 12 and marked the variant "oozing" in 22.

*1820* agrees with distinctive readings of the letter text in 6, 20, 22, and 31, but has Brown's heading, 8, 29, and 33, a new inversion in 4, and a new word in 17. If we suppose that Brown's transcript was the only MS at hand when Keats was preparing copy for the printer, then *1820*'s wording in 6, 20, 22, and 31—all in agreement with the letter—may have been supplied (with or without Keats's approval) by Woodhouse from $W^2$.

The present text is based on *1820*. Both Brown's and Woodhouse's transcripts (the latter in its initial state, without the subsequent corrections and variants) are included in the apparatus, even though they are derivative MSS, because of the likelihood that one or both of them influenced the wording of the final text.

17 Drows'd] The draft's "Dos'd" and Brown's "Dosed" are probably variant spellings of "Dozed"; see Textual Note to *The Jealousies* 692.

### *The Fall of Hyperion*

Begun as a revision of *Hyperion* probably at Shanklin toward the end of July 1819 and abandoned by 21 September (*Letters,* II, 132, 139, 167; Leonidas M. Jones, *SB,* 30 [1977], 120–135, argues that Keats wrote I.1–326 nearly a year earlier, in September–October 1818, but his case is much more speculative than that of the "respected authorities" whom he seeks to correct); the possibility of still later work on the poem has been suggested on the basis of Brown's remark that Keats was "remodelling" *Hyperion* at the same time that he wrote *The Jealousies* (*KC,* II, 72), but unfortunately we do not have a definite date for this latter poem. First published (all but I.187–210) by Milnes in *1857*—"Another Version of Keats's 'Hyperion,'" in *Miscellanies of the Philobiblon Society,* 3 (1856–57, with the spine date 1857)—and about the same time privately issued by Milnes as a separate pamphlet (see Garrod, pp. xxvii–xxviii; there is a copy at Keats House, Hampstead). The two publications are on the same paper and except for the manner of issue are bibliographically identical; it is not clear whether the pamphlet represents a small batch of offprints from the *Miscellanies,* or the *Miscellanies* (in which each item is separately paged) a binding-up of copies of the pamphlet. Milnes reprinted the work with a few corrections in an appendix in his one-volume *Life* of Keats in 1867. The omitted lines (I.187–210) were first published in de Selincourt's *Hyperion: A Facsimile* (Oxford, 1905).

The three extant MSS are complete transcripts by Woodhouse ($W^2$) and two of his clerks (Garrod's *T*) and a partial transcript by Charlotte Reynolds (I.1–326 only). In addition to these we have, in Keats's hand, I.1–11a, 61–86, II.1–4, 6 copied out in a letter to Woodhouse of 21, 22 September 1819 (MS at Harvard). On E. L. Lushington's "copy of Hyperion" in 1856 see Textual Note to *Hyperion.*

The lines quoted by Keats in his letter to Woodhouse lack the paragraph indention at I.81 and differ substantively from $W^2$ in I.64, 65, 69, 70, 83, and 85 (it is odd that Woodhouse did not record these letter variants in $W^2$; instead he marked the $W^2$ readings for I.64, 65, 69, and 70 in pencil on the letter holograph). These variant readings suggest that there may have been a draft of at least part of the poem prior to the now lost holograph from which all subsequent texts derive. $W^2$ has neither a date nor any indication of source, but there is clear evidence that it was copied from a MS in Keats's own hand (see the apparatus for I.10, 48 and the note below to I.167–168; Woodhouse also penciled "euewhie" in the margin beside I.179 to show how Keats wrote "erewhile" in the lost holograph, and noted that "Degraded" in I.322 was originally spelled "Degraged").

Charlotte Reynolds' partial transcript differs substantively from $W^2$ in I.7 ("the" for "they"), 10 ("chain"—presumably, as in the clerks' transcript, an attempt to make sense of $W^2$'s "cham"), 19 ("were" for "where"), 51 ("wrapt"—$W^2$ has "⟨w⟩rapt"), 69 (the same words as in $W^2$ but without Woodhouse's transposition marks), 75 (the omission of the line), 147 ("the" for "that"), 165–166 (the omission of "they have . . . here"), 185 (the omission of "love of"), 188 ("in" for "into"), 234 ("painted" for "paved"), 259 ("I" for "It"), 298 ("what"—$W^2$ has "was" with a penciled "what?" in the margin), 299 ("on" for "so"), and 319 ("footmark"). Except in I.10, 51, 69, and 298, these variants are all simple copying errors. The two transcripts are so strikingly close in accidentals that one of them almost surely had to have come from the other. Since it is not possible that Woodhouse copied Charlotte Reynolds' MS (she has only the first 326 lines, and some omissions within those), we must conclude that she took her lines from $W^2$ (see *Texts,* pp. vii–viii, 48–50, 260–261). It is not known when she made her transcript; if it postdates the publication of *Hyperion,* it is possible that she stopped with I.326, the end of a paragraph, on the realization that she was now copying lines already in print (see the separate note to I.294).

Toward the end of his life (on paper watermarked 1833) Woodhouse had the $W^2$ text copied for Brown by two of his clerks, the one writing Canto I, the other Canto II, and Woodhouse correcting the MS throughout, adding I.202b–204 (with "O far" for "far" in 204) and approving or overlooking substantive variants in I.10 ("chain"), 271 ("upwards"), 277 ("enwouned"), 308 ("sat"), 370 ("the" for "thy"), and II.41 ("cluster"). The clerks' MS was the source (via a now lost intervening copy made by Milnes or an amanuensis) of the first printed text, *1857,* which omitted I.187–210, added a line from *Hyperion* after II.22, reproduced the first clerk's readings in I.10 and 308, and introduced substantive changes and errors into more than fifty other lines ("high" for "light" in I.27, "As" for "When" in I.97, "had" for "hand" in I.344, "slumber's" for "slumbrous" in I.369, "reef" for "self" in II.10, "drear" for "dire" in II.18, "metal rich" for "metals sick" in II.33, "eye" for "eyes" in II.53, and "river" for "roar" in II.59 were all corrected in the second printing of the poem, in Milnes's *Life* of 1867; the rest of the corruptions are listed in Appendix II). Milnes's title above the text in *1857*—"Hyperion, a Vision"—is apparently based on his own words in *1848* ("still later recast it into the shape of a Vision," I, 244), which he undoubtedly took from the MS of Brown's "Life" of Keats ("remodelling . . . 'Hyperion' into a 'Vision,'" *KC,* II, 72).

The present text, based on $W^2$, contains substantive emendations in I.97 and 298.

I.4 these] It is not clear whether the deleted "that" before this word in $W^2$ represents Woodhouse's own error or a cancellation in the now lost holograph that he was copying. The same applies to the deletions and alterations recorded in the apparatus for I.14, 115, 138, 164, 166/167 (the substitution of "by" in the second canceled line), 217, 236, 317, 356, 382, II.38, 47.

I.69 toil'd . . . winds] The transpositions marked by Woodhouse in $W^2$ (and by him also, in pencil, in the letter holograph) may be his own revision rather than an authoritative change.

I.76 some] This word is marginally queried in pencil by Woodhouse in both $W^2$ and the clerks' transcript.

I.97 mid-May] The emendation here was first suggested by A. E. Housman, *TLS*, 8 May 1924, p. 286. Milnes in *1857* printed "midday."

I.167–168 do . . . To] Originally Woodhouse copied "do . . . Do" in $W^2$. He underscored "do" (167) in pencil and noted opposite, "This word sho$^{d}$ perhaps be omitted" and "The M.S. is as here"; then wrote "q *To*" beside "Do" (168); and finally changed "Do" in the text to "To." Clearly his holograph source had "do . . . Do."

I.187–210 Majestic . . . graves.] In both $W^2$ and the clerks' transcript these lines (minus 203–204 and with a different text in 202) are marked with a pencil line—in the margin of $W^2$ and vertically through the text in the clerks' copy—and there are notes by Woodhouse in both MSS to the effect that "Keats seems to have intended to erase this & the 21 follow$^{g}$ verses" ($W^2$). The fact that the lines were copied currently in the transcripts and the wording of Woodhouse's notes ("*seems* to have intended") make virtually certain that the passage was not marked for deletion or revision by Keats and that Woodhouse's notes represent critical conjecture (based on the partial repetition of 187, 194–198 in 211, 216–220) rather than textual information. Charlotte Reynolds copied 187–210 straight out, either ignoring Woodhouse's note in $W^2$ or else making her transcript before he wrote the note.

I.202–204 The . . . flown Apollo!] The fact that Woodhouse added the present 202b–204 on the opposite verso in $W^2$ (and also in the top margin of his clerks' MS) and did not include them in his count of "this & the 21 follow$^{g}$ verses" suggests that Keats may have later expanded the section that Woodhouse thought he "intended to erase" (see the preceding note), though it is also possible that Keats had already inserted the lines in his MS and that Woodhouse, intent on making an unusually faithful copy, entered them as an addition in imitation of the appearance of the holograph. Woodhouse in pencil suggested the insertion of "O" before "far" (204) in $W^2$—obviously to fill out the meter—and then wrote "O far" when he added the lines on the clerks' MS.

I.218 drooping] Woodhouse in pencil in $W^2$ suggested revision to "weeping" (presumably to avoid the repetition of the same word already used in 216).

I.272 mountain's] Woodhouse in pencil in $W^2$ suggested revision to "mountain."

I.294 Deep . . . vale,] This is the first of 134 lines that Keats took over more or less verbatim from the then unpublished *Hyperion.* The present I.294–296 correspond to *Hyperion* I.1–3; I.310b–330 to I.7b–25; I.339–365 to I.37–63; I.367–383 to I.67–72, 74–82, 85–86; I.386–387 to I.87–88; I.400–403 to I.89–92; I.412b–417 to I.106b–108, 110–112; I.432b–438a to I.127b–133a; II.7–48 to I.158–173, 175–182a, 186–204; II.54–56 to I.218–220; II.58–61 to I.214–217.

I.350 tune] Woodhouse penciled "q tone" in the margin of $W^2$.

I.395 every] Garrod (followed by Allott) emends to "ever" on the private suggestion of J. C. Maxwell. But Maxwell has since come upon the phrase "each day by day" in Hardy's *The Dynasts,* Part Second, II.vi.13, which he thinks supports the $W^2$ wording (see *John Keats: The Complete Poems,* ed. John Barnard, Harmondsworth, 1973, pp. 681–682).

I.462 waste] Woodhouse penciled "wa*n*st" above this word in $W^2$ and "q wait" on the opposite verso.

### *The day is gone, and all its sweets are gone*

Written in 1819 (so dated in Brown's transcript and Woodhouse's last transcript), possibly toward the end of the year, though the specific October datings by almost all scholars are not well grounded. First published in *PDWJ,* 4 October 1838, and then in *1848,* II, 304. The five extant MSS are Keats's original draft (in the Morgan Library), three transcripts by Woodhouse ($W^3$, $W^2$, and the Harvard copy that Garrod refers to as *T*), and a transcript by Brown.

The earlier of the two recoverable states of text is that of the extant draft. All of Woodhouse's transcripts reproduce this draft text. In the margins and between the lines of $W^3$ he noted canceled readings from the draft's 8–10 (and also provisionally revised 13 in pencil to correct the meter, altering "But as I" to "As I"), and below the text in $W^2$ he added an exact representation of the draft's 8–12, with all of Keats's cancellations and revisions. Probably both transcripts were made independently from the draft. Much later Woodhouse wrote out the *T* transcript from $W^2$.

The later state is represented by Brown's MS, which transposes the earlier version's second and third quatrains and shows further substantive changes in 3 and 13. Brown's source is not known, but there is a good possibility that this is one of the poems that he took from now lost (probably holograph) MSS in Fanny Brawne's possession (see *The Letters of Charles Armitage Brown,* Cambridge, Mass., 1966, p. 295—some or all of the next three poems also may have come from Fanny Brawne). Brown's MS was the source of the *PDWJ* text (which has "shade" for "shape" in 7 and "roof" for "woof" in 12, both copying or printing errors), and was printer's copy for *1848.*

The present text is based on Brown's MS.

### *I cry your mercy—pity—love!—aye, love*

Written in 1819 (so dated in Brown's transcript), perhaps toward the end of the year. First published in *1848,* II, 305. The single extant MS is a transcript by Brown, who probably took his text from a now lost MS in Fanny Brawne's possession (see Textual Note to the preceding poem). Brown's MS was printer's copy for *1848.*

### *What can I do to drive away*

Written probably in 1819 (Milnes, *1848,* II, 33, after quoting Keats's letter to Dilke of 1 October 1819, introduces these lines as "a fragment written about this date," and H. B. Forman, Lowell, and Garrod have turned this remark into a specific fact represented by Garrod's headnote, p. 504, "Dated: Oct. 1819 *1848*"; subsequent scholars, accepting October and even trying to determine *when* in October Keats composed the lines, overlook the fact that Milnes's approximate dating in the first place was a mere guess). First published in *1848,* II, 34–35. No MS has survived, and *1848* is our sole source. One may guess that this is another of the poems that Brown copied from MSS in Fanny Brawne's possession (see Textual Note to *The day is gone*), and that Milnes printed it in *1848* from a now lost Brown transcript. Of four substantive emendations proposed by H. B. Forman (see the notes below)—the first three in 1883 ed., II, 353 nn., and all four in Hampstead Keats, IV, 228–229 nn.—the second and fourth are incorporated into the present text.

3 Aye, an] Forman conjectures that Keats wrote "Aye, and an" or "Aye, but an," and that the word before "an" was inadvertently dropped in copying or printing. Garrod, p. 504 n., suggests that perhaps "Aye" should be omitted.

33 wretched] "Probably *wrecked* [the *1848* reading] should be *wretched.* There seems a want of aptness in making use of *wreck'd* (monosyllable) and *wrecked* (dissyllable) in such sharp counterpoint; and Keats would be quite likely to write *wreched* without the *t* and thus leave the word easy to mistake for *wrecked*" (Forman).

35 Ever] "I should think *Even* a likelier initial word here than *Ever*" (Forman).

42 flowers] "The word *bad* before *flowers* [in *1848*'s "bad flowers"] is questionable. Keats may have got as far as *bud* with the word *buds,* and then decided for *flowers* (dissyllable) and forgotten to strike out *bud*" (Forman).

### *To Fanny*

Written probably toward the end of 1819 or during the early months of 1820. First published in *1848,* II, 284–286. The two extant MSS are two and one-half leaves of Keats's original draft, at Harvard, and a complete transcript by Milnes.

The first leaf of Keats's draft, containing 1–8 and probably a canceled preliminary version of either 1–8 or 9–16, and the top half of the third leaf, containing 25–32, are missing. The surviving fragments consist of the second leaf (9–24), the bottom half of the third leaf (33–40), and all of the fourth leaf (41–56). Milnes's transcript, differing substantively from the extant portions of the draft in 12, 17, 45, 49, and 56, clearly came from another, later source than the draft (even though the draft, or at least the surviving parts of it, were once in Milnes's possession). We may conjecture that this is one more of the poems that Fanny Brawne permitted Brown to transcribe (see Textual Note to *The day is gone*), and that Milnes copied it from a now lost Brown transcript. Milnes's MS was printer's copy for *1848,* which introduced substantive corruptions, generally misreading Milnes's handwriting, in 8, 15, 46, and 56.

The present text is based on Milnes's MS.

33 my] This word is entirely missing from the draft (cut away with 25–32). It is possible that Milnes's alteration of "ah! Fanny" to "my Fanny!" is his own invention rather than an authoritative reading.

### *King Stephen*

Begun at Winchester late in August 1819 (just after the completion of *Otho*—*KC,* II, 67) and abandoned probably in November (the date after the title in

Brown's partial transcript). First published in *1848,* II, 204–214, though four short passages (I.i.16b–17, 29b–33, I.ii.12–15, 31–32) had appeared earlier as chapter epigraphs in Trelawny's *Adventures of a Younger Son* (1831), I, 318, III, 118, 124, 130. The two extant MSS, Brown's transcript of title, Dramatis Personae, and I.i.1–ii.19 and Keats's draft of I.ii.19b–iv.58 (at Harvard), together constitute our sole authoritative source for this fragment (they overlap only in "Now our dreaded Queen" in I.ii.19). In addition to these, Brown's copy of the extracts printed in Trelawny's *Adventures* is extant at the end of his transcript of that work now at Harvard.

Since Keats wrote from twenty-five to thirty lines per full page in the extant leaves of the draft MS, it is reasonable to suppose that the missing part of the draft, containing I.i.1–ii.19a, consisted of two leaves written on the recto sides only. The surviving leaves would then be leaves 3–7, with contents as follows:

| | *Recto* | *Verso* |
|---|---|---|
| Leaf 3 | I.ii.19b–44 | I.iii.1–18 |
| Leaf 4 | I.ii.45–54, followed by the heading, location, and opening s.d. for I.iii plus half a dozen canceled lines; the lower third of the page is blank | I.iii.19–45 |
| Leaf 5 | I.iii.46–47 plus s.d.; the rest of the page is blank | Blank |
| Leaf 6 | I.iv.1–29a (headed "Scene") | Blank |
| Leaf 7 | I.iv.29b–58 | Blank |

From the above it would appear that Keats drafted the first two scenes straight through, on the rectos of leaves 1–4, began and abandoned scene iii also on the recto of leaf 4, drafted part of an additional scene (scene iv in the present text) on leaves 6 and 7, and then went back to write the present scene iii on the versos of leaves 3 and 4 and the recto of an inserted leaf 5. Because he elsewhere (e.g., in the draft MS of *Otho*) sometimes used versos in the normal course of first composition, it is theoretically possible that he drafted scene iii on leaves 3v, 4v, and 5r before he wrote scene iv on the next two rectos. But the facts (a) that the canceled opening lines of scene iii on leaf 4r are followed by a third of a page of blank space, (b) that scene iv is headed simply "Scene," as if Keats did not know at the time how it would fit in with the others, and (c) that Brown's list of Dramatis Personae includes the named speakers of scenes i, ii, and iv, but omits De Kaims, who appears only in scene iii, all point to the conclusion that Keats added the forty-seven lines of the present scene iii after he wrote what we have of scene iv; there is no countering evidence to suggest that he wrote iii before iv. Pretty obviously, scene iii (which, as it stands, breaks off with the *entrance* of the Earl of Chester and his knights near the top of leaf 5r, after which the rest of the page is blank) and scene iv are both incomplete, and it may be a mistake to number the last scene "iv," as if Keats intended it to follow the last line of the unfinished scene iii.

It is not clear why Brown copied only the first two leaves of Keats's draft. One may guess either that, when he came to leaf 3, he could not reconstruct the proper order of passages, or else that Keats thought the rest, being incomplete, was not worth copying. In any case, from the two MSS that we have Brown supplied the four extracts that were used as chapter epigraphs in Trelawny's *Adventures,* and there is ample evidence, mainly in various peculiarities of accidentals and the understandable misreading of Keats's "mars" as "man" (I.ii.51), that both MSS together were the source of *1848*'s text. Since neither MS shows signs of having been directly used by the printer, one supposes that the work was set in type from Milnes's or an amanuensis' copy made from the two MSS. The *1848* text omits the Dramatis Personae and has substantive corruptions in eleven other lines besides the misreading mentioned above in I.ii.51.

The present text, based on Brown's transcript for heading, Dramatis Personae, and I.i.1–ii.19a and on Keats's draft for the remainder, corrects and adds to the second and fourth items of Brown's Dramatis Personae, adds "De Kaims" to the list as the fifth item, and takes over *1848*'s emendations in I.i.35, I.ii.28 (s.d. and text), I.ii.29 ff. s.p., and the numbering of the last scene.

I.ii.32 wounds] In copying 31–32 for the chapter epigraph in Trelawny's *Adventures* Brown wrote "harms."

I.iii.29 That . . . bow'd] Keats's draft has no punctuation in 28–31, but it seems better to take "That" to mean "So that" and "bow'd" to modify "presence chamber" (30) than to construe (in Allott's punctuation) 28–29 and 30–32a as separate clauses.

I.iv.32 Council] *1848,* followed by all subsequent editors, emended the draft's "council" to "counsel" (probably on the basis of I.iv.5–13), but in the seven instances of "counsel" and "council" elsewhere in holograph MSS Keats consistently uses "council" for the advisory group and "counsel" for the advice given.

### *This living hand, now warm and capable*

Written probably toward the end of 1819 (the lines were drafted or copied on the outside recto of a folded sheet on which, after turning it over and around, Keats drafted stanzas 45–51 of *The Jealousies*; they thus appear upside down on the page containing stanza 51 but predate at least the composition of stanza 45). First published in H. B. Forman's one-volume *Poetical Works of John Keats,* 6th ed. (1898), p. 417. The extant holograph (at Harvard) is our sole authoritative source. Modern editors usually follow Forman in emending "would" (5) to "wouldst."

### *The Jealousies*

Written probably toward the end of 1819 (Brown's reference in *KC,* II, 71–72, cannot be dated more precisely, and there is no other evidence for dating). Lines

217–256 first published in the *Indicator,* 23 August 1820, p. 368; lines 390–396, 415–423 first published (as chapter epigraphs) in Trelawny's *Adventures of a Younger Son* (1831), I, 326, II, 49; and a complete text (all but 793–794) first in *1848,* II, 215–251. The two principal MSS are Keats's original draft, of which 1–729 is extant in three places—the Morgan Library (1–72, 145–398, 460–729), the Huntington Library (73–108), and Harvard (109–144, 397–459)—and a complete transcript by Woodhouse ($W^2$). Brown's copy of the two extracts printed in Trelawny's *Adventures* is extant at the end of his transcript of that work now at Harvard.

What is lacking, apart from the remainder of Keats's draft (730–794), is a complete transcript by Brown. "I copied as he wrote," Brown tells in his "Life" of Keats (*KC,* II, 72), and there are various evidences of his transcript in the years after Keats's death: the extracts that he made for Trelawny's work; the specific reference to the poem as part of the "parcel containing all Keats's poems in my possession" that he sent Milnes in 1841 (*KC,* II, 98–99); and Milnes's publication of the poem in *1848* with a note on its incompleteness and lack of plan signed "Charles Brown" (see the first separate note below). It is virtually certain that Brown's now lost transcript was either printer's copy or the source of printer's copy for *1848*; and it is also likely that, when Keats gave Hunt the stanzas for the *Indicator* in August 1820 (at a time when Brown was in Scotland), he did so from Brown's copy, since the *Indicator* and *1848* agree substantively in seven lines against readings of Keats's draft.

Certain oddities of stanza-arrangement in the surviving nine-tenths of the untitled draft support Brown's statement that he copied the lines as Keats wrote them. For example, 208–243, 244–261, 262–279, and 289–315 were written on the versos of full sheets containing, respectively, 1–18, 37–54, 19–36, and 55–72; and 316–333 appear on the verso of a half-sheet containing 280–288. Obviously the draft never was intended to serve as a complete MS of the poem: Keats composed the stanzas on whatever sheets and half-sheets came to hand, Brown "copied as he wrote," and Keats subsequently used some of the blank versos for drafting new stanzas further on in the poem. He wrote the first eight stanzas without stanza numbers on sheets that he foliated "1" through "4"; the fifth full sheet (now separated into half-sheets that are at the Huntington and Harvard) has the foliation "5" and eight numbered stanzas (9–16, lines 73–144); thereafter Keats numbered the stanzas but did not foliate the leaves. The present stanzas 19–28 are numbered 17–26, and it is possible that the present stanzas 17 and 18, headed "17" and "18" from the beginning, are a later addition (see the note to 145–162, below).

Woodhouse's transcript, which has no indication of date or source, agrees substantively with *1848* against readings of the draft in fifty-five lines—23, 34, 135, 148, 159, 161, 170, 177, 192, 207, 208, 211, 214 ("repell'th"), 215, 216, 223, 225, 227, 233, 241–242, 246, 265, 304, 323, 365, 383 (punctuation), 387, 393, 407, 409, 415, 416, 419, 480, 491, 508, 509, 521, 522, 523, 526, 531 ("that minx"), 540, 549, 551, 562, 597, 613, 634, 641, 658, 666, 707, 708 (this list does not include differences owing to Keats's obvious slips of the pen)—and in such peculiarities as the error "dealers" in 208, the incompleteness of 522, and the inclusion of the notes to 365 and 403 (which are not present in the draft). Of the twenty-nine unique readings in $W^2$—in heading, 32, 40, 61, 91, 107, 120, 212, 286, 293, 307, 365 note, 371, 383, 391, 405, 437, 466, 468, 477, 485, 492, 527, 531 ("How"), 565, 582, 729, 730, 793–794—all but the first (the heading) and the last two (for which the draft has not survived) can be seen as either copying errors or Woodhouse's attempts to correct or improve the text. The seventeen unique readings in *1848*—in heading, 180, 214 ("powers"), 297, 347, 355, 391, 505, 544, 564, 568, 569, 574, 575, 576, 719, 730—can also, except in perhaps two instances (391, 730), be seen as either Milnes's emendations or printer's errors. With the likenesses between *1848* and $W^2$ so extensive, and their relatively few differences explainable in these ways, it would seem highly probable that Woodhouse copied the poem from *1848*'s source, Brown's lost transcript. (The principal but not insurmountable obstacle to this view is $W^2$'s reading in 422, which is discussed in a separate note below.)

If both $W^2$ and *1848* (as well as the *Indicator* and Trelawny extracts) came from the lost Brown transcript, then we have two basic texts of the poem, that of the original draft and that of Brown's transcript as represented by the agreement of the various texts deriving from it. There is still, however, the problem of the relationship between these two texts and especially their substantive differences in fifty-five lines not accountable in terms of Woodhouse's or Milnes's or the *1848* printer's alterations. It is unlikely (even if we take into account Brown's recent experience as coauthor of *Otho*) that Brown introduced all the changes on his own initiative, and it is also unlikely that the lost transcript was a different MS from the copy that Brown made while Keats was writing the poem (because, except for transcripts of two or three short poems for special purposes and probably some lost MSS written out for the *1820* and *PDWJ* printers, there is no evidence that Brown made more than a single copy of any poem). Consequently we must suppose that at least some and possibly all of the differences between the original draft and Brown's text recoverable via $W^2$ and *1848* are the results of Keats's revisions, either in his own hand or by his request, in the lost transcript.

The present text, based on *1848* (the more reliable representative of Brown's lost MS), contains substantive emendations in heading, 180, 184 (punctuation), 207, 208, 214, 297, 347, 355, 419, 505, 521, 522, 523, 544, 564, 568, 569, 574, 575, 576, 697–698 (punctuation), 719, and 793–794. Most of these emendations—all but 184, 207, 208, 419, 521, 522, 523, 697–698, 793–794—are based on the agreement of the draft and $W^2$ against *1848*. Those in 207, 419, 521, 522, 523 restore draft revisions that Keats seems to have made (unless Brown overlooked them) after Brown copied the lines. The rest are commented on in separate notes below.

*Heading* The . . . Lambeth] Woodhouse's title is here adopted as representing that in the lost Brown transcript. Brown says in his "Life" of Keats that the poem "was to be published under the feigned authorship of Lucy Vaughan Lloyd, and to bear the title of *The Cap and Bells,* or, which [Keats] preferred, *The Jealousies*" (*KC,* II, 72). Pretty clearly it was Milnes who preferred "The Cap and Bells," taking the title from Brown's "Life" just as he later (in *1857*) based another nonauthoritative title, "Hyperion, a Vision," on the same source. *1848* has a footnote to the main title: "This Poem was written subject to future amendments and omissions: it was begun without a plan, and without any prescribed laws for the supernatural machinery.—CHARLES BROWN."

23 Befitting] The draft's "Befeeling" is not recognized by the *OED,* but may be Keats's intentional coinage (= "feeling strongly") rather than a slip of the pen.

145–162 "I'll . . . Biancopany?] The present stanzas 19–28 are numbered 17–26 in the draft, and preliminary versions of the present stanzas 29 and 30 were originally headed "27" and "28." It may be, therefore, that stanzas 17 and 18 (lines 145–162), which have their present numbers unaltered, are a later addition to the MS, written around the time that Keats drafted stanza 30. But the matter is not perfectly clear. Stanzas 17–18 appear on the outside recto of a folded sheet containing, on the inside pages and the outside verso, the present stanzas 19–23, and we must suppose, if 17–18 are taken to be a later addition, that Keats originally left the outside recto blank and began his new sheet with the present 19 on an *inside* verso. It is perhaps more likely that he simply misnumbered the present 19–28, then realized his error and corrected accordingly when he was writing 30. (There is the further peculiarity that, while the preliminary version of stanza 29 is headed "27" altered to "29," it is followed on the next-written page by stanza 29 with the number unaltered and then, beneath it on the same page, the preliminary version of 30 originally headed "28." The explanation for this has to be that Keats did not number stanza 29 at all until he had written the preliminary lines below and then changed the number there from "28" to "30.")

184 slow‸] The *W²-1848* comma here produces a redundant apposition in 185 ("His speech, his only words"), and therefore the text is emended to the draft's adjectival phrase "slow / His speech."

207/208 (*apparatus*) ⟨His . . . Minster⟩] These canceled lines appear upside down on the page in the draft containing 316–333. They are given after 207 rather than at a later point in the apparatus because (a) 207 comes at the bottom of a verso page and these lines were written at what was originally the top of a new page, (b) the opening "His" follows from "The slave . . . He . . . " in 203–207, and (c) "wrapt," "cloak," and "In cognito" in the first two lines were all used shortly afterward in the poem (in 219–220). "Crimson" and "cloak" appear later on, in 267, and "pearl-built Minster" in 579.

208 houses] The *W²-1848* "dealers" obviously represents a copying error by Brown (probably based on an anticipatory glance at 210).

234 modern use] The *Indicator*'s unique "vile no-use" is probably Hunt's invention.

314 whelping] So the draft, *W²*, and *1848*. Modern editors usually follow H. B. Forman (1883 ed.) in emending to "yelping" (the dog is masculine in 312, 313, 315).

365 *note* is of] Woodhouse follows the *Spectator* (No. 317, 4 March 1712) in omitting "is." Possibly "is of" is an emendation in *1848* rather than the reading of Brown's lost transcript, but it seems equally likely that the scholarly Woodhouse remembered or checked the *Spectator*'s exact wording. Apparently J. H. Reynolds at one time agreed to provide notes for the poem (*Letters,* II, 268); Gittings, p. 370, suggests that he may have been responsible for this note and that to 403.

383 Pearl! What . . . whirl?] The original text in the draft was a straightforward declarative sentence, "'Tis Bertha Pearl that makes my Brains so whirl."

Keats then changed "that" to "what" but did not alter the punctuation, and he still may have intended a declaration rather than the exclamation and question in $W^2$-*1848*.

391 tiger's] The draft's "tigers" is ambiguous, and the choice here of *1848*'s "tiger's" over $W^2$'s "tigers'" is arbitrary (Brown's extract of 390–396 for Trelawny's *Adventures* has "tigers" and the printed chapter epigraph "tigers'").

419 and flit] In copying 415–423 for Trelawny's *Adventures* Brown wrote "or flit."

422 catch the treasure] $W^2$'s agreement with the draft against *1848* (and Brown's lost transcript—his extract for Trelawny has the *1848* wording) is difficult to explain if Woodhouse is supposed to have taken his text from Brown. One may conjecture that Brown's MS originally had "save 'the creature,'" and then "catch the treasure" substituted above it, and that Woodhouse, preferring the earlier reading (as he did occasionally elsewhere in his transcripts), copied the original instead of the revised text. While this may seem farfetched, it is easier to accept than the idea that Woodhouse copied the poem from some other source that we know nothing about.

547 pigsney] Woodhouse underscored the second syllable of this word in $W^2$ and penciled "q my" (i.e., "pigmy?") in the margin.

692 dozed] The draft's "dos'd" (like $W^2$'s and *1848*'s "dosed") was an acceptable spelling of "dozed" in Keats's time, and the emendation here (for clarity) is not substantive.

697–698 jokes:) . . . favour,] Though each of the three principal texts is punctuated differently, the emendation here accords with the essential agreement of the draft and $W^2$ in connecting "To . . . favour" with the rest of 698 and the first half of 699 rather than (as in *1848*) with 696–697.

730 o'er] The draft text is missing from 730 to the end. *1848*'s "o'er" is here preferred to $W^2$'s "through" on critical grounds (to avoid the repetition with "throughout" in 731) and also on the likelihood that the $W^2$ reading is a copying error based on an anticipatory glance at the next line.

735 Our] Woodhouse penciled "q *One*" in the margin of $W^2$.

738 wild-reefed] Woodhouse wrote "wild reefy" in $W^2$, then added "ed" in pencil in the margin and sometime afterward changed the second word in his text to "reefed."

759 scrape-graces] So $W^2$, *1848*. Modern editors usually emend to "scapegraces," but there is a fair chance that Keats intended a pun (scapegraces who bow and scrape).

793–794 Now . . . hall.] These lines (plus stanza number and asterisks) appear only in $W^2$, and were first published in Garrod's 1939 edition. *1848* ends with 792 followed by a row of asterisks and the parenthetical explanation "No more was written."

### *In after time a sage of mickle lore*

Written in 1820 (so dated in Brown's transcript; "the last stanza, of any kind, that [Keats] wrote before his lamented death" in *PDWJ*). First published in

*PDWJ,* 4 July 1839, and then in *1848,* I, 281. The single extant MS is a transcript by Brown written in his copy of Spenser's *Poetical Works* (8 vols., 1788) now at Keats House, Hampstead, in a blank space at the end of *The Faerie Queene* V.ii. This was made from a now lost holograph in another copy of Spenser (also at the end of V.ii) that Keats gave to Fanny Brawne. (The volume was lent to Fanny Keats in 1823, and subsequently "was lost in Germany"; see *Letters,* II, 302, and *Letters of Fanny Brawne to Fanny Keats,* ed. Fred Edgcumbe, New York, 1937, pp. 84, 86 n.) Presumably both the *PDWJ* and the *1848* texts derive from the extant transcript, which is also the basis of the present text.

8 grim] Here Brown's MS perhaps represents alternative readings in the lost holograph that he was copying.

APPENDIX I

# Editorial Emendations of the Copy-Texts

Several kinds of silent (i.e., unrecorded) change have been made to standardize the presentational features of this edition. The following apply generally to the texts, the record of variants and other readings in the apparatus, and the citation of texts and variants in the Textual Notes and appendixes:

(1) The typographical peculiarities of titles, division headings, first lines, and end-dates in printed sources (e.g., the use of Gothic or italic type and the combining of large and small capitals) are not preserved; printed titles entirely in capitals are regularized to conventional capitals and lowercase letters.

(2) Periods, dashes, and other meaningless marks after titles, epigraph sources, dedications, division headings, speech prefixes (when they are centered above the line), stanza numbers, and end-dates are omitted. Periods are added (where they are wanting) at the end of footnotes.

(3) Stanza numbers are regularized to arabic; all other division numbers—for books, cantos, parts, acts, and scenes—are regularized to cardinal roman. Ordinal for cardinal numbers (as in "2nd" for "II" in a scene heading) are not recorded as variants.

(4) Verse paragraphs are separated by line spaces, and all except the first in a series are indented; line spaces between parts of a sonnet are ignored, and indentions in sonnets and other stanzaic forms are regularized to conventional usage.

(5) Speech prefixes in poems are centered above the line and spelled out in full (abbreviations are not recorded as variants); speech prefixes in *Otho the Great* and *King Stephen* are placed at the beginning of the line and again spelled out in full, and they and the dramatis personae, scene locations, and stage directions are given a uniform style. Brown's repetitions of speech prefix following an interpolated stage direction in *Otho* are omitted.

(6) Ordinary quotation marks are regularized to double quotes; those enclosing quotations within quoted speech are regularized to single.

(7) Short dashes used as ordinary punctuation are represented by em dashes without spacing; longer dashes (e.g., in blank names and ellipses and at the end of interrupted speeches) are regularized to two-em.

(8) Lines or partial lines consisting of dots, x's, crosses, and other odd marks are represented by a series of asterisks.

(9) In texts and variants from transcripts and posthumous printings the ampersand is changed to "and"; "&c" with or without a period is changed to "etc.";

and "ag$^{t}$," "co$^{d}$," "tho'," "thro'," and "wo$^{d}$" are expanded to "against," "could," "though," "through," and "would" (Keats almost never used such abbreviations in his poetry MSS). In the apparatus and Textual Notes Woodhouse's "orig$^{y}$," "orig$^{l}$," and "or$^{l}$" are expanded to "originally."

(10) Elided forms are spaced or closed up according to conventional usage (e.g., "th' elect" is retained, but "'t is" is printed "'tis").

All other changes—emendations of wording, punctuation, spelling, capitalization, word-division, and paragraphing—are recorded in the lists below. The reading to the left of the bracket is that of the present edition, and the reading to the right is that of the copy-text. Where the heading has been emended, the copy-text heading is given in full in the first note.

*Imitation of Spenser*

12 fins‸] ~,
12 scalès] scales'
29 glassy] glossy

*On Peace*

1 Peace] peace
2 isle] Isle
8 mountain nymph] Mountain Nymph
13 kings] Kings
13 great;] ~‸
14 horrors] Honors

*Lines Written on 29 May, the Anniversary of Charles's Restoration, on Hearing the Bells Ringing*

Copy-text heading: —Lines— / written on 29 May.—the anniversary of Charles's Restoration.—On hearing the Bells ringing
3 patriots] Patriots
6 ear.] ~—

*Stay, ruby breasted warbler, stay*

Copy-text heading: Song, / (tune) Julia to the Wood Robin
A stanza number for the first stanza (only) has been added
2 eye;] Eye,
5 thee,] ~‸
6 love] Love
6 art;] ~,
7 plume] Plume
9 summer nights] Summer Nights
10 summer suns] Summer Suns
10 day,] ~;
11 notes‸] Notes,
13 eye's] Eye's
15 love] Love
18 destroy,] ~;
19 grove‸] ~,
20 joy.] ~—
21 love] Love
22 pleasure's tree] Pleasures Tree

*Fill for me a brimming bowl*

No heading (other than epigraph) in copy-text
Copy-text epigraph: What wondrous beauty! From this Mo[ ]fface from my Mind all Women. Terence's Eunuch. Act. 2.
S. 4 (*missing text lost through damage to MS*)
1 bowl] Bowl
2 soul] Soul
3 design'd‸] ~,
4 mind] Mind

5 stream] Stream
6 sense] Sense
7 But∧] ~,
9 breast] Breast
10 image] Image
11 eyes beheld,] Eyes ~∧
12 wand'ring fancy] wan'dring Fancy
13 chace∧] ~,
15 beaminess] beamminess
15 eyes] Eyes
16 breast, earth's] ~∧ Earth's
16 paradise] Paradise
17 blest,] ~∧
18 zest] Zest
20 page] Page
20 muse's] Muses
22 smile] Smile
23 relief,] ~∧
24 joy] Joy
24 grief] Grief
25 snow] Snow
28 halo] Halo
28 memory] Memory

*As from the darkening gloom a silver dove*

Copy-text heading: Sonnet
2 eastern] Eastern
9 quire] Quire
10 melodies∧] ~,
10 heaven] Heaven
12 omnipotent] Omnipotent

*To Lord Byron*

Copy-text heading: Sonnet / To Lord Byron
1 melody,] ~∧
2 tenderness,] ~∧
4 lute] Lute
4 by,] ~∧
5 Hadst] Had'st
8 halo] Halo
8 beamily;] ~.
9 veil,] ~∧
10 glow,] ~∧
12 flow.] ~∧
13 warble,] ~∧
13 tale,] ~∧

*Oh Chatterton! how very sad thy fate*

Copy-text heading: Sonnet
2 child] Child
2 sorrow! son] Sorrow! Son
2 misery] Misery
3 eye] Eye
4 genius] Genius
5 majestic∧] ~,
7 morning] Morning
8 ∧amate.*] [4]~.∧
8 *note* *Affright—Spenser] [4]affright—Spencer
9 past.] ~—
9 stars] Stars
10 heaven] Heaven
13 earth] Earth
13 man] Man
14 name] Name
14 tears] Tears

*Written on the Day That Mr. Leigh Hunt Left Prison*

Copy-text heading: III. / Written on the day that Mr. Leigh Hunt left Prison

*To Hope*

No emendations

*Ode to Apollo*

Copy-text heading: Ode. To Apollo
A stanza number for the first stanza (only) has been added
1 western halls] Western Halls
4 fate] Fate
9 western] Western

13 temple] Temple
29 master's] Master's
32 chorus] Chorus
33 chastity] Chastity
34 'Tis] $_{\wedge}$~
36 numbers] Numbers
38 youth] Youth
38 slumbers] Slumbers
43 powers] Powers
43 song] Song
46 evening] Evening

*To Some Ladies*

3 accents$_{\wedge}$ that,] ~, ~$_{\wedge}$
6 muse] rove
19 And, smiles$_{\wedge}$] ~$_{\wedge}$ ~,

*On Receiving a Curious Shell, and a Copy of Verses, from the Same Ladies*

Copy-text heading: On receiving a curious Shell, and a Copy of Verses, from the same Ladies
42 youth;] ~,

*O come, dearest Emma! the rose is full blown*

Copy-text heading: Song
1 come,] ~$_{\wedge}$
1 rose] Rose
1 blown,] bl[ ] (*text here and in the last word of 2 lost through damage to MS*)
2 riches] Riches
2 strown] s[ ]n
3 air] Air
4 west] West
4 beams] Beams
5 fair] Fair
6 seats] Seats
7 hymns] Hymns
8 sun-] Sun-
8 sylph] Sylph
9 bed] Bed
10 mosses] Mosses
10 head] Head
12 love] Love
14 think$_{\wedge}$] ~,
14 amorous zephyr] amourous Zephyr
17 why, . . . girl,] ~$_{\wedge}$ . . . Girl$_{\wedge}$
17 blisses] Blisses
18 mortal's] Mortal's
20 eyes] Eyes
20 voice] Voice

*Woman! when I behold thee flippant, vain*

No heading in copy-text
18 eyes$_{\wedge}$] ~,

*O Solitude! if I must with thee dwell*

Copy-text heading: VII

*To George Felton Mathew*

44 white;] ~.
53 Mathew,] ~$_{\wedge}$
73 muse] Muse
75 place":] ~:"

*Had I a man's fair form, then might my sighs*

Copy-text heading: II. / To * * * * * *

*Hadst thou liv'd in days of old*

Copy-text heading: To * * * *
15 hellebore] Hellebore

*I am as brisk*

No heading in copy-text
2 whisk-] Wisk-
4 milliner's thimble.] Milliner's ~—

*Give me women, wine, and snuff*

No heading in copy-text
1 women, wine,] ~∧ ~∧
2 "hold, enough!"] ∧~∧ ~∧
4 the] y[e]
4 resurrection;] ~∧
5 beard,] ~∧
6 Trinity.] ~∧

*Specimen of an Induction to a Poem*

19 knight] Knight
36 butts] buts
39–40 shield, . . . field?] ~? . . . ~.
46 steed] knight
47 knight∧] ~,

*Calidore*

Copy-text heading: Calidore. / A Fragment
35 sun∧] ~,
36 ever∧] ~,
44 window] windows
44 its] his
91 eye,] ~∧
96 cassia] Cassia

*To one who has been long in city pent*

Copy-text heading: X
5 heart's] hearts

*Oh! how I love, on a fair summer's eve*

Copy-text heading: Sonnet
2 west] West
3 zephyrs] Zephyrs
6 to] To
8 deceive.∧] ~.—
12 wing] Wing
14 eyes.∧] ~.—

*To a Friend Who Sent Me Some Roses*

Copy-text heading: V. / To a Friend who sent me some Roses

*Happy is England! I could be content*

Copy-text heading: XVII

*To My Brother George (sonnet)*

Copy-text heading: I. / To My Brother George

*To My Brother George (epistle)*

Repeated opening quotes have been omitted in 72–109
44 which∧] ~,

*To Charles Cowden Clarke*

Repeated opening quotes have been omitted in 129 and 130
5 Galaxy] galaxy
42 One^] ~,
82 misspent] mispent
114 fitting;] ~.

*How many bards gild the lapses of time*

Copy-text heading: IV

*On First Looking into Chapman's Homer*

Copy-text heading: XI. / On first looking into Chapman's Homer

*Keen, fitful gusts are whisp'ring here and there*

Copy-text heading: IX

*On Leaving Some Friends at an Early Hour*

Copy-text heading: XII. / On leaving some Friends at an early Hour

*To My Brothers*

Copy-text heading: VIII. / To My Brothers
9 -day,] -~^

*Addressed to Haydon*

Copy-text heading: XIII. / Addressed to Haydon

*Addressed to the Same*

Copy-text heading: XIV. / Addressed to the Same
4 archangel's] Archangel's
6 freedom's] Freedom's

*To G. A. W.*

Copy-text heading: VI. / To G. A. W.
13 Grace] grace

*To Kosciusko*

Copy-text heading: XVI. / To Kosciusko
7 Are] And
11 Alfred's^] ~,

*Sleep and Poetry*

The copy-text's epigraph (with square brackets just as in the present text) appears on a half title preceding the first page of text. Repeated opening quotes have been omitted in 2–5 of the epigraph
11 thee,] ~^
74 Meander] meander
151 intent,] ~^
181 schism] scism
234 poets] Poets
281 off,] ~^
282 who,] ~^
318 friendliness,] ~^

318 good;] ~.
323 -morrow—] -~.
359 futurity] Futurity
377 smoothness] smoothiness
379 weeds,] ~;

*I stood tip-toe upon a little hill*

No heading (other than epigraph) in copy-text
22 where] were
39 brethren] brethen
86 behaviours.] ~‸ (*defective period in copy-text*)
94 sweet‸] ~,
107 ¶What . . . ] *no indention, but new page in copy-text*
153 Fauns] Fawns
159 find‸] ~,
168 cool‸] ~,
233 other's] others'

*Written in Disgust of Vulgar Superstition*

Copy-text heading: Sonnet / Written in disgust of vulgar superstition
1 church] Church
3 dreadful] dreadfull
4 sermon's] Sermons
4 sound.] ~—
5 man] Man
8 crown'd.] ~—
9 damp,‸] ~,—
12 'tis] t'is
14 stamp.] ~—

*On the Grasshopper and Cricket*

Copy-text heading: XV. / On the Grasshopper and Cricket

*After dark vapours have oppressed our plains*

Copy-text heading: Sonnet
3 south] South
4 heavens] Heavens
5 month, . . . pains,] ~‸ . . . ~‸
10 autumn suns] Autumn Suns
11 eve] Eve

*To a Young Lady Who Sent Me a Laurel Crown*

Copy-text heading: Sonnet. To a young Lady who sent me a laurel crown
5 stars] Stars
6 sun's] Sun's
10 own] high
10 "Stand,"‸] "~‸";—
11 very] *blank space in copy-text*

*On Receiving a Laurel Crown from Leigh Hunt*

Copy-text heading: On receiving a laurel Crown from Leigh Hunt
3 labyrinth.] Labyrinth—
5 poet] Poet
7 sprigs] Sprigs
8 coronet] Coronet
11 trampling] Trampling
11 prizes,] ~‸
12 crowns] Crowns

*To the Ladies Who Saw Me Crown'd*

Copy-text heading: To the Ladies who saw me crown'd
1 earth] Earth
2 wreath] Wreath
3 halo] Halo
3 moon] Moon
4 lips] Lips
4 mirth] Mirth

6 roses] Roses
7 halcyon's] Halcyon's
7 sea] Sea
8 comparisons] Comparisons
8 worth.] ~—
11 breathes] breaths
11 life] Life
13 palm;] Palm—
14 reverence] Reverence
14 eyes.] ~—

*God of the golden bow*

No heading in copy-text
2 lyre] Lyre
3 hair,] ~^
4 fire,] ~^
6 year—] ~^
7 Where, where] ~? Wher
8 wreath—] Wreath?
9 laurel, . . . glory,] Laurel— . . . ~—
10 light] Light
10 story?] ~—
11 too] to
11 death,] ~—
13 and grasp'd,] ~ ~^
14 and frown'd;] ~ frownd^
15 eagle's] Eagle's
16 wrath] Wrath
18 under,] ~^
19 unbound.] ~^
20 worm] wom
21 lute] Lute
22 mute] Mute
24 Delphic] delphic
25 Pleiades] Pleides
25 up,] ~^
26 air;] ~^
27 earth] Earth
28 fare;] ~^
29 ocean, . . . neighbour,] ~^ . . . ~^
30 labor,] Labor^
31 who, who] ~—~
32 brow,] ~^
33 proudly,] ~^
35 now,] ~^
36 Delphic] delphic

*This pleasant tale is like a little copse*

Copy-text heading: Sonnet. Written on the blank space of a leaf at the end of Chaucer's tale of "The flowre and the lefe"

*To Leigh Hunt, Esq.*

Copy-text heading: Dedication. / To Leigh Hunt, Esq.
12 free,] ~^

*On Seeing the Elgin Marbles*

Copy-text heading: On seeing the Elgin Marbles
1 spirit] Spirit
1 mortality] Mortality
3 pinnacle] Pinnacle
4 godlike hardship^] Godlike Hardship,
5 eagle] Eagle
5 sky] Sky
6 luxury] Luxury
8 morning's] Morning's
10 heart] Heart
10 feud] Feud
11 wonders] Wonders
11 pain,] ~^
12 Grecian] grecian
13 time] Time
13 main] Main
14 sun] Sun
14 shadow] Shadow
14 magnitude] Magnitude

*To Haydon with a Sonnet Written on Seeing the Elgin Marbles*

Copy-text heading: To Haydon with a Sonnet written on seeing the Elgin Marbles
1 me, Haydon,] ~∧ ~∧
2 Definitively] Difinitively
3 eagle's] Eagle's
7 springs,] ~∧
9 numbers] Numbers
11 men] Men
12 idiotism—o'erweening phlegm—] Idiotism—oerweening Phlegm∧
14 star] Star
14 east] East

*On a Leander Which Miss Reynolds, My Kind Friend, Gave Me*

Copy-text heading: On a Leander which Miss Reynolds my kind friend gave me
1 maidens,] Maidens∧
2 Down-looking—aye,] Downlooking—~∧
2 light] Light
3 white—] ~∧
5 So] so
5 see,] ~∧
6 Untouch'd,] Untouchd∧
6 victim] Victim
7 spirit's night,] spirits Night∧
8 bewilder'd] bewilderd
8 sea:] Sea∧
9 'Tis] ∧~
9 death] Death
10 swooning,] ~∧
10 weary lips] weay Lips
11 Hero's] Heros
13 arms] Arms
13 awhile:] ~—
14 up bubbles] upbubbles
14 amorous breath.] amourous ~∧

*On* The Story of Rimini

Copy-text heading: On the Story of Rimini
7 night] Night
8 moon] Moon

*On the Sea*

1 whisperings] Whisperings
3 caverns] Caverns
7 fell,] ~∧
8 heaven] Heaven
9 tir'd,] ~∧
10 sea;] Sea∧
11 ears] Ears
11 rude,] ~∧
13 cavern's mouth] Cavern's Mouth
14 start,] ~∧
14 sea nymphs quired.] Sea Nymphs ~—

*Unfelt, unheard, unseen*

No heading in copy-text
1 Unfelt,] ~∧
1 unseen,] ~∧
2 queen,] Queen∧
3 arms] Ams
3 dying:] ~∧
4 touch,] ~∧
5 Who, who] ~? Who
6 madness] Madness
6 complying?] ~∧
7 sleek,] ~∧
8–9 speak, . . . quiet,] ~∧ . . . ~∧
11 burden dear,] Burden ~∧
12 love] Love
12 bounds."] ~∧"
13 monitors,] Monitors∧
14 laws:] ~∧
16 So, . . . ado,] ~∧ . . . ~∧
17 anew,] ~∧
18 morn.] ~∧

*Hither, hither, love*

No heading in copy-text
1 Hither, hither, love,] ~∧ ~∧ Love∧
2 'Tis] ∧~
2 mead;] Mead.
3 hither, love,] ~∧ Love∧
4 and feed.] ~ ~∧
5 Hither, hither, sweet,] ~∧ ~∧ ~∧
6 'Tis] ∧~
6 bed;] ~∧
7 Hither, hither, sweet,] ~∧ ~∧ ~∧
8 'Tis] ∧~
8 bespread.] bespead∧
9 Hither, hither, dear,] ~∧ ~∧ ~∧
10 life,] Life∧
11 Hither, hither, dear,] ~∧ ~∧ ~∧
12 wife.] ~∧
14 moment flies,] monent ~∧
16 moment] monent
17 pass'd—] pass'ed∧
18 near; (*end of line*)] ~∧
19 last,] ~∧
20 dear, . . . dear.] ~∧ . . . ~∧
21 Hither, hither, hither,] ~∧ ~∧ ~∧
22 sent;] ~∧
24 content.] ~∧

*You say you love; but with a voice*

Copy-text heading: Stanzas
7 September,] ~;
8 nun] Nun
9 Ember—] ~.
16 hand∧] ~,
17 returneth;] ~,
18 statue's] Statue's
19 mine] Mine
24 me—] ~∧

*Before he went to live with owls and bats*

Copy-text heading: Sonnet
3 housewife's] Housewife's
4 naumachia] Naumachia
9 nightmare] Nightmare
11 loggerheads] Loggerheads
11 chapmen] Chapmen

*The Gothic looks solemn*

Copy-text heading: On Oxford
3 bishop] Bishop
3 crosier] Crosier
5 larch,] ~∧
10 chantry] Chantry
11 steeple-] Steeple-
15 parsons] Parsons

*O grant that like to Peter I*

No heading in copy-text

*Think not of it, sweet one, so*

No heading in copy-text
8 die.] ~∧

*Endymion*

The copy-text's epigraph is on the title page, and the dedication to Chatterton on the next recto page following the title. The emendations in I.14, II.272, 748, 782, 960–961, 963, III.949, IV.151, 362, 537, 721, 876, 951–952 are specified by Keats in his letter to Taylor of 24 April 1818 (*Letters,* I, 272–273). His request for repeated opening quotes in I.944–959, III.430–443, 571–600 has not been followed in the present text
I.14 old, . . . young∧] ~∧ . . . ~,
I.55 autumn] Autumn
I.182 owlet's] owlets
I.263 faun] fawn

I.283 huntsmen] huntsman
I.293 "Be] ∧~
I.305 pæan] Pæan
I.306 Lycean!"] ~!∧
I.317 children's] childrens'
I.355 contemplating∧] ~,
I.404 stept—] ~.
I.486 cheered,] ~∧
I.550 tighten] lighten
I.680 moving,] ~∧
I.733 scathe∧] ~,
I.790 where] were
I.958 Echo] echo
II.39 chafing] chaffing
II.125 canst] cans't
II.175 spar'd∧] ~,
II.272 dim,] ~∧
II.282 raught] caught
II.318 the . . . among] among the zephyr-boughs
II.382 For, . . . wood,] ~∧ . . . ~∧
II.524 tighten'd] lighten'd
II.535 Love's] love's
II.602 beds,] ~;
II.631 heaven's] Heaven's
II.680 "Alas!"] "~!∧
II.704 hither, sleep,] ~∧ ~∧
II.705 Hither,] ~∧
II.748 delicious] my kindest
II.761 dov'd] lov'd
II.782 done't] done it
II.793 vailed] veiled
II.793 crystalline] crystaline
II.882 harbour] arbour
II.960–961 bane.∧ / ∧O] ~."— / "~
II.963 criminal.∧ ∧Alas] ~."—"~
II.973 eye] eyes
II.1016 lovers'] ~∧
II.1017 plains."] ~.∧
III.156 blithely] blithly
III.201 roar,] ~∧
III.202 Quicksand . . . shore] *not in copy-text*
III.286 humane] human
III.335 thin∧ pervading] ~-~
III.359 airy] aery
III.394 be—] ~∧ (*the dash is present, however, in another Illinois copy and in three of the nine copies at Harvard*)
III.537 Sighing,] ~∧
III.555 "That] ∧~
III.572 thee, my] ~∧ ~
III.744–745 commence," . . . "even] ~, ∧ . . . ∧~
III.811 Through] Though
III.949 lost∧] ~,
IV.97 for . . . twain] in twain for them
IV.151 is't] is it
IV.341 wide] wild
IV.362 ¶There . . . ] *no* ¶ *in copy-text*
IV.443 When] Where
IV.486 silverly] silvery
IV.537 longing!] ~.
IV.538 paradise] Paradise
IV.548 led] let
IV.558 masque] mask
IV.632 to] too
IV.721 doubt!"] ~?"
IV.858 sister] Sister
IV.876 heard?] ~!
IV.915 Vesper's] vesper's
IV.951–952 "Ha!∧ . . . ∧King] "~!" . . . "~

*In drear nighted December*

No heading in copy-text
1 December,] ~∧
2 tree,] ~∧
3 branches] Branches
6 them,] ~∧
7 glue] glew
8 prime.] ~—
9 December,] december∧
10 happy, . . . brook,] ~∧ . . . Brook∧
12 summer look;] Summer ~∧
14 fretting,] ~∧
15 Never, never] ~∧ ~
16 time.] ~∧
20 joy?] ~∧
21, 22, 23 it,] ~∧
23 steel] steal
24 rhyme.] ~∧

*Apollo to the Graces*

2 To-day] ~∧ ~
2 me?] ~∧
3 steeds] Steeds
3 thresholds] threshholds
3 morn:] Morn∧
5 To-day] ~∧ ~
6 kingdoms] Kingdoms
6 corn?] Corn∧
7 *s.p.* ∧The . . . answer∧] (~ . . . ~)
7 will, I—I—I—] ~∧ ~—~, ~∧
8 Apollo,] ~∧
8 thee;] the∧
9 will, I—I—I—] ~∧ ~, ~. ~∧
10 many, many] ~∧ ~
10 see,] ~∧
11 I—I—I—I—] ~∧ ~∧ ~∧ ~∧
12 lyre] Lyre
12 slacken'd string;] slackend ~∧
13 I—I—I—I—] ~∧ ~∧ ~∧ ~∧
14 sing.] ~—

*To Mrs. Reynolds's Cat*

Copy-text heading: To Mrs Reynoldse's Cat
1 grand climacteric] Grand Climacteric
2 rats] Rats
3 Destroy'd] Destroye'd
8 fish] Fish
8 mice] Mice
8 rats] Rats
9 Nay,] ~∧
10 wheezy asthma] weezy Asthma
12 maid have] Maid has
12 maul,] ~∧
14 enter'dst] enterd'st
14 wall.] ~—

*Lines on Seeing a Lock of Milton's Hair*

Copy-text heading: Lines on seeing a Lock of Milton's hair
1 numbers] Numbers
2 scholar] Scholar
2 spheres] Spheres
3 spirit] Spirit
10 melody] Melody
12 temple] Temple
18 Delian] delian
18 soul,] ~∧
19 lips] Lips
20 love] Love
23 vanish'd] vanishe'd
26 harmony] Harmony
27 life] Life
30 philosophy] Philosophy
35 power;] Power—
36–37 A . . . came,] A Lock of thy bright hair—sudden it came, (*one line*)
39 unaware;] ~—
41 Flood.] flood—

*On Sitting Down to Read* King Lear *Once Again*

Copy-text heading: On sitting down to read King Lear once again
1 golden-] Golden-
1 Romance] Ramance
1 lute] Lute
2 syren] Syren
2 queen] Queen
3 day,] ~∧
4 pages] Pages
5 dispute∧] ~,
6 damnation] Damnation
9 clouds] Clouds
14 phœnix wings] Phœnix Wings

*When I have fears that I may cease to be*

Copy-text heading: Sonnet
11 fairy] faiery

*O blush not so! O blush not so*

Copy-text heading: Song
9 not (*third word*)] no
20 apple] Apple

*Hence burgundy, claret, and port*

Copy-text heading: Song
1 burgundy, claret] Burgundy, Claret
1 port] Port
2 hock] Hock
2 madeira] Madeira
3 sport;] ~,
6 summer;] Summer,
10 pain—] ~∧

*God of the meridian*

No heading in copy-text
1 meridian] Meridian
2 east] East
8 fear.] ~—
10 Too] To
13 mother] Mother
14 infant] Infant
15 eagle's claws.] Eagle's ~—
16 cause] Cause
19 bear;] ~,
22 philosophy] Philosophy

*Robin Hood*

7 north] North
7 east] East
36 shawe";] ~;"

*Lines on the Mermaid Tavern*

1, 23 poets] Poets
2, 24 elysium] Elysium
19 old∧ sign] ~-~
22 zodiac] Zodiac

*Welcome joy, and welcome sorrow*

Copy-text heading: Fragment
Repeated opening quotes have been omitted in 2 and 3 of the epigraph
10 pantomime] Pantomime
18 music, music] Music, Music
30 yew] Yew
31 myrtles] Myrtles
32 lime-] Lime-

*Time's sea hath been five years at its slow ebb*

Copy-text heading: To ——
1 ebb;∧] ~;—
2 sand,∧] ~,—
12 Its] It's

*To the Nile*

Copy-text heading: Sonnet, / To the Nile
2 pyramid] Pyramid
2 crocodile] Crocodile
7 men] Men
10 'Tis] ∧~
11 itself:] ~,
13 -rise;] -~,
14 sea] Sea

*Spenser, a jealous honorer of thine*

No heading in copy-text
1 honorer] Honorer
2 trees,] ~∧
4 English] english

4 please.] ~—
6 earth] Earth
8 mirth] Mirth
12 blossoming.] ~—
13 summer] Summer
14 honor‸] ~,

*Blue!—'Tis the life of heaven—the domain*

Copy-text heading: Answer. J. Keats
1 heaven] Heaven
2 sun] Sun
11 queen] Queen

*O thou whose face hath felt the winter's wind*

No heading in copy-text
Quotation marks have been omitted at the beginning of 1 and the end of 14
1 winter's wind,] Winter's ~;
2 snow] Snow
2 mist,] Mist‸
3 stars,] Stars‸
4 spring] Spring
4 -time.] -~—
7 away,] ~‸
8 spring] Spring
8 morn.] ~—
9, 11 knowledge] Knowledge
9, 11 none,] ~‸
10 warmth;] ~‸
12 evening listens.] Evening ~—
13 idleness] Idleness
13 be] be be

*Extracts from an Opera*

[FIRST SONG]
2 godships] Godships
5 lady's] Lady's

DAISY'S SONG
1 sun] Sun
3 moon] Moon
5 spring . . . spring] Spring . . . Spring
6 king] King

FOLLY'S SONG
3 maidens] Maidens
13 pig] Pig
15 cheese] Cheese
17 lawyer] Lawyer
19 sawyer] Sawyer

[FOURTH SONG]
2 nightingale's] Nightingale's
3 pearl;] ~,
6 hand,] ~;
7 nurse] Nurse

[FIFTH] SONG
1, 5, 9, 15 stranger] Stranger
3, 7, 10, 13 lady('s)] Lady('s)
5 hall] Hall
10 But‸] ~,
12 lord's] Lord's
13 maid] Maid

[SIXTH SONG]
1 pearl] Pearl
3 heaven's] Heaven's

*Four seasons fill the measure of the year*

No heading in copy-text
1 seasons] Seasons
1 measure] Measure
2 seasons] Seasons
2 man] Man
3 spring,] ~‸
5 summer] Summer
7 soul dissolv'd,] Soul ~‸
8 autumn] Autumn
9 havens] Havens
11 mists] Mists
12 threshold] threshhold
13 winter] Winter
13 misfeature] Misfeature

*For there's Bishop's Teign*

No heading in copy-text
The copy-text's erratic stanza numbering (one vertical line for stanza 1, two vertical lines for each of the next

two stanzas, three vertical lines for stanza 5 and again for stanza 7, and four vertical lines for stanza 6, with no marking for stanza 4) has been replaced with conventional arabic numerals
1 there's] their's
1, 2, 3 Teign] teign
4 stream] Stream
6 spread] spead
6 bread.] ~—
8 Larch Brook,] larch ~∧
9 mill,] Mill∧
11 mouth,] ~∧
12 gill.] ~∧
13 Wood,] wood∧
14 mild] Mild
15 o'] ~∧
15 down,] ~∧
16 furze] furse
17 thin] than
18 catch] Catch
18 maiden's gown.] Maiden's ~∧
19 Newton Marsh] newton marsh
22 maidens] Maidens
24 revel.] ~∧
25 There's] Theres
25 barton] Barton
27 in,] ~∧
29 bee,] ~∧
30 wasp] Wasp
30 in.] ~∧
32 daisies blow,] Daisies ~∧
33 primroses] Primroses
33 waken'd,] ~∧
35 plight,] ~∧
36 end.] ~∧
38 Soho] soho
39 critics,] ~∧
42 prickets?] Prickets∧

*Where be ye going, you Devon maid*

No heading in copy-text
The words "nook" (13) and "on this willow" (14), which are run-over and underscored in the copy-text (see Textual Note), are here printed in roman
1 going,] ~∧
1 Devon maid,] devon Maid∧
2 i' the basket] ithe Basket
3 fairy, . . . dairy,] ~— . . . ~∧
4 it?] ~—
5 your meads] you Meads
5 flowers,] ~∧
6 mainly;] ~∧
7 more—] ~∧
8 not] no
9 hills] Hills
9 dales,] ~∧
13 basket] Basket
14 willow,] ~∧

*Over the hill and over the dale*

No heading in copy-text
The word "there" (13), which is run-over and underscored in the copy-text, is here printed in roman
1 dale,] ~.
3 gingerbread wives] Gingerbread Wives
3 sale,] ~∧
4 gingerbread] gingerbred
4 smallish.] ~—
5 hill,] ~∧
6 kick'd] kik'ed
6 petticoats fairly.] petticats ~∧
7 I,] ~∧
8 grass debonnairly.] Grass ~—
9 somebody (*fifth word*)] sombody
10 I,] ~∧
10 wind] Wind
10 parley.] ~∧
11 fuss,] ~∧
11 humming,] ~∧
12 debonnairly.] debonnaily—
14 Says I,] Say's ~∧
14 tongue,] ~∧
14 gipsey] Gipsey
16 tipsy.] ~—
17 wouldn't] would'nt
17 fair,] ~∧
18 wouldn't] would'nt
18 meadow?] Meadow∧
19 who] *not in copy-text*
19 there,] ~∧
20 do?] ~—

*Dear Reynolds, as last night I lay in bed*

Copy-text heading: To J. H. Reynolds Esq$^{r}$
3 shadows,] ~∧
3 remembrances] Remembrances
5 north] North
7 habergeon] Habergeon
10 Edgeworth's] Edgworth's
11 so∧ so] ~, ~
14 P'rhaps] P'erhaps
14 patient wings,] patent ~;
16 mermaid's] Mermaid's
17 pride,] ~;
19 life.] ~.—
23 cliff,] ~∧
25 mariners] Mariners
25 land.] ~.—
26 Castle—] ~∧
27 rock] Rock
27 border] Border
27 lake] Lake
28 trees] Trees
29 magic] Magic
30 Phœbus,] ~∧
31 castle] Castle
34 hall] Hall
35 isles] Isles
36 mountains] Mountains
37 animate,] ~∧
38 hate,] ~;
41 see] See
45 sun] Sun
46 witch] Witch
46 maudlin] Maudlin
52 westward] Westward
52 summer's] Summer's
54 poesies.] Poesies—
58 isles] Isles
59 shade] Shade
59 castle wall] Castle Wall
60 'tis] ∧~
65 music] Music
70 soul's] Soul's
71 night] Night
73 admiral] Admiral
75 ill,] ~∧
78 imagination] Imagination
80 purgatory] Purgatory
84 summer] Summer
85 nightingale] Nightingale
86 Reynolds,] ~.
88 lampit rock] Lampit Rock
88 weed] Weed
89 breakers.—] ~∧—
89 eve] Eve
98 happiness] Happiness
99 to-day] ~∧ ~
101 periwinkle] Periwinkle
103 shark] Shark
104 robin] Robin
105 worm.—] ~∧—
109 lurch.] ~—
111 moods] Moods
111 romance] Romance
112 refuge.—] ~∧—
112 centaine] Centaine
113 prose."∧] ~."—

*To J. R.*

1 week] Week
1 age,] ~∧
2 week;] ~∧
3 year] Year
3 be,] ~:
5 space;] ~∧
6 annihilate;] anihilate.
7 day's] days
8 joys,] ~∧
8 dilate.] ~—
9 Ind,] ~∧
10 Tuesday] tuesday
11 joys] Joys
11 bind,] ~∧
12 souls] Souls
13 morn, . . . friend,] ~∧ . . . ~∧
14 thought.] ~—

*Isabella*

Repeated opening quotes have been omitted in 28, 30, 38–40, 58–64, 66–68, 182–184, 186–188, 202–207, 298–304, 306–312, 314–320, 330–336, 349, 350, 504. "Basil" has been lowercased in 416, 423, 428, 458, 472, 473, 488, 490, 494, 496, 498, 504
456 noble's] Noble's
493 pilgrim] Pilgrim

*Mother of Hermes! and still youthful Maia*

No heading in copy-text
6 Seek,] ~‸
7 bards] Bards
10 primrose] Primrose
11 heaven] Heaven
11–13 ears / Rounded by thee, my . . . away, / Content as theirs,] ears rounded by thee‸ / My . . . away‸ content as theirs‸
14 day.‸] ~.—

*To Homer*

Copy-text heading: Sonnet, / To Homer
4 seas.] ~,
6 heaven] Heaven

*Give me your patience, sister, while I frame*

No heading in copy-text
1 patience, sister,] ~‸ Sister‸
2 capitals] Capitals
3 Apollo] apollo
7 kingdom] Kingdom
7 realms] Realms
8 heaven] Heaven
8 nurse‸] ~,
9 brotherhood] Brotherhood
10 Anthropophagi] Anthropopagi
10 Othello's mood,] Othelo's ~;
12 muse] Muse
14 incense] insence
14 laurel] Laurel
16 you,] ~‸
17 sister] Sister
19 wine,] ~‸
21 Sons, daughters,] ~‸ ~‸

*Sweet, sweet is the greeting of eyes*

No heading in copy-text
1 Sweet,] ~‸
3 adieux] Adieux
4 retreating.] ~—
5 hand,] ~‸
6 kiss] Kiss
6 brow] Brow
7 land] Land
8 plough] Plough

*On Visiting the Tomb of Burns*

Copy-text heading: On visiting the Tomb of Burns
1 town] Town
2 clouds] Clouds
2 seem,] ~‸
3 cold] Cold
3 dream‸] ~,
4 ago. Now . . . begun,] ~, now . . . ~‸
5 short-lived] shortlived
6 winter's] winters
6 hour's] hours
7 Though] Through
7 beam;] ~,
8 beauty] Beauty
9 relish,] ~‸
10 beauty] Beauty
11 Sickly] Fickly
12 Cast] *blank space in copy-text*
12 honour] honor
13 Great shadow,] great ~;
14 face—] ~,

*Old Meg she was a gipsey*

No heading in copy-text
1 gipsey,] Gipsey∧
2 moors;] Moors∧
3 turf,] ~∧
4 doors.] ~∧
5 blackberries,] ~∧
6 broom,] ~∧
7 rose,] ~∧
8 tomb.] ~∧
9 brothers] Brothers
9 hills,] ~∧
10 sisters] Sisters
12 please.] ~—
13 had] has
13 morn,] ~∧
14 noon,] ~∧
16 moon.] Moon—
17 every] evey
18 garlanding,] ~∧
19 yew] Yew
20 sing.] ~—
22 mats] Mats
22 rushes,] Rushes∧
23 cottagers] Cottagers
24 bushes.] Bushes—
28 on.] ~—

*There was a naughty boy*

No heading in copy-text
1 boy] Boy
6 knapsack] Knapsack
7 book] Book
15 stockings] Stockings
18 knapsack] Knapsack
20 rivetted] revetted
21 follow'd] followe'd
21 nose] Nose
22, 23, 25 north] North
33 pen] Pen
37 pother] Pother
42 postes] Postes
51 weather] wather
53 charm] cham
55 one's] ones
60 was] we
65 maid] Maid
66 afraid] affraid
67 granny-] Granny-
76 Tittlebat] Tittle bat
84 baby's] Baby's
88 fish] Fish
89 kettle—a kettle] Kettle—A Kettle
90 fish] Fish
91 kettle] Kettle
92, 93 boy] Boy
111 England] england
114, 115 wonder'd] wonderd

*Ah! ken ye what I met the day*

No heading in copy-text
2 mountains,] Mountains∧
4 An'] ~∧
4 fountains?] ~∧
5 Ah] A
5 Marie,] ~∧
8 expressing.] ~—
10 crosses,] ~∧
12 o' horses] ~∧ Horses
14 them,] ~∧
15 men,] Men∧
18 gallop—] ~∧
20 shallop.] ~—
22 mither,] Mither∧
24 togither.] ~—
27 wi'] ~∧
28 'Twixt] ∧Fwixt
28 waning.] ~—
29 oft,] ~∧
30 brithers] Brithers
31 bridegroom] Bridegroon
32 An'] ~∧
33 an'] ~∧
34 cheek—] ~∧
35 chick,] ~∧
36 speak.] ~—
37 Marie,] ~∧
37 ∧gane] '~
38 weather,] ~∧
39, 40 An'] ~∧
40 feather.] ~∧
41 Marie,] ~∧
44 shedding.] ~—

*To Ailsa Rock*

1 Hearken,] ~∧
2 voice,] ~∧
2 sea fowls'] Sea ~∧
3 streams] Streams
4 sun] Sun
5 is't] ist
5 power] Power
7 lap] Lap
7 thunder] Thunder
7 sunbeams] Sunbeams
8 coverlid?] Coverlid—
9 answer'st not,] answerst ~∧
9 asleep;] ~—
10 life] Life
10 eternities,] ~∧
11 air] Air
12 whales] Whales
12 eagle skies;] eglle ~—
13 earthquake] Earthquake
14 size] Size

*This mortal body of a thousand days*

Copy-text heading: Sonnet
5 barley-] Barley-

*All gentle folks who owe a grudge*

No heading in copy-text
2 thing,] ~∧
3 ears] earrs
3 trudge] tudge
4 sing.] ~—
5 gadfly] gad fly
5 sore—] ~∧
8 blue.] ~—
9 mare] Mare
10 legs] Legs
10 store?] ~∧
11 buttocks] Buttocks
12 four.] ~∧
13 lawyer] Lawyer
14 1743?] 17,43∧
15 lawyer's] Lawyer's
16 see.] ~∧
17 man] Man
18 Dumfounder'd] Dum founder'd
18 speech?] ~∧
20 breech.] ~∧
21 Lowther,] ~∧
22 day,] ~∧
23 mad'st] madst
24 say,] ~∧
25 gadfly] gad fly
26 a—e,] A—e∧
29 been,] ~∧
30 Mr. D——,] M[r] ~∧
31 too, . . . ween,] ~∧ . . . ~∧
32 Mr. V——.] M[r] ~∧
33 pray, . . . all,] ~∧ . . . ~∧
34 so;] ~∧
36 go.] ~—
38 novels,] ~∧
40 Lovels?] ~∧
42 pert—] ~∧
43 ring—] ~∧
44 wert.] Wert—
47 pray'd,] ~;
48 way?] ~—
49 gadfly's little] Gadfly's littl
52 rung.] ~∧
53 bo-] ~∧
54 conquering,] ~∧
55 mo∧] ~'
56 gadfly's] Gadfly's
56 sting.] ~∧

*Of late two dainties were before me plac'd*

No heading in copy-text
1 plac'd,] ~∧
2 Sweet, holy, pure, sacred, . . . innocent,] ~∧ ~∧ ~∧ ~∧ . . . ~∧
4 gods] Gods
4 particular taste.] particlar ~—
5 bag-pipe] ~∧ ~
5 haste;] ~∧
7 went;] ~∧
8 waste.] ~∧
9 bag-pipe,] Bag-~∧
9 away;] ~∧
10 Stranger,] ~∧
10 pipe] Pipe

10 charm;] ~∧
11 bag-pipe,] Bag∧ ~∧
11 didst] did'st
11 sway;] ~∧
12 gav'st] gave'st
13 heart,] ~∧
14 Mumchance] Mum chance
14 part.] ~—

*There is a joy in footing slow across a silent plain*

No heading in copy-text
1 plain,] ~∧
2 patriot battle] Patriot Battle
2 fought,] ~∧
2 glory] Glory
4 mantles] Mantles
5 spot∧] ~,
10 sea] Sea
11 castle] Castle
11 cot] Cot
13 hether-bells] Hether∧ ~
14 sun] Sun
14 lay] Lay
15 clear,] ~∧
16 heard,] ~∧
17 Blood-red] Bloodred
17 behind] bhind
18 caves] Caves
19 wing-wide] ~∧ ~
19 air] Air
22 palmer's] Palmer's
22 mid-desert] ~∧ ~
23 soul's] Soul's
23 child] Child
23 childhood] Childhood
23 brain;] ~∧
24 vain.] ~—
25 Aye,] ~∧
25 madman] Madman
27 man] Man
27 spirit] Spirit
28 bard's] Bard's
28 cradle] Cradle
29 bourn] Bourn
29 care] Care
31 steps,] ~∧
32 man] Man
34 brother's] Brother's
34 sister's brow] Sister's Brow
35 air, . . . move,] Air∧ . . . ~∧
35 portraiture intense,] Portraiture ~∧
36 painter's] Painter's
37 shapes] Shapes
38 grey,] ~∧
39 no, that] No∧ ~
39 cable's] Cable's
40 anchor] Anchor
40 strength.] ~—
41 hour, . . . ideot,] ~∧ . . . ~∧
42 soul's] Soul's
43 mountain's height,] Mountain's ~∧
44 hill's] Hills
45 anchor] Anchor
46 man] Man
46 lose] loose
46 mind on mountains] Mind [ ] Mountains (*middle word lost through damage to MS*)
47 after league] after League
47 birthplace] Berthplace
48 unblind.] ~—

*Not Aladdin magian*

No heading in copy-text
1 Aladdin] Aladin
2 began;] ~,
4 a] *not in copy-text*
4 see;] ~∧
5 St.] S[t]
5 Patmos' isle,] ~∧ ~∧
6 toil,] ~∧
7 seven,] ~∧
8 aisled,] ~∧
8 heaven,] ~∧
10 under,] ~∧
12 bare,] ~∧
15 rocks;] ~,
16 locks,] ~∧
17 main,] Main∧
18 again.] ~—
19 "What . . . thou?"] ∧~ . . . ~?∧
21 "What . . . this?"] ∧~ . . . ~?∧
23 spirit's] Spirits
24 trice] thrice
25 "I . . . Lycidas,"] ∧~ . . . ~∧

25 he,] ~∧
26–55 "Fam'd . . . dance."]
∧~ . . . ~.∧
26 minstrelsy.] Minstrelsey—
28 Oceanus;] ~∧
30 organs] Organs
30 day;] ~∧
31 all,] ~∧
32 palmers] palmer's
32 small,] ~∧
34 pearls] peals
34 strew.] ~∧
35 mortal] Mortal
36 ways,] ~∧
38 cathedral] Cathedral
38 sea.] Sea—
39 pontif] Pontif
40 waters] Waters
40 rest,] ~∧
42 ever;] ~—
43 mortal man;] Mortal Man.
44 sacristan] Sacristan
45 mortal] Mortal
46 rocky portal;] Rocky ~∧
48 taint,] ~∧
49 place.] ~—
50 face,] ~∧
51 boats,] ~∧
52 petticoats] Petticoats
53 sea] Sea
53 down,] down[ ] (*possible loss of punctuation through damage to MS*)
56 spirit's] Spirits

*Read me a lesson, Muse, and speak it loud*

No heading in copy-text
1 lesson, Muse] Lesson∧ muse
2 Nevis,] ~∧
2 mist] Mist
3 chasms,] Chasms∧
3 shroud] Shroud
5 hell] Hell
5 o'erhead,] ~∧
6 mist] Mist
7 heaven: mist] Heaven: Mist
8 earth] Earth
8 me;] ~—
8 such,] ~∧
9 man's] Man's
10 stones] Stones
11 that, . . . elf,] ~∧ . . . ~∧
13 crag] Crag
13 height,] ~∧
14 might.] ~—

*Upon my life, Sir Nevis, I am piqu'd*

No heading in copy-text
1, 33 *s.p.* Mrs.] M$^{rs}$
1 life, . . . Nevis,] Life∧ . . . ~∧
1 piqu'd] pique'd
2 panted, tugg'd,] ~∧ ~∧
6 Alas,] ~∧
7 mankind] Mankind
8 ones] one's
9 gentlemen immediately] Gentleman immediatly
11 baldpate,] Baldpate∧
11 disdain'd] disdaind
12 valleys] Valleys
12 not, . . . brain'd,] ~∧ . . . braind∧
13 Deserted] Deserrted
13 pickles] Pickles
13 preserves,] ~∧
14 china] China
14 nerves] Nerves
15 say, . . . ingrate,] ~∧ . . . ~∧
16 Left] Let
16 pot?] ~.
17 fates,] ~∧
18 shoemaker] Shoemaker
18 Mr.] M$^{r}$
19 Mr. Bates,] M$^{r}$ ~∧
20 dumb,] ~∧
*Prose after* 20 lady . . . whiskey . . . dashed it to . . . ground, . . . mountain . . . minutes] Lady . . . wiskey . . . dashed to . . . Ground∧ . . . Mountain . . . Minutes
21 mouth] Mouth
22 Disturb] Distur'd
22 slumber] Slumber
22 years?] ~—

23 secure,] secure[ ] (*possible loss of punctuation here and in 24, 37, 38 through damage to MS*)
24 endure.] endur[ ]
25 eagle's] Eagle's
26 damn'd] dam'd
26 dream,] ~∧
27 nightmare] Nightmare
27 What, madam,] ~∧ Madam∧
29 ∧Red-Crag,* my spectacles] *~-~,∧ My Spectacles
30 heavens, lady,] Heavens∧ Lady∧
31 sides] Sides
33 Nevis,] ~∧
34 Your] You
34 countenance] Countenance
34 above,] ~∧
36 bosom] Bosom
36 maid] Maid
37 treatment,] ~∧
37 sir;] sir[ ]
38 stir,] stir[ ]
39 No,] ~∧
39 stone,] Stone∧
40 bits,] ~∧
41 every day.] evey ~∧
42 cap, night] ~∧ ~
42 day,] ~∧
43 buss] Buss
44 Red-Crag] Reg∧ ~
44 What, madam,] ~∧ Madam∧
47 Red-Crag,] ~∧ ~∧
48 Red-Crag] ~∧ crag
49 sulphur] Sulphur
49 go, . . . Red-Crag,] ~∧ . . . ~∧ ~—
51 madam,] Madam∧
52 embrace] Embrace
53 ∧Blockhead,* . . . Blockhead,] *Block-head,∧ . . . ~∧
53 feel.] ~∧
53 *note* Another] another
54 leg's] legs
55 well, . . . boy,] ~∧ . . . ~∧
56 thither] thithers
56 joy.] ~∧
57 pines,] ~∧
58 phosphor] Phosphor
59 dragons' nest;] Dragons' ~∧
60 best,] ~∧
62 alligators, . . . span,] Aligators∧ . . . ~∧
64 whale;] ~—
65 Red-Crag] red∧ ~
66 back,] ~∧
67 breast.] ~∧
68 Blockhead,] ~∧
68 Muses,] ~∧
69 lady] Lady
69 dead,] ~∧
71 again. Soon] ~—soon
72 affrighted servants. Next day,] affrighed Servants—next ~∧
73 ground,] ~∧
74 late.] ~∧

*On Some Skulls in Beauley Abbey, near Inverness*

Copy-text heading: On some Skulls, in Beauley Abbey, near Inverness
In the copy-text MS Brown originally wrote the four lines of the two epigraphs as a single passage, with a semicolon at the end of the third line, and afterward inserted "Wordsworth" and "Shakspeare" above and below the end of the fourth line. In the present text quotation marks have been added, a long dash before the first line has been omitted, and the semicolon after "crossed" emended to a full stop
1 synod] Synod
4 ruin] Ruin
5 brethren's skulls] Brethren's Skulls
6 creed's] Creed's
10 orthodoxy] Orthodoxy
13 chronicles] Chronicles
14 revolutionist] Revolutionist
17 craniologist] Craniologist
25 toper] Toper
26 mass] Mass
27 lass] Lass
35 heaven] Heaven
37 churchman] Churchman
41 heathen] Heathen
41 sect] Sect
42 devil] Devil
43 skull] Skull
44 saint] Saint

45 missal] Missal
45 didst] did'st
59 superstition's] Superstition's
61 crime"!] ~!"
65 monkish pantomime] Monkish Pantomime
68 khan] Khan
72 heaven's lightning] Heaven's lightening
74 miser's] Miser's
75 Who, penitent‸] ~‸ ~,
77 And‸] ~,
77 heaven's] Heaven's
78 hell] Hell
79 ape] Ape
84 monkish] Monkish
85 porter] Porter
87 friars] Friars
94 reverend brothers] Reverend Brothers

*Nature withheld Cassandra in the skies*

No heading in copy-text
3 beauty] Beauty
3 dyes,] dies‸
4 peers.] ~‸
5 wings,] ~‸
7 kings] Kings
8 utter'd] uttere'd
8 sighs.] ~—
9 earth descend,] Earth ~‸
10 pains,] ~‸
11 pleasures,] ~—
11 life's end;] Lifes ~—
12 beauty] Beauty
12 veins.] ~‸

*Fragment of Castle-builder*

Copy-text heading: Fragment, of Castle-builder
1 *s.p.* Castle-builder] *not in copy-text*
2 convent] Convent
4 Garden] garden
6 lordship's] Lordship's
7 What,] ~‸
7 isle] Isle
9 *s.p.* Castle-builder] ~‸ ~
9 beast;] ~,
10 o'clock] o'Clock
11 cabbages] Cabbages
12 twelve] 12
15 hackney] Hackney
16 sir] Sir
21 friar] Friar
21 rake] Rake
24 To-night] ~‸ ~
45 passion-] Passion-
45 just] Just
47 phantasy] Phantasy
52 looking-glass] ~‸ ~
52 face,] ~‸
54 Tekel,] ~‸
58 'tis] ‸~
60 eye-sight] ~‸ ~
63 wrought,] ~‸
64 lama] Lama
70 wine] Wine
70 'tis] ‸~
71 friar] fryar

*And what is Love?—It is a doll dress'd up*

No heading in copy-text
9 Seven] seven
12 queens] Queens
12 soldiers] Soldiers
16 Egypt] Œgypt

*'Tis the "witching time of night"*

No heading in copy-text
1 ‸the "witching] "~ ‸~
1 night"—] ~"‸
2 moon] Moon
2 bright,] ~‸
3 stars] Stars
3 glisten, (*end of line*)] ~‸
4 listen.] ~‸
6 charm—] cham‸
7 alarm,] ~‸

8 moon] Moon
10 Moon,] ~∧
10 ears;] ~∧
11 Hearken, stars] ~∧ Stars
11 hearken, spheres;] ~∧ Spheres∧
12 Hearken,] ~∧
12 sky—] Sky∧
14 lullaby] Lullaby
15 listen (*second word*)] Listen
15 listen, (*end of line*)] ~∧
16 glisten, (*end of line*)] ~∧
17 lullaby!] ~?
18 rushes] Rushes
19 lake;] ~:
22 woollen] wollen
23 warm∧] wam,
24 Listen, stars'] ~∧ Stars∧
24 listen, (*end of line*)] ~∧
25 glisten (*second word*)] Glisten
25 glisten, (*end of line*)] ~∧
27 Child, . . . Child, . . . thee,] ~! . . . ~∧ . . . ~∧
29 Child, . . . Child, . . . thee,] ~∧ . . . ~∧ . . . ~∧
31 Child, I] ~∧ ~
31 more,] ~∧
32 *ever*more.] ~∧
33 see the] See the
33 lyre . . . lyre,] Lyre . . . Lyre∧
34 fire,] ~∧
36 flaring, (*end of line*)] ~.
38 sleep,] ~∧
41 amaze (*second word*)] Amaze
42 stares; (*end of line*)] ~∧
43 one dares;] ~ ~∧
49 child] Child
50 wild,] ~∧
52 endeavour,∧] ~.—
54 child] Child
55 wild,] ~∧

*Where's the Poet? Show him! show him*

Copy-text heading: Fragment
3 'Tis the man∧] ∧~ ~ ~,
4 king] King
8 'Tis] ∧~
11 lion's] Lion's
13 tiger's] Tiger's

*Fancy*

11 spring] Spring
35 autumn's] Autumn's

*Bards of passion and of mirth*

Copy-text heading: Ode
1, 37 passion] Passion
1, 37 mirth] Mirth

*Spirit here that reignest*

Copy-text heading: Song

*I had a dove, and the sweet dove died*

Copy-text heading: Song
1 sweet dove] sweet Dove
8 Why, . . . thing,] ~∧ . . . ~∧
9 pease;] ~,

*Hush, hush, tread softly, hush, hush, my dear*

Copy-text heading: Song
1 hush, (*sixth word*)] ~∧
2 well∧] ~,
3 jealous∧ old baldpate] ~, ~ Baldpate
3 hear,] ~∧
5 fairy's] fairies
7 Hush, hush . . . hush, hush,] ~∧ ~ . . . ~∧ ~∧
10 all's] Alls
11 care,] ~∧
15 gloom,] ~;
17 tenderly, sweet,] ~∧ ~∧
18 dead∧] ~,
18 chink.] ~∧
19 done—] ~,
19 seat:] ~∧

20 sleep,] dream^
20 wink;] ~^
21 shall] may
22 blown,] ~^
22 take;] ~^
23 coo,] ~^
24 melody,] ~^

*Ah! woe is me! poor Silver-wing*

Copy-text heading: Faery Song
2 lady's] Lady's
3 spring,] ~^
7 lady's] Lady's
8, 12 page] Page
18 spirit] Spirit
19 queen] Queen

*The Eve of St. Agnes*

Repeated opening quotes have been omitted in 99, 101–108, 116, 117, 119–126, 141–144, 147–153, 155–158, 174–180, 277–279, 308–315, 329–333, 335–342, 344–351
54 heaven] Heaven
56 god] God
61 retir'd, . . . disdain;] ~; . . . ~,
144 seem."] ~.^
292 mercy":] ~:"
301 deep:] ~^
315 love] Love
342 infidel.^] ~."

*The Eve of St. Mark*

Copy-text heading: The Eve of Saint Mark
1 Sabbath] sabbath
1 fell;] ~^
2 Sabbath bell,] sabbath ~;
3 prayer.] payer—
4 city] City
5 April rains, ] april ~^
8 unmatur'd] unmaturd
8 cold,] ~^
9 hedge,] ~^
10 springtide sedge,] spingtide ~^
11 primroses] Primroses
11 shelter'd rills,] shelterd ~^
12 daisies] dasies
12 hills.] ~—
13 Sabbath] sabbath
14 streets] Streets
15 companies,] ~^
16 Warm] Wam
16 orat'ries,] oratries^
18 prayer.] ~^
19 arched] ached
20 slow,] ~^
21 feet,] ~;
22 sweet.] ~—
23 bells] Bells
23 ceas'd] cea'd
23 begun,] ~^
25 volume, . . . torn,] ~^ . . . ~^
26 long, . . . morn,] ~^ . . . ~^
28 broideries;] ~—
30 stars] Stars
30 heaven,] ~^
30 angels'] ~^
31 blaze,] ~—
33 Aaron's breastplate] Aron's brestplate
34 heaven,] ~—
35 St. Mark,] S^t ~^
36 Covenantal Ark,] covenantal Arch^
38 mice] Mice
39 ¶Bertha . . . ] *no indention, but new page in copy-text*
42 antiquity,] ~—
43 bishop's] Bishop's
43 wall,] ~^
44 sycamores] Sycamores
44 tall,] ~^
45 Full . . . outstript,] *deleted in copy-text*
45 leav'd,] leave'd^
45 outstript,] outsript—
46 north] northe
46 nipt,] ~^
47 shelter'd] shelterd
47 pile^.] ~—.
48 awhile,] ~^

49 pane;] ~‸
50 tried, . . . again,] ~‸ . . . ~‸
52 legend] Legend
52 St.] S^t
54 chin,] ~‸
55 eyes,] ~‸
56 dazed] Dazed
56 imageries.] ~‸
57 ¶All . . . ] *no indention, but new page in copy-text*
57 silent all,] ~ ~‸
59 late,] ~—
60 gate.] ~—
61 daws,] ~‸
62 play,] ~‸
63 rest,] ~‸
64 nest,] ~‸
66 music] musick
66 chimes.] ~‸
67 silent,] ~—
67 gloom,] ~‸
68 Abroad] abroad
68 room;] ~—
69 sat, . . . soul,] ~‸ . . . ~‸
70 lamp] Lamp
71 hair,] ~‸
72 against] aginst
73 guise] guize
74 about, . . . size,] ~‸ . . . ~‸
75 ceiling] celinng
75 chair,] ~‸
76 parrot's] Parrots
76 square,] ~‸
77 warm] wam
77 screen,] screene‸
78 seen,] ~‸
79 Call'd doves] Calld Doves
79 mice,] Mice‸
80 paradise,] Paradise‸
81 Macaw,] ~‸
81 av'davat,] ~‸
82 furr'd Angora cat.] fur'd angora ~—
84 Glower'd] Glowerd
85 room] Room
85 shades,] ~‸
86 queens] Queens
87 back,] ~—
88 garments black.] gaments ~‸
89 legend] Legend
91 land] Land
91 seas] Seas
92 pains.] ~—
93 Sometimes] Somtimes
93 eremite,] Eremite‸
94 bright,] ~‸
96 crow-quill] crowquil
98 time:] ~‸
99 ——"Als] ——‸~
104 nativitie,] ~;
105 God] god
114 dethe."] ~".
115 ¶At . . . ] *no indention, but new page in copy-text*
116 martyrdom] Martyrdom
117 shrine,] shine‸

*Why did I laugh tonight? No voice will tell*

No heading in copy-text
2 god] God
2 demon] Deamon
2 response,] ~‸
3 hell.‸] Hell.—
7 darkness! darkness] Darkness! Darkness
7 moan,] ~‸
8 heaven] Heaven
8 hell] Hell
8 heart] Heart
9 lease—] ~‸
13 fame,] ~‸
13 beauty] Beauty
13 indeed,] ~‸
14 death . . . death] Death . . . Deaths
14 life's] Life's
14 meed.‸] mead."

*When they were come unto the Faery's court*

No heading in copy-text
1 court] Court
3 faeries do,] faery's ~‸
4 faeries] Faries
4 humans,] ~‸
4 true.] ~—

5 were,] ~∧
5 wild,] ~∧
6 robin] Robin
6 exil'd,] exild∧
7 afraid] affraid
9 home!"] ~!∧
9 Princess cry'd,] princess ~∧
10 dreary ride,] drery ~∧
11 cross,] ~∧
12 Persian] persian
12 toss,] ~∧
13 Ape,] ~∧
13 Fool,] ~∧
14 Otaheitan mule.] otahaietan ~∧
15 Dwarf,] ~∧
15 Fool,] ~∧
15 there?] ~∧
17 I'll] Ill
17 tear."] ~".
19 agape;] ~∧
20 switch,] ~∧
21 Dwarf] dwarf
22 Princess,] ~∧
23 too, . . . well?] ~∧ . . . ~∧
24 land?] ~∧
25 first, . . . Dwarf,] ~∧ . . . ~∧
25 understand—] ~∧
26 wand;] ~∧
27 company;] ~∧
28 last,] ~∧
28 three,] thee∧
29 home.] ~∧
30 prince . . . prince]
Prince . . . pince
31 see:] ~,
31 wand;] ~∧
33 prince . . . Fool, . . . prince,]
Pince . . . ~∧ . . . Prince∧
34 king's] King's
35 ball.] Ball—
36 prince] Prince
36 he, . . . thing,] ~∧ . . . ~∧
37 faery's boudoir] faerry's boudour
37 king,] King∧
38 ape. So] ~—so
38 awhile;] ~∧
39 indeed, we] ~∧ We
40 tomorrow."] ~—∧
42 Peel'd] Peal'd
42 white,] ~∧
43 apart,] ~∧
44 heart.] ~∧
45 mind,] ~∧
46 three] thee
47 but, . . . chance,] ~∧ . . . ~∧
48 dance,] ~∧
49 grinn'd] grin'd
49 ache.] ~—
50 sake,] ~∧
56 place.] ~∧
58 lovers, husbands,] Lovers∧ ~∧
58 expence.] ~∧
59 too:] ~∧
60 knew—] ~∧
61 though] tho'
62 faeries.] faries∧
63 Ape,] ~∧
63 won't] wont
63 to-day—] ~∧ ~∧
64 picklock, sirrah,] Picklock∧ ~∧
64 play."] ~—∧
66 rain.] ~—
68 picklock] Picklock
68 pocket] Pocket
68 jaw] Jaw
69 and, . . . straight,]
~∧ . . . straigh[ ] (*damage to MS*)
70 Tripp'd] Trip'd
71 wards;] ~,
71 door] Door
71 courteously] couteouly
72 three.] ~∧
76 prick'd] prick
76 ears∧] Ears—
76 ∧said, "Well done;] "~∧ ∧well ~,
77 least, . . . Prince,] ~∧ . . . ~∧
78 princess] Princess
79 king] King
79 Otaheitè—though] Othaietè—tho
79 mule,] Mule∧
80 king'—though∧] King'—tho—
80 fool,'] ~∧'
81 Mr.] M$^{r}$
81 said,] ~∧
82 head."] ~∧"
84 pollard] Pollard
85 rubb'd] rub
86 girths] Girths
87 bridle] Bridle
87 that,] ~∧
88 plait?] ~∧
89 sleep,] ~∧

90 monkies] Monkies
91 away.] ~∧
92 lay,] ~∧
93 Shamm'd] Sham'd
93 monkey-] Monkey-
93 descended,] ~∧
94 befriended] brefriended
95 bridle] Bridle
95 bough,] ~∧
96 off] of
96 went,] ~∧
96 how.] ~—

*As Hermes once took to his feathers light*

Copy-text heading: Sonnet, / On a Dream
2 slept,] ~;
5 eyes;] ~,
6 And,] ~∧
6 away—] ~,
9 hell] Hell
12 sorrows. Pale] ~,—pale

*Character of C. B.*

4 zephyr] Zephyr
16 pilgrim's] Pilgrim's
18 ofttimes] oftimes
20 Greek;] greek,
22 nantz] Nantz

*Bright star, would I were stedfast as thou art*

No heading in copy-text
1 star] Star
4 eremite] Eremite
7 mask] masque
8 moors;] ~—
9 unchangeable,] ~∧
14 death.] ~—

*Hyperion*

Copy-text heading: Hyperion. / A Fragment
Repeated opening quotes have been omitted in I.53–71, 96–134, 142–145, 151, 152, 228–250, 310–348, II.130–166, 174–243, 253–299, 310–324, 328–345, III.51–61, 63–79, 83–120
I.6 above] about
I.81 outspread,] ~∧
I.145 Chaos] chaos
I.176 bright,] ~∧
I.305 heaven] Heaven
II.38 heaven] Heaven
II.191 Chaos] chaos
II.191 Darkness] darkness
II.195 Light . . . Light] light . . . light
II.310 -foolish, Giant-Gods] -~∧ giant, Gods
II.375 east] East
III.111 mute (*fourth word*)] Mute
III.131 famed,] ~∧

*La Belle Dame sans Merci*

Copy-text heading: La belle Dame sans merci. / A Ballad
A repeated opening quote has been omitted in 40
1, 5 knight] Knight
7 squirrel's] Squirrel's
13 lady] Lady
14 child;] ~,
24 fairy's] Fairy's
37 kings] Kings
40 thrall!"] ~"!
47 lake] Lake

*Song of Four Fairies*

Copy-text heading: Song of four Fairies: / Fire, Air, Earth, and Water. Salamander, Zephyr, Dusketha and Breama
8 bat's] Bat's
27 self-same] ~$\wedge$ ~
28 asphodel] Asphodel
29, 30 Fire] fire
31 fairy,] faery$\wedge$
33 brim] Brim
34 cresses] Cresses
36 above] abovve
39 fairy true,] Faery ~$\wedge$
43 thee,] ~$\wedge$
45 far, far] ~$\wedge$ ~
47 sun] Sun
49 pallaces] Pallaces
51 star] Star
52 Vesper] vesper
55 fays] Fays
62 fairy] Fairy
64 fairies] Faries
65 lovers] Lovers
70 earth's] Earth's
72 thee,] ~$\wedge$
74 -wing'd$\wedge$] -~,
75 sprite,] Sprite$\wedge$
87 Dusketha] Dusketh
89 sky] Sky
90 them,] ~$\wedge$
90 sprite] Sprite
91 *s.p.* Zephyr and Breama] Zeph. *above* Brea. *bracketed in margin*
94 glooms,] ~$\wedge$
96 Blue-eyed] ~$\wedge$ ~
96 flowers] Flowers
97 May-] may-
97 lowers,] ~$\wedge$
98 Vesper, . . . whist,] ~$\wedge$ . . . wist$\wedge$
99 mist,] ~$\wedge$
100 bowers] Bowers

*Sonnet to Sleep*

5 Sleep] sleep
6 hymn,] ~$\wedge$
10 pillow,] ~$\wedge$
11 conscience,] ~$\wedge$
13 key] Key
13 wards,] ~$\wedge$
14 casket] Casket
14 soul.] ~—

*Ode to Psyche*

No emendations

*On Fame ("Fame, like a wayward girl")*

Copy-text heading: Sonnet on Fame
1 girl] Girl
3 boy] Boy
5 gipsey] Gipsey
7 jilt] Jilt
9 gipsey] Gipsey
11 bards] Bards
11 scorn;] ~,
12 artists] Artists
13 adieu;] ~,

*On Fame ("How fever'd is the man")*

Copy-text heading: Sonnet. / on Fame
*Epigraph* cake] Cake
1 man$\wedge$] Man,
5 rose] Rose
6 plum] Plum
8 gloom;] ~,
9 rose] Rose
9 briar] Briar
10 bees] Bees
11 plum] Plum
12 lake] Lake
12 space;] ~,
13 man,] Man$\wedge$
14 miscreed?] ~.

*If by dull rhymes our English must be chain'd*

Copy-text heading: Sonnet
2 sonnet] Sonnet
7 lyre] Lyre
12 crown;] ~,
13 muse] Muse

*Two or three posies*

No heading in copy-text
1 posies] Posies
3 noses] Noses
4 three] thee
6 ninnies] ninny's
13 cats] Cats
15 three] thee
16 great] gereat
19 three] thee
20 Mrs.] M$^{rs}$
21 smiles] Smiles
23 three miles] thee Miles

*Ode to a Nightingale*

No emendations

*Ode on a Grecian Urn*

17 lover] Lover
22 spring] Spring

*Ode on Melancholy*

No emendations

*Ode on Indolence*

Copy-text heading: Ode, / On Indolence
5, 7 urn] Urn
8 shades] Shades
10 vases] Vases
11 shadows] Shadows
12 masque] Masque
25 maid] Maid
29 maiden] Maiden
32 Love] love
33 Ambition—] ~∧
49 shadows] Shadows
51 ghosts] Ghosts
54 farce] Farce
56 urn] Urn
59 phantoms] Phantoms

*Shed no tear—O shed no tear*

No heading in copy-text
1 tear! (*end of line*)] ~∧
2 flower] Flower
2 year.] ~—
3 more! (*end of line*)] ~∧
4 core.] ~—
5 eyes! (*end of line*)] ~∧
7 melodies] Melodies
8 tear!] ~∧
9 head, (*end of line*)] ~∧
10 red.] ~—
12 bough.] bow—
13 me—] ~∧
14 ill.] ~—
15 tear! (*end of line*)] ~∧
16 year.] ~∧
17 adieu—I fly, adieu!] Adieu—~ ~∧ ~∧
19 Adieu, adieu!] ~∧ Adieu∧

*Otho the Great*

Copy-text heading: Otho the Great. / A Tragedy. / In Five Acts
Repeated opening quotes have been omitted in II.ii.56–61
I.i.1 *s.p.* Conrad.] *not in copy-text*
I.i.21 sister, slurring] Sister, sluring

I.i.23 child's] Child's
I.i.33 'Tis] ‸~
I.i.34 court-] Court-
I.i.38 son] Son
I.i.39 nobles] Nobles
I.i.50 empire's] Empire's
I.i.51 interest‸] ~—
I.i.53 ensigns] Ensigns
I.i.57 glad?] ~.
I.i.58 sister] Sister
I.i.88 brother] Brother
I.i.88 crown] Crown
I.i.89 queen's] Queen's
I.i.90 farewell,] ~‸
I.i.95 struck'dst] struck'd
I.i.100 -lords] -Lords
I.i.103 father] Father
I.i.104 son] Son
I.i.105 Emperor,] ~‸
I.i.107 camp] Camp
I.i.111 See‸] ~,
I.i.115 queen] Queen
I.i.131 sir] Sir
I.i.132 Lady! O] Lady! / O (*the first word by itself on a separate line*)
I.i.132 heaven] Heaven
I.i.136 ring] Ring
I.i.137 'Tis] ‸~
I.i.138 lady] Lady
I.i.140 you,] ~‸
I.i.141 sir] Sir
I.i.144 Auranthes"!] ~!"
I.i.146 brother] Brother
I.i.146 sister] Sister
I.i.148 heaven] Heaven
I.ii *opening s.d.* music . . . Knights, . . . the gate . . . banners] Music . . . ~‸ . . . the Gate . . . Banners
I.ii.1 herald] Herald
I.ii.3 banners] Banners
I.ii.6 victory] Victory
I.ii.12 hostess] Hostess
I.ii.13 soldiers] Soldiers
I.ii.13 ladies'] Ladies'
I.ii.19 daughter] Daughter
I.ii.20 kings] Kings
I.ii.21 son] Son
I.ii.23 lady] Lady
I.ii.24 lord] Lord
I.ii.32 boy] Boy
I.ii.35 liege] Liege
I.ii.37 *s.d.* Knights,] ~‸
I.ii.43 son's] Son's
I.ii.45 pagan's] Pagan's
I.ii.45 saints] Saints
I.ii.46 banquets] Banquets
I.ii.47 music] Music
I.ii.51 monarch] Monarch
I.ii.52 stranger's] Stranger's
I.ii.55 enemy's] Enemy's
I.ii.58 'tis] ‸~
I.ii.58 boy] Boy
I.ii.61 man] Man
I.ii.62 victory] Victory
I.ii.63 son] Son
I.ii.66 liege] Liege
I.ii.70 father's] Father's
I.ii.70 son] Son
I.ii.71 'tis] ‸~
I.ii.73 lord] Lord
I.ii.74 'tis] ‸~
I.ii.77 Will't] Wilt
I.ii.85 *s.d.* stage . . . soldiery] Stage . . . Soldiery
I.ii.85 prince] Prince
I.ii.87 prisoners] Prisoners
I.ii.87 prince] Prince
I.ii.92 captains] Captains
I.ii.97 gentlemen] Gentlemen
I.ii.100 kings] Kings
I.ii.100 princes] Princes
I.ii.102 palaces] Palaces
I.ii.103 monarch] Monarch
I.ii.104 princes'] Princes'
I.ii.116 prince] Prince
I.ii.116 soldier] Soldier
I.ii.118 lady] Lady
I.ii.125 battalions] Battallions
I.ii.133 king] King
I.ii.144 emperor] Emperor
I.ii.149 sire] Sire
I.ii.153 father's] Father's
I.ii.155 camp] Camp
I.ii.161 empire's] Empire's
I.ii.168 prince] Prince
I.ii.170, 172 lion] Lion
I.ii.175 power] Power
I.ii.185 benison] benizon
I.ii.185 heaven] Heaven
I.ii.187 conqueror] Conqueror
I.ii.188 joy] Joy
I.ii.191 maids] Maids
I.ii.192 heaven's] Heaven's

I.ii.194 enemy] Enemy
I.ii.196 camp] Camp
I.ii.198 sisterhood] Sisterhood
I.ii.200 saints] Saints
I.ii.202 music] Music
I.ii.202 *s.d.* scene] Scene
I.iii.3 Ludolph∧] ~,
I.iii.8 heaven] Heaven
I.iii.12 son] Son
I.iii.12 Mussleman∧] ~,
I.iii.15 greatness,] ~;
I.iii.16 castle-] Castle-
I.iii.17 warder] Warder
I.iii.18 son] Son
I.iii.24 swordsman] Sword's-man
I.iii.25 son] Son
I.iii.25 centurion] Centurion
I.iii.26 deeds∧] ~,
I.iii.29 sire] Sire
I.iii.30 lord] Lord
I.iii.38 father] Father
I.iii.38 son's] Son's
I.iii.51 boar] Boar
I.iii.54 -lords] -Lords
I.iii.61 lords] Lords
I.iii.65 courtier's missal] Courtier's Missal
I.iii.67 camp] Camp
I.iii.77 king] King
I.iii.78 lord] Lord
I.iii.82 father's] Father's
I.iii.86 truth;] ~,
I.iii.89 obstinate;] ~,
I.iii.95 son] Son
I.iii.96 loathes] loaths
I.iii.96 father's] Father's
I.iii.98 father] Father
I.iii.98 son] Son
I.iii.107 -influenced;] -~,
I.iii.113 sister, 'tis] Sister, ∧~
I.iii.115 father's] Father's
I.iii.119 grandchild] Grandchild
I.iii.122 messengers] Messengers
I.iii.123 you,] ~∧
I.iii.124 couriers] Couriers
I.iii.126 province] Province
I.iii.127 dignities] dignites
I.iii.128 *s.p.* Gonfrid] Gonfred
I.iii.129 you.] ~∧
I.iii.130 prude] Prude
I.iii.131 Come,] ~∧
I.iii.132 Friedburg castle.] friedburg Castle—
*After* I.iii.132 *copy-text has*: End of the first Act.
II.i.4 'tis] ∧~
II.i.6 antiroom] Antiroom
II.i.13 heavens] Heavens
II.i.17 nobles] Nobles
II.i.17 Well, sir] ~∧ Sir
II.i.19 son] Son
II.i.21 *s.d.* stage] Stage
II.i.23 he∧ . . . breathes∧] ~, . . . ~,
II.i.29 sire] Sire
II.i.31 diadem] Diadem
II.i.36 son] Son
II.i.39 same,] ~;
II.i.40 same, . . . shade,] ~; . . . ~;
II.i.46 father's] Father's
II.i.48 learn,] ~;
II.i.50 king's] King's
II.i.55 dukedom's] Dukedom's
II.i.63 son] Son
II.i.69 fool∧] ~,
II.i.73 sire] Sire
II.i.77 liege] Liege
II.i.78 son] Son
II.i.80 yours] your's
II.i.82 sir] Sir
II.i.85, 86 rebel] Rebel
II.i.88 boy] Boy
II.i.91 jailor] Jailor
II.i.99 father] Father
II.i.100 son's] Son's
II.i.101 parent's] Parent's
II.i.105 father] Father
II.i.108 counsellors] Counsellors
II.i.111 gods] Gods
II.i.111 liege] Liege
II.i.112 boy] Boy
II.i.113 father] Father
II.i.121 lord] Lord
II.i.122 father] Father
II.i.129 calf] Calf
II.i.132 soldiery] Soldiery
II.i.132 feast∧] ~,
II.i.135 god] God
II.i.136 father] Father
II.i.146 appalling,] ~∧
II.i.149 brother's daughter] Brother's Daughter
II.i.151 soldiers] Soldiers

II.ii.1 *s.p.* Erminia.] *not in copy-text*
II.ii.2 camp] Camp
II.ii.5 sun] Sun
II.ii.7 prisoner] Prisoner
II.ii.10 dame] Dame
II.ii.11 homage] hommage
II.ii.11 chiefs] Chiefs
II.ii.13 lady] Lady
II.ii.16 knight] Knight
II.ii.19 soldier] Soldier
II.ii.21 knight] Knight
II.ii.22, 24 man] Man
II.ii.25 monk] Monk
II.ii.26 gods] Gods
II.ii.27 prisoner] Prisoner
II.ii.28 beleaguer'd] beleager'd
II.ii.30 'tis] ‸~
II.ii.31 son] Son
II.ii.34 Well?] ~!
II.ii.35 court] Court
II.ii.35 camp] Camp
II.ii.44 maid] Maid
II.ii.46 niece] Niece
II.ii.48 men] Men
II.ii.49 knight] Knight
II.ii.57 yours] your's
II.ii.59 'Tis] ‸~
II.ii.59 *s.d.* (Reads.)] *not in copy-text*
II.ii.63 devil] Devil
II.ii.63 dragon] Dragon
II.ii.64 hell] Hell
II.ii.64 demon] Demon
II.ii.66 tent] Tent
II.ii.69 corslet] Corslet
II.ii.69 helm] Helm
II.ii.75 camp] Camp
II.ii.75 sisterhood] Sisterhood
II.ii.80 captains] Captains
II.ii.81 homage] hommage
II.ii.81 *s.d.* Enter Gersa] enters
II.ii.81 royal] Royal
II.ii.89 vestal] Vestal
II.ii.89 lord] Lord
II.ii.91 lady] Lady
II.ii.93 niece] Niece
II.ii.94 heavens] Heavens
II.ii.95 Erminia] Eminia
II.ii.96 Prythee, . . . lady,] ~‸ . . . Lady‸
II.ii.97 *s.p.* Erminia] Eminia
II.ii.97 soldiers] Solders
II.ii.97 *s.p.* Gersa] Gerza
II.ii.98 loveliness] Loveliness
II.ii.99 *s.p.* Erminia] Eminia
II.ii.99 Alas,] ~‸
II.ii.99 me!] ~‸
II.ii.100 indeed.] ~‸
II.ii.101 swan] Swan
II.ii.106 king] King
II.ii.112 sir] Sir
II.ii.117 lady] Lady
II.ii.117 'tis] ‸~
II.ii.118 father] Father
II.ii.120 daughter] Daughter
II.ii.122 virgin] Virgin
II.ii.123 false,] ~‸
II.ii.125 dove] Dove
II.ii.126 eagle] Eagle
II.ii.132 church] Church
II.ii.133 husbandmen] Husbandmen
II.ii.145 father] Father
II.ii.146 me,] ~‸
II.ii.149 daughter] Daughter
II.ii.151 lady] Lady
*After* II.ii.153 *copy-text has*: End of the Second Act.
III.i.1 *s.p.* Albert.] *not in copy-text*
III.i.9 boyhood] Boyhood
III.i.19 wind?] ~.
III.i.24 confessional?] ~!
III.i.26 woman's] Woman's
III.i.30 hell's] Hell's
III.i.34, 37 man] Man
III.i.38 gipsies] Gipsies
III.i.41 man] Man
III.i.49 heaven] Heaven
III.i.50 porters] Porters
III.i.54 duke] Duke
III.i.61 mitre] Mitre
III.i.64 -turn'd] -turnd
III.i.65 'Tis] ‸~
III.i.65 meteor.] ~—
III.ii.1 daughter] Daughter
III.ii.2 nuptial] nuptual
III.ii.4 liege] Liege
III.ii.5 bride] Bride
III.ii.5 love] Love
III.ii.12 lord] Lord
III.ii.13 beauty] Beauty
III.ii.17 king] King
III.ii.18 cities‸] Cities,
III.ii.22 children] Children

III.ii.25 lord] Lord
III.ii.27 sun] Sun
III.ii.28 heaven] Heaven
III.ii.28 son] Son
III.ii.29 music] Music
III.ii.30 soldier's] Soldier's
III.ii.33 heralds] Heralds
III.ii.33 royal] Royal
III.ii.34 knights] Knights
III.ii.36 lord] Lord
III.ii.36 tourney] Tourney
III.ii.38 heaven's] Heaven's
III.ii.41 car] Car
III.ii.44 earth] Earth
III.ii.44 palace] Palace
III.ii.44 room] Room
III.ii.48 romances] Romances
III.ii.49 He will] He 'll
III.ii.52 tourney] Tourney
III.ii.52 *s.d.* sennet] senet
III.ii.53 sirs] Sirs
III.ii.54 abbot] Abbot
III.ii.55 father] Father
III.ii.57 abbot] Abbot
III.ii.65 sister] Sister
III.ii.69 lord] Lord
III.ii.70 lady sister] Lady Sister
III.ii.72 barbarian] Barbarian
III.ii.73, 74 wife] Wife
III.ii.75 wife (*in Ludolph's speech*)] Wife
III.ii.76 priest] Priest
III.ii.82 demon's] Demon's
III.ii.83 lightning] lightening
III.ii.85 man] Man
III.ii.88 monk] Monk
III.ii.96 devil's] Devil's
III.ii.98 son] Son
III.ii.100 abbot's] Abbot's
III.ii.101 sire] Sire
III.ii.102 *s.d.* Ladies,] ~‸
III.ii.105 judge] Judge
III.ii.107 old] Old
III.ii.108 man] Man
III.ii.109 ambassador] Ambassador
III.ii.111, 112 abbot] Abbot
III.ii.117 innocent] Innocent
III.ii.122 this,] ~‸
III.ii.122 niece—] Niece?
III.ii.123 herbal, this] ~? This
III.ii.124 piety] Piety
III.ii.124 lady] Lady
III.ii.125 angel] Angel
III.ii.126 vails] veils
III.ii.126 pale—] ~,
III.ii.127 abbot] Abbot
III.ii.129 liege] Liege
III.ii.133 niece] Niece
III.ii.135 weeds‸ . . . hand‸] ~, . . . ~,
III.ii.139 lady] Lady
III.ii.141 -gallant] -Gallant
III.ii.144 head‸] ~,
III.ii.146 lady's] Lady's
III.ii.155 lady?] Lady.
III.ii.157 judge] Judge
III.ii.158 unread?] ~.
III.ii.159 sinner] Sinner
III.ii.160 monk] Monk
III.ii.164 virgin] Virgin
III.ii.165 brother] Brother
III.ii.170 priest] Priest
III.ii.171 lady] Lady
III.ii.176 man] Man
III.ii.178 son] Son
III.ii.180 man's] Man's
III.ii.180 heaven's] Heaven's
III.ii.183 man's] Man's
III.ii.186 clogg'd] clog
III.ii.187 miser] Miser
III.ii.189 knight] Knight
III.ii.196 dolt] Dolt
III.ii.204 sorcerer] Sorcerer
III.ii.209 man] Man
III.ii.214 daughter] Daughter
III.ii.216 liege] Liege
III.ii.218 monarch, 'tis] Monarch, ‸~
III.ii.219 -priest] -Priest
III.ii.220 awaken'd] awak'd
III.ii.223 lion] Lion
III.ii.223 gnat] Gnat
III.ii.228 moon] Moon
III.ii.233 night-] Night-
III.ii.233 man] Man
III.ii.237 monk] Monk
III.ii.244 physicians] Physicians
III.ii.245 guards] Guards
III.ii.248 court-] Court-
III.ii.252 man] Man
III.ii.255 heaven] Heaven
III.ii.268 drummer's] Drummer's
*After* III.ii.281 *copy-text has*: End of the Third Act.

IV.i.6 'tis] ^~
IV.i.22 woman] Woman
IV.i.34 women] Women
IV.i.34 taunted?] ~.
IV.i.36 pages] Pages
IV.i.51 sexton] Sexton
IV.i.51 man] Man
IV.i.55 castle] Castle
IV.i.61 Though] Thou
IV.i.62 sir] Sir
IV.i.68 host] Host
IV.i.69 lords] Lords
IV.i.71 brother's] Brother's
IV.i.73 thoughts.] ~—
IV.i.78 crown] Crown
IV.i.80 moon] Moon
IV.i.97 missal] Missal
IV.i.99 abbot] Abbot
IV.i.110 lady] Lady
IV.i.124 man] Man
IV.i.133 devil's] Devil's
IV.i.137 man] Man
IV.i.143 truth.] ~^
IV.i.143 traitor] Traitor
IV.i.151 soldier] Soldier
IV.i.151 queen] Queen
IV.i.152 provinces] Provinces
IV.i.153 cities] Cities
IV.i.159 traitor] Traitor
IV.i.160 hypocrite] Hypocrite
IV.i.164 them^] ~,
IV.i.165 lady] Lady
IV.i.165 emperor] Emperor
IV.i.166 autumn-sun] Autumn-Sun
IV.i.167 sir] Sir
IV.i.170 nightfall] Nightfall
IV.i.171 lady sister] Lady Sister
IV.i.172 castle] Castle
IV.i.184 *s.d.* apartment] Apartment
IV.ii.1 lord] Lord
IV.ii.11 diviner] divine
IV.ii.22 And, thoughtless!^] ~^ ~!—
IV.ii.36 nature's] Nature's
IV.ii.42 lion] Lion
IV.ii.45 sir] Sir
IV.ii.45 man] Man
IV.ii.55 soldier's] Soldier's
IV.ii.61 father] Father
IV.ii.62 banquet-] Banquet-
IV.ii.62 chiefs] Chiefs
IV.ii.74 sir] Sir
IV.ii.85 heaven] Heaven
IV.ii.88 devils] Devils
IV.ii.90 battailous] battaillous
IV.ii.92 boy] Boy
IV.ii.97, 99 sir] Sir
IV.ii.103 canst] can'st
IV.ii.105 wittol] Wittol
IV.ii.113 father] Father
IV.ii.113 coward] Coward
IV.ii.115 child] Child
IV.ii.115 lord] Lord
IV.ii.117 messenger] Messenger
IV.ii.126 lady] Lady
IV.ii.127 chamber's] Chamber's
IV.ii.132 boy] Boy
IV.ii.138 witch] Witch
*After* IV.ii139 *copy-text has*: End of the Fourth Act.
V.i.8 man] Man
V.i.10 heaven] Heaven
V.i.14 'Tis] ^~
V.i.16 boy] Boy
V.i.32 Now] How
V.ii.10 Shrive] Shrine
V.ii.22 soul"?] ~?"
V.ii.29 'Tis] ^~
V.ii.36 cockatrice] Cockatrice
V.ii.38 devil] Devil
V.ii.41 man] Man
V.ii.53 bride . . . bride . . . bride] Bride . . . Bride . . . Bride
V.ii.54 'tis] ^~
V.ii.56 halls] Halls
V.ii.58 canst] can'st
V.ii.59 lions] Lions
V.ii.59 lamb] Lamb
V.iii.1, 3, 9, 13, 14 *s.p.* Theodore] 1st Knight
V.iii.4 page's] Page's
V.iii.8, 12 lady] Lady
V.iii.12 abbot] Abbot
V.iii.13 'Tis] ^~
V.iv.1 boy] Boy
V.iv.1 son . . . son] Son . . . Son
V.iv.2 physicians] Physicians
V.iv.3 'Tis] ^~
V.iv.4 heaven] Heaven
V.iv.4 earth] Earth
V.iv.6 abbot] Abbot
V.iv.7 girl] Girl
V.iv.9 saints] Saints

V.iv.10 child] Child
V.iv.12 father's] Father's
V.iv.14 boy] Boy
V.iv.17 sire] Sire
V.iv.22 father] Father
V.iv.29 doctor] Doctor
V.iv.36 sire] Sire
V.iv.37 boy] Boy
V.iv.38 child] Child
V.iv.49 'Tis . . . 'tis] ^~ . . . ^~
V.iv.50 child] Child
V.iv.60 terrace] Terrace
V.v *location* Hall, . . . supper- . . . gold . . . silver . . . Gentlemen,] ~; . . . Supper- . . . Gold . . . Silver . . . ~^
V.v.5 seer] Seer
V.v.8 sir] Sir
V.v.10 soldiers] Soldiers
V.v.28 'Tis] ^~
V.v.28 men] Men
V.v.30 gods] Gods
V.v.36 heaven's] Heaven's
V.v.48 lord] Lord
V.v.49, 50, 51 'Tis] ^~
V.v.54 gods] Gods
V.v.69 'tis] ^~
V.v.73 heaven] Heaven
V.v.77 wife] Wife
V.v.78 music] Music
V.v.80 musicians] Musicians
V.v.80 *s.d.* music] Music
V.v.82 'Tis] ^~
V.v.85 presence] Presence
V.v.87 ladies] Ladies
V.v.87 lawn^] ~,
V.v.89 silks^] ~,
V.v.90 duchesses] Duchesses
V.v.90 margravines] Margravines
V.v.92 'tis] ^~
V.v.95 engender'd] engendur'd
V.v.107 raven] Raven
V.v.110 father] Father
V.v.117 father's] Father's
V.v.119 bride] Bride
V.v.125 Bacchus'] ~^
V.v.126 page] Page
V.v.133 prince] Prince
V.v.135 dragon] Dragon
V.v.137 sir] Sir
V.v.138 father] Father
V.v.139 *s.d.* Sigifred,] ~^
V.v.140 man] Man
V.v.141 conspirator] Conspiritor
V.v.147 judge's] Judge's
V.v.151 son] Son
V.v.152 father's] Father's
V.v.153 demon] Demon
V.v.154 temple-] Temple-
V.v.156 priest] Priest
V.v.156 justice] Justice
V.v.159 scorpion] Scorpion
V.v.161 father] Father
V.v.161 legions] Legions
V.v.164 son] Son
V.v.168 angel's] Angel's
V.v.171 man] Man
V.v.173 lord] Lord
V.v.179 son . . . son] Son . . . Son
V.v.183 lord . . . lord] Lord . . . Lord
V.v.186 *s.d.* doors] Doors
V.v.187 lord . . . lord] Lord . . . Lord
V.v.189 dagger] Dagger
V.v.192 nobles] Nobles
V.v.193 hand, father?—] ~—~^—

*Lamia*

Repeated opening quotes have been omitted in I.39–41, 69–80, 84–87, 90, 94–111, 118–122, 245, 246, 258–271, 273–286, 370, 372–374, 376, 377, II.43–45, 49–64, 86–91, 93–101, 165–169, 255, 278–290, 297, 298

I.27 ¶From . . . ] *no* ¶ *in copy-text*
I.377 dreams."] ~.^
II.213 ¶Soon . . . ] *no* ¶ *in copy-text*
II.298 prey?"] ~?^

*Pensive they sit, and roll their languid eyes*

No heading in copy-text
A repeated opening quote has been omitted in 20
1 eyes,] ~∧
2 toasts] tosts
3 night,] ~∧
4 appetite.] ~—
5 See,] ~∧
5 crew,] ~∧
7 Betty brings.] betty ~—
8 fly] Fly
10 No, no,] ~∧ ~∧
10 Mr.] m$^{r}$
10 spoon,] ~∧
11 handle,] ~∧
12 struggler, . . . dark,] ~∧ . . . ~∧
14 snuffers] Snuffers
14 handle;] ~∧
15 cauliflower] Cauliflower
15 candle,] ~—
17 No. 7,] no∧ ~∧
18 Alas,∧] ~∧"
18 coat] Coat
19 taylor live∧?"] Taylor ~"?"
20 then.∧] ~∧"
21 taylor] Taylor
22 tell. Let] ~—let
23 Wapping,] wapping∧
24 pleas'd."] ~∧

*To Autumn*

11 summer] Summer
23 spring] Spring

*The Fall of Hyperion*

Copy-text heading: The Fall of Hyperion / —A Dream
I.4 heaven] Heaven
I.5 Indian] indian
I.7 dream,] ~∧
I.10 charm] cham
I.12 poet] Poet
I.13 man] Man
I.17 poet's] Poet's
I.17 fanatic's] Fanatics
I.20 myrtle] Myrtle
I.21 plantane] Plantane
I.23 ears,] ~;
I.30 Which,] ~∧
I.31 angel] Angel
I.31 mother] Mother
I.37 Proserpine] proserpine
I.44 mortals] Mortals
I.44 world] World
I.47 elixir] Elixir
I.48 caliphat] Caliphat
I.49 monkish] Monkish
I.50 men] Men
I.67 cathedrals] Cathedrals
I.69 nature's rocks] Nature's Rocks
I.71 monument.] Monument—
I.80 jewelries.] ~—
I.84 south] South
I.85 eastward] Eastward
I.87 west] West
I.88 image] Image
I.97 -May] -way
I.97 east wind] East Wind
I.98 south] South
I.103 Maian] maian
I.115 universe] Universe
I.121 toil;] ~,
I.132 iced] ice'd
I.135 angels] Angels
I.139 I∧] ~,
I.143 That] that
I.145 purge] Purge
I.146 film."] ~"—
I.148 "But] ∧~
I.149 and] And
I.156 "Who] ∧~
I.166 they.] ~—
I.167 tribe,] ~∧
I.168 world] World
I.169 earth] Earth
I.171 Every] every
I.176 sins] Sins
I.180 temples] Temples
I.186 please,] ~∧
I.190 physician] Physician
I.190 men] Men
I.191 vultures] Vultures
I.192 eagles] Eagles

I.203 spleen,] ~‸
I.208 hectorers] Hectorers
I.213 image] Image
I.223 giant hierarchy] Giant Hierarchy
I.224 image] Image
I.227 priestess] Priestess
I.230 majesty] Majesty
I.241 less‸] ~,
I.250 mother's] Mother's
I.278 chambers] Chambers
I.282 sorrow.] ~—
I.285 temple] Temple
I.292 lips,] ~;
I.293 pine] Pine
I.296 eve's] Eve's
I.298 what] was
I.298, 299 image] Image
I.300 temple] Temple
I.302 realms."] ~‸"
I.309 eagle's] Eagle's
I.312 summer's] Summer's
I.316 divinity] Divinity
I.317 the] The
I.328 who‸] ~,
I.335 brood] Brood
I.345 there,] ~‸
I.355 one:] ~‸
I.356 *thou?* ] ~:
I.359 ocean] Ocean
I.361 majesty] Majesty
I.368 thoughtless] thoughless
I.371 weep."‸] ~."—
I.372 summer night] Summer Night
I.386 earth] Earth
I.387 feet;] ~.
I.392 moon] Moon
I.394 night,] ~‸
I.396 ghostly.] ~—
I.397 death] Death
I.397 vale] Vale
I.398 burthens.] ~—
I.401 kingdom] Kingdom
I.416 deity] Deity
I.421 sun] Sun
I.423 universe,] ~‸
I.424 of death] of Death
I.424 moan (*last word*)] Moan
I.426 palsy] Palsy
I.428 Weak as] Week as
I.430 moan (*second word*)] Moan
I.431 imps] Imps
I.434 heaven's] Heaven's
I.438 children."] ~‸"
I.440 man] Man
I.444 dolorous] dolourous
I.445 visions.] ~—
I.454 Thea] Thœa
I.465 antichamber] Antichamber
I.468 dare.‸] ~.—
*After* I.468 *copy-text has*: End of Canto 1.—
II.6 trees.] ~—
II.14 rule] Rule
II.14 majesty] Majesty
II.17 unsecure;] ~,
II.18 earth] Earth
II.20 even] Even
II.27 courts] Courts
II.34 west] West
II.39 hall . . . hall] Hall . . . Hall
II.45 trance,] ~‸
II.48 threshold] threshhold
II.48 west.‸] ~.—

*The day is gone, and all its sweets are gone*

Copy-text heading: Sonnet
10 holiday] Holiday
10 holinight] Holinight
13 missal] Missal

*I cry your mercy—pity—love!—aye, love*

Copy-text heading: Sonnet

*What can I do to drive away*

Copy-text heading: To ——
3 queen] Queen
4 Love] love
33 wretched] wrecked
34 pour‸] ~,
42 flowers] bad flowers

*To Fanny*

3 tripod] Tripod
5 theme! a theme] Theme! a Theme
7 thee] Thee
7 thou] Thou
9 love] Love
22 heart] Heart
27 wreathe,] ~;
31 heaven] Heaven
33 this, . . . Fanny!—] ~— . . . ~!^
35 'tis] ^~
35 new—] ~,
42 love,] ~^
46 love alone] Love alone
47 loveliest] Loveliest
47 free^] ~,
50 brief^] ~,
55 close,] ~^
56 Love,] ~^

*King Stephen*

Copy-text heading: King Stephen, / a fragment / of a Tragedy
*Dramatis Personae* Earl of Glocester] Duke of Glocester Earl Baldwin de Redvers] Earl Baldwin De Kaims] *not in copy-text*
I.i.1 soldier's] Soldier's
I.i.16 'Tis] ^~
I.i.16 enemy;] ~,
I.i.19 breathed] breath'd
I.i.26 lord] Lord
I.i.27 heaven] Heaven
I.i.28, 34 soldiers] Soldiers
I.i.35 Earls . . . Chester] Earl . . . Chesters
I.i.35 brow-beat] ~^ ~
I.ii.5 chroniclers] Chroniclers
I.ii.6 lord] Lord
I.ii.8 usurper's] Usurper's
I.ii.9 lord] Lord
I.ii.17 stag] Stag
I.ii.18 Welch] welch
I.ii.20 message] Message
I.ii.21 down,] ~^
I.ii.22 walls] Walls
I.ii.23 havock'd] havack'd
I.ii.23 feet.] ~—
I.ii.24 Glocester] Gloster
I.ii.24 heart,] ~^
I.ii.25 captains,] Captains^
I.ii.25 knights] Knights
I.ii.26 banquet] Banquet
I.ii.27 triumph] Triumph
I.ii.28 streets] Streets
I.ii.28 music] Music
I.ii.28 *s.d.* Enter Second Knight] a Knight
I.ii.28 Whence] When
I.ii.29, 31, 35, 45 *s.p.* Second Knight] Knight
I.ii.29 From Stephen,] ~ ~^
I.ii.30 name?] ~^
I.ii.31 think, . . . lord,] ~^ . . . Lord^
I.ii.31 man,] ~^
I.ii.32 demon] deamon
I.ii.33 Christian] christian
I.ii.34 soldier] Soldier
I.ii.35 victory] Victory
I.ii.36 swords] Swords
I.ii.37 aloof.] ~—
I.ii.38 battle] Battle
I.ii.38 sick,] ~^
I.ii.39 morion] Morion
I.ii.39 Flemish knight,] flemish Knight^
I.ii.40 short] shot
I.ii.41 vengeful] Vengeful
I.ii.42 Chester's horse,] Chesters ~^
I.ii.45 flew,] ~^
I.ii.46 Whom, . . . held,] ~^ . . . ~^
I.ii.47 breathe,] ~^
I.ii.50 sword] Swor'd
I.ii.50 snapp'd] snap'd
I.ii.51 lead] Lead
I.ii.51 Mars] mars
I.ii.54 salutation] Salutation
I.iii *opening s.d.* unarm'd] unam'd
I.iii.1 sword] Sword
I.iii.1 seize] sieze
I.iii.2 from] From
I.iii.2 armoury,] amoury^
I.iii.3 spears!] ~.
I.iii.4 my] *deleted in copy-text*
I.iii.4 enemies? Here, . . . hand,] Enemies? ~^ . . . ~^

I.iii.5 brood] Brood
I.iii.5 sword] Sword
I.iii.6 sword . . . sword] Sword . . . Sword
I.iii.7 hedge-stake] Hedge-Stake
I.iii.8 brawny vengeance,] brawy vengence^
I.iii.8 labourer] Labourer
I.iii.9 kingdom] Kindom
I.iii.10 plum'd,] ~^
I.iii.12 beard.] ~^
I.iii.13 *s.d.* De Kaims . . . Knights,] de Kaimes . . . ~^
I.iii.14 *s.p.* Kaims] Kimes
I.iii.15 unarm'd] unam'd
I.iii.15 us?] ~—
I.iii.16 Yield,] ~^
I.iii.16 sword's] Sword's
I.iii.17 traitor's] Traitor's
I.iii.18 it, . . . Kaims,] ~^ . . . ~^
I.iii.18 inch.] inch[ ] (*possible loss of punctuation through damage to MS*)
I.iii.19 Yes,] ~^
I.iii.19 madness] Madness
I.iii.19 meed] Meed
I.iii.20 *s.p.* Kaims] Kaimes
I.iii.20 dare,] ~^
I.iii.20 man disarm'd] Man disam'd
I.iii.21 lion] Lion
I.iii.22 me,] ~^
I.iii.22 price] Price
I.iii.23 glory] Glory
I.iii.23 day,] ~^
I.iii.24 king,] King^
I.iii.25 man] Man
I.iii.25 realm,] Realm^
I.iii.26 *s.p.* Kaims] Kains
I.iii.27 I,] ~^
I.iii.27 it, sir] ~^ Sir
I.iii.28 think'st] thinkst
I.iii.28 king,] King^
I.iii.29 That,] ~^
I.iii.29 court] Court
I.iii.29 haughty Maud,] hauty ~^
I.iii.30 presence] Presence
I.iii.31 whisper,] whiper^
I.iii.32 prisoner.] Prisoner—
I.iii.32 Certes, . . . Kaims,] ~^ . . . ~^
I.iii.33 one.] ~—
I.iii.33 true,] ~^
I.iii.34 And, Stephen,] ~^ ~^
I.iii.34 No, no—] ~. No.
I.iii.35 gorge,] ~^
I.iii.36 breast,] ~^
I.iii.37 knighthood] Knighhood
I.iii.38 lordship] Lordship
I.iii.39 need? Take] ~—take
I.iii.39 dastard] Dastard
I.iii.40 What,] ~^
I.iii.40 vulnerable] vulenable
I.iii.40 prisoner] Prisoner
I.iii.41 it,] ~—
I.iii.42 king] King
I.iii.43 'sdains] 'seigns
I.iii.43 yield] yeld
I.iii.43 peer,] Peer^
I.iii.44 title] Title
I.iii.44 deeds,] ~^
I.iii.45 Glocester.] ~—
I.iii.45 hilts, . . . Kaims,] ~^ . . . ~^
I.iv *heading* Scene IV] Scene
I.iv *opening s.d.* chair . . . state . . . Chester, . . . Attendants] Chair . . . State . . . ~^ . . . attendants
I.iv.1 Glocester,] ~^
I.iv.1 Boulogne] Boulougne
I.iv.3 hour,] ~^
I.iv.4 speech, . . . enough,] ~^ . . . eough^
I.iv.5 counsel] Counsel
I.iv.5 given,] ~^
I.iv.8 realm] Realm
I.iv.11 ear] Ear
I.iv.12 kingdom's] Kingdom's
I.iv.12 government] Goverment
I.iv.13 Not] not
I.iv.14 Advised, . . . school'd,] ~^ . . . ~^
I.iv.14 henceforth] hencefoth
I.iv.15 Spoken] spoken
I.iv.15 clear, plain,] ~^ ~^
I.iv.15, 16 terms,] ~^
I.iv.17 pardon, brother,] ~^ Brother^
I.iv.18 for, . . . said,] ~^ . . . ~^
I.iv.19 worldly pomp] wordly Pomp
I.iv.20 rebel] Rebel
I.iv.20 judge] Judge
I.iv.21 sentence] Sentence
I.iv.21 guilt.] ~—
I.iv.22 presence.] ~^
I.iv.24 is't] 'ist

I.iv.25 Boulogne,] Boulougne∧
I.iv.25 prisoner] Prisoner
I.iv.26 penance] Penance
I.iv.26 crimes] Crimes
I.iv.27 wholesome, sweet,] ~∧ ~∧
I.iv.28 Glocester's] Glocesters
I.iv.29 that, . . . Queen,] ~∧ . . . ~∧
I.iv.30 Earl,] ~∧
I.iv.32 Council] council
I.iv.32 books] Books
I.iv.34 play] Play
I.iv.34 Darius.] ~—
I.iv.35 last.] ~—
I.iv.36 Highness] higness
I.iv.37 courtesy] Courtesy
I.iv.38 rebel] Rebel
I.iv.39 ingrate] Ingrate
I.iv.40 lord] Lord
I.iv.40 sire,] Sire∧
I.iv.41 mishaps,] ~∧
I.iv.43 brow,] ~∧
I.iv.44 smile,] ~∧
I.iv.46 perjur'd] Perjur'd
I.iv.47 nay,] ~∧
I.iv.49 hours,] ~∧
I.iv.50 purgatory,] ~.
I.iv.51 bondage] Bondage
I.iv.52 feasts] Feasts
I.iv.52 music] Music
I.iv.52 shows] shous
I.iv.53 pageantry] Pageantry
I.iv.56 deeds.] ~—
I.iv.57 summer!] Summer.
I.iv.57 queen's] Queen's

*This living hand, now warm and capable*

No heading in copy-text
1 warm] wam
2 earnest] eanest
5 heart] heat
5 blood,] ~∧
7 -calm'd. See,] -~—see∧
7 is—] ~∧
8 you.] ~—

*The Jealousies*

Copy-text heading: The Cap and Bells; / Or, the Jealousies. / A Faëry Tale. Unfinished (the heading in the present text is based on that in $W^2$: The jealousies. / A faery Tale, / by / Lucy Vaughan Lloyd / of / China Walk, Lambeth)
Opening quotation marks have been added in 427, 642, 649, 658, 667, 676, 685, 694, 703, 712, 721, 730, 739, 748, 757, 766, 775, 784, and a closing quote in 787
40, 46 Princess] princess
61 rouse,"] ~;"
62 Princess] princess
83 Provence] Provençe
101 column∧ . . . B∧] ~, . . . ~.,
121 ease—] ~,
136 Prince] prince
180 felon] fellow
184 slow∧] ~,
207 For shortest] And for short
208 houses] dealers
214 power] powers
250 plodding,] ~∧
255 Who,] ~∧
257 monsieur] Monsieur
277 panel,] ~∧
284 and,] ~∧
295 paradise] Paradise
297 sly] slight
299 partial, . . . *nous,*] ~∧ . . . ~∧
307 magician] Magician
316 page] Page
330 page;] Page,
334 seer] Seer
347 treen] green
355 the] *not in copy-text*
365, 366 nantz] Nantz
366 seer] Seer
372, 373, 375 Berthas] Bertha's
408 Majesty] majesty
419 one] the
427 ottoman] Ottoman
434 mago] Mago
455 *I / do*] ~ ∧ ~
463 say∧] ~,
464 Highness] highness
474 Majesty] majesty
477 waist,] ~∧

487 Majesty] majesty
488 awake‸] ~,
492 swoon;] ~,
499 prize.] ~,
505 'gan] 'gan to
511 wool, . . . snow‸] ~‸ . . . ~,
520 alarm;] ~,
521 Uplift] But lift
522 palace, . . . fit."] palace. * * *
523 this] that
528 Emperor;] ~,
530 heavens] Heavens
543 Majesty] majesty
544 Whew!] Where?
546 Highness;] highness,
551 Ambassador's] ambassador's
564 get] yet
567 mignionette.‸] ~."
568 was] is
569 rang] ring
574 Came] Comes
575 Freckled] Freckles
576 blew] blow
587 janizaries] Janizaries
591 lords] Lords
600 hocus] Hocus
631 This‸ . . . falsehood‸] ~, . . . ~,
647 quite—] ~:
654 pun—] ~,
672 at—] ~,
673 Whoop!'—] ~!"‸
677 out—] ~,
692 dozed] dosed
697 jokes:)] ~,)
698 favour,] ~;
715 heaven] Heaven
719 her] his
739 they,] ~!
775 poet] Poet
775 court-clown's] Court-Clown's
778 prothalamion] Prothalamion
780 Where,'] ~!"
788 mago] Mago
793–794 Now . . . hall. (*plus stanza number*)] *not in copy-text* (*the text is taken from* $W^2$, *which has initial capitals in* authority, hubbub, *and* hall)

*In after time a sage of mickle lore*

No heading in copy-text
1 sage] Sage
2 giant] Giant
8 When,] ~‸

APPENDIX II

# Selective Historical Collations

This appendix lists substantive emendations and corruptions in MSS, nineteenth-century printed texts, and first printings of any date that are not recorded in the apparatus but nevertheless have been of some importance in the history of Keats's texts. The entries are selective in that they include only readings that have recurred in twentieth-century editions; readings that had no influence on modern texts are omitted here (though those in MSS and first printings are routinely detailed in the Textual Notes). The principal purposes are to specify the initial sources of emendations and errors of long-standing tradition and to make possible the identification of those that appear for the first time in twentieth-century reprintings. The intention is that any substantive reading in a modern text that differs from the text in the present edition will be one of three types: (1) an authoritative or possibly authoritative variant, in which case it will be in the apparatus of the present edition; (2) a nonauthoritative reading from a MS or a first or early printed text, in which case it will be in the appropriate list below; (3) an emendation or error originating in a twentieth-century reprinting, in which case it will be absent entirely from both the apparatus and this appendix. Thus Garrod's "Of" in *God of the golden bow* 6, a reading taken over from the draft, is recorded in the apparatus; his "while" in *Lines Written on 29 May* 4, a misreading repeated from Lowell's initial printing of the poem, is included in the second item of the first list below; and his "has" (for "is") in *La Belle Dame* 47, an emendation or corruption originating in his own edition, does not appear in either place.

With a few exceptions, only the first printing of a nonauthoritative reading is noted here (thus *1848* alone is cited for "the golden" in *To Lord Byron* 9, though the reading recurs throughout the rest of the nineteenth century and on into the twentieth); subsequent repetitions of the reading may be assumed to derive from the printed text cited. The following are used to abbreviate the names of transcribers:

| | |
|---|---|
| CCC | Charles Cowden Clarke |
| CP | Coventry Patmore |
| CR | Charlotte Reynolds |
| CWD | Charles Wentworth Dilke |
| JCS | J. C. Stephens |
| JHP | John Howard Payne |

| | |
|---|---|
| JJ | John Jeffrey |
| RMM | Richard Monckton Milnes |
| WC | Woodhouse's clerk |

The rest of the sigla are either abbreviations used throughout this volume or short references (by author, editor, or periodical title) to printings cited in the Textual Notes.

*Lines Written on 29 May, the Anniversary of Charles's Restoration, on Hearing the Bells Ringing*

1 will] while *Lowell*

4 Ah! when] Oh! while *Lowell*

*Fill for me a brimming bowl*

4 Woman] Women *WC, N&Q*

*As from the darkening gloom a silver dove*

12 Of . . . cleavest] O' . . . cleav'st *1876*

*To Lord Byron*

6 O'ershading] O'ershadowing *1876*

9 a golden] the golden *1848*

*Oh Chatterton! how very sad thy fate*

*Heading* Oh . . . fate] Sonnet. To Chatterton $W^2$, *WC*

4 wildly] mildly *1848*

6 murmurs] numbers *1848*

8 flower] flow'ret *1848*

*Ode to Apollo*

4 sung] sang $W^2$, *WC, 1848*

7 There] Here *1848*

*O come, dearest Emma! the rose is full blown*

*Heading* O . . . blown] Stanzas to Miss Wylie *Forman* (*1883*)

*Give me women, wine, and snuff*

*Heading* Give . . . snuff] Women, Wine and Snuff *Forman* (*1884*)

*Specimen of an Induction to a Poem*

33 lone] long *Galignani* (*1829*)

*Oh! how I love, on a fair summer's eve*

12 the] *omitted in CP, 1848*

*Sleep and Poetry*

234 clubs . . . poets‸] cubs . . . Poets' *Galignani (1829)—the first word earlier (and independently) as a query in Woodhouse's interleaved 1817*

*After dark vapours have oppressed our plains*

5 month, relieving] mouth, relieved *1848*

*To a Young Lady Who Sent Me a Laurel Crown*

11 very] mighty *1848*

*God of the golden bow*

*Heading* God . . . bow] Ode to Apollo *W*³, *W*², *W*¹, *CR, Woodhouse's copy for Severn, Western Messenger (the last independently of the others)*

23 I not] not I *Forman (1883)*

30 his] its *W*², *W*¹, *CR, Western Messenger (the last independently of the others)*

*This pleasant tale is like a little copse*

*Heading* This . . . copse] Sonnet / Written on a blank space at the end of Chaucer's tale "The flowre and the lefe" *W*¹

2 do] so *Clarke's "The Riches of Chaucer," CP, 1848 (the latter two independently of the first)*

*On Seeing the Elgin Marbles*

10 undescribable] indescribable *1848*

*To Haydon with a Sonnet Written on Seeing the Elgin Marbles*

*Heading* To . . . Seeing] Sonnet. To R. B. Haydon—with the foregoing Sonnet on *W*²

9 those] these *1848*

12 browless idiotism—] brainless idiotism and *1848*

13 the] the full *1848*

*On* The Story of Rimini

*Heading* On] On Leigh Hunt's Poem *1848 (from Milnes's expansion of the heading on Brown's transcript)*

*Unfelt, unheard, unseen*

*Heading* Unfelt . . . unseen] Lines *1848*

*You say you love; but with a voice*

19 for] to *TLS*

*Before he went to live with owls and bats*

6 pluck] pluck away *JCS, Nicoll and Wise*

8 Your] The *Nicoll and Wise*

10 valiant] motley *Nicoll and Wise*

11 Of] Most *JCS, Nicoll and Wise*

13 their] the *Nicoll and Wise*

*The Gothic looks solemn*

*Heading* The . . . solemn] Lines / Rhymed in a letter received (by J.H.R.) from Oxford *W*[1]

*Think not of it, sweet one, so*

*Heading* Think . . . so] To —— *W*[2], *W*[1], *CR*; On . . . . *CCC, 1848* (*CCC has 10 dots*)

7 drop^ then—It] ~, ~^ it *Forman (1883)*

*Endymion*

I.182 owlet's] owlets' *Galignani (1829)*
II.523 necks] neck *Forman (1883)*
II.749 Is . . . Who] Is it to be so? No! For Who *Taylor's alteration in the holograph fair copy*
II.974 thrush's] thrushes' *Woodhouse's alteration in his interleaved 1818, Forman (1883)*
III.918 my Cytherea] thou my Cythēra *Woodhouse's alteration in his interleaved 1818, Forman (1883)*

*Apollo to the Graces*

3 thresholds] threshold *TLS*

6 kingdoms] Kingdom *TLS*

*Lines on Seeing a Lock of Milton's Hair*

32 offerings] offering *CWD, Forman (1883)*

41 Methought] I thought *1848*

*O blush not so! O blush not so*

*Heading* O . . . so] Sharing Eve's Apple *Forman (1883)*
11 those . . . hips] these . . . lips *Forman (1883)—the last word earlier as a suggested revision in W*[3]

*Hence burgundy, claret, and port*

*Heading* Hence . . . port] A Draught of Sunshine *Forman (1883)*

*Welcome joy, and welcome sorrow*

*Epigraph* embryo] embryon *W*[1]
8 burn] are *CCC, 1848*

17 aspics] Aspic *JCS, CCC, 1848*

*Time's sea hath been five years at its slow ebb*

*Heading* Time's . . . ebb] To*—— *with a note added in Woodhouse's hand*: *the Lady whom he saw for some few moments at Vauxhall *WC*; *CP and 1848 reproduce this, changing* the Lady *to* A lady

4 thy] thine *Woodhouse's copy for Severn, CP, 1848* (*the latter two independently of the first*)

*Spenser, a jealous honorer of thine*

*Heading* Spenser . . . thine] Sonnet. To Spenser *Forman* (*1883*)

7 quell] quill *1848*

9 escape] 'scape *1848*

*Blue!—'Tis the life of heaven—the domain*

*Heading* Blue . . . domain] Answer—by J Keats to a Sonnet ending thus / "——Dark eyes are dearer far / "Than orbs that mock the hyacinthine bell." by J.H.R. *WC* (*all after* Keats *added in Woodhouse's hand*); *CP and 1848 reproduce most of this, omitting* by J Keats, *changing* orbs *to* those (*Woodhouse had written* ⟨those⟩ orbs *on the clerk's MS*), *and expanding* J.H.R. *to* J. H. Reynolds

9 to] of *CP, 1848*

*O thou whose face hath felt the winter's wind*

*Heading* O . . . wind] What the Thrush said: Lines from a Letter to John Hamilton Reynolds *Forman* (*1883*)

*Four seasons fill the measure of the year*

14 forget] forego *Galignani* (*1829*)

*For there's Bishop's Teign*

*Heading* For . . . Teign] Teignmouth: "Some Doggerel," Sent in a Letter to B. R. Haydon *Forman* (*1883*)

1 For] Here all the summer could I stay, / For *Tom Taylor*

3 Teign] Teign's *Tom Taylor*

13 There is] There's a *Tom Taylor*

19 There is] There's *Tom Taylor*

24 dusk] dark *Tom Taylor*

34 violet] violets *Tom Taylor*

35 Sits . . . plight] Sit . . . light *Tom Taylor*

36 bud's as . . . as] buds are . . . in *Tom Taylor*

39 dack'd] dark- *Tom Taylor*

42 prickets] crickets *Tom Taylor*

*Where be ye going, you Devon maid*

*Heading* Where . . . maid] The Devon Maid: Stanzas Sent in a Letter to B. R. Haydon *Forman* (*1883*)

1 ye] you *Tom Taylor*

2 i'] in *Tom Taylor*

14 And . . . this] Your shaw I'll hang on the *Tom Taylor*

*Over the hill and over the dale*

*Heading* Over . . . dale] Dawlish Fair *Forman* (*1883*)

8 sat] lay *Lowell*

11 and] or $W^3$, *Lowell*

19 would not] wouldn't *Lowell*

*Dear Reynolds, as last night I lay in bed*

19 Some,] ~‸ *1848*

29 magic‸like] ~-~ *1848*

38 Here] There *1848*

61 grate] -gate *1848*

73 to] so *1848*

75 lore] love *1848*

109 in] i' the *1848*

110–113 Do . . . prose."] *omitted in 1848*

*To J. R.*

*Heading* J. R.] J. H. Reynolds *1848*

*Mother of Hermes! and still youthful Maia*

*Heading* Mother . . . Maia] Fragment of an Ode to Maia, written on May Day 1818 *Forman* (*1883*)

7 in] on *1848*

*To Homer*

5 wast thou] thou wast *1848*

7 spumy] spermy *1848*

*Give me your patience, sister, while I frame*

*Heading* Give . . . frame] Acrostic: Georgiana Augusta Keats *Forman* (*1883*)

*On Visiting the Tomb of Burns*

4 ago. Now . . . begun,] ~, now . . . ~. *1848* (*reproducing JJ's punctuation except at the end of the line*)

8 done‸] ~: *1848*

13 have oft] oft have *1848*

*Old Meg she was a gipsey*

*Heading* Old . . . gipsey] Meg Merrilies *PDWJ* (*1840*); Old Meg *Hood's*

*There was a naughty boy*

*Heading* There . . . boy] A Song about Myself *Forman* (*1883*)

58 To . . . north!] To follow one's nose / To the north! (*two lines*) *Forman* (*1883*)

85 finger] fingers *Forman* (*1883*)

89 A . . . kettle] A Kettle— / A Kettle (*two lines*) *Forman* (*1883*)

96 There] Then *Forman* (*1883*)

112–113 So . . . in / His shoes] So . . . in his shoes (*one line*) *Forman* (*1883*)

116–117 his / Shoes and] his shoes / And *Forman* (*1883*)

*Ah! ken ye what I met the day*

30 thence] there *Forman* (*1883*)

32 An'] And *Forman* (*1883*)

*This mortal body of a thousand days*

*Heading* This . . . days] Sonnet. Written in the Cottage where Burns was born *Forman* (*1883*)

5 old] own *Milnes's "Life . . . of John Keats"* (*1867*)

*All gentle folks who owe a grudge*

*Heading* All . . . grudge] The Gadfly *Forman* (*1883*)

26 seat . . . a—e,] seat * * * *Forman* (*1883*)

41 wert] wort *Forman* (*1883*)

*Of late two dainties were before me plac'd*

*Heading* Of . . . plac'd] Sonnet. On hearing the Bag-pipe and seeing "The Stranger" played at Inverary *Forman (1883)*

*There is a joy in footing slow across a silent plain*

4 nettles] nettled *1848*
10 scurf] surf *1848*
46 on] in *1848*

*Not Aladdin magian*

*Heading* Not . . . magian] Staffa *1876*
55 every] each *W*[1]

*Upon my life, Sir Nevis, I am piqu'd*

9 gentlemen] Gentle man *Forman (1883)*
47 you] them *Forman (1883)*
58 where] when *Forman (1883)*
59 dragons'] Dragon's *Forman (1883)*

*On Some Skulls in Beauley Abbey, near Inverness*

19 wore] won *Colvin*
35 prayers] prayer *Colvin*
64 sadness] badness *Colvin*
65 their] this *Colvin*
71 here] how *Colvin*
80 mark] mask *Colvin*

*Nature withheld Cassandra in the skies*

*Heading* Nature . . . skies] Translation from a Sonnet of Ronsard *Forman (1883)*

*And what is Love?—It is a doll dress'd up*

10 Anthony] Antony *1876*

*'Tis the "witching time of night"*

*Heading* 'Tis . . . night"] A Prophecy / To His Brother George in America *1876*
1 time] hour *1848*
20 then] *omitted in 1848*
24 stars' light] starlight *Ladies' Companion, Ladies' Pocket Magazine, JHP, 1848*
50 the] th' *JHP, 1848*
55 the] th' *1848*

*Spirit here that reignest*

3 burneth] burnest *1848*
4 mourneth] mournest *1848*
13 danceth] dancest *1848*
14 pranceth] prancest *1848*

*I had a dove, and the sweet dove died*

5 would] should *RMM, 1848*
6 would] should *Forman (1883)*
7 on] in *RMM, 1848*
8 could] would *RMM, 1848*

*The Eve of St. Mark*

32 mid] and *1848*
40 the] th' *1848*
74 giant] giant's $W^2$
101 hem] him *1848*
115 eyelids] eye had $W^2$

*Why did I laugh tonight? No voice will tell*

6 Say, wherefore] I say, why *RMM, 1848*
11 could] would *1848*

*When they were come unto the Faery's court*

1 unto] into *Macmillan's*
46 A . . . three] And quaver'd like the *Forman (1890)*
53 and at] and [then] at *Forman (1890)*

*Character of C. B.*

*Heading* Character of C. B.] Spenserian Stanzas on Charles Armitage Brown *Forman (1883)*
3–4 in . . . the] a parle / It holds with *1848*
13 -herd] -head *1848*
23 hoarse] brave *JJ, 1848*

*Bright star, would I were stedfast as thou art*

*Heading* Bright . . . art] Keats's Last Sonnet *1848*; Sonnet. Written on a Blank Page in Shakespeare's Poems, facing "A Lover's Complaint" *Forman (1883)*
11 swell and fall] fall and swell *1848*

*If by dull rhymes our English must be chain'd*

*Heading* If . . . chain'd] On the Sonnet $W^1$

*Two or three posies*

27 dove's] dove *Forman (1883)*

*Ode on Indolence*

12 masque] mask *1848*
41 A . . . time] And once more *1848*

*Shed no tear—O shed no tear*

*Heading* Shed . . . tear] Fairy's Song *RMM*; Faery Song *1848*

*Otho the Great*

I.i.33 in] to *Forman (1883)*
I.i.37–38 rebel,— . . . Emperor$_{\wedge}$] ~$_{\wedge}$ . . . ~, *Forman (1883)*
I.i.83 ratio] ration *1848*
I.ii.81 No, no, no, no] No, no, no *1848*
I.ii.128 undistinguish'd, . . . friends$_{\wedge}$] ~, . . . ~, *1848*; ~ $_{\wedge}$ . . . ~, *Forman (1883)*
I.ii.172 -cates] -cakes *1848*
I.iii.51 a] the *1848*

I.iii.115 is^] ~— *1848*
II.i.126 ear^] ~. *1848*
II.ii.55 *s.d.* reads it] reading *1848*
II.ii.58 *s.d.* Aside] Speaks to himself *1848*
II.ii.128 In . . . name, I . . . demand of you] I' . . . name. I . . . demand *1848*
III.i.8 limbo] white limbs *1848*
III.i.64 Is] To *1848*
III.ii *opening s.d.* etc., etc., etc.] &c. *1876*
III.ii.15 receipt] recipe *1848*
III.ii.59 hangmen] hangman *1848*
III.ii.128 Whither, whither] Whither *1848*
III.ii.153 jaws] jaw *1848*
III.ii.160 tedious] hideous *1848*
III.ii.204 Bald] Bold *1848*
III.ii.279 mere] more *1848*
IV.i.168 prudence'] ~^ *1848*
IV.i.184 Oh! Oh! Oh!] *omitted in 1848*
IV.ii.22 thee] *omitted in Forman (1883)*
IV.ii.102 fresh] last new *1848*
IV.ii.127 answer] answers *1848*
V.i.27 dreary] dreamy *1848*
V.iv.4 can] to *1848*
V.iv.57 the] *omitted in 1848*
V.v.36 Hangings] Hanging *Forman (1883)*
V.v.59–60 We'll . . . fair;] *transposed to follow 72 in 1848*
V.v.193 Where . . . air!] *omitted in 1848*

*Lamia*

I.383 marble] marble's *Forman (1883)*

*Pensive they sit, and roll their languid eyes*

*Heading* Pensive . . . eyes] A Party of Lovers *Forman (1883)*
2 toasts] toast *World*
5 hapless] happy *World*
11 Inverts] Inserts *World*
12 struggler] straggler *World*

*The Fall of Hyperion*

*Heading* The . . . Dream] Hyperion, a Vision *1857*
I.10 charm] chain *CR, WC, 1857* (*the latter two independently of the first*)
I.24 Turning] Twining *1857*
I.55 sunk] sank *1857*
I.61 carved] curved *1857*
I.97 mid-May] midday *1857*
I.104 every thing] everything *1857*
I.144 thy] thine *1857*
I.161 They] Those *1857*
I.187–210 Majestic . . . graves.] *omitted in 1857* (*marked through in pencil in WC*)
I.204 far] O far *WC* (*Woodhouse's hand*)
I.216 linens] linen *1857*
I.217 Spake] Spoke *1857*
I.227 priestess of his] goddess of this *1857*
I.247 those] these *1857*
I.251 But] And *1857*
I.266 Soft^] ~, *1857*
I.276 ached . . . brain] asked . . . brow *1857*
I.277 enwombed] environed *1857*
I.307 At] Of *1857*
I.308 set] sat *WC, 1857*
I.315 voiceless] noiseless *1857*
I.320 farther] further *1857* (*this and the 1857 readings in I.348, 350, 356, 382, 436, II.13, 20, 21, 22 are taken over from the 1820 text of "Hyperion"*)
I.341 vanward] venom'd *1857*
I.348 hollow] *omitted in 1857*
I.349 spake] spoke *1857*
I.350 tune] -tone *1857*
I.356 cry] say *1857*
I.359 And] The *1857*
I.361 thine] thy *1857*
I.365 Scorches] Scourges *1857*
I.381 mat] net *1857*
I.382 those] these *1857*
I.409 in] of *1857*
I.410 spake] spoke *1857*

I.411 musings] moanings *1857*
I.415 above] upon *1857*
I.426 a shaking] an aching *1857*
I.436 let there] there shall *1857*
I.440 heard] hear *1857*
I.442 pleasant] *omitted in 1857*
II.13 our] the *1857*
II.17 unsecure] insecure *1857*
II.20 Nor . . . even] Not . . . hated *1857*
II.21 visitings] visiting *1857*
II.22 bell:] bell, / Or prophesyings of the midnight lamp; *1857*
II.25 glowing] shining *1857*
II.30 Flush] Flash *1857*
II.45 while] where *1857*
II.53 priestess-] priestess' *1857*
II.56 paved] -paned *1857*

*I cry your mercy—pity—love!—aye, love*

*Heading* I . . . love] Sonnet. To Fanny *Forman (1883)*

*What can I do to drive away*

*Heading* What . . . away] Lines to Fanny *Forman (1883)*

*To Fanny*

*Heading* To] Ode to *Forman (1883)*
8 out] not *1848*
15 a] *omitted in 1848*
46 has] his *1848*
56 last] lost *1848*

*King Stephen*

*Heading* Fragment . . . Tragedy] Dramatic Fragment *1848*
*Dramatis Personae (the entire list)*] *omitted in 1848*
I.i.36 *s.d.* Alarums] Alarum *1848*
I.ii.50 hilts] hilt *1848*
I.iii.5 comes] come *1848*
I.iii.16 dip] dips *1848*
I.iii.21 weapon] weapons *1848*
I.iii.45 hilts] hilt *1848*
I.iii.47 D'ye] Do you *1848*
I.iv.9 will I] I will *1848*
I.iv.20 a] *omitted in 1848*
I.iv.29 most] my *1848*
I.iv.32 Council] counsel *1848*

*This living hand, now warm and capable*

*Heading* This . . . capable] Lines Supposed to Have Been Addressed to Fanny Brawne *Forman (1898)*
5 would] wouldst *Forman (1898)*

*The Jealousies*

314 whelping] yelping *Forman (1883)*
452 These] Those *Forman (1883)*
615 me, by-] ~. By- *1876*

*In after time a sage of mickle lore*

*Heading* In . . . lore] Spenserian Stanza. Written at the Close of Canto II, Book V, of "The Faerie Queene" *Forman (1883)*

APPENDIX III

# The Contents of *1817* and *1820*

*1817*, printed by Charles Richards and published by Charles and James Ollier at the beginning of March 1817, consists of thirty-one items in four principal sections with a half title before each of the last three (the titles here accord with the headings used in the present edition):

Dedication: To Leigh Hunt, Esq.

Poems: I stood tip-toe upon a little hill
Specimen of an Induction to a Poem
Calidore
To Some Ladies
On Receiving a Curious Shell, and a Copy of Verses, from the Same Ladies
Hadst thou liv'd in days of old
To Hope
Imitation of Spenser
Woman! when I behold thee flippant, vain

Epistles: To George Felton Mathew
To My Brother George
To Charles Cowden Clarke

Sonnets:
I. To My Brother George
II. Had I a man's fair form, then might my sighs
III. Written on the Day That Mr. Leigh Hunt Left Prison
IV. How many bards gild the lapses of time
V. To a Friend Who Sent Me Some Roses
VI. To G. A. W.
VII. O Solitude! if I must with thee dwell
VIII. To My Brothers
IX. Keen, fitful gusts are whisp'ring here and there
X. To one who has been long in city pent
XI. On First Looking into Chapman's Homer
XII. On Leaving Some Friends at an Early Hour
XIII. Addressed to Haydon
XIV. Addressed to the Same

XV. On the Grasshopper and Cricket
XVI. To Kosciusko
XVII. Happy is England! I could be content

Sleep and Poetry

The title page contains an epigraph from *"Fate of the Butterfly.*—Spenser" (*Muiopotmos* 209–210)—"What more felicity can fall to creature, / Than to enjoy delight with liberty"—and beneath this a vignette profile of the head and shoulder of an Elizabethan male crowned with laurel (usually identified as Spenser but instead probably intended to represent Shakespeare—see Sperry, pp. 120–121). A note in square brackets appears on the verso page opposite the beginning of *I stood tip-toe*: "The Short Pieces in the middle of the Book, as well as some of the Sonnets, were written at an earlier period than the rest of the Poems." The half title preceding the Epistles contains an epigraph from William Browne's *Britannia's Pastorals* II.iii.748–750:

"Among the rest a shepheard (though but young
"Yet hartned to his pipe) with all the skill
"His few yeeres could, began to fit his quill."

Two other epigraphs in the volume are given above with the texts of *I stood tip-toe* and *Sleep and Poetry.*

*1820,* printed by Thomas Davison and published by Taylor and Hessey in the last week of June 1820, consists of thirteen items in five principal sections with a half title before each of the five:

Lamia

Isabella

The Eve of St. Agnes

Poems: Ode to a Nightingale
Ode on a Grecian Urn
Ode to Psyche
Fancy
Bards of passion and of mirth
Lines on the Mermaid Tavern
Robin Hood
To Autumn
Ode on Melancholy

Hyperion

Keats is identified on the title page as "Author of Endymion." An "Advertisement" dated 26 June 1820 appears on the first recto page after the title: "If any apology be thought necessary for the appearance of the unfinished poem of HYPERION, the publishers beg to state that they alone are responsible, as it was printed at their particular request, and contrary to the wish of the author. The poem was intended to have been of equal length with ENDYMION, but the reception given to that work discouraged the author from proceeding" (for Woodhouse's draft of an earlier version see *KC,* I, 115–116). In the Harvard copy that he presented to Burridge Davenport, Keats crossed through the whole of this note, explaining that "This is none of my doing—I w[as] ill at the time," and he also separately commented on the last twelve words of the final sentence ("but . . . proceeding"): "This is a lie" (see the facsimile in Lowell, facing II, 424).

There are trial layouts of the title page penciled near the front and again at the end of the $W^1$ book of transcripts; the one near the front has *Hyperion* as the second poem in the volume ("LAMIA / Hyperion, a Fragment, / ISABELLA / St. AGNES' EVE, / and other poems"), and the one at the end, which may have been written earlier, omits *Hyperion* altogether ("Lamia; / Isabella; / The Eve of S$^t$ Agnes; / ⟨with⟩ / & Other poems / by / John Keats"). Some pencil jottings on the verso of one of the leaves of the holograph fair copy of *Lamia* suggest that the publishers at one time planned to issue each of the five sections of the volume as a separate pamphlet (see Lowell, II, 426, and Gittings, p. 401).

APPENDIX IV

# The Original Preface to *Endymion*

Along with the fair copy of the text itself, Keats's MS of the original title page, dedication, and preface to *Endymion* is extant in the Morgan Library. The title page (with the same epigraph that was used on the *1818* title) is as follows:

Endymion,
a Romance

by John Keats—

The stretched metre of an antique song—
Shakespeare's Sonnets

The dedication (with "a bowed mind" quoted from the 1796–97 text of Coleridge's *Ode to the Departing Year* 6) reads:

Inscribed,
with every feeling of pride and regret,
and with "a bowed mind,"
To the memory of
The most english of Poets except Shakspeare,
Thomas Chatterton—

The original preface is given here in a reading text. Misspellings and slips of the pen are silently corrected; MS alterations and two editorial emendations of punctuation (40–41) are recorded in the apparatus following the text. The quotation in the first paragraph is from *Macbeth* V.iii.22, and that in the third paragraph from the end is from Marston's prefatory "To My Equal Reader" in *The Fawn* (1606).

Preface

In a great nation, the work of an individual is of so little importance; his pleadings and excuses are so uninteresting; his "way of life" such a nothing; that a preface seems a sort of impertinent bow to Strangers who care nothing about it—

5 A preface however should be down in so many words; and such a one that by an eye glance over the type, the Reader may catch an idea of an

Author's modesty, and non opinion of himself—which I sincerely hope may be seen in the few lines I have to write, notwithstanding certain proverbs of many ages' old which men find a great pleasure in receiving for gospel.

About a twelvemonth since, I published a little book of verses; it was read by some dozen of my friends, who lik'd it; and some dozen whom I was unacquainted with, who did not. Now when a dozen human beings, are at words with another dozen, it becomes a matter of anxiety to side with one's friends;—more especially when excited thereto by a great love of Poetry.

I fought under disadvantages. Before I began I had no inward feel of being able to finish; and as I proceeded my steps were all uncertain. So this Poem must rather be consider'd as an endeavour than a thing accomplish'd; a poor prologue to what, if I live, I humbly hope to do. In duty to the Public I should have kept it back for a year or two, knowing it to be so faulty: but I really cannot do so:—by repetition my favorite Passages sound vapid in my ears, and I would rather redeem myself with a new Poem—should this one be found of any interest.

I have to apologise to the lovers of Simplicity for touching the spell of Loveliness that hung about Endymion: if any of my lines plead for me with such people I shall be proud.

It has been too much the fashion of late to consider men biggotted and addicted to every word that may chance to escape their lips: now I here declare that I have not any particular affection for any particular phrase, word or letter in the whole affair. I have written to please myself and in hopes to please others, and for a love of fame; if I neither please myself, nor others nor get fame, of what consequence is Phraseology?

I would fain escape the bickerings that all Works, not exactly in chime, bring upon their begetters:—but this is not fair to expect, there must be conversation of some sort and to object shows a Man's consequence. In case of a London drizzle or a scotch Mist, the following quotation from Marston may perhaps stead me as an umbrella for an hour or so: "let it be the Curtesy of my peruser rather to pity my self hindering labours than to malice me."

One word more:—for we cannot help seeing our own affairs in every point of view—. Should any one call my dedication to Chatterton affected I answer as followeth:

"Were I dead Sir I should like a Book dedicated to me"—

Teignmouth March 19th 1818—

3 a preface] ⟨it nearly⟩ a preface  3 Strangers] ⟨an⟩ Strangers  4 it—] it —⟨However self pride is the less offended when⟩  6 Reader] ⟨Writer⟩ Reader  7 sincerely] ⟨hop⟩ sincerely  9 old] *interlined above* ⟨standing⟩  22 do so] *made out of* do it  23 I] *interlined above* ⟨as of such⟩  24 be] ⟨create any interest⟩ be  31 affair] ⟨matter⟩ affair  36 object] *successively* (*a*) object (*b*) objection (*c*) object  38 as] ⟨for⟩ as  40–41 me." . . . more:] *ed*; *the MS has* ~‸" . . . ~.  43 answer] ⟨say⟩ answer

Keats sent this preface (with the title page, dedication, and the fair copy of Book IV) to his publishers on 21 March, but they did not like it and, apparently through J. H. Reynolds, asked him to revise it (see *Letters,* I, 253, 266–267). He wrote a new preface on 10 April (it is so dated in *1818*) and sent it to Reynolds on the 17th (W. H. Bond, *K-SJ,* 20 [1971], 17–18). The MS of this new version has not survived; Keats's remark to Taylor on the 24th—"the preface is well without those thing[s] you have left out" (*Letters,* I, 272)—indicates that some cuts were made by the publishers.

APPENDIX V

# Summary Account of the Manuscripts

The following paragraphs briefly identify and evaluate the several groups of MSS and give locations of the transcripts. For a more detailed account see *Texts,* pp. 14–62. The arrangement here is alphabetical according to the name of the writer or copyist (unidentified transcripts are discussed after those of Isabella Jane Towers).

*Fanny Brawne.* Of Fanny Brawne's two extant transcripts—*Hush, hush, tread softly* in a copy of Hunt's *Literary Pocket-Book* for 1819 (1818) at Keats House, Hampstead, and *Bright star* in a copy of Volume I of H. F. Cary's 1814 translation of Dante's *Vision* at Yale—the former is probably our best representative of the latest state of the poem, and serves as copy-text in the present edition. The latter also represents a revised state of text—the same as that of the extant holograph fair copy, from which it was probably taken.

*Charles Brown.* Brown, who was Keats's closest associate from December 1818, when the poet moved in with him at Wentworth Place in Hampstead, until the summer of 1820, began copying Keats's poems during the walking tour that they took together through the Lake District and Scotland in the summer of 1818. By the spring of 1820 he had compiled "four MS books in my hand writing of Mr Keats' poems"—each, as he later explained to Milnes, to whom he gave the MSS in 1841, with a poem "of an exceptionable kind . . . written and copied for the purpose of preventing the young blue-stocking ladies from asking for the loan of his MS Poems" (*KC,* I, 261, II, 103). The "exceptionable" poems have not survived (unless *O blush not so* is one of them), but we do have forty-three texts by Brown, all but one of them in extant transcripts. Of these forty-three items (they are listed in *Texts,* pp. 51–52), thirty-nine are at Harvard. Brown's MS of *On Some Skulls in Beauley Abbey* is among Woodhouse's papers in the Morgan Library; his MSS of *Shed no tear* and *In after time a sage of mickle lore* are at Keats House, Hampstead; and his text of *The Gothic looks solemn* (for which the MS is no longer extant) survives via a letter printed in Forman (1883). The Harvard transcripts are all from the MS volumes that Brown gave Milnes except that of *Not Aladdin magian,* which is a MS acquired from a descendant of Joseph Severn.

Brown's extant transcripts, now a series of separate sheets, do not amount to anything like "four MS books." The volumes may have included some or all of the four long poems published in *1820*—*Lamia, Isabella, The Eve of St. Agnes, Hy-*

*perion*—and certainly included *The Jealousies.* From various references to "C.B." in Woodhouse's $W^2$ book we know that Brown copied *Fragment of Castle-builder, And what is Love, I had a dove,* and *Ode to a Nightingale*; and Brown's "Life" of Keats and his publication of poems in *NMM* and *PDWJ* indicate the former existence of transcripts of *Old Meg she was a gipsey, To Ailsa Rock, This mortal body of a thousand days, There is a joy in footing slow, Not Aladdin magian* (a different version from the one extant at Harvard), and *Read me a lesson, Muse.* In the absence of specific information about Milnes's sources for two poems to Fanny Brawne we may conjecture that Brown also transcribed *What can I do to drive away* and *To Fanny.* Doubtless there were others of which we have no hint.

The most significant fact about Brown's transcripts is that, with a single exception (*On "The Story of Rimini,"* which he may have taken from a copy by Leigh Hunt), his source in every instance was almost certainly a holograph, and more often than not a revised MS rather than an early draft. We know his sources for sure (because they are available for comparison) for only ten or a dozen poems, but Keats's letters and Brown's "Life" document the fact that Brown constantly had direct access to Keats's MSS (see *Letters,* I, 317, II, 104, 149; *KC,* II, 61, 72), and it is clear that he did not, as Woodhouse frequently did, copy other people's copies. In the one recorded instance where he acquired texts from someone other than the poet—in a letter to Fanny Brawne of 17 December 1829 he mentions "those poems addressed to you, which you permitted me to copy" (*The Letters of Charles Armitage Brown,* Cambridge, Mass., 1966, p. 295)—still his sources were very likely holographs. Some of his copies became the principal authorial MS versions after Keats gave away or discarded the holographs from which they were made. The presence of the poet's hand in half a dozen of them shows that he read over and used Brown's MSS for further revision, and it is probable that he wrote out at least some of the *1820* poems for the printer from these transcripts.

Brown's MSS were seen and copied by Dilke, George Keats, and Woodhouse, among others. Woodhouse in particular made extensive use, taking texts and noting headings, dates, and variants from more than thirty of them, extant and lost. After Keats's death Brown published poems from his MSS in *NMM,* the *Examiner, PDWJ,* and the *Plymouth, Devonport, and Stonehouse News,* and he provided his friend E. J. Trelawny with fifty-four extracts, eighteen of them from the unpublished *Otho, King Stephen,* and *The Jealousies,* to be used as chapter epigraphs in *Adventures of a Younger Son* (Brown's fair copy of *Adventures,* which was edited by Mary Shelley and others and then used as printer's copy for the 1831 first edition, is at Harvard, and the extracts there, placed all together at the end of the MS, constitute further partial transcripts of the three works). In 1841, after giving up his attempts to publish the "Life" of Keats and the poems in a volume of his own, he turned his MSS over to Milnes, who used them as the basis for the biographical narrative and a major portion of the texts in *1848.* All told, through his own publication of poems in periodicals and his gift of MSS to Milnes, Brown was responsible for the first publication of more than thirty pieces.

Because these transcripts were so frequently copied and drawn upon by others, they cannot be said to give us very many otherwise unknown versions, and they are our sole MS source for only three poems, *Ah! woe is me, I cry your mercy,* and *In after time a sage.* But they obviously have been important in the history of Keats's texts (and also in the history of Keats's reputation, which improved rapidly after the publication of *1848*). Twenty-four of Brown's texts (plus his partial transcript of *King Stephen*) serve as copy-texts in the present edition, and most of the others —all but *On "The Story of Rimini"* and *On Sitting Down to Read "King Lear" Once Again,* which do not vary substantively from the copy-texts—are collated in the apparatus.

*Charles Cowden Clarke.* Clarke, one of the earliest of Keats's close friends, is the writer of four of the extant transcripts—a copy of *To Ailsa Rock,* among Woodhouse's papers in the Morgan Library, which he made for Woodhouse from the published text in Hunt's *Literary Pocket-Book,* and copies of *Unfelt, unheard, unseen* (source unknown), *Think not of it* (from a now lost Woodhouse transcript), and *Welcome joy, and welcome sorrow* (probably from the MS now in the possession of Dorothy Withey), all three at Harvard, which he made for Milnes, who used them as printer's copy for the first published versions of the poems, in *1848*. The transcript of *Unfelt, unheard, unseen* is collated in the apparatus.

*Elizabeth Stott Clarke.* A copy of *1817* at Keats House, Hampstead, once belonging to one of C. C. Clarke's sisters, Isabella Towers (a printed copy not to be confused with the MS copy of *1817* and other poems that Clarke had made for Mrs. Towers in 1828—see below under J. C. Stephens), contains hitherto unidentified transcripts of *On the Sea* and *Blue!—'Tis the life of heaven* on blank pages preceding the Epistles and the Sonnets. The transcripts are in the same hand as the inscription at the front of the volume, "Isabella Jane Towers. / With her Sister's best love. / July 22nd 1846." Since Mrs. Towers had only one sister, it seems safe to identify that sister, Elizabeth Stott Clarke, as the writer of the two transcripts. As their substantive and accidental peculiarities make clear, both texts were taken from *1848*. It is difficult to square this fact with the date of the inscription, but fact and date are both certain; consequently we must suppose that Miss Clarke added the transcripts on a later occasion, two years or more after she gave the volume to her sister.

*James Freeman Clarke.* The American clergyman James Freeman Clarke (no relation of either of the preceding) published two of Keats's poems for the first time—*God of the golden bow* and *Not Aladdin magian*—in the *Western Messenger* in 1836 from holographs given or lent to him by George Keats, whom he knew in Louisville. He sent Milnes a copy of *God of the golden bow* in October 1845 (*KC,* II, 139–140), but Milnes printed the poem in *1848* from another source, and Clarke's transcript has not survived.

*Charles Wentworth Dilke.* Dilke, schoolfellow of Brown, co-owner of Wentworth Place, and a good friend of Keats until April 1819, when he moved away from Hampstead, transcribed seventeen poems on some blank leaves bound in at the end of his copy of *1818* now at Keats House, Hampstead (the items are listed in *Texts,* p. 56). Fifteen of the transcripts were made from sources now extant (Brown's MSS and two holographs at Harvard), and therefore have no textual significance. The remaining two, however, were taken from MSS that have since disappeared—*Fancy* from a holograph and *Ode to a Nightingale* from a Brown transcript—and because Dilke was an even more precise copyist than George Keats (who also transcribed *Nightingale* from the same Brown MS) they are our best representatives of those now lost sources.

*Benjamin Robert Haydon.* In November 1845 Haydon gave Edward Moxon, Milnes's publisher, copies of the two Elgin Marbles sonnets transcribed from the printed versions in *Annals of the Fine Arts,* where he had had them published from holograph MSS in 1818 (*KC,* II, 141–142). The two transcripts, at Harvard, have no independent authority, but probably were the source of Milnes's texts of the sonnets in *1848.* A third transcript, a copy of *Addressed to the Same* taken from an extant holograph, survives in a letter from Haydon to Wordsworth, 31 December 1816, in the Wordsworth Library, Grasmere. In addition to these a MS entitled "Sonnets addressed to & MS written by B. R. Haydon From 1817 to 1841 . . . Copied for Fun 1844" was sold at Sotheby's on 27 June 1972 to a Miss A. Folbare. According to the sale catalogue, "This manuscript contains all four of the sonnets addressed to Haydon by Keats (two transcribed by Haydon himself and two by his daughter)." Presumably these—*Addressed to Haydon, Addressed to the Same,* plus the Elgin Marbles sonnets—are similarly derivative texts. Attempts to identify Miss Folbare and locate the MS have so far been unsuccessful.

*James Augustus Hessey.* Hessey's transcript of *As Hermes once,* deriving from a Woodhouse copy and extant among Woodhouse's papers in the Morgan Library, appears to have been printer's copy for the version of the poem published in the *London Magazine* in 1821.

*Leigh Hunt.* Hunt made two transcripts of *On "The Story of Rimini,"* both at Harvard—the earlier in a copy of Galignani (1829) and the later on a separate sheet. Both derive from a holograph written in a now lost copy of *1817* that Keats presented to Hunt. The earlier transcript serves as copy-text in the present edition.

*John Jeffrey.* Jeffrey, the second husband of Georgiana Wylie Keats, copied fifteen of Keats's letters and sent the transcripts, now at Harvard, to Milnes in September 1845 (*KC,* II, 123). While omitting several other poems that Keats wrote or copied in these letters, the transcripts include texts of *On Sitting Down to Read "King Lear" Once Again, On Visiting the Tomb of Burns, Why did I laugh tonight, As Hermes once, Character of C. B.,* and *If by dull rhymes.* Jeffrey was perhaps the most unreliable of all the copyists, but his MSS are nevertheless of some significance. They were the bases, via Milnes's or an amanuensis' copies, of the texts of four poems published in *1848,* three of them for the first time. His text of the *King Lear* sonnet represents an otherwise unknown version, and the transcript containing *On Visiting the Tomb of Burns* is our sole MS source for that poem, and serves as copy-text in the present edition.

*George Keats.* George Keats wrote fifteen of the extant transcripts, six early ones in the Keats-Wylie Scrapbook, at Harvard (see below under Georgiana Augusta Wylie), and nine later ones in a notebook now in the British Library (MS. Egerton 2780). Of the MSS in the earlier group—*Stay, ruby breasted warbler, On Receiving a*

*Curious Shell, O come, dearest Emma, To one who has been long in city pent, To My Brother George* (sonnet), and *To My Brother George* (epistle)—the first and fourth appear to have been copied from Georgiana Wylie's extant transcripts, and the last was made from the extant holograph. The other three are assumed to be independent copies of now lost holographs.

George's nine transcripts in the British Library notebook were made during a three-week visit to London in January 1820 (they are listed in *Texts*, p. 23). Six of the texts clearly derive from extant transcripts by Brown, and hence have no independent authority, but the three others—*Robin Hood, The Eve of St. Agnes*, and *Ode to a Nightingale*—represent now lost sources of some importance (the first two are from lost holographs, the third from a lost Brown transcript). The transcript of *The Eve of St. Agnes* gives us the latest recoverable state of the poem before that of *1820*.

In addition to the above, an unidentified transcript of *Oh Chatterton* among Woodhouse's papers in the Morgan Library may also be by George, and we know of four other transcripts that once existed but have since disappeared—a version of *Hadst thou liv'd in days of old,* preserved in a series of Woodhouse transcripts, and texts of *'Tis the "witching time of night," As Hermes once,* and the first sonnet *On Fame,* all three copied in 1834 for John Howard Payne, who published the poems from George's MSS in the *Ladies' Companion* in 1837 and then recopied them himself in transcripts sent to Milnes in 1847.

*John Keats.* At present there exist 126 complete or partial holograph versions of ninety-seven poems (the locations of the holographs are given in the Textual Notes). The lists in *Texts,* pp. 16–19, are still accurate except that *Unfelt, unheard, unseen* should be removed from, and *Robin Hood* added to, the first (original drafts, pp. 16–17), and *To Hope* and another fair copy of *O Solitude* should be added to the second (later versions, pp. 18–19). The division between the two groups should continue to be viewed with some skepticism. As was explained earlier in connection with the lists, it is frequently difficult and sometimes impossible, when there is no external evidence (such as the indication of another, clearly earlier holograph), to decide whether a given holograph is an original draft or a version subsequent to a lost original. The appearance of a MS is not a consistently reliable indication of its status, because we have MSS known to be drafts that are cleanly written (where the words flowed readily or where Keats composed in his head before setting anything down on paper), and we also have some rather messy fair copies (where he was careless or where he undertook some complicated revisions). Of necessity, the discriminations between the two classes in the Textual Notes have been somewhat arbitrary, but the most difficult cases are discussed there and also specially noticed (with the phrases "arbitrarily cited as *D,*" "arbitrarily cited as *FC*") in the apparatus.

Fifty of the holographs serve as copy-texts in the present edition. Substantive alterations in these and all substantive variants and alterations in the rest of the holographs are recorded in the apparatus.

*Tom Keats.* Of the fifteen extant transcripts by Tom Keats, all of which are at Harvard, one is a separate item, *I stood tip-toe,* and the other fourteen are written in a notebook usually referred to as "Tom Keats's copybook" (they are listed in *Texts,* pp. 24–25). These MSS, made at the end of 1816, at the same time that Keats was preparing copy for the printer of *1817,* are relatively important. For four of the poems—*Imitation of Spenser, Had I a man's fair form, Specimen of an Induction,* and *Calidore*—they are the sole extant MSS apart from J. C. Stephens' copies taken from the *1817* printed texts, and for several others they represent the latest authoritative MS versions. Tom's text of *Written in Disgust of Vulgar Superstition,* the only one of the fifteen poems not included in *1817,* is the best that we have for this sonnet, and his MS serves as copy-text in the present edition.

*Thomasine Leigh.* Thomasine Leigh, of Sidmouth, an early friend of J. H. Reynolds, James Rice, and Benjamin Bailey, transcribed the two Elgin Marbles sonnets and the first twenty lines of *To Charles Cowden Clarke* in a commonplace book dated 1 January 1817 now at Keats House, Hampstead. Her source for all three items was Reynolds' review of *1817* in the *Champion* (9 March 1817, p. 78).

*Frederick Locker-Lampson.* The poet Locker-Lampson transcribed *Shed no tear* on a sheet inserted in a copy of *The Poetical Works of John Keats* (1841) now in the Berg Collection, New York Public Library. His source was the printed text in *1848.*

*William A. Longmore.* Longmore, a nephew of J. H. Reynolds, copied the extant draft of *Spenser, a jealous honorer of thine* and sent the transcript, now at Harvard, to Milnes in December 1870 (*KC,* II, 331–332). Milnes included a text based on it in a note to the poem in *1876.*

*Mary Strange Mathew.* Mary Mathew, a sister of G. F. Mathew, transcribed *On First Looking into Chapman's Homer* in an album that was extant in the early 1940s in the possession of T. G. Crump, of Reigate, Surrey (a photocopy of her album is among the Keats photostats in the University of Illinois Library). She copied the poem from *1817.*

*Richard Monckton Milnes.* Milnes made four transcripts extant at Harvard and probably a number of others that have since disappeared. The four known MSS —*I had a dove* (almost certainly from a lost Brown transcript), *Why did I laugh* (from Jeffrey's transcript), *Shed no tear* (from the extant holograph), and *To Fanny* (conjecturally also from a lost Brown transcript)—were used as printer's copy for *1848,* where three of the four poems were published for the first time. Milnes's text of *To Fanny* appears to be the best that we have for that poem, and serves as copy-text in the present edition.

*Coventry Patmore.* The poet Patmore, who in 1847 was employed by Milnes as an amanuensis, wrote twelve of the extant transcripts now at Harvard (the list in *Texts,* p. 61, should be corrected to include "two copies" in parentheses after *On the Sea*). All of these were taken from sources now extant—eleven from the late transcripts by Woodhouse's clerk (Garrod's *T*), and the recently discovered duplicate copy of *On the Sea* from the text in Woodhouse's letterbook. Eight of the transcripts were used as printer's copy for *1848,* and two others appear to have been the bases of new texts in *1876.*

*John Howard Payne.* Payne, the American actor and playwright, published three poems, two of them for the first time, in an article in the *Ladies' Companion* in 1837—*'Tis the "witching time of night," As Hermes once,* and the first sonnet *On Fame* —from texts that George Keats had written out for him in 1834 from Keats's letters (he also, in the same article, included *Hither, hither, love* from a holograph that George had given him). He recopied the three poems and sent the transcripts, now at Harvard, to Milnes in July 1847 (*KC,* II, 223–225). One of the transcripts, that of *'Tis the "witching time,"* was the basis of Milnes's text in *1848.*

*W. H. Prideaux.* Prideaux, a friend of William and Mary Howitt, copied a piece of Keats's draft of *I stood tip-toe* for Milnes in the 1840s (*KC,* II, 219–220). At the time, this fragment contained 111–112 plus four canceled lines on one side and 61–64 plus two uncanceled lines on the other. Subsequently the bottom two lines on each side were cut away, and this part of the draft MS has since disappeared. Prideaux's transcript, at Harvard, is currently our only source for these missing lines.

*Charlotte Reynolds.* The Reynolds-Hood Commonplace Book, in the Bristol Central Library, includes, in the hand of Charlotte Reynolds, the youngest of J. H. Reynolds' four sisters, complete or partial transcripts of sixteen poems by Keats (they are listed in *Texts,* pp. 47–48). At least nine of these were almost certainly copied from Woodhouse's $W^2$ transcripts, and there is a fair probability that all but three of the rest also derive from $W^2$ (see the discussion in *Texts,* pp. 48–50). The three that show some independence of Woodhouse's MSS are *You say you love, When I have fears,* and *Nature withheld Cassandra.* The first serves as copy-text in the present edition, and the other two are collated in the apparatus.

*John Hamilton Reynolds.* Reynolds was one of Keats's closest friends. Keats gave or sent him a great many of his poems, often just after he wrote them (some of them in response to Reynolds' own poems), and Reynolds made copies of them that he lent to various people including Taylor and Woodhouse. But except for Woodhouse's transcripts made from these copies and his and his clerks' transcripts of Keats's letters to Reynolds, along with a few holographs now at Harvard and in the Morgan Library (MSS that Keats presented to Reynolds), almost nothing of this exchange of poetry or of Reynolds' copies has survived. The one recoverable text of a Keats poem in Reynolds' hand—a version of *Blue!—'Tis the life of heaven* transcribed in a now lost copy of *The Garden of Florence* (1821) and published by A. J. Horwood in the *Athenaeum,* 3 June 1876, p. 764—is collated in the apparatus.

*J. C. Stephens.* Stephens, otherwise unknown but presumably a professional copyist, is the writer of a volume of transcripts that C. C. Clarke presented to his sister Isabella Jane Towers as a birthday present in 1828. The volume, at Harvard, contains the thirty-one poems of *1817,* written out from the printed texts in *1817,* plus six additional items (listed in *Texts,* p. 59) copied from other printed sources and from MSS in Clarke's possession. Stephens' sources are in every case extant, and none of his transcripts has independent textual authority.

*John Taylor.* A transcript by Taylor of *You say you love* is extant among Woodhouse's papers in the Morgan Library. This, as Woodhouse indicated when he recorded variants from it in $W^2$, derives from a MS that belonged to Isabella Jones, and it shows several substantive differences from the only other known text, that of the copies by Charlotte Reynolds and Woodhouse. It is collated in the apparatus.

*Isabella Jane Towers.* At the end of the MS volume that C. C. Clarke had Stephens write out in 1828 (see above under J. C. Stephens) Isabella Towers, the recipient of the volume, copied two additional poems, *This pleasant tale* (from the extant holograph that Keats gave Clarke) and *In drear nighted December* (from the text in Galignani's edition). Neither transcript has independent textual authority.

*Unidentified transcribers.* Most of the extant transcripts by unidentified hands are of no significance—copies of *There is a joy in footing slow* taken from the *Examiner* (bound into George Keats's notebook in the British Library) and *In drear nighted December* from the *Literary Gazette* (Keats House, Hampstead); a transcript of Keats's letter to Tom of 17–21 July 1818 containing *All gentle folks* and *Of late two dainties* (Harvard); and a transcript of an 1847 letter from Henry Stephens to G. F. Mathew containing the first four lines of *Give me women, wine, and snuff* (Harvard—see *KC,* II, 210). Unidentified copies of *Addressed to Haydon* and *Written in Disgust of Vulgar Superstition,* both in the same hand, on two sides of a sheet at Harvard, were the bases of printings in *Hood's Magazine* and *1876,* respectively (the latter representing the first publication of the poem); because their sources are unknown, these transcripts are collated in the apparatus. The one unidentified transcript of any consequence is that of *Oh Chatterton* among Woodhouse's papers in the Morgan Library. This may be in George Keats's hand, and in any case probably was Woodhouse's source for his own copy of the poem. It serves as copy-text in the present edition.

*Richard Woodhouse.* Woodhouse, a nearly lifelong friend and legal and literary adviser to Keats's publishers Taylor and Hessey, made or directed various clerks in making no fewer than 182 of the surviving transcripts of Keats's poems, and he was undoubtedly responsible for others that are now lost. The extant materials fall into eight groups (Garrod's sigla $W^3$, $W^2$, and $W^1$ are retained for the first three for reasons given in *Texts,* pp. 27–28).

(1) Twenty-nine of the transcripts, all in Woodhouse's hand and cited as $W^3$ in the apparatus and elsewhere in this edition, are in the Morgan Library. These once were part of a scrapbook, long since dismantled and the materials several times rearranged, that contained not only poems by Keats but a great many letters, poems, and other documents concerning or connected with Keats (including holograph fair copies of *Fill for me a brimming bowl, O come, dearest Emma,* and *O Solitude,* an unidentified transcript of *Oh Chatterton,* Taylor's transcript of *You say you love,* C. C. Clarke's transcript of *To Ailsa Rock,* and Brown's fair copy of *On Some Skulls in Beauley Abbey*). The transcripts by Woodhouse are a miscellaneous lot, in many cases (where there are duplicate transcripts and the chronological order among them can be established) the earliest extant copies that he made. In

general, though there are a number of exceptions, they seem to be a group of preliminary transcripts that were set aside after he recopied the poems in $W^2$.

(2) The $W^2$ book of transcripts, which survives intact at Harvard, contains—all in Woodhouse's hand—copies of seventy-three Keats poems and two sonnets by J. H. Reynolds, the English text of the Boccaccio story that Keats used for *Isabella,* and (at the end) a list of the $W^2$ contents, a selective record of cancellations and variants in the holograph fair copy of *Endymion,* and transcripts of the original title page, dedication, and preface intended for that work. This is the collection that Woodhouse took the most care with, entering variants, sources, dates, and annotations to the extent that it has the character of a variorum edition of the poems.

(3) The $W^1$ book of transcripts, also preserved intact at Harvard, contains thirty-four copies of Keats poems in Woodhouse's hand, copies of four of Reynolds' sonnets also by Woodhouse, and a transcript of *Hyperion* by two of his clerks. These appear to be a partial set of duplicates, perhaps for insurance against the loss of the $W^2$ copies. It is possible that they were kept by the publishers, for in a letter to Taylor Woodhouse speaks of writing out *Isabella* again in "the Book [at Taylor's] in which she was to be copied" (*KC,* I, 78–79), while in another letter, concerning Keats's revisions in *The Eve of St. Agnes,* he asks Taylor to "turn to it" (*Letters,* II, 163)—and both poems are included in $W^1$. There are trial layouts in pencil of the *1820* title page near the front and again at the end of the book. Since nine or ten of the transcripts demonstrably or very probably derive from the $W^2$ texts, and only one of them, *Hadst thou liv'd in days of old,* can be shown to derive from another source, it has been regularly assumed in the Textual Notes that Woodhouse and his clerks made these copies, with the exception of *Hadst thou liv'd,* from $W^2$.

(4) An interleaved copy of *1817* in the Huntington Library contains transcripts by Woodhouse of six Keats sonnets and a record of variants from a lost early version of *To Some Ladies.* Of the sonnet transcripts, that of *On the Sea* is distinctly different in several respects from the other five and seems to have been Woodhouse's first transcript of the poem. The other five are derivative copies, taken in two cases probably from $W^3$ transcripts and in the rest probably from $W^2$.

(5) An interleaved copy of *1818* in the Berg Collection, New York Public Library, contains an elaborate record of variants and canceled readings in the now lost original draft of *Endymion* Books II–IV—our only source of information about this important MS—and (at the end) a copy of Keats's draft of *Think not of it.*

(6) Woodhouse's letterbook, a notebook at Harvard in which Woodhouse and some clerks copied fifty-six of Keats's letters (seventeen of them now known only through these copies), includes as part of the letter transcripts six texts of Keats's poems by the clerks and two more by Woodhouse (as well as part of a third, the first four lines of *Over the hill*). Taylor, to whom Woodhouse bequeathed much of this material, handed over the letterbook to Milnes in the 1840s.

(7) Eight transcripts that Woodhouse wrote out for Severn in or after 1830 (the date of the watermark on the paper) are also at Harvard. The poems in this group are *After dark vapours, God of the golden bow, On Seeing the Elgin Marbles, To*

*Haydon with a Sonnet Written on Seeing the Elgin Marbles, On the Sea, When I have fears, Time's sea hath been,* and *Blue!—'Tis the life of heaven.* The texts could have come from $W^3$ and $W^2$ transcripts, but there are enough odd variants in them to suggest that Woodhouse may have written them from memory.

(8) A collection of transcripts that Woodhouse got together for Brown after he visited Brown in Florence in 1832 is again preserved at Harvard. These are on paper watermarked 1833 and are enclosed in a sheet bearing the inscription in Brown's hand, "Hyperion (remodelled) with minor poems"; Brown passed them on to Milnes with his own MSS in 1841 (and hence they are among the transcripts that Garrod designates *T*). Two of Woodhouse's clerks copied twenty poems, including *The Fall of Hyperion,* and Woodhouse added two others. The texts in every case were taken directly from $W^2$.

In addition to these materials we have Woodhouse's proof-sheets of *Lamia,* at Harvard, which in a sense deserve the same status as a transcript of the poem, since Woodhouse recorded variant readings in them in the same way that he did in the $W^2$ and other transcripts and clearly thought of them as a substitute for a transcript (*Lamia* is the only *1820* poem that he did not copy in the $W^2$ book). We also have the text of a now lost Woodhouse transcript of *On Some Skulls in Beauley Abbey,* printed by Colvin, pp. 553–556, and a facsimile of the first page of his shorthand transcript of *The Eve of St. Mark* (extant but in private ownership and unavailable for examination), included in A. Edward Newton's *A Magnificent Farce* (Boston, 1921), p. 121. In the preface to his English Men of Letters *Keats* (first published in 1887) Colvin mentions another Woodhouse notebook "containing personal notices and recollections of Keats" that "was unluckily destroyed in the fire at Messrs Kegan Paul and Co's. premises in 1883." This was probably Colvin's source for the text that he later gave of *On Some Skulls,* and it may have contained another transcript of *Isabella* (Woodhouse made four and only three are extant) and a transcript of *Otho the Great* (both Dilke and Severn report that he had a copy made of Brown's MS; it is possible that he himself destroyed it after Brown wrote to Taylor in March 1820, "Don't let any one take a Copy of Otho"—*Letters,* II, 276).

The comprehensive list of Woodhouse transcripts given in *Texts,* pp. 30–37, is still accurate but omits the eight copies made for Severn (group 7 above), which had been at Harvard since 1954 but were uncatalogued and unknown to the library staff when the present editor was collecting information in 1971–72.

Woodhouse began the $W^2$ book of transcripts in November 1818 with a series of ten poems that he took from texts "copied for my cousin [Mary Frogley] into a Volume of M.S. poetry, by Mr Kirkman, and said to be by Keats" (most of these, along with this headnote on the first page, were later cut out and transferred to the $W^3$ scrapbook, and six of the texts then recopied at the end of $W^2$— see *Texts,* pp. 39–42). He transcribed poems from "[J. H.] Reynolds's volume of Poetry," a now lost MS collection that he borrowed from Taylor also in November 1818 (*KC,* I, 63–64); from Brown's four MS volumes, made available to him through Taylor probably sometime between March 1820 and August 1821 (*Letters,* II, 276; *KC,* I, 261, 264); from Keats's letters to Benjamin Bailey, which he saw, again through Taylor, in or shortly after May 1821 (*KC,* I, 243–244); and from albums belonging to Charlotte Reynolds and at least one of her three sisters. Other texts came directly from J. H. Reynolds and C. C. Clarke. Woodhouse very helpfully specifies his initial source—"from Mary Frogley," "from JK's M.S.," "from C.B.," and the like—for more than half the poems that he copied. Where he does not provide such notes, his sources can be settled with certainty in some cases but have to be guessed at in others.

He went about his collecting with an admirable scholarliness, as may be seen in the care and frequency with which he recorded variants marginally and between the lines in many of the transcripts, especially those in $W^2$. He sometimes saw and made notes from as many as three or four different versions of a poem. He queried words, suggested improvements, and several times followed his own suggestions by incorporating them in later copies of the poems. He also seems to have occasionally penciled corrections, variants, and proposed revisions into other people's MSS that he was copying or collating—see the Textual Notes to *O come, dearest Emma, You say you love, Lines on Seeing a Lock of Milton's Hair, To the Nile, Isabella, Hyperion, Sonnet to Sleep, Ode on Melancholy, Otho the Great, To Autumn,* and *The Fall of Hyperion.*

Taken altogether, his MSS are an impressive assemblage of material. They represent the only surviving MS texts of seven of Keats's poems and provide distinctive early or revised versions that would otherwise be unknown for about twenty more. And they contain a wealth of information about the texts. Woodhouse's contributions to the final wording of *Isabella, Lamia,* and some shorter poems—for example, the substitution of "hoards" in *Sonnet to Sleep*—are determinable only through the transcripts (or, in the case of *Lamia,* through the proof-sheets), and his now lost copy of *On Some Skulls,* via the text that Colvin printed, is our only means of knowing which lines Keats was responsible for in that poem. Two of the $W^1$ transcripts—*Isabella* by Woodhouse and *Hyperion* by two of his clerks—served as printer's copy for *1820,* and various of the letterbook and $W^2$ texts, the latter through the late clerks' copies for Brown, were Milnes's source for sixteen of the poems that he published in *1848* as well as for *The Fall of Hyperion* in *1857* and two other poems in *1876.* Five additional poems (plus several in the "Questionable" category) were first published from Woodhouse's MSS in the twentieth century. Twenty of the transcripts serve as copy-texts in the present edition, and another fifty-six of the MSS are collated in the apparatus.

*William Pitter Woodhouse.* W. P. Woodhouse, brother of Richard, included two of Keats's poems in a commonplace book of July–August 1827 that is now at Harvard. The text of the first, *In drear nighted December,* incorporates Woodhouse's proposed revision of the entire third stanza (see *KC,* I, 64–65) and obviously was provided by Woodhouse. That of the second, *To G. A. W.,* was probably taken from *1817,* but is included in the apparatus as possibly deriving from another source now lost.

*Georgiana Augusta Wylie.* Georgiana Wylie, who married Keats's brother George in late May 1818 and emigrated with him to the United States a month later, is the writer of four of the earliest extant transcripts—complete copies of *Stay, ruby breasted warbler* and *To one who has been long in city pent* and partial copies of *On*

*Receiving a Curious Shell* and *To My Brother George* (epistle)—all four made probably during the latter half of 1816. These are in the so-called Keats-Wylie Scrapbook, at Harvard, which also contains a holograph fair copy of *To G. A. W.*, six transcripts of Keats poems by George Keats, and a sizable collection of MS and printed material unrelated to Keats. Georgiana's partial text of the epistle to George was taken from the extant holograph fair copy; the three others are assumed to derive from now lost holographs and therefore to have some textual value. The transcript of *Stay, ruby breasted warbler* serves as copy-text in the present edition.

APPENDIX VI

# Questionable Attributions

This appendix discusses and then gives reading texts (with accidentals emended silently) of six pieces that at one time or another have been assigned to Keats and, except for the last, usually appear in complete editions of his poems. (Two other pieces, *To Woman* [*from the Greek*] and *The Poet,* are omitted here, because their authorship by other writers is now firmly established by external evidence.) At present there is no reason to think that Keats wrote any of the first five, and only tenuous evidence for his having had a hand in the sixth. For more details see *Texts,* pp. 271–275.

*On Death,* first published by Forman (1883), II, 201, exists in a MS (dated 1814) by Georgiana Wylie in the Keats-Wylie Scrapbook, at Harvard. The poem is unassigned there, and as Garrod points out, pp. xlix–l, we have no evidence to indicate that Keats was the author (there are many non-Keats items in the scrapbook). The text below is based on Georgiana Wylie's MS.

*See, the ship in the bay is riding,* first published by Garrod in his 1939 edition, exists in two transcripts by Woodhouse in the Morgan Library. One of them, with "F" at the end, indicating that Woodhouse got the poem from a Kirkman copy in Mary Frogley's album, was originally written on fol. 3 of the $W^2$ book of transcripts, and was later cut out and transferred to the $W^3$ scrapbook. The second has "from Mary Frogley" in shorthand at the end. The transcripts are substantively the same, and in both Woodhouse left a space between 5 and 6, inserting a penciled comment on the lack of a rhyming line. Subsequently he added a note opposite the first transcript, "This piece K. said had not been written by him. He did not see it: but I repeated the first 4 lines to him." Finney, I, 47, thinks that it was "composed probably either by [G. F.] Mathew or by some member of his coterie." Garrod includes it (p. 539, from the second of the transcripts above) "with no belief in its authenticity" (p. lxxii). The text below, with heading editorially supplied, is based on the "F" transcript.

*Sonnet to A. G. S.,* first published by Garrod in *TLS,* 27 November 1937, p. 906, exists in a Woodhouse MS in the Morgan Library. No author's name is given, and the poem, like the next two below, has been assigned to Keats on the basis of Woodhouse's note on a leaf that once served as the title page of the $W^3$ scrapbook: "All that are not by Keats, have the names of the Authors added." But Mabel A. E. Steele has shown that this leaf was originally the title page of the $W^2$ book, and that the note almost surely was intended to refer to the $W^2$ transcripts rather than to those in $W^3$ (see *HLB,* 3 [1949], 232–256, and especially *K-SJ,* 5 [1956], 74 n.). If we discount the note, as we should, then there is no evidence for attributing the unassigned poems to Keats. "A. G. S." is Aubrey George Spencer, later the first bishop of Newfoundland, and Woodhouse also transcribed in the $W^3$ scrapbook the two poems by him referred to in the heading. Spencer was nine months older than Keats; "young bard" in the first line should have cast doubt on Keats's authorship from the beginning. Finney, II, 751, suggests that Woodhouse himself may have written the sonnet. The text below is based on Woodhouse's MS. The parenthetical "Miss Reynolds'" in the heading is in shorthand. Woodhouse wrote "And" in the margin beside "Yea" (which he underscored) at the beginning of 14.

*"The House of Mourning" written by Mr. Scott,* first published by Finney, II, 652, exists in a Woodhouse MS in the Morgan Library. This has the same status as the preceding, and again possibly is by Woodhouse himself. The text below, with heading editorially supplied, is based on Woodhouse's MS. The first line refers to John Scott's *The House of Mourning: A Poem, with Some Smaller Pieces* (1817).

*Gripus,* first published by Lowell, II, 535–544, exists in a Woodhouse MS in the Morgan Library and has the same status as the two preceding items. The few alterations in the MS—"thee" interlined above "⟨you⟩" in 40, "lady" deleted before "woman" in 79, "as I am handsome Lady" altered to "as ever I am Lady" in 100, "money" deleted before "beauty" in 185, "sober" interlined above "⟨prudent⟩" in 188—are the sort that one makes in composition rather than in copying. The text below, with heading, most of the speech prefixes, three stage directions (those in 37 and 156 and the last two words of that in 143), and a great deal of punctuation editorially supplied, is based on Woodhouse's MS.

*Love and Folly,* for which no MS survives, appeared in *NMM,* 5 (July 1822), 47–48, over the signature "S. Y."—the same initials used to sign Brown's and Keats's *On Some Skulls in Beauley Abbey* when it was published in the same magazine earlier in the same year. On this circumstantial evidence Walter E. Peck reprinted the poem and assigned it to Brown and Keats in *N&Q,* 25 February 1939, pp. 129–131. J. R. MacGillivray, *Keats: A Bibliography and Reference Guide* (Toronto, 1949), p. 76, thinks the attribution "probable," but it has never before been included in a modern edition. The text below reproduces that of *NMM.*

## *On Death*

Can death be sleep, when life is but a dream,
  And scenes of bliss pass as a phantom by?
The transient pleasures as a vision seem,
  And yet we think the greatest pain's to die.

5 How strange it is that man on earth should roam,
  And lead a life of woe, but not forsake
His rugged path; nor dare he view alone
  His future doom, which is but to awake.

### *See, the ship in the bay is riding*

See, the ship in the bay is riding;
  Dearest Ellen, I go from thee—
Boldly go, in thy love confiding,
  Over the deep and trackless sea.
5 When thy dear form no longer is near me,
This soothing thought shall at midnight cheer me:
  "My love is breathing a prayer for me."

When the thunder of war is roaring,
  When the bullets around me fly,
10 When the rage of the tempest, pouring,
  Blends the billowy sea and sky,
Yet shall my heart, to fear a stranger,
  Cherish its fondest hopes for thee—
This dear reflection disarming danger,
15   "My love is breathing a prayer for me."

### *Sonnet*

*To A. G. S. on Reading His Admirable Verses, Written in This (Miss Reynolds') Album, on Either Side of the Following Attempt to Pay Small Tribute Thereto*

Where didst thou find, young bard, thy sounding lyre?
  Where the bland accent, and the tender tone?
A sitting snugly by thy parlour fire,
  Or didst thou with Apollo pick a bone?
5 The muse will have a crow to pick with me
  For thus assaying in thy brightening path:
Who, that with his own brace of eyes can see,
  Unthunderstruck beholds thy gentle wrath?
Who from a pot of stout e'er blew the froth
10   Into the bosom of the wandering wind,
Light as the powder on the back of moth,
  But drank thy muses with a grateful mind?
Yea, unto thee beldams drink metheglin,
Yea, annisies, and carraway, and gin.

## The House of Mourning *written by Mr. Scott*

*The House of Mourning* written by Mr. Scott,
  A sermon at the Magdalen, a tear
  Dropt on a greasy novel, want of cheer
After a walk up hill to a friend's cot,

5 Tea with a maiden lady, a curs'd lot
Of worthy poems with the author near,
A patron lord, a drunkenness from beer,
Haydon's great picture, a cold coffee pot
At midnight when the muse is ripe for labour,
10 The voice of Mr. Coleridge, a French bonnet
Before you in the pit, a pipe and tabour,
A damn'd inseparable flute and neighbour—
All these are vile. But viler Wordsworth's sonnet
On Dover. Dover!—who *could* write upon it?

## *Gripus*

*Gripus.* And gold and silver are but filthy dross.
Then seek not gold and silver, which are dross,
But rather lay thy treasure up in heav'n!
*Slim.* Hem!
5 *Gripus.* And thou hast meat and drink and lodging too,
And clothing too, what more can man require?
And thou art single—
But I must lay up money for my children,
My children's children and my great-grandchildren;
10 For, Slim! thy master will be shortly married—
*Slim.* Married!
*Gripus.* Yea! married. Wherefore dost thou stare,
As though my words had spoke of aught impossible?
*Slim.* My lord, I stare not, but my ears play'd false—
Methought you had said married.
*Gripus.* Married, fool!
15 Is't aught unlikely? I'm not very old,
And my intended has a noble fortune.
*Slim.* My lord, 'tis likely.
*Gripus.* Haste, then, to the butcher's,
And ere thou go, tell Bridget she is wanted—
*Slim.* I go—gods! what a subject for an ode,
20 With Hymen, Cupids, Venus, Loves, and Graces! [*Exit.*
*Gripus* (*solus*). This matrimony is no light affair;
'Tis downright venture and mere speculation.
Less risk there is in what the merchant trusts
To winds and waves and the uncertain elements,
25 For he can have assurance for his goods
And put himself beyond the reach of losses—
But who can e'er ensure to me a wife
Industrious and managing and frugal,
Who will not spend far more than she has brought,
30 But be almost a saving to her husband?

But none can tell—the broker cannot tell
He is not cheated in the wares he buys;
And to judge well of women or the seas
Would oft surpass the wisest merchant's prudence,
35 For both are deep alike—capricious too—
And the worst things that money can be sunk in.
But Bridget comes—

*Enter* BRIDGET.

*Bridget.* Your pleasure, sir, with me?
*Gripus.* Bridget, I wish to have a little converse
Upon a matter that concerns us both,
40 Of like importance both to thee and me.
*Bridget.* Of like importance and concerning both?
What can your honour have to say to me?
O lord! I would give all that I am worth
To know what 'tis—
*Gripus.* Then pr'ythee rein thy tongue,
45 That ever battles with thine own impatience.
But to the point. Thou know'st, for twenty years
Together we have liv'd as man and wife,
But never hath the sanction of the church
Stamp'd its legality upon our union—
*Bridget.* Well, what of that?
50 *Gripus.* Why, when in wiser years
Men look upon the follies of their youth,
They oft repent, and wish to make amends,
And seek for happier in more virtuous days.
In such a case, and such is mine, I own,
55 'Tis marriage offers us the readiest way
To make atonement for our former deeds;
And thus have I determin'd in my heart
To make amends—in other words, to marry.
*Bridget.* O lord! how overjoy'd I am to hear it!
60 I vow that I have often thought myself,
What wickedness it was to live as we did!
But do you joke?
*Gripus.* Not so, upon my oath.
I am resolv'd to marry and beget
A little heir to leave my little wealth to.
65 I am not old, my hair is hardly grey,
My health is good—what hast thou to object?
*Bridget.* O dear, how close your honour puts the question!
I've said as much already as was fit
And incompatible with female modesty—
70 But would your honour please to name a day?
*Gripus.* To name a day! but hark, I hear a knock.

'Tis perhaps young Prodigal—I did expect him.
*Bridget.* But sir—a day?
*Gripus.* Zounds! dost thou hear the bell?
Wilt thou not run? He was to bring me money.
[*Exit* BRIDGET *and returns.*
75 *Bridget.* 'Tis he. I've shown him to the little study.
*Gripus.* Then stay thee here, and when I've settled him
I will return and hold more converse with thee. [*Exit.*
*Bridget* (*solus*). My head runs round—O what a happy change!
Now I shall be another woman quite.
80 Dame Bridget, then, adieu, and don't forget
Your Lady Gripus now that is to be—
Great Lady Gripus—O lord!
The lady of the old and rich Sir Gripus!
O how will people whisper, as I pass,
85 There goes my lady—what a handsome gownd,
All scarlet silk embroidered with gold—
Or green and gold will perhaps become me better—
How vastly fine—how handsome I shall be
In green and gold—besides, a lady too!
90 I'll have a footman too, to walk behind me.
Slim is too slender to set off a livery;
I must have one more lustier than him,
A proper man to walk behind his lady.
O how genteel—methinks I see myself
95 In green and gold and carrying my fan—
*Or perhaps I'd have a redicule about me.*
The lusty footman all so spruce behind me
Walking on tiptoes in a bran new livery;
And he shall have a favour in his hat,
100 As sure as ever I am Lady Gripus!

*Enter* SLIM.

*Slim.* Why how now, Bridget, you're turn'd actress sure!
*Bridget.* An actor, fellow, no. To something better,
To something grander and more ladylike!
Know I am turn'd—
*Slim.* A lunatic, 'tis plain.
105 But, lovee, leave this jesting for a while,
And hear thy servant, who thus pleads for favour.
*Bridget.* For favour, sirrah! but I must be kind.
I will forget your insolence this once,
And condescend to keep you in my service.
110 But no, I want a much more lustier man—
You are too slender to become my livery.
I must excard you—you must suit yourself.
*Slim.* Why how now, Bridget—

*Bridget.* You forget me, sure.
*Slim.* Forget thee, Bridget? Never from my heart
115 Shall thy dear image part.
Ah no,
I love you so,
No language can impart.
Alas! 'tis love that makes me thin,
120 I have a fiery flame within
That burns and shrivels up my skin—
'Tis Cupid's little dart,
And by this kiss I swear— [*Attempts to kiss her.*
*Bridget.* Ruffin, begone, or I will tell my lord.
125 Do you not care for difference of rank,
Nor make distinction between dirt and dignity?
*Slim.* Why Bridget, once you did not treat me thus—
*Bridget.* No, times are alter'd, Fortune's wheel is turn'd,
You still are Slim, but, though I once was Bridget,
130 I'm Lady Gripus now that is to be.
Did not his honour tell you he should marry?
*Slim.* Yea, to a lady of an ample fortune.
*Bridget.* Why that, you fool, he said in allegolly.
A virtuous woman, is she not a crown,
135 A crown of gold and glory to her husband?
*Slim.* Heav'ns, is it possible? I pray forgive me
That I could doubt a moment of that fortune
Which is but due to your assembled merits.
*Bridget.* Well, Slim, I do not wish to harbour malice,
140 But while you show a proper due respect
You may be certain of my condescension.
But hark! I hear his lordship on the stairs,
And we must have some privacy together.
[*Exit* SLIM. *Re-enter* GRIPUS.
O lord, how overjoy'd I am, your honour—
145 *Gripus.* Bridget, I thank thee for thy friendly zeal,
That seems to glory in thy master's bliss;
And much it grieves me that I can't requite it
Except by mere reciprocal good-wishes.
For, as a change in my domestic government
150 Will make thy place in future but a sinecure,
It grieves me much that I must warn you thus
To seek and get a situation elsewhere.
*Bridget.* O dear—O lord—O what a shock—O lord! [*Faints.*
*Gripus.* Ho! Slim—the devil's in the fool to faint.
155 Halloo!—what shall I do? halloo! halloo!
Ho! Slim, I say— [*Re-enter* SLIM.
Run, sirrah, for the brandy.
*Slim.* The brandy, sir? there is none in the house!

*Gripus.* No brandy! none! what, none at all, thou knave?
What, none at all? then, rascal, thou hast drunk it.
160 Why Bridget, Bridget,—what, no brandy, knave?
Zounds! what a fit—Where is my brandy, wretch!
Thou toping villain, say or I will slay thee—
[*Lets* BRIDGET *fall and collars* SLIM.
*Slim.* O lord, forgive me—Bridget had the wind,
And drank the brandy up to warm her stomach.
165 *Gripus.* A tipsy Bacchanal! then let her lie!
I'll not be drunken out of house and home.
Zounds! brandy for the wind—a cure indeed!
A little water had done just as well.
This is the way, then, when I want a drop—
170 I always find my cellar is stark naked.
But both shall go—yes, I discard ye, thieves!
Begone, ye thieves! [BRIDGET *jumps up.*
*Bridget.* No, not without my wages.
I'll have a month's full wages or my warning.
I'll not be left at nonplush for a place—
175 *Gripus.* A month's full warning! what, another month!
To sack, to ransack, and to strip the house,
And then depart in triumph with your booty!
Begone, I say!
*Bridget.* No, not without my wages!
And I'll have damages, you cruel man.
180 I will convict you of a breach of marriage.
*Gripus.* Begone, I say. Deceitful thing! begone—
Who ever dar'd to promise such a match
But thy own fancy, and thy lying tongue?
What, marry one as poor as a church mouse,
185 And equally devoid of rank and beauty!
Reason would sleep and prudence would be blind,
And Gripus then would be no longer Gripus,
But only fitting for more sober men
To lodge in Bedlam and to call a lunatic.

## *Love and Folly*

Among th' Olympian Chronicles I find—
No matter where I read them—it is stated
That Love was not, as we suppose, born blind;
He lost his eyes, so the account is dated,
5 Soon after man and Folly were created;
This story, quite an antiquarian treasure,
I shall set down, not as 'tis there related,

But tagg'd with rhyme, and here I feel great pleasure
While spoiling a good stanza in a slipshod measure.

10 Love who had often thought it pretty sport
To play with Folly half an hour or so,
Was lured by her at last to Plutus' court,
A place which Love, at that time, did not know;
And there was offer'd a fine golden bow,
15 And golden shafts, and peacock-feather'd wings,
And money-bags that glitter'd in a row,
Besides a thousand other hateful things,
Old parchments, rent-rolls, law-suits, jewels, chains, and rings.

Love laugh'd at all he saw; Folly look'd grave,
20 And preach'd about the wondrous riches there:
"Ha! ha!" says Love, "and are you Plutus' slave?—
I'm sorry,—for I liked you as you were,—
A hearty wench, buxom and debonair;
Farewell! I'm neither to be bought nor sold;—
25 Bless me! I feel a dampness in the air,—
A palace is a dungeon I am told,
And, faith! I half believe it, for I'm very cold.

"I'm off!" But Folly seized him by the head,
Threw gold-dust in his eyes, and quench'd their sight,
30 Alas! for ever! "Now, now," Folly said,
"We have him to ourselves,—here, day and night,
He shall do penance for our best delight!"
Stark nonsense! but what else could Folly say?
Meanwhile the poor blind boy, to left and right,
35 Sobbing and sighing, tried to grope his way,
But could not from that prison flee, ah! well-a-day!

Darkling he blunder'd, sad and sore distress'd,
And wander'd drearily from hall to hall;
Sometimes he tumbled in an iron chest,
40 And was lock'd up, or got a painful fall
Over some cash accounts, or, worse than all,
Whenever his escape by flight he tried,
He bruised his wings against the hard stone wall;
Till, wearied out, he sat him down and sigh'd
45 So heavily, it seem'd as if he must have died.

Heart-sick he pined and dwindled to a shade;
Folly too grieved, but Plutus' sons were glad
At his gaunt plight, because he might be weigh'd
Against the very smallest coin they had,
50 And be found wanting; this done, they forbad

His living any more at their expense,
And turn'd him out of doors, calling the lad
A vile impostor upon common sense,
With many ribald words which gave him great offence.

55 Poor Love was very ill, and his physicians,
Pleasure and Youth, day after day attended,
Night after night, with hourly repetitions
Of kissing draughts with ladies' fingers blended,
Sweetmeats, and heart's ease,—lord! how fast he mended!
60 And then they warm'd him to his heart's content
With Cyprus' wine, and lo! his sickness ended:
So Love revived, and now on vengeance bent,
He call'd aloud on Jove for Folly's punishment.

"Revenge!" he cried, "revenge me upon Folly!
65 Behold me, Jove, she has put out my eyes,
My happy eyes, now dark and melancholy!"
Jove listen'd to his little grandson's cries,
And cited the delinquent to the skies;
At first this heavenly summons made her wonder,—
70 Then she felt certain she was found too wise
To live on earth,—but, when she saw her blunder,
She trembled like a leaf, being much afraid of thunder.

Her fears, as usual, vanish'd presently;
Then, looking round her with a saucy face,
75 She ask'd if such a goodly company
Could find it worth their wisdom to disgrace
A girl like her, whose fault, in the first place,
Was but a slight one, and withal committed
Purely to serve her own dear human race:
80 "I grant," said she, "the boy is to be pitied,
Yet as he should be blind I ought to be acquitted.

"Think what a blessing it will be to man,
And woman too, made up of imperfection,
That Love no more can closely spy and scan
85 A blemish on the mind or the complexion;
Besides, as he must make a blind selection,
Pairing them off to fill his motley train
Just as his arrows take their chance direction,
How many a squinting nymph and loutish swain
90 May ogle and be spruce, nor find their frolics vain.

"Again, I'd have you know that Jove and all
The gods may be beholden—" "Hush!" says Jove,
"This argument grows somewhat personal;

Already hast thou said enough to prove
95 Thy guilt; in justice, therefore, to young Love
A grievous penalty shalt thou abide;
And as 'tis fit the little god should rove
Fearless throughout the world, thus we decide,—
Love shall for evermore have Folly for his guide."

# Index of Titles and First Lines

KING ALFRED'S COLLEGE
LIBRARY